Diamonds around the Globe

Diamonds around the Globe

The Encyclopedia of International Baseball

Peter C. Bjarkman

Greenwood Press
Westport, Connecticut • London

Library of Congress Cataloging-in-Publication Data

Bjarkman, Peter C.
    Diamonds around the globe: the encyclopedia of international
baseball / Peter Bjarkman.
    Includes bibliographical references and index.
    ISBN 0–313–32268–6 (alk. paper)
  1. Baseball—History. 2. Baseball—Cross-cultural studies. I. Title.
GV862.5.B43 2005
796.357'09—dc22   2004016511

British Library Cataloguing in Publication Data is available.

Library of Congress Catalog Card Number: 2004016511
ISBN: 0–313–32268–6

First published in 2005

Greenwood Press, 88 Post Road West, Westport, CT 06881
An imprint of Greenwood Publishing Group, Inc.
www.greenwood.com

Printed in the United States of America

The paper used in this book complies with the
Permanent Paper Standard issued by the
National Information Standards Organization (Z39.48–1984).

10 9 8 7 6 5 4 3 2 1

For my three Havana musketeers: **Ismael Sené**, who knows as much about Cuban baseball as anyone and who also maintains a remarkable ability to share his passions; **Martín Hachtoun**, whose presence at my side along the hidden byways of the Cuban baseball scene has made so much more out of the adventure; and my regular Havana traveling companion, **Bob Weinstein**, whose unparalleled position at the fulcrum of US-Cuban relations is widely acknowledged by all those truly in the know.

Contents

Acknowledgments

· ·

Any work of this scope entails a considerable litany of indebtedness and this one is no exception. On the international baseball scene, all of the following individuals require special mention: Omar Minaya, New York Mets and Montreal Expos general manager, for his constant support of all those genuinely interested in carrying the torch of international baseball; Ismael Sené, Cuba's number one baseball fan, for originally opening my eyes to the richness of Cuban baseball; Martín Hachtoun, a remarkable Havana journalist, for answering so many questions and proving such an irreplaceable companion on the international baseball scene; Jesús Suárez Valmaña, Cuban League public relations guru, who provided so much invaluable aid with current Cuban League statistics; Carlos (Carlitos) Rodríguez Acosta, Cuban League Commissioner, for opening doors and providing access during the 2003 World Cup in Havana and on countless earlier occasions; Mark Rucker, for companionship during early Cuban travels and for supplying much-needed photographs; Milton Jamail, for hours of discussion and insight concerning the Latin American baseball scene; and lastly Sigfredo Barros, longtime baseball beat writer for Havana's *Granma*, for his ongoing guidance in understanding the subtleties of Cuban baseball.

During editorial and production phases of the project, Judy Thurlow and Gundega Korsts, both of Capital City Press, proved invaluable in making this volume a far better book than it might otherwise have been. Judy guided the massive manuscript though a complicated production process with good humor and considerable vision; Gundega proved the most proficient and technically expert copy editor I have ever had the privilege to work with, and also a rare guiding light on both stylistic and baseball matters. And finally, much of the ultimate credit for this volume goes to my acquisition editor at Greenwood Press, Rob Kirkpatrick, who not only is responsible for suggesting the project in the first place, but who also displayed remarkable patience and faith when a number of unforeseen delays pushed the book beyond its original projected delivery date. Without Rob's unshaken faith in my ability to deliver, the book might never have seen the light of day. In the end, all errors and shortcomings must fall where they belong, on the shoulders of the author alone, but any successes are undeniably a result of a remarkable team effort.

Introduction

Birth of the International Pastime

· ·

When baseball is seen as American baseball, and when American baseball is seen as Major League Baseball (MLB), two disparate views tend to appear. In one case, fans happily accept expansion, rising attendance figures, and exciting home run races as evidence that all is well in this best of all possible baseball worlds. In the other case, the same evidence is seen as the desperate last flailings of a dying institution—or at least one on the edge of losing any recognizable character as the great American national pastime. Such pessimism (realism, the pessimists would of course call it) is not born of nostalgia alone, not even of the historically literate nostalgia that knows what the past was actually like. Much more, the bleak view of today's Major League Baseball is informed by experience and knowledge of competing baseball worlds. Different baseball worlds, and not necessarily inferior just for being outside of Major League Baseball. Baseball has long thrived in amateur and professional play around the world, especially in Latin America and the Asian-Pacific Rim. Other countries have made baseball their own, perhaps more deeply than we in the United States have.

This book is designed to present the rest of the world of baseball to U.S. fans. Found here are histories of skill and accomplishment, of contributions to the major leagues, of alternative visions of organized ball, of oddities and greatness. The book's aim is to preserve and restore memory, and especially to make wholly visible that amazing parallel universe that is Caribbean baseball, Asian-Pacific baseball, and Olympic-style international baseball. Its theme is the persuasive argument that "the most beautiful game ever invented" is by no defensible standard to be dismissed as being exclusively an American game.

Major League Baseball—seen with the bleak eye of the realist—seems to have contracted its fatal illness sometime during the late 1970s, perhaps even a handful of years sooner. The ravages of disease, already hinted at throughout the 1980s and early 1990s, came to full view as the new century approached. The game now sits before us disfigured and on life-support systems. Treatments invented in the late 1990s might serve to preserve an appearance of health for a short period. Among these are wildcard teams to expand excitement (and jack revenues) during postseason play and a combination of expansion-diluted pitching and juiced balls (and maybe juiced muscles) serving to cheapen long-sacred batting records. Luxurious retro-stadiums designed to capture the feel of bygone eras while maintaining luxury box seating double as shopping malls and full-scale electronic entertainment centers. A bottom-line assumption of each new innovation in the one-time American national pastime has been a realization that for late twentieth-century American audiences the game is no longer sufficient fare. (That itself is the undeniable proof of disease.) And, accordingly, baseball has increasingly receded into the background of American sports.

Big league baseball's decline was not at all instantaneous. It has been a long and slow process of step-by-step disintegration for the sport that was once unchallenged as the single anointed and cherished national game. Baseball has had many scares down through the decades and many critical battles with ill health. Some of these crises and narrowly averted disasters came early in the twentieth century, some even in the nineteenth century.

The National League was barely two years old when ace pitcher Jim Devlin and three teammates received life-long banishment for throwing games to cheat their Louisville club of its seemingly surefire 1877 pennant. The league (though not the franchise) survived relatively unscathed from that first close brush with tainted honesty, but Devlin lost his promising career and died destitute only six years later. The Black Sox scandal of 1919 and 1920 (with eight Chicago stars acquitted in a law court but nonetheless banned for life by newly installed Commissioner Kenesaw Mountain Landis) again threatened to destroy popular faith in the integrity of the professional big league game. The Second World War, with maimed and teenaged substitutes filling out club rosters, also weakened baseball's professional authenticity and economic health. But the recoveries were always rapid and inspired ones. Charismatic Babe Ruth and home run slugging followed on the heels of the 1919 World Series scandal. The war-ravaged 1940s gave long-overdue birth to racial integration and thus paved the way for the golden age 1950s of Mickey Mantle, Willie Mays, Hank Aaron, and the Casey Stengel dynasty Yankees.

This time around, there seems to be far less hope for such speedy recovery—or even for any substantial recovery at all. If the game is somehow kept alive in this current age of exploding scoreboards, exploding league rosters, home run derby slugging, astronomical salaries, and "rock star" ballplayer celebrities, and even if it continues to grip its diminishing fandom with an occasional thrilling pennant race or dramatic World Series, it seems sadly evident that our baseball will never again be, and be recognized as, what it once and for so long was.

Today, baseball is one of America's most heavily promoted prime-time television entertainments, alongside more action-packed professional NFL (National Football League) football and more celebrity-rich pro NBA (National Basketball Association) basketball. Yet it is foolishness to think that the Major League Baseball corporate enterprise still approximates America's cultural backbone or still lives at the nation's very spiritual heart and soul.

To the realist, all this doom-saying about America's bat-and-ball game is justified. It has the ring of truth. It is—despite the endless spin put on the sport by network play-by-play announcers and other representatives of Major League Baseball—the existing state of affairs. By no stretch of anyone's imagination is baseball qualified today to be called the American national game. That lofty nameplate was once merited, back in another time and place. There was a long era in American history—even a succession of eras—in which baseball did indeed reign supreme, but that era is gone. Today baseball is no longer special, nothing that stands apart from NFL football, NBA basketball, and NHL hockey. Like its fellow pro leagues, baseball exists as an entertainment spectacle for the service of television, the great mesmerizing force unleashed on the past several generations of contemporary Americans. But baseball no longer reflects daily American rhythms. The game is no longer at the heart of every barroom or village square debate, no longer on the lips of every citizen.

TELEVISION AND THE DECLINE OF AMERICA'S NATIONAL PASTIME

It was the institution of television itself, of course, that originally maimed the game of professional baseball.[1] Wall-to-wall electronic games beamed from big league cities into every town and village meant an eventual closing of local minor league parks and loss of the sport as a live neighborhood spectacle. Children in American cities and suburbs no longer take to the sandlots through-out the long summer weeks for spontaneous play, and a middle-aged sports fan who talks of nothing but baseball is now a true rarity. The game's remaining devotees focus increasingly if not exclusively on a hopelessly lost past. Theirs is a world of nostalgia, dimming memory, and longing for a game that no longer exists beyond childhood dreams. Newspaper sports-page big league box scores rarely share the morning breakfast table with coffee and the funny papers, and baseball heroes clearly do not hold the center stage of American popular culture as they once did, when they were truly the nation's icons. Few of today's youngsters know every detail of the game's endless numbers (many astoundingly know almost nothing of its substantial past). Perhaps most telling of all, the World Series, misnamed though it is, no longer brings an entire nation to a virtual halt in its daily activities each mid-October.

One most telling symptom of the current malaise is the near-universal notion that baseball (an entertaining spectacle, a community passion) and professional Major League Baseball (a profit-oriented business) are synonymous. Americans have always held this view to a degree, at least since the golden-era 1950s brought televised baseball into every corner of the nation and simultaneously launched the slow death throes of small-time professional and semi-pro teams and leagues all around the land. With the marriage of the game to the all-pervasive influence of television, the long arm of the new passive entertainment medium and the accompanying marketing strategies of Major League Baseball would work together, little by little, to rub out all competing baseball universes. Fans in outposts such as Des Moines or Albuquerque or Louisville could now tune into big league games in the comforts of the family den—weekly at first, then (especially with cable and satellite transmission) any or every day. As a result, the local leagues no longer seemed quite so attractive, and soon the hometown minor league or industrial league club was suffering a fatal blow to its nightly gate receipts. At the same time, local flesh-and-blood heroes were quickly replaced with larger-than-life electronic celebrities.

Negro league baseball was the first parallel baseball universe to be rubbed out, but that first catastrophe had very little to do with emerging television markets. When public attention around the land turned to Brooklyn's Jackie Robinson and a handful of other black big leaguers in the first years after integration, the Negro leagues around the South and the nation's heartland found their top stars overnight spirited away to the big leagues. Without their headliners (Larry Doby, Monte Irvin, Satchel Paige, Hank Aaron, Don Newcombe), the rarely solvent Negro circuits dwindled rapidly. Although scattered teams played on through the 1950s and the Negro American League lasted until 1960, it was 1948 that saw the end of the Negro National League and with it the last Negro World Series and All-Star games. What was once a vast enterprise and even a bedrock cultural institution of the African American community receded quickly into little more than a fleeting memory.[2]

The minor leagues of organized baseball (a term used here to designate the American professional baseball structure) were themselves rapidly reduced during the same decade to branch operations of the majors. As television eliminated distances, the local clubs no longer had much luster or any exclusive claim on fans previously too far from big city parks to develop major league loyalties. The once-distant big league outfits were now easier to identify with on a more intimate basis. As minor league clubs and leagues went out of existence, the surviving and reduced minor leagues also drastically changed. Class AAA and AA circuits increasingly looked more like the majors themselves, stripped of much of their local color. Families long accustomed to sitting in front of the television set rarely went to the local parks to see players of no great note nationally, and for several generations their kids had also abandoned the local sandlots in favor of watching television images—passive indoor consumers, no longer active participants outdoors. Other spectator games better suited to television—football and basketball—were also soon squeezing baseball further into a diminishing corner of the national consciousness. By the Vietnam years, referring to professional baseball as the American national pastime was already more of a cliché than a statement of fact. In the 1960s and 1970s, professional football (replete with its violence and metaphors of warfare) had already taken up that mythical title, de facto. Americans were left with largely a single baseball institution, that of the televised big leagues. This in itself was a clear prescription for eventual disaster.

The notion that Major League Baseball and baseball itself are synonymous endeavors is even now a delusion. Parallel baseball universes still exist, though one has to search more strenuously in today's shrinking world to find them. First, there has been a revival of late in minor league baseball, even if the minors today are mostly a reduced arm of the big league game. Then, too, college baseball is thriving and is perhaps more popular than it has ever been in the past.

Television has again played a role here. The annual June national championship tournament dubbed the College World Series—begun in the shadows of World War II as a mere four-team affair and moved to its present home in

Omaha in 1950—has become a minor television event. If it does not compete with the college basketball "March Madness" tournament phenomenon or the college football bowl season, at least the college diamond sport has broken into the awareness of the average American fan. ESPN began its broadcasts of the tournament's final round, and later the entire event, in the early 1980s; the College World Series eventually became such a popular television commodity that by 1989 ESPN could no longer afford the rights to air the national championship game.

Even in the largest stadiums in the most prosperous collegiate programs, spectators attending college games in person discover a thrilling return to some of the sport's roots, which can only foster an awareness of the malaise suffered by the big-time professional game. College baseball is also one of the more visible signals that alternative universes do indeed exist for the former national pastime.

The parallel baseball worlds exist in their greatest glory in places such as Cuba, the Dominican Republic, and Venezuela—indeed, throughout the Caribbean Basin and Central America. They also thrive with somewhat of a different local flavor in the distant corners of Asia, Australia, and the island nations of the South Pacific. Korea, for example, boasts an advanced eight-club pro circuit that has produced in slugger Seung-yeop Lee the latest candidate to reign as unmatched home run king. Taiwan had two competing pro leagues for a spell in the 1990s, and Hawaii enjoyed an experiment (1993–1997) with winter league play that briefly provided a supplement to traditional Caribbean venues and MLB's Arizona Fall League. Japan's pro baseball, of course, is universally accepted as being perhaps a step below the U.S. majors and has been running nonstop since the mid-1930s.

American-style baseball is even making small inroads with organized competitive leagues and tournaments in Europe. Especially in The Netherlands and Italy, the American sport had begun in the middle decades of the twentieth century to collect a small but enthusiastic contingent of European enthusiasts and promoters. Italy's pro league commenced play in 1948 and today operates with both a ten-team, fifty-four-game major circuit (A1) and a twenty-four-team minor (A2) division; the Mediterranean country has also played host to such prestigious world amateur championship events as the Intercontinental Cup (including the inaugural event of 1973) and Baseball World Cup (as early as 1978 and as recently in 1998). A Dutch pro league descending from the first amateur national championships of the 1920s has been even more successful. It is supplemented with the annual Haarlem International Baseball Week tournament, which for a quarter-century has been a showcase of world invitational competitions. The pro circuit operated by the Netherlands has been sufficiently strong to provide a number of prospects for American minor league rosters—and even a major league pitcher in right-hander Win Remmerswaal, who made a brief appearance (1979–1980) with the Boston Red Sox.

In most cases, these foreign ballplaying outposts—especially in the Caribbean countries and Japan—boast long and colorful histories. They offer healthy alternatives to what seems an increasingly distasteful North American professional baseball enterprise built upon top-dollar entertainment spectacles staged by multimillion-dollar celebrity athletes. And they are perhaps most vibrantly healthy and refreshing in those locales farthest removed and most thoroughly isolated from any big league influences. Japan's pro baseball leagues have of late abandoned insularity, increasing their business contacts with organized baseball; as a result, they now find their own operations increasingly denuded of top talent—such as Ichiro Suzuki (seven-time Pacific League batting champion and 2001 American League Rookie of the Year), Hideki Matsui (top Tokyo Giants slugger before escaping to the Yankees), and Kazuhiro Sasaki (all-time Japanese saves leader and recently the best American League closer with Seattle). The once-thriving winter circuits in the Dominican Republic, Venezuela, and Puerto Rico find themselves increasingly diminished by internal and external economic conditions, including MLB player contracts that restrict the off-season activities of big league pros. In contrast, the politically isolated Cuban circuit still enjoys nearly complete autonomy, with its homegrown talent still largely untouched, despite the occasional defections to the U.S. majors by a small handful of top Cuban League stars.

For all their promise as alternatives to a monolithic organized baseball structure that treats all other baseball countries only as cheap sources of underpriced talent, most foreign leagues today face major threats to their survival from the all-powerful U.S. big league operation. Homegrown talent is constantly weaned away at an early age by the promise of lucrative U.S. pro contracts. Expanding television of big league games to other corners of the world threatens to have the same dissipating effect that it had on midwestern and southern small-town markets in the 1950s and 1960s. Many of the existing overseas alternative baseball worlds seem to face an unpromising future in which their days are more than likely numbered.

If big league clubs have increasingly paid attention to the Caribbean and Asian–Pacific leagues as talent sources, U.S. fans have paid no notice. International baseball has been largely ignored in the United States, and international leagues (even Olympic-style tournaments) barely make the radar screen of the North American press. As in so much else, whatever does not serve obvious American interests is seen as altogether irrelevant. (In this case, "American interests" pretty much means the interests of Major League Baseball.)

In recent decades, baseball historians have celebrated the Caribbean leagues of the past century as a romanticized setting for Negro league play. On the contemporary scene, however, we tend to focus only on what we can see on the big league fields of play. We have thus acknowledged the Dominican Republic as a convenient resource for the mining of seemingly endless prospects for our increasingly talent-poor big league clubs. The same is today true of Japanese professional leagues and to a lesser extent those in Korea and Taiwan, where a handful of recruits are also beginning to emerge on major league rosters. Some outraged American media commentators and everyday fans, seeing the less attractive side of the coin, are beginning to lament the thinness of native talent and conclude that our extensive mining of Caribbean and Japanese sandlots apparently means that "foreign" players are taking over what was once unquestionably an American game. Baseball, which is purely an American invention only in myth, is increasingly now only nominally an American-dominated spectacle even at the highest professional levels.

Most recently, American press attention has focused on Cuba and its handful of big league defectors. Here we find the last remnants of a Cold War mentality, where defectors (a term rejected in Cuba for its political overtones) are celebrated as heroes. Americans are still in love with Hollywood-style stories of oppressed slaves escaping to freedom (and incidentally reaping the rewards of huge dollar-rich contracts). It is a perverted but powerful version of the perennial American Dream.

The problem with most of the stories surrounding Cuban baseball defectors such as "El Duque" Hernández and José Contreras (a pair of ace pitchers who both ended up starring for the Yankees) is that in most cases the tales have been colored by journalists and player agents. El Duque's desperate December 1997 "freedom flight" from Havana on a leaking raft was later exposed by *Sports Illustrated* (November 1998) to be a fictionalized version of how agent Joe Cubas arranged and carried out the star pitcher's clandestine removal from Cuba. Defector stories have also distorted the picture of baseball talent on the island of Cuba, forestalling any fully accurate portrait of the Cuban League as a legitimate alternative baseball universe.

Cuban baseball officials, not surprisingly, view the present situation from an opposite perspective. For them, big leaguers are baseball slaves no matter how highly they are rewarded. Major league players, contend the Cubans, are owned and traded as property—Cuban players never switch teams. The owners and athletes alike in U.S. organized baseball are viewed as selfishly motivated by excessive dollar profits alone and not by love of sport or the traditions of a national game.

The rest of world baseball goes entirely ignored by American fans and media and even by the big league baseball establishment itself. The 2000 Olympics in Sydney brought Team USA its first gold medal victory and a rare triumph over the perennially powerful Cubans, but the story was grossly underreported and consequently largely unnoticed. Television coverage of Olympic competitions does not accommodate team games with continuous action. Sports that lack the short segments of track and field, swimming, gymnastics, or ice skating do not fit conveniently between commercials. The gold medal showdown, with the Americans upending the Cubans 4–0 behind the brilliant hurling of big leaguer Ben Sheets, was televised back home only on a delayed and truncated basis. The story of America's top baseball moment in an international arena was flashed momentarily in the headlines and then forgotten almost overnight.

The prestigious Intercontinental Cup games staged in nearby Havana during Autumn 2002 (Cuba defeating South Korea in the finals) drew no notice at all among American fans. No Team USA contingent even attended, supposedly for reasons of political protest against the Castro communist regime. The same was true when Havana hosted the latest edition of the popular world amateur championships (now called the Baseball World Cup) in October 2003. The Americans sent only a B-level squad to compete and were unceremoniously ousted from the quarterfinals by Chinese Taipei. When the number one American squad, managed by Montreal Expos skipper Frank Robinson, was once again dumped in the quarterfinals of the Panama Olympic Qualifier a few weeks later, the short-lived page-two story in the States consisted merely of attacks against the existing format for Olympic baseball selection and cries for dumping Olympic baseball altogether and replacing it with an MLB-sponsored professional world cup event.

The American press does not cover most world baseball tournaments, perhaps because when U.S. teams do show up they rarely place among the winners (USA Baseball does not send top-flight American squads). These events often don't get even casual mention in the nation's sports pages. Though this has in some ways hurt the international game of baseball, yet it has in part also been its salvation.

The scene is now changing, however, with an emerging movement toward increased participation by professional players (so far, mostly AA and AAA minor leaguers, but beginning to include major leaguers). Starved for sources of new star-power talent and for avenues to widening fan support, MLB today seizes on the world popularity of baseball as an unexplored and underexploited territory that can only promise healthy new sources of revenue. Reportedly, MLB has considered plans for developing its own world tournament as an expanded revenue source, believing the games would bring millions of dollars in television rights and advertising contracts. The model would, of course, be the wildly popular World Cup of soccer, which MLB officials see (perhaps mistakenly) as a clear indicator of untold television profits. The upshot is that when U.S. interest in the world baseball community does expand under the guise of an organized baseball marketing scheme, the end results may prove to be anything but healthy for the rest of the baseball-playing world.

THE PAST: WORLD BASEBALL IN THE TWENTIETH CENTURY

More so than most games, baseball as a sport and as an institution thrives with myth and legend entrenched at its very core. Big league baseball, especially, has always been a world in which myth vies constantly with statistics and documentation as the historical foundation of the game. What tales are more cemented in the lore of the national pastime than Babe Ruth's "called" home run blast during the 1932 World Series, Fred Merkle's "bonehead" play that cost the New York Giants a 1908 National League pennant, Jackie Robinson's lonely one-man crusade as the first black man to play in the major leagues, or Abner Doubleday's miraculous "invention" of the sport on a sandlot in the picturesque village of Cooperstown? Yet all are, of course, either outlandish fabrications or minor distortions of documented reality. Ruth pointed at an enemy pitcher, not the bleachers; Merkle's Giants had several more shots at the pennant, which they squandered; Robinson's heroism is enmeshed in a complex and tangled story; and, as far as we can determine, Doubleday never even saw a baseball game.

No myth is quite as substantial or quite as misguided as the fundamental one, the claim that the sport of baseball as we know it today is both historically and inherently an exclusively red-white-and-blue American game. The notion first took hold for twentieth-century fans with the embellished legend of Doubleday, a fiction dreamed up by Albert G. Spalding, officially rubber-stamped in 1907 by Spalding's Mills Commission, and then quickly entrenched as one of the sport's first great marketing triumphs. Although all serious scholars have long since dismissed any connection between baseball's roots and either

Cooperstown or General Doubleday, the notion is nonetheless still deeply embedded in the American psyche.

The essentially American flavor of the game was unquestionably an invention of Spalding and other representatives of organized baseball in the early guise of the National League. An ex-professional ballplayer and later successful sporting goods entrepreneur, Spalding likely never appreciated any clear distinctions between his genuine love for the game and the economic opportunities represented by marketing bats, balls, and gloves to a nation of fans soon hooked on the new national pastime. But for all Spalding's proselytizing for baseball's American roots, many other forces also conspired to make the purity myth of American origins so appealing.

Baseball does not in fact trace its origins to any single inventor nor to any precise North American location or specific moment in time. There was instead a slow evolution and many competing sources from which the emerging game actually sprang. Admittedly, the primary origin of today's baseball was the so-called New York Game spawned during a single afternoon on the fields of Hoboken in New Jersey. That day, June 19, 1846, is the landmark date for a game staged between the New York and Knickerbocker nines at Hoboken's Elysian Fields playing grounds, for which Alexander Cartwright diagrammed a diamond-shaped playing field and drew up the rules (nine players to a side, three bases and home, three strikes and out, three outs for a side, runners put out by tagging and not "plugging") that defined the New York version of play. Competing early versions were the Massachusetts or Boston Game (a box-shaped rather than diamond-shaped field, wooden posts for bases, one out per inning, and runners put out by being hit or "plugged" with a thrown ball) and the Canadian or Ontario Game (eleven men to a side, five bases, and all eleven batters retired to end an inning).

Baseball's rapid spread across the rest of Canada, beyond the province of Ontario, came only after the Cartwright (New York) rules had been adopted. The earliest known versions of ball playing in Cuba also resembled the New York approach, with the single exception of an extra roaming outfielder. Thus, the type of baseball eventually played in Cuba, Canada, Japan, and all other countries derives directly or indirectly from Cartwright's unique New York–style game. Such an admission, however, should not be allowed to overshadow the extent to which other cultures have wholeheartedly adopted the diamond sport and shaped it to their own special needs. That would obliterate how deeply the sport is ingrained in the history and culture of a nation such as Cuba, or how thoroughly it was radically reshaped and nativized in Japan.[3]

The game that would eventually emerge as base-ball (its spelling throughout most of the nineteenth century) came to North America from Europe, probably from England. Its origins lie in the superficially similar British contests known as cricket and rounders. Cricket is still widely played today in England and many of its former colonies (from where recent immigrants are even bringing it back in a small way to the United States). Rounders is an old bat-and-ball game taking numerous forms but involving one base only, usually played on an individual rather than team basis and featuring runners being made out by striking them with a thrown ball. Early North American base-ball (or "base ball") sprang up in several competing forms around the Atlantic colonies during the early nineteenth century. There were also early versions played to the north in Canada, and one of those versions may have spawned the earliest recorded game that was anything like the orderly team sport we recognize today. The historic Beachville, Ontario, match of 1838 was a distinct form of baseball that featured the five bases and eleven-man sides associated with earliest Canadian play. Early American versions of "town ball" (that is, the Massachusetts Game or New England Game) were also quite distinct from modern-era play, with their violent plugging of base runners, odd-appearing four-foot high wooden base poles, and quirky rules ending games after 75 recorded tallies. At the least, it can be claimed that the Canadians were taking the game very much to heart equally as early as their neighbors to the south, and they have of course never relinquished their hold on it since.

Baseball arrived on Cuban shores in 1864 with apostles from the United States who had learned the infant game on American campuses—but those first apostles were Cuban natives (Havana students, such as Nemesio Guilló and Ésteban Bellán) and not the visiting American marines or longshoremen later so often reported. And once the Cubans took up the sport enthusiastically, baseball was so immediately connected with an emerging Cuban nationhood during the struggle for independence from imperial Spain that the American (as opposed to Spanish) sport quickly became even more of a national symbol than it would ever be back in North America. Several scholars have traced in detail the intimate early connections between the adopted sport of baseball and Cuba's anti-Spanish independence war during the 1870s and the two turbulent decades that followed (see especially my own *Baseball's Mysterious Island*, González Echevarría's *The Pride of Havana*, and Pérez's *On Becoming Cuban*). Nowhere was the spectacle of baseball more steadfastly connected with nationhood or with a people's evolved national identity than it was in late nineteenth and early twentieth-century Cuba.

The Cubans became the most dedicated apostles of baseball play throughout the Caribbean region, where the new American-style game flourished in the coming decades. The ongoing struggle for independence from Spain (the Ten Years War of 1868 to 1878, the War of 1895, and the Spanish-American War of 1898) led to several migrations of displaced Habaneros, who in turn transported baseball (along with a profitable Cuban sugar industry) to neighboring shores throughout the region. Cubans seeking refuge from turbulence at home during the early 1890s journeyed to the nearby Yucatán region of Mexico, where they soon instituted ballplaying traditions that would eventually establish that region as Mexico's most hardcore baseball hotbed. And Cubans first introduced the game to the Dominican Republic on the island of Hispaniola, also during the early stages of the Ten Years War, where it also took root overnight as a welcomed national institution long before U.S. Marines landed in 1916 to begin an eight-year occupation.

Cricket had arrived even earlier to the same Hispaniola outpost with the annual migrations of dark-skinned English-speaking Tortolan cane cutters known as Cocolos; these settlers—mostly in Santo Domingo and La Romana— paved the way for eventual adoption of the more modernized bat-and-ball contests imported by the Cubans. Cuban settlers would soon also be teaching

the game to eager disciples in Venezuela (where it was reportedly first introduced by a professional Cuban ballplayer named Emilio Cramer, who brought
his traveling all-star squad to Caracas in 1895) and in Puerto Rico (where during
the early 1890s the son of a Spanish diplomat, recently transferred from Havana,
taught the rudiments of the sport to local playmates around San Juan, and where
in 1898 a first reported organized match featured a team named Almendares in
honor of the popular professional Havana-based club). Cubans also transported
baseball westward, not only to the Yucatán portion of Mexico, but also to at least
one other Central American outpost. Nicaraguan baseball boasts distinct Cuban
roots: although the sport was introduced there in 1889 (at Bluefields) by
American businessman Albert Adlesberg, nonetheless the first visit of a touring
team from abroad was made by an all-star squad organized and led by a former
Cuban big leaguer named Manuel Cueto.

A noteworthy international flavor distinguished early American professional
baseball itself. There were far more than a mere handful of European-born big
leaguers in the nineteenth century—mostly Irish (30), English (14), and German
(11). A total of 58 Canadian-born athletes pulled on uniforms with various big
league clubs before 1900, including such notables as Tip O'Neill, who batted
a record .492 with American Association St. Louis in 1887; Bob Emslie, who
captured 32 on the hill with AA Baltimore in 1884; and Arthur Irwin, who pioneered
the then-novel fielder's glove. Some of the professional game's most important
founding figures were also British-born immigrants. Henry Chadwick, one of
baseball's most significant off-field innovators, was one of these; among his
myriad influences, Chadwick invented the box score and lobbied for such
innovations as extra-inning play and the infield-fly rule. And on the field of
play there was converted cricketer Harry Wright (organizing genius behind
the trailblazing 1869 Cincinnati Red Stockings) and his equally talented brother
George Wright (born in Yonkers, the son of a transplanted star British cricket
bowler). A pioneer at playing the difficult shortstop position, George Wright was
arguably the best all-around player in the entire country throughout the
1860s and 1870s.

Second- and third-generation Europeans contributed even more heavily in
the later decades of the game's first century. Subsequent waves of Irish (Mike
"King" Kelly and John "Mugsy" McGraw), German (Babe Ruth and Lou
Gehrig), Jewish (Hank Greenberg and Ed Reulbach), Italian (Joe DiMaggio and
Tony Lazzeri), and Slavic (Stan Musial and Ted Kluszewski) second-generation
immigrant sons were at the forefront of the national pastime throughout the
entire first half of the twentieth century. It was only baseball's racial integration
in the immediate aftermath of World War II that seemingly diminished the
importance of a star major leaguer's Old World ethnic lineage. For after
Jackie Robinson—but only after Robinson, with blacks and Latinos suddenly
emerging as more clearly defined ethnic heroes—all ballplayers of European
ancestry became reduced simply to homogeneous whites.

The true rise of baseball as a genuine international sport would come a half-
century after the crest of European immigration into the major leagues, on
the eve of World War II. Major league baseball had by then long since self-
righteously adopted the label of "world series" for its own season-ending
championships, and major leaguers had already carried the game to far corners of

the civilized world in several ballyhooed promotional tours. Baseball was already thriving sufficiently in Pacific locations such as Australia, Japan, and Hawaii—all stops on A. G. Spalding's grand 1888–1889 worldwide junket—for several stateside tours to have been arranged early in the century by college nines representing all three Pacific outposts. In 1905, a team representing Japan's Waseda University visited California and took on Stanford University and other college nines along the West Coast. Intrepid Australian baseballers made "The Disastrous Tour" in 1897, which included a match versus Boston old-timers (featuring Spalding himself) but which ended with the athletes penniless and hopelessly stranded in England. Beginning in 1910, Chinese Hawaiians representing the University of Hawaii in Honolulu made a series of annual treks to the American West Coast to do battle with assorted college, semi-pro, Pacific Coast League, and African-American teams. The first attempt at anything approximating a true worldwide competition, however, did not arrive until the late 1930s, in the guise of a pioneering "Amateur Baseball World Championship" tournament. This landmark event was at first an extremely limited effort, marked by few entrants and extremely shaky organization.

The first legitimate effort to stage a world baseball playoff was the event held in Havana, Cuba, in 1939; it involved only three amateur squads representing the United States, Nicaragua, and the host-country Cubans. Much credit for the affair goes to support by the newly elected government of Fulgencio Batista, but these first "amateur world series" matches were also the culmination of efforts by the U.S. Baseball Congress fronted by former big leaguer Leslie Mann to organize a world governing body for amateur baseball (the eventual International Baseball Federation or IBAF) on the heels of the Berlin Olympics. A similar event had already been staged by Mann in England a mere year earlier, with American and British teams as sole competitors; that makeshift tournament (won by the Brits) is still officially carried on the records as the debut of what is today known as the IBAF Amateur World Series (or Baseball World Cup). Of course the small-scale event promoted by Leslie Mann in London during August 1938 was not at all what it appeared to be. Most of the players were American soldiers stationed in Europe, and the host English team (made up mostly of practiced pros from a failed British league of a few years earlier) gave only the appearance of a genuine international event.

The first Havana affair at La Tropical Stadium in August 1939 was hardly more elaborate. The American club was laughably weak and didn't win a single game; its closest loss was 2–0 to Nicaragua. The impressive host squad, drawn from the powerful all-white Cuban amateur league, easily won all six of its own matches to claim the trophy. Over the next several years, a more substantial multinational tournament began to take shape among several of the world's top baseball-playing countries, with Venezuela, Mexico, Puerto Rico, and even Hawaii joining the 1940 fray, also staged in Havana. Havana remained the setting for three more years, and the Cubans remained the moving force behind the event when it moved on to Caracas for 1944 and 1945. The Cubans from the first represented the dominant on-field powerhouse in the sometimes annual and sometimes alternate-year event, which still thrives today (every other year) under the guise of a renamed and IBAF-sponsored Baseball World Cup.

Entering countries are now drawn from all serious baseball-playing nations of Latin and North America, Europe, Oceania, and the Far East.

Cuba did not only emerge as the regular victor in these earliest world amateur competitions. Throughout the first half of the twentieth century, the baseball-crazy island was also the undisputed showcase for winter-season baseball, the one place where big leaguers and minor leaguers, playing along-side banned black stars excluded from U.S. organized baseball, harmoniously honed their skills (and picked up valuable off-season cash in the bargain). In an era when winter barnstorming tours represented a showcase feature of the sport, Cuba had established itself by the first decade of the twentieth century as the reigning baseball paradise throughout the off-season winter months. Havana crowds that flocked to picturesque Almendares Park (the old version before 1916, the later version until 1926) were always enthusiastic and always knowledgeable. Cuban promoters (such as Abel Linares, who lured Babe Ruth to Havana in 1920) brought top white and black stars and entire big league teams to the island to satisfy the ravenous local baseball hunger. A professional winter league in Cuba supplemented the various series of barnstorming games between visiting American pros (including crack Negro leaguers) and both Cuban League outfits—mainly Almendares and Club Habana—and the most polished Cuban amateur ball clubs. Some of the latter teams, featuring upper-class white-skinned stars, were powerful enough to regularly trounce even the leading Cuban League pro squads. Best of all, the Havana-based Cuban League scene was one where whites and blacks could compete head-to-head as they could nowhere else, not in the North American professional leagues nor in the racially pure Cuban amateur circuit. Cuba thus remained throughout the 1910s, 1920s, and 1930s an altogether unrivaled stage for some of the world's sharpest baseball action.

Cuban players themselves migrated north to play professionally during summer months in the United States. Because most were quite obviously black or at least (to racially sensitized eyes) recognizably so in their facial features, these players were excluded under organized baseball's color bar. A few lighter-skinned Cubans did play in the majors after 1911 (which is when outfielders Armando Marsans and Rafael Almeida signed on with Cincinnati as the first modern-era Latino big leaguers), and a few became minor stars. Adolfo Luque was the most noteworthy, with 27 mound wins for Cincinnati in 1923 and a career victory total that eventually fell just short of 200. Catcher Miguel Angel González did yeoman journeyman work with the Cardinals, Cubs, and Giants for a couple of decades, managed a few games in St. Louis, and earned a permanent place in the game's lore when he invented the damning phrase "good field, no hit" (later so often applied to many of his own countrymen). It was in the Negro circuits that the Cubans were truly able to show their wares with the likes of Cooperstown Hall of Famer Martín Dihigo, who excelled at eight positions; Cristóbal Torriente, who briefly smacked Ruthian-like homers for Rube Foster's Chicago American Giants; and Luis "Lefty" Tiant (the elder Tiant), who reputably possessed baseball's best-ever pickoff move. Cubans also starred in winter circuits throughout the Caribbean region, with ace hurlers Dihigo (simultaneously a pitching and batting champion in 1938), Lázaro Salazar (Dihigo's only close rival as both batsman and mound ace), and Ramón

Bragaña (Mexico's only one-season 30-game winner) all leaving larger-than-life legacies in Mexican League annals.

Baseball was also flourishing in Japan by the middle of the twentieth century, though severe temporary setbacks accompanied the bombing of the island during World War II. There had never been much notice in the United States of the distant Japanese leagues, except when an occasional touring outfit of big leaguers made barnstorming tours of the Orient. Yet the game was already strongly embedded in the Japanese mentality by the early 1930s. When several contingents headed by Lefty O'Doul, Lefty Grove, Babe Ruth, and Lou Gehrig stopped off in the Land of the Rising Sun in 1931 and 1934, these fall barnstorming events brought out huge crowds (sometimes as many as 75,000) to witness the American stars perform against local university teams, commercial league nines, and Japanese pro all-star selections. Meanwhile, baseball was flourishing in Japan year around, with hugely popular high school tournaments and a thriving professional league that debuted in 1936 with both fall and spring seasons, and then split in 1950 into the still-thriving Central League and Pacific League. After midcentury, these two circuits (reminiscent of our own National and American leagues) met annually in a climactic Japan Series playoff with all the trappings of MLB's own misnamed World Series. The Japanese were also quite early developing their own legendary diamond stars, all of whom remained even more isolated from American media accounts than did the Cuban leaguers. Pro baseball's all-time home run king Sadaharu Oh (868), Japan's career base hits leader Isao Harimoto (3085), and the island's most popular star ever, slugging third baseman Shigeo Nagashima, all debuted before the end of the 1950s. The Japanese were also importing players from unlikely sources: Russian-born Victor Starffin wrote the island's greatest pitching legacy in the 1930s and 1940s and as the first Japanese hurler to win 200 and then 300 games he set numerous individual records that still stand almost a half-century later.

Baseball was on the upswing around the Caribbean Basin during decades between the two world wars. The Dominican Republic had launched a winter-season tradition with islandwide championship tournaments as early as 1912; two popular professional clubs, Licey and Escogido, were operating a full forty years before the first full-scale Dominican winter league (1955) aligned itself with organized baseball. Puerto Rican winter competitions (commenced as a formal league in 1938) were already a recognized Caribbean tradition before the onset of World War II, and by the late 1940s the Borinquen circuit was already rivaling a sagging Cuban League for prominence in the Caribbean region. Thanks to native sons such as Roberto Clemente and Vic Pellot Power and imports such as Willie Mays and Bob Thurman, Puerto Rican teams captured four of the first seven winter league wrap-up Caribbean series. During the same epoch (1937–1945), Mexico with its summer league developed arguably the strongest Latin circuit outside of Cuba. Indeed, the Mexican League had reached such potential by the mid-1940s that tycoon Jorge Pasquel indulged a brief dream and successfully raided big league rosters in the hopes of thus lifting his Mexican circuit to full parity with the top levels of U.S. organized baseball.

Venezuela and Panama also eventually got into the act during the winter of 1946 with pro winter leagues of their own. Panama's underfunded and fan-poor circuit did not survive, in its first incarnation, beyond the late 1960s; by the time Panama's military had deposed President Arnulfo Arías in 1968, the nearly moribund league had dwindled to but three struggling clubs. Winter league operations in Venezuela, however, flourished from the first and remained healthy. South America's top baseball nation would eventually begin to rival the Dominican Republic and Puerto Rico as a ripe source for big league talent. Only two Dominicans played in the majors before 1960 (Ozzie Virgil and Felipe Alou). Puerto Rico had already produced sixteen by that date (among them Clemente, Power, Orlando Cepeda, Rubén Gómez, Juan Pizarro, and Luis Arroyo). But Venezuela could boast of Chico Carrasquel, Pompeyo Davalillo, and Luis Aparicio. In the early 1940s, Venezuelan national teams with such stars as pitching ace Daniel Canónico and flashy shortstop José Casanova (Most Valuable Player of the 1941 Amateur World Series) were also consistently raising strong challenges to the reign of the overachieving Cubans as kings of world amateur baseball. Even Nicaragua, still without a professional winter league, featured national teams fronted by such heavy hitters as Chino Meléndez, Jonathan Robinson, and Stanley Cayasso (the first two being pitchers as well as fence-busting sluggers) that turned in impressive losing efforts versus Cuban juggernauts during the early 1939 and 1940 Amateur World Championship tournaments at Havana.

These Caribbean countries were not only idyllic settings for off-season leagues hosting big leaguers and Negro leaguers, they were also fostering their own remarkable stables of homegrown talent. While Cubans (led by Martín Dihigo, Lázaro Salazar, Ramón Bragaña, and Cocaína García) filled up rosters in the Dominican Republic, Mexico, and Puerto Rico, stars from those countries also not only flourished at home but found their way to the higher-profile leagues in Cuba and in Mexico. Perucho Cepeda (father of Orlando) and Francisco "Pancho" Coimbre authored substantial black-ball legends in Puerto Rico; Dominican Tetelo Vargas was a U.S. Negro leagues standout with the New York Cubans and also captured a 1944 batting crown in Puerto Rico; Venezuelan hurler Alejandro Carrasquel was already in the major leagues by 1939, as was Mexican outfielder Mel Almada a half-dozen seasons earlier. By the early 1950s, thriving winter circuits in four separate locations—Cuba, the Dominican Republic, Puerto Rico, and Venezuela—had made the diamond sport as central to the Caribbean sporting world as big league seasons were during summer months in the United States.

Healthy winter pro circuits would soon spawn a second major effort at a true "world series" playoff among nations, this time on the more visible professional level. With heightened competition for top players in the years immediately following World War II, roster raiding between winter circuits was a common practice until representatives from Cuba, Puerto Rico, Panama, and Venezuela met in Havana in August 1948 to enact agreements ending ballplayer pirating and to plan for a showcase season-ending interleague tournament. The so-called Caribbean World Series was hosted for the first time in Havana's Cerro Stadium in late February 1949 as a championship playoff between winning teams of the four operating winter circuits. Cuban League representative Almendares walked off with the title by beating each of the other three contenders twice. The following years saw six more Cuban victories (1952, 1956–1960), four wins by Puerto Rican teams (1951, 1953–1955), and one solo championship for Panama (1950). The series then ground to a temporary halt when pro baseball collapsed in Cuba in the aftermath of the Castro-led social revolution and the arrival of a communist system of state-controlled amateur sports.

The Caribbean series was never a tournament of play-downs pitting actual national teams. The all-star contingents or champion teams from each rival Caribbean winter league regularly included ballplayers who were not native sons of the country represented. These were games among league champions allowed to shore up their rosters with a few selections from other league teams. Major and minor league Americans were often involved, and occasionally Latin stars performed with winter league champions from countries other than their own. National pride was nonetheless at the forefront in these games— even if it was pride in the local winter circuit and not in the strictly native-born Olympic-style squad. Caribbean series traditions continued when the original series was revived in 1970, following the decade-long hiatus between the end of professional play in Cuba (robbing the event of its top winter circuit) and the launching of a second phase. The Dominican and Mexican leagues substituted for the departed Cubans and Panamanians. These week-long playoffs in early February (rotated annually among the four participating countries) have maintained their momentum for better than three decades, interrupted on only a single occasion by a contentious 1981 winter league players strike. If pro baseball's colorful Caribbean series seems to be slipping from hot stove notice of late, perhaps it is only because Caribbean winter league play is itself again experiencing a disturbing downward cycle.

More legitimate nation-versus-nation contests were cropping up in other guises after the 1950s. The Amateur World Series had actually been anticipated by more than a full decade by the Central American and Caribbean Games, a sports festival that limped out of the gate in Mexico City during late fall 1926 (with only Mexico, Cuba, and Guatemala participating) but gained steam once it was transferred to Havana in time to debut Cerveza Tropical Stadium. The 1930 Havana meet was promoted by faltering Cuban dictator Gerardo Machado as a means of distracting public attention from civil unrest and a sagging local economy; whatever the circumstances attached to their birth, these nation-versus-nation sports festivals featured the thriving Caribbean sport of baseball as a main showpiece and as a battleground for asserting national pride. The pitching- and hitting-rich Cubans were again the dominating team from 1926 on, winning the initial four tournaments and eventually claiming thirteen titles in the sixteen sessions the country has so far entered. These games, convened approximately every four years, had no North American or European or Asian entrants and thus have always seemed limited as tests of international baseball prowess. But, because the heart of international baseball from the 1930s through at least the 1960s fell squarely in the Caribbean Basin, the Central American Games matches in Cuba, Puerto Rico, Colombia, Panama, Mexico City, Jamaica, and elsewhere in the region were almost always highly competitive and far from insignificant.

A rival and somewhat more expansive venue debuted with the Pan American Games competitions launched at the century's midpoint. Again, as in the parallel Central American Games, baseball was a featured event and the sport that always drew top billing in those countries where it was either a national pastime or (as in Cuba and the Dominican Republic) the single unrivaled *"rey de deportes"*—King of Sports. Once more, here as elsewhere, powerful Cuban entrants owned the Pan American Games competitions, year in and year out—at least once the turmoil of the Cuban Revolution had subsided. It was at these games that Cuba, in fact, scored some of its first significant victories of the new sports regime under Fidel Castro. Cuba reentered the postrevolution amateur baseball arena by blasting all Amateur World Series competition in Costa Rica (although that win was in a weak field with no American, Dominican, or Puerto Rican representation) during the exact week that Fidel's army was coping with the United States–backed Bay of Pigs invasion at home.

Two years later in Brazil, a crack Cuban club laced with stars from a new amateur Cuban League (with ace hurlers Aquino Abreu, Manuel Alarcón, and Modesto Verdura at the forefront) rang up a pair of easy wins over the Americans in route to its first Pan American title under a banner of the island's new "revolutionary" baseball. With the advent of the Pan American Games, a normal Central American field was now expanded to include U.S. and Canadian clubs, a move guaranteed to spice competition with a veneer of Cold War propaganda battles between competing capitalist and socialist sporting systems (though not necessarily yielding an automatic improvement in the baseball action). A top highlight of this new venue came with the 1987 Indianapolis Games, which witnessed a dramatic Cuban gold medal game rally before a huge U.S. television audience. And the excitement experienced in Indianapolis was later outstripped at Winnipeg, in 1999, by one of the most thrill-packed international tournaments to date. Winnipeg's latest Pan American baseball games represented the first international matches in years using pro-style wooden bats instead of aluminum, as well as the first with professionals playing. Winnipeg play was also tinged with belated Cold War drama when a crucial semifinal match between favored Cuba and undefeated Canada was interrupted by an on-field political protester during the heat of tense ninth-inning action—with an Olympic slot in Sydney hanging in the balance.

Perhaps the most intriguing venue for world competitions is also the most recent, a thirty-year-old IBAF-sponsored tournament that periodically awards amateur baseball's prestigious Intercontinental Cup. This latest event was inaugurated in September 1973 by Italy's IBAF organization and has been renewed every second year since. Normally an eight- to twelve-team round-robin affair, it has been played in Europe, Cuba, Australia, and Canada but has yet to be staged in the United States or Asia. Here, the Cubans have remained as much in control of gold medal victories as in all the other major international events. But Cuba has also experienced some of its most shocking and embarrassing upset defeats in this particular tournament. Most dramatic among these was a 1997 humiliation suffered at the hands of Japan in Barcelona, in the immediate afterglow of the undefeated cakewalk in Atlanta's Olympiad. The 11–2 drubbing administered by the Japanese (now stocked with pro leaguers as well as collegiate amateurs) finally proved the Cubans mortal and beatable. It also sent shock waves throughout a Cuban baseball hierarchy back home in Havana. (National team coach Jorge Fuentes and technical director Miguel Valdés were quickly sacked in the aftermath of that loss, which ended nearly ten years without so much as a single game lost in top international venues.) A similar surprise defeat occurred only two year's later in Sydney, on the eve of the 2000 Australian-hosted Olympics. That second straight final-round Intercontinental Cup loss (this time 4–3, in extra innings to the Aussies) also provided a fore-shadow of the 2000 Olympic gold medal collapse that would occur less than twelve months later in the same Sydney stadium. With all its drama drawn from matching a truly international field of Asian, European, Latin American, and North American teams, the Intercontinental Cup remains arguably world base-ball's premier showpiece. It is also the only major world tournament—with a single exception of the Baseball World Cup itself—exclusively dedicated to America's national sport of bats and balls.

Baseball had actually appeared as an Olympic spectacle as early as the 1912 Games in Stockholm, when U.S. track athletes took a few days holiday to stage exhibitions matches with a group of amateur Swedish baseballers. These makeshift exhibition were repeated on several more occasions, highlighted by the 1936 Olympiad where a group of American college recruits unattached to the official U.S. Olympic squad entertained 90,000 bemused German track fans in a dimly lit Berlin Olympic Stadium. After Berlin a more organized formal movement was launched (thanks mostly to ex–big leaguer Leslie Mann) to establish baseball as a legitimate Olympic medal competition. But it was a movement that would prove excruciatingly slow in gaining any needed momen-tum. After renewed efforts at demonstrations in Melbourne (1956) and Tokyo (1964), Los Angeles finally featured a strong Olympic demonstration round-robin event in 1984 but one considerably diminished by the absence of any Cuban team. The same was true for the 1988 Olympiad in Seoul, Korea. Olympic baseball finally made its genuine debut in Barcelona in 1992 and by then the Cubans were back on board with a considerable vengeance. Four subsequent official Olympic baseball events have been marked by total Cuban domination; teams representing the communist island and its crack amateur league would win 21 straight matches before finally dropping an opening round game in Sydney to upstart Holland, then losing the 2000 finals to Team USA in an upset of major proportions. The gold medal victory in Sydney by Team USA repre-sented a single proud moment for the usually outclassed American forces. With a new round of games soon on tap for Athens (August 2004), the Americans had already slipped from the scene, ousted in the regional qualification tourna-ment in October 2003. USA Baseball watched from stateside while perennial powers Japan and Cuba, along with MLB-reinforced Australian and Canadian nines, did battle in a four-team race in Athens. And with MLB now making plans to launch its own televised World Cup event featuring U.S. and Caribbean Basin squads laced with big leaguers, the future of Olympic baseball itself now hangs very much in the balance.

THE PRESENT: WORLD BASEBALL AT THE MILLENNIUM

One defining feature of the 1990s, and also of the first decade of a new century and a new millennium, is the surprising fact that U.S. baseball interests have at long last paid at least minimal attention to the existence of a separate baseball universe found outside continental North America. Part of the

motivation—the part involving talent-rich baseball in Fidel Castro's Cuba—
has been embarrassingly political in tone. A recent showcase pair of contests
between the major league Baltimore Orioles and Fidel Castro's Team Cuba
carried all the overtones of a true Cold War–era pageant play. Major League
Baseball's never-ending lust for new revenue sources may be an even larger
part of such new-found interest. And the wounded pride of stateside fans—
and even more of big league officials—has also finally resulted in an American-
led initiative to place professionals on the rosters of teams competing in what
had always been world amateur tournaments. The precedent was launched a
decade earlier with the first U.S. Basketball Dream Team that was itself a response
to European and especially Russian usurping of Olympic titles in that other
acknowledged American national game. Baseball interests in the United States
would soon leap upon a parallel solution, and the world would be left with
little choice but to follow.

The first official Olympic baseball tournament in Barcelona during the fall
of 1992 was still exclusively a Cuban affair in which the longtime reigning
world amateur champions ran through nine games hardly breaking a sweat.
With future big league defectors Orlando Hernández, Osvaldo Fernández,
and Rolando Arrojo anchoring a pro-quality mound corps, the Cubans outscored
opposition teams 93–16 and cruised to a gold medal 11–1 rout of Chinese Taipei.
This was the first time that the sport had been a recognized part of the official
medals competitions at any Olympic venue. There had been demonstration
baseball in past Olympics, with Team USA fielding strong teams in both 1984
in Los Angeles (where a contingent featuring Mark McGwire, Will Clark, and
Barry Larkin somehow managed to lose the finals to a Japanese squad of college
all-stars) and in 1988 in South Korea (where the pitching of Jim Abbott and
slugging of Tino Martínez were enough to heap revenge on the Japanese entry).
But the Cubans had attended neither of these games, joining a Soviet boycott
of the Los Angeles event and a North Korean boycott of Seoul. When it came
time for an "official" showdown in Barcelona, the U.S. contingent was not at
all up to standard (despite such pros-in-waiting as Nomar Garciaparra, Jason
Giambi, Michael Tucker, and Jeffrey Hammonds) nor even up to the task at
hand. Cuba whipped the Americans 4–1 in the semis with slugger Victor Mesa
driving home all four deciding tallies.

Baseball returned to the Atlanta Olympics in the summer of 1996. With
competitions now held on U.S. soil and even staged in a major league ballpark,
greater American interest seemed in the offering. The tournament itself unfolded as one of the best international encounters in years. The Team USA
roster was more competitive this time around, with Travis Lee, Mark Kotsay,
Warren Morris, and A. J. Hinch in the batting order and Kris Benson, Jim
Parque, Billy Koch, and Jeff Weaver anchoring a talented mound corps. Yet
there was still little serious U.S. media coverage of baseball action, which took
an inevitable backseat to glamorous track and field stars such as Carl Lewis and
Michael Johnson and the celebrity-laced NBA Dream Team. Thousands of
American fans did pour through the turnstiles at Fulton County Stadium to
witness the international game in person and at its peak. A United States–
Cuba showdown in the opening round (the single televised game) was truly
a battle for the ages, with a barrage of slugging from both sides, numerous

lead changes, and the defending champs emerging unscathed by a 10–8 score. Again the Cubans were at the top of their game, despite a more vulnerable pitching corps weakened by the pretourney defection of ace Rolando Arrojo. A glamorous expected United States–Cuba gold medal face-off was averted when the Americans suffered a stunning semifinal loss to Japan that could not help but further the collapse of American interest in such international events. American fans want front runners, it seems, and most U.S. viewers focused attention on watching Charles Barkley, Shaquille O'Neal, David Robinson, and fellow NBA headliners easily slaughter the remainder of the world's premier basketball talent.

A third Olympic tournament four years down the road would provide still another shot at full redemption for U.S. baseball interests. Two years earlier (July 1999), the Pan American Games qualifying matches in Winnipeg launched the U.S.-backed experiment with professional players. Considerable interest had been stirred up once again for a United States–Cuba showdown by an Orioles–Cuba home-and-away series transpiring a few months earlier. Perhaps the Cubans were now ripe for beating under the new circumstances of wooden bats and with the U.S., Canadian, Dominican, Mexican, and Panamanian teams loaded with seasoned minor leaguers. It didn't turn out that way at all, despite some temporary bumps in the road for the Cubans, who dropped opening round games with the Canadians and Americans, suffered the defection of reserve pitcher Danys Báez, and had to endure disruptions by anti-Castro demonstrators during the tense final innings of a 3–2 semifinal squeaker with surprisingly potent host Canada. Again, few Americans followed the games or had television access to the event—which was a huge loss for American fans. The tournament turned out to be one of the most thrilling ever. American and Canadian squads both gave their best showings in years, the former qualifying for the Sydney Olympics with their 2–1 semifinal win versus Mexico, and the latter undefeated before dropping their own semifinal match with the gold medal Cubans. In the end, the Cuban on-field experience, and especially the seasoned pitching of José Contreras and José Ibar, once more paid dividends; veteran minor leaguers, novel wooden bats, bothersome MLB pro scouts, and even harassing political activists proved to be little more than sideshow distractions.

Cuba finally slumped—if a silver medal finish can be called a slump—in the Intercontinental Cup Olympic warm-up event staged the following autumn at Sydney. But it was the Australians and not the Americans who reaped the benefits with a 4–3 eleven-inning upset win over the favorites, which came on a rare final-frame misplayed fly ball by budding Cuban star Yasser Gómez. The Cubans did not send a very strong team to Sydney in November 1999 but opted instead to leave their seasoned veterans on the sidelines. The reasons why were not altogether obvious at the time. One explanation was simply an attempt to prepare some of the country's emerging young talent during what was seen as a less than crucial warm-up tournament. The Americans—who lost two preliminary round matches and then dropped a bronze medal showdown with Japan—didn't mount a truly competitive squad either, and here again it could be dismissed largely as the continued result of longstanding

American disdain for international competitions involving the supposed national pastime.

The highpoint for American participation in world baseball play came in September of 2000 with the staging of a third Olympic baseball tournament in Sydney, Australia. Team USA officials, assisted by MLB brass, had finally put together a top-flight squad for this occasion. The American club managed by Hall-of-Famer Tommy Lasorda included such headliners as touted Milwaukee Brewers pitching prospect Ben Sheets, Minnesota Twins first baseman Doug Mientkiewicz (who had actually taken a year off to focus on the Olympic squad), and former World Series Most Valuable Player catcher Pat Borders. The surprising result of such efforts at reinforcement was a much-anticipated date in the finals versus the omnipresent Cubans, who had earlier handed the Americans their only opening round setback. For the first time in baseball's brief Olympic history, Team USA now had the limelight. After being handled rather easily by the rival Cubans 6–1 in their qualifying-round encounter, the Americans benefited from a spectacular and well-timed pitching effort by Ben Sheets in the finale. A lengthy series might easily have fallen to the Cubans, who again seemed to boast the superior top-to-bottom lineup with veterans Linares, Kindelán, and pitcher José Contreras (who would soon be pitching for the New York Yankees). At any rate, there was perhaps a bit too much premature celebrating in the victorious American camp. Overconfident and less prepared four years later at the Olympic Qualifier in Panama City, the Americans (now managed by another Hall of Fame skipper, Frank Robinson) would fade once more in an early match against Mexico and thus fail to earn the right to defend their Olympic crown in Athens in 2004. This merely set the stage for Cuba to return to the top of the heap when the dust finally settled in Athens.

All the ups and downs of savage U.S. competitions with the Cubans during international tournaments sparked remarkably little keen interest among most fans on the American home front. There was the usual prejudice against such games, played by unrecognized stars without big league credentials or big league drawing power. There was also little media build-up for these events, nothing to arouse the passions of fans in North America. If the big leaguers—the sport's celebrity drawing cards—were not playing, then what was the point of watching? And what possible significance could the results have? When the big league ballplayers finally did take on the same Cubans—well, that perhaps would be more the stuff to stimulate a wide fan following. The opportunity for such a spectacle came and went during a few short weeks in the late spring of 1999, in the form of two celebrated exhibition showdowns between the vaunted Cuban national team, sparkling with all its Olympic medals, and the American League Baltimore Orioles, bright with all their million-dollar-a-year polished professionals.

There had been many failed attempts at détente between big league teams and Cuban squads representing the Castro government. For forty years, such games were proposed from time to time (often by Cuban native Preston Gómez, who once played and managed in the big leagues and later labored as a scout and front-office fixture with the California and Anaheim Angels), but the games themselves never materialized. They were always torpedoed at the eleventh hour by either big league brass or State Department honchos. It had been a long dry spell since the last visit in 1959 of big league clubs to the island of Cuba. The Los Angeles Dodgers and Cincinnati Reds had been the last pro teams to set foot on Cuban shores for a pair of spring training exhibitions only weeks after Fidel's fateful rise to power. It was the Cuban fans who were almost always the most enthusiastic about the possibilities of an eventual showdown with big leaguers: it might not only showcase the long-absent pro stars, but also test the true strengths of their own top heroes. Back in the States there were many who disapproved of such matches strictly on political grounds, because they might legitimize the Castro communist government and even pump dollars into its depleted coffers. Others saw them as the key to either baseball détente between two long-antagonistic governments or even as a tantalizing symbolic face-off between competing economic systems.

It was transparent political motives on both sides that ultimately brought the historic games in Havana and Baltimore to full fruition. They were suddenly a possibility largely because they now fit a preelection-year agenda of the Clinton administration and because Fidel had his own motives for the long-overdue confrontation with top American professionals. The opening game (March 28, 1999) in Havana's massive Latin American Stadium, whatever its causes, served to demonstrate both the high quality of Cuban baseball and the lingering political overtones of any such clash between contrasting baseball philosophies. Much was made in the States about the fact that average Cuban fans were kept out of the ballpark as Fidel filled the stands with 55,000 communist party loyalists. Yet the handpicked crowd does not necessarily condemn the Cuban system on the whole but only shows that it too has its warts. Certainly any similar five-star games in pro baseball (such as the MLB All-Star game or World Series matches) are also typically beyond the reach of average year-round fans, with most tickets available only to high rollers and special invitees. Those who did attend the well-played 3–2 Orioles victory in Havana (along with huge American and Cuban television audiences) witnessed an exciting extra-inning struggle proving beyond doubt that Cuban Leaguers belonged on the same field with seasoned big leaguers. Expectations were raised even a notch higher for the welcome rematch on American soil.

In Baltimore (May 3, 1999), there was perhaps even more at stake, especially for the prideful Cubans. For the big leaguers, the game was merely an off-day interruption and unwanted distraction. For the Cuban team, it was a shot at immortality. Certainly Fidel Castro saw it this way. Castro would later pronounce that the game in Baltimore was the one that truly mattered to Cuban baseball interests; in Havana, the issue had merely been to display a civilized Cuba to American television viewers (thus the handpicked *Estadio Latinoamericano* crowd). In Baltimore, it would be a matter of demonstrating (in Fidel's view) the clear superiority of baseball played for pride and socialist ideals over baseball played for dollars. If triumph on big league turf was the primary goal, the propaganda victories to be scored there for both the Cuban League and Cuban government were huge. In this second game, the Cubans ran roughshod over disinterested big leaguers, who didn't seem to want to play on a regular-season off-day; the 12–6 final score barely reflected the one-sided nature of a contest in which Cuban sluggers bombarded such second-tier Baltimore hurlers as Scott Kamieniecki, Doug Linton, Ricky Bones, and Mike Fetters.

It was again a demonstration of just how good the Cubans actually were. The visitors now had their full team on the field (in Havana, top players such as Germán Mesa, Antonio Pacheco, and Orestes Kindelán had been held back because their teams were still active in the Cuban postseason playoffs). It was indeed a sterling display of Cuban baseball potency, even if the big leaguers seemed unmotivated. Norge Vera baffled the big leaguers in seven innings of masterful relief, star third baseman Omar Linares was a perfect 4 for 4 at the plate, and DH Andy Morales socked a mammoth anticlimactic three-run ninth-inning homer into the distant centerfield bleachers. The biggest victory perhaps was one not reflected in the final score. When Andy Morales danced around the bases after his dramatic circuit blast, fans in both countries got to see and share the unfettered joy and unbridled enthusiasm that distinguish Cuban League baseball from its more restrained North American professional counter-part. Sadly, the big leaguers reportedly saw only an arm-waving bush league display, entirely missing the youthful joy. Postgame press conferences and the Baltimore press were laced with complaints by Orioles players about the Morales "stunt"—as they saw it to be. Yet the kid from rural Havana Province—playing for the first time on the Cuban national team—was merely carried away by his enthusiasms in the aftermath of an impossible dream—that of smacking a home run in a major league ballpark.

There seems to be little chance of another such Cuba–big league match-up anytime in the immediate future. Both sides had achieved both their stated and unstated goals. Fidel, in particular, had very little to gain and perhaps a good deal to lose by any quick rematches. The Cubans had, after all, won both their on-field (convincingly in Baltimore) and off-field (far more subtly in Havana) victories. There was nothing to be accomplished by playing again—perhaps versus the stronger Yankees or Angels or Dodgers—outside of risking some embarrassing losses. The big leaguers likewise seemed to have little to gain by returning to Havana, because they still could not actively scout any of the rich potential harvest of island talent.

The stateside interests in the Orioles–Cuba encounters were in the end largely the narrow interests of major league baseball. Scouts for big league teams have not been able freely to view Cuban talent against high-level pro competition. Omar Linares, Orestes Kindelán, José Ibar, and other top prospects on Cuban na-tional teams have always had to be measured against inferior opponents drawn from U.S. college squads or minor league–quality all-stars from second-rate Korean and Taiwanese leagues. Nor have they had the much-desired opening to visit the island itself in search of the presumed wealth of young players hidden there. Perhaps the two exhibitions of the spring of 1999 could be a first step toward breaking open the long-forbidden hunt for Cuban talent. That certainly seemed to be the game plan for the twenty-five teams that send delegations to Havana in March 1999 as part of the Baltimore Orioles cele-brated exhibition visit. These clubs would surely hope for more such exhibitions on the horizon.

The true colors of renewed American interest in world baseball are per-haps best revealed in MLB's recent stepped up recruitment of Japanese pros, Dominican teenaged prospects, and defecting Cuban national team stars. With continuous expansion of its roster of talent-hungry teams and the simultaneous precipitous drop in sandlot competitions among the nation's own youth, top-flight homegrown baseball talent seems increasingly scarce. More than ever, the big leagues are today looking abroad for the steady influx of foreign-bred talent required to fill the hundreds of major and minor league slots. The emphasis is not now—nor has it ever really been—on fostering the health of the sport in foreign parts. It is instead on reaping an inexpensive harvest of talent needed on the home shores. International ballplayers no longer simply add spice and flavor in the big league marketplace; in sad reality, they are absolutely necessary just to sustain it.

THE FUTURE: INTERNATIONAL BASEBALL IN THE 21ST CENTURY

It is perhaps ironic that international baseball seems to hold the keys to any deeply-desired salvation of the more aesthetic and commercial-free game of American baseball as we once knew it. Any such salvation will not come in the expected form, not as steady streams of foreign prospects shoring up depleted major league rosters. Hope lies instead in the preservation of distant leagues in the Far East and Latin America and Europe (and even in Africa or Oceania) as independent entities that can focus exclusively on their own growth and health as vibrant national cultural institutions.

In short, baseball's salvation depends on the continued existence of alternative baseball worlds, beyond the reach of a single behemoth professional circuit known as Major League Baseball. Throughout its history the sport has provided entertainment in many guises for fans who are not merely consumers of big league product marketing or boosters of one of the two dozen or more major league ball clubs. This entertainment has come at many diverse levels of thrilling competition, ranging from loosely organized youth leagues, to spontaneous sandlot play, to semi-pro or recreational leagues and on to scholastic and collegiate leagues, with finally the professional circuits operating at various levels of playing skill and entertainment value. The game has been played religiously if not always artfully in numerous corners of the world, either as a deeply entrenched national institution (Japan, Cuba, or Mexico) or as a newly imported minor sport with potential for entertaining thousands (Croatia, Poland, or South Africa). In most corners of this wider baseball universe, there has never been any confusion between baseball as recreational sport and Major League Baseball as profitable commercial entertainment.

If world baseball still retains its isolated pockets of independence, it has not been for lack of effort—especially in recent times—on the part of the marketing branches of Major League Baseball's governing bodies. The big league game has a lengthy history of exploiting lesser leagues for its own commercial interests and thus of eventually killing off the very corners of the game most likely to contain the best seeds for big league baseball's own future survival. The recruiting and marketing practices of the North American big leagues have been especially hard on the survival of coexisting leagues in most of the world's other top baseball-playing nations. Once fertile grounds for developing or fine-tuning big league talents, Caribbean winter leagues today stand near to final collapse. In the light of increasing defections of top Japanese stars to high-paying big league clubs, the fate of pro baseball in Caribbean baseball capitals such as Venezuela, Puerto Rico, and the Dominican Republic should raise strong storm signals for the long-standing Japanese Leagues. Surviving Korean, Taiwanese, and Cuban leagues face similar threats, which seem to promise the unfortunate repetition of an all-too old and familiar story.

Symptomatic of the fate of struggling local leagues faced with runaway player defections to higher-paying circuits is the crisis in the Korean Baseball Organization arising in the mid-1990s. Attendance in Seoul and elsewhere around the decade-old Korean league began to slip significantly after 1994. The foremost factor was the departure that season of ace pitcher Chan-ho Park to the Los Angeles Dodgers; suddenly Korean fans were focused on the Dodgers and not their own Haitai Tigers or Lotte Giants. On the heels of Park's defection came the departure of another top pitching favorite, Dong-yol Sun, who opted for greener grass in the stadiums of Japan. Batting champion Jeong-bum Lee quickly followed the same route. Such departures hit especially hard in any nation where it is already a struggle to find sufficient talent to maintain a vibrant national pro game. In both Korea and Taiwan, admitting rented foreign players has been a compromise unpopular with both fans and owners but a necessary one, if professional baseball is to keep going at all on the home front.

More than half a century ago, big league baseball killed off the thriving institution of Negro professional leagues, which were once an important social and economic pillar of black communities throughout the United States. Admittedly, the Negro leagues grew out of one of the darkest pages of American sports history. No argument could be justified, now or ever, for sustaining a world of racially segregated baseball. From any perspective, the Rickey–Robinson story was one of the brightest pages of both big league history and the nation's larger social history. And yet the folding of the Negro leagues on the heels of racial integration throughout organized baseball came with a terrible price. Players too old or not dazzling enough to make the few available big league roster spots were left with careers abruptly truncated. Fans who had flocked to community parks in Birmingham, Memphis, Indianapolis, Newark, Kansas City, and the thriving black neighborhoods of Chicago, Washington, and Pittsburgh now had only Jackie Robinson, Larry Doby, and a few others of their race to cheer for in the distant majors.

A similar saga was played out decades later in leagues throughout the Caribbean region. Here the circumstances were admittedly somewhat different and the details somewhat more complex. But indiscriminate big league player raiding of the top local talent and insensitivity to economic needs of the local leagues was again a central contributing factor in the diminished appeal of winter baseball circuits. Astronomically higher player salaries in the 1980s and 1990s meant less motivation for big leaguers to play winter ball. Eventually, big league contracts even blocked native Latino stars from returning home for off-season games with special clauses designed to limit a star ballplayer's off-season activities and thus protect the ball club's top-dollar investments from potential career-threatening injuries. Big league games televised to numerous Caribbean markets further eroded the gate appeal of the local winter leagues, especially once top major league stars were no longer appearing in San Juan, Caracas, or Santo Domingo. The decision of MLB to establish its own wintertime development league in Arizona has further undercut the

Caribbean's once flourishing culture of winter baseball. Disgruntled with supposedly "deteriorating conditions" in the traditional Caribbean winter circuits, MLB launched the Arizona Fall League in 1992 as a six-team circuit operating in the Phoenix area. The venture was designed to develop some of the game's top prospects without exposing raw rookies to the supposed pitfalls of playing in a "foreign" environment. As early as its second season, the new circuit was featuring such future front-line stars as Mike Piazza (Dodgers), Ryan Klesko (Braves), and Mike Lieberthal (Phillies). With all thirty big league organizations sending top prospects to Phoenix rather than to Latin ports of call, it seems that Latin-based winter ball has been hovering on life-support for much of the past decade.

The rapid decline of winter circuits throughout the Caribbean Basin is not all the doing of Major League Baseball. Sagging economic conditions in the Dominican Republic and the resulting severe shortages in electricity, potable water, and public transportation have often sabotaged league schedules and fan morale. In Puerto Rico in the early 1990s, economic conditions resulted in the curtailing of league schedules from 60 to 48 games and led to the folding of one long-prominent franchise. Bayamón threw in the towel on the eve of the 1992–1993 season, and that same winter unprecedented rains played havoc with what remained of the shortened league schedule. Venezuela has fared only slightly better. In 1999, devastating floods ravaged that country and shut down winter baseball play for five days in mid-December; in that same winter, two minor league prospects were shot and killed in separate savage armed robbery incidents. Despite difficult conditions in the leagues themselves, it has been above all the lack of hot prospects and known veterans on Dominican, Puerto Rican, and Venezuelan club rosters that has largely killed off once-thriving ballpark attendance. This absence of drawing cards in the Caribbean ballparks has only served to strengthen the situation in which many older Dominican and Puerto Rican ball fans have been spoiled by satellite transmissions and dish antennas bringing them four or five summertime big league games daily, while younger fans have been driven from the ballparks by competing forms of entertainment such as music videos, television, discos, American cinema, and even action-packed computer games.

Long before the collapse of winter circuits, major league baseball executed a more direct attack on competing rival leagues in both Mexico and Cuba. The pre–Jackie Robinson major league color line long aided Caribbean leagues by driving top black stars to seek winter employment in integrated circuits to the south. During the mid-1940s, recognizing that egalitarian winter baseball was likely the best baseball played anywhere at the time, Mexican League mogul Jorge Pasquel launched the one and only retaliatory raid on record against big league rosters, offering lucrative contracts to white big leaguers as well as Negro stars in the hopes of competing on an equal footing with the majors.

The result was a short-lived war with Major League Baseball that had a greater impact on the Cuban League than it did on the big league teams themselves. The Mexican League challenge was rather quickly repulsed, and the careers of only a handful of big leaguers were affected. A dozen recognized major leaguers—Sal Maglie and Max Lanier foremost among them—were handed suspensions (eventually revoked) for jumping to Mexican rosters.

The summer Mexican League itself dwindled overnight to its present diminished status as a top minor league. For winter baseball in Cuba, the immediate impact was more drastic: two separate Cuban circuits operated in both 1946–1947 and 1947–1948, with both Cuban and American players banned for signing with Pasquel now taking part in a separate *Liga Nacional* operating out of Tropical Stadium in direct competition with normal Cuban League play at Cerro Stadium. It was the entrée into Cuban and Caribbean winter baseball that big league owners had long desired. Soon, MLB negotiated agreements with Caribbean winter leagues (including the Cuban League) that regulated and controlled player flow between the majors and all winter circuits, essentially turning the latter into player-development leagues under MLB supervision. Less than a decade and a half later, a Cuban revolution would make the victory a moot point (as far as the Cuban League was concerned). Elsewhere, however, the direction and scope of winter league baseball had been drastically altered forever.

Major league baseball's devastating effect on competing forms of the sport has not been restricted to international leagues. The mere suggestion of business competition has never been a dynamic that organized baseball has relished or even for long tolerated. Often the monopolistic practices of MLB have even been directed squarely at members of its own extended family—that is, at minor league baseball. The spread of televised baseball into all corners of urban and rural America in the 1950s and 1960s was at the time a severe death blow for once thriving lower-level minor leagues and semi-pro or industrial leagues from coast to coast. Hometown teams—once the very center of the baseball universe for a majority of rural fans of the Far West, Midwest, and Deep South—faded from the scene, and the minor leagues as a whole suffered a depression at midcentury that further worked to change the face of baseball as we had long known it. In 1946, more than 32 million fans attended live minor league baseball, a postwar jump from less than 10 million a year earlier; before the end of the decade, attendance figures had reached more than 40 million. During the television boom of the 1950s, however, more than 300 cities would lose their minor league clubs. Forty-three separate leagues operated in 1952; in 1956, 27 leagues; and by the end of the decade, there were only 21 operating minor league circuits. Some overly pessimistic prophets were foreseeing the final collapse of minor league baseball altogether.

Clichés about history's penchant for repetition are not to be lightly dismissed in this case. With MLB now milking talent from lesser pro leagues in Korea and Taiwan and also beginning to raid the rosters of its foremost rival in Japan, Cuba with its touted amateur league stands alone in still resisting major league baseball's deadly incursions. Cuba stands as a genuine island (metaphorically as well as geographically) housing an anachronistic baseball culture. The baseball played there is something to be dearly treasured for its continued isolation. Here is a league that turns its back on selling players to organized baseball and thus continues to operate outside the clutches of the monopolistic enterprise represented by Major League Baseball. Cuba alone has managed to remain truly an alternative baseball universe.

The Cuban League has survived for some forty years, but it cannot survive much longer. Politics and United States–Cuba relations will see to that. The

Cuban League today lives on borrowed time. Defections of top stars have not as such destroyed the league, as some had long prophesized, but Cuba as a country cannot remain isolated from U.S. policies and economic domination for much longer. When a political détente is eventually reached, there will be few if any impediments to the baseball rapprochement certain to follow. Traffic between MLB and the Cuban League will most likely mirror the course of baseball history in other Latin American hotbeds. And the Cuban baseball world will change rapidly, to the likely eventual dismay of those same Cuban fans who now naïvely dream of seeing their stars move to the big leagues. The price for watching a next-generation Omar Linares or Orestes Kindelán slugging homers on television from Yankee Stadium or Wrigley Field will be severe: it will mean the absence of a crack national squad to cheer for during World Cup or Olympic tournaments, and the disappearance of top-flight local league play in Havana, Camagüey, or Santiago—the disappearance of Cuban League teams stocked with the very best talent the island has to offer.

In other corners of the globe, the future of baseball is less obvious at the outset of the twenty-first century. The Korean and Chinese (Taiwanese) leagues have no deep underpinnings in historical traditions to ward off growing pains and temporary economic crises. Taiwan's two circuits—the Chinese Professional Baseball League and the Taiwan Major League—together survived a devastating 1996 game-fixing scandal and several years of acrimonious competition, all of which ended in temporary truce with a 2003 league merger. Taiwanese pro baseball still suffers from such severe player shortages that importing foreign talent is the only immediate solution. Korea faces its own difficulties, in the form of mandatory military service interrupting the careers of most top stars and in the continuing drain of limited talent through defections to the higher-level Japanese circuit. Australian baseball has already seemingly run up against a wall: first, the once-thriving Australian Baseball League collapsed in ruin in 1999 after only a ten-year run, then a replacement International Baseball League Australia (intended as a winter developmental league) survived but two seasons. The future of the sport in Europe may not be a bright one either, not if international tournaments become a showcase television event under MLB management. Inevitably, participation would be reduced to just those countries able to staff their national rosters with scores of current seasoned major leaguers and top minor leaguers.

Perhaps most threatening to international baseball as a viable alternative to the institution of big league baseball is precisely these recent designs of MLB's marketing arm on control of the premier international tournament competitions. Here again MLB's motive is, as always, a transparently economic one. Part of the master plan for internationalizing the major league game (i.e., marketing of big league games to "foreign" consumers) is a glamorous World Cup–style event staged for television audiences and paralleling the wildly popular spectacle enjoyed every four years by international professional soccer. Such a plan has many flaws, foremost among them the untested assumption that the international frenzy accompanying the proposed Baseball World Cup would approach or equal that generated by European-style *fútbol*. Soccer, unlike baseball, has deep-rooted traditions as a surrogate for nation-versus-nation warfare, and the sport is already deeply entrenched in most corners of the globe.

But even if MLB's plan for its own World Cup might be overly ambitious and based in false expectations, it may nonetheless offer a serious threat to a neophyte Olympic baseball movement directed by the 65-year-old IBAF (International Baseball Federation), a movement that has itself barely gotten off the ground.

The chapters that follow trace in both broad outline and sharp detail the collective history of international baseball. The focus is both on the unique stories of the game's evolution in the major baseball-playing countries (apart from the United States) and on the saga of global competition in the form of both major amateur contests and professional international tournaments. In the process of sketching the story of baseball outside of U.S. borders, we also will uncover some important explanations for the precarious relationship between international leagues and the organized Major League forces of U.S. professional baseball. It is here that we find today's greatest threats to the health and status of the game as a truly international sport.

Laid before us, then, is baseball's greatest remaining untold story. In that story lie clues to both the future salvation and potential ruin of one of the sports world's most popular and intriguing team games. National baseball leagues around the world face continued threats of plunder by a Major League Baseball operation whose short-sighted game plan rarely stretches beyond the promise of new television markets, or the vision of limitless founts of fresh professional talent. But it is equally true that these same leagues, in their struggles for independent survival, contain the seeds for salvation of the diverse baseball universe we once knew in epochs before economic globalization (in baseball as in realms of any other corporate entities) became an undeniable and inescapable reality.

NOTES

1. Once radio proved that hearing instead of seeing a game is not only practical but a unique pleasure, the broadcasts were feared as the ultimate threat to major league baseball's prosperity. Why pay at the gate when you can hear the game at home? Instead, radio broadcasts expanded the local fan base for big league games across entire geographic regions, without immediately biting into support for local amateur and semi-pro teams. Radio invites an imaginative participation, and it is open to sharing in community. Radios were affordable after World War II; televisions were still pricey and bound down to the living room. One could walk down a summer street during a pennant race and—with every back yard or front porch tuned in to the game—not miss a pitch. Radio's place in the baseball world was sidelined with the advent of television, however, so we will never know how the listening–attending balance would have evolved, locally or nationally.

2. The Negro Leagues Baseball Museum in Kansas City, MO, founded in the early 1990s, has done much to restore, document, and preserve that memory, as have many devotees, scholars, and veterans of the black-ball era (both within and without the auspices of the Negro League Baseball Players Association).

3. Language provides a glimpse into the dual heritage of international baseball: foreign born but locally bred. In Latin America, the obviously North American term *béisbol* coexists comfortably with the fully native Spanish *pelota*. The Japanese, long saddled with the Americanism *besuboru*, have gratefully fallen upon *yakyū* (field ball) as a more honorable term.

BIBLIOGRAPHY

Bjarkman, Peter C. *Baseball's Mysterious Island: A True History of Baseball in Fidel Castro's Cuba.* Jefferson, NC, and London: McFarland & Company Publishers, forthcoming.

González Echevarría, Roberto. *The Pride of Havana: A History of Cuban Baseball.* New York: Oxford University Press, 1999.

Joseph, Gilbert. "Documenting a Regional Pastime: Baseball in Yucatán." In *Windows on Latin America: Understanding Society Through Photographs*, 77–89. Miami, FL: The University of Miami Press, 1987.

Pérez, Louis A., Jr. "Baseball and Becoming." In *On Becoming Cuban: Identity, Nationality and Culture*, 255–278. Chapel Hill and London: University of North Carolina Press, 1999.

Ruck, Rob. "The Crisis in Winter Baseball—Can It Survive?" *Baseball America* 10 (February 25–March 9, 1990): 8–9.

Wertheim, Jon, and Don Yaeger. "Fantastic Voyage—Three fellow refugees say the tale of Yankees ace Orlando (El Duque) Hernández's escape from Cuba doesn't hold water." *Sports Illustrated* 89:22 (November 30, 1998): 60–63.

List of Abbreviations

· ·

1B	first base, first baseman
2B	doubles; second base, second baseman
3B	triples; third base, third baseman
AA	American Association*
AB	at-bats
aka	also known as
AL	American League
BA	batting average
C	catcher
CF	center field, center fielder
CG	complete games
CS	caught stealing
DH	designated hitter
ERA	earned run average
FL	Federal League*
G	games
H	hits
HR	home runs
IF	infield, infielder
IP	innings pitched
L	losses; lost
LF	left field, left fielder
LHP	left-handed pitcher
LP	losing pitcher
MVP	Most Valuable Player
NA	National Association*
NL	National League
OF	outfield, outfielder
P	pitcher
PCT	percentage
PH	pinch hitter

PL   Players League*
PR   pinch runner
R   runs
RBI   runs batted in
RF   right field, right fielder
RHP   right-handed pitcher
SB   stolen bases
SO   strikeouts
SS   shortstop
T   ties; tied
U   utility player
UA   Union Association*
W   wins; won
WP   winning pitcher

* U.S. major leagues, nineteenth or early twentieth century.

CHAPTER 1

Cuba

Béisbol Paradiso

· ·

> *I had heard that Cubans are a deeply religious people. In two days here,*
> *I have learned that baseball is their religion.*
> —Sam Lacy (Negro leagues sportswriter and activist, ca. 1930)

Mystery has always been the operative byword of Cuba's epic baseball history. The mid-nineteenth-century origins of the sport here in the garden spot of the Caribbean are shrouded in confusion and enmeshed in a tangled web of contradictory accounts. Even the most recent era of Cuban baseball—the decades that followed the island's 1959 communist revolution—presents an equally misty mix of wild speculation and disingenuous misinformation. To round out this regrettable tale of verifiable fact buried under myth and propaganda, Cuba's rich historical connections with the North American Negro leagues across the quarter century separating two world wars arguably constitute baseball's most tragically lost story.[1] And even with the brief period of exposure to North American eyes during the 1950s and 1960s, the handful of Cuban big league heroes fronted by Camilo Pascual, Orestes "Minnie" Miñoso, "Pistol Pete" Ramos, Tony (born Pedro) Oliva, Tony Taylor, and Atanasio "Tany" (Tony) Pérez were more often undervalued, mislabeled, and misunderstood than celebrated as genuine headliners of the American and Cuban joint national game.

Cuba nonetheless stood in the vanguard of baseball's earliest twentieth-century Caribbean explosion. From the time of the American Civil War, baseball was already being played on Cuban sandlots, and in the third quarter of the nineteenth century it was Cubans (not Americans) who were the most energetic disciples and apostles of the new sport, spreading it almost everywhere throughout the rest of the Caribbean Basin. A long-held myth that visiting U.S. Marines brought baseball to Cuba has happily been thoroughly dispelled by a spate of solid academic histories of Cuban baseball published in the past half-dozen years (especially González Echevarría's *The Pride of Havana* and Rucker and Bjarkman's *Smoke*). It was, in reality, native sons of the island who themselves planted the first seeds, though it is true enough that they had themselves learned the sport while sojourning on North American soil. The first emissaries of Cuban baseball were thus American-trained but Havana-born schoolboys who adopted the new diversion during extended excursions to the United States (usually for university or secondary education and usually to New York) and then brought both equipment and knowledge of playing rules (as well as a serious case of infectious "baseball enthusiasm") back to their island homeland with them. Some of these earliest baseball emissaries have been treated kindly by history; the names of others have been hopelessly lost in time.

Baseball thus appeared in Cuba as early as the end of the U.S. Civil War and was thriving there only a few years later. Bats, balls, leather gloves, and rules for playing the new North American pastime were first carried to Havana by a pair of brothers, Nemesio and Ernesto Guilló, along with an intimate friend, Enrique Porto, when the three teenagers returned from a half-decade of high schooling at Alabama's Spring Hill College in 1864. Within mere days they were organizing rudimentary contests among companions in and around their populous Vedado neighborhood in downtown Havana. Less than four years later, the Guilló brothers and these same companions, now thoroughly dedicated to the novel ballplaying passion, had formed the Havana Base Ball Club—the same outfit that would travel to Matanzas in December 1874 for a landmark "first game" of Cuba's recorded baseball history. That celebrated Matanzas game—so often taken by later historians as the precise moment of baseball's spontaneous birth in Cuba—had in reality only climaxed a full decade of exploding baseball interest throughout the city of Havana and also in neighboring villages.

It was the local Guilló brothers (the name is sometimes spelled Guillot) who had first launched that interest and then painstakingly nurtured it to its first full flowerings. Nemesio—at eleven the youngest of the trio of Havana teens shipped to Alabama in 1858—would fare best in later historical accounts, often being named as a founding father of the national sport while the equally involved Ernesto Guilló and Enrique Porto were all but forgotten. The reason in large part is a surviving interview with Nemesio, published decades later in the Havana popular press (*Diario de la Marina*, January 6, 1924). It is there that Nemesio Guilló recounts in detail the early organization of neighborhood play in Vedado in late 1864; the founding of the Habana Base Ball Club in 1868; the club's first excursion that same year to Matanzas, where they encountered a friendly pickup game against crewmen from an American schooner anchored for repairs; the eventual total ban on ballplaying by Spanish authorities a mere year later with the outbreak of the savage Ten Years' War; the game's rapid reestablishment after the war's ending in 1878; and the subsequent inaugural league tournament (birth of the Cuban League) that same winter, also involving the newly founded Almendares ball club and the already existing Matanzas nine.

Today Nemesio and Ernesto Guilló (along with other founders of the Habana Base Ball Club, including Leopoldo de Sola, Enrique Canal, Alfredo Maruri, Ricardo Mora, and Francisco and Rafael Saavedra) have faded to near obscurity. Together, their claim on the parentage of the popular Cuban national game is little recognized in the annals of Cuba's baseball origins. Such are often the accidents and injustices in the recorded history of sport and other events in popular culture.

Two other, more prominent names do, nonetheless, remain before us to vie for the mythical honor of Father of Cuban Baseball, each with some legitimate claim to the title. In both cases, the baseball-playing careers of each of these men again begin (as with Nemesio and Ernesto Guilló) during teenage school days spent on the road up north, in the baseball cradle of the United States.

Ésteban Enrique Bellán has long been celebrated as Latin America's first representative to organized baseball. Dark-skinned "Steve" Bellán was perhaps the most accomplished of the dozen or more original Cuban players who received both their schoolbook education and their ballplaying education deep in Yankee territory. Bellán, however, was destined to become the first Latin American big leaguer, signing on with the National Association's Troy Haymakers fresh off the campus of Fordham University in 1871 and later playing a handful of games with the New York Mutuals in the same pioneering league. His professional career was hardly distinguished: parts of three seasons, 59 games with 288 official at-bats, 68 hits, a lame dead-ball-era batting average of only .236. Of Bellán's off-field life, little is known beyond the fact that he was born in Havana sometime in 1850 and died there on August 8, 1932. Cuban *fanáticos* now lionize him for a much more significant pioneering role as chief organizer of the first formal game, between his own hastily assembled Havana club and a team from Matanzas, played late in the year of 1874. Bellán also earned additional distinction as the first-ever player to connect for three home runs in a single Cuban game when he accomplished this rare dead-ball feat in that very first one-sided contest (Havana was victorious by a score of 51–9) on December 27, 1874. As one set of historians (Michael and Mary Oleksak, *Béisbol*, p. 6) has put it, if Guilló introduced the sport to island culture, Bellán performed the marriage between baseball and the Cuban people.

Bellán's rival in the earliest years of Havana-area baseball was fellow Habanero Emilio Sabourín. Like Bellán, Sabourín contributed as a player, yet made his greater mark on sporting history as a league organizer and club manager during the pioneering years of Cuban organized baseball. It was Emilio Sabourín (Rob Ruck in *Total Baseball*, 6th ed., overenthusiastically brands him the A. G. Spalding of Cuban baseball) who contributed heavily to founding a *Liga de Béisbol Profesional Cubana* and the first league tournament of 1878, the original launching pad for eight decades of pre–Castro era Cuban professional baseball (see *Total Baseball*, 6th ed., p. 536). Sabourín also took the field for that first historic game at Matanzas in December 1874. This game was obviously not the first ever played in Cuba; its fame rests on the fact that it was the first reported in the Cuban press and thus the first for which any concrete records exist. From those records, we gather that Bellán performed as the Havana catcher, hitting his 3 homers and scoring 7 runs for the winners. Sabourín played in the Havana infield and himself scored eight runs. Emilio Sabourín would then also go on to manage, once professional play began in Cuba a mere four years later. Again like Bellán (who managed or captained the Havana club to championships during the first three seasons of league tournament play—1879, 1880, 1883), Sabourín also claimed three titles as the bench leader for the same Havana ball club (in 1889, 1890, 1892).

Bellán's ballplaying and managerial rival was apparently a colorful character whose life away from the baseball diamond was immersed deeply in Cuban politics and in the ongoing independence struggle against Spain. A ten-year war for independence waged against the Spanish colonial government brought continuing chaos to the Cuban island between 1868 and 1878, which ceased only temporarily in the very winter when Emilio Sabourín, Ésteban Bellán, and others launched their first professional league tournament. Evidence that baseball and politics were already as inseparable in Cuba in the late nineteenth century as they have remained in the late twentieth century is found in the fact that revenues from this tourney were apparently funneled into the hands of those carrying on guerrilla rebellions against the hated Spanish overlords.

Eventually this mixture of baseball with anti-Spanish politics led to Sabourín's arrest in 1895 and a life sentence to a Moroccan prison, where the erstwhile baseball manager died of pneumonia and malnutrition only two years later. Sabourín's contributing baseball revenues to the anti-Spanish independence movement of José Martí not only cost the ballplaying patriot his own personal freedom but also resulted in a short-lived Spanish ban on the game throughout the island colony. Across their three final decades (1870s through 1890s) of control in Cuba, Spanish colonial authorities had always deeply distrusted rebellious Cuban students and likely assumed that the bats and balls used in the popular pastime of *pelota americana* were merely cleverly disguised implements of rebel warfare. Prison eliminated Sabourín himself, but the new sporting passion of the masses in the end proved far more difficult to eradicate.

Sabourín's claim on the parentage of Cuban baseball was destined to rest heavily upon his adjunct status as revolutionary hero—both at the dawn of the past century and especially again during the fervent patriotic times that would follow Fidel Castro's ascension to power a half-century later. Although a prominent player and manager in his own country, Sabourín had never played in any professional or amateur league in the United States and was thus more clearly a popularizer than an importer of the soon-beloved North American pastime. Sabourín's position as baseball founder in Havana is hardly as tenuous as that of Abner Doubleday in Cooperstown; nonetheless, it is a far stretch to see Bellán as the Cuban version of Alexander Cartwright or Sabourín as either the Cuban Henry Chadwick or (following Rob Ruck) an island resurrection of Albert Spalding. Both men indeed played significant roles in stabilizing and popularizing early Cuban professional baseball, yet neither could claim to have single-handedly launched the sport nor to have alone lifted it to prominence as the corner piece of a Cuban national identity.

There is, of course, one count on which Steve Bellán's fame is almost certain to outlast Sabourín's, even within Cuba itself. This is the mere fact that Bellán remains the first link between Cuba and the major leagues to the north—the one link that would etch Cuban ballplayers into the general North American consciousness. Great ballplaying feats back on the island would rarely reach North American eyes or ears. Black Cubans traveling northward were never more widely known to white stateside fans than were the hidden Negro leaguers of native U.S. origins. Few American fans ever heard of Martín Dihigo, easily Cuba's greatest diamond idol, and they knew nothing at all of Cristóbal

Torriente, the unparalleled black slugger whom touring big leaguers glimpsed in Havana and compared immediately to Babe Ruth, nor of the great fast-balling pitcher José Méndez, whom John McGraw considered a fair rival to his own crack ace Christy Mathewson. It was instead journeymen big leaguers such as Adolfo Luque, Mike González, and Armando Marsans who for more than half a century built all the exotic reigning stereotypes attached to Cuban ballplayers. Cubans were visible to Americans through the big leagues and not the winter leagues, and it was there that Steve Bellán most significantly blazed his own personal trails.

What must not be overlooked in any survey of baseball's early history on the Cuban island is the extreme degree to which the new sport was tied from the first to notions of nationhood and a distinctive Cuban (and, hence, anti-Spanish) identity. Adoption of the civilized North American game (and the simultaneous rejection of the barbaric Spanish sport of bull fighting) certainly had to do with far more than the manifold pleasures of invigorating recreation and exciting spectator entertainment. Baseball represented in the view of Cuban patriots all that was anti-Spanish and thus also all

José Méndez flashed meteor–like as Cuba's incomparable "Black Diamond." [Author's Cuban Collection]

that was natively Cuban in flavor. Many early league ballplayers were also rebel guerrillas active in the ongoing independence struggle for freedom from Spanish colonial control. Several gave their lives to the cause of the rebellion (including not only Emilio Sabourín but also champion pitcher José Pastoriza and early slugging star Ricardo Cabaleiro, both eventual Cuban Hall of Famers). Baseball matches were used to raise funds for the rebel cause, and such revenues were diverted to clothing, feeding, and arming rebel guerrilla bands. From the earliest years of Cuban championship play, the nation found its collective assessment of self-worth to be tied intimately to on-field baseball victories. The building of national pride on the battlefield that was the baseball diamond thus enjoys a rich history for Cubans that stretches back three-quarters of a century before the socialist revolution launched by Fidel Castro in the 1950s and 1960s. Baseball and the idea of a proud Cuban nation have indeed been intimately linked from the outset of Cuban national history in the 1870s and 1880s; the island's professional league and its status as sovereign nation were born hand in hand during the same decade. No other national institution so clearly reflects what most Cubans have long held sacred as constituting the very essence of what it means to be distinctly Cuban.

BÉISBOL PARADISO AND CUBA'S WINTER LEAGUE HERITAGE

Cuba's baseball saga falls neatly into three distinctive chapters and each is taken in some quarters (but not necessarily others) as being the lead story of the nation's ballplaying heritage. First and foremost—if only in chronology—is the seventy-five-year evolution of Cuba's celebrated professional league, which emerged somewhat tentatively in the final decades of the nineteenth century and was tied from the first to a unique brand of racially integrated winter ball that thrived throughout the long decades before organized baseball's sadly overdue admission of black athletes at the close of World War II. Often shifting its size and playing format across the years, the Cuban League was subject to many economic and aesthetic peaks and valleys, with numerous episodes of horrendous management and near collapse. It remained based almost exclusively in the capital city of Havana and reached a popular apex in the decade and a half separating World War II from the nation-changing 1959 communist revolution.

A second lesser-known chapter involves a thriving amateur tradition that grew up alongside Havana's pro league and that, for much of the first half of the twentieth century, actually outstripped the pro game in island-wide popularity and fan stature. Long before the arrival of Fidel Castro's social revolution, the Cuban amateur leagues and their star players (like Conrado Marrero, Natilla Jiménez, Quilla Valdés, Juan Ealo, and Julio Moreno) were already sustaining national triumphs with the first round of world championship tournaments launched in Havana in 1939 and soon hosted in other countries around the Caribbean throughout the 1940s and 1950s.

Chapter three of the Cuban baseball saga is the one now most heralded on the island itself and yet least known elsewhere. This is the tale of the drama-rich amateur Cuban League established by the Castro government in the early 1960s and still going strong four decades later (despite much-celebrated recent defections to professional organized baseball of a trickle of top star players, including ace pitchers Rolando Arrojo, José Contreras, and Orlando Hernández).

Throughout Cuba's isolation following the 1959 revolution, much of what has been written about Cuban baseball here in the United States has focused on nostalgia surrounding the final waves of Cuban big leaguers before the doors were slammed on baseball commerce with the post-1960 socialist-controlled island. Miami-based Cuban exiles long resident in the United States and poorly informed about many island realities of the past forty years fondly recall the glories of the long-absent Cuban pro circuit, but they do so through the cloudy perspective of a rosy nostalgia that exaggerates bygone glories and obliterates mid-century Cuban baseball's many warts. To read some recent commentators (Ángel Torres, especially), one has the impression that the glory years of Cuban baseball are limited to the four-team Havana circuit of the 1930s, 1940s, and 1950s, and it is often maintained that after pro ball was banned in Cuba the island's baseball culture virtually withered and died. This gross oversimplification is unfortunately largely a propaganda-driven distortion. Long before Castro, the Cuban pro circuit was often a shambles; many seasons were canceled due to financial crisis or lack of fan interest, and those that were played often drew scant attention from fans located outside the capital city. The island's biggest ballplaying heroes were often amateur stars who shunned the professional game as unrewarding and shamefully managed. Top amateur clubs (including semi-pro sugar mill teams, which quietly recruited visiting North American Negro leaguers) often easily beat the best Cuban League entries or pro all-star squads during popular exhibition games.

Once the Castro government formally banned an already sagging professional circuit (where attendance had steadily waned through the 1950s), the new nonprofessional chapter in the Cuban baseball saga would be anything but a total collapse of the Cuban national pastime. Cuba's baseball history following 1961 (the year the pro league was shut down) boasts all the glories and excitement normally attached to the top years of the earlier pro circuit. The contemporary Cuban League has the further bragging point that it represents the only truly island-wide national baseball of the country's century-plus sporting history—and it is this Cuban League of the past four decades which has also produced a new-generation of stars that have provided Cuba's grandest moments on the international baseball scene.

In the baseball heyday of the 1930s and 1940s, by almost any standard it was already the amateur game and not the celebrated professional version that represented the highest level of competition being staged anywhere on the island. Some of the best Cubans (bulldog pitcher Conrado Marrero and flashy shortstop Antonio "Quilla" Valdés, to cite but two outstanding cases) rejected pro contracts, in part because the pay wasn't good enough to be much of an enticement (far less rewarding than the cushy off-field jobs typically provided by social club or company-sponsored teams) but also because the pro circuit was widely seen as a cheap promotion-oriented spectacle run and staffed by Cubans (often black Cubans) of lesser social rank. There was also little perceived difference in level of talent: Cuban amateur and semi-pro ball clubs usually held their own and often even whipped clubs comprised of touring big leaguers or imported Negro leaguers, as well as all-star contingents of Cuban Leaguers.

Cuba's pro league is thus often exaggerated in stature when it comes to the chronicle of Cuba's national game, but it is nonetheless an important element of the island baseball story and a necessary opening chapter as seen from the historian's natural chronological orientation. The Havana pro league may not be the end-all or be-all of Cuba's national pastime, but it was certainly a vital starting point. Professional play on the island—as here in the United States—grew rapidly out of the sport's nineteenth-century roots among amateur social clubs (representing gentlemen of considerable social standing), which had taken up ballplaying at first for purely recreational and social ends.

The earliest seasons were not true seasons at all but rather brief championship tournaments lasting only a dozen or so games or sometimes even less, with play restricted to Sundays only and as few as two or three squads participating. This explains the unusual appearance of nineteen-century Cuban League stats, where so-called seasons may consist of as little as five or seven games for each club and champion batters often boast astronomical averages of .400 and higher. Today these early round-robins are lumped together with the full winter-long campaigns (which developed only in the early twentieth century, after hired professionals had come to rule the game).

The advent of playing for money after 1900 brought with it the popular spectator version of baseball; it also brought athletes of lower social rank, and these mercenary players were frequently from a poorer social class that usually included Cuban blacks. By the first decade of the twentieth century, the Cuban winter league was thoroughly integrated and also began to draw upon black stars imported from up north. At the same time, the Cuban amateur leagues and teams (often the island's most popular stars and teams) remained exclusively white: the elite social clubs that sponsored amateur clubs didn't allow nonwhites membership on their teams or participation in any club social events.

By the early twentieth century, then, Cuba had emerged as the cradle of winter baseball. This status was fostered by visits to the island by top American pro and amateur squads, including both big league clubs and crack Negro league nines. The surprising success of Cuban teams against these American invaders both elevated Cuban national pride and shored up the Cuban circuit's growing reputation. Landmark moments included the triumphs of black Cuban pitchers José Méndez (whose 8 wins against barnstorming big leaguers in 1908 to 1911 included a one-hitter versus National League Cincinnati) and Eustaquio Pedroso (author of a 1909 eleven-inning no-hitter versus American League Detroit) against overconfident big league nines. Cuba was soon a strong magnet for both black and white North American stars, who could supplement off-season incomes while performing against the very best competition offered, regardless of race.

The Cuban circuit quickly acquired a reputation for hosting the highest levels of interracial diamond competitions. This was all played out against a constant backdrop of often disorganized or shortened Cuban League seasons, which through the 1910s, 1920s, and 1930s suffered year in and year out from either political unrest in Havana or abominable management from moguls and promoters controlling Cuban League ball clubs.

The opening half-century of Cuban professional play (1880s–1930s) was especially noted for its remarkable pitching legends. First there was Adolfo Luján, who led the Cuban pro circuit in pitching victories for the first three seasons that such records were kept (1887–1889), and also Dominican import Enrique Hernández (known in his homeland as "Indio Bravo"), who possessed an unhittable curveball and soon shared domination of the hill with José Pastoriza (himself twice league leader in victories and three times in complete games during the 1890s). Next, at the turn of the century, came Carlos "Bebé" Royer, ace of the Habana club, who went 12–3 in 1901, 17–0 in 1902, and 13–3 in 1904. Royer was the Cuban League's first-ever 20-game winner in 1903 (21–12), and his single-season victory mark was not matched until Raymond Brown (an American Negro leaguer) also compiled 21 victories in 1937. Once Cuba's professional league finally closed its doors in the shadow of Castro's revolution it would still be Royer, remarkably, who held the records for consecutive wins in a season (17), consecutive victories over two campaigns (20 during 1902 and 1903), consecutive complete games (69, between 1901 and 1904), and consecutive complete games in a season (33 in 1903). This was, of course, still the epoch in which games were played once or twice weekly and a single star hurler took the ball for all of his team's scheduled games.

It was the unwarranted fate of these marvelous early Cuban pitchers to labor in almost complete island obscurity, however. José de la Caridad Méndez changed all that, if briefly, with his memorable performances against touring big leaguers, especially his first two startling shutouts against the visiting Cincinnati Reds during the 1908 Havana winter season. Méndez, known to history as "El Diamante Negro" ("The Black Diamond"), proved himself no mere flash in the pan as he continued his domination of Cuban League play with a record five seasons (between 1908 and 1914) as the circuit's biggest winner. An even more substantial boost in the stock of Cuban pitching talent came in the 1920s with the presence of light-skinned right-hander Adolfo "Dolf" Luque, who achieved a starring role in the North American big leagues (winning 27 games for Cincinnati in 1923) as well as posting stellar performances over almost three decades of Cuban winter play (leading the circuit four times in victories between 1916 and 1929). Other stars, if less legendary in status, included José Acosta (who tied Mendez's record as five-time champion pitcher between 1915 and 1925) and Oscar Tuero, owner of three solid post–World War I seasons with the National League St. Louis Cardinals. Of the few Cubans who made a small mark on the big leagues in the years before integration,[2] nearly all—with the single exception of catcher Miguel Ángel (Mike) González—earned their livelihood as rubber-armed pitchers.

The 1940s would also boast substantial diamond stars, again led primarily by the pitchers. Foremost were Ramón Bragaña—a headliner primarily in the black-ball leagues of North America—and diminutive left-hander Agapito Mayor. While Mayor would pace the Cuban circuit several times in victories during the World War II era, his indelible legend would—like Bragaña's—be earned outside Cuba. Mayor brought the island one of its greatest triumphs on the international scene with his 1949 stellar performance in the week-long inaugural Caribbean World Series (CWS), the first formal showdown between Caribbean winter league champions (Cuba, Venezuela, Panama, Puerto Rico). Mayor's gutsy performance of three victories in a single Caribbean series (one in a starting role and two via relief) has never again been equaled in forty-three subsequent seasons of annual CWS contests. Bragaña, by contrast, garnered much of his own fame in Mexico, setting a long string of Mexican Summer League hurling records between 1938 and the mid-1950s. Of "The Professor's" Mexican marks, none were more noteworthy than his 211 career victories, 222 complete games tossed, and 3,375 total innings pitched. Ramón Bragaña would also register a dozen winning seasons in Mexico and post a 2.58 ERA during the 1940 season.

Of all Cuba's diamond legends, however, none was more lofty, either at home or abroad, than that of Cuba's greatest all-around ballplayer of any era—the incomparable immortal ("El Inmortal") Martín Dihigo. Dihigo was one of the most versatile of Negro league stars and arguably the most complete all-around ballplayer ever to lace up spikes. Arriving on both the Cuban League and Negro league scenes in the early 1920s, the towering Negro athlete earned his grandest reputation in the middle and late 1930s. His special claims to fame are unparalleled performances on several occasions both in Cuba and Mexico as the league's top batter and hurler in one and the same season. His double feat in Mexico in 1938 (with a .387 batting average alongside an 18–2 pitching mark and 0.90 ERA) represents one of the greatest single-year performances anywhere on record. Dihigo was perhaps best as a pitcher, standing 109–59 across 20 seasons in the Cuban League and recording a lifetime 256–136 win–loss ledger outside his homeland. He was also a remarkable infielder and outfielder: an all-time black-ball team selected in the 1980s by surviving Negro leaguers tabbed Dihigo as the second baseman, but he also received numerous votes for outfield and at third base. Though he never displayed the slugging prowess of his contemporary Cristóbal Torriente, Dihigo hit with considerable power as a long-ball threat. He was also a remarkable manager, even at the height of his playing career; he directed a championship 1936 Santa Clara club (the same year he won a batting title) that is considered one of the best in Cuban League annals. At career's end, he even earned plaudits as an umpire and then later turned his talents to broadcasting. There was nothing on or near a baseball diamond that "El Inmortal" didn't perform with unmatched skill and with incomparable grace.

Another past legend today recalled by devotees of the Negro league era is Luis "Lefty" Tiant, master of the tantalizing fadeaway or popularly named screwball pitch. Tiant's only flaw as a topflight moundsman seemed to be that he was black-skinned and thus not available for big league service. While he twirled magic in the North American Negro leagues (starring for Alex Pompez's New York Cuban Giants and Cuban Stars), Tiant was also a year-after-year stalwart of winter league baseball back on his native soil. Five times between 1931 and 1941, Tiant (father of the better-known 1970s-era major leaguer, Luis Jr.) paced the Cuban circuit in shutouts, reaching a high-water mark of 12 in 1936–1937. Tiant's shutout skein today still stands as a record never surpassed during the era of Cuban professional play. This diminutive lefty's screwball magic was as effective in now largely forgotten tropical winter league play as it was in the shadows of the recently rediscovered North American Negro leagues. Twice he performed in the prestigious East–West All-Star game, the second time after posting a perfect 10–0 mark while leading the New York Cubans to a 1947 Negro National League pennant.

Pitchers were usually the hallmark of Cuban baseball, but there was also a legacy of fence-busting hitters, lionized batsmen such as Regino García, Armando Marsans, Alejandro Oms, Cristóbal Torriente, Pelayo Chacón, and the ubiquitous Martín Dihigo. Among these, none (except perhaps Dihigo) was quite as successful for quite so long as the versatile Silvio García. From 1931 through 1954, García worked his magic in the Cuban League as a solid hitter, an infield defensive stalwart, and even as a front-line pitcher. He would at career's end hold the Cuban record for lifetime base hits (891) and along the way capture two batting titles spaced a decade apart, in 1942 and 1951. His reputation as an all-around performer who could shift positions almost as freely as Dihigo went beyond the mere numbers he eventually recorded while playing for all four major Cuban clubs (Habana, Marianao, Cienfuegos, and Almendares). Little wonder that, when Branch Rickey's postwar search for a black ballplayer to integrate the majors turned to the untapped talent in Cuba, Silvio García (even though well past his prime at the end of World War II) was first among those recommended to The Mahatma by a host of veteran Cuban baseball watchers.

The legacy of pre-Castro Cuban baseball was thus indeed a rich one—perhaps the richest in all of Latin America—and the brightest stars from the 75 years separating Bellán from Castro fittingly found their way into the original Cuban Baseball Hall of Fame that was first established in Havana in 1936, the same year as the launching of major league baseball's more famous parallel shrine in Cooperstown. This original Cuban Hall of Fame is not to be confused with a much later copycat version established in 1962 by exiled Cuban players living in Miami, which began inducting waves of 1950s-era and postrevolution big leaguers at its annual banquets throughout the 1970s and 1980s. It is fitting testimony to the lengthy history of Cuban baseball that the genuine island-based Cuban Hall of Fame would initiate its first class of ten inductees in 1939 (see table at chapter's end), only three years after its Cooperstown counterpart elected its own inaugural quintet of Ty Cobb, Babe Ruth, Honus Wagner, Christy Mathewson, and Walter Johnson.

Notables enshrined in Havana include a veritable Who's Who of Cuban winter league stars, as well as three Cuban-born U.S. big leaguers (Rafael Almeida, Armando Marsans, and Jack Calvo) who equally distinguished themselves with solid spells of pre-1920 Cuban League play. The first class of inductees once held nearly the same stature on the island as the first Cooperstown class here in the United States; unfortunately, the decades-long official obliteration of Cuba's professional baseball tradition that followed the 1959 revolution has now rendered these earliest legends largely forgotten figures among all but the oldest fans back home in Cuba.

Among the initial group of stars inducted in Havana in 1939 were Negro league immortals Torriente and Méndez, big league Latin pioneers Almeida and Marsans, and a host of top performers from the earliest decades of Cuban League championship seasons. These include Luis Bustamante (judged by John McGraw as the greatest black shortstop before 1910), Antonio María García (four times a champion batter in the late nineteenth century), "Strike" González (the first great Cuban catcher, and battery mate of Méndez), Adolfo Luján (the top pitcher of the first several Cuban winter championships), and Carlos "Bebe" Royer (the Habana ace who won 17 games without tasting defeat in 1902). Notable by his absence until the time of his death in the late 1950s was the legendary ragtime-era Reds and Giants ace Adolfo Luque, perhaps because his performance at home in Cuba (he won but one pitching title, in 1928–1929) never quite matched the glories of his North American big league career.

In addition to enshrinement in Havana, several top Cuban stars also rest in the Mexican Baseball Hall of Fame (table at chapter's end), a fitting honor for their outstanding play in the Mexican League of the late 1930s and early 1940s. The unsurpassed Dihigo served nine seasons in Mexico (the first in 1937 and the last in 1947) and hurled the first-ever no-hitter (1937) witnessed on Mexican soil. Playing for five different Mexican League teams (Veracruz, Aguila, Mexico City, Torreón, and Nuevo Laredo), Dihigo distinguished himself as a hitter with the first six-for-six single-game batting performance and also set career pitching records for winning percentage (119–57, .676) and ERA (2.81) while recording a lifetime .317 batting average. Roberto Ortiz was a powerful slugging outfielder in the 1940s and 1950s, playing in Mexico City, Nuevo Laredo, and Yucatán. Ortiz authored a 35-game hitting streak in 1948 and was first to lead the Mexican circuit in homers four straight seasons. Ramón Bragaña won 30 games for Veracruz in 1944 and in the process became the only league pitcher ever to surpass the 30-victory mark. As a fleet-footed outfielder throughout the 1940s, Agustín "Pijini" Bejerano still reigns as the all-time Mexican stolen-base champion, with 313 total steals and an unsurpassed four-consecutive league base-stealing titles. The final notable Cuban immortal enshrined in Mexico was Lázaro Salazar, who established a superior pitching ledger

(113–77) and a .333 career batting average and yet eventually earned his greatest plaudits as the winningest Mexican League manager of all time. Salazar (a headliner as both pitcher and outfielder back home in Cuba) was the first to pilot three different teams (Veracruz, Córdoba, and Monterrey) to seven championships during a Mexican League managerial career.

In strictly baseball terms, Cuba first rocketed into North American consciousness at the time of the earliest off-season barnstorming tours of the island by big league teams. The earliest visit was that of the Cincinnati Reds in the fall of 1908, the big leaguers arriving along with the independent Brooklyn Royal Giants of the Negro circuit for a round-robin series with Almendares (its own roster staffed by American Negro leaguers) and Habana from the Cuban League. Although the first notable ballplaying junkets by big leaguers encountered considerable embarrassment at the hands of Cuban phenoms José Méndez and Eustaquio Pedroso during the winter seasons of 1908 and 1909, other such tours were soon to follow and each would create legends of its own. The Detroiters returned in 1910 with Ty Cobb and Sam Crawford in the lineup (both had missed the Tigers' 1909 visit) and fared somewhat better, winning seven of their dozen outings. The Phillies and Giants were visitors a year later and Christy Mathewson bested Méndez 4–0 in a brilliant head-to-head showdown. With each new vacation season tour to the "Gem of the Caribbean," it seems that an eloquent John McGraw or Frankie Frisch or some other big league manager would return home with glowing praise on his lips and lust in his heart for the talented black Cuban baseballers—players he might wish ever so much to see in his own lineup but could never hope to sign in a epoch still cursed by a so-called gentleman's agreement to shun ballplayers of color.

Decades later, Cuba would receive further headline-grabbing attention as spring training headquarters for the 1947 Brooklyn Dodgers, then featuring a sensational rookie named Jackie Robinson. It was ironic, indeed, that while Cuban stars perhaps suffered more than any single group under the exclusionary "gentleman's agreement" during the century's first half (for no where were there more talented black players obviously capable of immediate stardom on the big time circuit), it would be Cuba that would eventually offer the ideal stage for a prologue and opening act in Branch Rickey and Jackie Robinson's bold integration drama unfolding during the 1946 and 1947 seasons. Robinson had been first sheltered in Montreal during the 1946 minor league campaign, as French-speaking Canada seemingly provided a largely color-blind venue likely to accept the pioneering Negro star on the basis of ballplaying talent alone. If Montreal was largely free from the bigotry of most American big league cities, Havana was an even more ideal location for Robinson's final spring tune-up on the eve of his precedent-shattering 1947 campaign in Brooklyn.

Cuba had long been a winter diamond paradise. Throughout the entire first half of the century, this remarkable island retreat had showcased black and white ballplayers who mixed comfortably on the same field of play. And Cuba also meant a distant escape from the New York media glare, which would have been altogether unavoidable back in the United States, in the more normal spring training venues found anywhere in the Florida tropics or the deserts of Arizona.

In the decade following the Second World War, North American baseball would become a more regular visitor to Cuba, a country now restless under strong-arm military leader Fulgencio Batista. Cuba would at last offer something more to organized baseball than mere spring training tune-up sites or the occasional barnstorming tour by big league all-star outfits. In 1946, the North American minor leagues also arrived on the scene when the Havana Cubans franchise was placed in Havana's Gran Stadium as an operating member of the Class C (later Class B) Florida International League.

The new minor league operation had been founded by Papa Joe Cambria, a colorful island legend who had been working the Cuban trails as scout for the Washington Senators through the war years. Playing its first season in La Tropical Stadium, the ball club was sold after its maiden campaign to Cuban League promoter Bobby Maduro, who moved it to the new and larger Gran Stadium for the 1947 summer season. Featuring former amateur league star pitchers Conrado Marrero, Sandy Consuegra, and Julio "Jiqui" Moreno, the Havana Cubans were an immediate hit with Havana fans and also a runaway on-field success. The team captured several league pennants (four in a row, 1946 to 1950) and would survive eight campaigns before giving way

Cuba's Tomás de la Cruz crossed the National League color line three years before Jackie Robinson. [Author's Cuban Collection]

in 1954 to a new manifestation as Maduro upgraded his franchise to the Class AAA International League, the top echelon of minor league baseball. Called the Cuban Sugar Kings and again staffed with numerous homegrown talents, the new club would be affiliated with the National League Cincinnati Reds, long a fan favorite in Havana, ever since Dolf Luque had starred there in the 1920s. In a half-dozen seasons in the International League, the Sugar Kings would register only two regular-season finishes as high as third place (1955 and 1959), but the club would produce a steady stream of future big leaguers that included Rafael "Ray" Noble, Julio Becquer, Julio Moreno, Conrado "Connie" Marrero, Saul Rogovin, Pat Scantlebury, Raúl Sánchez, Clint Hartung, Sandalio "Sandy" Consuegra, Elio Chacón, Luis Arroyo, Carlos Paula, Cookie Rojas, Jim Pendleton, and Mike Cuéllar.

In all, it's a proud final chapter of the Cuban pro baseball saga that attaches to the minor league Havana Sugar Kings (1954–1960) and International League play during the years immediately preceding the rise to power of Fidel Castro's socialist revolution. Havana businessman Bobby Maduro (later special assistant to big league Commissioner Bowie Kuhn and also inspiration for a stadium bearing his name that housed minor league ball in Miami between the 1960s and 1990s) maintained ownership of the prosperous franchise and also sustained the dream that this entry into organized baseball would be but a first step toward eventually landing a major league team for baseball-crazy Havana. Unfortunately, however, the most famous incident surrounding the short-lived Havana International League ball club is itself now forever linked with the emerging Castro revolution, which soon put a sudden end to any further Cuban schemes or aspirations regarding organized baseball.

Fidel Castro took special pride in the presence of the Havana Sugar Kings in International League play. Always a rabid fan of the game (which he himself played as a schoolboy, though he was never a serious pro prospect, as press accounts often touted), the new Cuban president saw professional baseball on the island as an important source of both public morale at home and public relations abroad. But the political realities of the revolution he had created would stack the cards squarely against President Castro's hopes for maintaining a minor league or perhaps even major league presence in his Caribbean capital of Havana.

Castro nonetheless became a regular spectator at Sugar Kings games in the months following his sudden rise to power. He would often seemingly use the public arena of the ballpark as something of his own personal promotional stage. Such was the case when the former amateur schoolboy pitcher turned political leader took to the mound at Estadio Latinoamericano on July 24, 1959, for an exhibition contest staged to show off his reported considerable pitching talents. Fidel hurled two scoreless innings to lead his Cuban Army *Barbudos* (usually translated as "Bearded Ones"; in more modern parlance, "Men In Beards") to victory over a local Military Police ball club during preliminaries to an official International League match-up between the hometown Sugar Kings and visiting Rochester Red Wings. An action photo of the celebrity right-hander warming up—complete with sunglasses, the familiar beard, and a uniform emblazoned with the team name, "Barbudos"—was featured in the next day's edition of the Rochester (New York) *Democrat and Chronicle*. (This photo would take on a life of its own in subsequent years and has frequently been reprinted in stories repeating the stale and utterly false accounts of Fidel's pitching prowess, a talent that reputedly once attracted contract offers from a host of big league clubs.) The attached *Democrat and Chronicle* story reporting Fidel's brief mound appearance (with a bold headline reading "Castro Scores Smash Hit as Baseball Player") was carried in a prominent center-page position above the much smaller game report of that night's afterthought Red Wings–Sugar Kings league contest.

It was to be a final hurrah before disaster ironically undercut President Castro's innocent baseball fantasy a mere twenty-five hours later. Shortly after midnight on the evening of July 25–26, 1959, gunfire (reportedly the aimless discharge of rifles outside the stadium from a band of loyalists celebrating revolutionary fervor on the anniversary of Castro's aborted 1953 attack on a Santiago military installation) disrupted play as stray pellets fell in the infield and struck both Red Wings third base coach Frank Verdi (nicking his batting helmet) and Sugar Kings shortstop Leo Cárdenas (tearing his uniform sleeve). The night's play was immediately suspended with the game tied at 4–4 in the twelfth frame, and the badly shaken Rochester ball club hastily took the next day's first available flight out of the country. Havana's own team was subsequently forced by league officials to play out much of the remainder of its league schedule on the road, an inconvenience that failed to block the surprising Cuban team from claiming the International League pennant at the end of the summer with a postseason upset of major proportions. Finishing in third place at summer's end, the Cubans rallied to knock off first Columbus and later Richmond in tense playoff action, the final pennant-clincher coming at home before an enthusiastic throng in Havana's Gran Stadium.

Although play had returned to Havana long enough for the fall's "Little World Series" action in which Cuba's Sugar Kings (the surprise International League playoff winners) defeated the American Association champion Minneapolis Millers, the days of professional baseball in Cuba were now indeed severely numbered. The following season, on July 8, the International League board of governors (operating under unspecified political pressures from Washington officials seeking any available avenue to embarrass Fidel Castro) voted to immediately relocate the Cuban Sugar Kings franchise to Jersey City, New Jersey. With the team marooned on the road in Miami at the time of the fateful announcement, several team members (including manager Tony Castaño) opted to resign and return home while still others (Raúl Sánchez and Orlando Peña topped the list) remained abroad to pursue promising pro careers. With the overnight departure of Havana's showcase minor league franchise, a final curtain was rung down on nearly three quarters of a century of unparalleled Cuban baseball glory.

The showcase (even the central theme) of Cuban professional baseball would always remain the celebrated rivalry between the island's two most popular and legendary clubs—the blue-clad Scorpions (*Alacranes*) of Almendares and the red-clad Lions (*Leones*) of Habana (spelled throughout this chapter with "b" as it is spelled in Spanish, to distinguish the team name from the city).

President Fidel Castro's 1959 "Barbudos" pitching exhibition staged in Havana. [Author's Cuban Collection]

The rivalry began with the inaugural seasons of league tournament play in the late 1870s and early 1880s; it was already well established before the end of the nineteenth century, with the city's loyalties split down the middle and even families divided over their fanaticism for the Blues or the Reds. Between them the two teams would win most of the championship banners (53 out of a total of 73 contested) over the three-quarters of a century of competition. When the league folded operations in 1961, Habana had a slight edge, with 29 championships to 24 for Almendares, but this advantage was due in large part to the fact that the Reds triumphed nine times in the early short-duration tournament between 1879 and 1893 before the Blues garnered their first league trophy in 1894. Overall franchise win–loss records would in the end be nearly identical: Habana after the final 1961 season stood at 1608–1346 (.544 winning percentage) and Almendares at 1568–1308 (.545, over four fewer seasons).

These were the teams that enthralled almost all the rooters of Havana, still dividing even families in their passionate baseball loyalties. Among the Cubans who followed the national game as if it were a religion (and there were few who did not), each took an identity as clearly a *Habanista* or an *Almendarista*. There was no middle ground. The rivalry would perhaps peak in the 1940s and 1950s, especially between 1947 and 1955, when the annual slugfest fell five times to the Scorpions and on four occasions to the Lions. The 1947 season was especially dramatic, with Almendares capturing one of the most intense races in league history with a sizzling streak of 13 wins in the season's final 14 outings, overcoming an earlier Habana lead of six and a half games. Victory was ultimately seized by the Alacranes with two dramatic final weekend victories over the rival Lions on the strength of consecutive brilliant pitching performances by Agapito Mayor and American Max Lanier, a pair of stellar southpaws.

In the end, the intense Habana–Almendares rivalry was also the Cuban League's worst vulnerability. League promoters and moguls always felt the lack of a third and fourth strong team to spice competition and draw additional fan loyalties. In years when neither showcase team was strong and either Cienfuegos or Marianao or Santa Clara or another of the league's constantly shifting supporting cast rose to the fore, the result always seemed to be a precipitous drop in fan enthusiasm and gate support. When neither team played, Almendares Park, La Tropical, or (after 1946) Gran Stadium was often largely empty. Failure to find a viable third or fourth rival to arouse fan passions thus caused most of the circuit's economic problems across the years. But it was a glorious tradition as long as it lasted, and forty years after its final hurrah the two current Cuban League teams based in Havana (Industriales and Metropolitanos) still proudly sport blue and red jerseys in a not-so-subtle effort to appeal to fan loyalties that still stretch across the generations.

GLORIES OF POSTREVOLUTION CUBAN BASEBALL

Baseball did not dry up in Cuba after the doors to the island were closed tight on either side by Castro and by his Washington rivals. It might better be said that the sport underwent a strange and (for the outside world) largely silent rebirth in the form of an unprecedented level of amateur league play. On the international stage, Cuba has subsequently won sixteen of the nineteen world amateur baseball championships (World Cup) held since 1969, thus establishing the same grip on international amateur competitions that the island once exerted on Caribbean World Series professional play. The introduction in 1999 of professional players (mostly high-level minor leaguers) into these international events has not affected the Cuban stranglehold. The always-talented Cuban senior national team would, in fact, lose only 1 of 73 games it played against international competition during one peak 5-year stretch between the 1987 Pan American Games in Indianapolis and the 1992 Barcelona Olympics. Most prominent among the members of the powerhouse Cuban team during this era were pitcher René Arocha, the first Cuban player to defect during the Castro era and later a regular starter with the St. Louis Cardinals; mound ace José Ariel Contreras, perhaps the most talented of modern-era Cuban hurlers, who silenced the Baltimore Orioles in 1999 Havana exhibition play and also owned

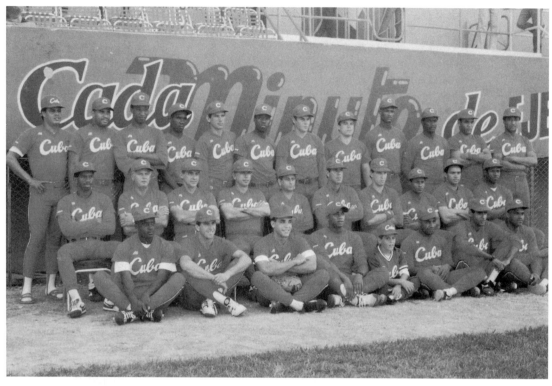

Cuban National Team, 1992 Olympic champions. [Author's Cuban Collection]

a perfect 13–0 international tournament record before his recent defection to the New York Yankees; and all-world third baseman Omar Linares, a complete-package slugger who was long considered by most observers (before his retirement to the Japanese pro league in 2002) as a can't-miss major leaguer and the best amateur baseball player in the world.

As already noted, an emphasis in Cuba on amateur baseball glories emerged long before Fidel Castro established himself on the scene and before top players had begun to flee their island home to pursue their professional ballplaying livelihoods. What the political and social changes of 1962 brought with them was the first steps toward an organized island-wide national league, something sorely missed till then in Cuban baseball. If the amateurs were already often the biggest stars in Cuba before 1960, now they would suddenly become the only game in town. Of course some might argue (and have argued) that the new league and its state-sponsored players were the equivalent of pro baseball found anywhere else. The players were compensated, after all, even if their wages were pathetically low and always controlled tightly by the National Institute of Sports, Physical Education, and Recreation, the government sports ministry known as INDER (Instituto Nacional de Deportes, Educación Física y Recreación). These were full-time players and not mechanics or office clerks merely playing for leisure-time recreation. At the same time, the new Cuban Leaguers were not professionals in the same sense as in organized baseball in the United States. The teams themselves were not capitalist franchises with private owners, business investments oriented toward turning profits from ticket sales, licensing, and especially television revenues. The sport was now run by the government, and the purpose of the league was not only to provide an entertaining season for spectators but also (and more importantly perhaps) to train top-level athletes who could represent the nation proudly in international games,which often took on the tone of pitched Cold War propaganda battles. What better advertisement for the revolution and its new social order than endless strings of high profile victories in the sporting arena? And what sweeter blows could be struck against the American enemies to the north than those that come of beating them repeatedly at their own national pastime?

This was the tradition, then, that continued uninterrupted after the revolution, with its island-wide banning of all professional sports and the inauguration of a new strictly amateur Cuban Baseball League during the winter season of 1961–1962. Perhaps it didn't matter that the rest of the mainstream baseball world (i.e., the U.S. baseball world) simply wasn't paying much attention any more to such events as a baseball World Cup or alternate-year Intercontinental Cup, events that most North American baseball fans have never even heard of, much less anticipate with any degree of enthusiasm. In Cuba, it was these annual competitions (along with the Pan American Games and Caribbean Games, and eventually the Olympic tournament after 1992) versus other countries also living on the fringes of organized baseball that would now supplant the annual visits by itinerant big leaguers that once held so much fan interest on the island.

On the home front, behind a wall of combined secrecy and isolation, the pace of Cuban amateur play would also continue unabated. From November through March, 450 ballplayers with an average age of 23 to 24 compete on sixteen teams in a 90-game national tournament series (season) designed to select Eastern (*Oriente*) and Western (*Occidental*) champions to match up in an April or May showdown seven-game final series. Each of the ball clubs in this highly competitive amateur league represents a different Cuban province, and thus regional pride and the socialist ideals of sportsmanship have replaced professional salaries as the driving force behind league play.

When the regular-season playoffs close down in May, a second league and a new schedule of games fills the void. The 45-game Selective Series provides an elaborate formalized tryout session which runs from late spring through midsummer. The second-season circuit is usually made up of only eight ball clubs (again representing provinces, but now with several provinces for each ball club) and features 225 of the island's top young athletes. The prize of the Selective Series is not so much a team championship (although that is awarded) but rather a spot for the two dozen best players on the nation's crack national team, formed annually to compete in Pan American, World Cup, and Olympic play. Players in the opening national series vie for slots on the more competitive Selective Series rosters; all-stars from the year's second season make their way into the forty or so coveted roster sports available on Team Cuba. At least this was always the structure before 1996, a year in which the Selective Series was finally abandoned in favor of a lengthy 90-game National Series that stretches into May or even June; a short second season was later reinstituted in 2002 as the now-renamed Cuban Super League.

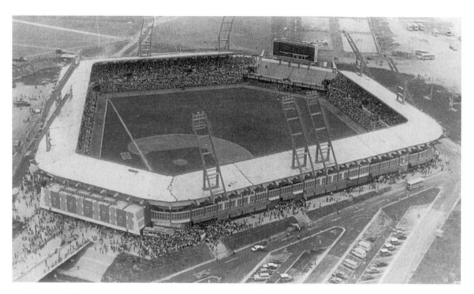

Holguín's Calixto García Stadium, a prototypical modern Cuban League ballpark. [Author's Cuban Collection]

The Cuban League established in 1962 would undergo numerous transformations in size and organizational structure over the next forty-plus years. The most dramatic changes came during the first couple of decades, as the league roster of teams and length of schedule slowly but steadily expanded. Play began with only four teams (Occidentales, Azucareros, Orientales, Habana) and was staged exclusively in Havana, reminiscent of the disbanded professional league that had just been replaced. Over the first dozen of so winters, there was slow movement toward a more truly national league and an island-wide championship. The Azucareros became the Havana-based Industriales in the second year of the league, giving birth to the ball club that would subsequently remain the most popular on the island. Two teams were added by 1966, and the league soon stretched out to 12 clubs (1968) and then to 14 (1973) and 18 (1978). The goal of a genuine national sport was thus reached during the 1970s. Even then there would be still more changes in format, the final major shift coming with the current separation of the league into geographical divisions (and thus several separate pennant races), which was launched in 1988 (National Series XXVII). With the exception of the two Havana-based teams, which are called Industriales and Metropolitanos, team names now signify only the province—but these have also varied from time to time. Pinar del Río was for a time represented by a club called Vegueros and the Santiago nine was for a time known as Mineros.

The most distinctive feature of today's Cuban baseball—one that has existed ever since the dawn of the revolution—is found in both the formal organization and the underlying operating assumptions of the modern-era Cuban League. Foremost, the National Series provides a genuine national competition, no merely fictitious regional representation. In practice and not just in name, teams literally represent each of the island's provinces and are thus truly local teams. Players perform only for their home provincial club; only in the rarest of occasions is permission granted for a ballplayer to shift residence and thus change his ball club in the process. There is no trading of ballplayers (a concession to the socialist ideal that athletes are never merchandise to be bought and sold like cattle), although there are occasional player shifts. It is not uncommon for promising rookies who start their careers with Metropolitanos to be reassigned to fan-favorite Industriales; players are also moved from other provinces to staff the lineup of the Isla de la Juventud (Isle of Youth) team, since this region of the country is too thinly populated to provide its own competitive roster. With stable rosters of homegrown stars, a strong rooting interest in the local nine is assured, as are rabid regional rivalries. The lack of player trading also avoids the problems that come with free agency, which seems for many to have spoiled current-era modern professional baseball at the big league level: in Cuban baseball, there are no free agents displaying loyalty only to the highest bidders and abandoning local fans to seek a heftier paycheck with some nearby rival team.

Across four decades now, the revamped Cuban League structure has continually assured that Cuban fans in all corners of the island (and not only those who can reach the ballpark in Havana) will have plenty of their own stars to replace the lost world of big league baseball, now only a distant memory. From the first, the Cuban League was producing a number of topflight stars who were measurably of big league skill level. As the size of the league expanded, there would also be regular memorable pennant races and the birth of numerous island homegrown legends to replace the stars of the departed and rejected professional epoch.

The two-tier Cuban season has existed for most years but not all. Despite shifts in the roster of competing teams, the National Series has remained a fixture since 1962 and recently completed its 42nd edition (the 2002–2003 campaign). It is the showcase National Series season, representing competition from all provinces, that is the staple of Cuban League baseball; this is what is usually meant when we discuss the Cuban League season. For more than a decade now, the four-division league structure and three rounds of postseason playoffs ending in a seven-game final series has closely resembled the organizational scheme of major league baseball.

The second season known as the Selective Series, always played immediately after the close of the National Series, was born in the mid-1970s. The format again changed slightly through the years, but in general the provincial teams were grouped into a smaller number of interprovince all-star squads. This superprovincial series was at times of greater length than the National Series itself, reaching a peak of 63 games (versus 44 or 48 in the National Series) between 1983 and 1991. That the Selective Series was deemed equivalent in stature to the National Series is demonstrated by the fact that all league records (and individual players' career statistics) include both seasons. The first Selective Series was played in 1975 and the final one was staged in 1995, before Cuban baseball underwent a brief period of overhaul, with emphasis on a single National Series expanded to 90 games. By summer 2002, the second-season format was being reintroduced, with the short campaign now labeled the Super League and reduced to a four-team, 30-game arrangement. The reason for this unique double-season structure follows quite obviously from the driving purpose behind contemporary Cuban League baseball—that of selecting national teams for prestigious international competitions like the World Cup and Pan American Games. The league seasons have been used from the outset as lengthy and highly efficient tryout or training seasons—almost an extended spring training, by big league standards. Nonetheless, the resulting pennant races themselves are always a main focus for Cuba's superbly informed and super-enthusiastic fans.

The strength of contemporary Cuban baseball has always been—since 1962—its function as an alternative universe, in contrast to the organized professional baseball played in the north and supported by neighboring Caribbean and Central American nations. Cuban baseball has, in fact, remained the only true alternative to an organized baseball system that views amateur and semi-professional leagues in other baseball-playing nations only as potential talent pools to be fished for replenishing rosters in the U.S. major leagues. In Cuba alone baseball has kept marching to its own rhythms and its own time clock. It has for decades remained a closed world, as free from major league interference as the outlaw Negro leagues once were in the days before baseball's tardy racial integration.

The isolated universe that is Cuban baseball is of course a fragile world, one that cannot be sustained much longer in its present circumstances. Change is everywhere on the horizon, with a sagging economy at home and amplified exposure to organized baseball feeding growing ballplayer dissatisfaction on the home front. The rate of defection of Cuban players from the island seems relatively stable and the number of true stars departing has remained minimal, but each loss of a José Contreras or Maels Rodríguez seems to signal a disintegrating Cuban baseball infrastructure. Cuba's current communist regime and its decades-long political and athletic isolation will likely not last forever. Eventually, there will be increased connections with the professional game on the U.S. mainland, so close to Cuba's shores. When it comes, this changing environment will bring some positives—especially expanded economic opportunities for Cuban ballplayers—but a large-scale movement of Cuban players to professional baseball will wreak the same havoc as was brought to the 1940s-era Negro leagues in the wake of Jackie Robinson and Branch Rickey. Change thus also promises to destroy a unique and thriving baseball world, one that is truly the last of its kind. The biggest losers, once such wholesale changes come, will be the devout Cuban baseball fans—though most of them probably do not now see it at all this way.

The tenuous future of Cuban baseball raises numerous questions that admit no easy answers. Do recent defections by Cuban ballplayers signal a groundswell of new available Cuban talent? If this is not merely a temporary aberration, will it be on the same order or beyond that which trickled into major league parks in the immediate aftermath of Branch Rickey and Jackie Robinson? Will Fidel Castro's government cave in to economic necessities and begin peddling front-line players to the highest major league bidders as Cuba's most valuable natural export? Are the top Cuban players truly of major league caliber, and if so, how many are actually future Miñosos, Pascuals, Luques, or Tony Olivas? Or will the (presumed) lack of first-rate competition in their own amateur league back home mean that the current crop of new Cuban stars will prove to be less than promising big league prospects? How will big league teams divide up Cuban talent—will the present draft lottery system prevent secret signings and other skullduggery?—and how will the new flock of Cuban ballplayers affect the recruiting of talent from other Caribbean nations? And, centrally, what will happen to baseball in Cuba once the island's best players again have access to major league careers? Only time holds the answers to what may indeed be the most exciting baseball questions in the first decade of the twenty-first century.

HAVANA AS THE AMATEUR BASEBALL CAPITAL OF THE WORLD

If any further proof were needed that Cuban baseball is very much alive and well—despite the ominous storm clouds—it came in spades with recent impressive international triumphs by the Cuban national team during late October and early November 2003 and again in August 2004 in Athens. First the Cubans continued their relentless domination of World Cup play, which they have all but owned for more than three decades. Next they partially avenged a 2000 Sydney setback with near-laughable ease at the Olympic Qualifier in Panama City. And most recently Cuban forces regained coveted Olympic gold they had let slip away in Sydney by wiping out a field in Athens that included a

Cuban National Team, 2003 World Cup champions. [Peter C. Bjarkman]

crack roster of Japan League pro all-stars, plus solid collections of minor leaguers and former big leaguers representing Canada (defeated 8–5 in the semis) and Australia (bested 6–2 in the finale).

Cuba has run roughshod over international baseball competition for much of the past century. The record of largely uninterrupted Cuban triumphs extends far back before the revolution, as we have already seen, and it is a record that is altogether unparalleled in either amateur or professional history. Cuban national team baseball arguably provides the greatest dynasty saga one can point to in any sport or any epoch. The string of Cuban victories was launched at the outset of the 1940s during the Havana-based amateur world series contests of 1939 and 1940. These were the settings for the first pair of competitions approximating true international tournaments, and only a pair of one-run losses marred the all-too-easy gold medal triumphs for the host country. The 1950s would see a brief lull in Cuban invincibility—not surprising, since the island spent the second half of that tumultuous decade fully embroiled in bloody revolutionary struggles between Fulgencio Batista's crumbling national army and Fidel Castro's grassroots peasant and student guerrilla movement. Shortly after the revolutionary dance finally subsided in 1960, the retooled Cubans were once more gobbling up prestigious baseball victories almost everywhere on the international scene. And, throughout the last four decades, Cuban teams have nearly made a mockery of these events—early on playing against strictly amateur (and often ill-trained) teams representing rival ballplaying nations and still more recently against more charged-up all-star squads of Puerto Rican, Japanese, Korean, Taiwanese, Dominican, Panamanian, Venezuelan, and American minor leaguers (with occasionally even a dose of talented big leaguers tossed into the mix).

The most recent victories have been perhaps the grandest of all. After losing their Olympic gold medal bragging rights in Sydney via a single showdown defeat at the hands of a rising major league star pitcher (Ben Sheets, who slammed the door on Cuba's bats in an upset 4–0 U.S. victory), Cuba's finest players rebounded with a steamroller-style gold medal triumph at the World Cup 2001 matches in Taipei. Next followed another Intercontinental Cup title in October 2002 on home turf in Havana (avenging shocking defeats in the finals of this event in both 1997 at Barcelona and 1999 in Sydney). And, for a final encore, there was a remarkable and even somewhat surprising double triumph in the fall of 2003, with a sweep of both the Havana World Cup matches and a more crucial Olympic Qualifier tournament held a week later in Panama. To put icing on the cake, a young Cuban team (inexperienced in pitching, with doubtful slugging prowess, and almost entirely retooled over the last two years) proved its unexpected toughness in August 2004 Athens medal-round victories over Team Canada (largely on the strength of a desperate eighth-inning 6-run comeback) and Australia (featuring a half-dozen former big leaguers and twice victorious over pretourney favorite Japan).

The 2003 doubleheader win and follow-up Athens successes were largely unexpected, because stars of the past decade such as Linares, Antonio Pacheco, Orestes Kindelán, and Germán Mesa were now retired, and the United States, especially, was expected to send a showcase team of big league prospects to the Olympic trials. The recent defection of top pitchers José Contreras and Maels

Rodríguez also seemed to work against Cuban prospects. The revitalized lineup of newly minted youngsters proved every bit as tough as the old guard, however, and not only did the Cubans coast past the opposition in Panama (after barely escaping with the World Cup title in Havana), but the vaunted U.S. squad crumbled in a disappointing quarterfinal loss against unheralded Mexico, which knocked the Americans straight out of the 2004 Athens Olympic field. In the end, recent player defections and retirements seem only to have helped the Cubans, who could now rush sterling rookies like Yulieski Gourriel and Frederich Cepeda into the lineup much earlier than expected. The Cubans not only charged right back to the top of the heap again; they did it with a surprisingly young and even inexperienced squad of unheralded up-and-coming replacements for their now absent big-name stars of the past decade.

Some in the press and also some connected with Team USA have repeatedly made much of the lack of competition faced by Cuban championship teams throughout most of the last several decades. First and foremost is the claim that other countries—especially the baseball-wealthy United States—do not take world amateur baseball events seriously and thus do not reserve top talent for what are perceived as back-burner events. There is also an argument that Cuban teams and players cannot be judged by their victories only, since the competition has always been laughably weak: time and again during the 1970s, 1980s, or 1990s, seasoned Cuban squads have trounced hastily arranged American clubs featuring college stars totally untrained in international competitions.

These charges might have had a good deal more merit before the 1999 Winnipeg Pan American Games. That gathering not only served as a North American qualifying event for the 2000 Sydney Olympics, but also for the first time both wooden bats (not used in Cuba since the mid-1970s) and top-level minor league professional players were part of the program. Suddenly the playing field was leveled, yet without an apparent derailing of Cuba's juggernaut. If the Cubans have now adjusted surprisingly well to the upgraded lineups of pros deployed the past several years by rival U.S., Japanese, Korean, Panamanian, and Dominican squads, the arguments about one-sided competitions seem largely defused. And there is another defense for long-standing Cuban achievement. The Cubans must, in fairness, be judged strictly by the playing field they have inherited. Even if past opposition was not up to professional-level standards, in the format used for Olympic-style tournament play (one single defeat in medal-round action and teams are sent packing) it is unlikely, if not nearly impossible, that the same nation will somehow win year in and year out, through each and every crucial elimination game. In baseball, a single brilliant pitching performance, plus a bad bounce or lucky blooper, can doom any powerhouse team on any given day. The most remarkable thing about Cuban national teams is that season after season, no matter the competition or their own lineup, they almost always find a way to win every single crucial showdown game.

The most glorious Cuban victories have come in World Cup tournaments; these began with a series of showcase events held in Havana in the early 1940s, during World War II. Details of Cuba's world amateur reign are treated more exhaustively in chapter 10, the part of this history devoted strictly to

Olympic-style world tournaments, but some capsule overview is in order here. It was the early multicountry tournaments of the 1940s, still known then as the Amateur World Series and attended by only a handful of Caribbean nations, which initially built Cuba's reputation as international baseball power-house. No events were any more dramatic than the pair of initial shootouts between Cuba and Venezuela in Havana's Tropical Stadium; these contests saw top island hero Conrado Marrero first lose a heartbreaking showdown with Venezuelan ace Daniel Canónico in the 1941 finale, then rebound to reclaim the prize during a rematch one year later. At the time, there were few Cuban big leaguers to bolster national identity in far-off professional venues. The greatest baseball stars on the island were the players still performing in the more popular amateur ranks. Now, with the new amateur world series event, the local heroes had been handed a chance to prove their skills on a larger and more spectacular international stage, and to uphold nationalistic pride in the bargain.

Cuba would enjoy perhaps its greatest World Cup performances in the years following the Castro revolution. These victories were now tinged with political and even blatantly propagandistic value, since they could be flaunted as demonstrations of the superiority of a socialist system that promoted athletics as a genuine right of the people and not as an entertainment spectacle driven by capitalist profit motive. Brand-new Cuban amateur stars wrote reams of history in tournaments stretched across the 1970s and 1980s. One was slugger Antonio Muñoz, an imposing southpaw swinger who blasted opposition pitching for a record 8 homers at the 1978 round-robin in Parma, Italy. Another was a young pitcher named José Huelga: Huelga earned instant hero-worship status back home by beating the rival Americans (and future big league knuckleballer Burt Hooton) in Cartagena, Colombia, late in 1970, at the height of Cold War posturing between Washington and Havana. Many times the sweetest victories—like the one anchored by Huelga—came against American forces, against those who had always boasted of baseball as their own genuine national game. But it was the Cubans who demonstrably now took the amateur game of baseball far more seriously. For Cuban ballplayers, especially, amateur sport had become an end in itself and not merely the convenient stepping stone to a lucrative professional career.

Cuba's reign has extended to other tournaments sometimes much more visible (at least to North Americans) than an often largely ignored World Cup venue. The most prestigious gathering has unarguably been the summer Olympic Games, though its history has been shamefully short: baseball did not become a sanctioned medal sport for the Olympic Games until 1992. In the first baseball Olympics at Barcelona, the Cubans immediately established their familiar invincibility in a new setting. The Barcelona Games found the Cubans hardly working up a sweat, breezing through nine matches unscathed and copping the gold with an 11–1 laugher versus Chinese Taipei. The victory run continued unmolested in Atlanta, with nine more wins (without defeat) and a convincing 13–9 clobbering of upstart Japan in the finale. The string was broken in Sydney, however, but only due to a rare stumble in one single game, when superior U.S. pitching by Sheets wiped out a previous convincing Cuban win against the same American squad during earlier qualification play. Here

Cubans celebrate a first-ever Olympic gold medal at Barcelona, 1992. [Author's Cuban Collection]

the format of world tournament baseball came heavily into account; it is likely that runner-up Cuba would have taken the measure of Team USA in any longer series, and Cuban manager Servio Borges probably squandered gold medal hopes by using ace pitcher José Contreras a day early in the semifinal match with Japan. The Cubans would benefit four years later from this same one-loss-and-out scenario, however, as the surprise upset of Team USA by Mexico in the 2003 Olympic Qualifier at Panama City meant that the planned return showdown between the 2000 Sydney finalists never materialized. Cuba was back as strong as ever to regain their crown at Athens in 2004, but the unlucky Americans were not there to defend their own surprise Sydney gold medal victory.

Cuba's easy romp through international baseball has also been played out in three other showcase tournaments. In Intercontinental Cup action—launched in 1973 but not attended by Cuba until its fourth reunion, in 1979—the record has been virtually the same: Cuba has captured a championship title in nine of the dozen events it has entered, winning an astounding 107 of 118 individual games. It was Cuba's inaugural Intercontinental Cup event hosted in Havana back in 1979 that provided one of the most sensational international performances ever witnessed from an amateur-level slugger, in this case Havana's Pedro José "Cheíto" Rodríguez, who broke down fences in his hometown ballpark that year with 7 homers, a .450 batting mark, and a 1.000 slugging average that together earned unanimous tourney Most Valuable Player honors.

In the Pan American Games, the Cubans have again been nearly invincible down through the years. Indeed, this tournament venue has supplied many of the island's loftiest triumphs, with eleven gold medal finishes to but one apiece for the Americans (1967), Dominicans (1955), and Venezuelans (1959).

In 1987, a 13–9 slugfest win by Cuba over Team USA in Indianapolis provided one of the most thrilling games ever between the two long-time rivals; it also launched a near-unbeaten string (only a single insignificant loss to Nicaragua during the 1991 Intercontinental Cup qualifying round) in international tournament play that would eventually stretch across ten years and nearly 100 games and not be snapped until 1997 Intercontinental Cup finals action in Barcelona.

When it comes to the Central American Games, the least noteworthy tournament on the list, generally weaker competition has meant still easier triumphs. In the sixteen Central American Games baseball tournaments (starting in 1926), Cuba has placed first thirteen times, second once, and third once—finishing out of medal contention on only a single rare occasion (Jamaica, 1962, when they dropped three of five games played).

It has been in these tournaments rather than in National Series seasons—especially since the heating up of Cold War standoffs with Washington in the early 1970s—that Cuba's greatest individual players have made their most memorable and lasting marks. Omar Linares and Orestes Kindelán were the biggest names in Cuban baseball at the end of the twentieth century, and if they are known anywhere off the island it is largely because of the home run barrages they unleashed at Fulton County Stadium during the 1996 Atlanta Olympics.

Before Linares and Kindelán, there were similar stars honing their skills in World Cup action or during tense battles for Pan American Games and Central American Games supremacy. Wilfredo ("El Hombre Hit") Sánchez was one such hero, ringing up a sterling lifetime .340 batting mark in international play (14 tourneys) that outstripped his already lofty .331 league mark earned back home. Agustín Marquetti (a .288 lifetime Cuban League batter) was another, blasting away at a .346 clip (with 31 homers) in his dozen international events. Great pitching feats by José Antonio Huelga were matched and then surpassed by 221-game Cuban League winner Braudilio Vinent throughout the 1970s and 1980s. A veteran of 17 world tournament competitions in his career, Vinent posted a remarkable lifetime 56–4 win–loss record and a 2.01 ERA that likely qualify him as the most invincible amateur pitcher even to perform on the worldwide stage.

In the past few years, great Cuban pitchers have reappeared with a vengeance. José Ariel Contreras, before his defection, won all thirteen international decisions, despite being repeatedly saved for the toughest assignments in semifinal and final showdown games. Norge Vera has now inherited the mantle from Contreras. Blanking the Baltimore Orioles in a long relief stint back in 1999, Vera reached his peak in the Havana World Cup in October 2003. His performance—pitching seven brilliant innings twice and earning crucial victories in both the semifinal and the gold medal games—was unprecedented in the long history of the prestigious World Cup event.

With its remarkable international tournament play, Cuba unquestionably has etched its baseball reputation in solid granite. That reputation alone has been sufficient—despite all the nay-saying and carping about watered-down competitions—to establish the island nation as the greatest baseball country in the world outside North American borders. The Dominicans boast their long

Cubans celebrate their 24th World Cup championship at Havana, October 2003. [Peter C. Bjarkman]

list of major leaguers and the Japanese own a pro league that some contend comes closest to big league standards, but the results of international play should be enough to clinch any argument that—had the politics of the Cold War only been a bit different—most big league scouts would long have been flocking not to the Dominican or Japan but instead to Cuba.

CUBA'S GREATEST PLAYERS

The tragedy of Cuban baseball is the isolation and obscurity suffered through the years by the island's genuine stars. First there were the racial barriers of organized baseball blocking access to major league stadiums for surefire all-stars the likes of Dihigo, Méndez, and Torriente. Later came Cold War tensions and a Washington–Havana standoff of forty-plus years, which assured that stardom on baseball's primary stage would also be denied to modern-vintage Cuban stalwarts such as Marquetti, Linares, and Kindelán. Without a major league venue to showcase their wares, Cuba's top-of-the-line players have for much of the past century largely remained unknown to baseball's biggest consumer market. All the same, there have indeed been a sufficient number of homegrown greats to rival those of any nation.

If the list of Cuban big leaguers has never been very large, even in the years following integration of the majors, it has certainly not been the result of any scarcity in genuine island-bred baseball talent. Once racial prejudice slid to the back burner, international politics would be quick to deal the next death blow to any Cuban aspirations for lucrative North American professional careers. With Uncle Tom finally and thankfully gone from the scene, Uncle Sam was quick to drive yet another wedge between Cuban ballplayers and the big league clubs that might have coveted them.

Nonetheless, there always remained at least occasional glimpses of the depth of ballplaying talents hidden behind a sugarcane curtain that isolated Fidel Castro's communist island. In the 1960s, 1970s, and 1980s, reports would from time to time leak out to the U.S. press about phenomenal sluggers with names like Agustín Marquetti and Antonio Muñoz, reputed near-clones of Tony Pérez or Tony Oliva; or about remarkable hurlers named Vinent and Huelga, who had handcuffed U.S. college stars and minor leaguers during little-noted world amateur tournaments. Establishment of baseball as an official medal event in Olympic competitions after 1992 meant that a wider U.S. audience would receive occasional four-year glimpses of a touted Cuban star named Linares, whom scouts had branded as a surefire Cooperstown candidate. And as the millennial turn of the century approached, a small wave of recent political defections by a half-dozen talented Cuban pitching aces capable of stepping directly onto the big league stage has further stoked rumors about buried Cuban talent waiting to be someday plucked by a voracious U.S. baseball enterprise.

The roster of first-order Cuban stars that follows is a representative sampling of big league heroes, once obscure Negro leaguers, and shadowy phenoms from the little-known postrevolution Cuban League scene. More detailed portraits are offered for the latter group of ballplayers simply because they are the least known off the island and thus the least covered (if covered at all) in other available published sources. Two renowned major leaguers with Cuban roots are given only summary treatments here, simply because of the tenuous nature of their joint claims on the Cuban baseball story. José Canseco and Rafael Palmeiro were both born on the island, of Cuban parents, yet both were raised in Florida (where they arrived as infants) and acculturated to baseball in a strictly North American setting; neither owns any life experiences or baseball experiences on the island of Cuba. They are downplayed here for the same reason that Alex Rodríguez—Yankees superstar—is missing from chapter 4 devoted to baseball in the Dominican Republic. To consider Canseco or Palmeiro as Cuba greats is equivalent to raising up Bobby Thomson as an illustration of the achievements of baseball in Scotland. Canseco and Palmeiro are mentioned here, nonetheless, in deference to their undeniable Cuban bloodlines and the pride they evoke among Cubans long exiled in the United States.

Dagoberto "Bert" Campaneris (b. March 9, 1942). Bert Campaneris filled a lengthy career with unique and unusual achievements, sometimes more recognizable for the curious than the substantial. Campy is one of three players to perform at all nine positions in a single big league contest. More significantly, he was also only the third player to homer twice in his debut big league game. Campaneris was also a lynchpin on the great Oakland world champion teams of the early 1970s. But beyond curiosities, Campy's career resume is almost the substantial stuff justifying a Cooperstown pretender. He lasted 19 seasons in the big time, was an American League basestealing champion on six different occasions (five times pilfering more than 50 and once even topping 60), participated in five All-Star games, rang up 2,249 base hits in 2,328 league games, and ranks fourteenth (with 649, more than either Maury Wills or Davey Lopes) on the career stolen base list. He was also for good measure a clutch performer on a pair of Oakland championship teams and a key postseason overachiever in both 1973 and 1974; in the former year he crushed two key American League Championship Series homers against Baltimore then assumed the role of Mr. Clutch in the World Series against the Mets by driving home the winning run in Game Three and hitting a two-run homer to help decide Game Seven. Not bad for a once unheralded prospect originally signed off Cuban sandlots by A's scout Felix Delgado for a piddling $500 bonus.

José Canseco (b. July 2, 1964).   Havana-born (but Miami-raised) José Canseco has approached the top echelons among Latin sluggers, surpassing the home run production of Hall-of-Famer Pérez and briefly (before Sosa and Palmeiro got in the way) reigning as Latin America's top all-time slugger; yet very few would see the well-traveled muscleman as one of the true greats of recent decades. Teamed with Mark McGwire as a member of the "Bash Brothers" for a few short years in Oakland, Canseco was in the late-eighties and early-nineties arguably one of baseball's handful of front-page headliners. Even at his peak, however, he was not nearly the complete package that Pérez and Palmeiro were—though even his particular case for immortality (446 homers and a half-dozen 100-plus RBI campaigns) is nothing flimsy or commonplace. Part of the problem was Canseco's off-the-field escapades (including such head-line-grabbing stunts as numerous speeding tickets, several arrests on weapons charges, sordid episodes of domestic violence involving his ex-wife, and a reported liaison with sex-symbol pop star Madonna) combined with his on-field swagger, the latter being especially distasteful to many of the sport's older Latino fans. Even such a staunch supporter as Cuban baseball historian Roberto González Echevarría—who in *The Pride of Havana* (p. 360) enigmatically anoints Canseco the best Cuban baseball player ever—must hasten to point out that old-timers in Havana rarely have warmed to Canseco as a national idol. González Echevarría (again p. 360) feels compelled to report that veteran Havana play-by-play broadcaster Eddy Martin labels Canseco *el pesado* ("the boor") and Miami-based Cuban sportswriting dean Fausto Miranda (brother of Cuban big leaguer Willie Miranda) once complained that Canseco had "the body of a superman and the brain of a baby." This is hardly the stuff of runaway hero worship among Cuba's own senior baseball community.

José Ariel Contreras (b. December 12, 1971).   José Ariel Contreras is today known to U.S. fans as one of the most successful and most highly compensated among the recent wave of Cuban baseball defectors. Like Orlando "El Duque"

Hernández, he gained substantial fame simply by having the luck or foresight to wind up on the roster of the perennial champion New York Yankees. So far in his short stay in New York (he was 7–2 in his debut 2003 campaign and became a regular starter in 2004 before being dealt to Chicago) he has already demonstrated that his substantial Cuban League reputation of the past half-dozen years was hardly exaggerated or inflated.

Contreras—the most recent big-time Cuban star to defect for major league riches and then actually reach the big time—is a statuesque, jet-black, muscular fireballer who turned numerous big league heads back in May 1999 while stifling the Baltimore Orioles in Havana and then did so again for an encore during crucial quarterfinal and final games at Winnipeg's Pan American Games tournament. On the latter occasion the stakes were raised measurably, with a Sydney Olympic bid hanging in the balance. First came the masterful eight-inning, two-hit relief performance in Havana's Estadio Latinoamericano, played out before a huge and curious ESPN television audience back in the States as well as fanatical radio and television throngs at home on the island. Three months later, Contreras followed up with his impressive domination (during a single 48-hour stretch) of big league and AAA hitters in Winnipeg's jam-packed Can West Global Park, clinching much-needed victories over the pesky Dominicans and formidable Americans.

The latter two contests featured the added pressures represented by team qualification for the Sydney Olympics and a coveted Pan American gold medal, both squarely on the line at the time. Legions of pro scouts were duly impressed in Winnipeg, even if most fans in the States saw or heard nothing of these genuinely clutch big-time performances. To truly appreciate Contreras's many achievements during his four brief seasons as pitching ace for the Cuban national team, one has only to apprehend the pressures surrounding Cuban players back in their homeland whenever coveted trips to the Olympics or gold medals in the Amateur World Series, Pan American Games, or Intercontinental Cup are ultimately the prizes at stake.

When El Duque Hernández was first grilled by the New York press corps about the awe-inspiring experience of debuting in legendary Yankee Stadium, the naïve refugee from the world's best amateur baseball had a ready-made answer. The American League playoffs or World Series were really nothing, explained El Duque, compared to facing arch-rival Santiago for his hometown Industriales club or playing before 55,000 screaming partisans at Havana's Latin American Stadium. For Yankee rookie José Contreras, the experience was altogether comparable: none among his several clutch 2003 outings versus the Boston Red Sox during an American League championship showdown could represent any more of a heart-stopping, gut-wrenching moment than taking the mound for seeming life-and-death games at Sydney or in Taiwan, with the shared hopes of an entire baseball-addicted nation hanging on his performance.

Contreras is a Lee Smith look-alike who—also reminiscent of the sure-bet Cooperstown reliever—is a truly dominant force when any big-stakes game is on the line. No other Cuban pitcher has been used in so many crucial tournament situations during the recent history of international play. It was Contreras who was called upon for long relief in Havana versus the Orioles; it was also Contreras who was handed the ball for starting assignments twice in less than

Cuban League defector Orlando "El Duque" Hernández, Havana, 1992. [Author's Cuban Collection]

two days, with Cuba's Olympic dreams about to crumble in Winnipeg; and it was inevitably the same Contreras who was asked to deliver crucial semifinal wins (and thus assure an expected gold medal appearance) in Sydney during the 2000 Olympics and at the 2001 World Cup in Taipei. The fireballer never failed on a single one of these pressure-packed occasions; his ability to deliver in such clutch outings is truly uncanny. It seems that of late Cuba's national team had lost the truly vital matches only when José Contreras was used up too early and thus was no longer available for the final championship test. At the time of his defection (October 2002 in Mexico), the Pinar del Río ace's international tournament mark remained unblemished (at 13–0) and it was a record that had been gained in a true test by fire.

Mike Cuéllar (b. May 8, 1937). Mike Cuéllar, who began as a pro with the triple-A Havana-based Sugar Kings, was the first Latin American pitcher ever to win the Cy Young Award (1969, when he split the honor with Denny McLain), and he was one of the last overachieving Cubans to escape to the majors before Castro's revolution closed the doors on professional baseball for future island hopefuls. By the time Cuéllar's decade-and-a-half career was done in Houston and Baltimore (he also pitched briefly for Cincinnati, St. Louis and California), he had won 185 games, topped 20 wins on four occasions, pitched in two major league midsummer classics, twice paced the American League in winning percentage, and led the circuit in complete games (21) as well as victories (24) during his peak Cy Young summer. His most notable characteristic throughout was his distinct lack of speed for an established big league starter; it was nonetheless a weakness soon turned to an advantage when it forced the wily Cuban to concentrate on a masterful variety of deliveries that included a wicked palm ball and a wide array of tantalizing breaking pitches. Cuéllar pitched in five different postseasons with Earl Weaver's powerhouse Baltimore teams and split eight decisions in his dozen playoff and World Series starts. If his pitching arsenal was never a standard one, Cuéllar's professional career also got its start in rather unlikely fashion when Cincinnati scouts discovered him during an impressive no-hit effort for a Cuban military team while serving in the army under soon-to-be-ousted Cuban dictator Fulgencio Batista.

Martín Dihigo (b. May 25, 1905; d. May 19, 1971).   Unlike some Negro leaguers eventually enshrined in Cooperstown, Martín Dihigo was no case of late admission into the Hall of Immortals driven more by sympathy or guilt than by balanced understanding of hard-earned achievements. Many rare distinctions marked Dihigo's résumé and thus fully justified his 1977 Cooperstown enshrinement. Dihigo, to begin with, claims unique distinction as one of the rare ballplayers elected to halls of fame in three separate nations—Cuba, Mexico, and the United States. "El Maestro" (his popular Mexican League moniker) performed like an all-star at eight different positions, failing only to earn distinction behind the plate because his value as a crafty pitcher, speedy infielder, and agile outfielder meant that he rarely donned the tools of ignorance. As if these unparalleled accomplishments in North American Negro league venues and on island barnstorming tours were not hefty credentials enough, Dihigo was an incomparable Mexican League legend, hurling that country's first-ever no-hitter (in 1937) while also incredibly pacing Mexican Leaguers in batting percentage the very next summer. Perhaps for icing—if icing were needed— so entrenched is Dihigo's stature on his native island, even today, that his living memory has even overcome 40 years of postrevolutionary efforts to belittle or stamp out altogether the earlier achievements of professional baseball from collective island memory. Thus, despite the many glories amassed by amateur baseball tradition in Cuba after the 1959 revolution, it is pre-Castro professional hero Martín Dihigo who still towers unsurpassed as the baseball-crazy nation's greatest diamond treasure.

Silvio García (b. October 11, 1914).   Silvio García was a Cuban black star who is today best remembered off the island for an unfortunate lack of personal discipline that may have robbed him of the chance to be a centerpiece for Branch Rickey's integration experiment. This hitting and pitching star of 1930s and 1940s Cuban League winter seasons nonetheless remains one of the true island greats. A better-than-average pitcher for four league teams (Marianao, Almendares, Cienfuegos, and Matanzas), García was more talented still as a classy shortstop and has been rated by many as the best Cuban ever at that position (no mean praise, in light of a host of top Cuban middle infielders ranging from Luis Bustamante at the dawn of the twentieth century to big league whiz Willie Miranda at mid-century). García logged 22 seasons in the Cuban League and batted above .300 on a half-dozen occasions, winning batting crowns in 1942 (.351) and again in a final hurrah season of 1950–1951 (.347). He was also a Negro league all-star with the New York Cubans in both 1946 and 1947. For all that, Silvio García's greatest fame (and notoriety) nonetheless comes from the widely circulated reports that Brooklyn's Branch Rickey approached him in the mid-1940s as a possible viable candidate for the integration role that eventually fell to Jackie Robinson. García's possible assignment with Brooklyn reportedly was quickly rejected when the moralistic Rickey learned of the Cuban's reputation for occasional heavy drinking and more frequent on-field displays of temper, which were hardly consistent with his ideal of a crusading black pioneer who could turn the other cheek and avoid any action that might potentially sabotage the risky plan for integration. One apocryphal anecdote even suggests that when Rickey (through his emissary Walter O'Malley) posed the inevitable question regarding a hypothetical possibility of García being spiked or bean-balled by a white player, the interviewee's reported response was immediate, if damning. "I kill him," fired back the indignant Cuban.

José Antonio Huelga (b. 1948; d. July 4, 1974).   The immensely talented José Antonio Huelga achieved legendary status even greater than that of Braudilio Vinent, but Huelga also easily owns the saddest among recent Cuban baseball legends. He burst on the scene of international play truly overnight and left a lasting impression despite the brevity of his tenure, just seven remarkable seasons. If his life and career would indeed be regrettably short, nonetheless his memory still looms larger than life among all but the most recent of island *aficionados*.

José Huelga could well have been Cuba's greatest pitching genius ever—and this includes any of the greatest big league hurlers or black-ball professionals from decades before the 1959 revolution. Some contend that this slender righty was indeed the best ever seen on the island, especially given the brevity of his brilliant career. José Antonio Huelga will assuredly live in Cuban baseball lore on the strength of his gutsy performances in the two unforgettable playoff games with Team USA that decided a 1970 Amateur World Series showdown in Cartagena, Colombia. The first of these games was the celebrated duel with Burt Hooton (a 3–1, eleven-inning Cuban win) that most veteran Cuban baseball watchers to this day still judge the most artistic game ever played during top-level international competitions. A mere day later, Huelga was again back on the field in a less familiar relief role to close out the deciding contest of the championship round. For these gritty performances, José Huelga was immediately proclaimed by Commander in Chief Fidel Castro to be the nation's new official "Hero of Cartagena."

Back home on the island, during his mere seven National Series seasons, Huelga earned further immortality with the lowest career ERA on record for a Cuban hurler. It remains an irony of his career, however, that he was never a single-season league leader in any major hurling category. Though he maintained remarkable consistency in the earned run department during an epoch of remarkable pitching, he was edged out each winter by the likes of Vinent (twice), Roberto Valdés, Rolando Castillo, Manuel Hurtado, Ihosvany Gallego, and Juan Pérez. During Huelga's career years, there was never a league ERA pacesetter with a mark higher than the 1.13 posted by Pérez in 1974. But a worse fate than mere on-field overshadowing awaited the young phenom from Sancti Spíritus. On July 4, 1974, Huelga died in an automobile accident on the open highway near Mariel, a dozen miles west of the capital city. He had pitched in a only handful more than 150 league contests, and his great victories in Cartagena were barely four years in the past. Today, nearly three decades after his most untimely demise, José Antonio Huelga is fittingly immortalized in his home province of Sancti Spíritus by the ballpark name which adorns a Cuban League Stadium located in that provincial capital.

Orestes Kindelán (b. November 1, 1964). The modern-era Cuban slugger whose hypothetical major league credentials are perhaps as difficult to assess as those of Agustín Marquetti would be 1990s fence-buster Orestes Kindelán. Performing for Santiago de Cuba, alongside the great second baseman and national team fixture Antonio Pacheco, Kindelán eventually obliterated all league records for long-ball slugging. His numbers are far more impressive than those of Marquetti, and even the shorter Cuban seasons do not cheapen his overall numbers—but Kindelán was not a solid all-around player (his defense at first base was adequate but hardly more), and any role in the majors would likely have depended on the existence of the controversial designated hitter. Those who saw him at the Atlanta Olympics were well enough aware of the explosive power in Kindelán's bat, whatever his defensive lapses, and he would continue to slug away in Cuba, even after wooden bats were introduced.

When it comes to debates about instant big league stardom, Cuba's all-time home run leader is indeed a difficult case to analyze. Kindelán's impressive string of Olympic homers in Atlanta in 1996 might well be discounted, due to less than big league–level pitching and use of rocket-launcher aluminum bats. As one *Sports Illustrated* writer cleverly summed it up, the Atlanta competition featured 133 often-mammoth home runs, nonstop pitching changes, and not a single broken-bat blooper. Kindelán is assuredly a big leaguer, nonetheless, even once one recognizes that the bulk of his batting feats were achieved with aluminum wands. Robin Ventura, for example, was hardly less of a true pro prospect when he emerged from the Oklahoma State campus simply because his collegiate 66-game batting streak was also the product of metal-assisted slugging. Kindelán's raw batting talent alone would seem sufficient to have guaranteed at least a major league trial during the years of his peak prowess. A case in point is the fact that organized baseball scouts made much of Habana Province third sacker Andy Morales when he defected from the island late in 1999, even though Morales was only an average everyday player in Cuban League circles and was never a hitter remotely approaching Kindelán's class.

By career's end, Orestes Kindelán had reached the elevated plateau of nearly 500 homers, all slugged in spacious stadiums and across a 21-year span that averaged between 75 and 90 annual games. Nobody in Cuba produced as much scoring: Kindelán himself tallied 1,379 times and is also the league's all-time top RBI producer with 1,511. Defensively he was usually solid if not spectacular at first base (and earlier as a catcher), and it is perhaps a tribute to his sufficient if not stellar defensive skills that the Santiago slugger was used in most international tournaments as well as the Orioles exhibition game at Baltimore as a position player and not a designated hitter. Few have ever hit balls as hard on a major league field as Kindelán did in Atlanta's Fulton County Stadium; one of his third-deck Olympic Games smashes was noted in the local press as easily the longest fly ball ever witnessed in the park's 30-year-plus history. No doubt any big league talent scout would have been thrilled to sign Kindelán, even in recent years when he was used exclusively as a designated batsman.

Kindelán has lately departed for Japan in official "retirement" and in 2002 was playing alongside Santiago teammate Antonio Pacheco on a Japanese amateur (industrial league) squad, on loan from Cuba for at least that season and the next. His impressive two-decade career in Cuba, now apparently relegated to history, can be matched for overall productivity throughout the 1980s and 1990s by no one except Linares. Kindelán has also come up big in international tournaments, season after season. He was the unrivaled slugging star in Atlanta during the 1996 Olympics and paced the tournament field both in both home run blasts (seven in preliminary round games and a pair in medal play) and RBI. And he has authored other moments of near-equal glory on the international scene, most notably the vital home run (stroked against Team USA during the deciding contest) that ended an extended slump at the Pan American Games Olympic qualifying tournament in Winnipeg. Several times Kindelán has been batting champion of showcase tournaments (1998 World Cup matches in Italy and the 1990 World Cup in Edmonton top the list). A ratio of 98 international homers in 735 official at-bats (one long ball smashed for every 7.5 times in the batter's box) puts him squarely into Ruthian or Aaronesque territory. In sum, his overall offensive stats for career international tournament play fall only a fraction short of the remarkable numbers that Omar Linares has posted.

Omar "El Niño" Linares (b. October 23, 1967). Among the most recent generation of Cuban ballplayers, Omar Linares stood out from the pack in the 1990s as the cover boy for Cuban League baseball talent. Son of an all-star outfielder who played in the earliest seasons of the postrevolution Cuban League, Linares has been widely celebrated across two decades by pro scouts, fans of Olympic-style baseball, and the Cuban sports ministry propaganda machine as the best third baseman on the planet not playing in the major leagues. Those who saw him perform at the plate and in the field during his prime (from the 1987 Indianapolis Pan American Games through the 1992 Barcelona and 1996 Atlanta Olympic Games) might easily and defensibly argue that there have been no obviously better all-around stars at the hot-corner position over the past twenty-odd years, not even on touchstone big league ball clubs.

A muscular black six-footer and right-hander who played most of his career weighing between 205 and 215 pounds, Omar Linares first broke onto Cuba's baseball scene in highly dramatic fashion, appearing on the 1982 national junior team roster at a most remarkable age of 14 and (despite his youth) batting a respectable .250 during the Juvenile World Championships staged in Barquisimeto, Venezuela. That same fall, the super-talented novice infielder surfaced as a raw Cuban League rookie prospect of apparently unlimited promise, appearing in 27 games for Vegueros (the team representing Pinar del Río province) before his sixteenth birthday. Two seasons later, during a second Junior World Cup tournament—this time in Kindersley, Canada—the young phenom, not yet 18 years old, first stunned international observers by crushing eight homers, blasting seven additional extra-base hits, and posting a remarkable .511 batting average to launch a burgeoning reputation as perhaps the greatest world amateur tournament player of all time. Elevated to senior national team status, Linares appeared first in the Intercontinental Cup games at Edmonton in 1985, where he once more slugged away at a remarkable .467 clip for the nine-game tournament span. He soon also lit up the Central American Games competitions held in the Dominican Republic the following year when he pounded the ball once more at a .497 clip; that same season he posted yet another glowing .457 mark in his first World Cup Series (11 games) staged at Haarlem in The Netherlands. A single year later at the late-summer Pan American Games in Indianapolis (while still a teenager, though now also a fully seasoned international veteran), he maintained that remarkable momentum with an eye-popping .520 average (including a pair of triples) to outstrip the entire field of tournament sluggers, among them potent future U.S. big leaguers such as Frank Thomas, Ty Griffin, Ed Sprague, and Tino Martínez. For an encore that same October, the prodigious teenager smashed 11 homers during Intercontinental Cup matches in Havana as the loaded Cuban contingent again ran roughshod over a yet another talented Team USA lineup, one mentored by University of Miami coaching legend Ron Fraser and boasting boasted future major leaguers Mickey Morandini, Chuck Knoblauch, and Scott Servais.

Cuba's Omar Linares might have been "The Greatest Third Baseman on the Planet." [Author's Cuban Collection]

The exploding Linares legacy grew largely from an amazing collection of unparalleled batting achievements which began in the 1980s and soon stretched across the decade of the 1990s. Twice, in 1990 and 1993, he batted over .400 for a full season consisting of both the longer National Series and shorter Selective Series campaigns; he completed four National Series schedules batting above the touchstone .400 plateau (admittedly all in the era of aluminum bats) and eventually reached 400-plus homers in only 1,700 games and 5,962 at-bats; his ratio of one round-tripper every 14.8 official at-bats rates favorably against the most legendary big league bashers. Using *Total Baseball's* Home Run Average (homers per ever 100 at-bats) as a good yardstick and comparing Linares to veteran major league stars—admittedly a futile, if entertaining, exercise—his 6.77 career mark would surpass all but those of Mark McGwire, Babe Ruth, Ralph Kiner, and Harmon Killebrew.

The Linares reputation grows also from the uncanny ability to deliver in almost all tense clutch situations. In the 1996 slugfest gold-medal shootout in Atlanta versus Japan, Linares saved the day with 3 booming homers, even after nearly proving a goat with his crucial early-game throwing error that had let Japan back into the contest. In the 1999 opening Cuba–Orioles match in Havana, despite coming off a season-long leg injury that had limited his National Series play to only 30 games, and despite the handicaps of hitting for the first time with wooden lumber and while debuting against major league pitchers, it was Linares who delivered the crucial game-tying eighth-inning single. (One is tempted to say 'unsurprisingly,' if such clutch hitting can ever be experienced as unsurprising.) A month later in Baltimore, during Cuba's 12–6 pasting of the big leaguers, the veteran slugger reached base in every plate appearance, recording three singles, a double, and a pair of walks. After slumping badly through most of the Pan Am Games in Winnipeg during August of that same year, Linares unloaded at just the right time (again against experienced professional hurling) with a vital homer in the do-or-die semifinal match versus Canada that clinched Cuba's hard-earned qualification for the 2000 Olympic Games in Sydney. The Winnipeg homer blasted off Canada's Mike Meyers was one of the most important long balls in recent Cuban national team history. Linares himself (in a 2002 biography released in Havana) recalls the Winnipeg circuit blast as his single brightest career moment, a landmark achievement among dozens and dozens of truly memorable clutch performances. And, finally, in 2002 Linares joined Orestes Kindelán and Antonio Pacheco as the first Cubans to play in Japan.

Adolfo "Dolf" Luque (b. August 4, 1890; d. July 3, 1957).   The list of memorable Cuban major leaguers begins win tough-as-nails pitcher Adolfo Luque, a two-decade National Leaguer who split his service among the Braves, Reds, Dodgers, and Giants. Luque's calling card was his 27 victories for the Cincinnati Reds in 1923 and his 194 lifetime big league wins. Yet today—if he is remembered at all—Luque carries the burden of an unjust reputation for hot-headed on-field and off-field behavior that all too neatly fits the stereotype of the fiery and undisciplined Latino ballplayer. Dolf Luque was indeed a rough customer, and his reputation for aggressive play was admittedly not all exaggeration. There was the famous (perhaps infamous) lapse when he charged the New York Giants bench and flattened Casey Stengel among a group of offending hecklers, but that event has been allowed to overshadow some remarkable mound work and a career noted for exceptional durability. The season enjoyed by Luque in 1923 (27–8, 1.93 ERA, 28 complete games) remains one of the most dominant in National League history. He salvaged a dramatic victory in the 1933 World Series when he relieved Hal Schumacher in Game Five and spun five scoreless frames to preserve the championship-clinching victory. He was a Hall-of-Fame manager in Cuba and still performed as a capable pitcher and batter well into his forties. Luque also did his share of significant groundbreaking: he was the first Latin to win 20 in a season, capture 100 victories in a career, and pitch in a World Series (1919) and also the first to lead a major league circuit in victories, winning percentage, and ERA. Before organized baseball's tardy integration on the heels of World War II, Adolfo Luque was arguably the foremost Latin American star performing on the major league scene.

Agustín Marquetti (b. 1955).   Agustín Marquetti was the first great Cuban slugger of the modern era. He was also the first Cuban Leaguer who left little doubt among the occasional professional bird dog who saw him perform about his unquestioned major league potential. A hulking black-skinned slugger who served Habana Province as first baseman but also did occasional outfield duty, Marquetti regularly dominated the Cuban League in individual offensive production throughout the late 1960s and early 1970s. He was best known for swatting towering home run blasts, and his 19 round-trippers in the 99-game National Series of 1969 stood as a record for several seasons until surpassed by Armando Capiró. The number of homers Marquetti blasted that top season may not seem overly impressive by big league standards—but his blasts all came in spacious league parks and were stroked during a era noted for an abundance of overpowering pitching. Existing photos of Marquetti's round-house swing suggest the awesome power that accounted for 207 homers across 22 short seasons (approximately 50 National Series games followed by an only slightly longer Selective Series campaign) played in an epoch largely dominated by pitching skill despite the presence of aluminum bats. By major league standards, Marquetti's homers were not particularly frequent (he hit one about every 32 at-bats), but some of them were truly gigantic. Marquetti saved some of his top slugging feats for important international tournament play (he registered 31 homers and compiled a .346 batting average in these events), where they always had the grandest impact. Lastly, he was a durable physical specimen who rarely suffered career-slowing injury, thus stretching out his talented career for 22 long winters and summers as one of the lengthiest tenures in Cuban League annals.

At the top of his fabulous career, Agustín Marquetti once fell victim to one of the strangest incidents ever witnessed during top-level baseball in any country. This came on a day when the young slugger knocked home a game-winning run with a blast to the outfield but then had that crucial single nullified with a rare play that can only recall the famed New York Giants goat, Bonehead Fred Merkle. After seemingly deciding a tense league game with his smack into right field, the 20-year-old rookie stood at home to embrace the teammate racing in with the winning tally. He was immediately gunned down at first by an alert opposition right fielder (nullifying both the hit and the run and extending the game to extra innings): a painful moment easily as embarrassing as any etched in Cuban League history.

Agapito Mayor (b. August 18, 1915).   Not all of the earliest Cuban stars were black Negro leaguers. Agapito Mayor was perhaps the best Cuban white pitcher of the 1940s and 1950s never to make his way into a major league roster. Star of the first Caribbean World Series (1949) and the only 3-game winner in a single series, Mayor's legacy would remain his achievements on the winter-ball circuits, altogether unknown to North American fans. He also carried one of baseball's stranger monikers, being known widely as "El Triple Feo" (The "Three-Times Ugly" Man) because his pointed nose, disappearing chin, and angular face presented anything but a movie idol profile. In his 14-year Cuban League pro career (1938–1953), the southpaw ace of the fan-favorite Almendares club had somewhat uneven results, posting only an overall 68–64 mark with 54 complete games. There were nonetheless some impressive showings against touring big league teams, topped by a 1940 four-hitter against the soon-to-be National League champion St. Louis Cardinals and an equally impressive 4–2 defeat two winters later of Leo Durocher's Brooklyn Dodgers. Mayor's special immortality in Cuba, however, was actually earned during the 1949 inaugural Caribbean series. It was there that three successful outings, including one start (a rout of Puerto Rico's Mayagüez Indians) and two relief victories, earned him tournament Most Valuable Player honors and a guaranteed spot in island lore. And there was also Mayor's career season of 1946–1947 which coincided with one of the most dramatic Cuban League pennant races ever. Almendares would triumph that year on the final two days of the nip-and-tuck battle with arch-rival Habana, thanks to a pair of brilliant pitching outings by Mayor and U.S. big leaguer Max Lanier.

José de la Caridad Méndez (b. 1888; d. October 31, 1928). Among the most notable island stars from the century's earliest decades was a brief and brilliant comet celebrated everywhere on the winter ball circuit as Cuba's "Black Diamond"—an epithet coined by none other than John McGraw. José de la Caridad Méndez first turned big league heads by kindling Cuban pride with his surprising dominations of John McGraw's Giants and Ty Cobb's Tigers during the barnstorming seasons of 1908 and 1909. The rubber-armed Méndez stood only 5′ 9″ and tipped the scales at a scrawny 155 pounds, but he flung a dancing fastball that appeared to even the most seasoned pro hitters to weigh almost more than the diminutive pitcher himself.

Méndez amazed the baseball world almost overnight in the winter of 1908 when first discovered by baseball's white establishment, much to the dismay of one set of big league batsmen who performed off-season duties that year for the Cincinnati Reds. When the visiting National League club arrived in Havana for their celebrated whirlwind tour, they could hardly have anticipated the rude greeting they would receive from an unheralded set of island blackball strikeout artists. Twenty-year-old Méndez was first to take the measure of the Cincinnati ball club, striking out nine, walking but two, and taking a no-hitter into the final frame of the November 15 outing in Almendares Park. The potential masterpiece was spoiled only by Miller Huggins's scratch single in the ninth. To prove that the first one-sided encounter was no fluke, Méndez hurled another seven shutout innings of relief versus the bedazzled Reds only two weeks after that first surprise blanking of big league bats. He then dramatically punctuated the issue with a second complete-game shutout (4–0, with eight strikeouts and no walks) a mere four days later. The final tally was twenty-five uninterrupted scoreless frames against a lineup that had limped home fifth in the National League only a few weeks before.

Trading in an Almendares jersey for the flannels of various barnstorming outfits, Méndez reportedly next continued his miraculous string of perfect outings with twenty more consecutive scoreless frames, though now admittedly toiling against somewhat lesser competition: a nine-inning shutout against a touring semi-pro outfit from Key West; a no-hitter during a return engagement against the same ball club back in Key West (in what was possibly the first racially integrated baseball game to be played within Florida); and finally two additional shutout innings for Almendares once Cuban League play resumed.

The magic which Méndez began against the shell-shocked Cincinnati ball club in 1908 continued against four additional big league visitors over the course of the next three winters. Things started a bit roughly for the celebrated Cuban ace the following winter, when the touring Detroit Tigers (without front-line stars Ty Cobb and Sam Crawford) administered a 9–3 drubbing. Although returning to form against Tigers ace Ed Willett (21–10 that summer in the American League), Méndez fell again, 4–0, despite yielding just six hits and one earned run but enduring four costly fielding errors committed behind him. Méndez did manage a victory against the Tigers in 1909, a 2–1 five-hitter in his third and final outing. The 1909 series against Detroit also saw a second supertalented black Cuban ace, Eustaquio Pedroso, dazzling the further humiliated big leaguers with his own eleven-inning no-hitter.

Manager McGraw desperately wanted Méndez for his own roster despite the Cuban's taboo dark skin, and the Giants manager even compared "El Diamante Negro" to the immortal Christy Mathewson—the current ace of his own National League staff back in New York. It was Dolf Luque, however, who offered perhaps the highest praise for the talents of the remarkable José Méndez. Returning to Havana for a public celebration marking his own twenty-seven-win 1923 National League campaign, the successful big leaguer spied Méndez lurking in the grandstand and approached the aging and now injury-riddled 36-year-old Negro leaguer with a most memorable greeting. "This parade should have been for you," said a humble and politic Luque. "Certainly you're a far better pitcher than I am."

Germán Mesa (b. May 12, 1967).   Not all recent top Cuban stars have been ace pitchers or muscular home run sluggers. Along with some flashy and daring base runners and aggressive outfielders there have been middle-infield glove wizards like Germán Mesa (no relation to Villa Clara stalwart Victor Mesa), long-time shortstop for Havana-based Industriales. Mesa fell into sudden if brief disfavor with INDER (Cuban sports ministry) officials in the mid-1990s but nonetheless strung together a remarkable 16-year career before and after his brief suspension from league and national team play that cost him a much-desired appearance in the Atlanta Olympics. Few Cuban players of the past quarter-century have stirred more debate about big league potential than glue-fingered Havana shortstop Germán Mesa. More than a handful of scouts have been thoroughly impressed by Mesa's stellar glove work on fields unmanicured to big league standards. Some observers have claimed Mesa a clear equal to Ozzie Smith. If the Ozzie Smith comparison is perhaps a stretch, few observers fail to peg Mesa a notch above former New York Mets stalwart Rey Ordóñez, who himself defected from Cuba precisely because Mesa blocked his route to National Team stardom.

Germán Mesa's temporary suspension and subsequent return were two of the biggest stories coming out of Cuba in recent seasons. The suspension—starting out as a full banishment but later rescinded as the result of a rare change of heart among top INDER officials—came under especially cloudy circumstances. Both Mesa, the top infield wizard, and Orlando Hernández, one of the country's leading hurlers, had been dropped from the national team for reported lackluster performance on the eve of 1996 Atlanta Olympic

Germán Mesa, Cuban National Team, 1992. [Author's Cuban Collection]

competition. In October (less than two months after the Cuban squad returned victorious from the Atlanta games), Mesa and El Duque, together with former national team catcher Alberto Hernández (no relation to Orlando or the already departed Liván) were all banished from further Cuban League play on the charges of having accepted undercover payments from an unidentified scout representing Miami-based player agent Joe Cubas. No further details were ever forthcoming, and Mesa quietly disappeared from the Cuban baseball scene for nearly two full years; El Duque, for his part, would soon make headlines with his much-heralded December flight from the island little more than a year later.

The subsequent saga of Mesa's surprising full reinstatement was nearly as shrouded in mystery and heavy intrigue as was his original harsh banishment. The dramatic return to action also provided an emotional moment for Havana fans: the talented Industriales stalwart was as universally beloved as any baseball figure on the island. The first Cuban ballplayer ever pardoned and reinstated after spawning such serious charges of disloyalty to INDER principles of amateur purity in sport, Germán Mesa may well have benefited as much from troublesome sagging fan support around the league as he did from his own apparent exemplary behavior while quietly suffering his career-threatening punishment. Whatever the reason for the turn-about reinstatement, it stirred as much excitement among fans in the capital city and elsewhere around Cuba as had any baseball event of the past several seasons. Mesa's celebrated reappearance came in Estadio Latinoamericano on opening day of National Series XXXVIII (October 18, 1998) and was the occasion for an emotional pregame infield scene where players from both Industriales and rival Pinar del Río rushed on the field to shake the resurrected star's hand moments before the season's opening pitch. At the same time, 40,000 patrons (the largest Havana opening game throng in many a National Series) rose in unison to shout out its own thunderous welcome. It was quite a remarkable spontaneous outpouring of love for Cuba's greatest modern-era shortstop.

Germán Mesa is indeed a rare sure-handed defender,[3] despite a reported lack of genuine motivation in recent seasons that now seems endemic to numerous ballplayers performing in Havana. There is increasing speculation among the most knowledgeable Havana fans that top players around the league seem to have little left to play for; with large collections of championship medals already in their pockets they nonetheless face little realistic prospect for improving their own financial hardships or those of their families, given their meager salaries paid out only in shrinking pesos. The situation seems especially difficult for Havana-based players, who are almost daily exposed to fellow Cubans employed in the tourist trade as waiters, taxi drivers, or hotel staffers who rake in substantial paychecks and tips consisting of highly valued American dollars. But whatever sharp drop in morale may exist, it is rarely visible to the untrained eye. Germán Mesa—even if he may not always be playing all out—is nonetheless a rare talent who makes the circus infield stop almost routinely game-in and game-out and who continuously amazes with both his range and whip-like throwing arm. He has no doubt slipped a notch since his forced retirement, but he still makes plays that would turn heads in any major league park, and he does so while performing on infields laced with pebbles ands ruts not found even on most crude sandlots diamonds up north.

Victor Mesa (b. February 20, 1960). Victor Mesa (unrelated to Germán Mesa) earned as much of a reputation for on-field craziness as he did for his brilliant play, a reputation that still dogs him today as one of the Cuban League's most colorful and controversial managers. On the field, he was one of the island's great hitters, one of its unparalleled base runners, and one of Cuba's greatest clutch performers in both league action and international tournament games.

Victor Mesa was known throughout his playing days above all else for his daring base running skills and his desire to always play the game with the utmost joy and the most outrageous flair for the dramatic and even the downright reckless. The Villa Clara native was a powerful and consistent hitter as well as a flashy outfielder. But he was also what the Cubans call a *postalita*—a "hot dog," in English parlance. His nickname "El Loco" ("The Crazy One") was an appropriate one, and throughout the 1980s and early 1990s he lived up to his derogatory moniker at each and every opportunity. Victor Mesa was the base-stealing champion a half dozen times in the National Series and several times more in the Selective Series played during early summer, but he ran the bases with a reckless style that had historically not been much appreciated in Cuba. The handsome and charismatic mulatto was an ever-present force who usually thrilled the home crowds in Santa Clara but was just as frequently a target of opposition fan wrath in Havana or Santiago or just about anywhere else around the sixteen-city Cuban circuit.

Victor Mesa was unquestionably one of Cuba's most colorful ballplayers of the recent epoch. He was also a dangerous opponent in world tournament play, which on several occasions turned him (despite his reported unpopularity in league cities outside Havana during National Series seasons) into something of a folk hero across all of Cuba. Such was the case in Brussels, Belgium, during late summer 1983 when Cuba dramatically reclaimed an Intercontinental Cup crown lost two years earlier and did so largely on the strength of impressive slugging by Mesa that featured a tournament-leading .576 batting average, plus the top totals for runs scored, base hits, and home runs.

Most recently "El Loco" has returned to the scene as a hugely successful manager with the team for which he played nearly twenty seasons. His pesky Villa Clara team was one of the big stories of the 2001 Cuban League season, though they did eventually collapse in the playoffs after posting the year's best regular-season mark. Many thought it was Mesa's brusque and highly emotional managerial style that best explained a year-end swoon, when his exhausted club surprisingly dropped three of four during quarterfinal action with weak-hitting Camagüey (a division rival Villa Clara outdistanced by six full games during the regular campaign). During 2002, Villa Clara again charged into the playoffs looking like a serious championship contender. And again they wilted under the heat of the semifinal series, versus a surprising destiny-driven team from Holguín. What made Mesa a star performer as a player now seems to be working against him on the manager's end of the bench. His moves are often the very epitome of overmanaging: he yanks relief pitchers prematurely, sometimes after only three or four tosses; on other occasions he punishes starters or relievers by leaving them on the mound when ineffective to suffer an ERA-destroying barrage of hits and runs; he shows up his players in full view of opponents and spectators by flamboyant sideline displays of displeasure at their failures or errors. In short, he repeatedly calls attention to himself as the club's leading star figure. There may be some truth to an oft-repeated speculation that Mesa's Villa Clara players have altogether little motive to sacrifice for the team or to go the extra proverbial mile for their unsupportive manager by the time postseason play rolls around.

Victor Mesa's career was marked from first to last by self-aggrandizing on-field displays, by a larger-than-life reputation for flamboyance, and by a personal ballplaying approach that always seemed largely out of sync with a normal smooth and controlled Cuban playing style. He was also a man unafraid of controversial words. Mesa even voiced his opinions freely to the North American press, something rare among Cuban athletes, who have little to gain and much to fear from extroverted comments to foreign reporters. The typical Cuban baseball player uses such interviews—as Omar Linares has so often done—to repeat what some would call a party line about the advantages and beauties of the Cuban amateur sports system. Mesa, however, was never afraid to step out of that mold. One such occasion occurred on the eve of the 1992 Barcelona Olympics, when his words appeared in an article by Jim Callis for *Baseball America*. When asked about his own prospects, and those of his teammates, as potential big league players, Victor Mesa boldly declared that the Cuban national team could win regularly on a major league diamond. Not at first perhaps, Mesa continued tongue in cheek, but "after a few years and with a little more pitching . . . perhaps with Nolan Ryan, with Roger Clemens, with Dwight Gooden, and the rest of who we have here, we would definitely win." It was the kind of playful understatement altogether rare among cautious Cuban athletes faced with what might easily appear to be a hostile U.S. sporting press.

Orestes "Minnie" Miñoso (b. November 29, 1922).   After Jackie Robinson the big league doors finally opened for Cuban blacks, and the first through those doors was Orestes "Minnie" Miñoso. Miñoso was the most exciting Latin major leaguer of the 1950s, at least before Roberto Clemente appeared on the scene with Pittsburgh. Miñoso is arguably the only Cuban-bred player ever to attain legitimate big league star status, given that Tony Pérez, Luis Tiant

Jr., and Mike Cúellar were all born on the island but participated in little of its baseball culture, while Camilo Pascual and Pete Ramos never quite elevated themselves into the highest echelon of big league headliners. A colorful and flamboyant performer in his years in Cleveland and Chicago, Miñoso was destined in the end to fall a bit short of most of the milestones that guarantee immortality, if not Cooperstown enshrinement. He came tantalizingly close to amassing 2,000 hits (1,962) and 200 homers (186) and was only a percentage point short of finishing up as a career .300-level hitter. Yet several misguided publicity stunts related to extending his career (cameo appearances in 1976 at age 54 and again in 1980, making him a five-decade player) in the end only tarnished a once glowing reputation. Of course Miñoso's big league numbers tell only half the story of a player who remained a winter league fixture for nearly three decades and logged 43 total seasons and better than 4,000 hits in aggregate major league, minor league, and winter league action. "The Cuban Comet's" legacy as a player thus perhaps remains a somewhat clouded one, despite his achievements and the infectious—even joyous—enthusiasm with which he always played. But never has baseball anywhere found a finer personal ambassador.

Antonio Muñoz (b. January 17, 1949).   If the New York Yankees had in Mantle and Maris their deadly M&M boys at the heart of the batting order in the early 1960s, so did the Cuban national teams later in the same decade, with Marquetti and Muñoz. Antonio Muñoz was the second great long-ball basher of the middle period of Cuban League history, and in reality Muñoz was a much more impressive home-run slugger than even Marquetti, especially if raw

Cuba's legendary slugger Antonio Muñoz in Latin American Stadium, Havana, 1975. [Author's Cuban Collection]

numbers and frequency of homers are to be valued over aesthetic impressions of mere distance brought on by brute power. Another black lefty of imposing stature, Muñoz labored for the Azucareros and Las Villas teams and, also like Marquetti, took up his defensive slot at first base. Marquetti pulled as many press headlines across the same era simply by having the advantage of playing in Havana, the nation's capital city in both politics and baseball, but it was Muñoz who rang up the much bigger numbers.

The statistics posted by Muñoz are his ultimate legacy, of course, and most of those numbers were for raw power hitting. His career totals for 24 seasons (National Series and Selective Series) would feature 370 homers, a .302 batting average, a .535 slugging mark, and 1,407 RBI. He garnered only two National Series home run titles and matched but never surpassed Marquetti's high of 19 in a single season, but he took individual honors six times in the spring–summer Selective Series, where his 25 dingers in 1979 fell three short of the record total of 28 achieved by teammate Cheíto Rodríguez, a mark which stood until Orestes Kindelán eventually surpassed it in the mid-1980s. Muñoz, affectionately branded by fans as "El Gigante del Escambray" (the Giant from Escambray), by career's end owned a lifetime home run per at-bats ratio of 1 in 18, almost twice as good as Marquetti, though considerably short of Cheíto (and also of both Omar Linares and Kindelán). Muñoz's career home run total stood as the league high-water mark until it was surpassed eventually in the late 1980s by Lázaro Junco and then again in the 1990s by both Kindelán and Linares. *Sports Illustrated* writer Ron Fimrite was especially impressed by Muñoz in his 1977 whirlwind tour of Cuban ballparks and described the towering southpaw slugger quite fittingly as being a near-clone left-handed version of fellow Cuban-born big leaguer and future Cooperstown honoree Atanasio "Tany" (Tony) Pérez.

Pedro "Tony" Oliva (b. July 20, 1940).   Pedro "Tony" Oliva (born in Pinar del Río and brother of a Castro-era Cuban League pitcher) was the only ballplayer ever to win batting titles in his first two major league seasons. He was also arguably Cuba's best-ever all-around hitter—at least among those who toiled as big leaguers. And Oliva was one of those many Latin ballplayers (like Minnie Miñoso and Vic Power) who spent an entire career playing under a name not his own (he was born Pedro, but entered the United States with an older brother's visa and name). The start of Oliva's career was indeed sensational, for in addition to his unprecedented debut as repeat batting champion, he also established a new American League rookie record for base hits, with 217. In his second season, he was also *The Sporting News* choice as big league player of the year. Over most of fifteen seasons he continued his remarkable slugging, slowed finally only by a string of late-career nagging injuries that left him with 220 homers and a .304 batting mark, painfully short of guaranteed Cooperstown numbers. Oliva in the end never quite measured up to Miñoso for pizzazz or Pérez for statistical production, but he was one of the finest hitters of his era and one of the finest players ever born on the island of Cuba.

Antonio Pacheco (b. June 4, 1964).   Antonio Pacheco, Santiago teammate to Orestes Kindelán, was a more complete ballplayer, one who set numerous

offensive milestones of his own over a parallel 22-season career. Next to Omar Linares,
Pacheco seemingly had the greatest potential as an everyday big leaguer. He was also
a team leader and an inspirational on-field
presence, which made him one of the island's most popular national team players. It
is as a clutch hitter, however—and a prolific
one to boot—that Pacheco will always be
best remembered on the island. His greatest
legacy will remain his rank as the Cuban
League's all-time base-hits leader, but he
also ranked at or near the top in numerous
other important offensive categories.

Pacheco has never enjoyed the enthusiastic press notices accorded Linares or
Kindelán. For one thing, he is not a flashy
performer and he doesn't boast big power
numbers or often slug towering fly balls.
Pacheco was a seasoned 10-year veteran of
international tournaments by age 28 and on
the eve of baseball's debut in the 1992 Barcelona Olympics. He had already come up
big for the Cuban juggernaut on numerous
occasions during tense international play.
In a 1992 Olympic preview essay carried
by *Baseball America*, Jim Callis refers to a
then-unknown Pacheco as "another lethal
hitter who would cause a bidding war

Antonio Pacheco, Cuban National Team, 1992. [Author's
Cuban Collection]

among U.S. teams if he were available." Perennial all-star second baseman
Antonio Pacheco was also a most durable (even indestructible) player. By the
time his career was winding down at the end of the 1990s, he had become Cuba's
all-time base hits leader (with 2,356) by a comfortable margin. He played for
years with a top-flight team (Santiago de Cuba owned five league titles during
his long service), and he himself largely made the difference between defeat
and victory in a handful of these championships seasons. Pacheco's balanced
offensive production has put him near the summit of a number of the Cuban
career top-ten lists: National Series played (third, with 22), runs scored (fifth,
1,258), doubles (second, 366), total bases (third, 3,700), at-bats (fourth, 7,045),
and batting average (fifth, .334).

Pacheco has rapidly risen in the Cuban League record books during recent
campaigns and has ultimately emerged as a kind of Cuban Pete Rose. Rarely
among the league's two or three top hitters in any given single year, he was also
never very far down the list. By sheer longevity, Pacheco would, like Rose,
eventually overtake all the great batsmen of past eras to emerge as Cuba's
career base hits pacesetter, outstripping Fernando Sánchez before the end of
the 2001 campaign. Like Kindelán, he is now finished as a player in Santiago
and has moved on to better-paying industrial league games in Japan, along

with Kindelán and Germán Mesa. Although Omar Linares grabbed most of the National Series headlines, Pacheco left behind a lasting legacy as one of the league's most solid all-around performers of the recent era. Given his vast popularity on the island and his reputation as an unflinchingly loyal team player most congenial to all his teammates, it is not unreasonable to imagine Antonio Pacheco as the Cuban national team manager some day not too far down the line.

Rafael Palmeiro (b. September 24, 1964).   Rafael Palmeiro—native of Havana but product of Miami—was hands down the most consistent first baseman in big league baseball throughout the decade of the 1990s, even if media darlings such as Mark McGwire, Mo Vaughn, and Frank Thomas drew far more attention from both press and public. One of the quietest revolutions of the last decade, in fact, was the one that the Baltimore Orioles and Texas Rangers standout worked on the baseball record books. At the start of the 2004 season, the 18-year veteran's 528 career homers, 2,780 hits, and 1,687 RBI put him among the elite sluggers of all baseball history—and he is not yet done, with 3,000 hits and 550 homers no longer that much of a stretch. Palmeiro's numbers certainly now stand at guaranteed Cooperstown proportions. With one Cuban first sacker, Tony Pérez, now lodged in Cooperstown, it is seemingly only a matter of time until a second, Palmeiro, follows.

It is not even that far off the mark, perhaps, to suggest that Palmeiro now looks like the greatest of all Cuban big leaguers. His near-550 home runs (in late-season 2004) and lifetime 1,700-plus RBI (in the top 20 all-time) are now the Cuban big league high-water marks. But, like José Canseco and even like Pérez, Palmeiro in the end can stir only limited pride for Cuban ball fans in either Havana or Miami. Canseco and Palmeiro are Cubans by birthright only; Miami raised and nurtured, they are truly North Americans when it comes to their baseball training and baseball experience. Palmeiro's Cooperstown enshrinement some day down the road will draw notice in Havana, to be sure, but it will not set off wild celebrations or be cause for any sanctioned national day of honor in a country that rarely acknowledges the pride of Miami as one of its own.

Camilo Pascual (b. January 20, 1934).   In the 1950s, it was a pair of white Cuban pitchers in Washington who kept the island's reputation sizzling, Camilo Pascual and Pete Ramos. Pascual was judged to possess the best curveball of an era that many still see as baseball's true golden age. Pascual retired in 1971 as the second-winningest big league Latin American hurler (174–170). He was also a prototype workhorse, who first labored ceaselessly with a truly mediocre team in Washington, then belatedly blossomed with an exceptional revamped ball club in Minnesota. From 1954 through 1959, Pascual suffered through a confidence-shattering .297 winning percentage while backed by an inept Washington squad that offered almost no support for one of the league's finest arms. Newly ensconced in the Twin Cities (after the first American League westward expansion move) and revived by a legitimate pennant contender, the once hapless Pascual now turned in sterling 20–11 (1962) and 21–9 (1963) campaigns, also leading the league in strikeouts for three straight seasons (1961–1963). During winter seasons in Cuba, however, the pitcher known as "Little Potato" enjoyed even more hefty achievement; he was a top Cuban League ace on several occasions in the uniform of the Cienfuegos Elephants. Perhaps his proudest moments came in the winter league showcase Caribbean series, where he earned a special reputation as one of the event's most dominating mound aces by capturing six games (two each visit in 1956, 1959, and 1960) without tasting defeat.

Atanasio "Tony" ("Tany") Pérez (b. May 14, 1942). Tony Pérez long ranked as the all-time big league home-run champion (with Orlando Cepeda) and RBI leader among Latin Americans. He banged out 379 career homers while also setting milestones among Latins for games played (2,777) and RBI production (1,652). His RBI total, his most prideful achievement, remains among the loftiest in big league history. And, if his slot as king of Cuban sluggers has now been taken by another native, Rafael Palmeiro, he can still claim a stronger connection to the island. Pérez, like Tony Oliva, lived considerably longer in the native homeland. But unlike Miñoso, Pérez never played organized baseball in Cuba. His Cuban identity, also, seemingly remains something of a technicality only.

Pérez was the first Cuban native to gain full-fledged Cooperstown credentials earned on major league diamonds but only because of the odious racial lines which kept the doors closed to the greatest of all Cubans, Martín Dihigo. But Pérez's Cooperstown status was certainly justified on its own merits. No Cuban slugger (or Latin slugger) before him reached such numbers in the power departments or performed so consistently for winning teams. Even if two fellow Cubans (José Canseco and Rafael Palmeiro) and one Dominican (Sammy Sosa) would eventually reach and overtake his home run numbers and even challenge his lead among top Latino RBI men.

Pedro "Pete" Ramos (b. April 28, 1935). Pedro Ramos, Camilo Pascual's team-mate, was never as successful either in the majors or back home on winter league diamonds. But "Pistol Pete" was equally talented (when it came to raw arm speed) and a good bit more colorful (when it came to both on-field and off-field antics). It was the color that often got in the way, especially during late-career and postcareer years. After departing the big time, the flamboyant Cuban ran afoul of the law on drug-trafficking and weapons charges and spent three years in a Miami prison. Ramos retired in 1970 with most big league losses (160) by a Latin American hurler. He was also one of the most generous pitchers in history when it came to giving up the long ball (yielding 315 dingers in 2,355 innings, one every 7.48 frames). If he gave up homers on a regular basis, he also served them up in prodigious proportions, including one to Mickey Mantle in May 1956 that missed by inches being the first ball ever hit completely over the Yankee Stadium roof. Ramos suffered in Washington as Pascual did and lost 18 or more games for four straight seasons between 1958 and 1961. Worse, he did not enjoy Pascual's good fortune of remaining with the revitalized franchise long enough to cash in on glory seasons in Minnesota. Some highlights came late in his career with the Yankees, where he was a leading figure (as a reliever) in the late-season 1964 pennant stretch run. Pete Ramos will perhaps always be remembered for the sideshow aspects of his career. As proud speedster, he once staged a celebrated pregame race against Mickey Mantle, and at one point late in his pitching career he even sought out a publicized moonlighting assignment as a B-movie Hollywood gunslinger. He also initiated an all-Cuban triple play on July 23, 1960 (with Senators shortstop José Valdivielso and first baseman Julio Becquer).

Maels Rodríguez (b. October 15, 1979).   Of all the recent pitching talent on the island, none has rung up more dollar signs in the eyes of lustful scouts and salivating agents than strapping right-hander Maels Rodríguez. Maels (Cubans tend to use his first name only) first turned the scouts' heads with his brief appearance in Winnipeg for the 1999 Pan American Games, where he uncorked blistering fastballs yet also demonstrated an obvious tendency toward wildness. He soon captured further headlines back home with phenomenal 2001 and 2002 campaigns that saw him obliterating most of the existing individual strike-out marks, mowing down enemy hitters and tossing pitch after blazing pitch at almost unimaginable speeds. The 2001 National Series season was Maels' anointed personal stage from one end straight through to the other. He rang up a new National Series strikeout mark with 263, only the third pitcher in forty years to cross the lofty 200 plateau. He was also the league ERA pacesetter and tied for top slot in starts. In 2002, for an encore he again struck down more than 200 enemy hitters and also lifted his unheralded Sancti Spíritus team straight into the league championship series for the first time in better than two decades. If he lost the big games at the end of the 2002 playoffs (taking the defeat in half of his team's championship-round four losses), this was perhaps understandable. Having hurled unscheduled exhibitions matches on two occa-sions in the middle of interrupted postseason action—once against visiting Mexican Leaguers, then again in the game staged to entertain former U.S. President Jimmy Carter—the exhausted Maels won two decisions and dropped a third in the playoff quarterfinals but won two more in the semis before two final starts in the championship face-off with Holguín. Maels started a playoff total of only four contests but ultimately appeared in eleven (mostly in long relief) and logged 46.2 total innings.

Maels (pronounced Miles) has been easily the biggest story of the first two years of 2000-era Cuban League baseball. In December 1999, the strapping youngster launched his relentless assault on league record books by per-forming the much-heralded feat of breaking a radar gun milestone with his 100-mile-per-hour clocking in official game action; no Cuban Leaguer had ever previously been measured above the century mark. Next came a perfect game versus Las Tunas barely two weeks later, also the first ever in league play. And finally there was the 2001 National Series countdown to a new single-season strikeout standard that gripped the island as it unfolded outing by outing near season's end. The only notable strikeout feat that somehow escaped Maels during the incredible run was a new single-game high of 22 posted the same winter by veteran Pinar del Río southpaw Faustino Corrales. The 2001 campaign naturally proved a hard act to follow, but Maels posted impressive numbers again in 2002 and this time around he also anchored a remarkably improved team that proved the surprise of the entire season. Sancti Spíritus would ride the arms of Rodríguez and two fellow aces (veteran Yovani Aragón and novice Ifreidi Coss) all the way to the league finals. Yet as just noted, the iron-willed Maels would ironically drop both his decisions in that luckless championship showdown. He was likely merely a twin victim of both an acknowledged overuse by his desperate manager and an inevitable law of averages now manifesting itself in a sudden run of bad luck on the field. Sancti Spíritus lost three one-run decisions to Holguín, with Maels, Aragón, and Coss each victimized once by a lack of timely run support.

Maels Rodríguez has been in recent seasons what José Antonio Huelga was for Cuban baseball in the 1960s and early 1970s. No Cuban pitcher of recent decades has flashed more dazzling potential or stimulated more buzz among the island's knowledgeable fans. Maels was the single story of the 2000 and 2001 Cuban seasons when he stood the league record books on end. Then came a series of troublesome arm problems which left the career of the Sancti Spíritus ace in serious doubt. Reduced to throwing a tame 85-mile-per-hour heater, the young star was left off the Team Cuba roster for both the World Cup and Olympic Qualifier games of October and November 2003. Disillusioned by his fate, Maels fled Cuba along with former national team infielder Yobal Dueñas on the eve of the October World Cup finals in Havana. Within days of his surprise departure, Maels was already generating press chatter in the United States about potential multimillion-dollar big league offers, with the Yankees mentioned prominently as the most serious suitor. Now that Maels Rodríguez has fled Cuba, it remains to be seen if he is indeed still healthy enough to fulfill his seemingly awesome major league potential.

Wilfredo Sánchez (b. 1958). Another potent Cuban batsman of note whose career overlapped with Marquetti and Muñoz was a still more devastating pure hitting wizard, even if he rarely ever knocked balls completely over the fences. Wilfredo Sánchez was Cuba's "Hit Man" ("El Hombre Hit"). Across his brilliant career, he rewrote the league's record books and left indelible memories as the island's greatest pure batsman. Wilfredo Sánchez was also a most potent force when it came to performances on the showcase stage of international tournaments. A lefty all the way, Sánchez was a born hitter who sprayed the ball to all fields and lined his smashes like frozen ropes. He did not hit a devastating long ball, but he was nevertheless a most extraordinary singles and doubles hitter. His career batting average (.331) today still ranks fifth on the all-time list, and his career total for base hits (2,174) also leaves him in fifth place lifetime. In his own era, Wilfredo Sánchez was the best natural hitter Cuba had ever produced with its postrevolution brand of amateur-style baseball. Only the career of Omar Linares may today be enough to challenge the once indisputable claim that "El Hombre Hit" was and is the best all-around pure hitter ever to represent the baseball-crazy Caribbean island.

Luis Tiant Jr. (b. November 23, 1940). Luis Tiant had quite a legend to live up to on the island nation he left during the years of the Castro revolution to seek out a professional ballplaying career in Mexico. Tiant Sr. (known colorfully as "Sir Skinny" on the Negro league circuit and more prosaically as Lefty back home on the winter circuit) appeared in two Negro league East–West All-Star games and was a mainstay for the New York Cubans of Alex Pompez in the 1930s and 1940s. He was best known for a devastating port-side pickoff move and a herky-jerky pitching motion that also became a trademark of his more widely celebrated big league offspring. The younger Tiant would carry on—even surpass—the considerable legacy of his famed father as one of the winningest pitchers (229–172, with 2,416 strikeouts) of Latin birthright in major league history. Unlike many of the others in the last wave of Cuban ballplayers to freely leave the island before the rupture between Fidel Castro and Washington, Tiant Jr. could claim the distinction (lost to Campaneris, Pérez, and Oliva, among others) of actually having pitched in the prerevolution Cuban League, where he enjoyed modest success in the final year of the doomed Havana pro circuit. For three seasons of the early 1960s, he also followed his father's path in the Mexican League before being discovered and inked to a big league contract by the Cleveland Indians, the club with which he spent his first half dozen summers in the majors and with which he had his first breakout season (21–9 with a sensational 1.60 ERA) in 1968. Three more times would the second Tiant post a 20-win season, all with Boston in the mid-1970s, and it was in Beantown that he would also post his second career sub-2.00 ERA (1.91 in 1972).

Tiant's earliest claim to fame as a big leaguer was not an exceptionally praiseworthy one, being the dubious distinction of having duplicated an unwanted feat of his famed countryman Adolfo Luque. For a brief while his hallmark achievement seemed destined to be the embarrassing fact that, like Luque, he had somehow managed to dovetail seasons in which he first won (Cleveland 1968) and then lost (Cleveland 1969) 20 games. Then came the fateful stop in Boston, which led directly to stardom and a niche as one of that tradition-rich franchise's most wildly popular players ever. During his run of spectacular Boston seasons (1973–1976, when he averaged 20 victories), Tiant was immortalized (like Stengel and Berra before him) by his colorful language ("Ees great to be weeth a weiner") and eccentric cigar puffing. Of course in this case—as with those of other Latins in the 1960s and 1970s—the image assuredly carried some heavy negative racial and ethnic overtones. Distinguished by a twisting mound delivery that rivaled his father's and never separated off the field from his huge Havana cigar, Tiant Jr. was exactly the kind of colorful and flamboyant figure on which the dominant myth of the eccentric Latino ballplayer has always regrettably thrived.

Cristóbal Torriente (b. 1895; d. 1938).   There was a black-ball star from Cuba—one named Cristóbal Torriente—who once out-slugged Babe Ruth during a memorable island visit by the Bambino (a visit noted most for the Babe's epic-style carousing). Much of Cristóbal Torriente's own legend is ironically founded not on his stellar decade of black-ball play (mostly with Rube Foster's Chicago American Giants) but upon his brief encounter with John McGraw's touring team of big leaguers (mostly New York Giants) in Havana during the late fall following the 1920 season. And no lesser figure played a key role in this memorable face-off than Babe Ruth himself, fresh from his stunning 54-homer debut with the Yankees the previous summer and enticed to perform in Havana by a then-incredible offer of $1,000 per game in hard cash from Cuban promoter Abel Linares. With regular Giants first baseman George "Highpockets" Kelly taking the mound for the big leaguers against the same Cuban Almendares club that had once featured José Méndez, Torriente seized the advantage by smashing booming back-to-back opposite field homers. When Ruth (who himself failed at the plate three times) assumed the hill (remember, Ruth was a pitcher first) to silence the Cuban slugger, he was greeted rudely enough by Torriente's third prodigious blow—a ringing double to left which nearly removed the legs from startled Giants third sacker Frankie Frisch.

The final count saw Torriente going four for five with three round-trippers and six runs batted home; Ruth stood zero for two, having walked twice and reached once on an error.[4] Frisch would later lionize "The Cuban Strongboy" when he remembered the particular blast that nearly amputated his limbs: "In those days Torriente was a hell of a player! Christ, I'd like to whitewash him and bring him straight up (to the majors)!"

Zoilo "El Zorro" Versalles (b. December 18, 1939; d. June 9, 1995).   Zoilo "El Zorro" ("The Fox") Versalles was Latin America's first American League Most Valuable Player (1965) and a solid mainstay for an American League Championship Minnesota ball club that same peak season. At the exact midpoint of his dozen-season big league sojourn, "El Zorro" enjoyed what might well have been the best single offensive performance by any shortstop up to that time: he paced the junior circuit in runs, triples, doubles, at-bats, and total bases, while also walking off with a Gold Glove and outdistancing teammate and fellow Cuban Tony Oliva by more than 100 ballots in the Most Valuable Player race. What came before and after wasn't much to crow about, however, and the back problems that cropped up the following season quickly sent his career on a final prolonged six-year downslide. He never topped 20 doubles again in his career, and his highs for homers and triples were an undistinguished 7 in each category. Though the first half-dozen seasons in the majors were a slow but steady climb to respectability for the Pinar del Río native, his early years in Washington were dogged by a series of offensive and defensive slumps and a damning reputation for moodiness. In his biography (James Terzian, *The Kid from Cuba*), Versalles would later explain his early malaise as being the direct result of homesickness and desperation over his wife's being unable to leave Cuba in the wake of the Castro revolution. Things took a decided turn for the better in July 1961 (the middle of his third season with the Senators–Twins, who had relocated to Minnesota earlier that year), when the broken family was reunited in Miami and the shortstop's batting average soared to .280 by year's end. When the rejuvenated Cuban won his first Gold Glove two years later he broke a five-year stranglehold on the award by Venezuelan great Luis Aparicio. And when he led the Twins into the World Series against the Koufax–Drysdale Dodgers in 1965, his performance in the fall classic (team best .286 BA, team-leading 8 hits, a key homer in the opener) was the easily overall best of any Cuban before the arrival of Luis Tiant (with the 1975 Bosox), Tony Pérez (with the 1976 Big Red Machine), or José Canseco (with the 1988 Oakland A's).

Braudilio Vinent (b. 1947).   Cuba has turned out some amazing pitchers in the past quarter-century, and it is no surprise that of the half-dozen or so recent political defectors who have enjoyed some big league success, all have been pitchers. But one of the best among Cuban mound stalwarts never left the island, except to dazzle international opponents in world tournaments over a fifteen-year span. Hard-throwing Santiago native right-hander Braudilio Vinent appeared on the scene in the late 1960s and starred in Cuban League play throughout the 1970s and 1980s. By the time he wrapped up a two-decade career, he had posted numerous pitching marks (such as 400 starts, 221 wins, 265 complete games, and 2,134 strikeouts) that became mountain peaks for all future stars to aim at, and he had constructed a lasting stature among postrevolution league icons that remains unassailable.

Aquino Abreu, Manuel Hurtado, José Huelga, Rogelio García, or even Santiago Mederos aside, the greatest revolutionary-era pitcher of them all was without doubt this durable right-hander from the Oriente who would before his 20-season tenure was complete break almost all existing records for individual pitching accomplishment. Braudilio Vinent, laboring over the years with four different National Series teams representing Santiago province, was the first Cuban hurler to appear in 20 different National Series seasons, the first to log 200 career victories, and also the first to hurl 3,000-plus innings. Several of these marks for endurance and unparalleled achievement have since been outstripped by successors, but his record total of 63 shutouts still seems safe from challenge. Rogelio García came nearest to Vinent, with 56 shutouts, and no active Cuban League hurler is much closer today than the half-way mark. Dubbed affectionately "The Meteor from La Maya," Vinent was not only the best league pitcher on the scene from the late 1960s through to the early 1980s, but he also performed brilliantly in dozens of international contests (making a record 96 total appearances) and owned a special and much appreciated penchant for dominating rival American squads in several celebrated gold medal showdowns. Vinent's international blue-ribbon outing came with Amateur World Series action in Managua in 1972, when he not only captured all four tournament appearances with a microscopic 0.62 ERA but also tossed an eight-hit complete-game whitewashing against a squad of tournament all-stars during special exhibition closing day action.

IN BRIEF

When comparisons are made with other Caribbean nations only in terms of raw numbers of big leaguers produced, the Cubans come out poorly. Even when it comes to stars, there are no Cubans to compare with Clemente, Sosa, Marichal, or even Fernando Valenzuela. But if the yardstick for assessing baseball talent or baseball accomplishment is found on the fields of play outside the realm of organized baseball, Cuba indeed stands unchallenged at the top of the heap. In the glorious hidden venues that were the Negro circuits of the first half of the twentieth century, none can overshadow top Cuban stars like Dihigo, Méndez, Torriente, Oms, and dozens more. This is equally true of the Caribbean winter circuits, where both pre- and postrevolution Cuban leagues have always been the magnet for all those seeking the purest of baseball entertainment. The Cubans in turn provided the bulk of truly immortal stars also found in other Latin leagues during the half-century before communist revolution and politics isolated the island from professional sports. And in the alternative universe of international amateur play, the Cubans have virtually had the playing field to themselves for nearly eight full decades. By all these measures and likely by any others that one could conceive, Cuba stands firm as a baseball country and baseball culture ranking a close second only to the United States itself.

SELECTED CUBAN RECORDS AND STATISTICS
Cuba's Major Leaguers

Cubans in the Major Leagues (1871–2003)

	Name*	Debut	Position	Debut Team	Seasons	Games	Career Statistics
1	Enrique Ésteban "Steve" Bellán	1871	IF	Troy Haymakers (NA)	3	60	.252 BA
2	Armando Marsans	1911	OF	Cincinnati Reds (NL)	8	655	.269 BA
3	Rafael Almeida	1911	OF	Cincinnati Reds (NL)	3	102	.270 BA
4	Mike (Miguel) González	1912	C	Boston Braves (NL)	19	1,042	.253 BA
5	Merito (Baldomero) Acosta	1913		Washington Senators (AL)	5	180	.255 BA
6	Jack (Jacinto) Calvo	1913	OF	Washington Senators (AL)	2	34	.161 BA
7	Ángel Aragón	1914	IF	New York Yankees (AL)	3	32	.118 BA
8	Adolfo "Dolf" Luque	1914	RHP	Boston Braves (NL)	20	550	194–179, 3.24 ERA
9	Emilio Palmero	1915	RHP	New York Giants (NL)	4	41	6–15, 5.17 ERA
10	Joseíto Rodríguez	1916	IF	New York Giants (NL)	5	58	.166 BA
11	Manolo (Manuel) Cueto	1917	OF	Cincinnati Reds (NL)	3	151	.227 BA
12	Eusebio González	1918	SS	Boston Red Sox (AL)	1	3	.400 BA
13	Oscar Tuero	1918	RHP	St. Louis Cardinals (NL)	3	58	6–9, 2.88 ERA
14	José Acosta	1920	RHP	Washington Senators (AL)	3	55	10–10, 4.51 ERA
15	Ricardo Torres	1920	C	Washington Senators (AL)	3	22	.297 BA
16	Pedro Dibut	1924	RHP	Cincinnati Reds (NL)	2	8	3–0, 2.70 ERA
17	Ramón (Mike) Herrera	1925	IF	Boston Red Sox (AL)	2	84	.275 BA
18	Oscar Estrada	1929	LHP	St. Louis Browns (AL)	1	1	0–0, 0.00 ERA
19	Roberto Estalella	1935	OF	Washington Senators (AL)	8	680	.282 BA
20	Mike (Fermín) Guerra	1937	C	Washington Senators (AL)	9	565	.242 BA
21	René Monteagudo	1938	LHP	Washington Senators (AL)	3	46	3–7, 6.42 ERA
22	Gilberto Torres	1940	IF	Washington Senators (AL)	4	44	.262 BA
23	Jack (Ángel) Aragón	1941	PR	New York Giants (NL)	1	1	.000 BA
24	Roberto Ortíz	1941	OF	Washington Senators (AL)	6	213	.255 BA
25	Chico (Salvador) Hernández	1942	C	Chicago Cubs (NL)	2	90	.250 BA
26	Mosquito (Antonio) Ordeñana	1943	SS	Pittsburgh Pirates (NL)	1	1	.500 BA
27	Nap (Napoleón) Reyes	1943	IF	New York Giants (NL)	4	279	.284 BA
28	Tommy (Tomás) de la Cruz	1944	RHP	Cincinnati Reds (NL)	1	34	9–9, 3.25 ERA
29	Preston (Pedro) Gómez	1944	IF	Washington Senators (AL)	1	8	.286 BA
30	Baby (Oliverio) Ortíz	1944	RHP	Washington Senators (AL)	1	2	0–2, 6.23 ERA
31	Luis Suárez	1944	3B	Washington Senators (AL)	1	1	.000 BA
32	Santiago (Carlos) Ullrich	1944	RHP	Washington Senators (AL)	2	31	3–3, 5.04 ERA
33	Roy (Rogelio) Valdés	1944	PH	Washington Senators (AL)	1	1	.000 BA
34	Jorge Comellas	1945	RHP	Chicago Cubs (NL)	1	7	0–2, 4.50 ERA
35	Sid (Isidoro) León	1945	RHP	Philadelphia Phillies (NL)	1	14	0–4, 5.35 ERA
36	Armando Roche	1945	RHP	Washington Senators (AL)	1	2	0–0, 6.00 ERA
37	Adrián Zabala	1945	LHP	New York Giants (NL)	2	26	4–7, 5.02 ERA
38	José Zardón	1945	OF	Washington Senators (AL)	1	54	.290 BA
39	Reggie (Regino) Otero	1945	1B	Chicago Cubs (NL)	1	14	.391 BA
40	Ángel Fleitas	1948	SS	Washington Senators (AL)	1	15	.077 BA
41	Moín (Ramon) García	1948	RHP	Washington Senators (AL)	1	4	0–0, 17.18 ERA
42	Enrique (Julio) González	1949	RHP	Washington Senators (AL)	1	13	0–0, 4.72 ERA
43	Minnie (Orestes) Miñoso	1949	OF	Cleveland Indians (AL)	17	1,835	.298 BA, 186 HR
44	Witto (Luis) Aloma	1950	RHP	Chicago White Sox (AL)	4	116	18–3, 3.44 ERA
45	Sandy (Sandalio) Consuegra	1950	RHP	Washington Senators (AL)	8	248	51–32, 3.37 ERA
46	Connie (Conrado) Marrero	1950	RHP	Washington Senators (AL)	5	118	39–40, 3.67 ERA
47	Limonar (Rogelio) Martínez	1950	RHP	Washington Senators (AL)	1	2	0–1, 27.00 ERA
48	Julio (Jiqui) Moreno	1950	RHP	Washington Senators (AL)	4	73	18–22, 4.25 ERA
49	Carlos Pascual	1950	RHP	Washington Senators (AL)	1	2	1–1, 2.12 ERA
50	Cisco (Francisco) Campos	1951	OF	Washington Senators (AL)	3	71	.279 BA

	Name*	Debut	Position	Debut Team	Seasons	Games	Career Statistics
51	Willie (Guillermo) Miranda	1951	SS	Washington Senators (AL)	9	824	.221 BA
52	Ray (Rafael) Noble	1951	C	New York Giants (NL)	3	107	.218 BA
53	Sandy (Edmundo) Amorós	1952	OF	Brooklyn Dodgers (NL)	7	517	.255 BA
54	Mike (Miguel) Fornieles	1952	RHP	Washington Senators (AL)	12	432	63–64, 3.96 ERA
55	Héctor Rodríguez	1952	3B	Chicago White Sox (AL)	1	124	.265 BA
56	Raúl Sánchez	1952	RHP	Washington Senators (AL)	3	49	5–3, 4.62 ERA
57	Carlos Paula	1954	OF	Washington Senators (AL)	3	157	.271 BA
58	Camilio Pascual	1954	RHP	Washington Senators (AL)	18	529	174–170, 3.63 ERA
59	Vicente Amor	1955	RHP	Chicago Cubs (NL)	2	13	1–3, 5.67 ERA
60	Julio Becquer	1955	1B	Washington Senators (AL)	7	488	.244 BA
61	Juan Delís	1955	3B	Washington Senators (AL)	1	54	.189 BA
62	Lino Donoso	1955	LHP	Pittsburgh Pirates (NL)	2	28	4–6, 5.21 ERA
63	Vince (Wenceslao) González	1955	LHP	Washington Senators (AL)	1	2	0–0, 27.00 ERA
64	Román Mejías	1955	OF	Pittsburgh Pirates (NL)	9	627	.254 BA
65	Pedro (Pete) Ramos	1955	RHP	Washington Senators (AL)	16	582	117–160, 4.08 ERA
66	José (Joe) Valdivielso	1955	SS	Washington Senators (AL)	5	401	.219 BA
67	Chico/Humberto Fernández	1956	SS	Brooklyn Dodgers (NL)	8	856	.240 BA
68	Evelio Hernández	1956	RHP	Washington Senators (AL)	2	18	1–1, 4.45 ERA
69	Cholly (Lazaro) Naranjo	1956	RHP	Pittsburgh Pirates (NL)	1	17	1–2, 4.46 ERA
70	René Valdez	1957	RHP	Brooklyn Dodgers (NL)	1	5	1–1, 5.54 ERA
71	Ossie (Oswaldo) Alvarez	1958	IF	Washington Senators (AL)	2	95	.212 BA
72	Pancho (Juan) Herrera	1958	1B	Philadelphia Phillies (NL)	3	300	.271 BA
73	Dan (Daniel) Morejón	1958	OF	Cincinnati Reds (NL)	1	12	.192 BA
74	Orlando Peña	1958	RHP	Cincinnati Reds (NL)	18	427	56–77, 3.71 ERA
75	Fernando (Fred) Rodríguez	1958	RHP	Chicago Cubs (NL)	2	8	0–0, 8.68 ERA
76	Tony (Antonio) Taylor	1958	IF	Chicago Cubs (NL)	19	2,195	.261 BA
77	Rudy (Rodolfo) Arias	1958	LHP	Chicago White Sox (AL)	1	34	2–0, 4.09 ERA
78	Mike (Miguel) Cuéllar	1959	LHP	Cincinnati Reds (NL)	15	453	185–130, 3.14 ERA
79	Zoilo Versalles	1959	SS	Washington Senators (AL)	13	1,400	.242 BA, 95 HR
80	Borrego (Rogelio) Alvarez	1960	1B	Cincinnati Reds (NL)	2	17	.189 BA
81	Joe (Joaquín) Azcue	1960	IF	Cincinnati Reds (NL)	11	909	.252 BA
82	Ed (Eduardo) Bauta	1960	RHP	St. Louis Cardinals (NL)	5	97	6–6, 4.35 ERA
83	Leo (Leonardo) Cárdenas	1960	IF	Cincinnati Reds (NL)	16	1,941	.257 BA
84	Mike (Miguel) de la Hoz	1960	IF	Cleveland Indians (AL)	9	494	.251 BA
85	Tony (Antonio) González	1960	IF	Cincinnati Reds (NL)	12	1,559	.286 BA, 103 HR
86	Héctor Maestri	1960	RHP	Washington Senators (AL)	2	2	0–1, 1.13 ERA
87	Leo (Leopoldo) Posada	1960	OF	Kansas City Athletics (AL)	3	155	.256 BA

(Suspension of Professional Baseball in Cuba)

	Name*	Debut	Position	Debut Team	Seasons	Games	Career Statistics
88	Berto (Dagoberto) Cueto	1961	RHP	Minnesota Twins (AL)	1	7	1–3, 7.17 ERA
89	Manny (Manuel) Montejo	1961	RHP	Detroit Tigers (AL)	1	12	0–0, 3.86 ERA
90	Héctor (Rodolfo) Martínez	1962	OF	Kansas City Athletics (AL)	2	7	.267 BA
91	Marty (Orlando) Martínez	1962	IF	Minnesota Twins (AL)	7	436	.243 BA
92	Orlando McFarlane	1962	C	Pittsburgh Pirates (NL)	5	124	.240 BA
93	Tony (Pedro) Oliva	1962	OF	Minnesota Twins (AL)	15	1,676	.304 BA, 220 HR
94	Cookie (Octavio) Rojas	1962	IF	Cincinnati Reds (NL)	16	1,822	.263 BA
95	Diego Seguí	1962	RHP	Kansas City Athletics (AL)	16	639	92–111, 3.81 ERA
96	José Tartabull	1962	OF	Kansas City Athletics (AL)	9	749	.261 BA
97	José Cardenal	1963	IF	San Francisco Giants (NL)	18	2,017	.275 BA, 138 HR
98	Marcelino López	1963	LHP	Philadelphia Phillies (NL)	8	171	31–40, 3.62 ERA
99	Tony (Gabriel) Martínez	1963	IF	Cleveland Indians (AL)	4	73	.171 BA
100	Aurelio Monteagudo	1963	RHP	Kansas City Athletics (AL)	7	72	3–7, 5.05 ERA
101	Dagoberto Campaneris	1964	SS	Kansas City Athletics (AL)	20	2,328	.259 BA
102	Tony (Atanasio) Pérez	1964	IF	Cincinnati Reds (NL)	23	2,777	.279 BA, 379 HR
103	Chico Ruiz	1964	IF	Cincinnati Reds (NL)	8	565	.240 BA
104	Luis Tiant Jr.	1964	RHP	Cleveland Indians (AL)	19	573	229–172, 3.30 ERA
105	Paul (Paulino) Casanova	1965	C	Washington Senators (AL)	10	859	.225 BA

(continued)

57

(continued)

	Name*	Debut	Position	Debut Team	Seasons	Games	Career Statistics
106	Tito (Rigoberto) Fuentes	1965	OF	San Francisco Giants (NL)	13	1,499	.268 BA
107	Jackie (Jacinto) Hernández	1965	SS	California Angels (AL)	9	618	.208 BA
108	Sandy (Hilario) Valdespino	1965	OF	Minnesota Twins (AL)	7	382	.230 BA
109	José Ramón López	1966	RHP	California Angels (AL)	1	4	0–1, 5.14 ERA
110	Minnie (Minervino) Rojas	1966	RHP	California Angels (AL)	3	157	23–16, 3.00 ERA
111	Hank (Enrique) Izquierdo	1967	C	Minnesota Twins (AL)	1	16	.269 BA
112	George (Jorge) Lauzerique	1967	RHP	Kansas City Athletics (AL)	4	34	4–8, 5.00 ERA
113	José Arcia	1968	IF	Chicago Cubs (NL)	3	293	.215 BA
114	Chico (Lorenzo) Fernández	1968	IF	Baltimore Orioles (AL)	1	24	.111 BA
115	José Martínez	1969	IF	Pittsburgh Pirates (NL)	2	96	.245 BA
116	Minnie (Rigoberto) Mendoza	1970	IF	Minnesota Twins (AL)	1	16	.188 BA
117	Oscar Zamora	1974	RHP	Chicago Cubs (NL)	4	158	13–14, 4.53 ERA
118	Orlando González	1976	1B	Cleveland Indians (AL)	3	79	.238 BA
119	Bobby (Roberto) Ramos	1978	C	Montreal Expos (NL)	6	103	.190 BA
120	Leo (Leonard) Sutherland	1980	OF	Chicago White Sox (AL)	2	45	.248 BA
121	Bárbaro Garbey	1984	OF	Detroit Tigers (AL)	3	226	.267 BA
122	José Canseco	1985	OF	Oakland Athletics (AL)	17	1,887	.266 BA, 462 HR
123	Rafael Palmeiro	1986	1B	Chicago Cubs (NL)	18	2,567	.291 BA, 528 HR
124	Orestes Destrade	1987	1B	New York Yankees (AL)	4	237	.241 BA
125	Nelson Santovenia	1988	C	Montreal Expos (NL)	7	297	.233 BA
126	Israel Sánchez	1988	LHP	Kansas City Royals (AL)	2	30	3–2, 5.36 ERA
127	Tony (Emilio) Fossas	1988	LHP	Texas Rangers (AL)	12	567	17–24, 3.90 ERA
128	Ozzie Canseco	1990	OF	Oakland Athletics (AL)	3	24	.200 BA
129	Tony Menéndez	1992	RHP	Cincinnati Reds (NL)	3	23	3–1, 4.97 ERA
130	René Arocha†	1993	RHP	St. Louis Cardinals (NL)	5	124	18–17, 4.11 ERA
131	Ariel Prieto†	1995	RHP	Oakland Athletics (AL)	5	67	15–24, 4.88 ERA
132	Osvaldo Fernández†	1996	RHP	San Francisco Giants (NL)	4	76	19–26, 4.93 ERA
133	Rey Ordóñez†	1996	SS	New York Mets (NL)	8	950	.248 BA
134	Liván Hernández†	1996	RHP	Florida Marlins (NL)	8	214	84–79, 4.22 ERA
135	Elieser (Eli) Marrero	1997	C	St. Louis Cardinals (NL)	7	525	.238 BA
136	Rolando Arrojo†	1998	RHP	Tampa Bay Devil Rays (AL)	5	158	40–42, 4.55 ERA
137	Orlando Hernández	1998	RHP	New York Yankees (AL)	6	124	53–38, 4.04 ERA
138	Vladimir Nuñez†	1998	RHP	Arizona Diamondbacks (NL)	6	208	17–29, 4.68 ERA
139	Jorge Toca†	1999	IF	New York Mets (NL)	3	25	.259 BA
140	Michael Tejera†	1999	LHP	Florida Marlins (NL)	3	100	11–12, 4.72 ERA
141	Adrian Hernández†	2001	RHP	New York Yankees (AL)	2	8	0–4, 5.46 ERA
142	Danys Báez†	2001	RHP	Cleveland Indians (AL)	3	155	17–23, 3.92 ERA
143	Edilberto Oropesa†	2001	LHP	Philadelphia Phillies (NL)	3	109	6–3, 6.94 ERA
144	Alex Sánchez	2001	OF	Milwaukee Brewers (NL)	3	286	.283 BA
145	Bill Ortega	2001	OF	St. Louis Cardinals (AL)	1	5	.200 BA
146	Hanzel Izquierdo†	2002	RHP	Florida Marlins (NL)	1	20	2–0, 4.55 ERA
147	José Ariel Contreras†	2003	RHP	New York Yankees (AL)	1	18	7–2, 3.30 ERA
148	Michel Hernández†	2003	C	New York Yankees (AL)	1	5	.250 BA

* First names follow major league practice. Where different, actual first names are given in parentheses. Nicknames are given in quotation marks.
† Played in post-1961 Cuban League before leaving Cuba (Cuban League defector).

58

Cuban League Record Book

Prerevolution Championship Team Records and Individual Batting Leaders (1878–1961)

Series	Year	Team	Records	Manager	Batting Champion	BA
1	1878–1879	Habana	4–0–1, 1.000	Ésteban Bellán*	No Official Records	
2	1879–1880	Habana	5–2, .714	Ésteban Bellán*	No Official Records	
	1880–1881	No Official Season				
	1882	Season Not Completed[†]				
3	1882–1883	Habana	5–1, .833	Ésteban Bellán*	No Official Records	
	1883–1884	No Official Season				
4	1885	Habana	4–3, .571	Ricardo Mora	Pablo Ronquilla	.350
5	1885–1886	Habana	6–0, 1.000	Francisco Saavedra	Wenceslao Gálvez	.345
6	1887	Habana	10–2, .833	Francisco Saavedra	Ricardo Martínez	.439
7	1888	Club Fé	12–3, .800	Antonio Utrera	Antonio María García	.448
8	1889	Habana	16–4–1, .800	Emilio Sabourín	Francisco Salabarría	.305
9	1889–1890	Habana	14–3, .824	Emilio Sabourín	Antonio María García	.364
10	1890–1891	Club Fé	12–6, .667	Luis Almoina y Meléndez	Alfredo Crespo	.375
11	1892	Habana	13–7, .650	Emilio Sabourín	Antonio María García	.362
12	1892–1893	Matanzas	14–9, .609	Luis Almoina y Meléndez	Antonio María García	.385
13	1893–1894	Almendares	17–7–1, .708	Ramón Gutiérrez	Miguel Prats	.394
	1894–1895	Season Not Completed[†]			Alfredo Arcaño	.430
	1895–1896	Season Canceled[†]				
	1896–1897	Season Canceled[†]				
	1897–1898	Season Not Completed[†]			Valentín González	.394
14	1898–1899	Habanista	9–3–1, .750	Alberto Azoy	Valentín González	.414
15	1900	San Francisco	17–10–1, .630	Patrocinio Silverio	Ésteban Prats	.333
16	1901	Habana	16–3–1, .842	Alberto Azoy	Julián Castillo	.454
17	1902	Habana	17–0–2, 1.000	Alberto Azoy	Luis Padrón	.463
18	1903	Habana	16–4, .800	Alberto Azoy	Julián Castillo	.330
19	1904	Habana	16–4, .800	Alberto Azoy	Regino García	.397
20	1905	Almendares	19–11, .633	Abel Linares	Regino García	.305
21	1905–1906	Club Fé	15–9–1, .625	Alberto Azoy	Regino García	.304
22	1907	Almendares	17–13–1, .567	Eugenio Santa Cruz	Regino García	.324
23	1908	Almendares	37–8–1, .822	Juan L. Sánchez	Emilio Palomino	.350
24	1908–1909	Habana	33–13–1, .690	Luis Someillán	Julián Castillo	.315
25	1910	Almendares	13–3–1, .812	Juan L. Sánchez	Julián Castillo	.408
26	1910–1911	Almendares	21–6–3, .714	Juan L. Sánchez	Preston Hill[‡]	.365
27	1912	Habana	22–12–1, .647	Eduardo Laborde	Emilio Palomino	.440
28	1913	Club Fé	21–11–2, .656	Agustín Molina	Armando Marsans	.400
29	1913–1914	Almendares	22–11–1, .667	Eugenio Santa Cruz	Manuel Villa	.351
30	1914–1915	Habana	23–11, .676	Mike González*	Cristóbal Torriente	.387
31	1915–1916	Almendares	30–12–3, .714	Alfredo Cabrera	Eustaquio Pedroso	.413
32	1917	Orientales	8–6–1, .571	Armando Marsans*	Adolfo Luque	.355
33	1918–1919	Habana	29–19, .604	Mike González*	Manuel Cueto	.344
34	1919–1920	Almendares	22–5–2, .815	Adolfo Luque*	Cristóbal Torriente	.360
35	1920–1921	Habana	21–9–5, .700	Mike González*	Pelayo Chacón	.344
36	1921	Havana	4–1, .800	Mike González*	Bienvenido Jiménez	.619
37	1922–1923	Marianao	35–19–1, .648	Baldomero Acosta*	Bernardo Baró	.401
38	1923–1924	Santa Clara	36–11–1, .766	Augustín Molina	Oliver Marcelle[‡]	.393
39	1924–1925	Almendares	33–16–1, .660	Joseíto Rodríguez	Alejandro Oms	.393
40	1925–1926	Almendares	34–13–2, .723	Joseíto Rodríguez	Johnny Wilson[‡]	.430
41	1926–1927	Habana	20–11, .645	Mike González*	Manuel Cueto	.398
42	1927–1928	Habana	24–13, .649	Mike González*	Jud "Johnny" Wilson[‡]	.424
43	1928–1929	Habana	43–12–1, .782	Mike González*	Alejandro Oms	.432
44	1929–1930	Cienfuegos	33–19–2, .635	Pelayo Chacón	Alejandro Oms	.389
	1930–1931	Season Not Completed[†]				
	1930–1931[§]	Almendarista	9–4–1, .692	Joseíto Rodríguez	Oscar Charleston[‡]	.373

(continued)

(continued)

Series	Year	Team	Records	Manager	Batting Champion	BA
45	1931–1932	Almendares	21–9–4, .700	Joseíto Rodríguez	Ramón Couto	.400
46	1932–1933	Almendares	13–9, .591	Adolfo Luque*	Mike González	.432
		Habana	13–9, .591	Mike González*		
	1933–1934	No Official Season				
47	1934–1935	Almendares	18–9–1, .667	Adolfo Luque*	Lázaro Salazar	.407
48	1935–1936	Santa Clara	34–14–1, .708	Martín Dihigo	Martín Dihigo	.358
49	1936–1937	Marianao	38–31–3, .551	Martín Dihigo	Harry Williams	.339‡
50	1937–1938	Santa Clara	44–18–4, .710	Lázaro Salazar	Sammy Bankhead	.366‡
51	1938–1939	Santa Clara	34–20–2, .630	Lázaro Salazar	Antonio Castaño	.371
52	1939–1940	Almendares	28–23–1, .549	Adolfo Luque*	Antonio Castaño	.340
53	1940–1941	Habana	31–18–5, .633	Mike González*	Lázaro Salazar	.316
54	1941–1942	Almendares	25–19–4, .568	Adolfo Luque*	Silvio García	.351
55	1942–1943	Almendares	28–20–1, .583	Adolfo Luque*	Alejandro Crespo	.337
56	1943–1944	Habana	32–16, .667	Mike González*	Roberto Ortiz	.337
57	1944–1945	Almendares	32–16–6, .667	Reinaldo Cordeiro	Claro Duany	.340
58	1945–1946	Cienfuegos	37–23–4, .617	Adolfo Luque*	Lloyd Davenport	.332‡
59	1946–1947	Almendares	42–24–2, .636	Adolfo Luque*	Lou Klein	.330‡
60	1947–1948	Habana	39–33–9, .542	Mike González*	Harry Kimbro	.346‡
61	1948–1949	Almendares	47–25, .553	Fermín Guerra*	Alejandro Crespo	.326
62	1949–1950	Almendares	38–34–4, .528	Fermín Guerra*	Pedro Formental	.336
63	1950–1951	Habana	41–32–1, .562	Mike González*	Silvio García	347
64	1951–1952	Habana	41–30–1, .577	Mike González*	Bert Haas	.323‡
65	1952–1953	Habana	43–29–1, .597	Mike González*	Edmundo "Sandy" Amorós	.373
66	1953–1954	Almendares	44–28–1, .611	Bobby Bragan*‡	Rocky Nelson	.352‡
67	1954–1955	Almendares	44–25–2, .638	Bobby Bragan*‡	Ángel Scull	.370
68	1955–1956	Cienfuegos	40–29–1, .580	Oscar Rodríguez	Forrest "Spook" Jacobs	.321‡
69	1956–1957	Marianao	40–28–1, .588	Napoleón Reyes*	Orestes "Minnie" Miñoso	.312
70	1957–1958	Marianao	43–32–1, .597	Napoleón Reyes*	Milton Smith	.320‡
71	1958–1959	Almendares	46–26–6, .639	Oscar Rodríguez	Tony Taylor	.303
72	1959–1960	Cienfuegos	48–24, .667	Antonio Castaño	Tony González	.310
73	1960–1961	Cienfuegos	35–31–1, .530	Antonio Castaño	Octavio "Cookie" Rojas	.322

Tie games are included in team records.
* Manager also a U.S. major leaguer at some point during his career.
† Season not completed or canceled: 1882, dispute between Habana and Club Fé; 1894–1895, playoffs suspended; 1895–1897, canceled
  during War of Independence; 1897–1898, suspended before playoffs; 1930–1931, suspended due to poor attendance.
‡ Non-Cuban player or manager.
§ Substitute "Campeonato Unico." (Alternate season arranged after regular championship suspended.)

Cuban Career and Season Individual Records (Prerevolution)

Category	Name	Record	Date
Batting			
Batting Average, Single Season	Bienvenido Jiménez	.619	1921 (Short Season)
Batting Average, Single Season. 100 or More ABs	Julian Castillo	.454	1901
Most Batting Titles Won	Antonio García	4	1887–88, 1889–90, 1891–92, 1892–93
	Julián Castillo	4	1901, 1903, 1908–1909, 1910
	Regino García	4	1904, 1905, 1906, 1907
Most Consecutive BA Titles	Regino García	4	1904, 1905, 1906, 1907
Most Seasons Batting .300-Plus	Manuel Cueto	11	
	Alejandro Oms	11	
Consecutive .300 Seasons	Alejandro Oms	8	1922–1923 through 1929–1930
Most RBI, Season	Pedro Formental	57	1952–1953
	Rocky Nelson	57	1954–1955

Category	Name	Record	Date
Most RBI, Game	Walt Moryn	8	Oct. 14, 1952
Most RBI, Career	Alejandro Crespo	362	
	Pedro Formental	362	
Most Seasons as RBI Leader	Leonard Pearson	3	1946–1947, 1948–1949, 1949–1950
Most Runs Scored, Season	Orestes Miñoso	67	1952–1953
Most Runs Scored, Game	Amado Ibáñez	6	Jan. 10, 1954
Most Runs Scored, Career	Pedro Formental	431	1942–1943 through 1954–1955
Most Seasons as Runs Leader	Cristóbal Torriente	4	1915, 1916, 1921, 1923
Most Base Hits, Season	Harry Kimbro	104	1947–1948
Most Base Hits, Game	Alejandro Oms	6	Dec. 30, 1928
	Antonio Castaño	6	Dec. 25, 1938
	Lloyd Davenport	6	Jan. 17, 1946
	Amado Ibáñez	6	Jan. 10, 1954
Most Career Base Hits	Silvio García	891	1931–1932 through 1953–1954
Most Seasons as Hits Leader	Valentín González	5	1893, 1895, 1899, 1902, 1905
Longest Hitting Streak	Alejandro Oms	30	Oct. 31 to Dec. 24, 1928
Most Home Runs, Season	Lou Klein	16	1952–1953
Most Home Runs, Game	James "Cool Papa" Bell	3	Jan. 1, 1929
	Dick Sisler	3	Jan. 24, 1946
Most Home Runs, Career, Righthanded	Pedro Formental	54	1942–1943 through 1954–1955
Most Home Runs, Career, Lefthanded	Roberto Ortíz	51	1939–1940 through 1954–1955
Pitching			
Seasons as Pitching Champion	José Méndez	5	1908, 1909, 1910, 1911, 1914
	José Acosta	5	1915, 1916, 1917, 1919, 1925
Most Games Won in Season	Carlos Royer	21	1903
	Raymond Brown	21	1936–1937
Consecutive Wins in Season	Carlos Royer	17	1902
Most Consecutive Wins	Carlos Royer	20	1902–1903
Most Career Victories	Martín Dihigo	105	1922–1923 through 1946–1947
Most Consecutive Relief Wins	Thomas Fine	9	1949–1950
Most Career Complete Games	Martín Dihigo	120	1922–1923 through 1946–1947
Consecutive Complete Games, Career	Carlos Royer	69	1901–1904
Consecutive Complete Games, Season	Carlos Royer	33	1903, with Playoffs
Most Games Pitched, Career	Adrián Zabala	331	1935–1936 through 1954–1955
Most Games Pitched, Season	Joe Coleman	44	1953–1954
Most Shutouts, Career	Adrián Zabala	83	1935–1936 through 1954–1955
Most Shutouts, Season	Enrique Rosas	14	1888–1889
Most Seasons Shutout Leader	Luis Tiant Sr.	5	1932, 1936, 1937, 1940, 1941
Most Strikeouts, Season	Carlos Royer	181	1903, including playoffs
Most Walks Allowed, Season	Robert Darnell	107	1953–1954
Most Hits Allowed, Season	Al Sima	209	1953–1954
Most Runs Allowed, Season	Carlos Royer	128	1903
Most Strikeouts, Game	George McCullar	21	Nov. 23, 1879
Strikeouts, Modern Game	Dave Barnhill	15	Jan. 10, 1948 (15 innings)
Consecutive Strikeouts	Adolfo Luque	7	Feb. 17, 1923
Other			
Cuban Unassisted Triple Play	Baldomero Acosta	1	Dec.2, 1918 (Havana vs. Almendares)

Cuban Professional League No-Hit Games Pitched

Pitcher	Series	Date	Score
Carlos Maciá	6	Feb. 13, 1887	Almendares 38, Carmelita 0
Eugenio de Rosas	8	July 14, 1889	Progreso 8, Cárdenas 0
Oscar Levis	39	Oct. 11, 1924	Habana 1, Almendares 0
Raymond "Jabao" Brown	49	Nov. 7, 1936	Santa Clara 7, Habana 0
Manuel "Cocaína" García	56	Dec. 11, 1943	Habana 5, Marianao 0
Tomás de la Cruz	57	Jan. 3, 1945	Almendares 7, Habana 0
Rogelio "Limonar" Martínez	62	Feb. 15, 1950	Marianao 6, Almendares 0
Antonio "Tony" Díaz	70	Nov. 23, 1957	Cienfuegos 2, Habana 0

Postrevolution (Amateur) Cuban League Statistics: Cuban Baseball Federation Records And Statistics (1962–2003)

National Series Championships and Batting Leaders (Provincial): Postrevolution Cuban League

Series	Year	Teams	Record	Play-offs*	Manager	Batting Champion	Team	BA
I	1962	Occidentales	18–9, .667		Fermín Guerra	Erwin Walter[†]	Occidentales	.367
II	1962–1963	Industriales	16–14, .533		Ramón Carneado	Raul González	Occidentales	.348
III	1963–1964	Industriales	22–13, .629		Ramón Carneado	Pedro Chávez	Occidentales	.333
IV	1964–1965	Industriales	25–14, .641		Ramón Carneado	Urbano González	Industriales	.359
V	1965–1966	Industriales	40–25, .615		Ramón Carneado	Miguel Cuevas	Granjeros	.325
VI	1966–1967	Orientales	36–29, .554		Roberto Ledo	Pedro Chávez	Industriales	.318
VII	1967–1968	Habana	74–25, .748		Juan Gómez	José Pérez	Azucareros	.328
VIII	1968–1969	Azucareros	69–30, .697		Servio Borges	Wilfredo Sánchez	Henequeneros	.354
IX	1969–1970	Henequeneros	50–16, .758		Mike Domínguez	Wilfredo Sánchez	Henequeneros	.351
X	1970–1971	Azucareros	49–16, .754		Pedro Delgado	Rigoberto Rosique	Henequeneros	.352
XI	1971–1972	Azucareros	52–14, .788		Servio Borges	Elpidio Mancebo	Mineros	.327
XII	1972–1973	Industriales	53–25, .679		Pedro Chávez	Eusebio Cruz	Camagüey	.341
XIII	1973–1974	Habana	52–26, .667		Jorge Trigoura	Rigoberto Rosique	Henequeneros	.347
XIV	1974–1975	Agricultores	24–15, .615		Orlando Leroux	Fermín Laffita	Cafetaleros	.396
XV	1975–1976	Ganaderos	29–9, .763		Carlos Gómez	Wilfredo Sánchez	Citricultores	.365
XVI	1976–1977	Citricultores	26–12, .684		Juan Bregio	Eulogio Osorio	Agricultores	.359
XVII	1977–1978	Vegueros	36–14, .720		José Pineda	Fernando Sánchez	Henequeneros	.394
XVIII	1978–1979	Sancti Spíritus	39–12, .765		Cándido Andrade	Wilfredo Sánchez	Citricultores	.377
XIX	1979–1980	Santiago de Cuba	35–16, .686		Manuel Miyar	Rodolfo Puente	Metropolitanos	.394
XX	1980–1981	Vegueros	36–15, .706		José Pineda	Amando Zamora	Villa Clara	.394
XXI	1981–1982	Vegueros	36–15, .706		Jorge Fuentes	Fernando Hernández	Vegueros	.376
XXII	1982–1983	Villa Clara	41–8, .837		Eduardo Martín	Juan Hernández	Forestales	.367
XXIII	1983–1984	Citricultores	52–23, .693		Tomás Soto	Wilfredo Sánchez	Citricultores	.385
XXIV	1984–1985	Vegueros	57–18, .760		Jorge Fuentes	Omar Linares	Vegueros	.409
XXV	1985–1986	Industriales	37–11, .771	6–0	Pedro Chávez	Omar Linares	Vegueros	.426
XXVI	1986–1987	Vegueros	34–13, .723	5–1	Jorge Fuentes	Javier Méndez	Industriales	.408
XXVII	1987–1988	Vegueros	39–9, .813	5–1	Jorge Fuentes	Pedro Luis Rodríguez	Habana	.446
XXVIII	1988–1989	Santiago de Cuba	29–19, .604	5–1	Higinio Vélez	Juan Bravo	Industriales	.414
XXIX	1989–1990	Henequeneros	37–11, .771	4–2	Gerardo Junco	Omar Linares	Vegueros	.442
XXX	1990–1991	Henequeneros	33–15, .688	6–1	Gerardo Junco	Lázaro Madera	Vegueros	.400
XXXI	1991–1992	Industriales	36–12 .750,	7–1	Jorge Trigoura	Omar Linares	Vegueros	.398
XXXII	1992–1993	Villa Clara	42–23, .646	8–3	Pedro Jova	Omar Linares	Pinar del Río	.446
XXXIII	1993–1994	Villa Clara	43–22, .662	8–5	Pedro Jova	Lourdes Gourriel	Sancti Spíritus	.395
XXXIV	1994–1995	Villa Clara	44–18, .710	8–2	Pedro Jova	Amado Zamora	Villa Clara	.395
XXXV	1995–1996	Industriales	41–22, .651	8–2	Pedro Medina	Luis Ulacia	Camagüey	.421
XXXVI	1996–1997	Pinar del Río	50–15, .769	8–0	Jorge Fuentes	José Estrada	Mantanzas	.391
XXXVII	1997–1998	Pinar del Río	56–34, .622	11–5	Alfonso Urquíola	Robelquis Videaux	Guantánamo	.393
XXXVIII	1998–1999	Santiago de Cuba	46–44, .511	11–7	Higinio Vélez	Yobal Dueñas	Pinar del Río	.418
XXXIX	1999–2000	Santiago de Cuba	61–28, .689	11–0	Higinio Vélez	Yorelvis Charles	Ciego de Ávila	.353
XL	2000–2001	Santiago de Cuba	55–35, .611	11–4	Higinio Vélez	Osmani Urrutia	Las Tunas	.431
XLI	2001–2002	Holguín	55–35, .611	11–6	Héctor Hernández	Osmani Urrutia	Las Tunas	.408
XLII	2002–2003	Industriales	66–23, .742	11–2	Rey Anglada	Osmani Urrutia	Las Tunas	.421

* Playoffs between Western and Eastern Zone winners to determine championship start with 1986 (National Series XXV).
[†] Also spelled Walters. Multiple spellings are not uncommon in Cuban baseball records.

Selective Series Champions and Batting Leaders in Postrevolution Cuban League

Series	Year	Team	Record	Playoffs*	Manager	Batting Champion	Team	BA
I	1975	Oriente	33–21, .612		José Carrillo	Alfonso Urquiola	Pinar del Río	.358
II	1976	Habana	34–20, .630		Roberto Ledo	Bárbaro Garbey	Industriales	.328
III	1977	Camagüeyanos	36–18, .667		Carlos Gómez	Wilfredo Sánchez	Matanzas	.381
IV	1978	Las Villas	35–25, .583	3–2*	Eduardo Martín	Pedro Jova	Las Villas	.372
V	1979	Pinar del Río	40–20, .667		José Pineda	Sixto Hernández	Las Villas	.368
VI	1980	Pinar del Río	39–20, .661		José Pineda	Héctor Olivera	Las Villas	.459
VII	1981	Orientales	38–22, .644		Carlos Martí	Luis Casanova	Pinar del Río	.363
VIII	1982	Pinar del Río	35–22, .614		Jorge Fuentes	Agustín Arias	Orientales	.404
IX	1983	Las Villas	42–18, .700		Eduardo Martín	Gerardo Simon	Orientales	.350
X	1984	Pinar del Río	28–15, .651		Jorge Fuentes	Luis Casanova	Pinar del Río	.391
XI	1985	Las Villas	26–19, .578		Eduardo Martín	Amado Zamora	Las Villas	.361
XII	1986	Serranos	41–22, .651		Frangel Reynaldo	Amado Zamora	Las Villas	.392
XIII	1987	Serranos	42–21, .667		Higinio Vélez	Luis Ulacia	Camagüeyanos	.384
XIV	1988	Pinar del Río	40–23, .635		Jorge Fuentes	Lourdes Gourriel	Las Villas	.430
XV	1989	Las Villas	45–18, .714	2–0*	Abelardo Triana	Amado Zamora	Las Villas	.413
XVI	1990	Ciudad Habana	46–17, .730		Servio Borges	Antonio González	Ciudad Habana	.416
XVII	1991	Pinar del Río	41–22, .651		Jorge Fuentes	Pedro Luis Rodríguez	Agropecuarios	.380
XVIII	1992	Serranos	36–27, .571	4–3*	Higinio Vélez	Omar Linares	Pinar del Río	.398
XIX	1993	Orientales	25–20, .556		Frangel Reynaldo	Gerardo Miranda	Occidentales	.390
XX	1994	Occidentales	27–18, .600		Jorge Fuentes	Juan Carlos Linares	Occidentales	.429
XXI	1995	Orientales	29–16, .644		Higinio Vélez	Rey Isaac	Orientales	.424
SuperL I	2002	Habaneros	16–11, .593	2–1*	Armando Johnson	Andy Zamora	Centrales	.391
SuperL II	2003	Centrales	13–7, .650	2–1*	Lourdes Gourriel	Frederich Cepeda	Centrales	.435

* Playoffs when necessary to determine championship.

Cuban League Career Leaders (National Series and Selective Series, 1962–2003)

Category	Name	Record
Batting		
Games	Fernando Sánchez	1,994
Innings	Sergio Quesada	16,702.1
At Bats	Sergio Quesada	7,528
Runs	Omar Linares	1,547
Hits	Antonio Pacheco	2,356
Batting Average	Omar Linares	.368
Doubles	Javier Méndez	381
Triples	Evenecer Godínez	81
Home Runs	Orestes Kindelán	487
Total Bases	Orestes Kindelán	3,893
Slugging percentage	Omar Linares	.644
Steals	Enrique Díaz	601
RBI	Orestes Kindelán	1,511
Sacrifice Bunts	Giraldo González	125
	Eduardo Cárdenas	125
Sacrifice Flies	Orestes Kindelán	91
Hit-By-Pitch	Gabriel Pierre	225
Pitching		
Games	Carlos Yanes	564
Games Started	Jorge Luis Valdés	414
Complete Games	Braudilio Vinent	265
Relief Appearances	Euclides Rojas	342

(*continued*)

(continued)

Category	Name	Record
Wins	Jorge Luis Valdéz	234
Losses	Carlos Yanes	184
Winning Percentage	Orlando Hernández	.728
Shutouts	Braudilio Vinent	63
Saves	Euclides Rojas	90
Innings Pitched	Braudilio Vinent	3,259.2
Strikeouts	Rogelio García	2,499
Bases on Balls	Faustino Corrales	1,138
ERA	José Huelga	1.50
Runs Allowed	Carlos Yanes	1,715
Wild Pitches	Faustino Corrales	206
Hits Allowed	Carlos Yanes	3,256

Cuban League (Amateur) No-Hit and No-Run Games (1962–2003)

No.	Series	Date	Location	No-Hit Pitcher	Game Line Scores, H–R–E
1	NAC 5	Jan. 16, 1966	Villa Clara	Aquino Abreu	Centrales 10–11–1, Occidentales 0–0–6
2	NAC 5	Jan. 25, 1966	Havana (EL)	Aquino Abreu	Centrales 7–8–0, Industriales 0–0–2
3	NAC 6	Feb. 14, 1967	Santiago de Cuba	Roberto Valdés	Orientales 12–16–0, Granjeros 0–0–6
4	NAC 7	Jan. 7, 1968	Havana (EL)	Leopoldo Valdés	Habana 5–12–0, Pinar del Río 0–0–0
5	NAC 7	Jan. 7, 1968	Artemisa	Jesús Pérez	Industriales 5–9–2, Vegueros 0–0–4
6	NAC 7	Jan. 14, 1968	Villa Clara	José Huelga	Azucareros 1–7–1, Granjeros 0–0–1
7	NAC 7	Jan. 25, 1968	Santiago de Cuba	Orlando Figueredo	Oriente 1–2–1, Azucareros 0–0–1
8	NAC 7	Apr. 4, 1968	Camagüey	Florentino González	Camagüey 1–8–0, Matanzas 0–0–2
9	NAC 8	Dec. 10, 1968	Havana	Raúl Alvarez	Pinar del Río 9–10–1, Camagüey 0–0–8
10	NAC 8	Feb. 4, 1969	Havana (EL)	Andrés Liaño	Industriales 8–8–1, Pinar del Río 0–0–6
11	NAC 8	Apr. 6, 1969	Villa Clara	Alfredo García	Henequeneros 1–5–3, Azucareros 0–0–0
12	NAC 9	Jan. 7, 1970	Havana (EL)	Rigoberto Betancourt	Industriales 1–3–2, Oriente 0–0–1
13	NAC 10	Jan. 16, 1971	Camagüey	Walfrido Ruíz (winner)[†]	Habana 10–9–2, Camagüey 0–0–6
15	NAC 12	Feb. 22, 1973	Camagüey	Juan Pérez	Camagüey 7–10–0, Serranos 0–0–3
16	NAC 13	Apr. 25, 1974	Santiago de Cuba	Juan Pérez	Camagüey 1–10–0, Oriente 0–0–1
17	NAC 14	Jan. 19, 1975	Camagüey	Juan Pérez	Ganaderos 2–7–0, Citricultores 0–0–0
18	SELS 1	May 4, 1975	Havana (EL)	Oscar Romero	Camagüey 4–11–1, Industriales 0–0–4
19	NAC 17	Dec. 27, 1977	Pinar del Río	Porfirio Pérez	Forestales 3–7–1, Habana 0–0–2
20	NAC 18	Feb. 18, 1979	Granma	Juan Gómaz (winner)[†]	Granma 14–18–3, Ciego de Ávila 0–0–2
21	SELS 5	Mar. 28, 1979	Villa Clara	Nivaldo Pérez	Las Villas 4–9–0, Camagüeyanos 0–0–1
22	NAC 20	Jan. 27, 1981	Ciego de Ávila	Omar Carrero	Ciego Avila 13–16–1, Las Tunas 0–0–4
23	NAC 21	Jan. 16, 1982	Havana (EL)	Ángel Leocadio Díaz	Industriales 2–6–3, Holguín 0–0–1
24	NAC 21	Feb. 11, 1982	Matanzas	Carlos Mesa	Citricultores 6–9–0, Habana 0–0–3
25	SELS	May 18, 1982	Havana (EL)	José Pedroso	Habana 1–5–0, Camagüeyanos 0–0–1
26	NAC 22	Dec. 30, 1982	Villa Clara	Mario Veliz	Villa Clara 3–11–1, Citricultores 0–0–2
27	SELS 9	Mar. 9, 1983	Pinar del Río	Julio Romero	Pinar del Río 2–9–0, Camagüey 0–0–1
28	NAC 23	Jan. 31, 1984	Villa Clara	Jorge Luis Valdés	Henequeneros 1–2–1, Villa Clara 0–0–3
29	SELS 13	Mar. 1, 1987	Camagüey	Rogelio García	Pinar 10–11–0, Camagüey 0–0–1 (KO)
30	SELS 13	Mar. 22, 1987	Pinar del Río	Rogelio García	Pinar del Río 3–5–2, Serranos 0–0–1
31	NAC 28	Dec. 10, 1988	Havana (EL)	Osvaldo Fernández G.	Metros 6–9–3, Citricultores 0–0–0
32	NAC 29	Dec. 13, 1989	Matanzas	Héctor Domínguez	Citricultores 2–3–1, Isla Juventud 0–0–1
33	SELS 16	Apr. 7, 1990	Matanzas	Orlando Hernández	Habana 11–15–0, Matanzas 0–0–4 (KO)
34	NAC 31	Nov. 19, 1991	Nueva Gerona	Faustino Corrales	Vegueros 7–10–1, Juventud 0–0–1
35	NAC 32	Nov. 29, 1992	Havana (EL)	Osvaldo Fernández R.	Holguín 10–11–0, Metros 0–0–2 (KO)

64

No.	Series	Date	Location	No-Hit Pitcher	Game Line Scores, H–R–E
36	NAC 32	Dec. 8, 1992	Granma	Ernesto Guevara	Granma 2–7–1, Industriales 0–0–0
37	NAC 37	Nov. 18, 1997	Las Tunas	Modesto Luis	Las Tunas 7–9–1, Granma 0–0–0
38	NAC 37	Nov. 22, 1997	Guantánamo	Geovanis Castañeda	Guantánamo 8–9–2, Las Tunas 0–0–2
39	NAC 38	Nov. 17, 1998	Havana (EL)	José Báez	Las Tunas 6–8–1, Metropolitanos 0–0–2
40‡	NAC 39	Dec. 22, 1999	Sancti Spíritus	Maels Rodríguez	Sancti Spíritus 1–9–0, Las Tunas 0–0–2
41	NAC 39	Dec. 25, 1999	Cienfuegos	Adiel Palma	Cienfuegos 4–8–1, Las Tunas 0–0–2
42	NAC 39	May 3, 2000	Nueva Gerona	Carlos Yanes	Isla Juventud 6–11–0, Villa Clara 0–0–1
43	NAC 40	Jan. 21, 2001	Havana	Norge Vera	Santiago de Cuba 3–5–1, Habana 0–0–1
44	NAC 40	Feb. 7, 2001	Villa Clara	Michel Pérez	Villa Clara 10–11–0, Las Tunas 0–0–0
45	SuperLg	Aug. 21, 2002	Havana (EL)	Maels Rodríguez	Centrales 1–4–0, Habaneros 0–0–0

Abbreviations: EL, Estadio Latinoamericano, Havana; KO, game terminated by the ten-run mercy rule after seven innings; NAC, National Series number; SELS, Selective Series number.
* With Elpidio Paez.
† With Pablo Castro and José Brizuela.
‡ Here Maels Rodríguez pitched the only perfect game (allowing no base runners) in Cuban League history, vs. Las Tunas.

Cuban Baseball Hall of Fame (Players, Founders, Officials Selected Before 1961)

Year of Induction	Names
1939	José de la Caridad Méndez, Luis Bustamante, Gervasio "Strike" González, Antonio María García, Armando Marsans, Valentín González, Adolfo Luján, Rafael Almeida, Cristóbal Torriente, Carlos "El Bebe" Royer
1940	Alfredo Arcaño, José Muñoz
1941	Regino García, Emilio Sabourín
1942	Agustín Molina, Alfredo "El Pájaro" Cabrera
1943	Luis Padrón, Heliodoro Hidalgo, Julián Castillo
1944	Carlos Maciá, Alejandro Oms
1945	Ramón Calzadilla, José "Juan" Pastoriza, Carlos Morán, Valentín Dreke, Bernardo Baró
1946	Wenceslao Gálvez, Arturo Valdés, Rogelio Valdés, Francisco Poyo, Ricardo Caballero
1947	None
1948	Juan Antiga, Antonio Mesa, Tomás Romañach, Jacinto Calvo, Rafael Hernández, Nemesio Guilló
1949	Eduardo Machado, Julio López, Pelayo Chacón, Gonzalo Sánchez, Manuel Villa
1950	Eugenio Jiménez, Eustaquio Gutiérrez, Rafael Figarola, Manuel Cueto, Ricardo Martínez
1951	José María Teuma, Alfredo Arango, Bienvenido Jiménez, Joseíto Rodríguez, Martín Dihigo
1952	None
1953	Moisés Quintero, Juan Violá, Carlos Zaldo
1954	Emilio Palmero, Pablo Ronquillo
1955	Baldomero "Mérito" Acosta
1956	Miguel Ángel González
1957	Emilio Palomino, Isidro Fabré
1958	Adolfo Luque
1959	Lázaro Salazar, José Acosta
1960	Ramón Bragaña, Armando Cabañas
1961	Oscar Rodríguez, Tomás de la Cruz

Cubans in the Mexican Baseball Hall of Fame

Year of Induction	Name
1964	Martín Dihigo ("El Maestro")
1964	Ramón Bragaña ("El Professor")
1964	Lázaro Salazar ("El Principe de Belén")
1972	Roberto Ortiz ("El Guajiro")
1972	Agustín Bejerano ("Pijini")
1974	Agustín Verde
1977	Santos Amaro
1979	Basilio Rosell ("Brujo")
1982	Mario Ariosa
1985	Adolfo Luque
1988	Lino Donoso
1990	Amado Maestri*
1992	Armando Rodríguez*
1993	René González
1996	Orestes Miñoso
1997	Andrés Ayón

* Umpire.

Cuba's Composite Record in International Baseball Championships

	Tournaments Entered	Championships Won	W–L	PCT	Shutout Victories	Shutout Losses
World Cup Championships	27	24	269–28	.906	88	5
Olympic Games	4	3	33–3	.917	6	1
Pre-Olympics (Pan American)	1	1	6–0	1.000	3	0
Intercontinental Cup	12	9	107–11	.907	25	0
Pan American Games	13	11	91–13	.875	22	0
Central American Games	16	13	100–14	.877	35	3
University World Cup	1	1	7–0	1.000	6	0
Totals	74	62	613–69	.899	185	9

NOTES

1. Recent literature has clarified much of the mythology surrounding the origins of ball-playing on the island of Cuba. Especially helpful here is the extensive treatment in Chapter 4 ("A Cuban *Belle Époque*") of Roberto González Echevarría's exhaustive *The Pride of Havana* (1999). My own two previous books (*Smoke* and the forthcoming *Baseball's Mysterious Island*) have addressed postrevolution Cuban League history at length, complete with the most detailed set of statistics available in English. Cuba's rich Negro League connections and black baseball legacy have been explored with varying thoroughness in all three books—and yet this last subject still demands much more thorough documentation.

2. Consider the costs of that era before integration. Most Cubans or Latins who merited star billing wore black skin and through the first half of the twentieth century could perform only in the back-page Negro circuits and in the Caribbean winter leagues. They would see the inside of a big league park only when Negro league games were staged there. A prime victim of this injustice was the incomparable Martín Dihigo,

Cuba's greatest all-around player. There was also a trio who would have starred in any big league lineup if given half a chance. Muscular Cristóbal Torriente spent his career in the black league, but not without occasionally turning the heads of John McGraw and other big leaguers who saw him. José Méndez was an unmatched pitcher for a few short years before his arm suddenly went dead when he was barely twenty-four and perhaps far short of his peak seasons. Before the lame arm cropped up, "The Black Diamond" was sensational enough that McGraw once ranked him as equal to his own immortal ace Christy Mathewson. And another slugging outfielder named Alejandro Oms carried a reputation on the Negro circuit that placed him alongside such unforgettables as countryman Torriente and the top American black outfielder Oscar Charleston.

3. On a personal note, this author never had the special good fortune to witness Germán Mesa play during his true peak of acrobatic performance in the late 1980s and early 1990s. But what I have observed since his return to action in late 1998 has been impressive enough to add my own acclaim to those of legions of boosters.

4. The legitimacy of this game has been challenged, under widespread rumors of gold-bricking by the Americans; the question has been widely discussed among Cuban baseball historians, especially Roberto González Echevarría (see *The Pride of Havana*, p. 161). It seems likely that Torriente's long homers came on gift pitches from a relaxed George Kelly.

BIBLIOGRAPHY

Books

Bjarkman, Peter C. *Baseball's Mysterious Island: A True History of Baseball in Fidel Castro's Cuba*. Jefferson, NC, and London: McFarland & Company Publishers, forthcoming.

González Echevarría, Roberto. *The Pride of Havana: A History of Cuban Baseball*. New York: Oxford University Press, 1999.

Jamail, Milton. *Full Count: Inside Cuban Baseball*. Carbondale and Edwardsville, IL: The Southern Illinois University Press, 2000.

Oleksak, Michael M., and Mary Adams Oleksak. *Béisbol—Latin Americans and the Grand Old Game*. Grand Rapids, MI: Masters Press, 1991.

Rucker, Mark, and Peter C. Bjarkman. *Smoke: The Romance and Lore of Cuban Baseball*. New York: Total Sports Illustrated, 1999.

Terzian, James. *The Kid from Cuba: Zoilo Versalles*. Garden City, NY: Doubleday, 1967.

Torres, Ángel. *La Leyenda del Béisbol Cubano, 1878–1997 (The Legend of Cuban Baseball, 1878–1997)*. Miami, FL: Review Printers (privately printed), 1996.

Articles

Bjarkman, Peter C. "Adolfo Luque: The Original 'Pride of Havana.'" *Elysian Fields Quarterly* 20:1 (Winter 2003): 21–38.

———. "The Cuban Comet (Minnie Miñoso)." *Elysian Fields Quarterly* 19:1 (Winter 2002): 22–36.

———. "Martín Dihigo: Baseball's Least-Known Hall of Famer." *Elysian Fields Quarterly* 18:2 (Spring 2001): 22–39.

———. "The Baseball Half-Century of Conrado Marrero." *Elysian Fields Quarterly* 17:1 (Winter 2000): 27–44.

———. "Fidel on the Mound: Baseball Myth and History in Castro's Cuba." *Elysian Fields Quarterly* 16:3 (Summer 1999): 31–41.

———. "Baseball and Fidel Castro." *The National Pastime: A Review of Baseball History* 18 (1998): 64–68.

Ruck, Rob. "Baseball in the Caribbean," in *Total Baseball*, 6th ed., 536–543, ed. John Thorn, Pete Palmer, et al. New York: Total Sports, 1999.

CHAPTER 2

Canada

Diamonds of the Frozen North

• •

In 1871, Fordham-educated but Cuban-born Steve Bellán launched what would mature a century later as the biggest foreign invasion ever witnessed in America's beloved national pastime: that by Latin American ballplayers. In the same year a Canadian, Mike Brannock, initiated a much quieter baseball infiltration. Brannock, a little-used infielder for the Chicago White Stockings, appeared in but five games spread over two summers in the National Association, pro baseball's first circuit boasting big league status. His legacy was even slighter than that of the light-hitting Cuban Bellán; the 5'8" Guelph native could boast only 23 at-bats during his 2 seasons and hit a most unhealthy .087 when he did manage to get a chance at the plate. As the first Canadian big leaguer, however, long-forgotten Brannock initiated a Canadian tradition on big league diamonds that has remained one of baseball's better kept secrets over ten-plus decades.

Canada's big league heritage is by almost all standards one of raw numbers more than excitement. For much of the game's history, the giant nation to the north could indeed boast of supplying major league rosters with the largest stockpile of non–U.S.-born athletes, though few of these were ever first-rate contributors. The greatest impact by Canadian players seemed to come in the late nineteenth century, with figures like Robert Emslie (an American Association pitcher, more renowned as a National League umpire), Tip O'Neill (the most successful single-season batter ever), and Arthur Irwin (the first Canadian to play for a National League pennant winner). These were admittedly somewhat minor figures on big league diamonds but substantial contributors nevertheless. Almost a full third of Canada's all-time big league roster comes from the earliest decades of the organized game (1870s, 1880s, and 1890s). True, the biggest Canadian names ever to grace the sport, Ferguson Jenkins and Larry Walker, are of quite recent vintage—but these two exceptions only seem to prove the rule of diminished Canadian big league influence just by being so noticeably exceptions.

The Dominican Republic (189 players through 1994) would eventually surpass Canada (with 187 that same year) as the then-largest supplier of foreign-born talent in what until about 1970 remained the U.S.-dominated major leagues—and Puerto Rico (154 players through 1994) threatened to do the same by the mid-nineties. Nonetheless, the impact of Canadian natives upon the North American big league scene would remain steadily productive, even if it often appeared largely inconsequential roster-filling. So far, Jenkins has been the only Canadian ballplayer to sport Cooperstown credentials, although Larry Walker may eventually amass hitting numbers sufficient to earn a second Canadian bronze plaque in baseball's American Valhalla. And yet Canadians have often supplied a rather colorful corner of the North American national pastime. It was a Canadian slugger (George Selkirk) who replaced Babe Ruth in the New York Yankees lineup of 1936. Another Canadian (Terry Puhl) holds the big league mark for fielding percentage among long-term outfielders, and still a third (John Hiller) made history by striking out six straight opposing batters at the start of an American League game. And back in June 1902 future journeyman big league catcher Jay "Nig" Clarke would earn an indelible spot in the minor league record books by stroking 8 homers for Corsicana of the Texas League during a single-game 51–3 rout of hapless Texarkana. That kind of exquisite "Ripley's Believe It or Not" moment has seemed to shadow Canadian ballplayers right down to the present.

Canadian baseball historians have been quick to point out hidden facts constituting the country's big league landmarks. Russ Ford of the New York Highlanders (debuting in 1910) is reported to have invented the emery-ball pitch, a soon-illegal scuffed-up toss with which he set a still-standing American League mark for rookie shutouts. Outfielder Jack Graney carved out a distinguished Cleveland career that included 1,400 games and 8 seasons with 100-plus hits, but he is more noted for two items of baseball trivia: that he once (1914) recorded the first big league base hit ever registered against the pitching of a Boston Red Sox southpaw phenom named Babe Ruth, and that he later was the first big leaguer to bat wearing a number on his uniform (when the Indians experimented with the novelty during a June 26, 1916, game versus the White Sox by wearing numerals on their jersey sleeves that corresponded to scorecard numbers indicating batting order positions). Ontario's Jeff Heath was the American League's first 20–20–20 (doubles–triples–homers) numbers man when he turned the trick for Cleveland in 1941; Dick Fowler, in turn, was one of the game's better unsung hurlers of the 1940s, winning 15 in back-to-back seasons with the also-ran Connie Mack A's. Tim Harkness, Montreal native, recorded the first-ever Shea Stadium base hit, and George "Twinkletoes" Selkirk was not only proud owner of one of baseball's more bizarre monikers, but he was also recipient of both Babe Ruth's right field position and the Babe's uniform number when Ruth finally left the Bronx Bombers. Terry Puhl from Saskatchewan became the game's most error-free defensive fly-chaser during his 14 seasons as a star in Houston (for another season he was briefly a replacement for George Brett as designated hitter in Kansas City). And southpaw John Hiller mowed down the first half-dozen Cleveland batters of the day in an early August game for the 1968 world champion Detroit Tigers.

Canadian ballplayers have often been a mere footnote to baseball history—but sometimes an eye-catching footnote nonetheless.

This is hardly a heritage that can compete with those of such baseball bastions as Cuba, the Dominican Republic, Puerto Rico, Japan, or hemisphere rival Mexico. Cuba unarguably lays claim to baseball's greatest ongoing fanaticism, even once the United States becomes part of the equation. The Dominican nation and the rest of the Caribbean have supplied not only quantity but quality (think of Juan Marichal, Sammy Sosa, and Albert Pujols just for starters) on big league diamonds since the middle of the twentieth century. Even Ferguson Jenkins—with his nearly 300 wins and 3,000-plus strikeouts—never made quite the same splash as did Mexico's Fernando Valenzuela, the Dominican's Marichal or Pedro Martínez, or Puerto Rico's Roberto Clemente. And if the Japanese are the Johnny-come-lately figures on the big league scene, nonetheless they have already provided such headline-grabbers as Ichiro, Nomo, and Matsui, while their own professional league points to a thriving baseball culture rarely identified with our hockey-playing neighbors to the north.

Canadian apologists for baseball north of the border have more solid ground for boasting when discussion turns away from the major leagues and focuses on the nineteenth-century game's multiple and sporadic North American origins. There is the celebrated case, for example, of the game held on public grounds in Beachville, Ontario, in June 1838. Canadians (especially Ontario boosters) point to Beachville to show that it was Canadians, not Americans, who supplied modern baseball's earliest inventive genius. Beyond the documented Beachville game—admittedly only a close cousin to the type baseball soon being played in New York or Massachusetts—Canada also boasts a significant history of early community recreational bat-and-ball play. Games and teams were reported popping up as early as the 1870s and 1880s in outposts as far removed from Ontario as Manitoba (where the way was paved by a popular Red River Valley entertainment called simply "bat"), Saskatchewan (where regional championships were claimed by a semi-pro Regina team in the late 1880s), Alberta (where amateur games were reported in 1886), and even the Yukon Territory (where heavy gambling on informal amateur matches was the rage from 1903 on).

In the sense of origins at least, as well as in terms of a vital lengthy history of semi-professional and amateur play, Canada does indeed qualify as still another of the handful of lands that can truly claim baseball as its own national game. There is sufficient reason for Canadian fans to balk at the constant mantra heard across the decades from down south, advertising America's self-appointed and self-sanctioned cultural ownership of "their" national game of baseball.

CAPSULE HISTORY OF EARLY CANADIAN BASEBALL

Of various candidates for a single landmark moment in Canadian baseball history, the best choice may be April 22, 1996—at least for Canadian fans themselves, weighed down by the northland's seemingly inherent national modesty complex. It was on that forgettable date that a pair of journeymen big league hurlers—Paul Quantrill with the Toronto Blue Jays and Rheal Cormier of the Montreal Expos—made history merely by taking the hill for starting assignments on the same afternoon; it marked the first time that both of Canada's two late-blooming big league franchises had Canadian-born pitchers starting on the same date. But of course that rather trivial milestone was much more of a culmination than a beginning. Canada's history with the "American" pastime actually stretches back a good deal farther than in any baseball-oriented nation of the Far East or any island hotbed in the Caribbean. Canadian enthusiasts may actually have taken up rudimentary versions of "base ball" even before Americans did so themselves. Canada may not be the foremost ballplaying or baseball-loving outpost, but it may well have been the first to adopt bat-and-ball play as a recreational sport (and perhaps also as novel spectator entertainment).

Those in Canada who might object to American claims concerning cultural and historical ownership of baseball often point to the historic town-ball-like game held in Beachville, Ontario, in June 1838, as evidence for Canada's own claim on baseball's primitive origins. The claims for Beachville as baseball's birthplace are persuasive but also somewhat tenuous. There is better documented evidence for the actual June 4, 1838, events in Beachville (for example, a letter by witness Adam Ford published almost fifty years later in *Sporting Life*, May 4, 1886) than for the claims regarding Doubleday and Cooperstown. The Beachville match was among the earliest manifestations of a game that approximates baseball as we know it today. But it was also an event that links only obliquely to the linear development of the sport we now practice. The game description provided by Ford—including later-verified names of participants and an intriguing diagram of the field of play—both parallels and differs from the historic 1845 game staged by Alexander Cartwright in Hoboken, NJ. Like Cartwright's diagram of the 1845 Elysian Fields game, Ford's contains fair and foul territory (a departure from cricket and town ball) and a separate home plate where the batter stood; the Beachville game differed from Cartwright's New York version in having five bases and in allowing the practice of "soaking" or hitting base runners with thrown balls to record outs. Beachville apparently launched (or at least represented) a version of the Canadian game that flourished for a couple of decades before Cartwright's American style of play was widely adopted north of the border.

What is certain is that a native Canadian tradition of ballplaying does indeed predate the mythical Cooperstown and Doubleday origins of America's pastime firmly fixed by (long-discredited) legend in the summer of 1839. It may even stretch back at least as far as any known form of the game played anywhere on U.S. soil. Both near and distant ancestors of modern baseball, such as rounders and cricket, were played both north and south of the U.S.–Canadian border at least as far back as the final decades of the eighteenth century. So, in a nutshell, the origins of baseball in both countries are equally ancient and equally murky.

Primitive bat-and-ball games played informally across Ontario during the first decades of the nineteenth century were mostly cricket matches or approximations of the increasingly popular Canadian game with its five bases and most often eleven defensive fielders. Another element of the game played only informally up north was that all batters had to be retired in order to end an inning and bring about a change in offensive and defensive sides. Once the more modern New York Game perfected by Cartwright's Knickerbockers was widely adopted as a standard by most Ontario nines, organized baseball play began spreading to other provinces. Between 1857 and 1860 Ontario baseballers also adapted such further innovations proposed by Knickerbockers club leader Daniel Adams as nine innings (rather than 21 tallies) to determine a game's length and 90 feet between bases. Quebec province, and especially Montreal, became a special hotbed for the sport by the time of the American Civil War, and in the mid-1860s local Montreal authorities even had to ban play in city parks and streets in the name of public safety.

As the popular new game spread westward, it found receptive homes all across the central Canadian plains. Play is documented in Manitoba as early as 1874, when it first supplanted an earlier version of bat-and-ball known around the Red River Valley region simply as "bat" and reportedly springing up at least three decades earlier. There was an unsuccessful attempt at a three-team league in Manitoba in the mid-1880s and later a more viable Winnipeg 1902 entry in the early pro North Dakota League. The Great Northern Railway Company and its local agent J. R. Smith were largely responsible for con-structing a playing field at the city's River Park and for initiating the North Dakota League team just after the turn of the century. A further connection between baseball's and the railroads' joint expansions into western provinces followed with completion of the Canadian Pacific Railway and the hiring of its sports representative, Joe Page. A former U.S. professional player with Indianapolis, Page quickly took the lead in sponsoring teams, games, and even local leagues all along the rail line, from Manitoba westward.

Alberta and Saskatchewan both experienced the westward expansion of the emerging diamond sport in the late 1880s, and Regina in the latter province hosted two regional championship teams during this era. Regina also boasted an 1887 touring semi-pro team that won a pair of regional trophies behind the ace pitching of Walter Scott (later first premier of Saskatchewan). Early settlers from Montana and perhaps eastern Canada brought baseball to Alberta's Lethbridge (near Calgary), where pick-up games were being played at least by 1886. After the turn of the century, recreational baseball had reached as far west and north as the Yukon Territory, where it was a popular excuse for heavy frontier gambling, and also into British Columbia, where in 1903 future big league headliner and miscreant Harold Homer "Prince Hal" Chase performed at first base for a Victoria ball club playing in a circuit operating mainly out of Washington state.

Organized baseball was itself a relatively early entry into Canada, which hosted a number of early pro teams and even boasted the 1877 International Association pennant winners in the guise of the Tecumsehs club from London, Ontario. Existing (if unverified) reports suggest that immediately after their pennant successes the Tecumsehs were offered a slot in the fledging National League. They promptly rejected an offer that would have put Ontario squarely in the center of the earliest versions of a major league map. Due to lack of fan support, the champion Tecumsehs actually disbanded only one season later.

Another nineteenth-century Canadian pennant winner in organized base-ball was the Toronto Canucks franchise of the then Eastern League during the 1887 season. The circuit itself would soon be better known as the International League, and for eight decades a Toronto-based ball club would remain one of the most solid and successful outfits in the venerable association. Toronto—dubbed the Maple Leafs after their second entry into the league in 1895—eventually claimed fifteen more league titles, some by posting regular-season first-place finishes and others with playoff victories. The string included back-to-back pennant flags in 1917 and 1918, 1956 and 1957, and finally in 1965 and 1966 (as Governor's Cup postseason champions under manager Dick Williams).

By the time Toronto's Maple Leafs had firmly established themselves as an International League powerhouse in the years separating two disastrous world wars, Montreal also was making inroads within the same circuit. The Montreal Royals (debuting in 1928) would eventually walk off with seven Governor's Cup titles of their own, all earned in the 1940s and 1950s. It was also in the mid-1940s that Montreal would play a major role in the long-overdue racial integration of professional organized baseball. Montreal's proud minor league heritage peaked in the shadows of World War II, and it is the 1946 Montreal Royals club that is best remembered—and far more for the presence of Jackie Robinson than for the only 100-win season in franchise history, or the 18.5-game victory margin over second-place Syracuse during the International League's first-ever season under its new AAA designation. It was fitting that organized baseball's odious segregation policies should be first corrected on Canadian soil, since it was there that the practice itself had taken final hold in 1899 when Bill "Hippo" Galloway was released after only a token 20-game appearance with the Woodstock (Ontario) club of the short-lived six-team Canadian League.

It did not take Robinson to legitimize a Canadian version of the American national pastime. Even before the curtain was finally rung down on the nineteenth century, Canadian baseball was flourishing and even becoming well integrated into the professional game already so wildly popular throughout American towns, villages, and cities. Ontario, Quebec, Manitoba, and other points north may have been little more than distant baseball outposts in the early 1900s—and it was perhaps already destined they should also remain so throughout much of the coming century—yet for all its bush league trappings, Canada has long enjoyed baseball as a shared national sport and can proudly claim its own thriving baseball culture and even its own deeply ingrained baseball traditions.

CANADA AND BASEBALL'S RACIAL INTEGRATION

Some have argued (perhaps a bit overenthusiastically) that Jackie Robinson's Brooklyn debut of 1947 was the proudest and maybe most glorious moment in all of baseball history. It seems easier still to defend the proposition that Robinson's appearance a season earlier in Montreal was without doubt the apex of Canada's numerous contributions to the North American professional game.

The story of Jackie Robinson and Branch Rickey and their crusade to integrate organized baseball is—like so much of baseball's grandest lore—surrounded with numerous half-truths and infused with substantial bald-faced fabrications. Robinson was not the first black man (that is, owner of any Negro blood, as was the operative definition at the time) during the twentieth century to cross the sport's odious racial barriers; Afro-Cubans (like Armando Marsans in 1911, Mike González in the 1920s, and Roberto Estalella after 1935) had played in the big leagues well before Jackie Robinson did. Nor was the Branch Rickey–inspired integration of Major League Baseball without its disastrous economic fallout for many thriving black neighborhoods in Kansas City, Pittsburgh, Birmingham, Indianapolis, and elsewhere that overnight lost their once-healthy professional franchises. But any historical distortions that would later warp an overinflated myth about Robinson's one-man barrier-busting were in 1945 still in the distant future; nothing at the time could make Robinson's heroic Montreal and Brooklyn performances of 1946 and 1947 any less impressive—nor his lonely pioneering road, first in Montreal and later in National League cities, any less difficult.

Canada can boast a major role in Jackie Robinson's integration of major league baseball. [Transcendental Graphics]

An important facet of the Robinson–Rickey legend would of course be played out first on Canadian soil in Montreal, not on U.S. turf in Brooklyn. Rickey cleverly elected to launch his experiment in Canada (and in French-speaking and multicultural Montreal in particular) for highly specific reasons. Foremost was the more relaxed racial atmosphere in multilingual and multiethnic Quebec; equally prominent was the physical separation of the city's International League club from the constant glare of a pestering and racially sensitized American press corps. There were also the hidden traditions surrounding occasional if infrequent earlier attempts to allow occasional black ballplayers into some of Canada's outlaw leagues and obscure rural minor league outposts. Such reasons also later prompted Rickey's National League team to hold its 1947 spring training in Havana, Cuba, during Robinson's historic debut on the big league level.

The baseball color line had already been broken in Canada—in the very same province of Quebec—as early as 1935, by a hard-hitting and hard-throwing pitcher and outfielder named Alfred Wilson. Wilson played late in that season with Granby of the then-outlaw Provincial League, operating outside the control of organized baseball, and he displayed his qualifications by hitting .392 throughout the final month-long stretch of the pennant drive. The same league had also sponsored an all-black Montreal-based club called the Black Panthers in both 1936 and 1937, its roster filled by teenaged prospects drawn mostly from distant Alabama and Mississippi. The result of the latter experiment was a short-lived rebellion by white Montreal Royals players scheduled for an exhibition match versus the Provincial League All-Stars with Black Panther outfielder Carl Logan penciled into the line-up. On the whole, however, Montreal was an easier location for baseball integration during the postwar years than any imaginable United States site might have been. The Quebec Hockey League had featured an all-black line on one of its clubs in the mid-1940s, and the Montreal Alouettes in 1946 (the year Robinson played for the Royals) also integrated the previously all-white Canadian Football League.

Jackie Robinson did not debut alone in Montreal but was accompanied by a pair of black teammates—journeyman pitchers John Wright and Roy Partlow. Of the three prospects, only Robinson—who was the league's top hitter at .349—made it big, both on the field and in the history books. Right-hander Wright, who had most recently been a star with the Homestead Grays, pitched only two no-decision games before being shipped off to Three Rivers of the Canadian American League (Can-Am, for short). Southpaw Partlow, another Homestead ace, replaced Wright and won both of his appearances before suddenly leaving the club under mysterious circumstances. Neither Negro league pitcher could apparently handle the off-field pressures even in racially tolerant Montreal, and both were subsequently dumped by the Brooklyn organization. The color line that Robinson and his pair of teammates crossed with varying degrees of success had remained the norm in Canada (at least outside the rebel Provincial League) since the brief Woodstock adventure of Bill Galloway a half-century earlier. After the high-profile Montreal appearances of Robinson, Partlow, and Wright, the doors quickly swung open upon further parallel experiments in social justice. Robinson was the only Negro to finish the International League season, but late that summer a teenage black shortstop named Vincent "Manny" McIntyre was signed by the Cardinals-affiliated Sherbrooke (Quebec) team of the Class C Border League.

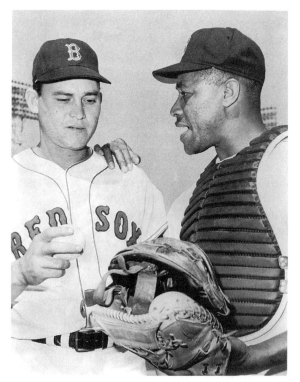

Elston Howard (right) prepped for his Yankees integration with Toronto's AAA Maple Leafs. [Transcendental Graphics]

Two additional black players also joined the ranks of the lesser Can-Am League for the subsequent 1947 season, the year that saw Robinson move on to lasting fame in Brooklyn. Future Hall of Famer Roy Campanella followed Robinson in the 1947 Montreal lineup, and still another milestone was crossed in 1951, when Sam Bankhead took the reins of the Provincial League Farnham (Quebec) team and in the process became the first black manager ever in the minor leagues.

If there were reasons aplenty for easing black ballplayers into organized baseball on the north side of the U.S.–Canadian border, this did not mean that such experiments in racial justice were smooth propositions. Other blacks traveling similar routes during the late 1940s and early 1950s still found the path pretty rocky. One troubled pioneer was supertalented and flamboyant first baseman Vic Power, native of Puerto Rico. Power was buried in the minors by the still racially intolerant New York Yankees, and part of his long road passed through Canada. It was in a Quebec town (Drummondville, in the Provincial League) that Power lost his family name. (His mother had already had her name, Pove, changed to Power by an I-know-best schoolteacher.) As Power would later tell it, he entered Drummondville still using his full name, *Victor Pellot Power*, but a French-speaking stadium public address voice would repeatedly pronounce *Pellot* with an "l" rather than more normal Spanish "y" sound, thus offering up what sounded like a crude French sexual term. The exasperated Puerto Rican youngster soon enough dropped *Pellot* from his ballplayer's resumé.

Another black pioneer with Canadian minor league roots was a second Yankees farmhand and one-time roommate of Power, highly touted catching prospect Elston Howard. The Yankees unloaded Power onto the Philadelphia franchise rather than risk him as a pioneering black in New York, but eventually they succumbed to mounting integration pressures and it was thus Howard who became the first black player to wear a New York Yankees big league uniform. Howard prepped for that role as an all-star International League receiver for the 1954 pennant-winning Toronto Maple Leafs—thereby keeping Montreal from hogging all of what would eventually be seen as integration glory. Elston Howard was twenty-five when he arrived at the Yankees' AAA affiliate: delayed by military service, the Yankees' foot-dragging on promoting a black ballplayer, and also the presence of Cooperstown-bound Yogi Berra in the New York starting lineup.

TRADITIONS OF MINOR LEAGUE BASEBALL NORTH OF THE U.S.–CANADA BORDER

Montreal's minor league tradition extends far beyond the saga of Jackie Robinson and the overdue integration of organized baseball. For years on end, Montreal was the jewel of the showcase International League, likely baseball's best circuit outside of the major leagues. Toronto, springboard to Elston Howard's more belated integration role with New York's American League franchise, had its own significant role to play in the long saga of the venerable International League. The Maple Leafs were for years (especially in the 1950s and 1960s) one of the strongest franchises of top-level minor league baseball.

Even at the highest levels of minor league baseball, the eventual big league venues that would come to Montreal (1969) and Toronto (1977) have not had the stage entirely to themselves, especially not after the large-scale expansions of the two major leagues (and the corresponding inflations of AAA farm clubs) that transpired throughout the two decades following the Dodgers and Giants joint escape to California. Four other AAA franchises have graced Canada's landscape in recent decades. The prestigious modern-era Pacific Coast League has for several decades been bolstered by the likes of the Calgary Cannons (1985–2002), Edmonton Trappers (1981–2003), and Vancouver Canadians (1978–1999). Vancouver enjoyed two earlier runs at fast-lane life in the Pacific Coast League [with the Mounties (1956–1962) and (1965–1969)], and the short-lived Winnipeg Whips (1970–1971) also briefly limped in and out of the same circuit. In recent seasons, the Ottawa Lynx have joined the expanded family of the still-standing International League, where they captured a surprising 1995 postseason championship trophy in only their third season of operation as a newly christened Montreal Expos AAA affiliate.

The 1990s saw a full half-dozen additional Canadian minor league franchises operating at various levels of organized baseball's ballooning structure. The London Tigers (Detroit Tigers affiliate) performed in the AA Eastern League between 1989 and 1993 and captured that circuit's 1990 postseason round-robin. There were three franchises in the short-season A-level New York–Pennsylvania League (St. Catherine's Blue Jays, Welland Pirates, and briefly the Hamilton Redbirds) and two others out west in the Rookie-class Pioneer League (Lethbridge Mounties, Medicine Hat Blue Jays). With its reborn Goldeyes, Winnipeg has lately boasted a highly successful franchise in the current version of the Northern League (an independent league based in the Upper Midwest and Manitoba).

Throughout the twentieth century, Canada has been proud host to more than this varied collection of minor league franchises in leagues largely based south of the border. There have also been a number of entire leagues that could for either brief or extended spells call Canada home base. Dating from the earliest years of the century, these scattered organizations included the Canadian League (1899–1900, 1905, 1911–1915), Eastern Canada League (Class B 1922–1923), Quebec–Ontario–Vermont League (Class B 1924), Quebec Provincial League (Class B 1940), Canadian-American League (Can-Am League; Class C 1936–1951, with teams in New York, Massachusetts, Ontario, and Quebec), and Provincial League (1922–1924, 1935–1955, 1958–1970). It was the last-named circuit that proved to be most colorful, willy-nilly moving in and out of organized baseball's realm over the years and at one time or another featuring such future or past big league and Negro league headliners as Max Lanier, Sal Maglie, Roland Gladu, Jean Pierre Roy, Vic Power, Buster Clarkson, Dave Pope, and Quincy Troupe.

The Provincial League boasted the longest and most lively history of the numerous Canadian-based minor league circuits, though it was a scrambled history, confused by constant shifts in league structures and names. Based mostly in Quebec and sometimes even referred to as the Quebec Provincial League, this constantly reborn and reshaped organization was launched with single seasons in 1894 and 1900, reemerged as the Ontario–Quebec–Vermont League of 1922 to 1924, and then took on a fourth and final chaotic life between 1935 and 1955. It was attached to organized baseball as a Class C four-team affair (later six teams) before finally collapsing in debt after the 1955 season—and then again found life as a struggling outlaw league throughout the 1960s. Like most Canadian circuits, the Provincial League was a direct product of Canadian Pacific Railway operations and that railway's energetic sports promoter, Joseph Page. As already noted, Page was instrumental in setting up leagues and teams almost everywhere that Canadian Pacific trains were scheduled to arrive and depart. He labored with former big league hurler Jean Dubuc to launch the Eastern Canada League in 1922, and later the Ontario–Quebec–Vermont League of 1924. (Dubuc was born on the Vermont side of the Quebec border.) And Page even had a hand, along with noted Canadian big leaguer Tip O'Neill, in assembling the Montreal Royals 1897 team that quickly won an 1898 Eastern League (later known as the International League) pennant.

Provincial League business interests grew most rapidly during the late 1930s: operating strictly outside organized baseball before 1940, the league discreetly recruited and illegally paid U.S. college players and briefly boasted a native Mohawk team from the Caughnawaga reservation. The Provincial League shut down during the lean wartime years, resumed operation in the late 1940s, and again collapsed in 1956 (a collapse coinciding with the general downturn in minor league baseball everywhere throughout North America). From 1958 to 1971, the league saw its last revival, this time in outlaw ball.

Best known as a progressive champion of native American and black players during its heyday as a preintegration rebel circuit, the Provincial League continued to house colorful off-beat ballplayers both during its later manifestation as a legitimate postwar Class C affiliated league and during its final return to outlaw baseball. Noted Provincial Leaguers include Maurice Richard (the Montreal Canadiens hockey great, who used baseball as a summer tune-up), Pete Gray (a one-armed outfielder who batted .283 for Trois-Rivières in 1938 before appearing with the 1944 American League St. Louis Browns), scholarly-appearing Montreal hurler Paul Calvert (who once lost 14 straight games with the Washington Senators), Adrian Zabala (a charismatic Cuban League southpaw who labored in 1938–1939 for Sherbrooke before his brief sojourns with Pasquel's rebel Mexican League and the big league New York Giants), cup-of-coffee native-son major leaguer Roland Gladu (who performed off and on with four different Provincial League teams between 1935 and 1951), and ex-big-leaguer Felix Mantilla (who was still hanging on as an outlaw leaguer three years after his 1966 retirement from the Houston Astros). The Provincial League's zenith unarguably came in the mid-1930s, however, as a haven for ostracized black players still struggling to crack organized baseball's long-standing color barrier.

The heftiest chapters of organized baseball in Canada will obviously remain those written by the Toronto and Montreal franchises, cornerstones of the International League for most of the first half of the twentieth century. Toronto appeared earliest on the scene, debuting in the then Eastern League in 1885 with a solid third-place finish, capturing a first-place banner in its third year, then sitting on the sidelines from 1891 through 1895 before taking up permanent residence as a league staple. The franchise had its ups and downs; the Maple Leafs (the Canucks, before 1890) eventually claimed 11 first place finishes during 79 active seasons but were also a basement-dwelling seventh or eighth on a dozen occasions through the years. There were several strings of championship runs highlighted by consecutive regular season titles in 1917 and 1918 and again in 1956 and 1957, and also triple back-to-back postseason crowns (1917 and 1918; 1956 and 1957; and once more in 1965 and 1966, the club's penultimate seasons). There were also memorable managers (Edward Barrow, Joe Kelley, Nap Lajoie, Steve O'Neill, Burleigh Grimes, Luke Sewell, Dixie Walker, Dick Williams) and players (Ned Crane, Bill Dinneen, Urban Shocker, Lajoie, Dolf Luque, Carl Hubbell, Dale Alexander, Ike Boone, Rip Collins, Dick Fowler, Connie Johnson, Rocky Nelson, Reggie Smith), many of whom made their way to later fame in the major leagues. And, as already noted, Toronto played its own small role in the big league integration story as training grounds for future Yankees great Elston Howard.

The Montreal Royals sported a proud tradition that stretched back considerably before the appearance of Jackie Robinson. The Royals never had the extended successes of the Maple Leafs, winning only one league championship over the first seventeen summers of ball club history before the end of World War II, yet they did have their later seasons in the spotlight. In the years surrounding Robinson (1945–1948), the club's advantage as top Brooklyn Dodgers farm team meant that many future Flatbush stars would bolster the Montreal roster throughout Brooklyn's "Boys of Summer" era. Such notable players as Roy Campanella, Junior Gilliam, Gino Cimoli, Bobby Morgan, Sandy Amoros, Jack Banta, Chico Fernández, Sam Jethroe, Rocky Nelson, Jim Pendleton, and Tommy Lasorda all cut their big league teeth with a final stop-over in Montreal. Throughout the war-shaken 1940s and the postwar boom-era 1950s, Montreal was indeed one of the showcase franchises of the entire minor league baseball world.

Expansion of the majors into Canada in 1969 (Montreal Expos) and 1977 (Toronto Blue Jays) also brought in its immediate wake an expansion of AAA-level baseball to prime locations north of the border. Vancouver on the West Coast was the first Canadian city to benefit, inheriting a Pacific Coast League club named the Mounties as early as the mid-1950s. The first Vancouver ball club lasted little more than a decade, playing twelve interrupted seasons in two stretches of 1956 to 1962 and 1965 to 1969. A Vancouver franchise was once more reborn in the late 1970s as the aptly named Canadians and enjoyed twenty-two seasons the second time around. In one of modern-era pro baseball's sad but not rare ironies, when the Vancouver Canadians celebrated a best-ever campaign in 1999 by winning both the Pacific Coast League post-season tournament and AAA Little World Series showdown with the American Association Charlotte Knights, it was also the club's final outing on Canadian soil. The Oakland A's AAA farm team was by that time already scheduled for relocation to Sacramento the following summer.

Edmonton (1981) and Calgary (1985) were not far behind Vancouver on the shifting Pacific Coast League scene. Edmonton's Trappers were a Pacific Coast League relocation franchise after the 1981 season, replacing Utah's Ogden club, and have remained a league fixture for nearly a quarter-century, most recently as a Montreal Expos affiliate. Four seasons later, Calgary's Cannons joined the growing stable of Pacific Coast League franchises, with a solid on-field second-place debut and second-best league attendance figure. Finally, in the early 1990s, Ottawa would get into the act over in the International League as the latest top-level Montreal farm team. Even Manitoba's Winnipeg made a too-brief International League appearance back in 1970 and 1971, but that ill-starred franchise never really got off the ground. The seemingly unwanted Whips were relocated from Buffalo to Winnipeg with the 1970 season already two-months old, then moved again to Virginia at the close of the 1971 season. The Ottawa Lynx were a much bigger immediate hit at the box office, though they have been largely mediocre on the field for much of their decade-long history. This top Montreal Expos 1993-to-2002 farm team (it switched affiliation to the Baltimore Orioles in 2003) enjoyed some surprising success in only its third season, when it pulled off an unexpected International League title in the historical Governor's Cup postseason playoffs.

This prestigious Governor's Cup victory was hardly the first for a Canadian franchise. Down through the years this top minor league prize, awarded annually since 1933 to the winner of postseason International League playoffs, has fallen to Canadian-based ball clubs on a dozen different occasions (see table at chapter's end). First to claim the trophy in 1934 were the Ike Boone–managed Toronto Maple Leafs, who slid past Rochester in the title round despite a third-place regular-season finish. Minor league legend Ike Boone was also that year's hitting star, with a league-best .372 average plus the International League Most Valuable Player trophy to spice his managerial triumphs.

It was the Montreal Royals in the following decade that early outdistanced the pack in postseason International League championship efforts. Montreal took home the Governor's Cup four times in the 1940s and three more times in the 1950s before Toronto would eventually reclaim the prize after a thirty-five-year dry spell. In one memorable season, in 1958, Montreal and Toronto even managed to conspire to provide International League fans with an unprecedented and especially exciting all-Canada championship showdown. Canada's two most venerable minor league clubs also reached the Governor's Cup final round series seven other times—Montreal in 1935, 1945, 1952, and 1954; Toronto in 1943, 1955, and 1956—but lost the ultimate championship battle on each of those less fortunate occasions.

Canada's lengthy minor league tradition has thus been from first to last a proud one. The Montreal Royals were for years a feeder system for the marvelous Brooklyn Dodgers "Boys of Summer" teams that ruled the National League throughout the golden age 1950s. The rival Ontario-based Toronto Maple Leafs played a similar role in the same decade, honing such notable future big leaguers as Reggie Smith, Ozzie Virgil, Sparky Lyle, Russ Nixon, Lou Johnson, Chuck Tanner, Faye Thronberry, Rocky Nelson, and Elston Howard. In recent years that tradition has been carried still farther in both the AAA International League and AAA Pacific Coast League, the only remaining top minor league circuits. The glory days of top-level Canadian minor league baseball are gone, but for most Canadians the loss seemed a small price to pay at the time for their long-awaited entry into the major league arena. That is not to say that with the recent woes surrounding the sagging Expos and Blue Jays—to say nothing of increased dilution and crass commercialization of the entire big league sport— diehard baseball purists may not today once again see it all very differently.

CANADA IN WORLD AMATEUR BASEBALL

Canada has made no great showing in world tournament play—less even perhaps than has the United States. The two countries with the most legitimate claims to the game's origins have rarely claimed gold medals in the sport's ranking amateur competitions. In the case of the Americans, this is largely explained by mere apathy and a single-minded focus on the more lucrative and commercial-friendly professional game. In Canada, it speaks more to a lack of depth in ballplaying talent and an absence of widespread focus on the grassroots sandlot game.

If Canada has rarely stood in the center stage spotlight of international tournaments as a powerhouse competitor, the country has played a vital role as gracious host to some memorable international matches down through the years. IBAF Amateur World Series play—a true World Series event, in more than name only—finally arrived on Canadian soil in August 1990, with a memorable fifteen days of round-robin action in Edmonton. Unfortunately, Team Canada's own entry assembled for World Cup XXXI won but two of nine matches and thus brought up the rear of the 12-team field. IBAF's Intercontinental Cup competitions made a much earlier appearance on Canadian turf back in 1975, when the second-ever edition was hosted by Montreal. A loaded United States club, behind the slugging of future big leaguer Ron Hassey, swept the field, but the Canadians were far more respectable this time out, with 4 victories and a narrow 7–5 semifinals loss to the Americans. When Intercontinental Cup play returned to Edmonton in 1981, the improving Canadians finally posted a winning record and even edged the champion Americans 9–7 in the opening round. Edmonton was again the host city for Cup play in 1985, but this time the home team was again embarrassed on the field with only 2 qualifying-round victories. Team Canada did manage to save some face by posting a repeat 9–7 win versus a much weaker 1985 edition of Team USA. To date, only Cuba (with four) has hosted more Intercontinental Cup reunions than Canada.

Canada's top international visibility has come with Pan American Games competitions, which began at mid-century. The first Canadian appearance in the hemisphere-wide event fell in 1967, when the matches (which include all summer sports, not just baseball) were hosted in Winnipeg, Manitoba. On the baseball diamond, the Canadian team again fared poorly—dead last among five teams, with a single win during a meaningless final opening-round game versus runner-up Cuba. But the tournament was quite noteworthy as a breakout occasion for U.S. amateur forces and also as a rare embarrassing stumble by the usually powerful Cuban contingent. The overconfident Cubans not only snoozed through a final opening-round game with Canada but dropped a rain-interrupted 2–1 thriller in the tie-breaker of a best-of-three finale. It was the first and only Pan American Games gold medal for the usually overmatched Americans. Perhaps the best Canadian team, until recent years and the introduction of seasoned pros, was one that reached a bronze medal showdown with Puerto Rico at the 1987 Pan American Games in Indianapolis. It was not a winning team in the end—taking four of nine overall—but a competitive one that managed to test talented Team USA (with slugger Tino Martínez and mound ace Cris Carpenter) during a narrow 7–6 semifinal loss.

The apex for Canadian national team achievement came near century's end, with the high-stakes tournament of the eighth Pan American Games in Winnipeg. This time around, the Canadians featured a balanced team that included seasoned young professionals like Todd Betts (AA Akron), Stubby Clapp (AAA Memphis), Jason Gooding (AA Wichita), Aaron Guiel (AAA Las Vegas), Jeremy Ware (AA Harrisburg), Ryan Radmanovich (AAA Tacoma), and Andy Stewart (AA Reading). The team manager (head coach) was a Canadian baseball icon named Ernie Whitt, who had recently starred in Toronto with the Blue Jays as one of that franchise's most popular all-time players. It seemed a team that might challenge either the Americans or the favored Cubans.

Easily meeting expectations, the July 1999 Winnipeg tournament soon proved perhaps the best world international tournament ever staged. Minor league pros were playing for the first time ever, and the sport had returned after decades of aluminum to the use of big league style wooden bats. The presence of minor leaguers meant that the rest of the field now had a chance to catch up with (perhaps even unseat) the always-dominant Cubans. The event also came on the heels of renewed American and Canadian interest in Cuban baseball, spurred by the ballyhooed Baltimore Orioles versus Cuban national team series of the previous spring. Team USA forces (for the first time operating in alliance with Major League Baseball) now believed they might finally dethrone the Cubans and thus gain an automatic Sydney 2000 Olympic invitation—this tournament's ultimate prize. Dominican and Canadian entries also harbored identical aspirations for reaching the finals and thus picking off one of the two coveted Sydney qualification slots available to western hemisphere teams. The Puerto Ricans and Venezuelans had stayed home on the sidelines due to debilitating turmoil within their own chaotic baseball federations.

The Canadians were the surprise of early tournament action. They trounced Brazil in a 16–4 knockout, upset Team USA in a 7–6 eleven-inning thriller (marred by coach Ernie Whitt's ejection over a rules technicality in the final frame), edged pesky Mexico, and blasted five top Cuban pitchers (including soon-to-be-defector Danys Báez) 8–1 to remain the single undefeated club in qualification-round play. It seemed the Cubans had been knocked back on their heels when they suffered one-sided opening-round losses to both upstart Canada and the strong American club (10–5). The Cubans also seemed to get more press attention off the field than on as the week-long games were permeated with excessive media interest in potential Cuban roster defections. With the wounded and so-far impotent Cubans needing to conquer the dangerous Dominicans in the quarterfinals and then overcome the hot Canadians in the semis, suddenly it appeared as if Team Canada and Team USA were together riding a fast track toward the finals and the coveted Olympic berth in Sydney.

The tournament's final weekend was one of the most thrill-packed in the decades-long history of world amateur tournaments. With their backs firmly against the wall, the gritty Cubans now put on a miraculous rush to the finish. Aces José Contreras (three years shy of his debut in Yankee Stadium) and Pedro Luis Lazo shut down the Dominicans and rode clutch homers by Luis Ulacia and Gabriel Pierre to easy victory. The semifinal match between Cuba and host Canada proved to be a game for the ages. It came down to a remarkable final inning—Cuba nursing a slim 3–2 advantage thanks to an Omar Linares homer— in which first an unwelcome anti-Castro protester stormed the field to disrupt play and heighten tensions, and then Lazo raced from the bullpen to relieve starter José Ibar and seal victory with two final strikeouts. The Cubans again had proved their true mettle. The finale was indeed anticlimactic, with Contreras returning to spin a neat four-hitter against the Americans, and Orestes Kindelán and Pierre providing all the necessary offense with two massive round-trippers. The Cubans were once more the toast of amateur baseball, locking up both their eighth consecutive Pan Am crown (their last loss had been in Winnipeg in 1967) and the opportunity to defend their Olympic title in Sydney. But Canada also finally showed some evidence that it could indeed be a competitive force on the world "amateur" (newly defined as "pros included") baseball stage.

If Canada was a surprise team on the field in Winnipeg, it was still a major disappointment in the final analysis that faced the hometown contingent. The bridesmaid had been left waiting on the outside as Cuba and Team USA headed off to do Olympic battle at Sydney. But there would be headier days waiting not that far down the road. The first Olympic event of the new century would bring with it a new system for qualification, and it was one that the Canadians would soon play to full advantage. At a special qualifying meet held in Panama during early November 2003, the Canadians were again no match for the hitting- and pitching-rich Cubans, losing a lopsided 5–0 gold medal match and garnering only four tame singles against their old nemesis, Pedro Luis Lazo. But they would nonetheless have their revenge against the archrival Americans. Team USA suffered its own more shocking defeat by a 2–1 count to Mexico (with former big leaguer Rigo Beltran on the mound) in the quarter-finals, a loss that dented American baseball pride and robbed the Americans of any chance to defend the gold they had finally won at Sydney. With the United States eliminated in shattering fashion, Team Canada filled the void in an unanticipated finale versus the nearly always invincible Cubans. The showdown was to be far more one-sided than it had been in Winnipeg: the Canadians never mustered a threat against Lazo, and Joan Pedroso's two-run homer in the seventh was enough to decide the issue. The truly big win for Canada had come a night earlier, in the semifinals, when Team Canada enjoyed a 10–1 laugher against the now-spent Mexicans. Canada had for the very first time qualified to compete for gold and glory in the baseball Olympiad. Athens 2004 now sat on the horizon as the potential apex in the unfolding saga of a heretofore always less-than-proud Team Canada. Even a disappointing fourth-place finish in Greece (losing 11–2 to Japan in a lopsided bronze medal match) barely slowed the momentum as Team Canada seemingly had finally risen above its longtime embarrassing also-ran status on the international baseball stage.

CANADA'S MAJOR LEAGUE CONNECTIONS

For baseball as it is played "north of the border," 1992 was both the best and the worst of times. Coming off the embarrassment of a season in which part of their stadium had collapsed and they had to complete their schedule with 26 straight taxing road games, the lackluster Montreal Expos opened to a largely empty house in April 1992. Part of the massive support structure for Olympic Stadium had tumbled to the ground just before the close of the 1991 campaign, necessitating the unprecedented month-long road trip and causing much speculation about whether the Expos would even call Montreal home in 1992. Baseball in Montreal had tumbled to such a lowly state that no local radio station would carry road games, and the local press no longer deemed it necessary to reserve a paid beat writer for the team's out-of-town contests. By the second half of 1992, however, under new field manager Felipe Alou, the revived Expos club was suddenly the surprise toast of the National League and immersed in the thick of a tense pennant race (where they also remained throughout 1993). Montreal's farm system was still one of the best, but the ball club's administration, headed by innovative General Manager Dave

Dombrowski, had already fled southward in droves to join the expansion Florida Marlins.

In anglophile Toronto, things were just as chaotic and ambivalent for the city's baseball boosters. Coming off a second divisional title in three seasons (and the second playoff crash landing as well), the underachieving Blue Jays were, on paper at least, the best club in all of baseball. But by late season they were floundering in a pennant race they should have dominated, and legions at the SkyDome were bracing for still another patented act of self-destruction. The much-lauded SkyDome itself was proving not to be the state-of-the-art pleasure palace it had once appeared to be; rather, the mammoth facility, already awash in a sea of red ink, was now displaying some structural damage of its own.

Off the field, things were even worse for Canadian baseball during the landmark summer of 1992—at least for those taking personal pride in the considerable baseball culture owned by a land better known for snow and hockey. Long the leading producer of non-American baseball talent (at least by big league measures), Canada was on the verge of falling from the lead in this category, about to be passed by the Dominican Republic and also pressed by the island "semi-nation" of Puerto Rico. And if matters were not bad enough in this regard, the once-thriving Canadian Baseball Hall of Fame—after several summers spent packed away in storage crates—seemingly collapsed in a mountainous heap of debt and hopeless void of corporate sponsorship. (It would revive, but at the time there was no predicting when or how or where.) If Canadians wanted to claim pride of place in the miniworld of baseball culture, this was not a very easy time to demonstrate it.

Nonetheless, for all the negatives of 1992, it was also a breakout year. For the rest of the world, and especially for many U.S. fans, Canadian baseball seemed to be born on October 14, 1992, with the clinching of a first American League pennant by the once lackluster Toronto Blue Jays. And perhaps even more on October 20, 1992, with the opening pitch of the first World Series game played on Canadian soil. But of course there had almost always been Canadian ballplayers, and the Canadian impact on big league play was always real enough, even if often buried in seeming insignificance. Ask the average fan about Canadian players and you'll likely get only one or two names—likely Fergie Jenkins or perhaps Larry Walker. Yet there were indeed other colorful Canadians in the big leagues from the earliest years of the nineteenth-century National League. Both the durable fielder Arthur Irwin and the great slugger Tip O'Neill stood out as early heroes, when the pro game was still in its infancy. A spate of journeyman pitchers—Phil Marchildon, Dick Fowler, "Frenchy" Raymond, Reggie Cleveland, and John Hiller—filled up the 1950s, 1960s, and 1970s. National League outfielder Terry Puhl enjoyed a long workman-like career and once even earned temporary celebrity as Canada's version of "Mr. October" with the 1981 Houston Astros, when he exploded for a .529 batting average in the National League Championship Series versus Philadelphia. By the early 1990s, a more recent flock of bright new potential stars (such as Larry Walker, Kirk McCaskill, Matt Stairs, and Kevin Reimer) seemed to promise renewed focus on the usually overshadowed Canadian ballplayer.

Some of the lesser-known Canadian big leaguers have enjoyed noteworthy careers, being sometimes authors of spectacular if little-noted events. Bob Emslie was the first Canadian diamond notable while a 30-game winner for American Association Baltimore during the mid-1880s. His notoriety, however, came much later as umpire "Blind Bob" Emslie, dubbed such by a disenchanted John McGraw. In this latter role Emslie was a central player in one of baseball's most remembered single games—even if his own part in the affair was soon enough universally forgotten. It was unfortunately Emslie who teamed up with Hank O'Day as the crew of much-maligned arbiters that ruled Fred Merkle onto the pages of baseball history, as the game's most infamous (and undeserving) "bonehead" goat. James "Tip" O'Neill was another early slugging star who left behind a memorable moniker to be later attached to generations of young ballplayers (and politicians) named O'Neill. Jeff Heath and Jack Graney earned outfield fame in Cleveland and Graney, like Emslie, went on to a second and more notable diamond career—not as umpire, but as the first ex-player to broadcast big league games on the radio. Another Canadian-bred outfielder, George Selkirk, was thrust by fate into the unenviable position of replacing the immortal George Herman Ruth in Yankee Stadium. While he failed predictably to erase Ruth's indelible memory (and that indeed was not his assignment), Selkirk did enjoy championship status and a much-deserved reputation as a more-than-adequate big league fly-chaser and equally potent slugger.

When it comes to truly immortal Canadian big league icons, Ferguson Jenkins stands in a class by himself. Pitching legend Jenkins is without dispute Canada's one legitimate Cooperstown Hall of Fame performer, and his induction in 1991 did almost as much as the Blue Jays first World Series appearance a year later to put all of Canadian baseball finally and squarely on the world's sports map.

And when the discussion turns to athletes representing ethnic, racial, or national minorities it seems as though Canadian big leaguers are the most undistinguished among any large-scale group. While jokes abound about the sparseness of Jewish big leaguers, nonetheless the fan with Jewish roots does retain boasting rights to such Goliaths of the mound and batter's box as Sandy Koufax with Los Angeles, Hank Greenberg with Detroit, and Chicago's dead-ball-era pitching ace Ed Reulbach, or present-day Dodgers slugger Shawn Green. European big leaguers, a shadowy-enough contingent, still feature Bobby Thomson (Scotland), Bert Blyleven (The Netherlands), Elmer Valo (Czechoslovakia), Moe Drabowsky (Poland), and Reno Bertoia (raised in Canada, but born in Italy), alongside famed pioneering arbiter Tom Connolly and reporter Henry Chadwick (both from England). The last named, inventor of the box score and candidate of many for canonization as "Father Chadwick," is the sport's most legitimate alternative to mythical Abner Doubleday. Furthermore, Latin ballplayers now rank everywhere among baseball's top superstars: Roberto Alomar, Mariano Rivera, Sammy Sosa, Rafael Palmeiro, Albert Pujols, Vladimir Guerrero, Pedro Martínez. When it comes to Canadians of star status, however, once we have dispensed with Ferguson Jenkins there is little to beat the drums about. Although Canada still led all "outside" nations in its total contribution of players to the American pastime as late as the 1994 season, the contribution was largely in terms of a roll call of journeymen.

Montreal Expos

Canada emerged in the consciousness of a general U.S. fandom only with the arrival of the Montreal Expos franchise in the twilight of the 1960s, and then again with American League expansion into Toronto slightly less than a decade later. Events surrounding launching of the Montreal Expos, and early ball club history as well, offered a good deal of promise for the first big league franchise placed outside of U.S. territory. Hoping for a fast start out of the gate, the initial Montreal management drafted a substantial number of veterans, including Manny Mota, Donn Clendenon (quickly traded for Rusty Staub), Jesús Alou, Maury Wills, Larry Jackson, Jim "Mudcat" Grant, and Carl Morton. That calculated move paid some early dividends. Base-stealing king Wills was the most notable early-round draft selection, a preseason trade corralled heavy-hitting outfielder Rusty Staub from Houston, and even if the club only won 52 games its first year out of the gate, it did excite fans prematurely by winning both road and home season's openers.

Slugger André Dawson models the tricolored uniform of Canada's first big league club. [Transcendental Graphics]

The first decade of Expos history was filled with a number of rare milestones, some bordering on the truly bizarre. The club's first no-hitter, by Bill Stoneman versus Philadelphia, was not only the first ever with an expansion team, but it miraculously came only three days after the debut of big league play on Canadian soil and in only the team's ninth outing ever. After a decade of rotating fourth, fifth, and sixth-place finishes, in 1979 the new-look Expos under third-year skipper Dick Williams boasted a club-record 95 wins for their ten-year anniversary season, finally positioning themselves as a National League powerhouse. To add to the joys of early Expos history, there was a unique outdoor stadium (Parc Jarry, with a swimming pool behind the right field fence) and perhaps the most colorfully outlandish tricolored uniforms ever donned by any big league club.

A brief spurt of glory seasons for the Montreal big league franchise came at the outset of the 1990s, despite some telltale signs externally of an oncoming franchise disintegration. Promotion of Felipe Alou to the manager's slot on May 1992 brought a late-season rally and jump to the second slot in the National League East, but the club nonetheless outreached only the ailing San Francisco Giants and Houston Astros in National League home attendance. A season later, a repeat second-place finish, 94 wins (second best in club history), and an exciting young roster featuring slugging outfielder Moises Alou, fireballer Ken Hill, and slick second baseman Delino DeShields was not enticing enough to Montrealers to boost baseball's second lowest attendance figure. As if to prove that disappointments do indeed come in triplicate, the 1994 player-strike-marred season would ironically coincide with the sudden rush to league prominence by a Montreal club that had been painstakingly built around the Alous (father and son) to challenge for the league title. All indications were that 1994 could finally be the Expos' pennant year—but the long-overdue flexing of Expos' muscles couldn't have come at a worse time. When big league parks closed prematurely on August 12th, Alou's club was running on a fast track toward its first franchise league title with a major league top victory total and a six-game bulge over the National League's second-best outfit in Atlanta. The Expos were not strangers to sudden surges during seasons short-ened by labor disputes; in 1981, they had reached the National League Cham-pionship Series during their one postseason visit but fell to the Dodgers on a ninth-inning Rick Monday homer in the deciding fifth game. If there was any poetic justice to the club's 1981 playoff failure or to the manner in which it was robbed of a likely 1994 National League title, it was only that there were few fans in Quebec to protest or mourn the lost opportunity of a phantom Montreal league pennant.

The sad plight of Montreal big league baseball in the late 1990s is certainly one of the true low points of Canada's century-plus connection with big league baseball. Never would the ill-starred franchise quite recover from the twin disasters of its 1991 stadium debacle and a fan-killing 1994-to-1995 Major League Baseball Players Association work stoppage. Constantly underfunded and with little hometown fan base, the Montreal management repeatedly shopped away players as soon as they were developed in the talent-rich Montreal farm system. The number of present and future stars passing through Montreal in the 1980s and 1990s today reads something like a who's who list for the decade. In a misguided effort at rebuilding in 1989, new General Manager Dave Dombrowski corralled Seattle flamethrower Mark Langston but only at the price of a future Hall of Famer, 6'10" Randy Johnson; Langston promptly departed via free agency to the California Angels after only a partial and disappointing season wearing a tricolored Montreal beanie. Early 1980s franchise star Gary Carter was shipped to the New York Mets on the heels of his career-best 1984 campaign; André Dawson, hero of the club's only charge to postseason play in the strike-defiled 1981 campaign, eventually followed the free-agency route into Chicago's Wrigley Field. Pedro Martínez was traded to Boston when he became unaffordable after a 1997 Cy Young campaign. Most recently, coveted slugger Vladimir Guerrero wound up with the deep-pocketed Anaheim Angels after a half-dozen seasons of dismantling National League pitching. And these are only the most prominent headliners who escaped Olympic Stadium and thus National League oblivion during the past quarter-century.

A nearly moribund Montreal franchise at the opening of the new century seems to be again playing out the identical scenario of the 1991 financially strapped Montreal club. This time it was total collapse of the local fan base and not of the aging Olympic Stadium superstructure that forced Expos management and National League brass to adopt a schedule that had the club playing an inordinate number of road dates. The franchise actually seemed headed for extinction, with widespread talk of a 2002 owner-backed plan for major league contraction; when that plan faltered (due largely to court action in Minneapolis to save the also-threatened Twins), franchise ownership was assumed by Major League Baseball's 29 other clubs and handed to a caretaker management headed by Commissioner-appointed General Manager Omar Minaya. Several home stands were scheduled for Hiram Bithorn Stadium in San Juan, Puerto Rico, with the result that the travel-weary team played 103 road dates, including 22 "home games" in San Juan. The ill-starred Expos seemingly had once more become like novelist Philip Roth's fictional wandering homeless team, the Ruppert Mundys (*The Great American Novel*)—and yet the young club somehow posted 83 wins in 2002 and hung in a wild-card race right down to the season's final week. From the start of the 2000s, each season has wound down with questions about where or even if the Expos would play the following spring. Midway through the summer of 2004, it is a question still very much in the air.

Toronto Blue Jays

Toronto's big league arrival came after several failed attempts at bringing the periodically expanding majors to Canada's largest city. In 1976, Toronto seemed on the verge of entering the National League, but a near-purchase of the San Francisco Giants franchise by Ontario interests collapsed at the eleventh hour. When it finally did come a year later, Toronto's big league debut was a mixed blessing. The spanking new American League team finally placed in the Queen City as a result of Major League Baseball's third expansion in two decades was a thoroughly predictable add-on club, woefully short on talented prospects and hopelessly without the resources to be truly competitive. For six seasons the overmatched Toronto club would predictably wallow in the junior circuit basement as a result of its haphazard birthright, but help was soon on the way in the form of such developing future franchise stars as pitchers Dave Stieb (the all-time Jays ace, with 175 victories and the club's first no-hitter) and Jim Clancy (winner of 128 games over 12 seasons with Toronto), slugging infielders Tony Fernández (several-time .300-plus batter in three tours with the team) and Fred McGriff (later also a hitting star with San Diego and Atlanta), and outfield bashers George Bell (1987 American League leader in RBI) and Jesse Barfield (1986 league home run king).

Lackluster but nonetheless colorful days in early Blue Jays history provided some of the more memorable moments, events, and figures of Canadian big league lore. If the 1970s to 1980s Blue Jays were never very successful, they were usually entertaining. To begin with, there was Rick Bosetti—a talent-poor outfielder known for outrageous off-field behavior and tabbed by one pair of authors (Bruce Nash and Allan Zullo) as among "the sorriest role models for American youth"—and third baseman Roy Howell—who never wore uniform shirt sleeves despite the often frigid conditions of Exhibition Stadium. The Blue Jays ballpark itself was a quaint throwback to earlier decades, with its unshaded

Venezuela's Luis Leál with the American League expansion Toronto Blue Jays, 1980. [Transcendental Graphics]

bleacher-style seats stretching between the foul poles and covered outfield grandstand. In this setting, the opening game of franchise history was itself a most memorable episode of big league action performed Canadian style. Toronto outlasted the visiting Chicago White Sox 7–3 before 40,000-plus chilled fans in near-blizzard conditions on a snow-covered field.

Glory seasons for the Blue Jays finally arrived in the late 1980s and early 1990s—and when they did, they would quickly surpass anything yet seen in the chaotic history of a rival ill-fated National League club in Montreal. Toronto's dizzying rise to prominence was marked by a trio of breakthrough American League East division titles in 1985, 1989, and 1991, each followed by disappointing American League Championship Series losses to Kansas City (after leading the series 3–1), Oakland, and Minnesota. The heartbreaking Jays also further smashed fan expectations by blowing two additional American League East crowns in 1987 and 1990 with disastrous final-week swoons. Finally, in 1992—bolstered by a $41 million roster that included both the previous year's Minnesota World Series pitching hero Jack Morris and Hall of Fame–bound slugger Dave Winfield—the retooled Jays survived an American League Championship Series rematch with Oakland to claim the first big league pennant ever to fly over a Canadian city.

In October 1992, Major League Baseball's World Series could finally erase its century-old misnomer status when Toronto's Blue Jays hosted a first-ever Fall Classic staged at least in part outside the territorial United States. The Toronto–Atlanta Series was a festive affair, sometimes colored with unavoidable political and cultural overtones, such as when a U.S. military honor guard callously paraded before the massive two-nation television audience with Canada's Maple Leaf national flag held upside down during the game one opening ceremonies in Atlanta. The ballgames themselves were highly entertaining, with the host Blue Jays positioning themselves for a victory by winning three of the first four and then clinching in Atlanta thanks to a clutch eleventh-inning two-run double by Winfield. The quick return of World Series action to Toronto a mere year later provided an opportunity for the Canadian-based club to capture its second championship directly on Canadian soil. Final victory in 1993 came with a special flair, when Joe Carter ended deciding game six by smashing a Series-ending walk-off homer, only the second in history. At least in nationalistic terms, however, the 1992 and 1993 Major League Baseball world championships provided only symbolic victory for Canadian-based fans. The club now had no native Canadian players, having traded off outfielder Rob Ducey midway through the first championship season. A standard joke voiced by Canadians at the time—that their Canadian Dominicans had defeated Atlanta's American Dominicans—held a painfully large element of truth.

The legacy of Toronto's marvelous SkyDome stadium-cum-shopping mall is perhaps one of Canada's biggest baseball boasting points. At the time of its June 1989 opening, the retractable-roof structure—complete with its 11,000-ton movable dome and battery of restaurants and hotel rooms above the outfield wall—was easily the plushest sports arena ever built. SkyDome signaled a new era for the major league's version of pleasure-dome athletic facilities. It also radically changed the big league game forever—many say for the worse— by converting a hometown ball yard into a commercial center and upscale entertainment complex having little in common with ballparks of that century-long epoch when the on-field game itself was the only necessary or expected entertainment fare. The short-haul payoff was nonetheless immense, as the Jays drew 3.4 million fans for the remainder of 1989, then saw attendance peak at 4 million-plus in 1991 and 1992.

The Canadian Ballplayer Pipeline

While major leaguers imported from south of the St. Lawrence and south of Miami and the Rio Grande paraded their talents in a Canadian venue after 1969, the road to the big time for Canadian-born players had always been an exceedingly tough one. Numerous factors have likely worked against Canadians reaching the majors and against their making much impact once a handful got there. The predominance in recent decades of pitchers among Canada's big leaguers is one such factor where weather and climate are surely involved. Pitchers can more easily hone their art with indoor practice during harsh Canadian winters, whereas outfielders, infielders, and catchers require lengthy summers and numerous apprenticeship games to fine-tune their complex physical skills. Other factors working against local player development also follow from climate and geography. Few Canadian high schools located outside the Toronto metropolitan area feature baseball programs with varsity teams, and Canada's sandlot baseball is now limited in scope—ever since the decline in activity in the late 1950s, when television killed off most town teams and rural outlaw leagues. This means there are few professional scouts from organized baseball fishing the more austere northern waters for Canadian talent. (One glimmer of hope—who knows, how sufficient—is the youth baseball camps and other promotional efforts of the recently renewed Canadian Hall of Fame in St. Mary's, Ontario.)

Canadians themselves have not been delinquent in identifying and honoring their own top baseball immortals. The land better known for hockey also has its own impressive Baseball Hall of Fame, an institution housed first in Toronto (where a home tied too closely to the old stadium nearly sunk the institution when the Blue Jays transferred to SkyDome) and now relocated in St. Mary's, Ontario. Like Cooperstown, St. Mary's is a rural setting, and if it is not itself of historical importance, it is fittingly near enough to Beachville, home of Canada's legendary first game. The Canadian version of Cooperstown took shape back in 1983 under the leadership of Bruce Prentice (brother of 1986 inductee Bobby Prentice, a minor league star in the Cleveland Indians organization during the late 1940s); its stated goal was to demonstrate that Canada indeed had a proud and substantial baseball history stretching back long before the birth of the Expos and Blue Jays, and its first Board of Directors contained such prestigious figures as Metro Toronto Chairman (mayor) Paul Godfrey, Blue Jays President Paul Beeston, Expos General Manager Murray Cook, and Technical Director for Baseball Canada, Bill Mackenzie.

An inaugural Hall of Fame induction ceremony was held in Toronto in 1983 to honor five memorable personalities from early Canadian baseball history. Two (Tip O'Neill and John Ducey) were pioneering ballplayers, two (Phil Marchildon and George Selkirk) were successful Canadian big leaguers of the era between the two great wars, and one (Frank Shaughnessey) was perhaps the country's most substantial contributor to the history of North American professional organized baseball. An American from Illinois, "Shag" Shaughnessey rebuilt the sagging Montreal International League club into a solid pennant winner in 1935 and a year later took over control of the entire circuit as league president. In the latter capacity, the far-sighted Shaughnessey developed a four-club playoff format (later leading to a Shaughnessey Cup trophy named in his honor), which some credit for saving not only the International League itself but perhaps the entire enterprise of minor league baseball.

The Canadian Hall within a few years could boast an impressive building and museum site adjacent to the city's lakefront major league ballpark, Exhibition Stadium. Among the showcase exhibits was the ball with which Babe Ruth slugged his only minor league home run at Toronto's Hanlan's Point Park in September of 1914. Most inductions included four or five figures, usually a couple of big leaguers from the past and equal numbers of the nation's earliest baseball pioneers or organizational contributors. Even former Prime Minister Lester Pearson, a one-time semi-pro player in Guelph, received a permanent plaque honoring his long-time support of the game in his homeland. (He may be the only Nobel Prize winner in any baseball hall of fame.)

Wider recognition came to the Canadian Hall of Fame in January 1991, when one of its own inductees, Ferguson Jenkins, stepped into the even more hallowed chambers at Cooperstown. Yet despite the role of Fergie Jenkins in expanding awareness for Canadian baseball, by the early 1990s the Canadian Hall of Fame looked to be something of a dying proposition. The most substantial blow came when the American League Blue Jays abandoned Exhibition Stadium and the adjacent Ontario Place exhibition grounds for a new downtown domed stadium; without the walk-in traffic brought by a site next door to a major league park, the well-stocked but small museum was doomed. By the time the Toronto Blue Jays had moved into their luxurious new home in SkyDome, the Canadian Hall was already packed away in storage crates. The annual inductions with gala banquets were suspended for 1993 and 1994, and many thought that Canada's Hall was to remain only a memory; however, inductions began again in 1995 with installation of slugging 1980s Houston outfielder Terry Puhl. The St. Mary's rebirth has been impressive though somewhat quiet. How widely known the reborn institution is even among Canadians themselves can be questioned. When reluctant-Canadian Kirk McCaskill was elected for enshrinement in 2003, he would observe, ingenuously, "I didn't know a lot about the Canadian Baseball Hall of Fame until I was nominated but I've come to learn a lot about it since and this is truly an honor."[1]

After the first quarter of the twentieth century had run its course, most of Canada's top players were earning their stripes in the United States, playing either in organized baseball's minors or on the grand major league stage. If after World War I there were relatively few native Canadians making truly big splashes in the majors, a few Canadian big leaguers were still popping up from time to time among the game's more memorable figures, at least when it came to unusual performances or oversized personalities.

For all the roadblocks, there were a substantial number of Canadians who made the late nineteenth-century and early twentieth-century big time, even if most didn't hang around very long. Jack Graney played in 1,402 games and surpassed 100 base hits on eight occasions; he also performed in the 1920 World Series with Cleveland. Russ Ford completed 76 percent of his career starts by laboring in an epoch of iron-man pitchers and won 26 games for the 1910 New York American Leaguers. George Gibson set a National League record by catching 133 straight games for the Pirates and later became the last Canadian big league manager (to date) when he served in the early 1920s and again in the 1930s with his former club in Pittsburgh. Switch-hitter William John "Bill" O'Neill manned an outfield post for Chicago's 1906 Hitless-Wonder White Sox and by virtue of his lucky assignment became the first among his countrymen to perform in a World Series. And Ontario's Bill Watkins was Canada's first big league manager when he rode the bench first with 1884 American Association Indianapolis (as a 26-year-old part-time player) and later with 1887 National League Detroit (where he also became Canada's first pennant-winning skipper).

There have even been some substantial Canadian big league stars over the years. James "Tip" O'Neill was the first, with his slugging and pitching feats during the nineteenth century. No pro batsman ever posted a higher mark than O'Neill's rule-assisted 1884 batting average of .492, which benefited from walks being registered as base hits. In the twentieth century, Jeff Heath was the earliest Canadian-born slugger of truly major reputation. In 1938, Heath barely missed a league batting title when he wilted under the pressure of Jimmie Foxx's onslaught in the final month. A decade later, he played a substantial role for the pennant-winning Boston Braves but missed the World Series due to a heartbreaking September injury. George Selkirk followed on the heels of Heath and could claim a certain measure of fame simply by being the novice who replaced Babe Ruth in the New York Yankees outfield. Goody Rosen, one of a small collection of talented Jewish ballplayers, also missed a batting title by a mere eyelash during the 1945 apex of his considerable National League career with Brooklyn. And Oscar Judd was a good-hitting if run-of-the-mill throwing pitcher who once worked his way onto the 1943 National League All-Star game roster.

Canada also produced a handful of quality pitchers at mid-century. Reggie Cleveland was eventually a 100-game winner and is arguably surpassed in stature among his countrymen only by Cooperstown-enshrined Fergie Jenkins.

Southpaw fireman John Hiller once set a big league mark for games saved out of the Detroit bullpen. Claude Raymond, another durable bullpen ace, is deserving of recognition as the most successful French-Canadian big leaguer. Toronto's Ron Taylor debuted in spectacular fashion for Cleveland with 11 shutout frames in Fenway Park, then hung around long enough to pile up 72 career saves; he was especially effective in his four World Series outings. John Rutherford earned distinction with the 1952 Brooklyn pennant winners as the first Canadian to pitch in the World Series. A decade earlier, Dick Fowler hurled the first no-hit big league game by a Canadian native. And, in the same wartime decade, Fowler's teammate Phil Marchildon was ace of Connie Mack's 1947 Philadelphia staff, winning 19 games and also pacing the junior circuit in strikeouts. At the outset of the 21st century, strapping Los Angeles reliever Eric Gagne (native of Montreal) has carried on tradition with a club record 55 saves for the 2003 Dodgers and a major league record for consecutive converted save opportunities that stretched well into the 2004 season.

Nearly a century transpired between the first Canadian big league player appearance and the arrival of the country's first (and so far only) certified Hall of Famer. Given Canada's role in integrating organized baseball, it was a fitting irony perhaps that the greatest Canadian ballplayer would be an Afro-Canadian. Ferguson Jenkins was thus a rarity on two counts when he debuted in 1965 with the Philadelphia Phillies. Half a dozen 20-win seasons later, he was already the one big-time ballplayer that Canadian fans could finally point to with real pride, instead of only a measured enthusiasm. There was always the added irony, of course, that very few American fans likely ever knew or really cared that this smooth black pitching ace with the late-1960s Chicago Cubs and mid-1970s Texas Rangers was actually a foreign-born Canadian.

In recent summers, British Columbia's muscular Larry Walker has carried the Canadian banner almost by himself, first in Montreal and later in Colorado and St. Louis. But then, the tradition he proudly represents has always been a largely hidden and understated one. There is, after all, something quite anomalous about ballplaying in a northern land where the winters are brutally long and the summers are tantalizingly short. Without question, Canadian love for the game is deep—but the role of baseball in the towns and cities of Quebec and Ontario, or on the plains of Manitoba and Saskatchewan, has also always been something of a second-class affair.

CANADA'S GREATEST PLAYERS

Any debate about great Canadian ballplayers (at least anywhere outside of Canada itself) reduces itself rather quickly to discussion of three long-faded nineteenth-century figures and two exceptional athletes from recent decades of major league play. Beyond that, there is little fuel to fire any hot stove discussion, even among the most dedicated diehards. Phil Marchildon and Reno Bertoia may be small icons of the golden age 1950s, but any fascination they generate rarely extends beyond our lust for exotic baseball trivia.

Reggie Cleveland (b. May 23, 1948). The argument can be made easily enough that Saskatchewan native Reggie Cleveland was the second-best pitcher ever to come out of Canada. He was the only Canadian big leaguer to win 100 games besides Jenkins, and he was also a 1971 *Sporting News* rookie pitcher of the year during his remarkable debut season in the rotation of the St. Louis Cardinals. His greatest claim on Canadian baseball history would result, however, from being the first of his countrymen ever tabbed as the starting pitcher for a World Series game. Cleveland's first full campaign in the big time saw him join a potent starting rotation with the second-place Cardinals that included 20-game winner Steve Carlton, 16-game winner Bob Gibson, and 14-game winner Jerry Reuss. Cleveland posted a 12–12 mark, hurled 10 complete games and struck out 148. The same summer, his countryman Ferguson Jenkins was topping the league in wins with 24 and walking off with a Cy Young trophy. The historic World Series start came in game five of the classic 1975 Boston–Cincinnati showdown, when Cleveland squared off with Don Gullett and lasted five-plus innings in the 6–2 Red Sox loss; 2 homers by Hall-of-Famer Tony Pérez were the big blows that spelled defeat for the workhorse right-hander. Reggie Cleveland actually appeared in three games of the seven-game Series, but the outing that remained most memorable was the one that made him the first of his countrymen (and still the only one) to both start and lose a game in the fall classic. Much earlier, Cleveland was also part of still another notable Canadian first when he dropped a September 1970 game in relief against the Montreal Expos; Claude Raymond was the victor in the contest, which is believed to be the first to witness Canadian hurlers earning both decisions.

Robert "Bob" Emslie (b. January 27, 1859; d. April 26, 1943). Canadian authorities don't always agree even among themselves about the true stature of some of their more memorable pioneering countrymen. William Humber (in "The Story of Canadian Ballplayers") begins his list of first-generation greats with Robert Emslie, but Jim Shearon (*Canada's Baseball Legends*) finds the same Emslie faded enough to ignore him entirely. Bob Emslie enjoyed a career noted for true longevity—six decades, divided up among playing, umpiring, and finally serving as a minor National League administrator; it was all enough to earn a cherished if tiny footnote in Cooperstown, where he was placed on a plaque honoring the game's Canadian forefathers. His role as a player was admittedly his least substantial achievement, and his long umpiring career has been reduced to the bitter memory of one decision (for which a bitter John McGraw hung on him the label of "Blind Bob").

Emslie was briefly a talented pitcher and he did win 32 games in 1884 for Baltimore in the American Association before a dead arm put a quick and unexpected end to phase one of his career. He later served long and well as a National League umpire (1891–1924), and it was there of course that he earned his greatest notoriety. Unfortunately Emslie's lasting legacy resulted from one of baseball's most infamous moments—that involving the sad saga of New York Giant Fred Merkle as arch-goat and unforgettable bonehead. The veteran Canadian umpire would thus have his most significant moment on the ball field during late September 1908, in New York's Polo Grounds, while officiating a vital Giants–Cubs game that was to have considerable consequence for the 1908 National League pennant race and still more for the otherwise noble career of then-rookie first sacker Fred Merkle. When Merkle trotted off the field rather than running to second on the apparent game-winning single by Al Bridwell, it was Emslie's umpiring partner Hank O'Day who ruled that Merkle was out, even though the rookie had followed the common practice of the day. Emslie concurred, and thus O'Day and Emslie would together be remembered for one of the most controversial of all umpiring decisions, while at the same time Merkle's career would be irreparably besmirched for all time—somewhat unjustly because that loss did not in itself (as legend has it) cost the Giants a 1908 pennant.

Like so many Canadian baseballers—like Selkirk, who replaced Ruth; Jeff Heath, whose injury kept him out of a World Series; or Dick Fowler, whose lone Canadian no-hitter is far less remembered than his complete helplessness every time he faced the Boston Red Sox—Emslie is today known only as a more-or-less regrettable footnote to larger events and more memorable figures.

Dick Fowler (b. March 30, 1921; d. May 22, 1972). Dick Fowler earned his own special niche in Canadian lore when he tossed the first and only no-hit game ever achieved in the big leagues by a Canadian-born hurler. The rare masterpiece outing came on September 9, 1945, in the second game of a doubleheader with the then-formidable St. Louis Browns. Fowler enjoyed other highlights during a 10-season career in the majors played out entirely with Philadelphia. Twice he won 15 games for the Mackmen, four times he logged more than 200 innings, and his 1947 ERA was fourth best in the league. Fowler, like teammate and fellow countryman Marchildon, also enjoyed a special date with history in 1941—the year of DiMaggio's record hitting streak and Ted Williams's memorable .406 batting performance. It was a raw rookie named Dick Fowler who faced Williams as the latter dueled with history and immortality in the first game of a doubleheader on the season's final day. Williams used Fowler's tasty deliveries as a springboard to a 6-hit afternoon, which clinched his hallmark as baseball's last-ever .400 hitter; in the first at-bat Ted smoked a scorching single off the Philadelphia rookie and the second trip he drilled a towering homer. Williams (who hit .366 off Fowler for his career) wasn't the only Boston thorn in Dick Fowler's side, however. In 28 starts against the Red Sox, the Canadian righty took home but 3 wins and was routed 21 times. For that period between 1941 and 1952, the eyes of Boston sluggers must have lit up each time they caught a glimpse of Dick Fowler.

Jeff Heath (b. April 1, 1915; d. December 9, 1975). Ontario-born Jeff Heath is best remembered for a shattering injury that robbed this heavy-hitting outfielder of a chance to play in a World Series and also likely robbed his team, the Boston Braves, of a championship. In 1948, Heath was in his 12th season and enjoying one of his finest summers playing for a winning outfit when he shattered his ankle sliding into home at Ebbets Field. It was a late September game and seemingly of little consequence to the Braves, who had already clinched their first National League pennant in 30 full seasons—but the consequences of that fateful home plate collision with Roy Campanella were to prove huge for Heath and his teammates. The Canadian slugger (the first American Leaguer to smash 20 doubles, 20 triples, and 20 homers during the same campaign) missed out on his only shot at postseason play; with one less potent bat in their lineup, Boston subsequently dropped the fall classic in six games to Heath's former club, the Cleveland Indians.

It was not the only near-miss for Heath. A decade earlier, in 1938, as an extraordinary Cleveland rookie he had put on such a sensational September batting surge that he closed the season trailing only a few points behind future Hall of Famer Jimmie Foxx for the league batting crown. In the end, however, Heath enjoyed some fine big league campaigns in his 14 productive seasons (1936–1949) with Cleveland, Washington, St. Louis, and Boston. His lifetime marks of 194 homers, 887 RBI, and a .293 batting average were unrivaled among his countrymen before Larry Walker came along. At the time his career wound down, Jeff Heath may have been the best player—hitter or pitcher—the Canadian sandlots had yet produced.

John Hiller (b. April 8, 1943).   If Jenkins and Cleveland outclass the remaining field as Canada's top duo of big league starting pitchers, John Hiller was without much doubt the country's finest among major league relief specialists (at least before Eric Gagne, with early 21st century editions of the Los Angeles Dodgers). The 6'1" Toronto southpaw even once picked up eleven votes in balloting for Cooperstown enshrinement—most ever for a Canadian until Jenkins became eligible. Spending all 15 big league seasons with Detroit in the American League, Hiller owns some impressive record performances and a small collection of notable firsts. In 1973, his eighth year in the big time, he not only paced the junior circuit in saves but set a new big league mark in the process when he successfully closed out games on 38 of 42 occasions. Five years earlier (in the 1968 championship season), he carved his name in the record books for the first time when he struck out six Cleveland hitters at the start of one August game. Hiller actually began his career as a starter and enjoyed a quietly productive year in the rotation (winning nine times) during Detroit's world championship run, though overshadowed by top aces Denny McLain and Mickey Lolich. Hiller's eventual move to the bullpen followed a miraculous return to action from a heart attack that nearly ended his career and his life in 1971. Only two years later, a feisty Hiller enjoyed one of the finest campaigns for a reliever in big league history: in addition to his then-record 38 saves, he worked 65 games and 125 innings, won 10, struck out 124, and sported the lowest ERA in the majors.

Arthur Irwin (b. February 14, 1858; d. July 16, 1921).   Toronto-born but Boston-raised Arthur Irwin qualifies as the third substantial hero of Canadian baseball's inaugural century. Irwin staked out his reputation as a slick-fielding shortstop during an epoch of crude, barehanded fielding. He starred with the Worcester team of the National League and played more than 300 games in the then-young circuit. If not one of the most skilled players of his era, he was certainly one of the most innovative. It was Irwin who first popularized the fielder's glove. Playing for Providence in the mid-1880s, Irwin decided to risk certain ridicule by purchasing an oversized buckskin glove and stuffing it with padding to protect two digits on his nonthrowing hand recently smashed by a wicked infield liner. He had other notable moments in the game, which included managing catcher Connie Mack (the later legendary Philadelphia manager/owner) while serving as playing skipper with Washington and also maintaining a leading role in the 1890 Players League revolt. When it comes strictly to Canadian play, Irwin's most lasting influence emerged only much later, through his significant role as part owner of the Toronto International League franchise. His suicide, by jumping overboard off a steamship in July 1921, left him as the only ballplayer whose official place of death is listed in the Macmillan *Baseball Encyclopedia* and its successor, *Total Baseball*, as "Atlantic Ocean."[3]

Ferguson "Fergie" Jenkins (b. December 13, 1943).   Only one Canadian ever enjoyed a big league career that was clearly destined to wind up in Cooperstown. Ferguson Jenkins has no rivals when it comes to selecting the single greatest Canadian ballplayer ever to don a major league uniform. The strapping Chatham right-hander pitched 19 seasons in the big time, won nearly 300 games, captured 20 victories in seven different seasons (during an eight-year stretch), garnered a Cy Young award, and struck out more than 3,000 enemy batters (reaching the milestone in 1982, the seventh to join the club Walter Johnson founded in 1923). Jenkins' 3,000-plus Ks were significantly achieved with fewer than 1,000 walks. In the course of his brilliant career he became a durable franchise star for both the National League Cubs in Chicago and the American League Rangers in Texas. The statistical record is sufficient for immortality. None of his countrymen can even come close: Reggie Cleveland is second in victories, with a mere 105, while John Hiller trails in strikeouts, falling more than 2,000 behind. It is fitting also that Canada's first Cooperstown honoree was a black athlete, given Canada's own substantial role in smashing organized baseball's color line in the 1940s.

Phil Marchildon (b. October 25, 1915; d. September 24, 1956).   Ace of the starting staff for Connie Mack's rather lackluster 1947 Philadelphia Athletics, Phil Marchildon was a 19-game winner that single summer and also finished among the top five American Leaguers in strikeouts. The right-hander known throughout his career as "Fidgety Phil" came to the big leagues when the Philadelphia club bought his contract in 1940 from the International League Toronto Maple Leafs. One legendary moment in Marchildon's modest career occurred when he allegedly came within a single toss of ending Joe DiMaggio's record 1941 hitting streak at 45 games (the streak of course stretched to 56 before it was eventually snapped). In the case of that one encounter, the story simply doesn't mesh with the historical facts. The legend has it that Marchildon faced the great DiMaggio in the ninth and had blown two strikes by Joe before wasting a high fastball that was clobbered into the outfield seats; the reality is that the fateful homer came in the first inning, off Marchildon's first pitch. Ironically, the Ontario native enjoyed what may have been his best overall performance during a 1948 campaign that saw him post what looked on the surface like his worst career numbers. Despite losing 15 games that year, Marchildon pitched more innings than any other Philadelphia mound performer and was indisputably Mack's one dependable workhorse for the entire dreadful also-ran season.

Kirk McCaskill (b. April 9, 1961). There is one other top Canadian pitcher in the big time during the modern era who has stirred plenty of pride among his original countrymen, but Kirk McCaskill of the Chicago White Sox and California Angels spent most of his big league career adamantly denying his native Canadian roots. On the playing field, McCaskill enjoyed his finest professional season during his 1986 sophomore campaign, when he struck out 202 batters while winning 17 games for the California Angels. He also hurled a one-hitter that season (spoiled by a homer off the bat of Texas Rangers infielder Steve Buechele) and followed up with yet another three years later versus the Toronto Blue Jays. But the bigger story seemed always to remain his native origins, as the talented right-hander time and again boasted of his American roots and hid his true Canadian birthright. Born in Kapuskasing, Ontario, Kirk McCaskill was raised as an American citizen, mostly in Tennessee. Son of a pro minor league hockey player, McCaskill himself took up the Canadian game as a youngster and was even tabbed by the NHL draft after starring in the winter game at the University of Vermont; baseball remained his prime focus, however, and while still in college he enjoyed his first summer of pro ball with Salem in the Northwest League. Throughout his early career as both amateur and pro athlete, the reluctant Canadian seemingly often misled members of the press regarding his nationality: One NHL official guidebook, reporting his drafting by the Winnipeg Jets, gave his birthplace as Arizona; baseball media guides during his early major league seasons often listed it as Vermont. The result, obviously, was a rather strange and contradictory legacy of competing birth data that dogged McCaskill's career as a professional athlete in two sports.

James Edward "Tip" O'Neill (b. May 25, 1858; d. December 31, 1915). The best all-around Canadian player of the nineteenth century was indisputably James Edward "Tip" O'Neill, a skilled pitcher and potent batter native to the baseball hotbed province of Ontario. With the National League's New York Gothams in 1883, O'Neill was the first Canadian to pitch in the majors, though with a 5–12 win–loss ledger he failed to live up to his promise. It was a season later with St. Louis that his career was actually jump-started, when he again hurled with modest results but eventually won a spot as a heavy-hitting outfielder with the club that was easily the best in the American Association. With the 1884 St. Louis Browns, O'Neill quickly emerged as one of the most colorful baseball personalities of his era and posted such eye-popping performances as a year-long .400-plus batting average that won an individual batting crown. O'Neill's big hitting year came in 1887, a season when it took four strikes to retire the batsman and walks were counted as base hits; with these advantages, the Canadian slugger rang up a batting average of .492, which remains the highest ever recorded in the major leagues. With bases on balls removed from the calculation, this astronomical mark would later be reduced to .435 in most baseball encyclopedias yet still remains an unmatched major league feat.[2] The stature of Canada's best nineteenth-century ballplayer was once so great both inside and outside his native land that it was commonplace to attach the moniker "Tip" to newborn males with the surname O'Neill. But it is also to be mentioned in passing that the Ontario native owned bigoted attitudes, not so unusual among white ballplayers of the day. On one infamous occasion in

1887, Tip O'Neill led his St. Louis teammates in presenting a petition objecting to an exhibition match with the touring black Cuban Giants.

Terry Puhl (b. July 8, 1956).   Another fine Canadian outfielder who never quite achieved the rewards he may have merited was Saskatchewan fly-chaser Terry Puhl, a steady if unspectacular performer for a decade and a half with the Houston Astros (1977–1990). Puhl was the very image of understated but steady performance on both offense and defense. He ended his career with a solid .280 average in more than 1,500 games, having played for a number of pennant-contending Houston teams. He also retired with a major league record for outfielders, having committed only 18 errors over his 15 full seasons in the big time.

Jean Claude "Frenchy" Raymond (b. May 7, 1937).   Being the first native son to play for Canada's first big league franchise was itself enough of a distinction to make any player memorable for fans north of the U.S. border, but right-hander Claude Raymond was also able to put up some very impressive performances to distinguish his 17 seasons of play in organized baseball. As a relief specialist, Raymond once logged 23 saves, turning the trick with a 1970 edition of the Montreal Expos. He had earlier been a dependable starter, turning in his only two career complete games for the Houston Astros during the 1965 National League pennant chase. But Raymond's biggest personal thrill undoubtedly came when he was named by Dodgers manager Walter Alston to a slot on the National League roster for the 1966 major league All-Star game slated for St. Louis. Claude Raymond was easily the most successful big leaguer ever to emerge from French-speaking Canada: at the end of a 12-year sojourn, mostly as a bullpen denizen, he could claim 46 victories next to his 53 major league losses, plus 83 games saved. That career of course earned its special niche when Raymond was sold in the middle of his 12-season tenure from the league-leading Atlanta Braves to the hometown expansion Montreal Expos. The move back to Quebec gave Raymond his second greatest big league thrill, as well as etching his name in the history books—even though at the time it meant leaving a front-running pennant contender to join a hopeless tail-ender expansion ball club.

Goodwin "Goody" Rosen (b. August 28, 1912; d. April 6, 1994).   There were also Canadian batsmen who labored to make the war decade of the 1940s one of the most productive for North Country big leaguers. Goodwin "Goody" Rosen was a proficient enough hitter against big league hurlers to post better than a base hit (557) for every career game (551) played. He also earned a special spot in the trivia books not only as the first near-miss major league batting champion of Canadian birth but also as the first Jewish big leaguer from Canada. Rosen was runner-up for a war-cheapened 1945 National League batting crown while performing as a serviceable outfielder with the Brooklyn Dodgers. Leading the circuit with a .363 mark in early August, the scrappy 5'10" lefty wilted down the stretch to finish a close third behind Phil Cavarretta of Chicago and Tommy Holmes of Boston. That same summer, Rosen came within three safeties of his only 200-hit season. These were not his only near-misses that season, though they were likely the most disappointing. The Brooklyn mainstay was also selected for that year's midseason All-Star game, the first Canadian to achieve such an honor, but lost his only crack at the big league's top showcase exhibition when the event was canceled due to a final round of wartime restrictions.

George Selkirk (b. January 4, 1908; d. January 19, 1987).   George Selkirk (saddled with the perplexing moniker of "Twinkletoes" for his unusual high-stepping gait when circling the bases) enjoyed a thrill-packed if not spectacular major league career (1934–1942) that included smashing a surprise home run off baseball's top pitcher (at that time) on his first-ever at-bat during a World Series game. That home run, stroked off Carl Hubbell, was only one slugging milestone for the stocky Ontario outfielder, who inherited one of baseball's most unenviable and difficult tasks ever—that of replacing Babe Ruth in the New York Yankees outfield. All in all, Selkirk would play in a total of six World Series with the dynasty Yankees of the Lou Gehrig and Joe DiMaggio era. On five different occasions, he was able to bat above .300 for a full season, and before his relatively short tenure was up he also played in two major league All-Star games. Perhaps the most memorable moment for Selkirk as a slugger came late in May of 1939, when he stroked 4 homers in two days; the outburst came in four straight at-bats against the same inept Bob Joyce, the Athletics' shell-shocked reliever. To round out a noteworthy career, Selkirk would later serve as playing manager for the Yankees' Newark farm team (1946), player personnel supervisor for the Kansas City Athletics (1957), and general manager of the Washington Senators (1964–1969).

Larry Walker (b. December 1, 1966).   Colorado's slugging outfielder Larry Walker has in recent summers emerged as the closest approximation since Fergie Jenkins to a true Canadian-bred big league superstar. The 6'3", 215-pound left-handed batter out of British Columbia may not yet be quite a Hall of Famer, but he owns one of the most booming bats seen in the National League over 15 recent seasons. The powerfully built Walker started his major league career on the fast track in Montreal, quickly becoming the first Canadian to smack 20 homers and steal 20 bases in a single season. After serving a half-dozen campaigns with Canada's premier big league club, Walker moved over to the expansion Colorado Rockies on the heels of a 1994 players strike; in the environment of Coors Field, the career ledger quickly became even more impressive. There were back-to-back batting titles in the final two seasons of the twentieth-century and a career year a season earlier, in 1997, when he paced the league in homers with 49, drove home 130 runs, and walked off with a landslide victory in the Most Valuable Player voting. Walker's slugging percentage (.720) that season was fifth highest in National League annals, and his 409 total bases were the most in the senior circuit since Stan Musial's 1948 total of 429. On the offensive side of the game, Larry Walker remains unrivaled among his countrymen, now easily outdistancing Jeff Heath as Canada's most productive slugging hero.

IN BRIEF

And here the lively discussion usually stops almost dead in its tracks. The number of Canadian big leaguers now stretches slightly above two hundred. Yet few have been more than cup-of-coffee walk-ons or run-of-the-mill journeymen enjoying their proverbial moment in the summer's sunshine. It is a rare big league season that has seen more than a half-dozen Canadians adorning big league rosters at any given time. Only a handful of notable Canadian ballplayers have made any substantial contributions as either pioneers or front-line stars, and theirs alone is the lightweight legacy of Canada's slim pages in the chronicle of major league baseball history.

SELECTED CANADIAN RECORDS AND STATISTICS

Canadians in the Major Leagues (1871–2003)

	Name	Debut	Position	Debut Team	Seasons	Games	Career Statistics
1	Michael "Mike" Brannock	1871	3B	Chicago White Sox (NA)	2	5	.087 BA
2	Thomas "Tom" Smith	1875	OF	Brooklyn Atlantics (NA)	1	3	.077 BA
3	William "Billy" Reid	1877	OF	Baltimore Orioles (AA)	2	43	.263 BA
4	William "Bill" Phillips	1879	1B	Cleveland Blues (NL)	10	1,038	.273 BA
5	Charles "Pop" Smith	1880	IF	Cincinnati Reds (NL)	12	1,112	.228 BA
6	Arthur "Doc" Irwin	1880	SS	Worcester Brown Sox (NL)	13	1,010	.251 BA
7	John Irwin	1882	IF	Worcester Brown Sox (NL)	8	322	.248 BA
8	Orrin "Bob" Casey	1882	IF	Detroit Tigers (NL)	1	9	.231 BA
9	John Doyle	1882	RHP	St. Louis Browns (AA)	1	3	0–3, 2.63 ERA
10	John "Tug" Thompson	1882	OF	Cincinnati Reds (AA)	2	25	.206 BA
11	James "Tip" O'Neill	1883	OF/RHP	New York Gothams (NL)	10	1,052	.326 BA/16–16
12	John Humphries	1883	C	New York Gothams (NL)	2	98	.143 BA
13	Robert "Bob" Emslie	1883	RHP	Baltimore Orioles (AA)	3	91	44–44, 3.19 ERA
14	James Pirie	1883	SS	Philadelphia Phillies (NL)	1	5	.158 BA
15	William "Medicine Bill" Mountjoy	1883	RHP	Cincinnati Reds (AA)	3	57	31–24, 3.25 ERA
16	James "Jim" McKeever	1884	C	Boston Reds (UA)	1	16	.136 BA
17	Milton "Milt" Whitehead	1884	SS	St. Louis Maroons (UA)	1	104	.207 BA
18	Charles "Chub" Collins	1884	IF	Buffalo Bisons (NL)	2	97	.196 BA
19	William Robert "Bill" Hunter	1884	C	Louisville Colonels (AA)	1	2	.143 BA
20	Jim "Darby" Knowles	1884	3B	Pittsburgh Alleghenys (AA)	5	357	.241 BA
21	Alexander "Alex" Gardner	1884	C	Washington Statesmen (AA)	1	1	.000 BA
22	Frederick "Fred" Wood	1884	C	Detroit Tigers (NL)	2	13	.065 BA
23	Jonas "Quiet Joe" Knight	1884	OF	Philadelphia Phillies (NL)	2	133	.309 BA
24	Henry Mullin	1884	OF	Washington Statesmen (AA)	1	36	.133 BA
25	Patrick Scanlan	1884	OF	Boston Reds (UA)	1	6	.292 BA
26	Jeremiah "Jerry" Dorsey	1884	LHP	Baltimore Unions (UA)	1	1	0–1, 9.00 ERA
27	Onesime Eugene "Gene" Vadeboncoeur	1884	C	Philadelphia Phillies (NL)	1	4	.214 BA
28	Joseph "Joe" Weber	1884	OF	Detroit Wolverines (NL)	1	2	.000 BA
29	Henry Oxley	1884	C	New York Giants (NL)	1	3	.000 BA
30	William "Bill" Watkins	1884	IF	Indianapolis Hoosiers (AA)	1	34	.205 BA
31	Jonathan "Jon" Morrison	1884	OF	Indianapolis Hoosiers (AA)	2	53	.241 BA
32	Frank Smith	1884	C	Pittsburgh Alleghenys (AA)	1	10	.250 BA
33	Stephen "Steve" Dunn	1884	IF	St. Paul White Caps (AA)	1	9	.250 BA
34	Peter "Pete" Wood	1885	RHP	Buffalo Bisons (NL)	2	27	9–16, 4.51 ERA
35	Wiman [Wyman] Andrus	1885	3B	Providence Grays (NL)	1	1	.000 BA
36	James "Jim" Hyndman	1886	OF/RHP	Philadelphia Athletics (AA)	1	1	.000 BA/0–1, 27.00 ERA
37	Fred [Frederick] "Tip" O'Neill	1887	OF	New York Mets (AA)	1	6	.308 BA
38	Samuel "Sam" LaRoque	1888	IF	Detroit Wolverines (NL)	3	124	.249 BA
39	George Walker	1888	RHP	Baltimore Orioles (AA)	1	4	1–3, 5.91 ERA
40	John "Spud" Johnson	1889	OF	Columbus Solons (AA)	3	331	.302 BA
41	Daniel "Dan" O'Connor	1890	1B	Louisville Colonels (AA)	1	6	.462 BA
42	Frederick "Fred" Osborne (b. USA?)	1890	OF/P	Pittsburgh Pirates (NL)	1	41	.238 BA/0–5, 8.38
43	Patrick "Pat" Lyons	1890	2B	Cleveland Spiders (NL)	1	11	.053 BA
44	Frederick "Fred" Demarais	1890	RHP	Chicago Cubs (NL)	1	1	0–0, 0.00 ERA
45	Michael "Mike" Jones	1890	LHP	Louisville Colonels (AA)	1	3	2–0, 3.27 ERA
46	James "Jim" [John] Gillespie	1890	OF	Buffalo Bisons (PL)	1	1	.000 BA
47	John O'Brien	1891	2B	Brooklyn Dodgers (NL)	6	501	.254 BA
48	Frederick "Fred" Lake	1891	C	Boston Pilgrims (NL)	5	48	.232 BA
49	August "Gus" Yost (b. USA?)	1893	RHP	Chicago White Sox (NL)	1	1	0–1, 13.50 ERA
50	William "Kid" Summers	1893	OF	St. Louis Browns (NL)	1	2	.000 BA
51	William "Bill" Pfann	1894	RHP	Cincinnati Reds (NL)	1	1	0–1, 27.00 ERA
52	Harley "Lady" Payne	1896	LHP	Brooklyn Dodgers (NL)	4	80	30–36, 4.04 ERA

(continued)

(continued)

	Name	Debut	Position	Debut Team	Seasons	Games	Career Statistics
53	William "Billy" Hulen (b. USA?)	1896	IF/OF	Philadelphia Phillies (NL)	2	107	.246 BA
54	Albert Johnson	1896	IF	Louisville Colonels (NL)	2	74	.238 BA
55	Patrick "Pat" Hannifan	1897	OF	Brooklyn Dodgers (NL)	1	10	.250 BA
56	William "Bill" Magee	1897	RHP	Louisville Colonels (NL)	5	107	29–51, 4.94 ERA
57	Frank "Cooney" Snyder	1898	C	Louisville Colonels (NL)	1	17	.164 BA
58	Emil Frisk	1899	OF/RHP	Cincinnati Reds (NL)	4	158	.267 BA/8–10
59	John "Larry" McLean	1901	C	Boston Red Sox (AL)	13	862	.262 BA
60	Winford "Win" Kellum	1901	LHP	Boston Red Sox (AL)	3	48	20–16, 3.19 ERA
61	William "Bunk" Congalton	1902	OF	Chicago Cubs (NL)	4	309	.292 BA
62	Clarence Currie	1902	RHP	Cincinnati Reds (NL)	2	53	15–23, 3.39 ERA
63	Louis "Pete" LePine	1902	OF	Detroit Tigers (AL)	1	30	.208 BA
64	Alex "Dooney" Hardy	1902	LHP	Chicago Cubs (NL)	2	7	3–3, 4.34 ERA
65	Nelson "Red" Long	1902	RHP	Boston Bees (NL)	1	1	0–0, 1.13 ERA
66	Ernie "Curley" Ross	1902	LHP	Baltimore Orioles (AL)	1	2	1–1, 7.41 ERA
67	Harry "Rube" Vickers	1902	RHP	Cincinnati Reds (NL)	5	88	22–27, 2.93 ERA
68	Ed "Peanuts" Pinnance	1903	RHP	Philadelphia A's (AL)	1	2	0–0, 2.57 ERA
69	William John "Bill" O'Neill	1904	OF	Boston Red Sox (AL)	2	206	.243 BA
70	James "Jimmy" Archer (b. Ireland)	1904	C	Pittsburgh Pirates (NL)	12	847	.249 BA
71	Jay "Nig" Clark	1905	C	Cleveland Indians (AL)	9	506	.254 BA
72	Jack "Happy" Cameron	1905	OF	Boston Bees (NL)	1	18	.180 BA
73	Eugene "Gene" Ford	1905	RHP	Detroit Tigers (AL)	1	7	0–1, 5.66 ERA
74	Arthur "Art" McGovern	1905	C	Boston Red Sox (AA)	1	15	.114 BA
75	William "Buffalo Bill" Hogg	1905	RHP	New York Yankees (AL)	4	116	37–50, 3.06 ERA
76	George "Moon" Gibson	1905	C	Pittsburgh Pirates (NL)	14	1,213	.236 BA
77	Frank "Yip" Owens	1905	C	Boston Red Sox (AL)	4	222	.245 BA
78	James "Jim" Cockman	1905	3B	New York Yankees (AL)	1	13	.105 BA
79	John "Happy Jack" Cameron	1906	Pitcher	Boston Braves (NL)	1	2	0–0, 0.00 ERA
80	Newton "Newt" Randall	1907	OF	Chicago Cubs (NL)	1	97	.211 BA
81	John "Jack" Graney	1908	OF	Cleveland Indians (AL)	14	1,402	.250 BA
82	Herbert "Bert" Sincock	1908	LHP	Cincinnati Reds (NL)	1	1	0–0, 3.86 ERA
83	William "Bill" O'Hara	1909	OF	New York Giants (NL)	2	124	.232 BA
84	Russell "Russ" Ford	1909	RHP	New York Yankees (AL)	7	199	99–71, 2.59 ERA
85	Roy "Doc" Miller	1910	OF	Chicago Cubs (NL)	5	557	.295 BA
86	David "Dave" Rowan	1911	1B	St. Louis Browns (AL)	1	18	.385 BA
87	Bill [William Dennis] "Midget" Jones	1911	OF	Boston Bees (NL)	2	27	.226 BA
88	Frank "Blackie" O'Rourke	1912	IF	Boston Bees (NL)	14	1,131	.254 BA
89	Andrew "Andy" Kyle	1912	OF	Cincinnati Reds (NL)	1	9	.333 BA
90	Thomas Daniel "Tom" Daly	1913	C	Chicago White Sox (AL)	8	244	.239 BA
91	Maurice "Shorty" Dee	1915	SS	St. Louis Browns (AL)	1	1	.000 BA
92	Robert "Bob" Steele	1916	LHP	St. Louis Cardinals (NL)	4	91	16–38, 3.05 ERA
93	Edmund "Ed" Wingo	1920	C	Philadelphia Athletics (AL)	1	1	.250 BA
94	James "Jim" Riley	1921	OF/IF	St. Louis Browns (AL)	2	6	.000 BA
95	Harry O'Neill	1922	RHP	Philadelphia Athletics (AL)	2	4	0–0, 1.80 ERA
96	Vincent "Vince" Shields	1924	RHP	St. Louis Cardinals (NL)	1	2	1–1, 3.00 ERA
97	John Melville "Mel" Kerr	1925	PR	Chicago Cubs (NL)	1	1	.000 BA
98	Augustin "Gus" Dugas	1930	OF	Pittsburgh Pirates (NL)	4	125	.206 BA
99	Vincent "Vince" Barton	1931	OF	Chicago Cubs (NL)	2	102	.233 BA
100	George Selkirk	1934	OF	New York Yankees (AL)	9	846	.290 BA, 108 HR
101	John Geoffrey "Jeff" Heath	1936	OF	Cleveland Indians (AL)	14	1,383	.293 BA, 194 HR
102	Joseph "Joe" Krakauskas	1937	LHP	Washington Senators (AL)	7	149	26–36, 4.53 ERA
103	Goodwin "Goody" Rosen	1937	OF	Brooklyn Dodgers (NL)	6	551	.291 BA
104	Ralph "Buck" Buxton	1938	P	Philadelphia Athletics (AL)	2	19	0–2, 4.25 ERA
105	Sherrard "Sherry" Robertson	1940	OF/IF	Washington Senators (AL)	10	597	.230 BA
106	Philip "Phil" Marchildon	1940	RHP	Philadelphia Athletics (AL)	9	185	68–75, 3.93 ERA
107	Oscar Judd	1941	LHP	Boston Red Sox (AL)	8	161	40–51, 3.90 ERA
108	Aldon Wilkie	1941	LHP	Pittsburgh Pirates (NL)	3	68	8–11, 4.59 ERA
109	Richard "Dick" Fowler	1941	RHP	Philadelphia Athletics (AL)	10	221	66–79, 4.11 ERA

Name	Debut	Position	Debut Team	Seasons	Games	Career Statistics
110	Earl Cook	1941	RHP	Detroit Tigers (AL)	1	1	0–0, 4.50 ERA
111	Henry "Bud" Sketchley	1942	OF	Chicago White Sox (AL)	1	13	.194 BA
112	Frank Colman	1942	OF	Pittsburgh Pirates (NL)	6	271	.228 BA
113	Paul Calvert	1942	RHP	Cleveland Indians (AL)	7	109	9–22, 5.31 ERA
114	Charles "Charlie" Mead	1943	OF	New York Giants (NL)	3	87	.245 BA
115	Roland Gladu	1944	OF/IF	Boston Braves (NL)	1	21	.242 BA
116	Byron "Ty" LaForest	1945	IF/OF	Boston Red Sox (AL)	1	52	.250 BA
117	Edson "Ed" Bahr	1946	RHP	Pittsburgh Pirates (NL)	2	46	11–11, 3.37 ERA
118	Jean-Pierre Roy	1946	RHP	Brooklyn Dodgers (NL)	1	3	0–0, 9.95 ERA
119	Ralph "Mack" McCabe	1946	RHP	Cleveland Indians (AL)	1	1	0–1, 11.25 ERA
120	Henry "Hank" Biasetti (b. Italy)	1949	1B	Philadelphia Athletics (AL)	1	21	.083 BA
121	Robert "Bob" Hooper	1950	RHP	Philadelphia Athletics (AL)	6	194	40–41, 4.80 ERA
122	Joseph "Joe" Erautt	1950	C	Chicago White Sox (AL)	2	32	.186 BA
123	Harry Fisher	1951	RHP	Pittsburgh Pirates (NL)	1	8	1–2, 6.87 ERA
124	John "Doc" Rutherford	1952	RHP	Brooklyn Dodgers (NL)	1	22	7–7, 4.25 ERA
125	Reno Bertoia (b. Italy)	1953	IF	Detroit Tigers (AL)	10	612	.244 BA
126	Camille Oscar "Ozzie" Van Brabant	1954	RHP	Philadelphia Athletics (AL)	2	11	0–2, 7.85 ERA
127	Tom "Tim" Burgess	1954	OF	St. Louis Cardinals (NL)	2	104	.177 BA
128	Robert "Bob" Alexander	1955	RHP	Baltimore Orioles (AL)	2	9	1–1, 10.64 ERA
129	Glen Gorbous	1955	OF	Cincinnati Reds (NL)	3	117	.238 BA
130	Eric MacKenzie	1955	C	Kansas City Athletics (AL)	1	1	.000 BA
131	William "Bill" Harris	1957	RHP	Brooklyn Dodgers (NL)	2	2	0–1, 3.12 ERA
132	Edward "Ted" Bowsfield	1958	LHP	Boston Red Sox (AL)	7	215	37–39, 4.35 ERA
133	Claude "Frenchy" Raymond	1959	RHP	Chicago White Sox (AL)	12	449	46–53, 3.66 ERA
134	Georges Maranda	1960	RHP	San Francisco Giants (NL)	2	49	2–7, 4.52 ERA
135	Kenneth "Ken" MacKenzie	1960	LHP	Milwaukee Braves (NL)	6	129	–10, 4.80 ERA
136	Ronald Piche	1960	RHP	Milwaukee Braves (NL)	6	134	10–16, 4.19 ERA
137	Thomas "Tim" Harkness	1961	1B	Los Angeles Dodgers (NL)	4	259	.235 BA
138	Ronald "Ron" Taylor	1962	RHP	Cleveland Indians (AL)	11	491	45–43, 3.93 ERA
139	Raymond "Ray" Daviault	1962	RHP	New York Mets (NL)	1	36	1–5, 6.22 ERA
140	Peter "Pete" Ward	1962	IF/OF	Baltimore Orioles (AL)	9	973	.254 BA, 98 HR
141	James "Jim" Lawrence	1963	C	Cleveland Indians (AL)	1	2	.000 BA
142	James Vernon "Vern" Handrahan	1964	RHP	Kansas City Athletics (AL)	2	34	0–2, 5.31 ERA
143	Peter "Pete" Craig	1964	RHP	Washington Senators (AL)	3	6	0–3, 11.50 ERA
144	Thomas "Tom" Harrison	1965	RHP	Kansas City Athletics (AL)	1	1	0–0, 9.00 ERA
145	John Hiller	1965	LHP	Detroit Tigers (AL)	15	545	87–76, 2.83, 125 S
146	Ferguson "Fergie" Jenkins	1965	RHP	Philadelphia Phillies (NL)	19	664	284–226, 3.34 ERA
147	Richard "Dick" Lines	1966	LHP	Washington Senators (AL)	2	107	7–7, 2.83 ERA
148	George Korince	1966	RHP	Detroit Tigers (AL)	2	11	1–0, 4.24 ERA
149	John Upham	1967	OF	Chicago Cubs (NL)	2	21	.308 BA
150	Michael "Mike" Kilkenny	1969	LHP	Detroit Tigers (AL)	5	139	23–18, 4.43 ERA
151	Ronald "Ron" Law	1969	RHP	Cleveland Indians (AL)	1	35	3–4, 4.99 ERA
152	Reginald "Reggie" Cleveland	1969	RHP	St. Louis Cardinals (NL)	13	428	105–106, 4.01 ERA
153	Harvey Shank	1970	RHP	California Angels (AA)	1	1	0–0, 0.00 ERA
154	David "Dave" Pagan	1973	RHP	New York Yankees (AL)	5	85	4–9, 4.96 ERA
155	Brian Ostrosser	1973	SS	New York Mets (NL)	1	4	.000 BA
156	John Balaz	1974	OF	California Angels (AL)	2	59	.241 BA
157	Kenneth "Ken" Crosby	1975	RHP	Chicago Cubs (NL)	2	16	1–0, 8.41 ERA
158	David "Dave" McKay	1975	IF	Minnesota Twins (AL)	8	645	.229 BA
159	Larry Landreth	1976	RHP	Montreal Expos (NL)	2	7	1–4, 6.64 ERA
160	William "Bill" Atkinson	1976	RHP	Montreal Expos (NL)	4	98	11–4, 3.42 ERA
161	Barry Cort	1977	RHP	Milwaukee Brewers (AL)	1	7	1–1, 3.33 ERA
162	Terry Puhl	1977	OF	Houston Astros (NL)	15	1,531	.280 BA
163	Sheldon Burnside (b. USA)	1978	LHP	Detroit Tigers (AL)	3	19	2–1, 6.00 ERA
164	Gordon "Gordie" Pladson	1979	RHP	Houston Astros (NL)	4	20	0–4, 6.04 ERA
165	Paul Hodgson	1980	OF	Toronto Blue Jays (AL)	1	20	.220 BA
166	Riccardo "Rick" Lisi	1981	OF	Texas Rangers (AL)	1	9	.313 BA

(continued)

(continued)

	Name	Debut	Position	Debut Team	Seasons	Games	Career Statistics
167	Douglas "Doug" Frobel	1982	OF	Pittsburgh Pirates (NL)	5	268	.201 BA
168	Kirk McCaskill	1985	RHP	California Angels (AL)	12	380	106–108, 4.12 ERA
169	David "Dave" Shipanoff	1985	RHP	Philadelphia Phillies (NL)	1	26	1–2, 3.22 ERA
170	Robert "Rob" Ducey	1987	OF	Toronto Blue Jays (AL)	12	646	.242 BA
171	Kevin Reimer	1988	OF	Texas Rangers (AL)	6	488	.258 BA
172	Stephen "Steve" Wilson	1988	LHP	Texas Rangers (AL)	6	205	13–18, 4.40
173	Larry Walker	1989	OF	Montreal Expos (NL)	15	1,806	.314 BA, 351 HR
174	Michael "Mike" Gardiner	1990	RHP	Seattle Mariners (AL)	6	136	17–27, 5.21 ERA
175	Denis Boucher	1991	LHP	Toronto Blue Jays (AL)	4	35	6–11, 5.42 ERA
176	David "Dave" Wainhouse	1991	RHP	Montreal Expos (NL)	7	85	2–3, 7.37 ERA
177	Rheal Cormier	1991	LHP	St. Louis Cardinals (NL)	12	472	61–54, 4.04 ERA
178	Vincent "Vince" Horsman	1991	LHP	Toronto Blue Jays (AL)	5	141	–2, 4.07 ERA
179	Peter Hoy	1992	RHP	Boston Red Sox (AL)	1	5	0–0, 7.36 ERA
180	Matthew "Matt" Stairs	1992	OF	Montreal Expos (NL)	11	1,046	.266 BA, 176 HR
181	Matthew "Matt" Maysey	1992	RHP	Montreal Expos (NL)	2	25	1–2, 5.55 ERA
182	Paul Quantrill	1992	RHP	Boston Red Sox (AL)	12	705	59–73, 3.65 ERA
183	Robert "Rob" Butler	1993	OF	Toronto Blue Jays (AL)	4	109	.243 BA
184	Joseph "Joe" Siddall	1993	C	Montreal Expos (NL)	4	73	.169 BA
185	Nigel Wilson	1993	OF	Florida Marlins (NL)	3	22	.086 BA
186	Paul Spoljaric	1994	LHP	Toronto Blue Jays (AL)	6	195	8–17, 5.52 ERA
187	Gregory "Greg" O'Halloran	1994	C	Florida Marlins (NL)	1	12	.181 BA
188	Derek Aucoin	1996	RHP	Montreal Expos (NL)	1	2	0–1, 3.38 ERA
189	Jason Dickson	1996	RHP	California Angels (AL)	4	73	26–25, 4.99 ERA
190	Richard "Rich" Butler	1997	OF	Toronto Blue Jays (AL)	3	86	.223 BA
191	Michael "Mike" Johnson	1997	RHP	Baltimore Orioles (AL)	5	81	7–14, 6.85 ERA
192	Daniel "Danny" Klassen	1998	SS	Arizona D-Backs (NL)	5	84	226 BA
193	Cordel "Corey" Koskie	1998	3B	Minnesota Twins (AL)	6	698	.285 BA
194	Ryan Dempster	1998	RHP	Florida Marlins (NL)	6	161	50–55, 5.01 ERA
195	Steven "Steve" Sinclair	1998	LHP	Toronto Blue Jays (AL)	2	45	0–3, 5.24 ERA
196	Eric Gagne	1999	RHP	Los Angeles Dodgers (NL)	5	212	17–18, 3.50, 107 S
197	Aaron Myette	1999	RHP	Chicago White Sox (AL)	5	42	6–12, 8.16 ERA
198	Jeffrey "Jeff" Zimmerman	1999	RHP	Texas Rangers (AL)	3	196	17–12, 3.27 ERA
199	Jordan Zimmerman	1999	LHP	Seattle Mariners (AL)	1	12	0–0, 7.88 ERA
200	Jason Green	2000	RHP	Houston Astros (NL)	1	14	1–1, 6.62 ERA
201	Steve Green	2001	RHP	California Angels (AL)	1	1	0–0, 3.00 ERA
202	Cody McKay	2002	C	Oakland A's (AL)	1	2	.667 BA
203	Eric Cyr	2002	LHP	San Diego Padres (NL)	1	5	0–1, 10.50 ERA
204	Aaron Guiel	2002	OF	Kansas City Royals (AL)	2	169	.259 BA
205	Erik Bedard	2002	LHP	Baltimore Orioles (AL)	1	2	0–0, 13.50 ERA
206	PierreLuc "Pete" LaForest	2003	C	Tampa Bay D-Rays (AL)	1	19	.167 BA
207	Jayson "Jay" Bay	2003	OF	San Diego Padres (NL)	1	30	.287 BA
208	James Richard "Rich" Harden	2003	RHP	Oakland A's (AL)	1	15	5–4, 4.46 ERA
209	Christopher "Chris" Mears	2003	RHP	Detroit Tigers (AL)	1	29	1–3, 5.44 ERA
210	Justin Morneau	2003	1B	Minnesota Twins (AL)	1	40	.226 BA

Several players listed here as having U.S. birthplaces (as in standard encyclopedias) may have been Canadian-born according to new evidence from Bill Humber's *Diamonds of the North*.

Canada's Professional Baseball Franchises

Montreal Expos, National League (1969–2003)

Year	Position	Record	Manager	Top Batter	BA	Top Pitcher	W–L	ERA
1969	6th East	52–110	Gene Mauch	Rusty Staub	.302	Bill Stoneman	11–19	4.39
1970	6th East	73–89	Gene Mauch	Ron Fairly	.288	Carl Morton	18–11	3.60

Year	Position	Record	Manager	Top Batter	BA	Top Pitcher	W–L	ERA
1971	5th East	71–90	Gene Mauch	Rusty Staub	.311	Bill Stoneman	17–16	3.14
1972	5th East	70–86	Gene Mauch	Ron Fairly	.278	Mike Torrez	16–12	3.33
1973	4th East	79–83	Gene Mauch	Ron Hunt	.309	Steve Renko	15–11	2.81
1974	4th East	79–82	Gene Mauch	Willie Davis	.295	Mike Torrez	15–8	3.58
1975	5th East	75–87	Gene Mauch	Larry Parrish	.274	Dale Murray	15–8	3.97
1976	6th East	55–107	Karl Kuehl	Tim Foli	.264	Woodie Fryman	13–13	3.37
1977	5th East	75–87	Dick Williams	Ellis Valentine	.293	Steve Rogers	17–16	3.10
1978	4th East	76–86	Dick Williams	Warren Cromartie	.297	Ross Grimsley	20–11	3.05
1979	2nd East	95–65	Dick Williams	Larry Parrish	.307	Bill Lee	16–10	3.04
1980	2nd East	90–72	Dick Williams	André Dawson	.308	Steve Rogers	16–11	2.98
1981	2nd East	60–48	Dick Williams	Warren Cromartie	.304	Steve Rogers	12–8	3.41
1982	3rd East	86–76	Jim Fanning	Al Oliver	.331*	Steve Rogers	19–8	2.40
1983	3rd East	82–80	Bill Virdon	Al Oliver	.300	Steve Rogers	17–12	3.23
1984	5th East	78–83	Bill Virdon	Tim Raines	.309	Charlie Lea	15–10	2.89
1985	3rd East	84–77	Buck Rodgers	Tim Raines	.320	Bryn Smith	18–5	2.91
1986	4th East	78–83	Buck Rodgers	Tim Raines	.334*	Andy McGaffigan	10–5	2.65
1987	3rd East	91–71	Buck Rodgers	Tim Raines	.330	Dennis Martínez	11–4	3.30
1988	3rd East	81–81	Buck Rodgers	Andrés Galarraga	.302	Dennis Martínez	15–13	2.72
1989	4th East	81–81	Buck Rodgers	Tim Raines	.286	Dennis Martínez	16–7	3.18
1990	3rd East	85–77	Buck Rodgers	Tim Wallach	.296	Bill Sampen	12–7	2.99
1991	6th East	71–90	Buck Rodgers	Ivan Calderón	.300	Dennis Martínez	14–11	2.39
1992	2nd East	87–75	Tom Runnells Felipe Alou	Larry Walker	.301	Dennis Martínez	16–11	2.47
1993	2nd East	94–68	Felipe Alou	Marquis Grissom	.298	Dennis Martínez	15–9	3.85
1994[†]	1st East	74–40	Felipe Alou	Moises Alou	.339	Ken Hill	16–5	3.32
1995	5th East	66–78	Felipe Alou	David Segui	.309	Pedro Martínez	14–10	3.51
1996	2nd East	88–74	Felipe Alou	Mark Grudzielanek	.306	Jeff Fassero	15–11	3.30
1997	4th East	78–84	Felipe Alou	David Segui	.307	Pedro Martínez	17–8	1.90
1998	4th East	65–97	Felipe Alou	Vladimir Guerrero	.324	Dustin Hermanson	14–11	3.13
1999	4th East	68–94	Felipe Alou	Vladimir Guerrero	.316	Dustin Hermanson	9–14	4.20
2000	4th East	67–95	Felipe Alou	Vladimir Guerrero	.345	Javier Vásquez	11–9	4.05
2001	5th East	68–94	Jeff Torborg	José Vidro	.319	Javier Vásquez	16–11	3.42
2002	2nd East	83–79	Frank Robinson	Vladimir Guerrero	.336	Tomo Ohka	13–8	3.18
2003	4th East	83–79	Frank Robinson	Vladimir Guerrero	.330	Liván Hernández	15–10	3.20

* National League batting champion.
† Postseason canceled by players strike.

Toronto Blue Jays, American League (1977–2003)

Year	Position	Record	Manager	Top Batter	BA	Top Pitcher	W–L	ERA
1977	7th East	54–107	Roy Hartsfield	Bob Bailor	.310	Dave Lemanczyk	13–16	4.25
1978	7th East	59–102	Roy Hartsfield	Rico Carty	.284	Jim Clancy	10–12	4.09
1979	7th East	53–109	Roy Hartsfield	Otto Velez	.288	Tom Underwood	9–16	3.69
1980	7th East	67–95	Bob Mattick	Al Woods	.300	Jim Clancy	13–16	3.30
1981	7th East	37–69	Bob Mattick	Dámaso García	.252	Dave Stieb	11–10	3.19
1982	6th East	78–84	Bobby Cox	Dámaso García	.310	Dave Stieb	17–14	3.25
1983	4th East	89–73	Bobby Cox	Barry Bonnell	.318	Dave Stieb	17–12	3.04
1984	2nd East	89–73	Bobby Cox	Rance Mullinks	.324	Dave Stieb	16–8	2.83
1985	1st East	99–62	Bobby Cox	Garth Iorg	.313	Doyle Alexander	17–10	3.45
1986	4th East	86–76	Jimy Williams	Tony Fernández	.310	Mark Eichhorn	14–6	1.72
1987	2nd East	99–66	Jimy Williams	Tony Fernández	.322	Jimmy Key	17–8	2.76
1988	3rd East	54–107	Jimy Williams	Rance Mulliniks	.300	Dave Stieb	16–8	3.04
1989	1st East	89–73	Cito Gaston	George Bell	.297	Dave Stieb	17–8	3.35

(continued)

(continued)

Year	Position	Record	Manager	Top Batter	BA	Top Pitcher	W–L	ERA
1990	2nd East	86–76	Cito Gaston	Fred McGriff	.300	Dave Stieb	18–6	2.93
1991	1st East	91–71	Cito Gaston	Roberto Alomar	.295	Jimmy Key	16–12	3.05
1992	WC	96–66	Cito Gaston	Roberto Alomar	.310	Jack Morris	21–6	4.04
1993	WC	95–67	Cito Gaston	John Olerud	.363*	Pat Hentgen	19–9	3.87
1994[†]	3rd East	55–60	Cito Gaston	Paul Molitor	.341	Pat Hentgen	13–8	3.40
1995	5th East	56–88	Cito Gaston	Roberto Alomar	.300	Al Leiter	11–11	3.64
1996	4th East	74–88	Cito Gaston	Otis Nixon	.286	Pat Hentgen	20–10	3.22
1997	5th East	76–86	Cito Gaston	Shawn Green	.287	Roger Clemens	21–7	2.05
1998	3rd East	88–74	Tim Johnson	Tony Fernández	.321	Roger Clemens	20–6	2.65
1999	3rd East	84–78	Jim Fregosi	Tony Fernández	.328	David Wells	17–10	4.82
2000	3rd East	83–79	Jim Fregosi	Carlos Delgado	.344	David Wells	20–8	4.11
2001	3rd East	80–82	Buck Martinez	Shannon Stewart	.316	Paul Quantrill	11–2	3.04
2002	3rd East	78–84	Carlos Tosca	Shannon Stewart	.303	Roy Halladay	19–7	2.93
2003	3rd East	86–76	Carlos Tosca	Vernon Wells	.317	Roy Halladay	22–7	3.25

Abbreviations: WC, world champions.
* American League batting champion.
[†] Postseason canceled by players strike.

Canadian Major League Milestones

Canadian Major League Batting and Pitching Leaders

Category	Name	Dates	Record
Batting			
Games Played, Career	Larry Walker	1988–2003	1,806
Base Hits, Career	Larry Walker	1988–2003	1,992
Base Hits, Season	Tip O'Neill	1887	225
Consecutive Game Hitting Streak	Pete Ward	June 7–24, 1963	18
	Terry Puhl	May 5–27, 1978	18
Runs Scored, Career	Larry Walker	1988–2003	1,238
Runs Scored, Season	Tip O'Neill	1887	167
Bases on Balls, Season	Jack Graney	1919	105
Strikeouts, Season	Larry Walker	1990	112
Home Runs, Career	Larry Walker	1988–2003	351
Home Runs, Season	Larry Walker	1997	49
Home Runs, Rookie Season	Pete Ward	1963	22
Runs Batted In, Career	Larry Walker	1988–2003	1,212
Runs Batted In, Season	Larry Walker	1997	130
Triples, Season	Jeff Heath	1941	20
Doubles, Season	Larry Walker	1997, 1998	46
Stolen Bases, Season	Larry Walker	1997	33
Pinch-Hit At-Bats, Career	Sherry Robertson	1940–1952	173
Pinch-Hits, Career	Sherry Robertson	1940–1952	35
	Pete Ward	1962–1970	35
Pinch-Hit At-Bats, Season	Tim Burgess	1962	43
Pinch-Hits, Season	Kevin Reimer	1990	12
Pinch-Hitting BA, Career	Jack Graney	1908–1922	.335
Pinch-Hitting BA, Season	Jeff Heath	1945	.409
Pitching			
Games Pitched, Career	Ferguson Jenkins	1965-1983	664
Games Pitched, Season	Eric Gagne	2003	77
Innings Pitched, Career	Ferguson Jenkins	1965–1983	4,498.2
Innings Pitched, Season	Ferguson Jenkins	1974	328.0

Category	Name	Dates	Record
Games Won, Career	Ferguson Jenkins	1965–1983	284
Games Won, Season	Russell Ford	1910	26
Consecutive Games Won	Russell Ford	Aug.–Oct. 1910	12
Games Lost, Career	Ferguson Jenkins	1965–1983	226
Games Lost, Season	Russell Ford	1912	21
Complete Games, Career	Ferguson Jenkins	1965–1983	267
Complete Games, Season	Russell Ford	1912	32
Shutouts, Career	Ferguson Jenkins	1965–1983	49
Shutouts, Season	Russell Ford	1910	8
Strikeouts, Career	Ferguson Jenkins	1965–1983	3,192
Strikeouts, Season	Ferguson Jenkins	1970	274
Strikeouts, Game	Ferguson Jenkins	June 27, 1970	14 vs. Pittsburgh Pirates
	Ferguson Jenkins	July 24, 1971	14 vs. Philadelphia Phillies
	Ferguson Jenkins	Sept. 19, 1971	14 vs. Philadelphia Phillies
Bases on Balls, Career	Ferguson Jenkins	1965–1983	997
Bases on Balls, Season	Phil Marchildon	1941	141
Saves, Career	John Hiller	1965–1980	125
Saves, Season	Eric Gagne	2003	55
No-Hit Games	Dick Fowler	1; Sept. 9, 1945	1–0 vs. St. Louis Browns

Canadian AAA Minor League Record Book

Canadian Governor's Cup Champions through the Years

Year	Champion	Manager	Governor's Cup Final Series Results
1934	Toronto Maple Leafs	Ike Boone	Defeated Rochester Royals, 4 games to 1
1941	Montreal Royals	Clyde Sukeforth	Defeated Newark Bears, 4 games to 3
1946	Montreal Royals	Clay Hopper	Defeated Syracuse Chiefs, 4 games to 1
1948	Montreal Royals	Clay Hopper	Defeated Syracuse Chiefs, 4 games to 1
1949	Montreal Royals	Clay Hopper	Defeated Buffalo Bisons, 4 games to 1
1951	Montreal Royals	Walter Alston	Defeated Syracuse Chiefs, 4 games to 1
1953	Montreal Royals	Walter Alston	Defeated Rochester Red Wings, 4 games to 0
1958	Montreal Royals	Clay Bryant	Defeated Toronto Maple Leafs, 4 games to 1
1960	Toronto Maple Leafs	Mel McGaha	Defeated Rochester Red Wings, 4 games to 1
1965	Toronto Maple Leafs	Dick Williams	Defeated Columbus Jets, 4 games to 1
1966	Toronto Maple Leafs	Dick Williams	Defeated Richmond Braves, 4 games to 1
1995	Ottawa Lynx	Pete Mackanin	Defeated Norfolk Tides, 3 games to 1

Toronto Maple Leafs, International League (1885–1967)*

Year	Finish	Record	Manager	Top Batter	BA	Top Pitcher	W–L
1885	3rd	24–20	Harrison Spence	*Not Recorded*		Jim McKinley	10–4
1886	3rd	53–41	John Humphries	Jon Morrison	.353	*Not Recorded*	
1887	1st	65–36	Charles Cushman	Ned Crane	.428	Ned Crane	33–13
1888	2nd	76–36	Charles Cushman	Harry Decker	.313	*Not Recorded*	
1889	5th	54–54	Charles Cushman	William Hoover	.333	Bill Serad	19–16
1890	3rd	30–20	Charles Maddock	*Not Recorded*		John Coleman	11–4
1891–1894	*No Team*						
1895	7th	43–76	Charles Maddock	Judson Smith	.373	*Not Recorded*	
1896	4th	59–57	Al Buckenberger	Jimmy Casey	.329	*Not Recorded*	
1897	2nd	75–52	Arthur Irwin	Buck Freeman	.357	Bill Dinneen	21–8
1898	3rd	64–55	Arthur Irwin	Buck Freeman	.347	Kirtley Baker	17–11

(continued)

(continued)

Year	Finish	Record	Manager	Top Batter	BA	Top Pitcher	W–L
1899	4th	58–57	Wally Taylor	Jim Bannon	.341	*Not Recorded*	
1900	5th	64–68	Edward G. Barrow	Charley Carr	.327	*Not Recorded*	
1901	2nd	76–50	Edward G. Barrow	Jim Bannon	.340	Pop Williams	19–13
1902	1st	85–42	Edward G. Barrow	Bill Massey	.313	Louie Bruce	18–2
1903	3rd	82–45	James Gardner	Louie Bruce	.356	Button Briggs	26–8
1904	6th	67–71	Richard Harley	Jack White	.277	Clarence Currie	18–10
1905	8th	48–89	Richard Harley	Jack White	.277	Fred Falkenberg	11–10
1906	8th	46–88	Edward G. Barrow	Jack Thoney	.294	Jim McGinley	15-13
1907	1st	83–51	Joseph Kelley	Jack Thoney	.329	Jim McGinley	22–10
1908	6th	59–79	Mike Kelley	Bill Phyle	.271	Dick Rudolph	18–12
1909	4th	75–68	Joseph Kelley	Myron Grimshaw	.309	Jim McGinley	22–13
1910	4th	80–72	Joseph Kelley	Jack Slattery	.310	Dick Rudolph	23–15
1911	3rd	94–59	Joseph Kelley	Jack Slattery	.342	Kid Mueller	17–8
1912	1st	91–62	Joseph Kelley	Benny Meyer	.343	Dick Rudolph	25–10
1913	7th	70–83	Joseph Kelley	Joe Schultz	.299	John Lush	17–13
1914	4th	74–70	Joseph Kelley	Robert Fisher	.311	Bull Wagner	13–7
1915	3rd	72–67	William Clymer	Maurice Rath	.332	Adolfo Luque	15–9
1916	5th	73–66	Joe Birmingham	Dawson Graham	.294	Urban Shocker	15–3
1917	1st	93–61	Larry Lajoie	Larry Lajoie	.380	Bunny Hearn	23–9
1918	1st	88–39	Dan Howley	Fred Lear	.345	Fred Hersche	21–6
1919	2nd	93–57	George Gibson	Eddie Onslow	.303	Fred Hersche	16–5
1920	2nd	108–46	Hugh Duffy	Benny Kauff	.343	Pat Shea	27–7
1921	4th	89–77	Larry Doyle	Jesse Altenburg	.346	Harry Thompson	15–9
1922	5th	76–88	Eddie Onslow	Eddie Onslow	.325	Billy Taylor	18–15
1923	4th	81–79	Dan Howley	Red Wingo	.352	Art Reynolds	11–5
1924	2nd	98–67	Dan Howley	Joe Kelly	.351	Walter Stewart	24–11
1925	2nd	99–63	Dan Howley	Joe Kelly	.340	Myles Thomas	28–8
1926	1st	109–57	Dan Howley	Bill Mullen	.357	Owen Carroll	21–8
1927	4th	89–78	Bill O'Hara	Dale Alexander	.338	Jim Faulkner	21–10
1928	3rd	86–80	Bill O'Hara	Dale Alexander	.380	Rip Collins	17–9
1929	2nd	92–76	Steve O'Neill	Ralph Shinners	.337	Phil Page	10–3
1930	4th	87–80	Steve O'Neill	Joe Harris	.333	Guy Cantrell	15–5
1931	5th	83–84	Steve O'Neill	Ken Strong	.340	Johnny Allen	17–6
1932	8th	54–113	Lena Blackburne	John Rothrock	.327	Arthur Smith	11–13
1933	5th	82–85	Dan Howley	Ike Boone	.357	Ralph Birkofer	16–8
1934[†]	3rd	85–67	Ike Boone	Ike Boone	.372	Gene Schott	18–9
1935	6th	78–76	Ike Boone	Ike Boone	.350	Jim Pattison	16–8
1936	5th	77–76	Ike Boone	George McQuinn	.329	Jake Mooty	12–8
1937	7th	63–88	Dan Howley	Don Ross	.305	Woody Davis	13–13
1938	5th	72–81	Jack Burns	Ted Petoskey	.289	Joe Sullivan	18–10
1939	8th	63–90	Tony Lazzeri	Bob Elliott	.328	Carl Fischer	11–9
1940	8th	57–101	Tony Lazzeri	John Tyler	.288	Carl Fischer	10–12
1941	8th	47–107	Lena Blackburne	Frank Colman	.295	Dick Fowler	10–10
1942	6th	74–79	Burleigh Grimes	Frank Colman	.300	Bill Brandt	15–11
1943	1st	95–57	Burleigh Grimes	Harry Davis	.291	Luke Hamlin	21–8
1944	3rd	79–74	Burleigh Grimes	Tony Castaño	.306	Al Jarlett	18–9
1945	3rd	85–67	Harry Davis	Ira Houck	.307	Woody Crowson	13–8
1946	6th	71–82	Bill Norman	Aus Knickerbocker	.294	Bill McCahan	11–7
1947	8th	64–90	Elmer Yoder	Ed Levy	.287	Luke Hamlin	15–6
1948	5th	78–76	Ed Sawyer	John Welaj	.315	Oscar Judd	14–8
1949	5th	80–72	Del Bissonette	John Welaj	.308	Jocko Thompson	14–5
1950	7th	60–90	Jack Sanford	John Mayo	.294	Jocko Thompson	10–14
1951	5th	77–76	Joe Becker	Grover Bowers	.291	Hal Hudson	16–5
1952	4th	78–76	Joe Becker	Ferrell Anderson	.299	John Hetki	13–7
1953	5th	78–76	Burleigh Grimes	Lew Morton	.307	Vic Lombardi	11–8
1954	1st	97–57	Luke Sewell	Elston Howards	.330	Rudy Minarcin	11–2
1955	2nd	94–59	Luke Sewell	Archie Wilson	.319	Connie Johnson	12–2

Year	Finish	Record	Manager	Top Batter	BA	Top Pitcher	W–L
1956	1st	86–66	Bruno Betzel	Archie Wilson	.301	Lynn Lovenguth	24–12
1957	1st	88–65	Dixie Walker	Mike Goliat	.296	Humberto Robinson	18–7
1958	2nd	87–65	Dixie Walker	Rocky Nelson	.326	Bob Tiefenauer	17–5
1959	8th	69–86	Dixie Walker	Archie Wilson	.294	Pat Scantlebury	12–5
1960[†]	1st	100–54	Mel McGaha	Don Dillard	.294	Riverboat Smith	14–6
1961	5th	76–79	Johnny Lipon	Lou Johnson	.286	Rip Coleman	10–7
1962	2nd	91–62	Chuck Dressen	Neil Chrisley	.317	Jim Constable	16–4
1963	2nd	76–75	Bill Adair	Lou Jackson	.315	Carl Bouldin	10–8
1964	5th	80–72	Sparky Anderson	Don Dillard	.288	Ron Piche	14–3
1965[†]	3rd	81–64	Dick Williams	Joe Foy	.302	Jack Lamabe	10–3
1966[†]	2nd	82–65	Dick Williams	Reggie Smith	.320	Ed Rakow	11–4
1967	6th	65–75	Eddie Kasko	John Ryan	.298	Dave Morehead	11–5

* The team name was Toronto Canucks from 1886 to 1890. The International League was originally named the Eastern League, through 1912.
† Governor's Cup league postseason champions.

Montreal Royals, International League (1928–1960)*

Year	Finish	Record	Manager	Attendance	League All-Stars
1928	6th	84–84	George Stallings	214,027	*None*
1929	4th	88–79	Eddie Holly	203,138	Billy Urbanski (SS), Elon Hogsett (P)
1930	3rd	96–72	Eddie Holly	207,757	Billy Urbanski (SS)
1931	6th	85–80	Eddie Holly	179,586	*None*
1932	4th	90–78	Eddie Holly	196,876	*None*
1933	4th N	81–84	Doc Gauthreau	179,396	Bennie Tate (C)
1934	6th	73–77	Frank Shaughnessy	158,997	Fresco Thompson (2B)
1935	1st	92–62	Frank Shaughnessy	234,115	Pete Appleton (P)
1936	6th	71–81	Frank Shaughnessy	162,977	*None*
1937	2nd	82–67	Rabbit Maranville	196,889	Marvin Duke (P)
1938	6th	69–84	Rabbit Maranville	166,068	*None*
1939	7th	64–88	Burleigh Grimes	135,733	*None*
1940	5th	80–80	Clyde Sukeforth	158,799	*None*
1941[†]	2nd	90–64	Clyde Sukeforth	182,024	*None*
1942	2nd	82–71	Clyde Sukeforth	183,841	Gene Moore, Les Burge
1943	4th	76–76	Fresco Thompson	206,507	*None*
1944	6th	73–80	Bruno Betzel	207,603	*None*
1945	1st	95–58	Bruno Betzel	338,409	Roland Gladu (3B)
1946[†]	1st	100–54	Clay Hopper	412,744	Jackie Robinson (2B)
1947	2nd	93–60	Clay Hopper	442,485	Ed Stevens, Roy Campanella (C)
1948[†]	1st	94–59	Clay Hopper	477,638	Jim Bloodsworth, Bobby Morgan (SS)
1949[†]	3rd	84–70	Clay Hopper	473,798	Bobby Morgan (SS), Sam Jethroe (OF)
1950	2nd	86–67	Walter Alston	391,001	*None*
1951[†]	1st	95–59	Walter Alston	391,107	Junior Gilliam, (2B) Héctor Rodríguez
1952	1st	95–56	Walter Alston	313,160	Junior Gilliam (2B), Jim Pendleton (OF)
1953[†]	2nd	89–63	Walter Alston	285,552	Rocky Nelson (1B), Sandy Amoros (OF)
1954	2nd	88–66	Max Macon	195,896	Rocky Nelson (1B), Chico Fernández (SS)
1955	1st	95–59	Greg Mulleavy	205,134	Rocky Nelson (1B), Gino Cimoli (OF)
1956	4th	80–72	Greg Mulleavy	191,624	Clyde Paris (3B), Bob Wilson (C)
1957	8th	68–86	Greg Mulleavy	176, 137	*None*
1958[†]	1st	90–63	Clay Bryant	213,475	Sparky Anderson (2B), Solly Drake (OF)
1959	6th	72–82	Clay Bryant	136,340	Curt Roberts (IF), Sandy Amoros (OF)
1960	8th	62–92	Clay Bryant	111,991	Joe Altobelli, (1B)

Abbreviations: N, Northern Division.
* International League was AA classification through 1945, AAA classification from 1945 to 1960.
† Governor's Cup league postseason champions.

Ottawa Lynx, International League (1993–2003)

Year	Finish	Record	Manager	Leading Hitter		Best Pitcher	ERA
1993	2nd E	73–69	Mike Quade	Curtis Pride	.302	Mario Brito	1.32
1994	3rd E	70–72	Jim Tracy	Tim Laker	.309	Heath Haynes	2.38
1995*	2nd E	72–70	Pete Mackanin	Kevin Castleberry	.294	Greg Harris	1.06
1996	5th E	60–82	Pete Mackanin	Steve Bieser	.322	Dave Leiper	1.93
1997	4th E	54–86	Pat Kelly	José Vidro	.323	Shayne Bennett	1.57
1998	5th E	69–74	Pat Kelly	Ray Holbert	.308	John DeSilva	2.61
1999	5th E	59–85	Jeff Cox	Trace Coquillette	.326	John DeSilva	2.89
2000	6th E	53–88	Jeff Cox/Rick Sweet	Milton Bradley	.304	Mike Johnson	2.10
2001	4th E	68–76	Stan Hough	Dave McKinley	.281	Sean Spencer	2.94
2002	3rd E	80–61	Tim Leiper	Endy Chavez	.343	Tim Drew	3.08
2003	2nd E	79–65	Gary Allenson	Eddy Garabito	.281	Sean Douglass	3.40

Abbreviations: E, Eastern Division.
* Won Governor's Cup League International League Championship (1995; defeating Norfolk 3 games to 1 in final series).

Winnipeg Whips, International League (1970–1971)

Year	Finish	Record	Manager	Attendance	League All-Stars
1970*	7th	52–88	Clyde McCullough	89,901	Ernest McAnally (P)
1971†	8th	44–96	Clyde McCullough	95,954	Dave McDonald (1B)

* Buffalo Bisons relocated as Winnipeg Whips on June 11, 1970.
† Franchise relocated as Peninsula Whips (Newport News and Hampton, VA) for the 1971 International League season.

Vancouver Mounties, Pacific Coast League (1956–1969)

Year	Finish	Record	Manager	Attendance	League All-Stars
1956	8th	67–98	Lefty O'Doul	152,893	*None*
1957	2nd	97–70	Charlie Metro	306,145	Buddy Peterson (SS), Lennie Green (OF)
1958	3rd	79–73	Charlie Metro	245,590	George Bamberger (P)
1959	2nd	82–69	Charlie Metro	238,970	Joe Taylor (OF)
1960	7th	68–84	George Staller	144,278	Chet Nichols (P)
1961	2nd	87–67	Billy Hitchcock	200,143	Ed Charles (3B), Denis Menke (SS)
1962	7th	72–79	Jack McKeon	88,075	*None*
1963	*No Team*				
1964	*No Team*				
1965	3rd W	77–69	Bob Hofman	124,048	*None*
1966	2nd W	77–71	Mickey Vernon	121,482	*None*
1967	3rd W	77–69	Mickey Vernon	143,541	*None*
1968	6th W	58–88	Mickey Vernon	82,028	*None*
1969	3rd N	71–73	Bob Lemon	62,666	*None*

Abbreviations: N, Northern Division; W, Western Division.

Vancouver Canadians, Pacific Coast League (1978–1999)

Year	Finish	Record	Manager	Attendance	League All-Stars
1978	3rd W	74–65	Jim Marshall	123,466	*None*
1979	1st N	79–68	John Felske	131,367	Lenn Sakata (2B), Mark Bomback (P)

Year	Finish	Record	Manager	Attendance	League All-Stars
1980	1st N	79–60	Bob Didier	150,758	*None*
1981	5th N	56–76	Lee Sigman	127,161	Larry Rush (3B)
1982	3rd N	72–72	Dick Phillips	158,767	Frank DiPino (P)
1983	5th N	60–80	Dick Phillips	179,337	Randy Ready (3B)
1984	2nd N	71–71	Tony Muser	147,599	Doug Loman (OF), Jaime Nelson (C)
1985*	1st N	79–64	Tom Trebelhorn	199,781	Mike Felder (OF), Carlos Ponce (DH)
1986	1st N	85–53	Terry Bevington	231,819	Glenn Braggs (OF), B. J. Surhoff (C)
1987	3rd N	72–72	Rocky Bridges	338,614	José Lind (2B), Mackey Sasser (C)
1988	1st N	84–57	Terry Bevington	386,220	Mike Woodard (2B)
1989*	2nd N	73–69	Marv Foley	281,812	*None*
1990	3rd N	74–67	Marv Foley	281,540	Jerry Willard (C), Grady Hall (P)
1991	5th N	49–86	Marv Foley	288,978	*None*
1992	2nd N	81–61	Rick Renick	333,564	Rod Bolton (P), Brian Drahman (P)
1993	2nd N	72–68	Max Oliveras	349,726	Eddie Pérez (3B)
1994	1st N	77–65	Don Long	320,863	Andrew Lorraine (P)
1995	1st N	81–60	Don Long	305,739	Don Long (Manager of the Year)
1996	4th N	68–70	Don Long	334,800	*None*
1997	3rd N	75–86	Bruce Hines	303,148	Todd Greene (C)
1998	4th N	53–90	Mitch Seoane	284,935	*None*
1999*†	1st N	84–58	Mike Quade	241,461	Frank Menechino (U), Brett Laxton (P)

Abbreviations: N, Northern Division; W, Western Division.
* Won Pacific Coast League Championship in postseason playoffs (1985, 1989, 1999).
† Won AAA Little World Series (1999, defeating Charlotte Knights 3 games to 2 in best-of-five series).

Edmonton Trappers, Pacific Coast League (1981–2003)

Year	Finish	Record	Manager	Attendance	League All-Stars
1981	4th N	62–74	Gordon Lund	187,501	John Loviglio (2B), Gary Holle (DH)
1982	4th N	70–74	Gordon Lund	233,044	Ron Kittle (OF), Gary Gray (OF)
1983	1st N	75–67	Moose Stubing	224,822	Dick Schofield (SS), Mike Brown (OF)
1984*	4th N	69–73	Moose Stubing	228,102	*None*
1985	4th N	66–76	Winston Llenas	229,112	Jack Howell (3B)
1986	3rd N	68–73	Winston Llenas	229,682	Gus Polidor (SS), Mark Ryal (DH)
1987	4th N	69–74	Tom Kotchman	229,381	Jim Eppard (1B)
1988	4th N	61–80	Tom Kotchman	243,419	*None*
1989	5th N	62–74	Tom Kotchman	230,728	*None*
1990	1st N	78–63	Max Oliveras	229,307	*None*
1991	2nd N	70–66	Max Oliveras	252,813	Ruben Amaro (OF), Kyle Abbott (P)
1992	3rd N	74–69	Max Oliveras	257,146	Tim Salmon (OF) (League MVP)
1993	3rd N	72–69	Sal Rende	261,361	Nigel Wilson (OF), David Weathers (P)
1994	4th N	67–75	Sal Rende	272,631	*None*
1995	3rd N	68–76	Gary Jones	462,012	Fausto Cruz (SS), George Williams (C)
1996*	1st N	84–58	Gary Jones	463,684	Gary Jones (Manager of the Year)
1997*	1st N	80–64	Gary Jones	432,504	*None*
1998	3rd N	76–67	Mike Quade	410,414	*None*
1999	3rd N	65–74	Carney Lansford	385,913	*None*
2000	3rd PN	63–78	Garry Templton	359,697	*None*
2001	4th PN	60–83	John Russell	372,244	*None*
2002	1st PW	81–59	John Russell	340,387	Javier Valentin (C), Michael Ryan (OF)
2003	1st AN	73–69	Dave Hubbert	333,792	Terrmel Sledge (OF)

Abbreviations: AN, American Conference North; N, Northern Division; PN, Pacific Conference North; W, Western Division.
* Won Pacific Coast League championship in postseason playoffs (1984, 1996, 1997).

Calgary Cannons, Pacific Coast League (1985–2002)

Year	Finish	Record	Manager	Attendance	League All-Stars
1985	2nd N	71–70	Bobby Floyd	272,322	Danny Tartabull (SS), John Moses (OF)
1986	5th N	66–77	Bill Plummer	288,197	Mickey Brantley (OF)
1987	1st N	84–57	Bill Plummer	304,897	Edgar Martínez (3B), Jim Weaver (OF)
1988	3rd N	68–74	Marty Martínez	332,590	Edgar Martínez (3B)
1989	4th N	70–72	Rich Morales	316,616	Bruce Fields (OF), Jim Wilson (DH)
1990	4th N	66–77	Tom Jones	312,416	Tino Martínez (1B), Tom Dodd (DH)
1991	1st N	72–64	Keith Bodie	325,965	Tino Martínez (1B) (League MVP)
1992	4th N	60–78	Keith Bodie	277,307	Bret Boone (2B), Mike Blowers (3B)
1993	4th N	68–72	Keith Bodie	278,140	*None*
1994	3rd N	71–72	Steve Smith	297,981	Marc Newfield (OF)
1995	5th N	58–83	Bobby Meacham	279,054	*None*
1996	3rd N	74–68	Trent Jewett	273,545	Jermaine Allensworth (OF)
1997	5th N	60–78	Trent Jewett	291,918	Manny Martínez (OF)
1998	1st PW	81–62	Tom Spencer	296,047	Mario Valdéz (1B)
1999	4th PW	57–82	Lynn Jones	269,002	*None*
2000	4th PN	60–82	Lynn Jones	270,682	*None*
2001	2nd PN	72–71	Chris Chambliss	246,991	Ramón Castro (C)
2002	3rd PW	67–71	Dean Treanor	182,831	Jason Wood (3B)

Abbreviations: N, Northern Division; PN, Pacific Conference North; PW, Pacific Conference West.

Canada's Hall of Fame

Canadian Baseball Hall of Fame, 1983–2004

	Name	Year	Claim to Fame
1	John Ducey	1983	Legendary Alberta Province amateur player, league umpire (1934–1945), and league administrator
2	Phil Marchildon	1983	Major league pitcher with American League Philadelphia Athletics
3	James "Tip" O'Neill	1983	Major league 19th-century batting champion with St. Louis Browns (American Association, 1887)
4	George Selkirk	1983	Major league outfielder with New York Yankees (1934–1942) who replaced Babe Ruth in New York lineup
5	Frank Shaughnessy	1983	International League president and Montreal Royals minor league manager (1934–1936)
6	Lester Bowles Pearson*	1983	Prime minister (1948–1957), Nobel Peace Prize winner (1957), and Canadian baseball supporter; played semi-pro baseball with Guelph Maple Leafs (1917)
7	Andrew Bilesky	1984	Legendary British Columbia Little League coach of four teams in Little League World Series
8	Charles Bronfman	1984	Founding major league owner of Montreal Expos; responsible for bringing 1982 All-Star game to Montreal
9	Jack Graney	1984	Major league outfielder with Cleveland Indians (1908–1922) and first big leaguer to wear a number on his uniform
10	Claude Raymond	1984	Major league pitcher with Montreal Expos (and four other clubs) who saved 23 games in 1970 (for Montreal)
11	Goody Rosen	1984	Major league outfielder with Brooklyn Dodgers who averaged better than one hit per game for six seasons
12	Carmen Bush	1985	Toronto amateur baseball entrepreneur and organizer instrumental in formation of several amateur leagues
13	Jack Kent Cooke	1985	Minor league owner of International League Toronto Maple Leafs during glory years of 1953 through 1961

	Name	Year	Claim to Fame
14	Dick Fowler	1985	Major league pitcher with Philadelphia Athletics who threw the only big league no-hitter by a Canada native
15	John Hiller	1985	Major league pitcher with Detroit Tigers whose 38 saves in 1973 were at the time a big league record
16	Ron Taylor	1985	Major league pitcher with Cleveland Indians and New York Mets who starred in two different World Series
17	Reggie Cleveland	1986	Major leaguer with Boston Red Sox and St. Louis Cardinals and first Canadian World Series starting pitcher
18	Bob Emslie	1986	Pioneering 19th-century big league pitcher and minor league umpire famed for role in Bonehead Merkle incident
19	Oscar Judd	1986	Major league pitcher with Boston Red Sox and Philadelphia Phillies (1941–1948); owned .263 batting average
20	Bob Prentice	1986	Minor league infielder (Cleveland Indians organization, 1949–1957) and major league scout for Toronto Blue Jays
21	Ferguson Jenkins	1987	Major league pitcher with Chicago Cubs and Texas Rangers elected to MLB Cooperstown Hall of Fame
22	George Gibson	1987	Major league catcher (1905–1919) and last Canadian-born big league manager with Pittsburgh Pirates (1932–1934)
23	Rocky Nelson	1987	American-born slugging major league first baseman with Pittsburgh Pirates; also International League MVP with both Montreal Royals (1953, 1955) and Toronto Maple Leafs (1958)
24	Reno Bertoia	1988	Ten-year major league utility infielder mostly with Detroit Tigers; born in Italy but raised in Ontario, Canada
25	Ted Bowsfield	1988	Major league pitcher with Boston Red Sox (team's top rookie in 1957), Cleveland Indians, and California Angels
26	Jeff Heath	1988	Major league outfielder with Cleveland Indians and Boston Braves twice named to American League all-star team
27	Bill Phillips	1988	First 19th-century Canadian major leaguer with Cleveland National League team in 1879; played 1,038 NL games
28	Ron Piche	1988	Seven-year major league pitcher with Milwaukee Braves and St. Louis Cardinals; also won 110 games in minors
29	Beachville and Zorra Amateur Teams[†]	1988	Two township amateur teams that met on June 4, 1838 for Canada's first recorded game in Beachville, Ontario
30	Bob Brown	1989	British Columbia sports entrepreneur and organizational pioneer widely known as Vancouver's "Mr. Baseball"
31	Russell Ford	1989	Major league pitcher with New York Yankees who employed a legal "spit-ball" to win 26 games in 1910
32	Arthur Irwin	1989	Pioneering 19th-century major league infielder and manager (Boston) who played more than 1,000 big league games
33	Jimmy Archer	1990	Irish-born early 20th-century big league catcher with pennant-winning Detroit Tigers (1907) and Chicago Cubs (1910) reputed to be first catcher to throw out base stealers from a squatting position behind the plate
34	Pete Ward	1991	Slugging major league third baseman with Chicago White Sox and 1963 American League rookie of the year
35	Jimmy Williams	1991	Major league coach with Houston Astros (1975) and Baltimore Orioles (1981–1987); also minor league outfielder
36	Jackie Robinson*	1991	American-born major league infielder/outfielder with Brooklyn Dodgers (1947–1956) who integrated organized baseball in 1946 with Montreal Royals and 1947 with Brooklyn Dodgers; MLB Cooperstown Hall of Fame member
37	Tim Burgess	1992	Big league outfielder and first baseman with NL St. Louis Cardinals (1954) and AL Los Angeles Angels (1962)
38	1991 Canadian Youth Team[†]	1992	Defeated Cuba, the United States, and Chinese Taipei during AAA World Youth Championships at Brandon, Manitoba
39	Terry Puhl	1995	Big league outfielder with Houston Astros (14 seasons) and Kansas City Royals; holds career fielding percentage record

(continued)

	Name	Year	Claim to Fame
40	Justin Jay "Nig" Clarke	1996	Played for 9 major league seasons (1905–1920)—interrupted by World War I—as catcher for Cleveland, Detroit, St. Louis (AL), Pittsburgh and Philadelphia (NL)
41	Father Ronald Cullen	1996	Coached and organized amateur baseball competitions in Windsor, Ontario, for 50 years
42	Frank O'Rourke	1996	Played 14 major league seasons between 1912 (age 17) and 1931 as infielder with Boston and Brooklyn in National League and Washington, Boston, Detroit, and St. Louis in American League
43	Pat Gillick	1997	Executive with Houston Astros, New York Yankees, Toronto Blue Jays (5 division titles, 2 World Series championships), Baltimore Orioles, and Seattle Mariners
44	John McHale	1997	Founding executive with the Montreal Expos; served as club General Manager from Oct. 1978 to Sept. 1984
45	Canadian AAGPBL players[†]	1998	64 Canadian women ballplayers who performed in the All-American Girls Professional Baseball League (1943–1954)
46	George Lee	1998	Played for 11 different amateur and semi-pro teams, managed 10 clubs, and had a vital role in development of at least six Canadian semi-pro and professional baseball leagues (1890s–1930s)
47	Ron Roncetti	1998	Player, manager, and big league scout over 4 decades (1930s–1960s); founded Leaside (Toronto) Baseball Association
48	Frank Colman	1999	Played half-dozen World War II-era major league seasons as outfielder with Pittsburgh Pirates and New York Yankees
49	Bobby Mattick	1999	Major league manager, scout, and front office executive (1940s–1980s); second Toronto Blue Jays manager (1980–1981)
50	George Sleeman	1999	"Father of Canadian Baseball" who organized first Canadian professional league (1876) and helped establish International Association (1877)
51	Jim Fanning	2000	Scout and executive with Montreal Expos franchise for 25 years; fourth Montreal Expos field manager (1982)
52	Gary Carter	2001	American-born All-Star who hit 220 of 324 career homers as catcher with the Montreal Expos; 2003 inductee to MLB Cooperstown Hall of Fame
53	Dave McKay	2001	Major league infielder; only Canadian player to take part in Toronto Blue Jays' inaugural game (April 7, 1977); played 8 seasons with the Minnesota Twins, Blue Jays, Oakland Athletics
54	Paul Beeston	2002	Executive with Toronto Blue Jays and with Major League Baseball Commissioner's Office
55	Cito Gaston	2002	Batting instructor and later manager with Toronto Blue Jays (4 division titles, 2 pennants, 2 World Series titles)
56	Don McDougall	2002	Founding director, Toronto Blue Jays
57	Dave Shury	2002	Baseball organizer, executive, historian, author (1950s–2000s)
58	Harry Simmons	2002	Executive, historian, writer, schedule maker, baseball rules authority; instrumental in obtaining Montreal Expos franchise for Canada
59	Bill Slack	2002	Brief-career minor league pitcher who later served 50 years as coach and minor league manager with Boston Red Sox, Atlanta Braves, Texas Rangers, and Kansas City Royals organizations
60	Richard Bélec	2003	Organizer of amateur baseball in Quebec and throughout Canada (also internationally) for more than 50 years
61	Joe Carter	2003	American-born slugger who played 6 of 16 major league seasons with Toronto Blue Jays; hero of 1993 World Series with walk-off game-winning home run in deciding game six at Toronto's SkyDome
62	Kirk McCaskill	2003	Pitched 12 seasons for California Angels and Chicago White Sox (after giving up minor league hockey career)
63	Vancouver Asahi[†]	2003	Famed Japanese–Canadian semi-pro team playing from 1914 until closed down by World War II internments
64	André Dawson	2004	American-born All-Star outfielder for 11 seasons with Montreal Expos (6 Gold Gloves); earned 10 additional Gold Glove fielding awards with the Chicago Cubs, Boston Red Sox, and Florida Marlins

	Name	Year	Claim to Fame
65	Peter Hardy	2004	Toronto Blue Jays front office executive; instrumental in acquiring Blue Jays franchise for Canada
66	Joseph "Joe" Lannin	2004	Boston Red Sox owner (1913–1916); born in Lac Beauport, Quebec
67	Jim McKean	2004	Major league umpire (American League, 1974–2000), born and raised in Montreal

No inductees in 1993 or 1994.
* Category: Honorary.
† Category: Honorary team. For individual names and career notes, see http://www.baseballhalloffame.ca under Inductees.

Canada's Amateur Game

Canadian Amateur National Champions

Year	Champion
1989	Québec
1990	Ontario
1991	Ontario
1992	Québec
1993	British Columbia
1994	Saskatchewan
1995	British Columbia
1996	British Columbia
1997	British Columbia
1998	Ontario
1999	Québec
2000	British Columbia
2001	Québec
2002	Alberta

NOTES

1. Quoted by Morris dalla Costa in his report in the *London Free Press* on the 2003 induction ceremony, available at http://www.canoe.ca/Slam030629/col_dallacosta-sun.html.

2. Major League Baseball's historians eventually decided to restore all nineteenth-century records, except where mistakes in arithmetic were uncovered. The present "final word" gives Tip O'Neill a .485 BA for 1887. For details, see Appendix D in the 2004 edition of *Total Baseball*.

3. Roberto Clemente's death in a plane crash off Puerto Rico is recorded as "at sea."

BIBLIOGRAPHY

Books

Bjarkman, Peter C. *The Toronto Blue Jays*. New York: Gallery Books (Brompton-Bison Books and W. H. Smith Publishers), 1990.

Cauz, Louis. *Baseball's Back in Town: From the Don to the Blue Jays, A History of Baseball in Toronto.* Toronto: Controlled Media Corporation, 1977.

Humber, William. *Diamonds of the North: A Concise History of Baseball in Canada.* New York and Toronto: Oxford University Press, 1995.

————— *Cheering for the Home Team: The Story of Baseball in Canada.* Erin, Ontario: The Boston Mill Press, 1983.

Nash, Bruce, and Allan Zullo. *The Baseball Hall of Shame II.* New York: Pocket Books, 1986.

Shearon, Jim. *Canada's Baseball Legends: True Stories of Canadians in the Big Leagues Since 1879.* Kanata, Ontario: Malin Head Press, 1994.

Turner, Dan. *Heroes, Bums and Ordinary Men: Profiles in Canadian Baseball.* Toronto: Doubleday Canada Limited, 1988.

Articles and Chapters

Barney, Robert Knight. "In Search of a Canadian Cooperstown: The Future of the Canadian Baseball Hall of Fame." *Nine: A Journal of Baseball History and Social Policy Perspectives* 1.1 (Fall 1992): 61–78.

Bjarkman, Peter C. "Montreal Expos: Bizarre New Diamond Traditions North of the Border." In *The Encyclopedia of Major League Team Histories—National League,* ed. Peter C. Bjarkman, 263–302. Westport, CT: Meckler Books, 1991.

—————. "Toronto Blue Jays: Okay, Blue Jays! From Worst to First in a Decade." In *The Encyclopedia of Major League Team Histories—American League,* ed. Peter C. Bjarkman, 445–486. Westport, CT: Meckler Books, 1991.

Bouchier, Nancy, and Robert Knight Barney. "A Critical Examination of a Source on Early Ontario Baseball: The Reminiscence of Robert E. Ford." In *Journal of Sport History* 15.1 (Spring 1998): 75–90.

Humber, William. "The Story of Canadian Ballplayers." In *The National Pastime: A Review of Baseball History* 12 (1992): 26–29.

Prentice, Bruce, and Merritt Clifton. "Baseball in Canada." In *Total Baseball: The Official Encyclopedia of Major League Baseball,* 544–548, 6th ed., ed. John Thorn, Pete Palmer, et al. New York: Total Sports Publishing, 1999.

CHAPTER 3

Japan

Besuboru Becomes *Yakyū* in the Land of *Wa*

• •

Amateur baseball competition in Japan dates to about the time the National League was born in the United States, and the country has had professional league play for more than half that span. Such an observation can be offered merely as a matter of perspective, a reminder that the game has had almost as long to develop a national character in Japan as it has in the United States. What was once known on the sprawling Pacific island nation as *besuboru*—a wholescale adaptation of the North American national pastime—has long since been reborn as *yakyū*—an indigenous term best translated "field ball" and less tied to Anglo perspectives on the culture and meaning of the adopted North American sport. But the transformation has been far more than merely linguistic. Japanese fanatics take enough pride in the local term to have enshrined its reported originator (Kanoe Chuma) in their own Cooperstown-like hall of fame. But they have also so thoroughly overhauled the game itself to make it—just like the altered name—something that is very much their own shaping.

Claims are often heard that Japan's professional leagues, now approaching three quarters of a century of continuous play, provide easily the best baseball found anywhere outside of the majors. Such efforts to compare baseball enterprises in various corners of the globe are always fanciful ventures at best, but in this case there seems to be little hard evidence to bolster such claims. Whether judging by mere aesthetics, or taking into account performances of either American pro players abroad or Japanese imports to the big leagues, it is difficult to find arguing points that would place Japan's version of the game ahead of that practiced on the island of Cuba. The problem here for those seeking a fair comparison is that Americans have not played in Cuba for nearly half a century. Nor have Cubans enjoyed much entrée to the U.S. majors during that identical span.

Japan nonetheless boasts a baseball tradition that quite undeniably ranks behind only those of North America (with Canada thrown into the mix) and Cuba in the pecking order of baseball-playing nations. The Dominican Republic has produced far more big league talent, but only because that island has no first-rate league to keep its talented prospects at home. Japan, like Cuba after its 1959 revolution, has preserved the identity of its national pastime by developing its own distinctive traditions in relative isolation from U.S. organized baseball and—at least until Ichiro Suzuki in 2001—keeping all of its biggest stars laboring before local fanatics on the home front.

Pro leagues and heroes have gotten most attention in Japan, at least since World War II, but the country's amateur tradition is (like Cuba's) the true cornerstone of Japan's baseball legacy. Japan has been a major player on the Olympic and World Cup scene of late, but the victories have not been as frequent or glorious as one might expect from a nation with such dedication to the professional version of the national pastime. But the same of course can be said of the United States, which boasts an even weaker history on the diamonds of international play. Japan's international reputation did not begin with Atlanta or Sydney Olympic showings; nor with the shocking upset (pulled off by a team of unheralded collegians) of a strong Team USA club at the 1984 Los Angeles Games. Nor was it launched with the visits of U.S. barnstormers to do battle with Japanese league clubs and university all-star nines between the two world wars. Long before Olympic competitions—either "official" or as a "demonstration" sport—Japanese teams were already scoring impressive victories on amateur fields that underscored both their affinity and their love for the Yankee bat-and-ball game.

ORIGINS OF AMERICA'S GAME IN THE LAND OF THE RISING SUN

A yearning for single inventive geniuses and single moments of creation has provided us with the enduring myth of Abner Doubleday as the inspiration for America's national pastime. Such inspired creators are all the more welcome if they happen to be Americans, as in the popular legend about marines landing on the shores of Cuba ready to instruct the locals in the art of ball-playing. The tale of Japanese baseball sprung entire as Horace Wilson's gift to the island in 1872 is very likely also a literary creation, if one with slightly greater basis in fact.

Wilson certainly had more to do with bringing baseball to Japan than General Doubleday ever did with inventing it in the first place, but he hardly did so single-handedly, as commonly reported. Cricket had been seen in Japan as early as 1864, when British army and navy recruits performed an exhibition match in Yokohama. In the early 1870s, there seem to have been a few American missionaries and teachers—and even one Brit—who tried their hands at teaching the finer points of the American game to their charges in Tokyo. G. H. Mudgett and Leroy James were the Americans who joined Horace Wilson in the enterprise of baseball instruction, and an Englishman named F. W. Strange also seems to have been active in such proselytizing. As in Cuba, however, some of the credit likely goes to local residents returning from study in the United States with the game and its equipment proudly in tow. Baseball in Japan seems to have received its first substantial boost not so much from Wilson and his fellow Americans as from local convert Hiraoka Hiroashi, a supervisor in the Ministry of Engineering and a former U.S. college student, who in 1878 organized Tokyo railway employees into what was probably the first active Japanese baseball team.

From its earliest days, the Japanese game was oriented toward college and high school teams. Japanese baseball was first discovered by Americans during early college tours, which took place in both directions. The game was introduced to the Japanese school system in the 1880s as an ideal form of physical training that also taught important cultural values of community spirit and team play. The competitive nature of the sport received a boost when students of the First Higher School (Ichiko) of Tokyo formed a team in 1890 and then challenged Americans at the Yokohama Athletic Club. Ichiko first embarrassed the Americans, 29–4. When the wounded pride of the Yokohama Athletic Club group drove them to recruit ringers from visiting U.S. naval vessels, the unfazed Japanese students simply won again—thus greatly contributing to both national pride and the emergence of baseball as a national passion.

Waseda Imperial University staged a landmark baseball tour in 1904. That summer, Waseda and Keio college teams both visited the United States to play on the West Coast against Stanford and other U.S. institutions of higher learning. Unfortunately, the tour served as much to reinforce stereotypes in the United States about Asians as it did to foster baseball diplomacy. Newspaper accounts of the tour on the West Coast quaintly described the Japanese players and marveled at their lack of sophistication concerning the proper wearing of spiked shoes. Back home in Japan, return tours of U.S. college clubs stimulated further interest in the game and at the same time fine-tuned local skills. A Tokyo Big Six University League was founded in 1925, and its highly competitive tournaments further bolstered the college-level enthusiasms for the sport.

Japan soon also became a favorite barnstorming venue for U.S. pro contingents in the early 1930s. Babe Ruth's celebrated tour with Lefty O'Doul and Lou Gehrig in 1934 is especially noteworthy. Huge crowds greeted the American delegation in Yokohama harbor, and it was a good guess that they were there more to see the Bambino than to catch a glimpse of even such famed fellow travelers as Gehrig, Charlie Gehringer, Earl Averill, Connie Mack, Lefty Gomez, and Jimmy Foxx. According to reports, more than a million later turned out for a cavalcade through the streets of Tokyo's Ginza district, with Ruth in the lead car. The crowds didn't subside when the games began, with more than 100,000 cramming their way into Tokyo's Meiji Stadium for one contest. The Americans again mostly breezed through 18 games. Ruth delighted fans by blasting 13 homers, as well as with such stunts as playing right field holding an umbrella during the torrential downpour that drenched one game. For Japanese fans, there was also one marvelous moment stoking national pride, when an unheard of 18-year-old native high schooler pinned back American ears by striking out the mighty Bambino three straight times and also mowing down future Cooperstown legends Gehringer, Ruth, Gehrig, and Foxx in succession. An instant folk hero, Eiji Sawamura lost his dream game in the seventh when Gehrig broke a 0–0 tie by smashing the novice's hanging curve into the bleachers. A marvelous diving catch by Bing Miller an inning later salvaged the 1–0 American victory. What started out as hero worship of Ruth

Colorful enthusiastic grandstand crowds add to the special flavor of Japanese *besuboro*. [Transcendental Graphics]

and Gehrig and their companions ended up with hundreds of thousands of newly minted Japanese ball fans celebrating a first genuine pitching hero of their very own.

It was Lefty O'Doul, a Pacific Coast League star slugger and National League batting champion with the Phillies in the 1920s, who gave Japanese baseball its biggest promotional boost. O'Doul made more than twenty trips to Japan, beginning in the 1930s (when, with his assistance, Matsutaro Shoriki founded the nation's first professional club) and culminating in his efforts to restore the Japanese sport in the aftermath of World War II. O'Doul's first visit to Japan came as part of a 1931 tour by big league all-stars who arrived in October after a two-week luxury cruise arranged by Shoriki, owner of the Yomiuri newspaper chain. Loaded with such familiar names as Gehrig, Lefty Grove, Mickey Cochrane, Frankie Frisch, Rabbit Maranville, and Al Simmons, the U.S. squad swept 17 games against university teams, commercial league teams, and an Nippon all-star team put together by Shoriki. One historical highlight was an injury to Gehrig, who was hit by a pitch in a 2–0 win over Keio University; the Yankees star was forced to sit out the rest of the barnstorming tour—the only games he would miss during his 15-year iron-man stint in the American League. Despite the 17 defeats in 17 games—some of them surprisingly close losses—the 1931 visit by O'Doul and Gehrig and company was a resounding success for Japanese baseball forces. More than 450,000 crammed sold-out stadiums, gate revenues, and newspaper sales soared during the tour, and the only real disappointment was that the greatest ball-playing idol of all, Babe Ruth, had turned down Shoriki's invitation to accompany the American team. When

Ruth relented and joined the next tour three years later, the final steps in converting the Japanese public to baseball fanaticism were all but assured.

An interesting legend also attaches to journeyman catcher and reputed undercover spy Moe Berg during O'Doul's second visit of 1932 to coach Big Six college teams. O'Doul had established his credentials with the Japanese by batting above .600 during the 1931 tour headlined by Gehrig. He now brought along catcher Berg and White Sox pitcher Ted Lyons to tutor young Tokyo college athletes in the finer points of the sport (O'Doul himself teaching batting). Berg appeared to fall in love with Japanese culture, quickly acquired the language (the intellectual backstop spoke a half-dozen tongues), and toured Tokyo's historical cites in his spare time. It was later rumored that the spy in baseball drag had also spent time photographing the city from the roof of St. Luke's International Hospital, photos said to have been a major intelligence source during bombing raids of the city at the height of World War II.

CAPSULE HISTORY OF THE JAPANESE PROFESSIONAL LEAGUES

Professional baseball in Japan began in 1934 with the birth of the Yomiuri Giants as a corporate team. Matsutaro Shoriki, the Yomiuri newspaper mogul, was the driving force behind founding the All-Japan team that would eventually evolve into the Tokyo Kyojin (Giants). The team toured widely, featuring the young Sawamura and another young pitcher, Victor Starffin. (Legend has it that Lefty O'Doul christened the club with the Giants name. Shoriki had wanted to call them the Great Japan Tokyo Baseball Club, until O'Doul intervened with a more fitting baseball name.) The All-Japan all-stars even paid a visit to American shores, when O'Doul assisted Shoriki in arranging an ambitious 110-game tour. The newly named Giants captured 75 games, played mostly against minor league clubs, and Shoriki reaped the benefits with elaborate play-by-play coverage in his newspapers back home. There had been earlier efforts at pro teams, but now, on the heels of O'Doul's three major league barnstorming tours (1931, 1932, and 1934), the environment was much improved. Shoriki was soon encouraging other businesses to form their own teams as well. The result was the pro league that in 1936 kicked off its first short season of play. The first few years saw both summer and winter campaigns. The league quickly settled into a circuit of between six and eight teams, which thrived until the final years of World War II.

Although the pro league shut down with the bombing of Tokyo in 1945, the American general Douglas MacArthur encouraged its reactivation in the postwar years. A big boost was provided when Lefty O'Doul returned in 1949, heading a Pacific Coast League All-Star club for yet another morale-boosting tour of Nippon ballparks. By the start of the 1950s, the new circuit was split into two rival leagues. With their Yomiuri Giants and their huge corporate advertising enterprises, the Central League became the fan favorite, but there were stars and competitive teams in the Pacific League as well.

Much of the history of the Japanese circuits in the 1950s and 1960s is the history of the Yomiuri Giants, who dominated the annual Japanese Series, first with slugger Tetsuharu Kawakami and later with Kawakami in the manager's seat and new stars Sadaharu Oh and Shigeo Nagashima in the lineup. Nagashima was the "Golden Boy" and always seemed to overshadow the even more productive Oh. The latter had to settle for the glory of merely breaking slugging records, because Nagashima reeled in the bulk of celebrity attention. Before the two decades were over, the Giants had achieved the unprecedented feat of nine straight Japanese Series wins, a string unrivaled in all professional sports.

Pitching has always outweighed hitting in Japanese baseball. This tradition was born early, with the heroic performance of Sawamura against big league sluggers in 1934, and was carried to the earliest pro seasons by Sawamura himself and also by Starffin. The dominance of pitching was especially evident in early league seasons during the late 1930s and throughout the 1940s. Thirty-game winners were not at all rare. Pitchers logged huge totals of innings, and many of them were eventually burned out in short order by such reckless overuse.

When there have been top hitters in Japan, they have often been spectacular. Lack of hitting power is a standard criticism of the Japanese style of play, but home run hitting has always been part of the game in smaller Japanese ballparks, and by the 1950s some strong sluggers with unique hitting styles were suddenly coming along. Kawakami was the first of the lot. Hiroshi Oshita and Futoshi Nakanishi also fit the mold in the late 1940s and on into the era of two separate leagues, but slow-footed catcher Katsuya Nomura was the first American-style home run basher. The tradition was thus well established by the time Nagashima joined the Giants lineup in 1958 and Oh signed on in 1959. Oh was originally a pitcher and then a converted first baseman with a flawed swing. His famed heron-style of one-leg batting came about in a disciplined effort to correct this flaw. The result was to unleash a Ruthian-style slugger on previously pitching-oriented Japanese baseball.

Joe DiMaggio and Lefty O'Doul honored during their 1951 Tokyo barnstorming tour. [Transcendental Graphics]

Big leaguers and other U.S. imports have had an important impact on the Japanese league record book. Most of the *gaijin* (as Japanese call the foreigners) have been huge disappointments, like Don Newcombe and Larry Doby in the 1960s and Joe Pepitone and Bob Horner in the 1970s and 1980s—but there have been some who flourished. Don Blasingame was a long-time regular. Daryl Spencer introduced a more aggressive playing style. And Leron Lee, Boomer Wells, and Randy Bass challenged the slugging records of Nagashima, Nomura, and Sadaharu Oh.

The homegrown heroes have always made the greatest legends, nonetheless, and there were plenty of these, even in the years before the interruptions caused by global war. Early landmark moments included Haruyasu Nakajima winning a first triple crown (1938) and Starffin ringing up remarkable pitching numbers in the late 1930s. Sawamura might well have matched Starffin, but he died nobly in the war. Japan's version of the Cy Young trophy was subsequently named in his honor.

The new strengths of the two pro leagues were soon evidenced by an increase in successes against big league barnstormers in the 1960s and 1970s. The World Champion Brooklyn Dodgers lost four games in 1956, a startling number (despite 12 wins) compared with earlier tours, which were nearly always sweeps for the big leaguers. The biggest breakthrough for Japanese forces came against the Dodgers—now in Los Angeles—when the big leaguers barely scraped out a series win, nine games to eight. Two years later the San Francisco Giants actually lost a series. In 1974, the Mets barely broke even in their tour, one year after reigning as National League champs.

A most special feature of *besuboru* Japanese league-style is an emphasis on ritual and conditioning—a strange component of the sport to most Americans. The conditioning regimen is so detailed that it seems to wear Japanese players down and to diminish performance, but the emphasis is always on factors of team unity and internal self discipline. The contrast in styles has had a strong impact on American *gaijin* struggling to fit into the Japanese game, and few American imports have successfully adapted to the ways of Japanese baseball.

For all its uniqueness, Japanese professional baseball has been slowly becoming Americanized in recent decades. This is not surprising, considering the long tradition of barnstorming visits by U.S. pro teams and also the increasing prevalence of U.S. imports on Japanese rosters. It was perhaps only a matter of time until the more practical American approaches to ruthless winning would begin to have their appeal over

International baseball's all-time home run king Sadaharu Oh, with his "heron stance." [Transcendental Graphics]

often self-defeating ritualistic approaches and gentlemanly sportsmanship.

The first major compromises with an American style of ball-playing seemed to have appeared in the 1960s, innovations copied from actions by *gaijin* performing on Japanese League teams. Former big leaguer Daryl Spencer is reputed to have spawned one of these minor revolutions when he introduced the take-out slide during his Japanese sojourn in the 1964 season. A few years later it was a Japanese pitcher, Masanori Murakami, seasoned by a cup-of-coffee trial with the San Francisco Giants, who threw what was reported to be the league's first-ever brush-back pitch. With the adoption of American approaches to the game, the Japanese version based on "scientific ball" and a strict code of ethics was quickly becoming supplanted by a far rougher approach.

The biggest changes came with the introduction of power hitting, also a product of the 1960s, and credited largely to the innovations of a single local slugging hero named Sadaharu Oh. Oh did for Japanese baseball in the 1960s what Babe Ruth had done in the Roaring Twenties in the big leagues—popularizing a new long-ball swinging style that converted the sport from one of pitching and "scientific play" to muscular fence busting. And, just like Ruth, Oh fostered a style that soon had its numerous disciples. Japanese parks are indeed smaller and favor the long ball at an especially high level, but still pitching had always ruled in Japan before Oh changed the tactics. Japanese baseball after Oh had left far behind its earlier Dead Ball Era.

Oh brought his new slugging style to the fore through an approach that was in strict accord with Japanese adaptations of the sport of baseball. Oh's slugging was based far more on his mental preparation than on any physical approach to the game. In this sense, he was the perfect prototype of genuine Japanese baseball.

One result of the changes in the Japanese playing approach after the 1960s was a far more balanced competition between Japanese all-stars and touring U.S. major league teams. The more competitive nature of Japanese baseball also extended to the amateur ranks, where a national team made history by sweeping a touring Team USA in summer 1999 barnstorming games. A second inevitable result has been increasing numbers of Japanese players ready for spots on major league rosters. These now include position players like Ichiro, So Taguchi, and Hideki Matsui—not just pitchers like Hideo Nomo, Kazuhiro Sasaki, and Makoto Suzuki. Japanese leagues today seem at a turning point, with continued MLB inroads both strengthening and weakening Nippon baseball. The fear of course is that increased peddling of televised major league games featuring expatriate Japanese players will eventually cut into Japanese League gate receipts.

JAPAN IN WORLD AMATEUR BASEBALL

At least since the mid-1990s, Japanese national teams have loomed as a far greater threat to continued Cuban dominance on the international scene than either Team USA or the strictly pro-baseball-oriented Dominicans. Japan had sent shock waves through Olympic baseball circles as early as 1984, when a team composed largely of unseasoned college players upended a powerful U.S. squad filled with future big leaguers in the Olympic gold medal game in Dodger Stadium. An unknown Atsunori Ito was the pitching hero of a 6–3 win decided by a three-run eighth-inning homer off the bat of first baseman Katsumi Hirosawa. It was only a demonstration match—baseball was still eight years from becoming an official Olympic event—and the victory was further muted by the fact that Cuba had remained on the sidelines as part of the Soviet Bloc boycott of the Los Angeles Games, but victory over an American squad that included the likes of Will Clark, Mark McGwire, Barry Larkin, Bobby Witt, and Billy Swift was heady stuff for the Japanese team of unknowns that did not include a single professional Japanese leaguer in its nearly anonymous lineup. It was apparently time for Team USA and the rest of the international baseball community to start taking the Japanese amateurs seriously.

Cuba would begin learning that lesson a decade later, though the full demonstration of latent Japanese power did not become apparent until the Intercontinental Cup matches of 1997 in Barcelona. Five years earlier, when Barcelona had hosted the first official Olympic baseball tournament, Japan had stumbled against Cuba and Taipei, and the retooled Japanese now took their revenge. The Cubans were still riding high after the 1996 Atlanta sweep that had maintained their decade-long undefeated string. All streaks end, however, and this one came crashing down against a previously unknown Japanese hurler in Barcelona's Intercontinental Cup finals.

The Intercontinental Cup has been an especially friendly venue for Japanese teams from the outset, beginning with the very first edition of this newest major international tournament, staged in Italy during the summer of 1973 and captured by a Japanese squad led by ace pitcher Kojiro Ikegaya. Ikegaya would develop as a major star for the Central League Hiroshima Carp, where he would pace the circuit with 20 victories only three years down the road. In Italy, Ikegaya won a pair of games and failed to give up an earned run as the Japanese contingent dropped only a single game (1–0 to the Americans) and finished at the top of the pack with a 6–1 ledger, a game better than the U.S. and Puerto Rican squads. Without Cuba in the field the victory might be seen as somewhat hollow, but it nonetheless launched a string of 1970s successes in the Intercontinental Cup games, including two eventual silver medals and one bronze. The Japanese would also ring up five more top-three finishes in the Intercontinental Cup before their startling Barcelona breakthrough against the Cubans in 1997.

In Barcelona, the Cubans looked as strong as ever when they twice defeated an ill-prepared U.S. team, but they collapsed in the finals under a 16-hit Japanese barrage. A big hero was young pitcher Kohji Uehara, whose performance in the finals against Cuban bats triggered a raft of pro offers. For Cuba, it was a devastating loss, one that promptly sent heads rolling back in Havana. The Cuban head coach and baseball commissioner were both sent packing—as was the national team's technical director—all on the heels of the single upset loss to underappreciated Japan.

Japan also fared well in the first three Olympics tournaments. Two losses to a surprisingly strong Taipei squad in Barcelona in 1992 left the Nippon team out of the gold medal hunt—Taipei's ace, after beating Japan in the semis, would sign on with the Hanshin Tigers—but a solid win over the Americans assured a bronze medallion on the final day of action. Atlanta in 1996 was a special high point for Japanese Olympic baseball. Going in, Team USA had expected to face-off with the rival Cubans, a dream that ended in the drubbing the Japanese administered to the home forces. Team Japan quickly knocked out future big leaguer Kris Benson to break American hearts. The finals against the

Cubans witnessed a tight game until the late innings, when Cuban bats awoke to settle the issue by a lopsided 13–9 count. In Sydney in 2000, Cuba defeated Japan on the path to the gold medal final with a special pitching performance from José Contreras, only two years before his surprise defection to the majors. Contreras had never lost an international game, and the Cubans selected him for the semifinals because they considered the Japan team a greater threat than the Americans—a plan that of course backfired. Japan meanwhile never recovered from the loss to the Cubans and let a bronze medal slip through their fingers against Korea, their first medal failure. In those first three Olympic Games, the Japanese squad was always in on the final medals competition.

Japan has never won a World Cup but did enter the field as early as 1972 in Nicaragua. Over the years, Team Nippon has broken into the medals field on four different occasions but only once (Korea in 1982) reached the gold medal showdown game. A major step forward for the Japanese program came when Tokyo hosted the World Cup event in 1980 and the locals captured a bronze, but the last few tournaments have been more disappointing. The most recent World Cup matches in Havana brought a particular subpar performance after the Japanese Federation left most of its best players at home to tune for an upcoming Olympic Qualifier. The end result was a semifinal loss to a good but not stellar Panama team.

Amateur baseball has always demanded devoted attention in Japan, with early traditions of strong college teams preceding the popularity of the post–World War II pro game. The semiannual national high school tournaments are still one of the showcases of the nation's sporting scene. School baseball has a grip in Japan that parallels U.S. collegiate football bowl games or the NCAA basketball tournament. There is extensive television coverage of school games, and many of the recruits into the Central and Pacific Leagues are signed off high school and college campuses. It is not at all surprising, then, that Japan has enjoyed success in the world amateur tournaments through the years. The country—like Cuba—does not have its sights set narrowly and exclusively on professional league versions of the sport.

Recent performances in world tourneys with pros now in the lineup have, ironically, cast some doubts concerning the current strength of the Japanese pro leagues. It might have been expected that the entry of baseball into Olympic tournaments (a move in the end largely orchestrated by the United States) would have benefited the Japanese every bit as much as it did the Americans, Dominicans, and Mexicans. The Sydney Olympics did not seem to point in that direction. Recently, Athens 2004 provided a still bigger disappointment when a top Japanese League all-star squad was knocked from the gold medal game with a 1–0 blanking at the hands of the previously tame Aussies. Even with players drawn from top pro rosters, the Japanese have not seemed so far to gain much if any ground on the still nominally amateur Cuban powerhouse teams.

JAPANESE BIG LEAGUE INVASION

Masanori Murakami was a man far ahead of his time when he appeared in nine games and fifteen innings with the San Francisco Giants during the 1964

National League season. A refugee from the Pacific League's Nankai Hawks, the slender 6' lefty was a controversial pioneer when he surfaced as the first-ever Japanese native in the U.S. majors. Murakami and two other Pacific League prospects had been innocently loaned that year to the Giants' Fresno farm club for seasoning, and when Masanori displayed more than expected promise he was called to the big club for a late-season trial. The Giants front office management was impressed enough to offer a renewed contract for 1965, but Nankai officials recalled their wayward pitcher. In subsequent wrangling over the prized lefty, Commissioner Ford Frick went so far as to sever relations with Japanese baseball. A compromise eventually returned Murakami to San Francisco for one additional season (during which he won four of five decisions and struck out 85 in only 45 frames) before he reentered Pacific League action for a largely mediocre late career interrupted by one stellar 1968 season (18–4, 2.38 ERA).

It would be 30 seasons before another native son of Japan would appear in the uniform of a big league ball club. Murakami's successes might have been an early foreshadowing of things to come in the form of Nomo, Ichiro, and a fireballing reliever named Kazuhiro Sasaki, but Japan's earliest gift to the majors disappeared swiftly from the scene and the promise was not realized for decades. The explanation of course is that Japan was not a cheap talent source like the Dominican Republic or Venezuela, where teenaged prospects could be found on sandlots ready to sign up for pocket change and desperately bent on seeking their athletic dreams in America. Japan's pro leagues have long resembled the Mexican circuit, with teams jealously guarding their franchise players and refusing to let talent simply slip through their fingers. A current working agreement with organized baseball—in effect since 1998—requires U.S. clubs to bid for rights to negotiate with Pacific League or Central League players and only then when permission or free agency is (it seems at whim) granted.

The divide between the majors and Japanese baseball is much greater still, because Japanese baseball is almost as far removed culturally from its American counterpart as cricket is from baseball or soccer from football.

Long after Murakami appeared as a blip on the baseball radar in San Francisco, it was a Los Angeles Dodgers 1995 rookie who belatedly launched the small Japanese invasion that has at long last begun to enrich major league baseball. Hideo Nomo arrived on the National League scene with a $2 million contract, made possible only because Nomo's Kintetsu team had carelessly released him in a salary dispute after four super-successful Pacific League seasons. The Osaka native with the unusual twirling right-handed delivery enjoyed overnight success in Los Angeles, conjuring up images of a another Dodger import of 14 years before, Fernando Valenzuela, and even launching a minor craze of parallel "Nomomania." Japanese photographers and journalists flooded U.S. ballparks to record and report every move of the hot rookie, who posted a stellar 13–6 freshman mark and even took the All-Star game mound as the National League starter. Nomo's blitz of National League batters continued for two additional seasons and included a remarkable feat of hurling a no-hitter at the powerful Colorado Rockies lineup in Denver's hitter-friendly Coors Field.

Arthroscopic surgery slowed Nomo's career after 1997, but the door had now been cracked open for other brave Nippon hopefuls. Between 1996 and 1998, four additional top pitchers escaped Japan via the free agent route into the major leagues. Kobe's right-hander Makoto "Mac" Suzuki was first on the scene but saw only limited duty over four years with Seattle before posting a more substantial 8–10 log in 2000 with Kansas City. Masato Yoshii signed as a high-priced free agent with the Mets after fulfilling his contract with the Central League champion Yakult Swallows. Two-time Pacific League ERA pacesetter Hideki Irabu created the biggest stir when he sat out a year in Japan while his contract expired with the Chiba Lotte Marines and then set off a bidding war between the Yankees and the San Diego Padres. Irabu never achieved much beyond journeyman status in six subsequent big league seasons with New York, Montreal, and Texas, posting a 34–35 losing ledger and a stratospheric 5.15 career ERA; nonetheless, he did attract enough media attention as a high-priced free agent acquisition to further gild the newly felt presence of a handful of Japanese big leaguers.

The Japanese invasion started with pitchers (Nomo, Mac Suzuki, Yoshii), but by 2001 the first position players had also graduated from the Japanese circuits into the majors. Ichiro Suzuki—seven-time batting champ with the Orix Blue Wave—created a large-scale furor with his hitting and fielding that dwarfed earlier "Nomomania" by a wide margin. And, although Ichiro broke new ground as opening-day right fielder in the Seattle Mariners lineup on April 2, 2001 (and would soon become American League Rookie of the Year), he didn't crack the position-player barrier all that much in advance of several other talented countrymen. Tsuyoshi Shinjo, formerly of the Central League Hanshin Tigers, took up a spot in the New York Mets lineup one day after Ichiro's debut in Seattle. A season later, another outfielder, So Taguchi (a former Blue Wave teammate of Ichiro), hit .400 in his opening 19-game trial with the St. Louis Cardinals. By 2003, the 29-year-old Yomiuri Giants slugger Hideki Matsui was walking off with runner-up honors for American League Rookie of the Year in the outfield of the league champion New York Yankees. But it was the 200-plus hits and American League batting crown garnered by Ichiro in 2001 that arguably made the single-name Seattle superstar the most significant among all Japanese recruits to date.

Closer Kazuhiro Sasaki has also recently added to Japanese luster in Seattle. If Sasaki had come onto the big league scene a bit earlier, he might have been a much bigger star than he now is likely to be. Number one on the all-time career saves list (with 210) when he departed from the Yokohama Bay Stars, Sasaki was already 33 when he took up a finisher's role in the Mariners bullpen, one in which he would earn 129 big league saves in just 4 seasons (2000–2003). Already flashing a 100-mile-per-hour fastball, a tantalizing forkball, and a reputation as nearly unhittable by the time he saved a record 45 games for Yokohama in 1998, the 6'4" power hurler had to bide his time back home for several seasons before free agent status would allow him to become a big leaguer. Sasaki returned to Japan and apparent retirement after the 2003 season, but his spot is about to be inherited by Japan's new all-time career saves leader, Shingo Takatsu, who recently signed a $1 million one-year deal with the Chicago White Sox.

Beyond these luminaries, Japanese who have made the grade have still been preciously few. At the start of the 2004 major league season, the inventory of Japanese-born big leaguers totaled twenty-five, seven of them Americans born in Japan. But the door opened by stars like Ichiro, Nomo, Matsui, and Sasaki can reasonably be expected soon to let through front-line Japanese League talent in ever-increasing numbers.

The threat of all this player movement across the Pacific to the future health of Japanese baseball is difficult to assess. Perhaps the traditional handful of *gaijin* players will balance out the superstar or two lost to higher-bidding American clubs, and perhaps the occasional big league game staged in the Tokyo Dome and the televising of big league matches to the Japanese islands will stimulate fan interest more than they deplete local ballpark attendance. Perhaps there will even someday be a major league team housed in Tokyo, as Major League Baseball runs out of expansion options in North America. But all this is still hard to imagine, let alone predict. Increased defection of top Japanese prospects could just as easily be disastrous for Central and Pacific League attendance (and thus for the overall health of the venerable national pastime) if fans tire of seeing their most exciting stars spirited away to play in a distant league in a distant land. Ichiro may yet prove either the salvation or the ruination of Japanese professional baseball.

It is clear that Japanese pro baseball today suffers a myriad of problems, most of them financial. League games now have a television rival in big league games featuring an increasingly large contingent of top Japanese stars performing on U.S. teams. A sagging economy has damaged player salaries, thus providing still more impetus for player defections. By the end of the 1990s, average Japanese league salaries approached $400,000 yen, but the wealthy Yomiuri Giants had a payroll topping that of the San Diego Padres or Pittsburgh Pirates, and three top stars—Sasaki, Ichiro, and Giants first baseman Kazuhiro Kiyohara—were each drawing over $2 million. There was also a troublesome imbalance between the strong Central League (featuring the crowd-pleasing Giants) and the weaker Pacific League (with small stadiums and fewer high-profile players). Proposals have recently been made to bring renewed health to the game. For example, to combat attendance inequities the Pacific League has repeatedly pushed for revenue sharing, interleague play, or even total merger of the two circuits—but the wealthier Central League clubs have rebuffed any suggestion of alterations in the traditional league power structure. Evidence so far is that Japanese club owners are no more willing to share their wealth or to compromise on rules of governance than narrow-sighted U.S. big league owners are.

JAPAN'S GREATEST PLAYERS

Despite the twin curses of pre-1947 racial segregation and post-1962 political isolation, Cuban League stars have far more currency among fans of the U.S. majors than do the legends of Japanese League action. After all, there were Cubans of some stature in the majors before Castro's closed-door policies took hold late in the 1960s and early in the 1970s: Tiant, Pérez, Campaneris, Cuéllar, and Oliva followed close on the heels of Miñoso, Ramos, Pascual, and Willie

Miranda. There was only a single little-noted cup-of-coffee visitor to the majors from the Land of the Rising Sun before Hideo Nomo swept over Los Angeles and the National League in 1995; the total roster of Japanese leaguers crossing the Pacific for major league assignments now—a decade after Nomo—barely outstrips the number of Cuban national team defectors over the same span.

Beyond Ichiro, Nomo, and Hideki Matsui, few casual American fans would likely recognize any Japanese baseball name other than Sadaharu Oh—and then they might have trouble placing Oh's accomplishment as baseball's greatest home run producer in its proper decade or identifying the legendary Central League team he played for. But even Sadaharu Oh is not the sum total of Japanese baseball lore, any more than Martín Dihigo is all of Cuban baseball or Héctor Espino the only boasting point of Mexican baseball. Hideo Nomo, for all his mastery of big league batters, would not likely make any all-time top-ten list of pro pitching legends back home. The Japanese League heroes profiled here (including American transplant Randy Bass) offer a perspective on a hidden corner of the world baseball saga as enthralling and inspiring and entertaining as any. Their accomplishments only serve to underscore the lost appreciations suffered by an American baseball fandom whose horizons are bordered by Boston on the east, Miami on the south, and Los Angeles on the western front. At the same time they provide further proof that parallel baseball universes are indeed alive and still doing exceedingly well.

Randy Bass (b. March 13, 1954).   Foreign ballplayers, or *gaijin*, have for years played a part in Japan's national pastime. Many of the biggest name major league retreads and washouts to visit Nippon, however, have been Japanese League disasters who earned only scorn and ridicule for their inability to adjust to the team-oriented Japanese game. Among the "U-turn" *gaijin* (as John Holway[1] once labeled them) were Joe Pepitone, Kevin Mitchell, Cecil Fielder, Bob Horner, and Pete Incaviglia, muscled sluggers all more famed in Tokyo as unproductive whiners or shameful roughnecks disrespectful of the genteel Japanese playing style. One clear exception was major league short-stinter Randy Bass, a cup-of-coffee San Diego Padres and Texas Rangers first base-man who in the mid-1980s reemerged in the Hanshin Tigers lineup as arguably the biggest-impact foreigner in Japanese league history, and perhaps also the most popular American ballplayer on the Japanese scene. The red-headed and bearded Bass earned his lasting fame in The Land of the Rising Sun when he broke out with back-to-back Central League triple crowns in the mid-1980s, the same season that native bad boy Hiromitsu Ochiai was pulling an identical feat over in the rival Pacific League. The first of these prolific seasons ended in dramatic controversy when Bass was walked four straight times in the season's finale by the Yomiuri Giants, managed by Sadaharu Oh—when Bass that particular day needed just one homer to tie Oh's single-season league record. Otherwise, Randy Bass's career total of 202 homers in Japan fell well short of Leron Lee's 283 mark, and his 743 career hits were about half of what Lee amassed. George Altman and Boomer Wells were other Americans who slugged more long balls than Bass on Japanese soil. But none matched Bass's popularity with the Japanese press and none earned the extensive commercial contracts that came to Bass on the heels of his double triple-crown feat. That

Randy Bass was never more than a journeyman in the majors is a fact that has often been used by those who would downplay the level of Japanese league competition—but that type of argument usually signals little of substance, as demonstrated by the hundreds of examples of big leaguers who soar in one league (Sammy Sosa, for example, after being transplanted from the Rangers and White Sox to the Cubs) after long treading water in the other.

Yutaka Fukumoto (b. 1947).   Fleet Hankyu Braves outfielder Yutaka Fukumoto was Japan's Rickey Henderson and Lou Brock on the basepaths as Nippon's unrivaled stolen base king. As a 1970 rookie, the 5'6" speedster launched a string of 13 straight base stealing titles that stands unparalleled in any known pro league; across that stretch, his steals-to-attempts ratio of nearly 80 percent (.781) was higher than marks which Ty Cobb, Maury Wills, or Brock rang up. He is also reported to have stolen six times in seven attempts versus Hall-of-Famer Johnny Bench during a Cincinnati Reds barnstorming tour against Japanese Leaguers in the late 1970s. Fukumoto's 1972 single-season record of 106 stands worthy of respect alongside Maury Wills's 104, Vince Coleman's 107—and even next to Brock's and Henderson's loftier totals, considering it was achieved in a much shorter 130-game schedule and with Fukumoto actually playing in only 122 contests that year. The Hankyu Greyhound topped the 90-steals level in two other seasons, and his career mark of 1,065 stood as an unofficial twentieth-century world record until it was finally overtaken in 1993 by Henderson. Fukumoto might very well still be placed on an exact par with Henderson as the most successful base stealer of all time when one considers that the Japanese speedster's 1,065 pilfers were logged in only 2,401 games (one steal per 2.25 games); it took Henderson an almost precisely equivalent 3,081 games to ring up his own much higher mark of 1,406 (one steal per 2.19 games).

Masaichi Kaneda (b. August 1, 1933).   In a land known for stellar pitchers, Masaichi Kaneda rewrote most of the pages of the Japanese league record books between 1950 and 1969 with a lifetime 400–298 ledger that includes still-standing marks for complete games (365), strikeouts (4,490), and innings pitched (5,526). One of only two Japanese league pitchers with better than 5,000 innings of work, Kaneda logged enough time on the hill to also hold the national record for bases on balls surrendered and to trail the immortal Victor Starffin by only a single whitewash in the career shutouts category. The slim 6'1" Korean-born southpaw—known widely during his career as "The Golden Arm" for reasons that are altogether transparent—is the only Japanese league hurler to amass 400 victories, an achievement that places him alongside Walter Johnson and Cy Young in one of pro baseball's most exclusive circles. Kaneda's unmatched career resumé also includes all of the following: Central League pacesetter in victories on three occasions, three Central League ERA crowns, a pair of no-hitters (one a perfect game), and three coveted Sawamura awards as Japan's top pitcher. Stuck in the rotation of the weak-sister Kokutetsu Swallows during his early career years, the incomparable Kaneda luckily joined the roster of the powerhouse and popular Yomiuri Giants in mid-career, a move which allowed him to contribute to 5 Central League pennant victories and 5 consecutive

Japanese Series crowns near career's end. Election to Japan's version of Cooperstown (in 1988) was a foregone conclusion for a pitcher whose one-time string of 64 consecutive shutout innings has never been equaled at any level of North American or Caribbean organized professional baseball.

Tetsuharu Kawakami (b. March 23, 1920). While Russian-born Vic Starffin was earning his unparalleled reputation on the hill, Giants teammate Tetsuharu Kawakami was constructing his own native legend as Japan's first great home-grown batting hero. Playing in a pitching-dominated era and practicing the mental art of Zen a decade before Sadaharu Oh, the self-proclaimed "God of Batting" slugged regularly over the .300 level with his magical red-colored lumber and in 1941 won a batting crown with a .310 mark (he was the league's only hitter above .270!). A two-decade career average of .313—still fifth best in seventy years of league annals—made the 5'9" lefty the first recognized world-class hitter created out of the new experiment of Japanese professional baseball. He hit over the high-water .300 mark thirteen times, captured five batting crowns, two home run titles, and three RBI titles alongside a trio of Most Valuable Player trophies. Upon retirement, he distinguished himself still further as Giants manager, leading a club with slugging stars Sadaharu Oh and Shigeo Nagashima—the country's two most popular players ever—to an almost unimaginable 11 Japan Series championships in a span of 14 years. And he did so steadfastly refusing to carry any foreign imports on his totally Japanese-flavored roster. In the end, it was Kawakami's fate nonetheless to be perhaps best remembered as the man replaced in the Yomiuri Giants lineup by Sadaharu Oh.

Sachio Kinugasa (b. 1947). If Oh seems to be some rare mythical combination of Babe Ruth and Hank Aaron, then Sachio Kinugasa (two-decade utility player with the Hiroshima Carp from the mid-1960s to the late 1980s) remains the Japanese iron-man version of Lou Gehrig grafted onto Baltimore's Cal Ripken Jr. An exceptionally durable performer, mostly at third and in the outfield, Kinugasa contributed as an offensive force with a 1984 RBI title and was also Most Valuable Player of the Central League that same season. Filling in anywhere he was needed, Kinugasa contributed substantially to five Central League pennants and three Hiroshima triumphs in the postseason Japan Series. But it was his iron-man feats that most impressed and that have been responsible for his niche in league history. Breaking into the starting lineup on October 18, 1970, and not retiring until 1987, the Carp workhorse rang up 2,215 consecutive games to outstrip Gehrig's celebrated durability feat almost a decade before Cal Ripken. Ripken's much celebrated surpassing of Gehrig on September 6, 1995 was a much needed feel-good event for Major League Baseball in the wake of an image-clouding 1994 player strike, but Baltimore's dependable shortstop did not become baseball's true iron man until he finally caught up to Kinugasa several months into the following 1996 season.

Shigeo Nagashima (b. February 20, 1936). Granting that Sadaharu Oh was Japan's most talented player and one of the best pure sluggers in any league in any corner of the globe, still Oh was never, for all his heroics, the biggest drawing card even on his own ball club. In this sense, his role might more fittingly parallel that of stolid Yankees hero Lou Gehrig than that of headline-loving Babe Ruth. Such parallels aside, Shigeo Nagashima (Oh's teammate and all-star third sacker for the dynasty Yomiuri Giants) was Japan's most popular player ever, and his fame began—but certainly didn't end—with smacking the most dramatic homer in the nation's sporting history, a game-winning ninth-inning blow in a special exhibition match staged with Emperor Hirohito and his empress looking on as guests of honor. That memorable homer in 1959 was one of nearly 450 that Nagashima blasted while hitting cleanup in a feared Yomiuri batting order, one slot behind teammate Oh. This remarkable "O–N Cannons" one–two punch propelled the fan-favored, Tokyo-based club to 13 pennants and 11 Japan Series titles during their joint glory-run of 18 seasons. His five Most Valuable Player campaigns fell only four short of teammate Oh's record nine such honors, but his six batting crowns topped Oh by one. Beyond all the numbers, the beloved third sacker was renowned for his clutch hitting—feats so celebrated they earned him the honored title of "Mr. Giant" even with the fabulous Oh always present alongside him in the same "Murderers' Row" Giants lineup.

Katsuya Nomura (b. June 29, 1935). Fukuoka and Nankai Hawks receiver Katsuya Nomura was the most durable backstop in the world across a quarter-century that stretched from the major league reigns of Roy Campanella and Yogi Berra to those of Carlton Fisk and Bob Boone. When it came to either power numbers or longevity records, the highly popular Nomura left all his major league rivals far back in the dust. His 657 career homers (second to Oh) outpace not only Mike Piazza, Johnny Bench, and Fisk by nearly 300 but rank ahead of every Cooperstown legend save Aaron, Ruth, Willie Mays, and Bonds. His Japanese record for games caught (2,918) over a 27-year tenure—remarkable for any player, let alone an abuse-suffering catcher—was nearly 500 (3 seasons!) beyond Fisk's corresponding big league total. His 3,017 total games and 10,472 at-bats are Japanese league milestones likely to long remain fixed in the untouchable category. Nomura's iron-man constitution was unequivocally demonstrated during one mid-career stretch in the 1960s when he spent every inning of every game lodged behind the plate for 6 straight seasons. And the old adage about the tools of ignorance taking their toll on the offensive production of even the most durable physical specimens simply didn't apply in the case of Nomura: he captured nine Pacific League home run crowns, including eight straight (four of these overlapping with Oh in the Central League, in 1965 to 1968). His 52 homers in 1963 long remained tied with the equal number stroked by Hiromitsu Ochiai in 1985 as the league record. (American Tuffy Rhodes finally shattered the mark with 55 in 2001.) He also claimed a single batting championship (1965), six straight RBI titles, and a 1965 triple crown, the first in Japanese pro baseball since 1938. The Japanese Hall of Famer also fell only 99 safeties short of the magical 3,000-hit landmark. Katsuya Nomura was by every conceivable measure one of Japan's heftiest all-time baseball legends.

Hiromitsu Ochiai (b. December 9, 1953). Lotte Orions three-time Pacific League triple crown winner Hiromitsu Ochiai was not only Japan's biggest star of the decade between Oh and Ichiro but also one of the biggest puzzles of contemporary Japanese baseball. A free spirit in a national sport that eschews individualism and selfish displays of disloyalty, Ochiai was Japanese baseball's top slugger of the 1980s and its top maverick of any decade stretching all the way back to the pioneering days of World War II. Retiring in 1998 with 2,300-plus career hits, 500-plus homers, and a .311 career average achieved during two decades of consistent on-field production, the irascible Ochiai also stood above the crowd for his "bad guy" displays that ran against the ingrained spirit of self-sacrifice for team values coloring Japan's version of the sport. As a rookie, he feuded with management over his preferred batting style and came out on top—much to his field manager's embarrassment; he later became the only player in regimented Japanese League structure to walk out on his membership in the mandatory players' union. Ochiai negotiated his own salary deals and wound up in 1987 with the first-ever 100-million-yen paycheck. And through all the distractions he posted a first triple crown in 1982 and two more in the 1985 and 1986 seasons. The latter two stellar campaigns included more than 50 homers each, batting averages twice above .360, and respective 146 and 116 RBI totals.

Sadaharu Oh (b. May 20, 1940).   Home run hero Sadaharu Oh ranks supreme as the Japanese player most widely known anywhere outside of that baseball-crazed nation and thus the default poster boy for the entire Japanese baseball enterprise. But Oh's international fame was itself only earned by a painfully slow process. Few stateside fans had ever heard of Oh before June 1974, when the *New York Times* reported on his record-setting career homer number 600 hit in Tokyo. The interest at the time was piqued of course by Hank Aaron's own rush past Babe Ruth's long-standing "world record" of 714 that same spring. Though he never became a household name in the United States, Oh's visibility would grow over the next half-dozen Japanese seasons as he elevated his own totals well beyond those of both American slugging icons, eventually logging 154 more round-trippers than Ruth and 113 more than Aaron in 467 fewer games. Oh was far more than a one-dimensional slugger, amassing a .301 career average on more than 2,700 hits in his 21-season Central League sojourn. His full resumé would eventually feature the single-season homer record of 55, fifteen home run titles (thirteen in a row), and thirteen RBI crowns; he was also a league batting champ on five occasions and fifteen times the leader in runs scored (a category in which he still owns Japan's top career total), and in the mid-1970s he walked off with back-to-back triple crowns.

Oh was a memorable figure also for his unique batting style, which he learned from master swordsman Hiroshi Arakawa and which resembled the stance of a heron or flamingo, with Oh balanced precariously on one foot while awaiting deliveries from enemy pitchers. The unique batting approach, which recalled 1930's New York Giants slugger Mel Ott, was founded upon Asian approaches to meditation and enhanced mental control over physical activity. Oh would actually practice his hitting technique by routinely balancing on his left leg with his bat tilted back over his head toward the pitcher and occasionally even touching his batting helmet. The unique style and its dedicated application created an unparalleled slugger of unmatched potency. So feared was Oh at the plate that, despite preceding equally fearsome slugger Shigeo Nagashima (444 career homers of his own) in the Giants batting order for nearly two decades, he still regularly also led the circuit in bases on balls, an underrated offensive category in which he today outdistances his nearest career rival by nearly a thousand free career passes. There may be argument among U.S. followers of baseball over what Oh's numbers might have looked like had he played in the U.S. majors, with heftier pitching and longer fences—but in Japan there is no argument anywhere that Sadaharu Oh was the Ruth–Gehrig–Mantle–Williams–McGwire–Sosa–Bonds of Japanese baseball all rolled up with that unique heron-like stance into a single super-disciplined batting artist of incomparable dimensions.

Victor Starffin (b. May 1, 1916; d. 1957).   Japan's first great diamond star was not even an island-born native son but rather an immigrant, and from Russia, surely one of the most unlikely of all places. Author Richard Puff[2]—in the only major U.S.-published article on Victor Starffin—has suggested that the Russian-born immigrant turned star Japanese league pitcher lived a life fit for a Hollywood script and amassed mound statistics appropriate for Cooperstown. Starffin's father, a top military officer under Czar Nicholas II, settled his refugee family in northern Japan in 1925 and the strapping 6'4" youngster first became a pitching force with his local school team on the island of Hokkaido. His agreeing to play on a national all-star squad (which would soon become the country's first pro team) not only launched his more visible pitching career but also averted his family's deportation and eventually earned a release from prison for Starffin's father, who was serving a trumped-up sentence for murder.

Russian-born Victor Starffin was Japanese pro ball's first big pitching legend. [Transcendental Graphics]

When a Japanese professional league was launched in 1936, Victor Starffin emerged alongside another early Japanese pitching legend, Eiji Sawamura, as one of the twin aces of the immensely popular and successful Tokyo Kyojin (Giants), which have been from the first the island's version of the New York Yankees. Sawamura tossed the league's first two no-hit games in 1936 and 1937 and Starffin authored the third, also in 1937. The powerful right-hander lasted on the Japanese pro circuit well into the modern two-league era, not retiring until 1955, by which time he had amassed more records (many still standing) than any hurler in league annals. He was the first Japanese leaguer to claim 300 wins and still stands among only a half-dozen to cross the plateau. He still owns the most consecutive seasons with 30-plus victories (3), most wins (42 in 1939) in a season, most career shutouts (83, one better than

Masaichi Kaneda), and a life-time 2.09 ERA. During his spectacular first half-dozen seasons he amassed 182 wins (better than 30 per year) against a mere 53 defeats and never allowed his ERA to soar above 1.70 (his 1937 mark). He might have been much better still, had it not been for personal demons: an early-career alcohol abuse problem likely brought on by public harassment received as a foreigner during World War II (a period when he was forced to take on a Japanese name, Hiroshi Suda) surfaced periodically throughout his later career, causing the breakup of his marriage and even his eventual death in a car wreck less than two years after his baseball retirement.

Ichiro Suzuki (b. October 22, 1973).   Ichiro (in full, Ichiro Suzuki), sporting a colorful single name and a magical hit-filled bat as his trademarks, burst on the American League scene in 2001 as the most exciting Asian big league import ever. As a diminutive 29-year-old slap-hitting rookie right fielder with the Seattle Mariners, Ichiro took American baseball by storm with a debut season unparalleled in the game's long annals. Pacing a revived and revamped Mariners club to a major league record 116 victories with both his relentless hitting and his stellar outfield defense, Ichiro not only won a league batting title but also overtook Shoeless Joe Jackson's 90-year-old major league rookie record with his 242 base hits and achieved an almost equally impressive milestone when he become the first player since Jackie Robinson in 1949 to capture the league title in both batting and stolen bases. The first Japanese position player to earn a spot in the majors, Suzuki was only taking up at Safeco Field the level of performance that had already made him a megastar in his homeland and that had almost become routine in such venues as the state-of-the-art dome stadiums of Tokyo, Fukuoka, Seibu, and Osaka. Prior to his departure from the Pacific League Orix Blue Wave, the lefty-swinging Ichiro had racked up a record seven straight batting titles across his first 7 pro seasons, marks that ranged from a low of .342 (1995) to a high of .387 (2000). For much of a decade, Ichiro had been the biggest thing to hit Japanese baseball since legendary sluggers Sadaharu Oh and Katsuya Nomura at the close of the 1970s. The celebrations of his arrival in Seattle were nearly matched at the opposite end of the scale by the gloom that his flight to America cast over ballparks all around the two Japanese professional circuits. The loss of Ichiro in Tokyo would be matched by further bad news for Japanese fanatics when, only two years later, four-time Central League home run king Hideki Matsui of the Yomiuri Giants was winging his way to the Bronx to join forces with George Steinbrenner's New York Yankees.

IN BRIEF

In the end, Japanese players still don't seem quite on a par with those coming to the big time from Cuba, the Dominican Republic, or even Venezuela and Puerto Rico. There is still the issue of physical size, for one thing; despite the recent exception of Hideki Matsui and the earlier stereotype-smashing examples of Sadaharu Oh and Katsuya Nomura, robust sluggers are still rare, and most Japanese hurlers get by on polished craft rather than raw physical power. And yet, during recent seasons—thanks mainly to the impact of the fiery Ichiro and the likes of such dominant hurlers as Hideo Nomo, Kazuhiro Sasaki, and Shigetoshi Hasegawa—Japanese pro baseball is at long last being taken as a serious equal to the high-level professional versions of the sport played in North America and throughout the islands of the Caribbean. The Japanese league and major league connections are now being forged, and doors to big league careers are rapidly opening to top Central and Pacific League stars. The jury is still very much out on whether this new direction for *yakyū* promises salvation or perhaps sounds an ultimate death knell for the deeply entrenched and culturally distinct Japanese national pastime.

SELECTED JAPANESE RECORDS AND STATISTICS

Japan's Major Leaguers

Japanese in the Major Leagues (1964–2003)

	Name	Debut	Position	Debut Team	Seasons (Games)	Career Statistics
1	Masanori Murakami	1964	LHP	San Francisco Giants (NL)	2 (54)	5–1, 3.43 ERA
2	Bobby Fenwick*	1972	IF	Houston Astros (NL)	2 (41)	.179 BA
3	Steve Chitren*	1990	RHP	Oakland Athletics (AL)	2 (64)	2–4, 3.58 ERA
4	Jim Bowie*	1994	1B	Oakland Athletics (AL)	1 (6)	.214 BA
5	Hideo Nomo	1995	RHP	Los Angeles Dodgers (NL)	9 (281)	114–90, 3.85 ERA
6	Jeff McCurry*	1995	RHP	Pittsburgh Pirates (NL)	5 (111)	3–12, 5.89 ERA
7	Makato (Mac) Suzuki	1996	RHP	Seattle Mariners (AL)	6 (117)	16–31, 5.72 ERA
8	Shigetoshi Hasegawa	1997	RHP	Anaheim Angels (AL)	7 (403)	40–34, 3.47 ERA
9	Hideki Irabu	1997	RHP	New York Yankees (AL)	6 (126)	34–35, 5.15 ERA
10	Takashi Kashiwada	1997	LHP	New York Mets (NL)	1 (35)	3–1, 4.31 ERA
11	Masato Yoshii	1998	RHP	New York Mets (NL)	5 (162)	32–47, 4.62 ERA
12	Masao Kida	1999	RHP	Detroit Tigers (AL)	3 (54)	1–1, 5.90 ERA
13	Tomokazu Ohka	1999	RHP	Boston Red Sox (AL)	5 (109)	30–37, 4.00 ERA
14	Dave Roberts*	1999	OF	Cleveland Indians (NL)	5 (309)	.261 BA
15	Keith McDonald*	2000	C	St. Louis Cardinals (NL)	2 (8)	.333 BA
16	Kazuhiro Sasaki	2000	RHP	Seattle Mariners (AL)	4 (228)	7–16, 3.14, 129 S
17	Ichiro Suzuki	2001	OF	Seattle Mariners (AL)	3 (473)	.328 BA
18	Tsuyoshi Shinjo	2001	OF	New York Mets (NL)	3 (303)	.245 BA
19	Kazuhisa Ishii	2002	LHP	Los Angeles Dodgers (NL)	2 (55)	23–17, 4.07 ERA
20	Satoru Komiyama	2002	RHP	New York Mets (NL)	1 (25)	0–3, 5.61 ERA
21	Takahito Nomura	2002	LHP	Milwaukee Brewers (NL)	1 (21)	0–0, 8.56 ERA
22	So Taguchi	2002	OF	St. Louis Cardinals (NL)	2 (62)	.290 BA
23	Hideki Matsui	2003	OF	New York Yankees (AL)	1 (163)	.287 BA
24	Stephen Randolph*	2003	LHP	Arizona Diamondbacks (NL)	1 (50)	8–1, 4.05 ERA
25	Micheal Nakamura	2003	RHP	Minnesota Twins (AL)	1 (12)	0–0, 7.82 ERA

* Non-Japanese born in Japan.

Japanese League Record Book

Championship Team Records and Individual Japanese Batting and Pitching Leaders (1936–2003)

Year	Champion	Record	Batting Champion (Team)	BA	Top Pitcher (Team)	ERA
Single Japanese League (1936–1949; split seasons 1936–1938)						
1936 (S)	Tokyo Senators	4–1–0	Not Recorded		Not Recorded	
1936 (F)	Tokyo Kyojin*	5–1–0	Yuki Nakane (Nagoya)	.376	Masaru Kageura (Tigers)	0.79
1937 (S)	Tokyo Kyojin	41–13–2	Kenjiro Matsuki (Tigers)	.338	Eiji Sawamura (Kyojin)	0.81
1937 (F)	Osaka Tigers	39–9–1	Masaru Kageura (Tigers)	.333	Yukio Nishimura (Tigers)	1.48
1938 (S)	Osaka Tigers	29–6–0	Haruyasu Nakajima (Kyojin)	.345	Yukio Nishimura (Tigers)	1.52
1938 (F)	Tokyo Kyojin	30–9–1	Haruyasu Nakajima (Kyojin)	.361	Victor Starffin (Kyojin)	1.05
1939	Tokyo Kyojin	66–26–4	Tetsuharu Kawakami (Kyojin)	.338	Tadashi Wakabayashi (Tigers)	1.09
1940	Tokyo Kyojin	76–28–0	Kazuco Kito (Lions)	.321	Jiro Noguchi (Tsubasa)	0.93
1941	Tokyo Kyojin	62–22–2	Tetsuharu Kawakami (Kyojin)	.310	Jiro Noguchi (Taiyo)	0.88
1942	Tokyo Kyojin	73–27–5	Ha Go (Kyojin)	.286	Yasuo Hayashi (Asahi)	1.01
1943	Tokyo Kyojin	54–27–3	Shosei Go (Kyojin)	.300	Hideo Fujimoto (Kyojin)	0.73
1944	Hanshin Tigers	27–6–2	Toshiaki Okamura (Kinki)	.369	Tadashi Wakabayashi (Hanshin)	1.56
1945	Season Canceled					
1946	Kinki Great Ring	65–38–2	Masayasu Kaneda (Hanshin)	.347	Hideo Fujimoto (Kyojin)	2.11
1947	Osaka Tigers	79–37–3	Hiroshi Oshita (Flyers)	.315	Giichiro Shiraki (Flyers)	1.74

Year	Champion	Record	Batting Champion (Team)	BA	Top Pitcher (Team)	ERA
1948	Nankai Hawks	87–49–4	Noboru Aota (Giants)	.306	Hiroshi Nakao (Giants)	1.84
1949	Yomiuri Giants	85–48–1	Makoto Kozuru (Stars)	.361	Hideo Fujimoto (Giants)	1.94

Japanese Central League (1950–2003)

Year	Champion	Record	Batting Champion (Team)	BA	Top Pitcher (Team)	ERA
1950	Taiyo-Shochiku Robins	98–35–4	Fumio Fujimura (Osaka)	.362	Nobuo Oshima (Shochiku)	2.03
1951	Yomiuri Giants	79–29–6	Tetsuharu Kawakami (Yomiuri)	.377	Kiyoshi Matsuda (Yomiuri)	2.01
1952	Yomiuri Giants	83–37–0	Michio Nishizawa (Nagoya)	.353	Tadayoshi Kajioka (Osaka)	1.71
1953	Yomiuri Giants	87–37–1	Tetsuharu Kawakami (Yomiuri)	.347	Takumi Otomo (Yomiuri)	1.85
1954	Chunichi Dragons	86–40–4	Wally Yonamine (Yomiuri)	.361	Shigeru Sugishita (Chunichi)	1.39
1955	Yomiuri Giants	92–37–1	Tetsuharu Kawakami (Yomiuri)	.338	Takehiko Bessho (Yomiuri)	1.33
1956	Yomiuri Giants	82–44–4	Wally Yonamine (Yomiuri)	.338	Shozo Watanabe (Osaka)	1.45
1957	Yomiuri Giants	74–53–3	Wally Yonamine (Yomiuri)	.343	Masaichi Kaneda (Kokutetsu)	1.63
1958	Yomiuri Giants	77–52–1	Kenjiro Tamiya (Osaka)	.320	Masaichi Kaneda (Kokutetsu)	1.30
1959	Yomiuri Giants	77–48–5	Shigeo Nagashima (Yomiuri)	.334	Minoru Murayama (Osaka)	1.19
1960	Taiyo Whales	70–56–4	Shigeo Nagashima (Yomiuri)	.334	Noboru Akiyama (Taiyo)	1.75
1961	Yomiuri Giants	71–53–6	Shigeo Nagashima (Yomiuri)	.353	Hiroshi Gondo (Chunichi)	1.70
1962	Hanshin Tigers	75–55–3	Katsuji Morinaga (Hiroshima)	.307	Minoru Murayama (Hanshin)	1.20
1963	Yomiuri Giants	83–55–2	Shigeo Nagashima (Yomiuri)	.341	Minoru Kakimoto (Chunichi)	1.70
1964	Hanshin Tigers	80–56–4	Shinichi Eto (Chunichi)	.323	Gene Bacque (Hanshin)	1.89
1965	Yomiuri Giants	91–47–2	Shinichi Eto (Chunichi)	.336	Masaichi Kaneda (Yomiuri)	1.84
1966	Yomiuri Giants	89–41–4	Shigeo Nagashima (Yomiuri)	.344	Tsuneo Horiuchi (Yomiuri)	1.39
1967	Yomiuri Giants	84–46–4	Toshio Naka (Chunichi)	.343	Masatoshi Gondo (Hanshin)	1.40
1968	Yomiuri Giants	77–53–4	Sadaharu Oh (Yomiuri)	.326	Yoshiro Sotokoba (Hiroshima)	1.94
1969	Yomiuri Giants	73–51–6	Sadaharu Oh (Yomiuri)	.345	Yutaka Enatsu (Hanshin)	1.81
1970	Yomiuri Giants	79–47–4	Sadaharu Oh (Yomiuri)	.325	Minoru Murayama (Hanshin)	0.98
1971	Yomiuri Giants	70–52–8	Shigeo Nagashima (Yomiuri)	.320	Kazuhiro Fujimoto (Hiroshima)	1.71
1972	Yomiuri Giants	74–52–4	Tsutomu Wakamatsu (Yakult)	.329	Takeshi Yasuda (Yakult)	2.08
1973	Yomiuri Giants	66–60–4	Sadaharu Oh (Yomiuri)	.355	Yakeshi Yasuda (Yakult)	2.02
1974	Chunichi Dragons	70–49–9	Sadaharu Oh (Yomiuri)	.332	Shitoshi Sekimoto (Yomiuri)	2.28
1975	Hiroshima Toyo Carp	72–47–11	Koji Yamamoto (Hiroshima)	.319	Sohachi Aniya (Hanshin)	1.91
1976	Yomiuri Giants	76–45–9	Kenichi Yazawa (Chunichi)	.355	Takamasa Suzuki (Chunichi)	2.98
1977	Yomiuri Giants	80–46–4	Tsutomu Wakamatsu (Yakult)	.358	Hisao Niura (Yomiuri)	2.32
1978	Yakult Swallows	68–46–16	Jitsuo Mizutani (Hiroshima)	.348	Hisao Niura (Yomiuri)	2.81
1979	Hiroshima Toyo Carp	67–50–13	Félix Millán (Yokohama)	.346	Masaji Hiramatsu (Yokohama)	2.39
1980	Hiroshima Toyo Carp	73–44–13	Kenichi Yazawa (Chunichi)	.369	Hiromu Matsuoka (Yakult)	2.35
1981	Yomiuri Giants	73–48–9	Taira Fujita (Hanshin)	.358	Suguru Egawa (Yomiuri)	2.29
1982	Chunichi Dragons	64–47–9	Keiji Nagasaki (Yokohama)	.351	Akio Saito (Yokohama)	2.07
1983	Yomiuri Giants	72–50–8	Akinobu Mayumi (Hanshin)	.353	Osamu Fukuma (Hanshin)	2.62
1984	Hiroshima Toyo Carp	75–45–10	Toshio Shinozuka (Yomiuri)	.334	Seiji Kobayashi (Hiroshima)	2.20
1985	Hanshin Tigers	74–49–7	Randy Bass (Hanshin)	.350	Tatsuo Komatsu (Chunichi)	2.65
1986	Hiroshima Toyo Carp	73–46–11	Randy Bass (Hanshin)	.389	Manabu Kitabeppu (Hiroshima)	2.43
1987	Yomiuri Giants	76–43–11	Toshio Shinozuka (Yomiuri)	.333	Masumi Kuwata (Yomiuri)	2.17
1988	Chunichi Dragons	79–46–5	Kozo Shoda (Hiroshima)	.340	Yutaka Ono (Hiroshima)	1.70
1989	Yomiuri Giants	84–44–2	Warren Cromartie (Yomiuri)	.378	Masaki Saito (Yomiuri)	1.62
1990	Yomiuri Giants	88–42–0	Jim Paciorek (Yokohama)	.326	Masaki Saito (Yomiuri)	2.17
1991	Hiroshima Toyo Carp	74–56–2	Atsuya Furuta (Yakult)	.340	Shinji Sasaoka (Hiroshima)	2.44
1992	Yakult Swallows	69–61–1	Jack Howell (Yakult)	.331	Koki Morita (Yokohama)	2.05
1993	Yakult Swallows	80–50–2	Tom O'Malley (Hanshin)	.329	Masahiro Yamamoto (Chunichi)	2.05
1994	Yomiuri Giants	70–60–0	Alonzo Powell (Chunichi)	.324	Genji Kaku (Chunichi)	2.45
1995	Yakult Swallows	82–48–0	Alonzo Powell (Chunichi)	.355	Terry Bross (Yakult)	2.33
1996	Yomiuri Giants	77–53–0	Alonzo Powell (Chunichi)	.340	Masaki Saito (Yomiuri)	2.36
1997	Yakult Swallows	83–52–2	Takanori Suzuki (Yokohama)	.335	Yutaka Ono (Hiroshima)	2.85
1998	Yokohama Bay Stars	79–56	Takanori Suzuki (Yokohama)	.337	Shigeki Noguchi (Chunichi)	2.34
1999	Chunichi Dragons	81–54	Bobby Rose (Yokohama)	.369	Koji Uehara (Yomiuri)	2.38
2000	Yomiuri Giants	78–57–0	Tatsuhiko Kinjo (Yokohama)	.346	Kazuhisa Ishii (Yakult)	2.60
2001	Yakult Swallows	76–58–6	Hideki Matsui (Yomiuri)	.333	Shigeki Noguchi (Chunichi)	2.46
2002	Yomiuri Giants	86–52–2	Kosuke Fukudome (Chunichi)	.343	Masumi Kuwata (Yomiuri)	2.22
2003	Hanshin Tigers	87–51–2	Makoto Imaoka (Hanshin)	.340	Kei Igawa (Hanshin)	2.80

(continued)

(continued)

Year	Champion	Record	Batting Champion (Team)	BA	Top Pitcher (Team)	ERA
Japanese Pacific League (1950–2003)						
1950	Mainichi Orions	81–34–5	Hiroshi Oshita (Tokyo)	.339	Atsushi Aramaki (Mainichi)	2.06
1951	Nankai Hawks	72–24–8	Hiroshi Oshita (Tokyo)	.383	Takeo Hattori (Nankai)	2.03
1952	Nankai Hawks	76–44–1	Shigeya Iijima (Daiei)	.336	Susumu Yuki (Nankai)	1.91
1953	Nankai Hawks	71–48–1	Isami Okamoto (Nankai)	.318	Tokuji Kawasaki (Nishitetsu)	1.98
1954	Nishitetsu Lions	90–47–3	Larry Raines (Hankyu)	.337	Motoji Takuwa (Nankai)	1.58
1955	Nankai Hawks	99–41–3	Futoshi Nakanishi (Nishitetsu)	.332	Takashi Nakagawa (Mainichi)	2.08
1956	Nishitetsu Lions	96–51–7	Yasumitsu Toyoda (Nishitetsu)	.325	Kazuhisa Inao (Nishitetsu)	1.06
1957	Nishitetsu Lions	83–44–5	Kazuhiro Yamauchi (Mainichi)	.331	Kazuhisa Inao (Nishitetsu)	1.37
1958	Nishitetsu Lions	78–47–5	Futoshi Nakanishi (Nishitetsu)	.314	Kazuhisa Inao (Nishitetsu)	1.42
1959	Nankai Hawks	88–42–4	Kohei Sugiyama (Nankai)	.323	Tadashi Sugiura (Nankai)	1.40
1960	Daimai Orions	82–48–3	Kihachi Enomoto (Daimai)	.344	Shoichi Ono (Daimai)	1.98
1961	Nankai Hawks	85–49–6	Isao Harimoto (Toei)	.336	Kazuhisa Inao (Nishitetsu)	1.69
1962	Toei Flyers	78–52–3	Jack Bloomfield (Kintetsu)	.374	Osamu Kubota (Toei)	2.12
1963	Nishitetsu Lions	86–60–4	Jack Bloomfield (Kintetsu)	.335	Masahiro Kubo (Kintetsu)	2.36
1964	Nankai Hawks	84–63–3	Yoshinori Hirose (Nankai)	.366	Yoshiro Tsumashima (Tokyo)	2.15
1965	Nankai Hawks	88–49–3	Katsuya Nomura (Nankai)	.320	Kiyohiro Miura (Nankai)	1.57
1966	Nankai Hawks	79–51–3	Kihachi Enomoto (Tokyo)	.351	Kazuhisa Inao (Nishitetsu)	1.79
1967	Hankyu Braves	75–55–4	Isao Harimoto (Toei)	.336	Mitsuhiro Adachi (Hankyu)	1.75
1968	Hankyu Braves	80–50–4	Isao Harimoto (Toei)	.376	Mutsuo Minagawa (Nankai)	1.61
1969	Hankyu Braves	76–50–4	Yozo Nagabuchi (Kintetsu)	.333	Masaaki Kitaru (Lotte)	1.72
1970	Lotte Orions	80–47–3	Isao Harimoto (Toei)	.383	Michio Sato (Nankai)	2.04
1971	Hankyu Braves	80–39–11	Shinichi Eto (Lotte)	.337	Hisashi Yamada (Hankyu)	2.37
1972	Hankyu Braves	80–48–2	Isao Harimoto (Toei)	.358	Toshihiko Sei (Kintetsu)	2.36
1973[†]	Nankai Hawks	68–58–4	Hideji Kato (Hankyu)	.337	Tetsuya Yoneda (Hankyu)	2.47
1974[†]	Lotte Orions	69–50–11	Isao Harimoto (Nippon)	.340	Michio Sato (Nankai)	1.91
1975[†]	Hankyu Braves	64–59–7	Jinten Haku (Taiheiyo)	.319	Choji Murata (Lotte)	2.20
1976[†]	Hankyu Braves	79–45–6	Satoru Yoshioka (Taiheiyo)	.309	Choji Murata (Lotte)	1.82
1977[†]	Hankyu Braves	69–51–10	Michiyo Arito (Lotte)	.329	Hisashi Yamada (Hankyu)	2.28
1978[†]	Hankyu Braves	82–39–9	Kyosuke Sasaki (Kintetsu)	.354	Keishi Suzuki (Kintetsu)	2.02
1979[†]	Kintetsu Buffaloes	74–45	Hideji Kato (Hankyu)	.364	Tetsuji Yamaguchi (Kintetsu)	2.49
1980[†]	Kintetsu Buffaloes	68–54	Leron Lee (Lotte)	.358	Isamu Kida (Nippon)	2.28
1981[†]	Nippon Ham Fighters	68–54	Hiromitsu Ochiai (Lotte)	.326	Noriaki Okabe (Nippon)	2.70
1982[†]	Seibu Lions	68–58–4	Hiromitsu Ochiai (Lotte)	.325	Satoshi Takahashi (Nippon)	1.84
1983	Seibu Lions	86–40–4	Hiromitsu Ochiai (Lotte)	.332	Osamu Higashio (Seibu)	2.92
1984	Hankyu Braves	75–45–10	Boomer Wells (Hankyu)	.355	Yutaro Imai (Hankyu)	2.93
1985	Seibu Lions	79–45–6	Hiromitsu Ochiai (Lotte)	.367	Kimiyasu Kudo (Seibu)	2.76
1986	Seibu Lions	68–49–13	Hiromitsu Ochiai (Lotte)	.360	Yoshinori Sato (Hankyu)	2.83
1987	Seibu Lions	71–45–14	Hiromasa Arai (Kintetsu)	.366	Kimiyasu Kudo (Seibu)	2.41
1988	Seibu Lions	73–51–6	Hideaki Takazawa (Lotte)	.327	Hirofumi Kono (Nippon)	2.38
1989	Kintetsu Buffaloes	71–54	Boomer Wells (Orix)	.322	Choji Murata (Lotte)	2.50
1990	Seibu Lions	81–45–4	Norifumi Nishimura (Lotte)	.338	Hideo Nomo (Kintetsu)	2.91
1991	Seibu Lions	81–43–6	Mitsuchika Hirai (Lotte)	.314	Tomio Watanabe (Seibu)	2.35
1992	Seibu Lions	80–47–3	Makoto Sasaki (Daiei)	.376	Motoyuki Akahori (Kintetsu)	1.80
1993	Seibu Lions	74–53–3	Hatsuhiko Tsuji (Seibu)	.319	Kimiyasu Kudo (Seibu)	2.06
1994	Seibu Lions	76–52–2	Ichiro Suzuki (Orix)	.385	Hiroshi Shintani (Seibu)	2.91
1995	Orix Blue Wave	82–47–1	Ichiro Suzuki (Orix)	.342	Hideki Irabu (Chiba Lotte)	2.53
1996	Orix Blue Wave	74–50–6	Ichiro Suzuki (Orix)	.356	Hideki Irabu (Chiba Lotte)	2.402
1997	Seibu Lions	76–56–3	Ichiro Suzuki (Orix)	.345	Satoru Komiyama (Chiba Lotte)	2.49
1998	Seibu Lions	70–61	Ichiro Suzuki (Orix)	.358	Hideo Kanemura (Nippon)	2.73
1999	Fukuoka Daei Hawks	78–54	Ichiro Suzuki (Orix)	.343	Kimiyasu Kudo (Fukuoka)	2.38
2000	Fukuoka Daei Hawks	73–60–2	Ichiro Suzuki (Orix)	.387	Nobuyuki Ebisu (Orix)	3.27
2001	Osaka Kintetsu Buffaloes	78–60–2	Kazuya Fukuura (Chiba Lotte)	.346	Nate Minchey (Chiba Lotte)	3.26
2002	Seibu Lions	90–49–1	Michihiro Ogasawara (Nippon)	.340	Masahiko Kaneda (Orix)	2.50
2003	Fukuoka Daei Hawks	82–55–3	Michihiro Ogasawara (Nippon)	.360	Kazumi Saito (Fukuoka)	2.83

Abbreviations: F, fall; S, spring.
* Kyojin is Japanese for Giants.
[†] Pacific League champion determined by best-of-five postseason playoff tournament (1973–1982). See next table.

Pacific League Championship Playoffs (1973–1982)

Year	Winning Team	Manager	Record	Losing Team	Manager	Series MVP
1973	Nankai Hawks	Katsuya Nomura	3–2	Hankyu Braves	Yukio Nishimoto	Michio Sato
1974	Lotte Orions	Masaichi Kaneda	3–0	Hankyu Braves	Toshiharu Ueda	Choji Murata
1975	Hankyu Braves	Toshiharu Ueda	3–1	Kintetsu Buffaloes	Yukio Nishimoto	Tokuji Nagaike
1976	Hankyu Braves	Toshiharu Ueda	—	No playoffs (Hankyu Braves won both halves of season)	—	—
1977	Hankyu Braves	Toshiharu Ueda	3–2	Lotte Orions	Masaichi Kaneda	Hisashi Yamada
1978	Hankyu Braves	Toshiharu Ueda	—	No playoffs (Hankyu Braves won both halves of season)	—	—
1979	Kintetsu Buffaloes	Yukio Nishimoto	3–2	Hankyu Braves	Takao Kajimoto	Tetsuji Yamaguchi
1980	Kintetsu Buffaloes	Yukio Nishimoto	3–0	Lotte Orions	Kazuhiro Yamauchi	Mitsuyasu Hirano
1981	Nippon Ham Fighters	Keiji Osawa	3–2	Lotte Orions	Kazuhiro Yamauchi	Juni Kashiwabara
1982	Seibu Lions	Tatsuro Hirooka	3–1	Nippon Ham Fighters	Keiji Osawa	Takuji Ota

Japanese Series Champions (1950–2003)

Year	Winning Team	Manager	League	Record	Losing Team	Manager
1950	Mainichi Orions	Yoshio Yuasa	Pacific	4–2	Shochiku Robins	Tokuro Konishi
1951	Yomiuri Giants	Shigeru Mizuhara	Central	4–1	Nankai Hawks	Kazuto Yamamoto
1952	Yomiuri Giants	Shigeru Mizuhara	Central	4–2	Nankai Hawks	Kazuto Yamamoto
1953	Yomiuri Giants	Shigeru Mizuhara	Central	4–2–1	Nankai Hawks	Kazuto Yamamoto
1954	Chunichi Dragons	Shunichi Amachi	Central	4–3	Nishitetsu Lions	Osamu Mihara
1955	Yomiuri Giants	Nobuyasu Mizuhara	Central	4–3	Nankai Hawks	Kazuto Yamamoto
1956	Nishitetsu Lions	Osamu Mihara	Pacific	4–2	Yomiuri Giants	Nobuyasu Mizuhara
1957	Nishitetsu Lions	Osamu Mihara	Pacific	4–0–1	Yomiuri Giants	Nobuyasu Mizuhara
1958	Nishitetsu Lions	Osamu Mihara	Pacific	4–3	Yomiuri Giants	Nobuyasu Mizuhara
1959	Nankai Hawks	Kazuto Yamamoto	Pacific	4–0	Yomiuri Giants	Nobuyasu Mizuhara
1960	Taiyo Whales	Osamu Mihara	Central	4–0	Daimai Orions	Yukio Nishimoto
1961	Yomiuri Giants	Tetsuharu Kawakami	Central	4–2	Nankai Hawks	Kazuto Yamamoto
1962	Toei Flyers	Shigeru Mizuhara	Pacific	4–2–1	Hanshin Tigers	Sadayoshi Fujimoto
1963	Yomiuri Giants	Tetsuharu Kawakami	Central	4–3	Nishitetsu Lions	Futoshi Nakanishi
1964	Nankai Hawks	Kazuto Yamamoto	Pacific	4–3	Hanshin Tigers	Sadayoshi Fujimoto
1965	Yomiuri Giants	Tetsuharu Kawakami	Central	4–1	Nankai Hawks	Kazuto Yamamoto
1966	Yomiuri Giants	Tetsuharu Kawakami	Central	4–2	Nankai Hawks	Kazuto Yamamoto
1967	Yomiuri Giants	Tetsuharu Kawakami	Central	4–2	Hankyu Braves	Yukio Nishimoto
1968	Yomiuri Giants	Tetsuharu Kawakami	Central	4–2	Hankyu Braves	Yukio Nishimoto
1969	Yomiuri Giants	Tetsuharu Kawakami	Central	4–2	Hankyu Braves	Yukio Nishimoto
1970	Yomiuri Giants	Tetsuharu Kawakami	Central	4–1	Lotte Orions	Wataru Nonin
1971	Yomiuri Giants	Tetsuharu Kawakami	Central	4–1	Hankyu Braves	Yukio Nishimoto
1972	Yomiuri Giants	Tetsuharu Kawakami	Central	4–1	Hankyu Braves	Yukio Nishimoto
1973	Yomiuri Giants	Tetsuharu Kawakami	Central	4–1	Nankai Hawks	Katsuya Nomura
1974	Lotte Orions	Masaichi Kaneda	Pacific	4–2	Chunichi Dragons	Wally Yonamine
1975	Hankyu Braves	Toshiharu Ueda	Pacific	4–0–2	Hiroshima Toyo Carp	Takeshi Koba
1976	Hankyu Braves	Toshiharu Ueda	Pacific	4–3	Yomiuri Giants	Shigeo Nagashima
1977	Hankyu Braves	Toshiharu Ueda	Pacific	4–1	Yomiuri Giants	Shigeo Nagashima
1978	Yakult Swallows	Tatsuro Hirooka	Central	4–3	Hankyu Braves	Toshiharu Ueda
1979	Hiroshima Toyo Carp	Takeshi Koba	Central	4–3	Kintetsu Buffaloes	Yukio Nishimoto
1980	Hiroshima Toyo Carp	Takeshi Koba	Central	4–3	Kintetsu Buffaloes	Yukio Nishimoto
1981	Yomiuri Giants	Motoshi Fujita	Central	4–2	Nippon Ham Fighters	Keiji Osawa

(continued)

(continued)

Year	Winning Team	Manager	League	Record	Losing Team	Manager
1982	Seibu Lions	Tatsuro Hirooka	Pacific	4–2	Chunichi Dragons	Sadao Kondo
1983	Seibu Lions	Tatsuro Hirooka	Pacific	4–3	Yomiuri Giants	Motoshi Fujita
1984	Hiroshima Toyo Carp	Takeshi Koba	Central	4–3	Hankyu Braves	Toshiharo Ueda
1985	Hanshin Tigers	Yoshio Yoshida	Central	4–2	Seibu Lions	Tatsuro Hirooka
1986	Seibu Lions	Masahiko Mori	Pacific	4–3–1	Hiroshima Toyo Carp	Junro Anan
1987	Seibu Lions	Masahiko Mori	Pacific	4–2	Yomiuri Giants	Sadaharu Oh
1988	Seibu Lions	Masahiko Mori	Pacific	4–1	Chunichi Dragons	Senichi Hoshino
1989	Yomiuri Giants	Motoshi Fujita	Central	4–3	Kintetsu Buffaloes	Akira Ogi
1990	Seibu Lions	Masahiko Mori	Pacific	4–0	Yomiuri Giants	Motoshi Fujita
1991	Seibu Lions	Masahiko Mori	Pacific	4–3	Hiroshima Toyo Carp	Koji Yamamoto
1992	Seibu Lions	Masahiko Mori	Pacific	4–3	Yakult Swallows	Katsuya Nomura
1993	Yakult Swallows	Katsuya Nomura	Central	4–3	Seibu Lions	Masahiko Mori
1994	Yomiuri Giants	Shigeo Nagashima	Central	4–2	Seibu Lions	Masahiko Mori
1995	Yakult Swallows	Katsuya Nomura	Central	4–1	Orix Blue Wave	Akira Ogi
1996	Orix Blue Wave	Akira Ogi	Pacific	4–1	Yomiuri Giants	Shigeo Nagashima
1997	Yakult Swallows	Katsuya Nomura	Central	4–1	Seibu Lions	Osamu Higashio
1998	Yokohama Bay Stars	Hiroshi Gondo	Central	4–2	Seibu Lions	Osamu Higashio
1999	Fukuoka Daiei Hawks	Sadaharu Oh	Pacific	4–1	Chunichi Dragons	Senichi Hoshino
2000	Yomiuri Giants	Shigeo Nagashima	Central	4–2	Fukuoka Daiei Hawks	Sadaharu Oh
2001	Yakult Swallows	Katsuya Nomura	Central	4–1	Kintetsu Buffaloes	Akira Ogi
2002	Yomiuri Giants	Tatsunori Hara	Central	4–0	Seibu Lions	Haruki Ihara
2003	Fukuoka Daiei Hawks	Sadaharu Oh	Pacific	4–3	Hanshin Tigers	Senichi Hoshino

Japanese Leagues Home Run Leaders (1950–2003)

	Central League				Pacific League		
Year	Player	Team	HR		Player	Team	HR
1950	Makoto Kozuru	Shochiku Robins	51		Kaoru Betto	Mainichi Orions	43
1951	Noboru Aota	Yomiuri Giants	32		Hiroshi Oshita	Tokyu Flyers	26
1952	Satoshi Sugiyama	Nagoya Dragons	27		Yasuhiro Fukami	Tokyu Flyers	25
1953	Fumio Fujimura	Osaka Tigers	27		Futoshi Nakanishi	Nishitetsu Lions	36
1954	Noboru Aota	Yosho Robins	31		Futoshi Nakanishi	Nishitetsu Lions	31
1955	Yukihiko Machida	Kokutetsu Swallows	31		Futoshi Nakanishi	Nishitetsu Lions	35
1956	Noboru Aota	Taiyo Whales	25		Futoshi Nakanishi	Nishitetsu Lions	29
1957	Noboru Aota	Taiyo Whales	22		Katsuya Nomura	Nankai Hawks	30
1958	Shigeo Nagashima	Yomiuri Giants	29		Futoshi Nakanishi	Nishitetsu Lions	23
1959	Takeshi Kuwata	Taiyo Whales	31		Kazuhiro Yamauchi	Daimai Orions	25
1960	Katsumi Fujimoto	Osaka Tigers	22		Kazuhiro Yamauchi	Daimai Orions	32
1961	Shigeo Nagashima	Yomiuri Giants	28		Katsuya Nomura	Nankai Hawks	29
1962	Sadaharu Oh	Yomiuri Giants	38		Katsuya Nomura	Nankai Hawks	44
1963	Sadaharu Oh	Yomiuri Giants	40		Katsuya Nomura	Nankai Hawks	52
1964	Sadaharu Oh	Yomiuri Giants	55		Katsuya Nomura	Nankai Hawks	41
1965	Sadaharu Oh	Yomiuri Giants	48		Katsuya Nomura	Nankai Hawks	42
1966	Sadaharu Oh	Yomiuri Giants	48		Katsuya Nomura	Nankai Hawks	34
1967	Sadaharu Oh	Yomiuri Giants	47		Katsuya Nomura	Nankai Hawks	35
1968	Sadaharu Oh	Yomiuri Giants	49		Katsuya Nomura	Nankai Hawks	38
1969	Sadaharu Oh	Yomiuri Giants	44		Tokuji Nagaike	Hankyu Braves	41
1970	Sadaharu Oh	Yomiuri Giants	47		Katsuo Osugi	Toei Flyers	44
1971	Sadaharu Oh	Yomiuri Giants	39		Katsuo Osugi	Toei Flyers	41
1972	Sadaharu Oh	Yomiuri Giants	48		Tokuji Nagaike	Hankyu Braves	41
1973	Sadaharu Oh	Yomiuri Giants	51		Tokuji Nagaike	Hankyu Braves	43
1974	Sadaharu Oh	Yomiuri Giants	49		Clarence Jones	Kintetsu Buffaloes	38
1975	Koichi Tabuchi	Hanshin Tigers	43		Masahiro Doi	Taiheiyo Lions	34
1976	Sadaharu Oh	Yomiuri Giants	49		Clarence Jones	Kintetsu Buffaloes	36

	Central League				Pacific League		
Year	Player	Team	HR		Player	Team	HR
1977	Sadaharu Oh	Yomiuri Giants	50		Leron Lee	Lotte Orions	34
1978	Koji Yamamoto	Hiroshima Toyo Carp	44		Bobby Mitchell	Nippon Ham Fighters	36
1979	Masayuki Kakefu	Hanshin Tigers	48		Charlie Manuel	Kintetsu Buffaloes	37
1980	Koji Yamamoto	Hiroshima Toyo Carp	44		Charlie Manuel	Kintetsu Buffaloes	48
1981	Koji Yamamoto	Hiroshima Toyo Carp	43		Hiromitsu Kadota	Nankai Hawks	44
1982	Masayuki Kakefu	Hanshin Tigers	35		Hiromitsu Ochiai	Lotte Orions	32
1983	Yasunori Oshima	Chunichi Dragons	36		Hiromitsu Kadota	Nankai Hawks	40
1984	Masayuki Kakefu	Hanshin Tigers	37		Boomer Wells	Hankyu Braves	37
1985	Randy Bass	Hanshin Tigers	54		Hiromitsu Ochiai	Lotte Orions	52
1986	Randy Bass	Hanshin Tigers	47		Hiromitsu Ochiai	Lotte Orions	50
1987	Rick Lancelloti	Hiroshima Toyo Carp	39		Koji Akiyama	Seibu Lions	43
1988	Carlos Ponce	Yokohama Whales	33		Hiromitsu Kadota	Nankai Hawks	44
1989	Larry Parrish	Yakult Swallows	42		Ralph Bryant	Kintetsu Buffaloes	49
1990	Hiromitsu Ochiai	Chunichi Dragons	34		Orestes Destrade	Seibu Lions	42
1991	Hiromitsu Ochiai	Chunichi Dragons	37		Orestes Destrade	Seibu Lions	39
1992	Jack Howell	Yakult Swallows	38		Orestes Destrade	Seibu Lions	41
1993	Akira Eto	Hiroshima Toyo Carp	34		Ralph Bryant	Kintetsu Buffaloes	42
1994	Yasuaki Taihoh	Chunichi Dragons	38		Ralph Bryant	Kintetsu Buffaloes	35
1995	Akira Eto	Hiroshima Toyo Carp	39		Hiroki Kokubo	Daiei Hawks	28
1996	Takeshi Yamazaki	Chunichi Dragons	39		Troy Neel	Orix Blue Wave	32
1997	Dwayne Hosey	Yakult Swallows	38		Nigel Wilson	Nippon Ham Fighters	33
1998	Hideki Matsui	Yomiuri Giants	34		Nigel Wilson	Nippon Ham Fighters	33
1999	Hideki Matsui	Yomiuri Giants	42		Tuffy Rhodes	Kintetsu Buffaloes	40
2000	Hideki Matsui	Yomiuri Giants	42		Norihiro Nakamura	Kintetsu Buffaloes	39
2001	Roberto Petagine	Yakult Swallows	39		Tuffy Rhodes	Kintetsu Buffaloes	55
2002	Hideki Matsui	Yomiuri Giants	50		Alex Cabrera	Seibu Lions	55
2003	Alex Ramírez	Yakult Swallows	40		Alex Cabrera	Seibu Lions	50

Japanese Leagues Most Valuable Players (1950–1998)

	Central League				Pacific League		
Year	MVP	Team	Position		MVP	Team	Position
1950	Makoto Kozuru	Shochiku Robins	OF		Kaoru Betto	Mainichi Orions	OF
1951	Tetsuharu Kawakami	Yomiuri Giants	1B		Kazuhito Yamamoto	Nankai Hawks	2B
1952	Takehiko Bessho	Yomiuri Giants	P		Susumu Yuki	Nankai Hawks	P
1953	Takumi Otomo	Yomiuri Giants	P		Isami Okamoto	Nankai Hawks	2B
1954	Shigeru Shugishita	Chunichi Dragons	P		Hiroshi Oshita	Nishitetsu Lions	OF
1955	Tetsuharu Kawakami	Yomiuri Giants	1B		Tokuji Iida	Nankai Hawks	OF
1956	Takehiko Bessho	Yomiuri Giants	P		Futoshi Nakanishi	Nishitetsu Lions	3B
1957	Wally Yonamine	Yomiuri Giants	OF		Kazuhisa Inao	Nishitetsu Lions	P
1958	Motoshi Fujita	Yomiuri Giants	P		Kazuhisa Inao	Nishitetsu Lions	P
1959	Motoshi Fujita	Yomiuri Giants	P		Tadashi Sugiura	Nankai Hawks	P
1960	Noboru Akiyama	Taiyo Whales	P		Kazuhiro Yamauchi	Daimai Orions	OF
1961	Shigeo Nagashima	Yomiuri Giants	3B		Katsuya Nomura	Nankai Hawks	C
1962	Minoru Murayama	Hanshin Tigers	P		Isao Harimoto	Toei Flyers	OF
1963	Shigeo Nagashima	Yomiuri Giants	3B		Katsuya Nomura	Nankai Hawks	C
1964	Sadaharu Oh	Yomiuri Giants	1B		Joe Stanka	Nankai Hawks	P
1965	Sadaharu Oh	Yomiuri Giants	1B		Katsuya Nomura	Nankai Hawks	C
1966	Shigeo Nagashima	Yomiuri Giants	3B		Katsuya Nomura	Nankai Hawks	C
1967	Sadaharu Oh	Yomiuri Giants	1B		Mitsuhiro Adachi	Hankyu Braves	P
1968	Shigeo Nagashima	Yomiuri Giants	3B		Tetsuya Yoneda	Hankyu Braves	P
1969	Sadaharu Oh	Yomiuri Giants	1B		Tokuji Nagaike	Hankyu Braves	OF
1970	Sadaharu Oh	Yomiuri Giants	1B		Masaaki Kitaru	Lotte Orions	P

(continued)

(continued)

	Central League			Pacific League		
Year	MVP	Team	Position	MVP	Team	Position
1971	Shigeo Nagashima	Yomiuri Giants	3B	Tokuji Nagaike	Hankyu Braves	OF
1972	Tsuneo Horiuchi	Yomiuri Giants	P	Yutaka Fukumoto	Hankyu Braves	OF
1973	Sadaharu Oh	Yomiuri Giants	1B	Katsuya Nomura	Nankai Hawks	C
1974	Sadaharu Oh	Yomiuri Giants	1B	Tomehiro Kaneda	Lotte Orions	P
1975	Koji Yamamoto	Hiroshima Toyo Carp	OF	Hideji Kato	Hankyu Braves	1B
1976	Sadaharu Oh	Yomiuri Giants	1B	Hisashi Yamada	Hankyu Braves	P
1977	Sadaharu Oh	Yomiuri Giants	1B	Hisashi Yamada	Hankyu Braves	P
1978	Tsutomu Wakamatsu	Yakult Swallows	P	Hisashi Yamada	Hankyu Braves	P
1979	Yutaka Enatsu	Hiroshima Toyo Carp	P	Charlie Manuel	Kintetsu Buffaloes	OF
1980	Koji Yamamoto	Hiroshima Toyo Carp	OF	Isamu Kida	Nippon Ham Fighters	P
1981	Suguru Egawa	Yomiuri Giants	P	Yukata Enatsu	Nippon Ham Fighters	P
1982	Takayoshi Nakao	Chunichi Dragons	C	Hiromitsu Ochiai	Lotte Orions	2B
1983	Tatsunori Hara	Yomiuri Giants	3B	Osamu Higashio	Seibu Lions	P
1984	Sachio Kinugasa	Hiroshima Toyo Carp	3B	Boomer Wells	Hankyu Braves	1B
1985	Randy Bass	Hanshin Tigers	1B	Hiromitsu Ochiai	Lotte Orions	3B
1986	Manabu Kitabeppu	Hiroshima Toyo Carp	P	Hiromichi Ishige	Seibu Lions	SS
1987	Kazuhiro Yamakura	Yomiuri Giants	C	Osamu Higashio	Seibu Lions	P
1988	Genji Kaku	Chunichi Dragons	P	Hiromitsu Kadota	Nankai Hawks	OF
1989	Warren Cromartie	Yomiuri Giants	OF	Ralph Bryant	Kintetsu Buffaloes	OF
1990	Masaki Saito	Yomiuri Giants	P	Hideo Nomo	Kintetsu Buffaloes	P
1991	Shinji Sasaoka	Hiroshima Toyo Carp	P	Taigen Kaku	Seibu Lions	P
1992	Jack Howell	Yakult Swallows	3B	Takehiro Ishii	Seibu Lions	P
1993	Atsuya Furuta	Yakult Swallows	C	Kimiyasu Kudo	Seibu Lions	P
1994	Masumi Kuwata	Yomiuri Giants	P	Ichiro Suzuki	Orix Blue Wave	OF
1995	Tom O'Malley	Yakult Swallows	OF	Ichiro Suzuki	Orix Blue Wave	OF
1996	Hideki Matsui	Yomiuri Giants	OF	Ichiro Suzuki	Orix Blue Wave	OF
1997	Atsuya Furuta	Yakult Swallows	C	Fumiya Nishiguchi	Seibu Lions	P
1998	Kazuhiro Sasaki	Yokohama Bay Stars	P	Kazuo Matsui	Seibu Lions	SS

Japanese League Career and All-Time Statistics

Japanese Career and Season Individual Records (1936–2003)

Category*	Player	Record	Years
Batting			
Games Played	Katsuya Nomura	3,017	1954–1980
At Bats	Katsuya Nomura	10,472	1954–1980
Runs Scored, Career	Sadaharu Oh	1,967	1959–1980
Runs Scored, Season	Makoto Kozuru	143	1950
Hits, Career	Isao Harimoto	3,085	1959–1981
Hits, Season	Ichiro Suzuki	210	1994
Batting Average	Leron Lee	.320	1977–1987
Doubles	Yutaka Fukumoto	449	1969–1988
Triples	Yutaka Fukumoto	115	1969–1988
Home Runs, Career	Sadaharu Oh	868	1959–1980
Home Runs, Season	Sadaharu Oh	55	1964
	Tuffy Rhodes	55	2001
RBI, Career	Sadaharu Oh	2,170	1959–1980
RBI, Season	Makoto Kozuru	161	1950
Slugging Percentage, Career	Sadaharu Oh	.634	1959–1980
Slugging Percentage, Season	Randy Bass	.777	1986

Category	Player	Record	Years
Stolen Bases, Career	Yutaka Fukumoto	1,065	1969–1988
Stolen Bases, Season	Yutaka Fukumoto	106	1972
Bases on Balls	Sadaharu Oh	2,390	1959–1980
Strikeouts	Sachio Kinugasa	1,587	1965–1987
Pitching			
Games Appeared	Tetsuya Yoneda	949	1956–1977
Complete Games, Career	Masaichi Kaneda	365	1950–1969
Complete Games, Season	Akira Bessho	47	1947
Wins, Career	Masaichi Kaneda	400	1950–1969
Wins, Season	Victor Starffin	42	1939
	Kazuhisa Inao	42	1961
Losses, Career	Masaichi Kaneda	298	1950–1969
Losses, Season	Masayoshi Nakayama	29	1940
Winning Percentage	Hideo Fujimoto	.697	1942–1955
Shutouts, Career	Victor Starffin	83	1936–1955
Shutouts, Season	Jiro Noguchi	19	1942
	Hideo Fujimoto	19	1943
Saves, Career	Shingo Takatsu	260	1991–2003
Saves, Season	Kazuhiro Sasaki	38	1997
	Sung Dong Yol	38	1997
Innings Pitched, Career	Masaichi Kaneda	5,526.2	1950–1969
Innings Pitched, Season	Yasuo Hayashi	541.1	1942
Strikeouts, Career	Masaichi Kaneda	4,490	1950–1969
Strikeouts, Season	Yutaka Enatsu	401	1968
Bases on Balls, Career	Masaichi Kaneda	1,808	1950–1969
Bases on Balls, Season	Tadashi Kameda	280	1939
ERA, Career	Hideo Fujimoto	1.90	1942–1955
ERA, Season	Hideo Fujimoto	0.73	1943
Hits Allowed	Tetsuya Yoneda	4,561	1956–1977

* Career records, unless specified as single-season record.

Japanese Special Miscellaneous All-Time Records

Category	Name	Record	Dates
Managerial Lifetime Wins	Kazuto Yamamoto	1,733	1946–1968
Consecutive Games Played	Sachio Kinugasa	2,215	Oct. 19, 1970–Oct. 22, 1987
Consecutive Game Hit Streak	Yoshihiko Takahashi	33	June 6, 1979–July 31, 1979
Consecutive Game HR Streak	Randy Bass	7	June 18, 1986–June 26, 1986
Consecutive Pitching Wins	Kazuhisa Inao	20	July 18, 1957–Oct. 1, 1957
Consecutive Pitching Losses	Masatoshi Gondo	28	July 9, 1955–June 2, 1957
Career Grand Slams	Sadaharu Oh	15	1959–1981
Grand Slams in Single Season	Michio Nishizawa	5	1950
Triple Crown Winners	Haruyasu Nakajima	.361 BA, 10 HR, 38 RBI	1938 Fall
	Katsuya Nomura (Pacific League)	.320 BA, 42 HR, 110 RBI	1965
	Sadaharu Oh (Central League)	.355 BA, 51 HR, 114 RBI	1973
	Sadaharu Oh (Central League)	.332 BA, 49 HR, 107 RBI	1974
	Hiromitsu Ochiai (Pacific League)	.325 BA, 32 HR, 99 RBI	1982
	Boomer Wells (Pacific League)	.355 BA, 37 HR, 130 RBI	1984
	Randy Bass (Central League)	.350 BA, 54 HR, 134 RBI	1985
	Hiromitsu Ochiai (Pacific League)	.367 BA, 52 HR, 146 RBI	1985
	Randy Bass (Central League)	.389 BA, 47 HR, 109 RBI	1986
	Hiromitsu Ochiai (Pacific League)	.360 BA, 50 HR, 116 RBI	1986

Career Statistics of Selected Japanese League Stars: Position Players

Player*	Position	Primary Team	Years	G	AB	R	H	HR	BA
Fumio Fujimura	3B	Hanshin Tigers	1936–1958	1,558	5,648	871	1,694	224	.300
Michio Nishizawa	U	Nagoya Dragons	1937–1958	1,704	5,999	750	1,716	212	.286
Shigeru Chiba	2B	Yomiuri Giants	1938–1956	1,512	5,643	981	1,605	96	.284
Tetsu Kawakami	1B	Yomiuri Giants	1938–1958	1,979	7,500	1,028	2,351	181	.313
Takeshi Doigaki	C	Hanshin Tigers	1940–1957	1,413	4,783	551	1,351	79	.282
Hiroshi Oshita	OF	Toei Flyers	1946–1959	1,547	5,500	763	1,667	201	.303
Wally Yonamine	OF	Yomiuri Giants	1951–1962	1,219	4,298	707	1,337	82	.311
Kazu Yamauchi	OF	Lotte Orions	1952–1970	2,251	7,702	1,218	2,271	396	.295
Yoshio Yoshida	SS	Hanshin Tigers	1953–1969	2,007	6,980	900	1,864	66	.277
Yasumitsu Toyoda	SS	Nishitetsu Lions	1953–1969	1,814	6,134	980	1,699	263	.277
Futoshi Nakanishi	3B	Nishitetsu Lions	1953–1969	1,388	4,116	673	1,262	244	.307
Katsuya Nomura	C	Fukuoka Hawks	1954–1980	3,017	10,472	1,509	2,901	657	.277
Masaaki Mori	C	Yomiuri Giants	1955–1974	1,884	5,686	392	1,341	81	.236
Kihachi Enomoto	1B	Tokyo Orions	1955–1972	2,222	7,763	1,169	2,314	246	.298
Yoshinori Hirose	OF	Nankai Hawks	1955–1977	2,190	7,631	1,205	2,157	131	.282
Shigeo Nagashima	3B	Yomiuri Giants	1958–1974	2,186	8,094	1,270	2,471	444	.305
Shinichi Eto	OF	Chunichi Dragons	1959–1976	2,084	7,156	924	2,057	367	.287
Sadaharu Oh	1B	Yomiuri Giants	1959–1980	2,831	9,250	1,967	2,786	868	.301
Isao Harimoto	OF	Toei Flyers	1959–1981	2,752	9,666	1,523	3,085	504	.319
Morimichi Takagi	2B	Chunichi Dragons	1960–1980	2,282	8,367	1,121	2,274	236	.272
Masahiro Doi	OF	Taiheiyo Lions	1962–1981	2,449	8,694	1,105	2,452	465	.282
Sachio Kinugasa	U	Hiroshima Carp	1965–1987	2,677	9,404	1,372	2,643	504	.270
Katsuo Osugi	1B	Toei Flyers	1965–1983	2,235	7,763	1,080	2,228	486	.287
Koichi Tabuchi	C	Hanshin Tigers	1969–1984	1,739	5,892	909	1,532	474	.260
Koji Yamamoto	OF	Hiroshima Carp	1969–1986	2,284	8,052	1,365	2,339	536	.290
Yutaka Fukumoto	OF	Hankyu Braves	1969–1988	2,401	8,745	1,656	2,543	208	.291
Hiromitsu Kadota	OF	Fukuoka Hawks	1970–1990	2,571	8,868	1,319	2,566	567	.289
Kenichi Yazawa	OF	Chunichi Dragons	1970–1986	1,931	6,818	847	2,062	273	.302
Tsuto Wakamatsu	U	Yakult Swallows	1971–1989	2,062	6,808	1,015	2,173	220	.319
Masayuki Kakefu	3B	Hanshin Tigers	1974–1988	1,625	5,673	892	1,656	349	.292
Yoshi Takahashi	SS	Hiroshima Carp	1975–1992	1,722	6,510	1,003	1,526	163	.280
Toshio Shinozuka	2B	Yomiuri Giants	1976–1994	1,651	5,572	739	1,696	92	.304
Hiromitsu Ochiai	OF	Lotte Orions	1979–1998	2,236	7,627	1,335	2,371	510	.311
Yutaka Takagi	2B	Taiyo Whales	1981–1994	1,628	5,782	—	1,716	88	.297
Takahiro Ikeyama	SS	Yakult Swallows	1984–2000	1,253	4,312	—	1,137	239	.264

* Chronological by player's debut season.

Career Statistics of Selected Japanese League Stars: Pitchers

Player*	Primary Team	Years	G	IP	W-L	CG	SO	SHO	ERA
Victor Starffin	Yomiuri Giants	1936–1955	586	4,075	303–175	350	1,950	83	2.09
Tad Wakabayashi	Osaka Tigers	1936–1950	528	3,559	240–141	263	1,000	57	1.99
Jiro Noguchi	Hankyu Braves	1939–1953	517	3,448	237–139	259	1,396	65	1.96
Takehiko Bessho	Yomiuri Giants	1942–1960	622	4,350	310–178	335	1,934	72	2.18
Hideo Fujimoto	Yomiuri Giants	1942–1955	367	2,628	200–87	227	1,177	63	1.90
Shigeru Sugishita	Chunichi Dragons	1949–1961	525	2,841	215–123	170	1,761	31	2.20
Masaichi Kaneda	Yakult Swallows	1950–1969	944	5,526	400–298	365	4,490	82	2.34
Masaaki Koyama	Hanshin Tigers	1953–1973	856	4,899	320–232	290	3,158	74	2.45
Tetsuya Yoneda	Hankyu Braves	1956–1976	949	5,130	350–285	262	3,388	64	2.41
Kazuhisa Inao	Seibu Lions	1956–1969	756	3,599	276–137	179	2,574	43	1.98
Minoru Murayama	Hanshin Tigers	1959–1972	509	3,050	222–147	192	2,271	55	2.09
Keishi Suzuki	Kintetsu Buffaloes	1966–1985	703	4,600	317–238	340	3,061	71	3.11
Yutaka Enatsu	Hanshin Tigers	1967–1984	829	3,196	206–158	154	2,987	45	2.49
Hisashi Yamada	Hankyu Braves	1969–1988	654	3,865	284–166	283	2,058	31	3.18

* Chronological by player's debut season.

Statistics of Selected Major League Batters in the Japanese Professional Leagues

Name	Birthplace	Japanese Leagues				Major Leagues			
		AB	H	HR	BA	AB	H	HR	BA
Matty Alou	Dom. Rep.	913	258	14	.283	5,789	1,777	31	.307
George Altman	USA	3,183	985	205	.309	3,091	832	101	.269
Mike Andrews	USA	389	90	12	.231	3,116	803	66	.258
Ken Aspromonte	USA	943	257	31	.273	1,483	369	19	.249
Don Blasingame	USA	1,356	371	15	.274	5,296	1,366	21	.258
Randy Bass	USA	2,208	743	202	.337	325	69	9	.212
Clete Boyer	USA	1,486	382	71	.257	5,780	1,396	162	.242
Glenn Braggs	USA	712	232	54	.326	2,336	601	70	.257
Ralph Bryant	USA	1,173	323	112	.275	1,997	515	30	.258
Don Buford	USA	1,779	480	65	.270	4,553	1,203	93	.264
Warren Cromartie	USA	2,961	951	171	.321	3,796	1,063	60	.280
Dick Davis	USA	1,703	564	117	.331	1,217	323	27	.265
Willie Davis	USA	797	237	43	.297	9,174	2,561	182	.279
Brian Dayett	USA	481	126	21	.262	426	110	14	.258
Orestes Destrade	Cuba	1,655	436	154	.263	635	157	21	.247
Mike Diaz	USA	943	288	72	.305	683	169	31	.247
Larry Doby	USA	240	54	10	.225	5,348	1,515	253	.283
Mike Easler	USA	517	156	26	.302	3,677	1,078	118	.293
Chuck Essegian	USA	300	79	15	.263	1,018	260	47	.255
Chico Fernández	Cuba	111	16	1	.144	2,778	666	40	.240
Adrian Garrett	USA	1,302	338	102	.260	276	51	11	.185
Wayne Garrett	USA	606	146	28	.241	3,285	786	61	.239
Davey Johnson	USA	660	159	39	.241	4,797	1,252	136	.261
Cecil Fielder	USA	384	116	38	.302	2,870	743	191	.259
Kent Hadley	USA	2,825	727	131	.257	363	88	14	.242
Mel Hall	USA	939	269	52	.286	4,212	1,168	134	.277
Vic Harris	USA	968	245	35	.253	1,610	349	13	.217
Jack Howell	USA	1,146	336	86	.293	2,268	535	84	.236
Clarence Jones	USA	3,182	762	246	.239	137	34	2	.248
Willie Kirkland	USA	2,323	559	126	.246	3,494	837	148	.240
Leron Lee	USA	4,934	1,579	283	.320	1,617	404	31	.250
Jim Lefebvre	USA	1,098	289	60	.263	3,014	756	74	.251
Norm Larker	USA	727	194	14	.267	1,953	538	32	.275
Johnny Logan	USA	254	48	7	.189	5,244	1,407	93	.268
Jim Lyttle	USA	3,319	945	166	.285	710	176	9	.248
Ken Macha	USA	1,699	516	82	.303	380	98	1	.258
Charlie Manuel	USA	2,127	644	189	.303	384	76	4	.198
Jim Marshall	USA	1,501	402	78	.268	852	206	29	.242
Carlos May	USA	1,397	431	70	.308	4,120	1,127	90	.274
Román Mejías	Cuba	52	15	0	.288	1,768	449	54	.254
Félix Millán	PR	1,139	348	12	.306	5,791	1,617	22	.279
Bobby Mitchell	USA	1,718	429	113	.250	617	150	3	.243
Don Money	USA	100	26	8	.260	6,215	1,623	176	.261
Tom O'Malley	USA	1,721	548	74	.318	1,213	310	13	.256
Don Newcombe	USA	279	73	12	.262	—*	—*	—*	—*
Bob Nieman	USA	355	107	13	.301	3,452	1,018	125	.295
Ben Oglivie	Panama	805	246	46	.306	5,913	1,615	235	.273
Steve Ontiveros	USA	2,458	768	82	.312	2,193	600	24	.274
Wes Parker	USA	482	145	14	.301	4,157	1,110	64	.267
Larry Parrish	USA	874	227	70	.260	6,792	1,789	256	.263
Stan Palys	USA	1,525	419	66	.275	333	79	10	.237
Joe Pepitone	USA	43	7	1	.163	5,097	1,315	219	.258
Jack Pierce	USA	291	66	13	.227	199	42	8	.211
Kevin Reimer	USA	470	140	27	.258	1,455	376	52	.258
Roger Repoz	USA	1,787	469	122	.262	2,145	480	82	.224

(*continued*)

(continued)

Name	Birthplace	Japanese Leagues				Major Leagues			
		AB	H	HR	BA	AB	H	HR	BA
Bombo Rivera	PR	541	130	37	.240	831	220	10	.265
Dave Roberts	Panama	2,774	764	183	.275	194	38	2	.196
Reggie Smith	USA	494	134	45	.271	7,033	2,020	314	.287
Tony Solaita	Am. Samoa	1,786	479	155	.268	1,316	336	50	.255
Daryl Spencer	USA	2,233	615	152	.275	3,689	901	105	.244
Gene Stephens	USA	232	52	5	.224	1,913	460	37	.240
Dick Stuart	USA	685	176	49	.257	3,997	1,055	228	.264
Gary Thomasson	USA	477	119	20	.249	2,373	591	61	.249
Bobby Tolan	USA	360	96	6	.267	4,230	1,121	86	.265
Jim Trabor	USA	495	150	24	.303	819	186	27	.227
Willie Upshaw	USA	653	160	39	.245	4,203	1,103	123	.262
Lee Walls	USA	343	82	14	.239	2,550	670	66	.262
Boomer Wells	USA	3,482	1137	231	.327	127	29	0	.228
Terry Whitfield	USA	1,407	406	85	.289	1,913	537	33	.281
Walt Williams	USA	952	264	44	.277	2,373	640	33	.270
Bump Wills	USA	633	164	16	.259	3,030	807	36	.266
George Wilson	USA	624	161	27	.258	209	40	3	.191
Gordy Windhorn	USA	1,966	501	86	.255	108	19	2	.176
Roy White	USA	1,229	348	54	.283	6,650	1,803	160	.271
Zoilo Versalles	Cuba	132	25	4	.189	5,141	1,246	95	.290
José Vidal	Dom. Rep.	122	27	2	.221	146	24	3	.164
George Vukovich	USA	754	193	32	.256	1,602	430	27	.268
Don Zimmer	USA	203	37	9	.182	3,283	773	91	.235

Abbreviations: Am., American; Dom., Dominican; PR, Puerto Rico; Rep., Republic; USA, United States.
* Pitching in the major leagues; no batting statistics given.

Statistics of Selected Major Leaguer Pitchers in the Japanese Professional Leagues

Name	Birthplace	Japanese League				Major Leagues			
		G	W–L	IP	ERA	G	W–L	IP	ERA
Bob Alexander	Canada	13	2–5	53	4.58	9	1–1	11	10.64
Rick Austin	USA	8	1–1	27	2.33	89	4–8	136	4.63
Andy Beene	USA	8	2–2	22	7.25	6	0–2	21	10.45
Pete Burnside	USA	57	10–22	282	3.10	196	19–36	567	4.81
Keith Comstock	USA	21	8–8	125	4.19	144	10–7	153	4.06
George Culver	USA	9	1–4	36	6.50	335	48–49	789	3.62
Paul Foytack	USA	18	2–3	58	3.16	312	86–87	1,498	4.14
Rich Gale	USA	33	13–8	191	4.30	195	55–56	970	4.54
Al Grunwald	USA	26	2–8	83	4.50	9	0–1	19	6.63
Leo Kiely	USA	6	6–0	45	1.80	209	26–27	523	3.37
Rick Krueger	USA	18	2–1	29	4.66	17	2–2	44	4.47
Fred Kuhaulua	HI	25	3–4	73	4.32	8	1–0	35	4.79
Terry Ley	USA	24	5–5	98	4.13	6	0–0	9	5.00
Glenn Mickens	USA	169	45–51	909	2.54	4	0–1	6	11.37
Phil Paine	USA	9	4–3	61	1.77	95	10–1	150	3.36
Ed Palmquist	USA	9	0–1	17	3.00	36	1–3	69	5.11
Dave Rajsich	USA	23	0–0	23	3.18	55	3–4	115	4.60
Bob Reynolds	USA	3	0–0	6	9.00	140	14–16	255	3.15
Steve Shirley	USA	50	5–7	118	4.17	11	1–1	13	4.26
Joe Stanka	USA	264	100–72	1,459	3.08	2	1–0	5	3.38
Dean Stone	USA	6	0–0	12	3.75	215	29–39	686	4.47
Thad Tillotson	USA	18	3–4	45	6.40	50	4–9	109	4.06
Clyde Wright	USA	59	22–18	340	3.97	329	100–111	1,729	3.50

Abbreviations: HI, Hawaii; USA, United States.

Japanese Single-League No-Hit Games Pitched (1936–1949)

Year	Date	Pitcher	Team	Game Score
1936	Sept. 25	Eiji Sawamura	Tokyo Kyojin	Kyojin 1, Tigers 0
1937	May 1	Eiji Sawamura	Tokyo Kyojin	Kyojin 4, Tigers 0
1937	July 3	Victor Starffin	Tokyo Kyojin	Kyojin 4, Eagles 0
1937	July 16	Mitsuhiko Ishida	Hankyu	Hankyu 6, Senators 0
1939	Nov. 3	Hiroshi Nakao	Tokyo Kyojin	Kyojin 1, Senators 0
1940	Mar. 18	Tadashi Kameda	Eagles	Eagles 5, Lions 0
1940	Apr. 14	Katsusaburo Asano	Hankyu	Hankyu 9, Hanshin 0
1940	July 6	Eiji Sawamura	Tokyo Kyojin	Kyojin 4, Nagoya 0
1940	Aug. 3	Satoru Miwa	Hanshin Tigers	Hanshin 1, Kyojin 0
1940	Aug. 22	Mitsuhiko Ishida	Hankyu	Hankyu 9, Lions 0
1941	Apr. 14	Tadashi Kameda	Kurowashi	Kurowashi 1, Hanshin 0
1941	July 16	Hiroshi Nakao	Tokyo Kyojin	Kyojin 3, Nagoya 0
1941	Oct. 27	Hirotaru Mori	Hankyu	Hankyu 2, Nagoya 0
1942	July 18	Michio Nishizawa	Nagoya	Nagoya 2, Hankyu 0
1943	May 2	Yoshio Tenpo	Hankyu	Hankyu 3, Nankai 0
1943	May 22	Hideo Fujimoto	Tokyo Kyojin	Kyojin 3, Nagoya 0
1943	May 26	Akira Bessho	Nankai	Nankai 2, Daiwa 0
1943	Oct. 12	Shinichi Ishimaru	Nagoya	Nagoya 5, Daiwa 0
1946	June 16	Shosei Go	Hanshin Gold Star	Hanshin 11, Senators 0
1948	Aug. 24	Tadayoshi Kajioka	Osaka Tigers	Tigers 3, Hawks 0
1948	Sept. 6	Shigeo Sanada	Taiyo Robins	Robins 3, Tigers 0 (Game 2)

Japanese Central League No-Hit Games Pitched (1950–2003)

Year	Date	Pitcher	Team	Game Score
1950	June 28	Hideo Fujimoto*	Yomiuri Giants	Giants 4, Pirates 0
1951	Sept. 5	Masaichi Kaneda	Kokutetsu Swallows	Swallows 1, Tigers 0
1952	May 7	Shigeo Sanada	Osaka Tigers	Tigers 12, Carp 0
1952	July 28	Takumi Otomo	Yomiuri Giants	Giants 17, Robins 0
1955	May 10	Shigeru Sugishita	Chunichi Dragons	Dragons 1, Swallows 0
1956	May 3	Teruo Owaki	Kokutetsu Swallows	Swallows 5, Dragons 0 (Game 2)
1956	Sept. 19	Toshitomo Miyaji*	Kokutetsu Swallows	Swallows 6, Carp 0 (Game 2)
1957	Aug. 21	Masaichi Kaneda*	Kokutetsu Swallows	Swallows 1, Dragons 0 (Game 2)
1957	Oct. 12	Hiroomi Oyane	Chunichi Dragons	Dragons 3, Tigers 0
1960	Aug. 11	Gentaro Shimada*	Taiyo Whales	Whales 1, Tigers 0 (Game 1)
1961	June 20	Yoshimi Moritaki*	Kokutetsu Swallows	Swallows 1, Dragons 0
1964	Aug. 18	Yoshiro Nakayama	Chunichi Dragons	Dragons 3, Giants 0
1965	June 28	Gene Bacque	Hanshin Tigers	Tigers 7, Giants 0
1965	Oct. 2	Yoshiro Sotokoba	Hiroshima Carp	Carp 2, Tigers 0
1966	May 1	Yoshiro Sasaki*	Taiyo Whales	Whales 1, Carp 0 (Game 2)
1967	Oct. 10	Tsuneo Horiuchi	Yomiuri Giants	Giants 11, Carp 0 (Game 1)
1968	May 16	Kunio Jonouchi	Yomiuri Giants	Giants 16, Whales 0
1968	Sept. 14	Yoshiro Sotokoba*	Hiroshima Carp	Carp 2, Whales 0
1970	May 18	Hidetake Watanabe	Yomiuri Giants	Giants 2, Carp 0
1970	June 9	Hiroshi Kito	Taiyo Whales	Whales 1, Atoms 0
1971	Aug. 19	Kazuhiro Fujimoto	Hiroshima Carp	Carp 6, Dragons 0 (Game 2)
1972	Apr. 29	Yoshiro Sotokoba	Hiroshima Carp	Carp 3, Giants 0
1973	Aug. 30	Yutaka Enatsu	Hanshin Tigers	Tigers 1, Dragons 0
1976	Apr. 18	Hajime Kato	Yomiuri Giants	Giants 5, Carp 0
1987	Aug. 9	Shinichi Kondo	Chunichi Dragons	Dragons 6, Giants 0
1992	June 14	Toshiro Yufune	Hanshin Tigers	Tigers 6, Carp 0
1994	May 18	Hiromi Makihara*	Yomiuri Giants	Giants 6, Carp 0
1995	Sept. 9	Terry Bross	Yakult Swallows	Swallows 4, Giants 0
1996	Aug. 11	Shigeki Noguchi	Chunichi Dragons	Dragons 5, Giants 0
1997	Sept. 2	Kazuhisa Ishii	Yakult Swallows	Swallows 3, Bay Stars 0

* Perfect game.

Japanese Pacific League No-Hit Games Pitched (1950–2003)

Year	Date	Pitcher	Team	Game Score
1952	Apr. 27	Giichi Hayashi	Daiei Stars	Stars 2, Braves 0 (DH game 1)
1954	Aug. 7	Noboru Yamashita	Kintetsu Pearls	Pearls 4, Unions 0
1955	June 4	Mamoru Otsu	Nishitetsu Lions	Lions 8, Pearls 0
1955	June 19	Fumio Takechi*	Kintetsu Pearls	Pearls 1, Stars 0 (DH game 2)
1958	July 9	Sadaaki Nishimura*	Seibu Lions	Lions 1, Flyers 0
1964	May 16	Yoshio Inoue	Seibu Lions	Lions 2, Braves 0
1966	May 12	Tsutomu Tanaka*	Seibu Lions	Lions 2, Hawks 0
1966	June 12	Toshihiko Sei	Seibu Lions	Lions 8, Buffaloes 0 (DH game 2)
1967	Sept. 17	Tadao Wakao	Seibu Lions	Lions 4, Braves 0 (DH game 2)
1968	Aug. 8	Keishi Suzuki	Kintetsu Buffaloes	Buffaloes 4, Flyers 0
1969	Aug. 16	Fumio Narita	Lotte Orions	Orions 1, Braves 0 (DH game 2)
1970	Oct. 6	Kiochiro Sasaki*	Kintetsu Buffaloes	Buffaloes 3, Hawks 0
1971	Aug. 21	Yoshimasa Takahashi*	Nittaku Home Flyers	Flyers 4, Lions 0
1971	Sept. 9	Keishi Suzuki	Kintetsu Buffaloes	Buffaloes 4, Lions 0
1973	June 16	Naoki Takahashi	Nittaku Home Flyers	Flyers 1, Buffaloes 0 (DH game 2)
1973	Oct. 10	Soroku Yagisawa*	Lotte Orions	Orions 1, Lions 0 (DH game 1)
1975	Apr. 20	Toshio Kanabe	Kintetsu Buffaloes	Buffaloes 1, Hawks 0 (DH game 2)
1976	May 11	Yoshinori Toda	Hankyu Braves	Braves 1, Hawks 0
1978	Aug. 31	Yutaro Imai*	Hankyu Braves	Braves 5, Orions 0
1985	June 4	Taigen Kaku	Seibu Lions	Lions 7, Ham Fighters 0
1985	June 9	Yukio Tanaka	Nippon Ham Fighters	Fighters 12, Buffaloes 0
1990	Apr. 25	Yasumitsu Shibata	Nippon Ham Fighters	Fighters 3, Buffaloes 0
1995	July 5	Yukihiro Nishizaki	Nippon Ham Fighters	Fighters 1, Lions 0
1996	Aug. 26	Yoshinori Sato	Orix Blue Wave	Blue Wave 7, Buffaloes 0
1996	June 11	Hisanobu Watanabe	Seibu Lions	Lions 9, Blue Wave 0

* Perfect game.

Baseball Tours of Japan by Major League and Other Professional Teams

Year	Team	Visitors Record, W–L–T
1908	Reach All-Americans	17–0–0
1913	New York Giants and Chicago White Sox	1–0–0
1920	Herb Hunter All-Americans	20–0–0
1922	Herb Hunter All-Americans	15–1–0
1927	Philadelphia Royal Giants (Negro Leagues)	23–0–1
1931	Major League All-Stars	17–0–0
1932	Philadelphia Royal Giants (Negro Leagues)	23–1–0
1934	Major League All-Stars	18–0–0
1949	San Francisco Seals	7–0–0
1951	Major League All-Stars	13–1–2
1953	Eddie Lopat All-Stars	11–1–0
1953	New York Giants	12–1–1
1955	New York Yankees	15–0–1
1956	Brooklyn Dodgers	14–4–1
1958	St. Louis Cardinals	14–2–0
1960	San Francisco Giants	11–4–1
1962	Detroit Tigers	12–4–2
1966*	Mexico City Tigers	0–13–0
1966	Los Angeles Dodgers	9–8–1
1968	St. Louis Cardinals	13–5–0
1970*	San Francisco Giants	3–6–0
1971	Baltimore Orioles	12–2–4
1974	New York Mets	9–7–2

Year	Team	Visitors Record, W–L–T
1978	Cincinnati Reds	14–2–1
1979	Major League All-Stars[†]	1–1–0
1981	Kansas City Royals	9–7–1
1984	Baltimore Orioles	8–5–1
1986	Major League All-Stars	6–1–0
1988	Major League All-Stars	3–2–2
1990*	Major League All-Stars	3–4–1
1991*	Korean All-Stars	2–4–0
1992	Major League All-Stars	6–1–1
1993*	Los Angeles Dodgers	0–2–0
1995	Korean All-Stars	2–2–2
1996	Major League All-Stars	4–2–2

* Series won by host Japanese Professional All-Stars.
[†] National League All-Stars defeated American League All-Stars in other matches, 4 games to 2 games.

Japan's Hall of Fame

Japanese Baseball Hall of Fame (1959–2004)

Order of Induction	Year Elected	Name	Electing Body
1	1959	Matsutaro Shoriki	Sportswriters Committee
2	1959	Hiroshi Hiraoka	Sportswriters Committee
3	1959	Yokio Aoi	Sportswriters Committee
4	1959	Isoo Abe	Sportswriters Committee
5	1959	Shin Hashido	Sportswriters Committee
6	1959	Kiyoshi Oshikawa	Sportswriters Committee
7	1959	Jiro Kuji	Sportswriters Committee
8	1959	Eiji Sawamura	Sportswriters Committee
9	1959	Michimaro Ono	Sportswriters Committee
10	1960	Victor Starffin (aka Hiroshi Suda)	Special Committee
11	1960	Chujun Tobita	Sportswriters Committee
12	1960	Atsushi Kono	Sportswriters Committee
13	1960	Yaichiro Sakurai	Sportswriters Committee
14	1962	Yutaka Ikeda	Special Committee
15	1962	Tadao Ichioka	Sportswriters Committee
16	1963	Haruyasu Nakajima	Special Committee
17	1964	Tadashi Wakabayashi	Special Committee
18	1964	Kiyoshi Miyahara	Sportswriters Committee
19	1965	Tetsuharu Kawakami	Special Committee
20	1965	Kazuto Tsuruoka (aka Kazuto Yamamoto)	Special Committee
21	1965	Nobori Inoue	Sportswriters Committee
22	1965	Saburo Miyatake	Sportswriters Committee
23	1965	Masaru Kageura	Sportswriters Committee
24	1966	Tsunetaro Moriyama	Sportswriters Committee
25	1967	Hisashi Koshimoto	Sportswriters Committee
26	1968	Sotaro Suzuki	Sportswriters Committee
27	1968	Munehide Tanabe	Sportswriters Committee
28	1968	Kobayashi. Ichizo	Sportswriters Committee
29	1969	Hisanori Karita	Special Committee
30	1969	Daisuke Miyake	Sportswriters Committee
31	1969	Takeo Tabe	Sportswriters Committee

(continued)

(continued)

Order of Induction	Year Elected	Name	Electing Body
32	1969	Jiro Morioka	Sportswriters Committee
33	1969	Zensuke Shimada	Sportswriters Committee
34	1969	Yoriyasu Arima	Sportswriters Committee
35	1970	Shun'ichi Amachi	Special Committee
36	1970	Nobuaki Nidegawa	Special Committee
37	1970	Komajiro Tamura	Sportswriters Committee
38	1970	Matsutaro Naoki	Sportswriters Committee
39	1970	Kanoe Chuma	Sportswriters Committee
40	1971	Tokuro Konishi	Sportswriters Committee
41	1971	Rihachi Mizuno	Sportswriters Committee
42	1972	Shuichi Ishimoto	Special Committee
43	1972	Takeji Nakano	Sportswriters Committee
44	1972	Shigeru Ota	Sportswriters Committee
45	1973	Kozo Utsumi	Sportswriters Committee
46	1973	Teiyu Amano	Sportswriters Committee
47	1973	Kenzo Hirose	Sportswriters Committee
48	1974	Sadayoshi Fujimoto	Special Committee
49	1974	Fumio Fujimura	Special Committee
50	1974	Seizo Noda	Sportswriters Committee
51	1976	Hideo Nakagami	Special Committee
52	1976	Shinzo Koizumi	Sportswriters Committee
53	1977	Shigeru Mizuhara	Special Committee
54	1977	Michio Nishizawa	Special Committee
55	1977	Shigeo Mori	Sportswriters Committee
56	1977	Yukio Nishimura	Sportswriters Committee
57	1978	Kenjiro Matsuki	Special Committee
58	1978	Shinji Hamazaki	Special Committee
59	1978	Yasuhiro Itami	Sportswriters Committee
60	1978	Masaki Yoshihara	Sportswriters Committee
61	1978	Genzaburo Okada	Sportswriters Committee
62	1979	Takehiko Bessho	Special Committee
63	1979	Ryozo Hiranuma	Sportswriters Committee
64	1979	Goro Taniguchi	Sportswriters Committee
65	1980	Hiroshi Oshita	Special Committee
66	1980	Makoto Kozuru	Special Committee
67	1980	Shigeru Chiba	Special Committee
68	1981	Tokuji Iida	Special Committee
69	1981	Yoshiyuki Iwamoto	Special Committee
70	1981	Tatsuo Saeki	Sportswriters Committee
71	1981	Shotaro Ogawa	Sportswriters Committee
72	1982	Ryuji Suzuki	Sportswriters Committee
73	1982	Mojuro Tonooka	Sportswriters Committee
74	1983	Osamu Mihara	Special Committee
75	1983	Yushi Uchimura	Sportswriters Committee
76	1984	Shinji Kirihara	Sportswriters Committee
77	1985	Shigeru Sugishita	Special Committee
78	1985	Katsumi Shiraishi	Special Committee
79	1985	Atsushi Aramaki	Special Committee
80	1985	Katsuo Tanaka	Sportswriters Committee
81	1985	Ikuji Yamanouchi	Sportswriters Committee
82	1986	Miyoshi Nakagawa	Sportswriters Committee
83	1986	Masao Matsukata	Sportswriters Committee
84	1987	Nobuo Fujita	Sportswriters Committee
85	1987	Minoru Yamashita	Sportswriters Committee
86	1988	Shigeo Nagashima	Special Committee
87	1988	Kaoru Betto	Special Committee

Order of Induction	Year Elected	Name	Electing Body
88	1988	Yukio Nishimoto	Special Committee
89	1988	Masaichi Kaneda	Special Committee
90	1988	Saburo Yokozawa	Sportswriters Committee
91	1988	Akeo Akuta	Sportswriters Committee
92	1988	Masaichi Nagata	Sportswriters Committee
93	1989	Hidenosuke Shima	Special Committee
94	1989	Katsuya Nomura	Special Committee
95	1989	Jiro Noguchi	Special Committee
96	1989	Tsuneo Ikeda	Sportswriters Committee
97	1989	Masao Date	Sportswriters Committee
98	1990	Juzo Sanada	Special Committee
99	1990	Isao Harimoto	Special Committee
100	1990	Isamu Saeki	Sportswriters Committee
101	1991	Shigeru Makino	Special Committee
102	1991	Osamu Tsutsui	Special Committee
103	1991	Kichiro Shimaoka	Special Committee
104	1991	Yoshio Nakazawa	Sportswriters Committee
105	1992	Tatsuro Hirooka	Special Committee
106	1992	Michinori Tsubouchi	Special Committee
107	1992	Yoshio Yoshida	Special Committee
108	1992	Masao Yoshida	Sportswriters Committee
109	1993	Kazuhisa Inao	Special Committee
110	1993	Minoru Murayama	Special Committee
111	1994	Sadaharu Oh	Special Committee
112	1994	Wally Kaname Yonamine	Special Committee
113	1994	Tomoo Hirooka	Sportswriters Committee
114	1995	Tadashi Sugiura	Special Committee
115	1995	Tokichiro Ishii	Special Committee
116	1995	Shosei Go	Sportswriters Committee
117	1995	Minoru Murakami	Sportswriters Committee
118	1996	Motoshi Fujita	Special Committee
119	1996	Sachio Kinugasa	Special Committee
120	1996	Naotaka Makino	Sportswriters Committee
121	1996	Makoto Hosaka	Sportswriters Committee
122	1997	Katsuo Osugi	Special Committee
123	1997	Eiichiro Yamamoto	Sportswriters Committee
124	1998	Hiroshi Nakao	Sportswriters Committee
125	1998	Shinjiro Iguchi	Sportswriters Committee
126	1999	Futoshi Nakanishi	Special Committee
127	1999	Yoshinori Hirose	Special Committee
128	1999	Takeshi Koba	Special Committee
129	1999	Sadao Kondo	Special Committee
130	1999	Ichiro Yoshikuni	Sportswriters Committee
131	2000	Shintaro Fukushima	Sportswriters Committee
132	2000	Tetsuya Yoneda	Special Committee
133	2001	Rikuo Nemoto	Special Committee
134	2001	Masaaki Koyama	Special Committee
135	2001	Tsutomu Takeda	Sportswriters Committee
136	2001	Ryohei Hasegawa	Sportswriters Committee
137	2002	Kazuhiro Yamauchi	Special Committee
138	2002	Keishi Suzuki	Special Committee
139	2002	Yutaka Fukumoto	Special Committee
140	2002	Kenjiro Tamiya	Special Committee
141	2002	Fujio Nakazawa	Sportswriters Committee
142	2002	Akihiro Ikuhara	Sportswriters Committee
143	2002	Frank O'Doul	Special Committee*

(*continued*)

(continued)

Order of Induction	Year Elected	Name	Electing Body
144	2002	Shiki Masaoka	Special Committee*
145	2003	Toshiharu Ueda	Special Committee
146	2003	Junzo Sekine	Special Committee
147	2003	Kohei Matsuda	Sportswriters Committee
148	2003	Horace Wilson	Special Committee*
149	2003	Sakae Suzuka	Special Committee*
150	2004	Akira Oogi	Sportswriters Committee
151	2004	Noboru Akiyama	Special Committee

Source: http://www.baseball-museum.or.jp/. See that Web page for career notes.
Japan's Hall of Famers include players, managers, owners, officials, and historical figures, including one poet (Shiki Masaoka).
* The same Special Committee, for the new category celebrating the advent of the new century.

Japan's Amateur Game
Japanese Amateur National Champions (Industrial Leagues)

Year	Winner
1990	Yamaha
1991	Toshiba Corporation
1992	Nippon Life Insurance
1993	Nippon Oil
1994	Honda Motors
1995	Nippon Oil
1996	Honda Motors
1997	Nippon Life Insurance
1998	Nissan Motors
1999	Toshiba Corporation
2000	Mitsubishi Motors
2001	Kawai Corporation
2002	Isuzu Motors

NOTES

1. Nagata and Holway, 1999, p. 528.
2. Puff, "The Amazing Story of Victor Starffin."

BIBLIOGRAPHY

Books

Graczyk, Wayne. *Americans in Japan: American Players in Japan Pro Baseball, 1950–1986.* 2nd ed. rev. Tokyo, Japan: self-published, 1986.
Johnson, Daniel E. *Japanese Baseball: A Statistical Handbook.* Jefferson, NC, and London: McFarland & Company Publishers, 1999.
Maitland, Brian. *Japanese Baseball: A Fan's Guide.* Rutland, VT: Charles E. Tuttle Publishers, 1991.
McNeil, William F. *Baseball's Other All-Stars.* Jefferson, NC, and London: McFarland & Company Publishers, 2000.

Oh, Sadaharu, and David Falkner. *Sadaharu Oh: A Zen Way of Baseball*. New York: Vintage Books (Random House), 1984.

Whiting, Robert. *You Gotta Have Wa: When Two Cultures Collide on the Baseball Diamond*. New York and London: Collier Macmillan Publishers, 1989.

Articles and Chapters

Fimrite, Ron. "Land of the Rising Fastball." *Sports Illustrated* (September 9, 1985): 62–76.

Ivor-Campbell, Frederick. "Sadaharu Oh's Place in Baseball's Pantheon." *The National Pastime: A Review of Baseball History* 12 (1992): 35–36.

Leutzinger, Richard. "Lefty O'Doul and the Development of Japanese Baseball." *The National Pastime: A Review of Baseball History* 12 (1992): 30–34.

Nagata, Yoichi, and John B. Holway. "Baseball in Japan." in *Total Baseball: The Official Encyclopedia of Major League Baseball*, 527–535. 6th ed. New York: Total Sports, 1999.

———. "Baseball in Japan." in *Total Baseball: The Official Encyclopedia of Major League Baseball*, 592–604. 1st ed. New York: Total Sports, 1989.

Puff, Richard. "The Amazing Story of Victor Starffin." *The National Pastime: A Review of Baseball History* 12 (1992): 17–19.

CHAPTER 4

The Dominican Republic

Cradle of Big League Shortstops

• •

When it comes to the individual star ballplayer, Latin nations have enjoyed a rotating ascendancy across the past five or so decades. In the 1950s, on the heels of racial integration, the Cubans were first to grab center stage when Minnie Miñoso, Camilo Pascual, Pete Ramos, and pudgy dervish Conrado Marrero provided the vanguard of the first Latin big league invasion. Puerto Ricans (Roberto Clemente, Orlando Cepeda, Vic Power, and Luis Arroyo) joined the new influx of Hispanic headliners alongside the still-swelling Cuban contingent (Mike Cuéllar, Zoilo Versalles, Tony Oliva, Bert Campaneris, and Luis Tiant) by the mid-1960s and early 1970s. Mexico eventually got into the act with a phenom named Valenzuela when the 1970s merged into the 1980s. The Dominicans also had their moment in the sun with Juan Marichal, Rico Carty, and the trio of Alou brothers in the turbulent 1960s, as did Venezuela a decade earlier with a pair of fleet-footed and sticky-gloved middle infielders named Luis Aparicio and Chico Carrasquel.

The parade of individual Latino superstars has been relentless for half a century, and each nation (even Cuba, with its doors slammed shut by the Castro revolution in 1959) has shared in the newfound opportunities for celebrity on North American diamonds. The argument might be made, however, that even such huge 1960s idols as Clemente and Marichal were still something of a sideshow on the big league stage, and that it was the "Fernandomania" of the 1981 strike-ruined season that actually first made mainstream celebrities of Hispanic big leaguers. Certainly the attention Valenzuela drew from a national media during that memorable rookie season (when he was both National League Rookie of the Year and Cy Young winner) provided something of a watershed for Latin ballplayers and the Latino fans alike. Fernando Valenzuela was undeniably the morning star, the single icon who glittered most brightly at the dawn of a renewed Latin American baseball invasion almost a quarter-century back. And if the 1980s Latin story was launched with Mexico's Valenzuela, the 1990s seemed in turn to rocket off the booming bats of Puerto Rico's Juan

González and Venezuela's Andrés Galarraga. At the end of one century and the start of another, the biggest Hispanic slugging stars are now Sammy Sosa, Albert Pujols, and the amazing ageless Rafael Palmeiro. Not since Orlando Cepeda and Tony Pérez have Latin sluggers been so prominent in the consciousness of everyday fans.

In the end, it was more a matter of the numbers on the big league census sheets than in the sports page stats columns. That is to say, it was more an issue of ceaseless supplies of foot soldiers than that of a well-publicized sprinkling of exotic superheroes. The Latin big league invasion finally became page one headlines rather than page two filler not precisely when Sosa joined McGwire in pursuit of Ruth and Maris, or even that same year (1998) when Sosa and Juan González walked off with the Most Valuable Player (MVP) trophies in their respective leagues. Nor did it transpire two decades earlier, when a media feeding frenzy pursued Valenzuela from coast to coast. It more likely is the case that the highest watermark for Latinos was reached instead when the midsummer classic All-Star game rosters of both leagues finally boasted more Spanish-speaking imports than Middle America native sons. Or perhaps even when MLB's sudden push for a professional-style baseball world cup, staffed exclusively by big leaguers (certainly the best way to eliminate, if not beat, the Cubans) began raising the uncomfortable prospect that such a revolutionary plan might easily do more to promote victory for the Dominicans than for Team USA.

But for all the rotating celebrity, the one dominant story underlying the Latin invasion of North American ballparks during the 1980s and early 1990s was that of the monsoon-proportioned Dominican Connection and the newfound baseball Mecca of San Pedro de Macorís. Merely ten years before, the average fan knew little more about the Caribbean baseball heritage than the flashy feats of Roberto Clemente or perhaps some overblown infamy attributed to a stereotypical hot-blooded Latino star cut in the mold of a gun-toting Dolf Luque or bat-wielding Juan Marichal. (The 1985 World series tantrums of Joaquín Andújar had bolstered the image foisted by an ignorant press on Marichal and his teammate Cepeda.) Since the late 1980s, by contrast, the literature of the national pastime has bulged with debates and speculations about the ever-fascinating phenomenon of the shortstop-spawning town of San Pedro.

As a storehouse of big league talent, the Dominican Republic long stood a distant third, behind Cuba and Puerto Rico. Cubans hit the big leagues in full force in the wake of Jackie Robinson, and both Mexico (Bobby Ávila, 1954) and Puerto Rico (Clemente, 1961) boasted major league batting champions before the demise of eight-team leagues with baseball's first expansion in 1961. Venezuela's Luis Aparicio and Cuba's Orestes Miñoso were already redefining big league base running by the time the first Dominicans (Ozzie Virgil [or Ossie, as he preferred], 1956, and Felipe Alou, 1958) appeared on the scene. In the 1960s and 1970s, the Dominican imports matched those of Puerto Rico body for body, and during the next twelve years (1980–1992) the big leagues welcomed 104 Dominicans, compared with only 67 Puerto Ricans, 38 Venezuelans, and 21 Mexicans. Since 1992, however, the flow of Latin talent has become a floodtide out of the Dominican nation. Dominican big leaguers down through the years now outstrip their closest rivals (the Puerto Ricans) by more than 30 percent

(361 to 211 is the current head count), and the gap is expanding at an increasing rate.

Broadscale recruitment throughout the Dominican cities, towns, and hinterland, launched in the wake of Marichal and the three Alou brothers (Felipe, Mateo, and Jesús), yielded a wave of new ballplayers, first propelling the Dominicans into a narrow first-place lead in the overall Latin talent race. This lead over the rapidly diminishing Venezuelan and Puerto Rican baseball pipelines would widen dramatically in coming summers, not least because the Dominican Republic seemed to possess a unique natural resource—the fecund baseball city of San Pedro de Macorís. By the end of the twentieth century, nearly 60 major leaguers had seen their first daylight and hit their first fastball (usually a top from a pop bottle, stroked with a sugarcane pole) on the dusty streets and side roads of San Pedro. This sprawling seaport town (100,000 population in a nation of 8 million) with its unparalleled baseball heritage is best known, of course, for its 1980s–1990s fleet of glue-fingered shortstops (Tony Fernández, Mariano Duncan, Manny Lee, José Offerman, and Rafael Ramírez, among others), but San Pedro has produced a bundle of fence-rattling sluggers as well (Rico Carty, Pedro Guerrero, George Bell, Julio Franco, Sammy Sosa, and Juan Samuel) and at least one dominating pitcher, Joaquín Andújar.

This unprecedented Dominican Phenomenon has generated considerable popular press and media attention, contributing heavily to the shifting of popular focus onto issues of Latin baseball and Latin ballplayers. Casual fans and earnest SABR (Society for American Baseball Research) historians alike now puzzle over hidden explanations for the disproportionate Dominican impact on the North American national pastime. One of baseball literature's voguish topics (along with Bill-Jamesian sabermetrics, astronomical player salaries, and endless nostalgia for lost eras of real-grass baseball in the 1940s and 1950s) is now the saga of those rare diamond urchins springing full-grown from the sugar mill towns of the Dominican.

Three important books of a decade back explore this topic from sociological, cultural, and economic perspectives. In *Sugarball: The American Game, the Dominican Dream*, Alan Klein focuses on how Dominican winter-season baseball fosters national pride and inspires fierce competition with a mistrusted North American neighbor. Klein's thesis, however, is that the Dominican national sport is far from anti-*yanqui* in spirit but rather promotes an acceptance (somewhat grudging, but an acceptance) of the North American presence felt throughout the island country. In *The Only Ticket Off the Island*, Canadian journalist Gare Joyce, using personalized player portraits (of George Bell, Rico Carty, and Dámaso García, among others) and finely etched evocations of Dominican ballpark atmosphere, creates a movingly detailed and lively picture (though now a bit dated) of the late twentieth-century Dominican baseball experience. And Rob Ruck, in *The Tropic of Baseball: Baseball in the Dominican Republic*, provides us with a most detailed and thoughtful look at the Dominican baseball heritage, one that suggests why a game ultimately imported from Yankee America has become this island nation's principal art form. Ruck's single chapter on Juan Marichal[1] is perhaps the most balanced and intimate personal portrait of a single Latin American player yet delivered to the North American baseball reading audience.

Ruck also comes closest among recent commentators to cracking the riddle of how a single tiny nation can provide such an abundance of baseball talent from such a parched soil of economic stagnation. The answer is partly historical and partly socioeconomic (as Ruck cleverly shows in his chapter entitled "Three Kings Day in Consuelo"). Like blacks in the ghettos of North America who bounce basketballs endlessly on the same playground pavements once occupied by inner-city culture heroes Isiah Thomas, Moses Malone, or Michael Jordan, hosts of Dominican youngsters without shoes or schoolbooks feel from their earliest years that sure-handed infield play and fearless skill when facing a big league fastball are their only tickets out of a life of poverty and obscurity. Embodiments of the baseball dream annually appear before their eyes when Tony Peña, Pedro Guerrero, Juan Samuel, Alfredo Griffin, and a fleet of other diamond stars (recently Sosa, Pedro Martínez, and Pujols) return to their own roots each winter, to bask luxuriously in the glow of a nation's limitless adulation. On one level then, the Latin baseball story might be read as the latest and most dramatic chapter of a century-long unfolding saga. It is a tale of baseball's role as the wide-eyed immigrant's most instantaneous key (if he can run like the wind and hit a breaking ball with grace) to unlocking the riches of the still bright American dream. Ignore for the moment the fact that U.S. immigration authorities keep a tight cap on this dream with a policy that restricts work visas for foreign ballplayers to a total of 500 per year throughout all of organized baseball.

The story of our national pastime in the Dominican Republic—as Rob Ruck has documented more thoroughly than any other scholar—stretches back through the full expanse of the twentieth century. And if there is a recurrent theme, then that theme is the role of the dominant Dominican sugarcane industry. And Dominican sugar even holds the key to the often-asked question about the true sources for today's Dominican baseball dominance.

The story of Dominican baseball actually begins with the story of Dominican cricket—and then is closely tied to the story of Cuban sugarcane production. The game of "bats and balls" in its most primitive form was inherited from the island's British rather than Hispanic side, so Dominican baseball is not strictly a direct import from Cuban sources alone. The Cubans did play a major role in transporting the American form of the game to the island of Hispaniola (now split between Haiti and the Dominican Republic), as well as to Puerto Rico and numerous other Caribbean ports of call—but what the Cubans brought that truly revolutionized life on Hispaniola was their sugarcane industry.

In the early 1870s, several thousand Cubans settled in Dominican coastal towns and villages, escaping from a destructive ten-year-long war at home for independence against the ruling Spaniards. That war had largely obliterated Cuba's thriving sugar production just as sugar emerged as an item of highest demand, due to a new working-class addiction throughout Europe and most of the western hemisphere. On the coastal plains surrounding San Pedro de Macorís and La Romana, the exiled Cubans were soon busily constructing the steam-powered mills that would turn the Dominican Republic from an economic and cultural backwater into a major player in the world sugar market.

In addition to transplanting a booming Cuban sugar trade, these expatriate settlers brought the game of baseball, which they were soon teaching to Hispaniola's coastal inhabitants. Once the sugar mills were up and operating, there was immediate need for a new and substantial labor force to carry out the menial tasks of cutting and processing on which the new industry depended. The small population of the Dominican Republic (then known as Dominicana) (less than a quarter million in the 1870s) itself had easy access to abundant land and thus little incentive to tackle the slave-like conditions of labor in the sugar mills and cane fields. The necessary labor was imported from overpopulated neighboring Caribbean islands, especially the British Virgin Islands and the Dutch Antilles, romantic places with names like Tortola, St. Kitts, Barbados, Jamaica, Trinidad, and Antigua. With these immigrants and migrants came a new breed of ballplayers, raised on the British game of cricket (the supreme pastime of Jamaica, Trinidad, and Barbados). By the dawn of the twentieth century, two new sporting traditions were thriving side by side in the sugar mill towns of the Dominican Republic. British Virgin Islanders were as dedicated to their own ancient game of cricket as the Cuban descendents were to their far younger North American version of rounders.

The labor backbone of the Dominican sugar industry in the last three decades of the nineteenth century was the Cocolos—dark-skinned, English-speaking Tortolans who first migrated in seasonal waves from the outer Caribbean islands to the Dominican sugar fields and then eventually stayed on as permanent settlers in the region of San Pedro and La Romana. While not all of these settlers were from British outposts (many hailed from French, Danish, and Dutch colonies), the Cocolos soon dropped their separate identities and began referring to themselves simply as the English. Their black skin, associated on Hispaniola with Haitian slave populations, and their distinctive culture marked by English language, Protestant religion, and higher levels of education all conspired to make the new laboring class the focus of considerable and continuing antagonism from the native Dominican population.

Overnight, the prosperous Dominican sugar industry had become a multinational affair: the operating capital was North American, the technical expertise was Cuban—only the land was Dominican. The labor was a strange mix of British language and culture and African origins, since Cocolos were direct descendents of those African slaves brought into the region by British and Dutch merchants in the seventeenth and eighteenth centuries. For a long time, the most visible symbol of this rare mixture were the Sunday afternoon cricket matches that became, in the early decades of the twentieth century, a San Pedro tradition.

British games and all things culturally English were doomed within a Hispanic sphere that was constantly becoming more ethnocentric. Even as the Cocolos proudly held on to their emotional link with the past by maintaining their cricket matches throughout the immediate pre–World War I era, their sons were soon enough turning their attention to the more native Cuban game. Barnstorming Negro league ball clubs, crack visiting Cuban teams, and even an occasional contingent of touring big leaguers also fueled interest in the increasingly more popular North American game. As the new Dominican fascination with baseball grew in the decades between the two world wars, it was the descendants of the Cocolo cricketers who would emerge as the new ballplaying stars of the San Pedro coastal regions.

Rob Ruck (*The Tropic of Baseball*, chapter 7) first underscored the fact that, while not all of today's Dominican big leaguers are of English–Cocolo descent, nonetheless the greatest concentrations of Dominican baseball talent today are found on those sugar mill estates of the San Pedro region that once boasted the most English populations and consequently the best cricket as well. The names themselves are a dead giveaway: Griffin (Alfredo), Bell (George), Offerman (José), Duncan (Mariano), Norman (Nelson), Lee (Manuel), Samuel (Juan), Carty (Rico). These future big leaguers had inherited from their cricket-playing fathers the key elements of a British sporting tradition and translated them into eventual baseball success: rigid family discipline, an uncompromising approach to sport, and a penchant for organization and structure—to say nothing of the genetic transfer of outstanding batting and hurling talents.

The Dominican professional version of the game was up and running not long after baseball emerged on Hispaniola as an amateur sport. Organized league competition as we know it today, however, did not begin until the early 1950s, when dictator Rafael Trujillo sanctioned a four-team summer circuit comprised of the long-standing Dominican amateur teams: Escogido, Licey, Estrellas Orientales (San Pedro de Macorís), and Aguilas Cibaeñas (Santiago). This first league would last four full seasons (two titles for Licey and one each for the Estrellas and the Aguilas) under the immediate and debilitating handicap of a summertime schedule of play. The circuit was operating head-to-head with major league baseball to the north, so the loss of any outstanding talent to the big leagues would deplete the quality of local play. With summer play, the Dominicans—unlike the Cubans, Puerto Ricans, Venezuelans, or Mexicans—could not root for the local heroes at home and again abroad during the same calendar year. These disadvantages became so obvious that the Dominican League was forced to reconstitute after only a brief trial at summer season play.

The most fabled teams of the new professional league—Licey and Escogido—already boasted a history stretching back four decades and more before the 1951 advent of a pro circuit on the island. The story of Dominican organized baseball begins, in fact, with the founding of the Licey baseball club and then closely parallels the growth and fortunes of that national baseball institution. What transpired between the earliest Cuban baseball invasions and the modern winter leagues was the great period stretching from the turn of the century to the late 1930s and today known to islanders as the Romantic epoch of Dominican baseball history (*béisbol romantico*).

Organized as a popular Santo Domingo club team in 1907 and dressed from the earliest years in blue and white striped flannels, the Licey baseball club ("Los Azules") fanned the sporting passions of the Dominican capital city in the years immediately preceding World War I. Island championship tournaments were soon being held, and the Nuevo Club captured the first in 1912. Four years later, the Ponce team from Puerto Rico would make the first barnstorming visit by a foreign ball club, and in 1921 Escogido ("Los Rojos") was organized to challenge the Licey team's island baseball superiority. The new team was actually a merger of three teams from the capital city (San Carlos, Delco-Light, and Los Muchachos). Five games were played between the new rivals that first year, with Licey taking a narrow 3–2 edge behind Puerto Rican slugging star Pedro Miguel Caratini and the first great Dominican

moundsman, Enrique ("Indio Bravo") Hernández. Another pioneering Dominican great was Juan "Tetelo" Vargas, a visiting star in the Cuban League and
later a Puerto Rican Hall of Famer who would earn batting and base stealing
championships on the latter island in the late 1930s and early 1940s as he
approached 40 years of age. A fleet-footed infielder, Vargas once smashed
7 consecutive homers in a 2-game span during 1931 Negro league play. He
later hit .404, in Puerto Rico in 1943–1944, and long starred with the barnstorming Havana Red Sox, New York Cubans, and New York Cuban Stars.

By the late 1920s, it had become fashionable to import high-priced Cuban
baseball mercenaries for the Dominican annual championship tournaments.
The rosters of Licey and Escogido were soon jammed with Cuban fixtures such
as batting champion Alejandro Oms, versatile hurler and hitter Martín Dihigo,
pitchers Ramón Bragaña and Cocaína García, and outstanding infielders
Pedro Arango and Pelayo Chacón. This escalation of talent and stakes reached
its great climax with the tense summer championship of 1937, in which president and dictator Rafael "Papa" Trujillo found his seat in power riding on the
prestige of his personally chosen "Los Dragones" ball club. Having renamed
Santo Domingo in his own image as Ciudad Trujillo, "El Jefe" also combined the
rosters of ancient rivals Licey and Escogido to do battle under his personal
banner against the rural Aguilas Cibaeñas and Estrellas Orientales. Trujillo
unleashed a torrent of under-the-table pesos to recruit his "super team" of
stellar Cubans and marquee blackballers, such as Josh Gibson, "Cool Papa"
Bell, and Satchel Paige. With an army of well-paid imports, Trujillo would
narrowly win his cherished championship during the most famous island
round-robin matchup of the (supposedly) amateur baseball years. Even that
memorable tournament, however, remains only slightly more than a footnote
played out against the backdrop of several decades of fierce Licey and Escogido
diamond rivalry.

THE DOMINICAN WINTER LEAGUE STORY

The great rivalries of the Dominican championship series have taken on a
fresh glow in the years since 1951, with Licey and Escogido combining for
28 titles in a half-century of subsequent league play. Dominican baseball had
gone into hibernation for more than a decade after 1937, but with Licey's first
professional island championship in 1951 the glory of the game came roaring
back. After the brief experiment with summer baseball, the Dominican winter
circuit kicked in with the 1955–1956 season, ready to grab its full share of
winter-ball headlines.

For a while, the new circuit was indeed one-sided. Escogido had not won
a single title in four years of summer play but took the first three winter
pennants and five of the first six. Big leaguers were now invited onto the
Dominican rosters, and the league thus displayed a wealth of talent comparable to competing winter circuits. It is not surprising that Escogido dominated
for the remainder of the 1950s. It was Trujillo's favored ball club, owned by
the dictator's own brother, and was thus assured of special clout for stock-
piling the best of local and important talent. Many Escogido stars of that first
decade are names familiar enough to big league fans: Matty, Felipe, and Jesús

Alou and Juan Marichal, Ozzie Virgil, Frank Howard, Stan Williams, Bill White, Willie Kirkland, André Rogers, Willie McCovey. And it is no accident that the Escogido club boasted a disproportionate number of New York and San Francisco Giants. Giants scout Alex Pompez (once owner of the New York Cubans Negro league ball club) had already signed the first two Dominican big league imports—Felipe Alou and Juan Marichal—and forty years of connections with the Latin baseball scene had earned him favor with Trujillo's special agent for Dominican ballplayers—the dictator's son, Ramfis.

Modern-day Dominican League action has spawned also a handful of heroes largely ignored outside of the island itself. Every Latin nation has its closet baseball legend or two—or three—with remembered and even cherished epic feats hidden from North American fans and the sporting press but nonetheless of truly mythic status back at home. In Cuba—at least in the pre-Castro epoch—José Méndez was always held in such esteem, and perhaps Cristóbal Torriente, as well as screwball master Luis Tiant the elder. In Mexico, there will always be Héctor Espino, the Latin Babe Ruth. In Venezuela, hero worship surrounds the elder Luis Aparicio as much as it does his major league son, and the pioneering moundsman Alejandro Carrasquel as much as his nephew who launched Venezuela's big league shortstop legacy. In Puerto Rico, barroom tales still feature Perucho Cepeda and Pancho Coimbre, and occasionally Canena Márquez or Luis Olmo. And in the Dominican Republic, the name that earns such reverence is that of Guayubín Olivo.

An ageless Dominican left-handed pitcher of the 1950s and 1960s, Guayubín Olivo made his major league debut at 41, largely unnoticed up in Pittsburgh, but with an entire nation proudly watching back home. Like Tony (Pedro) Oliva of Cuba and Vic Power (Pellot) of Puerto Rico, this Dominican hero came to the big leagues under quite another name than the one he wore back home. He was born as Diómedes Antonio Olivo in the tiny village of Guayubín, nestled in the province of Monte Cristi on the northwest side of the island. During his debut seasons of the early 1940s with a semi-pro club from Puerto Plata, Olivo was endlessly referred to by fans and press alike simply as "the great pitcher from Guayubín" and the designation stuck in shortened form, as such colorful handles so often do in the world of sport. Oblivious of the tradition, however, U.S. media and fans knew him simply by the given name of Diómedes Olivo—that is, if they paid him any attention at all.

Once he had arrived in the Show—his most productive early years tragically lost to the big league color barrier—Olivo made only a tiny impression on the collective baseball memory banks. It was a considerable impression at the time, however, for anyone hailing from either Pittsburgh or Hispaniola. Though Olivo was hardly a major factor in his first Pittsburgh relief appearance on the afternoon of September 5, 1960, yet over the final three weeks of the 1960 pennant chase the Dominican would enjoy four crucial mop-up assignments, all during the heat of a tense pennant race. He handled them brilliantly, recording a ten-inning 2.70 ERA and fanning ten enemy batters in the process. It would be an exaggeration to claim that Olivo actually saved a pennant in Pittsburgh that fall, but he certainly helped. For Dominican baseball watchers, it was all sweet vindication, recognition at last for the man who had been the greatest lefty of Dominican baseball throughout the 1950s and perhaps even of all time.

Guayubín Olivo merits his small niche in baseball history, if only for his distinction as baseball's oldest-ever rookie (this distinction hanging, of course, on Satchel Paige's true birth date), and his contribution, minimal as it was on the major league scene, amounts to more than mere barroom trivia. At age 43, during what constituted his official rookie season in 1962 (in terms of the minimum number of appearances to qualify for full rookie status), Olivo took the National League by storm, baffling hitters with a 5–1 record, 2.77 ERA, and seven important saves across 62 game appearances. It was a last proud hurrah, however, for a fading veteran with a spent fastball; the next year, Olivo lost all five of his decisions with the St. Louis Cardinals.

For Dominican fans, it hardly matters that Guayubín Olivo had only a brief moment in the North American sunshine. All the important records and feats in Dominican League history are fully the heritage of every Dominican *fanático*, just as the epic events of the major leagues are for the North American fan, and many of those feats involved Guayubín Olivo. As early as 1944, Olivo had starred on his country's team in the amateur world series staged in Caracas; two seasons later he did the same during Pan American Games competition in Barranquilla, Colombia. Outstanding as a batsman and fearsome as a moundsman, Guayubín played regularly in the outfield when not needed as a pitcher. In September 1947, he hurled a memorable no-hitter for Licey against the traditional rival Escogido in the Dominican capital city. Once organized professional play returned to the island in 1951, Olivo paced the same Licey club with league-best totals in wins (10), strikeouts (65), and ERA (1.90) during the maiden league season. While again leading the circuit in ERA in both 1952 and 1954, Guayubín also continued to make history with his bat, once breaking up a memorable scoreless duel (and no-hitter) between big leaguer Ewell Blackwell and Negro leaguer Johnny Wright with a clutch pinch-hit ninth-inning single. A week after this memorable pinch hit, Diómedes Olivo would hurl his own second Dominican no-hitter, again versus the rival Escogido ball club.

When the curtain finally dropped on his lengthy career this greatest of Dominican southpaws had left a truly impressive legacy in his wake. Included were lifetime league bests in ERA (2.11), winning percentage (86–46, .652), victories (86), and total strikeouts (742). A third career no-hitter was added to the portfolio during the 1963 International League season: tossed by—remember— a 44-year-old. Olivo's career ledger is as impressive as it is almost totally unknown to U.S. fans who thought of him merely as "one-year wonder" with the Clemente-led Pirates of the Bill Mazeroski and Bob Friend era. (These lost pitching records of Diómedes "Guayubín" Olivo are reproduced at the end of this chapter.)

In the end, of course, the Dominican League's greatest bragging point is its role as a major league farm system, stocked with a seemingly endless supply of fresh arms and potent bats. The trickle started with Olivo and Marichal and Alou. Ozzie Virgil was technically the first of his countrymen to reach the Promised Land when he donned a New York Giants uniform in 1956—but Virgil was raised in New York and qualifies as a Dominican ballplayer by birth certificate alone. It was the playgrounds of the Bronx, not the sugar fields of Santo Domingo or San Pedro, where Ozzie Virgil learned to hit, run, and field ground balls. In the 1970s and 1980s, the floodgates opened in full and Dominicans dotted almost every big league roster. By the early 1990s, the Dominican Republic had passed both Cuba and Canada in the race to supply the most foreign-grown U.S. baseball talent. In 1993, Canadians could slap each other on the back in celebration of two World Series triumphs by their beloved Toronto Blue Jays and point with pride to the fact that their *Canadian* Dominicans had finally beaten the opposition's *American* Dominicans.

Another point of pride for Dominicans remains their strength in the Caribbean World Series in its second phase (for series structure and history, see chapter 11). A Dominican League representative first entered the series in the year of its revival, 1970. The Dominicans were a substitute, along with Mexico, for the Cubans and Panamanians, the cream and the chaff of the first decade of play. Dominican performance in Caribbean World Series competition would quickly become a proper reflection of the general upgrade of their winter circuit and the quantum leap in the nation's big league talent parade during the same third of a century. In thirty-three winters of renewed play, the Dominican entrants captured the most games (121 through 2003), won the most tournament titles (14, compared with 10 for Puerto Rico in the same period), and established the highest overall winning percentage (outstripping the Puerto Ricans with 7 more games won and 13 fewer lost). Slowly but steadily have the Dominican League teams built their trophy stash, beginning with a first Caribbean World Series title in 1971, peaking with two straight victories during the 1990 and 1991 Miami-based experiments, and culminating with four more trophies in the 1990s and an additional pair since the turn of the new century. Despite missing out on the first eleven years of competition, the Dominican Leaguers by 1992 trailed only Puerto Rico (eight titles to eleven) in total tournament championships, having finally overtaken the Cubans (7), who had so dominated the first decade of Caribbean playoffs. During the next decade, the Dominicans would even up the score, knotting the tally in 2003 at 14 banners apiece.

In the 1980s and 1990s, the Dominican circuit has flourished as never before, despite an overall decline in winter ball's stature (due both to organized baseball's evolving restrictions on off-season activities of its high-priced and fragile stars and to the sport's spiraling salary structure, which has removed winter play as a necessity or even an attractive option for economically satisfied athletes). Those who have played in the circuit—mostly unheralded newcomers and rehabilitating veterans—have filled recent campaigns with some memorable and even landmark events. The 1993 season provided a transition of sorts, with Escogido tumbling to the back of the pack after reigning as league champion for four of the previous five years. The same campaign witnessed the first foreign batting champ, American Tom Marsh, in more than a decade. Marsh's .318 made him the first non-Dominican to pace the hit parade since Ken Landreaux back in 1981. The 1996 roller-coaster season was one of incredible highs and lows. Escogido rebounded with the best season's win–loss mark ever (34–14, .708) but collapsed during the playoffs, winning only five of eighteen in the four-team round-robin. That unexpected collapse was followed by yet another when the Dominican Dream Team (nominally league champ Aguilas, but staffed with the likes of Julio Franco, Raúl Mondesi, and Pedro Martínez) fell flat at home in the Caribbean series with a third-place finish. Bartolo Colón enjoyed a spectacular outing in 1997 with a new ERA record that washed away a venerable league standard established back in the mid-1950s. And in the two most recent seasons (2002 and 2003) Bernie Castro, a San Diego Padres second base prospect playing with Aguilas, has become the new hitting star on the horizon.

Recent seasons have witnessed exciting action on the Dominican League front, with a host of new stars coming to the fore and familiar powerhouse teams jockeying for championship honors. The same storied franchises are still annually at the top of the heap. Aguilas has enjoyed six regular-season first-place finishes in the decade since 1994, and the same club has also walked off with a half-dozen playoff victories (not all in pennant-winning years) and thus six trips to the climactic winter league Caribbean series. Traditional Aguilas rival Licey has three pennants and three playoff triumphs over the same stretch. Only in 1995 did the shared monotony get broken, when an upstart Azucareros club managed by Art Howe outdistanced Aguilas by a single game in the regular standings and then overcame the same club in the six-game finals. It was the first pennant ever for the Azucareros ("Sugarcane Cutters") and also ruined a career season for Aguilas first baseman and league MVP Domingo Martínez, who barely missed packing away a triple crown. Martínez fell short in the batting race, trailing Luis Mercedes (Estrellas) by 21 points. If familiar teams always seemed to come to the fore in the heat of pennant chases, the names and faces of top pitchers and sluggers regularly changed from year to year. When Bernie Castro (Aguilas) salted away a second straight batting crown in 2003, he became the first batsman to repeat since Stan Javier in the mid-1980s.

Another offshoot of stellar Dominican League competition in the 1990s has been the continued reign for the Dominicans in the annual Caribbean World Series showdown versus other winter circuits. Several recent seasons have seen the Dominicans own the field at this annual showdown precisely the way the Cubans once did a half-century back. The apex came with three consecutive championship trophies in 1997, 1998, and 1999, the first two earned by Aguilas and the third by Licey. The Dominicans have also come out on top in 1994 (Licey), 2001 (Aguilas), and 2003 (Aguilas). With six triumphs in ten outings, the Dominican forces have now finally knotted the overall championship tally versus Puerto Rico at fourteen apiece.

Due mainly to the virtual absence of Cuban Leaguers in the major league marketplace, the Dominican League (as well as a dozen MLB- and Japanese League–owned training academies for teenaged prospects signed directly off the sandlots) has remained a primary overseas source for future big league talent. With the prospects of an eventual thaw in United States–Cuba political relations flickering on the horizon, this situation may not continue very far into the future. Twenty Dominican-born rookies entered the majors in 2000, twenty-one more in 2001, and seventeen in 2003; twice that many now labor in the top three minor league levels of organized baseball. Venezuela, next in line for export of major leaguers, produced 13 rookies in 2001 and 11 each in 2002 and 2003—about half the Dominican contribution. But *Baseball America* correspondent Milton Jamail (*Full Count*, 1999), seeing the writing on the wall, raises a penetrating and almost rhetorical question when he inquires as follows: if the Dominican Republic with about three million fewer residents has 1,500 players currently signed to U.S. professional contracts, how many might Cuba produce with a much more highly organized existing baseball development system? Inevitable change in Cuba's long-frigid relationship with organized baseball will unquestionably go far to end the Dominicans' long-privileged status within the world of professional baseball.

All the same, the Dominican winter circuit has remained the most visibly healthy of four competing venues during recent decades of overall decline in winter baseball enterprises. Perhaps the game's biggest names no longer head south for island play once the World Series rings down its curtain, and even the local Dominicans and Puerto Ricans and Venezuelans are either reluctant or banned (by contract stipulations) from showing off directly in front of their worshipful countrymen—but the Dominican winter season is still one of baseball's richest spectacles. The Dominican teams seem to have Caribbean World Series title play in a vice grip of late. If San Juan was once an off-season launching pad for young big league aspirants, Santo Domingo and Santiago now seem to be far outstripping all rivals in that role. Licey is still the most successful team in Caribbean series history. And to polish the luster of Dominican winter baseball even more, *Baseball America*'s eighteenth annual winter league Player of the Year trophy for 2003 was awarded to a young Aguilas bullpen ace, Arnie Múñoz.

DOMINICANS IN WORLD AMATEUR PLAY

Professional Dominican ballplayers have pretty consistently done themselves proud every few years in winter-end Caribbean series pro tournament action. The triumphs have not been nearly so notable on the world amateur baseball stage. This may in large part be due—in recent decades certainly—to the ongoing big league exploitation of Dominican talent, which has usually left national teams (unlike those in Cuba) void of high-quality athletes or recognized prospects. The same is becoming equally true of late in Puerto Rico and in Venezuela, where teenage prospects are also snatched up by big league scouts and sent to baseball academies when they are as young as sixteen or seventeen. In amateur competition, Dominican teams have thus consistently brought up the rear among these three top Caribbean baseball nations, but no one seems to pay much attention back home: the nation's sporting pride is almost exclusively tied up with decades of native son big leaguers. This matter of focus is a likely and altogether simple explanation for the ongoing drought in the nation's Olympic-style diamond successes.

Blame must also be laid directly at the doorstep of poor administration by the Dominican Baseball Federation, which maintains a weak visibility (with no working website, for example) more appropriate to neophyte baseball nations like Croatia or Slovenia and reflects the low value placed on national teams competing anywhere outside of organized baseball. The great successes of Dominicans in reaching the majors and minors have buried any local interest in other levels of play that might be perceived as lesser in quality. (Here the Dominicans have become truly Americanized.) Rarely have the Dominicans put together competitive teams for the World Cup, the Pan American Games, or the Central American Games. They have almost never challenged the Cubans, and rarely since the World War II years have they even been competitive against other Latin American entrants. It was 1981 before a Dominican team showed up for an Intercontinental Cup tournament (IC V, Edmonton), and they didn't return again until 2002 (IC XV, Havana); both times they ran off with the bronze medal.

World Cup play has been an especially bleak venue for Dominican teams—twenty-two overall appearances, three silver medals (all before 1952), a pair of bronze medals (the last way back in 1962), two lowly finishes in twelfth and thirteenth place during the past two decades, and a single unexceptional 1948 championship when Cuba, the United States, Japan, Korea, and Venezuela all cheapened the field by staying at home. Only on a few rare occasions—one was the 1955 Pan American Games, when the gold medal winning lineup featured Santo Domingo University medical student Felipe Alou, whose eye-popping play in Mexico City brought immediate professional contract offers—has a strong contingent represented the nation. This has been especially true in the half-century since Dominicans began to make their way in ever greater numbers into organized baseball's professional big time.

There have been a few notable exceptions to the pattern of Dominican failure in world amateur competitions. Most of these have occurred when the country has hosted these events on its own soil (notably, World Cup XII, 1969, third place; also Pan American Games XIV, 2003, with the Dominicans holding on until the quarterfinals against champion Cuba). And most such uprisings are far in the past. Several were given a boost by the rare absence of usually dominant Cuban contingents. Such was clearly the case with Pan American Games II in Mexico City (1955), and also with Amateur World Series (World Cup) X in Managua, Nicaragua. At the former event, Felipe Alou and company captured six of eight games, dropping one-run decisions to both Mexico and Team USA. With the title decided simply by overall standings in the round-robin (all opponents facing each other twice), a 6–2 mark was good enough to outpace the four additional entrants (which included Venezuela and the Dutch Antilles). At the Managua tournament, the once-beaten Dominicans swept Puerto Rico in the two-game playoff to lock up their one and only world title. Victory came mainly thanks to MVP pitcher Ramón del Monte, who bolted down wins in all four appearances (half the team's winning total) and mystified opponents with an 0.34 ERA (one run allowed in 26.1 innings).

Most surprising perhaps has been a recent continuation of poor Dominican performances even after professional players began to be siphoned into the glamorous and once strictly amateur world tournaments. In the inaugural session including pro players, during the Summer 1999 Pan American Games in Winnipeg, the Dominicans managed to string together a barely respectable squad that included a smattering of future and past big leaguers: Pablo Ozuna (Marlins) at shortstop, Tilson Brito (Blue Jays) at third, Israel Alcantara (Red Sox) in the outfield, catcher César Devarez (Orioles), and pitchers Julio Manon (Expos) and José Martínez (Padres). The result was a quarterfinals elimination at the hands of a once-reeling Cuban team (already beaten by Canada and Team USA) and thus a failure to reach the 2000 Olympics. Things have only gone downhill rapidly from there. The Dominicans have been absent altogether from many recent tournaments, due reportedly to severe financial crises and administrative hassles relating to formation of a representative national team. They were no-shows at the World Cup in Havana in October 2003 and again at the Olympic Qualifier in Panama less than a month later. Kansas City Royals skipper Tony Peña was scheduled to manage a Dominican entry at both events, but bickering ensued over the make-up of the squad and also over monetary support. Peña eventually withdrew, collapsing the ill-fated effort entirely. When Dominicans did compete in the Pan American Games that they themselves hosted at Santo Domingo in late summer 2003, the results were altogether disappointing. While Mexico overachieved and even beat the eventual winners from Cuba by a lopsided 7–1 count in one preliminary round match, the host team, even though featuring such notable ex–big leaguers as outfielder Luis Polonia and pitcher Luis De los Santos, managed only to split four opening round contests and was then drummed out 10–0 by the Cubans in the quarterfinals.

In short, outside its role as a rich harvest for big league talent, the Dominican legacy in international baseball has been a poor one. It is not unfair even to say that the Dominicans have been the grandest failures on the international baseball scene. But given how little attention the world's top baseball nations—always excepting Cuba—pay to international competitions, Dominican failures have easily been pushed to the background by heady achievements from the island nation's endless stream of successful professional performers.

THE DOMINICAN MAJOR LEAGUE SAGA

Despite effusive attention from media and fans alike, Dominican baseball is still surrounded with numerous misconceptions. The foremost misunderstanding, of course, is a notion that the country is exclusively a proving grounds for shortstops and other weak-sticking infielders of the Pepe Frías and Mario Mendoza variety. None would dispute that it has been Dominican shortstops that have earned a large chunk of the island's fame in the popular imagination. All true baseball fanatics can recite the litany of at least a handful: Tony Fernández, Alfredo Griffin, Manuel Lee, Mariano Duncan, and Julio César Franco (a shortstop in his earliest years). To date, several dozen have reached the big leagues. But shortstops alone have not cornered the market of Dominican imports. The greatest island big leaguer—indeed the small nation's most noted sporting emissary—was a pitcher from the tiny village of Laguna Verde: Juan Marichal. Next in stature to the Dominican Dandy are the three Alou brothers, all outfielders by trade. Of more recent stars, perhaps the greatest have been outfielder César Cedeño (1970s), shortstop-turned-second sacker Julio Franco (1980s–1990s), outfield bashers Moises Alou and Sammy Sosa (1990s), and current novice headliners Vladimir Guerrero (outfielder) and Albert Pujols (first sacker).

Classy and durable Dominican big league infielder Julián Javier, 1960s. [Transcendental Graphics]

If nothing-but-shortstops is something of a misconception, so is the prominence of San Pedro de Macorís itself. The all-time roster of big leaguers born in San Pedro de Macorís (see the table at chapter's end) totaled thirty-eight through 1992 (when the phenomenon seemed at its height) and sixty-four through 2003—a very considerable number for any single city in any quarter of the globe. Missing from the San Pedro list, however, are five of the greatest Dominican players of all time—Marichal, Felipe Alou, Manny Mota, Vlad Guerrero, and Albert Pujols, and despite San Pedro's indelible reputation as the birthplace of shortstops, only a dozen Macorisanos have actually made it to the majors at this position (the last being Manny Alexander in 1992). The best of the lot, Julio Franco, was originally from the neighboring sugar mill village of Hato Mayor (although raised as a native son of San Pedro). And, though Franco broke into organized baseball as a shortstop, his big league tenure has since branded him a second baseman and (after injuries) a designated hitter. Also, catcher-turned-manager Tony Peña was raised in San Pedro and learned his baseball there (thus hiking the number of big league native sons to potentially 65 at last count), although Peña's birthplace is technically the nearby village of Monte Cristi.

Jesús Alou formed one-third of the San Francisco Giants all-Dominican and all-Alou outfield. [Transcendental Graphics]

The Dominican Republic has at any rate produced its fair portion of slugging and hurling heroes to go with its famous complement of vacuum-cleaner, glue-fingered middle infielders. The numbers actually suggest far more potent sluggers and hurlers than infield wizards—and among the true greats, Marichal, Mota, the elder Alou, Carty, George Bell, Sosa, Pujols (and perhaps even Pedro Guerrero, with his 215 career homers and .300 lifetime average) overshadow all others, even the most notable standard bearers, infielders Julio Franco and Tony Fernández.

The explosion of Dominican big leaguers in the past two-plus decades (since 1980) has expanded the roster of San Pedro players more than four and a half times (from 14 to 64), and it has also boosted the total Dominican roster by a still greater percentage (six-fold from 62 to 362). The Dominican now far outdistances all other countries in its production of big league athletes. Of course had Cubans found the same doors open to big league careers the story might have been somewhat different. But even so, the Dominican Republic would likely still have been at or very near the top. Only Cuba could have provided a serious rivalry.

This period (1980s–1990s) has also provided the two grandest among Dominican star big leaguers. Like Sandy Koufax, Pedro Martínez will never post the huge numbers through longevity that guarantee a Cooperstown plaque, and yet his place is secure among the immortals. With slugger Sammy Sosa likewise there is no question about a niche among the game's greatest long ball bashers. Sosa's records (nearly 600 homers) speak for themselves, though some may claim that it is a much different game with its inflated long ball numbers across the board that has lifted Sosa into his lofty standing among the near immortals.

Setting these great stars of the past aside, the future of Dominican baseball today seems to stand at a dangerous crossroads. The player pipeline shows no immediate signs of running dry, of course, and even the possible opening of Cuba does not suggest any immediate replacement for Dominican talent, but the winter league season that has been the heart and soul of the island sport today faces a wrenching economic crisis. Politics seems to disrupt each winter's play on the Dominican home front, along with an endless series of marketplace collapses that strip the pockets of potential fans and electricity shutdowns that dim stadium lights. Plans for an expanded wintertime Arizona league sponsored by Major League Baseball can only spell further trouble in the long term. Will the player talent still spew forth as it has in the past, once the island is robbed of its showcase display of highly competitive winter league action during coming decades? Will sugar mill youth still worship and emulate the nation's great ballplayers, once those heroes are dusty legends of the past and no longer contemporary flesh-and-blood inspirations? There's no telling. The jury is still out and likely to remain so for some time to come.

THE DOMINICAN REPUBLIC'S GREATEST PLAYERS

The number of Dominicans enshrined in Cooperstown has long been stuck at one—Juan Marichal. Of course it is true that Latin Americans of any origin have been an extreme rarity in Cooperstown until very recently, when the inductions of Orlando Cepeda and Tony Pérez signaled a slight diminution of old prejudices. Juan Marichal was technically the first Latino ever to be elected legitimately to the shrine (Clemente was enshrined outside the normal election procedure after his tragic death), giving Dominicans a semblance of permanent bragging rights. With current stars such as Sosa, Pedro Martínez, Vladimir Guerrero, and now Albert Pujols, Cooperstown's Latin count will likely soon move considerably higher—but even if Cooperstown honorees are something of a rarity, Dominican baseball has no real shortage of top candidates when it comes to tallying big league stars.

Felipe Alou (b. May 12, 1935).   When it comes to lasting legacies, Felipe Alou would most likely loom large in Dominican baseball lore solely on the strength of his rank as perhaps the finest of all Latin-born big league managers (Montreal Expos, 1992–2000). But there is much more to the saga of Felipe Alou, and most of it involves the heroism of landmark pioneering at the tail end of integrated big league baseball's first officially color-blind decade. Alou was actually the very first Dominican-raised big leaguer; only Ozzie Virgil preceded him to the Show. But Virgil was New York–raised and learned all his baseball on the sandlots of the Bronx and Brooklyn. The elder Alou was also the first true Dominican star in the big time and one of the earliest big league headliners among Latin ballplayers of any nation. His career line over 17 seasons would eventually read 2,101 hits, 206 homers, and a .286 average. His special niche was as a power-hitting leadoff man with the Braves in the mid-1960s. In that role he batted .327 with 31 homers in 1966, also leading the league with 218 hits and 122 runs scored. He opened games with homers on 20 different occasions, was one of the very few to repeat that trick in consecutive games, and was also first to bang consecutive-day game-opening homers twice. A final chapter of Alou's legacy is currently being written with his second successful managerial tenure, this one with the San Francisco Giants, and also with the career of his talented son Moises, who has already logged a dozen big league seasons and clubbed 239 major league round-trippers of his own.

Felipe Alou was the first Dominican-raised ballplayer to reach the major leagues. [Author's Cuban Collection]

Matty Alou (b. December 22, 1938).   Mateo Alou, middle member of three big league brothers, played most of his career deep in the shadows of his more accomplished older sibling—yet that never stopped the diminutive but swift-footed lefty-swinging outfielder from ringing up some hefty accomplishments of his own. Tops on Matty's personal resumé was a surprise 1966 National League batting championship in Pittsburgh, earned in part with special tutoring from Pirate skipper Harry "The Hat" Walker, who recommended a heavier bat and a more pronounced slap-hitting style. Under Walker, Alou raised his sagging batting average by more than one hundred points over the previous season (from .231 to .342) to walk off with the talented family's only major league batting crown. Earlier, Matty had joined his two brothers (Jesús was the youngest) on the roster of the San Francisco Giants and on September 10, 1963, they made history as the first all-sibling and all-Latin outfield trio. In their debut game together, the three Alous all came to the plate in the same inning against Mets hurler Carlton Willey, who promptly set them down in order. Matty was an accomplished big leaguer in his own right, even if his statistical numbers were slightly less spectacular and his career much shorter than his older and more famous brother's. Matty Alou rounded out his career with three summers in the Japanese Pacific League (1974–1976) and with a stint as manager (for Ciudad Trujillo) in the Dominican Winter League.

George Bell (b. October 21, 1959).   Another San Pedro de Macorís product who starred in the outfield and not at shortstop, George Bell was never a very popular ballplayer, despite his considerable and much celebrated on-field achievements. Part of the explanation lies in the rough road Bell had to travel simply to reach the big time. Stuck in the hinterlands (Helena in the Pioneer

League and Spartanburg in the Western Carolina League) during several minor league seasons, he struggled to learn enough English to survive, was repeatedly embarrassed by what seemed hostile press interviews, and battled loneliness and lingering racial discrimination. It was enough to create suspicion and bitterness when he reached the big time with the Blue Jays. Another factor working against Bell's popularity with fans and media alike was that his dour, chip-on-the-shoulder personality could not compare very favorably with the more popular Alou brothers or a more respected Juan Marichal. An unfortunate, if all too familiar, "Latino hothead" stereotype seemed to cling to Bell, not lightened in the least when he displayed such rash outbursts of anger as karate-kicking Boston hurler Bruce Kison after a knock-down pitch, or squawking loudly in the press when Toronto skipper Jimy Williams wanted to play him as the designated hitter. But Bell, despite all the negativity, rang up impressive slugging numbers while also playing for a talented championship team. He banged 265 career homers, walked off with an American League Most Valuable Player honor, and also won an American League RBI title.

Ricardo "Rico" Carty (b. September 1, 1939).   Rico Carty was blessed with reams of talent but cursed with boatloads of ill luck. The San Pedro de Macorís native was a powerful hitter, who might be best described for today's fans as an only slightly lesser version of Montreal slugger Vladimir Guerrero. Carty certainly had his moments of near greatness, especially during his initial seven seasons served with the Milwaukee and Atlanta Braves. He smacked the ball at a .330 clip as a raw rookie, continued to post marks above .300 in five of his first six seasons, and captured the 1970 National League batting title. But he never became a superstar or even a familiar household name. Perhaps he was somewhat ahead of his time: oozing with self-confidence and Latin pride, he often feuded with his managers (especially Eddie Mathews of the Braves and Whitey Herzog of the Rangers). With that trait, he earned quick tickets out of both Atlanta and Texas. His personality and talents might have been better suited to the current era, which has rewarded rather than sanctioned the sometimes colorful antics of both Sammy Sosa and Vladimir Guerrero. Instead, it was plain bad luck mixed with occasional bad judgment that tempered much of Carty's career. He initially signed naïvely with ten teams simultaneously, and it took a special ruling by National Association president George Trautman to place him with the Braves. He missed much of his second big league season with chronic back problems, and two years later a basepath collision with Ron Hunt again limited his productivity. He missed the entire 1968 season for treatment of tuberculosis, and the next year he dislocated his shoulder seven different times—but still batted .342. In the aftermath of his 1970 batting crown (.366), the ill-starred outfielder fractured a kneecap during winter league action and again missed all of the 1971 season. And to cap things off, he ended his career with a lifetime average a single point under .300. Carty's entire baseball career—both the penchant for disaster and the ability to always bounce back—was foreshadowed in a single minor league incident in Toronto in 1963: on that occasion he homered twice on the same at-bat. When his first blast was nullified because time had been called, Carty calmly stepped back into the batter's box and stroked the next pitch into the left field bleachers.

Tony Fernández (b. June 30, 1962). The marquee shortstop of Toronto Blue Jays franchise history, Tony Fernández made four different stops with the American League club that included parts of 12 different seasons and included several campaigns (1985–1987) as the best defensive and offensive shortstop in the junior circuit. The durable switch-hitting San Pedro de Macorís native also played for the Padres, Mets, Reds, Indians, Yankees, and Brewers—as well as the Japanese League Seibu Lions (in 2000)—over 18 years that also included tours at second base (in Cleveland) and third base (in Cincinnati). Ironically there was increased offensive production accompanying each defensive switch. Fernández was perhaps the best and, certainly by career's end, the most productive of the Dominican's long line of talented big league middle infielders. Most of his fame was earned in the middle 1980s with the steadily improving Toronto clubs he sparked to the franchise's first division titles. Late in his career Fernández became something of a true marvel of longevity when he batted .321 and .328 in his final two full-time seasons during his third stopover with his original club; at the time, he was 37 and 38 years of age. But, as is so often a ballplayer's dark fate, despite all his slugging and defensive wizardry (four Gold Gloves and a .980 career fielding mark), the slender Dominican is likely to be always linked in memory to an uncharacteristic boot of a routine grounder in the 11th frame of 1997 World Series game seven, a costly Cleveland miscue that flung open the doors on Edgar Rentería's dramatic championship-winning single for the expansion miracle Florida Marlins.

Julio César Franco (b. August 23, 1958). Julio Franco has more than matched his durable countryman, Tony Fernández, with 19 big league seasons, a similar one-year sojourn in the Japanese Pacific League (1998 with Chiba Lotte, at age 40), and a later-career return to the majors with Atlanta that continued his lifetime .300 hitting pace well after his 45th birthday. Distinguished by a unique corkscrew batting stance and a seeming ability to hit any pitcher—at any time, in any league, at any age—Franco is undoubtedly the most durable player ever to come from the cane fields of the Caribbean island nations. At least that is true among those who made it to the majors: Dihigo and Tetelo Vargas were likely his indestructible equals. Franco's career resumé today reads something like those of some of the greatest ancient Negro leaguers—John Henry "Pop" Lloyd comes first to mind—who somehow played well beyond normal career spans and magically continued to achieve at most remarkable ages. Nearing 46, Franco also still plays a most respectable first base—a position he learned only late in his career, when he had lost the range needed to continue contributing as a middle infielder or a swift fly-chasing outfielder. If Manny Mota could (in journalist Jim Murray's apt image) make contact fresh out of bed on Christmas morn (quoted under Mota's entry in *Baseball: The Biographical Encyclopedia*), Julio Franco could seemingly do it on any day of any week at any stage of his life, even after most mortal ballplayers would have been strolling the golf course or lounging in the hometown barroom, savoring well-earned retirement.

Vladimir Guerrero (b. February 9, 1976). Vladimir Guerrero is the closest thing to the Dominican version of Roberto Clemente—the same slashing, free-swinging batting style, the cannon arm in right field, the perfect combination of raw power and clutch productivity, the fast start in the majors, and the continued improvement in each subsequent season. The whole package seems to be there. With the sagging fortunes of the Expos in Montreal generating year-after-year talk of liquidation or franchise fire sales, Guerrero was the hottest property on the major league scene for some four or five seasons. Speculation was finally ended when Guerrero inked a huge free agent deal with the Anaheim Angels during the 2003–2004 off-season, and there seems to be no end in sight for the growing productivity of one of contemporary baseball's most fearsome batsmen. Signed as a hot 16-year-old off the Dominican sandlots in 1992, the muscular prospect with the rather unusual (for a Dominican) first name was tapped as *Sporting News* Minor League Player of the Year four summers later. Two consecutive batting titles in the lower minors were enough to promote Guerrero directly to Montreal in 1997, bypassing Triple A. Three trips to the disabled list ruined any prospects for National League Rookie of the Year status, but in only his second big league season he was already a full-blown 22-year-old superstar. He broke six franchise records in 1998 and was among senior circuit leaders in ten different offensive categories. Subsequent summers have seen no drop in talent or productivity. Guerrero smashed more than 40 homers in both 1999 and 2000, paced the National League in hits with 206 in 2002, earned four consecutive All-Star game berths between 1999 and 2002, and has maintained a lifetime .323 batting mark over

his first eight seasons. He opened his ninth major league campaign with Anaheim and was among the top American League hitters near season's end. The prospects are better than average in Anaheim that Vladimir Guerrero will soon be expanding his superstar stature by performing his heavy-hitting act on MLB's glamorous postseason stage.

Juan Antonio "Manito" Marichal (b. October 20, 1937).   The first Dominican idol was 1960s pitching legend Juan Marichal, winner of the most games by a Latin big leaguer until Dennis Martínez finally overtook him in 1998, and owner of a high-kicking delivery that remains one of the game's most identifiable trademarks. Marichal was, like so many others, victim to stereotypes surrounding Latino players, but he also paid an even stiffer price for a career-altering moment of his own sad indiscretion. And if this were not enough, he had the misfortune to play in the shadow of Koufax and Gibson, which cut into a large portion of his own potential glory. The moment Marichal would forever regret came in August 1965,

"Dominican Dandy" Juan Marichal paved the way for Hispanic pitchers in Cooperstown. [Transcendental Graphics]

when during the heat of a crucial pennant-race tussle with the rival Dodgers he clubbed LA's John Roseboro with his bat, knocking the catcher nearly senseless. The outrageous action brought a nine-day suspension (instrumental in costing the Giants a pennant) and a then-huge $1,750 fine as its short-term consequence; long-range implications were far greater, as lingering memories of the attack delayed "The Dominican Dandy's" Cooperstown election by two full years.

Marichal captured 20 games or more in six of seven heyday seasons, he pitched over 300 innings on four occasions, he earned 24 wins in 25 decision at Candlestick Park against the rival Dodgers, and he pitched in a record eight All-Star games. For all that dominance, however, he never earned a Cy Young trophy and only twice topped the National League victory list. Bob Gibson in St. Louis and Sandy Koufax in Los Angeles were both at their peak in the very same years that Juan Marichal was crafting his competing legend in San Francisco.

It was not entirely the single outburst in the Roseboro incident that permanently tarnished Marichal. The image of a less-than-complete moundsman (despite 243 career wins) was firmly etched in the popular imagination long before the regrettable incident. In his revealing autobiography, *A Pitcher's Story*, with sportswriter Charles Einstein, the Dominican Dandy would perhaps rightly place some of the blame on the inconsistency of his manager, Al Dark, who in one mood praised his ace as an athlete who "thrives on competition" and "always rises to the occasion," then in another humor blasted him as being "without guts" and careless with his talents (*A Pitcher's Story*, p.141, p.150). Dark once complained loudly to the Giants bench that if Marichal continued to strike out opponents using his screwball, he would soon be unable to lift his arm and thus be of no use to his teammates. Marichal's arm seemed to stay surprisingly healthy throughout his long career, but he was plagued by numerous other small injuries that (as with Clemente) unleashed a label of soft ballplayer who failed to look after his health.

Most damaging, perhaps, was Marichal's approach to the game, one that was hard to knock for its efficiency but almost guaranteed to turn off fans and a handful of traditional by-the-book managers alike. Frank Robinson, Cincinnati Reds slugger, once complained that you just couldn't appreciate Marichal (who threw his arsenal of varied pitches unpredictably and in all situations) the way you could Koufax (who relied on only a fastball and curve, yet still overpowered most batters). This was a complaint shared by most fans, who prefer powerhouse strikeout displays to any hidden or subtle mound craftsmanship (just as they prefer the .240-hitting home run slugger to the boring .300 singles hitter). While Sandy Koufax (and Bob Gibson as well) was a strikeout king, Marichal simply wasn't interested in how he got batters out so long as he did. His strategy was to throw the ball over the plate with uncanny accuracy, make the hitters put the horsehide into play, and avoid walks at all cost.

Pedro Martínez (b. October 25, 1971).   The career of Pedro Martínez perhaps most closely parallels that of Sandy Koufax—at least when it comes to awesome talent overshadowed by limited durability leading to less than expected career numbers. Few would deny that Martínez is among the two or three most talented major league pitchers of the past decade-plus. His headline-grabbing achievements include two 20-win seasons, three seasons atop the league strike-out leaders list, two seasons with better than 300 strikeouts, one Cy Young Award in the senior circuit and two more in the American League, and an out-of-sight .712 career winning percentage. But this is also a pitcher who has never accumulated large numbers of innings and never posted huge victory totals. The somewhat fragile Martínez logged better than 200 frames his last three years in Montreal and first two in Boston, but he has never again reached that total after 2000. It took him seven full seasons to first cross the 20-victory plateau, and his dozen-year average is a fraction under 14 per year. When he was used properly and at his peak, however, few hurlers have ever been more unhittable. Pedro's weaknesses were perhaps best seen up close during the postseason of 2003—an American League Championship Series showdown with the Yankees in which several on-camera outbursts threatened to brand him a hothead in the image of Rubén Gómez, Juan Marichal, or Joaquín Andújar. In the end, Martínez will surely go down as one of the most masterful pitchers of the late 1990s and early 2000s—but without climbing substantially above the career 200-victory high-water mark (in mid-2004, he was still some 20 short of 200), Pedro Martínez's once seemingly automatic admissions ticket to Cooperstown may not yet be stamped.

Manuel "Manny" Mota (b. February 18, 1938).   Some ballplayers are indelibly captured in a single unforgettable line of newsprint. *Los Angeles Times* columnist Jim Murray (quoted in *Baseball: The Biographical Encyclopedia*) once summed up Manny Mota and his unmatched penchant for delivering clutch pinch hits: "He could wake up on Christmas morning and rip a single into right field." Through the bulk of his twenty big league campaigns, Mota was the most reliable pinch batter in baseball annals; as a pinch-hitting specialist and part-time outfielder with the Dodgers (1969–1973), Mota hit over .300 in five consecutive seasons. He was also one of the nicest individuals ever to grace the game—courteous with fans, effusive with reporters (despite limited English), and popular with teammates during tours with four National League clubs. Above all else, he was a blessed natural hitter who found himself a special niche in the majors that would assure his eventual immortality. Though his records (150 pinch hits and a .297 pinch-hitting average) have now been over-taken by Lenny Harris, time has not diminished Manny Mota's standing as baseball's supreme pinch-hitting specialist. He is most remembered for his years on the bench as a talented reserve with the Los Angeles Dodgers, but Mota was also a lifetime overall .304 hitter who also served with the Giants, Pirates, and Expos. He was twice a bench coach at the major league level with the Dodgers and a six-year winter league manager back in the Dominican. He managed three clubs—Licey, Cambrioso, and Escogido—and was 1984 Manager of the Year with Cambrioso. And Mota left quite an additional legacy with his four talented baseball-playing sons, two of whom reached the majors in 1991 as infielders with Houston (Andy) and San Diego (José).

Diómedes "Guayubín" Olivo (b. January 22, 1919; d. February 15, 1977).
Diómedes "Guayubín" Olivo was never much of a big league star, though he

Guayubín Olivo earned notoriety in 1960 as the Pittsburgh Pirates "ancient" rookie. [Author's Cuban Collection]

had his few special moments when he briefly baffled rival hitters (5–1, 2.77) out of the Pittsburgh Pirates bullpen as a 43-year-old rookie. As a big leaguer, he was more a curiosity than anything else, something that seemed to run in the family; his brother, Chi Chi, also didn't draw attention in the big time with Atlanta until he was a youthful 38 and counting. Back home in winter league play it was quite a different story. There, as earlier noted, Olivo left the larger legacy of a true immortal. Four decades after his final game the colorfully named Diómedes (or Guayubín) still holds onto both career and single-season strikeout records in his native land and has never relinquished his lofty position as the biggest winner in Dominican Winter League annals.

Samuel Peralto "Sammy" Sosa (b. November 12, 1968). Sammy Sosa is easily today's biggest Dominican idol—though Albert Pujols is closing fast after only four seasons. He may well have become the biggest Latin baseball idol of all time—the gripping 1998 homer chase with Mark McGwire that transfixed the entire baseball universe took care of that. The attention surrounding Sosa during his head-to-head summer-long home run battle with McGwire, and with the shadows of Maris and Ruth, was an unparalleled phenomenon both in his proud homeland and also all across North America—and Sosa's amazing rise among the slugging immortals has only continued since then, and at a never-slackening pace. Sosa was already a solid player and a local star with the Cubs by the middle 1990s. He owned good speed and a rifle arm and routinely played with hustling enthusiasm. What he seemingly lacked was only discipline and patience at the plate. Once he developed these missing mental elements (and possibly also received a small boost from bodybuilding chemicals) in time for his tenth season, a top star was born for the rest of the baseball nation—for two nations—almost overnight.

Sosa was an also-ran of sorts in that breakout season, losing the home run race in the final days when McGwire smacked four long balls during a late Herculean finish on the last weekend. His consolation was the second highest homer tally ever and a league lead in RBI. McGwire soon quickly faded due to career-threatening injury after 1998, but Sosa was only getting started. He promptly became the first slugger with three 60-plus home run seasons and also the first to sock over 50 for four years running. He moved up on the all-time career list and today seems an easy bet for 600 and even a long shot for 700. He has become the most popular player ever in Wrigley Field, not a mean feat with a franchise so tradition-blessed. Sosa even became a much-admired national hero in his homeland (winner of the country's top civilian medal) after he exploited his new celebrity status to raise funds for victims of a devastating September 1998 hurricane. When it comes to hero status at home and abroad, few others can boast anything even remotely close.

Juan "Tetelo" Vargas (b. April 11, 1906; d. 1971).   Juan "Tetelo" Vargas never played in the big leagues, but that doesn't diminish his stature among long-in-the-tooth Dominican fanatics, who still often rate him among the nation's top handful of sports icons. The slender, wiry outfielder and shortstop of the 1930s and 1940s is without doubt the most accomplished Dominican native never to have spent a single day in the majors. This anomaly was of course due to the racial-segregation policies of organized baseball, which also sidelined the immortal Cuban Martín Dihigo and the incomparable Puerto Rican Perucho Cepeda. In the Caribbean winter leagues and the black-ball venues of the Negro National League, Vargas more than held his own against any of the greatest Cubans and Puerto Ricans, or against the visiting white big leaguers that he regularly faced year in and year out. Vargas began his Negro leagues career as a reserve shortstop with Alejandro Pompez's 1927 Cuban Stars, and by the early 1940s he was an outfield fixture for the New York Cubans. During winter months in the 1940s, he also starred in Puerto Rico, hitting as high as .410 in 1944. In 1946, at the astounding age of 46, he hit .355 in the summer Mexican League, then returned to Dominican parks for winter action and edged Ray Dandridge for a last-hurrah batting title. Tetelo Vargas played baseball at the highest levels in a half-dozen countries for more than a quarter-century and few played any better, either inside the lily-white major leagues or outside—where the pay and recognition was sparser but the competition was every bit as tough and then some.

IN BRIEF

The names of Dominican big leaguers are now so numerous that the country seems unrivaled as a continuing and perhaps limitless major league talent font. As the raw numbers of recruits keep coming, so do the gems in the rough. Most recently, Cardinals versatile outfielder–third baseman–first baseman Albert Pujols enjoyed the most sensational three-season debut within living memory, averaging a fraction under 200 hits and 40 homers per campaign, winning one league batting title, and averaging above .330 through almost 500 big league games. And Pujols is only the latest phenomenon to demonstrate that Dominican sandlots can still provide the pick of the crop, not just plain wheat and chaff. Megastars down through the decades such as Sammy Sosa, Vladimir Guerrero, Rico Carty, Pedro Martínez, Juan Marichal, and Felipe Alou ensure that the Dominican legacy will remain one of top-ranking stars and not one of raw numbers alone. The throw-away prospects and dependable journeymen have long been the shoal for some pretty big fish.

SELECTED DOMINICAN RECORDS AND STATISTICS
The Dominican Republic's Major Leaguers

Dominicans in the Major Leagues (1956–2003)

	Name	Debut	Position	Debut Team	Seasons	Games	Career Statistics
1	Osvaldo "Ozzie" Virgil	1956	IF/OF	New York Giants (NL)	9	324	.231 BA
2	Felipe Alou	1958	OF	San Francisco Giants (NL)	17	2,082	.286 BA, 206 HR
3	Matty Alou	1960	OF	San Francisco Giants (NL)	15	1,667	.307 BA, 1,777 H
4	Julián Javier	1960	2B	St. Louis Cardinals (NL)	13	1,622	.257 BA, 1,469 H
5	Juan Marichal	1960	RHP	San Francisco Giants (NL)	16	471	243–142, 2.89 ERA
6	Rudolph "Rudy" Hernández	1960	RHP	Washington Senators (AL)	2	28	4–2, 4.12 ERA
7	Diómedes "Guayubín" Olivo	1960	LHP	Pittsburgh Pirates (NL)	3	85	5–6, 3.10 ERA
8	Federico "Chi Chi" Olivo	1961	RHP	Milwaukee Braves (NL)	4	96	7–6, 3.96 ERA
9	Manuel "Manny" Jiménez*	1962	OF	Kansas City Athletics (AL)	7	429	.272 BA
10	Manuel "Manny" Mota	1962	OF	San Francisco Giants (NL)	20	1,536	.304 BA, 1,149 H
11	Amado Samuel*	1962	IF	Milwaukee Braves (NL)	3	144	.215 BA
12	Jesús Alou	1963	OF	San Francisco Giants (NL)	15	1,380	.280 BA
13	Pedro González*	1963	IF	New York Yankees (AL)	5	407	.244 BA
14	Ricardo "Rico" Carty*	1963	OF	Milwaukee Braves (NL)	15	1,651	.299 BA, 204 HR
15	Elvio Jiménez*	1964	OF	New York Yankees (AL)	1	1	.333 BA
16	Ricardo "Rick" Joseph*	1964	3B	Kansas City Athletics (AL)	5	270	.243 BA
17	Roberto Peña	1965	IF	Chicago Cubs (NL)	6	587	.245 BA
18	José Vidal	1966	OF	Cleveland Indians (AL)	4	88	.164 BA
19	Winston Llenas	1968	IF	California Angels (AL)	6	300	.230 BA
20	Rafael Robles*	1969	SS	San Diego Padres (NL)	3	47	.188 BA
21	Freddie Velázquez	1969	C	Seattle Pilots (AL)	1	6	.125 BA
22	Pedro Borbón	1969	RHP	California Angels (AL)	12	593	69–39, 3.52 ERA
23	Santiago Guzmán*	1969	RHP	St. Louis Cardinals (NL)	4	12	1–2, 4.50 ERA
24	César Gerónimo	1969	OF	Houston Astros (NL)	15	1,522	.258 BA
25	César Cedeño	1970	OF	Houston Astros (NL)	17	2,006	.285 BA, 199 HR
26	Teodoro "Teddy" Martínez	1970	IF	New York Mets (NL)	9	657	.240 BA
27	Tomás "Tom" Silverio	1970	OF	California Angels (AL)	3	31	.100 BA
28	Franklin "Frank" Taveras	1971	SS	Pittsburgh Pirates (NL)	11	1,150	.255 BA, 1,029 H
29	Elias Sosa	1972	RHP	San Francisco Giants (NL)	12	601	59–51, 3.32 ERA
30	Jesús "Pepe" Frías*	1973	IF	Montreal Expos (NL)	9	723	.240 BA
31	Rafael Batista*	1973	1B	Houston Astros (NL)	2	22	.280 BA
32	Mario Guerrero	1973	SS	Boston Red Sox (AL)	8	697	.257 BA
33	William "Bill" Castro	1974	RHP	Milwaukee Brewers (NL)	10	303	31–26, 3.33 ERA
34	Ramón De los Santos	1974	LHP	Houston Astros (NL)	1	12	1–1, 2.19 ERA
35	Arnulfo "Nino" Espinosa	1974	RHP	New York Mets (NL)	8	140	44–55, 4.17 ERA
36	Juan Jiménez	1974	RHP	Pittsburgh Pirates (NL)	1	4	0–0, 6.75 ERA
37	Miguel Diloné	1974	OF	Pittsburgh Pirates (NL)	12	800	.265 BA
38	José Sosa	1975	RHP	Houston Astros (NL)	2	34	1–3, 4.60 ERA
39	Jesús De la Rosa	1975	PH	Houston Astros (NL)	1	3	.333 BA
40	Alfredo "Al" Ignácio Javier*	1976	OF	Houston Astros (NL)	1	8	.208 BA
41	Samuel "Sam" Mejías	1976	OF	St. Louis Cardinals (NL)	6	334	.247 BA
42	Alejandro "Alex" Taveras	1976	IF	Houston Astros (NL)	3	35	.208 BA
43	Santo Alcalá*	1976	RHP	Cincinnati Reds (NL)	2	68	14–11, 4.76 ERA
44	Joaquín Andújar*	1976	RHP	Houston Astros (NL)	13	405	127–118, 3.58 ERA
45	Juan Bernhardt*	1976	OF/IF	New York Yankees (AL)	4	154	.238 BA
46	Alfredo Griffin	1976	SS	Cleveland Indians (AL)	18	1,962	.249 BA, 1,688 H
47	Mario Soto	1977	RHP	Cincinnati Reds (NL)	12	297	100–92, 3.47 ERA
48	Rafael Landestoy	1977	IF/OF	Los Angeles Dodgers (NL)	8	596	.237 BA
49	Luis Pujols	1977	C	Houston Astros (NL)	9	316	.193 BA
50	Silvio Martínez	1977	RHP	Chicago White Sox (AL)	5	107	31–32, 3.88 ERA
51	Ángel Torres	1977	LHP	Cincinnati Reds (NL)	1	5	0–0, 2.16 ERA
52	José Báez	1977	2B	Seattle Mariners (AL)	2	114	.245 BA

	Name	Debut	Position	Debut Team	Seasons	Games	Career Statistics
53	Pedro Guerrero*	1978	OF	Los Angeles Dodgers (NL)	15	1,536	.300 BA, 215 HR
54	Nelson Norman*	1978	SS	Texas Rangers (AL)	6	198	.221 BA
55	Domingo Ramos	1978	IF	New York Yankees (AL)	11	507	.240 BA
56	Luis Silverio	1978	OF	Kansas City Royals (AL)	1	8	.545 BA
57	Victor Cruz	1978	RHP	Toronto Blue Jays (AL)	5	187	18–23, 3.09 ERA
58	Arturo "Art" DeFreitas*	1978	1B	Cincinnati Reds (NL)	2	32	.208 BA
59	Dámaso García	1978	2B	New York Yankees (AL)	11	1,032	.283 BA, 1,108 H
60	Alberto Lois	1978	OF	Pittsburgh Pirates (NL)	2	14	.250 BA
61	Pedro Hernández	1979	IF/OF	Toronto Blue Jays (AL)	2	11	.000 BA
62	Rafael Vásquez	1979	RHP	Seattle Mariners (AL)	1	9	1–0, 5.06 ERA
63	Rafael Ramírez*	1980	SS	Atlanta Braves (NL)	13	1,539	.261 BA
64	José Moreno	1980	OF	New York Mets (NL)	3	82	.206 BA
65	Antonio "Tony" Peña	1980	C	Pittsburgh Pirates (NL)	18	1,988	.260 BA, 1,687 H
66	Julio Valdéz	1980	IF	Boston Red Sox (AL)	4	65	.207 BA
67	Pascual Pérez	1980	RHP	Pittsburgh Pirates (NL)	11	207	67–68, 3.44 ERA
68	Ésteban "Manny" Castillo	1980	3B	Kansas City Royals (AL)	3	236	.242 BA
69	Jesús Figueroa	1980	OF	Chicago Cubs (NL)	1	115	.253 BA
70	George (Jorge) Bell*	1981	OF	Toronto Blue Jays (AL)	12	1,587	.278 BA, 265 HR
71	Rufino Linares	1981	OF	Atlanta Braves (NL)	4	207	.270 BA
72	Alejandro Peña	1981	RHP	Los Angeles Dodgers (NL)	15	503	56–52, 3.11 ERA
73	Alejandro Sánchez*	1982	OF	Philadelphia Phillies (NL)	6	109	.229 BA
74	Rafael Belliard	1982	SS	Pittsburgh Pirates (NL)	17	1,155	.221 BA
75	Cecilio Guante	1982	RHP	Pittsburgh Pirates (NL)	9	363	29–34, 3.48 ERA
76	Carmelo "Carmen" Castillo*	1982	OF	Cleveland Indians (AL)	10	631	.252 BA
77	Juan Espino	1982	C	New York Yankees (AL)	4	49	.219 BA
78	Julio Franco*	1982	2B	Philadelphia Phillies (NL)	19	2,144	.300 BA, 2,358 H
79	Gilberto "Gil" Reyes	1983	C	Los Angeles Dodgers (NL)	7	122	.202 BA
80	Juan Samuel*	1983	IF/OF	Philadelphia Phillies (NL)	16	1,720	.259 BA, 161 HR
81	Rafael Santana	1983	SS	St. Louis Cardinals (NL)	7	668	.246 BA
82	José DeLeón	1983	RHP	Pittsburgh Pirates (NL)	13	415	86–119, 3.76 ERA
83	Julio Solano	1983	RHP	Houston Astros (NL)	7	106	6–8, 4.55 ERA
84	Octávio "Tony" Fernández*	1983	SS	Toronto Blue Jays (AL)	17	2,158	.288 BA, 2,276 H
85	Stanley "Stan" Javier	1984	OF	New York Yankees (AL)	17	1,763	.269 BA, 1,358 H
86	Victor "Vic" Mata	1984	OF	New York Yankees (AL)	2	36	.312 BA
87	Milciades "Junior" Noboa	1984	IF	Cleveland Indians (AL)	8	317	.239 BA
88	José Uribe González	1984	SS	St. Louis Cardinals (NL)	10	1,038	.241 BA
89	José Rijo	1984	RHP	New York Yankees (AL)	14	376	116–91, 3.24 ERA
90	José Román	1984	RHP	Cleveland Indians (AL)	3	14	1–8, 8.12 ERA
91	Ramón Romero*	1984	LHP	Cleveland Indians (AL)	2	20	2–3, 6.28 ERA
92	Denio "Denny" González	1984	IF/OF	Pittsburgh Pirates (NL)	5	98	.206 BA
93	Manuel "Manny" Lee*	1985	SS	Toronto Blue Jays (AL)	11	992	.255 BA
94	José González	1985	OF	Los Angeles Dodgers (NL)	8	461	.213 BA
95	Andrés Pérez Thomas	1985	SS	Atlanta Braves (NL)	6	577	.234 BA
96	Mariano Duncan*	1985	IF	Los Angeles Dodgers (NL)	12	1,279	.267 BA, 1,247 H
97	Rubén Rodríguez	1986	C	Pittsburgh Pirates (NL)	2	4	.125 BA
98	Wilfredo "Wil" Tejada	1986	C	Montreal Expos (NL)	2	18	.250 BA
99	Balvino Gálvez*	1986	RHP	Los Angeles Dodgers (NL)	1	10	0–1, 3.92 ERA
100	Manuel "Manny" Hernández	1986	RHP	Houston Astros (NL)	3	16	2–7, 4.47 ERA
101	Hipólito Peña	1986	LHP	Pittsburgh Pirates (NL)	3	42	1–7, 4.84 ERA
102	Sergio Valdéz	1986	RHP	Montreal Expos (NL)	8	116	12–20, 5.06 ERA
103	Juan Castillo*	1986	2B	Milwaukee Brewers (AL)	4	199	.215 BA
104	Luis Polonia	1987	OF	Oakland Athletics (AL)	12	1,379	.293 BA, 1,417 H
105	Nelson Liriano	1987	2B	Toronto Blue Jays (AL)	11	823	.260 BA
106	José Mesa	1987	RHP	Baltimore Orioles (AL)	17	762	70–91, 4.32, 249 S
107	Placido Polanco	1987	IF	St. Louis Cardinals (NL)	6	664	.294 BA
108	José Núñez	1987	RHP	Toronto Blue Jays (AL)	4	77	9–10, 5.05 ERA
109	Melido Pérez	1987	RHP	Kansas City Royals (AL)	9	243	78–85, 4.17 ERA

(continued)

(continued)

Name	Debut	Position	Debut Team	Seasons	Games	Career Statistics
110 Félix Fermín	1987	SS	Pittsburgh Pirates (NL)	10	903	.259 BA
111 Leo García	1987	OF	Cincinnati Reds (NL)	2	54	.241 BA
112 Félix José	1988	OF	Oakland Athletics (AL)	11	747	.280 BA
113 Gibson Alba	1988	LHP	St. Louis Cardinals (NL)	1	3	0–0, 2.70 ERA
114 José Bautista	1988	RHP	Baltimore Orioles (AL)	9	312	32–42, 4.62 ERA
115 Ravelo Manzanillo*	1988	LHP	Chicago White Sox (AL)	3	53	4–3, 4.43 ERA
116 Ramón Martínez	1988	RHP	Los Angeles Dodgers (NL)	14	301	135–88, 3.67 ERA
117 José Segura	1988	RHP	Chicago White Sox (AL)	3	22	0–2, 9.00 ERA
118 Silvestre "Sil" Campusano	1988	OF	Toronto Blue Jays (AL)	3	154	.202 BA
119 Luis De los Santos	1988	1B	Kansas City Royals (AL)	3	55	.209 BA
120 Juan "Tito" Bell*	1989	IF	Baltimore Orioles (AL)	7	329	.212 BA
121 Ramón Peña	1989	RHP	Detroit Tigers (AL)	1	8	0–0, 6.00 ERA
122 Sammy Sosa*	1989	OF	Texas Rangers (AL)	15	2,012	.278 BA, 539 HR
123 José Vizcaíno	1989	SS	Los Angeles Dodgers (NL)	15	1,504	.272 BA, 1,276 H
124 Joselito "José" Cano	1989	RHP	Houston Astros (NL)	1	6	1–1, 5.09 ERA
125 Gerónimo Berróa	1989	OF	Atlanta Braves (NL)	11	779	.276 BA, 101 HR
126 Francisco Cabrera	1989	C	Toronto Blue Jays (AL)	5	196	.254 BA
127 Junior Félix	1989	OF	Toronto Blue Jays (AL)	6	585	.264 BA
128 Andújar Cedeño	1990	SS	Houston Astros (NL)	7	616	.236 BA
129 Moises Alou (b. USA)	1990	OF	Pittsburgh Pirates (NL)	12	1,464	.300 BA, 239 HR
130 Luis Encarnación	1990	RHP	Kansas City Royals (AL)	1	4	0–0, 7.84 ERA
131 Ramón Manon	1990	RHP	Texas Rangers (AL)	1	1	0–0, 13.50 ERA
132 José Offerman*	1990	IF	Los Angeles Dodgers (NL)	13	1,488	.274 BA
133 Geronimo Peña	1990	2B	St. Louis Cardinals (NL)	7	378	.262 BA
134 Melaquides "Mel" Rojas	1990	RHP	Montreal Expos (NL)	10	525	34–31, 3.82, 126 S
135 Victor "Vic" Rosario	1990	SS	Atlanta Braves (NL)	1	9	.143 BA
136 Andrés Santana*	1990	IF	San Francisco Giants (NL)	1	6	.000 BA
137 Rafael Valdéz	1990	RHP	San Diego Padres (NL)	1	3	0–1, 11.12 ERA
138 Efrain Valdéz	1990	LHP	Cleveland Indians (AL)	3	26	1–1, 2.91 ERA
139 Héctor Wagner	1990	RHP	Kansas City Royals (AL)	2	7	1–3, 7.83 ERA
140 Ésteban Beltre	1991	SS	Chicago White Sox (AL)	5	186	.237 BA
141 Braulio Castillo	1991	OF	Philadelphia Phillies (NL)	2	56	.188 BA
142 Francisco De la Rosa	1991	RHP	Baltimore Orioles (AL)	1	2	0–0, 4.50 ERA
143 Antonio "Tony" Eusebio	1991	C	Houston Astros (NL)	9	598	.275 BA
144 Juan Guzmán	1991	RHP	Toronto Blue Jays (AL)	10	240	91–79, 4.08 ERA
145 Dionini "Johnny" Guzmán	1991	LHP	Oakland Athletics (AL)	2	7	1–0, 10.13 ERA
146 Josías Manzanillo*	1991	RHP	Boston Red Sox (AL)	10	241	10–12, 4.56 ERA
147 Luis Mercedes*	1991	OF	Baltimore Orioles (AL)	3	70	.190 BA
148 Andrés "Andy" Mota	1991	2B	Houston Astros (NL)	1	27	.189 BA
149 José Mota	1991	IF	San Diego Padres (NL)	2	19	.211 BA
150 Yorkis Pérez	1991	LHP	Chicago Cubs (NL)	9	337	14–15, 4.44 ERA
151 Rafael Bournigal	1992	IF	Los Angeles Dodgers (NL)	7	365	.251 BA
152 Bernardo Brito	1992	OF/DH	Minnesota Twins (AL)	3	40	.219 BA
153 Bienvenido "Bien" Figueroa	1992	IF	St. Louis Cardinals (NL)	1	12	.182 BA
154 Juan Guerrero	1992	IF	Houston Astros (NL)	1	79	.200 BA
155 César Hernández	1992	OF	Cincinnati Reds (NL)	2	6	.213 BA
156 Domingo Martínez	1992	1B	Toronto Blue Jays (AL)	2	15	.409 BA
157 Pedro Martínez	1992	RHP	Los Angeles Dodgers (NL)	12	355	166–67, 2.58 ERA
158 Julio Peguero	1992	OF	Philadelphia Phillies (NL)	1	14	.222 BA
159 Hipólito Pichardo	1992	RHP	Kansas City Royals (AL)	10	350	50–44, 4.44 ERA
160 Henry Mercedes	1992	C	Oakland Athletics (AL)	5	79	.247 BA
161 Bienvenido "Ben" Rivera*	1992	RHP	Atlanta Braves (NL)	3	67	23–17, 4.52 ERA
162 Henry Rodríguez	1992	OF	Los Angeles Dodgers (NL)	11	950	.259 BA, 160 HR
163 William Suero	1992	IF	Milwaukee Brewers (AL)	2	33	.233 BA
164 Pedro Borbon Jr.	1992	LHP	Atlanta Braves (NL)	9	368	16–16, 4.68 ERA
165 Pedro Astacio	1992	RHP	Los Angeles Dodgers (NL)	12	346	118–109, 4.58 ERA
166 Manny Alexander*	1992	SS	Baltimore Orioles (AL)	8	541	.234 BA

Name	Debut	Position	Debut Team	Seasons	Games	Career Statistics
167 Miguel Batista	1992	RHP	Pittsburgh Pirates (NL)	9	254	42–50, 4.39 ERA
168 Pedro Martínez	1993	LHP	San Diego Padres (NL)	5	122	7–4, 3.97 ERA
169 Manny Ramírez	1993	OF	Cleveland Indians (AL)	11	1,383	.317 BA, 347 HR
170 Julián Tavárez	1993	RHP	Cleveland Indians (AL)	11	491	63–48, 4.52 ERA
171 Ramón Caraballo	1993	2B	Atlanta Braves (NL)	2	40	.202 BA
172 Raúl Mondesi	1993	OF	Los Angeles Dodgers (NL)	11	1,450	.276 BA, 264 HR
173 Norberto Martín*	1993	IF	Chicago White Sox (AL)	7	354	.278 BA
174 Luis Ortiz	1993	INF/DH	Boston Red Sox (AL)	4	60	.228 BA
175 Roberto Mejía	1993	2B	Colorado Rockies (NL)	4	133	.219 BA
176 Domingo Cedeño	1993	IF	Toronto Blue Jays (AL)	7	429	.251 BA
177 Daniel "Danny" Bautista	1993	OF	Detroit Tigers (AL)	11	754	.268 BA
178 Domingo Jean*	1993	RHP	New York Yankees (AL)	1	10	1–1, 4.46 ERA
179 Salomon Torres*	1993	RHP	San Francisco Giants (NL)	7	114	20–31, 5.24 ERA
180 Héctor Carrasco*	1994	RHP	Cincinnati Reds (NL)	9	498	30–42, 4.22 ERA
181 José Martínez	1994	RHP	San Diego Padres (NL)	1	4	0–2, 6.75 ERA
182 José Lima	1994	RHP	Detroit Tigers (NL)	10	276	71–77, 5.13 ERA
183 Fausto Cruz	1994	IF	Oakland Athletics (AL)	3	39	.191 BA
184 Jesús Tavárez	1994	OF	Florida Marlins (NL)	5	228	.239 BA
185 José Oliva*	1994	3B	Atlanta Braves (NL)	2	89	.178 BA
186 Francisco Matos	1994	2B	Oakland Athletics (AL)	1	14	.250 BA
187 José Mercedes	1994	RHP	Milwaukee Brewers (AL)	8	145	33–39, 4.75 ERA
188 Armando Benítez	1994	RHP	Baltimore Orioles (AL)	10	564	30–31, 3.03, 197 S
189 Luis Andújar	1995	RHP	Chicago White Sox (AL)	4	35	3–10, 5.98 ERA
190 Félix Rodríguez	1995	RHP	San Francisco Giants (NL)	8	422	32–17, 3.43 ERA
191 Jorge Brito	1995	C	Colorado Rockies (NL)	2	26	.185 BA
192 César Devarez	1995	C	Baltimore Orioles (AL)	2	16	.091 BA
193 Ramón Morel	1995	RHP	Pittsburgh Pirates (NL)	3	42	2–2, 4.98 ERA
194 José Parra	1995	RHP	Los Angeles Dodgers (NL)	4	69	6–12, 6.33 ERA
195 Ángelo Encarnación	1995	C	Pittsburgh Pirates (NL)	3	76	.253 BA
196 Quilvio Veras	1995	2B	Florida Marlins (NL)	7	767	.270 BA
197 Freddy García	1995	OF/IF	Pittsburgh Pirates (NL)	4	175	.222 BA
198 Wilson Heredia	1995	RHP	Texas Rangers (AL)	2	16	1–1, 3.41 ERA
199 Sandy Martínez	1995	C	Toronto Blue Jays (AL)	7	214	.233 BA
200 Arquimedez Pozo	1995	IF	Seattle Mariners (AL)	3	26	.189 BA
201 José Herrera	1995	OF	Oakland Athletics (AL)	2	141	.264 BA
202 Rudy Pemberton	1995	OF	Detroit Tigers (AL)	3	52	.336 BA
203 Ramón Fermín	1995	RHP	Oakland Athletics (AL)	1	1	0–0, 13.50 ERA
204 Carlos Pérez	1995	LHP	Montreal Expos (NL)	5	142	40–53, 4.44 ERA
205 Carlos Valdéz	1995	RHP	San Francisco Giants (NL)	2	15	1–1, 5.00 ERA
206 Rafael Alberto "Al" Reyes	1995	RHP	Milwaukee Brewers (AL)	9	220	15–8, 4.06 ERA
207 Alberto Castillo	1995	C	New York Mets (NL)	9	343	.219 BA
208 Félix Heredia	1996	LHP	Florida Marlins (NL)	8	461	27–18, 4.27 ERA
209 Wilson Delgado	1996	IF	San Francisco Giants (NL)	8	211	.238 BA
210 Amaury Telemaco	1996	RHP	Chicago Cubs (NL)	7	170	23–32, 5.03 ERA
211 Manuel "Manny" Martínez*	1996	OF	Seattle Mariners (AL)	3	232	.245 BA
212 José Paniagua	1996	RHP	Montreal Expos (NL)	8	270	18–21, 4.49 ERA
213 Nerio Rodríguez*	1996	RHP	Baltimore Orioles (AL)	5	32	4–6, 6.32 ERA
214 Wilton Guerrero	1996	IF/OF	Los Angeles Dodgers (NL)	7	654	.283 BA
215 Neifi Pérez	1996	SS	Colorado Rockies (NL)	8	982	.271 BA
216 Rafael Quirico	1996	LHP	Philadelphia Phillies (NL)	1	1	0–1, 37.80 ERA
217 Dario Veras	1996	RHP	San Diego Padres (NL)	3	53	5–3, 4.67 ERA
218 Tilson Brito	1996	IF	Toronto Blue Jays (AL)	2	92	.238 BA
219 Pablo Martínez	1996	SS	Atlanta Braves (NL)	1	4	.500 BA
220 Vladimir Guerrero	1996	OF	Montreal Expos (NL)	8	1,004	.323 BA, 234 HR
221 Miguel Mejía*	1996	OF	St. Louis Cardinals (NL)	1	45	.087 ERA
222 Ésteban Yan	1996	RHP	Baltimore Orioles (AL)	8	327	28–32, 5.41 ERA
223 Leocadio "Tony" Batista	1996	IF/OF	Oakland Athletics (AL)	8	1,022	.253 BA, 182 HR

(continued)

(continued)

	Name	Debut	Position	Debut Team	Seasons	Games	Career Statistics
224	Luis Castillo*	1996	2B	Florida Marlins (NL)	8	856	.292 BA
225	Antonio Alfonseca	1997	RHP	Florida Marlins (NL)	4	400	23–30, 4.11 ERA
226	José Cabrera	1997	RHP	Houston Astros (NL)	6	198	19–17, 4.95 ERA
227	Abraham Orlando Núñez	1997	IF	Pittsburgh Pirates (NL)	7	518	.238 BA
228	Julio Santana*	1997	RHP	Texas Rangers (AL)	5	161	14–26, 5.33 ERA
229	Ramón Tatis	1997	LHP	Chicago Cubs (NL)	2	78	1–1, 6.82 ERA
230	Carlos Castillo (b. USA)	1997	RHP	Chicago White Sox (AL)	4	111	10–7, 5.04 ERA
231	Roberto Durán	1997	LHP	Detroit Tigers (AL)	2	31	0–1, 6.58 ERA
232	Melvin "Mel" Rosario	1997	C	Baltimore Orioles (AL)	1	4	.000 BA
233	Fernando Hernández	1997	RHP	Detroit Tigers (AL)	1	2	0–0, 40.50 ERA
234	Carlos Almanzar	1997	RHP	Toronto Blue Jays (AL)	6	137	6–10, 5.02 ERA
235	David Ortiz	1997	INF/DH	Minnesota Twins (AL)	7	583	.271 BA
236	Hanley Frías	1997	IF	Texas Rangers (AL)	4	173	.232 BA
237	Manuel "Manny" Aybar	1997	RHP	St. Louis Cardinals (NL)	7	186	17–18, 5.05 ERA
238	Robinson Checo	1997	RHP	Boston Red Sox (AL)	3	16	3–5, 7.61 ERA
239	Nelson Cruz	1997	RHP	Chicago White Sox (AL)	6	204	15–23, 5.04 ERA
240	Juan Encarnación	1997	OF	Detroit Tigers (AL)	7	752	.270 BA
241	Deivi Cruz	1997	SS	Detroit Tigers (AL)	7	1,006	.267 BA
242	Enrique Wilson	1997	IF	Cleveland Indians (AL)	7	447	.253 BA
243	José Guillén	1997	OF	Pittsburgh Pirates (NL)	7	750	.270 BA
244	Bartolo Colón	1997	RHP	Cleveland Indians (AL)	7	213	100–62, 3.86 ERA
245	Félix Martínez	1997	SS	Kansas City Royals (AL)	5	239	.214 BA
246	Miguel Tejada	1997	SS	Oakland Athletics (AL)	7	936	.270 BA, 156 HR
247	Fernando Tatis*	1997	3B	Texas Rangers (AL)	7	663	.261 BA
248	Odalis Pérez	1998	LHP	Atlanta Braves (NL)	5	114	38–37, 4.24 ERA
249	Willis Otañez	1998	3B	Baltimore Orioles (AL)	2	74	.236 BA
250	Ángel Peña*	1998	C	Los Angeles Dodgers (NL)	3	71	.209 BA
251	Mendy López	1998	IF	Kansas City Royals (AL)	6	172	.255 BA
252	Aramis Ramírez	1998	3B	Pittsburgh Pirates (NL)	6	622	.263 BA
253	Valerio De los Santos	1998	LHP	Milwaukee Brewers (NL)	6	189	8–10, 4.28 ERA
254	José Jiménez*	1998	RHP	St. Louis Cardinals (NL)	6	298	23–37, 4.66 ERA
255	Lariel González	1998	RHP	Colorado Rockies (NL)	1	1	0–0, 0.00 ERA
256	Carlos Febles	1998	IF	Kansas City Royals (AL)	6	506	.250 BA
257	Jesús Sánchez	1998	LHP	Florida Marlins (NL)	6	159	23–32, 5.26 ERA
258	Rafael Roque	1998	LHP	Milwaukee Brewers (NL)	3	56	5–8, 5.36 ERA
259	Guillermo García	1998	C	Cincinnati Reds (NL)	2	16	.200 BA
260	Marino Santana	1998	RHP	Detroit Tigers (AL)	2	10	0–0, 7.94 ERA
261	Adrian Beltre	1998	3B	Los Angeles Dodgers (NL)	6	810	.262 BA
262	Domingo Guzmán	1999	RHP	San Diego Padres (NL)	2	8	0–1, 19.50 ERA
263	Amaury García	1999	2B	Florida Marlins (NL)	1	10	.250 BA
264	Octavio Dotel	1999	RHP	New York Mets (NL)	5	289	30–23, 3.62 ERA
265	Rubén Mateo	1999	OF	Texas Rangers (AL)	5	244	.257 BA
266	Luis García	1999	IF	Detroit Tigers (AL)	1	8	.111 BA
267	Wilton Veras	1999	IF	Boston Red Sox (AL)	2	85	.262 BA
268	D'Ángelo Jiménez	1999	IF	New York Yankees (AL)	4	353	.269 BA
269	José Fernández	1999	IF	Montreal Expos (NL)	2	21	.143 BA
270	Héctor Ramírez	1999	RHP	Milwaukee Brewers (NL)	2	21	1–3, 5.40 ERA
271	Juan Sosa	1999	OF	Colorado Rockies (NL)	2	13	.200 BA
272	Ramón Ortiz	1999	RHP	Anaheim Angels (AL)	5	123	54–42, 4.63 ERA
273	Luis Vizcaino	1999	RHP	Oakland Athletics (AL)	5	200	11–8, 4.80 ERA
274	Julio Ramírez	1999	OF	Florida Marlins (NL)	4	72	.163 BA
275	Cristian Gúzman	1999	SS	Minnesota Twins (AL)	5	696	.264 BA
276	Guillermo Mota*	1999	RHP	Montreal Expos (NL)	5	252	11–14, 3.53 ERA
277	Juan Peña	1999	RHP	Boston Red Sox (AL)	1	2	2–0, 0.69 ERA
278	Alfonso Soriano*	1999	2B	New York Yankees (AL)	5	501	.284 BA
279	Willis Roberts	1999	RHP	Detroit Tigers (AL)	4	139	17–15, 4.62 ERA
280	Pascual Matos	1999	C	Atlanta Braves (NL)	1	6	.125 BA

	Name	Debut	Position	Debut Team	Seasons	Games	Career Statistics
281	Dámaso Marte	1999	LHP	Seattle Mariners (AL)	4	167	5–5, 2.97 ERA
282	Héctor Almonte	1999	RHP	Florida Marlins (NL)	2	50	1–4, 6.27 ERA
283	Francisco Cordero	1999	RHP	Detroit Tigers (AL)	5	191	10–13, 3.57 ERA
284	Timoniel "Timo" Pérez	1999	OF	New York Mets (NL)	4	372	.276 BA
285	Jesús Peña	1999	LHP	Chicago White Sox (AL)	2	48	2–1, 5.21 ERA
286	Julio Lugo	2000	SS	Houston Astros (NL)	4	483	.270 BA
287	Rafael Furcal	2000	SS	Atlanta Braves (NL)	4	520	.285 BA
288	Pedro Feliz	2000	IF	San Francisco Giants (NL)	4	264	.242 BA
289	Leoncio "Leo" Estrella	2000	RHP	Toronto Blue Jays (AL)	2	60	7–3, 4.46 ERA
290	Tomás De la Rosa	2000	SS	Montreal Expos (NL)	2	33	.284 BA
291	Lorenzo Barceló*	2000	RHP	Chicago White Sox (AL)	3	43	5–3, 4.50 ERA
292	Pablo Ozuna	2000	IF/OF	Florida Marlins (NL)	3	65	.261 BA
293	Santiago Pérez	2000	SS/OF	Milwaukee Brewers (NL)	2	67	.188 BA
294	Carlos Casimiro*	2000	DH	Baltimore Orioles (AL)	1	2	.125 BA
295	Elvis Peña*	2000	IF	Colorado Rockies (NL)	2	25	.245 BA
296	Juan Melo	2000	2B	San Francisco Giants (NL)	1	11	.077 BA
297	José Ortiz	2000	2B	Oakland Athletics (AL)	3	136	.243 BA
298	Yovanny Lara	2000	RHP	Montreal Expos (NL)	1	6	0–0, 6.35 ERA
299	Daniel "Danny" Mota	2000	RHP	Minnesota Twins (AL)	1	4	0–0, 8.44 ERA
300	Geraldo Guzmán	2000	RHP	Arizona Diamondbacks (NL)	1	13	5–4, 5.37 ERA
301	Israel Alcantara	2000	OF	Boston Red Sox (AL)	3	51	.270 BA
302	Yohanny Valera	2000	C	Montreal Expos (NL)	1	7	.000 BA
303	Lesli Brea*	2000	RHP	Baltimore Orioles (AL)	2	8	0–1, 12.27 ERA
304	Pasqual Coco	2000	RHP	Toronto Blue Jays (AL)	3	10	1–1, 6.05 ERA
305	Luis Saturria	2000	OF	St. Louis Cardinals (NL)	2	25	.100 BA
306	José Acevedo	2001	RHP	Cincinnati Reds (NL)	3	29	11–9, 5.22 ERA
307	Benito Báez	2001	LHP	Florida Marlins (NL)	1	8	0–0, 13–50 ERA
308	Pedro Santana*	2001	2B	Detroit Tigers (AL)	1	1	—
309	Erick Almonte	2001	SS	New York Yankees (AL)	2	39	.269 BA
310	Mario Encarnación	2001	OF	Colorado Rockies (NL)	2	23	.203 BA
311	Ángel Berroa	2001	SS	Kansas City Royals (AL)	3	193	.282 BA
312	José Antonio Núñez	2001	LHP	Los Angeles Dodgers (NL)	2	63	4–2, 4.50 ERA
313	Luis Pineda	2001	RHP	Detroit Tigers (AL)	2	42	1–4, 4.44 ERA
314	Victor Santos*	2001	RHP	Detroit Tigers (AL)	3	65	2–8, 5.48 ERA
315	Henry Mateo	2001	IF	Montreal Expos (NL)	3	127	.237 BA
316	Albert Pujols	2001	IF/OF	St. Louis Cardinals (NL)	3	475	.334 BA, 114 HR
317	Wilson Betemit	2001	SS	Atlanta Braves (NL)	1	8	.000 BA
318	Juan Uribe	2001	IF	Colorado Rockies (NL)	3	314	.258 BA
319	Jesús Colome*	2001	RHP	Tampa Bay Devil Rays (AL)	3	116	7–17, 5.10 ERA
320	Carlos Peña	2001	1B	Texas Rangers (AL)	3	268	.246 BA
321	Wascar Serrano	2001	RHP	San Diego Padres (NL)	1	20	3–3, 6.56 ERA
322	Joaquín Benoit	2001	RHP	Texas Rangers (AL)	3	43	12–10, 5.55 ERA
323	Juan Cruz	2001	RHP	Chicago Cubs (NL)	3	78	8–19, 4.43 ERA
324	Reynaldo García	2002	RHP	Texas Rangers (AL)	2	20	0–0, 11.25 ERA
325	Eddie Rogers*	2002	IF	Baltimore Orioles (AL)	1	5	.000 BA
326	Luis De los Santos	2002	RHP	Tampa Bay Devil Rays (AL)	1	3	0–3, 11.57 ERA
327	Jorge Sosa	2002	RHP	Tampa Bay Devil Rays (AL)	2	60	7–19, 5.01 ERA
328	Fernando Rodney	2002	RHP	Detroit Tigers (AL)	2	47	2–6, 6.04 ERA
329	Wily Mo Peña	2002	OF	Cincinnati Reds (NL)	2	93	.219 BA
330	Juan Brito	2002	C	Kansas City Royals (AL)	1	9	.304 BA
331	Duaner Sánchez	2002	RHP	Atlanta Braves (NL)	2	15	1–0, 12.75 ERA
332	Julio Mateo	2002	RHP	Seattle Mariners (AL)	2	62	4–0, 3.38 ERA
333	Miguel Olivo	2002	C	Chicago White Sox (AL)	2	120	.235 BA
334	Ricardo Rodríguez	2002	RHP	Cleveland Indians (AL)	2	22	5–11, 5.71 ERA
335	Miguel Asencio	2002	RHP	Kansas City Royals (AL)	2	39	6–8, 5.14 ERA
336	Francis Beltran	2002	RHP	Chicago Cubs (NL)	1	11	0–0, 7.50 ERA
337	Runelvys Hernández	2002	RHP	Kansas City Royals (AL)	2	28	11–9, 4.50 ERA

(continued)

	Name	Debut	Position	Debut Team	Seasons	Games	Career Statistics
338	Abraham Núñez	2002	OF	Florida Marlins (NL)	1	19	.118 BA
339	Alexis Gómez	2002	OF	Kansas City Royals (AL)	1	5	.200 BA
340	Ramón Santiago	2002	SS	Detroit Tigers (AL)	2	206	.231 BA
341	Franklyn Germán	2002	RHP	Detroit Tigers (AL)	2	52	3–4, 5.26 ERA
342	Rafael Soriano	2002	RHP	Seattle Mariners (AL)	2	50	3–3, 2.96 ERA
343	Ésteban Germán	2002	2B	Oakland Athletics (AL)	2	14	.205 BA
344	Wilkin Ruan	2002	OF	Los Angeles Dodgers (NL)	2	33	.231 BA
345	Luis Martínez	2003	LHP	Milwaukee Brewers (NL)	1	4	0–3, 9.92 ERA
346	Félix Sánchez	2003	LHP	Chicago Cubs (NL)	1	3	0–0, 10.80 ERA
347	José Valverde*	2003	RHP	Arizona Diamondbacks (NL)	1	54	2–1, 2.15 ERA
348	Luis Terrero	2003	OF	Arizona Diamondbacks (NL)	1	5	.250 BA
349	Edwin "Ed" Almonte	2003	RHP	New York Mets (NL)	1	12	0–0, 11.12 ERA
350	José Morban	2003	IF	Baltimore Orioles (AL)	1	61	.141 BA
351	Rodrigo Rosario	2003	RHP	Houston Astros (NL)	1	2	1–0, 1.13 ERA
352	Juan Domínguez	2003	RHP	Texas Rangers (AL)	1	6	0–2, 7.16 ERA
353	Jorge DePaula	2003	RHP	New York Yankees (AL)	1	4	0–0, 0.79 ERA
354	Jhonny Peralta	2003	SS	Cleveland Indians (AL)	1	77	.227 BA
355	Aquilino López	2003	RHP	Toronto Blue Jays (AL)	1	72	1–3, 3.42 ERA
356	Antonio Pérez	2003	IF	Tampa Bay Devil Rays (AL)	1	48	.248 BA
357	José Reyes	2003	SS	New York Mets (NL)	1	69	.307 BA
358	Francisco Santos	2003	OF	San Francisco Giants (NL)	1	8	.200 BA
359	Julio Manon	2003	RHP	Montreal Expos (NL)	1	23	1–2, 4.13 ERA
360	Claudio Vargas	2003	RHP	Montreal Expos (NL)	1	23	6–8, 4.34 ERA
361	Enrique Cruz	2003	3B	Milwaukee Brewers (NL)	1	60	.085 BA

* Born in San Pedro de Macorís.

San Pedro de Macorís Major League Roster through 2003

	Player	Position	Birth Date	Big League Debut Date	Debut MLB Team
1	Amado Samuel	SS	Dec. 6, 1938	Apr. 10, 1962	Milwaukee Braves (NL)
2	Rafael Robles	SS	Oct. 20, 1947	Apr. 8, 1969	San Diego Padres (NL)
3	Pepe Frías	SS	July 14, 1948	Apr. 6, 1973	Montreal Expos (NL)
4	Nelson Norman	SS	May 23, 1959	May 20, 1978	Texas Rangers (AL)
5	Rafael Ramírez	SS	Feb. 18, 1958	Aug. 4, 1980	Atlanta Braves (NL)
6	Tony Fernández	SS	Aug. 6, 1962	Sept. 2, 1983	Toronto Blue Jays (AL)
7	Mariano Duncan	SS	Mar. 13, 1963	Apr. 9, 1985	Los Angeles Dodgers (NL)
8	Manny Lee	SS	June 17, 1965	Apr. 10, 1985	Toronto Blue Jays (AL)
9	Tito Bell	SS	Mar. 29, 1968	Sept. 6, 1989	Baltimore Orioles (AL)
10	José Offerman	SS	Nov. 8, 1968	Aug. 19, 1990	Los Angeles Dodgers (NL)
11	Andrés Santana	SS	Feb. 5, 1968	Sept. 16, 1990	San Francisco Giants (NL)
12	Manny Alexander	SS	Mar. 20, 1971	Sept. 18, 1992	Baltimore Orioles (AL)
13	Pedro González	IF	Dec. 12, 1937	Apr. 11, 1963	New York Yankees (AL)
14	Rafael Batista	IF (1B)	Oct. 20, 1947	June 17, 1973	Houston Astros (NL)
15	Juan Bernhardt	IF	Aug. 31, 1953	July 10, 1976	New York Yankees (AL)
16	Art DeFreitas	IF (1B)	Apr. 26, 1953	Sept. 7, 1978	Cincinnati Reds (NL)
17	Julio Franco	IF (2B)	Aug. 23, 1958	Apr. 23, 1982	Philadelphia Phillies (NL)
18	Juan Castillo	IF	Jan. 25, 1962	Apr. 12, 1986	Milwaukee Brewers (AL)
19	Norberto Martín	IF	Dec. 10, 1966	Sept. 20, 1993	Chicago White Sox (AL)
20	José Oliva	IF (3B)	Mar. 32, 1971	July 1, 1994	Atlanta Braves (NL)
21	Luis Castillo	IF (2B)	Sept. 12, 1975	Aug. 8, 1996	Florida Marlins (NL)
22	Fernando Tatis	IF (3B)	Jan. 1, 1975	July 26, 1997	Texas Rangers (AL)
23	Alfonso Soriano	IF (2B)	Jan. 7, 1978	Sept. 14, 1999	New York Yankees (AL)
24	Elvis Peña	IF (2B/SS)	Mar. 29, 1967	Sept. 2, 2000	Colorado Rockies (NL)
25	Pedro Santana	IF (2B)	Sept. 21, 1976	July 16, 2001	Detroit Tigers (AL)
26	Eddie Rogers	IF	Aug. 10, 1978	Sept. 5, 2002	Baltimore Orioles (AL)

190

	Player	Position	Birth Date	Big League Debut Date	Debut MLB Team
27	Rick Joseph	IF/OF	Aug. 24, 1939	June 18, 1964	Kansas City Athletics (AL)
28	Pedro Guerrero	IF/OF	June 29, 1956	Sept. 22, 1978	Los Angeles Dodgers (NL)
29	Juan Samuel	IF/OF	Dec. 9, 1960	Aug. 23, 1983	Philadelphia Phillies (NL)
30	Manny Jiménez	OF	Nov. 11, 1938	Apr. 11, 1962	Kansas City Athletics (AL)
31	Rico Carty	OF	Sept. 1, 1939	Sept. 15, 1963	Milwaukee Braves (NL)
32	Elvio Jiménez	OF	Jan. 6, 1940	Oct. 4, 1964	New York Yankees (AL)
33	Al Javier	OF	Feb. 4, 1954	Sept. 9, 1976	Houston Astros (NL)
34	George Bell	OF	Oct. 21, 1959	Apr. 9, 1981	Toronto Blue Jays (AL)
35	Carmen Castillo	OF	June 8, 1958	July 17, 1982	Cleveland Indians (AL)
36	Alejandro Sánchez	OF	Feb. 14, 1959	Sept. 6, 1982	Philadelphia Phillies (NL)
37	Sammy Sosa	OF	Nov. 10, 1968	June 16, 1989	Texas Rangers (AL)
38	Luis Mercedes	OF	Feb. 15, 1968	Sept. 8, 1991	Baltimore Orioles (AL)
39	Rudy Pemberton	OF	Dec. 17, 1969	Apr. 26, 1995	Detroit Tigers (AL)
40	Miguel Mejía	OF	Mar. 25, 1975	Apr. 4, 1996	St. Louis Cardinals (NL)
41	Manny Martínez	OF	Oct. 3, 1970	June 14, 1996	Seattle Mariners (AL)
42	Luis Saturria	OF	July 21, 1976	Sept. 11, 2000	St. Louis Cardinals (NL)
43	Santiago Guzmán	P	July 25, 1949	Sept. 30, 1969	St. Louis Cardinals (NL)
44	Joaquín Andújar	P	Nov. 12, 1952	Apr. 8, 1976	Houston Astros (NL)
45	Santo Alcalá	P	Dec. 23, 1952	Apr. 10, 1976	Cincinnati Reds (NL)
46	Ramón Romero	P	Jan. 8, 1959	Sept. 18, 1984	Cleveland Indians (AL)
47	Balvino Gálvez	P	Mar. 31, 1964	May 7, 1986	Los Angeles Dodgers (NL)
48	Ravelo Manzanillo	P	Oct. 17, 1963	Sept. 25, 1988	Chicago White Sox (AL)
49	Josías Manzanillo	P	Oct. 16, 1967	Oct. 5, 1991	Boston Red Sox (AL)
50	Ben Rivera	P	Jan. 11, 1969	Apr. 9, 1992	Atlanta Braves (NL)
51	Domingo Jean	P	Jan. 9, 1969	Aug. 8, 1993	New York Yankees (AL)
52	Salomon Torres	P	Mar. 11, 1972	Aug. 29, 1993	San Francisco Giants (NL)
53	Héctor Carrasco	P	Oct. 22, 1969	Apr. 4, 1994	Cincinnati Reds (NL)
54	Nerio Rodríguez	P	Mar. 4, 1971	Aug. 16, 1996	Baltimore Orioles (AL)
55	Julio Santana	P	Jan. 20, 1973	Apr. 6, 1997	Texas Rangers (AL)
56	José Jiménez	P	July 7, 1973	Sept. 9, 1998	St. Louis Cardinals (NL)
57	Guillermo Mota	P	July 25, 1973	May 2, 1999	Montreal Expos (NL)
58	Lorenzo Barceló	P	Aug. 10, 1977	July 22, 2000	Chicago White Sox (AL)
59	Lesli Brea	P	Oct. 12, 1973	Aug. 13, 2000	Baltimore Orioles (AL)
60	Victor Santos	P	Oct. 2, 1976	Apr. 9, 2001	Detroit Tigers (AL)
61	Jesús Colome	P	Dec. 23, 1977	June 21, 2001	Tampa Bay Devil Rays (AL)
62	José Valverde	P	July 24, 1979	June 1, 2003	Arizona Diamondbacks (NL)
63	Ángel Peña	C	Feb. 16, 1975	Sept. 8, 1998	Los Angeles Dodgers (NL)
64	Carlos Casimiro	DH	Nov. 8, 1976	July 31, 2000	Baltimore Orioles (AL)

Players are grouped by field position and ordered by date of major league debut.

Dominican League Record Book

Dominican Republic League Teams and Managers, with Individual Batting Leaders (1951–2003)

Year	Champion	Manager	Batting Champion	BA	Home Run Leader	HR
Dominican Summer League						
1951	Licey	Félix Delgado	Luis Villodas	.346	Pedro Formental	13
1952	Aguilas	Rodolfo Fernández	Luis Olmo	.344	Alonzo Perry	11
1953	Licey	Oscar Rodríguez	Tetelo Vargas	.355	Alonzo Perry	11
1954	Estrellas	Ramón Bragaña	Alonzo Perry	.326	Bob Thurman	11
Dominican Winter League						
1955–1956	Escogido	Frank Genovese	Bob Wilson	.333	Willie Kirkland	9
1956–1957	Escogido	Red Davis	Ozzie Virgil	.312	Danny Kravitz	4
1957–1958	Escogido	Salty Parker	Alzono Perry	.332	Dick Stuart	14

(continued)

Year	Champion	Manager	Batting Champion	BA	Home Run Leader	HR
1958–1959	Licey	Joe Schultz	Felipe Alou	.351	Jim McDaniels	12
1959–1960	Escogido	Pete Reiser	Felipe Alou	.359	Frank Howard	9
1960–1961	Escogido	Pepe Lucas	Manny Mota	.344	Felipe Alou	4
1961–1962	*Season Not Completed*					
1962–1963	*League Suspended*					
1963–1964	Licey	Vern Benson	Manny Mota	.379	Orlando McFarlane	10
1964–1965	Aguilas	Al Widmar	Manny Mota	.364	Orlando McFarlane	8
1965–1966	*League Suspended*					
1966–1967	Aguilas	Pete Peterson	Matty Alou	.363	Winston Llanes	10
1967–1968	Orientales	Tony Pacheco	Rico Carty	.350	Bob Robertson	9
1968–1969	Escogido	Andy Gilbert	Matty Alou	.390	Nate Colbert	8
1969–1970	Licey	Manny Mota	Ralph Garr	.387	Winston Llenas	9
					Bobby Browne	9
1970–1971	Licey	Fred Hatfield	Ralph Garr	.457	César Cedeño	8
1971–1972	Aguilas	Ozzie Virgil	Ralph Garr	.388	Charlie Sands	10
1972–1973	Licey	Tommy Lasorda	Von Joshua	.358	Adrian Garrett	9
1973–1974	Licey	Tommy Lasorda	Dave Parker	.345	Rico Carty	9
1974–1975	Aguilas	Al Widmar	Bruce Bochte	.352	Bobby Darwin	8
					Rafael Batista	8
1975–1976	Aguilas	Tim Murtaugh	Wilbur Howard	.341	Larry Parrish	4
					Bill Nahorodny	4
1976–1977	Licey	Bob Rodgers	Mario Guerrero	.365	Pedro Guerrero	6
					Ike Hampton	6
1977–1978	Aguilas	Johnny Lipon	Omar Moreno	.345	Dick Davis	8
1978–1979	Aguilas	Johnny Lipon	Ted Cox	.319	Bob Beall	7
					Dick Davis	7
1979–1980	Licey	Del Crandall	Tony Peña	.317	Pedro Guerrero	3
					Leon Durham	3
1980–1981	Escogido	Felipe Alou	Ken Landreaux	.394	Tony Peña	7
1981–1982	Escogido	Felipe Alou	Pedro Hernández	.408	Dave Hostetler	9
1982–1983	Licey	Manny Mota	César Geronimo	.341	Howard Johnson	8
1983–1984	Licey	Manny Mota	Miguel Diloné	.343	Reggie Whittemore	12
1984–1985	Licey	Terry Collins	Junior Noboa	.327	Ralph Bryant	9
1985–1986	Aguilas	Winston Llenas	Tony Fernández	.364	Tony Peña	9
1986–1987	Aguilas	Winston Llenas	Stan Javier	.374	Ralph Bryant	13
1987–1988	Escogido	Phil Regan	Stan Javier	.363	Mark Parent	10
1988–1989	Escogido	Phil Regan	Julio Peguero	.326	Domingo Michel	9
1989–1990	Escogido	Felipe Alou	Ángel González	.434	Denio González	5
1990–1991	Licey	John Roseboro	Hensley Meulens	.338	Francisco Cabrera	8
1991–1992	Escogido	Felipe Alou	Luis Mercedes	.333	Gerónimo Berroa	4
					Sammy Sosa	4
1992–1993	Aguilas	Miguel Diloné	Tom March	.318	Domingo Martínez	6
1993–1994	Licey	Casey Parsons	Alex Arias	.371	Sil Campusano	7
1994–1995	Azucareros	Art Howe	Luis Mercedes	.352	Domingo Martínez	11
1995–1996	Aguilas	Terry Francona	Domingo Cedeño	.419	Sherman Obando	7
1996–1997	Aguilas	Mike Quade	Wilton Guerrero	.340	Domingo Martínez	6
1997–1998	Aguilas	Tony Peña	Julio Franco	.436	José Oliva	8
1998–1999	Licey	Dave Jauss	Luis Polonia	.336	Adrian Beltre	10
1999–2000	Aguilas	Tony Peña	Pablo Ozuna	.324	Isreal Alcantara	6
2000–2001	Aguilas	Tony Peña	Félix José	.376	Andy Barkett	11
2001–2002	Licey	Teddy Martínez	Bernie Castro	.349	Eric Byrnes	11
					Félix José	11
2002–2003	Aguilas	Tony Peña	Bernie Castro	.366	Rubén Mateo	10

The historic teams are Aguilas Cibaeñas, Escogido Lions, Licey Tigers, and Estrellas Orientales.

Dominican Republic League Postseason Results (1951–2003)

Year	Champion	Regular Season Record	Standing	Finals Opponent	Championship Results, Games
Dominican Summer League Split Season, First and Second Half					
1951	Licey	16–14; 15–8	2nd; 1st	Escogido	Licey 4, Escogido 1
1952	Aguilas	20–9; 12–12	1st; 3rd	Licey	Aguilas 4, Licey 3
1953	Licey	20–7; 16–11	1st; 2nd	Aguilas	Licey 4, Aguilas 1
1954	Estrellas	9–14; 22–5	3rd; 1st	Licey	Estrellas 4, Licey 1
Dominican Winter League					
1955–1956	Escogido	35–18	1st	Aguilas	Escogido 4, Aguilas 3
1956–1957	Escogido	31–21	2nd	Licey	Escogido 5, Licey 2
1957–1958	Escogido	31–20	1st	Estrellas	Escogido 5, Estrellas 1
1958–1959	Licey	30–29	2nd	Escogido	Licey 5, Escogido 4
1959–1960	Escogido	39–22	1st	Estrellas	Escogido 5, Estrellas 1
1960–1961	Escogido	20–19	1st	Aguilas	Escogido 5, Aguilas 2
1961–1962	*Season Not Completed*				
1962–1963	*League Suspended*				
1963–1964	Licey	28–30	3rd	Aguilas	Licey 5, Aguilas 3
1964–1965	Aguilas	27–26	3rd	Escogido	Aguilas 5, Escogido 0
1965–1966	*League Suspended*				
1966–1967	Aguilas	34–24	1st	Escogido	Aguilas 5, Escogido 3
1967–1968	Estrellas	38–19	1st	Escogido	Estrellas 5, Escogido 3
1968–1969	Escogido	31–17	1st	Estrellas	Escogido 5, Estrellas 2
1969–1970	Licey	30–20	1st	Aguilas	Licey 5, Aguilas 1
1970–1971	Licey	33–27	1st	Escogido	Licey 6, Escogido 1
1971–1972	Aguilas	28–31	3rd	Licey	Aguilas 5, Licey 3
1972–1973	Licey	32–23	1st	Aguilas	Licey 5, Aguilas 2
1973–1974	Licey	37–21	1st	Aguilas	Licey 5, Aguilas 2
1974–1975	Aguilas	28–28	2nd	Estrellas	Aguilas 5, Estrellas 4
1975–1976	Aguilas	36–26	2nd	Licey	Aguilas 5, Licey 2
1976–1977	Licey	24–26	2nd	Aguilas	Licey 5, Aguilas 2
1977–1978	Aguilas	32–27	2nd	Licey	Aguilas 5, Licey 2
1978–1979	Aguilas	36–24	1st	Escogido	Aguilas 5, Escogido 0
1979–1980	Licey	40–19	1st	Estrellas	Licey 5, Estrellas 1
1980–1981	Escogido	40–20	1st	Aguilas	Escogido 5, Aguilas 4
1981–1982	Escogido	37–23	1st	Estrellas	Escogido 5, Estrellas 1
1982–1983	Licey	29–30	2nd	Aguilas	Licey 5, Aguilas 2
1983–1984	Licey	40–29	2nd	Aguilas	Licey 4, Aguilas 3
1984–1985	Licey	40–20	1st	Azucareros	Licey 4, Azucareros 1
1985–1986	Aguilas	31–29	2nd	Licey	Aguilas 4, Licey 1
1986–1987	Aguilas	25–22	2nd	Estrellas	Aguilas 4, Estrellas 1
1987–1988	Escogido	32–28	3rd	Estrellas	Escogido 4, Estrellas 3
1988–1989	Escogido	30–29	3rd	Licey	Escogido 4, Licey 0
1989–1990	Escogido	27–21	2nd	Aguilas	Escogido 4, Aguilas 2
1990–1991	Licey	26–22	1st	Escogido	Licey 4, Escogido 1
1991–1992	Escogido	23–25	3rd	Estrellas	Escogido 4, Estrellas 1
1992–1993	Aguilas	29–17	2nd	Azucareros	Aguilas 4, Azucareros 1
1993–1994	Licey	26–22	1st	Aguilas	Licey 4, Aguilas 1
1994–1995	Azucareros	29–19	1st	Aguilas	Azucareros 4, Aguilas 2
1995–1996	Aguilas	26–21	2nd	Estrellas	Aguilas 4, Estrellas 1
1996–1997	Aguilas	32–16	1st	Escogido	Aguilas 4, Escogido 0
1997–1998	Aguilas	26–24	3rd	Licey	Aguilas 4, Licey 1
1998–1999	Licey	33–27	3rd	Escogido	Licey 5, Escogido 4
1999–2000	Aguilas	30–18	1st	Estrellas	Aguilas 4, Estrellas 3
2000–2001	Aguilas	32–18	1st	Escogido	Aguilas 4, Escogido 2
2001–2002	Licey	30–20	2nd	Aguilas	Licey 4, Aguilas 3
2002–2003	Aguilas	30–17	1st	Escogido	Aguilas 4, Escogido 0

Dominican League Pitching Leaders (1951–2003)

Year	Pitching Wins	W	ERA Leader	ERA	Strikeouts Leader	SO
Dominican Summer League						
1951	Guayubín Olivo	10	Guayubín Olivo	1.90	Guayubín Olivo	65
1952	Terry McDuffie	14	Guayubín Olivo	1.33	Luis Arroyo	101
1953	Emilio Cueche	13	Santiago Ullrich	1.98	Emilio Cueche	96
1954	Carrao Bracho	8	Guayubín Olivo	1.86	Julián Ladera	40
Dominican Winter League						
1955–1956	Fred Waters	11	Art Murray	0.57	Chuck Templeton	108
1956–1957	Pete Burnside	11	Pete Burnside	1.71	Pete Burnside	109
1957–1958	Fred Kipp	11	Vic Rehm	1.53	Stan Williams	96
1958–1959	Bennie Daniels	12	Octavio Acosta	1.66	Dom Zanny	86
1959–1960	Stan Williams	12	Fred Kipp	1.32	Stan Williams	105
1960–1961	Danilo Riva	13	Juan Marichal	1.41	Guayubín Olivo	160
1961–1962	*Season Not Completed*					
1962–1963	*League Suspended*					
1963–1964	Steve Blass	9	Juan Marichal	1.35	Gaylord Perry	106
1964–1965	Dick LeMay	8	Pete Richert	1.51	Gary Kroll	90
1965–1966	*League Suspended*					
1966–1967	Dock Ellis	9	Dave Hernández	1.67	Steve Bailey	101
1967–1968	Silvano Quezada	11	Chuck Taylor	1.69	Danny Coombs	90
1968–1969	Jay Ritchie	9	Leslie Scott	1.29	Santiago Guzmán	71
1969–1970	Gene Rounsaville	8	Sal Campisi	0.74	Santiago Guzmán	69
1970–1971	Rollie Fingers	9	Wade Blasingame	2.22	Archie Reynolds	79
1971–1972	Gene Garber	9	Pedro Borbón	1.68	Dick Tidrow	75
1972–1973	Pedro Borbón	9	Tom Dettore	2.30	Doug Rau	72
1973–1974	Rick Waits	8	Charlie Hough	1.29	Charlie Hough	73
1974–1975	J. R. Richard	8	J. R. Richard	1.64	J. R. Richard	103
1975–1976	Nino Espinosa	8	Kent Tekulve	1.00	J. R. Richard	88
1976–1977	Ángel Torres	10	Doug Bair	1.26	Odell Jones	70
1977–1978	*Three Tied*	7	Tom Hume	1.97	Mickey Mahler	80
1978–1979	Mike Proly	9	Bo McLaughlin	1.80	Frank Riccelli	82
1979–1980	Jerry Hannahs	9	Silvano Quezada	1.49	Mario Soto	62
1980–1981	Mario Soto	7	Steve Ratzer	1.24	Mario Soto	54
1981–1982	Pascual Pérez	10	Oscar Brito	1.85	Mario Soto	54
1982–1983	Pascual Pérez	9	Pascual Pérez	2.23	Juan Berenguer	59
1983–1984	Orel Hershiser	8	Orel Hershiser	1.51	Robin Fuson	61
1984–1985	Tom Filer	8	Craig Minetto	0.77	Ken Howell	71
1985–1986	Mickey Mahler	8	Andy Araujo	1.36	Chris Green	69
1986–1987	*Three Tied*	5	Gibson Alba	1.17	José Núñez	62
1987–1988	José Bautista	8	Dave Otto	1.27	José Núñez	85
1988–1989	Melido Pérez	8	Andy Araujo	1.09	Balvino Galvez	70
1989–1990	*Four Tied*	6	Jeff Edwards	2.17	Jeff Edwards	76
1990–1991	Francisco De la Rosa	7	Juan Guzmán	1.69	Francisco De la Rosa	49
1991–1992	José Núñez	6	Pedro Astacio	1.41	José Núñez	58
1992–1993	Julián Heredia	4	Julián Heredia	1.18	Pedro Borbón Jr.	37
1993–1994	Apolinar García	6	Vance Lovelace	1.55	Apolinar García	43
1994–1995	Hipólito Pichardo	6	Weston Weber	1.50	Wilson Heredia	58
1995–1996	Ramón Morel	5	Amaury Telemaco	1.31	Carlos Pérez	74
1996–1997	Dan Hubbs	6	Bartolo Colón	0.21	Everett Stull	44
1997–1998	Efrain Valdéz	8	Dan Hubbs	1.49	Josías Manzanillo	55
1998–1999	Nelson Cruz	6	Héctor Ramírez	1.18	Fernando Hernández	74
1999–2000	Fernando Hernández	6	Efrain Valdéz	1.17	Fernando Hernández	59
2000–2001	Fernando Hernández	7	Robert Ellis	1.55	Desi Wilson	56
2001–2002	Dámaso Marti	8	Odalis Pérez	1.88	Dámaso Marti	65
2002–2003	Alberto Reyes	5	Arnie Muñoz	1.55	Arnie Muñoz	74

Dominican League Career and Season Individual Records (1951–2003)

Category	Name	Record	Date
Batting			
Batting Average, Career	Manny Mota	.333	
	Matty Alou	.327	
Batting Average, Season	Ralph Garr	.457	1970–1971
Slugging Average	Alonzo Perry	.488	
Seasons Played	Manny Mota	20	
	Jesús Alou	20	
	Rafael Batista	20	
Games Played	Rafael Batista	946	
At-Bats	Rafael Batista	3,200	
	Winston Llenas	3,144	
Base Hits, Career	Miguel Diloné	866	
	Jesús Alou	865	
Base Hits, Season	Ralph Garr	105	1970–1971
Singles	Miguel Diloné	738	
	Jesús Alou	690	
Doubles	Rafael Batista	157	
	Jesús Alou	136	
	Winston Llenas	111	
Triples	Manny Mota	41	
	Miguel Diloné	40	
Home Runs, Career	Rico Carty	59	
	Winston Llenas	50	
	Alonzo Perry	49	
Home Runs, Season	Dick Stuart	14	1957–1958
RBI, Career	Rafael Batista	395	
	Winston Llenas	377	
	Jesús Alou	339	
RBI, Season	Alonzo Perry	53	1953 Summer
Runs Scored	Miguel Diloné	489	
Total Bases	Rafael Batista	1,160	
	Jesús Alou	1,098	
	Miguel Diloné	1,048	
Strikeouts, Batter	Rafael Batista	529	
Walks, Batter	Rafael Batista	379	
	Miguel Diloné	329	
Stolen Bases	Miguel Diloné	395	
Pitching			
Games Won	Diómedes "Guayubín" Olivo	86	
Winning Percentage	Mickey Mahler	.702 (40–17)	
ERA, Career	Juan Marichal	1.87 (57.1 IP)	
ERA, Season	Bartolo Colón	0.21	1996–1997
	Art Murray	0.57	1955–1956
Games Lost	Chi Chí Olivo	69	
Seasons Pitched	Silvano Quezada	21	
Games Started	Ramón De los Santos	364	
	Silvano Quezada	358	
Games Pitched, Season	Charlie Hough	35	1970–1971
Games Completed	Diómedes "Guayubín" Olivo	70	
Innings Pitched	Chi Chí Olivo	1,335.2	
	Silvano Quezada	1,198.1	
Innings Pitcher, Season	Fred Walters	163.1	1955–1956
Shutouts	Chi Chí Olivo	69	
Saves	Ramón Peña	80	
Strikeouts, Career	Diómedes "Guayubín" Olivo	742	
Strikeouts, Season	Diómedes "Guayubín" Olivo	160	1960–1961
Relief Strikeouts, Season	Arnie Múñoz	74	2002–2003
Walks, Career	Joaquín Andújar	382	
Walks, Season	Bennie Daniels	75	1956–1957

Guayubín Olivo's Dominican League Record

Year	Team	League	W–L	PCT	G	IP	ERA	SO	H
Dominican League									
1951	Licey	Dominican (S)	10–5	.667	16	107	1.90	65	107
1952	Licey	Dominican (S)	10–5	.667	19	115.1	1.33	79	93
1953	Licey	Dominican (S)	6–2	.750	19	96	2.34	57	104
1954	Licey	Dominican (S)	8–2	.800	13	87	1.86	33	75
1955–1956	Licey	Dominican (W)	8–3	.728	16	105.2	1.53	37	103
1956–1957	Licey	Dominican (W)	10–4	.714	16	107.2	1.84	45	89
1957–1958	Licey	Dominican (W)	4–8	.333	18	82.2	4.79	65	98
1958–1959	Licey	Dominican (W)	4–2	.667	21	17.2	2.13	66	65
1959–1960	Licey	Dominican (W)	7–6	.538	22	116	2.33	98	98
1960–1961	Licey	Dominican (W)	10–6	.625	20	142	1.58	160	95
1963–1964	Licey	Dominican (W)	9–3	.750	18	114	2.37	37	115
Dominican Totals			*86–46*	*.652*	*198*	*1,166.1*	*2.11*	*742*	*1,042*
Non-Dominican Leagues									
1955	Havana	Cuban (W)	0–1	.000	7	13	5.54	4	21
1955	Mexico City	Mexican	8–6	.571	28	141	4.91	120	151
1956	Mexico City	Mexican	15–8	.652	32	197	2.65	115	197
1957	Mexico City	Mexican	3–1	.750	5	36	2.00	29	27
1958	Mexico City	Mexican	8–6	.571	28	151	3.81	122	160
1959	Poza Rica	Mexican	21–8	.724	35	247	3.02	233	219
1960	Pittsburgh	National	0–0	.000	4	10	2.70	10	8
1961	Columbus	International	11–7	.611	66	130	2.01	118	100
1962	Pittsburgh	National	5–1	.833	62	84	2.79	66	88
1963	St. Louis	National	0–5	.000	19	13.1	5.40	9	16
*Major League Totals**			*5–6*	*.455*	*85*	*107.1*	*3.10*	*85*	*112*
Non-Dominican Totals			*71–43*	*.623*	*286*	*1,022.1*	*NA*	*826*	*987*

Abbreviations (league seasons): S, summer; W, winter.
* Major league totals are for 1960, 1962, and 1963 seasons.

Dominican Republic Amateur National Champions

Year	Champion
1994	Distrito Nacional
1995	Distrito Nacional
1996	Santiago
1997	Santiago
1998	Cotui
1999	San Francisco de Macorís
2000	Santiago
2001	Aguilas Cibaeñas
2002	Aguilas Cibaeñas

NOTE

1. The Marichal section appeared originally as an article: "Juan Marichal: Baseball in the Dominican Republic." *Baseball History 3: An Annual of Original Baseball Research*, ed. Peter Levine (Westport: Meckler, 1990), 49–70.

BIBLIOGRAPHY

Bjarkman, Peter C. *Baseball with a Latin Beat: A History of the Latin American Game.* Jefferson, NC, and London: McFarland & Company Publishers, 1994.

Jamail, Milton H. *Full Count: Inside Cuban Baseball.* Carbondale: Southern Illinois University Press, 2000.

Joyce, Gare. *The Only Ticket Off the Island.* Toronto: Lester & Orpen Dennys, 1990.

Klein, Alan. *Sugarball: The American Game, The Dominican Dream.* New Haven, CT: Yale University Press, 1991.

Marichal, Juan, with Charles Einstein. *A Pitcher's Story.* Garden City, NY: Doubleday, 1967.

Pietrusza, David, Matthew Silverman, and Michael Gershman, Editors. *Baseball: The Biographical Encyclopedia.* New York: Total Sports Illustrated, 2000.

Ruck, Rob. *The Tropic of Baseball: Baseball in the Dominican Republic.* 1st ed. Westport, CT, and London: Meckler Publishers, 1991.

———. *The Tropic of Baseball: Baseball in the Dominican Republic.* With a new afterword by the author. Lincoln: University of Nebraska Press, 1999.

CHAPTER 5

Venezuela

Stepchild of Latin American Baseball

• •

Things haven't been especially smooth lately in the Venezuela baseball universe. The final decade of the twentieth century was not a particularly heady time for Venezuelan Winter League interests nor, once the new century dawned, was it an especially good time to be a baseball fan back home in Caracas. Political unrest plaguing the Hugo Chávez government led to civil strife forcing cancellation of the entire 2002–2003 winter league season, and that debacle also meant the first absence of a Venezuelan entry at the Caribbean World Series in three decades. Things weren't much better only three seasons earlier, when most of the winter league headlines emanated from Caracas and almost all the news was exceptionally bad. Two promising minor league pitching prospects—one in the Atlanta Braves organization and the other a property of the Detroit Tigers—were shot and killed in separate incidents of armed robbery during the opening month of the 1999–2000 winter league campaign. Between those two tragedies, the entire Venezuelan circuit was shut down for five days in mid-December when devastating floods wracked the entire country.

And this was just the start of truly bad times on the Venezuela baseball scene. The nation's biggest modern-era star, slugger Andrés Galarraga, had his seemingly Cooperstown-bound career derailed for a nail-biting spell when a bout with cancer caused "The Big Cat" to miss the entire 1999 major league season. The country's faltering national amateur baseball federation suffered further embarrassments when the nonexistent Venezuelan national team sat home on the sidelines for the 2003 World Cup games in Havana, the November 2003 Western Hemisphere Olympic Qualifier in Panama, and even the 2003 Pan American Games in Santo Domingo. To cap off the string of relentless disasters and depressing setbacks, the Venezuelan entrants in recent editions of the winter league highlight Caribbean World Series have remained consistent also-rans since their last tournament victory way back in 1989—fifteen excruciatingly long years in the past.

If this has been a seemingly sour story, it has not been an altogether new one. Venezuelan baseball never seems to receive its deserved quota of untarnished respect. Neighbors on the north side of the Caribbean basin draw most of the headlines, whether for supplying Latin big leaguers or for the legends and achievements of winter league play. This oversight is especially evident and painful when the subject turns to Latin American stars performing in the U.S. major leagues. Cuba's Minnie Miñoso was a minor sensation of the 1950s; Roberto Clemente of Puerto Rico and Juan Marichal of the Dominican Republic grabbed headlines across the 1960s; Tony Pérez and Orlando Cepeda kept Cuban and Puerto Rican connections alive and thriving in the 1970s; Fernando Valenzuela was a media darling of the early 1980s; and the final decade of the twentieth century witnessed increasing fascination with fairytale sagas of Dominican shortstops from San Pedro de Macorís. In the first decade of the new century, the American press has become thoroughly enamored with politically tinged accounts of a scattered handful of defectors escaping Communist Cuba to reap their untold millions pursuing capitalist baseball dreams in the big leagues. Between Luis Aparicio's fancy fielding and adroit base running in the late 1950s and 1960s and the seemingly overnight superstar status of Andrés Galarraga in 1993, other Venezuelan major leaguers—such as Davey Concepción, Tony Armas, or Ozzie Guillén—have been relegated, quite un- justly, to the back pages of Latin baseball history.

Venezuela nonetheless sports its own lustrous and well-documented dia- mond tradition and has spawned its own batch of true big league heroes, both nearly at full parity with those of any of its Caribbean neighbors. Only Cuba (1871, 1911) and Mexico (1933) preceded Venezuela (with Alejandro "Alex" Carrasquel in 1939) in cracking big league player rosters; Puerto Rico (1942) and the Dominican Republic (1956) in fact lagged a full step or two behind the nation of Simón Bolivar in first denting the U.S. big league scene. The half- century-old Venezuelan Winter League circuit also boasts a lusty legacy that arguably matches any of its Caribbean Confederation rivals. And though the growing collection of Venezuelan major leaguers (in 2003 numbering 159, to Puerto Rico's 211, Cuba's 148, and Mexico's mere 97) may in raw numbers be overshadowed by the Dominican (364) as well as the Puerto Rican forces, when it comes to quality ballplayers of the most recent decade the issue is wide open for hearty debate.

It turns out that the coastal plain of Venezuela, not the island of Hispaniola, is the legitimate breeding grounds for major league shortstops. Here is the birthplace of Alfonso "Chico" Carrasquel, the first big leaguer at that position to earn wide distinction, and also the first Latin native to play in the National League versus American League All-Star midsummer classic. Aparicio, for his part, was not only arguably the best Hispanic shortstop ever to put on spikes and glove—at least until the arrival of American-raised Alex Rodríguez—but one of a tiny enclave of players at the game's most demanding position ever to earn Hall-of-Fame status. Davey Concepción and Ozzie Guillén were un- matched among Latin-born middle infielders of the 1970s and 1980s, respec- tively, and while Concepción may well be among Latin America's near-future Cooperstown choices, contemporary Cleveland star Omar Vizquel (latest in the line of stellar Caracas middle infielders) is at the outset of the twenty-first century repeatedly being compared to Ozzie Smith as one of the sport's unparalleled defensive stylists.

Venezuela's tally sheet reads one Hall of Famer (potentially two, assuming that Concepción will eventually join Aparicio in Major League Baseball's Valhalla) plus a hearty trio of nearly unmatched defensive greats (Carrasquel, Guillén, and Vizquel). Carrasquel and Aparicio may be credited with actually launching the popular image of the nonpareil Latino shortstop, an image that has long been at the heart of the Latin American baseball saga. For all the tribute paid Dominican shortstops during the final decade and a half of the twentieth century, it still remains indisputable that in Aparicio, Carrasquel, Concepción, Guillén, and Vizquel Venezuela already boasts five shortstops unrivaled by any other country—including baseball's self-anointed homeland, the United States itself.

There have also been muscular sluggers and spellbinding hurlers bred in Caracas and the oil-rich Venezuelan coastal plains. Tony Armas, for example, long ranked among the top home run producers of the region, trailing only Tony Pérez and Orlando Cepeda, though he has recently fallen far out of the upper echelons now that Andrés Galarraga and Manny Ramírez have surpassed 300, José Canseco and Juan González have topped 400, and Rafael Palmeiro and Sammy Sosa soar above the 500 plateau. Armas was nonetheless the first Latin fence-buster to win two home run titles (1981 with Oakland and 1984 with Boston), and though the first of these titles was tinged with the illegitimacy of a strike-shortened 1981 season, the second came via a most respectable 43 round-trippers that outdistanced all American League rivals. Armas was also RBI champion in the junior circuit in 1984 and narrowly missed home run crowns in 1980 (fourth, with 35) and 1983 (second to Jim Rice, with 36) that might have made him the first among his Latin countrymen to capture the most prestigious slugging honor on four different occasions.

Sluggers like Armas and Galarraga aside, it is Davey Concepción who so closely rivals Aparicio as the most noteworthy among Venezuelan big leaguers—and Concepción may well be one of the most overlooked of all Latin American superstars. Concepción's blessing as well as his bane is that he was never a flashy performer by Latin standards, and also that he quietly amassed Cooperstown-like numbers while seizing full advantage of playing on baseball's most powerful team of the early and mid-1970s. Wearing the unlucky uniform number "13" and showcasing consistent enough unrivaled glove work to earn five career Gold Gloves in the field across almost two decades, Davey Concepción stood out as one of the best major league shortstops of the 1970s and 1980s expansion era. Perhaps only Ozzie Smith was better. Mainstay of the Big Red Machine teams in Cincinnati, Concepción was elected team captain (1973) just in time to lead those powerhouse Reds outfits to a string of post-season successes between 1973 and 1976, culminating in back-to-back world championships.

He would play more than 100 games at the shortstop position for a dozen straight seasons (and also in 14 of the 15 years between 1971 and 1985), and he would retire only 44 games shy of Larry Bowa's National League record for games played at the most challenging infield position. When his career closed down, only five Latin Americans ranked ahead of him in career base hits, and only four Latinos (Luis Aparicio, Tony Pérez, Roberto Clemente, and Rod Carew) enjoyed more big league at-bats. It still seems only a matter of time before Davey Concepción is the next Latin American entrant welcomed through the hallowed portals of Cooperstown.

The Venezuelan pantheon holds other greats and near-greats. Wilson Alvarez blasted onto the scene as one of the best young Latin hurlers of the mid-1990s, until a series of arm injuries turned the potential Fernando Valenzuela clone into a gutsy hanger-on. For a brief spell, few left-handers were as dominating as the classy Alvarez, who had one of the smoothest deliveries and most accurate fastballs of recent times. Alvarez also holds the distinction of tossing a rare no-hitter in his first legitimate big league start (with Chicago's White Sox in August 1991, versus Baltimore). The Alvarez no-hitter in fact remains the only such masterpiece ever tossed by a Venezuelan in big league action.

Two pesky pitchers and a small host of exceptional middle infielders also added to the increasingly lustrous Venezuelan diamond saga during the middle and final decades of the twentieth century. Luis Leál was often erratic in his hot-and-cold career with Toronto's Blue Jays, once giving up a record five straight hits at the opening of a ball game and another time allowing a team-record single-game 10 earned runs. By the time of his 1985 release, however, Leál trailed only Jim Clancy and Dave Stieb among Toronto's career leaders in starts, innings, wins, losses, walks, and strikeouts. Ramón Monzant was a curveballing reliever for the venerable New York Giants of the golden age 1950s; his career like Leál's also exhibited erratic swings, yet he later started 16 games, hurled 150 innings, and won 8 contests during the Giants' maiden season of transplanted West Coast play. The best of the middle infielders during this same epoch included César Tóvar, César Gutiérrez, Alvaro Espinosa, and Fred Manrique. Tóvar and Gutiérrez, of course, will always be memorable to trivia buffs for their unique single-game feats. Tóvar once played all nine positions in a Minnesota Twins contest, while Gutiérrez once belied his "good field, no hit" image with a rather miraculous six singles and a double during seven at-bats in game two (12 innings) of a June 1970 doubleheader. Alvaro Espinosa and Fred Manrique were equally memorable players, displaying more quiet yet steady contributions during the 1990s. Espinosa held down regular shortstop positions for brief periods in New York and Cleveland, and Manrique anchored a slick Chicago White Sox double-play combination (in 1987 and 1988 with countryman Ozzie Guillén) that was cut squarely in the mold of those once featuring Carrasquel and Aparicio (both of whom played alongside Hall of Famer-to-be Nellie Fox).

Venezuelan baseball history and lore represent a most fertile ground for Latin American baseball enthusiasts, due in part to a fine collection of materials (mostly in Spanish) that have over the years found their way into print. Local on-the-scene reporters of Caribbean winter baseball history have been highly active in Venezuela, and though virtually all of these chronicles are in Spanish, they are not difficult to track down in the wide marketplace for used baseball books. A number of fine volumes document the Venezuelan baseball saga across fifty-seven seasons of winter league play and sixty-five summers of Venezuelan big league contributions. Among the best is a richly illustrated work by Alexis Salas, entitled *Momentos Inolvidables del Béisbol Profesional Venezolano, 1946–1984* ("Unforgettable Moments of Venezuelan Pro Baseball"). The book is a rare treat for anyone who can read his baseball history in Spanish. Hundreds of rare black and white action photos and player portraits supplement game-by-game accounts (complete with relevant box scores) for more than 150 incidents defining classic rivalries and heroic feats of one single ballplaying nation. Many of the reported events involve U.S. big leaguers such as Willie Mays, Bob Gibson, and Pete Rose, and a host of top Dominican and Cuban stars also receive extensive coverage. Smaller in scale than the Salas history— yet equally valuable to all those interested in Venezuelan big leaguers—is a compact paperback volume by Daniel F. Gutiérrez, published in 1990: *50 Años de Big Leaguers Venezolanos* ("Fifty Years of Venezuelan Big Leaguers"). This tome is packed full of portraits and anecdotes concerning each and every native son (through 1989) who had enjoyed even the briefest cup of coffee in a major league ballpark. Finally, Venezuela's proudest moments in world amateur competition are chronicled in fine detail in *Todos Fueron Héroes* ("All Were Heroes"), by Alí Ramos; this 1982 work is harder to find but is exquisitely valuable for its rare black and white vintage photographs of Venezuelan amateur games, ballparks, and ballplayers from the otherwise forgotten formative era preceding World War II.

When it comes to home front celebrations of the national game, a recent high note was struck with the June 2004 announcement of an inaugural class of nominees for the spanking new and long overdue Venezuelan Professional Baseball Hall of Fame. The city of Valencia has been selected as permanent site for the new museum, which formally opened its doors to the public with an elaborate installation ceremony (June 30, 2004) staged by the institution's commercial sponsor, the *Empresa Polar* soft drink distributor. Establishment of the much-needed museum represents not only a triumph for long-suffering Venezuelan baseball loyalists but also realizes a dream faithfully promoted over the years by popular journalist and local baseball historian Carlos Daniel Cárdenas Lares, himself a long-term champion of the Venezuelan national sport. The museum itself will eventually be housed in a newly constructed building of highly functional architectural design, featuring a domed roof decorated in the form of a gigantic baseball. Initial inductees were honored with bronze busts designed and executed by renowned Venezuelan sculptor Nelson García. These will eventually be accompanied by other large sculptures representing baseball action; the impressive statuary will be placed alongside interactive displays recounting the chronological development of the Venezuelan pastime. Museum director Javier González proudly announced at the initial installation ceremonies that future honorees will be drawn not only from the country's star players but also from other significant contributors, including managers, umpires, ball club officials, and the game's noted journalistic recorders and top historians.

The first class of immortal inductees boasts a dozen notables alongside a few frank surprises from Venezuela's illustrious baseball past. Pioneering big league shortstops Luis Aparicio and Chico Carrasquel and Big Red Machine standby Davey Concepción head the class of Cooperstown-level stalwarts, reflecting the country's substantial big league contributions, and José de la Trinidad "Carrao" Bracho, Luis "Camaleón" García, and Vidal López reflect a once-proud if lately sagging winter league heritage. Near-forgotten names such as league founder José Antonio Yánez and 1950s-era umpire standout Roberto Olivo represent fitting tributes to the foundational years of Venezuela winter seasons. The newfound Valhalla of Venezuelan baseball admittedly has a long way to go to match the long-established and heavily visited parallel Mexican institution in Monterrey, or even the Johnny-come-lately shrine now boasted by Caribbean neighbor Puerto Rico. But with an impressive roster of present and past greats from the big leagues (Andrés Galarraga, Omar Vizquel, Tony Armas, Manny Trillo, Bo Díaz, Bobby Abreu), winter leagues (Regino Otero, Ossie Virgil, Teolindo Acosta, Gustavo Gil, Luis Peñalver), Negro leagues (Martín Dihigo, Cocaína García, Lázaro Salazar), and amateur leagues (Daniel Canónico, Héctor Benítez) waiting in the wings for future nomination, the gap is likely to be closed considerably with only a handful of future enshrinements.

Venezuela's first experiments with baseball, like those of its Caribbean neighbors, stretch back well before the turn of the century, and the nation's first exposure to the game can again be traced at least tentatively to Cuban sources. These true apostles of Latin baseball arrived on Venezuelan shores only a few short years after they had transplanted their newly cultivated "American" sport elsewhere along the Caribbean island chain. Less than a decade after uprooted Cuban exiles (fleeing violent rebellions against Spanish overlords back home) offered demonstration matches in the Mexican Yucatán, and after Cuban sugar mill and plantation workers began competitions in the Dominican Republic, another Cuban baseball apostle was at work in Venezuela. In early 1895, Havana ballplayer Emilio Cramer and his touring contingent of itinerant pros reportedly first demonstrated the heretofore unknown game to curious spectators in metropolitan Caracas, and contagious "baseball fever" soon spread so rapidly among local youth that an active Caracas Base-ball Club was already formed and holding Sunday matches long before the end of the same year.

If baseball came quite early to Venezuela, it also developed quite a bit more slowly than elsewhere. It was 1938 before the country tested the larger waters of international competition with an entry in the Panama-hosted fourth reunion of the Central American Games, well after Cuba, Mexico, Panama, Nicaragua, El Salvador, Guatemala, and even Honduras had formed teams for the 1930 and 1935 Central American sports festivals. Venezuela next took up the Amateur World Series challenge two years later in Havana, winning 5 of 12 games and tying for fifth slot with a surprise entry from distant Hawaii. The Venezuelans were barely competitive in these initial outings, with a single victory in Panama and an out-of-the-money showing in Havana, but their presence and competitive fire did indicate that a half-century of amateur play at home had developed a fair mastery of the game and had indeed reached the high levels demanded for world-class competition. The emerging world of amateur baseball was hardly prepared, however, for the shock of seeing the Venezuelan entrant in the 1941 Amateur World Series not only sweep eight of nine contests but also upset heavily favored Cuba twice and walk away with championship laurels in only their third international competition ever. To prove that their sudden arrival at the top of the amateur scene was no mere fluke, Team Venezuela would soon also capture both the 1944 and 1945 wartime world amateur championship laurels.

True baseball respect seemingly comes only with the professional game, however, and it was these early amateur triumphs that lit the hunger for professional league play on the Venezuelan home front. A pro winter circuit modeled after those of Cuba and Mexico was thus founded in 1946, the year immediately following Venezuela's third Amateur World Series banner and the second straight on home soil. Four initial ball clubs filled their rosters with mostly local stars (Luis Aparicio Sr., Alejandro "Alex" Carrasquel, Dalmiro Finol, Alfonso "Chico" Carrasquel, Daniel "Chino" Canónico, and José Casanova), as well as a handful of imported U.S. Negro leaguers (Sam Jethroe, Roy Campanella, Roy Welmaker, and Quincy Trouppe). These inaugural teams represented Cervecería Caracas (sponsored by a leading brewery in the nation's capital and the only entrant with exclusively native players), Vargas (champion of the first two seasons), Magallanes (still existing today and partly owned by Luis Aparicio Sr. in the 1950s), and Club Venezuela (a short-lived, also-ran club destined never to win a league championship). Two of these teams (Caracas and Magallanes) had already been intense longtime semi-pro national rivals, whose regularly scheduled matches fueled emotions of the local fandom. Venezuelan professional play was thus launched with a respectable tradition of local competition already in place and a sufficient fan base to sustain the new circuit housed exclusively in the state-of-the-art, brewery-owned Estadio Cerveza Caracas.

THE VENEZUELAN WINTER LEAGUE STORY

The first two go-rounds of Venezuelan winter play featured much excitement and scattered the seeds of lasting legend. The first batter in the first league game of 1946 was fittingly the local favorite Luis Aparicio Sr., who promptly lined a solid base hit into right field. The elder Aparicio was in his own right a clever shortstop for Magallanes, but it was his identically named son who would later prove the greatest diamond star the homeland of Simón Bolivar would ever produce. The elder Aparicio never tasted a moment of big league action himself, but one of his Magallanes teammates already had tested the big-time: also pitching in that opening game was the first Venezuelan major leaguer, Washington Senator's workhorse Alejandro "Alex" Carrasquel. The elder Carrasquel braved racial taunts for a number of years around the American League circuit, a full decade before Jackie Robinson. In that January 1946 opening game in Caracas, he hurled the Magallanes nine to a historic and comfortable 5–2 victory over patriotically named Club Venezuela.

Pitcher Alejandro Carrasquel would never become much of a household name outside his native Caracas, but a more talented nephew would soon achieve precisely that distinction. That noteworthy relative was also on board for the inaugural Venezuelan pro season as a promising if untested 18-year-old shortstop on the roster of Cervecería Caracas. This Alfonso Carrasquel would four years later become much better known to North American fans as Chicago's "Chico" Carrasquel, an exciting rookie who lit up the 1950 American League season. In a dramatic debut in his hometown, Caracas, only five days after the opening league match featuring his uncle, the younger Carrasquel slugged a game-winning seventh-inning homer to cap his memorable debut professional contest. That blast launched him into immediate idol status among the nation's already superpassionate fans.

Venezuelan baseball first came to the notice of fans and observers of the major leagues during the second season of pro winter competitions. It was the spring training season of 1947 (at the very time when Jackie Robinson was preparing in Havana for his historic debut with Brooklyn), and the New York Yankees paid a barnstorming visit for a four-game tour of the Venezuelan countryside. With stars like Yogi Berra, Joe DiMaggio, Phil Rizzuto, Tommy Henrich, and Allie Reynolds, the Yankees would use the 1947 season as a springboard to their eventual two-decade domination of American League and World Series play. That springtime, the heavily loaded New York team won three of their four exhibition contests with Venezuelan League teams but did lose the opener on a ninth-inning homer struck by Vargas's Negro leagues import, Lloyd Davenport. Such exhibitions obviously held little importance for the touring big leaguers, and Venezuelan clubs (spiced with imports like Cuba's Cocaína García and black-ball star Ray Dandridge) only nominally represented the Latin country or its brand of native play—nonetheless, the single victory over the 1947 American League champion Yankees went very far toward boosting the home-front and stateside reputations of the new Venezuelan pro circuit.

Once regular Venezuelan migration to the big leagues began in earnest during the 1950s, this southernmost of the winter baseball circuits continued to enjoy steady if not always spectacular growth. Cervecería Caracas changed the name of its sponsored club to Caracas Lions by 1952: such outwardly visible sponsorship of the team was hurting sales of the beer among fans of other league ball clubs. By the mid-1950s, the circuit had expanded by six teams and split into Eastern and Western divisions. Eventual renewal in 1970 of a second phase of competitions in the showcase season-finale Caribbean series also brought the Venezuelan League back into direct postseason competition with its rival sister circuits. An inaugural Phase II Caribbean series February tournament—fortuitously staged in Caracas—provided the league its first Caribbean World Series title when Magallanes under Cuban manager Carlos Pascual swept aside the competition behind the slugging of native son César Tóvar and the pitching of imported Cubans Orlando Peña and Aurelio Monteagudo. Venezuela's annual Caribbean World Series representatives would also soon claim four more championship flags in 1979, 1982, 1984, and 1989. Able to escape the brutal acts of nature (floods and tropical storms) that eventually plagued Puerto Rican winter play of the late 1980s and also the worsening political instability that threatened Dominican League action during the same decade, the Venezuelan Winter League finally emerged as the most solid off-season circuit once the region entered the increasingly lean winter league years of the 1990s. It would be a short-lived heyday nevertheless, as eventually the wrath of both nature and politics would find its way also into Venezuela, with a rare vengeance.

Recent seasons have featured some outstanding individual and team performances. The best hitter in the early and mid-1990s was unquestionably Lara shortstop Luis Sojo, who earned his plaudits by capturing four batting crowns to equal the record total of Pompeyo Davalillo. The rotund Pirates, Blue Jays, and Yankees utility infielder spaced his four hitting titles in two pairs, separated by the intervening 1992 and 1993 seasons. Sojo soon clinched his place in league history with a fifth batting title in 2000. Luis Raven of Magallanes also proved a young hitting star, grabbing a pair of home run titles and busting out with 18 round-trippers in 1999. Emerging big league star Bobby Abreu batted well above .400 that same winter, and three years later Roberto Zambrano made headlines by smashing a record 19 homers to pace the circuit. By the late 1990s, Magglio Ordóñez had also arrived on the scene, with a 1997 Most Valuable Player (MVP) trophy earned by achieving two legs of a triple crown. Ordóñez belted only 7 homers during a long-ball-tame season but outdistanced the pack with 32 RBI and also posted a league-best 57 base hits.

The top team of the mid-1990s was the Magallanes Navigators, who claimed much of the thunder from their cross-city rivals, the Caracas Lions. Between them, the two clubs walked off with four postseason victories. Magallanes broke a string of back-to-back Zulia championships in 1994, then repeated itself in 1966 and 1997 with rousing playoff victories. Caracas broke through in the intervening season of 1995 by downing Zulia in a six-game final title-round set. It was the first championship since 1990 for the almost always potent but recently toothless Lions. The most thrilling of these mid-decade campaigns was probably the 1996 season. Magallanes, stocked that year mostly with Houston Astros prospects, underachieved during the regular campaign, sinking under .500 and finishing as a runner-up to rival Caracas for the fourth straight time. Thanks to the postseason mound heroics of late-year arrival Donne Wall, however, the Navigators pulled off a surprising belated charge that swept away Lara in seven games and left themselves with last-minute championship honors.

Another top story was the 1998 pitching staff of the league champion Lara Cardinals. Lara's exceptional mound corps featured three of the league's four biggest winners and also posted a cumulative league-best 3.01 ERA. Beiker Graterol (Toronto Blue Jays), Edwin Hurtado (Orix Blue Wave), and Giovanni Carrara (Seibu Lions) were the backbone of the talented crew that paced the Cardinals to a league-best overall record and a narrow final round 4–3 margin over the Caracas Lions. Lara's stellar mound crew would repeat their performance a year later, again overcoming Caracas during a six-game title series. Hurtado was the postseason star for Lara, with a 4–0 record and microscopic 1.76 ERA during the tense round-robin playoff series. Other great pitching performances were posted by Wilson Alvarez at the beginning and Omar Daal at the end of the 1990s. Alvarez recorded a brilliant string of 13 uninterrupted victories during the 1992 winter league campaign and in the process carried Zulia to a year-end Caribbean series berth. Daal matched Alvarez's earlier brilliance in 1997 by posting a league-best nine victories for the runner-up Caracas Lions. One year earlier, the big league–tested Daal claimed 10 wins for a Caracas team that had barely played break-even baseball. In both seasons, Daal's ERA also remained well below the coveted 2.00 mark.

Venezuelan teams have made surprisingly little noise in the Caribbean series during the 1990s or the early seasons of the new century. Zulia tied Puerto Rico's Mayagüez club during the 1992 round-robin but lost the decisive one-game playoff match in lopsided fashion. Since that near-miss, Venezuelan teams have in most years brought up the rear. Only in 2001 was Lara able to uphold some national pride with a break-even 3–3 record, tying Mexico for second place in the four-team field. More significantly, the league itself would suffer a truly disastrous season in 2000, marked by off-field tragedy and by a host of strange on-field events. In separate incidents only a month apart, two young prospects (pitchers Roger Blanco of Magallanes and Asdrubal Infante of Oriente) were shot and killed in Caracas during separate violent robbery attempts. In the month between these two untimely deaths, devastating floods swept the countryside and shut down league play entirely for five days in mid-December. The natural disaster also forced two of the league's more prominent clubs, the La Guaira Sharks and Caracas Lions, to play out the balance of the season on the road because their shared home venue of University Stadium in Caracas was pressed into emergency service as a flood-victim refugee center.

The new century saw further strong performances from within the Venezuelan League, with especially exciting postseason action marking both the 2001 and 2002 campaigns. Two finalists for the 2001 championship were determined only on the last day of semifinals action, thanks in part to the rarest of baseball events, a manager's protest of an umpire's decision that was actually upheld by the league's commissioner—Magallanes skipper Phil Regan protested successfully that Pastora closer Santos Hernández hadn't been properly listed on the postseason roster. Regan's club then swept a rescheduled doubleheader to knock Pastora out of finals contention and open the door for Lara's six-game championship sweep of Magallanes. Magallanes returned to claim the 2002 title after entering the year-end 16-game round-robin playoffs with a sub-.500 record; Magallanes's victim in the finals this time around was Aragua, another break-even club that had managed only a third place division finish during regular-season games. In the midst of such thrilling on-field play, Venezuelan baseball suffered a major setback when the 2003 season was canceled midstream due to renewed civil unrest involving the increasingly unpopular government headed by former ballplayer-turned-socialist Hugo Chávez. Despite recent chaos, there is still plenty of solid optimism surrounding this last strong bastion of Caribbean winter baseball. It has been easy to argue that of late, in the first few years of the new century, Venezuela possesses Caribbean baseball's most thriving and most competitive winter league venue.

VENEZUELA IN WORLD AMATEUR PLAY

If professional baseball has maintained consistent good health for more than six decades in the sport's northernmost South American venue, the same cannot be said for amateur versions. Venezuela has consistently taken a back seat behind the island nations of Cuba and the Dominican Republic—even behind Mexico and Nicaragua—when it comes to world tournament play. At the outset—in the early 1940s—the Venezuelans indeed seemed poised to position themselves alongside the mighty Cubans as a legitimate force in international baseball circles. A string of crack Venezuelan national teams battled the islanders tooth and nail during a pair of most memorable early international encounters, events which themselves served to kick-start growing interest in international baseball showdowns (at least within neighboring Caribbean regions). Caracas followed on the heels of Havana as an early host for world tournament matches that would eventually give birth to a six-decade world amateur championship heritage.

The peak moment for Venezuela as an international powerhouse in amateur baseball came early, with the dramatic 1941 and 1942 World Cup matches staged in Havana. In the first of these events, contested in La Tropical Stadium, the Venezuelans battled their hosts to a standstill in opening-round play. Both countries had exceptionally strong pitching: the Cuban mound corps was anchored by a pair of national treasures named Conrado Marrero and Natilla Jiménez. Marrero, a master of the junk ball, was headed down the road toward a memorable if short-lived big league career, but he was already a huge amateur star. The Venezuelans relied on their single ace, Daniel "Chino" Canónico, a portly right-hander with a sometimes unhittable fastball. Canónico had claimed all four of his starts in the preliminary round and had spun a magical 1.69 ERA across 32 innings. With both clubs tied at 7–1 after

Daniel Canónico (right), Venezuela's ace, poses with Cuba's Conrado "Connie" Marrero before their 1941 showdown. [Author's Cuban Collection]

more than two weeks of play, the visitors were ready to settle proudly for a tie result. The overconfident Cubans insisted on a deciding game, however, and even allowed a three-day break, which permitted ace Canónico (Venezuela's only substantial pitcher) to rest for one final showdown encounter. It was a fatal mistake for Cuba, with great consequences for baseball pride in both countries. On October 23, 1941, the now-fresh Venezuelan star pitched brilliantly in the extra playoff game, benefiting also from a slow start by Marrero, who gave up three first-inning runs. The final result of 3–1, assisted by some brilliant defensive plays from third baseman Romero and shortstop Casanova, was easily the greatest single victory in Venezuelan amateur baseball history. In an anticlimactic rematch a year later, again in Havana, the fired-up Cubans had their expected revenge against Canónico, who couldn't duplicate his masterful outing of a year earlier on the same field. In a preliminary-round rematch, Marrero cruised past Canónico 8–0 and Venezuela's defending champs could do no better than limp home with a 7–5 record and a most disappointing bronze medal third-place finish for 1942.

On the basis of this single great outing, Canónico emerged as perhaps the island's biggest star outside the major leagues. He was without doubt the greatest national team hero. For several years "Chino" Canónico remained a considerable homegrown icon, even becoming the subject of celebratory songs and poetic verse published periodically in the Caracas sporting press. A Caracas stadium was named in his honor more than three decades after his once-in-a-lifetime on-field achievement. By 1946, Canónico had turned professional in his homeland and continued a proficient but unexceptional mound career until his eventual 1953 retirement. His best season was a 10–3 outing in 1947 with the Gavilanes club of Maracaibo, but never again did he come close to matching that one glorious game versus the bedazzled Cubans in the world baseball capital of Havana.

If Venezuela's first Amateur World Series title had been earned by something of a fluke, its subsequent two crowns would be clouded by even more bizarre circumstances. Team Venezuela walked off with a much-disputed and tainted championship crown on its home turf in 1944. A seventh Amateur World Series might have been a showcase event, as the first multinational amateur tournament to be staged outside of Havana, but the round-robin competitions that began October 12th in Estadio Cerveza Caracas would soon all but collapse over the tense issue of questionable umpiring performances by highly partial hometown officials. Even the home Venezuelan squad was surprisingly robbed of an apparent victory by one of their own ill-trained umpires, who suspended a game on account of darkness and thus erased apparent winning runs tallied by his own countrymen in the top of the ninth. But true chaos finally broke out after a ruling in a Cuba–Venezuela game that allowed a Cuban runner to be tossed out at third when a sideline photographer retrieved an errant throw and returned it to the field of play; the incident was handled poorly enough (an umpire ruled that the photographer was a "baseball person" allowed to participate in live action) to send the Cubans packing in a storm of protest. Mexico (featuring future big leaguer Roberto Ávila) was next to withdraw from competition over a similar nasty incident. The suspended Mexico–Venezuela game was quickly ruled a forfeit by tournament organizers, and the hosts summarily proclaimed themselves as surviving tournament champions.

Venezuela's best overall showing came the following year, once more in Caracas—although this time the Cubans or Mexicans weren't around to offer any token opposition. The result was therefore another suspect championship victory, with a crack home squad running roughshod over the rest of a depleted six-team field. One embarrassing game saw the Venezuelans crush an inept El Salvador nine by the nightmarish count of 31–1, though a better-trained Nicaraguan squad put up much stiffer resistance during a final 4–3 match. Héctor Benítez was the heavy-hitting Venezuelan star: a .526 batting mark, 16 runs batted home, and another 16 runs scored. Mirno Zuloaga took up a mantle once worn by the departed Canónico and won four straight mound appearances, though he trailed far behind potent teammate Benítez in the individual MVP balloting.

With three championships before the end of World War II—tainted as they all were—Venezuela's forces stood a close second to the Cubans in the formal tally of world titles won. The victory sheet now read 4–3, Cuba still on top. In the sixty years to follow, the story has changed rather drastically. By 2003, the Cubans had raised their own count to 24 titles (in only 27 appearances); the forces of Venezuela remained in second place, but with only the same three early championships, all earned before 1946 (the year a pro winter league was launched in Caracas). Since the close of World War II, the only winners of the event not to wear Cuban jerseys have been the Colombians (twice) and the Dominicans, Puerto Ricans, South Koreans, and Americans (once each). In light of the immense distance between Cuba and everyone else, Venezuela's second-place standing in world cup competitions hardly seems to matter.

Venezuela also enjoyed a few heady moments in the 1950s, though the victories were already growing much fewer and the time between triumphs a good deal longer. A Venezuelan entry managed to walk off with the bronze medal for baseball in the second-ever Pan American Games, held in Mexico City in late March of 1955. It was an improvement over a fifth-place finish four years earlier during the first games, in Buenos Aires, though the 1955 Venezuelan club won only four games (the same as in 1951) and actually dropped one more contest. The jump to a medal-winning finish in 1955 could easily be accounted for by Cuba's failure to attend this second Pan American tournament.

In the Amateur World Series matches, Venezuela had another pair of runner-up performances, in 1951 (Mexico City) and 1953 (Caracas). In the first affair, the Venezuela nine matched Cuba with its 9–1 ledger in the opening round, then nipped the Cubans and the Dominicans in the final four-team round-robin, but soon enough they suffered a crushing 17–1 title-round pasting at the hands of gold medal-winning Puerto Rico. Two years later, back on home turf, the locals again matched the Cubans at 9–1 in preliminary contests but once more dropped the opening two games of a best-of-three title-round playoff. Ace Andrés Quintero won all four of his pitching decisions for the host club and walked off with the tournament's MVP honors. Quintero with his brilliant effort had resurrected at least some of the earlier glory of countryman Daniel Canónico.

Since the runaway emergence of the Cuban juggernaut after 1962—the first year of the Cuban League, which facilitates rather than competes with that country's national team efforts—Venezuela has remained an also-ran, with little claim on bragging rights. A final hurrah of sorts came with a surprise Venezuelan gold medal victory at the 1959 Pan American Games, staged in Chicago's Comiskey Park. This event featured future big leaguer and Cooperstown Hall of Famer-to-be Lou Brock in the Team USA lineup and up-and-coming young Cuban Leaguers Pedro Chávez and Urbano González performing for a Cuban squad that would improve by leaps and bounds over the next several seasons. Venezuela nonetheless ran off with three final-round games, though victories over the Americans and Cubans both came on shaky one-run margins. The Puerto Ricans limped home second and Team USA slipped by Cuba in a final clutch match to claim the consolation bronze. More significantly, this would be Venezuela's last first-place finish in any senior world tournament over the next half-century.

Recent seasons have witnessed a disastrous slip in Venezuela's national team play. Often, the country has not even entered a team in top tournaments. There was no Venezuelan representative, for example, competing in either Winnipeg's 1999 Pan American Games or the 2003 event at Santo Domingo. The Venezuelans have, in fact, not entered a Pan Am Games baseball meet since the 1987 Indianapolis round-robin nearly two decades back, after missing only one of the first ten Pan American matches. The last Venezuelan World Cup (Amateur World Series) team competed in 1990 at Edmonton and posted a disappointing last-place finish. The country has also never boasted an Olympic entrant in the proclaimed national sport, and only twice (1977 and 2002) has it ever sent a squad to the showcase Intercontinental Cup games. Team Venezuela's entrant at the 2002 Havana Intercontinental Cup event performed well enough to log a

4–4 win–loss tally on its overall ledger, but on the whole, Venezuela has been a virtual nonperformer of late on the amateur world baseball stage. Much of the explanation likely lies in the lack of financial support meted out by the current financially strapped Chávez government to the already floundering Venezuelan National Baseball Federation—but there is also the distinct absence of available young talent in a country now so heavily drained of its top emerging prospects by Major League Baseball's increasingly active scouting operations.

VENEZUELA'S GREATEST PLAYERS

Like all Latinos, Venezuelans are especially proud of the homegrown big league talent that Venezuelan League winter baseball has showcased through the years. Forty uninterrupted seasons of continuous Venezuela-based winter league play has featured many cherished heroes and not an insignificant number have been native sons who had already found their way into big league ballparks during summer months. For years, the big league career of Anzoátegui slugger Tony Armas (who spent 1976 to 1989 with the Athletics, Red Sox, Pirates, and Angels) was followed daily back home with an intensity almost rivaling that for national politics. A decade later, there was the equally intense media love affair during the 1993 National League season with native son Andrés Galarraga. As the wildly popular "Big Cat" chased after a senior circuit batting crown while playing for the expansion Colorado Rockies—and for more than two thirds of a season seriously flirted with hitting above .400—the local Venezuela press corps trumpeted each and every at-bat all along the way.

Venezuelan fans religiously followed Galarraga's every game on the National League circuit throughout the 1993 summer campaign with a national passion that evoked echoes of the earlier fanaticism surrounding the careers of such pioneering native sons as Chico Carrasquel, Luis Aparicio, and Tony Armas. Even if the ongoing saga of baseball action in Caracas and Maracaibo has not been as widely acclaimed in the North American press, Venezuelan partisans have remained as dedicated to their national pastime as have fans anywhere else in the Caribbean baseball-loving world.

Bob "Bobby" Abreu (b. March 11, 1974).   No big league club has mined Venezuelan talent more energetically or successfully than the National League Houston Astros, but front office management let one of the Astros' rarest Venezuelan treasurers slip through careless fingers. Slugging outfielder Bobby Abreu was *Baseball America*'s winter league player of the year for 1999, but by that time he had already been plucked from Houston's stable as third overall 1997 expansion draft selection, then promptly traded off by the Tampa Bay Devil Rays to the Philadelphia Phillies for eventual washout infielder Kevin Stocker. Having joined a rebuilding program with the Phillies, the handsome left-swinging batter promptly became both a solid offensive contributor and a genuine fan favorite. With Philadelphia, Abreu batted .300 in five of six campaigns (dipping to .289 in 2001), blasting 20 or more homers in all but one season across that same stretch (17 homers in 1998). Twice he knocked home better than 100 runs and twice surpassed the 180-hit mark. The 2002 season saw Abreu cross a special plateau when he became only the third Phillies batter in franchise history to reach 50 doubles in a single season, a figure that easily stood also as the league-best tally.

Edgardo Alfonzo (b. August 11, 1973). Versatile infielder and talented fence-buster Edgardo Alfonzo has never quite broken through as a big league super-star. But the former Mets third baseman has proven one of the most potent clutch hitters of the past decade (and thus a star surely, if not a superstar). A lifetime .288 hitter, Alfonzo batted above .300 in four different seasons with the Mets before finally moving via free agency to San Francisco for the 2003 season; he also slugged better than 25 homers twice, once topped the 100 RBI plateau, and in 1999 led National League second basemen in fielding as part of a crack Mets infield that included third sacker Robin Ventura, shortstop Rey Ordóñez, and first baseman John Olerud. It was a quartet that many rank among the best defensive contingents of all time. Alfonzo also displayed a gift for clutch hitting in the postseason, with several crucial National League Championship Series base knocks leading directly to the Mets 2000 Subway World Series date with the rival crosstown New York Yankees.

Wilson Alvarez (b. March 24, 1970). Arguably the best Venezuelan left-hander ever to reach the majors, Wilson Alvarez never quite lived up to an awesome potential displayed on more than one occasion during his earliest seasons with the Chicago White Sox. Traded in 1989 from the Rangers to Chisox (in the same deal as Sammy Sosa) and labeled as a budding southpaw prospect, Alvarez debuted with a bang two years later by tossing a no-hitter against the Orioles for one of his three rookie-season victories. Twice the portly southpaw won 15 games for the White Sox, yet he posted only three seasons of double-figure victories during his seven campaigns in the Windy City. Repeated nagging injuries sabotaged most of three comeback seasons with the expansion Tampa Bay Devil Rays between 1998 and 2002, and Alvarez was out of the big time altogether for two seasons, attempting to rehabilitate his faltering arm during 2000 and 2001. The 2003 season found him still hanging on with the Los Angeles Dodgers, still trying to gain the half-dozen more victories necessary to reach the elusive 100-win plateau.

Luis Aparicio Jr. (b. April 29, 1934). If Mexico has its Fernando Valenzuela, the Dominican Republic its Juan Marichal and later its Sammy Sosa, and Puerto Rico its Roberto Clemente, all firmly cemented atop the heap of national ballplaying heroes, for Venezuelan *aficionados* it is fleet-footed, base-pilfering short-stop Luis Aparicio who heads any list of native icons. Aparicio nearly by himself reinvented the lost art of base-stealing during a 1950s era devoted almost exclusively to offenses built around the base-clearing long ball. For nine seasons in a row Aparicio led the American League (and often the majors) in stolen bases, and though his career numbers in this department were not lofty by either earlier or later standards, he became nonetheless a modern-era prototype of the base-pilfering wizard. An unparalleled combination of foot speed and glove work made Aparicio an eight-time leader among shortstops in fielding percentage and also earned him nine American League Gold Gloves. With ballplaying talents inherited from his father (Luis Aparicio Sr.,

Luis Aparicio became a national hero as Venezuela's lone Cooperstown Hall of Famer. [Transcendental Graphics]

star shortstop and later part owner of the historic Magallanes club), young Luis starred first on the Venezuelan winter circuit and then in the majors, mostly with the White Sox and Orioles (but also briefly with Boston). He ultimately set the pattern for adept fielding, spray hitting, and swift base running, a model for infielders that in subsequent decades became a fixed major league prototype. His efforts and his achievements (including seven consecutive All-Star game appearances and ten overall) won Venezuela's first true big league star his ultimate reward in 1984 as only the second Latin American (after Marichal, one year earlier) voted into Cooperstown by normal election procedures. (Clemente had paved the way with 1973 special induction following his tragic death, and Cuban black-ball star Martín Dihigo entered in 1977 via the backdoor route of the Negro Leagues committee.) "Little Louie" remains to this day Venezuela's most treasured baseball icon.

Tony Armas (b. July 2, 1953). The 1980s-era slugger Tony Armas summoned up a perfect image of the one-dimensional outfielder, one who hit with substantial power when he connected and who did so frequently enough to merit his stature as a league leader in long-ball slugging and an always dangerous offensive force. But Armas's achievement was always somewhat muted, and he was blocked from the kind of stardom latter attached to countrymen Galarraga and Abreu by his atrocious batting eye, horrific command of the strike zone, and resulting anemic batting averages that blunted his ultimate offensive potential. Signed originally by Pittsburgh, Armas's career took flight only in March 1977, after he was one part of a massive player trade that helped revive Charlie Finley's Oakland Athletics. Armas won his first home run crown during a strike-shortened 1981 season, and he also appeared in that year's All-Star game, but he enjoyed his most productive Oakland campaign (.279, 35 HRs, 109 RBI) one summer earlier. A late-career highlight came in 1986 with Boston, when his clutch hitting helped fuel a late-season Red Sox American League pennant drive. His top performance, though, likely came in 1984 with Boston, when he slammed 43 homers and drove home 123 runners to pace the junior circuit in both departments. Tony Armas is also proud father to a current Montreal Expos hurler of the same name, who broke into the majors at the end of the 1990s and who, despite some early career detours (such as an arm injury that sabotaged the entire 2003 season), is still expected to display eventual big league greatness.

Alejandro "Alex" Carrasquel (b. July 24, 1912; d. August 18, 1969). Venezuela's ground-breaking big league pioneer was a charismatic pitcher named Alejandro "Alex" Carrasquel, who broke in with the Washington Senators in 1939 and stretched a modestly successful big league sojourn through the end of the 1940s, winning 50 games and posting a single double-figure victory season for Clark Griffith's club in 1947. Carrasquel—maternal uncle to 1950s big league shortstop Chico Carrasquel—saw his career dogged by continuing taunts from fans, teammates, and opponents regarding his dark skin and suspected African bloodlines. At one point the personable Venezuelan attempted quixotically to quiet this controversy by announcing a change of name to Alex Alexander, but local press in the nation's capital predictably responded by subsequently referring to the foreign import in print only as "Carrasquel the Venezuelan."

Alfonso "Chico" Carrasquel (b. January 23, 1926). When Luis Aparicio pulled on his White Sox flannels, he was not the first notable Venezuelan shortstop to do so; he had been anticipated by several seasons by an almost equally talented countryman, one whose substantial achievements he himself would eventually overshadow. Without Aparicio, Alfonso "Chico" Carrasquel might have earned somewhat wider fame as the true pioneering Latino shortstop wizard from the golden age 1950s. Carrasquel was not the best among the long line of seemingly rubber-stamped Venezuelan shortstops, but he does merit considerable distinction for being the first. His career was also substantial enough to earn four All-Star game berths and contain three separate finishes atop the list of best American League defensive shortstops. Originally signed by the Dodgers, Chico's career stalled early in Montreal, with little prospect of ever replacing the entrenched Peewee Reese in Brooklyn. The big league doors were soon thrown open with a trade to Chicago in 1950, and Carrasquel responded with a solid season for the White Sox as one of the American League's top three rookies (the other two were Boston's Walt Dropo and New York's Whitey Ford). His stellar rookie season also saw Carrasquel post a career-best 24-game hitting streak, and a year later he earned minor

Chico Carrasquel (nephew of Venezuela's first major leaguer, Alex Carrasquel) was the first Latin American to appear in a major league All-Star game. [Author's Cuban Collection]

immortality as the first Latin-born player ever to suit up for a big league All-Star classic. At the close of his solid 10-year career, Chico Carrasquel returned to his homeland as coach and eventual manager for the winter league Caracas Lions. He later blazed new career trails as a ten-year broadcaster for the Venezuelan Winter League and eventually a color commentator on Spanish-language broadcasts for his former big league club in Chicago.

David "Davey" Concepción (b. June 17, 1948). Seemingly the forgotten man on one of baseball's most legendary championship teams, Davey Concepción was infield defensive anchor for Cincinnati's 1970s-era Big Red Machine outfit headlined by current and future Hall of Famers Johnny Bench, Pete Rose, Tony Pérez, and Concepción's keystone partner, Joe Morgan. Cincinnati championship teams of 1975 and 1976 were known primarily for their considerable slugging prowess, but the clubs were anchored defensively by the wizardry of Concepción and Morgan in the middle of the infield. During franchise glory seasons (which included National League titles in 1970 and 1972), the dependable Venezuelan star claimed five Gold Gloves and might have even doubled that number if Cardinals Hall of Famer Ozzie Smith had not been in the league at precisely the same time. Concepción's contributions were not all

Venezuela's Davey Concepción was the defensive infield anchor of the Big Red Machine. [Author's Cuban Collection]

on the defensive end, either; a solid RBI producer, he normally posted quality batting averages in the .270 to .280 range and was equally adept as a daring but crafty base runner. The Aragua native took pride in wearing number "13" on his uniform, a universally supposed omen of ill luck that he in turn took as his own personal amulet. If there was any knock on this follower of Aparicio and Carrasquel and forerunner of Guillén and Vizquel (who also both later wore the number "13" in his honor), it was perhaps that he seemed to wear down after the Reds' extended string of championship seasons; at times late in his career Concepción did seem to perform with less than complete enthusiasm. Outside of Ozzie Smith, it is still hard to find a better shortstop from his era, and Concepción still merits considerable discussion each and every time Cooperstown balloting becomes the issue on the table.

Víctor "Vic" Davalillo (b. July 31, 1936). Pesky Vic Davalillo enjoyed a lengthy big league career that failed in the end to reach predicted stardom but never fell short of demonstrating time and again that the versatile Venezuelan was one of the game's most dependable bench players. And if genuine stardom was not in the cards for this 16-year veteran, career highlights certainly were. The small-stature outfielder and occasional first baseman paced the senior circuit in pinch hits with St. Louis in 1970, setting big league marks for pinch-hit doubles as well as triples. He won a coveted Gold Glove in 1964, played in the All-Star game a season later, and enjoyed playoff action on five different occasions. Not only did he taste the baseball postseason, but Davalillo contributed mightily in that special venue on several different occasions. Returning to the Los Angeles Dodgers bench from a Mexican League tour in late 1977, he keyed that club's pennant drive and played a huge role during a memorable National League Championship Series game three (when he ignited a desperate game-winning ninth-inning rally with a successful two-out drag bunt). He also batted .333 as a pinch hitter for the Pittsburgh Pirates 1971 World Series champions. Best remembered for his pinch hitting duties in Pittsburgh and elsewhere, Davalillo would eventually retire in sixth place on the all-time list in that often overlooked and underappreciated category of offensive specialization.

Baudilio "Bo" Díaz (b. March 23, 1953; d. November 23, 1990). Cua-born catcher Bo Díaz tragically suffered a most bizarre early demise but only after enjoying a hard-earned slice of big league glory achieved mainly via doggedly persistent workman-like habits. Without claiming any exceptionally lofty batting mark, Díaz displayed enough power in the clutch (87 career homers) and enough skill behind the plate to hang around in the majors for 13 seasons, with four different clubs. His top seasons offensively came with Cleveland, in the strike-interrupted 1981 summer and then a year later, when he slugged 18 homers and batted .288 as a regular with the Phillies. Unfortunately, there was very little life after baseball for Díaz. Less than a year after his 1989 retirement, he was killed instantly when struck by a lightning bolt while attempting to install a satellite dish atop his plush home on the outskirts of Caracas.

Andrés "Big Cat" Galarraga (b. June 18, 1961). If Luis Aparicio was the prototype of the Venezuelan infield speedster (later mirrored by Davey Concepción, Ozzie Guillén, and Omar Vizquel), Andrés Galarraga emerged during the final fifteen seasons of the twentieth century as similar archetype for the muscular Venezuelan slugger (an example anticipated by Tony Armas and soon enough reprised by Edgardo Alfonzo, Richard Hidalgo, and Bobby Abreu). Across the mid-1990s, the Big Cat captured in various seasons all three components of a triple crown, though without ever linking them all within a single campaign. He was first a National League batting champion in 1993 while performing in Colorado's hitter-friendly Coors Field. In that one brilliant season with the Rockies, he even flirted with a landmark .400 batting average for a large portion of the campaign. Three years down the road he would also capture a league home run title and then post back-to-back seasons as National League RBI champ (1996, 1997). The much-traveled first baseman (also a designated hitter, after interleague play set in) began his career laboring in Montreal, where he paced the league in both hits and doubles in 1988, and later played more briefly with St. Louis, Texas, Atlanta, and San Francisco. His career home run mark after 18 seasons stood only a pair of round-trippers short of 400, and his base-hit total was but one average season short of the 2,500 threshold. Perhaps the greatest power hitter Venezuela has ever produced, the personable Galarraga only added to his image as soft-spoken role model when he courageously battled back from a bout with kidney cancer, which caused him to miss the entire 1999 campaign as a result of chemotherapy treatments.

Oswaldo "Ozzie" Guillén (b. January 20, 1964). Third in the string of exceptional Venezuelan shortstops following in Aparicio's famed footsteps stands Ozzie Guillén, longtime Chicago White Sox stalwart of the 1990s and recently hired manager of the same club, with which he spent the bulk of his big league career. Breaking in as American League Rookie of the Year with the Chisox in 1985, Guillén built a solid career around making the challenging plays look routine and often even commonplace. Guillén worked his way to the majors in the San Diego organization and was the second outstanding shortstop prospect named Ozzie that the careless Padres front office let escape through their fingers in a brief two year span—the other being Ozzie Smith. Chicago's Ozzie was soon distinguished from the one in St. Louis by his reputation for quiet proficiency rather than gaudy flashiness. Off the field, Ozzie Guillén was a jovial character never at a loss for words and thus a darling of the Chicago media. Guillén was also a skilled enough hitter to fan only 25 times in 415 at-bats during the 1995 American League campaign. He rang up more than a dozen steals for five straight seasons at the end of the 1980s, and in 1989 he swiped a career-high 36 bases. But it was of course with the glove that he always contributed most heavily. His 1990 Gold Glove was earned with an impressive feat of committing only 17 errors while turning 100 double plays over the course of his league-leading 159 appearances. After several seasons as third base coach with expansion Tampa Bay, the always-popular Guillén was named manager in the 2003 off-season of a White Sox club hoping to reap heavy dividends from their former star's acknowledged career-long skills as an unparalleled clubhouse leader.

Richard Hidalgo (b. July 2, 1975).   Another underrated Venezuelan basher, Houston and later New York Mets outfield star Richard Hidalgo has been quietly posting, year in and year out, numbers the equal of those amassed by Bobby Abreu or Magglio Ordóñez. Hidalgo's breakthrough year was the summer of 2000, when he slugged 44 homers, knocked home 122 runs, and for an encore batted at a hefty .314 clip. His slugging percentage that year was also in the National League's top five, and in a special sabermetric "Fielding Runs" stat (first added to the encyclopedic *Total Baseball* with the 2004 edition) Hidalgo ranks during that same 2000 season as the most successful outfield defender in the senior circuit. Hidalgo's numbers dipped in an injury-plagued 2002 season, but the next year he was again matching his 2000 performance with another .300-plus batting mark and another 40-homer outburst.

Magglio Ordóñez (b. January 28, 1974).   The quietest Venezuelan star of recent years may well be dependable Chicago White Sox outfielder Magglio Ordóñez, a legitimate three-tool player with seemingly limitless batting and fielding potential. A Venezuelan Winter League Most Valuable Player back in 1997, Magglio broke in as a full-time outfielder with Chicago the following spring and began a steady offensive onslaught that has never slackened in a half-dozen subsequent seasons. Over five recent campaigns, he has averaged better than 30 homers, driven in 100-plus runs on all but one occasion (2003, when he missed by a single RBI), and relentlessly banged away at .300 and above. All this has been more or less quietly accomplished while playing in the huge shadows cast by franchise headliner Frank Thomas. But of late it has been the newcomer from Venezuela who has swung Chicago's heftiest bat. In 2002, he ranked among the league's top five in slugging, batting average (.320), doubles, and total bases. A year later, he was again on the league's top-five list in batting average for a second year running. And at age 30 (2003), the talented right fielder with a shotgun arm and heavy bat may have all his best seasons still stretching out before him.

César Tóvar (b. July 3, 1940).   Infielder and outfielder César Tóvar was not necessarily one of Venezuela's greatest ballplayers, but he nonetheless maintains an indelible spot in big league history, and he was anything but a mere second-rate journeyman in Minnesota, Texas, and Philadelphia. In a career that stretched for a dozen big league seasons he was, at different times, a league leader in triples, doubles, and base hits and he also rang up 226 career steals along the way. Tóvar's lasting legacy nonetheless comes down to a single afternoon in September 1968, when the durable Twins utility man became only the second player in big league history to perform the stunt of playing a single inning at each of the diamond's nine defensive positions. Opposition for that occasion was the Kansas City Athletics, and in a piece of fitting irony Tóvar faced Cuban Bert Campaneris as the first A's batsman during his one inning stint of mound duty; Campaneris himself had preceded Tóvar as the first to pull off this rare feat of virtuoso versatility. Tóvar also struck out Hall of Famer Reggie Jackson during his single frame as a hurler (itself perhaps not so unusual, given Jackson's stature as baseball's all-time career strikeout victim). For one final achievement in the baseball trivia category, this most memorable Venezuelan utility player was also the big league record holder in the department of breaking up no-hitters. Tóvar provided the only safety in five one-hitters tossed by Dave McNally, Miguel Cuéllar, Catfish Hunter, Barry Moore, and Dick Bosman.

César Tóvar became the second major leaguer ever to play all nine positions in a single game. [Transcendental Graphics]

Omar Vizquel (b. April 24, 1967). An argument increasingly heard from baseball cognoscenti is that Cleveland Indians standout Omar Vizquel has now finally outstripped Luis Aparicio as Venezuela's—perhaps even Latin America's—finest-ever defensive shortstop. Learning his defensive moves on rock-strewn fields in his native country, Vizquel debuted with Seattle as a 22-year-old in 1989 by posting the league's best ratio for double plays per innings played. His special talent for bare-handing hard-hit grounders first came to broad attention via a sensational play he made for the final out preserving Chris Bosio's April 1993 no-hitter. Later, in the mid-1990s with Cleveland, the flashy middle infielder cemented his reputation as the past decade's near-second-coming of Cardinals great Ozzie Smith. Over the years in Cleveland, Omar Vizquel improved as a solid hitter and also as an adept base-running threat. He has now stolen nearly 250 bases over the past decade, including a career high 43 in 1997 and 42 in 1999, and his batting average soared to a career-best .333 in 1999. When finally teamed with his defensive equal (Roberto Alomar) at second base in the late 1990s, Vizquel walked off with his seventh straight Gold Glove, a string that he would run to nine before eventually taking a backseat to New York native Alex Rodríguez as baseball's new acknowledged best contemporary defensive shortstop.

IN BRIEF

Venezuelan contributions to big league rosters have continued at a pace rivaling all but perhaps the Dominicans. A considerable number of young prospects now seem poised for future stardom: outfielder Alex Escobar (age 25) with the Cleveland Indians, southpaw pitcher Wil Ledezma (23) with the Detroit Tigers; righty pitcher Kelvim Escobar (28) with the Toronto Blue Jays, infielder Rey Olmedo (22) with the Cincinnati Reds, right-handed ace Victor Zambrano (29) with the Tampa Bay Devil Rays, and unrelated righty Carlos Zambrano (22) with the Chicago Cubs, just to touch the surface with prospects already graduated to the majors.

Foremost among these up-and-coming prospects are Florida Marlins versatile infielder and outfielder Miguel Cabrera and strong-armed pitcher Francisco Rodríguez of the revamped Anaheim Angels. Rodriguez flashed brilliance with the surprising World Champion Angels during their improbable 2002 postseason run past the Yankees (American League Championship Series) and Giants (World Series). Having appeared in only five regular-season contests without logging a decision, Rodríguez sparkled out of the postseason bullpen, earning five of the Angels' 11 playoff wins, striking out 28 in 19 postseason innings, and becoming the youngest pitcher (at 20) ever to win a World Series game.

A season later Miguel Cabrera enacted an eerie reprise of Rodríguez's eye-opening debut; anchoring third and filling emergency outfield duty for the equally Cinderella-like Marlins, Cabrera converted the 2003 postseason into a second straight showcase for young Venezuelan talent. With just 87 big league games under his belt after a late-June call-up, 20-year old Cabrera anchored left field (where he had logged only 3 minor league games and 55 National League contests before the 2003 playoffs) and slugged a crucial homer in pivotal World Series Game Four. And Cabrera had already flashed promise in winter league play the previous off-season as top prospect in the Venezuelan circuit back home, hitting .329 and displaying exceptional polish at bat and at third base rarely seen from a 19-year-old newcomer. Miguel Cabrera now appears ready to emerge as one of the best young sluggers in the National League and thus a potential all-star for the remainder of the current decade and perhaps beyond.

To complete an already bright picture, Tony Armas Jr. has also shown flashes of considerable potential on the mound with Montreal's Expos, especially with his nine victories in 2001 that featured 176 strikeouts and a club-leading 34 starts. But the stellar performances by Francisco Rodríguez and Miguel Cabrera in 2002 and 2003 World Series showcase games alone are sufficient to suggest that the country's immediate future is still quiet bright, at least on the proving-ground major league scene.

SELECTED VENEZUELAN RECORDS AND STATISTICS
Venezuela's Major Leaguers

Venezuelans in the Major Leagues (1939–2003)

	Name	Debut	Position	Debut Team	Seasons	Games	Career Statistics
1	Alejandro "Alex" Carrasquel	1939	RHP	Washington Senators (AL)	8	258	50–39, 3.73 ERA
2	Jesús "Chucho" Ramos	1944	OF	Cincinnati Reds (NL)	1	4	.500 BA
3	Alfonso "Chico" Carrasquel	1950	SS	Chicago White Sox (AL)	10	1,325	.258 BA, 1,199 H
4	Pompeyo "Yo-Yo" Davalillo	1953	SS	Washington Senators (AL)	1	19	.293 BA
5	Ramón Monzant	1954	RHP	New York Giants (NL)	6	106	16–21, 4.38 ERA
6	Luis Aparicio Jr.	1956	SS	Chicago White Sox (AL)	18	2,599	.262 BA, 2,677 H
7	Elio Chacón	1960	IF	Cincinnati Reds (NL)	3	228	.232 BA
8	Victor "Vic" Davalillo	1963	OF	Cleveland Indians (AL)	16	1,458	.279 BA, 1,122 H
9	César Tóvar	1965	IF	Minnesota Twins (AL)	12	1,488	.278 BA, 1,546 H
10	Nestor "Isaías" Chávez	1967	RHP	San Francisco Giants (NL)	1	2	1–0, 0.00 ERA
11	César Gutiérrez	1967	SS	San Francisco Giants (NL)	4	223	.235 BA
12	Roberto "Bobby" Rodríguez	1967	RHP	Kansas City Athletics (AL)	2	57	4–3, 4.81 ERA
13	José Herrera	1967	OF	Houston Astros (NL)	4	80	.264 BA
14	Gustavo "Gus" Gil	1967	IF	Cleveland Indians (AL)	4	221	.186 BA
15	Ángel "Remy" Hermoso	1967	IF	Atlanta Braves (NL)	4	91	.211 BA
16	Ángel Bravo	1969	OF	Chicago White Sox (AL)	3	149	.248 BA
17	Osvaldo "Ozzie" Blanco	1970	1B	Chicago White Sox (AL)	2	52	.196 BA
18	Dave "Davey" Concepción	1970	SS	Cincinnati Reds (NL)	19	2,488	.267 BA, 2,326 H
19	Enzo Hernández	1971	SS	San Diego Padres (NL)	8	714	.224 BA
20	Dámaso Blanco	1972	IF	San Francisco Giants (NL)	3	72	.212 BA
21	Gonzalo Márquez	1972	1B	Oakland Athletics (AL)	3	76	.235 BA
22	Manny Trillo	1973	IF	Oakland Athletics (AL)	17	1,780	.263 BA, 1,562 H
23	Pablo Torrealba	1975	LHP	Atlanta Braves (NL)	5	111	6–13, 3.27 ERA
24	Manny Sarmiento	1976	RHP	Cincinnati Reds (NL)	7	228	26–22, 3.49 ERA
25	Antonio Rafael "Tony" Armas	1976	OF	Pittsburgh Pirates (NL)	14	1,432	.252 BA, 251 HR
26	Baudilio "Bo" Díaz	1977	C	Boston Red Sox (AL)	13	993	.255 BA
27	Luis Aponte	1980	RHP	Boston Red Sox (AL)	5	110	9–6, 3.27 ERA
28	Luis Leál	1980	RHP	Toronto Blue Jays (AL)	6	165	51–58, 4.14 ERA
29	Luis Salazar	1980	3B	San Diego Padres (NL)	13	1,302	.261 BA
30	Fred Manrique	1981	IF	Toronto Blue Jays (AL)	9	498	.254 BA
31	Luis Mercedes Sánchez	1981	RHP	California Angels (AL)	5	194	28–21, 3.75 ERA
32	Leonardo "Leo" Hernández	1982	3B	Baltimore Orioles (AL)	4	85	.226 BA
33	Argenis "Angel" Salazar	1983	SS	Montreal Expos (NL)	5	383	.212 BA
34	Alvaro Espinoza	1984	SS	Minnesota Twins (AL)	12	942	.254 BA
35	Rafael Tobias "Toby" Hernández	1984	C	Toronto Blue Jays (AL)	1	3	.500 BA
36	Andrés Galarraga	1985	1B	Montreal Expos (NL)	18	2,250	.288 BA, 398 HR
37	Osvaldo "Ozzie" Guillén	1985	SS	Chicago White Sox (AL)	16	1,993	.264 BA, 1,764 H

(continued)

(continued)

Name	Debut	Position	Debut Team	Seasons	Games	Career Statistics
38 Gustavo "Gus" Polidor	1985	IF	California Angels (AL)	7	229	.207 BA
39 Urbano Lugo	1985	RHP	California Angels (AL)	6	50	6–7, 5.31 ERA
40 Alexis Infante	1987	SS	Toronto Blue Jays (AL)	4	60	.109 BA
41 Alfredo "Al" Pedrique	1987	IF	New York Mets (NL)	3	174	.247 BA
42 Miguel Ángel García	1987	LHP	California Angels (AL)	3	14	0–2, 8.41 ERA
43 Ubaldo Heredia	1987	RHP	Montreal Expos (NL)	1	2	0–1, 5.40 ERA
44 Lester "Les" Straker	1987	RHP	Minnesota Twins (AL)	2	47	10–15, 4.22 ERA
45 Carlos Quintana	1988	1B	Boston Red Sox (AL)	5	438	.276 BA
46 Antonio "Tony" Castillo	1988	LHP	Toronto Blue Jays (AL)	10	403	28–23, 3.93 ERA
47 Germán González	1988	RHP	Minnesota Twins (AL)	2	38	3–2, 4.11 ERA
48 Oswaldo Peraza	1988	RHP	Baltimore Orioles (AL)	1	19	5–7, 5.55 ERA
49 Ángel Escobar	1988	IF	San Francisco Giants (NL)	1	3	.333 BA
50 Carlos Martínez	1988	IF	Chicago White Sox (AL)	7	465	.258 BA
51 Johnny Paredes	1988	IF	Montreal Expos (NL)	3	60	.211 BA
52 Omar Vizquel	1989	SS	Seattle Mariners (AL)	15	1,990	.273 BA, 1,982 H
53 Wilson Alvarez	1989	LHP	Texas Rangers (AL)	12	294	94–82, 3.93 ERA
54 Julio Machado	1989	RHP	New York Mets (NL)	3	101	7–5, 3.12 ERA
55 Oscar Azocar	1990	OF	New York Yankees (AL)	3	202	.226 BA
56 Rich Garces	1990	RHP	Minnesota Twins (AL)	10	287	23–10, 3.74 ERA
57 Carlos García	1990	OF	Pittsburgh Pirates (NL)	10	610	.266 BA
58 Carlos Hernández	1990	C	Los Angeles Dodgers (NL)	10	488	.253 BA
59 Luis Sojo	1990	IF	Toronto Blue Jays (AL)	13	848	.261 BA
60 José Escobar	1991	IF	Cleveland Indians (AL)	1	10	.200 BA
61 Amalio Carreño	1991	RHP	Philadelphia Phillies (NL)	1	3	0–0, 16.20 ERA
62 Ramón García	1991	RHP	Chicago White Sox (AL)	3	95	17–16, 4.84 ERA
63 Cristóbal Colón	1992	SS	Texas Rangers (AL)	1	14	.167 BA
64 Danilo "Danny" León	1992	RHP	Texas Rangers (AL)	1	15	1–1, 5.89 ERA
65 Marcos Armas	1993	1B	Oakland Athletics (AL)	1	15	.194 BA
66 Omar Daal	1993	LHP	Los Angeles Dodgers (NL)	11	392	68–78, 4.55 ERA
67 Willie Canate	1993	OF	Toronto Blue Jays (AL)	1	38	.213 BA
68 Eddie Zambrano	1993	OF	Chicago Cubs (NL)	2	75	.263 BA
69 Pedro Castellano	1993	IF	Colorado Rockies (NL)	3	51	.161 BA
70 Roberto Petagine	1994	1B	Houston Astros (NL)	5	193	.225 BA
71 Juan Castillo	1994	RHP	New York Mets (NL)	1	2	0–0, 6.94 ERA
72 Carlos Pulido	1994	LHP	Minnesota Twins (AL)	2	26	3–8, 5.67 ERA
73 Robert Pérez	1994	OF	Toronto Blue Jays (AL)	6	221	.254 BA
74 Tomás Pérez	1995	IF	Toronto Blue Jays (AL)	8	502	.250 BA
75 Edwin Hurtado	1995	RHP	Toronto Blue Jays (AL)	3	43	8–9, 6.67 ERA
76 Felipe Lira	1995	RHP	Detroit Tigers (AL)	7	163	26–46, 5.32 ERA
77 Giovanni Carrera	1995	RHP	Toronto Blue Jays (AL)	7	174	17–11, 5.31 ERA
78 Eddie Pérez	1995	C	Atlanta Braves (NL)	9	474	.257 BA
79 Roger Cedeño	1995	OF	Los Angeles Dodgers (NL)	9	968	.275 BA
80 Edgar Caceres	1995	IF	Kansas City Royals (AL)	1	55	.239 BA
81 Ugueth Urbina	1995	RHP	Montreal Expos (NL)	9	448	35–37, 3.32, 206 S
82 Dilson Torres	1995	RHP	Kansas City Royals (AL)	1	24	1–2, 6.09 ERA
83 Edgardo Alfonzo	1995	3B	New York Mets (NL)	9	1,228	.288 BA, 133 HR
84 Bobby Abreu	1996	OF	Houston Astros (NL)	8	1,008	.306 BA, 136 HR
85 Miguel Cairo	1996	IF/OF	Toronto Blue Jays (AL)	8	707	.269 BA
86 Raúl Chávez	1996	C	Montreal Expos (NL)	6	53	.259 BA
87 Alex Pacheco	1996	RHP	Montreal Expos (NL)	1	5	0–0, 11.12 ERA
88 José Malave	1996	OF	Boston Red Sox (AL)	2	45	.226 BA
89 Alex Delgado	1996	C	Boston Red Sox (AL)	1	26	.250 BA

	Name	Debut	Position	Debut Team	Seasons	Games	Career Statistics
90	Robert Machado	1996	C	Chicago White Sox (AL)	8	216	.240 BA
91	Eddy Díaz	1997	IF	Milwaukee Brewers (AL)	1	16	.220 BA
92	Richard Hidalgo	1997	OF	Houston Astros (NL)	7	755	.280 BA, 130 HR
93	Magglio Ordóñez	1997	OF	Chicago White Sox (AL)	7	949	.307 BA, 178 HR
94	Henry Blanco	1997	C	Los Angeles Dodgers (NL)	6	424	.219 BA
95	Jorge Velandia	1997	IF	San Diego Padres (NL)	6	150	.151 BA
96	Giomar Guevara	1997	IF	Seattle Mariners (AL)	3	26	.207 BA
97	Jeremi González	1997	RHP	Chicago Cubs (NL)	3	68	24–27, 4.41 ERA
98	Oscar Henríquez	1997	RHP	Houston Astros (NL)	3	49	1–2, 6.06 ERA
99	Carlos Mendoza	1997	OF	New York Mets (NL)	2	28	.182 BA
100	Edgar Ramos	1997	RHP	Philadelphia Phillies (NL)	1	4	0–2, 5.14 ERA
101	Kelvim Escobar	1997	RHP	Toronto Blue Jays (AL)	7	301	58–55, 4.58 ERA
102	Luis Ordaz	1997	IF	St. Louis Cardinals (NL)	6	205	.219 BA
103	José Nieves	1998	IF	Chicago Cubs (NL)	5	212	.242 BA
104	Alexander "Alex" González	1998	SS	Florida Marlins (NL)	6	607	.244 BA
105	Alexander "Alex" Ramírez	1998	OF	Cleveland Indians (AL)	3	135	.259 BA
106	Carlos Guillén	1998	IF	Seattle Mariners (AL)	6	488	.264 BA
107	Melvin Mora	1999	OF	New York Mets (NL)	5	571	.262 BA
108	Antonio José Armas ("Tony Armas Jr.")	1999	RHP	Montreal Expos (NL)	5	86	30–37, 4.11 ERA
109	Horacio Estrada	1999	LHP	Milwaukee Brewers (NL)	3	15	4–1, 7.50 ERA
110	Wiklenman "Wiki" González	1999	C	San Diego Padres (NL)	5	269	.238 BA
111	Orber Moreno	1999	RHP	Kansas City Royals (AL)	2	14	0–0, 6.75 ERA
112	Liubiemithz "Liu" Rodríguez	1999	IF	Chicago White Sox (AL)	1	39	.237 BA
113	Freddy García	1999	RHP	Seattle Mariners (AL)	5	155	72–43, 3.97 ERA
114	Beiker Graterol	1999	RHP	Detroit Tigers (AL)	1	1	0–1, 15.75 ERA
115	Carlos Hernández	1999	IF	Houston Astros (NL)	2	18	.133 BA
116	Ramón Hernández	1999	C	Oakland Athletics (AL)	5	595	.253 BA
117	Clemente Alvarez	2000	C	Philadelphia Phillies (NL)	1	2	.200 BA
118	Rubén Quevedo	2000	RHP	Chicago Cubs (NL)	4	66	14–30, 6.15 ERA
119	Alexander "Alex" Cabrera	2000	1B	Arizona Diamondbacks (NL)	1	31	.262 BA
120	Darwin Cubillan	2000	RHP	Toronto Blue Jays (AL)	2	49	1–0, 7.09 ERA
121	Johan Santana	2000	LHP	Minnesota Twins (AL)	4	117	23–12, 3.97 ERA
122	Fernando Lunar	2000	C	Atlanta Braves (NL)	3	97	.224 BA
123	William "Willie" Martínez	2000	RHP	Cleveland Indians (AL)	1	1	0–0, 3.00 ERA
124	Luis Rivas	2000	IF	Minnesota Twins (AL)	4	397	.263 BA
125	Steven "Steve" Torrealba	2001	C	Atlanta Braves (NL)	2	15	.105 BA
126	Juan Rivera	2001	OF	New York Yankees (AL)	3	88	.262 BA
127	César Izturis	2001	SS	Toronto Blue Jays (AL)	3	339	.246 BA
128	Yorvit Torrealba	2001	C	San Francisco Giants (NL)	3	122	.271 BA
129	Alex Escobar	2001	OF	New York Mets (NL)	2	46	.248 BA
130	Carlos Hernández	2001	LHP	Houston Astros (NL)	2	26	8–5, 3.92 ERA
131	Jorge Julio	2001	RHP	Baltimore Orioles (AL)	3	149	6–14, 3.22 ERA
132	Juan Rinón	2001	RHP	Minnesota Twins (AL)	3	72	5–8, 4.43 ERA
133	Wilfredo Rodríguez	2001	LHP	Houston Astros (NL)	1	2	0–0, 15.00 ERA
134	Endy Chávez	2001	OF	Kansas City Royals (AL)	3	206	.254 BA
135	Carlos Zambrano	2001	RHP	Chicago Cubs (NL)	3	70	18–21, 3.57 ERA
136	Victor Zambrano	2001	RHP	Tampa Bay Devil Rays (AL)	3	112	26–20, 4.48 ERA

(continued)

(continued)

	Name	Debut	Position	Debut Team	Seasons	Games	Career Statistics
137	Juan Moreno	2001	LHP	Texas Rangers (AL)	2	49	3–3, 4.37 ERA
138	Donaldo Méndez	2002	SS	San Diego Padres (NL)	2	72	.183 BA
139	Antonio "Tony" Alvarez	2002	OF	Pittsburgh Pirates (NL)	1	14	.308 BA
140	Omar Infante	2002	IF	Detroit Tigers (AL)	2	87	.249 BA
141	Victor Martínez	2002	C	Cleveland Indians (AL)	2	61	.288 BA
142	Oscar Salazar	2002	IF	Detroit Tigers (AL)	1	8	.190 BA
143	Marcos Scutaro	2002	IF	New York Mets (NL)	2	75	.216 BA
144	Luis Ugueto	2002	DH/IF	Seattle Mariners (AL)	2	74	.214 BA
145	Félix Escalona	2002	SS	Tampa Bay Devil Rays (AL)	2	184	.212 BA
146	Alexander "Alex" Herrera	2002	LHP	Cleveland Indians (AL)	2	15	0–0, 5.11 ERA
147	Carlos Silva	2002	RHP	Philadelphia Phillies (NL)	2	130	8–1, 3.38 ERA
148	Francisco Rodríguez	2002	RHP	Anaheim Angels (AL)	2	64	8–3, 2.85 ERA
149	Wilfredo "Wil" Ledezma	2003	LHP	Detroit Tigers (AL)	1	34	3–7, 5.79 ERA
150	Rafael Betancourt	2003	RHP	Cleveland Indians (AL)	1	33	2–2, 2.13 ERA
151	Carlos Valderrama	2003	OF	San Francisco Giants (NL)	1	7	.143 BA
152	René Reyes	2003	OF	Colorado Rockies (NL)	1	53	.259 BA
153	Humberto Quintero	2003	C	San Diego Padres (NL)	1	12	.217 BA
154	Rosman García	2003	RHP	Texas Rangers (AL)	1	46	1–2, 6.02 ERA
155	Alejandro "Alex" Prieto	2003	2B	Minnesota Twins (AL)	1	8	.091 BA
156	Rainer "Rey" Olmedo	2003	IF	Cincinnati Reds (NL)	1	79	.239 BA
157	Carlos Méndez	2003	1B	Baltimore Orioles (AL)	1	26	.222 BA
158	Anderson "Andy" Machado	2003	PR	Philadelphia Phillies (NL)	1	1	—
159	Miguel Cabrera	2003	OF	Florida Marlins (NL)	1	87	.268 BA

Venezuelan League Record Book
Venezuelan Championship Teams, Managers, and Rookie or MVP Awards (1946–2003)

Year	Championship Team	Manager	Rookie of the Year (1946–1991) or MVP (1992–2003)	Team
1946	Vargas Sabios	Daniel Canónico	*Not Awarded*	
1946–1947	Vargas Sabios	Daniel Canónico	Alfonso "Chico" Carrasquel	Cervecería Caracas
1947–1948	Cervecería Caracas	José Casanova	*Not Awarded*	
1948–1949	Cervecería Caracas	José Casanova	José "Carrao" Bracho	Cervecería Caracas
1949–1950	Magallanes Navigators	Lázaro Salazar	Luis García	Magallanes
1950–1951	Magallanes Navigators	Lázaro Salazar	Emilio Cueche	Cervecería Caracas
1951–1952	Cervecería Caracas	José Casanova	*Not Awarded*	
1952–1953	Caracas Lions	Martín Dihigo	Pompeyo Davalillo	Caracas
1953–1954	Pastora Base Ball Club	Buster Mills	Luis Aparicio Jr.	Gavilanes
1954–1955	Magallanes Navigators	Lázaro Salazar	Dario Rubenstein	Magallanes
1955–1956	Valencia Industriales	Regino Otero	Elio Chacón	Valencia
1956–1957	Caracas Lions	Clay Bryant	Teodoro Obregón	Valencia
1957	Valencia Industriales	Regino Otero	José Ocanto	Oriente
1958–1959	Valencia Industriales	Regino Otero	Medardo Nava	Pastora

224

Year	Championship Team	Manager	Rookie of the Year (1946–1991) or MVP (1992–2003)	Team
1959	*Players Strike*	*Season Not Completed*	César Tóvar	Caracas
1960–1961	Valencia Industriales	Rudolfo Hernández	Dámaso Blanco	Pastora
1961–1962	Caracas Lions	Regino Otero	Héctor Urbano	Caracas
1962–1963	Valencia Industriales	Bobby Hoffman	Nelson Castellano	Oriente
1963–1964	Caracas Lions	Regino Otero	Juan Quintana	La Guaira
1964–1965	La Guaira Sharks	José Casanova	Isaias Chávez	Magallanes
1965–1966	La Guaira Sharks	Tony Pacheco	José Manuel Tóvar	Aragua
1966–1967	Caracas Lions	Regino Otero	Gustavo Sposito	Magallanes
1967–1968	Caracas Lions	Regino Otero	Carlos Santeliz	Lara
1968–1969	La Guaira Sharks	Wilfredo Calvino	Roberto Romero	La Guaira
1969–1970	Magallanes Navigators	Carlos Pascual	Virgilio Mata	Aragua
1970–1971	La Guaira Sharks	Dave García	Simón Barreto	Caracas
1971–1972	Aragua Tigers	Vern Rapp and Rod Carew	Jesús "Manny" Trillo	Caracas
1972–1973	Caracas Lions	Osvaldo "Ozzie" Virgil	Tony Armas	Caracas
1973–1974	*Players Strike*	*Playoffs Not Held*	Romo Blanco	La Guaira
1974–1975	Aragua Tigers	Osvaldo "Ozzie" Virgil	Félix Rodríguez	Magallanes
1975–1976	Aragua Tigers	Osvaldo "Ozzie" Virgil	Oswaldo Olivares	Magallanes
1976–1977	Magallanes Navigators	Don Leppert	Antonio García	Zulia
1977–1978	Caracas Lions	Felipe Alou	Alfredo Torres	Magallanes
1978–1979	Magallanes Navigators	Cookie Rojas	Williams Ereu	Lara
1979–1980	Caracas Lions	Felipe Alou	César Suarez	Zulia
1980–1981	Caracas Lions	Jim Leyland	Gustavo Polidor	La Guaira
1981–1982	Caracas Lions	Alfonso Carrasquel	Argenis Salazar	La Guaira
1982–1983	La Guaira Sharks	Osvaldo "Ozzie" Virgil	Norman Garrasco	La Guaira
1983–1984	Zulia Eagles	Rubén Amaro	Johnny Paredes	Zuila
1984–1985	La Guaira Sharks	Gustavo Gil	Omar Bencomo	Magallanes
1985–1986	La Guaira Sharks	José Martínez	Jesús Méndez	Aragua
1986–1987	Caracas Lions	Bill Plummer	Luis Sojo	Lara
1987–1988	Caracas Lions	Bill Robinson	Benigno Placeres	Lara
1988–1989	Zulia Eagles	Pete Mackanin	*Not Awarded*	
1989–1990	Caracas Lions	Phil Regan	Roberto Pérez	Lara
1990–1991	Lara Cardinals	Domingo Carrasquel	Juan Castillo	Magallanes
1991–1992	Zulia Eagles	Yo-Yo Davalillo	Carlos Quintana (MVP)	Zulia
1992–1993	Zulia Eagles (32–28, 7–5 Playoffs)	Yo-Yo Davalillo	Willie Canate (MVP)	Lara
1993–1994	Magallanes Navigators	Tim Tolman	Luis Soto (MVP)	Lara
1994–1995	Caracas Lions	Pompeyo Davalillo	Eddie Pérez (MVP)	Aragua
1995–1996	Magallanes Navigators	Tim Tolman	Roger Cedeño (MVP)	Caracas
1996–1997	Magallanes Navigators	John Tamargo	Magglio Ordóñez (MVP)	Oriente
1997–1998	Lara Cardinals (43–21, 10–6 Playoffs)	Omar Malavé	Alex Cabrera (MVP)	Occidente
1998–1999	Lara Cardinals (35–26, 10–6 Playoffs)	Omar Malavé	Bobby Abreu (MVP)	Caracas
1999–2000	Zuila Eagles (35–27, 10–6 Playoffs)	Rubén Amaro	Luis Sojo (MVP)	Lara
2000–2001	Lara Cardinals (37–23, 9–7 Playoffs)	Omar Malavé	Chris Jones (MVP)	La Guaira
2001–2002	Magallanes Navigators (30–32, 12–4 Playoffs)	Phil Regan	Roberto Zambrano (MVP)	Aragua
2002–2003	—*			

* Season suspended due to civil strife; two thirds of season completed.

Venezuelan League Individual Batting and Pitching Leaders (1967–2003)

Year	Season No.	Batting Leader	BA	Home Runs Leader	HR	Pitching Victories	W
1967–1968	23	Vic Davalillo	.395	Dave Roberts	10	*Two Tied*	12
1968–1969	24	Cito Gaston	.383	Brant Alyea	17	George Lauzerique	12
1969–1970	25	Cito Gaston	.360	John Bateman	9	Mike Corkins	11
1970–1971	26	Vic Davalillo	.379	Larry Howard	12	Bart Johnson	12
1971–1972	27	Rod Carew	.355	Brant Alyea	12	Bill Kirkpatrick	10
1972–1973	28	Enos Cabell	.371	Bobby Darwin	19	Jim Rooker	13
1973–1974	29	Al Bumbry	.367	Pete Koegel	18	Jim Todd	10
1974–1975	30	Al Bumbry	.354	Dave Parker	8	Tom House	10
1975–1976	31	Duane Kuiper	.357	Cliff Johnson	11	Scott McGregor	8
1976–1977	32	Dave Parker	.401	Mitchell Page	14	*Two Tied*	9
1977–1978	33	J. J. Cannon	.381	Clint Hurdle	18	Jerry Cram	13
1978–1979	34	Orlando González	.355	Tom Grieve	14	Tom Brennan	10
1979–1980	35	Eddie Miller	.368	Bo Díaz	20	Odell Jones	11
1980–1981	36	Tim Corcoran	.374	*Three Tied*	9	Porfirio Altamirano	8
1981–1982	37	Lloyd Moseby	.362	Bo Díaz	13	Tom Dixon	9
1982–1983	38	Tito Landrum	.345	Darryl Strawberry	12	Luis Leál	9
1983–1984	39	Alvin Davis	.342	*Two Tied*	8	Derek Botelho	9
1984–1985	40	Ossie Olivares	.352	Ron Shepherd	9	Bill Landrum	8
1985–1986	41	Joe Orsulak	.331	Andrés Galarraga	14	Ubaldo Heredia	8
1986–1987	42	Terry Francona	.350	Cecil Fielder	19	Stan Clarke	8
1987–1988	43	Cecil Fielder	.389	Leo Hernández	11	José Villa	9
1988–1989	44	Carlos Martínez	.331	Phil Stephenson	9	Julio Strauss	8
1989–1990	45	Luis Sojo	.351	Willie Magallanes	8	Jim Neidlinger	8
1990–1991	46	Luis Sojo	.362	Eddie Zambrano	11	Joe Ausanio	8
1991–1992	47	Chad Curtis	.338	Eric Anthony	5	Wilson Alvarez	8
1992–1993	48	Jeff Frye	.385	Scott Cepicky	13	Tony Castillo	9
1993–1994	49	Luis Sojo	.349	Luis Raven	7	Juan Carlos Pulido	11
1994–1995	50	Luis Sojo	.376	Marcos Armas	11	Fernando Mejías	7
1995–1996	51	Roger Cedeño	.340	Carlos Martínez	7	Omar Daal	10
1996–1997	52	Desi Wilson	.349	Magglio Ordóñez	7	Omar Daal	9
1997–1998	53	Raúl Marcano	.329	Alex Cabrera	8	Beiker Graterol	9
1998–1999	54	Bobby Abreu	.419	Luis Raven	18	Greg Beck	9
1999–2000	55	Luis Sojo	.384	Roberto Zambrano	6	Keith Evans	9
2000–2001	56	Antonio Alvarez	.359	Alex Cabrera	13	Edwin Hurtado	10
2001–2002	57	Ramón Hernández	.376	Roberto Zambrano	19	Jeff Farnsworth	7
2002–2003*	—*	Javier Colina	.355	Roberto Pérez	8	Bill Pulsipher	6

* Season suspended due to civil strife; two thirds of season completed.

Venezuelan League Career Batting and Pitching Leaders (1946–2003)

Category	Name	Record
Games Played	Vic Davalillo	1,249
	Teolindo Acosta	1,130
	César Tóvar	1,114
Base Hits	Vic Davalillo	1,505
	Teolindo Acosta	1,289
Runs Scored	Vic Davalillo	668
	César Tóvar	635
Home Runs	Tony Armas	91
	Leonardo Hernández	72
Runs Batted In	Luis García	531
	Vic Davalillo	477

Category	Name	Record
Stolen Bases	José Leiva	148
	César Tóvar	122
Innings Pitched	José "Carrao" Bracho	1,386
	Luis Penalver	1,317
Games Won	José "Carrao" Bracho	110
	Luis Penalver	84
Games Saved	Luis Aponte	73
	Roberto Múñoz	59
Strikeouts	Aurelio Monteagudo	894
	José "Carrao" Bracho	853

Modern-Era Venezuelan Individual Batting and Pitching Records (1965–2003)

Category	Name	Record	Date
Batting Average, Season	Dave Parker	.401	1976–1977
Most Batting Titles	Luis Sojo	5	1989–1990, 1990–1991, 1993–1994, 1994–1995, 1999–2000
	Vic Davalillo	2	1967–1968 and 1970–1971
	Cito Gaston	2	1968–1969 and 1969–1970
	Al Bumbry	2	1973–1974 and 1974–1975
Home Runs, Season	Bo Díaz	20	1979–1980
	Bobby Darwin	19	1972–1973
	Roberto Zambrano	19	2001–2002
Pitching Wins, Season	Jim Rooker	13	1972–1973
	Jerry Cram	13	1977–1978
Lowest ERA, Season	Mike Hedlund	0.75	1969–1970
Scoreless Innings, Consecutive	Mike Hedlund	38	Oct. 13, 1969 through Nov. 11, 1969
Strikeouts, Game	Lew Krausse	21	For Caracas vs. Lara, Nov. 3, 1965

Venezuelan League No-Hit, No-Run Games

Date	Pitcher (Country of Birth)	League Team	Game Line Scores and Results
Dec. 8, 1955	Leonard Yochim (USA)	Caracas Lions	Caracas 3–9–0, Magallanes 0–0–1
Nov. 18, 1963	Mel Nelson (USA)	Orientales (Magallanes)	Orientales 5–9–2, Caracas 0–0–1
Oct. 24, 1968	Howie Reed (USA)	Caracas Lions	Caracas 5–8–0, Magallanes 0–0–3
Nov. 14, 1971	Luis Tiant Jr. (Cuba)	La Guaira Sharks	La Guaira 3–5–0, Caracas 0–0–0
Jan. 6, 1973	Urbano Lugo (Venezuela)	Caracas Lions	Caracas 6–8–0, La Guaira 0–0–0
Nov. 10, 1981	Eric Rasmussen (USA)	Lara Cardinals	Lara 3–5–0, La Guaira 0–0–0
Jan. 24, 1987	Urbano Lugo, Jr. (Venezuela)	Caracas Lions	Caracas defeated La Guaira
Jan. 10, 1996	Donne Wall (USA), Oscar Henríquez (Venezuela), Dave Evans (USA)	Magallanes Navigators	Magallanes defeated La Guaira
Nov. 3, 1996	Dave Roberts (USA)	Magallanes Navigators	Magallanes defeated La Guaira
Nov. 21, 1996	Doug Creek (USA), José Villa, Luis Lunar (Venezuela)	Occidente Pastora	Pastora defeated Caribes
Oct. 16, 1998	Mike Romano (USA), Luis Silva, John Bale (USA)	Lara Cardinals	Lara defeated Magallanes
Jan. 13, 2000	William Martínez (Venezuela)	Oriente Caribbeans	Caribbeans defeated Pastora (7 in)
Dec. 3, 2000	Edwin Hurtado (Venezuela)	Lara Cardinals	Lara defeated Zulia (5.1 in)
Nov. 26, 2002	Josmir Romero (Venezuela), Steve Sinclair (USA), Beau Kemp, Richard Garcés	Aragua Tigres	Aragua 2, Magallanes 0

Venezuelan Professional Baseball Hall of Fame: Founding Class (2004 induction)

Name	Career Highlights
Luis Aparicio Montiel	Gold Glove fielding wizard and renowned base-stealing shortstop in 1950s major leagues with Chicago White Sox, Baltimore Orioles, and Boston Red Sox; Cooperstown Hall-of-Fame inductee held as model for adept fielding, spray hitting, and swift base running. Led American League in stolen bases first nine seasons; AL leader among shortstops in fielding percentage eight straight years.
Alfonso "Chico" Carrasquel	Another pioneering Latino shortstop wizard in 1950s major leagues, mostly with Chicago White Sox and Cleveland Indians. Returned home to coach and manage the Caracas Lions; later career as radio broadcaster in Venezuela and with Chicago White Sox. First Latin American to play in major league All-Star game (1951, in Detroit).
Alejandro "Patón" Carrasquel	First Venezuelan big leaguer when he debuted with Washington Senators in 1939; won 50 games for Washington during wartime decade of 1940s. Uncle of Hall-of-Fame inductee Chico Carrasquel.
José de la Trinidad "Carrao" Bracho	Considered greatest pitcher in Venezuelan Winter League history; led local winter league in victories four times, achieved most single-season wins (15 in 1961–1962), and also holds Venezuelan league records for most lifetimes victories (110), most years pitched (23), most complete games (93), and most innings pitched (1,386).
Luis "Camaleón" García	Legendary winter league infielder who played 518 consecutive games at third base (1949–1960); league Rookie of the Year in 1949–1950 with champion Magallanes. Played in eight Caribbean series winter league playoffs. All-time Series leader in doubles (23), runs scored (11), and games played (46). First player in Venezuelan League history to reach 1,000 career base hits.
Víctor Davalillo	Major leaguer (17 seasons) and Venezuelan Winter League star who was third to reach 1,000-hit plateau. First to bat .400 during Venezuela Winter League season (1962–1963); first to achieve 100-plus base hits in Venezuelan Winter League season (1979–1980).
César Tóvar	Played dozen years in major leagues and was at different times league leader in triples, doubles, and base hits; posted 226 career stolen bases in big league career, mostly with Minnesota and Texas in the American League. Most famed as second big leaguer to play all nine positions in a single game (for Minnesota, in Sept. 1968). Broke up major league no-hitters on a record five different occasions.
David Concepción	Arguably the best all-around Latin American shortstop in major league history and a strong candidate for eventual enshrinement in Cooperstown. Overshadowed star on one of baseball's greatest teams, the mid-1970s Cincinnati "Big Red Machine" club featuring Pete Rose, Tony Pérez, Joe Morgan, and Johnny Bench. Earned five National League Gold Gloves despite playing in same era as Cooperstown legend Ozzie Smith.
Vidal López	Pitcher–outfielder who headlined in Venezuelan Winter League as well as Mexican League (1943–1945 with Monterrey); starred as slugging outfielder and part-time hurler with Magallanes in 1940s and early 1950s; still considered one of the most versatile Venezuelan ballplayers ever produced. Famed as "El Muchachote de Barlovento" in his homeland.
Diego Seguí	Cuban-born Venezuelan Winter League star hurler who also pitched 15 seasons in majors (with 92–111) career record, earned mostly with Kansas City, Oakland, and Boston in the American League. Among the all-time career leaders in Venezuelan Winter League in the following departments: years pitched (14), games pitched (209), games started (155), complete games (72), wins (92), innings pitched (1,239) and strikeouts (900). Father of major league outfielder-first baseman David Seguí.

Name	Career Highlights
Abelardo Raidi	Longtime Caracas journalist and broadcaster covering Venezuelan Winter League and major league baseball; career stretched from 1950s through 1980s.
José Antonio Casanova	Pioneering Venezuelan Winter League manager who won league championships with both Cervecería Caracas (1947–1948, 1948–1949, 1951–1952) and La Guaira Sharks (1964–1965); also managed Venezuelan team in first-ever Caribbean series tournament in Havana (1949).
José Antonio "Yanesito" Yánez	League front office administrator in 1940s and 1950s and one of four original founders of Venezuelan Winter League in Dec. 1945.
Roberto Olivo	Venezuelan Winter League umpire of 1940s and 1950s best noted for controversial call in crucial sixth game of Caribbean series X (1958) that aided eventual victory for tournament champion Cuba over runner-up host Puerto Rico.

BIBLIOGRAPHY

Bjarkman, Peter C. *Baseball with a Latin Beat: A History of the Latin American Game.* Jefferson, NC, and London: McFarland & Company Publishers, 1994.

Gutiérrez, Daniel. *50 Años de Big Leaguers Venezolanos, 1939–1989 (Fifty Years of Venezuelan Big Leaguers, 1939–1989).* Caracas, Venezuela: Distribuidora Continental (self-published), 1990.

Mijares, Rubén. *Béisbol por Dentro (Inside Baseball).* Mérida, Venezuela: Editorial Alfa, no date given (circa 1989).

Ramos, Alí. *Todos Fueron Héroes (All Were Heroes).* Caracas, Venezuela: Venezuelan Ministry of Tourism and Information, 1982.

Salas, Alexis. *Los Eternos Rivales: Caracas-Magallanes, Pastora-Gavilanes, 1908–1988 (The Eternal Rivales: Caracas-Magallanes and Pastora-Gavilanes, 1908–1988).* Caracas, Venezuela: Grupo Editorial C.A., 1988.

———. *Momentos Inolvidables del Béisbol Profesional Venezolano, 1946–1984 (Unforgettable Moments in Venezuelan Professional Baseball, 1946–1984).* Caracas, Venezuela: Miguel Angel García and Sons, 1985.

CHAPTER 6

Puerto Rico

Big League Launching Pad

• •

Before Juan González and Rubén Sierra, there was Roberto Clemente (a fact well attested to by the choices of the two 1990s-era superstars to wear uniform number "21" in honor of the former 1960s icon whom they both idealized). Before Clemente, there were Negro leaguers Perucho Cepeda (father of Orlando Cepeda) and Pancho Coimbre (still the pick of more than a few *puertorriqueños* as the most naturally gifted island ballplayer ever). And even before Coimbre or Cepeda, there was Pedro Miguel Caratini, a legendary turn-of-the-century shortstop who transported the infant game of baseball all the way from his San Juan home to the environs of Santo Domingo in the Dominican Republic, and thus contributed mightily, if unknowingly, toward launching the sport's most improbable modern-day success story.

Puerto Rico's baseball origins stretch back nearly as far as those of any of its Caribbean rivals. The first known games on Borinquen (as the island is called by its natives) have been placed as early as 1897, the same year in which the long-time colony achieved independence from Spain. Of course the Cubans were the earlier proud possessors of the game and merit the bulk of the credit for bringing the sport to the ancient colonial city of San Juan and its environs in the first place. More recently, the neighboring Dominicans seem to have taken over the world of professional baseball as measured by winter league successes and the steady stream of Dominican big league headliners. Puerto Rico's historical roots, for all that, still run nearly as deep as those of its Caribbean neighbors. Borinquen could claim two major leaguers (Hiram Bithorn and Luis Olmo) before the color line fell, a number equal to Venezuela and only one behind Mexico, and the self-governing island commonwealth also boasts the oldest continuous winter league circuit still in annual operation. If San Juan is not Havana in baseball terms, neither is it Panama City or Managua.

If Puerto Rico seems to trail a step behind its Caribbean competition, Cuba and the Dominican Republic, in both historical tradition and big league impact, this is in many ways quite misleading. Puerto Rico's rosy winter league tradition is second to none, despite recent setbacks in both playing conditions and showcase talent. Its major league native sons still measure up to those of both Cuba and the Dominican, especially in the decades of the 1960s and 1970s (Orlando Cepeda, Juan Pizarro, Luis Arroyo, Vic Power) but also in the current epoch (Juan González, Robbie Alomar, Rubén Sierra, Pudge Rodríguez). And this island nation alone can boast in Clemente the greatest genuine icon among Latino ballplayers, the role model for generations of young Puerto Ricans, Dominicans, or Venezuelans reaching the majors and, for some, even the most gifted natural ballplayer ever captured in a pair of spikes. Yet in some respects Puerto Rico, caught between statehood and political sovereignty, has always indeed been forced to play second fiddle to its several baseball-proud regional rivals.

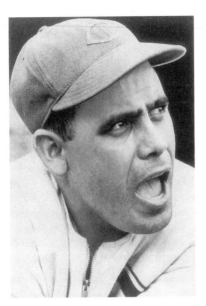

Hiram Bithorn, National League integration pioneer before Robinson as Puerto Rico's first big leaguer. [Author's Cuban Collection]

Perhaps poverty (its extent, as well as its mere presence or absence) has as much to do with this as anything. Like youngsters raised on the U.S. mainland, Puerto Rican youth have recently had other options to pursue beyond professional sports as their means of livelihood and as a pathway to fame and fortune. Unlike the ravaged Third World island of Hispaniola, locked in deep societal depression, Puerto Rico has bolted almost overnight from a sleepy agricultural society to a teeming extension of Miami and *Nueva York*. Baseball here has never been an exclusive ticket to the alluring Yankee dream of wealth and stardom; the youth of San Juan are not as bound in by hopeless crushing poverty as those living in the shadows of the sugar factories that rim the outskirts of San Pedro de Macorís.

If the level of talent and sheer numbers of Puerto Rican ballplayers has been tailing off of late, it is also true that the winter ball celebrated on the island has fallen on equally hard times. Long-time Puerto Rican baseball official Luis Rodríguez Mayoral has traced the malaise of the island's winter season to the sharp drop in big name talent that was already noticeable by the late 1970s. While Dominican stars like Tony Peña and Tony Fernández and Alfredo Griffin were still making at least token appearances in their hometown leagues during off-season months only a few years back, the same has rarely been true of Puerto Rico. Once, Roberto Clemente, Juan Pizarro, Orlando Cepeda, and Vic Power could be counted on to draw out the fans of San Juan and Mayagüez in record numbers during December and January; today's high-salaried native sons have little need to suit up once again after a tough major league grind has finally wound down in October. A mid-1950s outfield of the Santurce Crabbers once boasted Clemente, Willie Mays, and Bob Thurman. The same ball club in 1990 featured a triple-A outfield of no-names Albert Hall, Mark Ryal, and Osvaldo Sánchez. When Puerto Rico did finally field a "Dream Team" lineup for the 1995 Caribbean Series (with Alomar, Baerga, González, and Sierra all in uniform) it was only because of the anomaly of a strike-canceled big league campaign that left seasoned pros scrambling for ways merely to stay in shape.

Nonetheless, Puerto Rico—like the bulk of its neighbors—does still boast a glorious half-century professional baseball tradition. The amateur foundations of Puerto Rican ballplaying rest in the same final decade of the 19th century that brought baseball's discovery to almost all of Cuba's Caribbean neighbors. The first newspaper reports of an amateur contest on the island, for example, date from 1897 (the year of Puerto Rico's political break from Spain), and first accounts of an organized game complete with spectators appear in January of the following year. This landmark contest—played upon San Juan's grassy bicycle course, with patrons paying a 40-cent admission charge—was staged between a club called Borinquen (named for the island) and another christened Almendares (after an already-popular Cuban ball club). True baseball tradition fittingly intervened from the very first moment with a rainout after three innings, and thus the pioneering contest was not actually completed until three full weeks later—and then only after a second attempt at play was also washed out by the uncooperative elements.

THE PUERTO RICO WINTER LEAGUE SAGA

The recent difficulties of Puerto Rico Winter League baseball culminated in April 2004 with the announcement that the Santurce Crabbers had played their final season. The league's most prestigious franchise had been sold off to a group of investors consisting largely of former major leaguers, but the rights to the prestigious name had not been part of the sale. The Crabbers were now suddenly no more. It was another blow to fading tradition of a type that has dogged Puerto Rico's national pastime. In recent years, the league as a whole had withered to a mere shadow of its former self. The native heroes who had reached big league stardom were now rarely returning for showcase winter performances, and the financial structure of big league baseball meant that other major league regulars were longer on the scene, either. The league that had earlier showcased not only Clemente and Sandy Alomar (the elder) but also Mike Schmidt and Willie Mays was now a far less attractive venue, filled mostly with Double A prospects and fading big league hangers-on.

Professional play arrived in Puerto Rico in 1938 with the founding of the island nation's winter circuit, a league which has featured essentially the same franchises (Caguas, Ponce, Mayagüez, San Juan, Santurce, Bayamón, Guayama) throughout the circuit's entire uninterrupted sixty-six year history. Los Brujos ("The Witches") of Guayama would reign victorious in the first two league tournaments of 1938–1939 and 1939–1940. Ponce dominated in the early and mid-1940s, taking five league titles in the six seasons between 1942 and 1947. The 1950s witnessed the league's golden age, with such native stars as Vic Power, Roberto Clemente, Juan Pizarro, Orlando Cepeda, Luis Arroyo, and Rubén Gómez carving out memorable performances alongside such illustrious imports as Willie Mays, Bob Thurman, Willard Brown, Luke Easter, Sam Jones, Bobo Holloman, Earl Wilson, Wes Covington, George Crowe, Hank Aaron, Bob Cerv, and Bob Boyd. The strength of the Puerto Rican winter circuit during this epoch was fittingly measured not only by its illustrious lineups of front-line major leaguers but also by its four championships earned during the first seven years of Caribbean World Series competition.

Memorable stars of those lost eras of Puerto Rican league play were not limited to household-name big leaguers but included many island heroes and Negro league standouts in the mix. Most notable were Puerto Rico's two chief ballplaying idols from those earliest years before Roberto Clemente charged onto the scene. By the late 1920s and throughout the 1930s, Pedro "Perucho" Cepeda, father of the future big leaguer, carved out his special niche with barnstorming ball clubs performing throughout Puerto Rico, and in the Dominican Republic as well. In the very first season of Puerto Rican professional play

it was Cepeda who led all batsmen with a stratospheric .465 average, and again the next year in 1939–1940 Cepeda reigned as batting champion with a lofty .383 mark. In four more seasons with Guayama in the 1940s, the remarkable shortstop again compiled a composite .394 average (293 for 743) while posting a single-season hits record (81) that stood for the first full decade of island play. Francisco "Pancho" Coimbre matched Cepeda, feat for feat and hit for hit, throughout much of the pre-World War II period and himself captured league hitting titles in 1942–1943 and again in 1944–1945. Not to be outdone by his rival, Coimbre nearly matched Cepeda's 1939 campaign with a .425 average during the 1945 winter season. Only U.S. import Willard Brown (.347) would eventually hold a higher lifetime batting mark in the second oldest Caribbean winter circuit than the .337 career number posted by the talented Pancho Coimbre.

Pancho Coimbre, Puerto Rico's legendary Negro League and Winter League star. [Author's Cuban Collection]

Others carved out their own considerable reputations. Saturnino Escalera would one day be the first black player to wear a Cincinnati Reds uniform; but first the Santurce native would earn a solid winterball following with a credible .275 career hitting mark and more than 1,000 lifetime base hits. Nino Escalera still ranks third all-time in Puerto Rican league base hits and career runs scored, trailing only Luis "Canena" Márquez and Carlos Bernier in both categories. Canena Márquez himself was a dark-skinned outfielder who barely snuck into the big leagues for a journeyman's "cup of coffee" in the shadows of Jackie Robinson (recording 99 games and fewer than 150 at-bats with the Braves and Cubs in 1951 and 1954), and yet the brilliant Canena built a two-decade winter career that brought him 3,457 total hits and a .306 lifetime hitting ledger. The diminutive Juan "Felo" Guilbe, on the other hand, is still revered by old-timers as the island's greatest outfielder ever, a fly-chaser perhaps on a par with even Mays or the immortal Clemente himself. A star with Negro league clubs such as the New York Cuban Stars and

Indianapolis Clowns, Guilbe was a regular attraction on ball fields throughout Venezuela, the Dominican Republic, Colombia, the United States, and Canada across most of three decades. Big league star Juan Pizarro also paced the island circuit in strikeouts a remarkable five straight seasons as the 1950s merged with the 1960s. José Guillermo "Pantalones" Santiago's brief major league credentials (3–2 in three short seasons with Cleveland and Kansas City) cannot do even partial justice to his earlier triumphs back home as a winter season island pitching legend. And Carlos Bernier—cup-of-coffee outfielder and Clemente's teammate with the Pittsburgh Pirates—was another stateside journeyman who stood far taller and seemingly threw harder, ran faster, and swung a meatier bat during the winter months of play nourished by island home cooking.

Throughout the 1950s, the Puerto Rico Winter League earned a reputation as something of a launching pad for future major league stardom. Clemente, of course, first earned his wings on hometown turf in the uniform of the Santurce Crabbers. Luis Olmo would emerge from an illustrious Puerto Rican winter career that spanned fifteen seasons to earn unique distinction as the first Puerto Rican to stroke a home run in World Series play (earning this piece of Puerto Rican baseball history by connecting for Brooklyn in game 3 of the 1949 classic). Luis Arroyo would learn on his native island the craft that would eventually make him one of the most feared relievers of the 1960s with the American League Yankees. Arroyo, who led the island circuit in strikeouts with 145 in

Puerto Rico's pioneering big leaguer Luis Olmo (center) with the Brooklyn Dodgers, 1943. [Author's Cuban Collection]

1956–1957, would eventually post a league-best 29 saves for a powerhouse 1961 New York club forever immortalized by the record neck-and-neck home run onslaughts of Roger Maris and Mickey Mantle. The list of other big leaguers who cut their teeth during winter league action in San Juan, Ponce, and Mayagüez reads like the cast for a 1950s and 1960s-era highlight film: *norteamericanos* Roy Campanella, Johnny Logan, Bob Buhl, Jim Rivera, Brooks Lawrence, Lew Burdette, Bill Skowron, Billy Hunter, Henry Aaron, Bob Turley, Frank Robinson, Don Zimmer, Sandy Koufax, and Maury Wills; Puerto Ricans Roberto Clemente, Rubén Gómez, Juan Pizarro, Orlando Cepeda, and Vic Power; Cubans Tony Oliva, Luis Tiant Jr., and Tony Pérez; and Dominicans Manny Mota, Ozzie Virgil (the elder), and Julián Javier.

The league continued into the 1970s as an exceptional training ground for budding North American stars. Future Hall of Famer Mike Schmidt would eventually credit his adjustments to major league pitching to a 1973–1974 trip around the Puerto Rican winter circuit. The touted Phillies rookie had batted only .196 in his 1973 debut campaign, yet jumped nearly 100 points and paced the National League in round-trippers the very next season. Rickey Henderson also would hone his base running skills on the island in the mid-1970s—and he smashed all earlier base-running records for winter season play when he pilfered 44 bases in 1980–1981 (a 60-game season) during his second December–January visit with the Ponce Lions.

Many of the greatest feats of Puerto Rican league play were performed by outsiders, often Negro leaguers, like Willard "Ese Hombre" Brown, Bob Thurman, and Luke Easter. It was Brown who, during the late 1940s and early 1950s, became the brightest star in the Puerto Rican winter baseball firmament with two triple crowns, a record career .347 batting mark, and a season-record 27 round-trippers (1947–1948). An aging Luke Easter blasted winter pitching here for years as well and captured a home run crown (1955–1956) two years after his big league career with the Cleveland Indians had prematurely collapsed. The strapping black outfielder Bob Thurman also enjoyed several seasons on a par with those registered during the same decade by Willard Brown. Thurman would eventually overtake Brown's career home run record (finishing with 120), yet would capture only one individual long-ball title (shared with Brown in 1948–1949). Bob Thurman's big league career would also remain a disappointment, generating only 35 circuit blasts during five journeyman seasons in Cincinnati. Thurman's Puerto Rican stature was so elevated, however, that many island veterans still argue passionately that the 1954–1955 Santurce outfield of Thurman, Clemente, and Mays has to be the best ever seen upon any diamond—in any country in any year and by any standard, offensive or defensive.

The current drought for Puerto Rican baseball seems only to magnify the glories of the league's heyday, several decades back. The instabilities of government and shortfalls of currency that have threatened winter play in the Dominican Republic of late are not factors in the parallel downturn plaguing Puerto Rican winter ball. The absence of high-visibility North American or Dominican stars and high-salaried native heroes (such as Carlos Baerga or Rubén Sierra or Juan González) is the main culprit here, along with a severe assist from bad weather in several recent seasons. In January 1992, only about

450 spectators were on hand in 17,000-seat Hiram Bithorn Stadium to witness each of the league final games between the Mayagüez Indians and San Juan Metros. There was already legitimate concern in the early 1990s that the league might not be able to survive too many more winters of such shoddy fan support—but it is not apathetic fans or greedy and lazy ballplayers alone who are to blame for the sad state of affairs. Longtime Puerto Rican club official Luis Rodríguez Mayoral holds league and team managements themselves as largely responsible. Mayoral notes that stadium promotions are almost non-existent, corporate sponsorships are equally unknown, and league officials did next to nothing to counter the transfer of the 1990 and 1991 Caribbean World Series (CWS) tournaments onto U.S. soil in Miami.

If baseball in Puerto Rico has fallen on hard economic times and suffers waning interest, island love for the game and its long-standing traditions seems largely untarnished. Nowhere have Puerto Rican *fanáticos* better displayed their passion for the game and its island history than with the recent institution in the city of Ponce of a Puerto Rican Baseball Hall of Fame, meant to rival those of Havana, Mexico City, and Cooperstown. The roster of celebrated players during two initial induction banquets of 1991 and 1992 reads like a Puerto Rican baseball Who's Who culled from five decades of exciting winter play. Two North Americans and one Dominican take their places in the hall of honor alongside eighteen native islanders. With the new pantheon housed in Ponce, there is at least one Latin American baseball shrine not entirely dominated by the upstart Dominicans or by the Cubans who so long reigned as apostles of the Caribbean national pastime.

The Mayagüez Indians would reign as the dominant team during most of the 1990s, capturing four postseason titles—including three straight between 1997 and 1999—and also logging the top regular season record on a couple of other occasions. The club's four CWS appearances have featured a 1992 championship and two runner-up slots in 1998 and again the following winter. The apex season for the Indians was 1992, the year the Caribbean Baseball Confederation decided to honor tradition and return the tournament to a Latin American venue after two winters of disappointing experiment in Miami. Riding heavy hitting by American catcher Chad Kreuter (Detroit Tigers), the unanimous series Most Valuable Player (MVP), Mayagüez walked off with a thrill-packed event in Hermosillo by capturing an extra tie-breaker game with Venezuela's Zulia on the final night. The 8–0 win earned Puerto Rico's first title in five years. Manager Pat Kelly's lineup that year also included major leaguers Carlos Baerga, Eric Fox, and Héctor Villanueva (stars from other league teams all added as reinforcements for the CWS games) alongside regular-season Puerto Rican League MVP Wil Cordero of the Montreal Expos. The Mayagüez teams that won back-to-back-to-back league titles in 1997, 1998, and 1999 were all second- or third-place finishers that had miraculously rallied during postseason playoffs to earn their eventual admission tickets to CWS play.

The Caguas Criollos (Creoles) had been the dominant league team for most of the first four decades but did not maintain their long-time momentum into the 1990s or the first years of the new century. After a lengthy slump, Caguas did finally emerge in 2001 to edge Mayagüez in the regular season standings and then pick up their first league title in 14 winters with a 5–1 sweep in the best-of-nine postseason round-robin event. The biggest factor in the sudden rebirth of the Criollos was closer Courtney Duncan, who saved a league-high 17 games, then earned saves in all four of the team's semifinals sweep and duplicated the feat in the four championship-round wins. Duncan's value was underscored when he returned to the United States early after the Puerto Rican League shutdown. Without their dominant closer in the bullpen, the Caguas club slipped sadly in the subsequent Caribbean Series and finished at the very bottom of the heap.

The entire scenario surrounding the Puerto Rican winter league scene is well exemplified by the 2002 campaign, most especially by the fate that year of the eventual league postseason champion Bayamón Cowboys. The irony for both the team and the league was that off the field the season was an unending disaster from start to finish for the Bayamón club, but a resounding on-field success nonetheless. The Cowboys limped through a break-even season in fourth place, then came alive during the final weeks and swept through the postseason to an unexpected championship. During the course of the campaign a measly 200 fans per contest attended games at Bayamón Juan Ramón Loubriel Stadium. Former big league star Carlos Baerga headed a group that had recently purchased the franchise and doubled as player–owner, posting the second-best league batting mark despite his three-year absence from the big leagues. It was mainly Baerga's hitting—along with that of big leaguers Chris Hammonds and Brad Clontz—that paced the postseason upsurge for the club. Despite the late-year championship charge, the ball club had not been successful in building up a fan base after a disastrous first year in Bayamón in 2000–2001 (on the heels of relocation from Arecibo), when stadium renovations were delayed and the club was forced to perform much of the year strictly as a touring road team.

Puerto Rico has taken a back seat to the neighboring Dominican Republic during the last half-dozen or so years of post–winter league Caribbean Series action. Santurce's Crabbers did break through in 2000 with a championship victory that ended the three-year dominance that Dominican squads had held over the event in the final winters of the 20th century. Santurce's 2000 triumph at Santo Domingo didn't come easily, though. The Crabbers had entered the final game of the double elimination with an unblemished record but needed a victory over Aguilas Cibaenas to avoid an extra-game tie-breaker with the Dominicans. What they almost earned instead was the booby-prize distinction of one of the greatest eleventh-hour collapses in CWS history. Blowing a six-run lead in the eighth and ninth innings, Santurce avoided goats horns by escaping 11–10 in the eleventh, thanks to a title-winning homer stroked by White Sox shortstop José Valentín. A still greater highlight came in 1995 (during the midst of the labor unrest that had shut down the 1994 major league World Series), when Puerto Rico's Dream Team representing the San Juan Senators romped through CWS competition to earn a third post–winter league title for Borinquen clubs in the span of four years. Playing on home turf in San Juan, the Senators featured an invincible lineup—including the likes of Roberto Alomar, Carlos Baerga, Juan González, Rubén Sierra, and New York–born Edgar Martínez—that was the strongest since the CWS heydays of three decades earlier. Barely breaking a sweat, the heavy-hitting Puerto Ricans outscored their opponents

49–15 over the course of six straight easy victories. In more recent CWS events, however, the Puerto Rican bats have not been nearly as potent. In the three tournaments following Santurce's victory in 2000, Puerto Rican squads (including two in 2003, when Venezuela was forced out of the competition by political unrest on the home front), have managed only an 11–14 overall ledger, and for three years running a Puerto Rican team has filled the last-place spot in the four-team field.

PUERTO RICANS IN WORLD AMATEUR PLAY

In world amateur tournaments as elsewhere, Puerto Rico has never quite measured up to other Caribbean countries. Even though the professional clubs were frequently kings of the winter league Caribbean Series, both before and after Cuba's departure in the late 1950s, the same dominance has been almost totally absent in amateur arenas. Puerto Rico has yet to qualify for an Olympic Games baseball tournament, its only World Cup victory came more than half a century ago, it has reached the championship game of the Intercontinental Cup matches on only one occasion, and it owns no baseball gold medals in the Pan American Games. The most recent disaster came in the 2003 Panama Olympic Qualifier, where a subpar group of the country's minor leaguers reached the final field of four only to be humbled by the Cubans in a 10–0 knockout in the semifinals and equally embarrassed 10–1 by Mexico in the bronze medal conclusion.

Puerto Rico has been so far completely shut out of Olympic baseball, although this is due at least in part to the narrow selection rules that have also kept other top Latin and Caribbean baseball countries on the sidelines. Because only two teams can qualify from the entire baseball-rich North American and South American regions (including the Caribbean), it usually comes down to the Cubans and somebody else (of late, the Americans in 2000 and Canadians in 2004). A more significant explanation, however, lies in the skimming off of most amateur talent by the heavy pro signings on the island. And a somewhat inept national federation controlling Team Puerto Rico selections has not helped. Even with minor leaguers and a sprinkling of major leaguers now competing on national squads, Puerto Rico has seemed incapable of getting its act together and fielding a truly representative team.

In the Pan American Games, Puerto Rico twice displayed its mettle as runner-up but can boast of little else in the way of solid achievement at the hemisphere's main venue for amateur competition. The first silver medal for a Puerto Rican representative came back in 1959 at the Chicago-hosted games played in venerable Comiskey Park. This event was later remembered for the appearance of future Hall of Famer Lou Brock (at the time a Southwest Conference collegiate batting champ), who mustered only one single in ten at-bats, and also the presence of future Cuban League stars Pedro Chávez and Urbano González. It was a trio of unheralded and now little-remembered Puerto Ricans nonetheless who made most of the offensive noise: Irmo Figueroa was the tourney's top batsman with a .500 mark, Carlos Pizarro rang up the top hits total with a dozen, and Roberto Vázquez knocked home the most runs and tied American Al Hall for the home run crown (they each had two). Puerto

Rico claimed its silver medallion by beating Cuba (4–3) and the United States (9–5) in final-round action but lost the gold by stumbling against Venezuela (6–2). A second trip to the title game had to wait for 1991, on enemy grounds in Havana. A 7–1 victory over the Americans in the semis merely earned the right to be humiliated 18–3 by the heavy-hitting Cubans (featuring big league level stars Omar Linares, Victor Mesa, and Antonio Pacheco) in a title game mercifully shortened by the controversial ten-run knockout rule. For the last two Pan American events in Winnipeg (an Olympic qualifier tournament for Sydney 2000) and Santo Domingo (2003), the lately much-troubled Puerto Rican Federation would not even send a team to uphold the Commonwealth's sagging honor.

The Central American Games, stretching all the way back to the start of the 1930s, have displayed only slightly more of a Puerto Rican baseball presence. Puerto Rico's first entry—their first venture of any kind into international competitions—was at the 1938 Panama City event and brought a fourth place finish. It would be two decades before Commonwealth teams would make substantial noise in this less prestigious face-off between Caribbean and Southern Hemisphere rivals. The same Borinquen club that won Pan American silver in 1959 had also walked off with Central American gold at Caracas in January of that same year. There was a further pair of second-place finishes earned in the only two events (Jamaica, 1962; San Juan, 1966) staged in the 1960s. During the 1970s, Puerto Rico won bronze medals twice. In Santo Domingo in 1974, Puerto Rico (at 6–4) fielded the only winning team, outside of the champion Cubans (9–1) and runner-up host Dominicans (8–2). The only recent highlight for Puerto Rican amateur competitions was still another Central American Games silver medal finish in the final year of the century, this time in Mexico City. Overall the picture has not been very pretty for the Puerto Rican forces, even in action at the region's least celebrated international round-robin.

World Cup play has also been an unending disaster for Puerto Rican teams across most of the past quarter-century. In half of the Commonwealth's first six appearances in Amateur World Series play (as the tournament was officially called until the late 1990s), a trio of noticeably weak Puerto Rican squads finished no better than the eighth slot. The 1980s also brought a most embarrassing dry spell. An eighth-place finish in Tokyo (1980) that included a 23–1 lambasting by champion Cuba was followed up with similar finishes in Havana (1984) and The Netherlands (1986). The worst drubbing in Havana was 11–3 at the hands of the Japanese; the greatest embarrassment in Haarlem was the 11–1 opening-game pasting again administered by the usual strong Cuban contingent. Earlier in the 1980s, Puerto Rico had saved itself embarrassment by simply skipping World Cup XXVII in Seoul altogether. An all-time low was seemingly reached with the 1994 meeting of 16 countries in Nicaragua, where the lame Borinquen forces limped home stripped of all dignity (despite an upset of eighth-place Team USA) and sitting in eleventh place.

Some earlier moments of near-glory in World Cup tournaments were little noted at the time. A lone Borinquen first-place celebration took place in Mexico City (1951), on one of the rare occasions when the usually dominant Cubans entered a less-than-potent squad. Cuba matched Venezuela with but one loss in the ten-game opening round but then dropped a pair of close decisions to both the Venezuelans and Puerto Ricans in medal-round play to finish a surprising third. In addition to their slim victory against Cuba, the hot Puerto Ricans nipped the Dominican Republic (3–0) and mashed Venezuela (17–1) to claim the title. Ramón Maldonado (individual leader in doubles) and speedster Sotero Ortíz (stolen base king) were the individual stars on a team without big-name heroes. But Puerto Rican forces nonetheless had their one and only glory moment in the world baseball amateur spotlight.

Perhaps the most memorable moments involving a Puerto Rican team on the international baseball scene were those that transpired in 1966, during one of the most highly charged amateur athletic meets of recent memory. This was the tenth Central American Games event hosted in San Juan, in the midst of a highly charged political atmosphere, most of it involving the Communist nation of Cuba. Much of the excitement of this event didn't involve baseball at all. Cuba's beleaguered delegation, arriving on the renovated cargo ship *Cerro Pelado*, missed opening ceremonies and almost missed the entire proceedings when their vessel was detained by Puerto Rican immigration officials in San Juan harbor. Once on the baseball diamond, Cuba was victorious despite all the overt harassment. Fidel Castro's hand-picked team equaled the host club in winning five of six, then nipped Team Borinquen 6–2 in the extra playoff tie-breaking match. Puerto Rico had at least risen to the occasion and made one of its finest showings ever. A much later irony surrounding these historic 1966 matches unfolded as late as 1999, when the San Juan tournament's top pitching star—Cuban southpaw Rigoberto Betancourt—was the single political defector from an entourage of ex-players accompanying Cuba's national team when it faced off against the big league Baltimore Orioles.

PUERTO RICO'S GREATEST PLAYERS

For outsiders at least, or those with their eyes on the major leagues only, Puerto Rican baseball seems to begin and end with the island commonwealth's pair of Cooperstown Hall of Famers, Roberto Clemente and Orlando Cepeda. Though Perucho Cepeda and Pancho Coimbre stick out with almost equal luster in the memories of the diminishing population of aging island *fanáticos* who still remember mid-twentieth-century black-ball stars, both are almost completely unknown outside of island culture. There are contemporary Puerto Rican stars to be sure, but, whether in career numbers or visibility, Juan González and Javier Vázquez or Pudge Rodríguez or Carlos Delgado hardly seem to measure up to Sammy Sosa and Pedro Martínez, or even to Magglio Ordóñez and Bartolo Colón.

There is also a substantial Puerto Rican tradition of larger-than-life stars outside of the major leagues. One can start with the North American Negro circuits of the 1930s and 1940s and then turn to the winter leagues in Cuba, Mexico, and Puerto Rico itself, before Jackie Robinson initiated organized baseball's face-saving integration. Coimbre and the elder Cepeda certainly did not have an exclusive Borinquen corner on the winter-ball and black-ball markets. Tomás Quiñónez wrote pitching legends on native soil in the mid-1940s before touring with the Indianapolis Clowns. Luis Márquez was a versatile infielder and outfielder who reigned as 1954 winter-league batting champ alongside his major league cups of postintegration coffee with the Braves, Cubs, and

Pirates. Nonetheless, for most stateside fans Puerto Rico's popular image as a baseball hotbed is tied up with the inventory of major leaguers, and these have indeed been frequent in number and even occasionally awesome in stature.

Roberto Alomar (b. February 5, 1968). For most of the 1990s, there seemed little doubt anywhere that Roberto Alomar belonged eventually in Cooperstown, and there were many who touted his career as the best ever enjoyed by a big league second baseman. Those judgments seem of late to be coming under increased second-guessing. Until he joined the rebuilding New York Mets in 2002, Alomar was frequently mentioned without embarrassment in the same breath with either Rogers Hornsby or Joe Morgan. He was certainly worthy of designation as the best-ever Latin second baseman, and the statistical record was seemingly all on his side. Roberto Alomar captured ten Gold Gloves in eleven years (1991–2001) and played in ten straight major league All-Star games; he stole 20 or more bases on eight occasions, he batted above .300 nine times (six consecutively), and he also appeared in postseason play in exactly half of his first dozen big league seasons. Only a regrettable spitting incident involving umpire John Hirschbeck marred an otherwise brilliant career. At what seems to be the end of his career, however, Alomar's numbers have rapidly gone south. He hit in the .260s in one and a half seasons in New York and contributed even less in Chicago after being traded to the White Sox. Since 2000 his career batting average has slid from the impressive toward the near-mediocre; a career batting average that was safely above the universal standard of quality hitting (at .304 in 2000) only four years later threatens to dip below the touchstone .300 threshold. And the mediocre play of three late-career seasons is already dulling the memory of what was a few seasons back the best all-around keystone player anywhere in big league baseball.

Sandy Alomar Sr., distinguished sire to Puerto Rico's leading baseball family. [Author's Cuban Collection]

Santos "Sandy" Alomar Sr. (b. October 19, 1943). The elder Sandy Alomar was a fine utilityman who enjoyed an often productive decade-and-a-half journey of his own through the majors in the 1960s and 1970s, but his primary legacy would be that of sire to a pair of sons who wrote even larger legacies into pro baseball's substantial archives. Roberto, the youngest son, would emerge in the 1990s as one of the best-ever Latin-born middle infielders of the modern era. A namesake elder son (a standout catcher) today continues a solid 15-year big league sojourn, mostly with the Indians and White Sox, which has produced some solid offense including a 21-homer season in 1997 and more than 100 career long balls and 500-plus career RBI. Sandy Alomar Sr. contributed mostly as a valued bench player with the Braves, Mets, White Sox, Angels (for the longest tenure), and Yankees; but, he also performed well enough as an everyday infielder for the California Angels in 1970 to wind up on the American League All-Star squad.

Luis "Tito" Arroyo (b. February 18, 1927). The first Puerto Rican to reach the majors was a pitcher named Bithorn, but it took a few years more before the island commonwealth could produce a big league pitcher of more substantial quality, and then there were two: Rubén Gómez and Luis Arroyo. Arroyo exploded on the National League scene with the Cardinals in 1955 but slumped badly after a rookie-summer All-Star game selection; he reemerged in the public consciousness briefly in 1961 as a screwball-tossing Yankees bullpen fixture who posted a 15–5 mark of his own and saved many of the victories in Whitey Ford's first 20-win season. Like Gómez, Arroyo had moments of brilliance in the late 1950s—yet both were in the final analysis little more than commonplace journeyman hurlers.

Carlos Baerga (b. November 4, 1968). For a while it looked as if Carlos Baerga was destined to be one of Puerto Rico's greatest stars, but somewhere along the line Baerga took a wrong turn and nearly headed into oblivion. Breaking in with San Diego and then traded to Cleveland along with countryman Sandy Alomar Jr. for slugger Joe Carter, the pudgy second baseman who hit with power from both sides of the plate averaged better than 160 hits per year, with a .305 batting average across his first half-dozen seasons in the big time. He also earned a place in the trivia books as the first player to smack homers from both sides of the plate in the same inning (April 8, 1993). Baerga helped key Cleveland's rise in 1995 to its first World Series appearance in more than forty years. When limited range as a second base defender was accentuated by Baerga's tendency to add considerable weight to his already rotund form, the Cleveland star experienced a rapid career slide after that one mid-1990s World Series appearance. A trade to the New York Mets (where a few years later Roberto Alomar's career would also be disintegrating) brought a further collapse in Baerga's offensive numbers, and his batting average slid below .200. The late 1990s witnessed numerous attempts to climb back as a big league regular with St. Louis and Cincinnati, and again with both San Diego and Cleveland, but 1995 was indeed the apex, and by the time he turned thirty, Baerga's best seasons were all behind him.

Orlando Cepeda (b. September 17, 1937). Clemente at long last shares glories in Cooperstown with a Borinquen countryman whose own induction was delayed far longer than necessary by factors having nothing to do with on-field career achievement or diamond prowess. Dubbed "Baby Bull" (in homage to his father, the legendary Perucho), Orlando Cepeda was Puerto Rico's answer to Cuba's Atanasio "Tany" (Tony) Pérez. The difference was that Cepeda experienced both the jump start and the heavy millstone of having an illustrious

Orlando "Baby Bull" Cepeda was Puerto Rico's second Cooperstown Hall of Famer. [Transcendental Graphics]

national icon ballplayer for his own father. Cepeda's career was slow getting off the ground and along the way he had to overcome roadblocks that might have sabotaged any athlete of lesser character. Unfavorable comparisons to his legendary father almost forced him to quit the sport as a teenager, and his early years in U.S. pro ball were filled with racial prejudice that almost sent him packing. When Cepeda reached the Giants he was often in the doghouse of racist manager Alvin Dark, who openly admitted his skepticisms about the intestinal fortitude of blacks like Willie Mays and Latinos like Cepeda and Alou. In both San Francisco and St. Louis, however, he posted huge numbers and performed heroic feats, leading both clubs to National League pennants. "Cha Cha" Cepeda's career totals upon retirement in 1974 seemed to merit immediate Cooperstown enshrinement. His power stats compared favorably with the best sluggers of his era and set milestones to be aimed at by other Latinos: 370 HR (tied with Pérez as the top Latin total before Sosa, Palmeiro, and Canseco), 1,365 RBI, a .297 BA, 2,351 hits, one National League Most Valuable Player trophy, and a pioneering role as the first-ever Latin-born league home run champ and RBI leader (both in 1961)—but even after baseball, the dark fortunes that plagued his early career continued to dog him. Convicted for marijuana possession in 1975, Cepeda served a short prison term that subsequently (most would say unjustly) kept him outside Cooperstown's gates for nearly a quarter-century.

Perucho Cepeda (b. 1906; d. 1955). Despite the burden of expectations, Orlando Cepeda was seemingly assured greatness on the diamond by paternal bloodlines alone. If few outside the Commonwealth remember the elder ballplaying Cepeda, back home he remains an indelible icon. Perucho Cepeda (known as "The Bull") might have been a household name long before his slugging son, had the odious "gentlemen's agreement" not plagued organized baseball for quite so long, or had the elder Cepeda himself been willing to face the pitfalls and frequent hardships of playing Negro baseball away from home on the U.S. mainland. But it didn't and he wasn't. Inked by impresario Alejandro Pompez to a contract with the Negro National League New York Cubans, Cepeda defaulted on the deal and chose to avoid the U.S. black-ball circuit, where his inflammable temper and America's racial tensions might have proven a disastrous mix. He remained on his native island, where he starred at shortstop for league champion Guayama and paced the Puerto Rican winter circuit in batting in both of its first two seasons. In the two following campaigns, he elevated his slugging to .423 and .464 and yet lost his hitting crown to crack Negro leaguers Roy Partlow (.443) and Josh Gibson (.480). In late career he shifted to first base, and Puerto Rican old-timers still maintain that even at that position he had the distinct edge in raw talent over his Cooperstown-enshrined son.

Roberto Clemente (b. August 18, 1934; d. December 31, 1972). There is no debating that Roberto Clemente is hands down Puerto Rico's loftiest baseball star. Playing in a golden age that featured the likes of Mickey Mantle, Willie Mays, Hank Aaron, Ernie Banks, Frank Robinson, and Harmon Killebrew, Clemente has his supporters as one of the greatest ever to don steel spikes and leather glove. One-time headliner shortstop Billy Jurges, who played against Babe Ruth and Lou Gehrig and Rogers Hornsby and who managed Ted Williams, told this writer in 1995 that Clemente was simply the finest all-around individual player he had even seen on any ball field.

The young Roberto Clemente burst upon Forbes Field in April 1955, scooped up in a special draft from the Dodgers (who were unwilling to bring yet another black to the Brooklyn lineup and thus lost their chance for an outfield of Clemente, Duke Snider, and Carl Furillo, one that might have been the best in history). Over the next decade and a half, the Puerto Rican right fielder with baseball's best arm and one of its best bats inspired at least two distinctive mental images for baseball fans in all corners of North and South America. One image, predominant in much of the North, loomed large in the popular imagination, born of the U.S. press corps' endless fascination with the Pittsburgh star's frequent mood swings and colorful if outspoken "broken" English. It was an image of a shiftless malingerer who faked injuries and often showed little true desire to play through pain and adversity. This was the media's manufactured image of Clemente, who was time and again portrayed in the popular press as a crybaby and goldbrick, and it was an unfortunate and largely preposterous image that was to plague the Puerto Rican star's entire big league career—even if it could not keep him out of his preordained slot in the MLB Hall of Fame.

More on target was the competing image: that of the flashy and exciting ballplayer who would swing away at just about any pitch remotely near the plate, driving most deliveries to distant corners of the ballpark, and a ballplayer who ran the basepaths with nothing short of graceful abandon. The most exciting sight in baseball arguably is the triple, and the three-base hit was Clemente's personal trademark. In nine seasons (six in a row between 1965 and 1970) he reached double figures in triples, a truly rare feat in the modern baseball age of speedy outfielders, Astroturf, and symmetrical ballparks. The lost art of the three-base hit combines that special blend of pure foot speed and outlandish daring with raw hitting power. No baseball moment across the 1960s was more exciting than one featuring Clemente rounding second, arms flying, charging headlong into third with another three-bagger.

Francisco "Pancho" Coimbre (b. January 29, 1909; d. November 4, 1989). Francisco "Pancho" Coimbre is, like Perucho Cepeda, one of those top *Borinqueño* stars who were never major leaguers or even top stars in the U.S. Negro leagues. Before Clemente came on the scene, Coimbre was widely acknowledged to be the best Puerto Rican ballplayer ever. Like Clemente, the Coamo native was a graceful and speedy 5'11" outfielder who combined all the game's skills at their highest levels: he was a strong natural hitter who sprayed the ball to all fields, he could hit for power but reportedly rarely swung from the heels, he hustled on the basepaths and in the outfield with more than adequate foot speed, and he had an arm that perhaps didn't measure up to Clemente's but kept enemy base runners cautious and extended his reputation as a five-tool player. Too dark for the majors, Coimbre terrorized the opposition on the Puerto Rican winter circuit and after 1940 also starred for the New York Cubans of the Negro National League during summer months. In his first season on the U.S. black-ball circuit, Coimbre hit .330 out of the second slot in the batting order; a year later, he moved into the cleanup spot and jacked his average to .353. After a season out of Negro ball, the Puerto Rican star returned to New York in 1943 with a vengeance and rang up the highest batting mark (.436) of his exceptional career. He also hit .400-plus three times on the winter circuit: twice at home in Puerto Rico (1940, 1945) and once in Cuba (1944). Playing for Ponce throughout his heyday in the 1940s, the slugger finished with a .337 lifetime batting mark in his homeland (trailing only Willard Brown on the all-time list), established a league record by hitting safely in 22 straight games in 1941, and proved to be one of the hardest strikeouts in any league and any epoch. It was his ability to make contact (again like Clemente) that set Pancho Coimbre above most other hitters: across 13 seasons of Puerto Rican winter ball he was gunned down via the strikeout only 29 times in 1915 at-bats; for two straight winters between 1941 and 1943 he never fanned a single time. No lesser a figure than the loquacious Satchel Paige once called Puerto Rico's Pancho Coimbre the toughest out he ever faced. Given Paige's thousands of games against batters of both colors in leagues around the western hemisphere and during most of three decades, this statement alone would seem to constitute the ultimate compliment.

José Cruz (b. August 8, 1947).   Puerto Rico's big league hero garnering the least note or thinnest respect has to be José Cruz, long-term Houston Astros outfielder who posted numbers that stand up to many Hall of Famers both from his own era and from past decades of big league play. Part of the problem was that Cruz played the bulk of his career in Houston, out of the limelight of baseball's bigger markets and also off the stage of baseball's high-profile postseason. And playing in Houston's cavernous, pitcher-friendly Astrodome, prevented his substantial career offensive numbers from being as truly earth-shaking as they might otherwise have been. The Astrodome served to distort in negative ways the true achievements of Cruz as a potent batter: in a dozen year span from 1975 to 1987 he smacked only 40 homers in Houston but had twice as many on the road. Cruz did hit over .300 six different times after coming to the Astros from the Cardinals; he was voted the club's Most Valuable Player on four occasions; and in 1983 he topped the entire National League in base hits, falling just short of 200. The biggest career achievement for Cruz was amassing 2,251 base hits over 19 seasons, one of the highest figures for a Latin ballplayer. At the time of his retirement in 1988, he held the career top spot for the Astros in not only base hits but also at-bats, triples, and RBI. His legacy has also been extended by his son, the once highly promising José Cruz Jr., an outfielder mostly with Toronto who has himself never measured up to his father's record but has twice registered more than 30 homers in a single campaign.

Rubén Gómez (b. July 13, 1927; d. July 26, 2004).   Rubén Gómez was the starter and winner in the third game of the New York Giants 1954 World

Series sweep of the high-flying Cleveland Indians, and Gómez also started the first-ever major league game on the Pacific Coast when the same Giants relocated in 1958 to San Francisco. In the end, however, the erratic and temperamental right-hander would hang his lasting notoriety on a string of ugly bean-ball incidents involving Reds Hall of Famer Frank Robinson, Dodgers fly chaser Carl Furillo, and Braves slugger Joe Adcock, among others. Like Luque before, and Marichal and Andujar to follow, the temperamental Puerto Rican played directly into a convenient stereotype of the short-fused Latino more willing to sling his fists than his potent fastballs. But also like Luque and Marichal, there was far more to Rubén Gómez than his celebrated displays of epic tantrums. A mainstay of the 1954 world champions (for whom he posted a sparkling 17–9 ledger), he four times won in double figures and three times topped 100 strikeouts. His career stretched ten seasons and included 76 career wins, though his only league-leading performance came with a league-high 109 walks issued over the course of the 1954 championship season. In the vanguard of the earliest Puerto Rican pioneers on major league rosters, Gómez was one of the more memorable and dependable Latino hurlers of the golden age 1950s.

Juan González (b. October 20, 1969). Puerto Rico has never produced a more potent slugger than Juan González, bad-boy outfielder mostly with the Texas Rangers across fifteen seasons and counting. Not even Clemente and Cepeda can now match the power numbers put up by this two-time American League Most Valuable Player, and González isn't that far behind in more staid hitting categories such as batting average and on-base percentage, either. But a reputation for moodiness and self-aggrandizement along with a one-dimensional offensive game is likely to assure that González never is considered on quite the same level as his two highly respected Hall-of-Fame countrymen. The muscular right-handed outfielder has nonetheless slowly posted a most impressive offensive resumé: he captured a home run crown when only twenty-two, was league Most Valuable Player for the first time at twenty-seven, and two years later had crossed the 300 home run plateau before turning thirty. González enjoyed perhaps his best season in 1996 when, returning from a May spell on the disabled list to club 47 homers, he carried the Rangers to their first postseason in club history and edged Seattle's Alex Rodríguez in one of the closest American League Most Valuable Player races in history. At the end of the 1990s, he was unloaded on Detroit in a blockbuster deal that served as prelude to a career slump during one season in the Motor City. Free agent moves took him on to Cleveland and eventually back to Texas in a series of relocations that only fostered the popular image of the slugger as high-priced mercenary. His career has slowed with additional spans of inactivity on the disabled list, but Juan González still seems likely to end his career in the top five on anyone's all-time list of Latin American power hitters.

Guillermo "Willie" Hernández (b. November 14, 1954). The 70–63 big league win–loss record and 147 career saves achieved by Guillermo "Willie" Hernández, mostly with the Cubs and Tigers, doesn't look all that impressive as far as raw numbers go. The 6-3 lefty only once led the circuit in any recognized pitching category, with 80 appearances on the mound during his apex 1984 season in Detroit; he only once lost in double figures, but he never won more than nine game and only twice posted 30-plus saves. Hernández's lasting fame all boils down to a single peak season, when he made the remarkable transition from an ordinary set-up man in 1983 to bullpen ace of the World Champion 1984 Tigers of manager Sparky Anderson. Peaking at just the right time, Hernández utilized an assortment of sinking fastballs, screwballs, and sharp-breaking curves to baffle American League hitters while leading Detroit's pennant charge with a then record 32-straight successful save opportunities. He also won nine of twelve decisions and posted a stingy 1.92 ERA, all good enough for an unprecedented double coup as the league's Most Valuable Player and Cy Young Award winner. In the postseason that year, Hernández continued to carry the Tigers on his back, appearing in all three games during the American League Championship Series sweep of Kansas City, and then pitching in three of five World Series contests and saving a pair of them. After that, there were only two more stellar outings, with 31 and 24 saves over the next pair of seasons, the first number making the by-then fading veteran the first Tigers pitcher to record back-to-back 30-save campaigns. All in all, Willie Hernández was the poster child for baseball's always-growing list of surprising one (or two) season wonders.

After his years with the Cubs, Willie Hernández peaked in 1984 with simultaneous Cy Young and MVP trophies for the Tigers. [Transcendental Graphics]

Juan Pizarro (b. February 7, 1937). It was southpaw Juan Pizarro, a 19-year-old rookie with World Champion Milwaukee in 1957, who was Puerto Rico's first major big league pitching star—though that stardom was always limited by the venues in which Pizarro labored most of his career. The fireballing lefty gained most of his exposure in the 1960s with the Chicago White Sox and remains one of only a pair of hurlers to toss one-hitters for both Chicago teams. His performance pinnacles came in 1962 (a pair of two-hitters) and 1964 (19–9, 2.56 ERA). He once outdueled Mets ace Tom Seaver, and he himself smacked the Cubs' solo homer that preserved a 1–0 victory. It could be argued that no subsequent Borinquen hurler boasts any stronger big league resume; it is an even safer call that Juan Pizarro—with his 131 career wins and pair of major league All-Star game appearances—remains unrivaled down to the present in his lofty position as the island's best-ever fireballing southpaw.

Victor Pellot "Vic" Power (b. November 1, 1927).   When it comes to golden era 1950s baseball icons, none looms larger that Vic Power, an island hero both blessed and damned by a combination of black skin, seemingly unlimited all-around talent, and the most colorful playing style of his or almost any epoch. It is not exaggeration to suggest that back on his native island Vic Power is still the second most celebrated big league figure after the immortal Clemente—and that includes Hall of Famer Cepeda and modern-day heroes the likes of Roberto Alomar, Juan González, and Iván Rodríguez. But controversy was as much a part of Power's big league sojourn as was brilliant performance. Power also saw his career dogged by the unfortunate fact that he was never allowed to play under his own given name, a fate shared with several other Latino stars from the distant and not-so-distant past. The story of Power's name change during minor league days in Canada has already been related in Chapter 3. The saga of his status as a 1950s icon in Kansas City and Cleveland—where he revolution-ized first base play with his flamboyant one-handed style—remains one of Puerto Rico's most enduring baseball legends.

Victor Pellot, Gold Glove first baseman, played his entire career as Vic Power. [Transcendental Graphics]

Vic Power was certainly baseball flamboyance personi-fied. Never before or since has a first baseman played the game with quite the same inventive flair. During an era of two-handed defensive baseball, Power scooped ground balls and infield throws with a sweeping one-handed motion that was as ostentatious as it was deadly effective. Entrenched in the batter's box, he crouched from his patented stance and menacingly waved his bat at rival hurlers in bold pendulum style. Giving no quarter to hecklers or umpires, he seemed to breathe pure fire at anyone who would dare challenge his manliness. His line-drive slugging, impassioned base running (he once stole home twice in a game), and one-handed glove work were all flashy enough to have guaranteed huge celebrity status with New York's blacks and Hispanics had he been al-lowed to perform regularly in "the House that Ruth Built" and in a cast includ-ing Mickey Mantle, Yogi Berra, Whitey Ford, and Tony Kubek. But Power missed his chance to stand on center stage in the Bronx because of those very talents and unabashed style that would soon make his indelible mark upon the big league game. The staid New York Yankees under owners Dan Topping and Del Webb were not ready in 1953 to have a black star wearing their uniform, especially not one who called such attention to himself and his individualistic style of play. Power was quietly dealt from the Yankees minor league system to the Philadelphia Athletics in 1953; what Brooklyn exploited with Jackie Robinson, the Yankees let slip through their fingers with Vic Power.

Power was hardly a mere showboat—not if "showboat" means trading fiel-ding efficiency for the merely spectacular and risky. He was almost always spectacular, but he was also almost always nearly flawless. When sportswrit-ers first began handing out Gold Glove awards for fielding prowess in the junior circuit (1958), Puerto Rico's Vic Power was hands-down winner at the first base position for each of the first seven seasons (through 1964). Significantly, no American league first sacker has ever won that many in a row in the forty seasons since. And when he once admitted to manager Jimmy Dykes that perhaps he should give up his flashy one-handed fielding style and his exaggerated batting stance and thus court the goodwill of critical teammates and opponents, the Cleveland field boss would hear nothing of it. "Don't ever argue with success," was the warning from manager Dykes. The sage skipper had rightly assured Power that others carped about his playing style simply because he usually beat them with it.

Iván Rodríguez (b. November 27, 1971). Almost anyone's inventory of the game's greatest catchers—at least among modern-era big leaguers—either starts with Iván Rodríguez or arrives there very quickly. The prototype of the durable, power-hitting, shotgun-armed, team-leading receiver has had few if any better prototypes outside of perhaps Johnny Bench or Yogi Berra. Carlton Fisk doesn't come close as an offensive force, and Mike Piazza pales when compared to I-Rod on the defense side of the ledger. With the Texas Rangers, across the decade of the 1990s, Rodríguez provided the benchmark standard for versatile receivers by batting over .300 for eight straight seasons, blasting between 20 and 35 round-trippers annually, and completely shutting down enemy running games by nailing nearly half the runners attempting stolen bases on his watch. Nicknamed "Pudge" by his Rangers teammates as a complimentary link to Hall-of-Fame receiver Carlton Fisk, the solidly built righty was soon ringing up impressive offensive performances to complement his exceptional defensive tools: he slugged the most doubles (47) ever by a catcher in 1996; among backstops, only Hall of Fame Mickey Cochrane ever scored more runs in a season than the 116 that Iván Rodríguez posted in both 1996 and 1999. In that heady 1996 campaign, he also became the first major league backstop ever to collect 190 hits in a single campaign. And at the same time he was winning every Gold Glove and every American League All-Star berth for catchers between 1992 and the end of the decade. When he jumped to the rebuilding Florida Marlins as a free agent after a dozen American League years, he further bolstered his considerable Cooperstown credentials with a banner season and leadership role that carried his new club to a surprise wild-card berth and eventual World Series upset of the Yankees. Rodríguez has now moved to yet another rebuilding outfit in Detroit in a second free agent move aimed at again grabbing some of the magic of the 2003 "dream season" in Miami. Puerto Rico has never produced a better catcher—only Benito Santiago is even in the running—and some might argue that outside of Clemente and Cepeda it has never produced a more dedicated and productive ballplayer at any diamond position.

Benito Santiago (b. March 9, 1965). If it were not for Iván Rodríguez, Benito Santiago might well be on a path directly to Cooperstown. Certainly he would be the island's greatest backstop talent and one of its most memorable stars of the 1990s. As it was, Santiago has had to settle for the lesser reputation as one of baseball's best receivers at the end of the 1980s; by the close of the 1990s he was also one of the big leagues' most well-traveled receivers. And of course the two career labels are not entirely unrelated. After a few appearances in

1986, the Ponce native broke into the San Diego Padres lineup with a bang in 1987, earning National League rookie honors on the strength of a .300 BA, 18 homers, 21 steals, and a 34-game hitting streak to close out the season that was a new big league rookie record. He won three straight Gold Gloves the next trio of seasons and it was this ability as a defender—much more than hitting prowess—that put Santiago on four National League All-Star teams between 1989 and 1992. His arm was so strong that he was able to gun down potential base stealers from a kneeling position, a colorful style that not only thrilled fans but also earned respect from opponents all around the league; few opponents were willing to test his cannon. When offensive production began to decline in the 1990s, Santiago's reputation as a defender kept him moving to always available roster slots, first to the expansion Florida Marlins and later on to tours with the Cincinnati Reds, last-place Philadelphia Phillies, American League Toronto Blue Jays, and finally the Chicago Cubs. His return to the senior circuit with Chicago in 1999 came after a serious off-season auto wreck had forced the veteran backstop to miss almost the entire 1998 campaign. Four years later, the rugged 18-year veteran had passed through two more stops (back in Cincinnati and with the Giants in San Francisco), had made a fifth All-Star game appearance, and was closing in on 1,800 career hits, 220 homers, and 900 career RBI.

Rubén Sierra (b. October 6, 1965). A quieter version of Juan González is perhaps the best profile for durable Rubén Sierra, a switch-hitting slugger who has never achieved the greatness projected for him early on, but who has nonetheless hung around long enough to build a legacy now assured to last for decades. Sierra was not long ago described aptly by one prominent publication (*The Biographical Encyclopedia of Baseball*) as more of a shooting star than a superstar. His apex moment in the American League came in August 1992 not as a result of on-field performance but rather as feature player in a blockbuster trade that sent him from Texas to Oakland in exchange for another headlining Latin slugger, José Canseco. The careers of both would ironically sag after that much celebrated deal. The shooting-star reputation comes largely from Sierra's rapid and unsustained big league start: he blasted a career-high 30 homers at age twenty-two in only his second Texas season; at twenty-four, he led the league with his second 100-plus RBI campaign; and he made the American League All-Star team roster four times before turning thirty. Subsequent seasons saw him drift with little productivity from the Athletics to the Tigers, Blue Jays, White Sox, Reds, and Yankees (twice); by the age of thirty-two, he had played himself off a major league roster. By 2002, Sierra was nonetheless back with the Rangers for a second tour and capable of batting in the low .290s and socking 23 homers. Three years later, he was closing in on 300 career homers while again playing a valuable bench role with the New York Yankees in his eighteenth major league season.

Bernabe "Bernie" Williams (b. September 13, 1968). Few among casual big league fans likely even know that Yankees dependable and versatile center fielder Bernie Williams is a Latino ballplayer, native of San Juan; fewer still outside of New York are very likely to think of the 13-year Yankee veteran among the game's legitimate stars. But the fleet switch-hitter is indeed a product of Little League and Babe Ruth League youth competition on his native island, where he competed as a teenager against the likes of future Texas Rangers superstars Iván Rodríguez and Juan González. Williams was overshadowed at his position in the 1990s by Ken Griffey Jr. and in the history of his own ball club by the awesome shadows of Mickey Mantle and Joe DiMaggio. Nonetheless, his own considerable resumé has been sufficient to include an American League batting title (.339 in 1998), three Gold Gloves for defensive brilliance, and three World Series championship rings with the late-1990s dynasty Yankees under manager Joe Torre. The switch-hitter has even swung with power, blasting 20-plus homers on six occasions (including 30 homers during the 2000 world championship campaign). Few among Yankee stars have performed better in the clutch during postseason wars than Williams, who was the Most Valuable Player of the 1996 American League Championship Series and also socked a key home run in the final fifth game of the short 2000 Subway World Series with the crosstown Mets. Somewhat overshadowed by more glamorous teammates like Derek Jeter, Jason Giambi, and now Alex Rodríguez, Bernie Williams has been one of major league baseball's best kept secrets through much of the past decade.

IN BRIEF

When today's fan assesses the big league scene, it is impossible not to take note of the handful of established superstars who of late have carried on the proud tradition of Roberto Clemente. Argument can be made that, despite their lesser numbers (compared to Dominican and Venezuelan standouts), the recent handful of Puerto Rican stars has been the equal of those of any other nation. Juan González never quite filled his early promise as the game's future power-slugging nonpareil and fell short of his once assumed challenge to the 50 and perhaps even the 60 home run barrier. It would be Sosa and not Juan González who by the end of the 1990s was overhauling baseball's long-ball landmarks. Yet González (who entered 2004 with 429 homers and 1,387 RBI at age 35) will still almost assuredly wind up with power numbers sufficient for Cooperstown. Rubén Sierra (despite a dip in production after a trade from Texas to Oakland) remained for much of the 1990s the closest thing in two decades to Clemente himself. Iván Rodríguez and Benito Santiago are the two best Latin catchers ever to strap on the tools of ignorance, despite the defensive flair of Tony Peña and the clutch hitting of the late Venezuelan, Bo Díaz. No infielder anywhere was any better than Roberto Alomar in his lengthy prime when it came to either wielding a bat or knocking down enemy base hits. And switching-hitting Carlos Baerga in but three short seasons gave plenty of notice of a possible Hall-of-Fame career before mysteriously collapsing into obscurity. Whatever clouds may hang over Puerto Rico's winter-ball seasons, the island pipeline now open between San Juan and big league camps has never been filled with any richer flow of quality talent.

SELECTED PUERTO RICAN RECORDS AND STATISTICS
Puerto Rico's Major Leaguers

Puerto Ricans in the Major Leagues (1942–2003)

	Name	Debut	Position	Debut Team	Seasons	Games	Career Statistics
1	Hiram Bithorn	1942	RHP	Chicago Cubs (NL)	4	105	34–31, 3.16 ERA
2	Luis Rodríguez Olmo	1943	OF	Brooklyn Dodgers (NL)	6	462	.281 BA
3	Luis Márquez	1951	OF	Boston Braves (NL)	2	99	.182 BA
4	Rubén Gómez	1953	RHP	New York Giants (NL)	10	289	76–86, 4.09 ERA
5	Carlos Bernier	1953	OF	Pittsburgh Pirates (NL)	1	105	.213 BA
6	Vic Power (Victor Pellot)	1954	1B	Philadelphia Athletics (AL)	12	1,627	.284 BA, 1716 H
7	Saturnino "Nino" Escalera	1954	OF	Cincinnati Reds (NL)	1	73	.159 BA
8	José "Pantalones" Santiago	1954	RHP	Cleveland Indians (AL)	3	27	3–2, 4.66 ERA
9	Luis Arroyo	1955	LHP	St. Louis Cardinals (NL)	8	244	40–32, 3.93 ERA
10	Roberto Clemente	1955	OF	Pittsburgh Pirates (NL)	18	2,433	.317 BA, 3000 H
11	Roberto Vargas	1955	LHP	Milwaukee Braves (NL)	1	25	0–0, 8.76 ERA
12	Félix Mantilla	1956	SS/OF	Milwaukee Braves (NL)	11	969	.261 BA
13	Juan Pizarro	1957	LHP	Milwaukee Braves (NL)	18	488	131–105, 3.43 ERA
14	Valmy Thomas*	1957	C	New York Giants (NL)	5	252	.230 BA
15	Orlando Cepeda	1958	1B	San Francisco Giants (NL)	17	2,124	.297 BA, 379 HR
16	José Pagán	1959	IF	San Francisco Giants (NL)	15	1,326	.250 BA
17	Julio Gotay	1960	IF	St. Louis Cardinals (NL)	10	389	.260 BA
18	Ed Olivares	1960	OF	St. Louis Cardinals (NL)	2	24	.143 BA
19	Ramón Conde	1962	3B	Chicago White Sox (AL)	1	14	.000 BA
20	Félix Torres	1962	3B	Los Angeles Angels (AL)	3	365	.254 BA
21	Julio Navarro*	1962	RHP	Los Angeles Angels (AL)	6	130	7–9, 3.65 ERA
22	José Palillo Santiago	1963	RHP	Kansas City Athletics (AL)	8	163	34–29, 3.74 ERA
23	Santos "Sandy" Alomar Sr.	1964	2B	Milwaukee Braves (NL)	15	1,481	.245 BA, 1168 H
24	Santiago Rosario	1965	1B	Kansas City Athletics (AL)	1	81	.235 BA
25	Arturo "Art" López	1965	OF	New York Yankees (AL)	1	38	.143 BA
26	Héctor Valle	1965	C	Los Angeles Dodgers (NL)	1	9	.308 BA
27	Félix Millán	1966	2B	Atlanta Braves (NL)	12	1,480	.279 BA, 1617 H
28	Guillermo "Willie" Montañez	1966	1B	California Angels (AL)	14	1,632	.275 BA, 139 HR
29	(Ángel) Luis Alcaráz	1967	2B	Los Angeles Dodgers (NL)	4	115	.192 BA
30	Ramón Hernández	1967	LHP	Atlanta Braves (NL)	9	337	23–15, 3.03 ERA
31	Luis Alvarado	1968	IF	Boston Red Sox (AL)	9	463	.214 BA
32	Eliseo "Ellie" Rodríguez	1968	C	New York Yankees (AL)	9	775	.245 BA
33	Miguel "Mickey" Fuentes	1969	RHP	Seattle Pilots (AL)	1	8	1–3, 5.19 ERA
34	José "Coco" Laboy	1969	IF	Montreal Expos (NL)	5	420	.233 BA
35	Francisco "Frankie" Librán	1969	SS	San Diego Padres (NL)	1	10	.100 BA
36	Ángel Mangual	1969	OF	Pittsburgh Pirates (NL)	7	450	.245 BA
37	Julio "Jerry" Morales	1969	OF	San Diego Padres (NL)	15	1,441	.259 BA, 1173 H
38	José Ortíz	1969	OF	Chicago White Sox (AL)	3	67	.301 BA
39	Luis Peraza	1969	RHP	Philadelphia Phillies (NL)	1	8	0–0, 6.00 ERA
40	Juan Ríos	1969	IF	Kansas City Royals (AL)	1	87	.224 BA
41	José Cruz	1970	OF	St. Louis Cardinals (NL)	19	2,353	.284 BA, 2251 H
42	Rogelio "Roger" Moret	1970	LHP	Boston Red Sox (AL)	9	168	47–27, 3.66 ERA
43	Luis Meléndez	1970	OF	St. Louis Cardinals (NL)	8	641	.248 BA
44	Samuel "Sam" Parrilla	1970	OF	Philadelphia Phillies (NL)	1	11	.125 BA
45	Milton "Milt" Ramirez	1970	IF	St. Louis Cardinals (NL)	3	94	.184 BA
46	Jorge Roque	1970	OF	St. Louis Cardinals (NL)	4	65	.137 BA
47	Juan Beníquez	1971	OF	Boston Red Sox (AL)	17	1,500	.274 BA
48	Manny Muñíz	1971	RHP	Philadelphia Phillies (NL)	1	5	0–1, 6.97 ERA
49	Ángel "Jimmy" Rosario	1971	OF	San Francisco Giants (NL)	3	114	.216 BA
50	Rosendo "Rusty" Torres	1971	OF	New York Yankees (AL)	9	654	.212 BA
51	(José) Fernando González	1972	IF	Pittsburgh Pirates (NL)	6	404	.235 BA

(continued)

Name	Debut	Position	Debut Team	Seasons	Games	Career Statistics
52 José "Pepe" Mangual	1972	OF	Montreal Expos (NL)	6	319	.242 BA
53 David Rosello	1972	IF	Chicago Cubs (NL)	9	422	.236 BA
54 (Jesús Manuel) Orlando Álvarez	1973	OF	Los Angeles Dodgers (NL)	4	25	.157 BA
55 Héctor Cruz	1973	OF	St. Louis Cardinals (NL)	9	624	.225 BA
56 Cirilo "Tommy" Cruz	1973	OF	St. Louis Cardinals (NL)	2	7	.000 BA
57 Pedro García	1973	2B	Milwaukee Brewers (AL)	5	558	.220 BA
58 Eduardo Rodríguez	1973	RHP	Milwaukee Brewers (AL)	7	264	42–36, 3.89 ERA
59 Otto Velez	1973	OF	New York Yankees (AL)	11	637	.251 BA
60 Carlos Velásquez	1973	RHP	Milwaukee Brewers (AL)	1	18	2–2, 2.58 ERA
61 Benigno "Benny" Ayala	1974	OF	New York Mets (NL)	10	425	.251 BA
62 Iván DeJesús	1974	SS	Los Angeles Dodgers (NL)	15	1,371	.254 BA, 1167 H
63 Sergio Ferrer	1974	SS	Minnesota Twins (AL)	4	125	.242 BA
64 Eduardo "Ed" Figueroa	1974	RHP	California Angels (AL)	8	200	80–67, 3.51 ERA
65 Jesús Hernaíz	1974	RHP	Philadelphia Phillies (NL)	1	27	2–3, 5.88 ERA
66 Sixto Lezcano	1974	OF	Milwaukee Brewers (AL)	12	1,291	.271 BA, 148 HR
67 Luis Joaquín Quintana	1974	LHP	California Angels (AL)	2	22	2–3, 5.03 ERA
68 Jesús "Bombo" Rivera	1975	OF	Montreal Expos (NL)	6	335	.265 BA
69 Ramón Avilés	1977	IF	Boston Red Sox (AL)	4	117	.268 BA
70 Luis "Puchy" Delgado	1977	OF	Seattle Mariners (AL)	1	13	.182 BA
71 Gilberto "Gil" Flores	1977	OF	California Angels (AL)	3	185	.261 BA
72 Julio González	1977	IF	Houston Astros (NL)	7	370	.235 BA
73 Willie Hernández	1977	LHP	Chicago Cubs (NL)	13	744	70–63, 3.38 ERA
74 Edgar "Ed" Romero	1977	IF	Milwaukee Brewers (AL)	12	730	.247 BA
75 Luis Rosado	1977	1B	New York Mets (NL)	2	11	.179 BA
76 Manuel "Chico" Ruíz	1978	IF	Atlanta Braves (NL)	2	43	.292 BA
77 Antonio "Tony" Bernazard	1979	2B	Montreal Expos (NL)	10	1,071	.262 BA
78 Rafael Santo Domingo	1979	PH	Cincinnati Reds (NL)	1	7	.167 BA
79 Dickie Thon (b. USA)	1979	SS/IF	California Angels (AL)	15	1,387	.264 BA, 1176 H
80 Jesús Vega	1979	OF/IF	Minnesota Twins (AL)	3	87	.246 BA
81 Luis Aguayo	1980	IF	Philadelphia Phillies (NL)	10	568	.236 BA
82 Onix Concepción	1980	IF	Kansas City Royals (AL)	7	390	.239 BA
83 Orlando Isales	1980	OF	Philadelphia Phillies (NL)	1	3	.400 BA
84 Carlos Lezcano	1980	OF	Chicago Cubs (AL)	2	49	.186 BA
85 Mario Ramirez	1980	SS/IF	New York Mets (NL)	6	184	.192 BA
86 Osvaldo "Ozzie" Virgil	1980	C	Philadelphia Phillies (NL)	11	739	.243 BA
87 Juan Agosto	1981	LHP	Chicago White Sox (AL)	13	543	40–33, 4.01 ERA
88 Juan Bonilla	1981	2B	San Diego Padres (NL)	6	429	.256 BA
89 Luis DeLeón	1981	RHP	St. Louis Cardinals (NL)	7	207	17–19, 3.12 ERA
90 Candido "Candy" Maldonado	1981	OF	Los Angeles Dodgers (NL)	15	1,410	.254 BA, 146 HR
91 Adalberto "Bert" Peña	1981	IF	Houston Astros (NL)	6	88	.203 BA
92 Orlando Sánchez	1981	C	St. Louis Cardinals (NL)	4	73	.218 BA
93 Orlando Mercado	1982	C	Seattle Mariners (AL)	8	253	.199 BA
94 Adalberto "Junior" Ortíz	1982	C	Pittsburgh Pirates (NL)	13	749	.256 BA
95 Edwin Rodríguez	1982	IF	New York Yankees (AL)	3	11	.227 BA
96 Hediberto "Eddie" Vargas	1982	1B	Pittsburgh Pirates (NL)	2	26	.256 BA
97 Edwin Núñez	1982	RHP	Seattle Mariners (AL)	13	427	28–36, 4.19 ERA
98 James "Jaime" Cocanower	1983	RHP	Milwaukee Brewers (AL)	4	79	16–25, 3.99 ERA
99 Carmelo Martínez	1983	OF	Chicago Cubs (NL)	9	1,003	.245 BA, 108 HR
100 José Oquendo	1983	IF	New York Mets (NL)	12	1,190	.256 BA
101 Germán Rivera	1983	3B	Los Angeles Dodgers (NL)	3	120	.257 BA
102 Iván Calderón	1984	OF	Seattle Mariners (AL)	10	924	.272 BA, 104 HR
103 Francisco Melendez	1984	1B	Philadelphia Phillies (NL)	5	74	.214 BA
104 Danilo "Danny" Tartabull	1984	OF/DH	Seattle Mariners (AL)	14	1,406	.273 BA, 262 HR
105 Edwin Correa	1985	RHP	Chicago White Sox (AL)	3	52	16–19, 5.16 ERA
106 José Guzmán	1985	RHP	Texas Rangers (AL)	8	193	80–74, 4.05 ERA

Name	Debut	Position	Debut Team	Seasons	Games	Career Statistics
107 Carlos Ponce	1985	1B	Milwaukee Brewers (AL)	1	21	.161 BA
108 Juan Nieves	1986	LHP	Milwaukee Brewers (AL)	3	94	32–25, 4.71 ERA
109 Luis Aquino	1986	RHP	Toronto Blue Jays (AL)	9	222	31–32, 3.68 ERA
110 Rafael Montalvo	1986	RHP	Houston Astros (NL)	1	1	0–0, 9.00 ERA
111 Edgar Díaz	1986	SS	Milwaukee Brewers (AL)	2	91	.268 BA
112 Luis Quiñones	1986	IF	Oakland Athletics (AL)	8	442	.226 BA
113 Rey Quiñones	1986	SS	Boston Red Sox (AL)	4	451	.243 BA
114 Luis Rivera	1986	IF	Montreal Expos (NL)	11	781	.233 BA
115 Benito Santiago	1986	C	San Diego Padres (NL)	18	1,923	.263 BA, 211 HR
116 Rubén Sierra	1986	OF/DH	Texas Rangers (AL)	17	2,004	.270 BA, 285 HR
117 Joey Cora	1987	2B	San Diego Padres (NL)	11	1,119	.277 BA
118 Mario Díaz	1987	SS	Seattle Mariners (AL)	9	374	.256 BA
119 José Lind	1987	SS	Pittsburgh Pirates (NL)	9	1,044	.254 BA
120 Ulises "Candy" Sierra	1988	RHP	San Diego Padres (NL)	1	16	0–1, 5.53 ERA
121 Santos "Sandy" Alomar Jr.	1988	C	San Diego Padres (NL)	16	1,227	.275 BA, 109 HR
122 Luis Alicea	1988	2B	St. Louis Cardinals (NL)	13	1,341	.260 BA
123 Roberto Alomar	1988	2B	San Diego Padres (NL)	16	2,323	.301 BA, 206 HR
124 Juan González	1989	OF	Texas Rangers (AL)	15	1,655	.296 BA, 429 HR
125 Jaime Navarro	1989	RHP	Milwaukee Brewers (AL)	12	361	116–126, 4.72 ERA
126 Francisco Javier Oliveras	1989	RHP	Minnesota Twins (AL)	4	116	11–15, 3.71 ERA
127 Carlos Baerga	1990	2B	Cleveland Indians (AL)	12	1,458	.293 BA, 130 HR
128 Rafael Novoa (b. USA)	1990	LHP	San Francisco Giants (NL)	2	22	0–4, 5.06 ERA
129 Leo Gómez	1990	3B	Baltimore Orioles (AL)	7	611	.243 BA
130 José Meléndez	1990	RHP	Seattle Mariners (AL)	5	109	16–14, 3.47 ERA
131 Orlando Merced	1990	1B	Pittsburgh Pirates (NL)	13	1,391	.277 BA, 103 HR
132 Pedro Muñoz	1990	OF/DH	Minnesota Twins (AL)	7	517	.273 BA
133 Omar Olivares	1990	RHP	St. Louis Cardinals (NL)	12	349	77–86, 4.67 ERA
134 Michael "Mike" Pérez	1990	RHP	St. Louis Cardinals (NL)	8	313	24–16, 3.56 ERA
135 Julio Valera	1990	RHP	New York Mets (NL)	5	85	15–20, 4.85 ERA
136 Héctor Villanueva	1990	C	Chicago Cubs (NL)	4	191	.230 BA
137 Ricardo "Ricky" Bones	1991	RHP	San Diego Padres (NL)	11	375	63–82, 4.85 ERA
138 José Hernández	1991	IF/OF	Texas Rangers (AL)	12	1,323	.251 BA
139 Roberto Hernández	1991	RHP	Chicago White Sox (AL)	13	762	53–54, 3.30, 320 S
140 Iván Rodríguez	1991	C	Texas Rangers (AL)	13	1,623	.304 BA, 231 HR
141 Elam José "Rico" Rossy	1991	IF	Atlanta Braves (NL)	4	147	.211 BA
142 Rey Sánchez	1991	IF	Chicago Cubs (NL)	13	1,376	.273 BA, 1235 H
143 Bernabe "Bernie" Williams	1991	OF	New York Yankees (AL)	13	1,656	.305 BA, .241 HR
144 Wilfredo "Wil" Cordero	1992	IF/OF	Montreal Expos (NL)	12	1,191	.276 BA, 121 HR
145 Javier López	1992	C	Atlanta Braves (NL)	12	1,156	.287 BA, 214 HR
146 Melvin Nieves	1992	OF	Atlanta Braves (NL)	7	458	.231 BA
147 José Valentín	1992	SS	Milwaukee Brewers (AL)	12	1,309	.246 BA, 196 HR
148 Oreste Marrero	1993	1B	Montreal Expos (NL)	2	42	.225 BA
149 José Carlos "Charlie" Montoyo	1993	IF	Montreal Expos (NL)	1	4	.400 BA
150 Norberto "Tito" Navarro	1993	SS	New York Mets (NL)	1	12	.059 BA
151 Luis López	1993	IF	San Diego Padres (NL)	9	648	.245 BA
152 Carlos Delgado	1993	1B	Toronto Blue Jays (AL)	11	1,295	.284 BA, 304 HR
153 Ángel Miranda	1993	LHP	Milwaukee Brewers (AL)	5	116	17–21, 4.46 ERA
154 Roberto "Bobby" Muñoz	1993	RHP	New York Yankees (AL)	7	100	11–22, 5.17 ERA
155 Roberto Rivera	1995	LHP	Chicago Cubs (NL)	2	19	1–2, 4.50 ERA
156 Rafael Carmona	1995	RHP	Seattle Mariners (AL)	4	81	11–7, 4.94 ERA
157 Ricardo "Ricky" Otero	1995	OF	New York Mets (NL)	3	189	.256 BA
158 Jorge Posada	1995	C	New York Yankees (AL)	9	866	.270 BA, 135 HR
159 Rafael Carmona	1995	RHP	Seattle Mariners (AL)	4	81	11–7, 4.94 ERA
160 Yamil Benítez	1995	OF	Montreal Expos (NL)	4	169	.243 BA
161 José Alberro	1995	RHP	Texas Rangers (AL)	3	27	0–4, 7.41 ERA
162 Luis Antonio "Tony" Rodríguez	1996	SS/IF	Boston Red Sox (AL)	1	27	.239 BA

(continued)

(continued)

Name	Debut	Position	Debut Team	Seasons	Games	Career Statistics
163 Damon Mashore	1996	OF	Oakland Athletics (AL)	3	185	.249 BA
164 Pedro Valdés	1996	OF	Chicago Cubs (NL)	3	53	.247 BA
165 Felipe Crespo	1996	IF	Toronto Blue Jays (AL)	5	262	.245 BA
166 Raúl Casanova	1996	C	Detroit Tigers (AL)	6	332	232 BA
167 Iván Cruz	1997	1B	New York Yankees (AL)	4	41	.273 BA
168 José Vidro	1997	2B	Montreal Expos (NL)	7	863	.306 BA
169 José Santiago	1997	RHP	Kansas City Royals (AL)	7	225	17–22, 4.39 ERA
170 Javier Valentín	1997	C	Minnesota Twins (AL)	5	190	.228 BA
171 José Cruz Jr.	1997	OF	Seattle Mariners (AL)	7	905	.251 BA, 154 HR
172 José Alexander "Alex" Cora	1998	IF	Los Angeles Dodgers (NL)	6	546	.241 BA
173 Ricardo "Ricky" Ledee	1998	OF	New York Yankees (AL)	6	562	.243 BA
174 Edwin Díaz	1998	IF	Arizona Diamondbacks (NL)	2	7	.167 BA
175 Javier Martínez	1998	RHP	Pittsburgh Pirates (NL)	1	37	0–1, 4.83 ERA
176 Héctor Ortíz	1998	C	Kansas City Royals (AL)	4	93	.288 BA
177 Mike Lowell	1998	3B	New York Yankees (AL)	6	681	.274 BA, 108 HR
178 Carlos Beltrán	1998	OF	Kansas City Royals (AL)	6	726	.288 BA, 108 HR
179 Javier Vázquez	1998	RHP	Montreal Expos (NL)	6	192	64–68, 4.16 ERA
180 Armando Ríos	1998	OF	San Francisco Giants (NL)	6	419	.269 BA
181 Benjamin "Ben" Molina	1998	C	Anaheim Angels (AL)	6	500	.267 BA
182 Edgard Clemente	1998	OF	Colorado Rockies (NL)	3	114	.249 BA
183 Ramón Castro	1999	C	Florida Marlins (NL)	5	175	.232 BA
184 José Molina	1999	C	Anaheim Angels (AL)	4	107	.229 BA
185 Juan Carlos "J. C." Romero	1999	LHP	Minnesota Twins (AL)	5	185	14–13, 4.76 ERA
186 Robinson Cancel	1999	C	Milwaukee Brewers (NL)	1	15	.182 BA
187 Edwards Guzmán	1999	C	San Francisco Giants (NL)	3	127	.228 BA
188 Hiram Bocachica	2000	IF/OF	Los Angeles Dodgers (NL)	4	172	.216 BA
189 Héctor Mercado	2000	LHP	Cincinnati Reds (NL)	4	112	5–4, 4.55 ERA
190 José Rodríguez	2000	LHP	St. Louis Cardinals (NL)	2	12	0–1, 9.00 ERA
191 Ismael Villegas	2000	RHP	Atlanta Braves (NL)	1	1	0–0, 13.50 ERA
192 Javier Cardona	2000	C	Detroit Tigers (AL)	3	87	.206 BA
193 Raúl González	2000	OF	Chicago Cubs (NL)	4	161	.237 ERA
194 Joel Pineiro	2000	RHP	Seattle Mariners (AL)	4	94	37–20, 3.38 ERA
195 Alexander "Alex" Hernández	2000	IF/OF	Pittsburgh Pirates (NL)	2	27	.183 BA
196 Luis Matos	2000	OF	Baltimore Orioles (AL)	4	229	.265 BA
197 Ramón Vázquez	2001	IF	Seattle Mariners (AL)	3	261	.266 BA
198 Alexander "Alex" Cintrón	2001	SS	Arizona Diamondbacks (NL)	3	163	.302 BA
199 Ángel Santos	2001	IF	Boston Red Sox (AL)	2	41	.207 BA
200 Michael "Mike" Rivera	2001	C	Detroit Tigers (AL)	3	62	.218 BA
201 Dicky González	2001	RHP	New York Mets (NL)	1	16	3–2, 4.88 ERA
202 Felipe López	2001	IF	Toronto Blue Jays (AL)	3	193	.232 BA
203 César Crespo	2001	OF/IF	San Diego Padres (NL)	2	80	.203 BA
204 Pedro Feliciano	2002	LHP	New York Mets (NL)	2	29	0–0, 3.81 ERA
205 Wilbert Nieves	2002	C	San Diego Padres (NL)	1	28	.181 BA
206 Andrés Torres	2002	OF	Detroit Tigers (AL)	2	78	.214 BA
207 José Leon	2002	IF/OF	Baltimore Orioles (AL)	2	57	.245 BA
208 Javier López	2003	LHP	Colorado Rockies (NL)	1	75	4–1, 3.70 ERA
209 Carlos Rivera	2003	1B	Pittsburgh Pirates (NL)	1	78	.221 BA
210 Kiko Calero	2003	RHP	St. Louis Cardinals (NL)	1	26	1–1, 2.82 ERA

This list includes native-born Puerto Ricans only, with exception of island-raised Dickie Thon.
*Valmy Thomas and Julio Navarro also appear on list of Virgin Islands players (see p. 336).

Puerto Rican League Record Book

Puerto Rico Winter League Championship Teams and Managers (1938–2003)

Year	Playoff Champion	Manager or Playoff Record	Regular Season Champion	W–L	PCT
1938–1939	Guayama	Fernando García	Guayama	27–12	.692
1939–1940	Guayama	Fernando García	Guayama	39–17	.696
1940–1941	Caguas Criollos	José Seda	Caguas Criollos	27–15	.643
1941–1942	Ponce Lions	George Scales	Ponce Lions	30–13	.698
1942–1943	Ponce Lions	George Scales	Ponce Lions	19–16	.543
1943–1944	Ponce Lions	George Scales	Ponce Lions	37–7	.841
1944–1945	Ponce Lions	George Scales	Ponce Lions	28–11	.718
1945–1946	San Juan Senators	Robert Clark	Mayagüez Indians	24–16	.600
1946–1947	Ponce Lions	George Scales	Ponce Lions	38–22	.633
1947–1948	Caguas-Guayama	Quincy Trouppe	Mayagüez Indians	39–21	.650
1948–1949	Mayagüez Indians	Artie Wilson	Mayagüez Indians	51–29	.638
1949–1950	Caguas-Guayama	Luis Olmo	Caguas Criollos	47–31	.603
1950–1951	Santurce Crabbers	George Scales	Caguas Criollos	57–20	.740
1951–1952	San Juan Senators	Freddie Thon	San Juan Senators	43–29	.597
1952–1953	Santurce Crabbers	Buster Clarkson	San Juan Senators	45–27	.625
1953–1954	Caguas-Guayama	Mickey Owen	Caguas Criollos	46–34	.575
1954–1955	Santurce Crabbers	Herman Franks	Santurce Crabbers	47–25	.653
1955–1956	Caguas-Guayama	Ben Geraghty	Santurce Crabbers	43–29	.597
1956–1957	Mayagüez Indians	Mickey Owen	Santurce Crabbers	43–29	.597
1957–1958	Caguas-Guayama	Ted Norbert	Santurce Crabbers	36–28	.563
1958–1959	Santurce Crabbers	Monchile Concepción	San Juan Senators	38–24	.594
1959–1960	Caguas-Guayama	Vic Pellot "Power"	San Juan Senators	41–23	.641
1960–1961	San Juan Senators	Lum Harris	San Juan Senators	39–25	.609
1961–1962	Santurce Crabbers	Vern Benson	Mayagüez Indians	45–35	.563
1962–1963	Mayagüez Indians	Carl Ermer	Mayagüez Indians	42–28	.600
1963–1964	San Juan Senators	Less Moss	Caguas Criollos	41–29	.586
1964–1965	Santurce Crabbers	Preston Gómez	Santurce Crabbers	41–28	.594
1965–1966	Mayagüez Indians	Wayne Blackburn	Mayagüez Indians	42–28	.600
1966–1967	Santurce Crabbers	Earl Weaver	Ponce Lions	46–25	.648
1967–1968	Caguas-Guayama	Nino Escalera	Santurce Crabbers	47–22	.681
1968–1969	Ponce Lions	Rocky Bridges	Santurce Crabbers	49–20	.710
1969–1970	Ponce Lions	Jim Fregosi	Ponce Lions	44–25	.638
1970–1971	Santurce Crabbers	Frank Robinson	Caguas Criollos	41–29	.585
1971–1972	Ponce Lions	Frank Verdi	San Juan Senators	39–30	.565
1972–1973	Santurce Crabbers	Frank Robinson	Santurce Crabbers	45–25	.642
1973–1974	Caguas-Guayama	Bobby Wine	Ponce Lions	42–28	.600
1974–1975	Bayamón Cowboys	José Pagán	Caguas Criollos	43–27	.614
1975–1976	Bayamón Cowboys	José Pagán	Caguas Criollos	35–25	.583
1976–1977	Caguas Criollos	Doc Edwards	Caguas Criollos	40–20	.667
1977–1978	Mayagüez Indians	Rene Lachemann	Caguas Criollos	37–23	.617
1978–1979	Caguas Criollos	Félix Millán	Ponce Lions	33–27	.550
1979–1980	Bayamón Cowboys	Art Howe	Santurce Crabbers	36–24	.600
1980–1981	Caguas Criollos	Félix Millán	Bayamón Cowboys	39–21	.650
1981–1982	Ponce Lions	Edward Nottle	Caguas Criollos	37–23	.617
1982–1983	Arecibo Wolves	Ron Clarke	Santurce Crabbers	35–26	.574
1983–1984	Mayagüez Indians	Frank Verdi	Mayagüez Indians	38–22	.633
1984–1985	San Juan Senators	Mako Oliveras	Mayagüez Indians	38–22	.633
1985–1986	Mayagüez Indians	Nick Leyva	Caguas Criollos	33–21	.611

(continued)

(continued)

Year	Playoff Champion	Manager or Playoff Record	Regular Season Champion	W–L	PCT
1986–1987	Caguas Criollos	Tim Foli	Ponce Lions	34–19	.642
1987–1988	Mayagüez Indians	Jim Riggleman	Santurce Crabbers	31–21	.596
1988–1989	Mayagüez Indians	Tom Gamboa	San Juan Senators	35–25	.583
1989–1990	San Juan Senators	Mako Olivares	Ponce Lions	31–19	.620
1990–1991	Santurce Crabbers	Mako Olivares	San Juan Senators	33–25	.569
1991–1992	Mayagüez Indians	Pat Kelly	San Juan Senators	29–21	.580
1992–1993	Santurce Crabbers	Mako Oliveras	Santurce Crabbers	29–18	.617
1993–1994	San Juan Senators	Luis Meléndez	San Juan Senators	35–13	.729
1994–1995	San Juan Senators	5–3 over Mayagüez	Mayagüez Indians	33–21	.611
1995–1996	Arecibo Wolves	5–3 over Mayagüez	Mayagüez Indians	28–21	.571
1996–1997	Mayagüez Indians	5–3 over San Juan	Santurce and Mayagüez	28–22	.560
1997–1998	Mayagüez Indians	5–4 over San Juan	San Juan Senators	40–22	.645
1998–1999	Mayagüez Indians	5–1 over Ponce	Ponce Lions	29–18	.617
1999–2000	Santurce Crabbers	5–2 over Mayagüez	Mayagüez Indians	27–23	.540
2000–2001	Caguas Criollos	5–1 over Mayagüez	Caguas Criollos	30–19	.612
2001–2002	Bayamón Cowboys	5–3 over Santurce	Ponce Lions	31–22	.585
2002–2003	Mayagüez Indians	5–1 over Caguas	Caguas Criollos	32–18	.640

Puerto Rican Individual Batting Leaders (1938–2003)

Year	Batting Leader	BA	Home Run Leader	HR	Hits Leader	H
1938–1939	Perucho Cepeda	.465	Edward Stone	9	Perucho Cepeda	79
1939–1940	Perucho Cepeda	.383	Josh Gibson	6	Perucho Cepeda	81
1940–1941	Roy Partlow	.443	Roy Campanella	8	Perucho Cepeda	67
1941–1942	Josh Gibson	.480	Josh Gibson	13	Juan Sánchez	67
1942–1943	Francisco Coimbre	.342	Luis Olmo	4	Leonardo Chapman	49
1943–1944	Tetelo Vargas	.410	Juan Guilbe	2	Francisco Coimbre	60
1944–1945	Francisco Coimbre	.425	*Three Tied*	3	Juan Sánchez	61
1945–1946	Fernando Díaz Perozo	.368	Monte Irvin	3	Monte Irvin	56
1946–1947	Willard Brown	.390	Luis Márquez	14	Willard Brown	99
1947–1948	Willard Brown	.432	Willard Brown	27	Artie Wilson, Bob Thurman	102
1948–1949	Luke Easter	.402	Willard Brown	18	Artie Wilson	126
1949–1950	Willard Brown	.354	Willard Brown	16	Willard Brown	117
1950–1951	George Crowe	.375	Buster Clarkson	17	Bob Thurman	112
1951–1952	Bob Boyd	.374	*Three Tied*	9	Bob Boyd	114
1952–1953	George Freese	.330	*Three Tied*	9	George Freese	94
1953–1954	Luis Márquez	.333	Hank Aaron	9	Luis Márquez	94
1954–1955	Willie Mays	.395	Bob Cerv	19	Roberto Clemente	94
1955–1956	Victor Pellot "Power"	.358	Luke Easter	17	Vic Power, Wes Covington	87
1956–1957	Roberto Clemente	.396	Wes Covington	15	José García	94
1957–1958	Billy Harrell	.317	Vic Pellot "Power"	13	Orlando Cepeda	72
1958–1959	Orlando Cepeda	.362	Johnny Powers	17	Elmo Plaskett	81
1959–1960	Victor Pellot "Power"	.347	Jim McDaniels	10	Ramón Conde	79
1960–1961	Elmo Plaskett	.328	Elmo Plaskett	15	Elmo Plaskett	69
1961–1962	Miguel de la Hoz	.354	Orlando Cepeda	19	J. C. Martin	91
1962–1963	Joe Gaines	.352	John Herstein	14	Cookie Rojas	95
1963–1964	Tony Oliva	.365	José Cardenal	16	Danny Cater	82
1964–1965	Lou Johnson	.345	Fred Hopke	12	Jim Northrup	89

Year	Batting Leader	BA	Home Run Leader	HR	Hits Leader	H
1965–1966	Jim Northrup	.353	Dick Simpson	10	Jim Northrup	85
1966–1967	Tony Pérez	.333	Dick Simpson	12	Tony Pérez	87
1967–1968	Tony Taylor	.344	Degold Francis	14	Sandy Alomar	84
1968–1969	Félix Millán	.317	George Scott	13	Sandy Alomar	82
1969–1970	Félix Millán	.345	Nate Colbert	16	Sandy Alomar	88
1970–1971	Sandy Alomar	.343	Reggie Jackson	20	Sandy Alomar	86
1971–1972	Don Baylor	.324	Willie Montañez	15	Enrique Rivera	81
1972–1973	Richard Coggins	.352	Richie Zisk	14	Jerry Morales	80
1973–1974	George Hendrick	.363	Benigno Ayala	14	Mickey Rivers	90
1974–1975	Ken Griffey	.357	Danny Walton	14	Ken Griffey	84
1975–1976	Dan Driessen	.331	Benigno Ayala	14	José Morales	76
1976–1977	Sixto Lezcano	.366	Roger Freed	16	Orlando Álvarez	76
1977–1978	Ron LeFlore	.396	Roger Freed	17	José Moralez	78
1978–1979	José Cruz	.370	Jim Dwyer	15	José Cruz	78
1979–1980	Dennis Walling	.330	Dave Revering	9	Dennis Walling	70
1980–1981	Dickie Thon	.329	Candy Maldonado	10	Dickie Thon	82
1981–1982	Dickie Thon	.333	José Cruz	12	Dickie Thon	68
1982–1983	Brian Harper	.378	Carmelo Martínez	17	Brian Harper	87
1983–1984	Don Mattingly	.368	Jerry Willard	18	Steve Lubratick	68
1984–1985	Orlando Sánchez	.333	Jerry Willard	9	Milt Thompson	68
1985–1986	Wally Joyner	.356	Wally Joyner	14	Wally Joyner	67
1986–1987	Victor Rodríguez	.377	Iván Calderón	10	Tracy Woodson	63
1987–1988	Randy Milligan	.347	Iván Calderón	8	Roberto Alomar	60
1988–1989	Lonnie Smith	.366	Rickey Jordan	14	Doug Dascenzo	73
1989–1990	Edgar Martínez	.424	Greg Vaughn	10	Carlos Baerga	61
1990–1991	Héctor Villanueva	.347	Héctor Villanueva	12	Rod Brewer	71
1991–1992	Alonzo Powell	.339	Mike Simms	9	Alonzo Powell, Eric Fox	58
1992–1993	Wil Cordero	.304	Juan González	7	Wil Cordero	41
1993–1994	Kevin Báez	.348	Phil Hiatt	10	John Mabry	51
1994–1995	Rey Sánchez	.390	Carlos Delgado	12	Brian Johnson	72
1995–1996	Roberto Alomar	.362	Héctor Villanueva	8	Doug Glanville	66
1996–1997	Roberto Alomar	.347	Héctor Villanueva	11	Doug Glanville	56
1997–1998	Omar García	.375	José Hernández	20	Omar García	95
1998–1999	José Vidro	.417	Ernie Young	13	José Vidro	60
1999–2000	Raúl Casanova	.331	Lou Lucca	10	Darryl Brinkley	56
2000–2001	Victor Rodríguez	.364	Alex Cora	10	Yamil Benítez	52
2001–2002	Ramón Vázquez	.361	Miguel Correa	13	Ramón Vázquez	65
2002–2003	Gabby Martínez	.375	Omar García	15	Brian Roberts	57

Puerto Rican Individual Pitching Leaders (1938–2003)

Year	Pitching Victories	W	ERA Leader	ERA	Strikeouts Leader	SO
1938–1939	Rafaelito Ortíz	11	*Not Available*		José Figueroa	96
1939–1940	Satchel Paige	19	Silvio García	1.32	Satchel Paige	208
1940–1941	Billy Byrd	15	Roy Partlow	1.49	Dave Barnhill	193
1941–1942	Barney Brown	16	Raymond Brown	1.82	Leon Day	168
1942–1943	Ceferino Conde	10	Rafaelito Ortíz	1.83	Ceferino Conde	69
1943–1944	Rafaelito Ortíz	15	Tomás Quiñónez	1.69	Juan Santaella	86
1944–1945	Tomás Quiñónez	16	Tomás Quiñónez	2.52	Luis Cabrera	81
1945–1946	Tomás Quiñónez	10	Johnny Davis	2.42	Luis Cabrera	75

(continued)

Year	Pitching Victories	W	ERA Leader	ERA	Strikeouts Leader	SO
1946–1947	Barney Brown	16	Barney Brown	1.24	Dan Bankhead	179
1947–1948	Ford Smith	13	Rafaelito Ortíz	2.97	Johnny Davis	100
1948–1949	Royce Lynn	13	Royce Lynn	2.38	Gene Collins	157
1949–1950	Rubén Gómez	14	Cecil Kaiser	1.68	Dan Bankhead	131
1950–1951	Mike Clark	14	Mike Clark	2.10	Pete Wojie	116
1951–1952	Rubén Gómez	14	Earl Harris	1.24	Sam Jones	140
1952–1953	Bobo Holloman	15	Coot Deal	1.85	Rubén Gómez	123
1953–1954	Jack Harshman	15	Natalio Irizarry	1.49	Bob Turley	143
1954–1955	Sam "Toothpick" Jones	14	Sam Jones	1.88	Sam Jones	171
1955–1956	Steve Ridzik	14	Pete Wojie	2.46	Jim Owens	134
1956–1957	Marion Fricano	12	Bob Smith	1.94	Luis Arroyo	145
1957–1958	Juan Pizarro	14	Juan Pizarro	1.32	Juan Pizarro	183
1958–1959	Rubén Gómez	12	Lloyd Merritt	1.63	Juan Pizarro	139
1959–1960	Earl Wilson	15	Bob Bruce	1.98	Juan Pizarro	141
1960–1961	Phil Regan	11	Luis Arroyo	1.64	Juan Pizarro	122
1961–1962	Joe Horlen	13	Gordon Seyfried	1.67	Juan Pizarro	154
1962–1963	Bob Dustal	11	Bob Dustal	1.76	Bob Veale	104
1963–1964	Juan Pizarro	10	Joe Hoerner	1.21	John Boozer	132
1964–1965	Denny McLain	12	Fred Talbot	1.30	Denny McLain	126
	Mike Cuéllar	12				
1965–1966	John Boozer	15	Ferguson Jenkins	1.38	John Boozer	121
1966–1967	Nelson Briles	12	Dick Hughes	1.79	Grant Jackson	104
1967–1968	Darrell Osteen	12	Tom Timmerman	0.88	Juan Pizarro	108
1968–1969	Bill Kelso	10	Jerry Johnson	1.29	Bill Kelso, Rick Gardner	82
1969–1970	Wayne Simpson	11	Wayne Simpson	1.55	Wayne Simpson	114
1970–1971	Mike Weneger	9	Tom Kelly	2.04	William Parsons	97
1971–1972	Rogelio Moret	14	John Strohmayer	1.71	Rogelio Moret	89
1972–1973	Juan Pizarro	10	Bert Strom	1.65	Lynn McGlothen	130
1973–1974	Ed Figueroa	10	Ernie McAnnally	1.72	Ken Wright	147
1974–1975	Ed Figueroa	10	Richard Krueger	1.40	Roy Thomas	61
					Chris Zachary	61
1975–1976	Odell Jones	11	Tom Bruno	1.23	Odell Jones	77
1976–1977	Eduardo Rodríguez	9	José Martínez	1.91	Dave Lemanczyck	78
1977–1978	*Three Tied*	8	Scott McGregor	2.18	Bob Galasso	71
1978–1979	Steve McCatty	8	Steve McCatty	1.71	Johnny Morris	58
1979–1980	Dennis Kinney	9	Darrell Jackson	1.33	Frank LeCorte	56
1980–1981	Greg Harris	8	Dennis Martínez	1.39	Eric Show	62
1981–1982	Edwin Núñez	9	Edwin Núñez	1.72	Edwin Núñez	67
1982–1983	Ken Dayley	9	Ed Figueroa	2.93	Greg Harris	84
1983–1984	Rick Mahler	10	Kevin Hagen	1.92	Julián González	72
1984–1985	Francisco Olivares	8	José Guzmán	1.62	Randy Niemann	54
1985–1986	José Guzmán	7	José Guzmán	1.65	Tom Candiotti	53
1986–1987	*Five Tied*	6	Charles Corbell	2.21	Doug Jones	46
1987–1988	*Five Tied*	6	Miguel Alicía	0.93	Mike Kinnunen	54
1988–1989	Aris Tirado	9	Dave Rosario	1.32	Aris Tirado	67
1989–1990	Ricky Bones	8	Jeff Gray	1.24	Rick Reed	53
1990–1991	Kip Gross	7	Trevor Wilson	2.07	Rod Nichols	54
1991–1992	Turk Wendell	7	Gino Minutelli	0.90	Denny Naegle	64
1992–1993	José Lebron	7	Fernando Figueroa	0.63	Greg McMichael	40
1993–1994	Rafael Montalvo	7	Carlos Reyes	1.33	Rick White	38
					Randy Veres	38
1994–1995	Doug Brocail	7	Doug Brocail	1.70	Eric Gunderson	62
	Eric Gunderson	7				
1995–1996	Bronswell Patrick	6	Bronswell Patrick	1.66	Keith Shephard	63

Year	Pitching Victories	W	ERA Leader	ERA	Strikeouts Leader	SO
1996–1997	Rafael Montalvo	7	Rafael Montalvo	2.00	Julio Valera	42
1997–1998	Bart Evans	6	José Santiago	2.39	Jay Witasick	60
	Ricky Bones	6				
1998–1999	Pat Flury	6	Eric Ludwick	1.33	Doug Linton	56
1999–2000	Chuck Smith	6	Julio Valera	1.97	Eric Ludwick	66
2000–2001	J. D. Arteaga	7	Ricky Bones	1.13	Bubba Hardwick	50
2001–2002	J. C. Romero	6	Jon McDonald	1.72	Hideki Irabu	61
2002–2003	Jeff Wilson	8	Jon Albaladejo	0.68	Doug Linton	56

Puerto Rican Professional Baseball Individual Batting Records (1938–2003)

Category	Name	Record	Date
Batting			
Highest Season Batting Average	Josh Gibson	.480	1941–1942
Highest Career Batting Average	Willard Brown	.347	
	Francisco "Pancho" Coimbre	.339	
Individual .400 Averages	Josh Gibson	.480	1941–1942
	Perucho Cepeda	.465	1938–1939
	Roy Partlow	.443	1940–1941
	Willard Brown	.432	1947–1948
	Francisco "Pancho" Coimbre	.425	1944–1945
	Edgar Martínez	.424	1989–1990
	José Vidro	.417	1998–1999
	Tetelo Vargas	.410	1943–1944
	Luke Easter	.402	1948–1949
Most Batting Titles Won	Willard Brown	3	1946–1947, 1947–1948, 1949–1950
Batting Triple Crowns	Willard Brown	.432, 27 HR, 86 RBI	1947–1948
	Willard Brown	.354, 16 HR, 97 RBI	1949–1950
	Elmo Plaskett	.328, 15 HR, 45 RBI	1960–1961
	Wally Joyner	.356, 14 HR, 48 RBI	1985–1986
	Héctor Villanueva	.347, 12 HR, 44 RBI	1990–1991
Most Runs, Season	Luke Easter	81	1948–1949
Most Hits, Season	Artie Wilson	126	1948–1949
Consecutive Games Hit Streak	Francisco "Pancho" Coimbre	22	1940–1941
Most Doubles, Season	Luis Márquez	27	1946–1947
	Luke Easter	27	1948–1949
Most Triples, Season	Luis Olmo	10	1940–1941
	Quincy Trouppe	10	1941–1942
	Luis Márquez	10	1945–1946
	Luis Márquez	10	1949–1950
Most Home Runs, Season	Willard Brown	27	1947–1948
Most Home Runs, Career	Bob Thurman	120	
Most RBI, Season	Willard Brown	97	1949–1950
Most Stolen Bases, Season	Rickey Henderson	44	1980–1981
Pitching			
Most Games Won, Season	Satchel Paige	19	1939–1940
Lowest ERA, Season	Tom Timmerman	0.88	1967–1968
Most Strikeouts, Season	Satchel Paige	208	1939–1940
First Recorded No-Hit Game	Tomás Quiñónes	Ponce 8, Mayagüez 0	Dec. 3, 1944

Puerto Rican Baseball Hall-of-Fame Inductees (Players)

Name	Highlights
First Induction in Ponce, Oct. 1991	
Luis Ángel "Canena" Márquez	Puerto Rico Winter League batting champion (1954) and cup-of-coffee big leaguer (1951–1954)
Francisco "Pancho" Coimbre	Highest lifetime Puerto Rico Winter League average (.337) by Puerto Rican native and second highest overall
Pedro "Perucho" Cepeda	Winter League and U.S. black-ball barnstorming star of 1930s and 1940s who bypassed U.S. Negro leagues because of racial hostilities
Roberto Clemente	Puerto Rico's greatest baseball star and national hero and also first Latin American inducted into Cooperstown (elected 1973, Special Election)
Robert "El Mucaro" Thurman (USA)	Winter League slugging and pitching star of the 1940s and 1950s; five-season major leaguer
Willard "Ese Hombre" Brown (USA)	Highest lifetime Puerto Rico Winter League batting average (.347); brief major leaguer
Orlando "Peruchin" Cepeda	First Latin American major league home run and RBI champ (1961); Cooperstown Hall of Famer (elected 1999, Veterans Committee)
Victor Pellot "Power"	Big league star of the 1950s in Kansas City and Cleveland, known for fancy fielding at first base
Rubén Gómez	Fastballing right-hander with National League New York and San Francisco Giants who started first West Coast big league game (1958)
Juan "Terin" Pizarro	One of the winningest Latin Americans in major leagues before 1980s, with 131 career victories
Second Induction in Ponce, November 1992	
Luis "Tito" Arroyo	Eight-year big leaguer in 1950s (1955–1963) with 40–32 record; star bullpen ace for New York Yankees in year of Roger Maris's 61 homers
Carlos Bernier	Puerto Rico Winter League hero and brief big leaguer with National League Pittsburgh Pirates (1953)
Pedro Miguel Caratini	Slugging winter season outfielder during the 1920s while playing with original Ponce Lions; also pioneered baseball in Dominican Republic
Saturnino "Nino" Escalera	Puerto Rico Winter League hero and first black ballplayer with National League Cincinnati Reds (1954)
José "El Olímpico" Figueroa	Puerto Rico Winter League hero and Negro league star pitcher of the 1940s
Juan Guilbe	Puerto Rico Winter League hero and memorable Negro leagues pitcher and outfielder of the 1940s
Emilio "Millito" Navarro	Puerto Rico Winter League infielder and outfielder whose winter season career stretched from 1922 until 1942
Rafael "Rafaelito" Ortíz	Top Puerto Rico Winter League pitcher (1938–1948) with career 85–61 record in his native Commonwealth
Luis Rodríguez Olmo	Puerto Rico Winter League hero and decade-long big leaguer (1943–1951) who was second Puerto Rico native to reach the majors
Jorge "Griffin" Tirado	Puerto Rico Winter League hero, 1938–1951, who played on five league champions for the Ponce Lions
Juan Ésteban "Tetelo" Vargas (Dominican Republic)	Puerto Rico Winter League and Dominican League hero (1939–1946) who also starred with Negro National League New York Cubans (1938–1944) and in the Mexican League (1952–1953)

Puerto Rico Amateur National Champions

Year	Team
1940	Piratas
1941	Utuado
1942	Calvert
1943	Naval Air Station
1943	Piratas (Independent League)
1944	Ponce Cubans
1945	Cayey Bar Montañez
1946	Mayagüez Las Mesas
1947	Juncos
1948	Juncos
1949	Mayagüez Las Mesas
1950	Juana Díaz
1951	Humacao
1952	Juncos
1953	Juana Díaz
1954	Fajardo
1955	Santurce
1956	Juana Díaz
1957	Ponce
1958	Coamo
1959	Vega Baja
1960	Vega Alta
1961	Río Grande
1962	Vega Alta
1963	Vega Alta
1964	Juncos
1965	San Sebastián
1966	Aibonito
1967	Bayamón
1968	Río Grande
1969	Aguadilla
1970	Utuado
1971	Manati
1972	Manati
1973	Vega Baja
1974	Sabana Grande
1975	San Lorenzo
1976	Juana Díaz
1977	Cidra
1978	Juana Díaz
1979	Manati
1980	Yabucoa
1981	Sabana Grande
1982	Florida
1983	Juncos
1984	Manati
1985	Juncos
1986	Cayey
1987	Guayama
1988	Juana Díaz
1989	Juncos
1990	Juncos
1991	Juncos

(*continued*)

(continued)

Year	Team
1992	Santa Isabel
1993	Barranquitas
1994	Yabucoa
1995	Yabucoa
1996	Yabucoa
1997	San Lorenzo
1998	Cidra
1999	San Lorenzo
2000	San Lorenzo
2001	San Lorenzo
2002	San Lorenzo

BIBLIOGRAPHY

Bjarkman, Peter C. *Baseball with a Latin Beat: A History of the Latin American Game.* Jefferson, NC, and London: McFarland & Company Publishers, 1994.

———. *Roberto Clemente.* Chelsea House Baseball Legends Series. Philadelphia: Chelsea House Publishers, 1991.

Costa, Rafael. *Enciclopedia Béisbol, Ponce Leones, 1938–1987 (Baseball Encyclopedia, Ponce Lions, 1938–1987).* Santo Domingo, Dominican Republic: Editora Corripio, 1989.

Musick, Phil. *Who Was Roberto? A Biography of Roberto Clemente.* Garden City, New York: Doubleday and Company, 1974.

Van Hyning, Thomas E. *The Santurce Crabbers: Sixty Seasons of Puerto Rican Winter League Baseball.* Jefferson, NC, and London: McFarland & Company Publishers, 1999.

———. *Puerto Rico's Winter League: A History of Major League Baseball's Launching Pad.* Jefferson, NC, and London: McFarland & Company Publishers, 1995.

CHAPTER 7

Mexico

Traditions of Outlaw Baseball

· ·

Latino baseball, like Latin American politics, is largely an arena for overarching personalities; it is most often colorful men who shape the tenor of the game itself rather than the reverse. Mexican baseball history is thus dominated by three towering figures, each in equal parts a phenomenal triumph and a sensational failure. Tycoon Jorge Pasquel failed spectacularly in his grandiose project to bring major league status to a country battling a debilitating two-century-long inferiority complex. Slugger Héctor Espino built his legend in obscurity, blasting home runs on a par with Japan's Sadaharu Oh and America's Babe Ruth and yet remaining virtually unknown beyond his own nation's borders. And pudgy southpaw dervish Fernando Valenzuela captured imaginations both north and south of the border when he single-handedly launched the Latin American big league invasion of the 1980s. Unfortunately, Valenzuela's National League career never quite outstripped his sensational rookie season opening act. Each of these three odd baseball titans has in his own way mightily and ironically contributed to a persistent image of Mexican baseball as irrepressibly "minor league" in stature and overall accomplishment. Mexico even today continues to play out its baseball pageant in relative obscurity, always the poor cousin of the Caribbean baseball family.

If such failures were not enough, there is yet another and more forceful argument against any claim of baseball primacy in Mexico. The land of tacos, Pancho Villa, and Santa Anna is by any measure a country fanatically devoted to the world-dominant sport of *fútbol*—what the British and Americans call soccer. With the additional exception of the United States (where television's NFL version of football and Michael Jordan's NBA basketball have over recent decades pushed the one-time "national pastime" of baseball into the third slot among spectator entertainments), Mexico remains the one land among top baseball nations in which any other professional or amateur sport even comes close to rivaling diamond play as a monolithic national passion. Hockey is king in Canada, but Canada—without its own top-level league pro circuit—has never stood alongside Japan, Cuba, the Dominican Republic, Venezuela, or Puerto Rico as a true baseball hub. It is these last five locales that for most of a century and more have remained the world's handful of most exclusively baseball-devoted outposts. Mexico, like its sprawling neighbor to the north, has always been much more ambivalent about unambiguously embracing baseball as *el rey de los deportes* ("the king of sports").

Mexican League baseball does lay claim, nevertheless, to an impressive and sprawling history. Outside of Cuba, it is Mexico that boasts the longest and most stable tradition for international tournament play, and, after the Americans and Cubans, no one has operated a successful professional league that stretches back any further. Japan comes tantalizingly close in the national league department, having launched its own pro circuit actually one year earlier than the Mexicans—but Japan is a relative latecomer to world tournament play, while the Mexicans have been regularly locking horns with the Cubans, Dominicans, and Venezuelans from as far back as the late-1930s. Even if it remains true that Mexico has always been more of a soccer-crazy land than a first-rank baseball nation, Mexican baseball has also, for seven-plus decades, been an essential part of the nation's sporting fabric.

Crack Mexican ballplayers have long made their marks in amateur baseball circles. The country was an early participant in pioneering world amateur tournaments, even though its teams were usually not very successful on the field during these earliest encounters. In 1926, Mexico City hosted the first-ever Central American Games (at which the Cubans were the only other participant and won all three games that made up the entire competition). In the maiden years of a baseball World Cup competition (at first known as the Amateur World Series), the Mexicans were bronze medalists as early as 1941 and silver medal runner-ups in Havana in 1943; the second-place honor was earned merely by splitting the dozen games the Mexicans played—but that was still a better showing than either the Dominicans or Panamanians could muster. In 1955, Mexico City was also host to the second Pan American Games, at which its own baseball team limped home fourth with again only a break-even record. As a fascinating footnote to the 1955 games, a then-obscure visiting Argentine medical doctor by the name of Ernesto Guevara was hired as a staff photographer for the landmark event by a Latin American news agency known as *Agencia Latina* (now *Prensa Latina*); the same Guevara was later much less obscure under the adopted name Ché.

Mexican major leaguers have usually lagged far behind those of other Latin and Caribbean nations. The country boasts few native sons known widely either to big league fans or Negro league researchers; Jorge Orta or Aurelio Rodríguez will hardly stand comparison with Orestes Miñoso, Orlando Cepeda, Roberto Clemente, or Juan Marichal. When discussion turns to a roster of Mexican major league stars, Fernando Valenzuela has the field largely to himself—but Valenzuela was after all the page-one big league story coming out of all of Latin America during the 1980s. And the Mexican tradition of major leaguers is surprisingly deep, even if relatively few stars have captured the public's fancy.

Beyond the world amateur tournaments and the handful of memorable big leaguers, the Mexican baseball saga boils down to little more than colorful accounts of the three-quarter-century-old Mexican summer league. A more recent innovation, dubbed the winter league or Mexican Pacific League, has sometimes contested the older circuit for primacy, but Mexican winter league baseball is still pretty much a new kid on the block. The older and better established summer league outranks all but the two Cuban circuits (Havana's prerevolution professional league and today's postrevolution amateur *Serie Nacional*) and the Japanese pro leagues in the annals of international baseball. The Mexican League has nonetheless been somewhat diminished through recent decades by its official status as a "minor" league and also by its numerous movements in and out of organized baseball. Headier days were once the norm, back in an era when legendary Negro leaguers from both Cuban and U.S. shores regularly called Mexico's summer circuit their established home. In those proud yesteryears, it was indeed hard to find a league anywhere outside of organized baseball—with the single possible exception of Cuba—more jammed with color and teaming with drama. The Mexican circuit was more stable in many respects than its older Cuban counterpart; it didn't have occasional seasons cancelled like the Havana operation. The Mexican saga eventually peaked with mogul Jorge Pasquel's spectacular failures in his ambitious attempts to elevate Mexican baseball to still greater heights. Pasquel's salvos were aimed directly at the granddaddy American major leagues. For all the self-destruction they eventually rained down upon Mexican League baseball, these events now remain as one of the most intriguing chapters in the entire history of international baseball organizations.

THE STORY OF MEXICAN PROFESSIONAL BASEBALL

The origins in Mexico of *"el rey de los deportes"* remain obscure, and it is difficult, if not almost impossible, to pin down both Mexico's original baseball apostles and the dates or places for the earliest games played on Mexican soil.[1] At least three distinct sites vie for the honor of the country's baseball birthright, and none of them have enough support to stake any exclusive claims. Among leading candidates for the honor seem to be the city of Guaymas, in the state of Sonora; Nuevo Laredo, on the northern frontier of Tamaulipas; and Cadereyta de Jiménez, a small village in the state of Nuevo León. Renowned Mexican baseball historian Pedro Treto Cisneros (*The Mexican League: Comprehensive Player Statistics, 1937–2001*) briefly reviews the scattered evidence now attached to each of these contenders.

For starters, there is convincing documentation that sailors from an American ship (the *Montana*) docked at Guaymas in 1877 and staged a baseball contest witnessed by local residents. Another ship identified as the *USS Newborne* repeated the "baseball visit" only a few months later, and it was not long before there were even reports of local youngsters forming a baseball team of their own. At Nuevo Laredo, a rustic setting close to the U.S. border, it was American railroad construction bosses rather than American sailors who reputedly imported the game. During installation of railroad track and roadbed in Tamaulipas, American foremen were hired on to supervise Mexican day laborers and among them was a baseball *aficionado* named Johnny Tyson; Tyson is said to have held demonstrations of the new sport for interested native construction gangs. A pair of local nines were quickly formed (as legend has it), and the date reported for a first game staged between them is traditionally given as 1877, the very year of baseball's claimed debut in Guaymas.

In another region of Mexico, further to the south, Cubans seem to have been baseball's first apostles. Solid evidence exists that a Spanish war vessel christened *Ciudad Condal* transported a Cuban family named Urzaiz to a Yucatán port (a short sail from Cuban shores) in 1890; the Urzaiz family carried baseball equipment among the children's toys, and games were soon being organized by the recent immigrants that involved numerous youngsters drawn from the local population. Within a span of mere months, the previously unseen game of *béisbol* was rapidly catching hold as a most popular recreational activity among the citizens of Yucatán state.

The final and most persistent claim concerning Mexico's baseball origins comes out of Nuevo León, where the date of July 4, 1889, is commonly cited for the first documented contest witnessed on Mexican soil. Once again, American railroad workers were reportedly involved, and this time the story maintains that when Colonel Treadwell Ayres Robertson granted an Independence Day holiday to *gringo* laborers building a Monterrey–Tampico rail line, the men celebrated with a baseball match adjacent to the railroad station grounds in San Juan, smack on the boundary line with Cadereyta Jiménez County in Nuevo León. Although this final historic game is apparently documented by several sources, its claim to primacy as Mexico's "original" baseball contest is highly dubious, both because of the earlier claims involving Guaymas and because a "Mexico" ball club has been widely reported in other sources to have been founded in the capital city at least as early as 1887. This Mexico City team was an apparent forerunner of several eventual capital city teams bearing the name México (here spelled with the Spanish written accent, to distinguish the teams from the country) that have competed within the country's professional league—the league first founded in 1925 and still surviving down to the present day.

This is the sum and substance of Mexico's murky baseball prehistory. When the subject shifts from native origins to recorded professional competitions, the record isn't any less murky, especially regarding the foundational years of organized league play.

We do know that professional league baseball action debuted in Mexico precisely at the middle of the twentieth century's third decade, with five clubs organized in midsummer of 1925 for the country's inaugural championship tournament. This first formal Mexican summer season was largely the work of a single ambitious sportswriter, employed by the popular magazine *Toros y Deportes* (*Bulls and Sports*), who had returned to the Mexican capital earlier the same year from an American visit that had apparently left him overflowing with enthusiasm for the popular American pastime. Alejandro Aguilar Reyes—known to his readers by the pseudonym "Fray Nano"—had already devoted considerable attention to the thriving amateur baseball movement, by then already spreading like wild fire across Tamaulipas, Sonora, Veracruz, Yucatán, and elsewhere. Matches staged between local Mexican clubs and against visiting U.S. barnstormers were already a common practice. Aguilar Reyes soon approached still another baseball promoter, player, and club sponsor named Ernesto Carmona early in 1925 to explore what both sensed was the potential for an organized Mexican professional season. Carmona proved not only most enthusiastic about the plan but also fortuitously owned a baseball grounds that could serve as a perfect site for launching such a homegrown baseball season.

Carmona first took over the task of organizing and managing a ball club to be known as Agraria, and four other teams were also quickly formed to compete in the first formal season scheduled for that same summer. Fray Nano served as the first president of what was quite naturally labeled simply as the Mexican Baseball League. On the last Sunday of June, the historic first league contest was staged in Carmona's Franco Inglés Park, and it turned out to be a most memorable fourteen-inning classic struggle in which the Mexico club sponsored by Eduardo "Gualo" Ampudia outslugged and outlasted Carmona's own Agraria nine by an action-packed 7–5 score.

Details of the remainder of the first Mexican League season are quite sketchy, and the lack of documented results or team standings would prove the defining feature of the new circuit for most of the first dozen seasons of its existence. Cisneros, in his recent Mexican League encyclopedia, provides a casual summary of what details exist for these earliest seasons, and the account proves quite thin at best. We do know that the México team and another called 74th Regiment tied for first spot in the inaugural season, and a three-game playoff was then held to determine a league champion. Documentation for following seasons is even sketchier, and little exists beyond a list of pennant-winning ball clubs and their captains or managers. Win–loss records even for championship teams are unavailable for most years, and though we have some roster lists, for the most part these contain only family names. There is absolutely nothing in the way of statistical records for individual performers before the 1937 season—which for all practical purposes must therefore be adopted as the first year of a more or less fully documented Mexican League operation.

Facts can be gleaned from the earliest seasons of Mexican League action, even if these are more often the flimsy items of barroom trivia than the hard facts of genuine documentation. Games were held only on weekends during the first half-dozen or so seasons, and the third and fourth campaigns (1927 and 1928) reportedly began as early as January and were already over by midsummer. A particularly hard-fought three-game championship playoff was held in September 1929 between teams named Adams Chiclets and Delta "A." The star performer was a pitcher named Augusto Ascorve, who hurled two victories for the Chiclets ("Gummers," as they were called in local press accounts), including a 1–0 deciding masterpiece in which he himself scored the lone tally. That same year also saw the first league nine-man all-star team named at year's end, with unheralded American Charles Cortizzos selected as top pitcher. The 1935 season may have been the best, stretching from mid-June to early December and often interrupted for popular exhibitions in Mexico City between league clubs (especially one called Aztecas, operated by Homobono Márquez) and visiting barnstormers from both Cuba and the U.S. Negro leagues circuit. The most notable landmark of all, however, may have been a first-ever no-hitter tossed by Cuban immortal Martín Dihigo in 1937—quite fortuitously and fortunately the first year of detailed record keeping.

The period falling between 1925 and 1936, though somewhat better documented than the sport's nineteenth-century origins south of the Rio Grande, is still very much a part of Mexican baseball's lengthy prehistory. It remains an epoch laced with colorful legends, rarely substantiated with raw facts or numbers. It has become standard practice to divide Mexican League history into three distinct epochs. The first, or foundational, period runs from the first campaign of 1925 through the beginning of the 1940s and encompasses the first decade and a half of league competitions. It was an era in which most teams were reinforced with imported ballplayers, usually American Negro leaguers and especially legendary Cubans such as Martín Dihigo, Lázaro Salazar, Brujo Rosell, and Agustín Bejerano. The vital Cuban connection would remain strong throughout the 1940s with such memorable figures as Ramón Bragaña, Lino Donoso, Roberto Ortiz, Manuel "Cocaína" García, and the unrelated Silvio García. But the Cuban flavor of the Mexican League had already been at its height in the years preceding the outbreak of World War II.

A second phase of Mexican League history comprises the chaotic decade of the 1940s. This phase is intimately tied to the activities of the wealthy Pasquel brothers, especially dynamic millionaire ball club owner Jorge Pasquel, easily one of the most unforgettable figures in Mexican baseball annals. During this topsy-turvy era, Pasquel single-handedly tried to convert the Mexican League into a full-fledged big league operation that could compete on equal footing with the vaunted U.S. major leagues. Pasquel owned a team of his own, but his passion was league-wide and his Veracruz Azules (Blues) thus never did totally dominate league competition. The idea Pasquel had in mind was that of elevating talent across the entire league, not just for a single club; he was driven by motives that were highly nationalistic and stretched far beyond a mere passion for baseball alone. (The Pasquel story and the questions it generates are explored more fully in their own section, later in this chapter.) It was a project doomed in the end to certain failure. But for a few exciting summers the lavish spending and bold ballplayer raids orchestrated by Pasquel nearly pulled off a seemingly impossible pie-in-the-sky dream of Mexican baseball supremacy.

The final phase of Mexican League history was launched only after the sudden death of Jorge Pasquel in 1955; it consisted of steady-handed rebuilding of league fortunes under the capable direction of a new league management. The leadership change itself had come on the heels of a depression in league fortunes during the early 1950s, which in turn had predictably followed an expected collapse of Pasquel's grandiose plans for expansion. (Pasquel himself had given up the league's reins in 1951 once his own club finally won a championship.) The decades of the 1960s and 1970s, especially, were a heady period of league-wide prosperity, which included growth to as many as twenty teams by the close of the 1970s. During the 1960s, league management began to focus more intensely on the development of the native Mexican ballplayer, leading to an eventual minor surge in homegrown stars such as slugger Héctor Espino and future big leaguers Aurelio Rodríguez, Jorge Orta, and Francisco Barrios. A dreadful players strike interrupted the 1980 season and resulted in financial collapse for several league franchises, but since then growth has once again been steady across two decades. Visits by big league clubs for lucrative exhibitions and regular-season games in the late 1990s also renewed awareness of the Mexican League among North American baseball fans, who had unfortunately paid very little attention over most of the league's prior seven-decade history.

The Mexican League has been particularly famed as a refuge for imported players, most especially Negro stars from both Cuba and the United States. Martín Dihigo was perhaps the most renowned among early foreigners performing in Mexico and indeed may be the most legendary figure in the entire span of Mexican baseball history.

Arriving on the scene in 1937—fortuitously the first campaign in which league operatives maintained detailed individual player records—Dihigo starred as both ace pitcher and slugging outfielder until the end of the 1940s. He compiled a .676 winning percentage on the mound that still stands as the best-ever for a long-term Mexican League pitcher; he won 119 games, including 22 in the 1942 season; and at the same time he also batted at a .317 clip over the same 11 seasons. Dihigo was both a league batting champion and pitching all-star and once remarkably led the circuit in both hitting and ERA during the same summer. It was that 1938 campaign that became Dihigo's primary calling card; in that one season he was both the champion batsman and champion pitcher—an unlikely if not unparalleled double. Never, in fact, has a player enjoyed a finer season anywhere in professional baseball. (If Babe Ruth was superior as both slugger and hurler, he never was so in one and the same pennant chase.) And a single season earlier Dihigo had also earned considerable fame by tossing the league's first-ever no-hitter.

Cuban icon Martín Dihigo was the Mexican League's first great pitching and batting star. [Author's Cuban Collection]

Two additional Cuban pitchers, righty Ramón Bragaña and southpaw Lázaro Salazar, made equally big splashes in the Mexican League during the same early epoch graced by Dihigo. Bragaña indeed earned more plaudits in Mexico than in his own homeland (where he won only 47 games as a pro), laboring for 18 seasons and compiling a victory total of 212 that still places him seventh on the all-time Mexican League career list. The Havana native and owner of a wicked curve and hair-raising control is also the only pitcher ever to post 30 wins in a single season in Mexico, turning the trick in 1944 for Veracruz. "The Professor" was an early inductee to the Mexican Hall of Fame in Monterrey and must be included in any list of the top four or five pitchers ever to perform in Mexican professional baseball. Lázaro Salazar ("The Prince of Belén") was another two-way player like Dihigo; he was nearly as effective in Mexico in the 1940s as he was season after season back on the island of Cuba. Salazar won 112 games as a Mexican Leaguer and also compiled a .334 career batting mark over fifteen seasons as a slick first sacker and durable if not overly swift outfielder. (Roberto González Echevarría, in *The Pride of Havana*, points out that it was a fair assessment to consider Salazar a true left-handed Dihigo, even if he was a bit less powerful at bat and more limited in versatility as a lefty.)

Other Cubans contributed heavily, especially during the 1940s. Rangy if lead-footed and lead-gloved outfielder Claro Duany walked off with successive batting crowns in 1945 and 1946 while patrolling the pastures for Monterrey; Alejandro Crespo (who, González Echevarría reports, was once called the greatest Cuban League outfielder ever by nonpareil Cuban sportswriter Fausto Miranda) batted .320 across the entire decade with four different clubs. Silvio García wrote smaller legends on the mound and in the infield, again paralleling achievements on his home island; as a hurler he enjoyed but a single spectacular Mexican season in 1938, with Aguila (10–2, 1.68 ERA), yet batted .335 over seven campaigns as a shortstop and third baseman. And crafty ace Manuel "Cocaína" García (unrelated to Silvio) was equally as dazzling during the same World War II era, winning 19 games in 1942 and 18 games three seasons later. In 1966, a less heralded Cuban import, José Ramón López, achieved a dazzling single-season strikeout standard of 309, which left him the only hurler ever to fan as many as three hundred batters in a single Mexican professional campaign.

American blacks also had considerable impact south of the border in seasons surrounding World War II. Burnis "Wild Bill" Wright emerged as one of the most popular and certainly most productive ballplayers on the Mexican circuit during the early 1940s. Showing great offensive versatility, the fleet but powerful center fielder paced the league in doubles his first season on the scene in 1940; a summer later, he was not only batting champion but also topped the circuit in stolen bases. That same season, he was followed in the batting race by a pair of fellow American black legends, Cooperstown infielder Ray Dandridge ("Mamerto" to Mexicans) and all-universe catcher Josh Gibson. But it was in 1943 that Wright made his true splash by capturing a Mexican League triple crown, gaining that rare honor when he edged Dandridge in the batting race (.366 to .354) and nipped future Dodgers Hall of Famer Roy Campanella in the home run derby (13 to 12). Not to be outdone, however, Dandridge himself also carved a special niche in Mexico with his own several runs at the batting title; he captured the honor during his final season of 1948 and came close on a couple of other occasions, finishing behind Wright (1943) and Duany (who nipped him at the wire in 1945). Josh Gibson was also a brief force in the Mexican League, whaling the ball at .467 and .374 in his only two years on the scene; but black baseball's greatest catcher and slugger never reached the heights in Mexico that he achieved during summer sessions up north.

There were also some less canonized American blacks who became immortals and near-immortals in Mexico and even outstripped Dandridge, Wright, and Gibson in their ultimate stature there. Perhaps the most remarkable outfielder in Mexican annals was an otherwise forgotten American, Alfred Pinkston, a 215-pound black bomber who played only briefly and rather unspectacularly on the U.S. Negro circuit before finding his true home in the Mexican League. Among hitters at least, Pinkston (a strapping lefty swinger from Alabama) was the greatest foreign import ever. Not launching his Mexican League career until he had reached 40 years of age, Pinkston nonetheless managed to walk off with four consecutive batting crowns at the outset of the 1960s and retired after seven seasons with the highest league cumulative batting mark on record. Outfielder Jimmy Collins—a struggling .279 minor league hitter over a half-dozen summers—was yet another sensational import from Dixie (this time Mississippi) who posted spectacular campaigns in the late 1970s and also throughout much of the 1980s. Collins hit at a lofty .354 clip for his decade-plus exile career and captured batting crowns on three different occasions.

In the modern era, the Mexican League has also boasted numerous heroes of a strictly homegrown variety. Slugging first sacker Héctor Espino stood in the vanguard and might well be the best ballplayer Mexico has yet produced. Espino's personal decision to practice his diamond trade at home (after abandoning a brief early trial with AAA Jacksonville) left him a mystery man to fans in the rest of the baseball-playing world, much like recent Cuban star Omar Linares, who peaked in the 1990s, a decade after Espino. For Mexicans themselves, however, any debate concerning baseball talent or remarkable on-field performance begins and ends with Chihuahua-born Héctor Espino. Across three decades, Espino stood atop the league's rolls, season after season, in at least some if not most categories for heavy hitting. When he retired after 1984, he virtually owned the Mexican League record book in all departments that had to do with slugging. Today his records are slowly being eclipsed, and he has slid from the top spots on most career achievement lists; his sudden death of a heart attack in September 1997 (he was barely 58) seemed all the more incredible in light of the rugged durability of an athlete whose batting prowess seemed so unassailable for almost a quarter-century. Espino's legend endures, undiminished by the mere passage of time.

There have been still other slugging and hurling legends of only slightly lesser renown. Pitchers of rare note certainly include Ramón Arano, Miguel Solis, and Vicente Romo. Diminutive Arano won 334 games in the Mexican League (but never 20 in a season) and more than 400 when his Mexican Pacific League winter-season ledger is included as part of his remarkable resumé. More stunning still is the fact that the 5'8" right-hander toiled for 31 seasons, the final two coming after a decade of retirement when he was pushing 60 years of age. Arano is as easily compared with Satchel Paige in this regard as with Nolan Ryan or Jesse Orosco. Solis (1972–1989) was also a durable 200-game winner, who once enjoyed a 25–5 season (in 1979 with Saltillo, when he logged a 1.84 ERA) and rang up 11 campaigns with double-figure winning totals. Romo is better known to big league fans than Solis but is even more of a true legend back home. An eight-season break-even pitcher with five big league clubs, the feisty righty was a true record-buster down south, boasting the lowest-ever career ERA (2.49) and a number-three slot on the all-time list for shutouts, at 52.

In Mexico, it is the sluggers who always seem to write the biggest headlines. Andrés Mora was one Mexican heavy hitter familiar to at least a smattering of North American fans. Only a role player during four seasons in Baltimore and Cleveland, Mora was a shoo-in Hall of Famer back home with numbers that put him in the career top ten for homers (third, trailing only Nelson Barrera and Héctor Espino), base hits (sixth, with 2,259), and RBI (fourth, with 1,498). Ramón Montoya (known fittingly as *"El Diablo"* for both his tenacious play and long-time ball club affiliation) was a stellar defender in center field for the Mexico City Red Devils from the mid-1960s until 1980 and slugged above the .300 mark in all but three of his 15 stellar campaigns. Such other memorable performers as Miguel Suárez, Matías Carrillo, and Lázaro Acosta are equally household names among even casual Mexican fans. Acosta debuted at age 30 and then hit .300-plus for eight straight campaigns. Carrillo (veteran of 107 big league games) has recently written his name in the record book with his penchant for consistent hitting (running his string of .300-plus season past 15). And Nelson Barrera also claimed his rightful spot atop the heap of Mexican slugging immortals as the new all-time home run king (passing Espino at the end of a 25-year career) before a recent sad accident snuffed out his life even before his active playing days had completely wound down.

When it comes to individual ball clubs rather than individual players, the Mexico City *Diablos Rojos* and the Monterrey *Sultanes* seemingly boast the greatest traditions and the most rabid fan followings. The Red Devils carry a tradition that stretches back all the way to the founding years of Mexican professional baseball, although they didn't claim a first league pennant until 1956 (under the tutelage of Cuban manager Lázaro Salazar). Since then, the Devils have captured fourteen league championships, with half coming in the past two decades and the most recent pair during 2002 and 2003. In recent years, the popular club from the capital city has enjoyed a number of pitched pennant battles versus the crosstown Mexico City Tigers, also pennant winners on eight separate occasions. Monterrey has owned league championships an identical eight times, four under the banner of *Industriales* and four sporting the current club logo of *Sultanes*. The Sultans have been a top contender especially in recent campaigns, winning three banners across the 1990s and reaching the playoff semifinals in two of the past three summers. Since construction of their new state-of-the-art ballpark in 1990, the Monterrey Sultans arguably qualify as Mexico's true showcase professional franchise.

A special season of landmark proportions unfolded in 2001, an extraordinary campaign in which records fell by unprecedented proportions. The pennant chase itself was a memorable one, contested between teams from the capital city, with the Tigers besting the Red Devils in an emotional playoff series marked by a spate of high-scoring shootouts. The true highlight moments came with more individual batting displays. Veteran big leaguer Julio Franco from the Dominican Republic rang up one of the top Mexican League batting averages ever when he banged the ball at a season-long .437 clip. More important to native Mexican fans, the often overlooked Nelson Barrera at long last eclipsed Héctor Espino's most cherished record; now doubling as Oaxaca manager in his 25th season, Barrera stroked homer number 454 in the final contest of the season's first-half split schedule. It was a moment parallel to Hank Aaron overtaking Babe Ruth. Two other hitters, Daniel Fernández (Red Devils center fielder) and Matías Carrillo (Tigers first baseman), also chased down Espino in the Mexican League record book, with Fernández scoring his 1,506th run (to unseat Espino) but failing to extend his record-tying 14 straight seasons of .300 hitting when he slumped in the end to .290. Carrillo would gain his own most important niche a single season later, when he stretched his own streak of .300-plus seasons to 15; Carrillo, whose Mexican career was twice interrupted for short stints in the majors, has never hit under .300 back home and (as of this writing) his string continues.

The AAA-level Mexican League has remained a centerpiece for the nation's pro baseball scene, but diamond-based action has in fact been a year-round sport in Mexico for decades. The Mexican Pacific League has long been the showcase venue for winter league play, with its own traditions stretching back to an inaugural 1945–1946 season. There have actually been three versions of the circuit: the Mexican Pacific Coast League (1945–1958, 13 seasons), the Winter League of Sonora (1959–1970, 12 seasons), and the current Mexican Pacific League (1971–2003, 33 campaigns and still counting). It is the Mexican Pacific League that each February provides Mexico's entry for the celebrated Caribbean series, which matches champions of winter league circuits from Mexico, Venezuela, Puerto Rico, and the Dominican Republic in a week-long round-robin playdown for international professional bragging rights. Over the years, the November-to-January league has boasted anywhere from six to a dozen teams and has occasionally featured two divisions and a season split into first and second half campaigns (leading to postseason games to decide the championship). Hermosillo, Culiacán, Los Mochis, and Mazatlán have usually reigned as the circuit's showcase cities.

The Mexican Pacific League also boasts plenty of ballplayer legends of its own. Héctor Espino, for one, padded his summer AAA action with winter seasons, played mostly with the Hermosillo team, and his winter slugging feats proved every bit as spectacular as his summer lumber displays. The first sacker with the perfect swing claimed 13 winter batting titles; these included six straight over one stretch, along with three triple crown honors. Other Mexican League summer stars also continued to perform during winter campaigns. In the 1960s and 1970s, the Pacific League drew high-profile major leaguers and top minor leaguers from the United States, as seasoned professionals sought winter tune-ups or lucrative extra paychecks or both—and always some fading big leaguers found badly needed homes here in their efforts to extend careers on life-support that they simply could not force themselves to abandon. Minnie Miñoso was one of these refugees, winning a couple of Mexican Pacific League batting titles while already in his late forties. The list of big leaguers who have captured batting crowns in this circuit includes John Kruk, Davie Hollins, Canada's Matt Stairs, Ty Gainey, and Dimitri Young. Native Mexican big league hurlers of the stature of Vicente Romo, Teddy Higuera, Vicente Palacios, Fernando Valenzuela, and Sid Monge have also tuned up here during the major league off-season.

Like the other top baseball playing countries with histories in the sport stretching over most of the past century, Mexico claims its own national shrine of immortals where the game's past glories and traditions are celebrated in the proper tourist-enticing museum atmosphere. Mexico's Baseball Hall of Fame finds most of its enshrined members among homegrown champions of the professional game played within the country's borders, as well as a sprinkling of inductees chosen from the considerable inventory of visiting stars from neighboring nations. Foremost among the imports are the handful of Cuban greats who dominated league play during the earliest decades. The biggest displays, of course, are for native phenoms representing the highest pride of Mexico's native baseball legacy.

If the Mexican *Salón de Fama* seems little more than a small-scale knock-off of the true granddaddy shrine of professional baseball in Cooperstown, the parallels are more than merely superficial. Mexico's hall inducted its first class of immortals back in 1939, meaning that it traces its origins back exactly as far as the Cooperstown landmark—but the Mexicans didn't actually get around to constructing a physical plant to house their memorabilia and entertain visiting tourists until 1973, almost thirty-five years later. When an adequate museum building for a national shrine of heroes was belatedly erected, it was located fittingly in Monterrey, on the grounds of the Cuauntémoc Brewery. This was a natural choice, for Monterrey boasts perhaps the strongest claims to being at least the mythical home of Mexico's first reported baseball contest, thus providing still another unaccidental parallel with the cousin institution in Cooperstown.

Past legends of Mexican baseball therefore have their own fitting pantheon, and yet this small-scale shrine located on brewery grounds in Monterrey enjoys neither the pastoral setting nor the lush tourist trade of its Cooperstown inspiration. Mexico's "Hall" was actually inaugurated with a nationwide newspaper poll selecting Mexican greats back in 1939—an event staged to honor Cooperstown's own grand opening that same summer. Mexico's *Salón* not surprisingly shares a few black-ball icons with its Cooperstown counterpart—Roy Campanella, Josh Gibson, Cuba's Martín Dihigo, Monte Irvin, and Ray Dandridge. And one can also wander its limited halls and discover that black American unknown Alfred Pinkston somehow hit .372 during the late 1950s below the Rio Grande to post the highest career average in Mexican history, or that a decade earlier a more celebrated American black, Burnis "Wild Bill" Wright, carved out his own special niche as the "Black DiMaggio" of resounding Mexican fame.

Like Mexican baseball itself, however, Mexico's *Salón de Fama* in the end seems to be quite "minor league," if not "bush league," in both appearance and genuine baseball atmosphere. Perhaps this results in large part because among 82 ballplayers, managers, umpires, and sportswriters on display in its halls, the standout figure in the opinion of even the museum's director and staff is the great Cuban Martín Dihigo. It is as though Sadaharu Oh or Juan Marichal and not Babe Ruth or Walter Johnson or Christy Mathewson was the most treasured resident of hallowed Cooperstown. The Mexican equivalent to Abner Doubleday—at least by the institution's own accounting—appears to be American army colonel Treadwell Ayres Robertson (who, as legend has it, launched the reputed landmark match alongside fresh-laid tracks of the Monterrey–Tampico railway). Among the most prominent displays of the entire shrine is the bat with which Veracruz native Roberto "Beto" Ávila won an American League batting crown back in 1954 to become Mexico's first genuine big league star and record-setter. From first to last, the emphasis here is strongly on the symbiotic relationship between American and Mexican baseball history. If the Mexican Hall of Fame presents an argument through many of its displays that baseball is truly the "Game of the Americas" and not just an imported "American" game, that entire argument feels a bit more tenuous in Mexico than it does in Cuba or almost anywhere else throughout the Caribbean hotbed of Latin American baseball playing nations.

Jorge Pasquel and Mexico's War on Organized Baseball

The popular account of Jorge Pasquel's brazen postwar raid on big league rosters is one of the most familiar pieces of Latin baseball fact and folklore. The facts, to be sure, are familiar enough even to the game's most casual historians. It is the true motives and eventual strategies of the audacious Mexican mogul and promoter that still generate considerable controversy more than a half-century later.

Did Pasquel in 1946 and 1947 raid the U.S. majors in a selfish and overly ambitious effort to put Mexican professional baseball squarely on the map alongside the Cuban and North American circuits? Or was the entire episode merely an ostentatious display of personal power and an effort at base self-aggrandizement? Or is there some truth to various reports that Pasquel's grabbing at American ballplayers was connected with an underhanded effort to buy an upcoming presidential election for Miguel Alemán, a personal friend and benefactor of the powerful Pasquel family? Jorge Pasquel's deepest motives undoubtedly perished with their author in the March 1955 plane crash that snuffed out his flamboyant life. A reasonable explanation for events might suggest that both national and personal pride motivated the "Mexican baseball wars" far more than did any economic or political profit for Pasquel and his allies. One thing alone is certain: the whole sorry mess largely doomed both immediate and long-range futures for a once solvent circuit.

Jorge Pasquel, the Mexican mogul who challenged the major league monopoly after World War II. [Transcendental Graphics]

Some additional facts are plain enough. Jorge Pasquel was a wealthy Veracruz entrepreneur who, along with his brothers, rode herd over an expanding business empire built originally from their father's profitable cigar factory and customs brokerage firm. By the mid-1940s, it was estimated that the Pasquel family fortune numbered in the tens of millions of dollars and that much of this still-exploding revenue had been earned through Jorge's own astute (and quite often illegal) business dealings. By this same time, Pasquel and his brothers had already bought controlling interest in the Mexican League's Veracruz Blues and held at least partial ownership of several other league ball clubs. Pasquel's sway over Mexican League affairs crystallized when he was named president of the eight-team circuit (then consisting of Veracruz, Monterrey, Tampico, Torreón, Puebla, San Luis Potosí,

Nuevo Laredo, and Mexico City) in time for the 1946–1947 summer season. Pasquel's interest in Mexican baseball certainly seemed genuine enough; he had been a sandlot player as a youth and loved to take batting practice with the Veracruz club he directed. Like George Steinbrenner and dozens of modern big league club owners, Jorge Pasquel was apparently living out the fantasy of ball club ownership enjoyed by more than one wealthy businessman in possession of the ultimate grown boy's toy chest.

The newly installed Mexican League president was a man driven by nationalistic fervor and perhaps also by a smoldering hatred of *Yanqui* imperialist interests (fueled in large part by U.S. marine bombardments of Veracruz during his early childhood). His own personal retaliation against these Yankee affronts would soon come in the form of a clever if impractical plan to build the then prosperous Mexican League into a full-fledged rival for the major league circuits operating far to the north. Drawing upon some of the best among the black Cuban and American talent banned from organized baseball, Mexican baseball had begun to thrive during World War II years, at the very time when the majors suffered temporarily from severe wartime talent drains. Pasquel's influence and clever power-brokering was first apparent as early as 1943, when he arranged U.S. draft deferments for Negro league stars Theolic Smith and Quincy Trouppe, thus freeing them for Mexican League play. The Mexican business tycoon arranged these deferments by promising Washington a loan of 80,000 Mexican laborers to assist in worker-starved American war-industry efforts.

Further respectability was seized for Mexican baseball in 1944 and 1945, when Hall-of-Fame slugger Rogers Hornsby (just tabbed for Cooperstown in 1942) was lured south as a manager, and several lesser Latino big leaguers (among them Cuban catcher Sal "Chico" Hernández of the Chicago Cubs and Cuban pitcher Tomás de la Cruz of the Cincinnati Reds) also took their modest ballplaying talents southward. Encouraged by this small reverse migration of Latin American talent, Pasquel invested $285,000 in personal funds to tour big league and minor league facilities stateside for a firsthand look in 1944. It was this closer exposure to tempting opportunities that apparently hatched a scheme for throwing plenty of raw dollars (which the Pasquel clan certainly had) at ballplaying talent north of the border, in a full-blown effort to turn the Mexican circuit overnight into a rival third major league.

By 1946, Pasquel had decided to launch his full-scale raids on the majors. Among players seduced into abandoning big league status for truckloads of Mexican pesos were St. Louis Cardinals pitcher Max Lanier, Giants hurler Sal Maglie and infielder George Hausmann, Brooklyn catcher Mickey Owen, much-traveled slugger Lou Klein, colorful if inept Cuban outfielder Roberto Ortiz of the Washington Senators, and several dozen rather less talented but nonetheless seasoned major leaguers. Major League Commissioner Albert "Happy" Chandler—himself new to the scene—was quick to respond to such outrageous Mexican inroads by announcing lifetime bans against all ballplayers who departed for Pasquel's Mexican circuit, a ban which at least several dozen underpaid major leaguers were apparently well prepared to accept in exchange for promised earnings in Mexico. One potential highly prized recruit who did not rise to the lure was future Hall of Famer Stan Musial, of the 1944

World Champion St. Louis Cardinals. Pasquel's agents are widely rumored to have laid $50,000 in hard cash on Musial's spring training hotel room bed in St. Petersburg, Florida; whatever the true amount offered, it was not nearly sufficient to lure Stan the Man from his then-lofty $13,000-a-year perch in the St. Louis outfield.

Negro leaguers with little to lose by abandoning skimpy barnstorming deals back home proved far easier targets. Pasquel was no fool, and he wisely built his recruiting base with talented pitchers most likely to improve league quality almost instantly. Among the haul of American blacks were Chet Brewer (who returned to the Mexico City Devils in 1944, after earlier stints in the late 1930s), Raymond "Jabao" Brown (double-figure winner four straight times in the 1940s), and Leon Day (three-season ace with Veracruz and later Mexico City). Even bigger catches were a number of front-line Cubans who boasted either big league credentials (Adrian Zabala, New York Giants; Tommie de la Cruz, Cincinnati Reds; René Monteagudo, Washington Senators) or substantial Negro league reputations (Silvio García, Cocaína García, Lázaro Salazar).

A major motivation for Pasquel's raids on organized baseball talent may have been the upcoming presidential campaign faced by his business partner and childhood pal, Miguel Alemán. Alemán's election promised a windfall of preferential treatment for Pasquel's business interests, and any bolstering of big-time baseball by the Alemán–Pasquel camp could not fail to impress a baseball-crazed Mexican electorate. Lanier would later complain that such politicking was indeed squarely behind the entire scheme, and that furthermore, once Alemán had won the 1946 election, Pasquel began reneging everywhere on his promised contracts. Fabulous salaries tendered to imported players were cut by as much as half. The actual fact of the matter may only have been that Pasquel, for all his wealth, had largely overcommitted himself and was suddenly fresh out of pocket money to throw willy-nilly at baseball. No capital upgrades for the country's ancient stadiums had accompanied the high-priced player talent, the Mexican population for all its reported fervor was not large enough to support a big-time circuit, and gate revenues simply did not offset bloated player payrolls. In short, within a year after the arrival of Lanier, Owen, Hausmann, and company, the Mexican League began to self-destruct.

The U.S. talent flow was more like a trickle and was short-lived; it was completely ineffectual in launching anything like major league status. Dollar losses for the league were reported to be close to $400,000 for the 1947 and 1948 campaigns alone; league management was in disarray; the eight-team circuit crumbled to four franchises by July 1948, with all games held in Mexico City, which possessed the only sufficient fan population; players (North Americans and Cubans) left in droves; and by September 1948 the league had collapsed completely. Embarrassed big leaguers like Lanier and Maglie and Owen returned meekly home to find (to their relief) that the Commissioner's threatened lifetime ban fortunately had more bark behind it than true bite. Lanier served a mere one-year suspension and returned to the St. Louis Cardinals in 1949, although his career was now largely behind him; Maglie was back in the Polo Grounds by 1950, just in time to lead the National League in winning percentage; Mickey Owen was also back in uniform with the Chicago Cubs in 1949 and hung around the big leagues another half-dozen seasons.

Héctor Espino: Mexico's Babe Ruth

With the collapse of Pasquel's ambitious scheme came a parallel collapse of any grandiose dreams for a Mexican baseball tradition on a par with that in Cuba or the United States. That lofty dream would never materialize, despite total reorganization of the Mexican League after 1949 (with entirely new management, though Pasquel did retain his interests in the Veracruz ball club right up until his sudden death in 1955). Ironically, it was only months after Pasquel's passing that the Mexican League was fully accepted into the family of organized baseball as a sanctioned minor league circuit. Mexican baseball would continue to be largely provincial, however, with its stars and its events barely known beyond the borders of the country itself. This would continue even after the sudden and complete demise of Cuban professional baseball only a few years later and even after the arrival of Latin American talents such as Clemente, Marichal, Cepeda, and Pérez put Caribbean island and coastal nations squarely on the baseball map for hordes of American major league fans.

If Mexican baseball became more isolated after the early 1950s, it did still manage to produce two great heroes whose ballplaying feats became truly legendary both inside and outside Mexico. One talented native son burst on the scene nearly overnight after being blessed with an unexpected offer to head north and seek fortune and fame in big league ballparks. Screwball-throwing Fernando Valenzuela carried the Mexican banner so proudly in the early 1980s that he almost overshadowed all others from the growing Latin arena for an all-too-brief span of a half-dozen seasons. A second noteworthy Mexican star chose a far different path; nearly two decades earlier, a native son of Chihuahua with a booming bat had decided to remain sequestered at home and thus shun the limelight of the majors. His exploits are consequently not nearly so universally celebrated as those of Valenzuela. Yet for fans of Tijuana or Monterrey or Mexico City, the name of Héctor Espino is still easily the most magical Mexican baseball name of all.

Espino may well have been one of the game's greatest natural hitters. The stocky right-handed muscleman slugged home runs and posted batting averages across a 24-year career (1962–1984) that suggest he would surely have been a major league star of grandest proportions (see table containing Espino's career highlights at chapter's end). But no one ever knew much about Espino very far beyond the borders of Monterrey and Tijuana. Because he did not choose to appear in the majors when the opportunity arose, his legend will always remain generally suspect and his achievements will be overlooked or dismissed as somehow illegitimate. When Espino began slugging homers at a record clip in 1962 (one season after Yankee Roger Maris matched Babe Ruth), he was apparently doing so in tiny Mexican ballparks against inconsistent Mexican League pitching—AAA-caliber at best. And he was doing so without the headlines that cement legends in the North American sporting press. The fate of Espino thus largely parallels that of Japan's Sadaharu Oh or Cuba's Omar Linares, or even that of great Negro leaguers such as Cristóbal Torriente or Martín Dihigo in a previous generation, who also never played in the big time and thus were never credited with much legitimacy in the documented public record.

Héctor Espino's story is of course quite different from that of banned black Cubans like Dihigo or Torriente or the elder Luis Tiant. No onerous or immoral rules of on-field and off-field segregation slammed the doors of big league stardom on Espino. Rather, it was a matter of personal pride that kept Mexico's biggest attraction on the sidelines of pro baseball's prime venue. Espino, in his surprising decision to stay home once big league opportunity knocked squarely on his door, was similar in spirit to many of his fellow Latin Americans, equally distinguished by a proud sense of Latino dignity. The difference is that other rebels, such as Clemente and Cepeda, or Felipe Alou and George Bell, took their battles for personal respect smack into the center of the big league stage itself. Héctor Espino chose to play by an entirely different set of rules.

In the early 1960s, Espino was already being touted as a valued big league commodity. If North American fans knew nothing of his earliest exploits, the same could not be said for the big league bird dogs snooping around in Latin ports of call. The promising Mexican prospect was first scouted by the Dodgers, then signed by former Cuban Sugar Kings owner Bobby Maduro. Espino even had a brief cup of coffee in the minors when he played in 32 games with the 1964 Jacksonville Suns of the International League, posting a respectable short-term average of exactly .300 but banging only three round-trippers in 100 official at-bats. The prized Mexican recruit was not at all happy with the life of a U.S. minor leaguer, however, and had little motivation to return after his late-season debut in Jacksonville. Maduro would later report that it was largely an issue of homesickness and clashes of culture. In Maduro's assessment (quoted in a 1985 *Sport* magazine article penned by Leo Banks) Espino simply "couldn't adjust to things here, the food, the manner of living, anything." Other sources suggest that the real issue was the young slugger's horror of the incidents of racial discrimination he regularly encountered during his month-long sojourn in northern Florida. The whole experience seems only to foreshadow an equally inhospitable minor league road traveled by Toronto Blue Jays recruit George Bell (from the Dominican Republic) in hinterland Montana only a decade later.

Briefly put, Espino simply could not adjust and he seemed to look for any excuse not to continue. That excuse came almost immediately when his contract was sold to the St. Louis Cardinals and he thus fell subject to the same conditions as other Mexican League prospects plucked by teams based in the United States. Espino would receive a regular contract from the Cardinals, but his signing bonus (several thousand dollars) went directly to the Monterrey club owner. This was a long-standing agreement, first established between big league clubs and Mexican League officials after Pasquel's "player raids" had abruptly ended and a reconstituted Mexican circuit (AAA) had joined the ranks of organized baseball in the middle 1950s. Espino saw it only as ruthless exploitation. He demanded 10 percent of the signing bonus from Monterrey boss Anuar Canavati; when Canavati denied the request, Espino flatly refused to report for his Cardinals minor league reassignment. He would play for the hated Canavati in Monterrey, if necessary, but would not endure minor league bus rides in a hostile foreign land. Later Espino repeatedly claimed that he would have come back to the United States had he been more fairly compensated—but it seems like Espino's true desire was always to be a larger-than-life baseball icon back in his native homeland, rather than a possibly wealthy but always isolated and abused mercenary somewhere abroad.

For all the American dollars that dream may have cost him, the one-man protest bore substantial fruit on at least one count: there is no denying Espino became a larger-than-life hero on home turf. Over the next two decades, Héctor Espino reached new heights with each passing summer in the Mexican League, playing eventually with teams in Tampico and San Luis Potosí, as well as in Monterrey, where his career began and ended. He also tore up the winter-ball Mexican Pacific League each December and January. Espino would end up claiming five Mexican League batting titles (1964, 1966–1968, 1972) and four home run crowns (1964, 1968–1969, 1972). Just like Hank Aaron's, his homers mounted up over a quarter-century of consistency and longevity. Espino's total eventually reached 763 for combined summer and winter league play; his total of 453 Mexican Summer League round-trippers long stood as the minor league career record, and his 46 homers in 1964 remained a durable league record for 22 seasons.

Espino thus left a legacy quite comparable to that of Babe Ruth, Hank Aaron, or Willie Mays in the big leagues or Sadaharu Oh (professional baseball's all-time home run champion) in the Japanese leagues. In the process, he lived the comfortable (and comforting) life of a hometown hero with a more-than-modest income and the lasting adulation of his nation's fans, even if he had to sacrifice the potential glamour of big-time international baseball stardom. Today, many of Espino's records have fallen, and others are under immediate challenge, but the name and the legend nonetheless live on, every bit as indelible as ever.

Fernandomania

Won on a much grander stage, Valenzuela's status as Mexican national hero is almost as large as Espino's—but somehow Valenzuela was always more of a third-ring sideshow for Mexican baseball, and for big league baseball too. For one thing, his heroics were carried on far from the view of his own countrymen—a flickering image on the television set or a newspaper headline but never a crowd-pleasing spectacle in the local ballpark. An instant hero in Los Angeles in the early summer months of 1981, Fernando became more of a rallying point for North American *chicanos* than for native Mexican *fanáticos*. Compared with Clemente or Marichal or Cepeda or even Luis Aparicio, Valenzuela's instant fame as a big league superstar was short-lived indeed. It is much more than even money that Fernando Valenzuela will never sneak past the portals of immortality in Cooperstown.

Fernando Valenzuela was without dispute one of the best young pitchers of the early 1980s, and his 1981 triple-crown feat of combining Cy Young, Most Valuable Player, and Rookie of the Year honors in a single spectacular season earned the roly-poly Mexican southpaw a lasting niche in baseball's all-time annals. But Fernando was hardly ever a Cooperstown lock like Marichal, nor even a long-lasting season-in and season-out force like Cubans Dolf Luque (in the National League during the 1920s) and Luis Tiant Jr. (in the American League during the 1970s). The biggest downside of Valenzuela's flaming comet was perhaps the fact that it implanted a notion—for big league fans at any rate—that there has indeed been only one truly great Mexican ballplayer worth remembering or celebrating.

In the end, it is hard to say with Valenzuela which was the more notable story—his unprecedented rookie-season splash or his equally sudden lapse into almost total mediocrity? Few pitchers have ever turned as rapidly from being the spitting-image reapparition of Dizzy Dean or Cy Young into a disappointing approximation of Mike Moore or Bill Mombouquette. Part of the issue, of course, was that Valenzuela's remarkable debut was in some senses a matter of excessive hype by big league writers and a lot of premature celebration on the part of proud Hispanic supporters.

The first two or three seasons were meritorious enough (with a better than .600 winning percentage and some of the league's top numbers for games started and innings worked) and Valenzuela would claim league-bests in victories (21) and complete games (20) as late as 1986 (his seventh season and the last truly noteworthy one). His overall record, however, was not all that miraculous—an average of just 14 wins per summer over the full decade and but one 20-victory campaign. It must also be remembered in Valenzuela's case that a rookie sweep of pitching honors (gained on a 13–7 ledger with 180 strikeouts in 192 innings) was aided substantially by a bizarre and disruptive strike-plagued season. What started out looking like surefire Hall-of-Fame numbers, then, ended up no better than the middle of the pack among career Latin American pitching leaders.

A decade and a half later Valenzuela was still traveling the major league circuit—though he had migrated over to the American League. By 1991, his role was far more that of the nearly forgotten part-time role player than the celebrated franchise star. He nevertheless would eventually rebound from premature career "death" with an adequate and even surprising 1996 campaign back in the senior circuit with San Diego, when he won 13, pitched 170-plus innings, and lowered his ERA below 4.00 for the final time. All the same, by then it was clear that Fernando would never threaten Marichal or Tiant or even Dennis Martínez among all-time Latin aces. The plain truth was that for half his career (ten full years) Fernando Valenzuela never claimed more than 13 victories in a season, averaged less than 7 wins a year, and was weighed down with a mediocre winning percentage of .458 and a soaring ERA well above 4.50.

This is hardly the stuff of legend, or even respectability. Fernando Valenzuela— colorful author of West Coast Fernandomania—will likely be remembered more as a short-lived sensation than as a lasting icon. Any hope for a slot with the immortals for Mexico's top big league mound ace rests much more in Monterrey than it does in Cooperstown.

MEXICO IN WORLD AMATEUR BASEBALL

Mexico's track record in world tournament play is also anything but an exceptionally proud one. The country has never won a first prize in World Cup tournament play, and it has never sent a team to the Olympic baseball competitions. The Mexicans have not fared much better in the less-competitive Pan American Games, though they did enjoy a moment of moral victory in midsummer 2003 by handing the champion Cubans their only stinging (though ultimately insignificant) defeat during a rather meaningless preliminary round contest that carried nothing beyond temporary bragging rights.

The best outing for Mexican forces at any World Cup event came with a fourth renewal of the competitions that were still known ambitiously as a World Series of Amateur Baseball. The highlight achievement came during a 1941 tournament staged in Havana, one that was memorable largely for an almost legendary showdown duel between Cuba and Venezuela and their rival pair of star moundsmen—Cuba's future big leaguer Conrado "Connie" Marrero and Venezuela's fireballer Daniel "Chino" Canónico. Mexico finished in the third slot, with but two losses (one each to the two finalists), and was paced by its own star batsman named Gabe Prieto, who walked off with hitting honors (.545 BA) in the eight-game series. Two years later, again in Havana, Mexico actually claimed a silver medal and even upset the hosts 3–2 in the lidlifter; but after two rugged weeks of daily contests the outmanned Mexicans managed only to split their dozen games, owing their surprise runner-up slot primarily to the weak field of only four total entrants. When play next moved to Caracas in late 1944, the Mexicans and Cubans both made it to the championship round along with the host nation; but both challengers quickly withdrew amidst vicious disputes concerning biased local umpiring. There would not be another World Cup medal for the persistent Mexicans until they once again walked off with the runner-up prize in San José, Costa Rica, in 1961, nearly two decades later. Since then, it has all been largely downhill.

Even in older but less prestigious Central American Games the Mexicans have never walked off with a gold medal, though their participation dates back to the very origins of the event in 1926 on their own home turf in Mexico City. The Mexicans in fact launched Central American Games festivities when they squared off with the usually overpowering Cubans in an inaugural two-country, three-game playoff. The Cubans predictably won all three contests (the scores have long since been lost), launching what would soon become their own annual domination of the world amateur baseball scene. For their part, Mexican entries have won a grand total of seven Central American Games baseball medals: five silver trophies (1926, 1930, 1950, 1954, 1993) and two bronze (1962, 1970).

Over the years, teams representing Mexico in these world or regional tournament events have usually been little more than mediocre contingents of rank amateurs, not at all on a par with the professional nines that have filled the country's two professional leagues. At one match in Havana in the early 1970s— an international university competition—an inept squad representing Mexico was being so badly outclassed (26–0 in the fourth frame) that the Mexican team captain requested permission to address jeering fans at Havana's Latin American Stadium. With microphone in hand the brave captain apologized from the press box to knowledgeable local fans for his own club's sad incompetence, pointing out that his bumbling group of athletes had few real ballplayers among them since, after all, his nation was in reality devoted to European-style *fútbol* (soccer) and not to Cuba's national game of baseball.

If the Mexicans have fared rather badly across the years at the organized amateur level, they have more recently enjoyed a few sterling moments—now that professional players have been finally placed on team rosters for Olympic style events. There was a too-brief moment of glory attached to bashing Cuba 7–1 in Santo Domingo during the 2003 summer Pan American Games. Only a few months later, a far more satisfying and attention-getting upset would follow. Mexico's national team (carrying several former big leaguers) lost all three of its opening round games at the Olympic Qualifier of November 2003 at Panama City, but the limited field for the event allowed the winless Mexicans to garner a spot in the quarterfinals against a talented American team that was counting on a date in the finals with the favored Cubans (and thus also an automatic spot in Athens to defend the gold medal Team USA had finally won in Sydney). In one of the more shocking moments in international play from recent decades, the unheralded Mexicans completely shut down the vaunted Americans, behind a superlative pitching effort by major league reject Rigo Beltran (only a 2–3 lifetime big leaguer whose last outing was a winless 2000 appearance with Colorado). The stunning 2–1 Mexican upset abruptly ended any Olympic dreaming by the first overconfident and soon embarrassed Americans.

THE MAJOR LEAGUES VISIT MEXICO

Big league clubs never flocked to Mexico for off-seasons tours at anywhere near the rate with which they packed their trunks for barnstorming ventures to distant Japan, or even to nearby tropical Cuba. Perhaps Mexico was simply too close to home and not quite exotic enough to be an attractive magnet for vacation trips by barnstormers hoping to see the world or to test the competitive waters of baseball as played in other cultural venues.

The first Mexican tour staged by big leaguers occurred as early as 1906, when a handful of Charlie Comiskey's "Hitless Wonders" White Sox paid a brief visit on the heels of their second American League pennant and first World Series triumph over the crosstown "Tinker-to-Evers-to-Chance" Cubbies. Much later, another legendary owner–manager, Connie Mack, brought his Philadelphia Athletics south for spring training sessions in Mexico City and Veracruz during March 1937 preseason tune-up sessions. That second visit by North American pros spawned the first modest legend of Mexicans achieving tentative successes while playing against the seasoned big leaguers. This occurred with brilliant pitching outings unleashed against the Mackmen by a pair of unheralded Mexican hurlers named Carlos Rubio and Alberto Romo Chávez. The 1937 tour also gave a much-needed boost to the venture known as the Mexican League of Professional Baseball, which had already been operating in the shadows for less than a decade but was now about to establish itself as a first-rate national sporting institution.

There would not be another such visit by major league clubs until the Pittsburgh Pirates and their beloved Hispanic idol Roberto Clemente paid a brief autumn call in 1958 for several hot-ticket exhibition matches. Once the Pirates had renewed the practice, touring big league clubs soon began scheduling occasional spring training games as more regular March fare. The Los Angeles Dodgers were in Mexico in the spring of 1964, on the heels of a world championship sweep of the vaunted Mantle–Maris Yankees, and the New Yorkers (already well past their dynasty years) were also welcomed visitors four years later, before the 1960s had completely run their course. Media chatter surrounding the dream of luring big league baseball to Mexico on a more permanent basis multiplied in the aftermath of the Fernandomania craze that swept southern California and much of the United States in the early 1980s; one immediate result was the 1990 construction in baseball-crazed Monterrey of a modestly state-of-the-art stadium with certain big league pretensions (seating capacity of 26,000) that offered still further hopes for more regular stopovers by the major leaguers. Payoff for the Monterrey building efforts came in the form of a visit in spring 1990 by native-son Valenzuela and his Los Angeles Dodgers for community festivities inaugurating the showcase Monterrey ballpark. A memorable game was even played on that occasion, featuring Valenzuela himself hurling brilliantly against the National League rival Milwaukee Brewers (themselves boasting another native son, Teddy Higuera, but he was scratched by injury from a heavily promoted showdown versus Fernando).

Big league baseball finally came to Mexico in a big way in midsummer of 1996 when the city of Monterrey at long last hosted the first major league regular season contest ever staged anywhere outside the confines of United States or Canadian territory. The National League's San Diego Padres and New York Mets visited for a pair of weekend games that made big league history and also fanned flames surrounding the still-persistent fantasy of big league baseball eventually finding a permanent home on Mexican soil, the very dream that had first flared up with the adventures of Jorge Pasquel almost a half-century earlier. Within three years, the San Diego Padres would again stoke the fires of that dream when they returned to Monterrey along with the Colorado Rockies to stage the first big league season's opener held beyond U.S.–Canadian borders. It almost goes without saying, of course, that these ground-breaking visits were in large part motivated by transparent desires of Padres executives and Major League Baseball (MLB) brass to begin drawing upon potential marketplace profits represented by the nearby across-the-border Chicano fan base. The game plan now driving the Commissioner's office was likely from the first based far more on the notion of bringing Mexican fans across the border to San Diego than any expectation of putting a new or relocated franchise in Mexico City or even in Monterrey.

There seems to be very little realistic hope for a big league ball club setting up shop down in Mexico anytime in the near future. The economics of today's game just won't permit such a scenario. Mexican fans may be fanatic followers of the national game, but big league prices and a vital need for corporate sponsorship support do not seem compatible with an ever-sagging Mexican economy. Support for AAA baseball or winter league teams is a far cry from the economic underpinnings (complete with major television market) necessary to sustain a thriving big league operation. Nonetheless, when the near-moribund Montreal franchise, placed under control of a cartel of major league owners, began playing a portion of its regular schedule of home games in San Juan on the island of Puerto Rico, Monterrey's forces were once more inspired to renew their relentless courtship. Monterrey civic leaders made a strong if finally unsuccessful bid to convince the MLB Commissioner's office that the unorthodox 2004 Expos home schedule should include Monterrey as a secondary venue, rather than San Juan.

A pair of leading Monterrey businessmen—Carlos Bremer and José Maiz—continue to front an active movement to obtain major league status for the leading Mexican baseball city. The formal bid made by this enterprising pair began with their 2003–2004 courtship of the Montreal Expos. It now also includes an ambitious Website campaign utilizing the extensive MLB Internet facilities. Plans proposed include a renovation of the Monterrey stadium to bring it in line with recent big league specifications. The project may not have much hope for success in the short run. But the idea of big league games in Mexico is today anything but an entirely dead issue.

MEXICO'S GREATEST PLAYERS

When it comes to producing big leaguers, Mexico makes up a bit in quality what it has often lacked in quantity. Héctor Espino and Fernando Valenzuela stand in a class by themselves among homegrown stars, one having earned his glory strictly on the home front and the other on the more distant major league stage, but there have been plenty of other noteworthy Mexican diamond heroes to flesh out the native inventory, a few operating in the majors and considerably more showcasing their talents squarely on home turf.

One reason for the low numbers for Mexican big league talent likely results from the unique relationship that Mexican League baseball retains with the country's native-born ballplayers. Mexican players are owned outright by the Mexican League teams that originally signed them to contracts. Clubs in organized baseball must purchase the rights to any coveted Mexican prospects from the local franchise owning his original contract. The hefty fees almost always demanded by Mexican League clubs for their prospects are usually enough to send scouts to other Latin markets, where cheap talent can be corralled almost for the asking.

Legitimate Mexican stars in the majors have been surprisingly few, compared to those of neighboring countries around the Caribbean Basin. Three adequate infielders and two steady-if-unspectacular pitchers seem about all that stands above the rest of the crowd. Aurelio López (dubbed "Señor Smoke" for his unusually lively fastball) made a modest mark as a relief artist of more than minor stature, mostly by laboring for 1980s-era Detroit teams well into his thirties as a seasoned veteran with flair. Much of López's best stuff was left behind in Mexico, however, where he logged a dozen seasons and earned Most Valuable Player honors in 1977 for a sterling 19–8 (2.01 ERA) record in the uniform of the Mexico City Red Devils. Jorge Orta (White Sox and Royals) and Aurelio Rodríguez (Tigers) were solid big league infielders of the same decade. Orta, son to slugging Negro leaguer Pedro Orta (himself known in some circles as the "Babe Ruth of Mexican winter play"), etched a personal mark with his own potent bat, first by finishing second to Rod Carew in the American League batting race of 1974 and later by stroking a record-tying six base hits in a single game for Cleveland at the end of the same decade. Rodríguez was, by contrast, strictly a defensive standout who stretched his big league tenure out to almost two decades with a sticky glove that always more than compensated for his sawdust bat. For much of the 1970s with Detroit, the Sonoran remained friendly rival and near-equal to Baltimore's magical Brooks

Robinson as the junior circuit's slickest hot corner gloveman. Among this small pack of memorable "others" from baseball's golden age 1950s and 1960s, it is without doubt Bobby Ávila of the 1954 American League champion Cleveland Indians ball club who merited the biggest chunk of lasting fame. Ávila's claim to fame-as-notoriety would result as much from heated controversy surrounding his top achievement as from any indisputable prowess in the infield or batter's box.

Ramón Arano (b. August 31, 1939). Mexico's top pitching star on the home front scene is widely acknowledged to have been Ramón Arano, a diminutive 5'8", 160-pound right-hander who tasted only the briefest of trials in the U.S. minors. Arano today reigns undisputed as the all-time Mexican League pitching champion in a significant number of the sport's top hurling categories. For starters, he pitched an amazing total of 31 one seasons, in which he rang up the top marks for victories (334), games appeared (810), games started (675), innings pitched (4,770), shutouts (57), and also strikeouts (2,380). His starts outpace the runner-up by nearly 150, and his victory total is 79 better than second slot. He even came back for a brief swan song in the late 1990s (1995 and again in 1998) when he was a long-toothed senior citizen then pushing sixty! When winter league totals earned in the Mexican Pacific League are also added to the mix, the numbers (including 87 additional victories for an overall total of 421) become altogether astronomical.

Roberto [Bobby] "Beto" Ávila (b. June 7, 1926). If Mexican baseball and its heroes have most often been overshadowed or discredited by circumstance, nowhere is this more evident than with the strange case of Roberto Ávila, central figure in major league baseball's most controversial contest to determine a league batting champion. Bobby Ávila will long and rightly be remembered by most fans as the first Latin American native to earn a big league batting crown. Others will always contend that Ávila didn't so much "earn" the coveted title as swipe it from its rightful owner by virtue of a most bothersome technicality. Despite his career-best season in 1954, it was Ávila's rude fate to grab a crown tinged with persistent rumors of illegitimacy. Ávila spent the long summer season locked in a heated hitting duel with Boston's Ted Williams, with Williams eventually besting the Mexican infielder by a mere four percentage points. Williams had registered only 386 official at-bats, however, an insufficient amount to claim the title under rules then applicable. Controversy was spawned largely by the fact that the Boston slugger's low "at-bats" total had resulted in large part from a league-leading 136 free passes awarded to the "Splendid Splinter" by wary rival pitchers. It was this very dispute, in fact, that soon brought about a revision in the standards of batting leadership qualification. A substitution of "plate appearances" for "official at-bats" was almost immediately in the offing.

Although only a technicality rewarded Ávila in the end, it should also be noted for the record that Latin America's first hitting champion himself bravely played more than half the season with a broken thumb, a painful injury that would have slowed almost any other hitter and perhaps knocked out many. Some baseball encyclopedias adept at revisionist history (but not Thorn and

Chico Carrasquel (Venezuela) and Minnie Miñoso (Cuba) team with Beto Avila (Mexico) in Cleveland. [Transcendental Graphics]

Palmer's *Total Baseball*, 2001 edition) today list Ted Williams as the 1954 batting champ, despite contemporary rules and common-practice record-keeping of the era in question. But Bobby Ávila had gained another prize that season which neither Williams nor the historians could ever expunge from the record books. He had earned as well the rare opportunity (rare indeed for one playing in Cleveland) to perform on a championship ball club and thus to appear in major league baseball's World Series.

The legitimacy of Bobby Ávila as league batting champion or genuine baseball hero was never questioned for an instant in the talented second sacker's own native Mexico. Throughout his career, Ávila reigned as a national hero. And that sporting fame would also propel him to a lengthy career in the public eye once baseball days closed for the Veracruz native. Handsome, dapper, and personable, Ávila would return to Mexico at the end of his playing days in 1960 (after splitting his final season of 1959 among the Orioles, Red Sox, and Milwaukee Braves) to enter the wider business and political arenas, first serving as Mexican League president and later even enjoying a term as mayor of his home city.

Nelson Barrera (b. October 17, 1957; d. July 14, 2000).   Along with Jesús Sommers, Nelson Barrera is one of a modern pair of durable stars who, following in the path of Héctor Espino, earned their fame exclusively in their homeland and even overhauled significant portions of Espino's own legacy in the process. Barrera slugged away through the 1990s and eventually surpassed

Espino's top Mexican records for power categories (homers, RBI, extra base hits, and total bases). With 26 years of Mexican League play under his belt, and only months after he had supplanted the immortal Espino both as the all-time home run king and also as Mexico's leading RBI producer, Barrera died, electrocuted at home when an awning he was working on struck high-tension wires.

Vinicio "Vinny" Castilla (b. July 4, 1967). Héctor Espino is unchallenged as Mexico's top slugger on the home front, but it is Vinny Castilla of more recent vintage who stands unrivaled in the power department among his countrymen performing in the big leagues. After a 13-year sojourn that began in Atlanta in 1991, Castilla is still going strong and likely to hit more than 300 homers before his career is done. The 300 plateau is perhaps not a significant landmark when compared to the likes of Sammy Sosa, Rafael Palmeiro, and José Canseco, or even Orlando Cepeda and Tony Pérez. But Mexico's big league home run king has now left all other rivals among his countrymen far behind. The solidly built third sacker enjoyed his finest summers in hitter-friendly Coors Field in Denver with three straight seasons above 40 home runs during the late 1990s; only twice has he posted as many as 20 dingers when not wearing a Rockies uniform and enjoying the rarified mile-high Denver jet streams. But Castilla has also been a solid fill-in performer of late with perennial division winner Atlanta and is likely to hang around long enough to extend his homer total (at 268 entering 2004) to a healthy enough figure to leave next-generation Mexicans in awe for years to come.

Francisco "Paquín" Estrada (b. February 12, 1948). One of Mexico's top stars appeared in only a single big league game (with the New York Mets in 1971), but he managed to set a record for longevity at the catching position in Mexican League play that has few parallels anywhere in world's professional leagues. Francisco "Paquín" Estrada headlined behind the plate in Mexico's summer circuit for almost three decades, splitting his time among six teams. During that span he ran up the league record of nearly 2,500 games in which he wore the famed tools of ignorance. Paquín Estrada's final games-played mark of 2,747, which includes a few extra-duty winter league sessions on top of his summer triple-A play, stands second in the world behind the 2,918 total amassed by Japanese legend Katsuya Nomura. It also outstrips anything achieved in the big leagues by the likes of Yogi Berra, Johnny Bench, Gary Carter, Ted Simmons, or Carlton Fisk.

Teodoro "Teddy" Higuera (b. November 9, 1958). When it comes to earning stripes in the big time, Teodoro (Teddy) Higuera was without doubt Mexico's premier major league pitcher outside of 1980s rival portsider Fernando Valenzuela. Higuera may have been even better than Fernando, of course, if one considers raw talent alone or takes into account the difference between the Dodgers lineups that backed Valenzuela and the Milwaukee Brewers clubs that normally supported Higuera. In the end, the highly successful southpaw from Los Mochis fell a tad short of winning 100 games in the majors, with 94 career victories and a hefty .595 win–loss mark, but he did post one 20-game season (the same as Fernando) and had a second near-miss campaign (1987, at 18–10) in which he barely lost out on the recognized landmark for pitching excellence. Other career highlights include a sensational 1983 campaign for hometown Juárez (pacing the Mexican League in wins, complete games, innings, and strikeouts), the best rookie pitching season in Milwaukee Brewers annals (15–8, 3.90 ERA in 1985), and the considerable distinction attached to being Mexico's first-ever big league 20-game winner.

Aurelio López (b. September 21, 1948; d. September 22, 1992). For more than a half-dozen seasons of the early and mid-1980s, Tecamachalco's portly Aurelio López was one of the most successful relief pitchers in all of baseball. During much of this spell, López labored as Detroit's effective bull pen stopper, with 21 saves in consecutive seasons at the close of the 1970s; later, he would renew his career as the highly valued set-up man for Tigers star closer, Guillermo Hernández. The year he backed Hernández in a set-up role was the World Championship 1984 season, renowned for Hernández's own rare double as Cy Young and Most Valuable Player trophy winner. López hardly ever had to take a back seat to Hernández, however, or to anyone else in the Detroit pen, and on three different occasions he was able to ring up double-digit victory totals laboring exclusively with the Tigers talent-laden relief corps. López had nine Mexican seasons under his belt before he ever appeared in the majors, and in 1977 he was the Mexican League's Most Valuable Player with a sterling 19–8 performance (2.01 ERA) for Mexico City's Diablos Rojos.

Mario Mendoza (b. December 26, 1950). The most memorable baseball heroes of a nation are not always the ones that put up eye-catching performances or ring up awesome totals in hitting or pitching. Chihuahua infielder Mario Mendoza holds a special though unlikely spot in baseball lore. Mendoza was so consistent in his ineptitude as a major league batter from 1974 to 1982 that he was branded with the art of always hitting around the .200 level as his personal trademark. (A career .215 hitter, Mendoza labored two years at .198, close enough to a perfect inept .200 to fire the imaginations of fans and commentators.) If few fans of the big leagues know much of anything about Mendoza's actual career, they nevertheless have most likely heard of the "Mendoza line" as a baseball hallmark.[2] In this unintentional achievement, Mendoza seems to reflect the entire country's sometimes accidental baseball history. Houston Jiménez (four-year big leaguer with Minnesota, Pittsburgh, and Cleveland in the 1980s, who batted .185 across 158 games, compared with Mendoza's .215 mark across 686 games) actually came much closer to achieving the Mendoza line than did its actual namesake, but Jiménez lacked the memorable alliterative name and the same degree of colorful decade-long consistency. In Mexico itself, Mendoza is remembered chiefly for his fine fielding at short, which won him a spot in the Mexican Hall of Fame.

Andrés Mora (b. May 25, 1955). Héctor Espino was not alone among strapping Mexican League sluggers who flopped in organized baseball up north but proceeded to tear up the record books relentlessly back home on native soil. Andrés Mora had brief and largely unsuccessful trials in the U.S. minor leagues and also in the majors with the Baltimore Orioles; in both places, he showed a potential for power yet never made a memorable impact. For 16 seasons, however, Mora destroyed Mexican League pitchers, hitting over .300 on a dozen occasions and also winning four coveted league home run crowns. What was a blip on the radar in Baltimore was later a full-scale storm surge in Saltillo and Nuevo Laredo.

Jorge "Charolito" Orta (b. November 26, 1950). Mazatlán native Jorge Orta was Mexico's quietest big league batting star. Orta carried a significant legacy as offspring of Pedro "Charolito" Orta, a popular outfield talent born in Cuba who had consistently wrecked Mexican League pitching at a .300-plus clip between the mid-1940s and mid-1950s. The famed elder Orta was a huge star in his adopted homeland, and yet anything but a known figure anywhere outside of Mexico. The younger Orta once turned down a basketball scholarship to UCLA to stay at home and pursue baseball in the Mexican Pacific League. In the early 1970s, he was one of the league's top hitters and even won a winter batting crown in 1974 (a couple of years after his major league debut) with a hefty .370 average. He had joined the Chicago White Sox in 1972, where he became a starting second baseman and then hung around the majors for the next fourteen-plus years. Orta never hit well enough over the long haul to overcome some rather serious liabilities in the field; as a result, his big league career (130 HR, .278 BA) never measured up to the promise first flashed on local fields back home.

Jorge Orta, one of Mexico's top big league hitters, 1975. [Transcendental Graphics]

Aurelio Rodríguez (b. December 28, 1947; d. September 23, 2000). For Aurelio Rodríguez, fielding was the very hallmark of his polished game. Rodríguez continued to demand a paycheck for 17 seasons in the big leagues (mostly in Detroit) precisely because he was for most of that stretch just about the slickest fielding defender of the hot corner anywhere in the junior circuit—at least not counting the Baltimore Orioles lineup. When Aurelio Rodríguez won the 1976 American League Gold Glove at third, it was the first time since 1960 that the award had gone to anyone other than Baltimore's great Brooks Robinson. Aurelio Rodríguez back in his homeland enjoyed a brief six-year Mexican League stint wrapped around his 17 big league seasons (two years before and four after). He batted a shade over .300 in that span and only twice logged seasons of 100-plus games, facts sufficient to underscore any conclusion that his Mexican Hall-of-Fame credentials were all earned up north on big league diamonds.

Vicente "Huevo" Romo (b. April 12, 1943); Enrique Romo (b. July 15, 1947). Mexico turned out a small army of carbon-copy workman-like pitchers dispatched to the majors throughout the 1970s, and the brothers Vicente and Enrique Romo were as typical as any. Vicente Romo was perhaps the more successful of the pair, but only by the slimmest of margins (both are in the Mexican Hall of Fame). Vicente Romo enjoyed a sixteen-year career in the Mexican League (182–106, 2.49) and another eight seasons of productive work in the majors (32–33, 3.36, 52 saves). What pushed him slightly ahead of the pack is clearly his hometown Mexican League performances. The older Romo brother maintains the career record back home for lowest earned run average by a wide margin over American runner-up George Brunet (1973–1985, at 2.66). He also stands tied for third in career shutouts (52) and owns a share of another league record with ten whitewashes performed in a single season. In the majors, Enrique won more games in six seasons than his older brother in eight (44–33 won–lost in 350 games for Enrique, 32–33 in 335 games for Vicente), had the same number of saves (52), but had only a 3.45 ERA (compared with 3.36 for Vicente).

Jesús Sommers (b. November 11, 1949). Another slugging star who chased Héctor Espino's records, infielder Jesús Sommers lasted for nearly three decades with a contingent of Mexican League teams and put up numbers that made him both the nation's all-time base hits leader and also the first Mexican Leaguer to cross the milestone 3,000-hit landmark. Sommers would also finish his career as all-time leader in both games and seasons played (among position players), as well as the pacesetter in at-bats and doubles. In a remarkably durable 27-season career that opened in 1970 with Yucatán and closed in 1996 with Poza Rica, Sommers topped the .300 hitting plateau nine times—a somewhat surprisingly low total, perhaps, given his array of other impressive batting marks. Perhaps more surprising still is the fact that Mexico's only career 3,000-hit man never walked off with even a single league batting crown.

IN BRIEF

Beyond these few inspiring stories of limited big league successes, Mexican baseball has remained largely second class. The country's professional summer league has long held minor league status, yet is almost unknown even to dedicated followers of stateside AAA minor league play. Its winter circuit receives little press, compared with the Dominican and Venezuelan and Puerto Rico circuits, and thus draws only a leftover portion of the small group of big leaguers who still travel the wintertime circuit.

Mexico's professional baseball enterprise (like the semi-pro leagues and barnstorming circuits that preceded it) has celebrated more than a few exceptional moments in the sun since its quiet debut season in the summer of 1925. Here was the baseball birthplace of Fernando Valenzuela, Melo Almada (Mexico's pioneering first big leaguer, back in 1933), Teodoro Higuera, and Aurelio López. Héctor Espino created lasting long ball lore here, and James "Cool Papa" Bell and other exceptional U.S. black imports stopped just long enough to burn up the base paths for several summers of the late 1930s and early 1940s. Pitching legends have been carved out here as well by such illustrious winter-ball and Negro league stars as (among many others) Martín Dihigo, Ramón Arano, Ramón Bragaña, Adrian Zabala, and Vidal López.

Mexico, however, has in the end always been the place that fading ballplayers seemingly go to die, both figuratively and sometimes quite literally. Dihigo languished there at the tail end of a back-page black-ball career. The ageless Miñoso eventually disappeared into Mexico for a decade of seemingly washed-up play as a 40-plus-year-old journeyman who was more sideshow than main attraction—and yet Miñoso did win a pair of late-career batting titles in the Mexican Pacific League, proving that at age 48 he could still hit top-level minor-league pitching with considerable authority. Julio Franco recently repeated the scenario and used a pair of Mexican League batting titles as a springboard back to one final tour around the majors.

There was, of course, also the ill-fated exodus of that handful of mercenary ballplayers attracted by Pasquel's unrealistic expansion plan with its lure of truckloads of spare pesos. And there was Hi Bithorn, shot to death on New Year's Day of 1952 while attempting a futile comeback in Mexico City—and Dolf Luque, still laboring as a minor league manager in the 1940s and tutoring Sal Maglie in the art of the brushback pitch that Luque himself had once used so effectively to terrorize enemy hitters from New York to Havana. There was Francisco Barrios, as well, dying in his homeland of a drug overdose at the tender age of 29, in the ghostly shadows of a failed big league career. And there were Luke Easter and Tommy de la Cruz and Jerry Hairston Sr. all chasing elusive baseball dreams from Tampico to Monterrey to Hermosillo, long after their fragile talents had left them. All looked to Mexico as a final refuge and all seemingly vanished forever once they quietly slipped below the border.

SELECTED MEXICAN RECORDS AND STATISTICS

Mexicans in the Major Leagues (1933–2003)

	Name	Debut	Position	Debut Team	Seasons	Games	Career Statistics
1	Baldomero "Melo" Almada	1933	OF	Boston Red Sox (AL)	7	646	.284 BA
2	José "Chili" Gómez	1935	IF	Philadelphia Phillies (NL)	3	200	.226 BA
3	Jesse Flores	1942	RHP	Chicago Cubs (NL)	7	176	44–59, 3.18 ERA
4	Roberto "Beto" Ávila	1949	2B	Cleveland Indians (AL)	11	1,300	.281 BA, 80 HR
5	Procopio "Tito" Herrera	1951	RHP	St. Louis Browns (AL)	1	3	0–0, 27.00 ERA
6	Felipe Montemayor	1953	OF	Pittsburgh Pirates (NL)	2	64	.173 BA
7	Vinicio "Chico" García	1954	2B	Baltimore Orioles (AL)	1	39	.113 BA
8	Robert "Bob" Greenwood	1954	RHP	Philadelphia Phillies (NL)	2	12	1–2, 3.92 ERA
9	Guillermo "Memo" Luna	1954	LHP	St. Louis Cardinals (NL)	1	1	0–1, 27.00 ERA
10	Rubén Amaro	1958	IF	St. Louis Cardinals (NL)	11	940	.234 BA
11	Marcelino Solis	1958	LHP	Chicago Cubs (NL)	1	15	3–3, 6.06 ERA
12	Belran "Benny" Valenzuela	1958	3B	St. Louis Cardinals (NL)	1	10	.214 BA
13	Jorge Rubio	1966	RHP	California Angels (AL)	2	10	2–3, 3.19 ERA
14	Aurelio Rodríguez	1967	3B	California Angels (AL)	17	2,017	.237 BA, 124 HR
15	Horacio Piña	1968	RHP	Cleveland Indians (AL)	8	314	23–23, 3.25 ERA
16	Vicente Romo	1968	RHP	Los Angeles Dodgers (NL)	8	335	32–33, 3.36 ERA
17	Carlos "Bobby" Treviño	1968	OF	California Angels (AL)	1	17	.225 BA
18	Héctor Torres	1968	3B	Houston Astros (NL)	9	622	.216 BA
19	José Peña	1969	RHP	Cincinnati Reds (NL)	4	61	7–4, 4.97 ERA
20	Miguel Puente	1970	RHP	San Francisco Giants (NL)	1	6	1–3, 8.20 ERA
21	Francisco Estrada	1971	C	New York Mets (NL)	1	1	.500 BA
22	Rodolfo "Rudy" Hernández	1972	2B	Chicago White Sox (AL)	1	8	.190 BA
23	Jorge Orta	1972	2B	Chicago White Sox (AL)	16	1,755	.278 BA, 130 HR
24	Sergio Robles	1972	C	Baltimore Orioles (AL)	3	16	.095 BA
25	Celerino Sánchez	1972	IF	New York Yankees (AL)	2	105	.242 BA
26	Cecilio "Cy" Acosta	1972	RHP	Chicago White Sox (AL)	4	107	13–9, 2.66 ERA
27	Máximo "Max" León	1973	RHP	Atlanta Braves (NL)	6	162	14–18, 3.71 ERA
28	Luis Gómez	1974	SS	Minnesota Twins (AL)	8	609	.210 BA
29	Francisco Barrios	1974	RHP	Chicago White Sox (AL)	7	129	38–38, 4.15 ERA
30	Aurelio López	1974	RHP	Kansas City Royals (AL)	11	459	62–36, 3.56 ERA
31	Mario Mendoza	1974	SS	Pittsburgh Pirates (NL)	9	686	.215 BA
32	Isidro "Sid" Monge	1975	LHP	California Angels (AL)	10	435	49–40, 3.56 ERA
33	Carlos López	1976	OF	California Angels (AL)	3	237	.260 BA
34	Andrés Mora	1976	OF	Baltimore Orioles (AL)	4	235	.223 BA
35	Enrique Romo	1977	RHP	Seattle Mariners (AL)	6	350	44–33, 3.45 ERA
36	Alex Treviño	1978	C	New York Mets (NL)	13	939	.249 BA
37	Germán Barranca	1979	IF	Kansas City Royals (AL)	4	67	.290 BA
38	Fernando Valenzuela	1980	LHP	Los Angeles Dodgers (NL)	17	453	173–153, 3.54 ERA
39	Angel Moreno	1981	LHP	California Angels (AL)	2	21	4–10, 4.02 ERA
40	Ernesto Escarrega	1982	RHP	Chicago White Sox (AL)	1	38	1–3, 3.67 ERA
41	Salomé Barojas	1982	RHP	Chicago White Sox (AL)	5	179	18–21, 3.95 ERA
42	Houston Jiménez	1983	SS	Minnesota Twins (AL)	4	158	.185 BA
43	Alfonso Pulido	1983	LHP	Pittsburgh Pirates (NL)	3	12	1–1, 5.19 ERA
44	Teodoro "Teddy" Higuera	1985	LHP	Milwaukee Brewers (AL)	9	213	94–64, 3.61 ERA
45	Vincente Palacios	1987	RHP	Pittsburgh Pirates (NL)	8	134	17–20, 4.43 ERA
46	José Ceceña	1988	RHP	Texas Rangers (AL)	1	22	0–0, 4.78 ERA
47	Germán Jiménez	1988	LHP	Atlanta Braves (NL)	1	15	1–6, 5.01 ERA
48	Tony Perezchica	1988	2B	San Francisco Giants (NL)	4	69	.228 BA
49	Rosario Rodríguez	1989	LHP	Cincinnati Reds (NL)	3	34	2–2, 4.80 ERA
50	Narciso Elvira	1990	LHP	Milwaukee Brewers (AL)	1	4	0–0, 5.40 ERA
51	Matías Carrillo	1991	OF	Milwaukee Brewers (AL)	5	107	.251 BA
52	Vinicio "Vinny" Castilla	1991	3B	Atlanta Braves (NL)	13	1,477	.281 BA, 268 HR
53	Héctor Fajardo	1991	RHP	Pittsburgh Pirates (NL)	4	30	5–9, 6.95 ERA

(continued)

Name	Debut	Position	Debut Team	Seasons	Games	Career Statistics
54 Everardo Magallanes	1991	IF	Cleveland Indians (AL)	1	3	.000 BA
55 Armando Reynoso	1991	RHP	Atlanta Braves (NL)	11	196	68–62, 4.68 ERA
56 Carlos Rodríguez	1991	SS	New York Yankees (AL)	3	85	.278 BA
57 José Tolentino	1991	3B	Houston Astros (NL)	1	44	.259 BA
58 Guillermo Velásquez	1992	1B	San Diego Padres (NL)	2	94	.223 BA
59 Benjamin "Benji" Gil	1993	IF	Texas Rangers (AL)	8	604	.237 BA
60 Ismael Valdéz	1994	RHP	Los Angeles Dodgers (NL)	10	277	88–94, 3.93 ERA
61 Juan Acevedo	1995	RHP	Colorado Rockies (NL)	8	366	28–40, 4.33 ERA
62 Andres Berumen	1995	RHP	San Diego Padres (NL)	2	40	2–3, 5.66 ERA
63 Octavio Alvarez	1995	RHP	Montreal Expos (NL)	2	19	3–6, 5.40 ERA
64 Noé Muñoz	1995	C	Los Angeles Dodgers (NL)	1	2	.000 BA
65 Antonio Osuna	1995	RHP	Los Angeles Dodgers (NL)	9	376	34–28, 3.58 ERA
66 Juan Castro	1995	SS	Los Angeles Dodgers (NL)	9	557	.222 BA
67 Karim García	1995	OF	Los Angeles Dodgers (NL)	9	403	.243 BA
68 Isidro Marquez	1995	RHP	Chicago White Sox (AL)	1	7	0–1, 6.75 ERA
69 Ésteban Loaiza	1995	RHP	Pittsburgh Pirates (NL)	9	269	90–82, 4.58 ERA
70 Francisco Córdoba	1996	RHP	Pittsburgh Pirates (NL)	5	166	42–47, 3.96 ERA
71 Elmer Dessens	1996	RHP	Pittsburgh Pirates (NL)	7	199	38–43, 4.46 ERA
72 José Silva	1996	RHP	Toronto Blue Jays (AL)	5	116	21–25, 5.37 ERA
73 Ricardo Rincón	1997	LHP	Pittsburgh Pirates (NL)	7	418	19–22, 3.42 ERA
74 Rigoberto "Rigo" Beltran	1997	LHP	St. Louis Cardinals (NL)	4	76	2–3, 4.34 ERA
75 Mario Valdéz	1997	OF	Chicago White Sox (AL)	3	91	.238 BA
76 Dennys Reyes	1997	LHP	Los Angeles Dodgers (NL)	7	268	15–21, 4.77 ERA
77 Gabriel "Gabe" Alvarez	1998	3B	Detroit Tigers (AL)	3	92	.222 BA
78 Roberto Ramírez	1998	LHP	San Diego Padres (NL)	2	53	2–5, 7.69 ERA
79 David Cortez	1999	RHP	Atlanta Braves (NL)	2	6	0–0, 8.10 ERA
80 Erubiel Durazo	1999	1B	Arizona Diamondbacks (NL)	5	441	.270 BA
81 Miguel Del Toro	1999	RHP	San Francisco Giants (NL)	2	27	2–0, 4.61 ERA
82 Luis Rivera	2000	RHP	Atlanta Braves (NL)	1	6	1–0, 1.23 ERA
83 Daniel Garibay	2000	LHP	Chicago Cubs (NL)	1	30	2–8, 6.03 ERA
84 Rodrigo López	2000	RHP	San Diego Padres (NL)	3	65	22–22, 4.81 ERA
85 Humberto Cota	2001	C	Pittsburgh Pirates (NL)	3	24	.262 BA
86 Geronimo Gil	2001	C	Baltimore Orioles (AL)	3	196	.239 BA
87 Mario Valdéz	2001	OF	Oakland A's (AL)	1	32	.278 BA
88 Oliver Pérez	2002	LHP	San Diego Padres (NL)	2	40	8–15, 4.65 ERA
89 Alfredo Amezaga	2002	SS	Anaheim Angels (AL)	2	49	.246 BA
90 Luis Garcia	2002	IF	Baltimore Orioles	1	6	.333 BA
91 Rodrigo López	2002	P	Baltimore Orioles (AL)	1	33	15–9, 3.57 ERA
92 Victor Alvarez	2002	LHP	Los Angeles Dodgers (NL)	2	9	0–2, 7.31 ERA
93 Luis Ayala	2003	RHP	Montreal Expos (NL)	1	65	10–3, 2.92 ERA
94 Juan Cerros	2003	LHP	Cincinnati Reds (NL)	1	11	0–0, 4.85 ERA
95 Edgar González	2003	RHP	Arizona Diamondbacks (NL)	1	9	2–1, 4.91 ERA
96 Miguel Ojeda	2003	C	San Diego Padres (NL)	1	61	.234 BA
97 Oscar Villarreal	2003	RHP	Arizona Diamondbacks (NL)	1	86	10–7, 2.57 ERA

Mexican League Record Book

Mexican League Baseball (AAA Summer) Championship Teams, Cities, and Managers (1925–2003)

Year	Champions	Record	City	Manager
1925	74 Regimento	NA	Puebla	Jesús Valdéz
1926	Ocampo	NA	Jalapa	José Mancisidor
1927	Gendarmería	NA	Mexico City	Jesús Valdéz

Year	Champions	Record	City	Manager
1928	Policía	NA	Mexico City	Horacio Hernández
1929	Chiclets Adams	NA	Mexico City	Agustín Suárez Peredo
1930	Comintra	19–16	Mexico City	Manuel Oliveros
1931	Tráfico	NA	Mexico City	Gregorio Valdéz
1932	Obras Publicas	NA	Mexico City	Ernesto Carmona Verduzco
1933	Comintra	NA	Mexico City	Manuel Oliveros
1934	Monte de Piedad	NA	Mexico City	Ernesto Carmona Verduzco
1935	Agrario	NA	Mexico City	Salvador Teuffer
1936	Agrario	NA	Mexico City	Salvador Teuffer
1937	Aguila	NA	Veracruz	Agustín Verde
1938	Aguila	NA	Veracruz	Agustín Verde
1939	Cafeteros	NA	Córdoba	Lázaro Salazar
1940	Azules de Veracruz	61–30	Mexico City	Jorge Pasquel
1941	Azules de Veracruz	67–35	Mexico City	Lázaro Salazar
1942	Union Laguna	48–40	Torreón	Martín Dihigo
1943	Industriales	53–37	Monterrey	Lázaro Salazar
1944	Azules de Veracruz	52–37	Mexico City	Ramón Bragaña
1945	Alijadores	52–38	Tampico	Armando Marsans
1946	Alijadores	56–41	Tampico	Armando Marsans
1947	Industriales	50–47	Monterrey	Lázaro Salazar
1948	Industriales	50–35	Monterrey	Lázaro Salazar
1949	Industriales	52–33	Monterrey	Lázaro Salazar
1950	Union Laguna	48–36	Torreón	Guillermo Garibay
1951	Azules de Veracruz	40–35	Mexico City	Jorge Pasquel and Angel Castro
1952	Aguila	57–33	Veracruz	Santos Amaro
1953	Tecolotes	43–33	Nuevo Laredo	Adolfo Luque
1954	Tecolotes	56–24	Nuevo Laredo	Adolfo Luque
1955	Tigres	55–47	Mexico City	George Genovese
1956	Diablos Rojos	83–37	Mexico City	Lázaro Salazar
1957	Leones de Yucatán	68–52	Merida	Oscar Rodríguez
1958	Tecolotes	75–45	Nuevo Laredo	José "Cheo" Ramos
1959	Petroleros	84–62	Poza Rica	Luis García
1960	Tigres	77–66	Mexico City	Guillermo Garibay
1961	Aguila	77–57	Veracruz	Santos Amaro
1962	Sultanes	77–53	Monterrey	Clemente Carrera
1963	Pericos	80–52	Puebla	Antonio Castaño
1964	Diablos Rojos	82–58	Mexico City	Tomás Herrera
1965	Tigres	82–57	Mexico City	José Luis García
1966	Tigres	79–62	Mexico City	Ricardo Garza
1967	Jalisco	85–55	Guadalajara	Guillermo Garibay
1968	Diablos Rojos	82–58	Mexico City	Tomás Herrera
1969	Broncos	91–63	Reynosa	Miguel Sotelo
1970	Aguila	87–63	Veracruz	Enrique Izquierdo
1971	Jalisco	82–65	Guadalajara	Benjamín Reyes
1972	Cafeteros	72–61	Córdoba	Mario Pelaez
1973	Diablos Rojos	79–55	Mexico City	Wilfredo Calviño
1974	Diablos Rojos	75–61	Mexico City	Benjamín Reyes
1975	Alijadores	73–62	Tampico	Benjamín Valenzuela
1976	Diablos Rojos	75–63	Mexico City	Benjamín Reyes
1977	Tecolotes	77–75	Nuevo Laredo	Jorge Fitch Díaz
1978	Rieleros	89–62	Aguascalientes	Jaime Fabela
1979	Angeles	86–51	Puebla	Jorge Fitch Díaz
1980*	Saraperos	52–47	Saltillo	Gregorio Luque
1981	Diablos Rojos	75–47	Mexico City	Winston Llenas
1982	Indios	73–55	Ciudad Juárez	José Guerrero

(*continued*)

(continued)

Year	Champions	Record	City	Manager
1983	Piratas	70–44	Campeche	Francisco Estrada Soto
1984	Leones de Yucatán	65–51	Merida	Carlos Paz
1985	Diablos Rojos	80–52	Mexico City	Benjamín Reyes
1986	Angeles Negros	88–41	Puebla	Rodolfo Sandoval
1987	Diablos Rojos	75–49	Mexico City	Benjamín Reyes
1988	Diablos Rojos	82–45	Mexico City	Benjamín Reyes
1989	Dos Laredos	NA	Laredo/Nuevo Laredo	José Guerrero
1990	Bravos	NA	León	Francisco Estrada
1991	Sultanes	NA	Monterrey	Aurelio Rodríguez
1992	Tigres	76–52	Mexico City	Gerardo Gutierrez
1993	Olmecas de Tabasco	66–59	Villahermosa	Juan Navarrette
1994	Diablos Rojos	73–40	Mexico City	Marco Antonio Vazquez
1995	Sultanes	65–49	Monterrey	Derek Bryant
1996	Sultanes	82–33	Monterrey	Derek Bryant
1997	Tigres	77–40	Mexico City	Dan Firova
1998	Guerreros	68–50	Oaxaca	Nelson Barrera
1999	Diablos Rojos	74–43	Mexico City	Marco Vazquez and Tim Johnson
2000	Tigres	74–44	Mexico City	Dan Firova
2001	Tigres	74–43	Mexico City	Dan Firova
2002	Diablos Rojos	74–36	Mexico City	Bernie Tatis
2003	Diablos Rojos	68–40	Mexico City	Bernie Tatis

Abbreviations: NA, not available.
* The 1980 season was interrupted and then extended due to a players union strike.

Mexican League Batting Leaders (1937–2003)

Year	Batting Champion	BA	Home Run Leader	HR	RBI Leader	RBI
1937	Alfonso Nieto	.476	Carlos Galina	6	Roberto Cabal	31
1938	Martín Dihigo	.387	Angel Castro	9	Angel Castro	40
1939	Lázaro Salazar	.374	Angel Castro	9	Angel Castro	50
1940*	James "Cool Papa" Bell	.437	James "Cool Papa" Bell	12	James "Cool Papa" Bell	79
1941	Burnis (Bill) Wright	.390	Josh Gibson	33	Josh Gibson	124
1942	Monte Irvin	.397	Monte Irvin	20	Silvio García	83
1943*	Burnis (Bill) Wright	.366	Burnis (Bill) Wright	13	Burnis (Bill) Wright	70
1944	Alberto Hernández	.395	Salvador Hernández	13	Salvador Hernández	97
1945	Claro Duany	.375	Roberto Ortiz	26	Claro Duany	100
1946	Claro Duany	.364	Roberto Ortiz	25	Roberto Ortiz	108
1947	Roberto (Beto) Ávila	.346	Roberto Ortiz	22	Alejandro Crespo	96
1948	Ray Dandridge	.369	Roberto Ortiz	19	Roberto Ortiz	74
1949	Adolfo Sánchez	.379	Jesús Díaz	13	Jesús Díaz	83
1950	Lorenzo Cabrera	.354	Jesús Díaz	10	Angel Castro	68
1951*	Angel Castro	.354	Angel Castro	22	Angel Castro	79
1952*	René González	.370	René González	21	René González	84
1953	René González	.343	Héctor Lara	13	René González	63
1954	René González	.359	René González	21	Fernándo Pedrozo	80
1955	Leonardo Rodríguez	.385	Mario Ariosa	22	Alonso Perry	122
1956*	Alonso Perry	.392	Alonso Perry	28	Alonso Perry	118
1957	Aldo Salvent	.359	Earl Taborn	27	Alonso Perry	107
1958	Pablo Bernard	.371	Edward Moore	32	Herminio Cortes	98
1959	Alfred Pinkston	.369	Aldo Salvent	29	Marvin Williams	109
1960	Alfred Pinkston	.397	Aldo Salvent	36	Alfred Pinkston	144

Mexican League Batting Leaders (1937–2003)

Year	Batting Champion	BA	Home Run Leader	HR	RBI Leader	RBI
1961	Alfred Pinkston	.374	Witremundo Quintana	23	Witremundo Quintana	89
1962	Alfred Pinkston	.381	Rolando Camacho	25	Héctor Espino	105
1963	Vinicio García	.368	Rolando Camacho	39	Ronaldo Camacho	108
1964	Héctor Espino	.371	Héctor Espino	46	George Prescott	123
1965	Emilio Sosa	.368	George Prescott	39	Jaime Favela	109
1966	Héctor Espino	.369	George Prescott	41	George Prescott	122
1967	Héctor Espino	.379	Elrod Hendricks	41	Winston Llenas	113
1968	Héctor Espino	.365	Héctor Espino	27	George Prescott	84
1969	Teolindo Acosta	.354	Héctor Espino	37	Ronaldo Camacho	116
1970	Francisco Campos	.358	Rogelio Alvarez	33	Ildefonso Ruíz	99
1971	Teolindo Acosta	.392	Humberto García	23	Victor Torres	107
1972	Donald Anderson	.362	Héctor Espino	37	Gabriel Lugo	106
1973	Héctor Espino	.377	Rommel Canada	26	Héctor Espino	107
1974	Teolindo Acosta	.366	Byron Browne	32	Jorge Roque Vargas	90
1975	Patrick Bourque	.372	Andrés Mora	35	Andés Mora	109
1976	Lawrence Fritz	.355	Jack Pierce	36	Jack Pierce	118
1977	Vic Davalillo	.384	Ismael Oquendo	34	Reggie Sanders	119
1978	Rommel Canada	.366	Harold King	28	Harold Kings	114
1979	James Collins	.438	Luis Angel Alcaraz	24	Earl Williams	112
1980†	James Collins	.380	Jack Pierce	7	James Collins	31
1981	Willie Norwood	.365	Andrés Mora	23	Andrés Mora	93
1982	Robert Smith	.357	Andrés Mora	25	Andrés Mora	80
1983	Ricardo Durán	.377	Carlos Soto	22	Enrique Aguilar	89
1984	James Collins	.412	Derek Bryant	41	Ramón Antonio Lora	127
1985	Oswaldo Olivares	.397	Andrés Mora	41	Ricardo Renteria	125
1986	Willie Mays Aikens	.454	Jack Pierce	54	Willie Mays Aikens	154
1987	Orlando Sánchez	.415	Nelson Barrera	42	Nelson Barrera	134
1988	Nick Castañeda	.374	Leo Hernández	36	Nelson Barrera	124
1989	Willie Mays Aikens	.395	Leo Hernández	39	Willie Mays Aikens	131
1990	Nick Castañeda	.388	Alejandro Sánchez	28	Dave Stockstill	109
1991	Ricardo Renteria	.442	Roy Johnson	37	Lawrence See	129
1992	Raúl Pérez Tóvar	.416	Ty Gainey	47	Ty Gainey	133
1993	Nelson Simmons	.382	Matías Carrillo García	38	Matías Carrillo García	125
1994	Adam Casillas	.367	Héctor Villanueva	30	Héctor Villanueva	108
1995*	Ty Gainey	.411	Ty Gainey	27	Ty Gainey	115
1996	Matías Carrillo García	.368	Sam Horn	30	Guillermo Velazquez	112
1997	Cornelio García	.382	Ty Gainey	25	Ty Gainey	108
1998	Luis Polonia	.381	Charles Smith	29	Nelson Barrera	110
1999	Julio Franco	.423	Mike Meggers	28	Boi Rodríguez	105
2000	Warren Newson	.386	Eduardo Jiménez Castillo	45	Julian Yan	129
2001	Julio Franco	.437	Boi Rodríguez	33	Boi Rodríguez	100
2002	Willie Romero	.388	Roberto Saucedo	32	Félix José	102
2003	Félix José	.377	Guillermo García	28	Guillermo García	95

* Year with a triple crown winner.
† The 1980 season was interrupted and then extended due to a players union strike.

Mexican League Pitching Leaders (1937–2003)

Year	ERA Leader	ERA	Win–Loss Leader	W–L	PCT	Strikeouts Leader	SO
1937	Alberto Chávez	0.78	Alberto Chávez	8–0	1.000	Basilio Rosell	71
1938	Martín Dihigo	0.90	Martín Dihigo	18–2	.900	Martín Dihigo	184
1939	John Taylor	1.19	John Taylor	11–1	.917	Martín Dihigo	202
1940	Ramón Bragaña	2.58	William Jefferson	22–9	.710	Edward Porter	232

(*continued*)

(continued)

Year	ERA Leader	ERA	Win–Loss Leader	W–L	PCT	Strikeouts Leader	SO
1941	Jesús Valenzuela	3.12	Robert Cabal	9–1	.900	Edward Porter	133
1942	Martín Dihigo	2.53	Martín Dihigo	22–7	.759	Martín Dihigo	211
1943	Vidal López	2.08	Manuel Fortes	18–6	.750	Martín Dihigo	134
1944	Adrian Zabala	2.74	Adrian Zabala	10–2	.833	Ramón Bragaña	144
1945	Juan Guerrero	2.87	Juan Guerrero	11–1	.846	Agapito Mayor	156
1946	Max Lanier	1.94	Martín Dihigo	11–4	.733	Booker Daniels	171
1947	Santiago Ulrich	2.65	Armando Torres	14–6	.700	Booker Daniels	127
1948	Guillermo López	2.37	Pedro Ramírez	9–2	.818	Agapito Mayor	92
1949	Alfonso Ramírez	2.35	Vicente Torres	13–5	.722	Wilfredo Salas	158
1950	Pedro Antuñez	1.87	William Creason	10–1	.909	Barney Brown	157
1951	Lino Donoso	2.55	James Lamarque	19–6	.760	Lino Donoso	197
1952	Vicente Torres	2.43	Guadalupe Ortegón	8–3	.727	Lino Donoso	235
1953	Jesús Moreno	1.63	Jesús Moreno	18–3	.857	Lino Donoso	162
1954	Humberto García	2.29	Tomás Arroyo	15–1	.938	Raul Galata	118
1955	Fred Waters	2.09	Fred Waters	18–3	.857	Fred Walters	126
1956	Francisco Ramírez	2.25	Francisco Ramírez	20–3	.870	Francisco Ramírez	148
1957	Edward Locke	3.20	Lino Donoso	8–2	.800	Julian Ladera	136
1958	Julio Moreno	2.70	Romeo Cadena	7–1	.875	Juan Piedra	159
1959	Roberto Vargas	2.55	Roberto Vargas	13–3	.813	Diómedes Olivo	233
1960	Silvio Castellanos	3.24	Luis Tiant	17–7	.708	Silvio Castellanos	122
1961	Julio Moreno	3.01	Ramón Arano	11–3	.786	Juan Piedra	171
1962	Ramón Arano	2.60	Ramón Arano	17–6	.739	Miguel Cuéllar	124
1963	Arturo Cacheux	2.69	Ramón Arano	13–4	.765	Miguel Sotelo	208
1964	Alberto Osorio	2.56	Andrés Ayon	16–5	.762	José Ramón López	213
1965	Frank Barnes	1.58	Frank Barnes	13–5	.722	José Ramón López	201
1966	Waldo Velo	2.01	Waldo Velo	17–4	.810	José Ramón López	309
1967	Juan Suby	2.36	Andrés Ayon	25–6	.806	Frank Maytorena	175
1968	James Horsford	1.59	Celso Contreras	14–6	.700	James Horsford	212
1969	Salvador Sánchez	1.84	Manuel Lugo	14–6	.700	James Horsford	199
1970	Alfredo Mariscal	1.85	Blas Mason	13–5	.722	Felipe Leál	170
1971	Andrés Ayon	1.22	José Soto	10–3	.769	Felipe Leál	223
1972	Alfredo Meza	1.83	Andrés Ayon	22–3	.880	Alvin Martin	166
1973	Manuel Lugo	1.60	Silvano Quezada	22–2	.917	José Peña	195
1974	Juan Pizarro	1.57	Aurelio Monteagudo	12–0	1.000	Antonio Pollorena	183
1975	Ricardo Sandate	1.42	Miguel Pereyra	8–0	1.000	José Peña	199
1976	Gary Ryerson	1.52	Enrique Romo	20–4	.833	Enrique Romo	239
1977	Horacio Piña	1.70	Roberto Verdugo	8–2	.800	Byron McLaughlin	221
1978	Michael Nagy	1.64	Carlos Sosa	9–1	.900	Aurelio Monteagudo	222
1979	Rafael García	1.69	Miguel Solis	25–5	.833	Rafael García	222
1980*	Gilberto Rondón	1.44	Pilar Rodríguez	9–0	1.000	Luis Mercedez	155
1981	Vicente Romo	1.40	Rafael García	20–5	.800	Rafael García	187
1982	Ernesto Cordova	1.58	José Peña	10–1	.909	Santos Alcala	192
1983	Arturo González	1.92	Maximino León	13–1	.929	Teodoro Higuera	165
1984	Salvador Colorado	2.20	Miguel Solis	17–4	.810	Jesús Ríos	194
1985	Jesús Ríos	2.52	Eleazar Beltran	18–3	.857	Ramón Serna	200
1986	Barry Bass	2.03	Octavio Orozco	13–2	.867	Rafael García	155
1987	Robin Fuson	2.67	Luis Leál	15–2	.882	Jesús Ríos	200
1988	Dave Walsh	1.73	Dave Walsh	14–1	.933	Jesús Ríos	195
1989	Mercedes Esquer	1.98	Idelfonso Velazquez	20–6	.769	Adolfo Navarro	150
1990	Guy Normand	2.08	Luis Castillo	9–1	.900	Armando Reynoso	170
1991	Odell Jones	2.67	Salome Barojas	10–1	.909	*Several Tied*	
1992	Mercedes Esquer	2.24	Francisco Esquer	18–4	.818	Jesús Ríos	186
1993	Manuel Hernández	2.20	Francisco Córdoba	9–2	.818	Urbano Lugo	164
1994	Leobardo Mesa	1.67	Francisco Montaño	19–1	.950	*Several Tied*	
1995	Cecilio Ruíz	1.71	Francisco Córdoba	13–0	1.000	Angel Moreno	108
1996	Sixto Báez	1.54	Rafael Díaz	14–1	.933	Will Flynt	137

Year	ERA Leader	ERA	Win–Loss Leader	W–L	PCT	Strikeouts Leader	SO
1997	Emigdio López	1.91	Eleazar Mora	16–3	.842	Jesús Ríos	121
1998	Angel Moreno	1.96	Bernardo Cuervo	11–1	.917	Ravelo Manzanillo	144
1999	Juan Jesús Alvarez	2.20	Héctor Heredia	9–1	.900	Narciso Elvira	133
2000	Luis Fernández Morales	2.04	José López	8–2	.800	Ravelo Manzanillo	183
2001	Ravelo Manzanillo	1.52	Ravelo Manzanillo	16–3	.842	Ravelo Manzanillo	202
2002	Edwin Hurtado	1.38	Eleazar Mora	15–6	.714	Francisco Campos	125
2003	Dan Serafini	1.59	José Mercedes	14–6	.700	Bo Magee	155

* The 1980 season was interrupted and then extended due to a players union strike.

Individual Mexican League Batting and Pitching Records (1937–2003)

Category	Name	Record	Date
Batting			
Seasons Played	Jesús Sommers	27	1970–1996
Games Played, Career	Jesús Sommers	2,908	1970–1996
Games Played, Season	Rolando Camarero	161	1969
Consecutive Games Played	Gerardo Sánchez	1415	1984–1999
Batting Average, Career	Alfred Pinkston	.372, 1,204 hits	1959–1965
Batting Average, Season	Willie Mays Aikens	.454	1986
Lowest BA for Batting Champ	Roberto "Beto" Ávila	.346	1947
Most Batting Titles Won	Héctor Espino	5	1964, 1966, 1967. 1968, 1973
Most Seasons Batting .300	Matías Carrillo	15	1989–2003
Most At-Bats, Career	Jesús Sommers	10,327	1970–1996
Most At-Bats, Season	Pedro Cardenal	649	1959
Most Seasons as At-Bats Leader	Gonzalo Villalobos	4	1965, 1968, 1975, 1978
Runs Scored, Career	Daniel Fernández	1,506	1983–2001
Runs Scored, Season	Nicholas Castañeda	141	1986
Runs Scored, Game, 9 innings	Alfred Pinkston	6	May 8, 1960
	Teolindo Acosta	6	Apr. 15, 1970
	Humberto García	6	Apr. 3, 1973
Most Seasons as Runs Leader	Héctor Espino	4	1962, 1964, 1969, 1972
Base Hits, Career	Jesús Sommers	3,004	1970–1996
Base Hits, Season	Miguel Suárez López	227	1977
Most Seasons as Hits Leader	Ray Dandridge	3	1943, 1947, 1948
	Alfred Pinkston	3	1959, 1960, 1962
	Miguel Suárez López	3	1971, 1976, 1977
Consecutive Base Hits	Héctor Espino	11	1980
	Danny García	11	1982
	Willie Mays Aikens	11	1986
Hitting Streak, Games	Roberto Ortiz	35	1948
Doubles, Career	Jesús Sommers	488	1970–1996
Doubles, Season	Vinicio García	49	1961
	Roberto Vizcarra Acosta	49	1979
Triples, Career	Gonzalo Villalobos	132	1963–1980
Triples, Season	Albino Díaz	19	1975
	Leonardo Valenzuela	19	1979
Home Runs, Career	Nelson Barrera	455	1977–2002
Home Runs, Season, Right-handed	Héctor Espino	46	1964
Home Runs, Season, Left-handed	Jack Pierce	54	1986
Most Seasons as HR Leader	Angel Castro	4	1938, 1939, 1950, 1951
	Roberto Ortiz	4	1945, 1946, 1947, 1948
	Héctor Espino	4	1964, 1968, 1969, 1972
	Andres Mora	4	1974, 1981, 1982, 1985

(*continued*)

(continued)

Category	Name	Record	Date
Home Runs, Game, 9 innings	Derek Bryant	4	May 14, 1985
Runs Batted in, Career	Nelson Barrera	1,928	1977–2002
Runs Batted In, Season	Willie Mays Aikens	154	1986
Total Bases, Career	Nelson Barrera	4,872	1977–2002
Total Bases, Season	Willie Mays Aikens	384	1986
Total Bases, Game	Derek Bryant	19	May 14, 1985, four HRs and triple
Extra Base Hits, Career	Nelson Barrera	972	1977–2002
Stolen Bases, Career	Antonio Briones Luna	490	1971–1988
Stolen Bases, Season	Michael Cole	100	1989
Stolen Bases, Game, 9 innings	Antonio Briones Luna	7	June 2, 1980
Strikeouts, Career	Nelson Barrera	1,457	1977–2002
Strikeouts, Season	William Parlier	131	1970
Walks, Career	Rolando Camacho	1,411	1956–1975
Intentional Walks, Career	Héctor Espino	408	1962–1984
Pitching			
Seasons Pitched	Ramón Arano	31	1959–1986, 1995, 1998
Games Won, Career	Ramón Arano	334	1959–1986, 1995, 1998
Games Won, Season	Ramón Bragaña	30	1944
Games Lost, Career	Ramón Arano	264	1959–1986, 1995, 1998
Games Lost, Season	Ramón Ramos	21	1957
ERA, Career	Vicente Romo	1.49	2535.2 innings
ERA, Season	Martín Dihigo	0.90	167 innings, in 1938
Winning Percentage, Career	Martín Dihigo	.676	119–57
Winning Percentage, Season	Francisco Córdoba	1.000	13–0, in 1995
Games Pitched, Career	Ramón Arano	810	1959–1986, 1995, 1998
Games Pitched, Season	Roberto Osuna	75	1997
Complete Games, Career	Ramón Arano	297	1959–1986, 1995, 1998
Complete Games, Season	James Horsford	30	1969
Games Started, Career	Ramón Arano	675	1959–1986, 1995, 1998
Games Started, Season	William Jefferson	39	1940
Saves, Career	Antonio Pulido Leál	197	1979–1993
Saves, Season	Luis Ignacio Ayala	41	1997
Shutouts, Career	Ramón Arano	57	1959–1986, 1995, 1998
Shutouts, Season	Gary Ryerson	10	1976
	Luis Mere Gómez	10	1977
	Vicente Romo	10	1979
Consecutive Scoreless Innings	James Horsford	51	July 12, 1968 thru Aug. 7, 1968
Innings Pitched, Career	Ramón Arano	4,770	1959–1986, 1995, 1998
Innings Pitched, Season	Ramón Bragaña	325.1	1944
Strikeouts, Career	Ramón Arano	2,380	1959–1986, 1995, 1998
Strikeouts, Season	José Ramón López	309	1966
Strikeouts, Season, Relief	Aurelio López	165	1977
Strikeouts, Game	Martín Dihigo	22	June 4, 1938, in 13 innings
Strikeouts, Game, 9 innings	Martín Dihigo	18	Aug. 5, 1939
	Lefty Glover	18	June 30, 1940
	Lino Dinoso	18	Mar. 21, 1951
	Ricardo Sandate	18	May 6, 1974
Bases on Balls, Career	Daniel Ríos	1,441	1939–1964
Bases on Balls, Season	Booker McDaniels	176	1946
Bases on Balls, Game, 9 innings	Carlos Hidalgo	16	June 27, 1982, in 5.2 innings
Balks Committed, Career	Ernesto Carlos Kuk Lee	21	1972–1982
Balks Committed, Season	Peter Bonfils	6	1978
Wild Pitches, Career	José Peña	150	1962–1984
Wild Pitches, Season	Rafael García	30	1988
Wild Pitches, Game, 9 innings	Cecilio Acosta	6	June 28, 1979

Mexican League Rookie of the Year (1937–2000)

Year	Name	Team
1937	Alfonso Nieto	Agricultura
1938	Angel Castro	Tampico
1939	Epitacio Torres	Monterrey
1940	Laureano Camacho	Veracruz
1941	Guillermo Garibay	Union Laguna
1942	Jesús Díaz	Union Laguna
1943	Roberto "Beto" Ávila*	Puebla
1944	Jorge Bravo	Mexico City
1945	Juan Conde	Puebla
1946	Guillermo Alvarez	Puebla
1947	Tomás Arroyo	Tampico
1948	Felipe Montemayor*	Monterrey
1949	Leonard Rodríguez	Union Laguna
1950	Francisco Ramírez Conde	San Luis
1951	Fernando García	San Luis
1952	Jaime Abad	Aguila
1953	Pecas Serrano	Monterrey
1954	Alejandro Moreno	Laredo
1955	Roman Ramos	Aguila
1956	Jesse Durán	Mexico City Tigers
1957	Mario Luna	Mexico City Reds
1958	Alberto Palafox	Mexico City Reds
1959	Ramón Arano	Poza Rica and Aguila
1960	Mauro Ruíz Rubio	Mexico City Tigers
1961	Pablo Montes de Oca	Aguila
1962	Héctor Espino	Monterrey
1963	Vicente Romo*	Mexico City Tigers
1964	Elpidio Osuna	Poza Rica
1965	Héctor Barnetche	Mexico City Tigers
1966	Abelardo Balderas	Mexico City Reds
1967	Francisco Maytorena	Reynosa
1968	Francisco Campos*	Jalisco
1969	Luis Lagunas	Jalisco
1970	Ernesto Escarrega	Mexico City Reds
1971	Miguel Suárez	Mexico City Reds
1972	Rodolfo Hernández	Jalisco
1973	Francisco Barrios*	Jalisco
1974	Guadalupe Salinas	Reynosa
1975	Juan Martínez Cordero	Monterrey
1976	Alfonso Jiménez	Puebla
1977	Abraham Rivera	Puebla
1978	Joel Pérez	Durango
1979	Fernando Valenzuela*	Yucatán
1980	*No Election*	
1981	Teddy Higuera*	Ciudad Juárez
1982	Matías Carrillo	Poza Rica
	Nelson Matu	Tabasco
1983	Ramón Serna	Ciudad Juárez
	Jesús Antonio Barrera	Laredo
1984	Jesús Ríos	Mexico City Tigers
	Carlos de los Santos	Córdoba
1985	Pablo Machiria	Tamaulipas
	Florentino Vásquez	Monclova
1986	Eduardo Torres	Saltillo
	Lorenzo Retes	Mexico City Tigers

(continued)

(continued)

Year	Name	Team
1987	Miguel Angel Valencia	Mexico City Tigers
1988	Marco Antonio Romero	Jalisco
	Andrés Cruz	Yucatán
1989	Germán Leyva	Monclova
1990	Lázaro Tiquet	Tabasco
	David Sinohui	León
1991	Oscar Romero	Córdoba
1992	Antonio Osuna*	Mexico City Tigers
1993	Ismael Valdés*	Mexico City Tigers
1994	Elemer Dessens*	Mexico City Red Devils
	Fernando Rodríguez	Torreón
1995	Bernardo Cuervo	Campeche
	Raúl Paez	Mexico City Red Devils
1996	Francisco Campos	Campeche
1997	Erubiel Durazo*	Monterrey
1998	Luis Mauricio Suárez	Mexico City Tigers
1999	Luis Carlos García	Mexico City Tigers
2000	Pablo Ortega	Mexico City Tigers

* U.S. Major leaguer.

Mexican League No-Hit Games Pitched (1937–2000)

	Year	Date	Pitcher	Teams and Score (Game Innings)	Location
1	1937	Sept. 16	Martín Dihigo*	Aguila 4, Nogales 0 (9)	Veracruz
2	1939	May 29	Chet Brewer†	Tampico 6, Comintra 0 (9)	Tampico
3	1939	July 23	John Taylor†	Córdoba 4, Monterrey 0 (9)	Córdoba
4	1939	Aug. 12	Chet Brewer†	Tampico 1, Santa Rosa 0 (9)	Tampico
5	1948	Apr. 10	Cocaína García*	Tampico 2, Veracruz 0 (9)	Tampico
6	1955	Aug. 13	Jaime Ochoa	Tigres 15, Aguila 0 (7)	Mexico City
7	1959	Sept. 20	Charlie Gorin†	Austin 2, Mexico City 0 (9)	Austin, TX
8	1961	July 14	Roman Ramos	Poza Rica 11, Austin 0 (9)	Poza Rica
9	1961	July 15	Larry Maxie†	Austin 5, Nogales 0 (9)	Poza Rica
10	1966	June 25	Andrés Ayon*	Puebla 7, Jalisco 0 (9)	Puebla
11	1966	Aug. 10	Evelio Hernández	Monterrey 2, Puebla 0 (7)	Puebla
12	1970	July 11	José Ramón López	Monterrey 1, Jalisco 0 (7)	Guadalajara
13	1970	July 29	Héctor Madrigal	Poza Rica 2, Jalisco 0 (9)	Poza Rica
14	1971	June 9	Alejo Ahumada	Tampico 4, Poza Rica 0 (7)	Poza Rica
15	1974	Apr. 29	Anastacio Velazquez	Aguila 1, Chihuahua 0 (9)	Veracruz
16	1974	May 4	Alfredo Meza	Mexico City Tigres 3, Tampico 0 (9)	Mexico City
17	1974	June 14	Eduard Kelly	Jalisco 3, Coahuila 0 (9)	Monclova
18	1975	May 1	Horacio Pina	Aguascalientes 1, Ciudad Juárez 0 (7)	Ciudad Juárez
19	1975	May 20	Roger Hambright†	Ciudad Juárez 4, Tampico 0 (7)	Tampico
20	1975	July 8	Tom Miali	Coahuila 1, Chihuahua 0 (7)	Chihuahua
21	1975	July 21	Héctor Valenzuela	Coahuila 3, Tampico 0 (9)	Tampico
22	1977	May 26	Arturo Casas	Tampico 1, Córdoba 0 (7)	Tampico
23	1977	June 20	George Brunet†	Poza Rica 5, Durango 0 (9)	Poza Rica
24	1978	June 28	Arturo González	Monterrey 2, Torreón 0 (9)	Monterrey
25	1978	July 12	Michael Paul†	Ciudad Juárez 1, Monterrey 0 (7)	Ciudad Juárez
26	1979	Apr. 13	Tomás Armas	Saltillo 5, Monterrey 0 (9)	Saltillo
27	1979	May 19	Aurelio Monteagudo*	Coahuila 10, Laredo 0 (7)	Sabinas
28	1979	July 1	Roberto Ochoa	Tabasco 2, Aguila 0 (5)	Villahermosa
29	1979	July 8	Fernándo López	Puebla 2, Durango 0 (7)	Durango
30	1979	Aug. 17	Peter Bonfils	Poza Rica 2, Tampico 0 (5)	Poza Rica

	Year	Date	Pitcher	Teams and Score (Game Innings)	Location
31	1980	May 20	Joe Henderson	Coatzacoalcos 3, Monterrey 0 (9)	Coatzacoalcos
32	1981	Mar. 27	Ramón de los Santos	Torreón 4, Chihuahua 0 (7)	Chihuahua
33	1981	Apr. 12	Rolando Menendez	Saltillo 2, Reynosa 0 (7)	Saltillo
34	1981	May 17	Rafael García	Ciudad Juárez 3, Coatzacoalcos 0 (7)	Ciudad Juárez
35	1981	May 25	Gary Beare[†]	Laredo 2, Mexico City Diablos 0 (7)	Laredo
36	1982	May 6	Herminio Domínguez	Campeche 2, Mexico City Tigres 0 (7)	Campeche
37	1982	July 3	Alvaro Soto	Yucatán 2, Aguila 0 (7)	Veracruz
38	1982	July 7	Jesse Jefferson[†]	Laredo 9, Chihuahua 0 (7)	Chihuahua
39	1982	July 15	Jesús Hernaiz	Coatzacoalcos 11, Yucatán 0 (9)	Mérida
40	1982	July 18	Leonel García	Laredo 5, Reynosa 0 (7)	Reynosa
41	1983	May 12	Héctor Madrigal	Aguila 7, Ciudad Juárez 0 (9)	Veracruz
42	1983	July 21	Alvaro Soto	León 5, Monterrey 0 (7)	Monterrey
43	1984	May 12	Jesús Ríos	Mexico City Tigres 2, Córdoba 0 (9)	Mexico City
44	1985	June 4	Salvador Colorado	Córdoba 4, Monterrey 0 (7)	Córdoba
45	1985	June 8	Carlos Sosa	Tampico 4, Puebla 0 (9)	Tampico
46	1986	May 4	Kenneth Angulo	Yucatán 8, Mexico City Tigres 0 (7)	Médida
47	1986	May 25	Herminio Domínguez	Campeche 12, Aguila 0 (7)	Veracruz
48	1987	May 17	Armando Pruneda	Monclova 1, Nogales 0 (7)	Monclova
49	1987	May 24	Isaac Jiménez	Yucatán 6, Nogales 0 (9)	Mérida
50	1988	May 2	Isidro Morales	San Luis 2, Tabasco 0 (7)	San Luis
51	1990	July 4	Israel Velazquez	León 5, Mexico City Tigres 0 (7)	Mexico City
52	1990	July 20	Armando Reynoso	Saltillo 1, Nogales 0 (7)	Saltillo
53	1990	Aug. 4	Lauro Cervantes	Torreón 4, Nogales 0 (9)	Torreón
54	1991	June 5	Antonio Félix	Mexico City Diablos 7, Monterrey 0 (9)	Mexico City
55	1992	Apr. 1	Ernesto Barraza	Laredo 5, Córdoba 0 (7)	Córdoba
56	1992	July 18	Andrés Cruz	Yucatán 8, Jalisco 0 (9)	Mérida
57	1993	Mar. 21	Arturo Olmos	Saltillo 2, Aguascalientes 0 (7)	Aguascalientes
58	1993	June 13	Leobardo Meza	Aguila 3, Laredo 0 (9)	Laredo
59	1993	June 19	Israel Velazquez	Minatitlan 2, Campache 0 (7)	Campeche
60	1994	Mar. 17	Francisco Montaño	Monclova 3, Industriales 0 (7)	Monclova
61	1995	June 6	Roberto Ramírez	Mexico City Diablos 2, Tabasco 0 (7)	Mexico City
62	1995	June 20	Julio Hernández	Aguila 1, Mexico City Diablos 0 (7)	Mexico City
63	1995	July 1	John Henry[†]	Puebla 3, Aguila 0 (7)	Puebla
64	1995	July 2	Bernardo Cuervo	Campeche 4, Minatitlan 0 (7)	Ciudad Carmen
65	1996	July 10	Roberto Ramírez	Mexico City Diablos 2, Tabasco 0 (9)	Villahermosa
66	1997	Mar. 24	Rob Mattson[†]	Aguascalientes 2, Poza Rica 0 (9)	Poza Rica
67	1997	Apr. 20	Héctor Fajardo	Monclova 3, Torreón 0 (7)	Monclova
68	1998	June 26	Jaime Orozco	Córdoba 5, Aguascalientes 0 (7)	Córdoba
69	1998	Aug. 4	Obed Vega	Laredo 7, Saltillo 0 (9)	Laredo
70	1999	Mar. 20	Narciso Elvira	Campeche 5, Cancún 0 (9)	Cancún
71	1999	June 10	Narciso Elvira	Campeche 1, Laredo 0 (9)	Campeche

* From Cuba.
† From the United States.

Mexican League Perfect Games Pitched (1937–2000)

	Year	Date	Pitcher	Teams and Score (Game Innings)	Location
1	1953	Aug. 14	Ramiro Cuevas	Laredo 1, Mexico City Diablos 0 (9)	Mexico City
2	1972	June 30	Andres Ayon	Saltillo 9, Monterrey 0 (7)	Monterrey
3	1978	June 21	Diego Segui*	Córdoba 5, Laredo 0 (7)	Córdoba
4	1978	July 12	Horacio Piña	Aguascalientes 3, Mexico City Diablos 0 (9)	Aguascalientes
5	1981	Apr. 26	Victor García	Laredo 1, Ciudad Juárez 0 (7)	Laredo
6	1984	June 10	Jairo Valenzuela	Saltillo 5, Córdoba 0 (7)	Córdoba

(continued)

	Year	Date	Pitcher	Teams and Score (Game Innings)	Location
7	1985	Apr. 14	Herminio Domingüez	Campeche 1, Córdoba 0 (7)	Campeche
8	1992	June 2	Don Heinkel[†]	Campeche 7, Mexico City Diablos 0 (7)	Campeche
9	1971	Mar. 24	Francisco Maytorena (3 IP) Héctor Manuel Díaz (3 IP) Nicolas García (1 IP)	Mexico City Tigres 3, Aguila 0 (7)	Mexico City

* From Cuba.
[†] From the United States.

Career of Héctor Espino, the Mexican Babe Ruth

Héctor Espino's Profile

Leagues	Mexican League (Summer); Mexican Pacific League (Winter)
League Teams	Monterrey Sultanes (ML); Tampico Alijadores (ML); San Luis Potosí Tuneros (ML); Hermosillo Naranjeros (MPL)
Seasons	24 (1962–1984)
Career Home Runs (Total)	763 (Sadaharu Oh, 868, Hank Aaron, 744, Babe Ruth, 714)
Career Home Runs, ML	453
Career Home Runs, MPL	310
Career Batting Average	.335
Career Runs Batted In	1,573 (Mexican League); 2,693 (both leagues)
Hall of Fame	Mexican Baseball Hall of Fame
Died	Sept. 7, 1997, age 53, heart attack, in Monterrey, Mexico

Héctor Espino's Ten Greatest Career Moments

1962	Named Mexican League Rookie of the Year with 23 HR, 105 RBI, and .358 BA
1964 (May 10)	Hits 4 homers and double for Monterrey Sultans in contest versus Poza Rica
1964	Sets Mexican League record of 46 home runs (breaking old mark of 39) in single season
1969 (Apr. 27)	Receives four intentional walks in doubleheader opener against Mexico City
1969 (Apr. 27)	Also collects career base hit number 1,000 in game two of same doubleheader
1969 (May 15–19)	Smashes record 8 homers in six-game period for Monterrey Sultans
1972	Wins record fourth Mexican League home run crown
1976	Leads Hermosillo team to Mexico's first Caribbean World Series title in Santo Domingo
1982	Appears in fifth and final Caribbean World Series at Hermosillo's Héctor Espino Stadium
1984	Retires as all-time home run champion (with 453) of Mexican League history

Abbreviations: ML, Mexican League; MPL, Mexican Pacific League.

Statistics of Select Cuban, Latin American, and U.S. Stars Playing in the Mexican League: Batters

Name	Country	Years	Seasons	AB	H	HR	RBI	BA
Josh Gibson	USA	1940–1941	2	450	177	44	162	.393
Willie Mays Aikens	USA	1986–1991	6	2,328	867	170	657	.372
James "Cool Papa" Bell	USA	1938–1941	4	1,189	436	27	168	.367
Vic Davalillo	Venezuela	1974–1981	6	2,190	782	35	302	.357
Alonzo Perry	USA	1955–1963	7	3,122	1,107	138	721	.355
Rico Carty	Dominican	1974	1	401	142	11	72	.354

Name	Country	Years	Seasons	AB	H	HR	RBI	BA
Dan Driessen	USA	1989	1	436	153	12	82	.351
Ray Dandridge	USA	1940–1948	8	2,714	943	34	447	.347
César Tóvar	Venezuela	1977–1978	2	539	185	2	70	.343
Luis Márquez	Puerto Rico	1962–1963	2	861	290	41	163	.337
Burnis "Bill" Wright	USA	1940–1951	10	2,891	969	67	504	.335
Silvio García	Cuba	1938–1948	7	2,344	786	52	440	.335
Lázaro Salazar	Cuba	1938–1952	15	2,103	977	31	407	.334
Marvin Williams	USA	1945–1949	6	1,362	455	68	314	.334
Buck Leonard	USA	1951–1953	3	758	247	27	173	.326
Willie Wells	USA	1940–1944	4	1,354	437	26	237	.323
Harry "Suitcase" Simpson	USA	1963–1964	2	757	241	35	140	.318
Martín Dihigo	Cuba	1937–1950	11	1,917	607	55	370	.317
Orestes Miñoso	Cuba	1965–1973	9	2,254	715	56	377	.317
Roberto Ortiz	Cuba	1945–1956	7	1,715	600	106	418	.317
Buster Clarkson	USA	1940–1947	4	927	293	46	196	.316
Santos Amaro	Cuba	1939–1955	17	4,267	1,339	32	705	.314
Héctor Villanueva	Puerto Rico	1994–1999	9	1,623	504	96	347	.311
Willie Crawford	USA	1978–1979	2	556	171	13	90	.308
Fermín "Mike" Guerra	Cuba	1943, 1955	2	423	132	8	72	.306
Sandy Amorós	Cuba	1962	1	403	123	13	71	.305
Andrés Flietas	Cuba	1945–1947	3	1,126	342	6	138	.304
Von Joshua	USA	1978–1982	3	1,285	386	20	197	.300
Héctor Rodríguez	Cuba	1943–1963	11	3,476	1,040	19	374	.299
Lou Klein	USA	1946–1949	3	638	186	10	85	.292
Roy Campanella	USA	1942–1943	2	423	123	14	69	.291
George Hausmann	USA	1946–1949	3	928	263	2	100	.283
Bernie Carbo	USA	1982	1	306	85	6	47	.278
Danny Gardella	USA	1946	1	378	104	13	64	.275
LeRon Lee	USA	1976	1	400	110	15	57	.275
Ed Armbrister	USA	1979–1980	2	517	137	14	79	.265
José Tartabull	Cuba	1972	1	336	85	5	27	.253

Statistics of Select Cuban, Latin American, and U.S. Stars Playing in the Mexican League: Pitchers

Name	Country	Years	Seasons	G	W–L	SO	BB	ERA
Ramón Bragaña	Cuba	1938–1955	18	542	211–162	1,372	1,406	3.57
George Brunet	USA	1973–1985	14	327	132–127	1,483	722	2.66
José Ramóm López	Cuba	1963–1974	11	349	130–138	1,701	746	3.34
Julio "Jiqui" Moreno	Cuba	1945–1966	12	360	124–99	883	627	3.85
Martín Dihigo	Cuba	1937–1950	11	213	119–57	1,109	465	2.84
Lino Donoso	Cuba	1950–1962	11	327	118–84	1,230	609	2.92
Lázaro Salazar	Cuba	1938–1952	14	270	112–78	786	912	3.43
Aurelio Monteagudo	Cuba	1974–1981	8	240	106–85	1,025	415	2.93
Agapito Mayor	Cuba	1942–1954	8	254	98–76	762	524	3.79
Diego Segui	Cuba	1978–1985	9	193	96–61	1,015	364	2.91
Manuel "Cocaína" García	Cuba	1941–1949	8	233	96–68	532	519	3.83
Ed Bauta	Cuba	1969–1974	6	209	64–66	475	187	2.55
Vicente López	Cuba	1955–1964	9	193	62–70	535	440	4.44
Diómedes Olivo	Dominican	1955–1959	5	128	55–29	599	226	3.38
Alejandro Carrasquel	Venezuela	1946–1956	8	159	53–36	195	282	3.60
Ray "Jabao" Brown	USA	1946–1949	4	119	51–36	313	342	3.31
Luis Tiant Jr.	Cuba	1959–1983	5	141	48–51	524	400	4.23

(continued)

Name	Country	Years	Seasons	G	W–L	SO	BB	ERA
Sal Maglie	USA	1946–1947	2	86	40–25	223	200	3.55
Tomás de la Cruz	Cuba	1945–1948	4	106	40–26	237	168	2.60
Adrian Zabala	Cuba	1944–1947	3	106	40–30	224	242	3.78
Juan Pizarro	Puerto Rico	1974–1976	3	63	38–21	391	183	2.04
Santiago "Sandy" Ullrich	Cuba	1943–1954	4	120	34–39	201	259	3.87
Chet Brewer	USA	1938–1944	3	76	32–24	317	174	3.03
Dan Bankhead	USA	1953–1966	10	134	29–18	213	188	4.67
Vidal López	Venezuela	1943–1945	3	65	29–27	227	211	3.01
Jesse Jefferson	USA	1982–1985	4	54	28–15	187	114	3.41
Limonar Martínez	Cuba	1948–1955	3	66	27–20	108	102	3.72
Leon Day	USA	1940–1948	3	60	24–20	141	203	4.04
Terry McDuffie	USA	1940–1947	5	79	21–33	238	166	4.29
Roy Walmaker	USA	1940–1941	2	64	20–24	214	177	4.75
Rubén Gómez	Puerto Rico	1964–1971	5	65	19–21	215	112	2.58
Tracy Stallard	USA	1971–1973	3	60	19–24	220	97	2.72
Mike Kekich	USA	1976–1981	4	43	15–17	219	143	3.11
Jorge Comellas	Cuba	1941–1946	2	53	15–22	116	120	3.88
Miguel "Mike" Cuéllar	Cuba	1962, 1979	2	44	13–10	154	73	3.54
Steve Stone	USA	1984–1985	2	60	11–6	92	61	3.51
Silvio García	Cuba	1938–1945	5	17	10–2	89	28	1.64
John "Blue Moon" Odom	USA	1977–1978	2	19	9–8	64	62	3.78
Luis Tiant Sr.	Cuba	1941–1948	2	34	6–9	52	70	5.26
Max Manning	USA	1951–1953	2	23	5–9	72	66	3.70
Shawn Hillegas	USA	1994	1	8	4–3	15	12	3.51
Juan Berenguer	Panama	1993–1994	2	42	2–7	1,109	465	4.27
Juan Agosto	Puerto Rico	1995	1	17	1–4	18	15	6.15
René Arocha	Cuba	1999	1	12	1–7	47	14	4.55
René Monteagudo	Cuba	1946–1948	3	6	0–1	3	10	6.97

Mexican Winter League Professional Baseball Championship Teams, Cities, and Managers (1945–2003)

Year	Season	Playoff Champions	Record	City	Manager
Mexican Pacific Coast League					
1945–1946	I	Mazatlán	30–24	Mazatlán	Manolo Fortes
1946–1947	II	Hermosillo	33–21	Hermosillo	Art Lilly
1947–1948	III	Guaymas	38–22	Guaymas	Héctor Leál
1948–1949	IV	Culiacán	39–21	Culiacán	Manuel Arroyo
1949–1950	V	Culiacán	34–26	Culiacán	Manuel Arroyo
1950–1951	VI	Guaymas	37–23	Guaymas	Luis Montes de Oca
1951–1952	VII	Culiacán	35–25	Culiacán	Manuel Arroyo
1952–1953	VIII	Mazatlán	39–18	Mazatlán	Guillermo Garibay
1953–1954	IX	Mazatlán	48–32	Mazatlán	Guillermo Garibay
1954–1955	X	Mazatlán	NA	Mazatlán	Guillermo Garibay
1955–1956	XI	Culiacán	33–25	Culiacán	Manuel Arroyo
1956–1957	XII	Hermosillo	40–20	Hermosillo	Hub Kittle
1957–1958	XIII	Mazatlán	NA	Mazatlán	Guillermo Garibay
Winter League of Sonora					
1958–1959	I	Ostioneros	22–14	Guaymas	Manuel Magallon
1959–1960	II	Ostioneros	31–16	Guaymas	Manuel Magallon
1960–1961	III	Naranjeros	35–19	Hermosillo	Virgilio Arteaga
1961–1962	IV	Naranjeros	39–21	Hermosillo	Virgilio Arteaga
1962–1963	V	Ostioneros	32–28	Guaymas	Guillermo Frayde
1963–1964	VI	Naranjeros	47–33	Hermosillo	Leonardo Rodríguez

Year	Season	Playoff Champions	Record	City	Manager
1964–1965	VII	Ostioneros	47–33	Guaymas	Guillermo Frayde
1965–1966	VIII	Yaquis	48–32	Obregón	Manuel Magallon
1966–1967	IX	Tomateros	55–31	Culiacán	Vinicio García
1967–1968	X	Ostioneros	58–36	Guaymas	Ronaldo Camacho
1968–1969	XI	Cañeros	35–27	Los Mochis	Benjamín Valenzuela
1969–1970	XII	Tomateros	36–27	Culiacán	Vinicio García
Mexican Pacific League					
1970–1971	XIII	Naranjeros	56–30	Hermosillo	Maury Wills
1971–1972	XIV	Algodoneros	38–31	Guasave	Vinicio Garcia
1972–1973	XV	Yaquis	45–40	Obregón	Dave García
1973–1974	XVI	Venados	44–39	Mazatlán	Ronaldo Camacho
1974–1975	XVII	Naranjeros	50–32	Hermosillo	Benjamín Reyes
1975–1976	XVIII	Naranjeros	49–37	Hermosillo	Benjamín Reyes
1976–1977	XIX	Venados	29–36	Mazatlán	Alfredo Ortiz
1977–1978	XX	Tomateros	42–31	Culiacán	Raúl Cano
1978–1979	XXI	Mayos	41–32	Navojoa	Chuck Goggin
1979–1980	XXII	Naranjeros	51–23	Hermosillo	Benjamín Reyes
1980–1981	XXIII	Yaquis	50–34	Obregón	Lee Stigman
1981–1982	XXIV	Naranjeros	54–36	Hermosillo	Tom Harmon
1982–1983	XXV	Tomateros	37–33	Culiacán	Francisco Estrada
1983–1984	XXVI	Cañeros	43–31	Los Mochis	Vinicio García
1984–1985	XXVII	Tomateros	37–34	Culiacán	Francisco Estrada
1985–1986	XXVIII	Aguilas	39–32	Mexicali	Benjamín Reyes
1986–1987	XXIX	Venados	35–27	Mazatlán	Carlos Paz
1987–1988	XXX	Potros	38–19	Tijuana	Jorge Fitch
1988–1989	XXXI	Aguilas	49–35	Mexicali	Dave Machemer
1989–1990	XXXII	Naranjeros	46–23	Hermosillo	Tim Johnson
1990–1991	XXXIII	Potros	41–27	Tijuana	Joel Serna
1991–1992	XXXIV	Naranjeros	37–37	Hermosillo	Tim Johnson
1992–1993	XXXV	Venados	36–29	Mazatlán	Ramón Montoya
1993–1994	XXXVI	Naranjeros	37–31	Hermosillo	Marv Foley
1994–1995	XXXVII	Naranjeros	28–28	Hermosillo	Derek Bryant
1995–1996	XXXVIII	Tomateros	29–27	Culiacán	Francisco Estrada
1996–1997	XXXIX	Tomateros	38–24	Culiacán	Francisco Estrada
1997–1998	XL	Venados	30–32	Mazatlán	*Not Available*
1998–1999	XLI	Aguilas	35–32	Mexicali	*Not Available*
1999–2000	XLII	Mayos	39–28	Navojoa	*Not Available*
2000–2001	XLIII	Naranjeros	40–28	Hermosillo	Derek Bryant
2001–2002	XLIV	Tomateros	41–27	Culiacán	Francisco Estrada
2002–2003	XLV	Cañeros	28–33	Los Mochis	*Not Available*

Mexican Pacific League Batting Leaders (1945–2003)

Year	Batting Leader	BA	Home Run Leader	HR	RBI Leader	RBI
Mexican Pacific Coast League						
1945–1946	Manuel Arroyo	.375	Manuel Magallon	6	Manuel Arroyo	42
1946–1947	Félix McLaurin	.371	*No Records Available*		*No Records Available*	
1947–1948	Epitacio Torres	.362	Jack Graham	13	Barney Serrell	61
1948–1949	José "Pepe" Bache	.319	Pete Hughes	8	Angel Castro	44
1949–1950	Clint Courtney	.371	Pedro Ramírez	7	Pedro Ramírez	33
1950–1951	Pedro Ramírez	.343	Pedro Ramírez	10	Pedro Ramírez	47
1951–1952	Claudio Solano	.386	Marvin Williams	17	Mario Ariosa	52

(continued)

(continued)

Year	Batting Leader	BA	Home Run Leader	HR	RBI Leader	RBI
1952–1953	Vernal Jones	.377	Angel Castro	16	Angel Castro	56
1953–1954	Héctor Mayer	.355	Dick Hall	20	Claudio Solano	54
1954–1955	Benji Valenzuela	.385	Luke Easter	20	George Schmees	76
1955–1956	Joe Brovia	.352	Jim Lemon	19	Bob Bowman	51
1956–1957	Benji Valenzuela	.367	Earl Averill	15	Benji Valenzuela	60
1957–1958	Benji Valenzuela	.324	Duke Carmel	18	Angel Castro	45
Winter League of Sonora						
1958–1959*	Ronaldo Camacho	.317	Ronaldo Camacho	7	Ronaldo Camacho	21
1959–1960	David García	.345	Claudio Solano	8	Sal Villegas	33
1960–1961	Héctor Espino	.380	Héctor Espino	10	Juan Villarreal	41
1961–1962	Héctor Espino	.344	Sal Villegas	12	Sal Villegas	51
1962–1963	Héctor Espino	.402	Felipe Montemayor	14	Felipe Montemayor	52
1963–1964	Héctor Espino	.379	Ronaldo Camacho	27	Héctor Espino	77
1964–1965*	Héctor Espino	.382	Héctor Espino	25	Héctor Espino	62
1965–1966	Héctor Espino	.346	Héctor Espino	19	Ronaldo Camacho	52
1966–1967	Orestes Miñoso	.344	Héctor Espino	25	Héctor Espino	63
1967–1968	Héctor Espino	.342	Ronaldo Camacho	18	Arturo Bernal	45
1968–1969	Gabriel Lugo	.309	Rogolio Alvarez	20	Bill Parlier	50
1969–1970	Orestes Miñoso	.359	Héctor Espino	19	Celerino Sánchez	67
Mexican Pacific League						
1970–1971*	Héctor Espino	.348	Héctor Espino	22	Héctor Espino	62
1971–1972	Héctor Espino	.372	Bobby Darwin	27	Héctor Espino	75
1972–1973*	Héctor Espino	.415	Héctor Espino	26	Héctor Espino	83
1973–1974	Jorge Orta	.370	Roger Freed	20	Roger Freed	56
1974–1975	Jerry Hairston	.311	Jack Pierce	14	Héctor Espino	50
1975–1976	Héctor Espino	.319	Andrés Mora	18	Jack Pierce	54
1976–1977	Nicolas Vázquez	.345	Charlie Sands	13	Willie Mays Aikens	53
1977–1978	Mike Easler	.341	Willie Mays Aikens	14	Héctor Espino	48
1978–1979	Héctor Espino	.344	Andrés Mora	15	Eddie Gates	45
1979–1980	Neil Fiala	.364	Andrés Mora	11	Gary Gray	53
1980–1981	David Green	.321	Jeff Leonard	14	Wayne Cage	57
1981–1982	Junior Moore	.325	Mark Funderburk	17	Jeff Leonard	54
1982–1983	Héctor Espino	.316	Enrique Aguilar	8	Andrés Mora	36
1983–1984	Jimmy Collins	.314	Chuckie Canady	14	Jimmy Collins	46
1984–1985	Roy Johnson	.337	Nelson Barrera	15	Nelson Barrera	68
1985–1986	Eddie Brunson	.335	Carlos Soto	17	Gary Gray	61
1986–1987	John Kruk	.385	Willie Mays Aikens	24	Wllie Mays Aikens	64
1987–1988	Darrell Brown	.360	Nelson Barrera	16	Chris Knabenshue	48
1988–1989	Nelson Simmons	.353	Willie Mays Aikens	22	Willies Mays Aikens	73
1989–1990	Dave Hollins	.327	Alejandro Ortiz	16	Guillermo Velazquez	74
1990–1991	Matt Stairs	.330	Eduardo Jiménez	14	José Tolentino	55
1991–1992	Ty Gainey	.353	Ty Gainey	20	Jim Wilson	68
1992–1993	Matías Carrillo	.404	Nelson Simmons	16	Nelson Simmons	52
1993–1994	Ted Wood	.308	Nelson Simmons	18	Nelson Simmons	62
1994–1995	Marquiz Riley	.351	J. R. Phillips	17	Guillermo Velazquez	54
1995–1996	Dimitri Young	.356	Eduardo Jiménez	18	Eduardo Jiménez	49
1996–1997	Darryl Brinkley	.369	Tony Barron	13	Eddie Pearson	47
1997–1998	Matt Stark	.372	Bubba Smith	12	Derrick White	43
1998–1999	Matt Stark	.349	Bubba Smith	14	Erubiel Durazo	48
1999–2000	Juan Canizales	.336	Eduardo Jiménez	21	Morgan Burkhart	55
2000–2001	Bry Nelson	.330	Hensley Meulens	15	Chris Hatcher	61
2001–2002	Ramón Orantes	.313	Bubba Smith	19	Tony Zuniga	55
2002–2003	Heber Gómez	.353	Bubba Smith	24	Bubba Smith	64

* Season with triple crown winner.

Mexican Pacific Coast League Pitching Leaders and Award Winners (1945–1958)

Year	W–L Leader	W–L	PCT	League MVP	Rookie of the Year
1945–1946	Theolic Smith	6–1	.857	Daniel Ríos (Mazatlán)	Aureo Espiricueta (Guaymas)
1946–1947	*No Records Available*			Manuel Echevarría (Hermosillo)	Jesús Estrada (Guaymas)
1947–1948	Teolic Smith	11–4	.733	Barney Serrell (Guaymas)	Luis Castro (Guaymas)
1948–1949	Walter McCoy	11–3	.786	Walter McCoy (Obregón)	Filo Hernández (Los Mochis)
1949–1950	Alfonso Ramírez	16–5	.762	Alfonso Ramírez (Culiacán)	Miguel Gaspar (Guaymas)
1950–1951	Alfonso Ramírez	13–6	.684	Daniel Ríos (Mazatlán)	Cisco Higuera (Los Mochis)
1951–1952	Tomás Arroyo	12–5	.706	Claudio Solano (Guaymas)	Gregorio Figueroa (Obregón)
1952–1953	Daniel Ríos	14–4	.778	Angel Castro (Mazatlán)	Refugio Bernal (Hermosillo)
1953–1954	Amado Guzmán	15–5	.750	Claudio Solano (Hermosillo)	Armando Sánchez (Culiacán)
1954–1955	Jaime Ochoa	15–5	.750	Luke Easter (Culiacán)	Alfredo Ríos (Mazatlán)
1955–1956	Tomás Arroyo	9–2	.818	Marvin Williams (Navojoa)	Mike Rodríguez (Navojoa)
1956–1957	Pete Meza	13–2	.867	Benji Valenzuela (Obregón)	Arturo Cacheux (Mazatlán)
1957–1958	Dick Hall	10–3	.769	Dick Hall (Mazatlán)	Rafael Cruz (Hermosillo)

Winter League Pitching Leaders (1958–2003)

Season	ERA Leader	ERA	W–L Leader	W–L	PCT	Strikeout Leader	SO
Winter League of Sonora							
1958–1959	Manuel Estrada	1.11	Jesús Bustamante	6–1	.857	Manuel Estrada	48
1959–1960	César Gutierrez	1.26	Emilio Ferrer	13–5	.722	Emilio Ferrer	76
1960–1961	Emilio Ferrer	1.24	Miguel Sotelo	17–3	.850	Miguel Sotelo	114
1961–1962	Tomás Arroyo	1.21	Tomás Arroyo	8–2	.800	Miguel Sotelo	146
1962–1963	Arturo Cacheux	1.54	José Peña	9–3	.750	Miguel Sotelo	156
1963–1964	Francisco Ramírez	2.32	Mauro Ruíz	10–4	.714	Francisco Ramírez	145
1964–1965	Vicente Romo	1.47	Horacio Solano	15–5	.750	Ramón Arano	151
1965–1966	Mario Pelaez	1.35	Mario Pelaez	10–3	.769	Felipe Leál	195
1966–1967	Efrain Arano	1.36	Efrain Arano	8–2	.800	José Leyva	203
1967–1968	Vicente Romo	1.10	Enrique Romo	15–4	.789	Vicente Romo	171
1968–1969	Vicente Romo	1.54	Don Secrist	15–3	.833	Jerry Hinsley	171
1969–1970	René Paredes	1.20	Salvador Sánchez	11–2	.846	Bob Johnson	130
Mexican Pacific League							
1970–1971	Vicente Romo	1.60	Maximino León	7–1	.875	Felipe Leál	134
1971–1972	Mark Ballinger	2.13	Eduardo Acosta	7–2	.778	Mark Ballinger	144
1972–1973	Saul Montoya	1.89	Saul Montoya	8–2	.800	Dyar Miller	150
1973–1974	Eduardo Acosta	1.51	Francisco Maytorena	8–1	.889	Rafael García	159
1974–1975	César Díaz	1.40	Enrique Romo	12–2	.857	Don Kirkwood	117
1975–1976	Carlos Carrasco	1.45	Enrique Romo	12–2	.857	George Brunet	117
1976–1977	Maximino León	1.47	Maximino León	9–3	.750	Roberto Castillo	109
1977–1978	José Peña	1.33	José Peña	14–1	.933	John D'Aguisto	116
1978–1979	Byron McLaughlin	1.05	Angel Moreno	7–1	.875	Byron McLaughlin	143
1979–1980	Maximino León	0.87	José Peña	6–1	.857	George Brunet	85
1980–1981	Alejandro Ahumada	1.42	Eleno Cuen	14–4	.778	Fernando Valenzuela	184
1981–1982	Mike Paul	1.32	Jaime Orozco	14–2	.875	Mercedes Esquer	129
1982–1983	Salvador Colorado	0.53	Salvador Colorado	11–3	.786	Mercedes Esquer	82
1983–1984	Ramón Villegas	1.10	Alfonso Pulido	7–1	.875	Vicente Romo	100
1984–1985	Teodoro Higuera	1.24	Arturo González	12–2	.857	Teodoro Higuera	114
1985–1986	Félix Tejada	1.25	Guillermo Valenzuela	13–3	.813	Jaime Orozco	125
1986–1987	Vicente Palacios	2.31	Alfonso Pulido	6–1	.857	Vicente Palacios	109
1987–1988	Tim Leary	1.30	Tim Leary	9–0	1.000	Arturo González	86
1988–1989	Mercedes Esquer	2.09	Mercedes Esquer	13–3	.813	Mercedes Esquer	110
1989–1990	Narciso Elvira	1.41	Arturo González	10–1	.909	Narciso Elvira	94
1990–1991	Cecilio Ruíz	1.87	Rosario Rodríguez	7–1	.875	Cecilio Ruíz	91

(*continued*)

(continued)

Season	ERA Leader	ERA	W–L Leader	W–L	PCT	Strikeout Leader	SO
1991–1992	Tim Burcham	1.63	Alfonso Pulido	7–2	.778	Tim Burcham	92
1992–1993	Blaine Ilsley	1.88	Ezequiel Cano	9–1	.900	Jesús Ríos	90
1993–1994	Héctor Heredia	1.64	Emigdio López	10–2	.833	Antonio Osuna	90
1994–1995	Aaron Acosta	1.69	Isidro Marquez	8–0	1.000	Vicente Palacios	87
1995–1996	Juan Palafox	1.29	Aaron Quiroz	7–0	1.000	Enrique Couch	73
1996–1997	Vicente Palacios	1.59	Blaine Beatty	9–3	.750	Raúl Rodríguez	80
1997–1998	Julio Miranda	1.59	Ricardo Osuna	7–1	.875	Vicente Palacios	64
1998–1999	José Hernández	2.00	Salvador Rodríguez	8–4	.666	Daniel Garibay	77
1999–2000	Angel Moreno	2.39	Leobardo Mesa	9–2	.818	Luis Rivera	89
2000–2001	Eleazar Mora	1.45	Randy Galvez	8–4	.666	Danny Magee	78
2001–2002	Francisco Campos	1.66	Rodrigo López	10–2	.833	Francisco Campos	89
2002–2003	Edgar González	1.89	Edgar González	8–1	.889	Francisco Campos	76

Mexican Pacific League No-Hit, No-Run Games Pitched (1961–1996)

	Year	Date	Pitcher (IP)	Teams and Score (Game Innings)	Location
1	1961	Nov. 19	Vicente Romo (7.0) Emilio Ferrer (2.0)	Guaymas 3, Obregón 0 (9)	Guaymas
2	1962	Dec. 8	Miguel Sotelo	Hermosillo 2, Navojoa 0 (9)	Hermosillo
3	1963	Feb. 9	Blas Arredondo	Hermosillo 2, Navojoa 0 (9)	Hermosillo
4	1965	Dec. 28	Ramón Arano	Obregón 1, Mazatlán 0 (9)	Obregón
5	1967	Nov. 28	Simón Betancourt	Los Mochis 1, Mazatlán 0 (9)	Los Mochis
6	1970	Nov. 28	Steve Bailey	Guasave 3, Guaymas 0 (9)	Guaymas
7	1971	Jan. 13	Kenneth Frailing	Mazatlán 2, Los Mochis 0 (9)	Mazatlán
8	1972	Dec. 23	Dyar Miller	Navojoa 3, Guasave 0 (9)	Guasave
9	1975	Nov. 16	Peter Bonfils	Los Mochis 3, Obregón 0 (9)	Los Mochis
10	1976	Jan. 7	René Chávez	Guaymas 3, Mazatlán 0 (9)	Guaymas
11	1976	Nov. 3	George Brunet	Guasave 1, Guaymas 0 (9)	Guasave
12	1977	Dec. 22	Kevin Stanfield	Los Mochis 6, Navojoa 0 (9)	Los Mochis
13	1978	Oct. 12	John Fulghman	Hermosillo 1, Mazatlán 0 (9)	Hermosillo
14	1978	Dec. 7	Byron McLaughlin	Guaymas 2, Mazatlán 0 (9)	Guaymas
15	1979	Dec. 3	Fernando López	Guaymas 1, Mazatlán 0 (9)	Mazatlán
16	1980	Nov. 29	Rafael García	Guasave 2, Mexicali 0 (9)	Mexicali
17	1980	Nov. 30	Will McEnaney	Mexicali 1, Guasave 0 (9)	Mexicali
18	1981	Jan. 16	Jim Gott	Guaymas 10, Obregón 0 (9)	Guaymas
19	1981	Nov. 1	Allan Fowlkes	Mexicali 5, Guaymas 0 (7)	Mexicali
20	1982	Jan. 3	Alejandro Vidaña	Los Mochis 7, Mazatlán 0 (9)	Los Mochis
21	1982	Jan. 8	Fernando Valenzuela	Navojoa 1, Culiacán 0 (7)	Navojoa
22	1982	Nov. 25	Carlos Ibarra	Hermosillo 5, Obregón 0 (7)	Hermosillo
23	1982	Nov. 26	Fernando Arroyo	Guasave 2, Mexicali 0 (7)	Guasave
24	1982	Nov. 27	Eleno Cuén	Guaymas 6, Guasave 0 (9)	Guasave
25	1982	Dec. 27	Larry Feola	Guasave 2, Culiacán 0 (9)	Guasave
26	1983	Dec. 16	Arturo González	Navojoa 4, Mazatlán 0 (9)	Navojoa
27	1985	Nov. 12	Ray Chadwick	Tijuana 2, Obregón 0 (7)	Tijuana
28	1985	Dec. 7	Kent Angulo	Guaymas 3, Hermosillo 0 (9)	Navojoa
29	1986	Oct. 26	Lorenzo Retes	Hermosillo 4, Navojoa 0 (7)	Guaymas
30	1986	Dec. 9	Rafael García	Mazatlán 1, Obregón 0 (9)	Mazatlán
31	1987	Dec. 6	Carlos Ibarra	Navojoa 6, Obregón 0 (9)	Navojoa
32	1988	Nov. 10	Curt Schilling	Hermosillo 2, Culiacán 0 (9)	Hermosillo
33	1989	Oct. 11	Ildefonso Velasquez	Guaymas 11, Hermosillo 0 (9)	Guaymas
34	1990	Jan. 14	Andrés Cruz	Mazatlán 2, Navojoa 0 (9)	Mazatlán
35	1991	Oct. 27	Isaac Jiménez	Mexicali 3, Guasave 0 (7)	Mexicali

	Year	Date	Pitcher (IP)	Teams and Score (Game Innings)	Location
36	1991	Oct. 27	Timber Mead	Guasave 3, Mexicali 0 (7)	Mexicali
37	1992	Oct. 23	Timber Mead	Guasave 8, Los Mochis 0 (9)	Los Mochis
38	1992	Nov. 18	Armando Valdéz	Guasave 10, Obregón 0 (9)	Guasave
39	1993	Nov. 2	Lorenzo Retes (6.1) Andrés Berúmen (1.2)	Guasave 2, Mexicali 0 (8)	Guasave
40	1994	Jan. 12	Vicente Palacios (1.0) Joe Eishen (6.0) Andrés Berúmen (2.0)	Mexicali 12, Hermosillo 0 (9)	Hermosillo
41	1994	Dec. 22	Antonio Osuna	Hermosillo 2, Los Mochis 0 (9)	Hermosillo
42	1995	Nov. 26	Enrique Couch	Mexicali 3, Guasave 0 (7)	Mexicali

Mexican Pacific League Additional No-Hit Games, with Runs (1961–1996)

	Year	Date	Pitcher	Teams and Score (Game Innings)	Location
1	1961	Oct. 13	Rubén Rendón	Obregón 4, Guaymas 1 (9)	Obregón
2	1962	Dec. 15	Alfredo Mariscal	Empalme 6, Los Mochis 1 (9)	Empalme
3	1963	Oct. 26	Francisco Ramírez	Los Mochis 2, Obregón 1 (9)	Obregón
4	1967	Date Unknown	Horacio Piña	Culiacán 2, Guaymas 1 (9)	Culiacán
5	1971	Nov. 17	Thor Skogan	Guasave 2, Mazatlán 1 (9)	Guasave
6	1986	Dec. 5	Pablo Ruíz	Obregón 8, Navojoa 1 (9)	Obregón

Mexican Pacific League Perfect Games Pitched (1961–1996)

	Year	Date	Pitcher	Teams and Score (Game Innings)	Location
1	1971	Jan. 5	Vicente Romo	Obregón 12, Guaymas 0 (9)	Guaymas
2	1989	Oct. 19	Jesús Moreno	Los Mochis 1, Obregón 0 (9)	Obregón

Members of Mexican Baseball Hall of Fame (1939–2004)

	Name	Year Elected	Birthplace	League Affiliation	Career Span*
1	Lucas "El Indio" Juárez	1939	Mexico	Veracruz League	1903–1918
2	Antonio Delfin	1939	Mexico	Mexican Semi-Pros	1914–1925
3	Julio "Diamante Blanco" Molina	1939	Mexico	Mexican Semi-Pros	1910–1926
4	Leonardo "Najo" Alanis	1939	Mexico	Mexican League	1924–1932
5	Fernando Barradas	1939	Mexico	Mexican League	1936–1944
6	Angel Castro	1964	Mexico	Mexican League	1936–1957
7	Martín Dihigo	1964	Cuba	U.S. Negro Leagues	1937–1950
8	Epitacio Torres	1964	Mexico	Mexican League	1939–1957
9	Lázaro Salazar	1964	Cuba	Mexican League	1938–1952
10	Ramón Bragaña	1964	Cuba	U.S. Negro Leagues	1938–1955
11	Genaro Casas	1964	Mexico	Mexican Semi-Pros	1907–1927
12	Roberto "Beto" Ávila	1971	Mexico	U.S. Major Leagues	1943–1947, 1960
13	José "Chili" Gómez	1971	Mexico	U.S. Major Leagues	1937–1954
14	Baldomero Almada	1971	Mexico	U.S. Major Leagues	1933–1939[†]
15	Alberto Romo Chávez	1971	Mexico	Mexican League	1932–1946
16	Jesús Valenzuela	1971	Mexico	Mexican League	1938–1948

(continued)

	Name	Year Elected	Birthplace	League Affiliation	Career Span*
17	Alejandro Aguilar Reyes	1971	Mexico	Sportswriter/Founder	1920s
18	Jorge Pasquel	1971	Mexico	Owner/Official	1940s–1950s
19	Ernesto Carmona	1971	Mexico	Manager/Official	1920s–1930s
20	Roy Campanella	1971	USA	U.S. Major Leagues	1942–1943
21	Josh Gibson	1971	USA	U.S. Negro Leagues	1940–1941
22	Monte Irvin	1971	USA	U.S. Major Leagues	1942
23	Daniel "La Coyota" Ríos	1973	Mexico	Mexican League	1939–1963
24	Roberto Ortiz	1973	Cuba	U.S. Major Leagues	1945–1956
25	Agustín Bejerano	1973	Cuba	Mexican League	1937–1954
26	Anuar Canavati	1973	Mexico	Club President	1949–1965
27	Lázaro Penagos	1973	Mexico	Official	1930s–1950s
28	Manuel Oliveros	1973	Mexico	Manager	1928–1939
29	Alfred Pinkston	1974	USA	Mexican League	1959–1965
30	Ramiro Cuevas	1974	Mexico	Mexican League	1949–1959
31	Agustín Verde	1974	Mexico	Manager	1914–1938
32	Guillermo Alvarez	1976	Mexico	Mexican League	1946–1961
33	Luis Montes de Oca	1976	Mexico	Mexican League	1937–1954
34	Fernando "Fray Kempis" Campos	1976	Mexico	Sportswriter	1910–1974
35	Santos "Canguro" Amaro	1977	Cuba	Mexican League	1939–1955
36	Guillermo Garibay	1977	Mexico	Mexican League	1941–1952
37	Felipe Montúfar	1978	Mexico	Mexican League	1927–1939
38	Basilio "Brujo" Rosell	1979	Cuba	Mexican League	1937–1947
39	Jesús "Chanquilón" Díaz	1979	Mexico	Mexican League	1942–1960
40	Leonardo Rodríguez	1980	Mexico	Mexican League	1949–1971
41	Eduardo Orvañanos	1980	Mexico	Broadcaster/Writer	1942–1960
42	Carlos Alberto González	1980	Mexico	Umpire	1950–1978
43	Ramón Montes de Oca	1980	Mexico	Mexican League	1925–1933
44	Vinicio García	1981	Mexico	Mexican League	1944–1970
45	Tomás Arroyo	1981	Mexico	Mexican League	1947–1959
46	Salvador Castro	1981	Mexico	Umpire	1955–1975
47	Apolinar Pulido	1981	Mexico	Mexican League	1937–1949
48	Manuel "Cicl"on" Echeverría	1982	Mexico	Mexican League	1939–1953
49	Burnis "Wild Bill" Wright	1982	USA	U.S. Negro Leagues	1940–1951
50	Francisco "Panchillo" Ramírez	1982	Mexico	Mexican League	1950–1970
51	Horacio López Díaz	1982	Mexico	Director/Official	1962–1981
52	Mario Ariosa	1982	Cuba	Mexican League	1947–1972
53	Felipe Montemayor	1983	Mexico	Mexican League	1948–1966
54	Claudio "El Sordo" Solano	1983	Mexico	Mexican League	1948–1961
55	Ronaldo Camacho	1983	Mexico	Mexican League	1956–1975
56	José Bache	1983	Mexico	Mexican League	1946–1963
57	Rafael Reyes Nájera	1983	Mexico	Broadcaster/Writer	1940s–1970s
58	Alejo Peralta	1983	Mexico	Director/Official	1970s–1980s
59	Guillermo "Memo" López	1984	Mexico	Mexican League	1946–1963
60	Alfonso "La Tuza" Ramírez	1984	Mexico	Mexican League	1942–1952
61	Miguel "Becerril" Fernández	1984	Mexico	Mexican League	1956–1974
62	Gabriel Atristain	1984	Mexico	Umpire	1920s–1943
63	Manuel González	1984	Mexico	Broadcaster	1938–1960s
64	Porfirio "Chico" Martínez	1985	USA	Mexican League	1923–1935
65	Adolfo Luque	1985	Cuba	Manager	1950s
66	Miguel Sotelo	1985	Mexico	Mexican League	1956–1967
67	Marcos "Bugarini" Valdéz	1986	Mexico	Mexican League	1921–1939
68	Benjamín Valenzuela	1986	Mexico	Mexican League	1954–1966
69	Moises Camacho	1986	Mexico	Mexican League	1951–1975
70	Rubén Amaro	1986	Mexico	U.S. Major Leagues	1958–1969[†]
71	Manuel Chávez	1987	Mexico	Mexican League	1920s–1930s
72	Jesús "Jesse" Flores	1987	Mexico	U.S. Major Leagues	1942–1950[†]

	Name	Year Elected	Birthplace	League Affiliation	Career Span*
73	Guillermo "Memo" Luna	1987	Mexico	Mexican League	1948–1961
74	Raúl Mendoza	1987	Mexico	Sportswriter	1945–1980s
75	Juan Ley Fong	1987	Mexico	Director/Official	1960s
76	Antonio Ramírez Muro	1987	Mexico	League President	1962–1982
77	Lino Donoso	1988	Cuba	Mexican League	1950–1962
78	Horacio Piña	1988	Mexico	Mexican League	1967–1984
79	Arnulfo Rodríguez	1988	Mexico	Director/Official	1956–1972
80	Abel "Pancho" Cano	1988	Mexico	Sportswriter	1936–1980s
81	Héctor Espino	1988	Mexico	Mexican League	1962–1984
82	Pedro "El Mago" Septién	1988	Mexico	Broadcaster	1950s–1960s
83	Ray Dandridge	1989	USA	U.S. Negro Leagues	1940–1948
84	José "Zacatillo" Guerrero	1989	Mexico	Mexican League	1949–1974
85	Teodoro Mariscal	1989	Mexico	Founder/Director	1940s
86	Oscar Esquivel	1989	Mexico	Broadcaster/Writer	1960s
87	Ramón "Diablo" Montoya	1990	Mexico	Mexican League	1962–1983
88	Alfredo "Yaqui" Ríos	1990	Mexico	Mexican League	1956–1971
89	Alfonso Robinson Bours	1990	Mexico	League President	1950s
90	Amado Maestri	1990	Cuba	Umpire	1940s
91	Tomás Morales	1990	Mexico	Broadcaster	1950s–1960s
92	Jaime Corella	1991	Mexico	Mexican League	1958–1976
93	Antonio Pollorena	1991	Mexico	Mexican League	1965–1985
94	Chara Mansur	1991	Mexico	Director/Official	1950s–1970s
95	Agustín de Valdéz	1991	Mexico	Broadcaster	1947–1980s
96	Juan Lima	1991	Mexico	Umpire	1960s–1970s
97	Benji "Cananea" Reyes	1992	Mexico	Manager	1960s–1980s
98	Vicente Romo	1992	Mexico	U.S. Major Leagues	1963–1986
99	José "Peluche" Peña	1992	Mexico	Mexican League	1962–1984
100	Armando Rodríguez	1992	Cuba	Umpire	1960s–1970s
101	Jorge Blanco	1992	Mexico	Broadcaster	1950s–1980s
102	René González	1993	Cuba	Mexican League	1947–1956
103	Oscar Rodríguez	1993	Mexico	Mexican League	1957–1969
104	Ramón Arano	1993	Mexico	Mexican League	1959–1998
105	Aurelio López	1993	Mexico	U.S. Major Leagues	1968–1977
106	Alfredo Ortiz	1993	Mexico	Mexican League	1963–1987
107	Homobono Márquez	1993	Mexico	Official	1920s–1930s
108	Humberto Galaz	1993	Mexico	Sportswriter	1946–1980s
109	Miguel "Pilo" Gaspar	1994	Mexico	Mexican League	1951–1977
110	Celerino Sánchez	1994	Mexico	Mexican League	1964–1979
111	Miguel Suárez	1994	Mexico	Mexican League	1971–1987
112	Carlos Galina	1994	Mexico	Mexican League	1937–1954
113	Jaime Pérez Avellá	1994	Mexico	Director/Official	1970s–1980s
114	Aurelio Rodríguez	1995	Mexico	U.S. Major Leagues	1965–1966, 1984–1989
115	William Berzunza	1995	Mexico	Mexican League	1957–1979
116	Arnoldo "Kiko" Castro	1995	Mexico	Mexican League	1960–1983
117	Rodolfo "Botete" Alvarado	1995	Mexico	Mexican League	1949–1970
118	Jorge "Charolito" Orta	1996	Mexico	U.S. Major Leagues	1972–1987†
119	César Díaz	1996	Mexico	Mexican League	1969–1989
120	Orestes "Minnie" Miñoso	1996	Cuba	U.S. Major Leagues	1949–1980†
121	Juan Manuel Ley López	1996	Mexico	Director/Official	1950s–1960s
122	Jorge "Sonny" Alarcón	1996	Mexico	Broadcaster/Writer	1960s–1980s
123	Andrés Ayón	1997	Cuba	Mexican League	1964–1979
124	Maximino Léon	1997	Mexico	Mexican League	1968–1991
125	Alfonso Araujo	1997	Mexico	Broadcaster	1970s–1980s
126	Victor Sáiz	1997	Mexico	Umpire	1965–1992
127	Eugenio Garza Sada	1998	Mexico	Hall of Fame Official	1970s
128	Juan Navarette	1998	Mexico	Mexican League	1970–1990

(continued)

(continued)

	Name	Year Elected	Birthplace	League Affiliation	Career Span*
129	Marcelo Juárez	1998	Mexico	Mexican League	1967–1984
130	Miguel Solis	1998	Mexico	Mexican League	1972–1989
131	George Brunet	1999	USA	Mexican League	1973–1985
132	Gregorio Luque	1999	Mexico	Mexican League	1963–1980
133	Francisco Maytorena	1999	Mexico	Mexican League	1967–1982
134	Pedro Treto Cisneros	1999	Mexico	Writer/Historian	1980s–1990s
135	Francisco "Paquín" Estrada	2000	Mexico	Mexican League	1966–1994
136	Mario Mendoza	2000	Mexico	U.S. Major Leagues	1982–1990
137	Gabriel Lugo	2000	Mexico	Mexican League	1966–1983
138	Roberto Méndez	2000	Mexico	Mexican League	1965–1984
139	Jorge Fitch	2001	Mexico	Mexican League	1957–1975
140	Jack Pierce	2001	USA	Mexican League	1974–1987
141	Pedro "Charrascas" Ramírez	2001	Mexico	Mexican League	1942–1955
142	Rodolfo "Rudy" Sandoval	2001	Mexico	Mexican League	1955–1980
143	Salomé Barojas	2002	Mexico	Mexican League	1976–1996
144	Ernesto Escárrega	2002	Mexico	Mexican League	1970–1989
145	Mario Hernández Maytorena	2002	USA	Club President	1960s–1970s
146	José Maiz García	2002	Mexico	Executive	1980s
147	Roberto Mansur Galán	2002	Mexico	Club Official	1980s–1990s
148	Jesús Sommers	2002	Mexico	Mexican League	1970–1996
149	Nelson Barrera	2003	Mexico	Mexican League	1977–2002
150	Andrés Mora	2003	Mexico	Mexican League	1972–1997
151	Enrique Romo	2003	Mexico	U.S. Major Leagues	1968–1976
152	Fermín "Burbuja" Vázquez	2003	Mexico	Mexican League	1939–1955
153	Enrique Kerlegand	2003	Mexico	Writer/Historian	1960s–1990s
154	Isidro "Sid" Monge	2004	Mexico	U.S. Major Leagues	1975–1984[†]
155	Elpidio Osuna	2004	Mexico	Mexican League	1964–1983
156	Francisco "Chico" Rodríguez	2004	Mexico	Mexican League	1965–1985
157	Ismael Ruiz	2004	Mexico	Umpire	1969–1990s

* Career span refers to seasons played or served in the Mexican League; exceptions are noted with [†].
[†] Career years in U.S. Major Leagues (for several players with little or no service in Mexico).
For each inductee, biography and career details are available at http://www.salondelafama.com.mx.

Mexican Amateur National Champions

Year	Team
1994	Baja California
1995	Nueva León
1996	Chihuahua
1997	Nueva León
1998	Chihuahua
1999	Nueva León
2000	Chihuahua

NOTES

1. Mexico's territory is far larger than for any Caribbean island country, and larger also than Venezuela. Small wonder then that there seem to be multiple points of origin.

2. As commonly used, the threshold Mendoza line is usually fixed at the imagined and aesthetically neat .200 figure, but sometimes at Mendoza's own .215 career mark, a confusion that cannot be blamed on Mario Mendoza himself.

BIBLIOGRAPHY

Books

Cisneros, Pedro Treto. *The Mexican League: Comprehensive Player Statistics, 1937–2001.* Jefferson, NC, and London: McFarland & Company Publishers, 2002.

Phillips, John. *The Mexican Jumping Beans: The Story of the Baseball War of 1946.* Perry, GA: Capital Publishing Company, 1997.

Articles and Chapters

Banks, Leo. "Babe Ruth of Mexico (Héctor Espino)." *Sport* 80 (February 1958): 70.

Beezley, William. "The Rise of Baseball in Mexico and the First Valenzuela." *Studies in Latin American Popular Culture* 4 (1985): 3–23.

Joseph, Gilbert. "Documenting a Regional Pastime: Baseball in Yucatán." in *Windows on Latin America: Understanding Society Through Photographs*, 77–89, ed. Robert M. Levine. Miami, FL: The University of Miami Press, 1987.

LaFrance, David G. "Labor, the State, and Professional Baseball in Mexico in the 1980s." *Journal of Sport History* 22:2 (Summer 1995): 111–134.

Vaughn, Gerald F. "Jorge Pasquel and the Evolution of the Mexican League." *The National Pastime: A Review of Baseball History* 12 (1992), 9–13.

———. "George Hausmann Recalls the Mexican League of 1946–47." *The Baseball Research Journal* 19 (1990): 59–63.

CHAPTER 8

The Caribbean Basin

Baseball's Hidden Sandlots

● ●

Not all the Latin-born big leaguers have come from the familiar talent fonts in Cuba, the Dominican Republic, Puerto Rico, Venezuela, or Mexico. There also exist other more distant and much less recognized outposts. Miami's instant World Series hero of 1997, Edgar Rentería, learned his ballplaying skills on the north coast of Colombia, a minor ballplaying country that also produced a first Latin-born big leaguer of the twentieth century (Jud Castro). It was not Team USA or Korea or Japan that squared off against the Cubans in the finals of the 2003 World Cup, but rather a team representing Panama and boasting a lineup strewn with ex-big-leaguers. When it comes to top Latin hitters, it is still hard to think of any that could possibly rank far ahead of Canal Zone–born Rod Carew. And among the region's most celebrated current-generation big league stars, few have resumés more hefty than Atlanta's Andruw Jones, a native son of the island of Curaçao.

These lesser countries of the Caribbean Basin region have also made occasional noise in world amateur competitions. Not only did Panama play in the World Cup finals in 2003, but that country also hosted the same year's Americas Region Olympic Qualifier tournament. Nicaragua, and not Venezuela or the Dominican Republic, sent a team to the Atlanta Olympics in 1996, and Nicaragua also boasts Latin America's winningest big league pitcher ever (Dennis Martínez). Only three countries have won multiple first-place trophies in the 60-year-old Baseball World Cup (originally the Amateur World Series)—thanks mainly to Cuba's relentless collecting of 24 titles and counting—and one of them is Colombia.

Baseball's origins also go back deep into the past in some of Latin America's more distant baseball outposts. Organized teams were playing in Nicaragua as early as 1889 and perhaps well before. Panama was entering the Central American Games competitions almost from the start, with a 1935 debut (the sport had begun there at the turn of the century). With both Nicaragua and Panama, the baseball apostles were not Cubans but rather North Americans.

Panama's Avelino Asprilla turns a double play against Cuba at the 2003 Havana World Cup finals. [Peter C. Bjarkman]

Even in El Salvador and Honduras, baseball was already a popular enough activity for those two countries to enter teams for the Central American Games when competitions heated up in the early and mid-1930s. Beyond the hotbed Caribbean Basin, as the tables at chapter's end reveal, amateur baseball is also played at the very tip of South America (in Argentina and Chile) and also along the spine of the Andes (in mountainous Ecuador and Peru).

COLOMBIA

Jud Castro remains one of baseball's most mysterious figures, and part of the mystery involves his roots as a native Colombian. Castro—born Luis Castro—had the most minor of big league sojourns, appearing in only 42 games with the Philadelphia Athletics of the infant American League (AL) during the summer of 1902, but it was enough to make history. Castro became the first Latin major leaguer in the twentieth century and the first in the National or American Leagues—today's big league circuits. What remains a mystery is the place of Castro's birth. Colombia seems to have nearly as much right to claim the first Latin big leaguer (with Jud Castro) as does Cuba (with Ésteban Bellán); on the other hand, because the region of Colombia where Castro may have been born is part of today's Panama, the latter country could exercise the same weak claim.

Baseball came early to Colombia but, ironically, not any earlier than Colombia made its own debut in the majors. The first organized games appear to have been played around 1903, which would be a year later than Jud Castro's season with the Philadelphia club. It is likely that the earliest games were played along the coast, probably in the cities of Barranquilla and Cartagena, but not enough is known to flesh out this shadowy history. What is known is that the game had advanced enough in several decades for Colombia to enter international competitions for the first time in 1944, winning two of its seven games at the Amateur World Series matches staged in nearby Caracas.

Colombia has never had the professional tradition of its neighbor, Panama, but there have been some efforts at establishing a professional game. After a surprising Colombian success in the 1947 Amateur World Series in Barranquilla, the idea was floated for a pro league in the country. A league called "Licobal," which used mostly imported players, was tried in 1948 but with only moderate success. The experiment stretched out for nearly ten years before the circuit was disbanded altogether. Most of the players participating had been low-level minor leaguers looking for winter employment. A considerable number were Americans. Jim Gentile, Jim Pisoni, Joe Lonnett, Ryne Duren, Wayne Causey, Earl Wilson, and Mudcat Grant all played briefly in Colombia in the late 1950s. For twenty years after the collapse of the first Colombian league, there was no effort at any revival. A second phase of pro baseball in Colombia was finally launched in 1979; this time around, the circuit lasted for a half-dozen winter seasons. The main product of the second effort was Colombian native Jackie Gutiérrez, who eventually broke into the big time via a quality rookie campaign with the 1984 Boston Red Sox. Other future big leaguers who performed briefly in Colombia during their early minor league careers include all of the following: U.S.-born Jim Presley, Joe Orsulak, Curtis Wilkerson, Jerry Willard, Steve Lyons, Brad Komminsk, Cecil Fielder, Glenn Davis, John Shelby, Oil Can Boyd, Howard Johnson, Mike Marshall, Tim Teufel, Jesse Barfield, Billy Hatcher, Willie McGee, and Harold Reynolds; Dominicans Mariano Duncan, Juan Samuel, Rafael Belliard, and Tony Fernández; Cuban Tony Fossas; Honduran Gerald Young; and German-born Craig Lefferts.

Colombia's impact, limited as it is, has been far greater in international amateur baseball. In 1947, three years after an initial appearance at Caracas, the Colombians hosted the ninth reunion of the Amateur World Series and surprised all by walking off with the title. The Cubans had not come, but the victory was nonetheless impressive. In 1965, again on its home turf, Colombia won another surprise title, also aided by Cuba's absence. The two victories provide an interesting anomaly. Only three countries have captured what is now known as the baseball IBAF World Cup two or more times. Cuba owns 24 crowns. Venezuela has won three titles, at least one and perhaps two of them being very tainted. Colombia is the third country boasting repeat championships. The expected baseball powers, such as Mexico, Puerto Rico, Venezuela, and the Dominican Republic, aren't on the list.

Colombia also provided the stage for one of the best Amateur World Series showdowns ever, held in Cartagena in November 1970. This time the Cubans attended and, as expected, they were the major players. Before they were over, the competitions provided the most dramatic Cold War face-offs ever between the front-running Cubans and their archrivals, the underachieving Americans. The tournament in the end was noted for a pair of pitching masterpieces (see chapter 10) and especially a showdown between an immortal Cuban ace (José Antonio Huelga) and a future big league star (Burt Hooton).

Obscure world amateur play aside, for most Americans, Colombia's blip on the baseball map is because of a single memorable big leaguer named Edgar Rentería, who enjoyed his moment of fame in the 1997 World Series. Baseball in Colombia is played exclusively in the coastal regions around Barranquilla and Cartagena, and it was there that Rentería learned the game and was eventually found by a persistent big league scout. That precisely three countrymen preceded the current St. Louis Cardinals infielder to the big time, and three others have followed, is a piece of trivia almost too arcane for even the most ardent fan.

NICARAGUA

Mention Nicaragua and almost any U.S. baseball enthusiast will make an immediate connection with Dennis Martínez, the Orioles and Expos star pitcher. Martínez is certainly a featured player in Nicaragua's obscure century-and-a-quarter baseball saga, but he is hardly the whole story. Baseball was played in Nicaragua almost as early as it was in Mexico, and a good deal earlier than in Panama or nearby Colombia. A century after baseball's arrival in this Central American nation, traditions were strong enough to account for the Nicaraguans having a team in the 1996 Atlanta Olympics—while the Dominicans, Venezuelans, Panamanians, and Puerto Ricans sat home on the sidelines.

Nicaragua owns a proud baseball tradition that goes beyond its few big leaguers. The game came to the country late in the nineteenth century (1889), when an American businessman, Albert Adlesberg, was horrified to see the British tradition of cricket putting down roots in the coastal city of Bluefields. Nicaragua is thus one of the few places in the region where the baseball origins were clearly American and not Cuban. Within a few years, clubs had been formed in Managua and Granada as well as in Bluefields. The country's most famous and beloved amateur team, Boer, began play only a few years into the twentieth century. In 1912, Boer would win its first national tournament title (the first ever contested in Nicaragua). A near century later, Club Boer is still winning national titles.

Although it might be hard to see it from the distant vistas of North America, especially given the relative sparseness of the country's major league heritage, it is obvious to any visitor that Nicaraguan baseball passions run almost as deep as they do in Cuba or the Dominican Republic. Writer Jay Feldman has led "Baseball for Peace" tours to the country with his 40-and-over team and experienced the ingrained passions first hand, writing about them in a series of mostly self-published essays and newsletters over the years. In an article for *Whole Earth Review*, Feldman describes baseball as "a passion in Nicaragua, a profound expression of the local character" and points to a popular national saying that every boy in the country is born with a glove and ball in his hand—*Nació con un guante y una bolla en la mano*. It sounds amazingly like Cuba. It also leaves one wondering about the intimate connections between this supposedly most American of games and the passions it arouses in Communist (Castro's Cuba) or socialist (Nicaragua under the *Sandinistas* and Venezuela under Leftist President Hugo Chávez) countries.

Two occupations by U.S. Marines (1912–1925 and 1926–1933) left baseball even more firmly rooted in the land. Later, during the 1940s and 1950s, there were direct broadcasts of big league games in Managua. The soil was thus ripe when in the 1950s and 1960s the Somoza government subsidized an ill-fated professional league. Today's fans in the renamed Managua Stadium (once Somoza Stadium) still talk of a 500-foot blast that future Amazin' Mets big leaguer Marv Throneberry once slugged there. The circuit consisted of an eight-team first division, with seven clubs sponsored by corporate businesses and the eighth, known as Cinco Estrellas (Five Stars), representing the widely despised national guard of the ruling dictator, Anastasio Somoza. The other Managua team, Boer, was the popular favorite among fans in the capital city, who could take out their frustrations with the government in few ways beyond rooting against Cinco Estrellas. The pro league tumbled in the late 1960s, when cotton (the main national crop) lost its value on the international market and Somoza withdrew his support for pro baseball. The gap would nonetheless be quickly filled by a thriving amateur game.

Having made an appearance in official Olympic baseball competition, Nicaragua can boast a distinction in world amateur play that neither Mexico nor Puerto Rico nor Venezuela can claim. The Dominican Republic has also tasted the Olympic scene but finished more poorly in Barcelona than the Nicaraguans did in Atlanta. Once they arrived in Atlanta, the Nicaraguans did themselves proud. The club coached by Cuban big league legend Luis Tiant Jr. was the surprise of the Atlanta event. In the semifinals, they put up a brief struggle against Cuba before losing in lopsided fashion 8–1. No match for Cuba in the end, Nicaragua had nonetheless earned the right to play Team USA for the bronze medal. The loss was disappointing, but merely reaching medals-round play showed indisputably that Nicaragua was holding its own against the larger baseball powers.

Nicaraguan slugger Erasmo Baca prepares to bat at the Atlanta Olympics, 1996. [Transcendental Graphics]

There have been a few other high spots for Nicaragua in world amateur play. In the 1980s and 1990s, there were two silver medal finishes in the Pan American Games tournament. These wins in Caracas (1983) and Mar del Plata, Argentina (1995) were the true highlights of the nation's baseball history—at least in cutthroat amateur international competitions. And there have also been a pair of bronze medals (1975, 1991) won in the baseball-only Intercontinental Cup. Take away the early successes of the Venezuelans in the 1940s, and Nicaragua can point to as healthy a world tournament record as anyone in the region (always excepting the invincible Cubans).

For most outside observers, however, the baseball legacy of Nicaragua remains that involving its sprinkling of big leaguers. Dennis Martínez was easily the most noteworthy, but there have been a few others. David Green, a journeyman outfielder of the 1980s, was one. Al Williams, a pitcher who won 11 games for the Minnesota Twins in 1983, was yet another. With the inspiration of Dennis Martínez now laid out before them—as well as the successes of the 1996 Olympic team—more Nicaraguan big leaguers can perhaps be expected to soon be on the way.

PANAMA

Panama was a surprise performer in the October 2003 World Cup tournament staged in Havana's venerable *Estadio Latinoamericano*. A dark horse competitor at best, few would have envisioned the Panamanians staying in the hunt for medal contention against the likes of Cuban, U.S., Japanese, Korean, and Taiwanese squads—all of them tuning up for the Olympic qualification showdowns two weeks down the road in Tokyo and Panama City. Stocked with a half-dozen of the country's journeyman big leaguers and ex–big leaguers and managed by former Pittsburgh Pirates outfielder Omar Moreno, the gritty Panama squad survived opening round play with a 5–2 ledger, easily eliminated Nicaragua 5–0 in their quarterfinal match, then stunned the overconfident Japanese 4–1 in the tournament semifinal game. The defeat of the Japanese, who had admittedly left their best players in Tokyo to prepare for the Asian Olympic Qualifier, came on the strength of a strong mound outing by former Florida Marlin Rafael Medina. Panama's breeze through the quarter and semifinals was all the more sweet in the light of the ouster of Team USA in its quarterfinal match versus Taipei, as well as Cuba's severe scare in the same round, where the hosts barely edged the upstart Brazilians. In the finals, Team Panama was at last overmatched, yet still came within a pair of late-inning homers by Cuba's Frederich Cepeda of also winning the title showdown against heavily favored Cuba.

Perhaps dizzied by such overachievements on the road in Havana, the Panamanians collapsed altogether a mere week later on their own turf in the Olympic Qualifier, where they didn't make it into the medal round, despite another early elimination of the Americans. Back home in Panama City, the native arms went limp and the bats went ice cold. But Panama's strongest national team in years had nonetheless given clear signals throughout the month of reemerging as one of the region's legitimate baseball powers.

The rebirth of the Panamanian baseball forces in the fall of 2003 revived a Panamanian baseball tradition that has deep roots and considerable boasting points. In the late 1940s, the country featured a strong winter league affiliated with organized baseball. Panama's winter pro circuit was launched in 1946, immediately after the close of World War II, and the Panamanian League made its mark in early Caribbean series tournaments. Though the league did not last, Panama was now on the baseball map, and immediately after World War II a scattering of big league teams even visited for spring training exhibitions.

The mid-1940s also produced the country's first substantial baseball hero and its first major contributor in professional circuits on foreign soil. By 1947, Patricio "Pat" Scantlebury, a robust southpaw boasting a big league curve and fastball, was an established Negro leagues star, with the Negro National league champion New York Cubans. Bob Feller described the Panamanian's spitball as "a pigeon coming out of a barn." Scantlebury was a minor star in the Caribbean World Series, where he won three games and lost three over several competitions and also recorded victory in the very first Caribbean World Series game ever played. The lefty also posted several quality seasons in winter league action, both in Puerto Rico and Cuba. When integration came, Scantlebury snuck into the majors for a brief taste of the big time in Cincinnati. By the time he reached the majors, however, he was already 38 and only a shadow of what he had earlier been.

Three other Panamanians actually beat Pat Scantlebury into the U.S. majors. Humberto Robinson was first to break the barrier, with the Milwaukee Braves, and hung around for parts of five seasons. Héctor López was Panama's first big league regular. López, by playing with the visible Yankees, first established the presence of Panamanian baseball for most American fans. Webbo Clarke also slipped into the majors with the Senators in 1955 but slipped back out just as quickly. Clarke was another lefty who accumulated a substantial Negro leagues resumé before testing the waters in the majors.

Rod Carew arrived in Minnesota a dozen years after Humberto Robinson had blazed a trail as the first Panamanian big leaguer. There were thirteen big leaguers from the land of the famed canal before Carew's debut, and thirty of his countrymen have followed him, but none were more noted or more talented than the hitting machine born in the Canal Zone and raised in New York City. Carew left one of the largest major league resumés of any Latin star. Before the century-end bumper crop of future Hall of Famers that includes Sammy Sosa, Rafael Palmeiro, Juan González, and Ivan Rodríguez, only Roberto Clemente could match Carew's Cooperstown numbers. The year that brought Carew's debut also brought Manny Sanguillén to the majors. Sanguillén was not among the most talented Latins in the big time, but he was among the most colorful and most beloved.

More recently, Panamanians in the majors are headed by a pair of talented New York Yankees relief pitchers. The argument is solid that Mariano Rivera is baseball's most talented and successful pressure closer ever. Rivera's reputation has been largely constructed in the cauldron of postseason championship baseball and is all the more impressive for that fact alone. Ramiro Mendoza has also enjoyed a solid if slightly less remarkable career, which is now winding down in Boston. In addition, Carlos Lee by 2003 was beginning to make headlines as a slugger in Chicago's Comiskey Park.

A decade or two earlier, the roster of Panamanian big leaguers had been extended by Ben Oglivie, Rennie Stennett, and Juan Berenguer. Oglivie was a slugger who shone brightly but for only a very few seasons in Milwaukee; Stennett is best remembered for one outstanding batting performance (a 7-hit game); and Berenguer was a workhorse reliever years before Mariano Rivera and Ramiro Mendoza.

Panama's Audes De León blasts a game-tying homer in the 2003 Havana World Cup finals. [Peter C. Bjarkman]

Panama's role in world amateur tournaments, by contrast, has been something of a mixed story. The 2003 World Cup finals in Havana unquestionably provided the highpoint of this saga. In previous decades, the Panamanians made little noise on the world stage; they were rarely ever even noticeable players. The country did send a weak national team to World Cup tournament action as early as 1940, though only with predictably unsatisfying results. The one medal victory in the Amateur World Series before 2003 came way back in 1945, in the eighth World Cup event in Caracas. Panama has also appeared in Pan American Games tourneys on three occasions over the past two decades but again always with less than inspiring results.

The biggest story in Panama of late involved the 2001–2002 reestablishment of a professional winter league, with plans to slowly merge the circuit into the existing four-country professional Caribbean Confederation. On the field, the first season was a modestly successful one. Four teams participated, sporting colorful names (Carta Vieja, Cerveza Panama, Cerveza Atlas, Azuero) that recall the country's professional baseball past. Furthermore, the league's four top hitters (Olmedo Sáenz, Carlos Lee, José Macías, Roberto Kelly) were all names that underscore Panama's recent major league contributions. Olmedo Sáenz came close to a triple-crown feat, which would have duplicated two stellar winter league performances (Joe Atkins, 1951 and Héctor López, 1954) seen in the early 1950s. But for all these on-the-field successes, the experiment was a temporary failure. Financial backing was unavailable for a second season, and the winter of 2002–2003 saw the ballparks again quiet in Panama City and Colón.

VIRGIN ISLANDS

No other baseball outpost quite so small has produced quite as many big leaguers. For all its insignificance in size, the Virgin Islands boast a most eye-catching baseball tradition. There have been no pro leagues there, the major league clubs do not visit for exhibitions, and the islands have not had a national team in prestigious world tournaments—but the islands have produced a small, steady stream of big leaguers emanating from one of baseball's least noted talent sources.

Exactly how the diamond sport was originally transported to this island paradise remains something of a mystery. As elsewhere, the Cubans certainly played a major role. Bat-and-ball games here actually began with the arrival of cricket, but as Virgin Islanders began seeking work as sugarcane cutters in both Cuba and the Dominican Republic, the baseball connections were also quickly established, and well before the end of the nineteenth century.

Among the earliest professional stars from the Virgin Islands, one was a Negro leaguer who never played on a major league diamond. Alfonso Gerard left a most impressive legacy nonetheless. Gerard played for 14 years in Puerto Rico, and it was there that a young Clemente broke in behind him in right field on the same Santurce team. In the 1940s, Gerard had already tried his hand in the U.S. Negro circuits, where he was once a touted prospect with the New York Black Yankees, but his performance in New York never lived up to expectations.

Valmy Thomas, the first big leaguer from the region, was not in truth a native son but rather an import from nearby Puerto Rico, yet one who can certainly claim his roots in the Virgin Islands baseball tradition. Thomas was born in Santurce and would later launch his baseball reputation there, but as a youngster he lived in the Virgin Islands and was weaned on cricket, which his father played with great skill. His pro career got its first jump-start when he was Puerto Rican winter league top rookie in 1951 with Santurce. In that same year, Thomas was a racial pioneer in the Canadian Provincial League, with a team in St. Jean. He also played in the Dominican circuit, with Escogido. He spent five years in the big leagues, with two clubs in each league. His service was limited to fill-in duty in only 250 games, but he was a pioneer nonetheless, regardless of the slight impact his big league numbers (a .230 BA) may have had.

Valmy Thomas, native son of both Puerto Rico and the Virgin Islands. [Transcendental Graphics]

Due to Thomas's Puerto Rican birthright, among purists Joe Christopher gets the bulk of the credit as the island's true major league pioneer. Christopher was the first native-born Virgin Islander to pull on a big league uniform. He played with a championship club in the majors when he rode the bench and played some as a reserve with the 1960 Pittsburgh Pirates. He also played for several Puerto Rican winter league winners, as well as in both the Dominican Republic and Venezuela. Among American baseball watchers he will always be best remembered—if remembered at all—as a member of the original Amazin' New York Mets managed by Casey Stengel.

Perhaps the most notable Virgin Islands big leaguer so far has been Elrod "Ellie" Hendricks, longtime backup receiver and eventual coach with the 1960s and 1970s Baltimore Orioles. No one among Virgin Islanders has made a bigger overall contribution to the sport of baseball. As player and coach, Hendricks has worn the Baltimore Orioles uniform longer than any man alive. He played for a dozen seasons and then continued on as a bull pen coach for more than a quarter-century. As a player, Hendricks was hardly a front-line star, but his career did have its highlights. He played in four World Series, three with Baltimore and the last with the 1976 Yankees. He even socked a homer in the fall classic, something that not everyone can claim. And he was also involved in at least three most memorable World Series moments. The first, in 1969, featured a miraculous catch of one of his blasts by Tommie Agee. A mixed-up fielding play in that same series involving Hendricks and Pete Richert featured prominently in the Amazin' Mets upset win. The final moment was a controversial call at the plate involving a missed tag by Hendricks in the opening game of the 1970 series with Cincinnati.

There have been a scattered handful of other big leaguers from the Virgin Islands region. José Morales played in the big time for two decades. Elmo Plaskett won a triple crown while playing in Puerto Rico and later enjoyed a brief stop in Pittsburgh with the Pirates. Jerry Browne put in noteworthy service as a utility man. Horace Clarke was a workhorse for the New York Yankees during some of the franchise's leanest years. And Al McBean pitched admirably for a full decade, mostly with the Pittsburgh Pirates. In the top highlight seasons of his professional career in the National League (NL), his victory totals reached double figures on two occasions.

To complete the record of the Virgin Islands big league heritage, there are also a pair of special cases involving Puerto Rico—those of Julio Navarro and Henry Cruz. Here the pattern was reversed from that set by Valmy Thomas. Julio Navarro is a most special case as the only *viequense* (native of the Spanish Virgin Islands, now incorporated into Puerto Rico) to make the majors. Navarro actually learned his baseball playing on the island of St. Croix. Originally signed by the Giants after a February 1955 Puerto Rico tryout that also featured Orlando Cepeda and José Pagán, Navarro eventually spent parts of six seasons in the majors and also pitched for 22 winters in Puerto Rico—third most in island history. Nicknamed El Látigo ("Whiplash") for his sidearm fastball, Julio Navarro produced a son, Jaime (born in Puerto Rico), who since 1989 has enjoyed his own even more substantial big league pitching career. Henry "Papo" Cruz was born in Christiansted in the Virgin Islands but grew up in Puerto Rico after his family moved there when he was only a youngster. Signed as an outfielder off the campus of San Germán's Inter-American University, Cruz was a productive backup for the Los Angeles Dodgers and Chicago White Sox for a brief span of only four short summers. If his big league sojourn was hardly more than a long cup of coffee, Papo Cruz experienced some top-level baseball service elsewhere, spending 13 winter seasons in Puerto Rico and later posting some hefty offensive numbers for the Mexican League club in Saltillo.

THE CARIBBEAN BASIN'S GREATEST PLAYERS

This smallest and least noted of the world's baseball playing regions boasts quite an unexpected heritage when it comes to producing memorable and even star-quality major leaguers. These less noted Caribbean Basin countries can boast in Rod Carew one native-son Hall of Famer, and in Dennis Martínez another near-immortal who is almost a sure bet for eventual Cooperstown enshrinement, as well as several more memorable and colorful ballplayers among the current bright crop of emerging young Latino and island stars. Though only Panama ranks very far up the list of total big leaguers produced, the total region (with 90 major leaguers to its credit) nearly equals the output of traditional baseball powerhouse Mexico. And even Panama still considerably outranks Japan in its current inventory of successful major leaguers. Japan may well host a pro league and deep-rooted baseball tradition second to none outside of North America (unless Cuba is added in the mix), but the Japanese are still Johnny-come-lately newcomers on the big league scene compared to the Panamanians or even to the whole expanse of Central America at large.

Rod Carew (Panama) (b. October 1, 1945). There have been few better pure hitters in baseball history than Panama's Rod Carew, in Latin America or anywhere else. Batting above the magic .300 mark for fifteen straight seasons, the Colón native carved out a niche that at the time of his retirement only five immortal lumbermen had ever duplicated. The decade and a half of uninterrupted .300 hitting elevated Carew to the rare company of Ty Cobb, Cap Anson, Honus Wagner, Stan Musial, and Ted Williams. For this fact alone Rod Carew is unquestionably Panama's most notable diamond product, though at age 16 he emigrated to New York City and thus learned almost all his baseball skills stateside and not in the land of his birth. Even Carew's actual Panamanian birthplace evokes something of a sense of irony: he was born on a train passing through the U.S. operated Canal Zone while his mother, in labor, was en route to a hospital in the nearby Panamanian city of Colón. Carew's promising rookie season—in which he batted .292 for the Twins, collected 150 hits, and walked off with the American League top rookie award—gave only small indication of how stellar his later performances would be. He won the first of six batting crowns two years later and registered

Rod Carew, Panama's celebrated hit magician and Cooperstown Hall of Famer. [Transcendental Graphics]

over 200 base hits on four separate occasions. The sweet-swinging left-hander crossed the 3,000-hit plateau in his nineteenth and final season (1985) while wearing the uniform of the California Angels. His first-ballot Hall of Fame selection in 1991 made him only the fifth Latin American player (the fourth who had played in the majors) to earn baseball's highest honor. Much better remembered for his unparalleled handling of the bat, Carew early in his career was (like Ty Cobb) a daring base runner who pilfered home seventeen times—a record seven times in the single 1969 season alone.

Charles "Chili" Davis (Jamaica) (b. January 17, 1960). Jamaican-born but Los Angeles–raised Chili Davis is another of the substantial list of Caribbean region athletes—include Tony Taylor (Cuba), George Bell (Dominican Republic), Vic Power and Bernie Williams (Puerto Rico), and Andruw Jones (Curaçao) in the mix—whose name obscures his status as a non- *norteamericano* big league headliner. Davis was rarely at the top of any of the National or American League categories for individual slugging—something that would have established his rank as a first-rate star during his years with the Giants, Angels, Twins, Royals, and Yankees—but he did hang around long enough and was potent enough with the bat to amass 2,380 hits, 350 homers, and 1,372 RBI, and also to earn three All-Star game selections and three World Series rings. During seven initial seasons with San Francisco, the dependable switch-hitting outfielder was celebrated for both his speed and power; throughout a final dozen junior circuit seasons (mostly in Anaheim and Minnesota), Davis reshaped his image as a durable and dependable designated hitter (DH) capable of regular 20-homer and 85-RBI contributions year in and year out. Davis's career highlight was arguably the 1991 World Series, when he homered twice for the Twins during a seven-game championship victory over the Atlanta Braves. His potentially best season unfortunately coincided with the 1994 players union strike; the August shutdown left the Angels DH stuck on 26 homers, 84 RBI, and a .311 batting mark with nearly two months left to play.

Andruw Jones (Curaçao) (b. April 23, 1977). Multitalented Atlanta Braves outfielder Andruw Jones, native of Curaçao, broke into the majors with something resembling a sonic boom. A late-season callup with barely 30 big league games and 100 at-bats under his belt, the 19-year-old prospect rewrote the history books at Fulton County Stadium in the opening game of the 1996 World Series. Blasting an Andy Pettitte fastball into the left-field seats in the second frame, Jones became the youngest man ever to smash a homer in the fall classic; an inning later he joined Gene Tenace (Oakland, 1972) as the second player ever to homer in his first two trips to the plate in World Series play. For an encore, he merely finished the series with a .400 batting average across the six-game Atlanta loss to the New York Yankees. In his first official rookie season the following summer, Jones slipped a notch, with a .231 average and 18 homers; yet as both a center fielder and right fielder the cannon-armed fly-chaser proved himself one of the league's best defenders. He also finished fifth in National League Rookie of the Year balloting, stole 20 bases, and was now barely 20 years old. From there, it has been an steady climb. Across his subsequent half-dozen seasons, he has quietly posted numbers that if continued for another dozen years would lock down an invitation to Cooperstown. Jones has averaged 33 homers, 99 RBI, 32 doubles, and 16 stolen bases across the span. He has also walked off with six straight National League Gold Glove awards for unparalleled outfield defense, a string that makes him the league's only outfielder to earn the award the past six years running (1998–2003). Ask about modern-day Latin-born or foreign-born outfielders, and most fans can recite the names of Manny Ramírez, Juan González, Sammy Sosa, and perhaps even Magglio Ordóñez. As with the case of Bernie Williams, Jones's non-Spanish-sounding name seems to hide his status as one of the sport's biggest international stars— but it's hard to imagine putting together an all-star outfield today without including Curaçao's Andruw Jones.

Héctor López (Panama) (b. July 9, 1929). One of the earliest black ballplayers to don a New York Yankees uniform was Héctor López, a flashy third sacker and converted outfielder from Panama who lasted a dozen years in the big leagues and peaked in 1959 with 22 homers and 93 RBI. It was that stellar 1959 season that found López switching from his post as the regular third sacker with cellar-dwelling Kansas City to an outfield role with the perennial champion New York Yankees. López was almost a third-base equivalent of Vic Power, another flashy black-skinned Latino who starred during the same decade at first base (and whom Yankees management let escape in the opposite direction, to the Philadelphia, soon to be Kansas City, Athletics). Power was apparently deemed a bit too flashy as a potential racial pioneer for the staid Yankees organization, whereas López must have seemed a good deal more acceptable: a quiet overachiever who rarely called attention to himself with either off-field carousing or flamboyant on-field defensive play. Defense was not at all López's forte, and he led American League third basemen in errors in each of his four full seasons with Kansas City. But his batting eye was sound and complemented by frequent displays of power: he batted .290 as a rookie, banged 27 doubles and 19 homers his second year in the majors, and enjoyed his biggest moment with the Yankees when he drove home five runs with a round-tripper and a triple in the final game of the 1961 World Series.

Dennis Martínez (Nicaragua) (b. May 14, 1955). The winningest Latin pitcher in big league history is not Juan Marichal, Dolf Luque, or Pedro Martínez. It is surprisingly Nicaragua's favorite native son, 23-year veteran right-hander Dennis Martínez who, among his countrymen, is often honored with the moniker " *El Presidente*"—the chief executive, presiding on the mound. Martínez earned his place among the greats more via the route of longevity than lofty star-quality performances. Only once did he lead his league in pitching victories, and that was with only 14, during the strike-shortened season of 1981. His only additional league-leading performances came with 39 starts, 18 complete games, and 292 innings logged in 1979 for Baltimore, and also with five shutouts and a 2.39 ERA in 1991 for Montreal. Never did he manage to win 20 in a season, post an ERA below 2.35, or strike out more than 156 enemy batters in a single campaign. But, still toiling in Atlanta at age 43, he managed his career victory number 244 on August 12, 1998, passing Juan Marichal on the all-time list. Three seasons before his retirement, El Presidente had been urged by top

Nicaraguan politicos to return home and attempt a serious run at the nation's top political office, an invitation he rejected in favor of a few additional summers of big league pitching. If Martínez never was able to register big single-season numbers, he did achieve one of baseball's rarest pitching feats: on July 28, 1991, he hurled a perfect game for Montreal in historic Dodger Stadium.

Ben Oglivie (Panama) (b. February 11, 1949). Like Carew, Ben Oglivie was born in Panama (Colón) yet raised in New York City—in the Bronx—where all his baseball skills were acquired. His clumsy defensive and base-running styles and exceptionally quiet personality served to brand the young outfielder as an unexceptional platoon player during early seasons with both the Red Sox and Detroit, and Oglivie seemed to be going nowhere fast until a lucky trade moved him to Milwaukee. Replacing an injured Larry Hisle in the Brewers outfield in 1979 proved to be the career break Oglivie needed, and he busted out with a three-homer game in July and an eventual 29 circuit blasts (alongside 81 RBI) for the season. Oglivie's "career year" followed in 1980, when he smacked a league-best total of 41 round-trippers, trailed only teammate Cecil Cooper in the RBI race with 118, and earned the first of three eventual All-Star game selections. Ben Oglivie's big league career wound down in 1986, after 16 seasons and a total of 235 lifetime homers, but he still had enough pop left in his bat to log two more campaigns in Japan with the Kintetsu Buffaloes. Enjoying one final hurrah in the Far East, the nearly 40-year-old big league transplant again slugged more than 20 homers and batted above .300 in both those swan song seasons.

Edgar Rentería (Colombia) (b. August 7, 1976). Colombia's Edgar Rentería will always be celebrated for a highlight World Series moment, especially in the memories of fans in South Florida. Just the fourth of his countrymen to make it to the majors, Barranquilla-born Rentería wasted little time establishing himself as a national hero along the baseball-loving northern Colombia coast. But he became an even bigger overnight idol in the Latino-dominated region of Miami as events unfolded surrounding the surprising 1997 championship run of the Florida Marlins. The slim righty-swinger had posted solid .309 and .277 batting marks during his first two campaigns as the Marlins everyday shortstop. His solid debut campaign had earned a runner-up slot for National League top rookie honors in 1996, and his 22-game hitting streak that summer was the longest by a rookie since Chicago's Jerome Walton had rung up 30 in 1989. But it was the postseason of 1997 that elevated Rentería to full hero status. He set the tone when he drove in the winning run in the bottom of the ninth of the National League Championship Series opener, but that feat was topped and then some when Rentería poked the season-ending game seven 11th-inning single that unleashed a frenzied World Championship celebration for the Marlins in only the fifth year of the club's existence. On the strength of those postseason heroics, Edgar Rentería set off a frenzy of only slightly lesser proportions back home, where he was voted Colombia's 1997 Man of the Year and was also toasted with a prestigious San Carlos Cross of the Order of the Great Knight, the country's highest civic honor.

Mariano Rivera (Panama) (b. November 29, 1969).   Yankees bullpen closer par excellence Mariano Rivera will never represent Panama's greatest big league contribution—Rod Carew has closed the door on that honor—but he is certainly the most successful pitcher the country ever produced. He is also a lock someday to become the first Panamanian-raised ballplayer to walk through the portals of major league baseball's greatest shrine in Cooperstown. Rivera's casual and surgical style of shutting down opponents in the late innings does not draw the attention that attaches to some of the game's more histrionic relief aces; his career total of 283 saves ranks only eighteenth on the all-time list (tied with Troy Percival and trailing Rod Beck; and his season's best mark of 50 (in 2001) leaves him in only the ninth spot in that career category. But hardly anyone will argue strongly against the choice of Rivera as the greatest clutch-situation closer in baseball history. That reputation has been earned primarily in postseason play, where Mariano Rivera has been frequently tested as the bullpen version of such earlier Yankees mound greats as Whitey Ford, Allie Reynolds, and Vic Raschi. His two saves and one win during the season's finale against the Atlanta Braves earned the slim-built, hard-throwing Panamanian the 1999 World Series Most Valuable Player award. That honor capped a marvelous campaign in which Rivera did not allow a single earned run across the final three months of regular relief work—and with nearly all of his appearances coming with ball games on the line. The same peak season featured a major-league-best 45 saves and left opponents hitting a meager .176 against his deliveries across the entire summer.

Manny Sanguillén (Panama) (b. March 21, 1944).   Puerto Rico's Roberto Clemente was Pittsburgh's undisputed inspirational leader on and off the field throughout the 1950s and 1960s, but Panama's Manny Sanguillén provided the emotional glue that actually held those sometimes overachieving Pirates ball clubs together, year after year. For most of a decade, Sanguillén was one of the most respected catchers in the National League—though that was never to say that he was the best catcher in terms of either raw talent or polished performance. Sanguillén overcame substantial defensive liabilities in his early seasons to emerge as a proficient enough backstop to keep a spot in the everyday lineup and allow his heavy bat to earn most of his daily keep. His lifetime .296 batting average was one of the highest for catchers in his own or any other era, and his slugging also earned Manny Sanguillén an outfield slot once his defensive value behind the plate began to slide. While Clemente was always known for brooding intensity, Sanguillén uplifted the Pirate clubs of his era with his contrasting infectious optimism and enthusiasm. Pittsburgh won five division titles with their Panamanian backstop in the lineup. In 1976, an unusual trade shipped Sanguillén along with $100,000 to Oakland in exchange for manager Chuck Tanner, but a year later Sanguillén was back in Pittsburgh and again contributed as a reserve catcher on the 1979 World Championship team. When Clemente was lost at sea off the coast of San Juan in a plane crash, it was his friend Sanguillén who spent hours diving in the treacherous waters searching for the never-recovered body. And it was also Sanguillén who convinced Pittsburgh management to let him open the 1973 season in the right field slot left vacant by Clemente's disappearance.

IN BRIEF

Rod Carew, Dennis Martínez, and Andruw Jones aside, baseball (especially organized professional baseball) played on the fringes of the Caribbean Basin and around Central America holds little of the glamour and almost none of the renown attached to the sport in such primetime winter league venues as Cuba, Puerto Rico, the Dominican Republic, or Venezuela. Panama may not rank all that far behind Mexico as a big league recruiting center, and Rod Carew provides every bit as much bragging rights as Fernando Valenzuela or Andrés Galarraga. Over the past decade, Panama and even Nicaragua have outmuscled such heavyweights as Mexico, Puerto Rico, and the Dominican Republic on the fields of world tournament play. Without a winter league organization affiliated with U.S. organized baseball, these second-tier nations always seem to live far from the limelight surrounding the world of major league baseball. But their story is not to be bypassed or ignored. If baseball—amateur or professional—is ever to claim legitimacy as a truly worldwide game, then it is precisely here on the frontiers that the sport's long-term health and growth inevitably resides.

SELECTED CARIBBEAN BASIN RECORDS AND STATISTICS

Caribbean Basin Players in the Major Leagues

Name	Debut	Position	Debut Team	Seasons	Games	Career Statistics
Aruba (Curaçao, Netherlands Antilles): 9 Big Leaguers						
1 Hensley Meulens	1989	OF	New York Yankees (AL)	7	182	.220 BA
2 Ralph Milliard	1996	2B	Florida Marlins (NL)	3	42	.172 BA
3 Andruw Jones	1996	OF	Atlanta Braves (NL)	8	1,137	.269 BA. 221 HR
4 Calvin Maduro	1996	RHP	Philadelphia Phillies (NL)	5	68	10–19, 5.78 ERA
5 Eugene Kingsale	1996	OF	Baltimore Orioles (AL)	7	211	.251 BA
6 Randall Simon	1997	1B	Atlanta Braves (NL)	6	445	.297 BA
7 Radhanes Dykhoff	1998	LHP	Baltimore Orioles (AL)	1	1	0–0, 18.00 ERA
8 Sidney Ponson	1998	RHP	Baltimore Orioles (AL)	6	177	58–65, 4.54 ERA
9 Ivanon Coffie	2000	IF	Baltimore Orioles (AL)	1	23	.217 BA
Bahamas: 5 Big Leaguers						
10 André "Andy" Rodgers	1957	SS	New York Giants (NL)	11	854	.249 BA
11 George Anthony "Tony" Curry	1960	OF	Philadelphia Phillies (NL)	3	129	.246 BA
12 Percival Edmund Wentworth "Wenty" Ford	1973	RHP	Atlanta Braves (NL)	1	4	1–2, 5.51 ERA
13 Edison "Ed" Armbrister	1973	OF	Cincinnati Reds (NL)	5	224	.245 BA
14 Wilfred "Wil" Culmer	1983	OF	Cleveland Indians (AL)	1	7	.105 BA
Belize (British Honduras): 1 Big leaguer						
15 Reyenaldo Ignacio "Chito" Martínez	1991	OF	Baltimore Orioles (AL)	3	158	.259 BA
Colombia: 7 Big Leaguers						
16 Luis "Jud" Castro	1902	IF	Philadelphia Athletics (AL)	1	42	.245 BA
17 Orlando Ramírez	1974	SS	California Angels (AL)	5	143	.189 BA
18 Joaquín "Jackie" Gutiérrez	1983	SS	Boston Red Sox (AL)	6	356	.237 BA
19 Edgar Rentería	1996	SS	Florida Marlins (NL)	8	1,147	.289 BA
20 Orlando Cabrera	1997	SS	Montreal Expos (NL)	7	801	.269 BA
21 Jolbert Cabrera	1998	OF/IF	Cleveland Indians (AL)	6	448	.253 BA
22 Yamid Haad	1999	PH	Pittsburgh Pirates (NL)	1	1	.000 BA
Honduras: 1 Big Leaguer						
23 Gerald Young	1987	OF	Houston Astros (NL)	8	640	.246 BA
Jamaica: 3 Big Leaguers						
24 Charles "Chili" Davis	1981	OF	San Francisco Giants (NL)	19	2,436	.274 BA, 350 HR
25 Devon White	1985	OF	California Angels (AL)	17	1,941	.263 BA, 208 HR
26 Rolando Roomes	1988	OF	Chicago Cubs (NL)	3	170	.254 BA
Nicaragua: 8 Big Leaguers						
27 Dennis Martínez	1976	RHP	Baltimore Orioles (AL)	23	692	245–193, 2149 SO
28 Silvio "Tony" Chévez	1977	RHP	Baltimore Orioles (AL)	1	4	0–0, 12.38 ERA
29 Albert "Al" Williams	1980	RHP	Minnesota Twins (AL)	5	120	35–38, 4.24 ERA
30 David Green	1981	OF	St. Louis Cardinals (NL)	6	489	.268 BA
31 Porfirio Altamirano	1982	RHP	Philadelphia Phillies (NL)	3	65	7–4, 4.03 ERA
32 Marvin Benard	1995	OF	San Francisco Giants (NL)	9	891	.271 BA
33 Vicente Padilla	1999	RHP	Arizona Diamondbacks (NL)	5	147	35–32, 3.61 ERA
34 Oswaldo Mairena	2000	LHP	Chicago Cubs (NL)	2	33	2–3, 6.06 ERA
Panama (including Canal Zone): 44 Big Leaguers						
35 Humberto Robinson	1955	RHP	Milwaukee Braves (NL)	5	102	8–13, 3.25 ERA
36 Héctor López	1955	IF/OF	Kansas City Athletics (AL)	12	1,450	.269 BA, 136 HR
37 Vibert "Webbo" Clarke	1955	LHP	Washington Senators (AL)	1	7	0–0, 4.64 ERA
38 Patricio "Pat" Scantlebury*	1956	LHP	Cincinnati Reds (NL)	1	6	0–1, 6.63 ERA
39 Thomas "Tom" Hughes*	1959	RHP	St. Louis Cardinals (NL)	1	2	0–2, 15.75 ERA
40 George "Bobby" Prescott	1961	OF	Kansas City Athletics (AL)	1	10	.083 BA
41 David "Dave" Roberts	1962	1B	Houston Colt 45s (NL)	3	91	.196 BA
42 Ruperto "Rupe" Toppin	1962	RHP	Kansas City Athletics (AL)	1	2	0–0, 13.50 ERA
43 Ivan Murrell	1963	OF	Houston Colt 45s (NL)	10	564	.236 BA

(continued)

(continued)

Name	Debut	Position	Debut Team	Seasons	Games	Career Statistics
44 Gil Garrido	1964	IF	San Francisco Giants (NL)	6	334	.237 BA
45 Adolfo Phillips	1964	OF	Philadelphia Phillies (NL)	8	649	.247 BA
46 Ruthford "Chico" Salmón	1964	IF	Cleveland Indians (AL)	9	658	.249 BA
47 Osvaldo "Ossie" Chavarría	1966	IF	Kansas City Athletics (AL)	2	124	.208 BA
48 Rod Carew*	1967	IF	Minnesota Twins (AL)	19	2,469	.328 BA, 3053 H
49 Manuel "Manny" Sanguillén	1967	C/OF	Pittsburgh Pirates (NL)	13	1,448	.296 BA, 1500 H
50 Allan "Al" Lewis	1967	OF	Kansas City Athletics (AL)	6	156	.207 BA
51 Ramón "Ray" Webster	1967	1B	Kansas City Athletics (AL)	5	380	.244 BA
52 William "Bill" Heywood	1968	RHP	Washington Senators (AL)	1	14	0–0, 4.70 ERA
53 Eduardo "Ed" Acosta	1970	RHP	Pittsburgh Pirates (NL)	3	57	6–9, 4.05 ERA
54 Benjamin "Ben" Oglivie	1971	OF	Boston Red Sox (AL)	16	1,754	.273 BA, 235 HR
55 Renaldo "Rennie" Stennett	1971	2B	Pittsburgh Pirates (NL)	11	1,237	.274 BA
56 Omar Moreno	1975	OF	Pittsburgh Pirates (NL)	12	1,382	.252 BA, 1257 H
57 Edward Michael "Mike" Eden*	1976	IF	Atlanta Braves (NL)	2	15	.080 BA
58 Juan Berenguer	1978	RHP	New York Mets (NL)	15	490	67–62, 3.90 ERA
59 Roberto Kelly	1987	OF	New York Yankees (AL)	14	1,337	.290 BA, 124 HR
60 Carlos Maldonado	1990	RHP	Kansas City Royals (AL)	3	38	2–2, 5.65 ERA
61 Fernando Ramsey	1992	OF	Chicago Cubs (NL)	1	18	.120 BA
62 Enrique Burgos	1993	LHP	Kansas City Royals (AL)	2	10	0–1, 8.78 ERA
63 Sherman Obando	1993	OF	Baltimore Orioles (AL)	4	177	.239 BA
64 Orlando Miller	1994	SS	Houston Astros (NL)	4	297	.259 BA
65 Olmedo Sáenz	1994	IF/DH	Chicago White Sox (AL)	5	352	.264 BA
66 Rubén Rivera	1995	OF	New York Yankees (AL)	9	662	.216 BA
67 Mariano Rivera	1995	RHP	New York Yankees (AL)	9	512	43–29, 2.49, 283 S
68 Einar Díaz	1996	C	Cleveland Indians (AL)	8	557	.259 BA
69 Ramiro Mendoza	1996	RHP	New York Yankees (AL)	8	314	57–39, 4.32 ERA
70 Julio Mosquera	1996	C	Toronto Blue Jays (AL)	2	11	.233 BA
71 Manuel Barrios	1997	RHP	Houston Astros (NL)	2	5	0–0, 6.75 ERA
72 Bruce Chen	1998	LHP	Atlanta Braves (NL)	6	155	20–19, 4.59 ERA
73 Rafael Medina	1998	RHP	Florida Marlins (NL)	2	32	3–7, 5.96 ERA
74 Fernando Seguignol	1998	OF/IF	Montreal Expos (NL)	5	178	.249 BA
75 José Macías	1999	IF/OF	Detroit Tigers (AL)	5	449	.255 BA
76 Carlos Lee	1999	OF	Chicago White Sox (AL)	5	727	.284 BA, 121 HR
77 Julio Zuleta	2000	1B	Chicago Cubs (NL)	2	79	.247 BA
78 Roger Deago	2003	LHP	San Diego Padres (NL)	1	2	0–1, 7.84 ERA
Virgin Islands: 12 Big Leaguers						
79 Valmy Thomas	1957	C	New York Giants (NL)	5	252	.230 BA
80 Joseph "Joe" Christopher	1959	OF	Pittsburgh Pirates (NL)	8	638	.260 BA
81 Alvin "Al" McBean	1961	RHP	Pittsburgh Pirates (NL)	10	409	67–50, 3.13 ERA
82 Elmo Plaskett	1962	C	Pittsburgh Pirates (NL)	2	17	.200 BA
83 Julio Navarro‡	1962	RHP	Los Angeles Dodgers (NL)	6	130	7–9, 3.65 ERA
84 Horace Clarke	1965	IF	New York Yankees (AL)	10	1,272	.256 BA
85 Elrod "Ellie" Hendricks	1968	C	Baltimore Orioles (AL)	12	711	.220 BA
86 José Morales	1973	C/DH	Oakland Athletics (AL)	12	733	.287 BA
87 Henry Cruz	1975	OF	Los Angeles Dodgers (NL)	4	171	.229 BA
88 Jerome "Jerry" Browne	1986	2B	Texas Rangers (AL)	10	982	.271 BA
89 Midre Cummings	1993	OF	Pittsburgh Pirates (NL)	9	436	.256 BA
90 Calvin Pickering	1998	IF/DH	Baltimore Orioles (AL)	3	53	.217 BA

* Born in Canal Zone.
† Born in Puerto Rico, raised in Virgin Islands.
‡ Born in Vieques (Spanish Virgin Islands portion of Puerto Rico).

Panamanian Professional Winter League

Panamanian Winter League (1949–1960)

Year	Champion	Manager	Caribbean Series Results (Location)
1949	Spur Cola	Leon Treadway	Third (2 wins, 4 losses) (Havana)
1950	Carta Vieja	Wayne Blackburn	Champion (5 wins, 2 losses) (San Juan)
1951	Spur Cola	Leon Kellman	Fourth (1 win, 5 losses) (Caracas)
1952	Carta Vieja	Al Leap	Third (3 wins, 3 losses) (Panama City)
1953	Chesterfield	Graham Stanford	Third (2 wins, 4 losses) (Havana)
1954	Carta Vieja	Joe Tuminelli	Third (3 wins, 3 losses) (San Juan)
1955	Carta Vieja	Al Kubski	Fourth (1 win, 5 losses) (Caracas)
1956	Chesterfield	Graham Stanford	Second (3 wins, 3 losses) (Panama City)
1957	Club Balboa	Leon Kellman	Second (3 wins, 3 losses) (Havana)
1958	Carta Vieja	Wilmer Shantz	Second (3 wins, 3 losses) (San Juan)
1959	Coclé	Lester Peden	Fourth (0 wins, 6 losses) (Caracas)
1960	Marlboro	Wilmer Shantz	Second (3 wins, 3 losses) (Panama City)

Major League Baseball's Panama Winter League

Year	First Place	Second Place	Batting Champion	Pitching Champion
2002	Carta Vieja Roneros	Cerveza Panama	Olmedo Sáenz (.331)	Miguel Gómez (5–0)

Caribbean Basin and South American Amateur National Champions

Argentina National Champions (Amateur)

Year	Champion
1957	Capital
1958	Provincia
1959	Provincia
1960	Gran Buenos Aires
1961	Liga Metropolitana
1962	Liga Metropolitana
1963	Liga Metropolitana
1964	Liga Metropolitana
1965	Liga Metropolitana
1966	Liga Metropolitana
1967	Liga Metropolitana
1968	Liga Metropolitana
1970*	Liga Metropolitana
1971	Liga Metropolitana
1972	Liga Metropolitana
1973	Liga Salteña
1974	Liga Metropolitana
1975	Asociación Rosarina
1977*	Liga Metropolitana
1999*	Salta

(continued)

(continued)

Year	Champion
2002*	Salta

Existing records indicate that formal baseball activities began in Buenos Aires in 1888, with formation of a Buenos Aires Baseball Club by expatriate Americans living in Argentina's capital city. George Newberry and George MacNally are the names of two Americans known to have heavily proselytized for the new sport. Several American-owned refrigeration firms formed company teams for informal competitions in 1918 and 1919, and a newly established Argentine Baseball Federation staged annual tournaments between 1925–1926 and 1930–1931; these events were followed by more elaborate competitions under the auspices of the Argentina Baseball League, beginning in 1932 (with an inaugural trophy being won by a club representing Standard Oil Company). Argentina's debut on the international tournament scene arrived with an eighth-place (0–7) finish at the inaugural 1951 Pan American Games held, fittingly, on home soil in Buenos Aires.

* Note interruption. National championships were not held during those years missing from the summary list.

Aruba (Dutch Antilles) National Champions (Amateur)

Year	Champion
1986	Marlboro Sport Club
1987	Marlboro Sport Club
1988	Marlboro Sport Club
1989	Marlboro Sport Club
1990	Marlboro Sport Club
1991	Marlboro Sport Club
1992	Marlboro Sport Club
1993	Marlboro Sport Club
1994	Marlboro Sport Club
1995	Marlboro Sport Club
1996	*None*
1997	Coastal Baseball Organization
1998	Coastal Baseball Organization
1999	Coastal Baseball Organization
2000	Spuiters Baseball Club
2001	Spuiters Baseball Club

Aruba and Curaçao, rival islands that long fought for baseball supremacy in the Netherlands Antilles, finally joined forces to enter a Dutch Antilles national team for the first time in Amateur World Series XIII (1952) in Havana. The confederation subsequently competed in three World Cup events in the 1960s—Costa Rica (1961), Colombia (1965), and the Dominican Republic (1965)—thus fixing the islands among the world's serious baseball-playing regions. Ballplaying reportedly became popular in Aruba and Curaçao early in the twentieth century due to the close proximity of Venezuela; little documentation survives on early games or players.

Chile National Champions (Amateur)

Year	Champion
1953	Santiago
1954	Tocopilla
1955	Santiago
1956	Iquique
1957	Santiago
1958	Tocopilla
1960*	Santiago
1961	Tocopilla
1963	Tocopilla
1965	Tocopilla
1966	Tocopilla
1967	Tocopilla
1968	Tocopilla

Year	Champion
1969	Tocopilla
1971	Tocopilla
1974*	Tocopilla
1975	Tocopilla
1976	Tocopilla
1977	Tocopilla
1978	Tocopilla
1980	Tocopilla
1982	Tocopilla
1983	Santiago
1984	Tocopilla
1985	Tocopilla
1996*	Antofagasta
1997	Tocopilla
2000	Tocopilla

Chile hosted the second annual South American Championships at Santiago in 1961 but, as last-place finisher, failed to win a single contest. At South American Championships VII (1970), again held on Chilean soil in Antofagasta and Tocopilla, the hosts again finished dead last but won their first international game. National amateur championships have been held in the country intermittently since the early 1950s.
* Note interruption. National championships were not held during those years missing from the summary list.

Colombia National Champions (Amateur)

Year	Champion
1948	Bolivar
1950*	Bolivar
1953*	Bolivar
1954	Bolivar
1955	Bolivar
1957	Bolivar
1958	Magdalena
1959	Bolivar
1960	Bolivar
1963*	Bolivar
1964	Atlantico
1965	Atlantico
1966	Atlantico
1967	Antioquia
1968	Bolivar
1969	Bolivar
1970	Antioquia
1972*	Bolivar
1973	Bolivar
1974	Bolivar
1975	Bolivar
1977	Bolivar
1978	Bolivar
1979	Bolivar
1980	Bolivar
1981	Bolivar
1983	Bolivar
1984	Bolivar
1985	Bolivar

(continued)

(continued)

Year	Champion
1986	Bolivar
1987	Sucre
1988	Córdoba
1989	Bolivar
1990	Atlantico
1991	Bolivar
1992	Bolivar
1994	Bolivar
1995	Bolivar
1996	Atlantico
1998	Bolivar
1999	Cartagena
2000	Córdoba
2001	Bolivar

Colombia witnessed its earliest baseball games at the same time as Panama, in 1903, with the beginning of Panama Canal construction. The earliest games were played by U.S. construction crews in regions of Colombia that are today within the borders of Panama. The country's lasting distinction in early baseball history rests with native son Jud Castro (who may actually have been born in Venezuela), the first twentieth-century Latin American major leaguer. Colombia made its debut in World Cup play as early as 1944 and boasts a small number of Amateur World Series titles (2) and big league products (7), both seemingly out of proportion with its small baseball-playing population. Popularity of the game is restricted exclusively to coastal regions around Barranquilla and Cartagena.

* Note interruption. National championships were not held during those years missing from the summary list.

Costa Rica National Champions (Amateur)

Year	Champion
1960	Gigantes
1961	Hopec
1962	Hopec
1963	Hopec
1964	Soto López
1965	Motive Power
1966	M-27
1967	Numar
1968	Ludeja
1969	Gulf
1970	Gulf
1971	Limón
1972	Limón
1973	Universidad de Costa Rica
1974	Glidden
1975	Glidden
1976	Glidden
1977	Fertica
1978	Glidden
1979	Datsun
1980	*Championship Series Not Held*
1981	Universidad de Costa Rica
1982	CEQSA
1983	Limón
1984	Limón
1985	Piratas
1986	Limón
1987	Cachorros

Year	Champion
1988	Limón
1989	Limón
1990	Limón
1991	Santo Domingo
1992	Universidad Internacional de Las Américas
1993	Fibrolit
1994	Universidad Internacional de Las Américas
1995	Universidad Internacional de Las Américas
1996	Universidad Internacional de Las Américas
1997	Fibrolit
1998	Universidad Internacional de Las Américas
1999	Universidad Internacional de Las Américas
2000	Universidad Internacional de Las Américas
2001	Santo Domingo
2002	Poliflex

One year after inaugurating its own national amateur tournament, Costa Rica hosted World Cup XV in San José, thus helping the International Baseball Federation (IBAF) to revive the amateur world championship competitions that had lain dormant for eight years. The hosts won only a single contest, but the tournament itself held historic significance in that it marked Cuba's first appearance on the world scene after its 1959 socialist revolution, thus providing the stage for launching Cuba's modern-era world baseball dynasty.

El Salvador National Champions (Amateur)

Year	Champion
1972	Acero
1973	Acero
1974	Acero
1975	Acero
1976	Acero
1977	Acero
1978	Acero
1979	Acero
1980 W	Acero
1980 S	Picalas Pizarrines
1980–1981	Pirmar
1981	Acero
1982	La Centroamericana
1983	Eveready
1984	Hispanoamérica
1985	Autosal Mitsubishi
1985–1986	Hispanoamérica
1986	Gramoxone
1987	Gramoxone
1988	La Centroamericana
1989	Klerat
1990	Klerat
1991	Hispanoamericana
1992	Klerat
1993	Klerat
1994	Kerns
1996*	Universidad Tecnológica

(*continued*)

(continued)

Year	Champion
1997	Coca Cola
1998	Didelco
1999	Didelco
2000	Universidad Tecnológica
2001	Didelco
2002	Universidad Tecnológica

With youth baseball (especially in high schools in the capital city of San Salvador) already growing in popularity in the small Central American nation during the 1920s and 1930s, El Salvador made an early debut on the international scene in the 1941 Havana Amateur World Series. The Salvadorans appeared twice more in World Cup play in the 1940s, winning only a pair of games, but did manage on one occasion to upset a powerful Mexican national team. The country's finest individual product has undoubtedly been Jorge Aguilar, a talented pitcher who toiled with much success in the Mexican League during the 1940s.
Abbreviations: S, summer; W, winter.
* Note interruption. National championships were not held during those years missing from the summary list.

Guatemala National Champions (Amateur)

Year	Champion
1971	Municipal
1972	Municipal
1973	Municipal
1974	Suzuki
1975	Municipal
1976	Municipal
1977	Municipal
1978	Municipal
1979	Suzuki
1980	Universidad San Carlos
1981	Universidad San Carlos
1982	Lifeboy
1983	Universidad San Carlos
1984	Universidad San Carlos
1985	Universidad San Carlos
1986	Universidad San Carlos
1987	Universidad San Carlos
1988	Universidad San Carlos
1989	Universidad San Carlos
1990	Universidad San Carlos
1991	Municipal
1992	Universidad San Carlos
1993	Pumas
1994	Universidad San Carlos
1995	Universidad San Carlos
1996	Municipal Gold Star
1997	Pumas
1998	Universidad San Carlos
1999	Municipal Gold Star

The introduction of baseball to Guatemala is usually placed in the year 1920 and normally is credited to American businessman Monty Morency. Colorful legend suggests that Morency imported a large supply of bats, gloves, balls, chest protectors, and face masks to Guatemala City only to face stiff scrutiny from puzzled customs officials who had no idea of the purpose of such military-looking gear. Morency was reportedly still alive in Guatemala City in 1979, when he received special homage from the country's baseball officials and sportswriters as Guatemala's "Father of Baseball." Guatemala's earliest appearances on the world baseball scene occurred with the second Central American Games (Havana) in 1930, the third Central American Games (San Salvador) in 1935 (where Guatemala won their first international game), and the ninth Amateur World Series (Colombia) in 1947 (where they managed a single 1–0 win versus El Salvador).

Honduras National Champions (Amateur)

Year	Champion
1990	Medias Verdes
1991	Medias Verdes
1992	Medias Verdes
1993	Medias Verdes
1994	Medias Verdes
1994	Medias Verdes
1995	Medias Verdes
1997	Tío Rico
1998	Olimpia Pepsi
1999	Olimpia Pepsi

Honduras has produced only a single big leaguer, and its national teams attracted little notice in the second half of the twentieth century, but the Central American country bordering baseball-crazy Nicaragua did muster a team for the Central American Games as early as 1935 (where its squad lost all five games) and did make five World Cup appearances between 1950 and 1973. Two Cuban players, pitcher Isidro Fabré and catcher Mágaro Gómez, took up residence in Tegucigalpa in 1932 and did much to foster interest in the game; a strong tradition of national championships was also fostered in the 1930s. Though most records of these early competitions are lost, it is known that top professionals from neighboring Nicaragua (e.g., Alfredo "Chiquirín" García, Chino Meléndez, and Jonathan Robinson) regularly took part.

Nicaragua National Champions (Amateur)

Year	Champion
1912	Boer
1913	Granada
1914	Granada
1915	Managua
1916	Managua
1917	Boer
1918	Boer
1919	Boer
1920	Managua
1921	Managua
1922	Managua
1923	Managua
1929*	Managua
1930	Managua
1931	Managua
1932	Boer
1933	General Somoza
1934	General Somoza
1935	General Somoza
1936	Granada
1937	Chinandega
1938	Boer
1939	León
1940	Boer
1942*	San Fernando
1943	Roberto Debayle
1944	Cinco Estrellas
1945	Cinco Estrellas
1946	Cinco Estrellas
1947	Cinco Estrellas
1948	Cinco Estrellas

(continued)

(continued)

Year	Champion
1949	Cinco Estrellas
1950	Boricuas
1951	Cinco Estrellas
1952	Granada
1953	Cinco Estrellas
1954	Cinco Estrellas
1955	Boer
1957*	San Carlos
1958	Cabo Mejía
1959	San Carlos
1960	San Felipe
1961	Siuna
1962	San Felipe
1963	San Felipe
1964	San Felipe
1965	Alfredo Pellas
1966	Reyes Cubs
1967	San Felipe
1969*	San Felipe
1970	Chinandega
1971	Chinandega
1972	Granada
1973 W	León
1973 S	Flor de Caña
1974 W	Chinandega
1974 S	Mets de León
1975 W	Búfalos del Boer
1975 S	Cinco Estrellas
1976 W	Búfalos del Boer
1976 S	Mets de León
1977 W	Búfalos del Boer
1977 S	Granada
1978	Granada
1979	Quedó Desierto
1980	Rivas
1981	León
1982	Rivas
1982–1983	León
1983–1984	León
1984–1985	Dantos
1985–1986	León
1986–1987	Dantos
1987–1988	Dantos
1988–1989	Costa Atlantica
1989–1990	León
1990–1991	Dantos
1991–1992	San Fernando
1992–1993	Granada
1993–1994	San Fernando
1994–1995	Boer
1995–1996	Boer
1996–1997	León
1997–1998	Boer
1998–1999	León
1999–2000	Norte
2000–2001	León

Year	Champion
2001–2002	Boer
2002–2003	León

American businessman Albert Adlesberg staged baseball exhibitions and donated equipment in 1889 at the port city of Bluefields. The effort was reported to be an attempt by the patriotic American to head off the growing popularity of British cricket in the region. Later that same year, there are reports of two organized teams in the region called Club Southern and White Rose. When the Recreational Society of Managua created its own baseball team in 1891 (called simply Managua) they relied on star pitcher David Arellano, who had earlier hurled for Fordham University in New York. In July 1891, the Managua team played another pioneering nine from Granada, and in 1905 the historic Boer team was founded, the same club that would win a first national championship in 1912 and its twelfth national title 90 years later in 2002.

Abbreviations: S, summer; W, winter.

* Note interruption. National championships were not held during those years missing from the summary list.

Panama National Champions (Amateur)

Year	Champion
1944	Panama
1945	Herrera
1946	Panama
1947	Panama
1948	Panama
1949	Colón
1950	Panama
1951	Panama
1952	Panama
1953	Colón
1954	Panama
1955	Panama
1956	Colón
1957	Colón
1958	Colón
1959	Colón
1960	Panama
1961	Bocas del Toro
1962	Colón
1963	Panama
1964	Panama
1965	Herrera
1966	Herrera
1967	Herrera
1968	Panama
1969	Panama
1970	Panama
1971	Panama
1972	Los Santos
1973	Panama
1974	Los Santos
1975	Panama
1976	Los Santos
1977	Herrera
1978	Chiriquí
1979	Chiriquí
1980	Herrera
1981	Panama

(continued)

(continued)

Year	Champion
1982	Herrera
1983	Panama
1984	Veraguas
1985	Herrera
1986	Herrera
1987	Coclé
1988	Herrera
1989	Herrera
1990	Desierto
1991	Chiriquí
1992	Chiriquí
1993	Chiriquí
1994	Panama
1995	Los Santos
1996	Chiriquí
1997	Herrera
1998	Chiriquí
1999	Chiriquí
2000	Chiriquí
2001	Panama
2002	Chiriquí
2003	Herrera

The American national sport of baseball came to Panama along with the famed canal that remains the nation's most enduring symbol. During the 1903–1914 building of the giant waterway, North American sailors and construction gangs slowly established ballplaying habits among the local residents of Colón and Panama City. By 1912, the first amateur league had been organized and included five teams: Mateo Iturralde (the first champion), Tigrillo, Tosanía, Walk Over, and Palais Royal. Only three seasons later, the country had already produced its first recognized star player, batting champion Miguel Navas. That same 1915 season also witnessed the first recorded Panamanian triple play, performed by Club Tin Ortega.

Peru National Champions (Amateur)

Year	Champion
1991	Club Yamanaschi
1992	Club Yamanaschi
1993	Club Yamanaschi
1994	Club Yamanaschi
1995	Club Yamanaschi
1996	Club Taiyo
1997	Club Yamanaschi
1998	Club Taito
1999	Club Yamanaschi
2000	Club Taiyo
2001	Club Taiyo
2002	Club Leones

Baseball play seems to have made its way to the coast of Peru in the second decade of the twentieth century—thanks mainly to visiting North American sailors, who staged exhibitions at the main port near Lima. *Spalding Baseball Guides* of 1916 and 1917 report such games, including in particular one in the harbor town of El Callao involving crewmen of the *USS Marblehead*. Money from this historic 1916 contest was donated to the Peruvian Red Cross, and pitcher Ramírez and catcher Rafael León are reported to have distinguished themselves on the field. Most of the country's early ballplayers were descendants of Japanese immigrants to the Peruvian capital city of Lima.

BIBLIOGRAPHY

Books

Bjarkman, Peter C. *Baseball with a Latin Beat: A History of the Latin American Game.* Jefferson, NC, and London: McFarland & Company Publishers, 1994.

Costello, Rory S. *Baseball in the Virgin Islands.* New York: Hungry Joe Publishing [self-published], 2000 (available at http://members.aol.com/vibaseball).

García, Carlos J. *Baseball Forever! (Béisbol Para Siempre!).* Mexico City, Mexico: [self-published], 1980.

Oleksak, Michael M., and Mary Adams Oleksak. *Béisbol: Latin Americans and the Grand Old Game.* Grand Rapids, MI: Masters Press, 1991.

Pastrian, Héctor. *Béisbol: Reseña histórica internacional y argentina (Historical Review and Outline of International and Argentinean Baseball).* Buenos Aires: Argentinean Baseball Federation, 1977.

Articles and Chapters

Feldman, Jay. "Baseball in Nicaragua." *Whole Earth Review* (Fall 1987): 40–45.

———. "Hot Corner: A Nicaraguan Baseball Adventure." Unpublished manuscript (circa 1985).

CHAPTER 9

Europe, Africa, and the Pacific Rim

Rounding the Global Bases

• •

The internationalization of baseball, America's celebrated national pastime, had begun before the bat-and-ball sport was even out of its infancy. American exporting of baseball was launched with two adventurous international tours, both dreamed up by nineteenth-century pitching ace Albert Spalding. The first ballplaying expedition arrived in England in 1874, with optimistic prospects for drawing on that country's demonstrated penchant for novel bat-and-ball games. Accompanied by Boston and Philadelphia clubs from the National Association, the pioneering big leaguer and future sporting goods mogul staged sparsely attended exhibitions at Lord's Cricket Grounds in London. Spalding's trip had been inspired by an earlier visit the same year of British cricketers to the United States and Canada. Cricket players on either side of the Atlantic apparently saw little merit in the novel Yankee versions of their own sport, however. There was not much advance publicity for Spalding's friendship matches, and the short British tour stirred hardly a noticeable ripple.

The second brash effort at export came with Spalding's Asian–Pacific ventures fifteen years later, which turned rather unexpectedly into a full-blown world tour. Before the junket was over, Spalding and his two touring clubs of Chicago White Sox and other assorted big league stars would play exhibitions in Hawaii and Australia, continuing on to a worldwide circuit that would also include Ceylon, Egypt, Italy, France, England (again), and Ireland. Spalding had not been daunted by the failures of his earlier British adventure, which had received mostly a cold shoulder and thus should hardly have inspired further efforts at baseball imperialism. He was now bolstered, however, by several decades of wild growth of the new pastime at home, as well as the ongoing spread of *béisbol* throughout Caribbean nations (mainly as a consequence of Cuban efforts). Again, results were mixed at best. The 1888 to 1889 junket

Ireland's ambidextrous pitcher Tony Mullane won 284 big league games in the 1880s and 1890s. [Transcendental Graphics]

(like that of 1874) was something of a public relations bonanza back in the United States, but like its forerunner it did little to convert Asians (or Europeans) into enthusiastic ball-playing fanatics.

If the seeds were planted firmly in rich soil anywhere, it was perhaps in Australia, but even here the evidence was slim that there would be any immediate baseball enthusiasm. That baseball was growing in some quarters in Australia was signaled best with an early tour by Australians (most of them cricket stars, retrained) through-out the United States in 1897. By the new century's third decade, Australia also had its own popular headline series in the form of Claxton Shield tournaments (between state teams from New South Wales, South Australia, and Victoria) to crown annual national champions. Nonetheless, full-scale professional play and serious amateur national teams representing the country at major international events had to await Olympic baseball and the short-lived Australian Baseball League in the last decades of the twentieth century.

Promotional tours would continue in the early twentieth century and some would even include top pro players on winter barnstorming holidays. Most notable were the visits to Cuba by both big league and Negro league barnstormers at the dawn of the new century: John McGraw and Connie Mack, among others, took reduced big league rosters to Havana in the 1900s and 1910s, only to suffer a small string of embarrassing whitewashings by crack black Cuban aces like Eustaquio Pedroso and José de la Caridad Méndez. And there were also the notable exploits of Babe Ruth, Lou Gehrig, Lefty O'Doul, Jimmie Foxx, and others during 1934 in Japan, where the Sultan of Swat blasted long homers that thrilled crowds in Tokyo, but where 18-year-old high schooler Eiji Sawamura made the biggest international headlines by striking out Gehringer, Ruth, Gehrig, and Foxx in succession.

It is likely that less-publicized tours and exhibitions by enthusiastic ama-teurs did the most to stimulate enthusiasm for the American game. Sailors, and also railroad workers, were the game's earliest apostles in the Caribbean (both Cuba and the Dominican Republic) and Mexico, even if their pioneering role has often been clouded by myth. American railroad construction gangs along the U.S.–Mexico frontier provided one of the two early fronts for importa-tion of baseball south of the border; sailors loading sugar at the northern port city of Matanzas provided early demonstrations and equipment for Cubans, although native students returning to Havana had already pioneered the game in the capital city two years earlier. Visits by baseball-playing sailors on American fleet ships at Sydney in 1908 and in Victoria in 1905 accomplished every bit as much as had A. G. Spalding in bringing baseball enthusiasms to pre–World War I Australia.

If Babe Ruth and company received wildly enthusiastic responses in Japan in the 1930s, it was perhaps only because the seeds had already been firmly planted by touring amateur clubs representing schools and universities. The tours went in both directions throughout the early part of the century and were marked by occasional noteworthy successes and failures for the neophyte Japanese. A huge lift was given to the game, first introduced to Tokyo University students in 1872, when local youth began to test their new-found skill against the island's American imperialist visitors. A first known game between Japanese and American nines took place as early as 1896, when a local school team challenged American Athletic Club recreational players in Yokohama and promptly whipped them 29–4; the Japanese youngsters also easily won a rematch, despite the American club's underhanded recruitment of older reinforcements from Yokohama-based U.S. battleships. Waseda University students also visited California in 1905 to compete against American college clubs, and the highlight of their tour (at least for a jingoistic California press) was a game with Stanford University in which the diamond-naïve Japanese showed up with spikes attached backwards to their makeshift baseball footwear.

The Japanese experience of the late nineteenth century offers an eerie parallel with events in other countries where baseball was becoming rapidly nativized. Cubans had latched onto baseball at almost the same time, as a symbol of revolt against the despised colonial Spanish government. At first the new allegiance in 1870s Cuba was to anything either pro-American or anti-Spanish: baseball was futuristic and thus desirable; bullfighting was crudely backward-looking and therefore rejected. By 1898, with the Spanish gone and the Americans suddenly entrenched as the new occupiers, it was victories over the *gringos* that now carried heavy nationalistic overtones. Baseball's roots were planted so deep in Cuban soil largely because of the victories of native Cuban League squads in the new century's first two decades over both visiting big league barnstormers (Tigers, Giants, Athletics, Reds, and Phillies) and winter league outfits staffed mainly by imported U.S. Negro leaguers. The first great Cuban icons of the diamond were born in these matches, and none was bigger than José de la Caridad Méndez when he befuddled the Cincinnati and New York National Leaguers. Cuban League schedules of the first several decades after 1900 were even structured to accommodate these nationalistic fervors, with preseason October visits by the big leaguers and black all-stars to square off against either already popular Almendares or its rival Club Habana.

In Japan, by contrast, the local pros were not nearly as advanced as Cuban counterparts and had far fewer successes against seasoned American pros, once big league clubs began touring the Far East. The visiting big leaguers rarely lost even a single contest: an inaugural group known as Reach All-Stars rolled through 17 games undefeated in 1908; combined Giants and White Sox squads won three games without blemish in 1913; the Herb Hunter All-Stars were 20–0 in 1920 and 15–1 two years later; and the black Philadelphia Royal Giants were only once tied in two dozen 1927 contests. On amateur diamonds, however, things changed after the earliest encounters. A pair of Japanese school teams beat the visiting University of Washington club in four of ten 1908 contests. And unparalleled successes a decade earlier by Ichiko (First Higher School) students in Tokyo against the various squads representing Yokohama's American Athletic Club fanned patriotic fervor all across the land. These games literally soothed the soul of a proud nation on the heels of the Russo-Japanese War (1904–1905). There was nothing quite comparable to beating the Yanks at their own native game, as the Cubans also gleefully learned. Thus, baseball and nascent nationalism were as quickly entwined in Japanese outposts as they had been at outposts across the Caribbean.

Perhaps the failures of baseball in Europe and the contrasting successes in Cuba and Japan are explained by such matters of international culture and politics. The major overseas hotbeds for America's game were found in two lands where the United States was for some time an occupier and not just an occasional and welcome visitor—which certainly had as much to do with building anti-American sentiment as it did with promoting any happy imitations based on a passion for all things American. The two nations that took most wholeheartedly to the American sport were also the two that rebuilt and refined it in their own image. Cuba and Japan both made baseball uniquely their own, both in spirit and in the style and strategy of play. Both would seize baseball not only as their own national game but as a vital element of the emerging national culture. Indeed, Cuba and Japan by the end of the twentieth century would both outstrip America itself as locations where baseball is truly a reigning national pastime. This is no small theme in the history of international sports.

BASEBALL IN EUROPE

"The Giants win the pennant! The Giants win the pennant! The Giants win the pennant!" The recorded voice of New York Giants radio announcer Russ Hodges is burned into the nation's consciousness for all who experienced firsthand or later heard repeated the final moments of the greatest pennant race in National League history. No legitimate baseball fan is entirely unaware of the game's most cherished historical moment, when Bobby Thomson stroked the "shot heard round the world" to dramatically clinch a 1951 pennant playoff versus the rival crosstown Brooklyn Dodgers.

In this, perhaps the most famous moment of all of baseball history, the prime actor would prove to be an athlete who was not an American native son, nor even an import from neighboring Canadian or Latino turf. Bobby Thomson was a native of Scotland, one of the few European-born ballplayers to reach the big time after the third decade of the twentieth century. It is ironic indeed that America's national game should find one of its most cherished moments authored by such a foreign-born athlete—but since 1492 this has been a land of immigrants, so perhaps there is little irony after all. Leave aside the fact that Thomson was American by every measure possible but his birth certificate, and that he had learned his baseball on American soil. It would still be a few years yet before any significant portion of the game's stars would be welcomed from overseas. And when that began happening, the major talent fonts would now be found nearby in the Caribbean and not far across the Atlantic in Old World Europe.

Thomson gained more fame than all the others, but he was just one of a small handful of European-born immigrants to North American shores who performed well enough at pitching or fielding and hitting to make it onto a big league club. Most European-born big leaguers arrived and left in the nineteenth century, and most of those were hardly more than journeymen and thus have long ago disappeared into the cracks of history. A small trickle continued to fill rosters well into the twentieth century. Elmer Valo (native of Ribnik, Czechoslovakia) was one of these curiosities of a more modern period; the heavy-hitting and slick-fielding fireplug outfielder performed mostly with the Philadelphia Athletics and is likely most noteworthy as one of the few four-decade big leaguers. Italian-born Reno Bertoia (actually raised in Toronto, Canada) was yet another who served with the Detroit

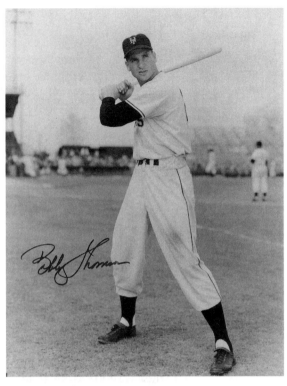

Scotland's Bobby Thomson, the most celebrated European-born major leaguer. [Transcendental Graphics]

Tigers as one of the more dependable among seemingly countless interchangeable 1950s-era infield sparkplugs. Finally, there were also the 1966 World Series mound heroics of Poland's Moe Drabowsky with the Baltimore Orioles, which proved almost as memorable (and certainly as vital) as the pennant-winning blast of Bobby Thomson.

Together, these players were only part of Europe's (especially England's and Germany's) big league heritage, which today remains largely unnoticed. In the earliest years, the biggest contributions often came off the field of play. England's Harry Wright is one of the strongest claimants to a legitimate crown as Father of Baseball; however, in the eyes of many of his countryman, Henry Chadwick has even greater hold upon that same mythical title. Son of a notable British cricketer who had emigrated to America after signing on as star bowler for the New York Cricket Club, 23-year-old Wright first took up baseball as pitcher and outfielder with the famed pioneering Knickerbockers club of New York; ten years later he would form and direct Cincinnati's Red Stockings nine, the first all-salaried outfit, which launched professional baseball with its celebrated 1869 and 1870 East Coast tours (producing 60 consecutive victories). It was as clever pioneer of playing tactics, however, that Wright was most extraordinary: he is credited with such innovations as fielders backing up teammates on defensive tosses, pregame batting practice, the fungo drill, hand signals, defensive positioning of infielders and outfielders to counteract hitters'

British-born Harry Wright holds major claims on the title of "Father of American Baseball." [Transcendental Graphics]

strengths, the double steal and the hidden-ball trick, face-masks for catchers, and gloves for all fielders. Himself a convert to baseball from its ancestor, British cricket, Wright was thus a major transitional figure linking American baseball with its older forerunner. Chadwick, for his part, stood equally tall in formulating the American version of the sport we know today. A sportswriter who covered New York cricket matches before he first grew enthused about a new American-style of play resembling town ball, Chadwick labored to codify baseball's original rules and also contributed mightily to the game's future statistical veneer by devising the invaluable record-keeping device known as the box score. He later devoted years of writing in the New York and national press to popularizing baseball as the nation's newest showcase professional sport. It was Chadwick who in 1895 first staked the claim for the deceased Harry Wright as baseball's founding father; many since then have pinned the label on "Father Chadwick" himself.

Another outstanding pioneering figure of the 1880s was Germany's Chris von der Ahe, a prosperous immigrant St. Louis tavern owner who was anything but a true baseball man and who admittedly understood almost nothing of the intricacies of the sport. Native to Hille, Germany, Von der Ahe would for all his baseball naïveté nonetheless produce one of the greatest teams of the national pastime's formative epoch. When the new American Association circuit opened for business in 1882, Von der Ahe bought controlling interest in the St. Louis entrant that would play at Sportsman's Park, adjacent to his prosperous saloon; since the new circuit was to be based in part on the sale of beer and liquor and on Sunday baseball (both banned at the time by a rival National League), the mere business opportunities represented by this new-fangled baseball seemed outstanding enough to the profit-minded tavern mogul. As flamboyant boss of the powerful American Association St. Louis Browns (captained and managed by future Chicago White Sox owner Charles Comiskey, and soon winner of four straight pennants), Von der Ahe for more than a decade contributed financial support and staged ingenuous promotions that did more than almost anything else to cement professional baseball in St. Louis as first-order American entertainment. Some recent historians (Gerlach, Hetrick) have cleverly described Von der Ahe's successful promotional tactics as a foreshadowing of Bill Veeck, and his less admirable tendencies to meddle naïvely with on-field club operations as an early prefiguring of George Steinbrenner. Chris Von der Ahe thus remains one of the most colorful and pivotal figures in early professional baseball history.

Baseball proved popular for Europe's native sons in America, but it was never a grand hit anywhere on European soil itself. Efforts to bring the game to English territory as early as the late nineteenth century met with mostly indifference and sometimes even outright hostility. Spalding's return to England and Ireland at the end of his 1889 world tour turned even fewer heads than his first foray a decade and a half earlier. When George Bernard Shaw watched touring U.S. professionals demonstrate the new American version of ball-playing, he could bless the performance with only the most damning form of praise. Baseball was superior to cricket, Shaw noted, because the games were over much faster than they were with the British bat-and-ball sport (Humber, 1989).

Similar fates awaited the American game elsewhere, especially in sunny Mediterranean Italy. Italy had not proven very receptive baseball territory at first, despite some noteworthy pioneering efforts by native enthusiasts. An Italian transplant to the United States named Max Otto (born Massimiliano Ottino) returned to his native Turin in 1923 loaded down with baseball equipment and began his lengthy effort to promote the sport, work that he would carry past World War II. A professor in Rome, Guido Graziani, organized the first known game in June 1920, featuring two pick-up Italian teams. These early attempts failed to generate or sustain any real momentum, however, and interest was at a low ebb between the wars. Equally unproductive were the export ventures of a few Italian enthusiasts who carried the sport eastward into Yugoslavia. But things would change quite a bit after World War II.

Italy would eventually prove one of baseball's most fertile fields in Europe. The game would never have quite the popularity on the shores of the Mediterranean or the Adriatic that it enjoyed in the Caribbean or in certain Pacific outposts. But the Italians did eventually prove somewhat receptive, especially after World War II. Max Otto and Guido Graziani had been early pioneers of baseball in the 1920s, and both returned after World War II to continue their efforts. While Graziani focused efforts chiefly on softball, Otto organized the first Italian Baseball League in March 1948 at Milan. The professional league that grew out of Otto's efforts has had a sporadic existence throughout, yet has been a late-career refuge for a handful of U.S. pros unable to reach major league status. The Italian League even eventually produced a major leaguer in 1979 when U.S.-born but Italian League–trained Craig Minetto reached the roster of the Oakland Athletics. Italy has more significantly served as a frequent home to international tournaments, hosting the Intercontinental Cup competitions twice (1973, 1993) and the amateur world championships on three occasions (1978, 1988, 1998). The first-ever Intercontinental Cup was contested at two Italian sites in Parma and Bologna, and the first European hosting of the Baseball World Cup was also by Italy (at Parma, Bologna, and Rimini). Italian national teams have been frequent if not overly successful visitors to international tournaments after first appearing at the 1970 World Cup matches in Colombia. Italy's own greatest professional star was Giulio Glorioso, who in January 2004 was awarded the Star of Rome, a medal presented each year to a native Roman with distinguished career achievements. Glorioso ended his 20-year Italian League career back in 1974 with 226 wins, 2,711 innings pitched, 2,092 career strikeouts, and a lifetime 1.82 ERA. These were most impressive career numbers, whatever the league.

Baseball received significant outside boosts in European locales between the two world wars. Several semisuccessful tours by American pros particularly aided the cause during the 1920s. McGraw's Giants and Comiskey's White Sox carried out a grand tour in 1924 that featured a series of exhibitions staged in the Paris Olympic Stadium. While some French clubs had been reportedly organized as early as 1910 to 1913, thousands of American soldiers stationed on French soil during and immediately after World War I staged matches between army units that couldn't fail to spur some local curiosity if not clear-cut interest. A Paris Baseball Association (directed by American Frank B. Ellis) was formed in order to hold a 1918 tournament in which at least twenty clubs participated. But it was the big leaguers in 1924 that had the most effect and on the heels of their visit the French Baseball Association (now incorporating the earlier Paris League) was formed. A team representing the French association would pay a visit to Barcelona in 1929, and a 10–6 win on that occasion over the host Spanish club represented France's first attempt at international competition. By the end of the decade, there was also small-scale tournament play in a number of additional European nations.

The Dutch took to the bat-and-ball sport with wide open arms, and when European competitions began in earnest on the eve of World War II, the Dutch were already in the forefront. They had taken up club play in 1911 and started crowning annual national champions in 1922, with the first tournament won by the Quick Club of Amsterdam. By the 1950s, the situation in the Netherlands was somewhat parallel to that in Mexico. Soccer was king, but baseball had made major inroads. The Dutch would continue to be the showcase venue for European baseball, entering their first European championship contender in 1956 and then finishing either first or second in twenty-three of the next twenty-four events (they didn't compete in 1967). The Netherlands would also send the first European-trained ballplayer to the majors in 1979, when pitcher Win Remmerswaal debuted with the Boston Red Sox. Bert Blyleven (with 287 wins over 22 seasons) was easily the most talented among European-born major leaguers of the modern era, far outstripping 1951's pennant hero Bobby Thomson (in career achievement, if not in any one single flash of glory).

To complete their impressive resumé, the Dutch would soon have the best pro league in Europe. A descendant of the amateur national tournaments first held in the 1920s, the circuit is now known as the Dutch Major League and of late consists of six teams playing a 47-game season followed by semifinals and finals in postseason play (along with six additional clubs in a 20-game Pool B "minor league" season). Rotterdam-based Neptunus has been the recent league powerhouse (five titles in a row), and the Amsterdam Pirates recently had a loose, four-year working agreement with the Montreal Expos. It is also the Dutch who have established the one European event that provides a regular stop on the international baseball circuit. The Haarlem Baseball Week, played for nearly a quarter-century in attractive compact Pim Mulier Stadium, began attracting college teams from around the world in the 1980s and would eventually also receive semiregular visits from the vaunted Cuba national team when it occasionally toured Europe to tune up for bigger world tournaments like the Intercontinental Cup.

The Dutch have long represented Europe most proudly in world tournament play. They own the second stoutest European heritage when it comes to World Cup play, joining Italy for a 1970 debut performance in Colombia and posting an overall 7–6 record in the two most recent events. The Dutch have participated in all but the first Baseball Olympiad (Spain bumped them in 1992 as the automatically entered host nation). They have played well, even if they have not

The Moscow University baseball team dressed for action, 1985. [Author's Collection]

won much, with victories over Australia and Italy at the Atlanta Games and a startling upset of Cuba in Sydney. The apex of Dutch baseball clearly came with the single remarkable outing at Sydney in 2000 when Team Holland stunned the powerhouse Cubans 4–2 in a preliminary game of ultimately little significance but much headline grabbing potential.

Spain did not regularly host local baseball matches until at least 1920, when interest cropped up simultaneously in both Madrid and Barcelona. Despite Olympic play in 1992 and the Intercontinental Cup matches five years later also in Barcelona, there seems little indication of any national baseball craze in this soccer-mad country, which peaked early with a single European championship won nearly a half-century ago.

France has an even more limited baseball heritage than Spain and has yet to produce teams that could compete seriously with the Italians or Dutch. But the sport has not been without its brief outbursts even in France, where thirty teams were playing at senior and junior levels in the early 1980s with more than 1,000 registered players. If there has never been a French pro circuit or strong French national team entered in World Cup play, there are nonetheless hundreds of enthusiastic amateur players spread around the country and a French Baseball–Softball–Cricket Association crowning annual national champions over the past five years. And in Charlie Lea, there is even a French-born major leaguer (one of several).

Even the Russians boast some limited baseball enthusiasm. For a while, many thought that the Russians (then the Soviet Union) would soon take up the American game of baseball with the same dedication they had given to Canada's sport of hockey, then use their Spartan training techniques to improve with stunning speed and to score international propaganda victories in Olympic venues. This vision never materialized, and the collapse of the Soviet Union has done little to improve the prospects. The lack of Russian baseball appreciation may seem all the stranger since the country does boast a traditional national bat-and-ball game called *lapta*, which the former Soviets were once fond of promoting as the true origin for the American national pastime. That Russian baseball has not come very far was proven dramatically during the October 2003 World Cup event in Havana, where the national squad was belted in five of six outings and embarrassed 20–1 by the Cubans. But for all their slowness to adapt, the Russians have made some progress with the game and can now point proudly to a surprise win versus seemingly unmotivated Chinese Taipei in their final 2003 World Cup match.

Europe indeed plays another important role on the international baseball scene. With nearly three dozen federations, and a good number of them actively competing, the continent has long been a major player in the international amateur baseball movement. Numerous international matches have been staged over the decades in Italy, Spain, Belgium, and the Netherlands. Spain boasts the first Olympic baseball tournament under official sanction, and in 2004 Greece hosted what may prove (if Major League Baseball succeeds in supplanting Olympic baseball with a full-fledged professional World Cup of its own) to be the last of these events. Finally, the governing body of international baseball known as the IBAF has long been housed on European soil (Lausanne, Switzerland), led admirably since 1993 by its Italian president, Aldo Notari.

AUSTRALIA'S SUBSTANTIAL BASEBALL TRADITIONS

Baseball in Australia goes back as far as almost anywhere. The first known (or at least reported) game was played in 1857 and therefore predates any record of baseball play in such bastions of the sport as Cuba, Japan, or Mexico. The founding influence in Australia was without question American; at the outset of the 1850s, American profiteers were reportedly staging pick-up games on the gold-rush fields near Ballarat. Like the famous pioneering Canadian game of June 1838 held in Beachville, Ontario, this earliest known Australia experiment yielded a strange game, indeed. *Bell's Life* magazine carried accounts of a three-inning match on February 28, 1857, between teams representing Richmond and Collingwood. Conflicting reports suggested that each team either batted until an entire side was retired or perhaps that runs were counted for every base crossed. The victory thus fell easily to the Collingwood side by the astronomical tally of 350–230. The event may have been far more cricket than it was modern-era baseball.

Americans made other attempts to foster their emerging national game over the next twenty odd years. A first Australian club team known as the St. Kilda Baseball Club held exhibitions in 1879 versus Hicks's Original Georgia Minstrels, a touring troupe of black American musicians (the teams split two games and tied a third), and informal club matches were also noted during the 1870s in Sydney. It was not until big leaguer Albert Spalding's memorable world tour of 1888 to 1889 passed by Australian shores that the American version of bat-and-ball play grabbed anything like a firm hold on the Down Under population. Spalding had already met considerable resistance from a wary cricket establishment in England back in 1874. The popular impression was that his whirlwind visit to Britain (accompanied by cricketer-turned-baseballer

Harry Wright and other members of the Boston National Association club) was motivated in large part by a desire to undermine and even supplant established local cricket traditions. But Al Spalding's actual intentions seem to have been otherwise. The former pitcher and novice sporting goods entrepreneur was by all accounts motivated by a genuine love for baseball and his passions almost constituted a missionary's zeal. He was also something of a P. T. Barnum promoter, traveling to Asia and the South Pacific with a full entertainment package in tow that included a baton-twirling and dancing Negro as mascot and a daredevil high-wire act, all part of a spectacular roving entertainment caravan.

During Spalding's second major junket during 1888 and 1889 to promote American-style baseball on foreign soil, the entourage included two seasoned clubs of professionals; one was the Chicago White Sox team of Charles Comiskey, the other was a pickup squad of pros playing under the convenient name of "All-America." Games included matches with Melbourne and Sydney cricket squads, to spice a three-ring-style entertainment spectacle. Professor Bartholomew performed his daredevil balloon and parachute feats in Sydney and Melbourne before crashing on a rooftop and injuring both legs in Ballarat. Ed "Cannonball" Crane entertained throngs in Melbourne by besting the Australian distance record for throwing a cricket ball. And some locally hired Aborigines provided a demonstration of boomerang throwing and rope skipping on New Year's Day of 1889 as the tour wound down in Melbourne. Returning to Chicago by April, Spalding announced that Australia boasted the best overseas possibility yet seen for serious baseball inroads.

Upon his departure, Albert Spalding left behind hand-picked local baseball missionary Harry Simpson to carry on the task of proselytizing for the still young American pastime. More than up to the task, native-son Simpson spent the next five years developing the new game in every available corner of his continent-sized country. Popularity of ballplaying spread so rapidly that within three years several intracolonial tournaments were being staged between "sides" representing South Australia, Victoria, and New South Wales.

The Australians soon returned the favor of missionary zeal as the first foreign baseballers to tour in the United States. Former Melbourne cricket club manager Harry Musgrove (who had already brought his cricket group to America a year earlier) traveled to San Francisco in early 1870 to arrange travel plans and scheduling details, but he soon advised the hand-picked Australian squad that they would be better off remaining on home soil and avoiding likely financial hardships. The warning was ignored. Despite its uncontested historical significance, the Aussie club's tour begun in April 1897 would become known chiefly as the "Disastrous Tour," since it quickly proved a colossal financial failure. Musgrove's enthusiastic group mixed many baseball exhibitions in California, Denver, Chicago, and eventually New York with long bouts of sightseeing and carousing that left the team repeatedly in desperate financial straights. One feature of the whirlwind tour was an old-timers' game in Boston that included an appearance on the field by Al Spalding (who hit well but could no longer get around the bases) and also saw Henry Chadwick officially scoring the match. The bold Aussies continued mixing ball games and tourism until July and eventually moved on to England. There they were finally hopelessly stranded when their exasperated and now unscrupulous promoter, Harry Musgrove, disappeared with the small bundle of remaining funds.

The next important landmark for Australian baseball was a 1914 tour by big league teams that proved highly successful in rekindling at least temporary interest. The New York Giants and Chicago White Sox arrived in Brisbane on New Year's Day of that year, carrying with them such noted stars as Tris Speaker, Buck Weaver, Sam Crawford, Fred Merkle, and Olympian-turned-major leaguer Jim Thorpe. Nine games in all were played (four were special exhibitions between the pro clubs and all-star selections representing New South Wales and Victoria), and the matches were in every way a resounding success; several of the games proved especially thrilling on the field, as well as having their desired effect in promoting improved international relations. Then, in just a few short years, World War I would set the game back everywhere on Australian soil.

Modern-era semi-pro and professional play had its roots in the Claxton Shield matches, which were inaugurated in the early 1930s. This competition was the showcase of Australian baseball between the two world wars, with the five states of South Australia, New South Wales, Victoria, Queensland, and Western Australia entered in an annual tournament for a coveted trophy donated by Norm Claxton, a prominent Australian Rules footballer, cricketer, and base-baller, who had also served for many years as president of the amateur South Australian Baseball League. The original plan was to offer the shield only until one state team retired it with three consecutive victories; when South Australia captured the initial three tournaments of the mid-1930s, however, it was decided to make the suddenly popular competition an ongoing annual affair. One of the most exciting days of Australian baseball history came at the outset of Claxton Shield matches in 1935, when a pair of extra-inning thrillers clinched the trophy for the South Australia side. A pitching hero of that special day, South Australia's Ron Sharpe, was later honored with an annual medal presented to each year's best Claxton Shield individual player.

While the diamond sport was progressing in fits and starts during the long history of the Claxton Shield matches, the Aussies were also finally taking their first tentative steps in the arena of international tournament competitions. Several brief sorties into the amateur world championships—one in Italy in 1978 and others in Japan and South Korea in 1980 and 1982—proved the country's earliest national squads to be easily overmatched, and the best outing was only a miserable eighth slot and a 4–7 record, posted at Tokyo. A major break-through finally came with the 1997 Intercontinental Cup series at Barcelona, where a surprising Australian entrant (with Paul Gonzalez leading the field in batting and gaining the Most Valuable Player trophy) swept six of seven opening round games and upended Team USA in a bronze medal third-place game. There was reason for optimism on the eve of the showcase 2000 Sydney-based Olympic Games. As part of Olympic preparations, Australia proudly hosted Intercontinental Cup matches in November 1999 at Sydney's Homebush Stadium and amazingly reached the finals versus a reduced Cuban entrant consisting largely of up-and-coming Cuban League prospects. The hosts claimed victory in the gold medal match on a late-game Cuban error by hot-prospect outfielder Yasser Gómez, and there was not only wild celebrating but much optimism about challenging for an Olympic medal a year later. The Aussies seemed to have come a long way, and almost overnight, from their makeshift 1996 Olympic squad, which had shown a great deal of offense in Atlanta but little adequate pitching. The optimism nonetheless proved unwarranted. The Aussies collapsed badly in the September 2000 Olympiad, winning only two games (versus Korea and South Africa) and thus finishing well out of the medal chase. Four years later, with a number of ex–big league hurlers in tow (Adrian Burnside, Graeme Lloyd, John Stephens) there would be yet another rebound, this time strong enough to shock favored Japan twice and bring home an Athens silver medal after once more falling to the pesky Cubans.

Australian baseball took a significant turn once a pro-style league replaced the lengthy Claxton Shield tradition of state-versus-state competitions. The league enjoyed a rather turbulent ride during the decade of the 1990s, while functioning as a Far East equivalent of traditional winter baseball held through-out the Caribbean. The circuit began with an initial season in 1989–1990, boasting eight teams, a 40-game schedule, and a best-of-five postseason playoff won by regular-season leader Waverley. Essentially the same format continued for exactly a decade and featured some exciting play with exclusively homegrown Australian talent. The Perth Heat were a dominant team in the early going, winning the second postseason and then reigning as regular-season pacesetter for two more years. Big league catcher Dave Nilsson (Milwaukee Brewers) returned to make his managerial debut with the Brisbane Bandits in 1997 and guided them as a player–skipper to the runner-up spot. A year later, Melbourne's Reds enjoyed a surprising worst-to-first season and became the first team (after having started their history in Waverley) to capture three Australian Baseball League (ABL) titles. The crucial turning point for the league came on the eve of the 2000 Sydney Olympics, when the circuit was sold to a group fronted by Milwaukee Brewers catcher Dave Nilsson; the plan was to continue with a six-team circuit, with hopes for future expansion. In reality, the new organization—renamed the International Baseball League of Australia and for the first time featuring foreign imports—limped through one schedule of only seventeen games and then contracted to only four teams for its second and final outing. The final winter pitted clubs called the Internationals, Taiwan, Australians, and MLB All-Stars in a 43-game pennant race that was sparsely attended. It marked at least a temporary swan song for efforts at developing Australian professional baseball.

Perhaps a true measure of Australian baseball progress lies in the successes enjoyed by the country's small population of native major leaguers. Graeme Lloyd and Dave Nilsson are the biggest names, but there have been more than a few others. Craig Shipley was surprisingly the first twentieth-century Australian big leaguer; he signed on with the Los Angeles Dodgers in 1984 and debuted two years later. Joseph Quinn owns nineteenth-century pioneering rights, starting his career in 1884 with St. Louis in the long-gone Union Association. Mark Hutton earned distinction with the New York Yankees in 1993 as the first Australian-born hurler to start a major league game, then pitched with the Florida and Colorado expansion clubs before his five-year stint was over. Shayne Bennett was more successful on the mound with Boston and Montreal but has never matched his ABL stature, where he was once Reliever of the Year and also acquired the quirky record of five strikeouts in a single inning. Together, these expatriate Aussie players and a handful more have kept Australia at least on the edges of the U.S. baseball limelight. It remains to be seen if the game Down Under has already peaked, and if so, whether the decline is only temporary.

THE EMERGING KOREAN BASEBALL STORY

Korea (and South Korea is understood here) has long played second fiddle in Asian baseball. For decades, the Koreans have trailed far behind the Japanese when it comes to almost any measure of baseball growth. Their own clubs have rarely rivaled the Japanese teams in any international competitions. Their few pro stars have played in Japanese pro circuits and then mostly as journeymen and fill-ins and not true stars. The Korean nation does not have a strong native baseball tradition like the Japanese nor even one to measure up to the sport's considerable stature in Taiwan (now known as Chinese Taipei). There have been very few inspired triumphs in world tournament games or in Olympic matches. Of late, Korean teams have even fallen far behind the upstart Taiwanese with their 1992 Olympic silver medal and pair of equally potent pro circuits. Nonetheless, there have been a few Korean major leaguers over the past decade to boost the country's baseball playing reputation. A growing big league presence is about the only area in which Korea can rival the Japanese or outstrip the Taiwanese when it comes to competitive bragging rights.

Korea does boast a showcase professional league that has experienced both promising highs and disappointing lows since the early 1980s. The circuit known as the Korean Baseball Organization (KBO) began in a flurry of political motivation that recalls Jorge Pasquel's use of Mexican League baseball as a political platform in the mid-1940s, or dictator Rafael Trujillo's similar efforts at propagandistic baseball triumphs during rigged election campaigns in the Dominican Republic back in the 1930s. A half-century after Trujillo and four decades after Pasquel, then-president Chun Du-hwan (giving the family name first, in Korean style, for this public figure) sought to salvage his own sinking popularity and bury worsening political chaos with the public enthusiasm likely to become attached to a competitive professional baseball league. The plan was put into operation with a 1982 KBO season featuring six teams (Lotte Giants, Samsung Lions, Haitai Tigers, OB Bears, MBC Dragons, and Sammi Superstars), 126 games, and a postseason culminating in the 7-game Korean Series. Following the typical Asian model, KBO teams are all sponsored by and named after huge business conglomerates. The number of teams has now doubled, but little else has changed across twenty-two summers.

Once underway, the KBO would soon be producing dozens of homegrown stars and even some thrilling pennant competitions. Unique postseason play pits third- and fourth-place finishers in a best-of-three, the winner next advancing to a 5-game showdown with the league's runner-up. Thus, the regular-season leader waits in the wings for a finale versus the survivor of the first two play-down rounds. The Korean League season finally peaks with the best-of-seven, winner-take-all Korean Series at year's end. The showcase event has been dominated most years by a single team that appears to be a Korean version of the Yankees, Giants, Cubs, and Red Sox all rolled into one. The Haitai Tigers captured nine of the first sixteen Korean Series; they then slipped temporarily to the league cellar for a few late-1990s campaigns before acquiring a brand new corporate identity as the Kia Tigers and rebounding to one of the league's top regular-season ledgers in 2002. The Haitai and Kia Tigers have also produced some of the league's top stars, led by eight-time ERA champ Dong-yol Sun (for ballplayers the family name is here given last, American-style, as befits candidates for American rosters and statistical lists), who was signed out of the Tigers hometown city of Kwangju. The parade of Tigers all-stars has lately featured the emergence of starter Dae-jin Lee and closer Chang-young Im on the strong Haitai staff of the late 1990s. Other teams have boasted their substantial heroes, and one of the biggest of late has been Samsung Lions first baseman Seung-yeop Lee, a slugger who rang up impressive numbers in only his second season in the league (.329 BA, 170 hits, 114 RBI, 32 homers in 1997).

A highlight of South Korean baseball, as well as a small measure of the nation's diamond progress, has been the Korea–Japan Supergame series. This is a string of friendly games between national all-star teams staged every four years, starting in 1992, with the Japanese first visiting Korea and the host country then alternating thereafter. The second series in 1996, with its even 4-game split, showed that the Koreans were becoming more competitive. The series was notable also for its encounter between rival batting champions, Japanese idol Ichiro Suzuki (then of the Orix Blue Wave and later of the Seattle Mariners) and Jeong-bum Lee of the Haitai Tigers. If that second Supergame match was an unqualified success, the following year brought Korea's biggest baseball fiasco during yet another exhibition of teams from the two rival Asian baseball nations. The much-ballyhooed return of Korean star Dong-yol Sun from Japan (where he had escaped to the Chunichi Dragons) proved to be a promotional disaster when a scheduling miscalculation put the games smack up against a simultaneous event featuring the Japanese and Korean national soccer teams. With Koreans caught up in a frenzy of anticipation for upcoming World Cup Soccer 2002 (scheduled to be cohosted by Korea and Japan), the soccer match proved the hottest ticket in town. The baseball game, billed as a special new Korea–Japan Golden Series, was to be played in a stadium adjacent to the soccer venue. Fewer than 2,000 saw the two baseball games and embarrassed Korean star Dong-yol Sun even refused to appear in the first sparsely attended contest and pitched only a single inning in the second. The disaster led to a quick dropping of any ideas about again soon playing a renewal of the experimental Golden Series versus the Japanese League stars.

Another recent headline feature of Korean baseball has been the record-setting slugging of Samsung infield star Seung-yeop Lee, Asia's newest version of Henry Aaron and Korea's answer to Sadaharu Oh. At age 27, the powerful right-hander rewrote history during the recent 2003 KBO season by becoming the youngest player in world baseball annals to reach the 300 plateau for career round-trippers. Smashing 56 long balls during the historic campaign (as well as hitting at a .301 clip and knocking home 144 runs), Lee overhauled the existing Asian record of 55 held by Japan's Oh. He also stirred up something of a crazed fan following in his homeland, reminiscent of the 1998 major league season revolving around Mark McGwire and Sammy Sosa in the United States. Lee's retrieved 300th career smash sold at auction for the equivalent of $100,000 in U.S. dollars, and fans jammed outfield bleachers at season's end toting butterfly nets and gloves in the hope of cashing in on historic homer number 56. The ultimate record breaker came on the season's final day and set off a mad spectator scramble identical to those outside Wrigley Field's left field wall that greeted many of Sosa's September and October blasts in 1998 and 1999. Lee became a free agent at the end of the 2003 season and is expected to be seen in the U.S. major leagues before very much longer.

Korea's few major league stars have risen in reputation far beyond what might have been expected from their rather slim numbers. With his nearly 100 National League wins, Chan-ho Park has been the most notable Korean big leaguer. Park's performances with the Los Angeles Dodgers may not have raised the same furor inspired by Hideo Nomo with his sensational debut season and hordes of trailing Japanese media—but in subsequent seasons Park has proven an equally effective major league hurler. Park has so far stood at the top of the Korean heap, but he has been joined of late by Diamondbacks (later Red Sox) reliever Byung-hyun Kim and Cubs (now Marlins) slugging first baseman Hee-seop Choi, both of whom initially enjoyed rather mixed results. Kim flashed promise as a side-arming closer before collapsing in the 2002 World Series versus the Yankees. Choi was touted as a replacement for popular Cubbie Mark Grace; he started slow against big league pitching, however, and was dealt to Florida (where his hopes for a career revival soon took another detour to Los Angeles).

There have been no Korean versions of Ichiro; there is no KBO-exile Hideo Nomo, Hideki Irabu, or Hideki Matsui. Korean big leaguers are not followed like rock stars by an adoring and frenzied national press corps, as are the Japanese players, and Korean athletes coming to the majors or even playing pro ball in the closer-to-home venues of Japan face a serious obstacle in the form of national military obligations. Much heated controversy has raged throughout the country over this issue of late: it seems an excessive and ruinous requirement that pro baseballers (like all other Koreans) must devote 26 months to army duty at the height of their athletic prime. Still, the Koreans have had a rather surprising impact on the majors, for all the stumbling blocks so far thrown in their paths. This is especially true given the notable weakness of their national teams when stacked up against the Japanese and even lately against the forces from Chinese Taipei.

Korean teams have generally disappointed in their numerous forays into World Cup, Asian Championship, or Olympic play. Japan and Taiwan have shut them out of several Olympic tournaments (Barcelona and Athens) as the only pair of Asia-region qualifiers. There have also been preciously few highlight moments in World Cup or Intercontinental Cup play. But there was a long-anticipated period of pride and glory in the fall of 2000, when KBO play shut down for three weeks during September so that a crack contingent of league stars could staff the Korean national team at the Sydney Olympics. It was a most successful venture, as the Korean nine rebounded from a slow four-and-three preliminary round to shut down archrival Japan 3–1 in the bronze

Korea's Ji-hwan Son turns a double play against Japan in their 2003 World Cup showdown. [Peter C. Bjarkman]

medal playoff. The triumph was only momentary, however, for the Koreans faltered badly with a second-level squad at the 2003 Havana World Cup and also with their top club at the Asian Olympic Qualifier during that same October. Korean baseball is still very much a developing work in progress.

BASEBALL IN TAIWAN AS A JAPANESE INSTITUTION

Taiwan is one place where baseball's apostles are not actually the automatically expected culprits. Taiwanese baseball is not stepchild to the American game, as one might expect; nor was it a mainland Chinese import, even though China itself had already discovered American-style baseball by the late nineteenth century. Taiwan's adopted national sport is instead a strictly Japanese phenomenon in both flavor and historical development, and this fact is reflected in just about every single feature of the Taiwanese game as it is today played religiously at all age levels everywhere around the large island nation.

Japanese origins for baseball on the Taiwanese island have had many ramifications. During the earliest Japanese occupation at the beginnings of the twentieth century, baseball was a game taught exclusively to Japanese immigrant children attending numerous Japanese-sponsored schools. The adult version of play caught on rather sporadically during the century's second decade. Postal workers and army personnel established the first adult teams at the southern outpost of Tainan in 1910; five years later, the Taiwanese Baseball Association established the first league play (with mostly Japanese ethnic players and only a handful of native Taiwanese athletes, though there were reported to be fifteen initial active amateur teams). American pros also made two brief visits, one during each of the next two decades. Both of these visits were actually attached to tours of Japan by the big leaguers, the first in 1921, when a group of seasoned professionals faced off with a Japanese squad in Taipei. The great Bambino Babe Ruth himself, accompanied by the likes of Lou Gehrig, Charlie Gehringer, Lefty Gomez, and Connie Mack, appeared on the island (again at Tainan) during a brief 1934 stopover en route to a celebrated series of wildly successful exhibitions throughout Japan.

The year 1921 would also mark a true birth of the Japanese–American sport as a native game with something of visible local traditions. Hualien resident Chia-hsing Lin spotted and organized untrained enthusiastic youngsters playing with only sticks and rocks, and inside a year he had shaped them into a proficient technical school squad. This "Nengkao" team of indigenous teenagers drawn from the Ami aboriginal population along the country's east coast soon achieved remarkable successes against their Japanese overlords. During a 1925 government-sponsored tour of Japan, the Nengkao nine shocked both their hosts and their homeland with an opening 28–0 win and a later advancement to the title game of the prestigious Japanese Koshien high school tournament. The Nengkao not only built up local baseball enthusiasm and considerable national pride, but they also planted more firmly the soon ingrained traditions surrounding aboriginal athletes in Taiwan's baseball development. Within three years, a second popular school team called Chia-nung and representing ethnic Chinese residents of the island would perform similar, parallel roles in spreading what had once been a strictly Japanese sport. Most of the Chia-nung (a Chinese abbreviation for the Chiayi School for Agriculture and Forestry) success again came in Japan, once more with the Koshien tournament. In 1931 Chia-nung was the first school team composed of native Taiwanese to capture Taiwan's own qualifying tournament preceding the Osaka-based Koshien high school championships; that same year they advanced to the title game in Japan. A new generation of skilled players and coaches drawn largely from this club would soon be playing a most significant role in Taiwan's own rapid developments in the sport both at home and abroad.

Before World War II, there was no pro league to spark further interest and foster the game for potential Taiwanese fans, but some of the island's best native players made their marks nonetheless, playing with established pros to the north in Japan. In the very first Japanese League season of 1936, two able recruits from the 1921 Nengkao squad performed proficiently with the Tokyo Senators. Both Tao-hou Luo and Tien-sung Lan were native Ami players, and their appearance in the new Japanese professional circuit successfully opened doors for a number of their countrymen. A third Nengkao team member, Tien-sung Ye, joined the Nankai Hawks in 1940 and soon after captured a 1944 Japanese League batting title with a lofty .369 mark. Chia-nung school team members of ethnic Chinese backgrounds (Ami are ethnic Polynesians) also enjoyed parallel success. Pu-chiang Ching was a member of the original Hanshin Tigers and also won a 1937 fall season batting title, the first Taiwanese-born star to be Japan's top hitter. Hsin-heng Wu enjoyed a productive season as well with the 1944 Yomiuri Giants, batting above .300 (fourth in the league) and shining as a top base stealer. And there were others to follow during these formative seasons of Japanese professional league baseball. Chang-cheng Wu won hitting crowns in 1942 and 1943 for the Yomiuri Giants, a time when most top Japanese players had been called to wartime duties. Wu eventually burned his left foot during an American bombing raid on Osaka but made a remarkable recovery to return as a pitcher and toss a league no-hitter. Hiroshi Oshita was a native Japanese raised in Taiwan who belted better than 200 homers in his postwar Japanese League career.

Taiwanese baseball has never been known in the United States for professional stars coming to the majors (as with Japan, for example) or for national team triumphs in world amateur senior-level play (as with Cuba). Rather, Taiwan earned its stripes in the United States primarily through a sudden and startling involvement in Little League baseball. Taiwan's Little league successes in Williamsport date back to the late 1960s and are still talked about today. The first surprising victory came when the Taichung Golden Dragons team walked off with a 1969 Williamsport championship, after first emerging as Far East Regional winner in the inaugural year of Taiwan's National Youth Baseball Association.

The Golden Dragons were admittedly a national contingent and as such not properly representative of the true spirit of Little League competitions, which are based on advancement by local squads of community all-stars. The Taiwanese association would quickly have to modify its approaches to continue competing in the international youth arena. This was accomplished with few hitches, and the Tainan City Giants captured a second crown for the Asian representatives only two years later. In the process, these early youth teams became celebrated national heroes at home and were toasted with festive parades and presidential audiences. Questions were always lurking about the ages of the players from Taiwan, however, as well as reports circulating abroad (mainly in the United States) that local officials altered identities and changed birthdates. Age was a contentious issue even back on the island itself. On the heels of the Golden Dragons' impressive triumph, one manager and one coach were handed prison sentences for forging birth documents of several Hung Yeh school players. There was other bending of the rules and even some scandal involving gambling on youth matches; pressure on local school teams to win youth tournaments and qualify players for prestigious national squads led to such practices as payment to coaches by local booster clubs (a clear violation of international rules) and even payment to preteenage athletes for winning key games. In the face of such embarrassing revelations and continuing difficulties in certifying the ages of their players, Taiwan would eventually (by the late 1990s) choose to withdraw altogether for a time from the international Little League movement.

Theories abound concerning the successes of Taiwanese youth teams. Certainly age was a factor, but that doesn't explain enough about the high degree of baseball skills among the nation's youth. There was obviously the factor of national pride combined with the local prestige and benefits (including travel opportunities) offered by a slot on the top youth teams. Quite important was the matter of dedicated training and the use of skilled paid coaches (the latter being another blatant violation of Little League rules and spirit of competition). A narrow and even obsessive dedication to the unrivaled national sport by officials, coaches, fans, and players alike is most likely the best explanation of all.

There is a common notion still afloat that Taiwanese ballplayers simply disappear from the scene once their years of Little League eligibility have expired. This is an absurdity that ignores the realities of Taiwanese baseball. Some stars continued to travel to Japan in the four decades that separated World War II and the first efforts at pro ball on the Taiwanese home front. The most notable expatriate star was Yuan-chih Kuo, a member of the Golden Dragons Little League champions who won 106 games on the mound with the Chunichi Dragons after breaking in with a loud splash as Japan's 1982 Rookie of the Year. Another was Yi-hsin Chen (also an Ami, like Kuo), who returned to his homeland in 1992 after three Japanese seasons and eventually won Most Valuable Player (MVP) honors in both of the newly founded Taiwanese pro circuits.

Taiwan belatedly launched its own pro league in 1990. Before the decade was out, there were actually two competing leagues operating. The first season of the Chinese Professional Baseball League (CPBL) had four teams: President Lions, Brother Elephants, Weichuan Dragons, and Mercury Tigers; the teams represented the large corporations that sponsored them, rather than home cities. A 90-game schedule was played with teams barnstorming all around the island. Expansion after three years to first seven and then eight teams meant it was necessary almost from the start to bring in foreign pros in order to sustain the ambitious CPBL in the face of rather severe local player shortages. And Taiwanese professional baseball was almost ruined before it had hardly gotten off the ground when a major betting and game-fixing scandal rocked the CPBL in its seventh year of operations. Once the smoke cleared on the 1996 campaign, it was revealed that nearly two dozen players and coaches—perhaps many more—individually made as much as $120,000 in U.S. dollars to throw games on which there had been heavy wagering. The result was arrest and imprisonment of a number of top stars, including pitcher Chin-hsing Kuo, a former MVP. One of the league's premier clubs collapsed when the Chinese Times Eagles suffered nineteen player suspensions, lost star reliever Chien-chien Kuo to a thirty-month prison sentence, played out the second half of 1997 with mostly replacement players, and finally suspended operations for the 1998 campaign.

That very year of 1997 also witnessed the formation of a rival Taiwan Major League (TML), and subsequently Taiwanese baseball has continued to limp along despite the sport's severe dip in credibility among local fans and supporters. League expansion itself came in a cloud of acrimony, first resulting from a CPBL dispute with the government over television cable rights, then from wholesale raiding of CPBL players by newcomer TML ball clubs. The two warring leagues were finally merged successfully in 2003, and the future is recently looking a little brighter for the whole Taiwanese baseball operation.

A prime venue for top adult players has increasingly been the country's sometimes powerful national amateur teams. Taiwan joined Japan in 1972 as the first-ever Asian World Cup teams during that year's championships in Managua. Disputes quickly followed, however—contentious issues involving the right of the now-independent island nation to compete in Olympic-style events and to continue using "Republic of China" as its national designation. The mainland People's Republic of China had returned actively to the world sporting scene and was orchestrating Taiwan's temporary ouster from Olympic venues. After a brief period on the sidelines, the Taiwanese were readmitted to IBAF-sponsored events just in time to show up for the 1982 Seoul-hosted World Cup championships. From this point on, Taiwanese entrants in all sports would play under the banner of Chinese Taipei. There were some truly impressive performances after this reemergence in international play: at the 1984 World Cup in Havana, Chinese Taipei defeated the vaunted Cubans 7–4 and Puerto Rico 4–2 in medal-round games while en route to an impressive silver medal finish. Two years later in Amsterdam, Chinese Taipei once again upset Cuba, handing them their last World Cup individual game loss until 2001, five tournaments later. At the 1984 demonstration Olympics matches in Dodger Stadium, a solid Chinese Taipei team finished third, a feat diminished only slightly by the absence of Cuba. Three years later, the country claimed its first Asian championships on hostile grounds in Tokyo. The zenith came with a silver medal performance (losing in the finals to Cuba, of course) at the first fully official Olympic baseball tournament in Barcelona.

The story doesn't seem to be over. During the 2003 World Cup in Havana, an underrated Taipei club shocked overconfident Team USA in a 2–1 pitchers-duel quarterfinals but then lost the bronze medal match to its nemesis, Japan. Two years earlier, the same event was held for the first time in Taipei itself, and the host country celebrated with a rousing third-place victory over the same rival Japanese. The Taiwanese—coming off their World Cup momentum in Havana—edged out Korea in the October 2003 Asian championships and thus qualified to join neighboring Japan in a proud return to Olympic play in Athens.

The most recent development for baseball in the country now called Chinese Taipei (at least for sporting competitions) was the 2003-season merger of the two pro baseball leagues that had previously existed side-by-side with only an uneasy truce. Betting scandals have now also been left in the past, but a continuing problem is the staffing of a full contingent of pro league

Chinese Taipei infielder Chin-wei Shih in 2003 Havana World Cup semifinals action. [Peter C. Bjarkman]

teams with players from less than two dozen national amateur clubs. The rechristened Taiwan Professional League will likely continue to struggle for legitimacy (even after the 2003 merger) as long as it remains so heavily reliant on imported athletes to man its half-dozen rosters. There are also issues of national prestige involving insignificant numbers of Taiwanese players making the big leagues, especially given the relative successes of the national team when stacked up against the Koreans or Japanese. There are reasons for Taiwan's absence from the big leagues. Taiwanese stars prefer Japanese pro baseball, for cultural reasons; Japanese ties are still strong in a land where many from an earlier generation were educated by the former colonial Japanese system. The military obligation of 18 months compulsory service facing young players (as in Korea) is also a factor. CPBL lifetime contracts and a ban on free agency have proved further obstacles to league jumping. And only recently has there been a solid pro league at home to train young stars and prepare them early for the highest competition levels. Such explanations are sound enough, but offer small consolation.

Nonetheless, the first few Taiwanese big leaguers are indeed beginning to appear on the horizon. Chien-ming Wang is a promising right-handed pitcher who recently went 7–6 as a starter at Trenton (AA) in the talent-stocked New York Yankees chain. Another righty, Chin-hui Tsao, split his three decisions with the Colorado Rockies during his rookie 2003 season and thus became the first among his countrymen to both win and lose a big league game. And promising outfielder Chin-feng Chen earlier became the first-ever Taiwanese-born position player in the majors when he appeared in several contests with the Los Angeles Dodgers, first in 2002 and again in 2003. There will likely soon be more to bolster the challenges by Chinese Taipei to both Japan and Korea as a legitimate font for future oriental major league stars.

EUROPEAN AND PACIFIC RIM COUNTRIES IN WORLD AMATEUR TOURNAMENTS

Asian countries were latecomers to world tournament play, which has traditionally been dominated by the invincible Cubans and a slim supporting cast of North American (United States, Mexico, Canada), Caribbean (Puerto Rico, the Dominican Republic, Venezuela), Central American (Nicaragua, Panama), and European (Netherlands, Italy) nations. The Japanese and Taiwanese first entered World Cup matches in the early 1970s, both debuting with solid if unspectacular inaugural outings during the 1972 Nicaragua-based event. Korea made its first bow in the premier international tournament four years later, in Colombia, splitting ten games to finish sixth in a field of eleven.

When three Asian teams entered the world baseball arena as amateur combatants, they did so at first with only limited success. Two early highlights were a pair of impressive performances by the Taiwan team against the vaunted Cubans of the 1980s. Playing under the banner of Chinese Taipei—after a bitter dispute about international Olympic sanction with the People's Republic of China—the former Republic of China embarrassed the Cubans on their home field in Havana during a 1984 second-round game and thus walked off with a surprising silver medal finish; two years later, they replicated the feat in Amsterdam, with the 4–3 win that represented Cuba's last defeat in individual World Cup games for a stretch covering the next fifteen years (46 individual games). Japan also eventually made several strong showings in World Cup events by claiming its first medal (bronze) in 1976 and peaking with a 1982 second-place finish in Seoul (first place going to neighboring South Korea, with Cuba sitting out the event back home). The Koreans themselves anticipated their 1982 gold medal with a 1978 bronze (in Italy) and the 1980 runner-up slot in Tokyo, and the first two official Olympic tournaments found teams from Asia (Chinese Taipei in Barcelona and Japan in Atlanta) embarrassing American squads by advancing to the finals before suffering one-sided thrashings in gold medal face-offs with the still-invincible Cubans.

There had been a demonstration version of baseball in the Olympics as early as the 1912 Games, hosted by Sweden in Stockholm. On that occasion, a pair of U.S. teams comprised of track and field athletes rolled over a squad of Swedish amateurs 13–3 on a makeshift field otherwise used for equestrian events; a day later, a second exhibition featured American track athletes only (including future big leaguer Jim Thorpe) and matched two clubs dubbing themselves "Finlands–West" and "Olympics–East" for the occasion. The experiment was tried again with only mixed results at Berlin in 1936; there, another crude diamond with no mound and little lighting saw a night contest featuring two squads of U.S. collegians who were not part of the official U.S. Olympic contingent. The teams were labeled "World Champions" and "U.S. Olympics" and played a seven-inning match that reportedly drew 90,000 baseball-innocent curiosity seekers. These were hardly legitimate world tournaments; if anything, they set back the world baseball movement a full step or two.

An even more ambitious foray into baseball as a true world sport occurred in England two years after the Berlin Games. It was a precedent-setting event that later would be recorded perpetually in IBAF yearbooks as the first Baseball World Cup (then called the Amateur World Series). In actuality, it was little more than a staged exhibition in which mostly American soldiers took part. Dreamed up by American Leslie Mann, organizer of the 1936 exhibition match in Berlin and relentless early promoter of baseball as an Olympic sport, the August 1938 London matches featured a squad of Europe-based American soldiers and a contingent of former English pros (veterans of a short-lived league existing in the Manchester area in the mid-1930s) battling for a trophy named after John Moore, founder of the British Amateur Baseball Federation. England claimed a world championship when its team swept four of five games, but a championship that in no way implied or reflected any British adoption of the American national game. More legitimate if still primitive world tournament play did not begin until a year later in Havana, Cuba, when a small field of Cuban, Nicaraguan, and U.S. squads at least represented formal "national teams" representing thriving amateur competitions in their own countries.

When the notion of Olympic baseball once again cropped up nearly a quarter-century later the Asians countries for the first time took a more substantial role. A strong U.S. baseball squad of collegiate all-stars, led by University of Southern California coach Rod Dedeaux and with eight future big leaguers on board, visited the 1964 Tokyo Olympics to do a one-game battle with Japanese amateur all-stars before 50,000 in Tokyo Olympic Stadium. A more ambitious demonstration tournament at the 1984 Los Angeles Olympics was notable mainly because the powerful Cubans—joining the Soviet boycott of the event—were not present to compete. This was nonetheless the first Olympic demonstration in which the combatants were actual national all-star teams and not collections of nonbaseballers from other sports. Surprisingly enough, a group of Japanese university student all-stars behind pitcher Atsunori Ito embarrassed the host Americans (including Will Clark, Mark McGwire, Barry Larkin, and Bobby Witt) in the tense title game 6–3 and walked off with the cherished, if unofficial, Olympic gold. Four years later, a similar event would be hosted by Korea when the Olympic Games moved to Seoul, their second-ever Asian stopover. The Cubans were absent again (now joining a North Korean boycott), but this time a crack American squad came out on top when one-handed southpaw Jim Abbott rode 2 homers by Tino Martínez to a 5–3 revenge-laced title win over the Japanese. The 1988 unofficial U.S. Olympic squad was staffed by such additional future big leaguers as Ben McDonald, Robin Ventura, and Andy Benes. It may have been the best U.S. international tournament team ever assembled, but it came four years early, before baseball was finally anointed as a legitimate medal-round Olympic sport.

When baseball did debut a full-fledged Olympic event in the early 1990s, the long-reigning Cuban world champions were predictably back on the scene. And when there were any challenges to the Cubans, they would come from the Asian clubs and not from the suddenly impotent Americans, who had apparently peaked a bit too early in amateur baseball circles. In Barcelona in August 1992, it was Chinese Taipei that made a surprising appearance in the final match for the gold medal. The Cubans breezed 11–1, but Taiwan had now resoundingly entered the world of ranking baseball nations with their 5–2 upset of Japan in the semifinals. Team USA did boast future big leaguers Nomar Garciaparra, Jason Giambi, and Michael Tucker but, nevertheless, tumbled 6–1 to Cuba in the semifinals. In Atlanta four years later, it would be the Japanese who would suddenly rise up to oust the Americans in the semis (11–2) and thus challenge the Cubans for the gold medal. A team of Japanese industrial league stars made it two silver medals in a row for the Asians, despite being run off the field 13–9 by the slugging Cubans with Omar Linares and Orestes Kindelán in the title match. Teams from Italy, the Netherlands, and Australia also showed surprising strength at moments: the slugging Italians offered little pitching and won only twice but did defeat Korea and score a dozen runs in besting Australia. Australia won a game over runner-up Japan, and the Dutch in turn beat the Aussies by a 16–6 count. All three teams at times demonstrated some heavy hitting, but with little pitching to keep them truly competitive.

The only real Olympic boasting point so far for any European team would be authored by the talented but inexperienced squad representing the Netherlands at the September 2000 Sydney Games. That came in the form of a single surprising day of glory during an otherwise meaningless opening round contest with the defending champion and talent-laced Cubans. Riding a strong pitching performance by Rob Cordemans, the Dutch (managed by Arizona State head coach Pat Murphy and including Caribbean players from the Netherlands Antilles) pulled off a 4–2 upset that represented the first Olympic loss ever suffered by a Cuban squad, which had previously coasted through nine games in Barcelona, nine more in Atlanta, and the first three outings at Sydney. Unable to sustain their momentum, the apparently equally shocked Dutch team (also an earlier winner over host Australia) quickly collapsed themselves in a game against the baseball-naïve South Africans (3–2) and so finished with a losing ledger. But the uprising against the Cubans was certainly enough to grab brief attention of world baseball watchers. Unfortunately, there has been little positive connected with European teams to follow that single delightful moment of baseball aberration. Italy, like the Netherlands, finished up on the losing end (2–5) in Sydney. In subsequent World Cup events in Taipei (2001) and Havana (2003), teams from Italy, France, the Netherlands, and Russia have proved little more than predictably weak also-rans. Russia's single upset win over Chinese Taipei in Havana and a Dutch winning ledger (4–3) at Taipei are the less-than-arresting high points. France limped through an embarrassing 0–14 cumulative experience in the two prestigious tournaments and even dropped one shortened knockout game in Taipei 17–0 (themselves getting only one hit) to the barely motivated Americans.

The Japanese, Taiwanese, and Korean teams were also left by the wayside in Sydney in 2000 and again in Intercontinental Cup and World Cup matches in Havana in 2002 and 2003. The Japanese were knocked from the limelight in Sydney's medal round by a strong Cuban pitching performance from future big league defector José Contreras (a 3–0 six-hitter) in the semifinal match. The Japanese entrant that year was one of the country's strongest ever and had been an odds-on gold medal favorite; the team featured 20-year-old pitching sensational Daisuke Matsuzaka and Kintetsu Buffaloes slugging third baseman Norihiro Nakamura. In recent years, however, despite rosters now laced with such homegrown Japanese League professionals, the Japanese squads have somehow never measured up to expectations. Their biggest disappointment may have been in the 2003 World Cup, where they missed the title game after dropping the semifinals to Panama and former big league washout Roberto Medina; Japan's consolation bronze medal came despite a relatively weak field outside of the host Cubans. Japanese officials had admittedly left their best performers at home to prepare for the Asian Olympic Qualifier that would clinch their 2004 reservation at the Athens Olympiad. There, the Japanese and Taiwanese were planning once more to try to snap Cuba's firm stranglehold on top world baseball events.

A true highlight moment for Asian baseball forces came most recently, when an unheralded Chinese Taipei team (the country's top squad had been left home to prepare for the Asian Olympic Qualifier) scored a stunning upset of the unprepared American club during the 2003 Havana World Cup quarterfinals. Admittedly it was not a top U.S. team, since the Americas (as also the Japanese and Koreans) were playing in Havana with B squads while A-level teams practiced at home for the Olympic selection matches scheduled only a month later. Also, the Taiwanese team was quickly bounced two nights later by the Cubans, dropping a one-sided semifinal game. But the defeat of Team USA was impressive enough to show that Japanese, Taiwanese, and even Korean clubs were no longer ever a force to be taken lightly in top world tournament events.

But most recent notes for Asian baseball have been sour ones indeed. Athens 2004 was a nightmare event for Pacific Rim countries by almost any measure.

The Koreans were home on the sidelines during the fourth Baseball Olympiad and both the Chinese Taipei and Japanese contingents might have wished for a similar fate. Taipei embarrassingly missed out on the medal round by inconceivably tripping in a preliminary round match with last-place Italy; a victory in that contest would have left the Taiwanese tied for fourth slot with the eventual runner-up Aussies and thus a medal-round qualifier due to their 3–0 victory in head-to-head play between the two. And despite their heftiest Olympic lineup ever, the underachieving Japanese League professional all-stars tripped twice against the same over-achieving Aussies—the second time 1–0 in the semifinals—and thus had to settle for an embarrassing bronze medal.

BASEBALL IN HAWAII, AFRICA, AND OTHER DISTANT GLOBAL OUTPOSTS

Elsewhere, baseball has grown only by minimal fits and starts. While a number of African nations have attempted to join the world baseball movement as productive members (Nigeria, Ghana, Uganda, and Zimbabwe tops among them), the progress has been sporadic at best on that vast continent. Hawaii made a too-brief and quickly aborted attempt in the mid-1990s at joining the world of organized professional baseball with an ill-fated Major League Baseball-sponsored winter circuit. Ukrainian and Lithuanian national teams demonstrated some progress and faced-off for the 2003 title in a European Inter-League Open championship staged in Belarus during early September, but a long-discussed emergence of baseball in Russia, the core of the former Soviet Union, has never seemed to materialize.[1] Russia's ill-prepared entry in the 2003 World Cup in Havana offered sufficient proof that post-Soviet baseball was developing on a slow track, if on any track at all. Upsetting Chinese Taipei in their final game with a strong pitching performance by ace Alexei Valyaline, a punchless Russian team was knocked around by Cuba (20–1) and all its other opponents.

Some Eastern European countries among the former Soviet Bloc nations have taken to the sport more enthusiastically. Croatia is probably the best example, though there (as also in, for example, Lithuania) professional basketball and not baseball is the one non-European game that seriously rivals soccer for national attention. National championships have been held for more than a dozen years in the Adriatic coastal nation that was once part of Yugoslavia. Poland, an early provider of both star (Stan Musial) and journeyman (Ray Jablonski and Rip Repulski) big leaguers among its American immigrant families, has also witnessed considerable efforts to foster the American-style game through efforts of imported U.S. pro and collegiate coaches. And the Czech Republic has of late proven to be something of a minor baseball hotbed with three straight appearances (fifth place in 2001) at European Federation tournaments. In another Eastern European outpost, the Blagoevgrad Buffaloes recently walked off with a Bulgarian national championship for the eleventh consecutive year.

Africa as a continent is now making noticeable progress toward becoming a legitimate part of an expansive IBAF international effort. October 2003, for example, witnessed an eighth edition of an All-Africa baseball tournament, staged in Abuja, Nigeria. Competition director for the ambitious event was

Silvano Ambrosioni, former manager of the Italian national team, and the tournament took on special significance because its winner from a six-team field would play Oceania champion Australia in November for a final slot in the 2004 Athens Olympics. South Africa not so surprisingly claimed the crown in Abuja with a final-day 15–0 rout of host Nigeria in the title match. Zimbabwe defeated Uganda 17–4 for the less-significant bronze medal, with the score again indicating the still-primitive level of even the best African play. Defensive and pitching shortcomings of the top African squads were again demonstrated in early February 2004, when Australia breezed over South Africa in three straight games (by lopsided scores of 8–1, 6–4, 13–1) in Sydney's Blacktown Olympic Park to clinch the final Athens Olympic invitation. South Africa's one-sided loss in Australia meant that the African region would not yet enjoy a second Olympic visit as springboard to advancing baseball interest throughout the continent. At the 2000 Games in Sydney, the same South African team was part of the prestigious field representing Oceania–Africa, since the stronger Australians that year enjoyed automatic participation as host nation. But the South Africa team quickly proved in Sydney how badly it was overmatched, finishing dead last in the field and losing all but one of its games (including such blowouts as 16–0 versus Cuba, 13–0 versus Italy, and 13–3 versus Korea). Perhaps the surprise game of the entire Olympic tournament that year unfolded when South Africa edged a veteran Netherlands team (3–2) soon after the Dutch handed runner-up Cuba its only qualifying round defeat; to further stamp this small claim to legitimacy, when the South Africans lost to gold medal winner Team USA, it was by a count of only 6–2.

Hawaii represents still another significant baseball outpost, with its few major leaguers down through the years and recent abortive attempts at jump-starting a new professional winter league circuit. Hawaii's baseball tradition is much more closely tied to the saga of Asian or Asian-Pacific baseball than it is to the sport's evolution in the mainland United States. There have nonetheless been some Hawaiian big leaguers of note staking out an American connection. Mike Lum debuted with Atlanta's Braves in 1967 and lasted for 15 years as a soft-hitting (.247) big league outfielder. Far more significant are a trio of top pitchers: Charlie Hough, Sid Fernandez, and Ron Darling. Hough both won and lost over 200 games during a lengthy tenure (split between the American and National leagues) as a tenacious knuckleball hurler with numerous clubs. Fernandez and Darling both starred as New York Mets in the 1980s and early 1990s and each won more than 100 big league contests. The island state also boasted a AAA minor league club in the Pacific Coast League during the 1960s, 1970s, and most of the 1980s (1961–1987), and a top California Angels affiliate christened the Hawaii Islanders peaked with a 98-win first-place finish in 1970 (losing that year's championship playoffs to Spokane). In both 1975 and 1976, under veteran manager Roy Hartsfield, the Islanders won the Pacific Coast League title outright (at the time doing service as the top farm club of the San Diego Padres).

Minor league baseball in a less ambitious form returned to the island in 1993 to fill the gap on the local baseball scene created when the Islanders franchise folded up its 27-year operation in the late 1980s. A new winter circuit debuted in autumn 1993 as organized baseball's third alternative to traditional

Caribbean winter leagues and the newer Arizona Fall League. Its history was a painfully short one, but it did provide for a brief integration of U.S. and Asian players (mainly from Japan) paralleling the Latin–U.S. mixture that was long a noted feature of winter play. Highlights of the short-lived circuit included appearance of some top Japanese stars, a few recognizable big leaguers, and even some players from the U.S. women's professional circuit. Brad Fullmer (much-traveled slugger with Montreal, Toronto, and the Anaheim Angels) won a batting title in the penultimate 1996 season. Other big leaguers of note performing in Hawaii included Aaron Boone (later the Yankee home run hero of the 2003 American League Championship Series versus Boston), highly regarded Florida Marlins outfield prospect Preston Wilson, and native son Benny Agbayani (briefly a New York Mets regular). High-profile Japanese star and future big league phenom Ichiro Suzuki also made a token appearance for a single season. But the most headline-worthy imports were a pair of female stars who had played previously with the touring Colorado Silver Bullets. Julie Croteau and Lee Ann Ketchum made history in the winter of 1994 when they suited up for the Maui Stingrays as the first women ever to perform on a regular basis for a men's professional team. But for all its innovations, the island circuit was never very prosperous as a gate attraction and lasted but five seasons. The same year as its demise, the St. Louis Cardinals and San Diego Padres played a regular season National League series (April 1997) that drew 77,432 total fans to Aloha Stadium in Honolulu. But it was a bittersweet swan song for U.S. pro baseball, given that no big leaguers have performed on the island during five subsequent seasons.

There has been much heavy complaining—especially in the United States and Cuba—about the imbalanced fields for world Olympic-style tournaments. It seems to make little sense in the eyes of those representing powerful baseball countries located mostly in the Western Hemisphere or in the Far East to reserve regular spots for two European teams (the number open to North America and the Caribbean region combined) in the Olympics or to have a weak entrant like South Africa qualifying for the 2000 event at Sydney, while at the same time only two slots remain available to be split between the United States, Canada, and the numerous baseball powerhouses of the Caribbean (namely Cuba, Puerto Rico, Venezuela, and the Dominican Republic). But there are two sides to this as to any other argument. It can also be easily maintained that the existing structure for international tournaments fosters legitimate growth for baseball as a world sport, providing real opportunities and constant motivation to nations where baseball is still in a raw developmental stage. An annual or occasional world championship limited to American, Cuban, Dominican, and Japanese or Korean entrants would do little to encourage the hopes of smaller European or Oceania national teams, no matter how much it might accomplish in assuring a more legitimate world champion.

Easily the stronger position seems to be the argument that final (medal) round play in world tournaments should be expanded to double or triple elimination play, following a pattern established by the annual U.S. collegiate world series staged at Omaha. Today's long-standing format of single-elimination playoffs results more often than necessary in lamentable upsets based on off-days or unpredictable one-time pitching gems—such as the United

States loss to Mexico (at the hands of revenge-minded ex–big leaguer Rigo Beltran) in the 2003 Olympic Qualifier, or Ben Sheets's whitewash of favored Cuba during Sydney's Olympic Gold Medal showdown—that unjustly sabotage superior clubs. Baseball is one sport where endurance and consistency is always more highly valued than lucky bounces or one-time aberrations in on-field performance.

One more controversy looms. A World Cup event sponsored by Major League Baseball—which some suggest lies not far down the road—will probably do very little to foster, or even to replace, IBAF efforts at advancing a legitimate world baseball movement. Certainly the reported Major League Baseball plan would be a big step forward for those who believe that either young pro leagues or select national teams from European, African, Latin American, and Asian nations exist primarily for purposes of raising future talent for the U.S.-based professional leagues. The motivation of major league officials, however disguised, transparently lies in this domain of baseball imperialism. And the Major League Baseball Commissioner's Office is also driven by an apparent belief that full-scale World Cup frenzy equal to that sustaining European-style soccer would inevitably provide a financial bonanza of television dollars to be poured into Major League Baseball coffers. There has also been a long-standing feeling among U.S. fans and Major League Baseball brass alike that stateside baseball can only regain its rightful prestige with the introduction of top professionals fully able to repeatedly thrash the opposition from Cuba or Venezuela or the Dominican, thus assuring a regular floodtide of coveted gold medals. It was the same jingoistic motivation on the heels of a humiliating basketball loss to the Russians at the 1972 Munich Games that eventually dragged a National Basketball Association Dream Team into Olympic basketball tournaments. It may all make perfectly logical sense to Americans to see Derek Jeter, Alex Rodríguez, and Barry Bonds squaring off against the best pitching that Cuba or the Netherlands can hope to muster. (Of course big league Dream Team rosters would likely only supplant Team Cuba with the Dominican Republic—featuring an immediate lineup anchored by Albert Pujols, Sammy Sosa, Vladimir Guerrero, Bartolo Colón, and Pedro Martínez—as surefire World Cup Gold Medal shoo-in.) Such one-sided stacking of either U.S. or Dominican rosters will do little for inspiring or sustaining baseball's now far-scattered distant international outposts.

SELECTED BASEBALL RECORDS AND STATISTICS FOR EUROPE, AFRICA, AND THE PACIFIC RIM (WITH OCEANIA)

Africa is here represented only by one table, with amateur championship results for the Republic of South Africa. There are at least fourteen other baseball-playing countries in that vast continent, though none have lengthy traditions of holding national amateur tournaments. Similarly, Australia is not the only country in Oceania that plays amateur baseball; there are also, for example, Micronesia, Palau, the Fiji Islands, and New Zealand. For a complete list, see the 2003 IBAF membership roster (Appendix B).

European Players in the Major Leagues (1871–2003)

Name	Debut	Position	Debut Team	Seasons	Games	Career Statistics
Austria: 2 Big Leaguers						
1 Frank Rooney	1914	1B	Indianapolis Hoosiers (FL)	1	2	.200 BA
2 Kurt Krieger	1949	RHP	St. Louis Cardinals (NL)	2	3	0–0, 12.60 ERA
Belgium: 1 Big Leaguer						
3 Brian Lesher	1996	OF	Oakland Athletics (AL)	5	108	.224 BA
Czechoslovakia: 4 Big Leaguers						
4 Amos Cross	1885	C	Louisville Colonels (AA)	3	117	.268 BA
5 Joseph "Joe" Hovlik	1909	RHP	Washington Senators (AL)	3	16	2–0, 3.62 ERA
6 Elmer Valo	1940	OF	Philadelphia Athletics (AL)	20	1,806	.282 BA, 1420 H
7 Carl Linhart	1952	PH	Detroit Tigers (AL)	1	3	.000 BA
Denmark: 1 Big Leaguers						
8 Olaf "Swede" Henriksen	1911	OF	Boston Red Sox (AL)	7	321	.269 BA
England: 30 Big Leaguers						
9 William Henry "Harry" Wright	1871	OF/RHP	Boston Red Stockings (NA)	7	180	.276 BA, 4–4 W–L
10 Samuel "Sam" Jackson	1871	IF/OF	Boston Red Stockings (NA)	2	20	.216 BA
11 Alfred "Al" Reach	1871	IF/OF	Philadelphia Athletics (NA)	5	83	.247 BA
12 George Hall	1871	OF	Washington Olympics (NA)	7	365	.322 BA
13 Richard "Dick" Higham	1871	C/OF	New York Mutuals (NA)	8	372	.307 BA
14 Albert "Al" Thake	1872	OF	Brooklyn Atlantics (NA)	1	18	.295 BA
15 Robert "Bobby" Clack	1874	OF/RHP	Brooklyn Atlantics (NA)	3	82	.154 BA, 0–0 W–L
16 Edward "Ed" Cogswell	1879	1B	Boston Red Caps (NL)	3	109	.294 BA
17 Thomas "Tom" Brown	1882	OF/RHP	Baltimore Orioles (AA)	17	1,788	.265 BA, 2–2 W–L
18 James "Jim" Halpin	1882	SS	Worcester Brown Stockings (NL)	3	63	.165 BA
19 Timothy "Tim" Manning	1882	IF	Providence Grays (NL)	4	200	.189 BA
20 Dennis Fitzgerald	1890	SS	Philadelphia Athletics (AA)	1	2	.250 BA
21 Alfred "Al" Lawson	1890	RHP	Boston Pilgrims (NL)	1	3	0–3, 6.63 ERA
22 Martin "Marty" Hogan	1894	OF	Cincinnati Reds (NL)	2	40	.241 BA
23 Harry Smith	1901	C	Philadelphia Athletics (AL)	10	343	.213 BA
24 Alfred "Al" "Shoddy" Shaw	1901	C	Detroit Tigers (AL)	4	181	.200 BA
25 David "Dave" Brain	1901	IF	Chicago White Stockings (AL)	7	679	.252 BA
26 Edward "Ed" Walker	1902	LHP	Cleveland Bronchos (AL)	2	4	0–2, 4.50 ERA
27 Walter Carlisle	1908	OF	Boston Red Sox (AL)	1	3	.100 BA
28 Thomas "Tom" Tuckey	1908	LHP	Boston Beaneaters (NL)	2	25	3–12, 3.49 ERA
29 Edward "Ned" Crompton	1909	OF	St. Louis Browns (AL)	2	16	.154 BA
30 Armstrong "Klondike" Smith	1912	OF	New York Yankees (AL)	1	7	.185 BA
31 Charles "Charlie" Hanford	1914	OF	Buffalo Blues (FL)	2	232	.280 BA
32 Samuel "Sam" White	1919	C	Boston Beaneaters (NL)	1	1	.000 BA
33 James "Jim" "Jiggs" Wright	1927	RHP	St. Louis Browns (AL)	2	4	1–0, 5.79 ERA
34 Leslie "Les" Rohr	1967	LHP	New York Mets (NL)	3	6	2–3, 3.70 ERA
35 Keith Lampard	1969	OF	Houston Astros (NL)	2	62	.238 BA
36 Paul Marak	1990	RHP	Atlanta Braves (NL)	1	7	1–2, 3.69 ERA
37 Lance Painter	1993	LHP	Colorado Rockies (NL)	10	314	25–18, 5.24 ERA
38 Danny Cox	1993	RHP	St. Louis Cardinals (NL)	11	278	74–75, 3.64 ERA
Finland: 1 Big Leaguer						
39 John Michaelson	1921	RHP	Chicago White Sox (AL)	1	2	0–0, 10–13 ERA

Name	Debut	Position	Debut Team	Seasons	Games	Career Statistics
France: 7 Big Leaguers						
40 Lawrence "Larry" Ressler	1875	OF	Washington Blue Legs (NA)	1	27	.194 BA
41 Joseph "Joe" Woerlin	1895	3B	Washington Nationals (NL)	1	1	.333 BA
42 Edward "Ed" Gagnier	1914	SS	Brooklyn Tip-Tops (FL)	2	115	.195 BA
43 Duke Markell (b. Henry Duquesne Markowsky)	1951	RHP	St. Louis Browns (AL)	1	5	1–1, 6.33 ERA
44 Bruce Bochy	1978	C	Houston Astros (NL)	9	358	.239 BA
45 Charles "Charlie" Lea	1980	RHP	Montreal Expos (NL)	7	152	62–48, 3.54 ERA
46 Larry Steven "Steve" Jeltz*	1983	SS	Philadelphia Phillies (NL)	8	727	.210 BA
Germany: 37 Big Leaguers						
47 John Martin "Marty" Swandell	1872	IF/OF	Brooklyn Eckfords (NA)	2	16	.213 BA
48 Joseph "Joe" Miller	1872	2B	Washington Nationals (NA)	2	29	.139 BA
49 Emil Geis	1882	RHP	Baltimore Orioles (AA)	1	13	4–9, 4.80 ERA
50 William "Bill" "Willie" Kuehne	1883	3B	Columbus Buckeyes (AA)	10	1,085	.232 BA
51 Gus Shallix (b. August Schallick)	1884	RHP	Cincinnati Reds (AA)	2	36	17–14, 3.56 ERA
52 Charles "Charlie" "Pretzels" Getzein	1884	RHP	Detroit Wolverines (NL)	9	296	145–139, 3.46 ERA
53 George Meister	1884	3B	Toledo Blue Stockings (AA)	1	34	.193 BA
54 Edward "Ed" Eiteljorge	1890	RHP	Chicago Colts (NL)	2	9	1–6, 6.68 ERA
55 John "Jack" Katoll	1898	RHP	Chicago Orphans (NL)	4	47	17–22, 3.32 ERA
56 Frederick "Fritz" Buelow	1899	C	St. Louis Perfectos (NL)	9	431	.192 BA
57 Skel Roach (b. Rudolf Charles Weichbrodt)	1899	RHP	Chicago Orphans (NL)	1	1	1–0, 3.00 ERA
58 William "Bill" Miller	1902	OF	Pittsburgh Pirates (NL)	1	1	.200 BA
59 Otto "Pep" Deininger	1902	OF/LHP	Boston Red Sox (AL)	3	58	.263 BA, 0–0 W–L
60 Bernard "Ben" Koehler	1905	OF	St. Louis Browns (AL)	2	208	.233 BA
61 Frederick "Fred" Gaiser	1908	RHP	St. Louis Cardinals (NL)	1	1	0–0, 7.71 ERA
62 Emil "Reggie" Richter	1911	RHP	Chicago Cubs (NL)	1	22	1–3, 3.13 ERA
63 Martin "Marty" Krug	1912	OF	Boston Red Sox (AL)	2	147	.278 BA
64 Robert "Bun" Troy	1912	RHP	Detroit Tigers (AL)	1	1	0–1, 5.40 ERA
65 Frederick "Fritz" Mollwitz	1913	1B	Chicago Cubs (NL)	7	534	.241 BA
66 William "Bill" Zimmerman	1915	OF	Brooklyn Robins (NL)	1	22	.281 BA
67 Frederick "Dutch" Schliebner	1923	1B	Brooklyn Robins (NL)	1	146	.271 BA
68 Anton "Tony" Welzer	1926	RHP	Boston Red Sox (AL)	2	76	10–14, 4.78 ERA
69 Charles "Dutch" Schesler	1931	RHP	Philadelphia Phillies (NL)	1	17	0–0, 7.28 ERA
70 Heinz "Harry" "Dutch" Becker	1943	1B	Chicago Cubs (NL)	4	152	.263 BA
71 Ralph Robert "Mickey" Scott*	1972	LHP	Baltimore Orioles (AL)	5	133	8–7, 3.72 ERA
72 Robert "Rob" Belloir	1975	SS	Atlanta Braves (NL)	4	81	.216 BA
73 Glenn Hubbard*	1978	2B	Atlanta Braves (NL)	12	1,354	.244 BA
74 Ronald "Ron" Gardenhire*	1981	SS	New York Mets (NL)	5	285	.232 BA
75 Stefan Wever	1982	RHP	New York Yankees (AL)	1	1	0–1, 27.00 ERA
76 Craig Lefferts	1983	LHP	Chicago Cubs (NL)	12	696	58–72, 3.43 ERA
77 Thomas "Tom" McCarthy*	1985	RHP	Boston Red Sox (AL)	3	40	3–2, 3.61 ERA
78 Michael "Mike" Blowers*	1989	3B	New York Yankees (AL)	11	761	.257 BA
79 Robert "Bob" Davidson*	1989	RHP	New York Yankees (AL)	1	1	0–0, 18.00 ERA
80 David "Dave" Pavlas*	1990	RHP	Chicago Cubs (NL)	4	34	2–0, 2.65 ERA
81 William "Will" Ohman*	2000	LHP	Chicago Cubs (NL)	2	17	1–1, 7.80 ERA
82 Steven "Steve" Kent*	2002	LHP	Tampa Bay Devil Rays (NL)	1	34	0–2, 5.65 ERA
83 Edwin Jackson*	2003	RHP	Los Angeles Dodgers (NL)	1	4	2–1, 2.45 ERA
Greece: 1 Big Leaguer						
84 Alexander "Al" Campanis (b. Alessandro Campani)	1943	IF	Brooklyn Dodgers (NL)	1	7	.100 BA
Ireland: 38 Big Leaguers						

(continued)

(continued)

Name	Debut	Position	Debut Team	Seasons	Games	Career Statistics
85 James "Jimmy" Hallinan	1871	IF/OF	Fort Wayne Kekiongas (NA)	5	170	.287 BA
86 Andrew "Andy" Leonard	1871	OF	Washington Olympics (NA)	9	501	.297 BA
87 Hugh Campbell	1873	RHP	Elizabeth Resolutes (NA)	1	19	2–16, 2.84 ERA
88 Mathew "Mike" Campbell	1873	IF	Elizabeth Resolutes (NA)	1	21	.143 BA
89 Thomas "Tommy" Bond	1874	RHP	Brooklyn Atlantics (NA)	8	322	193–115, 2.25 ERA
90 John McGuinness	1876	1B	New York Giants (NL)	3	66	.244 BA
91 Charles "Curry" Foley	1879	OF/LHP	Boston Beaneaters (NL)	5	305	.286 BA, 27–27 W–L
92 Patrick "Pat" McManus	1879	RHP	Troy Trojans (NL)	1	2	0–2, 3.00 ERA
93 Anthony "Tony" Mullane	1881	RHP/OF	Detroit Wolverines (NL)	13	784	284–220, 3.05 ERA
94 Thomas "Sleeper" Sullivan	1881	C	Buffalo Bisons (NL)	4	97	.184 BA
95 Hugh Daily	1882	RHP	Buffalo Bisons (NL)	6	165	73–87, 2.92 ERA
96 Michael "Mike" Muldoon	1882	3B	Cleveland Blues (NL)	5	495	.233 BA
97 Cornelius "Conny" Doyle	1883	OF	Philadelphia Phillies (NL)	2	31	.254 BA
98 Michael "Mike" Hines	1883	C/OF	Boston Beaneaters (NL)	4	120	.202 BA
99 Timothy "Ted" Sullivan	1884	OF	Kansas City Unions (UA)	1	3	.333 BA
100 John Horan	1884	RHP	Chicago Browns (UA)	1	13	3–6, 3.49 ERA
101 Bernard "Barney" McLaughlin	1884	OF/RHP	Kansas City Unions (UA)	3	178	.243 BA, 1–3 W–L
102 Joseph "Reddy" Mack	1885	IF	Louisville Colonels (AA)	6	550	.254 BA
103 Daniel "Cyclone" Ryan	1887	1B	New York Metropolitans (AA)	2	9	.212 BA
104 William "Billy" Collins	1887	C	New York Metropolitans (AA)	4	5	.167 BA
105 John "Jocko" Fields	1887	OF/C	Pittsburgh Pirates (NL)	6	341	.271 BA
106 John Tener	1888	RHP	Chicago White Stockings (NL)	3	61	25–31, 4.30 ERA
107 Samuel "Sam" Nicholl	1888	OF	Pittsburgh Pirates (NL)	2	22	.128 BA
108 John "Jack" Doyle	1889	IF/OF/C	Columbus Solons (AA)	17	1,569	.299 BA, 1811 H
109 Peter "Pete" Daniels	1890	LHP	Pittsburgh Pirates (NL)	2	14	2–8, 4.79 ERA
110 Charles "Charlie" McCullough	1890	RHP	Brooklyn Bridegrooms (AA)	1	29	5–23, 4.88 ERA
111 Patrick "Patsy" Donovan	1890	OF	Boston Beaneaters (NL)	17	1,824	.301 BA, 2256 H
112 Thomas "Tom" Dowse	1890	OF	Cleveland Blues (NL)	3	160	.243 BA
113 Michael "Mike" Flynn	1891	C	Boston Red Stockings (AA)	1	1	.000 BA
114 Cornelius "Con" Lucid	1893	RHP	Louisville Colonels (NL)	5	54	23–23, 6.02 ERA
115 Michael "Mike" O'Neill	1901	LHP	St. Louis Cardinals (NL)	4	85	32–44, 2.73 ERA
116 John "Jack" O'Neill	1902	C	St. Louis Cardinals (NL)	5	303	.196 BA
117 James "Jimmy" Archer	1904	C	Pittsburgh Pirates (NL)	12	847	.249 BA
118 Henry "Irish" McIlveen	1906	OF	Pittsburgh Pirates (NL)	3	53	.215 BA
119 Patrick "Paddy" O'Connor	1908	C	Pittsburgh Pirates (NL)	6	108	.225 BA
120 James "Jimmy" Walsh	1912	OF	Philadelphia Athletics (AL)	6	541	.232 BA
121 John "Johnny" O'Connor	1916	C	Chicago Cubs (NL)	1	1	—
122 Joseph "Joe" Cleary	1945	P	Washington Senators (AL)	1	1	0–0, 189.00 ERA
Italy: 6 Big Leaguers						
123 Louis "Lou" Polli	1932	RHP	St. Louis Browns (AL)	2	24	0–2, 4.68 ERA
124 Julio Bonetti	1937	RHP	St. Louis Browns (AL)	3	46	6–14, 6.03 ERA
125 Marino Pieretti	1945	RHP	Washington Senators (AL)	6	194	30–38, 4.53 ERA
126 Rinaldo "Rugger" Ardizoia	1947	RHP	New York Yankees (AL)	1	1	0–0, 9.00 ERA
127 Henry "Hank" Biasetti	1949	1B	Philadelphia Athletics (AL)	1	21	.083 BA
128 Reno Bertoia	1953	IF	Detroit Tigers (AL)	10	612	.244 BA
Netherlands [Holland]: 8 Big Leaguers						
129 Rynie (Reinder) Wolters	1871	RHP	New York Mutuals (NA)	3	45	19–23, 3.75 ERA
130 Frank Houseman	1886	RHP	Baltimore Orioles (AA)	1	1	0–1, 3.38 ERA
131 John Houseman (b. Holland)	1894	IF/OF	Chicago Colts (NL)	2	84	.253 BA
132 John Otten (b. Holland)	1895	C/OF	St. Louis Cardinals (NL)	1	26	.241 BA
133 Rik Aalbert "Bert" Blyleven	1970	RHP	Minnesota Twins (AL)	22	692	287–250, 3.31 ERA
134 Win Remmerswaal	1979	RHP	Boston Red Sox (AL)	2	22	3–1, 5.50 ERA
135 Rikkert Faneyte	1993	OF	San Francisco Giants (NL)	4	80	.174 BA
136 Robert Eenhoorn	1994	IF	New York Yankees (AL)	4	37	.239 BA

Name	Debut	Position	Debut Team	Seasons	Games	Career Statistics
Norway: 3 Big Leaguers						
137 John Anderson	1894	OF	Brooklyn Bridegrooms (NL)	14	1,636	.290 BA
138 James "Jimmy" Wiggs	1903	RHP	Cincinnati Reds (NL)	3	13	3–4, 3.81 ERA
139 Arndt "Art" Jorgens	1929	C	New York Yankees (AL)	11	307	.238 BA
Poland: 4 Big Leaguers						
140 Henry "Pep" Peploski	1929	OF	Boston Bees (NL)	1	6	.200 BA
141 John Clarence "Nap" Kloza	1931	OF	St. Louis Browns (AL)	2	22	.150 BA
142 John "Johnny" Reder	1932	1B	Boston Red Sox (AL)	1	17	.135 BA
143 Myron "Moe" Drabowsky	1956	RHP	Chicago Cubs (NL)	17	589	88–105, 3.71 ERA
Russia and the Ukraine: 7 Big Leaguers						
144 Jacob "Jake" Gettman	1897	OF	Washington Nationals (NL)	3	197	.278 BA
145 William "Bill" Cristall*	1901	LHP	Cleveland Blues (AL)	1	6	1–5, 4.84 ERA
146 Jacob "Jake" Livingstone	1901	RHP	New York Giants (NL)	1	2	0–0, 9.00 ERA
147 Alexander John "Rube" Schauer[†] (b. Dimitri Ivanovich Dimitrihoff)	1913	RHP	New York Giants (NL)	5	93	10–29, 3.35 ERA
148 Reuben Ewing[†]	1921	SS	St. Louis Cardinals (NL)	1	3	.000 BA
149 Isidore "Izzy" Goldstein[†]	1932	RHP	Detroit Tigers (AL)	1	16	3–2, 4.47 ERA
150 Victor Cole*	1992	RHP	Pittsburgh Pirates (NL)	1	8	0–2, 5.48 ERA
Scotland: 8 Big Leaguers						
151 David Abercrombie	1871	OF	Troy Haymakers (NA)	1	4	.000 BA
152 James "Jim" McCormick	1878	RHP	Indianapolis Browns (NL)	10	492	265–214, 2.43 ERA
153 Malcolm "Mac" MacArthur	1884	RHP	Indianapolis Hoosiers (AA)	1	6	1–5, 5.02 ERA
154 Michael "Mike" Hopkins	1902	C	Pittsburgh Pirates (NL)	1	1	1.000 BA
155 Michael "Mike" McCormick	1904	3B	Brooklyn Bridegrooms (NL)	1	105	.184 BA
156 George Chalmers	1910	RHP	Philadelphia Phillies (NL)	7	121	29–41, 3.41 ERA
157 Robert "Bobby" Thomson	1946	OF	New York Giants (NL)	15	1,779	.270 BA, 264 HR
158 Thomas "Tom" Waddell	1984	RHP	Cleveland Indians (AL)	3	113	15–11, 4.30 ERA
Spain: 4 Big Leaguers						
159 Alfredo "Al" Cabrera	1913	IF	St. Louis Cardinals (NL)	1	1	.000 BA
160 Bryan Oelkers	1983	LHP	Minnesota Twins (AL)	2	45	3–8, 6.01 ERA
161 Alberto "Al" Pardo	1985	C	Baltimore Orioles (AL)	4	53	.132 BA
162 Danny (Daniel) Ríos	1997	RHP	New York Yankees (AL)	2	7	0–1, 9.31 ERA
Sweden: 4 Big Leaguers						
163 Charles "Charlie" Hallstrom	1885	RHP	Providence Grays (NL)	1	1	0–1, 11.00 ERA
164 Charles "Charlie" "Dutch" Bold	1914	OF	St. Louis Browns (AL)	1	2	.000 BA
165 Eric Erickson	1914	RHP	New York Giants (NL)	7	145	34–57, 3.85 ERA
166 Axel Lindstrom	1916	RHP	Philadelphia Athletics (AL)	1	1	0–0, 4.50 ERA
Switzerland: 1 Big Leaguer						
167 Otto Hess	1902	OF/LHP	Cleveland Bronchos (AL)	10	280	.216 BA, 70–90 W–L
Wales: 2 Big Leaguers						
168 Edward "Ted" Lewis	1896	RHP	Boston Pilgrims (NL)	6	183	94–64, 3.53 ERA
169 James "Jimmy" Austin	1909	3B	New York Highlanders (AL)	18	1,580	.246 BA

* U.S. citizen born abroad.
[†] Born in Odessa, Ukraine.

History of Pacific Rim Countries with Players in the Major Leagues (1884–2003)

Country of Birth	First Player	Debut	Total
Afghanistan	Jeff Bronkey*	1993	1
American Samoa	Tony Solaita	1968	1
Australia	Joe Quinn	1884	15
China	Harry Kingman*	1914	1
Hawaii[†]	Johnnie Williams	1914	28

(*continued*)

(continued)

Country of Birth	First Player	Debut	Total
Japan‡	Masanori Murakami	1964	25
Korea, South	Chan Ho Park	1994	9
Okinawa	Bobby Fenwick*	1972	2
Philippines	Bobby Chouinard	2003	1
Singapore	Robin Jennings*	1996	1
Taiwan (Chinese Taipei)	Chin-feng Chen	2002	4
Vietnam	Danny Graves	2002	1

* Players of other nationality but born in this country.
† Hawaii became a state on August 21, 1959; players born before and after that date are grouped together in figures for Hawaii.
‡ See Chapter 3 for full coverage of Japanese baseball.

Pacific Rim Players in the Major Leagues (1884–2003)

Name	Debut	Position	Debut Team	Seasons	Games	Career Statistics
Afghanistan: 1 Big Leaguer						
1 Jacob Jeffrey "Jeff" Bronkey	RHP	P	Texas Rangers (AL)	3	45	2–2, 4.04 ERA
American Samoa: 1 Big Leaguer						
2 Tolia "Tony" Solaita	1968	1B	New York Yankees (AL)	7	525	.255 BA
Australia: 15 Big Leaguers						
3 Joseph "Joe" Quinn	1884	IF	St. Louis Maroons (UA)	17	1,769	.262BA, 1800 H
4 Craig Shipley	1986	SS	Los Angeles Dodgers (NL)	11	582	.271 BA
5 David "Dave" Nilsson	1992	C	Milwaukee Brewers (AL)	8	837	.284 BA, 105 HR
6 Mark Hutton	1993	RHP	New York Yankees (AL)	5	84	9–7, 4.75 ERA
7 Graeme Lloyd	1993	LHP	Milwaukee Brewers (AL)	10	568	30–36, 4.04 ERA
8 Mark Ettles	1993	RHP	San Diego Padres (NL)	1	14	1–0, 6.50 ERA
9 Shayne Bennett	1997	RHP	Montreal Expos (NL)	3	83	5–7, 5.87 ERA
10 Trent Durrington	1999	2B	Anaheim Angels (AL)	3	59	.238 BA
11 Jeffrey "Jeff" Williams	1999	LHP	Los Angeles Dodgers (NL)	4	37	4–1, 7.49 ERA
12 Luke Prokopec	2000	RHP	Los Angeles Dodgers (NL)	3	56	11–17, 5.30 ERA
13 Cameron Cairncross	2000	LHP	Cleveland Indians (AL)	1	15	1–0, 3.86 ERA
14 Grant Balfour	2001	RHP	Minnesota Twins (AL)	2	19	1–0, 5.02 ERA
15 Bradley "Brad" Thomas	2001	LHP	Minnesota Twins (AL)	2	8	0–3, 9.00 ERA
16 Damian Moss	2001	LHP	Atlanta Braves (NL)	3	69	22–18, 4.22 ERA
17 John Stephens	2002	RHP	Baltimore Orioles (AL)	1	12	2–5, 6.09 ERA
China: 1 Big Leaguer						
18 Henry "Harry" Kingman	1914	1B	New York Yankees (AL)	1	4	.000 BA
Okinawa: 2 Big Leaguers						
19 Robert "Bobby" Fenwick	1972	IF	Houston Astros (NL)	2	41	.179 BA
20 Craig House	2000	RHP	Colorado Rockies (NL)	1	16	1–1, 7.24 ERA
Philippines: 1 Big Leaguer						
21 Robert "Bobby" Chouinard	1996	RHP	Oakland A's (AL)	5	111	11–8, 4.57 ERA
South Korea: 9 Big Leaguers*						
22 Chan-Ho Park	1994	RHP	Los Angeles Dodgers (NL)	10	253	90–65, 4.09 ERA
23 Jin-Ho Cho	1998	RHP	Boston Red Sox (AL)	2	13	2–6, 6.52 ERA

Name	Debut	Position	Debut Team	Seasons	Games	Career Statistics
24 Byung-Hyun Kim	1999	RHP	Arizona Diamondbacks (NL)	5	292	29–27, 3.24 ERA
25 Sang-Hoon Lee	2000	LHP	Boston Red Sox (AL)	1	9	0–0, 3.09 ERA
26 Sun-Woo Kim	2001	RHP	Boston Red Sox (AL)	3	43	3–3, 5.66 ERA
27 Hee-Seop Choi	2002	1B	Chicago Cubs (NL)	2	104	.210 BA
28 Jung-Keun "Jung" Bong	2002	LHP	Atlanta Braves (NL)	2	45	6–3, 5.29 ERA
29 Jae-Weong Seo	2002	RHP	New York Mets (NL)	2	33	9–12, 3.80 ERA
30 Thomas "Tommy" Phelps	2003	LHP	Florida Marlins (NL)	1	27	3–2, 4.00 ERA
Singapore: 1 Big Leaguer						
31 Robin Jennings	1996	OF	Chicago Cubs (NL)	4	93	.244 BA
Chinese Taipei (Taiwan): 2 Big Leaguers*†						
32 Chin-feng Chen	2002	OF	Los Angeles Dodgers (NL)	2	4	.000 BA
33 Chin-hui Tsao	2003	RHP	Colorado Rockies (NL)	1	9	3–3, 6.02 ERA
Vietnam: 1 Big Leaguer						
34 Danny Graves (b. Vietnam)	1996	RHP	Cleveland Indians (AL)	8	397	39–36, 3.89, 131 S

* Following the standard English-speaking pattern, Chinese and Korean names are listed with the given name first (usually two parts or two syllables) and the family name second (usually a single syllable). At home, these players would write it the other way around.
† As of midseason 2004, Taiwan has two pitchers waiting in the minor league wings: Chien-ming Wang (RHP) for the New York Yankees and Hong-chih Kuo (LHP) for the Los Angeles Dodgers.

Hawaiian Players in the Major Leagues

Name	Debut	Position	Debut Team	Seasons	Games	Career Statistics
1 John "Johnnie" Williams*	1914	RHP	Detroit Tigers (AL)	1	4	0–2, 6.35 ERA
2 Tony Rego (b. Antone De Rego)*	1924	C	St. Louis Browns (AL	2	44	.286 BA
3 Prince Oana*	1934	OF/RHP	Philadelphia Phillies (NL)	3	30	3–2, 3.77 ERA
4 Michael "Mike" Lum*	1967	OF	Atlanta Braves (NL)	15	1,517	.247 BA, 90 HR
5 John Matias*	1970	OF	Chicago White Sox (AL)	1	58	.188 BA
6 Charles "Charlie" Hough*	1970	RHP	Los Angeles Dodgers (NL)	25	858	216–216, 3.75 ERA
7 Milton "Milt" Wilcox*	1970	RHP	Cincinnati Reds (NL)	16	394	119–113, 4.07 ERA
8 Ryan Kurosaki*	1975	RHP	St. Louis cardinals (NL)	1	7	0–0, 7.62 ERA
9 Len Sakata*	1977	IF	Milwaukee Brewers (AL)	11	565	.230 BA
10 Fred Kuhaulua*	1977	LHP	California Angels (AL)	2	8	1–0, 4.79 ERA
11 Douglas "Doug" Capilla*	1976	LHP	St. Louis Cardinals (NL)	6	136	12–18, 4.34 ERA
12 Joseph "Joe" DeSa	1980	1B	St. Louis Cardinals (NL)	2	35	.200 BA
13 Carlos Diaz*	1982	LHP	Atlanta Braves (NL)	5	179	13–6, 3.21 ERA
14 Ronald "Ron" Darling	1983	RHP	New York Mets (NL)	13	382	136–116, 3.87 ERA
15 Charles Sidney "Sid" Fernandez	1983	LHP	Los Angeles Dodgers (NL)	15	307	114–96, 3.36 ERA
16 Brian Fisher	1985	RHP	New York Yankees (AL)	7	222	36–34, 4.39 ERA
17 Jessie Reid	1987	OF	San Francisco Giants (NL)	2	8	.100 BA
18 Tanner Joe "Joey" Meyer	1988	DH/IF	Milwaukee Brewers (AL)	2	156	.251 BA
19 Michael "Mike" Huff	1989	OF	Los Angeles Dodgers (NL)	7	369	.247 BA
20 Steven "Steve" Cooke	1992	LHP	Pittsburgh Pirates (NL)	6	104	26–36, 4.31 ERA
21 Benny Agbayani	1998	OF	New York Mets (NL)	5	383	.274 BA
22 Onan Masaoka	1999	LHP	Los Angeles Dodgers (NL)	2	83	3–5, 4.23 ERA
23 Keith Luuloa	2000	SS	Anaheim Angels (AL)	1	6	.333 BA
24 Brandon Villafuerte	2000	RHP	Detroit Tigers (AL)	4	71	1–4, 4.14 ERA
25 Justin Wayne	2002	RHP	Florida Marlins (NL)	2	7	2–5, 6.52 ERA
26 Jerome Williams	2003	RHP	San Francisco Giants (NL)	1	21	7–5, 3.30 ERA
27 Shane Victorino	2003	OF	San Diego Padres (NL)	1	36	.232 BA
28 Dane Sardinha	2003	C	Cincinnati Reds (NL)	1	1	.000 BA

* Born before Hawaii achieved statehood.

Australian Professional League Champions

Claxton Shield Winners

Year	Champion State	Helms Ron Sharpe Player Medal*
1934	South Australia	—
1935	South Australia	—
1936	South Australia	—
1937	New South Wales	—
1938	New South Wales	—
1939	New South Wales	—
1940–1945	—†	—
1946	New South Wales	—
1947	Victoria	—
1948	Victoria	—
1949	Victoria	—
1950	New South Wales	—
1951	New South Wales	—
1952	Western Australia	—
1953	New South Wales	—
1954	Victoria	—
1955	New South Wales	—
1956	Victoria	—
1957	South Australia	—
1958	Victoria	—
1959	South Australia	—
1960	South Australia	—
1961	South Australia	—
1962	Victoria	Anthony Strand (New South Wales)
1963	New South Wales	Kevin Cantwell (New South Wales)
1964	South Australia	Adrian Pearce (South Australia)
1965	Victoria	Graeme Deany (Victoria)
1966	South Australia	Kevin Greatrex (South Australia)
1967	South Australia	Garry Thompson (South Australia)
1968	Victoria	John Swanson (Victoria)
1969	South Australia	Neil Page (South Australia)
1970	South Australia	Paul Russell (New South Wales)
1971	South Australia	Ron McIver (Victoria)
1972	Victoria	Donald Knapp (Western Australia)
1973	Victoria	David Mundy (South Australia)
1974	Victoria	Neil Buszard (Victoria)
1975	Western Australia	Laurence Home (Queensland)
1976	South Australia	Alan Albury (Queensland)
1977	Western Australia	Ronald Owen (Victoria)
1978	Western Australia	Ray Michell (Western Australia)
1979	Western Australia	Brian Wonnacott (Victoria)
1980	South Australia	John Galloway (South Australia)
1981	Victoria	John Hodges (Victoria)
1982	Queensland	Geoffrey Martin (Queensland)
1983	Queensland	Doug Mateljan (Western Australia)
1984	Victoria	Brett Ward (Victoria)
1985	Western Australia	Tony Stall (Western Australia)
1986	Victoria	Lindsay Orford (Victoria)
1987	Queensland	Dave Nilsson (Queensland)
1988	Queensland	Tony Adamson (Western Australia)
1989	New South Wales	Richard Vagg (Victoria)
2003‡	Queensland	—
2004	New South Wales	—

* The Helms Ron Sharpe Player Medal was not awarded before 1962 or after 1989.
† Claxton Shield competition was canceled during World War II.
‡ A Claxton Shield series was renewed in 2003, after the pro league had disbanded.

Australian Baseball League (1989–1999)

Year	Regular Season Winner	Record	PCT	Playoff Winner (Games Won)	Record
1989–1990	Waverley Reds	34–6	.850	Waverley Reds defeated Melbourne	3–1
1990–1991	Gold Coast Dragons	31–9	.775	Perth Heat defeated Gold Coast	3–2
1991–1992	Perth Heat	36–11	.765	Gold Coast Dragons defeated Perth	3–1
1992–1993	Perth Heat	30–18	.625	Melbourne Monarchs defeated Perth	2–0
1993–1994	Sydney Blues	35–19	.648	Brisbane Bandits defeated Sydney	2–0
1994–1995	Waverley Reds	44–14	.750	Waverley Reds defeated Perth	2–0
1995–1996	Brisbane Bandits	29–16	.644	Sydney Blues defeated Melbourne	2–0
1996–1997	Perth Heat	40–20	.666	Perth Heat defeated Brisbane	2–1
1997–1998	Melbourne Reds	32–20	.615	Melbourne Reds defeated Gold Coast	2–0
1998–1999	Adelaide Giants	28–17	.622	Gold Coast Cougars defeated Sydney	2–0

International Baseball League of Australia

Year	Regular Season Winner	Record	PCT	Playoff Winner	Games Won
1999–2000	Victorian Aces	11–6	.647	Western Heelers defeated Queensland	2–1
2000–2001	Internationals	25–15–3	.616	Internationals defeated Australia	2–1

Korea, Taiwan, and Hawaii

Korean Professional League Series Champions and Seasonal Leaders

Year	League Champion			Individual Leader			
	Team	Record	Season MVP	Batting	BA	Pitching	W–L
1982	OB Bears	56–24–0	Chul-soon Park	In-chun Baek	.412	Chul-soon Park	24–4
1983	Haitai Tigers	55–44–1	Man-su Lee	Hyo-jo Chong	.369	Myung-bu Chong	30–16
1984	Lotte Giants	50–48–2	Dong-won Choi	Man-su Lee	.340	Dung-won Choi	27–13
1985	Samsung Lions	77–32–1	Song-han Kim	Hyo-jo Chong	.373	Shi-jin Kim	25–5
1986	Haitai Tigers	67–37–4	Dong-yol Sun	Hyo-jo Chong	.329	Dong-yol Sun	24–6
1987	Haitai Tigers	55–48–5	Hoi-jo Kim	Hyo-jo Chong	.387	Shi-jin Kim	23–6
1988	Haitai Tigers	68–38–2	Song-han Kim	Sang-hoon Kim	.354	Hak-kil Yoon	18–10
1989	Haitai Tigers	65–51–4	Dong-yol Sun	Won-bu Ko	.327	Dong-yol Sun	21–3
1990	LG Twins	71–49–0	Dong-yol Sun	Dae-hwa Han	.349	Dong-yol Sun	22–6
1991	Haitai Tigers	79–42–5	Jung-hoon Chang	Jeong-hoon Lee	.348	Dong-yol Sun	19–4
1992	Lotte Giants	71–55–0	Jong-hoon Chang	Jeong-hoon Lee	.360	Jin-woo Song	19–8
1993	Haitai Tigers	81–42–3	Song-rae Kim	Jun-hyuk Yang	.341	Gye-hyun Gho	17–6
1994	LG Twins	81–45–0	Jeong-bum Lee	Jeong-bum Lee	.396	Sang-hoon Lee	18–4
1995	OB Bears	74–47–5	Sang-ho Kim	Kwang-rim Kim	.337	Sang-hoon Lee	20–5
1996	Haitai Tigers	73–51–2	Dae-song Ku	Jun-hyuk Yang	.346	Dae-song Ku	18–3
1997	Haitai Tigers	75–50–1	Seung-yeop Lee	Ki-tae Kim	.344	Hyun-uk Kim	20–2
1998	Hyundai Unicorns	81–45–0	Tyrone Woods*	Jun-hyuk Yang	.342	Young-su Kim	18–6
1999	Hanwha Eagles	72–58–0	Seung-yeop Lee	Hae-yong Ma	.372	Min-tae Chong	20–7
2000	Hyundai Unicorns	91–40–2	Tom Quinlan*	Jong-ho Park	.340	Sun-dong Im	18–4
2001	Doosan Bears	65–63–5	Tyrone Woods*	Joon-hyuk Yang	.355	Yoon-ho Shin	15–6
2002	Samsung Lions	82–47–4	Hae-young Ma	Seong-ho Chang	.343	Narciso Elvira*	13–6
2003	Hyundai Unicorns	80–51–2	Seung-yeop Lee	Jong-soo Shim	.355	Shane Bowers*	13–4

Following the standard English-speaking pattern, Korean names are listed with the given name first (usually two parts or two syllables) and the family name second (usually a single syllable).

* Foreign imported player. Foreign players have been employed by the Korean Baseball Organization beginning with the 1998 season.

Taiwanese Professional League (Chinese Taipei)

Year	Champion Team	Record	Batting Champion	BA	Pitching Leader	W–L
Chinese Professional Baseball League						
1990	Weichuan Dragons		Not Recorded		Not Recorded	
1991	President Lions		Not Recorded		Not Recorded	
1992	Brother Elephants		Not Recorded		Not Recorded	
1993	Brother Elephants		Not Recorded		Not Recorded	
1994	Brother Elephants		Not Recorded		Not Recorded	
1995	President Lions	62–36–2	Ángel González*	.354	Chin-hsing Kuo	20–7
1996	President Lions		Not Recorded		Not Recorded	
1997[†]	Weichuan Dragons	46–46	Ted Wood*	.373	Chun-liang Wu	15–6
1998	Sinon Bulls	58–45–2	Jay Kirkpatrick*	.387	Yuan-chih Kuo	14–3
1999	China Trust Whales	60–29–2	Chi-feng Hung	.333	Kevin Henthorne*	15–5
2000	Sinon Bulls	50–38–1	Chung-yi Huang	.354	Mark Kiefer*	20–3
2001	Brother Elephants	44–39–7	Min-ching Luo	.357	John Burgos*	18–4
2002	Brother Elephants	53–33–4	Chien-wie Chen	.334	Chao-chi Sung	16–8
Taiwan Major League						
1997	Chia-nan Luka	53–42–0	Epy Guerrero*	.361	Yi-hsin Chen	19–11
1998	Kao-ping Fala	62–45–1	Luis de los Santos*	.357	Don August*	19–5
1999	Taipei Suns	48–33–3	Brad Strauss*	.387	Hisanobu Watanabe*	18–7
2000	Taipei Gida	52–30–2	Manny Estrada*	.362	Takehiro Ishii*	16–5
2001	Taichung Agan	43–16–1	Kun-han Lin	.368	Chin-chih Huang	7–3
2002	Taichung Agan	47–24–1	Roberto Mejia*	.332	Chin-chih Huang	16–2
Taiwan Professional League						
2003	Brother Elephants	63–31–6	Cheng-min Peng	.355	Yokota Hisanori*	16–3

Following the standard English-speaking pattern, Chinese names are listed with the given name first (usually two parts or two syllables), the family name second (usually a single syllable).
* Foreign imported player. Foreign players have been employed by Taiwanese professional baseball beginning with the 1990 season.
[†] The Chinese Professional Baseball League 1997 season was interrupted and discredited by major game-fixing and gambling scandals following the 1996 campaign.

Hawaii Winter League Professional Champions and Individual Leaders

Year	Champion Team	Record	Runner-Up	Batting Champion	BA	Pitching Leader	W–L
1993	Hilo Stars	26–22	Honolulu Sharks	Chad Fonville	.336	Brian Harrison	5–3
1994	Kauai Emeralds	29–21	Maui Stingrays	Hiroki Kokubo	.370	Hidekazu Watanabe	8–0
1995	Maui Stingrays	25–28	Honolulu Sharks	D. J. Boston	.347	Ryan Hancock	5–1
1996	Maui Stingrays	25–24	Honolulu Sharks	Brad Fullmer	.333	Masahiro Sakumoto	5–0
1997	Honolulu Sharks	27–27	Hilo Stars	Nobuhiko Matsunaka	.372	Keith Evans	4–3

Europe, Africa, Pacific Rim, and Oceania Amateur National Champions
Austria National Champions (Amateur)

Year	Champion
1985	WBV Homerunners
1986	WBV Homerunners
1987	WBV Homerunners

Year	Champion
1988	WBV Homerunners
1989	WBV Homerunners
1990	BC (Vienna Wanderers)
1991	Sportunion Wien (Vienna Bulldogs)
1992	WBV Homerunners (Vienna Lions)
1993	Sportunion Wien (Vienna Bulldogs)
1994	WBV Homerunners (Vienna Lions)
1995	SC Schwaz Tigers
1996	WBV Homerunners (Vienna Lions)
1997	Sportunion Wien (Vienna Bulldogs)
1998	SC Schwaz Tigers
1999	Dornbirn Indians
2000	Vienna Bulldogs
2001	Hard Bulls
2002	Kufstein Vikings
2003	Dornbirn Indians

Austria has never entered European Federation championship matches (fourteen other countries have), but the country has staged its own national tournament since 1985 and historically also shares with Germany a primitive bat-and-ball game known as *Schlagball* (literally, hitball or even beatball), which some have cited as a true baseball ancestor.

Belarus National Champions (Amateur)

Year	Champion
1999	Gsducor-1 (Minsk)
2000	Gsducor-1 (Minsk)
2001	Sdushor Minsk
2002	Sdushor Minsk

Belarus is one region of the former Soviet Union that has made recent efforts at developing youth leagues and staging national senior-level tournaments, all with its eye on more ambitious European championship international matches. Belarus has yet to enter a national team in any serious international tournaments. In September 2003, a European Inter-League Open international tournament was staged in Brest, with a host team (Brest Zubry) trailing squads from the Ukraine, Lithuania (three clubs), and Russia in a six-team field.

Belgium National Champions (Amateur)

Year	Champion
1947	General Motors
1948	General Motors
1949	General Motors
1950	Luchtball Greys
1951	Spalding Kendalls
1952	General Motors Giants
1953	Brussels Senators
1954	Spalding Haecht
1955	Borgerhout Squirrels

(*continued*)

(continued)

Year	Champion
1956	Luchtball Greys
1957	Borgerhout Squirrels
1958	Brussels Senators
1959	Brussels Senators
1960	Berchem Cristals
1961	Luchtball Greys
1962	Pioneers
1963	Luchtball Greys
1964	Luchtball Greys
1965	Luchtball Greys
1966	Luchtball Greys
1967	Luchtball Greys
1968	Luchtball Greys
1969	Brasschaat
1970	Pioneers
1971	Luchtball Greys
1972	Luchtball Greys
1973	Luchtball Greys
1974	Luchtball Greys
1975	Luchtball Greys
1976	Luchtball Greys
1977	Luchtball Greys
1978	Luchtball Greys
1979	Luchtball Greys
1980	Berchem
1981	Berchem
1982	Berchem
1983	Antwerp Eagles
1984	Antwerp Eagles
1985	Antwerp Eagles
1986	Antwerp Eagles
1987	Antwerp Eagles
1988	Antwerp Eagles
1989	Luchtball Greys
1990	Luchtball Greys
1991	Antwerp Eagles
1992	Brasschaat Braves
1993	Brasschaat Braves
1994	Brasschaat Braves
1995	Brasschaat Braves
1996	Brasschaat Braves
1997	Brasschaat Braves
1998	Namur Angels
1999	Brasschaat Braves
2000	Mortsel Stars
2001	Brasschaat Braves
2002	Brasschaat Braves

Belgium entered a national team for the first time during 1978 World Cup play staged in Italy and lost all ten games. The origins of the sport in this northern European country date back to the early 1920s, when Japanese sailors practiced baseball in their free time during visits to the port city of Antwerp. A local club called Antwerp Black Cats was formed in 1923 to play exhibition matches against these Japanese visitors. Two other such clubs were soon organized (General Motors in 1927 and Bell Telephone in 1930), which resulted in informal tournaments and the 1936 founding of a Belgium Baseball Federation. Organization of formal national championships after World War II gave a huge lift to the sport in Brussels, and the Belgians claimed their first international gold medal with a victory in the 1967 European championship tournament.

Brazil National Champions (Amateur)*

Year	Champion
1990	Presidente Prudente
1991	Londrina
1992	São Paulo
1993	Blue Jays
1994	Presidente Prudente
1995	Blue Jays
1996	Mogi das Cruzes
1997	Blue Jays
1998	Mogi das Cruzes
1999	Blue Jays
2000	Nippon Blue Jays
2001	Nippon Blue Jays
2002	Nippon Blue Jays

Brazil appeared in World Cup play for the first time in Nicaragua in 1972 and won enough games (4–11) to finish ahead of Italy, Costa Rica, El Salvador, and Germany. Between the late 1950s and early 1970s, this soccer-crazy nation also fielded strong enough teams to win five South American championships (which don't include strong Caribbean baseball countries like Cuba or the Dominican Republic). Most Brazilian players are drawn from the nation's considerable Japanese population, and it was an ethnic Japanese pitcher named Kleber Tomita (a professional pitcher during the summer in Japan's Industrial League) who nearly paced the Brazilian club to a stunning upset of the Cubans during a recent 2003 World Cup quarterfinal match in Havana.

* Geographic logic aside, Brazil has been placed in this chapter's catchall list of world amateur champions and not in Chapter 8 (Caribbean baseball), which does include results for such Andean countries as Argentina, Chile, Ecuador, and Peru. The reason, in part, is that as a Portuguese-speaking nation Brazil does not seem a comfortable fit with Hispanic baseball-playing countries; furthermore, most players on recent Brazilian national teams have been descendents of Japanese immigrants and carry distinctly Japanese names. At any rate, placing Amazonian Brazil in a chapter about the Caribbean would have been an equally uncomfortable fit.

Bulgaria National Champions (Amateur)

Year	Champion
1990	Academics Sofia
1991	Academics Sofia
1992	Academics Sofia
1993	Blagoevgrad Buffaloes
1994	Blagoevgrad Buffaloes
1995	Blagoevgrad Buffaloes
1996	Blagoevgrad Buffaloes
1997	Blagoevgrad Buffaloes
1998	Blagoevgrad Buffaloes
1999	Blagoevgrad Buffaloes
2000	Blagoevgrad Buffaloes
2001	Blagoevgrad Buffaloes
2002	Blagoevgrad Buffaloes
2003	Blagoevgrad Buffaloes

Bulgaria also has remained largely outside European Federation tournament competitions but has staged its own trophy games annually around the Sofia region for more than a decade. In these annual matches, the Blagoevgrad club has now won 11 straight. That same city will host (with Rouen, France) games during European Cup Pool B championship play in June 2004, a further step in the nation's European baseball visibility.

China National Champions (Amateur)

Year	Champion
1979	Beijing
1980	Gansu
1981	Beijing
1982	Shanghai
1983	Tianjin
1984	Beijing
1985	Sichuan
1986	Sichuan
1987	Sichuan
1988	Tianjin
1989	Tianjin
1990	Beijing
1991	Beijing
1992	Beijing
1993	Beijing
1994	Beijing
1995	Beijing
1996	Beijing
1997	Beijing
1998	Beijing
1999	Beijing
2000	Tianjin
2001	Tianjin
2002	Tianjin

Japanese college teams and one Japanese little league club visited China for goodwill tours during the late 1970s, and in January 1980 IBAF-sponsored coaches held instructional clinics in the world's most populous country. At the same time China launched its own national championship tournament and the Chinese also participated in BFA Asian championships for the first time in 1985 at Perth, Australia, finishing dead last as could be expected. Recently, former big leaguers Jim Lefebvre (manager) and Bruce Hurst (pitching coach) directed China's national team that competed against Japan, Korea, and Chinese Taipei in an October 2003 All-Asia Olympic Qualifier tournament.

Chinese Taipei (Taiwan) National Champions (Amateur)

Year	Champion
1990 Spring	Military
1990 Autumn	Zong-Kong
1991 Spring	Military
1991 Autumn	China Times
1992 Spring	Sampo
1992 Autumn	China Times
1993 Spring	Sampo
1993 Autumn	Cooperative Bank
1994 Spring	China Trust
1994 Autumn	Sampo
1995 Spring	China Trust
1995 Autumn	China Trust
1996 Spring	China Trust
1996 Autumn	China Trust
1997 Spring	Military
1997 Autumn	Military
1998 Spring	Military

Year	Champion
1998 Autumn	Taipei Sports College
1999 Spring	Taipei Sports College
1999 Autumn	Cooperative Bank
2000 Spring	Military
2000 Autumn	Mei Fu Giants
2001 Spring	Military
2002	Taiwan Cultural University

The island nation long known as the Republic of China (ROC) began competing in senior-level international tournaments with the 1972 Nicaragua World Cup matches. Major breakthroughs came with a silver medal finish at 1992's first official Olympic tournament in Barcelona, and then with Taiwan's role in hosting the 2001 World Cup games, but the country's baseball stature comes largely from remarkable Little League successes beginning at the end of the 1960s (but which also sparked heated controversy about the use of overage and professionally trained youth players). Taiwan's game has clear Japanese roots, which has colored all elements of baseball history there.

Croatia National Champions (Amateur)

Year	Champion
1992	Nada Split
1993	Zagreb Zagreb
1994	Olimpija Karlovac
1995	Olimpija Karlovac
1996	Zagreb Zagreb
1997	Olimpija Karlovac
1998	Olimpija Karlovac
1999	Olimpija Karlovac
2000	Olimpija Karlovac
2001	Kelteks Karlovac
2002	Kelteks Karlovac
2003	Kelteks Karlovac

Croatia can boast that their baseball stretches back to the beginnings of the nation's history—for the Croatian Baseball Federation (and its national tournament) were both inaugurated in the first year of a new nation established near the end of the horrific civil wars in Yugoslavia during the 1980s and 1990s. Baseball was first introduced to the former Yugoslavia during World War I and reemerged after World War II under strong Italian influence.

Czech Republic National Champions (Amateur)

Year	Champion
1979	Tempo Praha
1980	Tempo Praha
1981	Sokol Krc
1982	Sokol Krc
1983	Kovo Praha
1984	Kovo Praha
1985	Kovo Praha
1986	Kovo Praha
1987	Kovo Praha
1988	Sokol Krc
1989	Kovo Praha
1990	Technika Brno
1991	Technika Brno
1992	Kovo Praha
1993	Technika Praha

(continued)

(continued)

Year	Champion
1994	Technika Praha
1995	Draci Brno
1996	Draci Brno
1997	Draci Brno
1998	Draci Brno
1999	Draci Brno
2000	Draci Brno
2001	Draci Brno
2002	Draci Brno
2003	Draci Brno

Baseball came relatively late to this sports-loving nation which is only half of the former Czechoslovakia (but includes the main baseball center of Prague). Play apparently began informally in 1964, when members of the Prague-based Vojenskéstavby Softball Club decided to experiment with baseball. The country made its first three appearances in the European championships in 1997 France (7th, 4–4), 1999 Italy (8th, 4–4, lost quarterfinals to Russia), and 2001 Germany (5th, 4–3, lost quarterfinals to France). During an inaugural 1997 appearance at Paris, the Czechs showed considerable promise, thrashing Germany 14–4 in their first-ever match and winning half of their eight contests.

Denmark National Champions (Amateur)

Year	Champion
1978	HBSK Hoersholm
1979	HBSK Hoersholm
1980	HBSK Hoersholm
1981	Munkene Gentofte
1982	HBSK Hoersholm
1983	HBSK Hoersholm
1992	Copenhagen Fighters
1993	HBSK Hoersholm
1994	Ballerup Vandals
1995	Copenhagen Fighters
1996	Copenhagen Fighters
1997	Copenhagen Fighters
1998	Copenhagen Fighters
1999	Copenhagen Fighters
2000	Warriors
2001	Warriors
2002	Copenhagen Fighters
2003	Copenhagen Fighters

A Danish Baseball and Softball federation was established in 1978, with 150 participating individuals and a handful of active clubs (many more of them for softball than for baseball). All play here continues to be located near the capital city of Copenhagen and on the island of Zeeland. Early hopes for fostering the sport came from a reported close personal friendship between Danish Baseball Federation founder and first president, Svend Ericksen, and then Los Angeles Dodgers President and international baseball supporter Peter O'Malley. So far, this hope has never been realized.

Estonia National Champions (Amateur)

Year	Champion
1989	Estonians Tallinn
1990	Estonians Tallinn
1991	Estonians Tallinn

Year	Champion
1992	Kairos Keila
1993	Kairos Keila
1994	Kairos Keila
1995	Kairos Keila
1996	Kairos Keila
1997	Kairos Keila
1998	Baseball Club of Keila

Active associations and federations throughout the 1990s in both the Ukraine and Estonia have advanced the cause of baseball's adoption by nations once part of the former Soviet Union. Ukrainian teams have enjoyed far more on-field successes in recent European Interleague open play (as in Belarus in September 2003), but Estonia reports a decade long effort at crowning national champion clubs within its own borders.

Finland National Champions (Amateur)

Year	Champion
1981	Hawks
1982	Wranglers
1983	Puumat
1984	Puumat
1985	Kintaro
1986	EBSC
1987	Puumat
1988	Devils
1989	Devils
1990	Devils
1991	Puumat
1993	Puumat Helsinki
1994	Piraijat Riihimaki
1995	Puumat Helsinki
1996	Athletics
1997	Athletics
1998	Athletics
1999	Puumat Helsinki
2000	Athletics
2001	Athletics
2002	Icebreakers

Finland claims a popular parallel pastime known as *pesäpallo*, which seems to offer hope for eventual development of the American-style sport of baseball. The popular local game was invented decades back by native Finn Lauri Phkala, presumably after his return from many years residence in the United States; it was reportedly supported by close to 80,000 active players during the 1970s. Informal teams from Finland and neighboring Sweden (a regular competitor in European championships since 1962) played friendly games throughout the 1970s and 1980s, and they have continued the practice on an irregular basis in more recent decades.

France National Champions (Amateur)

Year	Champion
1998	Montpellier
1999	Savigny
2000	PUC Paris

(continued)

(continued)

Year	Champion
2001	Savigny sur Orge
2002	Savigny sur Orge
2003	Rouen

Over the years (at least since U.S. soldiers debuted the game during World War I), France has evidenced several bursts of enthusiasm for the American sport as a strictly recreational activity. American students in France also spread their pastime to regions outside Paris, especially to Bordeaux, and a French Baseball Federation existed as early as 1918 (when the first local tournament was held with equipment donated by the YMCA and the U.S. Sailors Club). The country has provided no strong national teams, however, and no organized pro or semi-pro leagues. France did begin periodically entering sanctioned national teams in the European championships after 1955, but in 17 overall appearances across the second half of the century they have finished as high as third (1999, when the matches were hosted in Paris) on only one occasion.

Germany National Champions (Amateur)

Year	Champion
1951	Stuttgart Baseball Club
1952	Frankfurt Juniors
1953	Frankfurt Juniors
1954	Mannheimer Baseball Club
1955	Frankfurt Juniors
1956	MEV München
1957	Mannheimer Baseball Club
1958	Mannheimer Baseball Club
1959	Mannheimer Baseball Club
1960	TB Germania Mannheim
1961	TB Germania Mannheim
1962	TB Germania Mannheim
1963	TB Germania Mannheim
1964	TB Germania Mannheim
1965	FVR Mannheim
1966	FVR Mannheim
1967	Darmstadt Colt 45
1968	Darmstadt Colt 45
1969–1981	*Championship Not Played*
1982	Mannheim Tornadoes
1983	Mannheim Amigos
1984	Mannheim Tornadoes
1985	Mannheim Tornadoes
1986	Mannheim Tornadoes
1987	Mannheim Tornadoes
1988	Mannheim Tornadoes
1989	Mannheim Tornadoes
1990	Köln Cardinals
1991	Mannheim Tornadoes
1992	Mannheim Amigos
1993	Mannheim Tornadoes
1994	Mannheim Tornadoes
1995	Trier Cardinals
1996	Trier Cardinals
1997	Mannheim Tornadoes
1998	Köln Dodgers

Year	Champion
1999	Paderborn Untouchables
2000	Lokstedt Stealers
2001	Paderborn Untouchables
2002	Paderborn Untouchables
2003	Paderborn Untouchables

Germany made its surprise first visit to true international competition at the 1972 World Cup (Amateur World Series) in Managua, where it lost 15 straight games. This excursion quickly led to the building of a small stadium (dedicated to and named after Roberto Clemente) on German soil a year later. Berlin had hosted a demonstration tournament during the 1936 Olympiad, and the country played a role in the 1954 founding of the European Baseball Federation and the European championship tournament. In these European championships after 1954, Germany had some small successes early on, even finishing second at the 1957 event held in Mannheim (losing only to gold-medal Netherlands in its four matches). In recent European championships, the Germans have been far outclassed, coming home in tenth place in both 1997 and 1999, when they were able to defeat only weak Slovenia and inexperienced Croatia.

Great Britain (England) National Champions (Amateur)

Year	Champion
1890	Preston North End
1892	Middlesborough
1893	Thespian London
1894	Thespian London
1895	Derby
1896	Wallsend-on-Tyne
1897	Derby
1898	Derby
1899	Nottingham Forest
1906	Tottenham Hotspur
1907	Clapton Orient
1908	Tottenham Hotspur
1909	Clapton Orient
1910	Brentford
1911	Leyton
1934	Hatfield Liverpool
1935	New London
1936	White City London
1937	Hull
1938	Rochdale Greys
1939	Halifax
1948	Liverpool Robins
1949	Hornsey Red Sox
1950	Burtonwood Bees
1951	Burtonwood Bees
1959	Thames Board Mills
1960	Thames Board Mills
1961	Liverpool Tigers
1962	Liverpool Tigers
1963	East Hull Aces
1964	Hull Aces
1965	Hull Aces
1966	Stetford Saints
1967	Liverpool Yankees
1968	Hull Aces

(continued)

(continued)

Year	Champion
1969	Watford-Sun Rockets
1970	Hull Royals
1971	Liverpool Tigers
1972	Hull Aces
1973	Burtonwood Yanks
1974	Nottingham Lions
1975	Liverpool Tigers
1976	Liverpool Trojans
1977	Golders Green Sox
1978	Liverpool Trojans
1979	Golders Green Sox
1980	Liverpool Trojans
1981	London Warriors
1982	London Warriors
1983	Cobham Yankees
1984	Croydon Blue Jays
1985	Hull Mets
1986	Cobham Yankees
1987	Cobham Yankees
1988	Cobham Yankees
1989	London Warriors
1990	Enfield Spartans
1991	Enfield Spartans
1992	Leeds City Royals
1993	Humberside Mets
1994	Humberside Mets
1995	Humberside Mets
1996	Menwith Hill Patriots
1997	London Warriors
1998	Menwith Hill Patriots
1999	Brighton Buccaneers
2000	London Warriors
2001	Brighton Buccaneers
2002	Brighton Buccaneers

Britain's biggest boast on the international baseball scene is its victory in what is now traditionally billed as the first-ever amateur world series of August 1938; this contest for a John Moore Trophy (named for the founder of the British Baseball Federation) featured a five game face-off between U.S. soldiers stationed in Europe (nominally the American team) and a squad of Brits (some of whom may have been associated with several attempts at a British pro circuit during the 1930s). National amateur championships were held with mixed success as early as the late nineteenth century, and a first significant ragtag pro league (that reportedly drew only 400 to 500 spectators per contest) operated in the mid-1930s in and around Manchester (with eight teams: Belle Vue Tigers, Oldham Greyhounds, Manchester North End Blue Sox, Hurst Hawks, Salford Reds, Hyde Grasshoppers, Rochdale Greys, Bradford Northern—the last two being strictly amateur clubs).

Hungary National Champions (Amateur)

Year	Champion
1992	Budapest Islanders
1993	Budapest Islanders
1994	Budapest Islanders
1995	Budapest Islanders
1996	Nasskanizsa Ants Thùry
1997	Nasskanizsa Ants Thùry

Year	Champion
1998	Szentendre Sleepwalkers
1999	Szentendre Sleepwalkers
2000	Szentendre Sleepwalkers
2001	Nagykanisza

Hungary is yet to debut in the European championships or any other senior men's international tournament competitions. With a successful decade of uninterrupted in-country tournaments and both baseball and softball club-level recreational play, Hungary now shows prospects of catching up with its neighbors in such minor hotbed locations as those in Croatia, the Czech Republic, Slovenia, and Slovakia.

India National Champions (Amateur)

Year	Champion
1985 A	Delhi Team
1985 B	Delhi Team
1986	Delhi Team
1987	Delhi Team
1988	Karnataka Team
1989	Delhi Team
1990	*Not Held*
1991	Andhra Pradesh Team
1992	Rajasthan
1993	*Not Held*
1994	Andhra Pradesh Team
1995	Madhya Pradesh Team
1996	*Not Held*
1997	*Not Held*
1998	Andhra Pradesh Team
1999	Madhya Pradesh Team
2000	Madhya Pradesh Team
2001	Madhya Pradesh Team and Haryana
2002	Delhi Team
2003	Madhya Pradesh Team

India, like Pakistan, remains a baseball and softball backwater, where American bat-and-ball playing has enjoyed little popularity in the face of British cricket and popular field hockey. India's Baseball Federation staged its 15th National men's and women's championships with 41 participating clubs in February 2004, with the frequent winner Madhya Pradesh Team again capturing a gold medal prize in a tight 3–2 win over rival Goa.

Italy National Champions (Professional)

Year	Champion
1948	Libertas Bologna
1949 A	Firenze (Lib)
1949 B	Lazio (Fibs)
1950	Libertas Roma
1951	Nettuno BC
1952	Nettuno BC
1953	Nettuno BC
1954	Nettuno BC
1955	Lazio
1956	Chlorodont Nettuno

(continued)

Year	Champion
1957	Chlorodont Nettuno
1958 A	Cus Milano
1958 B	Algida Nettuno
1959	Coca Cola Roma
1960	Seven-Up Milano
1961	Europhon Milano
1962	Europhon Milano
1963	Simmenthal Nettuno
1964	Simmenthal Nettuno
1965	Simmenthal Nettuno
1966	Europhon Milano
1967	Europhon Milano
1968	Europhon Milano
1969	Montenegro Bologna
1970	Europhon Milano
1971	Glen Grant Nettuno
1972	Montenegro Bologna
1973	Glen Grant Nettuno
1974	Montenegro Bologna
1975	Cercosti Rimini
1976	Germal Parma
1977	Germal Parma
1978	Biemme Bologna
1979	Derbigum Rimini
1980	Derbigum Rimini
1981	Parmalat Parma
1982	Parmalat Parma
1983	Barzetti Rimini
1984	BeCa Bologna
1985	World Vision Parma
1986	Grohe Grosseto
1987	Trevi Rimini
1988	Lenoir Rimini
1989	Mamoli Grosseto
1990	Scac Nettuno
1991	Parma Angels
1992	Telemarket Rimini
1993	CFC Nettuno
1994	Cus Capriparma
1995	Cus Capriparma
1996	Danesi Nettuno
1997	Cus Capriparma
1998	Danesi Nettuno
1999	Semenzato Rimini
2000	Semenzato Rimini
2001	Danesi Nettuno
2002	Semenzato Rimini
2003	Bologna

Italy has deeper baseball roots and a more active baseball culture than any European country save The Netherlands (Holland). The sport's introduction in 1919 is credited to Massimiliano Ottino (aka Max Otto), whose return to Turin from years of living in the United States included some equipment and a newfound passion for the American pastime. It was also Otto who later organized the Italian Baseball League at Milan in 1948, thus founding an institution that has survived for half a century as Europe's top pro baseball circuit. Italy has now also joined Spain (Barcelona) and The Netherlands (Atlanta, Sydney, and Athens) as Europe's representative at all four official Olympic Baseball tournaments.

Democratic People's Republic of Korea (North Korea) National Champions (Amateur)

Year	Champion
1985	Kikwancha Sport Club
1986	Kikwancha Sport Club
1987	Kikwancha Sport Club
1988	Kikwancha Sport Club
1989	Kikwancha Sport Club
1990	Kikwancha Sport Club
1991	Kikwancha Sport Club
1992	Kikwancha Sport Club
1993	Kikwancha Sport Club
1994	Kikwancha Sport Club
1995	Kikwancha Sport Club
1996	Kikwancha Sport Club
1997	Kikwancha Sport Club
1998	Kikwancha Sport Club
1999	Kikwancha Sport Club
2000	Kikwancha Sport Club
2001	Kikwancha Sport Club

Korean baseball is centered mostly in the South Korean nation, with its greater western orientations and stronger Japanese cultural ties. Play to the north has been restricted largely to military squads. Only on one occasion has North Korea taken part in Asian Baseball Federation championships, in 1993 sending an ill-prepared club to Perth (in Australia) that limped home in sixth place, ahead of only the Philippines.

Republic of Korea (South Korea) National Champions (Amateur)

Year	Champion
1955	Korean Army
1955 (2)*	Korean Army
1956	Korean Air Force
1956 (2)*	Korean Army
1957	Korean Army
1958	Korean Army
1958 (2)*	Korean Army
1960	Traffic Department
1961	Nonghyup
1962	Nonghyup
1963	Nonghyup
1964	Sangup Bank
1965	Crown
1966	Hanil Bank
1967	Korean Army
1968	Korean Army
1969	Korean Army
1970	Hanjon
1971	Hanjon
1972	Hanil Bank
1973	Chell Bank
1974	Chell Bank
1975	Korean Army
1976	Hanil Bank
1977	Korean Cosmetios
1978	Korean Air Force
1979	Sungmu
1980	Sangup Bank

(continued)

(continued)

Year	Champion
1981	Chell Bank
1982	Inha University
1983	Hanyang University
1984	Hanyang University
1985	Hanyang University
1986	Sangmu
1987	Dongkuk University
1988	Kyungsung University
1989	Hanyang University
1990	Dankuk University
1991	Sangmu
1992	Yonsei University
1993	Hanyang University
1994	Korea University
1995	Korea University
1996	Korea University
1997	Korea University
1998	Youngnam University
1999	Korea University
2000	Yonsei University
2001	Dankook University
2002	Dongeui University

Korea became a noted site on the world's baseball map with the Seoul Olympic competitions in 1988, when baseball appeared as a demonstration sport for the final time. The game arrived in about 1915, a decade after the Russo–Japanese War, and was thus a product—as in Taiwan—of Japanese military and political occupation. The last two decades of the twentieth century have been notable both for a showcase professional league (complete with imported Japanese, Latin American, and even U.S. players), along with some surprisingly strong international performances by the Korean national team (highlighted by an Olympic bronze medal in Sydney and the runner-up slot at Italy's 1998 World Cup).
* Split seasons were played for the years 1955, 1956, and 1958, with competitions in both the spring and fall. The designation (2) here indicates the champion for the second, fall season.

Lithuania National Champions (Amateur)

Year	Champion
1988	Auda Kaunas
1989	Auda Kaunas
1990	Zalgiris Vilnius
1991	Panerys-Deka Vilnius
1992	Panerys Vilnius
1993	Klevas Vilnius
1994	Kaunas Kaunas
1995	Klevas Vilnius
1996	Vikingas Vilnius
1997	Vikingas Vilnius
1998	Kaunas Kaunas
1999	Vikingas Vilnius
2000	Vikingas Vilnius
2001	Vikingas Vilnius
2002	Lituanica Kaunas

Lithuania, a notable basketball-playing country, continues experiments with building a strong base for amateur softball and baseball play. Recent performances by several Lithuanian club teams suggest that the country is making significant steps toward greater representation in European championship play. At a recent September 2003 European Interleague Open tournament hosted by Brest (in Belarus), the defending national champion Lituanica Kaunas lost the title game 8–1 to Kirovograd Ukraine, with two additional Lithuanian clubs—Judoasis Vikingas Vilnius (third) and Vanagai Vilnius (fifth)—also competing in a six-team field.

Malta National Champions (Amateur)

Year	Champion
1994	Marsa Slammers
1995	Mellieha Northenders
1996	Marsa Mustangs
1997	Mellieha Northenders
1998	Mellieha Northenders
1999	Marsa Mustangs
2000	Mellieha Northenders
2001	Gozo Tornadoes
2002	Gozo Tornadoes
2003	Gozo Tornadoes

The island nation of Malta, like the even smaller but land-locked San Marino, boasts strong Italian baseball influences and features several dozen amateur club teams among its small but enthusiastic baseball community. To date still a nonparticipant in senior-level international matches, Malta nonetheless posts an active baseball website and stages national championships that now stretch back more than a decade.

Netherlands National Champions (Amateur–Professional)

Year	Champion
1922	Quick Amsterdam
1923	Blauw-Wit Amsterdam
1924	Ajax Amsterdam
1925	Quick Amsterdam
1926	AGHC Amsterdam
1927	AGHC Amsterdam
1928	Ajax Amsterdam
1929	SC Haarlem
1930	SC Haarlem
1931	Blauw-Wit Amsterdam
1932	Blauw-Wit Amsterdam
1933	VVGA Amsterdam
1934	SC Haarlem
1935	Quick Amsterdam
1936	HHC Haarlem
1937	Blauw-Wit Amsterdam
1938	Blauw-Wit Amsterdam
1939	Seagulls Amsterdam
1940	SC Haarlem
1941	SC Haarlem
1942	Ajax Amsterdam
1943	Blauw-Wit Amsterdam
1944	Blauw-Wit Amsterdam
1945	Blauw-Wit Amsterdam
1946	Blauw-Wit Amsterdam
1947	Schoten Haarlem
1948	Ajax Amsterdam
1949	OVVO Amsterdam
1950	OVVO Amsterdam
1951	OVVO Amsterdam
1952	OVVO Amsterdam
1953	OVVO Amsterdam
1954	EHS Haarlem
1955	OVVO Amsterdam
1956	Schoten Haarlem
1957	Schoten Haarlem

(continued)

(continued)

Year	Champion
1958	EDO Haarlem
1959	EHS Haarlem
1960	Schoten Haarlem
1961	Schoten Haarlem
1962	EHS Haarlem
1963	Sparta Rotterdam
1964	Sparta Rotterdam
1965	Haarlem Nicols
1966	Sparta Rotterdam
1967	Sparta Rotterdam
1968	Haarlem Nicols
1969	Sparta Rotterdam
1970	Haarlem Nicols
1971	Sparta Rotterdam
1972	Sparta Rotterdam
1973	Sparta Rotterdam
1974	Sparta Rotterdam
1975	Haarlem Nicols
1976	Haarlem Tetramin Nicols
1977	Haarlem Tetramin Nicols
1978	Wera Kinheim Haarlem
1979	Amsterdam Amstel Tijgers
1980	Amsterdam Amstel Tijgers
1981	Kok Juwelier Neptunus Rotterdam
1982	Haarlem Nicols
1983	Haarlem Nicols
1984	Haarlem Nicols
1985	Haarlem Nicols
1986	Amsterdam Cleo Tijgers
1987	Amsterdam Tas Detach Pirates
1988	Haarlem Opel Nicols
1989	Haarlem Opel Nicols
1990	Amsterdam Tas Detach Pirates
1991	Levi's Neptunus Rotterdam
1992	Install Data ADO Den Haag
1993	Levi's Neptunus Rotterdam
1994	Boom Planeta Kinheim Haarlem
1995	Levi's Neptunus Rotterdam
1996	Mr. Cocker HCAW Bussum
1997	Minolta Pioniers Hoofddorp
1998	Mr. Cocker HCAW Bussum
1999	Door Training Neptunus Rotterdam
2000	Door Training Neptunus Rotterdam
2001	Door Training Neptunus Rotterdam
2002	Door Training Neptunus Rotterdam
2003	Door Training Neptunus Rotterdam

By just about any measure imaginable the Netherlands (Holland) is Europe's reigning baseball capital. As evidence of a long baseball history, five Dutch teams have played 1,000 games or more: Neptunus Rotterdam reached the mark in 2004, joining Sparta/Feyenoord, HCAW, ADO/Tornados, and Kinheim. The Dutch have made the best showings in world tournaments, even beating Cuba 4–2 in one 2000 Sydney Olympic opening-round contest. The country's handful of native major leaguers include Win Remmerswaal (the first big leaguer who developed in Europe, as well as being born there) and 287-game winner Bert Blyleven, a potential hall-of-famer. A showcase annual Haarlem International Baseball Week tournament has been staged for more than two decades in historic Pim Mulier Stadium near Amsterdam; it attracts many top national squads, often including the Cuban national team whenever it tours Europe in preparation for Intercontinental Cup, World Cup, or Olympic tournament play. Dutch teams have dominated European championship competition from the outset, claiming seventeen gold medals (Italy is second, with eight) including ten medals in eleven outings between the mid-1950s and mid-1970s. Highlights of Dutch international play have been a first-ever appearance in World Cup play in Colombia in 1970, a sixth-place finish at the 1980 Korea World Cup event, and appearances in three official Olympic baseball tournaments (Atlanta, Sydney, Athens).

Norway National Champions (Amateur)

Year	Champion
1991	Oslo Pretenders BBK
1992	Oslo Pretenders BBK
1993	Oslo Pretenders BBK
1994	Oslo Pretenders BBK
1995	Oslo Pretenders BBK
1996	Oslo Ballkam Alligators
1997	Bekkestua Dragons
1998	Oslo Ballkam Alligators
1999	Oslo Ballkam Alligators
2000	Oslo Pretenders BBK
2001	Oslo Pretenders BBK
2002	Oslo Pretenders BBK

Stronger amateur baseball movements in other Scandinavian nations (Sweden, Denmark, and Finland) largely overshadow efforts at baseball development in Norway, despite a decade of small-scale national tournaments staged since the early 1990s in Oslo. (Long ago, in the 1890s, a Norwegian-born but U.S.-raised ballplayer named John Anderson did appear in the Brooklyn National League outfield in the 1890s.) Long, harsh winters have limited the growth of Norwegian baseball, which is restricted almost exclusively to the region near Oslo.

Pakistan National Champions (Amateur)

Year	Champion
1992	Punjab
1993	Pakistan Police
1994	Pakistan Army
1995	Pakistan Wapda
1996	Pakistan Police
1997	Pakistan Wapda
1998	Pakistan Police
1999	Pakistan Army
2000	Pakistan Army
2001	Pakistan Army
2002	Pakistan Army

Fifty-plus club teams competing in different age categories were already reported by international baseball chronicler Carlos García (*Baseball Forever!*) as existing in Pakistan in the late 1970s. Here, as also in India, however, cricket and field hockey remain far too strong as the local national sports for any serious inroads by foreign bat-and-ball games without clear British roots. Another relatively weak neophyte baseball country, China, drubbed Pakistan 19–0 at Japan's Sapporo Dome to claim a special qualifying round in Asia's 2003 Olympic Qualifier Tournament.

Poland National Champions (Amateur)

Year	Champion
1984	Rybnik KS Silesia
1985	Rybnik KS Silesia
1986	Rybnik KS Silesia
1987	Rybnik KS Silesia
1988	Stal Kutno
1989	Stal Kutno
1990	Warszawa RKS Skra
1991	Stal Kutno
1992	Stal Kutno
1993	Warszawa RKS Skra

(*continued*)

(continued)

Year	Champion
1994	Warszawa RKS Skra
1995	MKS Kutno
1996	MKS Kutno
1997	MKS Kutno
1998	BK Jastrzebie
1999	BK Jastrzebie
2000	BK Jastrzebie
2001	BK Jastrzebie
2002	MKS Kutno

Polish senior-level teams and even some competitions with neighboring Czechoslovakia existed by the mid-1960s, and the country was also a European Federation member as early as January 1960, despite its continued absence from Federation tournament events. If Poland has little baseball tradition to date, there are early reports of recreational play of the similar German–Austrian game called *Schlagball* (literally, hitball or even beatball).

Russia National Champions (Amateur)

Year	Champion
1989	Moscow CSKA PVO Balashiha
1990	Moscow Krasnije Diavoly
1991	Moscow Krasnije Diavoly
1992	Moscow Krasnije Diavoly
1993	Moscow Krasnije Diavoly
1994	Moscow Krasnije Diavoly
1995	Moscow Krasnije Diavoly
1996	Moscow CSKA PVO Balashiha
1997	Moscow CSKA PVO Balashiha
1998	Moscow CSKA PVO Balashiha
1999	Moscow VATU of Zhukovskiy
2000	Moscow CSKA PVO Balashiha
2001	CSC WWS Balashiha
2002	Moscow Tornado MGU
2003	Tornado Balashiha

Despite repeated reports that Russian coaches in the 1970s and 1980s were putting the same intensity into baseball training that underpinned their sudden rise as a world power in Canadian-style hockey and in U.S.-style basketball—and despite the prediction by a top Cuban journalist in 2001 (Sigfredo Barros, writing in the pages of the Communist Party newspaper *Granma* on the eve of the tournament) that Russia's entrant would be a surprise of that year's Taipei World Cup (they won only one game, versus the Philippines)—baseball has made modest progress (at least on a national team level) in the heart of the former Soviet Union. Russia's biggest moment so far was the shocking 4–1 triumph over normally strong Chinese Taipei in the final opening round match of the 2003 Havana World Cup. Alexei Valyaline allowed a single run in 8.2 strong innings; but less than a week earlier the otherwise winless Russians were humiliated 20–1 (a seven-inning knockout) by a Cuban team that was merely going through the motions of a preliminary-round game.

San Marino National Champions (Amateur)

Year	Champion
1997	Caravantours San Marino Baseball Club
1998	Factory Outlet San Marino Baseball Club
1999	Factory Outlet San Marino Baseball Club
2000	T & A San Marino Baseball Club

One of Europe's smallest and least known republics also boasts one of the region's most active and unusual baseball histories. Close to the Italian baseball hotbed of Rimini (host to the 1978 Baseball World Cup), the influence of Italian baseball is strong here. A new member of the European Federation in 1971, San Marino was a surprise entrant in that year's European championships (staged in nearby Parma) and an even more surprising fifth-place finisher with upset victories over Great Britain (13–10) and Spain (6–4).

Slovakia National Champions (Amateur)

Year	Champion
1991	Bratislava Ekonom Indians
1992	Trnava White Angels
1993	Bratislava STU Tronet Spiders
1994	Bratislava STU Tronet Spiders
1995	Bratislava STU Tronet Spiders
1996	Bratislava STU Tronet Spiders
1997	Bratislava STU Tronet Spiders
1998	Bratislava STU Tronet Spiders
1999	Trnava White Angels
2000	Trnava White Angels
2001	Kranjski Lisjaki
2002	Trnava White Angels

As a sports-loving country, the former Czechoslovakia temporarily joined the European Federation in the mid-1960s and reported some club activities but to date has never entered any teams in European tournaments. Most activity had been based in the Prague area (see table for Czech Republic), now separated from Slovakia.

Slovenia National Champions (Amateur)

Year	Champion
1991	Ljubljana Golovec
1992	Ljubljana Golovec
1993	Ljubljana Zajcki
1994	Ljubljana Zajcki
1995	Ljubljana Zajcki
1996	Ljubljana Zajcki
1997	Ljubljana Zajcki
1998	Ljubljana Jezica
1999	Kranjski Lisjaki
2000	Kranjski Lisjaki
2001	Kranjski Lisjaki
2002	Ljubljana Jezica
2003	Wilson Jezica

This region of the former Yugoslavia entered the European championships with a national team for the first three times in 1995, 1997, and 1999, finishing dead last on all occasions. The Slovenian team lost all 21 of its games in these three outings, often by embarrassingly large scores.

South Africa National Champions (Amateur)

Year	Champion
1997	Western Province
1998	KwaZulu Natal
1999	KwaZulu Natal
2000	Western Province
2002	KwaZulu Natal
2003	Easterns

Baseball's only serious African development so far seems to have taken place in South Africa. Capturing the All-Africa tournament in October 2003, South Africa's national team qualified to face off with Oceania champion Australia for the final Athens Olympic slot. Filling the final spot in the 2000 Sydney Olympiad, South Africa captured only one of its seven games, with a 3–2 upset of The Netherlands. Apartheid slowed early baseball development and also worked against South African participation in international matches, although the national team did for the first time attend the 1974 amateur world championships in Florida.

Spain National Champions (Amateur)

Year	Champion
1982	Viladecans
1983	Viladecans
1984	Viladecans
1985	Viladecans
1986	Viladecans
1987	Viladecans
1988	Viladecans
1989	Viladecans
1990	Viladecans
1991	Viladecans
1992	Viladecans
1993	Viladecans
1994	Viladecans
1995	Viladecans
1996	Viladecans
1997	Viladecans
1998	Viladecans
1999	Viladecans
2000	Viladecans
2001	Viladecans
2002	Viladecans

During the 1920s, ballplaying in Spain began sporadically, in both Madrid and Barcelona. The Piratas Baseball Club was formed in Madrid in 1927 (coincidentally, the year Pittsburgh's Pirates made a rare World Series appearance). A 1929 Barcelona International Exposition hosted the first documented international games (with an informal French national team besting a Spanish pickup squad 10–6, and a group of Paris-based Americans also defeating the same local club, 11–4); that same year, a four-team semi-pro league lasted briefly in Barcelona. An early attempt at a national championship was staged in 1944 (Club Español was the winner), and the Spanish Baseball Federation was organized in May 1945. Regular national tournaments date only from the 1980s, however, and a single club has won all trophies over two decades.

Sweden National Champions (Amateur)

Year	Champion
1963	Solna Basebollklubb
1964	Leksand
1965	Wasa
1966	Wasa
1967	Leksand
1968	Leksand
1969	Leksand
1970	Leksand
1971	Leksand
1972	Leksand
1973	Bagermossen
1974	Bagermossen
1975	Leksand
1976	Bagermossen
1977	Bagermossen
1978	Leksand
1979	Leksand
1980	Bagermossen
1981	Leksand
1982	Leksand

Year	Champion
1983	Leksand
1984	Sundbyberg Heat
1985	Sundbyberg Heat
1986	Sundbyberg Heat
1987	Leksand
1988	Leksand
1989	Skelleftea
1990	Skelleftea
1991	Skelleftea
1992	Skelleftea
1993	Skelleftea
1994	Skelleftea
1995	Skelleftea
1996	Leksand
1997	Leksand
1998	Leksand
1999	Skelleftea
2000	Alby
2001	Rattvik
2002	Rattvik
2003	Sundbyberg Heat

Swedish baseball origins can be traced to 1910, with reports existing of sandlot games played that year in both Gothenburg (where the origins are unknown) and Stockholm (where rules and equipment may have been provided by a local businessman named Sigfrid Edström). The Stockholm Olympiad two years later featured demonstration matches between a local Västeras Club team and a pick-up squad of athletes from the United States track and field team. U.S. military personal revived interest throughout Sweden in the aftermath of World War II, and in 1963 a Swedish Baseball Federation was finally organized and immediately staged its first championship tournament.

Yugoslavia (Serbia and Montenegro) National Champions (Amateur)

Year	Champion
1993	Belgrade Kings
1994	Belgrade Dogs
1995	Belgrade Dogs
1996	Belgrade Dogs
1997	Beograd 96
1998	Beograd 96
1999	Beograd 96
2000	Belgrade Dogs

Baseball had brief and unsuccessful trials immediately after both World Wars, with the presence of occupying U.S. and British allied forces being at least a small factor in attempts at organizing games. Italians were the primary importers of the sport in this region, however, and by 1973 some contests were played by local clubs against visiting Italian teams. Most recent baseball activity has been restricted to the region of the former Yugoslavia that is now Croatia, around Zagreb (see table for Croatia).

NOTE

1. Of the seven major league players born in what was then Russia or the Soviet Union, four are from Odessa, in the Ukraine, not Russia as such. See table on p. 381.

BIBLIOGRAPHY

Ardolino, Frank. "The Hawaii Winter League, 1993–1997." *The National Pastime: A Review of Baseball History* 20 (2000): 42–45.

Carino, Peter. "Baseball in Translation: The Italian Professional League." *Nine: A Journal of Baseball History and Social Policy Perspectives* 7:2 (Spring 1999): 49–59.

Cava, Pete. "Baseball in the Olympics." *The National Pastime: A Review of Baseball History* 12 (1992): 2–8.

García, Carlos J. *Baseball Forever!* (*Béisbol Para Siempre!*) Mexico City, Mexico: [self-published], 1980.

Gerlach, Larry R. "German Americans in Major League Baseball: Sport and Acculturation." *The American Game: Baseball and Ethnicity*, 27–54, ed. Lawrence Baldassaro and Richard A. Johnson. Carbondale, Illinois: Southern Illinois University Press, 2002.

Hetrick, Richard Egenriether. "Chris Von der Ahe: Baseball's Pioneering Huckster." *Nine: A Journal of Baseball History and Social Policy Perspectives* 7:2 (Spring 1999): 14–39.

Holway, John. "Taiwan Little Leaguers Grow into Big Leaguers." *The National Pastime: A Review of Baseball History* 12 (1992): 48–50.

Humber, William. *Let's Play Ball! Inside the Perfect Game.* Toronto, Ontario: Lester & Orpen Dennys, 1989.

Juhase, Kim Steven, and Blair A. Ruble. "Soviet Baseball: History and Prospects." *The National Pastime: A Review of Baseball History* 12 (1992): 45–47.

Laidlaw, Robert. "Baseball in Australia." in *Total Baseball: The Official Encyclopedia of Major League Baseball*, 549–558, 6th ed., ed. John Thorn, Pete Palmer, et al. New York: Total Sports, 1999.

Porter, David. "Untold Saga of Europe's Big-Leaguers." *The National Pastime: A Review of Baseball History* 12 (1992): 70–76.

Reaves, Joseph A. "Silk Gowns and Golden Gloves: The Forgotten History of Chinese Bat Ball." *Nine: A Journal of Baseball History and Social Policy Perspectives* 7:2 (Spring 1999): 60–74.

St. John, Thomas. "History of the Korean Baseball Organization." in *Total Baseball: The Official Encyclopedia of Major League Baseball*, 559–562, 6th ed., ed. John Thorn, Pete Palmer, et al. New York: Total Sports, 1999.

Wilson, Jeffrey. "Baseball in Taiwan." in *Total Baseball: The Official Encyclopedia of Major League Baseball*, 563–569, 6th ed., ed. John Thorn, Pete Palmer, et al. New York: Total Sports, 1999.

CHAPTER 10

Baseball's Olympic Movements

World Amateur Competition

• •

> *Opera in English is, in the main, just about as sensible as baseball in Italian.*
> —H. L. Mencken

North Americans have historically paid little or no attention to the showcase events of international baseball. Rarely have American teams—those sponsored by the nation's governing body for national amateur play known officially as "USA Baseball"—won these tournaments, and almost as rarely has USA Baseball ever fielded respectable or even competitive squads. Over the past four decades, the situation for the Americans has become more galling in light of the remarkable domination by teams representing socialist Cuba. Repeated Cuban victories have spurred a flurry of U.S. excuses that either downplay or dismiss Cuban triumphs as meaningless because they have not been earned against "true American talent," which is all presumed to be lodged in the professional game. These sour rebuttals usually run as follows: (1) Olympic-style world amateur tournaments have never represented a legitimate measure of on-field supremacy in the sport, since professional athletes—the acknowledged best players—don't perform there. (2) The Castro government has brazenly exploited the international baseball scene in its effort to manipulate sport in the service of gaining Cold War propaganda victories. (3) As with the Olympic basketball tournament, where NBA stars now perform (largely assuring a string of uninterrupted smashing U.S. victories), the Olympic baseball movement might as well go ahead and include big league players. (After all, the argument goes, Cuba's players are amateurs only by government decree: professionals in amateur dress.) Undeniably, the motive behind all these complaints has been the large-scale embarrassment caused by humiliating defeats of Team USA. In terms of national prestige, at least, baseball is still considered our anointed national pastime. For many, there is indeed something rather unsettling about watching Fidel Castro orchestrate repeated blows against the American system by means of what is famous as the quintessentially American game.

It must be remembered here that the movement to bring NBA stars into Olympic basketball competitions itself came on the heels of strengthening among rival international teams representing, in particular, the former Soviet Union and the then-also-communist nation of Yugoslavia. The straw that broke the camel's back was the 1988 Olympic tournament in Seoul, where (with the exception of the boycotted 1980 games in Moscow) Team USA sat on the sidelines for the first time ever during an Olympic gold medal men's finale. The increasing commercialization of the Olympic Games as a made-for-television spectacle also proved a strong motive for including front-line NBA stars. (The thinking was that Michael Jordan or Magic Johnson ought to be able to sell the Olympics to millions of cable viewers just as they had so successfully sold the NBA itself.) But there are many who now argue that the Dream Team phenomenon of invincible pro U.S. squads has also ruined the competitiveness and the historic traditions of the once-thrilling Olympic basketball competitions. Admittedly, the argument may have been somewhat muted by failures of a recent USA NBA Dream Team at the 2004 Athens Olympiad; yet if Olympic basketball appears after Athens to again be slightly more competitive, it nonetheless clearly remains a competition now reserved for the handful of nations boasting a considerable collection of NBA superstars.

A parallel movement toward using top professional athletes in baseball is now rumored to be in progress. Spurred on largely by organized baseball (Major League Baseball) and its ever expanding television interests, International Baseball Federation (IBAF) officials have already begrudgingly admitted pros into showcase world baseball tournaments including recent Olympiads and Pan American Games matches. The transition began with the 1999 Pan American Games in Winnipeg, which served as that year's Olympic Qualifier for North, Central, and South American entrants in the 2000 Sydney Olympics. The experiment continued with recent World Cup, Intercontinental Cup, and Pan American Games matches, as well as the Sydney Games themselves. So far, the pros performing on U.S., Canadian, Mexican, and other regional national teams (Australia and Canada) have been only upper-level minor leaguers, with a small sprinkling of washed-up major leaguers. No one ever seriously proposed entering a National League all-star team—or perhaps the Pittsburgh Pirates or the Kansas City Royals—in the 2004 Athens games. But the main difficulty here, of course, is that (unlike the NBA) only about half of today's top big league stars are actually native-born Americans in the first place.

With baseball, the results in Sydney and Winnipeg, or in the 2003 Havana World Cup or 2003 Panama-based Olympic Qualifier, have so far not at all paralleled the basketball Dream Team phenomenon. Foremost has been the fact that Major League Baseball has not cooperated to the same degree as did the National Basketball Association. Another factor is timing: Olympic and World Cup tournaments always come during the heart of the major league and minor league seasons. It is not practical for the majors to release large numbers of the best players to staff rosters for several different competing countries.

There are also the self-evident economic considerations that control Major League Baseball motives; organized baseball would sooner rather than later like to have its own World Cup—one exclusively of its own making and control. The result so far has been the staffing of U.S. teams and those of a handful of

Cubans celebrate 2003 World Cup gold in Havana as Panamanians taste defeat. [Peter C. Bjarkman]

other nations (such as Puerto Rico, the Dominican Republic, Canada, Australia, and Venezuela) with squads of AA and AAA players and a handful of big league prospects or washouts. Japan of late has turned to crack professionals of its own, and the 2004 Japanese Olympic squad was a true "Dream Team" lineup of Central League and Pacific League all-stars. Even with this talent source made available to countries harboring big leaguers, the Cuban domination of top tournaments has been little slowed, if in any way affected. Cuba won in Winnipeg in 1999, lost the 2000 gold medal game in Sydney on a day when its own bats went quiet, and ran off with the next two World Cup trophies in 2001 and 2003 as if nothing had changed. The besieged Cubans qualified (along with Canada) for Athens 2004; the AAA-rich American squad did not. And in Athens the Cuban League squad of nominal "amateurs" again proved superior in semifinal and final medal-round games against Canadian and Australian squads laced with journeymen ex–big leaguers. Japan's lustrous pro all-stars were in turn stunned by the Aussies in semifinal action. One lesson has already seemed to emerge. Baseball talent has a much broader international base than basketball does, so it is not at all clear that rampant use of big leaguers would

Cuban Luis Casanova is greeted at the plate during an Intercontinental Cup V match versus Australia. [Author's Cuban Collection]

strengthen Team USA any more than it would the squads of a handful of other nations. Even in basketball, the 2004 Athens Olympiad seemed to reveal that the rest of the world has caught up, especially in the NBA, which boasts a far smaller foreign population than major league baseball.

For the world's other baseball nations—some utter newcomers to the sport, such as Croatia, and others boasting traditions that rival U.S. adaptations of the game—it is these Olympic-style events, much more than the institutions of professional organized baseball, that have stood since the middle of the twentieth century as the true highlight of each baseball year. For the Cubans, especially, international baseball has always been the central focus of their deeply ingrained passion for the national sport. And from the earliest years of amateur world tournament play in the late 1930s and early 1940s the Cubans have virtually owned the international baseball scene.

Since the game of baseball achieved official medal-awarding status with the Barcelona Olympics in 1992, the Olympic tournament has been international baseball's showcase event. Several parallel tournaments nonetheless boast lengthy and remarkably rich historical traditions, and the Olympic event staged only every fourth year is in some senses a Johnny-come-lately attraction in world amateur competition. Less publicized events such as the highly competitive Intercontinental Cup matches (a fixture in odd-numbered years since 1973) and the round of Olympic Qualifiers (an innovation in 2003) offer equally thrilling competitions with more expansive and competitive fields (the Olympics remains a restricted affair with only eight prequalified entrants). All are showcase events instituted and refined by the IBAF—world baseball's primary governing administrative body, currently housed in Lausanne, Switzerland.

That international baseball is alive and well was demonstrated beyond doubt with two showcase tournaments during the 2003 fall season. In both the 2003 World Cup and the Olympic Qualifier that followed on its heels, the Cubans demonstrated that their place atop the heap was still secure. The U.S. involvement in these games was, as in the past, only minimal. There were the usual disappointments (a pair of quarterfinal-round losses) for Team USA squads that hardly represented America's finest, although part of the problem seemed to be an overconfidence on the part of those guiding USA Baseball, an overconfidence resulting perhaps from the American gold medal triumph in the 2000 Sydney Olympics. Whether Team USA underachieved or was sabotaged by Major League Baseball, the result was the same. No USA team appearing in Athens for the 2004 Olympiad meant a new hue and cry from USA forces for either revamping or scrapping Olympic baseball.

With increased meddling by Major League Baseball and with the always increasing commercialization of the Olympics themselves, there are of course evergrowing threats to the world of international baseball as we have long known it. Ever on the lookout for new markets and for further monopoly control of the sport

Taipei's Yung-chi Chen forces Cuba's Frederich Cepeda during 2003 World Cup action. [Peter C. Bjarkman]

and its worldwide talent sources, Major League Baseball has of late launched a movement to replace Olympic competitions with its own Major League Baseball–controlled soccer-style baseball World Cup. (The notion has naturally gained more widespread support in the United States on the heels of the embarrassing American losses in October and November 2003.) The line has been more or less as follows: if the United States cannot participate in the 2004 Athens Olympics, then the whole Olympic baseball event might just as well be jettisoned.

If such a movement by Major League Baseball is successful, it will have some obvious effects—if not entirely negative, certainly not entirely positive. The most obvious, perhaps, is the devastating impact on the international baseball movement as a healthy alternative to the professional world of organized baseball. To convert world tournaments into another branch of Major League Baseball's commercial enterprise—one aimed at mining the talent of all nations for incorporation into big league and minor league rosters—will likely mean an end to thriving national leagues in a number of the world's top

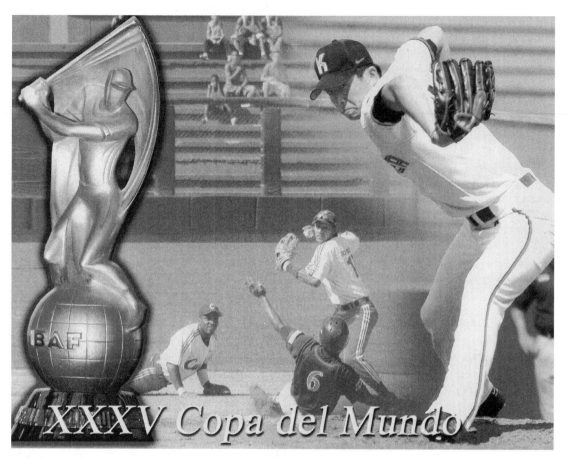

Korean hurler Kwan-sik Kang and Cuban infielder Yulieski Gourriel in a 2003 World Cup collage. [Peter C. Bjarkman]

baseball-playing nations. The Cuban League, the Japanese Central and Pacific leagues, the Korean Baseball Organization, and the Taiwan Major League—as well as four Caribbean Winter Leagues—may all truly be living on borrowed time.

Whatever the storm clouds on the horizon, it seems inevitable that change is in the offing. Olympic and World Cup tournaments under the control of the IBAF may not exist much longer, not as we have for decades known them. Baseball as an Olympic sport is of course also threatened by forces outside of U.S. organized baseball. It may soon be abandoned by the International Olympic Committee, along with other team sports such as women's softball, women's soccer, and team handball—all events open to the charge that they are not universally played or widely followed in the world of international sport. An envisioned MLB World Cup would likely also put out of business the six-decade-old IBAF-sponsored event of the same name. We may soon arrive at a purer measure of which country can claim the best of the best in baseball talent—but in the process, we likely will not continue to foster increased vigor of the international sport in the newest of developing (or underdeveloped) baseball nations. No matter what happens in the near future, however, baseball as a world sport already carries an impressive and often dramatic history. The on-field record of that history is largely contained within the detailed accounts of the handful of worldwide and regional competitions that have defined the international game for the last three-quarters of a century.

SUMMARIES OF WORLD AMATEUR BASEBALL CHAMPIONSHIPS

Provided here are the most extensive and complete summaries anywhere available on year-by-year international amateur tournaments. The rosters of Cuban teams are as complete as existing data permits, and individual statistical leaders as well as final team standings are here offered for all years and for all five major tournaments: Amateur World Series (World Cup), Olympic Games, Intercontinental Cup, Pan American Games, and Central American Games (in that order). Lesser data is also given for some of the more minor tournaments on the international baseball scene: the Asian Federation Championships (1954–2001), European Championships (1954–2001), and Oceania Confederation Championships (1999–2003). Country abbreviations in the statistical summaries follow the three-letter codes used by the International Olympics Committee and the IBAF (see Appendix B for an alphabetical listing).

Much of what follows reads like a reprise of Cuban baseball history, but this is inevitable. The Cubans have won so often and so consistently that there are few years or few tournaments where their performances have not been the page one story. Tournaments in which Cuba was eligible but did not compete are marked as such. Complete Cuban ballplayer rosters are provided, as well as game-by-game Cuban team scores and scores for championship teams other than Cuba.

World Cup Championships (Amateur World Series), 1938–2003

What started off being called the Amateur World Series (or just the "world championships" in countries without an established professional league) has been of late renamed the World Cup in official IBAF (International Baseball Federation) media materials. (For simplicity, the term *World Cup* will typically be used for this event, even though that was not the designation when the earlier tournaments were being staged.) Part of the motivation for the name change was certainly the overtures of Major League Baseball toward establishment of a "world cup" baseball tournament of their own sponsorship and control. Major League Baseball moguls see such an event as replacement for Olympic Games baseball play (where Team USA is rarely successful) and also as a huge revenue producer paralleling the model of World Cup soccer.

Cuba was largely responsible for launching and nursing along this showcase event, first under the government of Fulgencio Batista in the 1940s, when its earliest competitive events coincided with the apex of prerevolution amateur teams and leagues on the island. Without Cuba's support, neither the oldest and most durable international tournament nor the IBAF itself would likely be around today.

Cuba's Overall Performance: Tournaments (24 of 27 Tournament titles won, plus one second place and one third place); Games (269 Won and 28 Lost, .906 Pct.).

U.S. batter strikes out at first Amateur World Series at Havana, October 1939. [Author's Cuban Collection]

Country-by-Country Championships Won: Cuba (24 of 27 tournaments entered), Venezuela (3), Colombia (2), Dominican Republic (1), Puerto Rico (1), South Korea (1), USA (1), and England (1).

Note: In 1944 (World Championship VII held at Caracas) Cuba (7–4) withdrew in the final round and forfeited its final game (Mexico also withdrew from the championship round). In 1976 (World Championship XXIV held at Cartagena) Cuba was declared champion when Puerto Rico withdrew and thus forfeited an earlier win against the Cubans. Cuba did not participate in the following eight events: 1938 (England), 1945 (Venezuela), 1947 (Colombia), 1948 (Colombia), 1965 (Colombia), 1973 (Managua, Nicaragua), 1974 (St. Petersburg, Florida), and 1982 (South Korea). This tourney was known for years as the Amateur World Series but is now officially named The Baseball World Cup.

1938 Baseball World Cup I (London, England, August 13–18)

World championship play is inaugurated with a two-team and 5-game series that is the brainchild of American businessman Leslie Mann. "The John Moore Trophy" (honoring the founder of the English Baseball Association) is presented to a winning squad representing England, but both teams actually consist of American soldiers currently on duty at European military bases, along with a smattering of native British baseballers from an earlier experimental, short-lived British professional league.

Champion: England

Teams and Final Standings: England (4–1), USA (1–4).

Individual Statistical Leaders: No statistics are available for this tournament.

Game Scores: England beat USA 3–0, England beat USA 8–6, USA beat England 5–0, England beat USA 4–0, England beat USA 5–3.
Cuba Did Not Participate

1939 Baseball World Cup II (Havana, Cuba) (August 12–26)

The pastoral setting of Havana's La Tropical Stadium hosts the first "legitimate" international tournament consisting of amateurs representing three countries. Outfielder Juan Torres paces undefeated Cuba with a decisive game-winning hit in the opening match versus Nicaragua. Nicaragua boasts heavy hitting by black stars Stanley Cayasso and Jonathan Robinson, who slug the only 2 homers of the week-long event. A winless U.S. team is exceptionally weak and only serves to round out the three-team field.
Champion: Cuba (6–0)
Teams and Final Standings: Gold: Cuba (6–0), Silver: Nicaragua (3–3), Bronze: USA (0–6).
Individual Statistical Leaders: **BA**: Sam Garth (NCA) .500; **Runs**: Ésteban Maciques (CUB) 7; **Hits**: Sam Garth (NCA), G. Toyo (CUB) 9; **2B**: Ernesto Estévez (CUB), Stanley Cayasso (NCA) 2; **3B**: Wenceslao González (CUB), Bernardo Cuervo (CUB) 2; **HR**: Stanley Cayasso (NCA), Jonathan Robinson (NCA) 1; **RBI**: Bernardo Cuervo (CUB) 6; **SB**: C. Newell (NCA) 4; **Wins**: Pedro "Natilla" Jiménez (CUB) 2–0; **MVP**: Juan J. Torres (CUB).
Cuba Roster: **Manager**: León Rojas. **Batting** (AB, H, BA): Wenceslao González (6, 3, .500), Conrado Marrero (4, 2, .500), Eliecer Alvarez (4, 2, .500), Ésteban Estévez (18, 7, .389), G. Toyo (27, 9, .333), A. González (6, 2, .333), M. Tamayo Saco (3, 1, .333), Kiko Gutiérrez (7, 2, .286), Clemente González (15, 4, .267), Ésteban Maciques (16, 4, .259), L. Minsal (22, 5, .227), Bernardo Cuervo (20, 4, .200), Mario Fajo (10, 2, .400), Juan J. Torres (23, 4, .174), Andrés Fleitas (12, 2, .167), Natilla Jiménez (7, 1, .143), D. Pérez (2, 0, .000), N. Carbo (0, 0, .000). **Pitching** (W, L, ERA): Pedro "Natilla" Jiménez (2, 0, 0.95), Wenceslao González (2, 0, 5.14), Eliecer Alvarez (1, 0, 2.00), Conrado Marrero (1, 0, 3.00), M. Tamayo Saco (0, 0, 0.00).
Cuba Game Scores: Round-robin: Cuba beat Nicaragua 4–3, Cuba beat USA 13–3, Cuba beat Nicaragua 3–2, Cuba beat USA 8–3, Cuba beat Nicaragua 9–1, Cuba beat USA 12–7.

1940 Baseball World Cup III (Havana, Cuba) (September 14–October 6)

The field increases to seven teams, including distant Hawaii (featuring several Japanese players), but Cuba is again dominant despite more balanced competition and a more representative U.S. entrant. Robinson and Cayasso repeat their heavy-hitting displays for Nicaragua; but Cuba's pitching—especially Marrero, Jiménez, and Parra—is the deciding factor. Two notable players appearing in this tournament are U.S. pitcher Stubby Overmire (later a ten-year major leaguer with Detroit) and Cuban black infielder Pedro "Charolito" Orta, father of Mexican-born future major leaguer Jorge Orta.
Champion: Cuba (10–2)
Teams and Final Standings: Gold: Cuba (10–2), Silver: Nicaragua (9–3), Bronze: United States (9–3), Venezuela (5–7), Hawaii (5–7), Mexico (2–10), Puerto Rico (2–10).
Individual Statistical Leaders: **BA**: Jonathan Robinson (NCA) .444; **Runs**: Jonathan Robinson (NCA) 14; **Hits**: Stanley Cayasso (NCA) 19; **2B**: José Pérez (VEN), J.N. Vallecino (NCA) 4; **3B**: José Pérez (VEN) 3; **HR**: Jonathan Robinson (NCA) 1; **RBI**: J.N. Vallecino (NCA) 10; **SB**: L. Kunihisha (HAW) 7; **Wins**: José "Chino" Meléndez (NCA) 3–0; **MVP**: Conrado Marrero (CUB).
Cuba Roster: **Manager**: Reinaldo Cordeiro. **Batting** (AB, H, BA): Eliecer Alvarez (4, 3, .750), Segundo "Guajiro" Rodríguez (30, 13, .433), Natilla Jiménez (12, 5, .417), Tomás Hechevarría (10, 4, .400), Antonio Ruiz (43, 16, .372), Mario Fajo (41, 14, .341), Manuel

"Chino" Hidalgo (38, 12, .316), Napoleón Reyes (37, 11, .297), Virgilio Arteaga (45, 13, .289), Pedro Orta (39, 11, .282), Pedro "Kiko" Gutiérrez (18, 5, .278), C. Ramos (30, 7, .233), F. Sánchez (22, 5, .227), Ésteban Maciques (19, 4, .211), Conrado Marrero (12, 2, .167), Carlos Colás (32, 5, .156), J.R. López (22, 3, .136), Daniel Parra (4, 0, .000). **Pitching** (W, L, ERA): Conrado Marrero (3, 2, 1.15), Tomás Hechevarría (2, 0, 1.16), Eliecer Alvarez (1, 0, 1.26), Antonio "Loco" Ruiz (1, 0, 1.29), Natilla Jiménez (2, 0, 1.91), Daniel Parra (1, 0, 2.77).

Cuba Game Scores, Double round-robin: Cuba beat Hawaii 3–1, Cuba beat Mexico 6–0, Cuba beat Nicaragua 8–5, Cuba beat Venezuela 11–1, Cuba beat Puerto Rico 10–4, Cuba beat Hawaii 6–5, USA beat Cuba 2–1, Cuba beat USA 3–2, Cuba beat Puerto Rico 19–3, Cuba beat Venezuela 7–1, Cuba beat Mexico 6–2, Nicaragua beat Cuba 5–4.

1941 Baseball World Cup IV (Havana, Cuba) (September 27–October 22)

One of the most hotly contested and highly memorable tournaments of international baseball history is again staged in La Tropical Stadium. Cuba and Venezuela deadlock with 7–1 records; an unscheduled deciding match is thus a last-minute addition. Allowed extra days of rest for their ace pitcher Daniel "Chino" Canónico, Venezuela surprises favored Cuba with three first-inning runs against Marrero in the dramatic finale. Venezuela behind Canónico holds on to win, despite superb seven-inning relief from Cuban southpaw Natilla Jiménez and a ninth-inning rally by the home club that falls two runs short of victory.

Champion: Venezuela (8–1)

Teams and Final Standings: Gold: Venezuela (8–1), Silver: Cuba (7–2), Bronze: Mexico (6–2), Panama (5–3), Dominican Republic (5–3), USA (2–6), Nicaragua (2–6), Puerto Rico (1–7), El Salvador (1–7). *Venezuela defeated Cuba 3–1 in tie-breaking single playoff game for championship.

Individual Statistical Leaders: **BA**: G. Prieto (MEX) .545; **Runs**: Antonio "Mosquito" Ordeñana (CUB) 14; **Hits**: Clemente González (CUB) 17; **2B**: Víctor Manuel Canales (MEX) 5; **3B**: Héctor Romero Benítez (VEN) 3; **HR**: Leon Kellman (PAN) 1; **RBI**: Bernardo Cuervo (CUB) 10; **SB**: Carlos "Pinchón" Navas (NCA) 6; **Wins**: Daniel Canónico (VEN) 4–0; **MVP**: José Casanova (VEN).

Cuba Roster: **Manager**: Joaquín Viego. **Batting** (AB, H, BA): Bernardo Cuervo (30, 12, .400), Clemente González (43, 17, .395), Andrés Fleitas (37, 14, .378), Nap Reyes (35, 12, .343), D. Galvez (6, 2, .333), Conrado Marrero (6, 2, .333), Segundo "Guajiro" Rodríguez (31, 10, .323), Carlos Pérez (37, 10, .270), Antonio Ordeñana (43, 11, .256), Rafael Cabrera (32, 5, .156), Rogelio "Limonar" Martínez (12, 0, .000), Julio Moreno (7, 0, .000), Natilla Jiménez (6, 0, .000), Ramón Roger (3, 0, .000), Tomás Hechevarría (4, 0, .000), P.A. Fernández (0, 0, .000), Rouget Avalos (0, 0, .000), Daniel Parra (0, 0, .000). **Pitching** (W, L, ERA): Rogelio "Limonar" Martínez (2, 0, 0.00), Natilla Jiménez (0, 0, 0.00), Conrado Marrero (3, 0, 0.46), Tomás Hechevarría (1, 0, 1.00), Julio "Jiqui" Moreno (1, 1, 1.29), Ramón Roger (0, 0, 2.08). (*Team Cuba stats do not include extra playoff game).

Venezuela Game Scores: Round-robin: Venezuela beat Puerto Rico 12–1, Venezuela beat El Salvador 8–2, Venezuela beat Mexico 5–2, Venezuela beat USA 12–1, Venezuela beat Panama 7–2, Venezuela beat Nicaragua 6–0, Dominican Republic beat Venezuela 4–2, Venezuela beat Cuba 4–1. Playoff: Venezuela beat Cuba 3–1.

Cuba Game Scores: Round-robin: Cuba beat El Salvador 16–0, Cuba beat Dominican Republic 4–2, Cuba beat USA 5–4, Cuba beat Nicaragua 7–0, Cuba beat Panama 9–0, Cuba beat Puerto Rico 7–0, Cuba beat Mexico 11–1, Venezuela beat Cuba 4–1. Playoff: Venezuela beat Cuba 3–1.

1942 Baseball World Cup V (Havana, Cuba) (September 26–October 20)

Cuba avenges the disappointing loss of a year earlier, with Marrero this time besting Canónico 8–0 in a one-sided opening-round rematch. Cuban catcher Andrés Fleitas enjoys a career highlight as tourney MVP and batting leader and both Julio Moreno and Isidoro León post 3–0 pitching records and sub 2.00 ERAs. The tournament trophy is now designated as the "Copa Presidente Batista" (The Batista Presidential Cup), and wartime restrictions limit the field to five teams (with the U.S. team pulling out early and forfeiting several matches). A memorable moment involves a near grandstand riot inspired by the antics of colorful Dominican Republic manager Burrolote ("Big Donkey") Rodríguez. Luis Aparicio Sr., father of the future Cooperstown Hall of Famer, plays at shortstop for Venezuela.

Champion: Cuba (10–2)

Teams and Final Standings: Gold: Cuba (10–2), Silver: Dominican Republic (9–3), Bronze: Venezuela (7–5), Mexico (3–9), USA* (1–11). *USA withdrew before tournament's completion and lost four games by forfeit.

Individual Statistical Leaders: **BA**: Andrés Fleitas (CUB) .405; **Runs**: Carlos Pérez (CUB) 20; **Hits**: Antonio "Quilla" Valdés (CUB) 16; **2B**: Juan Ealo (CUB) 4; **3B**: Pedro Echevarría (CUB), Carlos Pérez (CUB) 1; **HR**: Francisco "Chito" Quicutis (CUB), Carlos Pérez (CUB), Quilla Valdés (CUB) 2; **RBI**: Quilla Valdés (CUB) 14; **SB**: Carlos Pérez (CUB) 4; **Wins**: Julio Moreno (CUB), Isidoro León (CUB) 3–0; **MVP**: Andrés Fleitas (CUB).

Cuba Roster: **Manager**: León Rojas. **Batting** (AB, H, BA): Luis Suárez (19, 11, .579), José R. Hernández (25, 12, .480), Villa Cabrera (14, 6, .429), Andrés Fleitas (37, 15, .405), Juan Ealo (40, 15, .375), Pedro Echevarría (35, 13, .371), F.P. Sánchez (15, 5, .333), Conrado Marrero (3, 1, .333), Antonio "Quilla" Valdés (53, 16, .302), Carlos Pérez (52, 15, .288), José Luis García (26, 7, .269), Eraso del Monte (13, 3, .231), Remigio Vega (25, 5, .200), Daniel Parra (5, 1, .200), Julio Moreno (16, 3, .188), Chito Quicutis (34, 6, .176), Mario Fajo (32, 4, .125), Isidoro León (9, 1, .111). **Pitching** (W, L, ERA): Erasmo "Coco" del Monte (2, 1, 0.94), Julio Moreno (3, 0, 1.36), Isidoro León (3, 0, 1.93), Daniel Parra (1, 0, 2.38), Conrado Marrero (1, 1, 3.09).

Cuba Game Scores: Multiple round-robin: Dominican Republic beat Cuba 7–6, Cuba beat Dominican Republic 5–2, Cuba beat USA 11–1, Cuba beat Venezuela 8–0, Cuba beat USA 20–0, Cuba beat Mexico 8–0, Cuba beat USA 17–0, Cuba beat Venezuela 9–2, Cuba beat Mexico 11–3, Cuba beat Venezuela 11–4, Dominican Republic beat Cuba 4–3, Cuba beat Mexico 7–6.

1943 Baseball World Cup VI (Havana, Cuba) (September 25–October 19)

Cuba wins for the fourth time during five straight tournaments played in Havana. Pitching dominates during an event that saw no home runs hit during 24 games in Tropical Stadium. Julio Moreno with three victories and Natilla Jiménez with no earned runs allowed in two outings are the top pitching stars, with Jiménez chosen as tourney MVP. Unheralded infielder Ángel Fleitas (brother of catcher Andrés Fleitas) is Cuba's offensive hero and the tournament's batting champion. Conrado Marrero sat out this tournament, having been temporarily stripped of his amateur status by the Cuban Baseball Federation.

Champion: Cuba (9–3)

Teams and Final Standings: Gold: Cuba (9–3), Silver: Mexico (6–6), Bronze: Dominican Republic (5–7), Panama (4–8).

Individual Statistical Leaders: **BA**: Ángel Fleitas (CUB) .371; **Runs**: Gil Garrido (PAN) 10; **Hits**: Luis Suárez (CUB) 17; **2B**: José Luna (MEX) 5; **3B**: Luis Suárez (CUB), Luis

Báez (DOM) 2; **HR**: None; **RBI**: Luis Suárez (CUB) 9; **SB**: Luis Báez (DOM) 7; **Wins**: Julio Moreno (CUB) 3–1; **MVP**: Pedro "Natilla" Jiménez (CUB).

Cuba Roster: **Manager**: León Rojas. **Batting** (AB, H, BA): Ángel Fleitas (35, 13, .371), Luis Suárez (48, 17, .354), Rouget Avalos (15, 5, .333), Alberto Morera (41, 12, .292), Sandalio Consuegra (7, 2, .286), Ernesto Estévez (43, 13, .279), Rogelio Valdés (23, 5, .217), Antonio "Quilla" Valdés (50, 10, .200), Pedro "Natilla" Jiménez (15, 3, .200), Félix del Cristo (28, 5, .179), Virgilio Arteaga (41, 6, .146), Julio Moreno (14, 2, .143), Rogelio Martínez (8, 1, .125), Chito Quicutis (33, 2, .061), Armando "Jojo" Báez (11, 1, .091), Leandro Pazos (11, 1, .091), Bautista Aristondo (1, 0, .000), Isidoro León (5, 0, .000), Agustín Cordeiro (1, 0, .000). **Pitching** (W, L, ERA): Pedro "Natilla" Jiménez (1, 1, 0.00), Isidoro León (1, 0, 0.00), Julio "Jiqui" Moreno (3, 1, 0.70), Rogelio "Limonar" Martínez (3, 0, 0.96), Sandalio Consuegra (1, 1, 3.44).

Cuba Game Scores: Multiple round-robin: Mexico beat Cuba 2–1, Cuba beat Mexico 3–2, Dominican Republic beat Cuba 1–0, Cuba beat Panama 2–1, Cuba beat Dominican Republic 5–4, Cuba beat Panama 5–3, Cuba beat Mexico 7–0, Cuba beat Dominican Republic 3–0, Cuba beat Panama 5–3, Cuba beat Dominican Republic 3–0, Cuba beat Mexico 6–0, Panama beat Cuba 7–0.

1944 Baseball World Cup VII (Caracas, Venezuela) (October 12–November 18)

The first legitimate Amateur World Series (later to be called the World Cup) held outside of Havana turned into a nightmare of controversy and lasting ill will when incompetent and overly partial umpiring in three late-round games resulted in acrimonious withdrawal by both Cuban and Mexican teams. Hometown umpires cost host Venezuela one victory when a game was unaccountably suspended by darkness after a late Venezuelan rally, the game thus reverting to an earlier inning with the Dominicans declared winners. The next contest saw the Cubans leaving the field in protest after a Cuban base runner was thrown out with an assist from a sideline photographer who interfered with on-field play. A similar dispute also sent Mexico packing several days later. The final suspended playoff match between Mexico and Venezuela was ruled a forfeit and the host team declared a much-disputed victory in its own favor.

Champion: Venezuela (7–3)

Elimination-Round Teams and Final Standings: Gold: Venezuela (2–1), Silver: Mexico* (2–1), Bronze: Cuba* (2–1), Panama (0–3). *Cuba and Mexico both withdraw in protests over umpiring and host Venezuela then declares its own team to be champion.

Qualifying-Round Teams and Final Standings: Mexico (6–1), Panama (5–2), Venezuela (5–2), Cuba (4–3), Dominican Republic (4–3), Colombia (2–5), Nicaragua (1–6), Puerto Rico (1–6).

Individual Statistical Leaders: **BA**: Leonard Roberts (PAN) .478; **Runs**: Guillermo Vento (VEN) 14; **Hits**: Antonio Briñez (VEN) 19; **2B**: Stanley Cayasso (NCA), Guillermo Vento (VEN) 5; **3B**: P. Miranda (COL), P. García (CUB) 2; **HR**: A. González (VEN), B. López (MEX), J. Diaz (MEX) 2; **RBI**: Dalmiro Finol (VEN) 15; **SB**: José Araujo (COL) 4; **Wins**: Mirno Zuloaga (VEN), F. Alcaraz (MEX) 3–0.

Cuba Roster: **Manager**: Pipo de la Noval. **Batting** (AB, H, BA): A. Rodríguez (11, 6, .545), Félix del Cristo (12, 6, .500), Sandalio Consuegra (2, 1, .500), Ángel Fleitas (38, 13, .342), Rogelio "Limonar" Martínez (3, 1, .333), Carlos Pérez (37, 11, .297), J.L. García (34, 10, .294), Pablo García (36, 10, .278), F. Fernández (11, 3, .273), Antonio "Quilla" Valdés (24, 6, .250), Amado Ibáñes (12, 3, .250), Julio Moreno (12, 3, .250), Juan Ealo (34, 7, .206), Conrado Marrero (10, 2, .200), Ángel Torres (17, 3, .176), Tango Suárez (18, 3, .167), Isidoro León (6, 1, .167), Rouget Avalos (15, 1, .067), Antonio Estrella (0, 0, .000), A. Gallart (0, 0, .00). **Pitching** (W, L, ERA): Sandalio Consuegra (1, 0, 1.00), Conrado Marrero (2, 1, 2.20), Isidoro León (1, 0, 2.70), Antonio Estrella (0, 0, 3.00), Julio Moreno (2, 2, 3.80), Rogelio "Limonar" Martínez (0, 1, 3.86).

Venezuela Game Scores: Qualifying Round: Panama beat Venezuela 3–2, Venezuela beat Puerto Rico 15–3, Dominican Republic beat Venezuela 2–0, Venezuela beat Nicaragua 10–0, Venezuela beat Colombia 3–2, Venezuela beat Mexico 6–0, Venezuela beat Cuba 7–2. Finals: Venezuela beat Mexico 8–4, Cuba beat Venezuela 9–7, Venezuela beat Panama 12–7. Playoff: Venezuela beat Mexico 10–9, Venezuela beat Mexico 9–0 (forfeit).

Cuba Game Scores: Qualifying Round: Cuba beat Puerto Rico 6–0, Cuba beat Colombia 4–0, Cuba beat Nicaragua 6–3, Panama beat Cuba 6–3, Mexico beat Cuba 2–0, Cuba beat Dominican Republic 2–1, Venezuela beat Cuba 7–2. Playoffs: Cuba beat Dominican Republic 3–2. Finals: Cuba beat Panama 8–0, Cuba beat Venezuela 9–7, Mexico beat Cuba 4–1.

1945 Baseball World Cup VIII (Caracas, Venezuela) (October 27–November 18)

With Cuba and Mexico still sitting on the sidelines after the previous year's debacle in Caracas, Venezuela stages a less controversial defense of its tainted championship by cruising through a depleted six-team field. Héctor Benítez is the heavy hitter for undefeated Venezuela, batting over .500, knocking in 16 runs, and scoring another 16 himself. Mirno Zuloaga wins four pitching decisions for the victors but trails teammate Benítez in the MVP voting. Mexico and Puerto Rico will return for the next tournament (1947) and the Dominican Republic will reenter and also win in 1948, but Cuba will remain on the sidelines until the beginning of the next decade.

Champion: Venezuela (10–0)

Teams and Final Standings: Gold: Venezuela (10–0), Silver: Colombia (7–3), Bronze: Panama (6–4), Nicaragua (5–5), El Salvador (1–9), Costa Rica (1–9).

Individual Statistical Leaders: **BA**: Héctor Benítez (VEN) .526; **Runs**: Héctor Benítez (VEN) 16; **Hits**: Ramón Fernández (VEN) 21; **HR**: L. Kellman (PAN) 2; **RBI**: Héctor Benítez (VEN) 16; **SB**: Luis Romero Petit (VEN) 9; **Wins**: Mirno Zuloaga (VEN) 4–0; **MVP**: Héctor Benítez (VEN). No additional statistics available.

Venezuela Game Scores: Double round-robin: Venezuela beat Costa Rica 11–1, Venezuela beat Colombia 3–0, Venezuela tied Panama 2–2, Venezuela beat El Salvador 10–1, Venezuela beat Nicaragua 3–0, Venezuela beat Costa Rica 15–1, Venezuela beat Colombia 12–0, Venezuela beat Panama 8–4, Venezuela beat Nicaragua 13–9, Venezuela beat El Salvador 31–1, Venezuela beat Nicaragua 4–3.

Cuba Did Not Participate

1947 Baseball World Cup IX (Barranquilla, Colombia) (November 29–December 20)

With Cuba again a notable absentee, host Colombia bests Puerto Rico and Nicaragua in the playoff round to capture its first title. Stanley Cayasso is still a slugging presence for Nicaragua and captures the RBI crown. This is Colombia's second consecutive strong showing and comes with balanced team play, as the Colombians have only one player in 1945 or 1947 who leads in any individual statistical category (Armando Crizón with 14 steals in 1947). Timoteo Mena earns three pitching victories for third-place Nicaragua.

Champion: Colombia (7–2)

Teams and Final Standings: Gold: Colombia (6–2), Silver: Puerto Rico (6–2), Bronze: Nicaragua (6–2), Mexico (5–3), Venezuela (5–3), Panama (3–5), El Salvador (2–6), Costa Rica (2–6), Guatemala (1–7). *In final playoff round, Puerto Rico eliminated Nicaragua (6–1 score) and Colombia defeated Puerto Rico (6–5 score) to decide cup championship.

Individual Statistical Leaders: **BA**: Fausto Fuenmeyer (VEN) .483; **Runs**: Eduardo Green (NCA), J. Hernández (NCA) 14; **3B**: O. Lara (ESA) 3; **HR**: E. Pessuey (PAN) 2; **RBI**: Stanley Cayasso (NCA) 12; **SB**: Armando Crizón (COL) 6; **Wins**: Timoteo Mena (NCA) 3–0. No additional statistics available.

Colombia Game Scores: Qualifying Round: Colombia beat Costa Rica 9–2, Colombia beat Mexico 4–3, Venezuela beat Colombia 4–1, Colombia beat Panama 3–1, Puerto Rico beat Colombia 7–0, Colombia beat Guatemala 8–0, Colombia beat El Salvador 13–0, Colombia beat Nicaragua 4–0. Playoffs: Colombia beat Puerto Rico 5–0.
Cuba Did Not Participate

1948 Baseball World Cup X (Managua, Nicaragua) (November 20–December 12)

Cuba stays on the sidelines for the third straight tournament, with most of the country's top amateur players now holding pro contracts. Cuba's Juan Ealo does direct the host Nicaragua team but is fired by Nicaraguan dictator Anastasio Somoza after a close loss to Mexico. Somoza himself then manages the Nicaragua squad, which not surprisingly still finishes far out of the running. The Dominicans edge Puerto Rico in a brief playoff series to capture their first and only world title. Ramón del Monte of the Dominican Republic posts a perfect 4–0 pitching record as the tournament MVP.
Champion: Dominican Republic (8–1)
Teams and Final Standings: Gold: Dominican Republic* (6–1), Silver: Puerto Rico (6–1), Bronze: Colombia (5–2), Mexico (5–2), Panama (3–4), Guatemala (2–5), Nicaragua (1–6), El Salvador (0–7). *In playoff round, Dominican Republic defeated Puerto Rico (11–1 and 2–1) in first two games of best-of-three series.
Individual Statistical Leaders: **BA**: Manuel Caceres (DOM), Luis Morales (COL) .522; **Runs**: Elias Farias (DOM) 9; **Hits**: Manuel Caceres (DOM), Luis Morales (COL), Miguel Corrales (MEX) 12; **2B**: F. Arrieta (MEX), M. Ruiz (PUR) 4; **3B**: R. Baldiris (COL), B. Arias (DOM), M. Ruiz (PUR) 2; **HR**: Miguel Corrales (MEX) 3; **RBI**: Eduardo Green (NCA) 11; **SB**: Nugent Josephs (PAN) 9; **Wins**: Ramón del Monte (DOM) 4–0; **ERA**: Ramón del Monte (DOM) 0.34; **MVP**: Ramón del Monte (DOM).
Dominican Republic Game Scores: Qualifying Round: Puerto Rico beat Dominican Republic 1–0, Dominican Republic beat Panama 8–3, Dominican Republic beat Colombia 7–1, Dominican Republic beat Mexico 7–3, Dominican Republic beat Nicaragua 9–5, Dominican Republic beat Guatemala 11–0, Dominican Republic beat El Salvador 9–0. Finals: Dominican Republic beat Puerto Rico 11–1, Dominican Republic beat Puerto Rico 2–1.
Cuba Did Not Participate

1950 Baseball World Cup XI (Managua, Nicaragua) (November 18–December 10)

In another tournament wrapped in controversy, Cuba finishes in a three-way tie with the Dominican Republic and Venezuela and enters a round-robin playoff that is finally won by the Dominicans. This playoff is annulled the following October when a special IBAF meeting disqualifies Puerto Rico for using professional players and thereby names Cuba champion. An opening round 13–11 loss to Puerto Rico is thus changed to a Cuban victory, amending the team's record from 9–2 to 10–1. Several outstanding individual performances highlight an event for which most statistical records unfortunately have been lost. Cuba's Juan Izaguirre set tournament (21) and game (7) marks for runs batted in, Cecilio Miller of Panama stole 14 bases, and Mexico's Nicolas Genestas posted a perfect 4–0 pitching ledger.
Champion: Cuba (10–1) (including forfeit victory over Puerto Rico)
Teams and Final Standings: Gold: Cuba* (9–2), Silver: Dominican Republic (9–2), Bronze: Venezuela (9–2), Panama (8–3), Nicaragua (7–4), Colombia (6–5), Mexico (6–5), Puerto Rico (5–6), El Salvador (3–8), Guatemala (2–9), Costa Rica (2–9), Honduras (0–11). *Cuba declared champion when Puerto Rico is sanctioned for using professional players and Puerto Rico's victory over Cuba is changed to forfeit win for the Cubans, breaking a tie between Cuba, Dominican Republic, and Venezuela.

Individual Statistical Leaders: **BA**: Eduardo Green (NCA) .487; **Runs**: Juan Izaguirre (CUB) 16; **Hits**: Eduardo Green (NCA) 19; **2B**: Candelario Guevara (VEN), Eduardo Green (NCA) 7; **3B**: Fernando García (MEX) 2; **HR**: Juan Izaguirre (CUB) 4; **RBI**: Juan Izaguirre (CUB) 21; **SB**: Cecilio Miller (PAN) 14; **Wins**: Nicolas Genestas (MEX) 4–0; **ERA**: Nicolas Genestas (MEX) 1.13.

Cuba Partial Roster: Position Players: Juan Izaguirre (4 HR, 21 RBI, 16 R), L. Seijo, D. Domínguez, Gilberto Soto, E. Muñoz, A. Armas, Juan Mir. Pitchers (W–L): Erasmo "Coco" del Monte (2–1), C. Cossio (3–1), Juan Ravelo (2–0), Marcelo Fernández (2–0). No additional roster names or statistics available.

Cuba Game Scores: Round-robin: Cuba beat Costa Rica 9–7, Cuba beat Venezuela 7–1, Cuba beat Honduras 26–0, Cuba beat El Salvador 9–5, Cuba beat Panama 5–4, Cuba beat Guatemala 5–0, Puerto Rico beat Cuba 13–11 (Cuba later declared forfeit winner, 9–0), Mexico beat Cuba 5–1, Cuba beat Colombia 7–1, Cuba beat Nicaragua 7–2, Cuba beat Dominican Republic 11–2.

1951 Baseball World Cup XII (Mexico City, Mexico) (November 1–19)

After matching Venezuela with a 9–1 record and first-place standing in preliminary round play, an undistinguished Cuba team dropped a pair of one-run decisions to Venezuela and Puerto Rico in the playoffs and limped home in third place. Statistical records from the only Amateur World Series ever played in Mexico are hopelessly sparse, although a complete listing of game scores does survive. This is only the third time (in eight tournaments attended) that Cuba does not claim first place. Nicaragua's unheralded Bert Bradford was the top hitter while playing for a team that did not make the final round. After this debacle in Mexico, Cuba would proceed to win each and every renewal of the World Amateur Series it attended over the next half-century (which would amount to eighteen of the twenty-two tournaments staged).

Champion: Puerto Rico (10–3)

Final Round Teams and Standings: Gold: Puerto Rico (3–0), Silver: Venezuela (2–1), Bronze: Cuba (1–2), Dominican Republic (0–3).

Preliminary Round Teams and Standings: Cuba (9–1), Venezuela (9–1), Puerto Rico (7–3), Dominican Republic (7–3), Nicaragua (6–4), Costa Rica (5–5), Panama (5–5), Colombia (4–6), Mexico (2–8), Guatemala (1–9), El Salvador (0–10).

Individual Statistical Leaders: **BA**: Bert Bradford (NCA) .481; **Runs**: Sotero Ortiz (PUR) 21; **Hits**: Bert Bradford (NCA) 25; **2B**: Ramón Maldonado (PUR) 8; **3B**: Reinaldo Grenald (PAN) 4; **HR**: Walter James (DOM) 3; **SB**: Sotero Ortiz (PUR) 10. No additional statistics available.

Cuba Final Round Scores: Cuba defeated Dominican Republic 14–1 (WP: Puentes); Venezuela defeated Cuba 7–6 (LP: García); Puerto Rico defeated Cuba 7–6 (LP: Naranjo).

Cuba Preliminary Round Scores: Puerto Rico defeated Cuba 13–12 (LP: Naranjo); Cuba defeated Panama 8–2 (WP: Puentes); Cuba defeated Dominican Republic 8–7 (WP: García); Cuba defeated Venezuela 6–2 (WP: Brull); Cuba defeated Mexico 5–5 (WP: Puentes); Cuba defeated Guatemala by forfeit; Cuba defeated Colombia 5–0 (WP: Naranjo); Cuba defeated Nicaragua 5–4 (WP: García); Cuba defeated El Salvador 4–0 (WP: Erasmo del Monte); Cuba defeated Costa Rica 6–1 (WP: Isidro Brull).

Cuba Roster: Pitchers (W–L): Naranjo (1–2), Puentes (3–0), García (2–1), Isidro Brull (2–0), Erasmo del Monte (1–0). No further data or statistics available for Cuban player roster in this tournament.

Puerto Rico Game Scores: Preliminary Round: Puerto Rico beat Cuba 13–12, Puerto Rico beat El Salvador 13–8, Puerto Rico beat Nicaragua 9–6, Colombia beat Puerto Rico 4–0, Venezuela beat Puerto Rico 10–0, Puerto Rico beat Dominican Republic 9–4, Puerto Rico beat Guatemala 20–3, Panama beat Puerto Rico 31–14, Puerto Rico beat Mexico

8–1, Puerto Rico beat Costa Rica 25–5. Finals: Puerto Rico beat Venezuela 17–1, Puerto Rico beat Dominican Republic 3–0, Puerto Rico beat Cuba 7–6.

Cuba Game Scores: Preliminary Round: Puerto Rico beat Cuba 13–12, Cuba beat Panama 8–2, Cuba beat Dominican Republic 8–7, Cuba beat Venezuela 6–2, Cuba beat Mexico 5–4, Cuba beat Guatemala 9–0 (forfeit game), Cuba beat Colombia 5–0, Cuba beat Nicaragua 5–4, Cuba beat El Salvador 4–0, Cuba beat Costa Rica 6–1. Finals: Cuba beat Dominican Republic 14–1, Venezuela beat Cuba 7–6, Puerto Rico beat Cuba 7–6.

1952 Baseball World Cup XIII (Havana, Cuba) (September 6–26)

Cuba's iron-clad fifty-year grip on amateur world championships began in Havana in September 1952, six months after strongman Fulgencio Batista grabbed power (March 10) and suspended constitutional government. No Cubans appear in the list of individual statistical leaders, but the pitching of Isidro Brull, Alejandro Eiriz, and J. Suárez in the final round sustained crucial wins over Panama (10–9), the Dominican Republic (9–5), Nicaragua (6–2), and Venezuela (5–4) to wrap up a gold medal. Existing team photographs reveal that black ballplayers now held five slots on the Cuban team roster as the slow process of amateur baseball racial integration continued.

Champion: Cuba (9–2)

Final Round Standings: Gold: Cuba (4–1), Silver: Dominican Republic (3–2), Bronze: Puerto Rico (2–2), Panama (2–2), Nicaragua (2–3), Venezuela (1–4).

Group A Preliminary Standings: Cuba (5–1), Puerto Rico (5–1), Nicaragua (4–2), Mexico (3–3), Dutch Antilles (2–4), El Salvador (2–4), Honduras (0–6).

Group B Preliminary Standings: Venezuela (4–1), Dominican Republic (4–1), Panama (4–1), Colombia (2–3), Costa Rica (1–4), Guatemala (0–5).

Individual Statistical Leaders: **BA**: E. Marte (DOM) .436; **Runs**: A. Martínez (DOM), Sotero Ortiz (PUR) 13; **Hits**: E. Marte (DOM) 17; **2B**: J. Ortiz (NCA), Sotero Ortiz (PUR) 4; **3B**: W. Figueredo (PUR) 3; **HR**: J.R. García (PUR) 2; **RBI**: O. Hardy (PAN) 12; **SB**: J.R. García (PUR) 7; **Wins**: E. Evangelista (DOM) 4–1. No additional statistics available.

Cuba Roster: **Manager**: Clemente "Sungo" Carreras. **Batting** (AB-H-BA): Alejandro Eiriz (4–2–.500), R. Navarrete (5–2–.400), Juan Mir (15–5–.333), L. Estrada (22–7–.318), A. Armas (34–10–.294), Antonio Suárez (7–2–.286), J. Barrios (7–2–.286), C. González (37–10–.270), Rouget Avalos (37–10–.270), E. Ferrer (34–9–.265), E. Marcos (27–7–.259), J. Suárez (4–1–.250), L. Olivares (13–3–.231), Manolo García (10–2–.200), Alfonso Suárez (35–6–.167), Isidro Brull (8–1–.125), I. Rodríguez (9–0–.000), G. Pérez (3–0–.000). **Pitching** (W–L): Isidro Brull (2–0), Alejandro Eiriz (2–0), R. Navarrete (1–0), Antonio Suárez (1–0), J. Suárez (3–1), G. Pérez (0–1).

Cuba Game Scores: Preliminary round-robin: Cuba beat Mexico 2–1, Cuba beat Dutch Antilles 8–1, Cuba beat El Salvador 11–3, Cuba beat Puerto Rico 7–4, Nicaragua beat Cuba 6–2, Cuba beat Honduras 6–0. Finals: Cuba beat Dominican Republic 9–5, Puerto Rico beat Cuba 7–1, Cuba beat Panama 10–9, Cuba beat Nicaragua 6–2, Cuba beat Venezuela 5–4.

1953 Amateur World Series XIV (Caracas, Venezuela) (September 12–October 9)

Cuba defended its 1952 title by sweeping Venezuela in the best-of-three final-round playoffs. Despite owning the most balanced team (with Alfonso Suárez and Manolo García both hitting above .400 and Antonio Suárez, along with Alejandro Eiriz, again providing formidable pitching), Cuba once more had no individual statistical pacesetters. The only loss for the champions came in the tournament's most exciting opening-round game, a 3–2 pitchers' duel between Antonio Suárez and Venezuela's tournament MVP Andrés Quintero.

Champion: Cuba (11–1)
Teams and Final Standings: Gold: Cuba (9–1), Silver: Venezuela (9–1), Bronze: Nicaragua (7–3), Dominican Republic (7–3), Panama (6–4), Puerto Rico (5–5), Colombia (3–7), Guatemala (3–7), Mexico (3–7), Dutch Antilles (2–8), El Salvador (1–9). *Cuba defeated Venezuela (4–2 and 4–0) in first two games of best-of-three championship playoffs.
Individual Statistical Leaders: **BA**: Domingo Vargas (DOM) .455; **Runs**: L. Cumberbatch (PAN), Dario Rubenstein (VEN) 16; **Hits**: O. Alvarado (NCA) 18; **2B**: Juan A. Pérez (AHO) 4; **3B**: A. Castillo (PAN) 4; **HR**: Conrado Griffith (PAN) 2; **RBI**: F. Torres (PUR) 15; **SB**: Dario Rubenstein (VEN) 10; **Wins**: Andrés Quintero (VEN) 4–0; **ERA**: M. Estrada (MEX) 0.00; **MVP**: Andrés Quintero (VEN).
Cuba Roster: **Manager**: Osvardo Castellanos. **Batting** (AB, H, BA): Alfonso Suárez (36, 15, .417), Manolo García (37, 15, .405), M. González (33, 11, .333), J. M. Fernández (33, 10, .303), C. Cordova (30, 9, .300), L. Olivares (42, 11, .262), A. López (Not Available), F. Foyo (NA), G. de Cárdenas (NA), J. Figarola (NA), L. Seijo (NA), E. Cruz (NA), Antonio Suárez (NA). **Pitching** (W, L, ERA): Antonio Suárez (2, 1, 0.87), L. Fiuza (3, 0, 1.78), J. Suárez (2, 0, 2.35), Alejandro Eiriz (1, 0), Ricardo Diaz (1, 0), C. Pérez (0, 0). No additional statistics available.
Cuba Game Scores: Preliminary Round: Cuba beat Puerto Rico 3–2, Cuba beat Dominican Republic 8–4, Venezuela beat Cuba 3–2, Cuba beat Dutch Antilles 9–1, Cuba beat Nicaragua 1–0, Cuba beat Mexico 3–1, Cuba beat El Salvador 6–2, Cuba beat Colombia 1–0, Cuba beat Guatemala 5–0, Cuba beat Panama 10–7. Playoffs: Cuba beat Venezuela 4–2. Cuba beat Venezuela 4–0.

1961 Baseball World Cup XV (San José, Costa Rica) (April 7–21)

Mass tryouts in Havana produced an exceptionally strong Cuban team for the first international competition after the installation of Fidel Castro's revolutionary government. In a quirk of timing, the Cuban entry ran roughshod over five other participating teams at precisely the same moment as Fidel's army was repulsing a U.S.-backed home-front invasion at the Bay of Pigs. Alfredo Street, a lanky black right-hander from Oriente Province and a holdover from the National Amateur League of the final years of the Batista era, won three games without defeat and José M. Pineda (2–0) allowed only one earned run in eighteen innings of work. Pedro Chávez, another key transitional figure in the transfer from prerevolution professional to postrevolution amateur leagues, provided most of the team's heavy hitting with tournament-best figures in both RBI and base hits.

Champion: Cuba (9–0)
Final Round Standings: Gold: Cuba (5–0), Silver: Mexico (4–1), Bronze: Venezuela (3–2), Panama (2–3), Costa Rica (1–4), Guatemala (0–5).
Group A Preliminary Standings: Panama (4–0), Venezuela (3–1), Costa Rica (2–2), Honduras (1–3), El Salvador (0–4).
Group B Preliminary Standings: Cuba (4–0), Mexico (3–1), Guatemala (1–3), Nicaragua (1–3), Dutch Antilles (1–3).
Individual Statistical Leaders: **BA**: Mario González (CUB) .500; **Runs**: J. Fernández (CUB) 20; **Hits**: Pedro Chávez (CUB), J. Fernández (CUB) 17; **2B**: José Parcero (MEX) 5; **3B**: eight players with one each; **HR**: Williams Proutt (PAN) 6; **RBI**: Pedro Chávez (CUB) 19; **SB**: J. Fernández (CUB) 5; **Wins**: Luis García (MEX) 4; **ERA**: José M. Pineda (CUB), 0.50.
Cuba Roster: **Manager**: Clemente "Sungo" Carreras. **Batting** (AB, H, BA): Mario González (32, 16, .500), Jorge Trigoura (23, 11, .478), Pedro Chávez (37, 17, .459), Eladio Sauquet (18, 8, .444), J. Fernández (41, 17, .415), René Díaz (25, 10, .400), Ángel Fuentes (33, 12, .364), Raúl Ortega (30, 8, .267), Antonio González (12, 3, .250), Urbano

González (28, 7, .250), Ricardo Lazo (27, 6, .222), D. Blanco (10, 2, .200), José M. Pineda (9, 3, .333), Santiago Pérez (3, 1, .333), Alfredo Street (10, 3, .300), Rolando Pastor (7, 1, .143), Ricardo Díaz (8, 1, .125), Jacinto Blanco (2, 0, .000). **Pitching** (W, L, ERA): Jacinto Blanco (0, 0, 0.00), José M. Pineda (2, 0, 0.50), Ricardo Díaz (1, 0, 0.72), Alfredo Street (3, 0, 1.15), Rolando Pastor (2, 0, 1.50), Santiago Pérez (1, 0, 3.60).

Cuba Game Scores: Preliminary Round: Cuba beat Dutch Antilles 18–0, Cuba beat Nicaragua 16–0, Cuba beat Guatemala 25–0, Cuba beat Mexico 11–1. Finals: Cuba beat Panama 12–3, Cuba beat Guatemala 13–2, Cuba beat Mexico 13–1, Cuba beat Costa Rica 12–2, Cuba beat Venezuela 9–3.

1965 Baseball World Cup XVI (Cartagena, Colombia) (February 12–27)

Colombia's right-wing government denied visas to the favored Cuban contingent, striking a Cold War blow against the new communist island government and leaving the powerhouse defending champions sitting at home on the sidelines. Colombia and Mexico finished in a dead heat in the play-down round, necessitating a championship series swept by the hosts in two straight. Two notable pitching feats marked this tournament: a perfect game (and the first Amateur World Series no-hitter) by Mexican hurler David García against Guatemala (February 14) and a single-game World Series strikeout record by Puerto Rico's Efraín Contreras (19 Ks) versus the Dutch Antilles (February 22).

Champion: Colombia (9–2)

Teams and Final Standings: Gold: Colombia* (7–1), Silver: Mexico (7–1), Bronze: Puerto Rico (5–3), Panama (4–4), Nicaragua (4–4), Guatemala (3–5), Dutch Antilles (2–6), El Salvador (0–8). *After losing opening playoff game (4–2), Colombia defeated Mexico twice (11–5 and 4–0) in best-of-three championship finals round.

Individual Statistical Leaders: **BA**: Andrés Cruz (PUR) .485; **Runs**: Luis de Arcos (COL) 12; **Hits**: Andrés Cruz (PUR) 16; **2B**: José Parcero (MEX) 4; **3B**: seven players with 2 each; **HR**: five players with one each; **RBI**: Andrés Cruz (PUR) 8; **SB**: Urbano Camarena (PAN) 5; **Wins**: Arturo Hudson (NCA), David García (MEX) 3; **ERA**: Arturo Hudson (NCA) 0.00.

Colombia Game Scores: Preliminary Round: Colombia beat Dutch Antilles 3–0, Colombia beat El Salvador 15–1, Colombia beat Panama 2–1, Puerto Rico beat Colombia 3–2, Colombia beat Guatemala 9–0, Colombia beat Nicaragua 4–0, Colombia beat Mexico 5–4, Colombia beat Dominican Republic 3–2. Final Playoffs: Mexico beat Colombia 4–2, Colombia beat Mexico 11–5, Colombia beat Mexico 4–0.

Cuba Did Not Participate

1969 Baseball World Cup XVII (Santo Domingo, Dominican Republic) (August 15–26)

Played under considerable political tension in Santo Domingo (due to strong anti-American feeling spawned by the U.S. invasion of the Dominican Republic four years earlier), the 1969 World Cup Series was a landmark event for postrevolutionary Cuban baseball. Cuba returned after their 1965 banishment from Colombia, and the United States fielded a team for the first time since their debacle performance of 1942: both teams moved undefeated through the field and squared off in a dramatic gold medal showdown. Gaspar Pérez was the hero of the finale, pitching brilliantly in relief, driving in the crucial tying run, and also scoring the eventual winning tally. The 2–1 Cuban victory was witnessed by 20,000 pro-Cuba spectators, of whom almost one third were reported to be armed soldiers and military police on hand to control potential anti-American hostilities.

Champion: Cuba (10–0)

Teams and Final Standings: Gold: Cuba (10–0), Silver: USA (9–1), Bronze: Dominican Republic (7–2), Venezuela (7–3), Panama (4–6), Puerto Rico (4–6), Colombia (4–6), Nicaragua (4–6), Mexico (2–7), Guatemala (1–8), Dutch Antilles (1–8).

Individual Statistical Leaders: **BA**: Owen Blandino (CUB) .500; **Runs**: Owen Blandino (CUB) 13; **Hits**: Owen Blandino (CUB) 20; **2B**: Luis Mercado (PUR) 6; **3B**: Fermín Laffita (CUB), E. Ruiz (MEX), Luis Mercado (PUR) 3; **HR**: Fermín Laffita (CUB) 3; **RBI**: Fermín Laffita (CUB) 16; **SB**: Carlos Urriola (VEN) 5; **Wins**: Gaspar Pérez (CUB) 4–0; **ERA**: G. Rodríguez (DOM) 0.00; **MVP**: Gaspar Pérez (CUB).

Cuba Roster: **Manager**: Servio Borges. **Batting** (AB, H, BA): Owen Blandino (40, 20, .500), Luis Pérez (25, 12, .480), Fermín Laffita (43, 19, .442), Féliz Isasi (21, 9, .429), Felipe Sarduy (38, 16, .421), Rigoberto Rosique (14, 5, .357), Agustín Marquetti (32, 11, .344), Andrés Telémaco (27, 9, .333), Antonio González (11, 3, .273), Silvio Montejo (45, 12, .267), Rodolfo Puente (24, 4, .167), Ramón Hechavarría (13, 2, .154), Gaspar Pérez (11, 6, .545), Lázaro Santana (6, 2, .333), Rolando Macías (7, 2, .286), José Antonio Huelga (4, 1, .250), Roberto Valdés (5, 1, .200), Santiago "Changa" Mederos (5, 1, .200). **Pitching** (W, L, ERA): Santiago "Changa" Mederos (1, 0, 1.00), Gaspar Pérez (4, 0, 0.35), José Antonio Huelga (1, 0, 0.75), Roberto Valdés (1, 0, 0.96), Rolando Macías (1, 0, 2.20), Lázaro Santana (2, 0, 2.45).

Cuba Game Scores: Round-robin: Cuba beat Venezuela 9–0, Cuba beat Nicaragua 10–1, Cuba beat Panama 8–0, Cuba beat Guatemala 17–0, Cuba beat Dominican Republic 10–3, Cuba beat Colombia 9–3, Cuba beat Puerto Rico 9–1, Cuba beat Mexico 5–3, Cuba beat Dutch Antilles 12–1, Cuba beat USA 2–1.

1970 Baseball World Cup XVIII (Cartagena, Colombia) (November 18–December 4)

The 1970s are arguably the showcase decade for postrevolution Cuban amateur baseball, and the era opened with a truly spectacular international tournament win. Cuba's only opening round loss came at the hands of an exceptionally strong U.S. club and the knuckle-ball pitching of future big league stalwart Burt Hooton. When the same two teams opened a best-of-three championship round, Hooton was matched up against young Cuban ace José Antonio Huelga in a classic mound duel, which finally fell to the Cubans 3–1 after eleven hard-fought innings. Cuban southpaw ace Santiago "Changa" Mederos started the second playoff game and received stellar relief support from Manuel Alarcón—and once again from José Antonio Huelga—in the 5–3 win that clinched Cuba's tenth world championship crown.

Champion: Cuba (12–1)

Teams and Final Standings: Gold: Cuba (10–1), Silver: USA (10–1), Bronze: Puerto Rico (9–2), Colombia (8–3), Venezuela (7–4), Dominican Republic (6–5), Nicaragua (4–7), Dutch Antilles (3–8), Italy (1–9), Canada (1–9), Netherlands (1–10). *Cuba wins championship cup with two straight wins (3–1 and 5–3) over USA in best-of-three championship round.

Individual Statistical Leaders: **BA**: Abel Leal (COL) .477; **Runs**: Félix Isasi (CUB), Wilfredo Sánchez (CUB), Abel Leal (COL), W. Pérez (DOM) 12; **Hits**: Abel Leal (COL) 21; **2B**: Luis Hernández (VEN), Luis Gaviria (COL) 5; **3B**: five players with two each; **HR**: Ramón Ortiz (PUR) 3; **RBI**: Félix Isasi (CUB) 15; **SB**: Orlando Ramírez (COL) 8; **Wins**: five pitchers with three each; **IP**: A. Jaramillo (COL) 32.2; **Strikeouts**: Burt Hooton (USA) 44; **ERA**: Burt Hooton (USA) 0.00. **MVP**: Abel Leal (COL).

Cuba Roster: **Manager**: Servio Borges. **Batting** (AB, H, BA): Felipe Sarduy (28, 12, .429), Wilfredo Sánchez (46, 19, .413), Félix Isasi (48, 19, .396), Fermín Laffita (39, 14, .359), Vicente Diaz (27, 9, .333), Rigoberto Rosique (31, 10, .323), Ramón Hechavarría (19, 6, .316), Rodolfo Puente (27, 8, .296), Urbano González (27, 8, .296), Luis Pérez (18, 4, .222), Armando Capiró (21, 4, .190), Agustín Marquetti (18, 3, .167), Antonio González (12, 2, .167), Raul Reyes (8, 1, .125), José Antonio Huelga (3, 2, .667), Oscar Romero (8, 3, .375), Emilio Salgado (6, 2, .333), Manuel Hurtado (5, 0, .000), Santiago "Changa" Mederos (6, 0, .000), Gaspar Legón (9, 0, .000). **Pitching** (W, L,

ERA): Emilio Salgado (2, 0, 0.00), Manuel Hurtado (2, 0, 0.00), José Antonio Huelga (1, 0, 0.00), Gaspar Legón (3, 0, 0.43), Oscar Romero (2, 0, 0.50), Santiago "Changa" Mederos (2, 1, 1.59).

Cuba Game Scores: Preliminary Round: Cuba beat Canada 12–0, Cuba beat Puerto Rico 10–0, Cuba beat Dominican Republic 11–1, Cuba beat Italy 9–1, Cuba beat Netherlands 10–1, Cuba beat Venezuela 8–1, Cuba beat Dutch Antilles 7–0, USA beat Cuba 3–1, Cuba beat Guatemala 4–0, Cuba beat Nicaragua 10–0, Cuba beat Colombia 6–0. Playoffs: Cuba beat USA 3–1, Cuba beat USA 5–3.

1971 Baseball World Cup XIX (Havana, Cuba) (November 21–December 4)

World Cup Series action returned to Havana in December with games played all around the island and the hosts easily sweeping a weakened field that had no U.S. representative. Rodolfo Puente (batting champion and MVP) and Elpidio Mancebo were the hitting stars for Cuba, while Armando Capiró (that year's National Series RBI champion) and Rigoberto Rosique (National Series batting leader) both slumped badly throughout the 9-game tournament. Nelson García of Colombia tossed the second-ever World Cup no-hitter when he shut down Italy 7–0 in Pinar del Río. Santiago "Changa" Mederos pitched flawlessly for Cuba; Antonio Jiménez, Oscar Romero, and José Antonio Huelga also each won a pair of games. Huelga tossed a two-hit shutout in Cuba's 6–0 win over a tournament all-star squad in the event finale.

Champion: Cuba (9–0)

Teams and Final Standings: Gold: Cuba (9–0), Silver: Colombia (7–2), Bronze: Nicaragua (6–3), Puerto Rico (6–3), Panama (5–4), Dominican Republic (4–5), Canada (4–5), Italy (2–7), Mexico (2–7), Dutch Antilles (0–9).

Individual Statistical Leaders: **BA**: Rodolfo Puente (CUB) .429; **Runs**: Elpidio Mancedo (CUB) 12; **Hits**: Ruperto Cooper (PAN) 14; **2B**: Ramón Greene (DOM), Alvin Fleming (AHO), Eduardo Ruiz (MEX) 5; **3B**: A.T. Wester (AHO), Ramón Greene (DOM), Luis Gaviria (COL) 2; **HR**: Luis Escoba (COL), Rick Cruise (CAN) 7; **RBI**: Ruperto Cooper (PAN) 11; **SB**: Orlando Ramírez (COL) 7; **Wins**: Carlos Lowell (PUR) 3; **ERA**: Santiago "Changa" Mederos (CUB) 0.00; **MVP**: Rodolfo Puente (CUB).

Cuba Roster: **Manager**: Servio Borges. **Batting** (AB, H, BA): Rodolfo Puente (21, 9, .429), Luis Pérez (27, 11, .407), Eulogio Osorio (5, 2, .400), Elpidio Mancebo (34, 13, .382), Wilfredo Sánchez (33, 12, .364), Raul Reyes (18, 6, .333), Owen Blandino (16, 5, .313), Félix Isasi (33, 9, .273), Urbano González (11, 3, .273), Antonio González (4, 1, .250), Rigoberto Rosique (33, 8, .242), Armando Capiró (23, 5, .217), Ramón Hechevarría (6, 1, .167), Vicente Díaz (17, 2, .118), José Antonio Huelga (5, 2, .400), Roberto Valdés (3, 1, .333), Antonio Jiménez (8, 2, .250), Santiago "Changa" Mederos (6, 1, .167), Oscar Romero (6, 0, .000), Rolando Macías (0, 0, .000). **Pitching** (W, L, ERA): Santiago "Changa" Mederos (2, 0, 0.00), Roberto Valdés (1, 0, 0.00), Antonio Jiménez (2, 0, 0.51), Oscar Romero (2, 0, 0.53), José Antonio Huelga (2, 0, 0.75), Rolando Macías (0, 0, 2.70).

Cuba Game Scores: Round-robin: Cuba beat Dominican Republic 16–2, Cuba beat Canada 4–0, Cuba beat Mexico 4–1, Cuba beat Panama 5–1, Cuba beat Puerto Rico 7–0, Cuba beat Nicaragua 2–0, Cuba beat Dutch Antilles 9–0, Cuba beat Italy 16–0, Cuba beat Colombia 3–0.

1972 Baseball World Cup XX (Managua, Nicaragua) (November 15–December 5)

Cuba wins for a fourth straight time over the largest field to date, with 16 nations competing in November at Managua. Braudilio Vinent was the pitching star, with a perfect 4–0 slate (0.62 ERA); Wilfredo Sánchez slugged at a .414 clip and Armando Capiró (making up for his slump a year earlier) knocked home 21 runs. Cuba's 5–3 victory over the United States accounted for the difference in the standings between the top two teams. The only loss suffered by the champions was a 2–0 whitewashing at the hands of Nicaragua. In an additional all-star contest matching the champion Cubans with top stars drawn from other participating nations, Cuba was again victorious, 6–0, with Vinent pitching an eight-hit complete-game victory and Armando Capiró slugging a three-run first-inning homer. The tournament also featured no-hitters by Puerto Rico's Sandalio Quiñónez (versus Costa Rica) and Panama's Ronaldo Montero (versus Germany).

Champion: Cuba (14–1)

Teams and Final Standings: Gold: Cuba (14–1), Silver: USA (13–2), Bronze: Nicaragua (13–2), Japan (11–4), Panama (10–5), Dominican Republic (9–6), Puerto Rico (9–6), Taiwan (9–6), Canada (8–7), Guatemala (5–10), Honduras (4–11), Brazil (4–11), Costa Rica (4–11), El Salvador (4–11), Italy (2–12), German Federal Republic (0–15).

All-Star Game (December 5, 1972): Cuba 6, World Cup All-Stars 0 (WP: Braudilio Vinent).

Individual Statistical Leaders: **BA**: Masaru Oba (JPN) .415; **Runs**: Wilfredo Sánchez (CUB) 22; **Hits**: Wilfredo Sánchez (CUB) 29; **2B**: Félix Isasi (CUB) 8; **3B**: Wilfredo Sánchez (CUB), Armando Capiró (CUB), Manuel Estrada (USA) 3; **HR**: René Mena (GUA) 4; **RBI**: Armando Capiró (CUB) 21; **SB**: Masaru Oba (JPN) 4; **Wins**: Jay Smith (USA), Richard Smith (USA), Braudilio Vinent (CUB) 4; **IP**: Tan Shing-Ming (TPE) 51.1; **Strikeouts**: Tan Shing-Ming (TPE) 53; **ERA**: Zengo Ikeda (JPN) 0.00.

Cuba Roster: **Manager**: Servio Borges. **Batting** (AB, H, BA): Evelio Hernández (20, 10, .500), Wilfredo Sánchez (77, 29, .414), Lázaro Pérez (34, 14, .412), Armando Capiró (61, 23, .377), Arturo Linares (14, 5, .357), Félix Isasi (55, 19, .345), Urbano González (38, 12, .316), Rodolfo Puente (42, 13, .310), Fermín Laffita (43, 13, .302), Rigoberto Rosique (31, 9, .290), Owen Blandino (33, 8, .240), Agustín Marquetti (54, 15, .278), Agustín Arias (19, 7, .368), Braudilio Vinent (8, 4, .500), Oscar Romero (4, 2, .500), Orlando Figueredo (10, 4, .400), Antonio Jiménez (8, 1, .125), Bernardo González (1, 0, 0.00), Santiago "Changa" Mederos (1, 0, .000), José Antonio Huelga (10, 1, .100). **Pitching** (W, L, ERA): Bernardo González (1, 0, 0.00), Santiago "Changa" Mederos (0, 0, 0.00), Braudilio Vinent (4, 0, 0.62), José Antonio Huelga (3, 1, 0.79), Orlando Figueredo (3, 0, 0.86), Oscar Romero (3, 0, 1.17), Antonio Jiménez (1, 0, 1.35).

Cuba Game Scores: Round-robin: Cuba beat Germany 10–0, Cuba beat Panama 13–2, Cuba beat Costa Rica 19–0, Cuba beat Brazil 13–3, Cuba beat Japan 2–0, Cuba beat Honduras 3–0, Cuba beat El Salvador 16–0, Cuba beat Puerto Rico 4–2, Cuba beat Chinese Taipei 10–1, Cuba beat Dominican Republic 14–0, Cuba beat Italy 19–1, Cuba beat Canada 5–1, Cuba beat USA 5–3, Cuba beat Guatemala 7–2, Nicaragua beat Cuba 2–0.

1973 Baseball World Cup XXI (Havana, Cuba) (November 25–December 9)

Another undefeated Cuban squad was one of the strongest ever in World Cup play, featuring a pitching staff that logged 110 consecutive innings without allowing a single earned run—Cuba was scored upon in only three of its fourteen outings. One highlight moment of this stellar two-week pitching performance came when Juan Pérez tossed a no-hitter against Venezuela, the first ever "perfecto" for Cuba in World Cup play. On the hitting front, Fermín Laffita smacked 2 homers in the same inning against Mexico, Marquetti collected the most base hits of the tournament, and three Cubans shared home run hitting honors. Despite these remarkable performances by Laffita and Pérez, it was the consistent Marquetti who walked off with the tournament MVP honors.

Champion: Cuba (14–0)

Teams and Final Standings: Gold: Cuba (14–0), Silver: Puerto Rico (10–3), Bronze: Venezuela (10–4), Dominican Republic (7–6), Panama (6–8), Mexico (5–9), Dutch Antilles (3–11), Netherlands (0–14).

Individual Statistical Leaders: **BA**: J. Fontánez (PUR) .432; **Runs**: Félix Isasi (CUB) 20; **Hits**: Agustín Marquetti (CUB) 25; **2B**: F. Rodríguez (MEX) 6; **HR**: Evelio Hernández (CUB), Armando Capiró (CUB), Félix Isasi (CUB) 3; **RBI**: Agustín Marquetti (CUB) 21; **SB**: Wilfredo Sánchez (CUB) 9; **Wins**: Julio Romero (CUB), Luis Barreiro (CUB), E. Ovalles (VEN) 3–0; **IP**: E. Ovalles (VEN) 27.0; **Strikeouts**: Luis Barreiro (CUB) 34; **ERA**: Julio Romero (CUB) 0.00; **MVP**: Agustín Marquetti (CUB).

Cuba Roster: **Manager**: Servio Borges. **Batting** (AB, H, BA): Evelio Hernández (21, 11, .524), Rigoberto Rosique (10, 5, .500), Agustín Marquetti (60, 25, .417), Rodolfo Puente (48, 17, .354), Armando Capiró (57, 21, .368), Lázaro Pérez (28, 9, .321), Wilfredo Sánchez (55, 20, .364), Félix Isasi (52, 17, .327), Julian Villar (21, 6, .286), Alfonso Urquiola (14, 4, .286), Ubaldo Alvarez (10, 2, .200), Alfredo García (7, 1, .143), Luis Barreiro (13, 3, .231), Julio Romero (13, 1, .077), Mario Fernández (4, 0, .000), Antonio Jiménez (5, 0, .000), Juan Pérez Pérez (5, 0, .000), Braudilio Vinent (2, 0, .000). **Pitching** (W, L, ERA): Julio Romero (3, 0, 0.00), Alfredo García (2, 0, 0.00), Antonio Jiménez (2, 0, 0.00), Luis Barreiro (3, 0, 0.00), Mario Fernández (2, 0, 0.00), Braudilio Vinent (1, 0, 0.00), Juan Pérez Pérez (1, 0, 0.95).

Cuba Game Scores: Round-robin: Cuba beat Dominican Republic 8–2, Cuba beat Mexico 7–0, Cuba beat Dutch Antilles 8–1, Cuba beat Netherlands 14–0, Cuba beat Venezuela 4–0 (no-hitter by Juan Pérez), Cuba beat Dominican Republic 11–0, Cuba beat Puerto Rico 10–0, Cuba beat Panama 8–0, Cuba beat Mexico 13–0, Cuba beat Dutch Antilles 7–0, Cuba beat Netherlands 7–0, Cuba beat Venezuela 6–0, Cuba beat Puerto Rico 3–2, Cuba beat Panama 13–0.

1973 Baseball World Cup (FEMBA) XXII (Managua, Nicaragua) (November 22–December 5)

Political infighting among members of amateur baseball's governing body, the International Baseball Federation (IBAF), leads to a meeting in Bologna, Italy, where delegates from 24 countries announce a rival organization, FEMBA (Federación Mundial de Béisbol Amateur; World Federation of Amateur Baseball). While FIBA holds its own 1973 tournament as scheduled in Havana, FEMBA also orchestrates a rival event in earthquake-devastated Nicaragua, with eleven countries participating. Team USA claims the FEMBA title, followed by Nicaragua in the runner-up slot. In the final game, Team USA clinches the trophy in a thrilling 1–0 pitchers duel between two future big leaguers, Dick Wortham (USA) and Dennis Martínez (Nicaragua).

Champion: USA (10–0)

Teams and Final Standings: Gold: USA (10–0), Silver: Nicaragua (8–2), Bronze: Puerto Rico (8–2), Colombia (7–3), Taiwan (7–3), Canada (4–6), Honduras (4–6), Costa Rica (3–7), Guatemala (3–7), Mexico (1–9), Germany (0–10).

Individual Statistical Leaders: No statistics are available from this tournament.

USA Game Scores: Double round-robin: USA beat Mexico 4–0, USA beat Germany 4–0, USA beat Chinese Taipei 4–2, USA beat Guatemala 4–0, USA beat Colombia 7–1, USA beat Canada 8–1, USA beat Puerto Rico 7–0, USA beat Costa Rica 9–0, USA beat Honduras 8–0, USA beat Nicaragua 1–0.

Cuba Did Not Participate

1974 Baseball World Cup (FEMBA) XXIII (St. Petersburg, Florida, USA) (September 13–23)

FEMBA member countries attempt a second alternative Amateur World Series (World Cup), this time staged in the United States, with the Americans again claiming a championship. Cuba remains on the sidelines until the next FIBA event scheduled for 1976 at Cartagena, Colombia. Subsequent World Cup tournaments sponsored by FIBA will recognize the two FEMBA tournaments as World Cup XXII and World Cup XXIII in order to preserve the consecutive numbering system already in use.

Champion: USA (9–1)

Teams and Final Standings: Gold: USA (7–0), Silver: Nicaragua (7–0), Bronze: Colombia (5–3), Canada (3–5), Italy (3–5), Chinese Taipei (3–5), Dominican Republic (3–5), Puerto Rico (3–5), South Africa (1–7). *USA defeated Nicaragua twice (5–4 and 9–2) in best-of-three championship playoff round.

Individual Statistical Leaders: **BA**: J. Cuaresma (COL) .470; **HR**: P. Llamas (COL), D. Comm (USA) 3; **RBI**: C. Jarquin (NCA) 10; **Wins**: Six pitchers with two wins each; **ERA**: P. Altamirano (NCA) 0.50. No additional player data or statistics are available, as all other records appear to be lost; spelling of names for non–Latin American players also are questionable.

USA Game Scores: Double round-robin: USA beat Mexico 4–0, USA beat Germany 4–0, USA beat Chinese Taipei 4–2, USA beat Guatemala 4–0, USA beat Colombia 7–1, USA beat Canada 8–1, USA beat Puerto Rico 7–0, USA beat Costa Rica 9–0, USA beat Honduras 8–0, USA beat Nicaragua 1–0.

Cuba Did Not Participate

1976 Baseball World Cup XXIV (Cartagena, Colombia) (December 3–19)

The world of amateur international baseball returns more or less to normal as FEMBA disbands and FIBA renews its series of tournaments held in alternate years. FIBA will henceforth be known as AINBA or IBA (International Association of Amateur Baseball). Normality also reigns on the playing field, with Cuba again a walk-away champion, although Cuba and Puerto Rico actually finish with identical 8–2 records and victory comes to the defending champs when Puerto Rico withdraws and forfeits its playoff-round contests. Armando Capiró and Agustín Marquetti are the big guns in the Cuban lineup and Omar Carrero logs four pitching victories.

Champion: Cuba (10–2)

Teams and Final Standings: Gold: Cuba (8–2), Silver: Puerto Rico (8–2), Bronze: Japan (7–3), Nicaragua (7–3), South Korea (5–5), Taiwan (5–5), Dominican Republic (5–5), Colombia (4–6), Panama (3–7), Mexico (2–8), Netherlands (1–9). *Cuba awarded gold medal with two forfeit victories over Puerto Rico in playoffs.

Individual Statistical Leaders: **BA**: Manuel Cabrejas (DOM) .521; **Runs**: Armando Capiró (CUB) 17; **Hits**: Manuel Cabrejas (DOM) 25; **2B**: Agustín Marquetti (CUB) 7; **3B**: Douglas Moody (NCA) 4; **HR**: Armando Capiró (CUB) 5; **RBI**: Agustín Marquetti (CUB) 20; **SB**: A. Rosario (DOM) 5; **Wins**: Omar Carrero (CUB) 4–0; **IP**: Omar Carrero (CUB) 29.2; **Strikeouts**: Kuo Yuan Chin (TPE) 41; **ERA**: J.L. de León (PUR) 0.00.

Cuba Roster: **Manager**: Servio Borges. **Batting** (AB, H, BA): Elpidio Osorio (9, 6, .667), Evelio Hernández (9, 9, .667), Agustín Marquetti (42, 21, .500), Rodolfo Puente (39, 18, .462), Armando Capiró (45, 19, .422), Lázaro Pérez (31, 12, .387), Wilfredo Sánchez (44, 17, .381), Pedro Jova (6, 2, .333), Bárbaro Garbey (18, 6, .333), Félix Isasi (16, 5, .313), Antonio Muñoz (26, 8, .308), Fermín Laffita (32, 9, .281), Rey Anglada (22, 5, .227), Pedro José Rodríguez (44, 9, .205). **Pitching** (W, L, ERA): Omar Carrero (4, 0, 0.61), Santiago "Changa" Mederos (1, 0, 1.80), Rogelio García (0, 1, 1.80), Braudilio Vinent (2, 1, .2.84), Oscar Romero (0, 0, 5.00), Julio Romero (1, 0, 6.75).

Cuba Game Scores: Round-robin: Cuba beat Netherlands 27–1, Cuba beat Mexico 15–1, Dominican Republic beat Cuba 13–12, Cuba beat Panama 7–3, Cuba beat Chinese Taipei 6–2, Cuba beat South Korea 13–2, Cuba beat Japan 4–0, Nicaragua beat Cuba 5–0, Cuba beat Puerto Rico 8–1, Cuba beat Colombia 7–5.

1978 Baseball World Cup XXV (Parma, Bologna and Rimini, Italy) (August 25–September 6)

World Cup play returns to Europe for the first time since the initial two-team event of 1938. Cuba once more outdistances the field, winning the crucial showdown match with Team USA. A pair of no-hitters are authored by César Monge of Nicaragua (against Belgium) and Yasuyuki Yamamoto of Japan (against the same hapless Belgians); both transpire in seven innings via the 10-run mercy rule. Australia and Belgium participate for the first time and finish in the final two spots in the standings. Antonio Muñoz establishes a new tournament record for home runs with eight; not surprisingly, he wears the crown as tournament MVP.

Champion: Cuba (10–0)

Teams and Final Standings: Gold: Cuba (10–0), Silver: USA (9–1), Bronze: South Korea (8–2), Japan (7–3), Nicaragua (5–5), Italy (5–5), Netherlands (4–6), Mexico (3–7), Canada (2–8), Australia (2–8), Belgium (0–10).

Individual Statistical Leaders: **BA**: Roberto Espino (NCA) .500; **Runs**: Antonio Muñoz (CUB), T. Wallace (USA) 14; **Hits**: Roberto Espino (NCA), Fernando Sánchez (CUB) 16; **2B**: Fernando Sánchez (CUB) 5; **3B**: J. Simon (USA), Terry Francona (USA) 2; **HR**: Antonio Muñoz (CUB) 8; **RBI**: Antonio Muñoz (CUB) 18; **SB**: M. Kobayashi (JPN) 13; **Wins**: Mori Shigekazu (JPN), D. Wong Choi (KOR) 4; **IP**: D. Wong Choi (KOR) 33.1; **Strikeouts**: D. Wong Choi (KOR) 44; **ERA**: M. Thurman (USA) 0.00; **MVP**: Antonio Muñoz (CUB).

Cuba Roster: **Manager**: Servio Borges. **Batting** (AB, H, BA): Agustín Marquetti (20, 9, .450), Luis Casanova (36, 16, .444), Fernando Sánchez (37, 16, .432), Pedro Jova (19, 8, .421), Antonio Muñoz (32, 13, .406), Pedro Medina (19, 6, .316), Rodolfo Puente (36, 13, .361), Alfonso Urquiola (37, 11, .297), Armando Capiró (28, 9, .321), Wilfredo Sánchez (17, 4, .235), Pedro José Rodríguez (37, 8, .216), Alfonso Martínez (13, 2, .154), Rey Anglada (1, 0, .000). **Pitching** (W, L, ERA): Rogelio García (1, 0, 0.00), Juan Carlos Oliva (2, 0, 0.00), Omar Carrero (0, 0, 0.00), Lázaro Santana (2, 0, 0.69), Julio Romero (1, 0, 1.00), Braudilio Vinent (3, 0, 1.80), Félix Pino (1, 0, 2.70).

Cuba Game Scores: Round-robin: Cuba beat Italy 6–0, Cuba beat Japan 3–2, Cuba beat Australia 10–3, Cuba beat Nicaragua 7–2, Cuba beat Canada 5–1, Cuba beat Netherlands 12–1, Cuba beat USA 5–3, Cuba beat Mexico 11–1, Cuba beat Belgium 16–0, Cuba beat South Korea 11–0.

1980 Baseball World Cup XXVI (Tokyo, Japan) (August 22–September 5)

Servio Borges serves as World Cup winning manager for the eighth time (without defeat), a record that will likely stand for decades. Lourdes Gourriel again proved his mettle during international competition with a game-winning hit in the showdown with Team USA, but the Cubans were rarely challenged in sweeping through eleven games without defeat. This was the first tournament staged in Asia, and Japanese fans had plenty to cheer about with the host country and Korea both winning nine games apiece. Antonio Muñoz again hit over .400 and again locked up MVP honors, tying teammate Gourriel for the home run crown. Braudilio Vinent anchored the pitching corps with three more victories in his penultimate World Cup tournament appearance.

Champion: Cuba (11–0)

Teams and Final Standings: Gold: Cuba (11–0), Silver: South Korea (9–2), Bronze: Japan (9–2), USA (8–3), Canada (6–5), Italy (5–6), Venezuela (4–7), Puerto Rico (4–7), Colombia (4–7), Australia (4–7), Mexico (1–10), Netherlands (1–10).

Individual Statistical Leaders: **BA**: Eusebio Moreno (COL) .448; **Runs**: Kim Kwon (KOR) 18; **Hits**: Fernando Sánchez (CUB) 21; **2B**: Stan Edmonds (USA) 6; **3B**: A. Romero (USA) 3; **HR**: Antonio Muñoz (CUB), Luis Casanova (CUB) 7; **RBI**: Antonio Muñoz (CUB) 19; **SB**: Kim Kwon (KOR) 18; **Wins**: Lee Sung Hee (KOR) 4; **IP**: Lee Sung Hee (KOR) 40.1; **Strikeouts**: Choi Dong Won (KOR) 43; **ERA**: José Luis Alemán (CUB) 0.00; **MVP**: Antonio Muñoz (CUB).

Cuba Roster: **Manager**: Servio Borges. **Batting** (AB, H, BA): Alfonso Martínez (9, 7, .778), Carmelo Pedroso (12, 6, .500), Lourdes Gourriel (42, 19, .452), Pedro Medina (31, 14,

.452), Fernando Sánchez (47, 21, .447), Alfonso Urquiola (32, 13, .406), Antonio Muñoz (45, 18, .400), Luis Casanova (47, 17, .362), Rodolfo Puente (36, 13, .361), Héctor Olivera (26, 9, .346), Pedro Jova (18, 6, .333), Pedro José Rodríguez (46, 13, .263), Wilfredo Sánchez (8, 2, .250). **Pitching** (W, L, ERA): José Luis Alemán (2, 0, 0.00), Félix Pino (0, 0, 0.00), Jesús Guerra (1, 0, 1.33), Braudilio Vinent (3, 0, 1.38), José Darcourt (2, 0, 2.16), Julio Romero (1, 0, 2.45), Juan Carlos Oliva (2, 0, 3.24).

Cuba Game Scores: Round-robin: Cuba beat Italy 10–2, Cuba beat Puerto Rico 23–1, Cuba beat Australia 3–1, Cuba beat Colombia 25–0, Cuba beat Canada 15–1, Cuba beat Venezuela 11–3, Cuba beat South Korea 9–3, Cuba beat Mexico 10–0, Cuba beat Netherlands 8–0, Cuba beat Japan 1–0, Cuba beat USA 5–4.

1982 Baseball World Cup XXVII (Seoul, South Korea) (August)

Cuba remains on the sidelines while South Korea hosts and wins the second straight World Cup staged in the Orient. Japanese, Taiwanese, and Korean hitters and pitchers also thoroughly dominate the individual tournament leaders lists. For only the third time in thirty years (not counting the two FEMBA events), a team other than Cuba celebrates a championship. Cuba will win all the remaining World Cup tournaments of the twentieth century (eight straight, beginning in 1984 and extending through 2003).

Champion: South Korea (8–1)

Teams and Final Standings: Gold: South Korea (8–1), Silver: Japan (7–2), Bronze: USA (6–3), Chinese Taipei (6–3), Canada (5–4), Netherlands (3–6), Panama (3–6), Dominican Republic (3–6), Italy (2–7), Australia (2–7).

Individual Statistical Leaders: **BA**: Chen Sin Chang (TPE) .531; **Runs**: R. Cobb (USA) 10; **Hits**: Chen Sin Chang (TPE) 17; **2B**: Chen Sin Chang (TPE) 7; **3B**: four players with three each; **HR**: K. Takssue (JPN) 4; **RBI**: K. Takssue (JPN) 18; **SB**: M. Kobayashi (JPN) 7; **ERA**: Sun Dong Yul (KOR) 0.00; **MVP**: Sun Dong Yul (KOR). No additional player data or statistics are available, as all other records appear to be lost; spelling of names for non–Latin American players are also questionable.

South Korea Game Scores: Double round-robin: Italy beat Korea 2–1, Korea beat USA 2–1, Korea beat Netherlands 11–0, Korea beat Chinese Taipei 6–0, Korea beat Panama 4–2, Korea beat Canada 5–1, Korea beat Dominican Republic 3–0, Korea beat Australia 7–6, Korea beat Japan 5–2.

Cuba Did Not Participate

1984 Baseball World Cup XXVIII (Havana, Cuba) (October 14–28)

The first World Cup Series held in Cuba in eleven years is surrounded with expected propaganda and pageantry as Fidel Castro visits opening game festivities with West German president Willie Brandt. Ceremonies honor Cuba's legendary nineteenth-century players, and 1950s-era star Connie Marrero throws a ceremonial first pitch to postrevolution Cuban League legend Rodolfo Puente. Key hits by Lourdes Gourriel and Alfonso Urquiola avoid a potentially embarrassing opening round loss to Italy, and Cuba then rolls to its seventeenth world title and the first of what will eventually become the current string of seven straight. Victor Mesa was the MVP. Early shaky pitching was quickly corrected, with Romero, Costa, and Valdés all posting perfect 3–0 records. Future major league home run king Barry Bonds played for the third-place U.S. squad as a skinny 19-year-old outfielder.

Champion: Cuba (11–2)

Teams and Final Standings: Gold: Cuba (11–2), Silver: Chinese Taipei (7–5), Bronze: USA (8–4), Japan (8–5), Panama (7–5), Venezuela (6–4), Puerto Rico (6–7), South Korea (5–7), Nicaragua (5–8), Dutch Antilles (4–6), Dominican Republic (3–6), Italy (3–7), Netherlands (1–8).

Individual Statistical Leaders: **BA**: Victor Mesa (CUB) .475; **Runs**: Victor Mesa (CUB) 17; **Hits**: Victor Mesa (CUB) 28; **2B**: Lourdes Gourriel (CUB) 7; **3B**: four players with two each; **HR**: Pedro José Rodríguez (CUB), Luis Casanova (CUB) 6; **RBI**: Lourdes Gourriel (CUB), Barry Bonds (USA) 16; **SB**: Victor Mesa (CUB) 8; **Wins**: H. Nagatomi (JPN), J. Moya (NCA) 4; **ERA**: S. Deng Ryeul (KOR) 0.00; **MVP**: Victor Mesa (CUB).

Cuba Roster: **Manager**: Pedro Chávez. **Batting** (AB, H, BA): Juan Castro (31, 14, .452), Alfonso Martínez (16, 4, .250), Pedro Medina (25, 5, .200), Alfonso Urquiola (49, 22, .449), Antonio Muñoz (33, 14, .424), Pedro José Rodríguez (49, 11, .229), Antonio Pacheco (35, 15, .429), Pedro Jova (25, 6, .240), Rolando Verde (4, 0, .000), Lourdes Gourriel (55, 17, .309), Victor Mesa (59, 28, .475), Luis Casanova (55, 20, .364), Lázaro Junco (40, 15, .375). **Pitching** (W, L, ERA): Julio Romero (3, 0, 2.03), Rogelio García (0, 1, 4.61), Reinaldo Costa (3, 0, 1.65), Jorge Luis Valdés (3, 0, 2.21), Braudilio Vinent (1, 0, 6.97), José Sánchez (0, 0, 16.00), Ángel Leocadio Diaz (1, 1, 2.89).

Cuba Game Scores: Qualifying Round: Cuba beat Italy 6–5, Puerto Rico beat Cuba 5–4, Cuba beat Venezuela 13–0, Cuba beat Dutch Antilles 9–2, Cuba beat Nicaragua 10–0, Cuba beat Japan 3–1. Finals: Cuba beat Panama 10–6, Cuba beat South Korea 5–0, Cuba beat Japan 14–4, Cuba beat Nicaragua 16–7, Chinese Taipei beat Cuba 7–4, Cuba beat Puerto Rico 7–5, Cuba beat USA 10–1.

1986 Baseball World Cup XXIX (Haarlem, The Netherlands) (July 19–August 2)

Nineties-era heroes Linares and Kindelán appear in their first World Cup with this transitional Cuban team that also features Victor Mesa and Luis Casanova, two celebrated Cuban sluggers of the mid-1980s. This is the final national team managed by Pedro Chávez before Jorge Fuentes arrives on the scene. Casanova captures his second of three straight home run crowns in the "Mundiales," and Mesa, Pacheco, and Linares all bat above .500 for the tournament. Pablo Miguel Abreu is the Cuban ace with three wins, and future big leaguer René Arocha also pockets two victories.

Champion: Cuba (10–1)

Teams and Final Standings: Gold: Cuba (10–1), Silver: South Korea (8–3), Bronze: Chinese Taipei (8–3), USA (7–4), Japan (6–5), Italy (6–5), Puerto Rico (5–6), Venezuela (5–6), Netherlands (5–6), Colombia (3–8), Dutch Antilles (2–9), Belgium (1–10).

Individual Statistical Leaders: **BA**: G. Carelli (ITA) .478; **Runs**: R. Biachi (ITA) 18; **Hits**: G. Carelli (ITA) 22; **2B**: R. Chung (KOR) 8; **3B**: M. Fujoshi (JPN) 3; **HR**: Luis Casanova (CUB) 6; **SB**: R. Santana (PUR) 6; **Wins**: Pablo Miguel Abreu (CUB), P. Dong Hec (KOR) 3; **ERA**: K. Ming Shan (TPE) 0.35. No additional statistics available.

Cuba Roster: **Manager**: Pedro Chávez. **Batting** (AB, H, BA): Victor Mesa (44, 18, .409), Antonio Pacheco (46, 21, .457), Omar Linares (46, 21, .457), Orestes Kindelán (46, 18, .391), Luis Casanova (44, 18, .409), Lourdes Gourriel (42, 15, .357), Antonio Muñoz (39, 15, .385), Juan Castro (23, 7, .304), Luis Ulacia (39, 13, .333), Pedro Medina (8, 2, .250), Jorge García (2, 1, .500), Juan Padilla (3, 2, .667), Lázaro Vargas (3, 1, .333). **Pitching** (W, L, ERA): Pablo Miguel Abreu (3, 1, 1.55), Omar Carrero (1, 0, 0.00), Félix Nuñez (1, 0, 3.68), Jorge Luis Valdés (1, 0, 0.00), René Arocha (2, 0, 2.13), Luis Tissert (1, 0, 1.35), Rogelio García (1, 0, 2.25).

Cuba Game Scores: Round-robin: Cuba beat Puerto Rico 11–1, Cuba beat Dutch Antilles 15–3, Cuba beat Colombia 11–0, Cuba beat USA 11–0, Cuba beat Netherlands 12–1, Cuba beat Venezuela 9–3, Cuba beat Belgium 21–3, Cuba beat South Korea 10–2, Cuba beat Italy 15–5, Cuba beat Japan 4–2, Chinese Taipei beat Cuba 4–3.

1988 Baseball World Cup XXX (Parma and Rimini, Italy) (August 23–September 7)

Future major league all-star Robin Ventura swung a big bat for the United States and led the field in several power-hitting categories. Another future big leaguer of note,

Tino Martínez, also swung a heavy stick for the Americans, and Ben McDonald (a rookie with the Orioles the next spring) was the tournament's most outstanding pitcher. Jim Abbott was another hurler on one of the strongest-ever U.S. contingents. But Cuba remains undefeated with a gold medal victory over talent-laden Team USA. Despite the likes of Ventura and Martínez, it is Antonio Pacheco of Cuba who turns the most heads by leading in hitting and earning a selection as the tourney's top defensive performer. Cuba would avoid another showdown with nearly the same U.S. squad by conveniently boycotting the demonstration baseball tournament held at the Olympic Games in Seoul, South Korea, later this same year.

Champion: Cuba (13–0)

Finals: Cuba beat USA 4–3 (Gold Medal), Chinese Taipei beat Japan 4–2 (Bronze Medal).

Semifinals: Cuba beat Japan 7–3, USA beat Chinese Taipei 6–3.

Preliminary Round Standings: Cuba (11–0), USA (10–1), Chinese Taipei (8–3), Japan (7–4), Canada (7–4), Puerto Rico (6–5), Nicaragua (5–6), South Korea (5–6), Italy (4–7), Netherlands (2–9), Dutch Antilles (1–10), Spain (0–11).

Individual Statistical Leaders: **BA**: Antonio Pacheco (CUB) .500; **Runs**: Omar Linares (CUB), T. Griffith (USA) 17; **Hits**: Antonio Pacheco (CUB) 21; **2B**: Robin Ventura (USA) 8; **3B**: J. Kokas (CAN), T. Kajima (JPN) 3; **HR**: Luis Casanova (CUB) 7; **RBI**: Robin Ventura (USA) 28; **SB**: J. Medina (NCA), K. Tomashino (JPN) 6; **Wins**: four pitchers with three each; **ERA**: Ben McDonald (USA) 0.00; **MVP**: Tino Martínez (USA).

Cuba Roster: **Manager**: Jorge Fuentes. **Batting** (AB, H, BA): Antonio Pacheco (42, 21, .500), Lourdes Gourriel (26, 13, .500), Luis Casanova (43, 18, .419), Luis Ulacia (37, 14, .378), Omar Linares (47, 17, .362), Victor Mesa (40, 14, .350), Ermidelio Urrutia (30, 10, .333), Alejo O'Reilly (35, 11, .314), Orestes Kindelán (44, 13, .295), Pedro Luis Rodríguez (26, 13, .500), Juan Castro (13, 3, .231), Juan Padilla (6, 1, .167), Lázaro Vargas (15, 4, .267). **Pitching** (W, L, ERA): Lázaro Valle (2, 0, 1.50), Omar Ajete (1, 0, 2.07), Jorge Luis Valdés (1, 0, 4.36), José Luis Aleman (2, 0, 2.59), René Arocha (1, 0, 6.56), Orlando Hernández (1, 0, 5.19), Euclides Rojas (3, 0, 0.93).

Cuba Game Scores: Preliminary Round: Cuba beat Italy 11–1, Cuba beat South Korea 9–5, Cuba beat Canada 18–0, Cuba beat Chinese Taipei 7–3, Cuba beat Spain 11–0, Cuba beat Puerto Rico 7–6, Cuba beat Dutch Antilles 10–3, Cuba beat Japan 3–2, Cuba beat Nicaragua 11–1, Cuba beat Netherlands 15–5, Cuba beat USA 10–9. Playoffs: Cuba beat Dominican Republic 3–2. Semifinals: Cuba beat Japan 7–3. Finals: Cuba beat USA 4–3.

1990 Baseball World Cup XXXI (Edmonton, Canada) (August 4–19)

Orestes Kindelán was the tournament's hitting star as he rang up a triple crown with the leadership in homers and RBI and also a spot as champion batter. An easy team victory was the fourth straight World Cup Series success for Team Cuba in a string that now stretches through seven tournaments dating back to 1984 (a period in which Cuba has lost only four individual games of seventy-seven played). This was perhaps Cuba's easiest international victory ever, with runner-up Nicaragua winning only half as many games and with little serious challenge from the usual rivals Puerto Rico, Japan, and Team USA. A dozen Cuban players bat above .333, and Lázaro Valle is virtually unhittable in his three tournament pitching starts.

Champion: Cuba (10–0)

Teams and Final Standings: Gold: Cuba (10–0), Silver: Nicaragua (5–5), Bronze: South Korea (5–4), Puerto Rico (7–2), Japan (6–3), USA (5–4), Chinese Taipei (4–5), Netherlands (3–5), Italy (3–5), Mexico (2–6), Canada (2–7), Venezuela (1–7).

Individual Statistical Leaders: **BA**: Orestes Kindelán (CUB) .581; **Runs**: Orestes Kindelán (CUB) 23; **Hits**: Orestes Kindelán (CUB) 25; **2B**: Orestes Kindelán (CUB) 7; **3B**: five players with three each; **HR**: Orestes Kindelán (CUB) 9; **RBI**: Orestes Kindelán (CUB) 25; **SB**: M. Naito (JPN) 6; **Wins**: Lee Chien Fu (TPE) 4; **ERA**: Lázaro Valle (CUB) 0.00; **MVP**: Orestes Kindelán (CUB).

Cuba Roster: **Manager**: Jorge Fuentes. **Batting** (AB, H, BA): Pedro Luis Rodríguez (29, 10, .345), Alberto Hernández (3, 1, .333), Antonio Pacheco (37, 13, .351), Omar Linares (32, 18, .563), Luis Ulacia (8, 2, .250), Juan Padilla (2, 1, .500), Germán Mesa (32, 16, .500), Orestes Kindelán (34, 20, .588), Lourdes Gourriel (33, 17, .515), Victor Mesa (33, 13, .394), Javier Méndez (23, 8, .348), Luis Casanova (13, 6, .462), Ermidelio Urrutia (23, 9, .391). **Pitching** (W, L, ERA): Jorge Luis Valdés (2, 0, 3.95), Omar Ajete (2, 0, 0.64), Osvaldo Fernández Rodríguez (2, 0, 0.95), Lázaro Valle (3, 0, 0.00), Orlando Hernández (0, 0, 0.00), Euclides Rojas (1, 0, 0.00), Reinaldo Santana (0, 0, 4.50).

Cuba Game Scores: Qualifying Round: Cuba beat Italy 18–2, Cuba beat Nicaragua 7–3, Cuba beat South Korea 26–1, Cuba beat Mexico 11–0, Cuba beat Japan 8–2, Cuba beat Chinese Taipei 16–3, Cuba beat South Korea 5–1, Cuba beat USA 23–1. Playoffs: Cuba beat Nicaragua 14–0, Cuba beat Nicaragua 11–5.

1994 Baseball World Cup XXXII (Managua, Nicaragua) (August 3–14)

Again Cuba finishes undefeated and largely unchallenged in a tournament featuring the hitting of Lourdes Gourriel, Ermidelio Urrutia, Kindelán, and Pacheco and the pitching of a balanced staff that included four future major leaguers (Liván Hernández, Orlando Hernández, Osvaldo Fernández, and Rolando Arrojo). It was the third World Series title for manager Jorge Fuentes and the fourth straight for Cuban teams boasting Linares and Kindelán in the lineup. At the halfway point between the Barcelona and Atlanta Olympics, the Cubans again looked as invincible as ever. They had now not lost a single World Cup ball game since eight years earlier in Haarlem.

Champion: Cuba (10–0)

Finals: Cuba beat South Korea 6–1 (Gold Medal), Japan beat Nicaragua 8–1 (Bronze Medal).

Semifinals: Cuba beat Nicaragua 13–1, South Korea beat Japan 9–0.

Quarterfinals: Cuba beat USA 15–2, Japan beat Chinese Taipei 6–5, Nicaragua beat Panama 10–4, South Korea beat Italy 13–2.

Group A Preliminary Round: Cuba (7–0), Nicaragua (6–1), Italy (4–3), Chinese Taipei (4–3), Australia (3–4), Colombia (2–5), Dominican Republic (2–5), France (0–7).

Group B Preliminary Round: Japan (6–1), South Korea (5–2), Panama (5–2), USA (4–3), Netherlands (3–4), Puerto Rico (3–4), Sweden (1–6), Canada (1–6).

Individual Statistical Leaders: **BA**: Ermidelio Urrutia (CUB) .667; **Runs**: Lourdes Gourriel (CUB) 13; **Hits**: Lourdes Gourriel (CUB), Omar Linares (CUB), D. López (COL) 15; **2B**: G. Jenkins (USA), H. Park (KOR), H.M. Matsumoto (JPN) 4; **3B**: I. Ho (TPE), Lourdes Gourriel (CUB), R. Hunter (NCA) 2; **HR**: Orestes Kindelán (CUB) 5; **RBI**: Antonio Pacheco (CUB) 13; **SB**: S. Moreno (NCA) 5; **Wins**: several pitchers with two each; **ERA**: M. Santana (DOM), 0.00; **MVP**: Lourdes Gourriel (CUB).

Cuba Roster: **Manager**: Jorge Fuentes. **Batting** (AB, H, BA): Alberto Hernández (21, 6, .286), Antonio Pacheco (31, 11, .355), Eduardo Paret (1, 0, .000), Ermidelio Urrutia (21, 14, .667), Germán Mesa (24, 10, .417), Jorge Luis Toca (3, 2, .667), José Estrada (26, 8, .308), Juan Carlos Linares (8, 1, .125), Juan Manrique (2, 0, .000), Juan Padilla (1, 0, .000), Lourdes Gourriel (30, 15, .500), Omar Linares (30, 15, .500), Orestes Kindelán (26, 11, .423), Pedro Luis Rodríguez (4, 2, .500), Victor Mesa (32, 7, .219). **Pitching** (W, L, ERA): Faustino Corrales (1, 0, 1.80), Lázaro Valle (1, 0, 0.00), Liván Hernández (1, 0, 0.00), Omar Ajete (0, 0, 0.00), Orlando Hernández (1, 0, 0.00), Osvaldo Fernández Rodríguez (2, 0, .150), Luis Rolando Arrojo (1, 0, 1.80).

Cuba Game Scores: Preliminary Round: Cuba beat France 24–0, Cuba beat Colombia 7–1, Cuba beat Italy 14–1, Cuba beat Dominican Republic 12–0, Cuba beat Chinese Taipei

7–1, Cuba beat Nicaragua 12–1, Cuba beat Australia 7–3. Quarterfinals: Cuba beat USA 15–2. Semifinals: Cuba beat Nicaragua 13–1. Finals: Cuba beat South Korea 6–1.

1998 Baseball World Cup XXXIII (Parma and Rome, Italy) (July 22–August 2)

Cuba captured its twenty-second overall world title and sixth in a row by breezing undefeated through ten games in Italy in late July. The victory string also stretched out to 41 straight games for the Cubans, who have now not lost a single World Cup Series contest since the 1986 event in Holland. This time the victim in the gold medal game was South Korea, by a lopsided 7–1 score. José Contreras (who didn't allow a single earned run during his two outings) went the distance in the finale, striking out thirteen and tossing a five-hitter. The other medal-round contests were even more lopsided routs for the champions: 14–2 over Nicaragua in the semifinals and 12–1 over The Netherlands in the quarterfinals match-up. Although this World Cup tournament was for the first time open to professional ballplayers, no major leaguers performed and the only competing teams with professionals (minor leaguers in this case) on their rosters were Panama and the Dominican Republic.

Champion: Cuba (10–0)

Finals: Cuba beat South Korea 7–1 (Gold Medal), Nicaragua beat Italy 5–1 (Bronze Medal).

Semifinals: Cuba beat Nicaragua 14–2, South Korea beat Italy 8–2.

Quarterfinals: Cuba beat Netherlands 12–1, Italy beat Australia 9–8, Nicaragua beat Dominican Republic 12–4, South Korea beat Japan 8–5.

Group A Preliminary Round: Cuba (7–0), Japan (6–1), Dominican Republic (5–2), Italy (3–4), Panama (3–4), Spain (2–5), China (2–5), South Africa (0–7).

Group B Preliminary Round: Nicaragua (5–2), Australia (5–2), South Korea (4–3), USA (4–3), Netherlands (4–3), Chinese Taipei (3–4), Canada (3–4), Russia (0–7).

Individual Statistical Leaders: **BA**: Orestes Kindelán (CUB) .560; **Runs**: Robelquis Videaux (CUB) 15; **Hits**: Robelquis Videaux (CUB), R. Padilla (NCA) 15; **2B**: R. Padilla (NCA), Sh. Abe (JPN) 5; **3B**: G. Cibati (ITA) 3; **HR**: F. Chon Chin (TPE) 5; **RBI**: Antonio Pacheco (CUB) 14; **SB**: D. Rigol (ITA) 5; **Wins**: several pitchers with two each; **IP**: E. Yano (JPN) 18.0; **ERA**: José Ariel Contreras (CUB), D. Ricci (ITA) 0.00.

Cuba Roster: **Manager**: Alfonso Urquiola. **Batting** (AB, H, BA): Ariel Benavides (8, 2, .250), Robelquis Videaux (31, 15, .484), Danel Castro (21, 9, .429), Loidel Chapelli (27, 12, .444), Orestes Kindelán (25, 14, .560), Omar Linares (22, 11, .500), Oscar Machado (24, 10, .417), Oscar Macías (3, 0, .000), Yosvany Madera (10, 4, .400), Juan Manrique (17, 9, .529), Javier Méndez (3, 1, .333), Juan Carlos Moreno (7, 2, .286), Antonio Pacheco (25, 11, .440), Gabriel Pierre (8, 3, .375), Carlos Tabares (30, 10, .333). **Pitching** (W, L, ERA): Yovani Aragón (2, 0, 1.13), José Ariel Contreras (2, 0, 0.00), José Ibar (2, 0, 2.25), Pedro Luis Lazo (2, 0, 0.00), Omar Luis (1, 0, 1.08), Walberto Quesada (0, 0, 0.00), Norge Vera (1, 0, 4.70).

Cuba Game Scores: Preliminary Round: Cuba beat Spain 14–2, Cuba beat South Africa 14–1, Cuba beat Italy 20–0, Cuba beat Japan 9–0, Cuba beat China 10–0, Cuba beat Dominican Republic 9–2, Cuba beat Panama 8–5. Quarterfinals: Cuba beat Netherlands 12–1. Semifinals: Cuba beat Nicaragua 14–2. Finals: Cuba beat South Korea 7–1.

2001 Baseball World Cup XXXIV (Taipei, Taiwan) (November 6–17)

The uninterrupted string of World Cup victories continued for Cuba with their seventh straight crown and twenty-third title in twenty-six tournaments entered. Veteran outfielder Luis Ulacia—likely making his final appearance for Team Cuba—was the undisputed series hero, with a remarkable .512 batting average and tourney MVP honors to his credit. Championship victory came with an emotional 5–3 defeat of Team USA in the gold medal showdown, with unheralded Camagüeyano Vicyohandri Odelín pitching brilliantly in relief of starter José Ibar. This was the second championship victory in three years against U.S. squads using major league and minor league professional players. Again (as in the Sydney Olympics) José Contreras was selected for the crucial semifinal outing versus Japan; he fanned eleven in a tight eleven-inning 3–1 victory. Norge Vera and Ciro Silvino Licea pitched brilliantly as well, in two outings apiece. Veteran stars Omar Linares, Antonio Pacheco, Orestes Kindelán, and Germán Mesa appeared in what seemed likely to be their final time in international tournament play.

Champion: Cuba (9–1)

Finals: Cuba beat USA 5–3 (Gold Medal), Chinese Taipei beat Japan 3–0 (Bronze Medal).

Semifinals: Cuba beat Japan 3–1, USA beat Chinese Taipei 4–1.

Quarterfinals: Cuba beat Dominican Republic 3–1, USA beat Panama 7–2, Chinese Taipei beat Netherlands 2–0, Japan beat South Korea 3–1.

Group A Preliminary Round: Chinese Taipei (6–1), South Korea (5–2), USA (5–2), Dominican Republic (5–2), Nicaragua (4–3), Italy (2–5), South Africa (1–6), France (0–7).

Group B Preliminary Round: Japan (7–0), Cuba (6–1), Panama (5–2), Netherlands (4–3), Australia (3–4), Canada (2–5), Russia (1–6), Philippines (0–7).

Individual Statistical Leaders: **BA**: Luis Ulacia (CUB) .512; **Runs**: Yoshinobu Takahashi (JPN) 10; **Hits**: Luis Ulacia (CUB) 18; **2B**: Hae Young Ma (KOR) 5; **3B**: Chin Feng Cheng (TPE) 4; **HR**: Evert-Jan T. Hoen (NET) 3; **RBI**: Chin Feng Cheng (TPE), Jayane Valera (DOM) 11; **SB**: Ralph Milliard (NET) 7; **Wins**: Chin Chia Chang (TPE) 3–0; **ERA**: Samuel Meaurant (FRA) 0.00; **MVP**: Luis Ulacia (CUB). Statistics do not include medal round games.

Cuba Roster: **Manager**: Higinio Vélez. **Batting** (AB, H, BA): Luis Ulacia (43, 22, .512), Antonio Scull (8, 4, .500), Orestes Kindelán (33, 12, .364), Michel Enríquez (28, 10, .357), Antonio Pacheco (34, 12, .353), Giorvis Duvergel (6, 2, .333), Yobal Dueñas (21, 7, .333), Omar Linares (25, 8, .320), Rolando Meriño (13, 4, .308), Yasser Gómez (25, 6, .240), Ariel Pestano (21, 5, .238), Eduardo Paret (13, 3, .231), Germán Mesa (19, 4, .211), Oscar Macías (29, 6, .207), José Estrada (6, 1, .167), Osmani Urrutia (13, 1, .077). **Pitching** (W, L, ERA): Ciro Silvino Licea (2, 0, 0.00), José Ariel Contreras (2, 0, 0.00), Norge Vera (2, 0, 0.47), Vicyohandri Odelín (1, 0, 0.79), Pedro Luis Lazo (2, 0, 1.08), Lamey de la Rosa (0, 0, 4.50), Maels Rodríguez (0, 0, 4.66), José Ibar (0, 1, 6.75).

Cuba Game Scores: Preliminary Round: Cuba beat Canada 1–0, Cuba beat Philippines 17–0, Cuba beat Australia 9–5, Japan beat Cuba 5–3, Cuba beat Panama 8–0, Cuba beat Netherlands 6–2, Cuba beat Russia 11–1. Quarterfinals: Cuba beat Dominican Republic 3–1. Semifinals: Cuba beat Japan 3–1. Finals: Cuba beat USA 5–3.

2003 Baseball World Cup XXXV (Havana, Cuba) (October 12–25)

Back on home turf for the first time since 1984, Cuba's impressive juggernaut ran its record of uninterrupted World Cup titles to eight straight, posting a fifth unblemished record over that stretch. The impressive home field performance came against a backdrop of defections by a pair of top Team Cuba stars—fastballing pitcher Maels Rodríguez and slugging outfielder Yobal Dueñas. Tournament highlight moments were a dramatic game-saving ninth-inning homer by Kendry Morales during the quarterfinal round, a pair of important solo round-trippers by Frederich Cepeda in the title showdown with Panama, and the record-setting clutch pitching of veteran ace Norge Vera. Morales's blast saved Cuba from disaster against upstart Brazil and their ace pitcher, Kleber Tomita. Cepeda starred alongside youngsters Morales and Yulieski Gourriel in a Cuban lineup that averaged but 22 years of age. Vera became the first pitcher in World Cup history to post wins (with two stellar seven-inning outings) in both the semifinal and final games. With Pan American and Asia Pre-Olympic Qualifying tournaments scheduled for the following week, traditional powerhouses Japan, South Korea, Canada, and the United States sent B-level squads to Havana; nevertheless Cuba's victory in the finals came against a Panama team that featured seven players in its lineup boasting previous major league experience.

Champion: Cuba (9–0)

Finals: Cuba beat Panama 4–2 (Gold Medal), Japan beat Chinese Taipei 7–3 (Bronze Medal).

Semifinals: Cuba beat Chinese Taipei 6–3, Panama beat Japan 4–1.

Quarterfinals: Cuba beat Brazil 4–3, Chinese Taipei beat USA 2–1, Panama beat Nicaragua 5–0, Japan beat Korea 2–0.

Group A Preliminary Round: Cuba (6–0), Nicaragua (4–2), Chinese Taipei (3–3), South Korea (3–3), Canada (3–3), Italy (1–5), Russia (1–5).

Group B Preliminary Round: Japan (7–0), USA (5–1), Panama (5–2), Brazil (4–3), Netherlands (3–3), Mexico (2–5), China (1–6), France (0–7).

Individual Statistical Leaders: **BA**: Michel Enríquez (CUB) .571; **Runs**: Omar Moreno (PAN) 11; **Hits**: Michel Enríquez (CUB) 12; **2B**: Akihide Shimuzu (JPN) 5; **3B**: 15 players with 1 each; **HR**: Takashi Yoshiura (JPN) 5; **RBI**: Takashi Yoshiura (JPN) 16; **SB**: Eduardo Paret (CUB) 7; **Wins**: 7 pitchers with 2 each; **ERA**: Vichohandri Odelín (CUB) 0.00; **MVP**: Takashi Yoshiura (JPN). Statistics do not include medal round games.

Cuba Roster: **Manager**: Higinio Vélez. **Batting** (AB, H, BA): Ariel Pestano (23, 4, .174), Roger Machado (5, 1, .200), Eriel Sánchez (1, 0, .000), Joan Carlos Pedroso (2, 1, .500), Kendry Morales (34, 9, .265), Yulieski Gourriel (38, 14, .368), Eduardo Paret (30, 10, .333), Danel Castro (25, 7, .280), Michel Enríquez (33, 14, .424), Yorelvis Charles (1, 0, .000), Ariel Benavides (3, 1, .333), Osmani Urrutia (23, 7, .304), Carlos Tabares (23, 11, .478), Robelquis Videaux (16, 1, .063), Frederich Cepeda (32, 13, .406). **Pitching** (W, L, ERA): Adiel Palma (1, 0, 0.00), Vicyohandri Odelín (1, 0, 2.12), Yadel Martí (0, 0, 3.46), Norge Vera (3, 0, 1.22), Ormari Romero (1, 0, 1.10), Yovani Aragón (0, 0, 2.25), Jonder Martínez (2, 0, 1.29), Ifredi Coss (0, 0, 0.00), Pedro Luis Lazo (1, 0, 1.13).

Cuba Game Scores: Preliminary Round: Cuba beat Chinese Taipei 6–3, Cuba beat Korea 4–0, Cuba beat Russia 20–1, Cuba beat Italy 7–0, Cuba beat Canada 8–0, Cuba beat Nicaragua 7–1. Quarterfinals: Cuba beat Brazil 4–3. Semifinals: Cuba beat Chinese Taipei 6–3. Finals: Cuba beat Panama 4–2.

OLYMPIC GAMES BASEBALL CHAMPIONSHIPS, 1992–2004

Despite a half-dozen attempts at demonstration tournaments to showcase the American sport in Olympic Games venues reaching all the way back to Stockholm in 1912, the history of baseball in the Olympics started little more than a decade ago—Barcelona 1992. Some of baseball's Olympic prehistory (namely, Stockholm 1912 and Berlin 1936) amounts to little more than silly exhibitions staged among U.S. track and field athletes or other recreational players and thus hardly qualified as serious competitions (and certainly not as international competitions). At least two pre-Barcelona events, however, did come close to full-scale Olympic-style matches. The 1984 Los Angeles games staged in Dodger Stadium showcased perhaps the best version of Team USA ever put on a field for amateur competitions. The Rod Dedeaux–coached squad featuring Will Clark, Barry Larkin, Mark McGwire, and Bobby Witt (among other big leaguers-in-training) was first disappointed by the absence of the powerhouse Cubans, who withdrew to honor a Soviet boycott; they were then

One of Cuban slugger Orestes Kindelán's frequent home run trots at the 1996 Atlanta Olympics. [Transcendental Graphics]

shocked by an underrated team of Japanese collegians who ended the Americans undefeated string (in demonstration games) stretching back to Stockholm. Four years later, in Seoul, the United States entered another equally potent contingent (now coached by Mark Marquess), but any hopes of finally squaring off with the vaunted Cubans and avenging a tough intervening gold medal loss at the Indianapolis Pan American Games was quickly squelched when the Cubans again boycotted, this time in sympathy with their fellow communist regime in North Korea. But the Americans did taste revenge against the Japanese in a rematch of the 1984 Los Angeles finals.

Now that the stage had been set for legitimate and fully sanctioned competitions, with baseball finally on the same footing as other official Olympic team sports (such as basketball, soccer, ice hockey, and water polo), the theme of the competitions shifted 180 degrees: from American efforts to stimulate baseball interest to Cuban efforts to add still another prestigious stage for their own ongoing total domination of a game they also embraced as a national pastime. The entire story of official Olympic baseball has been first and last the story of the invincible Cuban team, with perhaps a single exception of one sterling pitching performance by American ace Ben Sheets during the 2000 finals at Sydney. The Cubans didn't lose a single contest while breezing to two gold medals in Barcelona and Atlanta. The unbeaten string was finally snapped with a monumental upset sprung by a mediocre Dutch team during an otherwise meaningless opening round game. Cuba's more vital loss to Team USA in the Sydney championship shootout was in part the story of Ben Sheets, who shut down Cuban bats on but three hits, and in part a matter of the law of averages: Cuba had lost less than a half-dozen times in more than 200 games in international ventures over a half-dozen seasons. The Cuban loss of gold in Sydney may also have resulted as much as anything from a tactical error in using seasoned ace José Contreras (later a defector to the New York Yankees) in the semifinal showdown with Japan and not in the championship tussle versus the Americans. But it was only an apparent bump in the road for the Cubans. A rude ouster of Team USA in the November 2003 Panama Olympic Qualifier (Cuba and Canada grabbing the region's two available Olympic slots) suggested that Cuba again would have the field largely to itself when the next Olympic round-robin opened at Athens in August 2004. And this quickly proved to be the case, despite Japan's entry of a pro all-star roster and solid Australian and Canadian teams filled with talented minor leaguers and a substantial number of seasoned major league veterans.

Olympic Baseball Prehistory

1912 Stockholm (Sweden)

A staged exhibition pits an American nine (mainly members of the U.S. track team) against a Swedish club called Vesteras who compete with a pitcher and catcher borrowed from the Americans. The final count was USA 13, Sweden 3. The following day the American East and West clubs (called "Finland" and "Olympic" for the occasion) stage a second exhibition. Olympic (East) wins 6–3; future big leaguer Jim Thorpe (a U.S. track star) plays in this second game.

1936 Berlin (Germany)

American Leslie Mann (a 16-year big league outfielder) attempts to arrange demonstration matches which several countries initially agree to support. When no other teams show up a U.S. amateur squad traveling with the U.S. delegation (but not sanctioned Olympic athletes) is split into two squads for an exhibition witnessed by between 90,000 and 125,000 in Berlin Stadium, spectators who had arrived early for prime seats at the track events scheduled later in the evening. The squad called "World Champions" defeated the U.S. Olympics club 6–5 when Floridian Les McNeese smacked a homer to end the game shortened (to great applause) to seven innings.

1940 Tokyo (Japan)

Baseball's new popularity in Japan (a pro league there had begun in 1936, after several successful visits of barnstorming big leaguers) caused the Japanese to institute baseball as a recognized if not sanctioned part of the scheduled 1940 Games, but with World War II underway the Tokyo Olympics were canceled.

1952 Helsinki (Finland)

Baseball was again tried as an exhibition event, pitting a national champion Finnish team against a makeshift American group from the Olympic Village coached by the manager of the U.S. soccer team. Tuning up with a 14–6 victory over a volunteer group of athletes from Venezuela (both teams had to borrow equipment from the Finnish squad), the Americans then routed the inept Finns 19–1. Charlie Colombo, member of the U.S. soccer team, reportedly slugged a homer over the roof of an adjacent building to the delight of about 4,000 curious but novice Finnish spectators.

1956 Melbourne (Australia)

Military personnel from the U.S. Far East Command Post engage a select squad of Australians in yet another 1-game exhibition match. As the evening's scheduled track events grew near, the crowd swelled to nearly 100,000 in the Olympic Stadium, but few were very interested in the ball game reaching its conclusion on the field below. The U.S. soldiers posted an easy 11–5 victory and Americans thus could boast they had still never lost an "Olympic" baseball match.

1964 Tokyo (Japan)

The last of the single-game-style exhibitions featured a U.S. collegiate all-star team coached by University of Southern California mentor Rod Dedeaux and actually hand-picked and trained for the occasion. The Americans even toured against a Far East All-Star team of Japanese amateurs to prepare for the Tokyo appearance. Team USA (the first actual American Olympic baseball "team") was successful 6–2 against some seasoned Japanese amateurs and semipros.

1984 Los Angeles (USA)

Gold: Japan; Silver: USA; Bronze: Chinese Taipei
The first tournament format for Olympic baseball drew 385,000 to Dodger Stadium in Los Angeles. The American club, bursting with future big league prospects, was a heavy favorite in Cuba's absence. Japan was 2–1 in the opening round before edging Chinese Taipei 2–1 in a ten-inning semifinal thriller. The Japanese hero was unknown college hurler Atsunori Ito, who was matched against U.S. ace John Hoover. First baseman Katsumi Hirosawa smacked an eighth-inning tie-breaking homer to seal the 6–3 upset of Mark McGwire, Oddibe McDowell, Barry Larkin, and company.

1988 Seoul (South Korea)

Gold: USA; Silver: Japan; Bronze: Puerto Rico
Ten players returned from the American squad that had lost a heartbreaker to the Cubans at Indianapolis in 1987, and this time there would be no upset of Team USA (nor of the Cubans, who stayed at home as part of the Communist Bloc's boycott of the Seoul Olympics). Breezing past Puerto Rico 7–2 in the semis behind the strong pitching of Ben McDonald (soon of the Baltimore Orioles), coach Mark Marquess sent one-handed sensation Jim Abbott to the hill for the rematch with Japan. Abbott hurled a strong complete game, and Tino Martínez socked a pair of homers to seal the 5–3 gold medal win.

Olympic Baseball History

Cuba's Overall Performance: Tournaments (3 gold medals and one silver medal in four Olympic tournaments held); Games (33 Won and 3 Lost, .917 Pct.).

Country-by-Country Championships Won: Cuba (3 of 4 tournaments entered) and USA (1).

Note: Cuba has lost only three games total in Olympic competition: to The Netherlands (4–2) in preliminary round at Sydney 2000, to USA (4–0) in gold medal game at Sydney 2000, and to Japan (6–3) in preliminary round at Athens.

1992 Olympic Baseball Championships (Barcelona, Spain) (July 26–August 5)

Cuba establishes the same dominance over the first-ever Olympic Games field that it has traditionally held in all other international tournaments. A showdown semifinal game between Cuba and Team USA (featuring future big league stars Nomar Garciaparra, Jason Giambi, Michael Tucker, Charles Johnson, Darren Dreifort, and Jeffrey Hammonds) fell to the Cubans 4–1, with Victor Mesa driving home all four tallies for the proud winners. Giorge Díaz hurled a four-hit complete-game masterpiece in the finale, aided by three Cuban homers to spice the 11–1 routing of Chinese Taipei. Cuba scored in seven of nine innings during the gold medal match. Victor Mesa and Omar Linares were overall batting stars, and future defector (and big leaguer) Osvaldo Fernández was the tournament's most effective pitcher.

Champion: Cuba (9–0) (Silver Medal: Chinese Taipei; Bronze Medal: Japan)
Finals: Cuba beat Chinese Taipei 11–1 (Gold Medal), Japan beat USA 8–3 (Bronze Medal).
Semifinals: Cuba beat USA 4–1, Chinese Taipei beat Japan 5–2.
Preliminary Round Standings: Cuba (7–0), Chinese Taipei (5–2), Japan (5–2), USA (5–2), Puerto Rico (2–5), Dominican Republic (2–5), Italy (1–6), Spain (1–6).
Individual Statistical Leaders: **BA**: Victor Mesa (CUB) .545*; **Runs**: Omar Linares (CUB) 13; **Hits**: Omar Linares (CUB) 16; **2B**: Ermidelio Urrutia (CUB) 5; **3B**: 17 players with one each; **HR**: Koji Tokunaga (JPN) 4; **RBI**: Koji Tokunaga (JPN) 13; **SB**: Calvin Murray (USA) 9; **Wins**: four pitchers with two each; **IP**: Lee Chien-Fu Kuo (TPE) 20; **ERA**: Osvaldo Fernández (CUB) 0.00. *Mesa's batting title (plus all other stats here) based on preliminary round only and does not include medal-round games.
Cuba Roster: **Manager**: Jorge Fuentes. **Batting** (AB, H, BA): José Raúl Delgado (8, 3, .375), Alberto Hernández (26, 8, .308), Lourdes Gourriel (39, 16, .410), Antonio Pacheco (40, 14, .350), Omar Linares (40, 20, .500), Germán Mesa (26, 10, .385), Juan Padilla (5, 3, .600), Lázaro Vargas (37, 17, .459), Luis Ulacia (5, 0, .000), Orestes Kindelán (30, 11, .367), Victor Mesa (30, 15, .500), Ermidelio Urrutia (36, 14, .389), José Estrada (5, 1, .200). **Pitching** (W, L, ERA): Jorge Luis Valdés (1, 0, 5.14), Omar Ajete (1, 0, 0.00), Orlando "El Duque" Hernández (1, 0, 5.40), Osvaldo Fernández Rodríguez (2, 0, 0.57), Rolando Arrojo (1, 0, 0.00), Juan Carlos Pérez (1, 0, 1.04), Giorge Díaz (2, 0, 1.00).
Cuba Game Scores: Preliminary Round: Cuba beat Dominican Republic 8–0, Cuba beat Italy 18–1, Cuba beat Japan 8–2, Cuba beat USA 9–6, Cuba beat Spain 18–0, Cuba beat Puerto Rico 9–4, Cuba beat Chinese Taipei 8–1. Semifinals: Cuba beat USA 4–1. Finals: Cuba beat Chinese Taipei 11–1.

1996 Olympic Baseball Championships (Atlanta, Georgia USA) (July 20–August 2)

Omar Linares's 3 homers in the gold medal slugfest with Japan was the tournament highlight as Cuba defended its Barcelona title and remained seemingly invincible, despite considerable signs of vulnerability in the usually brilliant Cuban pitching corps. Defection by Rolando Arrojo on the eve of the tournament may have added to the Cuban pitching jitters, but remaining aces José Contreras and Omar Ajete were soundly spanked by opposing hitters. Orestes Kindelán supplemented the slugging of Linares with tournament-high totals in both homers and RBI. Kindelán also shared the leadership in base hits with Linares. Team USA proved a disappointment before enthusiastic home crowds, losing a hard-fought preliminary round match with the Cubans (10–8) and dropping the semifinal game versus Japan (11–2). Cuba's overall Olympic record would now stand at eighteen games won without a single defeat.

Champion: Cuba (9–0) (Silver Medal: Japan; Bronze Medal: USA)
Finals: Cuba beat Japan 13–9 (Gold Medal), USA beat Nicaragua 10–3 (Bronze Medal).
Semifinals: Cuba beat Nicaragua 8–1, Japan beat USA 11–2.

Preliminary Round Standings: Cuba (7–0), USA (6–1), Japan (4–3), Nicaragua (4–3), Netherlands (2–5), Italy (2–5), Australia (2–5), South Korea (1–6).

Individual Statistical Leaders: **BA**: L. Carroza (ITA) .571; **Runs**: Omar Linares (CUB) 17; **Hits**: Omar Linares (CUB), Orestes Kindelán (CUB) 16; **2B**: F. Casolari (ITA) 5; **3B**: Jacque Jones (USA), T. Igustzi (JPN) 2; **HR**: Orestes Kindelán (CUB) 7; **RBI**: Orestes Kindelán (CUB) 14; **SB**: Luis Ulacia (CUB) 3; **Wins**: Omar Luis (CUB) 3; **IP**: R. Cabalisti (ITA) 19.2; **ERA**: P. Nanne (ITA) 0.00.

Cuba Roster: **Manager**: Jorge Fuentes. **Batting** (AB, H, BA): Miguel Caldés (34, 11, .324), José Estrada (44, 13, .295), Alberto Hernández (9, 2, .222), Rey Isaac (14, 9, .643), Orestes Kindelán (43, 19, .442), Omar Linares (42, 20, .476), Juan Manrique (26, 11, .423), Antonio Pacheco (39, 14, .359), Juan Padilla (1, 1, 1.000), Eduardo Paret (32, 12, .375), Antonio Scull (5, 2, .400), Luis Ulacia (27, 15, .556), Lázaro Vargas (35, 12, .343). **Pitching** (W, L, ERA): Omar Ajete (0, 0, 4.00), José Ariel Contreras (1, 0, 6.23), Jorge Fumero (1, 0, 8.53), Pedro Luis Lazo (1, 0, 5.40), Eliecer Montes de Oca (1, 0, 10.13), Omar Luis (3, 0, 5.71), Ormari Romero (2, 0, 7.11).

Cuba Game Scores: Preliminary Round: Cuba beat Australia 19–8, Cuba beat Japan 8–7, Cuba beat Netherlands 18–2, Cuba beat South Korea 14–11, Cuba beat Italy 20–6, Cuba beat USA 10–8, Cuba beat Nicaragua 8–7. Semifinals: Cuba beat Nicaragua 8–1. Finals: Cuba beat Japan 13–9.

2000 Olympic Baseball Championships (Sydney, Australia) (September 17–27)

Legendary veteran national team manager Servio Borges returns to the helm for the first time in several years and receives considerable second-guessing from many quarters after he uses ace José Contreras in a semifinal match with Japan, thus expending his best hurler before the gold medal showdown with improved Team USA. USA (under major league Hall of Fame manager Tommy Lasorda) pulls off the championship upset when big leaguer Ben Sheets blanks the stunned Cubans on but three hits in the finale. Cuba had dominated the U.S. squad in a preliminary round match 5–1 behind masterful pitching from José Ibar. Cuba's first-ever defeat in an Olympic Games outing also came in the preliminary round with a stunning 4–2 loss to unheralded Holland.

Champion: USA (8–1) (Silver Medal: Cuba; Bronze Medal: South Korea)

Finals: USA beat Cuba 4–0 (Gold Medal), South Korea beat Japan 3–1 (Bronze Medal).

Semifinals: Cuba beat Japan 3–0, USA beat South Korea 3–2.

Preliminary Round Standings: Cuba (6–1), USA (6–1), South Korea (4–3), Japan (4–3), Netherlands (3–4), Italy (2–5), Australia (2–5), South Africa (1–6). *USA beat Cuba (4–0) in gold medal game and South Korea beat Japan (3–1) in bronze medal game.

Individual Statistical Leaders: **BA**: Dave Nilsson (AUS) .565; **Runs**: Miguel Caldés (CUB), Omar Linares (CUB), Mike Neill (USA) 8; **Hits**: Dave Nilsson (AUS), So Taguchi (JPN), Bill Abernathy (USA) 13; **2B**: Bill Abernathy (USA) 5; **3B**: several players with one each; **HR**: eight players with two each; **RBI**: Danilo Sheldon (ITA), Orestes Kindelán (CUB), Norihiro Nakamura (JPN) 8; **SB**: J. Soo-Keun (KOR) 5; **Wins**: Robert Frankly (USA) 3; **IP**: Daisuke Matsuzaka (JPN) 19; **ERA**: José Ibar (CUB) 0.00. *Statistics based on preliminary round and not medal-round games.

Cuba Roster: **Manager**: Servio Borges. **Batting** (AB, H, BA): Ariel Pestano (19, 4, .211), Juan Manrique (10, 2, .200), Orestes Kindelán (34, 12, .353), Antonio Scull (9, 3, .333), Antonio Pacheco (26, 10, .385), Oscar Macías (29, 10, .345), Omar Linares (33, 11, .333), Gabriel Pierre (1, 0, .000), Germán Mesa (22, 8, .364), Daniel Castro (5, 1, .200), Javier Méndez (3, 1, .333), Luis Ulacia (36, 11, .306), Yobal Dueñas (18, 6, .333), Yasser Gómez (24, 6, .250), Miguel Caldés (30, 10, .333), Rolando Meriño (DNP). **Pitching** (W, L, ERA): José Ariel Contreras (2, 0, .0.86), Pedro Luis Lazo (1, 1, 4.26), Omar

Ajete (0, 0, 2.45), José Ibar (2, 0, 1.69), Lázaro Valle (1, 0, 0.00), Yovani Aragón (0, 0, 7.50), Maels Rodríguez (0, 0, 0.00), Norge Vera (1, 1, 1.23).

USA Game Scores: Preliminary Round: USA beat Japan 4–2, USA beat South Africa 11–1, USA beat Netherlands 6–2, USA beat Korea 4–0, USA beat Italy 4–2, Cuba beat USA 6–1, USA beat Australia 12–1. Semifinals: USA beat Korea 3–2. Finals: USA beat Cuba 4–0.

Cuba Game Scores: Preliminary Round: Cuba beat South Africa 16–0, Cuba beat Italy 13–5, Cuba beat South Korea 6–5, Netherlands beat Cuba 4–2, Cuba beat Australia 1–0, Cuba beat USA 6–1, Cuba beat Japan 6–2. Semifinals: Cuba beat Japan 3–0. Finals: USA beat Cuba 4–0.

2004 Olympic Baseball Championships (Athens, Greece) (August 15–25)

Athens 2004 was a tournament marked by seemingly endless surprises, not the least of which was the fact that no team took the field representing the USA. Cuba, despite fielding its youngest and perhaps weakest team yet for Olympic competitions, again proved too much for the field and remained unscathed in the end, suffering only a single opening-round defeat at the hands of pretourney favorite Japan. The Japanese arrived with a stellar team of pro league all-stars and swept everything in sight but the Australians, tumbling from contention with a shocking 1–0 semifinal loss to the Aussies. Canada held up well with its roster of minor league veterans and made it to the medal round. Chinese Taipei somehow managed to drop a game to the otherwise winless Italians, an unaccountable loss that kept the Taiwanese on the sidelines for medal-round action. And Australia was the biggest surprise of all, rebounding from a disastrous tourney four years earlier in Sydney to reach the gold medal contest. Cuba's victory was highlighted by the hitting of veteran catcher Ariel Pestano, brilliant pitching from rising star Adiel Palma, and a miraculous eighth-inning six-run comeback against Team Canada in the semifinal. The gold medal showdown was marred by an egregious umpiring call on a fly ball "caught" by outfielder Carlos Tabares to squelch an early Aussie rally; but in the end, the blown call was a mere footnote that had little impact on yet another impressive Cuban championship victory.

Champion: Cuba (8–1) (Silver Medal: Australia; Bronze Medal: Japan)

Finals: Cuba beat Australia 6–2 (Gold Medal), Japan beat Canada 11–2 (Bronze Medal).

Semifinals: Cuba beat Canada 8–5, Australia beat Japan 1–0.

Preliminary Round Standings: Cuba (6–1), Japan (6–1), Canada (5–2), Australia (4–3), Chinese Taipei (3–4), Netherlands (2–5), Greece (1–6), Italy (1–6). *Cuba beat Australia (6–2) in gold medal game and Japan beat Canada 11–2 in bronze medal game.

Individual Statistical Leaders: **BA**: Ariel Pestano (CUB) .512; **Runs**: Kosuke Fukudome (JPN) 11; **Hits**: Ariel Pestano (CUB), Shinya Miyamoto (JPN) 18; **2B**: Ariel Pestano (CUB), Kenji Jojima (JPN) 5; **3B**: several players with one each; **HR**: four players with three each; **RBI**: Ariel Pestano (CUB) 14; **SB**: Cheng-min Peng (TPE) 5; **Wins**: Adiel Palma (CUB) 3; **IP**: Adiel Palma (CUB) 19.1; **ERA**: Chris Oxspring (AUS), Hiroki Kuroda (JPN) 0.00. *Statistics for both preliminary round and medal-round games.

Cuba Roster: **Manager**: Higinio Vélez. **Batting** (AB, H, BA): Frederich Cepeda (33, 15, .455), Michel Enríquez (38, 10, .263), Yulieski Gourriel (35, 12, .343), Danny Miranda (16, 3, .188), Eduardo Paret (34, 10, .294), Ariel Pestano (35, 18, .514), Alexei Ramírez (18, 5, .278), Carlos Tabares (25, 4, .160), Osmani Urrutia (33, 11, .333), Yorelvis Charles (3, 0, .000), Roger Machado (0, 0, .000), Eriel Sánchez (25, 9, .360), Antonio Scull (17, 3, .176), Yoandri Urgelles (3, 1, .333). **Pitching** (W, L, ERA): Pedro Luis Lazo (0, 0, 4.92), Jonder Martínez (0, 0, 27.00), Adiel Palma (3, 0, 1.40), Danny Betancourt (1, 0, 3.46), Norge Luis Vera (1, 0, 0.69), Norberto González (1, 0, 0.75), Vicyohandri

Odelín (0, 1, 6.75), Manuel Alberto Vega (0, 0, 2.70), Luis Borroto (2, 0, 0.00), Frank Andy Montieth (0, 0, 0.00).

Cuba Game Scores: Preliminary Round: Cuba beat Australia 4–1, Cuba beat Greece 5–4, Japan beat Cuba 6–3, Cuba beat Chinese Taipei 10–2, Cuba beat Netherlands 9–2, Cuba beat Canada 5–2, Cuba beat Italy 5–0. Semifinals: Cuba beat Canada 8–5. Finals: Cuba beat Australia 6–2.

2003 Pan American Pre-Olympic Qualifying Tournament (Panama City, Panama) (October 30–November 10)

Defending Olympic champion Team USA is shocked in its quarterfinal game by Mexico (0–3 in the qualifying round) and thus loses a chance to defend its 2000 title in Athens. A young and seemingly invincible Cuban squad, fresh off its World Cup victory one week earlier in Havana, continues to roll with another unblemished ledger and three straight shutout victories (behind starters Norge Vera, Vicyohandri Odelín, and Adiel Palma) during medal round competitions. Yulieski Gourriel and Frederich Cepeda again supply the long ball action in a 5–0 quarterfinal win over Brazil, Puerto Rico is eliminated with a surprising 10–0, seven-inning knockout victory, and a two-run round-tripper by first sacker Joan Carlos Pedroso alongside a two-run triple by veteran catcher Ariel Pestano provide the muscle in gold medal action versus Canada. Cuba is now again poised to win back its Olympic gold medal so embarrassingly lost in 2000 at Sydney.

Champion: Cuba (6–0) (Silver Medal: Canada; Bronze Medal: Mexico)

Finals: Cuba beat Canada 5–0 (Gold Medal), Mexico beat Puerto Rico 10–1 (Bronze Medal).

Semifinals: Cuba beat Puerto Rico 10–0, Canada beat Mexico 11–1.

Quarterfinals: Cuba beat Brazil 5–0, Canada beat Colombia 14–6, Puerto Rico beat Panama 5–3, Mexico beat USA 2–1.

Group A Preliminary Round: Cuba (3–0), Canada (2–1), Puerto Rico (1–2), Mexico (0–3).

Group B Preliminary Round: USA (3–0), Panama (3–1), Colombia (2–2), Brazil (1–2), Nicaragua (0–4).

Individual Statistical Leaders: **BA**: Eriel Sánchez (CUB) .571, Angerl Pagán (PUR) .500, Omar García (PUR) .500, Eduardo Paret (CUB) .500, Ariel Pestano (CUB) .500, Ernest Young (USA) .500; **ERA**: Claudio Yamada (BRA) 0.00 (9.0 innings), Jason Stanford (USA) 0.00 (7.0 innings), Rafael Medina (PAN) 0.00 (6.0 innings), Isidro Márquez (MEX) 0.00 (5.0 innings), Ryan Madson (USA) 0.00 (5.0 innings), Horacio Ramirez (USA) 0.00 (5.0 innings). *Statistics based on preliminary round and do not include medal-round games.

Cuba Roster: **Manager**: Higinio Vélez. **Position Players**: Eduardo Paret (SS), Michel Enríquez (3B), Yulieski Gourriel (2B), Eriel Sánchez (DH, C), Frederich Cepeda (OF), Ariel Pestano (C), Robelquis Videaux (OF), Joan Carlos Pedroso (1B), Danel Castro (SS), Carlos Tabares (OF), Roger Machado (C), Yorelvis Charles (IF), Ariel Benavides (OF, DH), Osmani Urrutia (OF). **Pitchers:** Adiel Palma (L), Yovani Aragón (R), Jonder Martínez (R), Norge Vera (R), Pedro Luis Lazo (R), Vicyohandri Odelín (R), Yadel Martí (R), Ifredi Coss (R), Ormari Romero (R).

Cuba Game Scores: Preliminary Round: Cuba beat Puerto Rico 4–2, Cuba beat Mexico 5–4, Cuba beat Canada 7–2. Quarterfinals: Cuba beat Brazil 5–0. Semifinals: Cuba beat Puerto Rico 10–0. Finals: Cuba beat Canada 5–0.

INTERCONTINENTAL CUP BASEBALL CHAMPIONSHIPS, 1973–2002

If Cuba's overall record in this baseball-only event appears slightly less spectacular when viewed from afar—four other countries have claimed six titles versus the dozen won by the tried and true world champions—this is only because Cuban teams did not participate until the fourth event was staged in 1979 at Havana. Since their debut, Cubans have been bumped but three times. They dropped an extra-inning thriller to the Americans in the 1981 Edmonton event; they were shocked by the Japanese in Barcelona in 1997, thus ending a miraculous decade-long unbeaten skein; and they were again rudely upset by host Australia in the 1999 Olympic tune-ups at Sydney, once more in extra innings. To frame it another way, since entering the fray in 1970, the Cubans have played in the Intercontinental Cup gold medal game twelve straight times. Cuba owns this tournament every bit as much as it does all the others. Intercontinental Cup venues have also been scene for some of the most heroic individual performances by a host of top Cuban ballplayers. Most memorable among these are Luis Casanova's triple crown at Edmonton in 1981 (in a losing cause), Victor Mesa's slugging two years later in Brussels, Omar Linares's debut as an 18-year-old "international rookie" at Edmonton (1985), sensational hitting by Lourdes Gourriel during the 1989 Puerto Rico games, and finally Yobal Dueñas's mammoth homer in Latin American Stadium (Havana) to clinch the 2002 title contest.

Cuba's Overall Performance: Tournaments (9 of 12 Tournament titles won, plus three second place finishes); Games (107 Won and 11 Lost, .907 Pct.).

Country-by-Country Championships Won: Cuba (9 of 12 tournaments entered), Japan (2), USA (2), South Korea (1), and Australia (1).

Note: Cuba did not participate in the following three tournaments: 1973 (Italy), 1975 (Canada), and 1977 (Nicaragua).

1973 Intercontinental Cup Championship I (Parma and Rimini, Italy) (September 1–8)

Squabbling within amateur baseball's governing body (FIBA, International Federation of Baseball, now known as IBAF, International Baseball Federation) reaches a climax at the group's annual meeting in Bologna, Italy, with the resulting formation of a rival organization (FEMBA, World Federation of Amateur Baseball) that boasts 24 member countries. This meeting in late August coincides with the first Intercontinental Cup baseball championships organized by Italy's FIBA delegation and featuring national teams from eight countries representing Europe (Italy), Asia (Japan and Taiwan), and the Americas (Puerto Rico, United States, Nicaragua, Canada, and Argentina). Japan claims the first title of the FEMBA event that was initially planned for alternate years.

Champion: Japan (6–1)

Teams and Final Standings: Gold: Japan (6–1), Silver: Puerto Rico (5–2), Bronze: USA (5–2), Nicaragua (4–3), Canada (4–3), Italy (4–3), Chinese Taipei (1–6), Argentina (0–7).

Individual Statistical Leaders: **BA**: J. Ortiz (PUR) .417; **Runs**: D. Simon (CAN) 8; **Hits**: N. Morales (PUR) 11; **2B**: P. Lepage (CAN) 4; **3B**: Y. Hosaya (JPN) 2; **HR**: N. Morales (PUR) 4; **RBI**: N. Morales (PUR) 12; **SB**: H. Naito (JPN) 8; **Wins**: four pitchers with two each; **ERA**: Kojiro Ikegaya (JPN) 0.00.

Japan Game Scores: Single round-robin: Japan beat Chinese Taipei 10–1, Japan beat Puerto Rico 1–0, Japan beat Argentina 25–0, Japan beat Italy 11–5, Japan beat Nicaragua 10–0, USA beat Japan 1–0, Japan beat Canada 1–0.

Cuba Did Not Participate

1975 Intercontinental Cup Championship II (Montreal, Canada) (August 14–31)

FEMBA sponsors a second Intercontinental Cup competition—this time located in Montreal, Canada—and the United States earns the championship trophy while Cuba once again sits on the sidelines. South Korea and Colombia replace Taiwan and Nicaragua in the eight-team field. Team USA features future major leaguer catcher Ron Hassey as its top slugger and breezes through its nine games undefeated, with defending champion Japan, a two-time loser, in the runner-up slot. Only the top two teams record winning records.

Champion: USA (9–0)

Teams and Final Standings: Gold: USA (9–0), Silver: Japan (7–2), Bronze: Nicaragua (4–5), Canada (4–5), Puerto Rico (3–4), South Korea (3–4), Italy (2–5), Colombia (0–7).

Individual Statistical Leaders: **BA**: T. Mirakami (JPN) .588; **Runs**: Ron Hassey (USA) 9; **Hits**: Ron Hassey (USA), Y. Mackawa (JPN) 14; **2B**: J. Mondalto (USA) 4; **3B**: C. Jarquín (NCA) 2; **HR**: Y. Mackawa (JPN) 3; **RBI**: Y. Mackawa (JPN) 11; **SB**: L. Mc. Chong (KOR) 4; **Wins**: S. Anderson (USA), I. Osborne (CAN) 2–0; **IP**: K. Ho Joong (KOR) 26.0; **ERA**: S. Anderson (USA) 0.60.

USA Game Scores: Preliminary Round: USA beat Puerto Rico 10–3, USA beat Italy 12–0, USA beat Nicaragua 4–1, USA beat Korea 5–2, USA beat Canada 6–0, USA beat Japan 1–0, USA beat Colombia 12–2. Finals: USA beat Canada 7–5, USA beat Japan 8–0.

Cuba Did Not Participate

1977 Intercontinental Cup Championship III (Managua, Nicaragua) (November 10–20)

The field is expanded to nine teams for the third Intercontinental Cup championship tournament in Managua, and a preliminary round and championship round format is adopted. South Korea edges the United States in a thrilling tie-breaker to claim the first-place trophy. The FIBA–FEMBA split has now been resolved and this and all remaining tournaments are held under the auspices of AINBA (International Amateur Baseball Association). For the third and final time, Cuba sits out the Intercontinental Cup—an event that it will soon come to dominate.

Champion: South Korea (10–4)

Championship Round Final Standings: Gold: South Korea (4–1), Silver: USA (4–1), Bronze: Japan (3–2), Nicaragua (3–2), Colombia (1–4), Puerto Rico (0–5). *South Korea beat USA (5–4) in tie-breaking playoff game.

Preliminary Round Standings: USA (8–0), South Korea (5–3), Japan (4–4), Nicaragua (4–4), Colombia (4–4), Puerto Rico (3–5), Chinese Taipei (3–5), Canada (3–5), Venezuela (2–6). *Top six teams qualified for final round.

Individual Statistical Leaders: **BA**: Kim Jae Bak (KOR) .426; **Runs**: E. López (NCA) 12; **Hits**: Kim Jae Bak (KOR) 23; **2B**: E. Moreno (COL), Pablo Juárez (NCA) 6; **3B**: T. Bogenez (USA), Kim Jae Bak (KOR), W. Taylor (NCA) 2; **HR**: J. Cuaresma (NCA), E. López (NCA) 5; **RBI**: L. Percey (USA), J. Cuaresma (NCA) 12; **SB**: N. Kobayashi (JPN) 11; **Wins**: Shicekazu Mori (JPN) 4–0; **IP**: Sun Hee Lee (KOR) 48.2; **ERA**: Jack Lazorko (USA) 0.00.

South Korea Game Scores: Preliminary Round: USA beat Korea 5–4, Korea beat Puerto Rico 4–0, Korea beat Venezuela 8–2, Japan beat Korea 1–0, Korea beat Colombia 7–0, Korea beat Nicaragua 8–1, Chinese Taipei beat Korea 2–1, Korea beat Canada 3–1. Playoff Round: USA beat Korea 3–0, Korea beat Nicaragua 13–3, Korea beat Colombia 4–1, Korea beat Puerto Rico 4–2, Korea beat Japan 3–2. Finals: Korea beat USA 5–4.

Cuba Did Not Participate

1979 Intercontinental Cup Championship IV (Havana, Cuba) (December 15–26)

The fourth Intercontinental Cup tournament heralds its fourth different champion as Cuba hosts the event for the first time and charges through the field undefeated. Japan earns a silver medal, with Team USA collecting the bronze. Team USA's appearance marks the first visit of an American amateur team to Cuban soil in 37 years. Cuban third sacker Pedro José "Cheíto" Rodríguez turns this tournament into his own personal showcase with his .450 BA, 1.000 slugging average (more total bases than times at bat), 17 RBI, and seven circuit blasts. Manager Servio Borges again leads the Cuban forces; for Borges, this tournament marks ten years of uninterrupted international victories.

Champion: Cuba (10–0)

Teams and Final Standings: Gold: Cuba (10–0), Silver: Japan (8–2), Bronze: USA (6–4), Nicaragua (3–7), Puerto Rico (3–7), Panama (0–10).

Individual Statistical Leaders: **BA**: Pedro Medina (CUB) .462; **Runs**: Pedro José Rodríguez (CUB) 15; **Hits**: Pedro José Rodríguez (CUB) 18; **2B**: P. Dobson (USA) 6; **3B**: Alfonso Urquiola (CUB) 2; **HR**: Pedro José Rodríguez (CUB) 7; **RBI**: Pedro José Rodríguez (CUB) 17; **SB**: M. Kobayashi (JPN) 7; **Wins**: seven pitchers with two each; **IP**: I. Kido (JPN) 22.2; **ERA**: José Luis Aleman (CUB) 0.00.

Cuba Roster: **Manager**: Servio Borges. **Batting** (AB, H, BA): Pedro Medina (26, 12, .462), Alfonso Martínez (8, 5, .624), Antonio Muñoz (38, 7, .184), Agustín Marquetti (33, 5, .152), Alfonso Urquiola (42, 14, .333), Rodolfo Puente (30, 11, .367), Pedro Jova (27, 4, .148), Pedro José "Cheíto" Rodríguez (40, 18, .450), Leonardo Goire (2, 1, .500), Fernando Sánchez (29, 10, .345), Luis Casanova (40, 15, .375), Lourdes Gourriel (34, 10, .294), Wilfredo Sánchez (15, 5, .333). **Pitching** (W, L, ERA): Braudilio Vinent (2, 0, 2.18), Jesús Guerra (2, 0, 2.51), Carlos Mesa (0, 0, 0.00), José Luis Alemán (2, 0, 0.00), Rogelio García (1, 0, 0.90), Juan Carlos Oliva (2, 0, 0.75), Rafael Castillo (1, 0, 0.82).

Cuba Game Scores: Double round-robin: Cuba beat Japan 7–1, Cuba beat Puerto Rico 7–1, Cuba beat Nicaragua 4–0, Cuba beat Panama 16–0, Cuba beat USA 6–4, Cuba beat Japan 4–1, Cuba beat Puerto Rico 9–1, Cuba beat Nicaragua 10–1, Cuba beat Panama 6–1, Cuba beat USA 7–4.

1981 Intercontinental Cup Championship V (Edmonton, Canada) (August 6–16)

Luis Casanova enjoys his finest international tournament, walking off with the batting triple crown as the home run, RBI, and batting champion. But the overconfident Cuban squad managed by Servio Borges suffers a humiliating and eye-opening defeat when Team USA captures its second and final Intercontinental Cup (both won in Canada). After the strong Cuban contingent led by the bats of Casanova, Muñoz, Fernando Sánchez, and Victor Mesa crushed the United States in opening round action, two unaccountable setbacks were suffered at the hands of Canada and the Dominicans. Rogelio García matched up with future big leaguer Ed Vosberg in the title game; Braudilio Vinent pitched heroically in relief on one day's rest; and veteran Pedro Medina's clutch homer tied the contest in late innings; but Team USA nonetheless pulled out a tense 6–5 victory in the tenth frame.

Champion: USA (7–2)

Finals: USA beat Cuba 6–5 (10 innings) (Gold Medal), Dominican Republic beat South Korea 4–3 (15 innings) (Bronze Medal).

Semifinals: Cuba beat South Korea 9–1, USA beat Dominican Republic 5–3.

Preliminary Round Standings: USA (5–2), Cuba (5–2), South Korea (5–2), Dominican Republic (4–3), Canada (4–3), Japan (3–4), Panama (1–6), Australia (1–6).

Individual Statistical Leaders: **BA**: Luis Casanova (CUB) .517; **Runs**: Luis Casanova (CUB) 12; **Hits**: Luis Casanova (CUB) 15; **2B**: J. Gerbar (DOM) 5; **3B**: twelve players with one each; **HR**: Luis Casanova (CUB) 6; **RBI**: Luis Casanova (CUB) 19; **SB**: M. Kobayashi (JPN) 8; **Wins**: Dong Won Choi (KOR) 2–0; **IP**: Dong Won Choi (KOR) 27.1; **ERA**: P. Lychak (CAN) 0.66.

Cuba Roster: **Manager**: Servio Borges. **Batting** (AB, H, BA): Carmelo Pedroso (0, 0, .000), Francisco Javier Carbonell (0, 0, .000), Alfonso Martínez (16, 7, .438), Luis Casanova

(37, 19, .514), Antonio Muñoz (35, 15, .429), Pedro Jova (37, 12, .324), Victor Mesa (7, 3, .429), Pedro Medina (14, 5, .357), Lourdes Gourriel (37, 11, .297), Alfonso Urquiola (41, 11, .268), Héctor Olivera (35, 11, .314), Fernando Sánchez (32, 11, .344), Rodolfo Puente (35, 7, .200). **Pitching** (W–L): Julio Romero (2, 0), Rogelio García (0, 0), Juan Carlos Oliva (0, 0), Braudilio Vinent (3, 1), José Darcourt (1, 1), José Luis Alemán (0, 0), Rafael Castillo (0, 1).

USA Game Scores: Preliminary Round: USA beat Korea 6–4, USA beat Dominican Republic 10–5, USA beat Panama 3–2, USA beat Australia 14–2, USA beat Japan 6–1, Canada beat USA 9–7, Cuba beat USA 14–3. Semifinals: USA beat Dominican Republic 5–3. Finals: USA beat Cuba 6–5 (10).

Cuba Game Scores: Preliminary Round: Cuba beat Australia 5–0, Cuba beat Japan 10–8, Canada beat Cuba 2–1, Dominican Republic beat Cuba 8–4, Cuba beat South Korea 8–0, Cuba beat Panama 23–12, Cuba beat USA 14–3. Semifinals: Cuba beat South Korea 9–1. Finals: USA beat Cuba 6–5 (10).

1983 Intercontinental Cup Championship VI (Brussels, Belgium) (July 13–25)

Cuba reclaims the Intercontinental Cup championship lost two years earlier in Edmonton, winning mainly on the strength of offensive displays provided by slugging outfielder Victor Mesa. Mesa was tournament leader in most major offensive categories (including BA, hits, runs scored, and home runs). Veterans Antonio Muñoz (with 14 RBI), Lourdes Gourriel (with a .400-plus BA), and Antonio Pacheco (batting .378) also swung potent bats. Rogelio García (at three) and Braudilio Vinent (with two) claimed the bulk of the pitching victories. Former national team pitching star José Pineda took over for Servio Borges as manager and claimed the first of what would eventually be seven straight Cuban first-place finishes in this event.

Champion: Cuba (8–2)

Championship Round Standings: Cuba (1–0), USA (1–1), Chinese Taipei (0–1).

Playoff Round Standings: Cuba (2–1), USA (2–1), Chinese Taipei (2–1), Netherlands (0–3).

Elimination Round Standings: Cuba (5–1), USA (5–1), Chinese Taipei (3–3), Netherlands (3–3), South Korea (3–3), Nicaragua (1–5), Canada (1–5).

Individual Statistical Leaders: **BA**: Victor Mesa (CUB) .567; **Runs**: Victor Mesa (CUB) 13; **Hits**: Victor Mesa (CUB) 17; **2B**: Lourdes Gourriel (CUB) 4; **3B**: Antonio Pacheco (CUB) 2; **HR**: Victor Mesa (CUB), Eric Foxx (USA) 5; **RBI**: Antonio Muñoz (CUB) 14; **SB**: W. Fu Lien (KOR) 4; **Wins**: Chen Chiu (TPE) 3–0; **IP**: Zon Dong Liu (KOR) 31.0; **ERA**: Bill Swift (USA) 0.00.

Cuba Roster: **Manager**: José M. Pineda. **Batting** (AB, H, BA): Victor Mesa (42, 20, .476), Pedro Jova (41, 17, .415), Antonio Muñoz (44, 17, .386), Lourdes Gourriel (42, 18, .429), Pedro José Rodríguez (45, 17, .378), Fernando Sánchez (39, 15, .385), Fernando Hernández (18, 5, .278), Antonio Pacheco (37, 14, .378), Anselmo Martínez (31, 7, .389), Luis Casanova (18, 7, .389), Pedro Medina (11, 5, .455), Alfonso Urquiola (4, 1, .250), Leonardo Goire (6, 3, .500). **Pitching** (W, L, ERA): Rogelio García (3, 1, 3.32), Braudilio Vinent (2, 1, 4.36), Lázaro de la Torre (0, 0, 6.24), Mario Veliz (1, 0, 6.24), Jorge Luis Valdés (0, 0, 7.60), Anselmo Martínez (0, 0, 37.95), Julio Romero (2, 0, 0.50).

Cuba Game Scores: Preliminary Round: Cuba beat South Korea 17–2, Cuba beat USA 6–1, Cuba beat Netherlands 17–7, Cuba beat Chinese Taipei 12–3, Canada beat Cuba 12–11, Cuba beat Nicaragua 8–4. Playoffs: Cuba beat Netherlands 11–0, Chinese Taipei beat Cuba 13–1, Cuba beat USA 4–1. Finals: Cuba beat USA 8–4.

1985 Intercontinental Cup Championship VII (Edmonton, Canada) (August 8–18)

Eighteen-year-old Omar Linares made his first Intercontinental Cup appearance and batted .467 as the starting third baseman. Established stars Lourdes Gourriel and Luis

Casanova provided the biggest bats in the Cuban lineup, however, with Gourriel hitting over .400 and Casanova blasting 6 homers. Veteran right-hander José Luis Alemán earned victories in relief in both playoff games (over South Korea and Chinese Taipei) and was fittingly named tournament MVP. This was the first international tournament in which the dependable trio of Linares, Kindelán, and Pacheco (who would together dominate world tournaments for the next 15-plus years) appeared together in the same Cuban lineup.

Champion: Cuba (8–1)

Finals: Cuba beat South Korea 4–3 (Gold Medal), Japan beat Chinese Taipei 4–2 (Bronze Medal).

Semifinals: Cuba beat Chinese Taipei 8–7, South Korea beat Japan 4–3.

Preliminary Round Standings: Cuba (6–1), Japan (6–1), South Korea (5–2), Chinese Taipei (5–2), Canada (2–5), USA (2–5), Nicaragua (1–6), Australia (1–6).

Individual Statistical Leaders: **BA**: Ch. Tai Chuang (TPE) .531; **Runs**: Ch. Tai Chuang (TPE) 12; **Hits**: Ch. Tai Chuang (TPE) 17; **2B**: P. Meyers (USA), Antonio Muñoz (CUB) 6; **3B**: six players with two each; **HR**: Luis Casanova (CUB) 6; **RBI**: Luis Casanova (CUB) 14; **SB**: T. Hirose (JPN) 3; **Wins**: K. Bum Kim (KOR), H. Nagatomi (JPN) 3–0; **IP**: K. Bum Kim (KOR) 20.1; **ERA**: Reinaldo Costa (CUB) 0.00; **MVP**: José Luis Alemán (CUB).

Cuba Roster: **Manager**: José M. Pineda. **Batting** (AB, H, BA): Juan Castro (17, 5, .294), Orestes Kindelán (6, 2, .333), Antonio Pacheco (29, 11, .379), Antonio Muñoz (28, 11, .393), Rolando Verde (4, 0, .000), Pedro Jova (31, 7, .226), Lázaro Vargas (1, 0, .000), Omar Linares (30, 14, .467), Lourdes Gourriel (29, 12, .414), Fernando Sánchez (10, 1, .100), Lázaro Contreras (26, 10, .385), Luis Casanova (28, 12, .429), Fernando Hernández (10, 3, .300). **Pitching** (W, L, ERA): Luis Tissert (2, 0, 2.57), Julio Romero (1, 0, 3.24), Jorge Luis Valdés (1, 0, 2.00), Reinaldo Costa (1, 0, 0.00), Lázaro de la Torre (0, 0, 3.00), José Luis Alemán (3, 0, 1.00), José Ramón Riscart (0, 1, 6.75).

Cuba Game Scores: Preliminary Round: Cuba beat Nicaragua 17–3, Cuba beat Chinese Taipei 8–4, Japan beat Cuba 3–2, Cuba beat Australia 9–2, Cuba beat Canada 11–4, Cuba beat South Korea 7–1, Cuba beat USA 3–2. Semifinals: Cuba beat Chinese Taipei 8–7. Finals: Cuba beat South Korea 4–3.

1987 Intercontinental Cup Championship VIII (Havana, Cuba) (October 10–18)

Tournament play is staged in Havana for second time (the first was in 1979). Cuba scores one of its most lopsided victories, winning 13 games without defeat. Future major leaguers Chuck Knoblauch and Mickey Morandini play on Team USA, which finishes in the runner-up slot. Linares slugs 11 homers for an Intercontinental Cup tournament record and walks off with MVP honors. Jorge Fuentes debuts as Cuban manager, and a trio of pitchers (Jorge Luis Valdés, Rogelio García, and future big leaguer René Arocha) win three games apiece.

Champion: Cuba (13–0)

Teams and Final Standings: Gold: Cuba (13–0), Silver: USA (8–5), Bronze: Japan (10–3), Chinese Taipei (8–5), Canada (4–9), South Korea (6–7), Nicaragua (2–6), Mexico (2–6), Italy (1–7), Aruba (1–7).

Individual Statistical Leaders: **BA**: Alejo O'Reilly (CUB) .553; **Runs**: Omar Linares (CUB) 22; **Hits**: L. Chu Ming (TPE) 25; **2B**: Mickey Morandini (USA) 3; **3B**: Antonio Pacheco (CUB) 3; **HR**: Omar Linares (CUB) 11; **RBI**: Omar Linares (CUB) 26; **SB**: Chuck Knoblauch (USA) 7; **Wins**: Rogelio García (CUB), Jorge Luis Valdés (CUB) 3–0; **IP**: H. Ping Yang (TPE) 30.1; **ERA**: Pablo Miguel Abreu (CUB) 0.00.

Cuba Roster: **Manager**: Jorge Fuentes. **Batting** (AB, H, BA): Orestes Kindelán (47, 23, .469), Juan Castro (20, 1, .050), Pedro Luis Rodríguez (9, 2, .222), Alejo O'Reilly (38,

21, .553), Antonio Muñoz (7, 1, .143), Antonio Pacheco (48, 19, .396), Omar Linares (51, 23, .451), Lázaro Vargas (27, 10, .370), Luis Ulacia (45, 13, .289), Lourdes Gourriel (49, 16, .327), Ermidelio Urrutia (18, 8, .444). **Pitching** (W, L, ERA): Jorge Luis Valdés (3, 0, 1.29), Omar Ajete (1, 0, 0.69), Luis Tissert (1, 0, 0.75), Pablo Miguel Abreu (2, 0, 0.00), Rogelio García (3, 0, 0.81), René Arocha (3, 0, 1.64).

Cuba Game Scores: Multiple round-robin: Cuba beat Mexico 10–0, Cuba beat Italy 4–1, Cuba beat Canada 28–2, Cuba beat South Korea 12–1, Cuba beat Mexico 14–1, Cuba beat Canada 10–0, Cuba beat Italy 15–3, Cuba beat South Korea 8–1, Cuba beat Japan 11–5, Cuba beat South Korea 7–2, Cuba beat Canada 11–1, Cuba beat USA 5–0, Cuba beat Chinese Taipei 3–2.

1989 Intercontinental Cup Championship IX (San Juan, Puerto Rico) (August 16–27)

Cuba rings up an 8–2 victory over Japan in the title game to claim a fourth straight cup and also finishes its second consecutive tournament with an undefeated ledger. Lourdes Gourriel hits .435 (with a .913 slugging percentage) to walk off with MVP honors, punctuating his performance with four RBI in the final contest. Cuba's semifinal victory was a 14–0 rout of South Korea behind five hits (including a triple and a homer) by outfielder Luis Ulacia. The highlight of this tournament, however, came in the opening round when Lázaro Valle pitched an eight-inning perfect game (ended at 11–0 by the 10-run mercy rule) over South Korea, striking out 13 of the 24 batters he faced.

Champion: Cuba (8–0)

Finals: Cuba beat Japan 8–2 (Gold Medal), Puerto Rico beat South Korea 3–2 (Bronze Medal).

Semifinals: Cuba beat South Korea 14–0, Japan beat Puerto Rico 5–4.

Preliminary Round Standings: Cuba (6–0), Japan (4–2), Puerto Rico (3–3), South Korea (3–3), Chinese Taipei (3–3), USA (1–5), Italy (1–5).

Individual Statistical Leaders: **BA**: T. Matsui (JPN) .500; **Runs**: Orestes Kindelán (CUB) 10; **Hits**: T. Matsui (JPN) 13; **2B**: M. Mieske (USA) 4; **3B**: Ch. Tai Chuang (TPE) 2; **HR**: Orestes Kindelán (CUB) 5; **RBI**: Orestes Kindelán (CUB) 11; **SB**: H. Son Lee (KOR) 2; **Wins**: T. Yoda (JPN) 2–0; **IP**: D. Sung Gu (KOR) 18.2; **ERA**: Lázaro Valle (CUB) 0.00; **MVP**: Lourdes Gourriel (CUB).

Cuba Roster: **Manager**: Jorge Fuentes. **Batting** (AB, H, BA): Pedro Luis Rodríguez (15, 3, .200), José Raul Delgado (5, 1, .200), Alejo O'Reilly (15, 5, .333), Antonio Pacheco (24, 8, .333), Juan Padilla (2, 0, .000), Omar Linares (23, 11, .478), Germán Mesa (10, 1, .100), Victor Mesa (22, 9, .409), Luis Ulacia (13, 5, .385), Ermidelio Urrutia (5, 2, .400), Orestes Kindelán (20, 9, .450), Lourdes Gourriel (23, 10, .435), Ivan Rojas (20, 8, .400). **Pitching** (W, L, ERA): Lázaro Valle (2, 0, 0.00), José Luis Aleman (1, 0, 1.29), Jorge Luis Valdés (1, 0, 0.00), Pablo Miguel Abreu (1, 0, 3.00), Euclides Rojas (1, 0, 2.16), Osvaldo Duvergel (0, 0, 0.00), Omar Ajete (0, 0, 2,70).

Cuba Game Scores: Preliminary Round: Cuba beat Italy 16–0, Cuba beat Chinese Taipei 7–3, Cuba beat USA 13–2, Cuba beat South Korea 11–0, Cuba beat Japan 4–2, Cuba beat Puerto Rico 12–4. Semifinals: Cuba beat South Korea 14–0. Finals: Cuba beat Japan 8–2.

1991 Intercontinental Cup Championship X (Barcelona, Spain) (July 2–13)

Team Cuba now makes it five Intercontinental Cup titles in a row with an exciting extra-inning defeat of the strong challengers from Japan in the tournament finale. Southpaw ace Omar Ajete made an early exit from the championship game: 2 homers sent Cuba's starter to the showers in the fourth inning. Hiroshi Shintani held Cuba to a single run until the ninth frame, when two runs knotted the score. Japan tallied again in the tenth, but a bases-loaded single by catcher José Delgado brought home the Cuban victory.

Ajete shut out Japan in the preliminary round on the strength of 2 homers by second baseman Juan Padilla. The site for the tournament was Hospitalet Stadium on the grounds prepared for the upcoming 1992 Barcelona Olympics.

Champion: Cuba (10–1).

Finals: Cuba beat Japan 5–4 (Gold Medal), Nicaragua beat Chinese Taipei 4–3 (Bronze Medal).

Semifinals: Cuba beat Chinese Taipei 2–1, Japan beat Nicaragua 4–3.

Preliminary Round Standings: Cuba (8–1), Japan (7–2), Nicaragua (6–3), Chinese Taipei (6–3), South Korea (6–3), Mexico (5–4), Italy (4–5), Spain (2–7), Russia (1–8), France (0–9).

Individual Statistical Leaders: **BA**: Y. Yamoda (JPN) .500; **Runs**: José Estrada (CUB) 16; **Hits**: Carlos Manrique (MEX) 17; **2B**: H. Roa (NCA), R. Blandi (ITA), Y. Yamoda (JPN) 6; **3B**: seven players with two each; **HR**: Ramón Padilla (NCA), Luis Casanova (CUB) 4; **RBI**: Carlos Manrique (MEX) 17; **SB**: Y. Teing Chang (TPE) 10; **Wins**: D.S. Gu (KOR) 3–0; **IP**: Epifanio Pérez (NCA) 23.2; **ERA**: Omar Ajete (CUB), R. Sánchez (NCA) 0.00. Statistics based on preliminary round only.

Cuba Roster: **Manager**: Gerardo Junco. **Batting** (AB, H, BA): Evenecer Godinez (30, 9, .300), Juan Padilla (32, 10, .313), Gabriel Pierre (29, 9, .310), Luis Casanova (26, 10, .385), Miguel Zayas (4, 0, .000), Carlos Kindelán (5, 2, .400), Victor Bejerano (13, 2, .154), Lázaro Madera (21, 10, .476), Lázaro Junco (34, 14, .353), José Raul Delgado (26, 7, .269), Manuel Morales (5, 0, .000), Julio Germán Fernández (34, 13, .382), José Estrada (34, 14, .412). **Pitching** (W, L, ERA): Osvaldo Duvergel (1, 0, 4.00), Leonardo Tamayo (2, 0, 1.13), Ariel Cutiño (1, 0, 1.29), Wilson López (1, 0, 1.69), Felipe Fernández (0, 0, 13.50), Omar Ajete (2, 0, 0.00), Jorge Martínez (1, 1, 5.06).

Cuba Game Scores: Preliminary Round: Cuba beat France 10–0, Cuba beat South Korea 7–4, Cuba beat Japan 3–0, Cuba beat Italy 13–1, Cuba beat Chinese Taipei 4–2, Cuba beat Russia 11–1, Cuba beat Mexico 15–0, Cuba beat Spain 12–2, Nicaragua beat Cuba 10–5. Semifinals: Cuba beat Chinese Taipei 2–1. Finals: Cuba beat Japan 5–4.

1993 Intercontinental Cup Championship XI (Northern Italy) (June 23–July 4)

Cuba ran its string of consecutive Intercontinental Cup titles to six by defeating top rival Team USA 9–4 in the gold medal contest. Japan whitewashed Nicaragua 9–0 in the bronze medal game. Play was hosted in several northern Italian cities: Macerata, Rimini, Bologna, Verona, Navara, Modena, Reggio Emilia, and Parma. A crucial early-round game saw Cuba defeating Japan 4–3 in ten innings after a game-tying late-inning homer by Japan's Hidenori Taniguchi. Team USA also pushed the Cubans to the limit before losing 5–2 in an early-round meeting of the eventual finalists. Omar Linares clubbed 6 homers for the winners, and Orestes Kindelán walked off with the individual RBI crown; Linares again was the batting champion.

Champion: Cuba (11–0)

Finals: Cuba beat USA 9–4 (Gold Medal), Japan beat Nicaragua 9–0 (Bronze Medal).

Semifinals: Cuba beat Nicaragua 10–1, USA beat Japan 6–3.

Preliminary Round Standings: Cuba (9–0), Japan (8–1), USA (6–3), Nicaragua (5–4), South Korea (5–4), Australia (5–4), Mexico (3–6), Italy (2–7), Spain (2–7), France (0–9).

Individual Statistical Leaders: **BA**: Omar Linares (CUB) .576; **Runs**: Omar Linares (CUB) 16; **Hits**: Omar Linares (CUB) 19; **2B**: Ermidelio Urrutia (CUB), H. Kokibo (JPN), Todd Walker (USA) 5; **3B**: A. Fau (FRA) 3; **HR**: Omar Linares (CUB) 6; **RBI**: Orestes Kindelán (CUB), Hidenori Taniguchi (JPN) 16; **SB**: T. Ido (JPN), T. Nishi (JPN) 5; **Wins**: H. Watanabe (JPN) 2–0; **IP**: J. Woong Shin (KOR) 26.0; **ERA**: H. Watanabe (JPN) 0.00.

Cuba Roster: **Manager**: Jorge Fuentes. **Batting** (AB, H, BA): José Estrada (43, 18, .419), Antonio Pacheco (44, 17, .386), Omar Linares (40, 22, .550), Orestes Kindelán (42, 16, .381), Lourdes Gourriel (42, 16, .381), Victor Mesa (44, 16, .364), Ermidelio Urrutia (44, 18, .409), Adrian Hernández (25, 8, .320), Germán Mesa (34, 15, .441), Juan Padilla (1, 0, .000), Miguel Caldés (1, 0, .000), Juan Carlos Bruzón (2, 1, .500), Daniel Lazo (3, 3, 1.000), Juan Manrique (3, 1, .333), José Raul Delgado (9, 1, .111). **Pitching** (W, L, ERA): Orlando "El Duque" Hernández (1, 0, 2.08), Giorge Díaz (2, 0, 0.00), Lázaro Valle (1, 0, 1.93), Omar Ajete (1, 0, 1.17), Luis Rolando Arrojo (2, 0, 0.82), Jorge Luis Valdés (1, 0, 0.00), Osvaldo Fernández Rodríguez (1, 0, 1.93).

Cuba Game Scores: Preliminary Round: Cuba beat Australia 12–2, Cuba beat South Korea 11–0, Cuba beat Italy 12–0, Cuba beat Mexico 10–0, Cuba beat USA 5–2, Cuba beat Japan 4–3, Cuba beat Spain 8–0, Cuba beat France 14–2, Cuba beat Nicaragua 6–1. Playoffs: Cuba beat Dominican Republic 3–2. Semifinals: Cuba beat Nicaragua 10–1. Finals: Cuba beat USA 9–4.

1995 Intercontinental Cup Championship XII (Havana, Cuba) (October 26–November 5)

Cuba plays host for the third time, a record number of twelve teams participate in preliminary and playoff rounds, and Team Cuba runs its string of Intercontinental Cup championships to seven straight (the final two without losing a single game). This will be the last Cuban championship triumph in this event for the 1990s. An irony of this tournament is that Cuba does not boast a single leader in individual statistics but does get strong performances from pitcher Omar Luis (3–0, 0.86 ERA) and sluggers Omar Linares, Rey Isaac, and José Estrada, who all bat over .400 for the 9-game stretch.

Champion: Cuba (9–0)

Finals: Cuba beat Japan 4–1 (Gold Medal), Nicaragua beat South Korea 10–5 (Bronze Medal).

Playoffs: Cuba beat South Korea 6–5, Japan beat Nicaragua 4–2, Cuba beat Nicaragua 7–6, Japan beat South Korea 16–3, Cuba beat Japan 7–6, South Korea beat Nicaragua 10–2.

Group A Preliminary Round Standings: Cuba (5–0), Nicaragua (4–1), Netherlands (2–3), Chinese Taipei (2–3), Brazil (2–3), Spain (0–5).

Group B Preliminary Round Standings: Japan (5–0), South Korea (4–1), Puerto Rico (3–2), South Africa (1–4), Mexico (1–4), Italy (1–4).

Individual Statistical Leaders: **BA**: S. Yusuyuki (JPN) .692; **Runs**: O. Hideaki (JPN) 8; **Hits**: C. Jeffrey (NET) 11; **2B**: O.R. Hidemi (BRA) 6; **3B**: thirteen players with one each; **HR**: J.C. Rodríguez (PUR) 4; **RBI**: M. Nobuhike (JPN) 11; **SB**: L. Byoung Kyu (KOR) 6; **Wins**: D. Miranda (NCA) 2–0; **IP**: D. Miranda (NCA) 16.0; **ERA**: R. Rivera (PUR) 0.00.

Cuba Roster: **Manager**: Jorge Fuentes. **Batting** (AB, H, BA): Adrian Hernández (24, 9, .375), Juan Manrique (4, 1, .250), Jorge Luis Toca (36, 11, .306), Orestes Kindelán (35, 11, .314), Antonio Pacheco (27, 7, .259), Omar Linares (37, 17, .459), Germán Mesa (36, 10, .278), Juan Padilla (12, 2, .167), Eduardo Paret (1, 0, .000), Lourdes Gourriel (1, 0, .000), Victor Mesa (36, 10, .278), Rey Isaac (29, 13, .448), José Estrada (39, 16, .410), Luis Piloto (5, 1, .200), Michel Perdomo (DNP). **Pitching** (W, L, ERA): José Ibar (2, 0, 3.75), José Ariel Contreras (0, 0, 0.00), Lázaro Valle (0, 0, 2.84), Rolando Arrojo (1, 0, 3.27), Orlando Hernández (2, 0, 4.00), Pedro Luis Lazo (1, 0, 1.23), Omar Luis (3, 0, 0.86).

Cuba Game Scores: Preliminary Round: Cuba beat Netherlands 12–2, Cuba beat Nicaragua 4–3, Cuba beat Chinese Taipei 6–1, Cuba beat Brazil 12–2, Cuba beat Spain 10–0. Playoffs: Cuba beat South Korea 6–5, Cuba beat Nicaragua 7–6, Cuba beat Japan 7–6. Finals: Cuba beat Japan 4–1.

1997 Intercontinental Cup Championship XIII (Barcelona, Spain) (August 1–10)

A string of seven straight Intercontinental Cup titles for Cuba finally comes to an end with a shocking 11–2 defeat at the hands of Japan during the finals in Barcelona. Kohji Uehara is the winner for Japan in a contest put well out of reach by three runs in the first frame and three more in the second. The title game defeat would be the first single game loss in international tournament play for the Cubans since an early-round defeat during the 1991 Intercontinental Cup, also staged in Barcelona. Shockwaves from this defeat would cause immediate shake ups throughout Cuban baseball, with firings of national team manager Jorge Fuentes and national team technical director Miguel Valdés.

Champion: Japan (6–3)

Finals: Japan beat Cuba 11–2 (Gold Medal), Australia beat USA 7–6 (Bronze Medal).

Semifinals: Cuba beat USA 7–1, Japan beat Australia 10–5.

Preliminary Round Standings: Cuba (7–0), Australia (6–1), Japan (4–3), USA (4–3), Nicaragua (4–3), Italy (2–5), France (1–6), Spain (0–7).

Individual Statistical Leaders: **BA**: Paul Gonzalez (AUS) .588; **Runs**: Orestes Kindelán (CUB) 10; **Hits**: J. Tyner (USA) 13; **2B**: five players with four each; **3B**: José Estrada (CUB), Y. Takahashi (JPN) 2; **HR**: Orestes Kindelán (CUB) 6; **RBI**: Paul Gonzalez (AUS) 14; **SB**: Luis Ulacia (CUB) 3; **Wins**: José Ariel Contreras (CB), A. Shiamizu (JPN) 2–0; **IP**: S. Meurant (FRA) 15.0; **ERA**: Kohji Uehara (JPN) 0.00.

Cuba Roster: **Manager**: Jorge Fuentes. **Batting** (AB, H, BA): José Estrada (34, 10, .294), Luis Ulacia (35, 12, .343), Omar Linares (30, 11, .367), Orestes Kindelán (32, 11, .344), Antonio Pacheco (33, 12, .364), Yobal Dueñas (29, 8, .276), Gabriel Pierre (29, 12, .414), Juan Manrique (24, 8, .333), Miguel Caldés (32, 10, .313), Danel Castro (3, 0, .000), Lázaro Vargas (6, 2, .333), Juan Carlos Linares (2, 1, .500), Yosvany Madera (1, 0, .000), Rey Isaac (2, 1, .500). **Pitching** (W, L, ERA): José Ariel Contreras (2, 0, 2.61), Pedro Luis Lazo (2, 0, 1.23), Oscar Romero (1, 0, 10.29), Lázaro Garro (0, 0, 0.00), Ciro Silvino Licea (1, 1, 2.92), Wilson López (0, 0, 0.00), Leonides Turcás (0, 0, 1.80), Abel Madera (2, 0, 0.00).

Japan Game Scores: Preliminary Round: Japan beat USA 9–6, Japan beat Spain 12–2, Australia beat Japan 7–4, Japan beat France 9–1, Japan beat Italy 7–0, Nicaragua beat Japan 3–2, Cuba beat Japan 7–3. Semifinals: Japan beat Australia 10–5. Finals: Japan beat Cuba 11–2.

Cuba Game Scores: Preliminary Round: Cuba beat France 14–0, Cuba beat Australia 9–6, Cuba beat Spain 15–0, Cuba beat USA 4–1, Cuba beat Nicaragua 6–0, Cuba beat Italy 6–3, Cuba beat Japan 7–3. Semifinals: Cuba beat USA 7–1. Finals: Japan beat Cuba 11–2.

1999 Intercontinental Cup Championship XIV (Sydney, Australia) (November 3–14)

Cuba lost its second consecutive Intercontinental Cup with a subpar gold medal game performance, this time falling to host Australia in extra innings on a misplayed fly ball by outfielder Yasser Gómez in the eleventh frame. Australia was paced by Milwaukee Brewers catcher Dave Nilsson, whose timely slugging and eleven RBI earned tournament MVP honors. Cuban selections for the all-tournament team were veteran pitcher Faustino Corrales, second baseman Oscar Macías, shortstop Danel Castro, and outfielder Yobal Dueñas. Veteran stars such as Linares, Kindelán, Pacheco, Contreras, and Germán Mesa were left off this slightly subpar Cuban roster in favor of youngsters such as Gómez, Dueñas, Ciro Silvino Licea, and catcher Ariel Pestano.

Champion: Australia (8–1)

Finals: Australia Beat Cuba 4–3 (11 innings) (Gold Medal), Japan beat USA 6–0 (Bronze Medal).

Semifinals: Cuba beat USA 7–0, Australia beat Japan 2–0.

Preliminary Round Standings: Australia (6–1), Cuba (5–2), Japan (5–2), USA (5–2), Chinese Taipei (3–4), South Korea (2–5), Italy (2–5), Netherlands (0–7).

Individual Statistical Leaders: **BA**: A. Wamura (JPN) .483; **Runs**: A. Burton (AUS) 8; **Hits**: A. Wamura (JPN) 14; **2B**: Dave Nilsson (AUS), Danel Castro (CUB) 4; **3B**: C. Pan (TPE) 3; **HR**: Oscar Macías (CUB) 3; **RBI**: Dave Nilsson (AUS) 11; **SB**: Y. Hyung Ahn (KOR), B. Ralph (USA) 4; **Wins**: seven pitchers tied with two each; **IP**: T. Chong (KOR) 18.1; **ERA**: T. Fujita (JPN) 0.00; **MVP**: Dave Nilsson (AUS).

Cuba Roster: **Manager**: Carlos Martí. **Batting** (AB, H, BA): Ariel Pestano (25, 7, .280), Oscar Machado (2, 2, 1.000), Michel Abreu (4, 0, .000), Loidel Chapelli (23, 7, .304), Danel Castro (28, 8, .286), J.C. Moreno (1, 1, 1.000), Oscar Macías (25, 6, .240), Michel Enríquez (30, 10, .333), Gabriel Pierre (24, 5, .208), Michel Perdomo (21, 2, .095), Yobal Dueñas (26, 10, .385), Robelquis Videaux (12, 3, .250), Yasser Gómez (1, 0, .000), Isaac Martínez (12, 4, .333). **Pitching** (W, L, ERA): Yosvani Pérez (1, 0, 1.00), Faustino Corrales (2, 0, 0.00), Maels Rodríguez (0, 0, 13.50), Carlos Yanes (0, 1, 1.59), Leonides Turcás (1, 0, 1.42), Jorge Luis Machado (0, 0, 0.00), Ciro Silvino Licea (2, 0, 3.46), Yoide Castillo (0, 1, 5.40).

Australia Game Scores: Preliminary Round: Australia beat Netherlands 3–1, Australia beat Italy 9–1, Australia beat USA 12–2, Australia beat Chinese Taipei 11–3, Japan beat Australia 6–1, Australia beat Korea 3–0, Australia beat Cuba 5–1. Semifinals: Australia beat Japan 2–0. Finals: Australia beat Cuba 4–3 (11).

Cuba Game Scores: Preliminary Round: South Korea beat Cuba 4–3, Cuba beat Chinese Taipei 1–0, Cuba beat Netherlands 7–2, Cuba beat Japan 4–1, Cuba beat Italy 14–2, Cuba beat USA 5–1, Australia beat Cuba 5–1. Semifinals: Cuba beat USA 7–0. Finals: Australia beat Cuba 4–3 (11).

2002 Intercontinental Cup Championship XV (Havana, Cuba) (November 8–20)

Not surprisingly, Cuba regained its Intercontinental Cup supremacy when play returned to island home turf in a tournament staged in both Matanzas and Havana and featuring the youngest Cuban international squad in more than two decades. The host team races through its opposition largely untested in both the preliminary (5-game round-robin) and championship rounds (double-elimination), after the United States fails to send a team to Cuba for largely political reasons. Yobal Dueñas is ultimately the hitting star, with a mammoth seventh-inning two-run homer to decide a hard-fought 2–1 gold medal victory over South Korea (Cuba's only severe test). New third-base star Michel Enríquez proves an adequate replacement for Omar Linares as the tourney's leading hitter, and veteran hurler José Ibar proves largely unhittable in two eight-inning outings. The successful tournament also sets the stage for World Cup competition scheduled to return to Havana in November 2003.

Champion: Cuba (10–0) (Silver Medal: South Korea; Bronze Medal: Dominican Republic).

Playoff Finals Phase: Cuba beat South Korea 2–1, South Korea beat Panama 8–0, Cuba beat Dominican Republic 11–0.

Playoff Semifinals Phase: Cuba (3–0), South Korea (2–1), Dominican Republic (2–1), Panama (2–1), Venezuela (1–2), Japan (1–2), Chinese Taipei (1–2), Italy (0–3).

Group A Elimination Round: Cuba (5–0), Venezuela (3–2), Japan (3–2), Dominican Republic (2–3), Netherlands (2–3), China (0–5).

Group B Elimination Round: South Korea (4–1), Chinese Taipei (4–1), Panama (3–2), Italy (2–3), Brazil (1–4), Mexico (1–4).

Individual Statistical Leaders: **BA**: Michel Enríquez (CUB) .526; **Runs**: Frederich Cepeda (CUB), Michel Enríquez (CUB) 7; **Hits**: Luis Iglesias (PAN) 11; **2B**: Carlos Muñoz (PAN) 5; **3B**: Germain Chirinos (VEN) 2; **HR**: Katsuaki Furuki (JPN), Feng-An Tsai (TPE) 4; **RBI**: Yobal Dueñas (CUB), Feng-An Tsai (TPE) 10; **SB**: Daniel Matsumoto (BRA)

3; **Wins**: Ifreidi Coss Gómez (CUB) 2; **IP**: Chi-Hsien Ho (TPE) 12.2; **ERA**: José Ibar (CUB) 0.00; **MVP**: Bárbaro Cañizares (CUB). *Official tournament statistics include preliminary round qualification games only.

Cuba Roster: **Manager**: Héctor Hernández. **Batting** (AB, H, BA): Michel Enríquez (34, 17.500), Yasser Gómez (26, 7, .269), Eduardo Paret (31, 11, .355), Frederich Cepeda (26, 6, .231), Bárbaro Cañizares (34, 14, .412), Kendry Morales (37, 10, .270), Oscar Macías (7, 1, .143), Amaury Casañas (26, 11, .423), Ariel Pestano (32, 7, .219), Robelquis Videaux (7, 1, .143), Yobal Dueñas (32, 11, .344), Yunieski Gourriel (3, 0, .000), Yorelvis Charles (5, 2, .400), Giorvis Duvergel (7, 1, .143), Roger Machado (5, 0, .000). **Pitching** (W, L, ERA): José Ibar (2, 0, 0.46), Pedro Luis Lazo (0, 0, 2.84), Vicyohandri Odelín (1, 0, 4.97), Orelvis Ávila (1, 0, 0.00), Yadel Martí (2, 0, 2.25), Norge Vera (1, 0, 1.42), Ifreidi Coss Gómez (2, 0, 0.00), Maels Rodríguez (1, 0, 1.42), Yosvani Pérez (0, 0, 9.00). *Cuba roster statistics complete for preliminary round and medal round games.

Cuba Game Scores: Elimination Round: Cuba beat Netherlands 5–0, Cuba beat Japan 8–7, Cuba beat Venezuela 15–2, Cuba beat Dominican Republic 14–5, Cuba beat China 12–1. Semifinals Phase: Cuba beat Dominican Republic 3–2. Semifinals: Cuba beat Japan 5–0, Cuba beat Italy 11–0, Cuba beat Panama 7–1. Finals Phase: Cuba beat Dominican Republic 11–0, Cuba beat South Korea 2–1.

PAN AMERICAN GAMES BASEBALL CHAMPIONSHIPS, 1951–2003

An inaugural Pan American Games event in Buenos Aires (March 1951)—especially its showcase baseball competitions—was surrounded by a boatload of ominous and even bizarre circumstances, as well as strong flavorings of things to come. The U.S. baseball team traveling to Argentina for the tournament was not the usual select all-star group, but rather a ragtag varsity ball club from Wake Forest University. The multisport games themselves had been in the works for about a dozen years but had been put off for a decade on account of World War II. These particular games were almost swept away by severe storms that raked the Argentine capital city on the eve of the event and forced several days of postponement for repairs to damaged venues. The on-field baseball round-robin—once underway—quickly set a pattern that would remain very much the norm down to the present. It was the familiar scenario of Cuba on the champion's platform and a small handful of the region's other baseball worshipping nations (in this case, Mexico and the United States deadlocked in second) shaking off also-ran status to scrap for the remaining consolation prizes. After winning the lidlifter, Cuba would fall out of the championship picture only in 1955 and 1959—a period preoccupied at home with the revolution against Fulgencio Batista, and again in 1967, when it suffered one of its most embarrassing letdowns ever in the finals with archrival Team USA. The Pan American tournament reached a zenith at Winnipeg in 1999, doubling as the qualifying event for the 2000 Sydney Olympics. The most exciting shootout was arguably the one in 1987 at Bush Stadium in Indianapolis, which matched the Cubans and Team USA in a hard-fought finale viewed by a large stateside television audience. Since their second place finish in Winnipeg in 1967, the Cubans have lost four times—four individual games that is, while winning seventy.

Cuba's Overall Performance: Tournaments (11 of 13 Tournament titles won, plus one second place and one fourth place); Games (91 Won and 13 Lost, .875 Pct.).

Country-by-Country Championships Won: Cuba (11 of 13 tournaments entered), Venezuela (1), Dominican Republic (1), and USA (1).

Note: Cuba finished in fourth place in 1959 tournament at Chicago (USA); it was Cuba's only nonmedal finish in 12 tournaments attended. Cuba did not participate in 1955 Pan American Games (held in Mexico City, Mexico).

1951 Pan American Games Championship I (Buenos Aires, Argentina) (February 27– March 6)

Cuba captures the first-ever Pan American Games baseball title by defeating a surprisingly strong U.S. college contingent from Wake Forest University in the final round-robin game by an 8–1 score. Mexico matched the Americans' overall record but fell to the United States in their head-to-head match-up. Violent windstorms delayed the opening of the Games and adversely affected playing-field conditions. Standing-room-only crowds of 4,000 to 5,000 attended every game, with 8,000 packed into the host stadium (most of them standing) for the Cuba–United States showdown. Future minor leaguer Ángel Scull was the hitting star for Cuba and tied for the home run lead with U.S. slugger Frank Wehner.

Champion: Cuba (6–1) (Silver Medal: USA; Bronze Medal: Mexico)

Teams and Final Standings: Gold: Cuba (6–1), Silver: USA (5–2), Bronze: Mexico (5–2), Nicaragua (4–3), Venezuela (4–3), Colombia (3–4), Brazil (1–6), Argentina (0–7). Note: USA defeated Mexico (9–3) during round-robin play to earn silver medal.

Individual Statistical Leaders: **BA**: Fernando García (MEX) .423; **Runs**: Frank Wehner (USA) 13; **Hits**: Juan Izaguirre (CUB), Israel Arredondo (VEN) 13; **2B**: Israel Arredondo (VEN) 5; **3B**: five players with two each; **HR**: Ángel Scull (CUB), Frank Wehner (USA) 3; **RBI**: Ángel Scull (CUB) 14; **SB**: Ángel Scull (CUB) 4; **Wins**: Stanley Johnson (USA) 3–0; **Strikeouts**: Stanley Johnson (USA) 25; **IP**: Stanley Johnson (USA) 30; **ERA**: Juan Ravelo (CUB), 0.00.

Cuba Roster: **Manager**: Fabio de la Torre. **Position Players**: M. Díaz, A. Brito, Juan Izaguirre (13 H), D. Jácome, O. Orgelles, J. Silva, L. Feijo, G. Delgado, Ángel Scull (3 HR, 11 RBI, 4 SB), Juan Vistuer, A. Herrera. **Pitchers** (W–L): N. Campbell (1–0), G. Martínez (1–0), L. Fiuza (2–0), Juan Ravelo (1–0), C. Oviedo (1–1). No additional data or player statistics are available.

Cuba Game Scores: Round-robin: Cuba beat Mexico 3–0, Cuba beat Colombia 5–2, Cuba beat Nicaragua 6–5, Venezuela beat Cuba 4–3, Cuba beat Argentina 18–0, Cuba beat USA 8–1, Cuba beat Brazil 24–3.

1955 Pan American Games Championship II (Mexico City, Mexico) (March 13–24)

Action took place at the 30,000-seat Social Security Baseball Park in downtown Mexico City and featured a double round-robin format involving five teams. The surprising Dominican squad lost once in the opening round to Team USA and again in the second round to Mexico, but held on to edge the USA (which lost three straight in the second round) by a single game in the standings. Top prospect in the Dominican lineup was a Santo Dominigo University medical student named Felipe Alou, who would soon be the first Dominican-raised player to make it to the major leagues. Cuba sat on the sidelines, the bulk of its best amateur talent recently having been funneled off to the Class B Havana Cubans (1946–1953), Class A Cuban Sugar Kings (after 1954), and minor league clubs in the United States.

Champion: Dominican Republic (6–2) (Silver Medal: USA; Bronze Medal: Venezuela)

Teams and Final Standings: Dominican Republic (6–2), USA (5–3), Venezuela (4–4), Mexico (4–4), Dutch Antilles (1–7). Note: Venezuela defeated Mexico (8–2) in playoff game for bronze medal.

Individual Statistical Leaders: **BA**: Domingo Vargas (DOM) .453; **Runs**: Pablo Tineo (DOM) 13; **Hits**: Domingo Vargas (DOM) 16; **2B**: J. Faillo (DOM), J. Matos (VEN), James Temp (USA) 4; **3B**: four players with three each; **HR**: J. Schoolmaker (USA) 3; **RBI**: James Temp (USA) 14; **SB**: Pablo Tineo (DOM), J. Chico (MEX) 5; **Wins**: Rafael Quesada (DOM) 3–0; **Strikeouts**: R. Quesada (DOM), Paul Ebert (USA) 18; **IP**: Juan Julián (AHO) 23; **ERA**: F. Barranca (MEX), 1.59.

Dominican Republic Game Scores: Double round-robin: Dominican Republic beat Venezuela 4–3, Dominican Republic beat Mexico 8–7, USA beat Dominican Republic 6–5, Dominican Republic beat Dutch Antilles 15–6, Dominican Republic beat Venezuela 10–8, Mexico beat Dominican Republic 8–6, Dominican Republic beat USA 10–7, Dominican Republic beat Dutch Antilles 13–8.

Cuba Did Not Participate

1959 Pan American Games Championship III (Chicago, Illinois, USA) (August 27–September 7)

Cuba returns to action but suffers a disappointing fourth-place finish, mustering only two opening-round wins and losing three straight in championship play. Nine teams took part in the event staged in Comiskey Park and the large field necessitated a "two group" structure for opening round games. A final-round 3–2 U.S. victory over Cuba clinched a bronze medal for the winners. Southwest Conference batting champion and future major league Hall-of-Fame hero Lou Brock garnered only a single base hit in ten at-bats. Future postrevolution Cuban Leaguers Pedro Chávez and Urbano González led an uneven Cuban lineup that boasted few other recognizable names or all-star performers.

Champion: Venezuela (6–1) (Silver Medal: Puerto Rico; Bronze Medal: USA)

Teams and Final Standings: Gold: Venezuela (6–1), Silver: Puerto Rico (5–1), Bronze: USA (4–3), Cuba (2–4), Mexico (3–2), Costa Rica (3–3), Nicaragua (2–4), Dominican Republic (2–3), Brazil (0–6). Note: Cuba qualified for four-team medal round as second-place finisher in preliminary round Pool A.

Individual Statistical Leaders: **BA**: Irmo Figueroa (PUR) .500; **Hits**: Carlos Pizarro (PUR) 12; **2B**: Roberto Coto (MEX) 5; **3B**: José Flores (VEN) 3; **HR**: R. Vázquez (PUR), A. Hall (USA) 2; **RBI**: R. Vázquez (PUR) 10; **Wins**: M. Ruiz (MEX), M. Pérez (VEN), L. Peñalver (VEN) 2–0; **ERA**: Charles Davis (USA) 0.69.

Cuba Roster: **Manager**: M. de la Fuente. **Batting** (AB, H, BA): R. Bringas (12, 3, .250), Pedro Carvajal (21, 4, .181), A. Castillo (19, 2, .105), A. Crespo (25, 7, .280), Pedro Chávez (9, 5, .556), R. Díaz (9, 2, .222), Urbano González (11, 4, .363), Antonio Jiménez (12, 4, .333), M. González (18, 3, .167), P. Moret (15, 3, .200), T. Ramos (2, 1, .500), J. Torres (10, 3, .300), O. Flores (16, 4, .250), O. Albelo (6, 2, .333), R. Pérez (4, 0, .000), A. Rodríguez (3, 0, .000), F. Sanfeliz (4, 2, .500), Alfredo Street (4, 1, .250). **Pitching** (W, L): R. Pérez (1, 0), O. Albelo (0, 1), A. Rodríguez (1, 0), F. Sanfeliz (0, 2), Alfredo Street (0, 1).

Venezuela Game Scores: Preliminary Round: Venezuela beat USA 11–6, Mexico beat Venezuela 3–0, Venezuela beat Brazil 14–1, Venezuela beat Costa Rica 14–2. Finals Phase: Venezuela beat Cuba 6–5, Venezuela beat USA 3–2, Venezuela beat Puerto Rico 6–2.

Cuba Game Scores: Preliminary Round: Cuba beat Dominican Republic 9–3, Puerto Rico beat Cuba 9–1, Cuba beat Nicaragua 5–4. Finals Phase: Venezuela beat Cuba 6–5, Puerto Rico beat Cuba 4–3, USA beat Cuba 3–2.

1963 Pan American Games Championship IV (San Paulo, Brazil) (April 21–May 1)

Paced by a pitching staff of veteran Cuban Leaguers Aquino Abreu, Manuel Alarcón, and Modesto Verdura, along with the booming bats of Urbano González, Pedro Chávez, and Antonio González, Cuba climbed back to the top of the heap by winning seven of eight contests. Team USA lost twice to the champions by 13–1 and 3–1 counts. Alarcón, Verdura, and Abreu each registered two pitching wins and Cuban hitters paced most individual batting categories (all but doubles, triples, and stolen bases). Only one member of the strong Cuban pitching staff registered an ERA as high as 3.00.

Champion: Cuba (7–1) (Silver Medal: USA; Bronze Medal: Mexico)

Teams and Final Standings: Gold: Cuba (7–1), Silver: USA (5–3), Bronze: Mexico (4–4), Venezuela (2–6), Brazil (2–6).

Individual Statistical Leaders: **BA**: Urbano González (CUB) .485; **Runs**: Antonio González (CUB) 13; **Hits**: Urbano González (CUB) 16; **2B**: Archie Moore (USA), Wilson Parma (USA) 4; **3B**: Ángel Méndez (VEN) 4; **HR**: Miguel Cuevas (CUB) 3; **RBI**: Pedro Chávez (CUB) 13; **SB**: Alan de Jardin (USA) 4; **Wins**: Manuel Alarcón (CUB), Modesto Verdura (CUB), Aquino Abreu (CUB) 2–0; **Strikeouts**: Oscar Ogassawara (BRA) 19; **IP**: Luis García (MEX) 27.1; **ERA**: Aquino Abreu (CUB) 0.50.

Cuba Roster: **Manager**: Gilberto Torres. **Batting** (AB, H, BA): Miguel Cuevas (17, 9, .529), Urbano González (33, 16, .485), Pedro Chávez (32, 14, .438), Daniel Hernández (31, 11, .355), Ramón Hechavarría (18, 6, .333), Raul Ortega (6, 2, .333), Ricardo Lazo (16, 5, .313), Jorge Trigoura (32, 9, .281), Fidel Linares (30, 7, .233), Lázaro Pérez (19, 4, .211), Santiago Scott (11, 2, .182), Antonio González (28, 5, .179). **Pitching** (W, L, ERA): Aquino Abreu (2, 0, 0.50), Modesto Verdura (2, 0, 1.00), Antonio Rubio (0, 1, 1.42), Manuel Alarcón (2, 0, 1.50), Rolando Pastor (0, 0, 2.25), Franklyn Aspillaga (1, 0, 3.00).

Cuba Game Scores: Double round-robin: Cuba beat USA 13–1, Cuba beat Brazil 11–2, Mexico beat Cuba 5–2, Cuba beat Venezuela 13–3, Cuba beat USA 3–1, Cuba beat Brazil 17–3, Cuba beat Mexico 7–3, Cuba beat Venezuela 6–4.

1967 Pan American Games Championship V (Winnipeg, Canada) (July 23–August 6)

In a breakout year for U.S. amateur baseball interests, the Americans captured their only Pan American Games title, defeating defending champion Cuba in the first and third games of a showdown final series. The only two U.S. losses in the preliminaries also came at the hands of the Cubans. High drama marked the final game, when rain showers delayed the top of the ninth frame of a 1–1 tie, setting the stage for a clutch two-run game-winning single by George Greer off Cuban ace Manuel Alarcón. For the first time, Team USA was the Pan American champion—but it would also be the final time. Across the next three decades and eight tournaments, Cuba would come home winners each and every time.

Champion: USA (8–3) (Silver Medal: Cuba; Bronze Medal: Puerto Rico)

Playoffs: USA beat Cuba 8–3, Cuba beat USA 7–5, USA beat Cuba 2–1.

Preliminary Round Standings: Cuba (7–1), USA (6–2), Puerto Rico (4–4), Mexico (2–6), Canada (1–7).

Individual Statistical Leaders: **BA**: Allan Robertson (CAN) .467; **Runs**: Steve Sogge (USA) 11; **Hits**: Allan Robertson (CAN) 14; **2B**: George Greer (USA) 6; **3B**: José Báez (PUR) 2; **HR**: Steve Sogge (USA) 3; **RBI**: Félix Isasi (CUB) 10; **SB**: Fermín Laffita (CUB) 5; **Wins**: Rigoberto Betancourt (CUB), Roberto Valdés (CUB), T. Plodinet (USA) 2–0; **Strikeouts**: Joe Sanderfeld (USA), R. Stead (CAN) 23; **IP**: R. Stead (CAN) 23.1; **ERA**: Joe Sanderfield (USA) 0.75.

Cuba Roster: **Manager**: Roberto Ledo. **Batting** (AB, H, BA): Elpidio Mancebo (17, 6, .353), Felipe Sarduy (26, 9, .346), Fermín Laffita (42, 14, .333), Antonio González (36, 11, .306), Félix Rosa (7, 2, .286), Ricardo Lazo (21, 6, .286), Urbano González (36, 10, .278), Féliz Isasi (46, 10, .217), Pedro Chávez (46, 10, .217), Miguel Cuevas (16, 3, .188), Antonio Jiménez (22, 4, .182), Lázaro Pérez (19, 2, .105). **Pitching** (W, L, ERA): Rigoberto Betancourt (2, 0, 2.45), Roberto Valdés (2, 0, 2.81), Jesús Torriente (2, 0, 1.17), Manuel

Alarcón (1, 2, 2.33), Gaspar Pérez (0, 0, 2.70), Felipe Sarduy (0, 0, 3.60), Alfredo Street (1, 1, 6.14).

USA Game Scores: Preliminary Round: Cuba beat USA 4–3, USA beat Mexico 4–1, USA beat Puerto Rico 8–3, USA beat Canada 14–10, Cuba beat USA 9–2, USA beat Mexico 6–3, USA beat Puerto Rico 7–3, USA beat Canada 14–2. Playoffs: USA beat Cuba 8–3, Cuba beat USA 7–5, USA beat Cuba 2–1.

Cuba Game Scores: Preliminary Round: Cuba beat USA 4–3, Cuba beat Mexico 4–1, Cuba beat Puerto Rico 3–0, Cuba beat Canada 6–4, Cuba beat USA 9–2, Cuba beat Mexico 6–5, Cuba beat Puerto Rico 6–5, Canada beat Cuba 10–9. Playoffs: USA beat Cuba 8–3, Cuba beat USA 7–5, USA beat Cuba 2–1.

1971 Pan American Games Championship VI (Cali, Colombia) (July 31–August 9)

The defending champion Americans took their title defense quite seriously in 1971 and played a 30-game exhibition schedule before arriving in Cali with a team that included future major leaguers Fred Lynn and Alan Bannister. A key match-up was the third opening round game, in which the confident Americans lost to Cuba 4–3, despite solo home runs by outfielders Fred Lynn and Jerry Mims and first baseman Jerry Tabb. A standing-room-only crowd of 11,000 watched this headline contest, which provided the only close call for the undefeated Cuban team. Cuba's victory accomplished the first of a string of eight straight Pan American Games gold medals that extends down to the present moment.

Champion: Cuba (8–0) (Silver Medal: USA; Bronze Medal: Colombia)

Teams and Final Standings: Gold: Cuba (8–0), Silver: USA (6–2), Bronze: Colombia (4–4), Canada (4–4), Puerto Rico (3–5), Venezuela (3–5), Dominican Republic (3–5), Nicaragua (3–5), Mexico (2–6). Note: Colombia defeated Canada (7–6) during round-robin play to claim bronze medal.

Individual Statistical Leaders: **BA**: Luis Escobar (COL) .552; **Runs**: six players with eight each; **Hits**: Luis Mercado (PUR) 16; **2B**: Félix Isasi (CUB) 6; **3B**: Wilfredo Sánchez (CUB), C. Errington (NCA) 2; **HR**: Fred Lynn (USA) 4; **RBI**: Wilfredo Sánchez (CUB), Armando Capiró (CUB) 10; **SB**: Miguel Dilone (DOM) 3; **Wins**: six players with two each; **Strikeouts**: J. Smith (USA) 21; **IP**: J.J. Tineo (DOM) 20.1; **ERA**: Antonio Herradora (NCA) 0.00; **MVP**: Alan Bannister (USA).

Cuba Roster: **Manager**: Servio Borges. **Batting** (AB, H, BA): Lázaro Martínez (2, 1, .500), Rigoberto Rosique (20, 10, .455), Lázaro Pérez (32, 14, .438), Urbano González (7, 3, .429), Agustín Marquetti (31, 12, .387), Féliz Isasi (34, 13, .382), Wilfredo Sánchez (39, 13, .333), Rodolfo Puente (27, 9, .333), Armando Capiró (35, 11, .314), Vicente Díaz (25, 7, .280), Silvio Montejo (8, 1, .125). **Pitching** (W, L, ERA): Rolando Macías (2, 0, 0.59), Emilio Salgado (1, 0, 0.90), Braudilio Vinent (1, 0, 1.35), José Antonio Huelga (2, 0, 1.72), Walfrido Ruiz (1, 0, 7.45), Oscar Romero (1, 0, 0.00).

Cuba Game Scores: Round-robin: Cuba beat Dominican Republic 4–0, Cuba beat Puerto Rico 15–1, Cuba beat Nicaragua 4–1, Cuba beat USA 4–3, Cuba beat Canada 7–4, Cuba beat Venezuela 6–0, Cuba beat Mexico 6–2, Cuba beat Colombia 10–4.

1975 Pan American Games Championship VII (Mexico City, Mexico) (October 13–24)

Cuba's successful and undefeated title defense came largely on the strength of a stellar pitching staff that included Braudilio Vinent, Juan Pérez, Santiago "Changa" Mederos, Julio Romero, Oscar Romero, and Oscar Carrero. Four of the Cuban triumphs (half their tournament total) were shutouts. Cuba assured its victory in the final two games with a come-from-behind 4–3 conquest of the Americans and a 3–0 whitewashing of host Mexico. Runner-up United States also boasted a stellar mound corps, with future big leaguers Bob Owchinko, Pete Redfern, Rich Wortham, Scott Sanderson, and Mike Scott,

all still collegians at the time. The U.S. roster also featured additional big league prospects Ron Hassey (catcher), Wayne Krenchicki (infielder), and Steve Kemp (outfielder).
Champion: Cuba (8–0) (Silver Medal: USA; Bronze Medal: Venezuela)
Teams and Final Standings: Gold: Cuba (8–0), Silver: USA (6–2), Bronze: Venezuela (5–3), Dominican Republic (5–3), Mexico (5–3), Colombia (3–5), Canada (2–6), Puerto Rico (2–6), El Salvador (0–8). Note: Venezuela defeated Mexico (8–2) and Dominican Republic (9–3) in round-robin series to determine bronze medal.
Individual Statistical Leaders: **BA**: Luis Mercado (PUR) .500; **Runs**: Luis Bravo (VEN), David Stegman (USA) 8; **Hits**: J. Hernández (VEN) 14; **2B**: Gustavo Bastardo (VEN), Agustín Marquetti (CUB) 4; **3B**: Osvaldo Oliva (CUB) 3; **HR**: nine players with one each; **RBI**: Ron Hassey (USA) 9; **SB**: J. Hernández (VEN) 6; **Wins**: Bob Owchinko (USA) 3–0; **Strikeouts**: Bob Owchinko (USA) 28; **IP**: V. Cruz (DOM) 26; **ERA**: Juan Pérez (CUB) 0.00.
Cuba Roster: **Manager**: Servio Borges. **Batting** (AB, H, BA): Pedro José Rodríguez (5, 3, .600), Félix Isasi (10, 5, .500), Agustín Marquetti (25, 12, .480), Evelio Hernández (26, 12, .462), Osvaldo Oliva (29, 13, .448), Fermín Laffita (24, 9, .375), Alfonso Urquiola (287, 9, .333), Rodolfo Puente (24, 8, .333), Fernando Sánchez (6, 2, .333), Armando Capiró (32, 10, .323), Lázaro Pérez (4, 1, .250), Agustín Arias (2, 0, .000), Antonio Muñoz (20, 4, .200), Wilfredo Sánchez (21, 4, .190). **Pitching** (W, L, ERA): Braudilio Vinent (2, 0, 3.44), Juan Pérez (2, 0, 0.00), Santiago "Changa" Mederos (1, 0, 1.38), Julio Romero (1, 0, 2.08), Omar Carrero (0, 0, 2.16), Oscar Romero (2, 0, 1.80).
Cuba Game Scores: Round-robin: Cuba beat Canada 9–8, Cuba beat Dominican Republic 4–3, Cuba beat Puerto Rico 6–3, Cuba beat El Salvador 6–0, Cuba beat Venezuela 2–0, Cuba beat Colombia 12–0, Cuba beat USA 4–3, Cuba beat Mexico 3–0.

1979 Pan American Games Championship VIII (San Juan, Puerto Rico) (July 2–11)

Team USA was shut out of a Pan American baseball medal for the first time in eight tries while the Cubans rang up their third gold medallion in a row and fifth overall. One of the best U.S. teams ever—featuring future big league pitchers Tim Leary and Craig Lefferts and solid hitters Terry Francona and Mike Gallego—slumped in the late going and finished in fourth slot. Vinent again led the Cuban pitching with four victories (and 0.44 ERA) and Pedro José (Cheíto) Rodríguez continued his slugging onslaught from earlier Intercontinental Cup matches in Havana with five more round-trippers. Cheíto and Armando Capiró also both hit an even .500 to pace the tournament in batting.
Champion: Cuba (8–0) (Silver Medal: Dominican Republic; Bronze Medal: Puerto Rico)
Teams and Final Standings: Gold: Cuba (8–0), Silver: Dominican Republic (7–1), Bronze: Puerto Rico (6–2), USA (5–3), Bahamas (3–5), Venezuela (3–5), Colombia (2–6), Canada (1–7), Mexico (1–7).
Individual Statistical Leaders: **BA**: Pedro José Rodríguez (CUB), Armando Capiró (CUB) .500; **Runs**: Fernando Sánchez (CUB) 11; **Hits**: Luis Casanova (CUB), Agustín Marquetti (CUB), Terry Francona (USA) 13; **2B**: J. Cazáeez (MEX) 5; **3B**: Luis Casanova (CUB), Terry Francona (USA) 3; **HR**: Pedro José Rodríguez (CUB) 5; **RBI**: Agustín Marquetti (CUB) 13; **SB**: A. Romero (DOM), Y.A. Morrillo (VEN) 3; **Wins**: Braudilio Vinent (CUB) 4–0; **Strikeouts**: J. Feliciano (PUR) 22; **IP**: Braudilio Vinent (CUB), R. Seymour (BAH) 20.1; **ERA**: O. de León (DOM) 0.00.
Cuba Roster: **Manager**: Servio Borges. **Batting** (AB, H, BA): Armando Capiró (22, 11, .500), Pedro José Rodríguez (22, 11, .500), Alfonso Urquiola (2, 1, .500), Rey Anglada (31, 9, .290), Pedro Jova (18, 5, .278), Luis Casanova (35, 13, .371), Agustín Marquetti (32, 13, .406), Antonio Muñoz (35, 11, .314), Fernando Sánchez (30, 12, .400), Fernando Hernández (5, 1, .200), Pedro Medina (24, 9, .375), Rodolfo Puente (27, 10, .370), Wilfredo Sánchez (13, 3, .231), Alberto Martínez (1, 0, .000). **Pitching** (W, L, ERA):

Braudilio Vinent (4, 0, 0.44), Jesús Guerra (2, 0, 2.45), Rogelio García (0, 0, 5.40), Juan Carlos Oliva (1, 0, 3.00), Lázaro Santana (0, 0, 6.23), Rafael Castillo (1, 0, 2.70).
Cuba Game Scores: Round-robin: Cuba beat Dominican Republic 9–0, Cuba beat Bahamas 12–0, Cuba beat Colombia 12–1, Cuba beat Mexico 9–6, Cuba beat Canada 9–8, Cuba beat Venezuela 8–7, Cuba beat USA 7–1, Cuba beat Puerto Rico 11–3.

1983 Pan American Games Championship IX (Caracas, Venezuela) (August 15–26)

For the fourth straight time Cuba blasted through the Pan American tournament field undefeated and it was beginning to look like the Cubans might never lose another game to hemisphere opponents. Team USA—with future big leaguers Jeff Ballard, Tim Belcher, Mark McGwire, and B. J. Surhoff—also cruised undefeated through the first round before stumbling against Nicaragua and then being blitzed 8–1 by Cuba with the title squarely on the line. The Cuba–United States game saw a precarious 1–0 American lead through six, before catcher Juan Castro's homer ignited a Cuban rally in the late innings. Cuba's Pedro Medina posted a scorching .667 batting average to claim the individual hitting title.

Champion: Cuba (9–0) (Silver Medal: Nicaragua; Bronze Medal: USA)
Finals Round Standings: Cuba (5–0), Nicaragua (3–2), USA (3–2), Dominican Republic (2–3), Venezuela (2–3), Panama (0–5). Note: Nicaragua beat USA 9–5 in Finals Round to determine Silver Medal, Bronze Medal.
Pool A Preliminary Round: USA (5–0), Nicaragua (3–2), Dominican Republic (3–2), Canada (3–2), Puerto Rico (1–4), Brazil (0–5).
Pool B Preliminary Round: Cuba (4–0), Venezuela (2–1), Panama (2–1), Colombia (1–3), Dutch Antilles (0–4).
Individual Statistical Leaders: **BA**: Pedro Medina (CUB) .667; **Runs**: Pedro Medina (CUB) 9; **Hits**: Tom Nelson (CAN) 12; **2B**: Luis Fontanez (PUR) 5; **3B**: six players with 1 each; **HR**: Pedro Medina (CUB), Mark McGwire (USA) 4; **RBI**: B.J. Surhoff (USA) 11; **SB**: John Ivan (USA), A. Delgado (NCA), C. García (NCA) 2; **Wins**: Julio Moya (NCA) 2–0; **Strikeouts**: Julio Moya (NCA) 12; **IP**: Julio Moya (NCA) 18; **ERA**: John Hoover (USA) 0.00.
Cuba Roster: **Manager**: José M. Pineda. **Batting** (AB, H, BA): Amado Zamora (7, 1, .143), Pedro Jova (1, 0, .000), Victor Mesa (17, 5, .294), Antonio Muñoz (16, 3, .167), Lourdes Gourriel (19, 10, .526), Pedro Medina (15, 10, .667), Ramón Otamendi (16, 8, .500), Antonio Pacheco (16, 8, .500), Juan Castro (10, 7, .700), Fernando Hernández (10, 4, .400), Alfonso Urquiola (18, 4, .222), Alberto Martínez (6, 2, .333), Leonardo Goire (1, 0, .000). **Pitching** (W, L, ERA): Braudilio Vinent (2, 0, 0.00), Rogelio García (3, 0, 0.00), Julio Romero (0, 0, 4.50), Jorge Luis Valdés (3, 0, 13.51), Félix Nuñez (1, 1, 3.44), Mario Veliz (1, 0, 0.00), Lázaro de la Torre (DNP).
Cuba Game Scores: Preliminary Round: Cuba beat Dutch Antilles 12–2, Cuba beat Venezuela 5–4, Cuba beat Panama 5–0, Cuba beat Colombia 24–5. Finals Round: Cuba beat Nicaragua 8–3, Cuba beat Dominican Republic 15–3, Cuba beat Panama 11–0, Cuba beat Venezuela 13–3, Cuba beat USA 8–1.

1987 Pan American Games Championship X (Indianapolis, Indiana USA) (August 9–22)

Cuba finally lost a single game but remained invincible by again winning a clutch contest head-to-head with Team USA. The Cuban loss was at the hands of an American team (on a dramatic homer by Ty Griffin) that breezed undefeated through the preliminary round. An August 22nd showdown for the top prize matched the tournament's two perennial powerhouses and found the Americans leading 9–8 in the sixth inning with Cris Carpenter suddenly being called upon to protect a late lead for the second

day in a row. Two Cuban runs in the eighth and three more in the ninth against the overworked Carpenter provided the final victory margin for the defending champions.
Champion: Cuba (8–1) (Silver Medal: USA; Bronze Medal: Puerto Rico)
Finals: Cuba beat USA 13–9 (Gold Medal), Puerto Rico beat Canada 12–2 (Bronze Medal).
Semifinals: Cuba beat Puerto Rico 6–5, USA beat Canada 7–6.
Elimination Round Standings: USA (7–0), Cuba (6–1), Puerto Rico (5–2), Canada (4–3), Nicaragua (3–4), Aruba (1–6), Venezuela (1–6), Dutch Antilles (1–6).
Individual Statistical Leaders: **BA**: Efrain García (PUR) .533; **Runs**: Ty Griffin (USA) 14; **Hits**: Efrain García (PUR) 16; **2B**: Bill Byckowski (CAN) 6; **3B**: Omar Linares (CUB), Greg Duce (CAN) 2; **HR**: Orestes Kindelán (CUB) 7; **RBI**: Orestes Kindelán (CUB), Tino Martínez (USA) 19; **SB**: Rick Hirstenstener (USA) 5; **Wins**: Cris Carpenter (USA) 3–0; **ERA**: Cris Carpenter (USA) 0.00. *Statistics do not include metal round games.
Cuba Roster: **Manager**: Higinio Vélez. **Batting** (AB, H, BA): Luis Casanova (21, 9, .429), Juan Castro (22, 4, .181), Jorge García (13, 2, .153), Giraldo González (2, 0, .000), Lourdes Gourriel (28, 9, .321), Orestes Kindelán (28, 14, .500), Omar Linares (25, 13, .520), Pedro Medina (6, 2, .333), Victor Mesa (24, 7, .281), Alejo O'Reilly (10, 6, .600), Antonio Pacheco (26, 12, .481), Luis Ulacia (23, 12, .521), Lázaro Vargas (6, 4, .667). **Pitching** (W, L, ERA): Pablo Miguel Abreu (2, 1, 1.08), Omar Ajete (2, 0, 0.00), Rogelio García (1, 0, 2.84), Euclides Rojas (0, 0, 0.00), Luis Tissert (0, 0, 0.00), Jorge Luis Valdés (2, 0, 5.40), Lázaro de la Torre (DNP).
Cuba Game Scores: Elimination Round: Cuba beat Dutch Antilles 12–1, Cuba beat Puerto Rico 1–0, Cuba beat Aruba 13–2, Cuba beat Venezuela 13–1, USA beat Cuba 6–4, Cuba beat Nicaragua 17–1, Cuba beat Canada 15–4. Semifinals: Cuba beat Puerto Rico 6–5. Finals: Cuba beat USA 13–9.

1991 Pan American Games Championship XI (Havana, Cuba) (August 4–17)

Cuba was again champion and again undefeated in the eleventh Pan American Games venue, staged once more in Havana. The new batch of Cuban slugging stars—Pacheco, Victor Mesa, Linares, Kindelán, and Gourriel—dominated the statistics in almost all categories. Cuba appeared weakened before the tourney with an injury to starter Lázaro Valle (reportedly a blood clot in his pitching arm) and the defection of top hurler René Arocha. The Cubans were actually stronger than ever, thrashing Puerto Rico 18–3 in the finale (with 3 homers by Ermidelio Urrutia). As a team, Cuba scored 136 runs and batted .400 over the ten-game stretch; five of Cuba's ten victories came with the 10-run knockout rule. Jorge Luis Valdés also pitched the first no-hit, no-run game in Pan American Games history, blanking Canada 14–0 and striking out twelve in the mercy rule–shortened seven-inning contest.
Champion: Cuba (10–0) (Silver Medal: Puerto Rico; Bronze Medal: USA)
Finals: Cuba beat Puerto Rico 18–3 (Gold Medal), USA beat Dominican Republic 2–1 (Bronze Medal).
Semifinals: Cuba beat Dominican Republic 14–5, Puerto Rico beat USA 7–1.
Elimination Round Standings: Cuba (8–0), USA (7–1), Puerto Rico (5–3), Dominican Republic (5–3), Nicaragua (4–4), Mexico (3–5), Aruba (2–6), Canada (1–7), Dutch Antilles (1–7).
Individual Statistical Leaders: **BA**: Antonio Pacheco (CUB) .545; **Runs**: Victor Mesa (CUB), Antonio Pacheco (CUB), Omar Linares (CUB), Germán Mesa (CUB) 13; **Hits**: Antonio Pacheco (CUB) 18; **2B**: four players with five each; **3B**: 14 players with one each; **HR**: Lourdes Gourriel (CUB), Orestes Kindelán (CUB), Chris Roberts (USA) 4; **RBI**: Antonio Pacheco (CUB) 15; **SB**: Chris Wimmer (USA) 8; **Wins**: Félix Nova (DOM) 3–0; **Strikeouts**: Félix Nova (DOM) 23; **ERA**: Jorge Luis Valdés (CUB) 0.73; **MVP**: Antonio Pacheco (CUB).

Cuba Roster: **Manager**: Jorge Fuentes. **Batting** (AB, H, BA): Alberto Hernández (9, 1, .111), José Raúl Delgado (20, 10, .500), Omar Linares (29, 12, .414), Lourdes Gourriel (31, 13, .419), Antonio Pacheco (33, 18, .545), Lázaro Vargas (8, 4, .500), Germán Mesa (27, 11, .407), Luis Ulacia (24, 12, .500), Victor Mesa (27, 11, .407), Orestes Kindelán (31, 11, .355), Ermidelio Urrutia (15, 5, .333), Romelio Martínez (22, 9, .409), Pedro Luis Rodríguez (DNP). **Pitching** (W, L, ERA): Jorge Luis Valdés (3, 0, 0.73), Euclides Rojas (0, 0, 9.82), Osvaldo Fernández Guerra (1, 0, 3.27), Osvaldo Duvergel (1, 0, 4.50), Leonardo Tamayo (2, 0, 0.90), Omar Ajete (2, 0, 3.86), Osvaldo Fernández Rodríguez (1, 0, 0.82).

Cuba Game Scores: Elimination Round: Cuba beat Nicaragua 14–6, Cuba beat Mexico 22–0, Cuba beat Canada 14–0, Cuba beat Dutch Antilles 8–3, Cuba beat Puerto Rico 16–2, Cuba beat Aruba 20–1, Cuba beat USA 3–2, Cuba beat Dominican Republic 16–5. Semifinals: Cuba beat Dominican Republic 14–5. Finals: Cuba beat Puerto Rico 18–3.

1995 Pan American Games Championship XII (Mar del Plata, Argentina) (March 11–24)

Another undefeated Cuban championship squad featured a pitching staff (Osvaldo Fernández, Omar Ajete, Rolando Arrojo, Orlando "El Duque" Hernández, José Ibar, Elicer Montes de Oca, and Pedro Luis Lazo) with no single ERA as high as one run per nine-inning game. If previous Cuban entries rarely lost a single game, this one rarely gave up an earned run. Montes de Oca earned the ERA title with most innings pitched, and the top hitters for Cuba were Lourdes Gourriel (.464 BA), José Estrada (tournament leader in hits, runs, and homers), and Victor Mesa (the top RBI producer).

Champion: Cuba (9–0) (Silver Medal: Nicaragua; Bronze Medal: Puerto Rico)

Finals Round Standings: Cuba (5–0), Nicaragua (4–1), Puerto Rico (2–3), Mexico (2–3), Panama (1–4), Argentina (1–4). Note: Puerto Rico earned bronze medal by defeating Mexico during medal-round play.

Group A Preliminary Round: Mexico (4–0), Argentina (3–1), Puerto Rico (2–2), Guatemala (1–3), USA (0–4).

Group B Preliminary Round: Cuba (4–0), Panama (3–1), Nicaragua (2–2), Brazil (1–3), Dutch Antilles (0–4).

Individual Statistical Leaders: **BA**: Lourdes Gourriel (CUB) .464; **Runs**: José Estrada (CUB) 14; **Hits**: José Estrada (CUB) 18; **2B**: Alonso Reyes (MEX) 5; **3B**: Omar Linares (CUB), Jaime Roque (PUR) 4; **HR**: José Estrada (CUB) 2; **RBI**: Victor Mesa (CUB) 16; **SB**: Mariano Cadiz (ARG) 3; **Wins**: Elicer Montes de Ocha (CUB), Luis Miranda (NCA) 3–0; **ERA**: Elicer Montes de Ocha (CUB) 0.00.

Cuba Roster: **Manager**: Jorge Fuentes. **Batting** (AB, H, BA): Pedro Luis Rodríguez (4, 0, .000), Juan Manrique (29, 12, .414), Orestes Kindelán (32, 10, .313), Lourdes Gourriel (28, 13, .464), Jorge Luis Toca (8, 3, .375), Antonio Pacheco (32, 14, .438), Juan Padilla (4, 1, .250), Germán Mesa (25, 11, .440), Eduardo Paret (6, 1, .167), Omar Linares (32, 12, .375), Victor Mesa (33, 13, .394), Ermidelio Urrutia (38, 13, .342), José Estrada (30, 18, .462), Luis Ulacia (4, 2, .500), Daniel Lazo (5, 0, .000). **Pitching** (W, L, ERA): Osvaldo Fernández Rodríguez (2, 0, 0.00), Omar Ajete (0, 0, 0.50), Luis Rolando Arrojo (2, 0, 0.69), Orlando "El Duque" Hernández (2, 0, 0.00), José Ibar (0, 0, 0.00), Elicer Montes de Oca (3, 0, 0.00), Pedro Luis Lazo (0, 0, 0.00).

Cuba Game Scores: Preliminary Round: Cuba beat Panama 16–6, Cuba beat Brazil 22–4, Cuba beat Dutch Antilles 9–0, Cuba beat Nicaragua 11–0. Finals Round: Cuba beat Panama 11–0, Cuba beat Argentina 10–0, Cuba beat Puerto Rico 6–1, Cuba beat Nicaragua 6–1, Cuba beat Mexico 8–0.

1999 Pan American Games Championship XIII (Winnipeg, Canada) (July 25–August 2)

One of the best-played and hardest fought international tournaments on record resulted from the first such event in which teams (with the exception of Cuba) drew their rosters from AA and AAA minor league players representing organized baseball. In addition, for the first time in more than two decades wooden bats were reintroduced for international tournament matches. Cuba surprisingly lost to both Team USA and Team Canada in the preliminary round and seemed on the verge of blowing an expected trip to the 2000 Sydney Olympics (only the two finalists would qualify for Sydney). The veteran Cuban team came alive in the medal round, however, largely on brilliant pitching by José Ariel Contreras in the quarterfinal match with the Dominican Republic and again in the gold medal collision (two days later) versus Team USA. José Ibar (with Pedro Luis Lazo in ninth-inning relief) also shut down Canada in the crucial semifinal match that assured an Olympic berth. Little-used and previously unheralded reliever Danys Báez defected from the Cuban contingent in Winnipeg and would emerge several years later as a big league star in Cleveland.

Champion: Cuba (5–2) (Silver Medal: USA; Bronze Medal: Canada)

Finals: Cuba beat USA 5–1 (Gold Medal), Canada beat Mexico 9–2 (Bronze Medal)

Semifinals: Cuba beat Canada 3–2, USA beat Mexico 2–1. Note: Semifinal winners (Cuba, USA) both qualify for 2000 Olympic Games Tournament.

Quarterfinals: Cuba beat Dominican Republic 3–1, Canada beat Guatemala 12–2, Mexico beat Nicaragua 5–1, USA beat Panama 5–2.

Group A Elimination Round: Canada (4–0), USA (3–1), Cuba (2–2), Mexico (1–3), Brazil (0–4)

Group B Elimination Round: Dominican Republic (2–1), Nicaragua (2–1), Panama (2–1), Guatemala (0–3)

Individual Statistical Leaders: **BA**: Héctor Alvarez (MEX) .625; **Runs**: Andy Stewart (CAN) 8; **Hits**: Andy Stewart (CAN) 12; **2B**: Jeromy Ware (CAN) 4; **3B**: Lee Delfino (CAN), Orlando Miller (PAN) 1; **HR**: Andy Stewart (CAN), Marcus Jensen (USA) 3; **RBI**: Andy Stewart (CAN) 12; **SB**: David Roberts (USA), Félix Martínez (DOM) 3; **Wins**: Yan Lachapelle (CAN) 2; **ERA**: Steve Green (USA), 0.00.

Cuba Roster: **Manager**: Alfonso Urquiola. **Batting** (AB, H, BA): Ariel Pestano (21, 7, .333), Juan Manrique (0, 0, .000), Orestes Kindelán (28, 6, .214), Germán Mesa (17, 3, .176), Danel Castro (9, 1, .111), Omar Linares (25, 4, .160), Gabriel Pierre (14, 4, .286), Michel Enriquez (3, 1, .333), Javier Méndez (6, 1, .167), Yobal Dueñas (18, 4, .222), Daniel Lazo (6, 1, .167), Robelquis Videaux (11, 0, .000), Luis Ulacia (26, 8, .308), Isaac Martínez (22, 9, .409). **Pitching** (W, L, ERA): José Ariel Contreras (2, 0, 0.98), Pedro Luis Lazo (0, 0, 1.13), Norge Vera (1, 0, 2.25), José Ibar (1, 0, 1.74), Maels Rodríguez (1, 1, 8.53), Ciro Silvino Licea (0, 1, 12.47), Ormari Romero (0, 0, 7.73), Faustino Corrales (0, 0, 3.38), Danys Báez (0, 0, 0.00).

Cuba Game Scores: Elimination Round: Cuba beat Mexico 5–1, Cuba beat Brazil 10–1, USA beat Cuba 10–5, Canada beat Cuba 8–1. Quarterfinals: Cuba beat Dominican Republic 3–1. Semifinals: Cuba beat Canada 3–2. Finals: Cuba beat USA 5–1.

2003 Pan American Games Championship XIV (Santo Domingo, Dominican Republic) (August 2–12)

Surviving a shocking preliminary round 7–1 pasting by Mexico, a young Cuban squad bounced back to sweep the Dominican Republic, Nicaragua, and Team USA in medal play and thus capture the country's eleventh Pan American gold medal in only thirteen outings. The victory also ran Cuba's overall Pan American Games ledger to 91 victories in 104 contests. Veteran mound ace Norge Vera was the gold medal hero, with his brilliant complete-game two-hit shutout versus an American roster laced with minor league professional players. Catcher Ariel Pestano provided the offensive punch in the deciding game, stroking a double and a homer and knocking home two of Cuba's three tallies. Another sterling pitching performance was provided in the semifinal match with Nicaragua by Vicyohandri Odelín, who logged 8.1 shutout innings after relieving starter

Yovani Aragón in the opening frame. Nineteen-year-old second baseman Yulieski Gourriel and outfielder Osmani Urrutia represented the champion Cubans on the tournament all-star squad.

Champion: Cuba (5–1) (Silver Medal: USA; Bronze Medal: Mexico)

Finals: Cuba beat USA 3–1 (Gold Medal), Mexico beat Nicaragua 6–2 (Bronze Medal).

Semifinals: Cuba beat Nicaragua 2–1, USA tied Mexico 2–2 (13 innings). Note: USA earns Championship Finals on basis of better Preliminary Round record.

Quarterfinals: Cuba beat Dominican Republic 10–0, Nicaragua beat Panama 5–2, Mexico beat Guatemala 6–0, USA beat Brazil 7–0.

Group A Preliminary Round: Cuba (2–1), Mexico (2–1), Brazil (1–2), Panama (1–2).

Group B Preliminary Round: Nicaragua (4–0), USA (3–1), Dominican Republic (2–2), Guatemala (1–3), Bahamas (0–4).

Individual Statistical Leaders: **BA**: Mario Santana (MEX) .571; **Runs**: Jesús Taváres (DOM), Eric Patterson (USA) 6; **Hits**: Jim González (NCA) 9; **2B**: Ramón Martínez (MEX), Osmani Urrutia (CUB), Daniel Putnam (USA) 3; **3B**: Luis García (MEX) 2; **HR**: Roberto Saucedo (MEX), Jonathan Vega (PAN), Eduardo Romero (NCA), Jim Greene (USA) 1; **RBI**: Eduardo Romero (NCA) 6; **SB**: Amilcar Estrada (GUA) 3; **Strikeouts**: Yosvani Aragón (CUB) 9; **ERA**: Cairo Murillo (NCA) 0.00 (9.0 innings).

Cuba Roster: **Manager**: Higinio Vélez. **Batting** (AB, H, BA): Ariel Benavides (1, 1, 1.000), Frederich Cepeda (12, 1, .083), Michel Enríquez (12, 1, .083), Yulieski Gourriel (10, 5, .500), Roger Machado (4, 1, .250), Javier Méndez (11, 3, .273), Eduardo Paret (10, 3, .300), Joan Carlos Pedroso (12, 3, .250), Ariel Pestano (6, 2, .333), Alexander Ramos (0, 0, .000), Carlos Tabares (11, 3, .273), Osmani Urrutia (12, 5, .417), Robelquis Videaux (0, 0, .000). **Pitching** (W, L, ERA): Yovani Aragón (1, 0, 0.00), Orelvis Ávila (0, 0, 0.00), Yadel Martí (0, 0, 2.57), Vicyohandri Odelín (0, 1, 6.00), Norge Vera (1, 0, 0.00). **Note**: Statistics for Preliminary Round games only.

Cuba Game Scores: Preliminary Round: Cuba beat Panama 5–0, Cuba beat Brazil 4–0, Mexico beat Cuba 7–1. Quarterfinals: Cuba beat Dominican Republic 10–0. Semifinals: Cuba beat Nicaragua 2–1. Finals: Cuba beat USA 3–1.

CENTRAL AMERICAN AND CARIBBEAN GAMES CHAMPIONSHIPS, 1926–1998

This granddaddy of international tournaments began modestly in Mexico City in 1926 with a Mexico–Cuba 3-game set that also marks the beginning of Cuba's long reign over international amateur baseball. Four years later, Cuban strongman Gerardo Machado seized on a second edition of the Games as an opportunity to deflect public attention from his government's growing unpopularity. The second Central American Games tournament is notable for its role in inaugurating Havana's La Tropical Stadium (built for the occasion), one of the most picturesque locales for international tournaments and winter professional league action throughout the 1930s and early 1940s. Cuba again has not surprisingly proved dominant year in and year out in this lesser version of the Pan American Games, on only one occasion (of those it attended) failing to earn a gold, silver, or bronze medal. The Dominican Republic (with two medals) is the only other Latin American or Central American nation to come away from this event victorious on more than a single occasion.

Cuba's Overall Performance: Tournaments (13 of 16 Tournament titles won, plus one second place and one third place); Games (100 Won and 14 Lost, .877 Pct.).

Country-by-Country Championships Won: Cuba (13, out of 16 tournaments entered), Dominican Republic (2), Venezuela (1), Colombia (1), and Puerto Rico (1).

Note: Cuba finished in fourth place (2–3 record) in 1962 tournament at Kingston (Jamaica), for their only nonmedal finish in 16 tournaments attended. Cuba did not participate in the 1954 Central American Games (held in Mexico City), 1959 Central American Games (held in Caracas, Venezuela), nor 2002 CA Games (staged in El Salvador).

1926 Central American Games Championship I (Mexico City, Mexico) (October 12–November 2)

The first Central American Games marked both Cuba's first participation in amateur international baseball competition and also its first championship in what would soon be a regular flood tide of world amateur baseball crowns. The games in Mexico City attracted only three participants, and Guatemala arrived without a baseball team. In the 3-game set with Mexico for the baseball medal, the Cubans were unchallenged and blanked the Mexicans 12–0 in the opener behind Lalo Rodríguez. The Cuban squad contained mostly players from the amateur league powerhouse Vedado Tennis Club team, including star pitcher Antonio Casuso, who had earlier whitewashed a pro outfit in Cuba during a pretournament warm-up match. Players from the Police Club, Havana Yacht Club, Loma Tennis Club, and the University of Havana filled out Team Cuba's ragtag roster.

Champion: Cuba (3–0)
Teams and Final Standings: Cuba (3–0), Mexico (0–3).
Individual Statistical Leaders: **BA**: Joaquín del Calvo (CUB) .714; **Runs**: C. Hernández (CUB) 6; **Hits**: Joaquín del Calvo (CUB) 5; **HR**: J. Echarri (CUB) and C. Hernández (CUB) 1. No additional stats available for this tournament.
Cuba Roster: **Manager**: Horacio Alfonso. **Batting** (BA): Miguel Aguilera (.000), Gustavo Alonso (.333), Joaquín del Calvo (.714), Antonio Castro (.571), R. Puig (.181), P. Ruíz (.333), C. Vietti (.400), Gustavo Consuegra (.500), J. Echarri (.333), Jorge Consuegra (.500), Cándido Hernández (.300), Rafael Inclán (.429), Porfirio Espinosa (.400). **Pitching** (W–L): T. Minguillón (1–0), Lalo Rodríguez (1–0), Antonio Casuso (1–0). No additional statistics available.

1930 Central American Games Championship II (Havana, Cuba) (March 15–April 5)

Strongman president Gerardo Machado organized a second Central American Games in Havana, to divert attention from growing domestic unrest on the island. These games also took on significance as the maiden event staged in the new Cerveza La Tropical Stadium, a facility built specifically for the occasion. A significant appearance was made by Cuba's first National Leaguer, Rafael Almeida, who served as Team Cuba manager. The only loss for the host team was a 2–1 nail-biter with Mexico, and most of the five wins were laughable routs (including 15–1 over Guatemala). University of Havana outfielder Porfirio Espinosa hit .429 and also won the javelin throw competition, while Cuban pitcher Juan Mendizabel earned a track and field gold medal in the shot put. Narciso Picazo, star hurler with the National Amateur League powerhouse Club Teléfonos, was the tournament's most effective pitcher.

Champion: Cuba (5–1) (Silver Medal: Mexico; Bronze Medal: Panama)
Teams and Final Standings: Cuba (5–1), Mexico (4–2), Panama (3–3), Guatemala (0–3), El Salvador (0–3).
Individual Statistical Leaders: **BA**: M. Chávez Méndez (MEX) .500; **Runs**: R.E. Ruiz (PAN) 8; **Hits**: P. Espinosa (CUB) 8; **HR**: J.A. Antadilla (PAN) 3; **SB**: F. Torrijos (MEX), J. Torrijos (MEX) 5; **Wins**: Narciso Picazo (CUB) 2–0.
Cuba Roster: **Manager**: Rafael Almeida. **Batting** (BA): Gustavo Consuegra (.500), Carlos Fleites (.500), Porfirio Espinosa (.429), Francisco Espiñeira (.429), M. Morera (.333),

Gustavo Alfonso (.278), A. Paituni (.250), Cándido Hernández (.250), Miguel Aguilera (.238), Jorge Consuegra (.235), A. Arredondo (.143), Luis Romero (.090), Oscar Reyes (.000). **Pitching** (W–L): Narciso Picazo (2–0), Juan Mendizábal (1–0), J. Montero (1–0), Manuel Domínguez (1–1), F. Clavel (0–0). No additional statistics available.

1935 Central American Games Championship III (San Salvador, El Salvador) (March 24–April 7)

Hurricane damage delayed the opening of the next games nearly a full year and built anticipation for a Cuba–Mexico showdown on neutral grounds. When Cuba protested that the Mexican baseball roster was filled with professionals, the Mexicans hastily withdrew. Teams from Panama and Nicaragua (both teams also accused by the Cubans of using pros—and some players were in fact Cubans under assumed names) offered the main opposition. Used to playing seasoned professionals at home, Team Cuba with National Amateur League pitching stars Manuel Fortes (also a heavy hitter) and Naciso Picazo breezed through the field almost unchallenged.

Champion: Cuba (8–1) (Silver Medal: Panama and Nicaragua, with no bronze medal)
Championship Round Final Standings: Cuba (3–1), Panama (1–2), Nicaragua (1–2).
Opening Round Teams and Final Standings: Cuba (5–0), Panama (4–1), Nicaragua (3–2), El Salvador (2–3), Guatemala (1–4), Honduras (0–5).
Individual Statistical Leaders: **BA**: F. Hernández (CUB) .444; **Runs**: José Luis García (CUB) 13; **HR**: José Luis García (CUB), H. Carter (NCA) 5; **SB**: José Luis García (CUB) 6; **Wins**: Manuel Fortes (CUB) 3–0. No additional statistics available for this tournament.
Cuba Roster: **Manager**: León Rojas. **Batting** (BA): F. Fernández (.154), Carlos Fleites (.211), Manuel (Manolo) "Chino" Fortes (.357), E. García (.359), José Luis García (.395), F. Hernández (.444), Ésteban Maciques (.316), Conrado Morales (.187), F. López (.338), M. López (.400), A. Izquierdo (.297), Antonio Palencia (.269), Jorge Santacruz (.364). **Pitching** (W–L): Narciso Picazo (2–0), Felo Suárez (0–1), Adrian Zabala (1–0), Manuel (Manolo) "Chino" Fortes (3–0), F. Fernández (2–0). No additional statistics available.

1938 Central American Games Championship IV (Panama City, Panama) (February 11–23)

Mexico returned to the baseball wars, still using at least some of its Mexican League pros, and Puerto Rico and Venezuela entered for the first time. Club Atlético's manager León Rojas directed Team Cuba for the second time and fielded a formidable squad headed by the pitching of Agapito Mayor (Fortuna), Juan Decall (Vedado Tennis Club), and Natilla Jiménez (Hershey). Mayor was almost the whole story, winning four games in a combination of starting and relief appearances, a feat not duplicated before or since in this long-standing tournament. The deciding game saw Natilla Jiménez blank hapless El Salvador and also smack a mammoth homer to cap his own winning performance.

Champion: Cuba (5–1) (Silver Medal: Panama; Bronze Medal: Nicaragua)
Teams and Final Standings: Cuba (5–1), Panama (4–2), Nicaragua (4–2), Puerto Rico (4–2), Mexico (3–3), Venezuela (1–5), El Salvador (0–6). *Panama, Nicaragua, and Puerto Rico played extra round-robin series to determine second through fourth place.
Individual Statistical Leaders: **BA**: E. Lanuza (PAN) .556; **HR**: O. Arleuwite (PAN) 2; **Wins**: Agapito Mayor (CUB) 4–0. No additional statistics available from this tournament.
Cuba Roster: **Manager**: León Rojas. **Batting** (BA): M. Fajo (1.000), Carlos Fleites (.174), A. Gómez (.174), Ésteban Maciques (.275), J. Nápoles (.200), R. Ortiz (.000), Antonio Palencia (.087), David Pérez (.294), Segundo "Guajiro" Rodríguez (.200), Jorge Santacruz (.370), José Luis "Cocoliso" Torres (.200), Antonio "Quilla" Valdés (.333), Remigio Vega (.318). **Pitching** (W–L): Agapito Mayor (4–0), Pedro "Natilla" Jiménez

(1–0), Juanito Decall (0–1), J. Valdés (0–0), E. Aguirre (DNP). No additional names or statistics available for Cuban roster.

1946 Central American Games Championship V (Barranquilla, Colombia) (December 9–28)

Future Cuban League great and slick-fielding big league shortstop Willie Miranda (later of the New York Yankees and Baltimore Orioles) made his first appearance on Team Cuba in these games staged in Barranquilla. Miranda's Cuban career began in the years 1942 to 1947 as an amateur star with powerhouse Club Teléfonos. With little hitting and less than their usual pitching strength, Cuba dropped both final-round games, to Colombia and the Dominicans, and failed to defend its Central American crown for the first time. It was the beginning of what would prove a brief dry spell in Cuban amateur play, brought on largely by increased pro signings of amateur stars in the wake of the 1946–1947 racial integration of organized baseball in the United States.

Champion: Colombia (8–1) (Silver Medal: Dominican Republic; Bronze Medal: Cuba)
Championship Round Final Standings: Colombia (2–0), Dominican Republic (1–1), Cuba (0–2).
Preliminary Round Final Standings: Colombia (6–1), Cuba (6–1), Dominican Republic (4–3), Venezuela (3–3), Puerto Rico (3–3), Mexico (2–5), Costa Rica (0–7).
Individual Statistical Leaders: **BA**: C. González (PUR) .478; **HR**: five players tied with one each; **Wins**: R. Rodríguez (COL) 3–0. No additional statistics available from this tournament.
Cuba Roster: **Manager**: Vitico Muñoz. **Batting** (BA): Rouget Avalos (.091), Bernardo Cuervo (.200), Julio Delgado (.000), Mario Díaz (.250), A. Domínguez (.130), Galate Gómez (.441), Hiram González (.200), José Luis García (.207), Guillermo "Willie" Miranda (.250), Mario Pérez (.211), Ramiro Ramírez (.320), Gilberto Soto (.143). **Pitching** (W–L): Nicaragua Chacón (0–0), Ignacio Ferrer (1–0), Catayo González (1–2), Miguel Montiel (1–0), René "Tata" Solis (1–1), Curricán Stable (2–0). No additional statistics available.

1950 Central American Games Championship VI (Guatemala City) (February 25–March 12)

Cuba reversed its brief slump and reclaimed the Central American Games baseball title lost four years earlier in Colombia. Another eye-popping debut occurred when future Brooklyn Dodgers World Series hero Edmundo "Sandy" Amorós, a recent product of the Juveniles (the youth leagues), slammed 6 homers in seven games to thoroughly dominate tournament headlines. Amorós and pitcher Justiniano Garay were two initially token blacks carried on Team Cuba's roster as racial integration slowly and quietly arrived within Cuban amateur baseball circles.

Champion: Cuba (7–0) (Silver Medal: Mexico; Bronze Medal: Nicaragua)
Teams and Final Standings: Cuba (7–0), Mexico (6–1), Nicaragua (4–3), Colombia (4–3), Costa Rica (3–4), El Salvador (2–5), Honduras (1–6), Guatemala (1–6). *Nicaragua beat Colombia during round-robin matchup to earn third place.
Individual Statistical Leaders: **BA**: M. Jacques (MEX) .474; **HR**: Edmundo Amorós (CUB) 6; **Wins**: D. Reatiga (MEX) 3–0. No additional statistics available from this tournament.
Cuba Roster: **Manager**: Oscar Reyes. **Batting** (BA): Derubin Jácome (.423), Edmundo Amorós (.370), E. Ballester (.370), Ángel Scull (.344), E. Tamayo (.308), Antonio González (1.000), Alfonso Suárez (1.000), L. Seijo (.500), M. Hernández (.333), L. Estrada (.333), C. Balvidares (.222). **Pitching** (W–L): Erasmo del Monte (2–0), L. Fiuza (2–0), Justiniano Garay (2–0), G. Martínez (0–0), R. Contreras (1–0). No additional statistics available.

1954 Central American and Games Championship VII (Mexico City, Mexico) (March 6–20)

With Cuban amateur baseball now in a precarious state (due to mass signings of young players by professional teams both in Cuba and abroad), Team Cuba is absent from the

Central American Games for the very first time. Venezuela seizes the opportunity and edges host Mexico for first-place honors. The four-team field is the smallest since the first edition of the tournament back in 1926. Nicaragua is the only entrant to win neither a medal nor a single game.

Champion: Venezuela (5–1) (Silver Medal: Mexico; Bronze Medal: Dominican Republic)

Teams and Final Standings: Venezuela (5–1), Mexico (4–2), Dominican Republic (3–3), Nicaragua (0–6).

Individual Statistical Leaders: **BA**: J. Matos (VEN) .455; **Runs**: J. Matos (VEN), D. Rubenstein (VEN), E. Reveron (VEN), A. Ríos (MEX) 9; **HR**: C. Duarte (MEX) 3; **RBI**: R. Caballero (MEX), J. Matos (VEN), E. Reveron (VEN) 10; **SB**: P. Colina (VEN) 4; **Wins**: Ángel Guillen (VEN) 3–0; **ERA**: Ángel Guillen (VEN) 1.29. No additional statistics available.

Cuba Did Not Participate

1959 Central American Games Championship VIII (Caracas, Venezuela) (January 6–18)

With political turmoil back home during the month when Fidel Castro and Che Guevara's Sierra Maestra-based rebels finally seize government authority from President Fulgencio Batista, Cuba is absent from the tournament for a second straight session. Puerto Rico thus emerges as champions of the still-small five-team field, with the host country losing in the crucial tie-breaking title game. This is the last time in the twentieth century that Cuba misses this tournament; in the forty years that follow, the Cubans will be outright champions eight times and runners-up on one of the other two occasions.

Champion: Puerto Rico (8–1) (Silver Medal: Venezuela; Bronze Medal: Panama)

Teams and Final Standings: Puerto Rico (7–1), Venezuela (7–1), Panama (4–4), Mexico (2–6), Dutch Antilles (0–8). *Puerto Rico defeated Venezuela in tie-breaker playoff game to earn gold medal.

Individual Statistical Leaders: **BA**: L. Sanjur (PAN) .500; **Runs**: M. Mendible (VEN) 13; **HR**: four tied with one each; **RBI**: F. Sánchez (PAN) 11; **SB**: B. Hoftjzer (AHO) 5; **Wins**: F. Castilleros (PAN), J.E. Marrero (PUR), R. Molina (PUR), P. Higuerey (VEN), J. Pérez (VEN) 2–0; **ERA**: P. Pérez (PUR) 0.00. No additional statistics available.

Cuba Did Not Participate

1962 Central American Games Championship IX (Kingston, Jamaica) (August 11–26)

Cuba returns to the games and finishes far out of medal contention for the only time in sixteen visits to Central American action. This would be largely the same Cuban team that would score a major triumph in the 1963 Pan American Games—a selection of all-stars from the new National Series that would include manager Gilberto Torres, infielders Urbano González and Jorge Trigoura, outfielders Fidel Linares and Erwin Walter, and pitchers Aquino Abreu, Modesto Verdura, Alfredo Street, and Manuel Alarcón. Several heartbreaking losses plagued a team that had not yet fully come together.

Champion: Dominican Republic (4–1) (Silver Medal: Puerto Rico; Bronze Medal: Mexico)

Teams and Final Standings: Dominican Republic (4–1), Puerto Rico (3–2), Mexico (3–2), Cuba (2–3), Venezuela (2–3), Colombia (1–4). *Puerto Rico defeated Mexico in round-robin play and thus awarded second place.

Individual Statistical Leaders: **BA**: A. Méndez (VEN) .500; **HR**: four players tied with one each; **Wins**: S. Vázquez (MEX) 2–0; **ERA**: S. Vázquez (MEX) 0.00. No additional statistics available from this tournament.

Cuba Roster: **Manager**: Gilberto Torres. **Batting** (AB, H, BA): Urbano González (24, 10, .417), Fidel Linares (13, 5, .385), Jorge Trigoura (21, 8, .381), Ricardo Lazo (16, 6, .375), Daniel Hernández (18, 6, .333), Ramón Hechevarría (3, 1, .333), Julio Becquer (8, 2, .250), Mario González (18, 4, .222), Erwin Walter (20, 5, .250), Juan Emilio Pacheco (23, 3, .130), Miguel Cuevas (5, 0, .000), Antonio González (1, 0, .000), Aquino Abreu (2, 2, 1.000), Modesto Verdura (2, 1, .500), Manuel Alarcón (5, 2, .400), Alfredo Street (3, 1, .333), A. Rubio (3, 0, .000). **Pitching** (W, L, ERA): Aquino Abreu (0, 0, 1.50), Alfredo Street (1, 0, 1.80), Modesto Verdura (0, 1, 2.70), Manuel Alarcón (1, 1, 2.25), Antonio Rubio (0, 1, 2.57), Francisco Salcedo (DNP).

1966 Central American Games Championship X (San Juan, Puerto Rico) (June 11–25)

Postrevolution political troubles surrounding Cuban sports were again in evidence as the cargo ship *Cerro Pelado* carrying Cuban athletes was detaining upon entering San Juan harbor and most of the Cuban delegation missed the opening ceremonies. Anti-Castro exiles threw stones at Cuban ballplayers during several matches, and tensions remained high. A series of dramatic close games included Aquino Abreu's 5–2 opening day win over Puerto Rico, Gaspar Pérez's heartbreaking 1–0 loss to Venezuela (resulting from his own fielding error), and a 1–0 blanking of the Dominicans won with Miguel Cuevas's clutch double. Southpaw Rigoberto Betancourt, top pitcher of this tournament, would eventually become a celebrated defector thirty-three years later during the Cuba–Orioles exhibition match staged in Baltimore.

Champion: Cuba (6–1) (Silver Medal: Puerto Rico; Bronze Medal: Panama)

Teams and Final Standings: Cuba (5–1), Puerto Rico (5–1), Panama (4–2), Dominican Republic (3–3), Venezuela (3–3), Mexico (1–5), Dutch Antilles (0–6). *Cuba beat Puerto Rico (6–2) in extra playoff game for gold medal.

Individual Statistical Leaders: **BA**: Pedro Chávez (CUB) .444; **Runs**: six players tied with five each; **Hits**: Pedro Chávez (CUB) 12; **2B**: R. Ortiz (PUR) 5; **3B**: nine players tied with one each; **HR**: four players tied with one each; **RBI**: Pedro Chávez (CUB) 6; **SB**: Antonio González (CUB), J. Santos (PUR) 5; **Wins**: E. Castillo (PAN) 2; **Strikeouts**: Rigoberto Betancourt (CUB) 18; **ERA**: A. Villamil (VEN) 0.00.

Cuba Roster: **Manager**: Gilberto Torres. **Batting** (AB, H, BA): Ramón Hechavarría (5, 3, .600), Pedro Chávez (27, 12, .444), Miguel Cuevas (23, 10, .435), Urbano González (29, 8, .276), Lino Betancourt (27, 7, .259), Ricardo Lazo (21, 5, .238), Felipe Sarduy (19, 4, .211), Antonio González (28, 6, .214), Rafael Herrera (26, 5, .192), Antonio Jiménez (7, 1, .143), Rigoberto Betancourt (2, 1, .500), Aquino Abreu (5, 2, .400), Jesús Torriente (4, 1, .250), Gaspar Pérez (5, 1, .200), Alfredo Street (4, 0, .000), Raúl López (2, 0, .000), Agustín Arias (0, 0, .000). **Pitching** (W, L, ERA): Gaspar Pérez (1, 1, 0.00), Jesús Torriente (1, 0, 0.00), Alfredo Street (1, 0, 0.00), Raúl López (1, 0, 0.00), Rigoberto Betancourt (1, 0, 1.80). Aquino Abreu (1, 0, 3.29).

1970 Central American Games Championship XI (Panama City, Panama) (February 28–March 14)

The Cubans successfully defended their title under new manager Servio Borges. This victory was preliminary to the more dramatic World Cup showdown near year's end with Team USA in Colombia. As in Cartagena in December, young phenom José Antonio Huelga was the pitching star, with two nearly perfect outings. Wilfredo Sánchez, Rodolfo Puente, Silvio Montejo, and Félix Isasi all chipped in with batting averages above .350, but Fermín Laffita was the biggest offensive hero with top tournament marks for RBI, homers, and stolen bases.

Champion: Cuba (7–1) (Silver Medal: Dominican Republic; Bronze Medal: Mexico)

Teams and Final Standings: Cuba (7–1), Dominican Republic (6–2), Mexico (6–2), Colombia (5–3), Venezuela (4–4), Panama (4–4), Puerto Rico (3–5), Nicaragua (1–7), Dutch Antilles (0–8). *Dominican Republic defeated Mexico in round-robin play to earn silver medal.

Individual Statistical Leaders: **BA**: W. Pietersz (AHO) .560; **Runs**: T. Moreno (COL) 11; **Hits**: W. Pietersz (AHO) 14; **2B**: T. Moreno (COL) 6; **3B**: C. Rosales (NCA) 3; **HR**: Fermín Laffita (CUB), Urbano González (CUB) 2; **RBI**: Fermín Laffita (CUB) 11; **SB**: Fermín Laffita (CUB), Wilfredo Sánchez (CUB), Félix Isasi (CUB) 5; **Wins**: O. García (COL) 3–0; **ERA**: José Antonio Huelga (CUB) 0.00.

Cuba Roster: **Manager**: Servio Borges. **Batting** (AB, H, BA): Armando Capiró (15, 10, .667), Wilfredo Sánchez (33, 13, .394), Rodolfo Puente (23, 9, .391), Silvio Montejo (29, 11, .379), Fermín Laffita (32, 12, .375), Félix Isasi (28, 10, .357), Urbano González (23, 7, .304), Owen Blandino (13, 4, .308), Felipe Sarduy (30, 9, .300), Ramón Hechavarría (10, 3, .300), Agustín Arias (11, 2, .182), L. Pérez (18, 3, .167), José Antonio Huelga (6, 3, .500), Santiago Mederos (6, 0, .000), Braudilio Vinent (5, 0, .000), Gaspar Pérez (4, 0, .000), Manuel Hurtado (2, 0, .000), Gregorio Pérez (2, 0, .000). **Pitching** (W, L, ERA): José Antonio Huelga (2, 0, 0.00), Manuel Hurtado (1, 0, 0.00), Santiago Mederos (2, 0, 0.50), Gaspar Pérez (1, 0, 0.96), Braudilio Vinent (1, 1, 3.48), Gregorio Pérez (0, 0, 5.40).

1974 Central American Games Championship XII (Santo Domingo, Dominican Republic)

A new generation of sluggers named Antonio Muñoz, Agustín Marquetti, and Armando Capiró joined Rodolfo Puente and Wilfredo Sánchez to spark the potent offense of yet another unbeatable Servio Borges–managed Cuban team. The predictable result was a third straight Central American Games title, with only a single opening defeat in nine total games. Juan Pérez was the anchor of a pitching staff that also featured a young Braudilio Vinent. The latter would be heard from in many international tournaments to come, though he did not earn a decision here in his fifth national team outing.

Champion: Cuba (9–1) (Silver Medal: Dominican Republic; Bronze Medal: Puerto Rico)

Teams and Final Standings: Cuba (9–1), Dominican Republic (8–2), Puerto Rico (6–4), Venezuela (4–5), El Salvador (1–8), Virgin Islands (1–9). *One game between Venezuela and El Salvador was canceled.

Individual Statistical Leaders: **BA**: Rodolfo Puente (CUB) .500; **Runs**: A. Louis (DOM) 13; **Hits**: A. Louis (DOM) 20; **2B**: Agustín Marquetti (CUB), J. Guerrero (DOM) 4; **3B**: Armando Capiró (CUB) 3; **HR**: A. Louis (DOM), E. Maldonado (PUR), A. López (PUR) 1; **RBI**: Armando Capiró (CUB) 15; **SB**: Wilfredo Sánchez (CUB), J. Hernández (VEN), P. Ávila (VEN) 4; **Wins**: Juan Pérez (CUB), H. Flores (PUR) 3; **Strikeouts**: S. Martínez (DOM) 29; **ERA**: Juan Pérez (CUB) 0.00.

Cuba Roster: **Manager**: Servio Borges. **Batting** (AB, H, BA): Rodolfo Puente (28, 14, .500), Ubaldo Alvarez (10, 5, .500), Lázaro Pérez (14, 6, .429), Alfonso Urquiola (24, 10, .417), Evelio Hernández (30, 11, .357), Fermín Laffita (24, 8, .333), Agustín Arias (12, 4, .333), Armando Capiró (37, 12, .324), Agustín Marquetti (38, 12, .316), Germán Aguila (34, 10, .294), Félix Isasi (14, 4, .286), Wifredo Sánchez (40, 11, .275), Julian Villar (16, 4, .250), Rigoberto Rosique (18, 3, .167), Luis Barreiro (8, 5, .625), Alfredo García (6, 3, .500), Juan Pérez (8, 1, .125), Mario Fernández (4, 0, .000), Julio Romero (2, 0, .000). **Pitching** (W, L, ERA): Juan Pérez (3, 0, 0.00), Luis Barreiro (2, 0, 0.00), Mario Fernández (2, 0, .061), Alfredo García (2, 0, 0.73), Braudilio Vinent (0, 0, 2.00), Julio Romero (0, 1, 2.08).

1978 Central American Games Championship XIII (Medellín, Colombia)

Cuba dominates the field to make it four straight Central American Games titles. The Cubans had an offensive field day in their opening round victory over Puerto Rico, setting numerous offensive team records (31 runs, 32 hits, 30 RBI, 7 doubles, 11 home runs, 19 extra base hits). First baseman Antonio Muñoz posted 20 hits in 28 appearances for a hefty .714 BA during the full ten games, while outfielders Armando Capiró (.614) and Luis Casanova (.606) also both logged stratospheric .600-plus batting averages. Third baseman Pedro Luis Rodríguez added to the onslaught with a tournament record fifteen round-trippers while Rogelio García and Juan Carlos Oliva both rang up unblemished 3–0 pitching marks.

Champion: Cuba (10–0) (Silver Medal: Nicaragua; Bronze Medal: Puerto Rico)

Second Round Team Standings: Cuba (5–0), Puerto Rico (4–2), Nicaragua (4–2), Dominican Republic (3–3), Venezuela (2–4), Dutch Antilles (1–4), Colombia (1–5). *Cuba and Dutch Antilles did not play each other in second round.

First Round Team Standings: Cuba (5–0), Nicaragua (5–1), Puerto Rico (3–3), Venezuela (3–3), Dominican Republic (2–4), Colombia (2–4), Dutch Antilles (0–5). *Cuba vs. Dutch Antilles rained out and not rescheduled.

Individual Statistical Leaders: **BA**: Antonio Muñoz (CUB) .714*; **Runs**: Pedro José Rodríguez (CUB), Armando Capiró (CUB) 23*; **Hits**: Armando Capiró (CUB) 27*; **2B**: Luis Casanova (CUB), A. Llenas (DOM) 5; **3B**: G. Villegas (COL), D. Abrahams (AHO), M. González (VEN) 2; **HR**: Pedro José Rodríguez (CUB) 15*; **RBI**: Pedro José Rodríguez (CUB) 37*; **SB**: H. Jones (AHO) 3; **Wins**: Rogelio García (CUB), Juan Carlos Oliva (CUB) 3–0; **Strikeouts**: O. Valentín (PUR), **IP**: R. Colin (VEN) 27, **ERA**: J. Moya (NCA) 0.75. *Starred items are tournament records.

Cuba Roster: **Manager**: Servio Borges. **Batting** (AB, H, BA): Antonio Muñoz (28, 20, .714), Armando Capiró (44, 27, .614), Luis Casanova (33, 20, .606), Pedro José Rodríguez (45, 25, .556), Pedro Jova (32, 16, .500), Alfonso Urquiola (11, 5, .455), Fernando Sánchez (47, 21, .447), Agustín Marquetti (42, 18, .429), Pedro Medina (39, 15, .385), Rey Anglada (34, 12, .353), Alberto Martínez (3, 1, .333), Wilfredo Sánchez (21, 6, .286), Rodolfo Puente (21, 6, .286). **Pitching** (W, L, ERA): Félix Pino (1, 0, 0.00), Juan Carlos Oliva (3, 0, 2.25), Rogelio García (3, 0, 4.50), Braudilio Vinent (2, 0, 4.95), Lázaro Santana (1, 0, 5.40), Gaspar Legón (0, 0, 7.71), Santiago "Changa" Mederos (0, 0, 22.50).

1982 Central American Games Championship XIV (Havana, Cuba)

Cuba's disappointing runner-up outing interrupted two separate streaks of four consecutive Central American Games titles. Young Lázaro de la Torre would share top pitching honors for Cuba with veteran Braudilio Vinent; the pair would later emerge as two of only four Cuban League pitchers with 200 career National Series victories. (A third 200-game winner, Jorge Luis Valdés, was also a member of this same Cuban pitching staff.) Cuba would not lose another championship in this event over the next twenty-year stretch.

Champion: Dominican Republic (5–1) (Silver Medal: Cuba; Bronze Medal: Panama)

Teams and Final Standings: Dominican Republic (5–1), Cuba (4–2), Panama (3–3), Dutch Antilles (3–3), Nicaragua (2–4), Puerto Rico (2–4), Venezuela (2–4).

Individual Statistical Leaders: **BA**: J. Cartagena (VEN) .523; **Runs**: Antonio Muñoz (CUB), R. Valbuena (VEN) 6; **Hits**: J. Cartagena (VEN) 11; **2B**: Antonio Muñoz (CUB) 4; **3B**: six players tied with one each; **HR**: Pedro José Rodríguez (CUB), R. Machado (PUR), A. Cruz (NCA) 2; **RBI**: Pedro José Rodríguez (CUB), Lourdes Gourriel (CUB) 6; **SB**: O. Cuarrero (DOM) 6; **Wins**: M. Quiñones (PUR), O. Torres (VEN) 2–0; **ERA**: Lázaro de la Torre (CUB), 0.00.

Cuba Roster: **Manager**: Servio Borges. **Batting** (AB, H, BA): Pedro Medina (8, 3, .375), Juan Castro (16, 2, .125), Antonio Muñoz (24, 8, .333), Juan Luis Baró (11, 5, .455), Pedro Jova (23, 8, .348), Pedro José Rodríguez (21, 4, .190), Agustín Arias (5, 2, .400),

Wilfredo Hernández (0, 0, .000), Giraldo González (18, 4, .222), Victor Mesa (28, 7, .250), Fernando Hernández (25, 8, .320), Lázaro Junco (1, 0, .000), Fernando Sánchez (14, 5, .357), Lourdes Gourriel (23, 5, .217). **Pitching** (W, L, ERA): Félix Pino (0, 1, 3.00), Braudilio Vinent (2, 0, 0.54), Lázaro de la Torre (2, 0, 0.00), Octavio Galvez (0, 0, 10.13), Alfonso Ilivanes (0, 0, 3.00), Jorge Luis Valdés (0, 1, 2.25).

1986 Central American Games Championship XV (Santiago de los Caballeros, Dominican Republic)

Cuba regained its winning touch under new manager Pedro Chávez and left the field far behind with a perfect 7-game record. Orestes Kindelán emerged as yet another Cuban international slugging star, with a .533 batting average and the top spot in the tournament for homers and RBI as well as base hits. Omar Linares fell a single base hit shy of a .500 BA; Lourdes Gourriel and Luis Casanova also weighed in as .500 hitters. An unheralded team from the Dutch Antilles provided a major surprise with their silver medal finish, ahead of such traditional baseball powers as Venezuela, Puerto Rico, Nicaragua, and the host Dominicans.

Champion: Cuba (7–0) (Silver Medal: Dutch Antilles; Bronze Medal: Venezuela)

Teams and Final Standings: Cuba (7–0), Dutch Antilles (4–3), Venezuela (4–3), Puerto Rico (4–3), Nicaragua (3–4), Dominican Republic (2–5), Colombia (2–5), Panama (2–5).

Individual Statistical Leaders: **BA**: C. Rodríguez (COL) .556; **Runs**: Luis Casanova (CUB) 16; **Hits**: Orestes Kindelán (CUB) 16; **2B**: Luis Ulacia (CUB) 5; **3B**: L. Tavera (DOM) 3; **HR**: Orestes Kindelán (CUB) 7; **RBI**: Orestes Kindelán (CUB) 20; **SB**: several players with one each; **Wins**: D. Raudez (NCA) 3–0; **ERA**: Omar Carrero (CUB) 0.00.

Cuba Roster: **Manager**: Pedro Chávez. **Batting** (AB, H, BA): Juan Castro (9, 3, .333), Orestes Kindelán (30, 16, .533), Pedro Medina (18, 6, .333), Antonio Muñoz (24, 9, .375), Antonio Pacheco (29, 13, .440), Omar Linares (27, 11, .497), Luis Ulacia (32, 15, .469), Lázaro Vargas (5, 3, .600), Juan Padilla (2, 1, .500), Lourdes Gourriel (21, 11, .524), Luis Casanova (26, 13, .500), Victor Mesa (33, 12, .364), Jorge García (1, 1, 1.000). **Pitching** (W, L, ERA): Omar Carrero (1, 0, 0.00), Rogelio García (2, 0, 4.50), Pablo Abreu (1, 0, 2.16), René Arocha (1, 0, 1.13), Jorge Luis Valdés (0, 0, 4.50), Félix Nuñez (1, 0, 0.90), Luis Tissert (1, 0, 0.00).

1990 Central American Games Championship XVI (Mexico City, Mexico)

Cuba defends its 1986 title with yet another perfect record in Mexico during November, while Orestes Kindelán puts on a one-man power show as first-ever Central American Games triple crown winner (7 homers, 18 RBI, .533 batting average). Servio Borges returns as manager of the Cuban national team, making his fifth Central American Games appearance in that capacity. Veteran southpaw Jorge Luis Valdés (soon to be a 200-game winner in National Series action) is the tournament pitching star, throwing three consecutive shutouts and not allowing a single earned run in his trio of super-successful starts.

Champion: Cuba (8–0) (Silver Medal: Puerto Rico; Bronze Medal: Dominican Republic)

Final Round Team Standings: Cuba (2–0), Puerto Rico (1–1), Dominican Republic (1–1), Mexico (0–2).

Preliminary Round Team Standings: Cuba (6–0), Puerto Rico (4–2), Mexico (4–2), Dominican Republic (3–3), Dutch Antilles (3–3), El Salvador (1–5).

Individual Statistical Leaders: **BA**: Orestes Kindelán (CUB) .533; **Runs**: Orestes Kindelán (CUB) 12; **Hits**: Orestes Kindelán (CUB), Antonio Pacheco (CUB) 16; **2B**: C. Rostran (ESA) 4; **3B**: J. Vera (DOM) 3; **HR**: Orestes Kindelán (CUB) 7; **RBI**: Orestes Kindelán

(CUB) 18; **SB**: S. Andriano (AHO) 3; **Wins**: Jorge Luis Valdés (CUB) 3–0; **ERA**: A. Bonavacia (AHO) 0.00.

Cuba Roster: **Manager**: Servio Borges. **Batting** (AB, H, BA): Germán Mesa (31, 7, .226), Antonio Pacheco (33, 16, .485), Omar Linares (32, 11, .344), Orestes Kindelán (30, 16, .533), Lourdes Gourriel (28, 12, .429), Javier Méndez (25, 5, .200), Ermidelio Urrutia (31, 13, .419), Pedro Luis Rodríguez (27, 11, .407), Victor Mesa (30, 11, .368), Lázaro López (3, 0, .000), Juan Carlos Millán (4, 3, .750), Luis Ulacia (6, 1, .167), José Raúl Delgado (3, 0, .000). **Pitchers** (W, L, ERA): Ivan Alvarez (1, 0, 1.04), Eucildes Rojas (0, 0, 0.96), Osvaldo Fernández Rodríguez (0, 0, 4.50), Lázaro Valle (1, 0, 3.00), Jorge Luis Valdés (3, 0, 0.00), Omar Ajete (2, 0, 1.32), René Arocha (1, 0, 0.82).

1993 Central American Games Championship XVII (Ponce, Puerto Rico)

Another undefeated victory for the Cubans, this one under the directorship of replacement national team manager Jorge Fuentes. Future major leaguers Rolando Arrojo (Tampa Bay and Boston), Osvaldo Fernández (Giants and Reds), and Orlando "El Duque" Hernández (New York Yankees) headline a brilliant Cuban pitching staff, along with second-tier aces Omar Ajete, Lázaro Valle, and Ernesto Guevara. Position players Antonio Pacheco, Lourdes Gourriel, and Omar Linares all bat over .400 to pace the expected Cuban hit parade.

Champion: Cuba (7–0) (Silver Medal: Mexico; Bronze Medal: Puerto Rico)

Teams and Final Standings: Cuba (7–0), Nicaragua (5–2), Puerto Rico (4–3), Mexico (4–3), Panama (2–5), Venezuela (2–5), Aruba (2–5), Dutch Antilles (2–5).

Individual Statistical Leaders: **BA**: Rigoberto Aparicio (PAN) .579; **Runs**: Antonio Pacheco (CUB) 10; **Hits**: Lourdes Gourriel (CUB) 12; **2B**: Omar Linares (CUB) 4; **3B**: seven players tied with one each; **HR**: Antonio Pacheco (CUB), Orestes Kindelán (CUB) 3; **RBI**: J.R. Padilla (NCA) 9; **SB**: S. Moreno (NCA), R. Aparicio (PAN) 5; **Wins**: Rolando Arrojo (CUB), R. Santiago (PUR), J. Huazequi (MEX) 2; **ERA**: M.J. Zelaya (NCA) 0.00.

Cuba Roster: **Manager**: Jorge Fuentes. **Batting** (AB, H, BA): Alberto Hernández (21, 2, 0.95), Ángel López (2, 1, .500), José Raúl Delgado (2, 2, 1.000), Orestes Kindelán (26, 8, .308), Lourdes Gourriel (27, 12, .444), Antonio Pacheco (25, 10, .400), Juan Padilla (1, 0, 0.00), Omar Linares (28, 12, .429), Gabriel Pierre (1, 0, .000), Germán Mesa (25, 10, .400), Eduardo Paret (1, 0, .000), Victor Mesa (30, 9, .300), Ermidelio Urrutia (28, 10, .333), Juan Carlos Linares (3, 1, .333). **Pitchers** (W, L, ERA): Omar Ajete (1, 0, 0.00), Jorge Luis Valdés (0, 0, 2.70), Osvaldo Fernández Rodríguez (1, 0, 0.00), Luis Rolando Arrojo (2, 0, 0.00), Lázaro Valle (1, 0, 0.00), Ernesto Guevara (1, 0, 0.00), Orlando "El Duque" Hernández (1, 0, 0.00).

1998 Central American Games Championship XVIII (Maracaibo, Venezuela)

Cuba wins a fourth consecutive Central American Games title during the late-August event and extends its individual-game unbeaten streak through four consecutive tournaments. Former national team star infielder Alfonso Urquiola becomes the third Cuban manager to capture a team title in this event during the decade of the 1990s. First baseman Orestes Kindelán (.588 BA), catcher Juan Manrique (the surprise home run and RBI leader), and outfielder Loidel Chapelli (pacesetter in homers, along with Manrique, and also in runs scored) provide the major offense, while mound stars Omar Luis and José Contreras each capture two pitching victories.

Champion: Cuba (6–0) (Silver Medal: Nicaragua; Bronze Medal: Venezuela)

Teams and Final Standings: Cuba (6–0), Nicaragua (5–1), Venezuela (4–2), Panama (4–2), Dominican Republic (3–3), Puerto Rico (2–4), Dutch Antilles (1–5), Colombia (1–5), Virgin Islands (0–4). *Cuba beat Nicaragua (13–3) in gold medal game and Venezuela beat Panama (5–4) in bronze medal game.

Individual Statistical Leaders: **BA**: Orestes Kindelán (CUB) .588; **Runs**: Loidel Chapelli (CUB) 13; **Hits**: J. Solis (PAN) 13; **HR**: Juan Manrique (CUB), Loidel Chapelli (CUB), J. León (COL) 3; **RBI**: Juan Manrique (CUB), E. Agnoly (PAN) 12; **SB**: A. Rodríguez (PUR), S. Martínez (DOM) 3; **Wins**: I. Ávila (VEN), Omar Luis (CUB), José Ariel Contreras (CUB) 2–0; **Strikeouts**: J. Ávila (VEN) 19, **IP**: O. Clemencia (AHO), J. Ávila (VEN) 21.1, **ERA**: J. Viñas (DOM) 1.04.

Cuba Roster: **Manager**: Alfonso Urquiola. **Batting** (AB, H, BA): Ariel Benavides (3, 2, .667), Danel Castro (21, 8, .381), Loidel Chapelli (20, 10, .500), Orestes Kindelán (17, 10, .588), Omar Linares (14, 6, .429), Oscar Machado (18, 3, .167), Oscar Macías (6, 4, .667), Yosvani Madera (2, 0, .000), Juan Manrique (21, 7, .333), Javier Méndez (6, 4, .667), Juan Carlos Moreno (3, 0, .000), Antonio Pacheco (15, 4, .267), Gabriel Pierre (5, 1, .200), Carlos Taberas (23, 9, .391), Robelquis Videaux (25, 12, .480). **Pitchers** (W, L, ERA): Yovani Aragón (1, 0, 1.13), José Ariel Contreras (2, 0, 4.61), José Ibar (0, 0, 2.70), Pedro Luis Lazo (1, 0, 1.35), Omar Luis (2, 0, 1.38).

Asia Baseball Federation Championships, 1954–2001

Composite Standings of Championships: Japan 12 (1955, 1959, 1962, 1965, 1967, 1969, 1973, 1985, 1989, 1991, 1993, 1995); **South Korea** 6 (1963, 1971, 1975, 1983, 1997, 1999); **Chinese Taipei** 2 (1987, 2001); **Philippines** 1 (1954).

1954 Asia Baseball Federation Championship I (Manila, Philippines)
Champion: Philippines
Final Standings: Philippines (Gold), Japan (Silver), Korea (Bronze), Chinese Taipei.

1955 Asia Baseball Federation Championship II (Manila, Philippines)
Champion: Japan
Final Standings: Japan (Gold), Chinese Taipei (Silver), Korea (Bronze), Philippines.

1959 Asia Baseball Federation Championship III (Tokyo, Japan)
Champion: Japan
Final Standings: Japan (Gold), Korea (Silver), Chinese Taipei (Bronze), Philippines.

1962 Asia Baseball Federation Championship IV (Taipei, Taiwan)
Champion: Japan
Final Standings: Japan (Gold), Chinese Taipei (Silver), Korea (Bronze), Philippines.

1963 Asia Baseball Federation Championship V (Seoul, South Korea)
Champion: South Korea
Final Standings: Korea (Gold), Japan and Chinese Taipei (Silver), Philippines.

1965 Asia Baseball Federation Championship VI (Manila, Philippines)
Champion: Japan
Final Standings: Japan (Gold), Korea (Silver), Chinese Taipei (Bronze), Philippines.

1967 Asia Baseball Federation Championship VII (Tokyo, Japan)
Champion: Japan
Final Standings: Japan (Gold), Korea (Silver), Chinese Taipei (Bronze), Philippines.

1969 Asia Baseball Federation Championship VIII (Taipei, Taiwan)
Champion: Japan
Final Standings: Japan (Gold), Chinese Taipei (Silver), Philippines (Bronze), Korea.

1971 Asia Baseball Federation Championship IX (Seoul, South Korea)
Champion: South Korea
Final Standings: Korea (Gold), Japan (Silver), Philippines (Bronze), Australia, Chinese Taipei.

1973 Asia Baseball Federation Championship X (Manila, Philippines)
Champion: Japan

Final Standings: Japan (Gold), Korea (Silver), Chinese Taipei (Bronze), Philippines, Australia.

1975 Asia Baseball Federation Championship XI (Seoul, South Korea)
Champion: South Korea

Final Standings: Korea (Gold), Japan (Silver), Australia (Bronze), Chinese Taipei, Philippines.

1983 Asia Baseball Federation Championship XII (Seoul, South Korea)
Champion: South Korea

Final Standings: Korea (Gold), Chinese Taipei and Japan (Silver), Australia, Philippines.

1985 Asia Baseball Federation Championship XIII (Perth, Australia)
Champion: Japan

Final Standings: Japan (Gold), Korea (Silver), Chinese Taipei (Bronze), Australia, China.

1987 Asia Baseball Federation Championship XIV (Tokyo, Japan)
Champion: Chinese Taipei

Final Standings: Chinese Taipei (Gold), Japan (Silver), Korea (Bronze), Guam, Australia, China, India.

1989 Asia Baseball Federation Championship XV (Seoul, South Korea)
Champion: Japan

Final Standings: Japan (Gold), Korea and Chinese Taipei (Silver), China, Guam, Philippines, India.

1991 Asia Baseball Federation Championship XVI (Beijing, China)
Champion: Japan

Final Standings: Japan (Gold), Chinese Taipei (Silver), Korea (Bronze), Australia, Philippines, China, Guam.

1993 Asia Baseball Federation Championship XVII (Perth, Australia)
Champion: Japan

Final Standings: Japan (Gold), Korea (Silver), Chinese Taipei (Bronze), Australia, China, North Korea, Philippines.

1995 Asia Baseball Federation Championship XVIII (Kurashiki, Japan)
Champion: Japan

Final Standings: Japan (Gold), Korea (Silver), Chinese Taipei (Bronze), China, Philippines, Thailand.

1997 Asia Baseball Federation Championship XIX (Taipei, Taiwan)
Champion: South Korea

Final Standings: Korea (Gold), Japan (Silver), Chinese Taipei (Bronze), China, Thailand, Philippines.

1999 Asia Baseball Federation Championship XX (Seoul, South Korea)
Champion: South Korea

Final Standings: Korea (Gold), Japan (Silver), Chinese Taipei (Bronze), China, Philippines, Thailand.

2001 Asia Baseball Federation Championship XXI (Taipei, Chinese Taipei)
Champion: Chinese Taipei

Final Standings: Chinese Taipei (Gold), Korea (Silver), Japan (Bronze), Philippines, Indonesia.

European Baseball Championships, 1954–2001

Composite Standings of Championships: Netherlands 17 (1956, 1957, 1958, 1960, 1962, 1964, 1965, 1969, 1971, 1973, 1981, 1985, 1987, 1993, 1995, 1999, 2001); **Italy** 8 (1954, 1975, 1977, 1979, 1983, 1989, 1991, 1997); **Spain** 1 (1955); **Belgium** 1 (1967).

1954 European Championship I (Antwerp, Belgium) (June 26–27)
Champion: Italy
Final Standings: Italy (Gold), Spain (Silver), Belgium (Bronze), Germany.
Italy Game Scores: Italy beat Belgium 6–1, Italy beat Spain 7–4.

1955 European Championship II (Barcelona, Spain) (July 5–10)
Champion: Spain
Final Standings: Spain (Gold), Belgium (Silver), Germany (Bronze), Italy, France.
Spain Game Scores: Spain beat France 21–3, Spain beat Germany 9–0, Spain tied Italy 0–0, Spain beat Belgium 2–0.

1956 European Championship III (Rome, Italy) (July 10–15)
Champion: Netherlands
Final Standings: Netherlands (Gold), Belgium (Silver), Italy (Bronze), Spain, Germany.
Netherlands Game Scores: Netherlands beat Italy 13–2, Netherlands beat Belgium 1–0, Netherlands beat Spain 6–4, Netherlands beat Germany 3–2.

1957 European Championship IV (Mannheim, Germany) (July 7–13)
Champion: Netherlands
Final Standings: Netherlands (Gold), Germany (Silver), Italy (Bronze), Spain, Belgium.
Netherlands Game Scores: Netherlands beat Germany 9–0, Netherlands beat Italy 3–1, Netherlands beat Belgium 14–0.

1958 European Championship V (Amsterdam, Netherlands) (June 5–12)
Champion: Netherlands
Final Standings: Netherlands (Gold), Italy (Silver), Germany (Bronze), Belgium, Spain, France.
Netherlands Game Scores: Netherlands beat Italy 6–5, Netherlands beat Germany 4–3, Netherlands beat Italy 5–2.

1960 European Championship VI (Barcelona, Spain) (September 22–25)
Champion: Netherlands
Final Standings: Netherlands (Gold), Italy (Silver), Spain (Bronze), Germany.
Netherlands Game Scores: Netherlands beat Italy 1–0, Netherlands beat Germany 12–1, Netherlands beat Spain 1–0.

1962 European Championship VII (Amsterdam, Netherlands) (July 21–29)
Champion: Netherlands
Final Standings: Netherlands (Gold), Italy (Silver), Spain (Bronze), Belgium, Germany, France, Sweden.
Netherlands Game Scores: Netherlands beat France 20–1, Netherlands beat Sweden 14–0, Netherlands beat Spain 7–2, Netherlands beats Belgium 8–2, Netherlands beats Italy 9–4.

1964 European Championship VIII (Milan, Italy) (August 29–September 6)
Champion: Netherlands
Final Standings: Netherlands (Gold), Italy (Silver), Spain (Bronze), Sweden, France.
Netherlands Game Scores: Netherlands beat Spain 10–0, Netherlands beat Sweden 19–4, Netherlands beat France 30–0, Netherlands beat Italy 3–1.

1965 European Championship IX (Madrid, Spain) (August 29–September 5)
Champion: Netherlands
Final Standings: Netherlands (Gold), Italy (Silver), Germany (Bronze), Spain, Sweden.
Netherlands Game Scores: Netherlands beat Sweden 19–0, Netherlands beat Spain 15–0, Netherlands beat Italy 16–0, Netherlands beat Germany 7–0.

1967 European Championship X (Antwerp, Belgium) (August 6–12)
Champion: Belgium
Final Standings: Belgium (Gold), Great Britain (Silver), Germany (Bronze), Spain, Sweden.
Belgium Game Scores: Belgium beat Spain 11–0, Belgium beat Sweden 18–6, Belgium beat Great Britain 13–2, Belgium beat Germany 8–3.

1969 European Championship XI (Wiesbaden, Germany) (July 27–August 3)
Champion: Netherlands
Final Standings: Netherlands (Gold), Italy (Silver), Spain (Bronze), Germany, Belgium, Sweden, France.
Netherlands Game Scores: Netherlands beat Belgium 9–0, Netherlands beat Belgium 9–3, Netherlands beat Italy 9–5.

1971 European Championship XII (Parma and Bologna, Italy) (September 5–12)
Champion: Netherlands
Final Standings: Netherlands (Gold), Italy (Silver), Germany (Bronze), Belgium, San Marino, Spain, Great Britain, Sweden, France.
Netherlands Game Scores: Qualification round-robin: Netherlands beat Spain 1–0, Netherlands beat Belgium 20–1, Netherlands beat Sweden 14–0, Netherlands beat France 21–0, Netherlands beat Italy 4–2. Finals: Italy beat Netherlands 1–0, Netherlands beat Italy 7–3.

1973 European Championship XIII (Haarlem, Netherlands) (June 30–July 8)
Champion: Netherlands
Final Standings: Netherlands (Gold), Italy (Silver), Spain (Bronze), Belgium, Sweden, France.
Netherlands Game Scores: Netherlands beat Spain 7–0, Netherlands beat Belgium 16–0, Netherlands beat Sweden 16–1, Netherlands beat France 21–0, Netherlands beat Italy 7–6, Netherlands beat Belgium 8–0, Netherlands beat Spain 10–2, Netherlands beat Italy 6–2.

1975 European Championship XIV (Barcelona, Spain) (July 25–August 3)
Champion: Italy
Final Standings: Italy (Gold), Netherlands (Silver), Germany (Bronze), Spain, Sweden, France.
Italy Game Scores: Italy beat Spain 9–0, Italy beat France 13–0, Netherlands beat Italy 2–0, Italy beat Netherlands 7–1, Italy beat Netherlands 5–1, Netherlands beat Italy 9–4, Italy beat Netherlands 9–4.

1977 European Championship XV (Haarlem, Netherlands) (July 23–31)
Champion: Italy
Final Standings: Italy (Gold), Netherlands (Silver), Belgium (Bronze), Sweden, Spain.
Italy Game Scores: Italy beat Sweden 29–0, Italy beat Spain 22–0, Italy beat Belgium 27–0, Netherlands beat Italy 6–5, Netherlands beat Italy 2–1, Italy beat Netherlands 4–1, Italy beat Netherlands 1–0.

1979 European Championship XVI (Trieste, Italy) (August 11–19)
Champion: Italy
Final Standings: Italy (Gold), Netherlands (Silver), Belgium (Bronze), Sweden.

Italy Game Scores: Italy beat Sweden 6–0, Italy beat Belgium 21–5, Italy beat Netherlands 5–4, Italy beat Netherlands 14–1, Italy beat Netherlands 5–0, Italy beat Netherlands 8–4, Netherlands beat Italy 8–5.

1981 European Championship XVII (Haarlem, Netherlands) (July 11–19)
Champion: Netherlands
Final Standings: Netherlands (Gold), Italy (Silver), Sweden (Bronze), Belgium.
Netherlands Game Scores: Netherlands beat Sweden 6–5, Italy beat Netherlands 3–1, Netherlands beat Belgium 19–1, Netherlands beat Sweden 14–2, Netherlands beat Belgium 13–1, Netherlands beat Italy 8–3, Netherlands beat Italy 11–7, Netherlands beat Italy 8–1.

1983 European Championship XVIII (Florence, Italy) (July 28–August 7)
Champion: Italy
Final Standings: Italy (Gold), Netherlands (Silver), Belgium (Bronze), Spain, Sweden, France.
Italy Game Scores: Italy beat Netherlands 9–5, Italy beat Belgium 7–0, Italy beat Spain 21–0, Italy beat France 32–0, Italy beat Netherlands 14–1, Italy beat Netherlands 3–2, Italy beat Netherlands 8–2, Netherlands beat Italy 14–4.

1985 European Championship XIX (Haarlem, Netherlands) (July 6–14)
Champion: Netherlands
Final Standings: Netherlands (Gold), Italy (Silver), Belgium (Bronze), Sweden, Spain, San Marino.
Netherlands Game Scores: Netherlands beat Sweden 31–2, Netherlands beat Italy 5–4, Netherlands beat Belgium 11–1, Netherlands beat Spain 12–1, Netherlands beat San Marino 18–7, Netherlands beat Italy 6–4, Netherlands beat Italy 12–4, Netherlands beat Italy 11–8, Netherlands beat Italy 8–6.

1987 European Championship XX (Barcelona, Spain) (July 17–26)
Champion: Netherlands
Final Standings: Netherlands (Gold), Italy (Silver), Spain (Bronze), Belgium, Sweden, France, Germany.
Netherlands Game Scores: Netherlands beat Sweden 11–1, Netherlands beat Spain 22–0, Netherlands beat France 27–0, Netherlands beat Belgium 19–4, Netherlands beat Italy 7–6, Netherlands beat Italy 7–4, Italy beat Netherlands 13–4, Italy beat Netherlands 5–4, Netherlands beat Italy 16–1.

1989 European Championship XXI (Paris, France) (September 6–15)
Champion: Italy
Final Standings: Italy (Gold), Netherlands (Silver), Spain (Bronze), Sweden, France, Belgium, Great Britain, Germany.
Italy Game Scores: Italy beat Netherlands 5–4, Netherlands beat Italy 15–2, Netherlands beat Italy 10–6, Italy beat Netherlands 8–0, Italy beat Netherlands 7–5, Italy beat Spain 7–0, Italy beat Germany 24–4, Italy beat France 15–3, Italy beat Sweden 12–0.

1991 European Championship XXII (Rome, Italy) (August 2–11)
Champion: Italy
Final Standings: Italy (Gold), Netherlands (Silver), Spain (Bronze), France, Belgium, USSR, Sweden, Great Britain.
Italy Game Scores: Italy beat Sweden 26–6, Italy beat France 15–1, Italy beat USSR 10–0, Italy beat Spain 7–1, Italy beat Netherlands 12–3, Italy beat Netherlands 12–1, Italy beat Netherlands 9–2, Italy beat Netherlands 3–1, Italy beat Netherlands 3–2.

1993 European Championship XXIII (Stockholm, Sweden) (July 9–18)
Champion: Netherlands
Final Standings: Netherlands (Gold), Italy (Silver), Sweden (Bronze), France, Spain, Belgium, Germany, Russia.
Netherlands Game Scores: Netherlands beat Sweden 12–5, Netherlands beat Spain 9–1, Netherlands beat Russian 6–2, Netherlands beat France 10–2, Netherlands beat Italy 7–1, Netherlands beat Italy 7–2, Netherlands beat Italy 11–2, Italy beat Netherlands 21–7, Netherlands beat Italy 11–0.

1995 European Championship XXIV (Haarlem, Netherlands) (July 7–16)
Champion: Netherlands
Final Standings: Netherlands (Gold), Italy (Silver), Belgium (Bronze), Spain, France, Germany, Sweden, Russia, Ukraine, Slovenia.
Netherlands Game Scores: Netherlands beat Ukraine 10–2, Netherlands beat France 15–8, Netherlands beat Spain 23–3, Netherlands beat Russia 11–3, Netherlands beat Belgium 10–0, Italy beat Netherlands 12–9, Netherlands beat Italy 13–7, Netherlands beat Italy 13–10, Netherlands beat Italy 7–4.

1997 European Championship XXV (Paris, France) (August 30–September 6)
Champion: Italy
Final Standings: Italy (Gold), Netherlands (Silver), Spain (Bronze), Russia, France, Belgium, Czech Republic, Sweden, Great Britain, Germany, Ukraine, Slovenia.
Italy Game Scores: Italy beat Slovenia 25–8, Italy beat Germany 11–1, Italy beat Sweden 12–0, Italy beat Belgium 21–4, Italy beat Czech Republic 6–5, Italy beat France 17–12, Italy beat Russia 15–5, Italy beat Netherlands 4–2.

1999 European Championship XXVI (Parma and Bologna, Italy) (July 23–31)
Champion: Netherlands
Final Standings: Netherlands (Gold), Italy (Silver), France (Bronze), Russia, Spain, Belgium, Sweden, Czech Republic, Great Britain, Germany, Croatia, Slovenia.
Netherlands Game Scores: Preliminary Round: Netherlands beat Germany 8–1, Netherlands beat Czech Republic 9–0, Netherlands beat Belgium 9–1, Netherlands beat Spain 8–1, Netherlands beat Slovenia 15–2. Quarterfinals: Netherlands beat Sweden 6–0. Semifinals: Netherlands beat Russia 7–0. Finals: Netherlands beat Italy 3–0.

2001 European Championship XXVII (Bonn and Cologne, Germany) (July 28–August 5)
Champion: Netherlands
Final Standings: Netherlands (Gold), Russia (Silver), Italy (Bronze), France, Czech Republic, Spain, Germany, Croatia, Belgium, Great Britain, Ukraine, Sweden.
Netherlands Game Scores: Preliminary Round: Netherlands beat Great Britain 27–0, Netherlands beat Spain 6–3, Netherlands beat Czech Republic 5–1, Russia beat Netherlands 4–3, Netherlands beat Ukraine 6–0. Quarterfinals: Netherlands beat Croatia 8–7. Semifinals: Netherlands beat France 5–1. Finals: Netherlands beat Russia 4–0.

Oceania Baseball Confederation, 1999–2003

1999 Baseball Confederation of Oceania Championships (Guam) (May 31–June 9)
Champion: Guam
Final Standings: Guam (Gold), American Samoa (Silver), Micronesia (Bronze), Palau, CNMI, New Caledonia.
Guam Game Scores: Guam beat Micronesia 10–0, Guam beat Palau 21–4, Guam beat New Caledonia 27–0, Guam beat CNMI 16–6, Guam beat American Samoa 13–3. Finals: Guam beat American Samoa 6–5.

2000 Baseball Confederation of Oceania Championships (Guam) (June 12–16)
Champion: Guam

Final Standings: Guam (Gold), American Samoa (Silver).

Game Scores: American Samoa beat Guam 3–2, American Samoa beat Guam 11–6, Guam beat American Samoa 15–11, Guam beat American Samoa 5–4, Guam beat America Samoa 9–2.

2003 Oceania World Cup Qualifier (Guam) (April 26–29)
Champion: Australia

Final Standings: Australia (Gold), Guam (Silver).

Game Scores: Australia beat Guam 12–1, Australia beat Guam 12–1, Guam beat Australia 8–2, Australia beat Guam 5–1.

2003 South Pacific Games (Fiji Islands) (June 30–July 9)
Champion: Guam

Final Standings: Guam (Gold), American Samoa (Silver), Micronesia (Bronze), Palau, New Caledonia, Solomon Islands, Fiji Islands.

Guam Game Scores: Guam beat Micronesia 6–1, Guam beat Fiji Islands 14–1, Guam beat New Caledonia 15–0, Guam beat Palau 3–1, Guam beat Solomon Islands 19–0. Semifinals: Guam beat Palau 4–0. Finals: Guam beat American Samoa 11–3.

WORLD UNIVERSITY CHAMPIONSHIPS, 2002

2002 World University Championship I (Messina, Italy) (August 2–11)

Although there have been numerous world university games competitions over the years, a baseball-exclusive college tournament was staged for the first time in the summer of 2002, under sponsorship and management of the International University Sports Federation and the IBAF (International Baseball Federation). Not at all surprisingly, Cuba swept the competition, with the United States and Japan trailing in the medal hunt. Cuba was scored upon in one of its seven games.

Champion: Cuba (7–0) (Silver Medal: USA; Bronze Medal: Japan)

Teams and Final Standings: Cuba (7–0), USA (5–2), Japan (5–2), Chinese Taipei (3–4), South Korea (3–3), Italy (3–3), China (3–3), Czech Republic (1–5), Canada (1–4), France (0–5).

Final Round Game Scores: Cuba Beat USA 6–0 (Gold Medal), Japan beat Chinese Taipei 5–0 (Bronze Medal), South Korea beat Italy 12–2 (Fifth Place), China beat Czech Republic 9–0 (Seventh Place), Canada beat France 3–0 (Ninth Place).

Semifinal Round Game Scores: Cuba beat Chinese Taipei 2–0, USA beat Japan 2–1.

Quarterfinal Round Game Scores: Cuba beat China 3–0, Japan beat South Korea 6–1, USA beat Czech Republic 14–1, Chinese Taipei beat Italy 14–3.

Pool A Preliminary Round Game Scores: USA beat Italy 10–0, China beat Canada 5–1, Italy beat South Korea 2–0, USA beat Canada 9–1, Italy beat Canada 14–3, South Korea beat China 7–3, China beat USA 4–3, South Korea beat Canada 14–2, USA beat South Korea 16–2, Italy beat China 2–1.

Pool B Preliminary Round Game Scores: Japan beat France 13–0, Cuba beat Chinese Taipei 7–4, Chinese Taipei beat Czech Republic 5–0, Cuba beat France 7–0, Cuba beat Czech Republic 14–0, Japan beat Chinese Taipei 1–0, Chinese Taipei beat France 8–6, Japan beat Czech Republic 11–1, Czech Republic beat France 4–0, Cuba beat Japan 1–0.

BIBLIOGRAPHY

Casa, Edel, Jorge Alfonso, and Alberto Pestana. *Viva y en juego (Alive and Playing)*. Havana, Cuba: Editorial Científico Técnica, 1986.

Cava, Pete. "Baseball in the Olympics." *The National Pastime: A Review of Baseball History* 12 (1992): 2–8.

González Echevarría, Roberto. *The Pride of Havana: A History of Cuban Baseball*. New York: Oxford University Press, 1999.

Humber, William. *Diamonds of the North: A Concise History of Baseball in Canada*. New York and Toronto: Oxford University Press, 1995.

CHAPTER 11

The Caribbean and Baseball's Real World Series

The Heyday of Latin Winter Ball

• •

Summer afternoon—summer afternoon. To me those have always been the two most beautiful words in the English language.

—Henry James

Almost any North American youngster—raised anywhere from the crowded suburbs of Boston to the spacious farming plains of Salinas, Kansas—would be quick to provide a hearty cheer and a slight twist of focus for those immortal words of novelist Henry James. While our staid middle-aged and expatriate author (himself not a fan of ball games) pined perhaps for quietly sociable afternoon teas and leisurely contemplative walks through shaded English gardens, for thousands upon thousands of bat-and-glove-toting youth the thought of a summer afternoon holds more robust images: towering outfield flies, dramatic dashes around the basepaths, the dangers of a slide.

Baseball neither requires the English language nor insists on a sleepy winter. Across the blue of the Caribbean, the calendar peels its leaves backwards and the time clock ticks at a more southerly pace. Each crisp autumn season, at the conclusion of prime time televised World Series excitement, when baseball in the United States seems to roll up its battered basepaths and pack away its barren bull pens to silently disappear into hibernation for the long winter months ahead—then, unnoticed by casual observers, the national pastime also migrates south of the border for several more weeks of exciting big league–caliber winter-ball competition.

Winter baseball, in fact, has reigned for decades as the revered national sport in such tropical paradise settings as the island nations of Cuba, Puerto Rico, and the Dominican Republic, and it is a safe bet that General Abner Doubleday's mythically quaint and marvelous pastoral game enjoys a very real and present popularity throughout Central American strongholds in Mexico, Nicaragua, and Panama as well. It is one of the triumphs of the Latin invasion of the 1980s and 1990s that few stateside fans now remain uninformed about the big league impact of such slick Latino infielders as Tony Fernández, Manny Lee, or Roberto Alomar, or the slugging heroics of present and past Hispanic stars like Albert Pujols and Orlando Cepeda. Unaccountable, then, that so few are aware of the thriving tropical baseball world that flowers during each Caribbean winter season.

Stateside fans are left during winter's harsher months with only memories and dreams and hot-stove scuttlebutt about the hometown nine—or, more likely today, with the steady diet of financial bulletins concerning baseball's exploding list of instant millionaires that seems to have replaced debate over fresh outfield phenoms or long-of-tooth and lame-armed mound veterans. South of the border, baseball does not hibernate. Caribbean islanders seize their moment to thrill to the crack of ash wood on horsehide and to hear the infectious daily cries of *"plei bol!"* or *"jonrón!"* spread across two delightful months of *béisbol* celebration—Caribbean style!

The bread and butter of this hidden Caribbean season remains today the four Winter League pennant races that now operate in the Dominican Republic, Puerto Rico, Venezuela, and Mexico—the last-named nation also serving as home to the AAA Mexican League for traditional summer-season play. The crown jewel is the exciting weeklong championship playoff series—the *Serie del Caribe,* as it is known to Latin *fanáticos*—an intense 12-game round-robin battle held between the four Winter League champions each February as culmination to the ten-week Caribbean season. Far more than a mere tourist attraction to boost the local economy of participating host countries, this four-nation Winter League season, along with the Caribbean Series with which it concludes, has been the spawning grounds for numerous future big league stars over the past four or more decades.

Puerto Rico's Vic Power (Pellot) holds the Caribbean World Series record for career hits, with 50 hits in eight years. [Transcendental Graphics]

Retired 1980s home run king Mike Schmidt, the game's greatest-ever third baseman, is one baseball immortal who publicly traces his sudden sophomore successes of 1974 to a largely invisible winter league education the year before in Puerto Rico. A winter league experience ignored or forgotten by the media, perhaps, but not by Schmidt. Two decades before Schmidt's Puerto Rican trial by fire, there were other future big league stars such as Sandy Koufax, Orlando Cepeda, Roberto Clemente, Charlie Neal, Rubén Gómez, Hank Aaron, Luke Easter, Vic Power, and Bob Buhl—Spanish- and English-speaking prospects alike—honing their skills in hotly contested ball games spread across the face of Puerto Rico. Winter ball has thus long been the familiar off-season stomping grounds for dozens of travel-weary big league scouts and player personnel directors seeking out the elusive untouted prospect or perhaps supervising extra work details for scores of sore-armed rehabilitating pitchers, overanxious youthful batsmen with landing-strip strike zones, and shaky journeyman infielders struggling to perfect a big league double-play pivot.

This is not to suggest that Caribbean winter ball is any mere diamond meat market or boot camp for untutored minor leaguers. Winter ball—with all its salsa music, fiesta-like trappings, and unbridled nationalistic fervor—is also an incomparable baseball culture unique unto itself. Here one uncovers a rich universe of Latin-flavored *mano-a-mano* diamond play, which actually looms larger and more important—at least for thousands of *fanáticos* spread throughout a half-dozen Caribbean Basin countries—than major league play itself. And these same Caribbean fans who show such enthusiasm for winter ball each December and January know their big league history quite as well as their stateside counterparts do. Local sports pages follow the daily exploits of Latino big leaguers religiously throughout the summer months (every 1993 at-bat of Andrés Galarraga was replayed as front-page news in Caracas), radio transmissions of major league contests were beamed to Cuba regularly in the days before Castro's revolution, and Roberto Clemente remains perhaps the greatest national hero (both inside and outside of the sporting world) the island community of Puerto Rico has ever produced.

The 1992 Mexican-based Caribbean series, contested in Hermosillo's plush stadium, marked the thirty-fourth renewal of this colorful winter baseball ritual, a joyous baseball festival that has witnessed a checkered if often lively past history. The first phase (*Primera Etapa*), launched in the Gran Stadium of Havana in the spring of 1949, lasted through 1960 and was dominated in the final years by the strong Cuban entrants, who won seven of the twelve round-robins and finished as runner-up on three additional occasions. Only Venezuela failed to capture a single tourney in the first dozen years of play, a period that saw Puerto Rico take four crowns and Panama eke out a single title in 1950. The Primera Etapa was the scene for such legendary events of the Latin diamond as Agapito Mayor's unmatched three mound victories for host Cuba in 1949, American Tommy Fine's unique no-hitter (the only one in CWS play to date) of 1952, and Willie Mays's dramatic game-winning circuit clout during the 1955 final round.

A full decade of suspended play followed, brought about by a combination of economic difficulties in the region and the disappearance of reigning powerhouse Cuba from Winter League play. Caribbean baseball, like Caribbean life and economic life in general, suffered an inevitable fallout of Cold War mentality in the wake of damaged relations between Washington and Castro's rebellious Cuba. The Series was renewed in 1970 (*Segunda Etapa*) and has been played each year since (except for a second brief players-strike suspension in 1981), with the island nations of the Dominican Republic and Puerto Rico (thirteen titles between them) continuing to dominate championship play. Venezuela has subsequently won four Caribbean titles; Mexico (Panama's replacement in the second phase) has captured two; and the talent-rich Dominican Republic, as if standing in Cuba's abandoned shoes, has hoisted eight championship banners during the renewed phase of the competition.

Phase Two of this 35-year baseball extravaganza has also provided its own special unmatched treasure trove of records, statistics, legends, lore, and memorable baseball feats. (Summaries for much of this history appear later in this chapter, drawing largely on Spanish-language sources.[1])

For all its glory, Latin America's Caribbean World Series remains among the forgotten lore of American baseball. Today, the true triumphs and glories of play "south of the border" are an even more desperately lost segment of our baseball past than even the black-ball world of Negro league play. Satchel Paige and Josh Gibson have long been household names for literate baseball fans, while Martín Dihigo, Napoleón Reyes, Agapito Mayor, Héctor Espino, and Willard Brown are lost in the shadows of the pantheon.

THE HEYDAY OF LATIN WINTER BALL

A ballpark is a place of pure and unrivaled magic, as are so many commonplace sites first discovered in childhood. The ballpark is at the same time one of the truly rare locations where such magic persists into adulthood, and even cynical adulthood. This experience is as well known to the Caribbean patron as it is to hardened ball fans anywhere in U.S. towns and cities.

Though born of the same magic, Winter League play, and especially the February Caribbean Series, boasts an appearance entirely unique to the Latin American baseball world. This is no mere Grapefruit League or Cactus League campaign transported to quaint island ballparks in a sunnier clime. Each game is instead a small but joyous festival and a true celebration of national pride and spirit. No matter what happens on the field of play, no one sits on his or her hands in the grandstands of Hermosillo, Caracas, Caguas, or Santo Domingo.

Mariachi bands blare from the grandstand and inebriated fans dance throughout nine innings in a constant fandango. Aromatic feasts, strange to North American taste buds, are constantly served up throughout the teeming bleachers. On-field play is often wild, woolly, and totally unparalleled on most big league diamonds—reminiscent, at times, of the old slapstick St. Louis Brownies or 1930s-era Daffiness Dodgers, before the former escaped east of the Mississippi to staid Baltimore and the latter exchanged Babe Herman for Duke Snider and Wilbert Robinson for Jackie Robinson. Sometimes young children race into the outfield for autographs between pitches; local beauty queens, resplendent team mascots, often sit stoically in the home team dugout; sportswriters and television crews scour the benches for cherished interviews between innings and even sometimes while the ball is still in play. This ongoing collage of color and action makes even the informalities of spring training play (pitchers running wind sprints in the outfield, or sea gulls alighting upon the infield) seem somehow structured and staid.

It is not charm, delight, or spectacle alone. Legendary baseball feats have been accomplished through the years in ballparks spread from Santiago to Santurce to Tijuana to Mexicali. What dedicated Dominican or Mexican or Venezuelan *fanático* could ever forget Jesús "Chiquitín" Cabrera's .619 batting average, which stunned fans at the 1951 Venezuela Series? Cabrera's heroic single-series batting exploits took place in Caracas and still inspire the same enthusiasm around that Venezuelan capital city as those of Ted Williams or Bobby Doerr might evoke among 1950s-era fans anywhere New England. And what long-time fan of the Caribbean pastime does not also relish the memory of Texan Tommy Fine's delicate no-hitter, twirled for Cuba at Panama City in 1952—still the only perfect pitching masterpiece ever recorded in Caribbean Series play?

Memory thrives likewise on the legendary home run feats, such as those compiled through the years by Latin big leaguers Tony Armas (Venezuela) and Rico Carty (Dominican Republic), Mexican leaguer Héctor Espino, and North America's own journeyman minor league hero Phil Stephenson. Or Barry Jones's record 5 homers struck in the misshapen Orange Bowl during a more recent campaign, when the 1990 Series inaugurated a brief two-year residence for Caribbean Series play here on U.S. soil. (From here on, Caribbean Series and the richly deserved alternative, Caribbean World Series, or CWS, will be used interchangeably.)

Willie Mays, Roberto Clemente, the three Alou brothers, Tony Armas, Camilo Pascual, Monte Irvin, Don Baylor, Luís Aparicio, Chico Carrasquel. Through the Caribbean Series, such famed big league names—and these are but a handful out of many more—have left their lasting marks on local play as well, in the process blazing indelible sporting legends into the rich baseball traditions of Venezuela, Mexico, Panama, and the Caribbean island nations of Puerto Rico and the Dominican Republic. So too have largely obscure major league toilers, such as Tommy Fine, Chuck (born Kevin) Connors, and Dan Bankhead (major league baseball's first African American pitcher); Negro league immortals such as Satchel Paige, Wilmer Fields, and Luke Easter; and local Latin heroes such as Héctor Espino (Mexico), Héctor Rodríguez (Cuba), and José "Carrao" Bracho (Venezuela). Fabled Winter League exploits on the order of Juan Pizarro's 17 strikeouts in a single 1958 contest and Rico Carty's 5 towering homers during four consecutive games of the 1977 Caribbean Series stand among the game's great moments in Spanish-speaking lands—while remaining at the same time entirely lost to summertime fans residing north of the border.

For a sampling of the most glorious moments from more than four decades of Caribbean Series play, there is no better place to begin than 1949 in Havana, Cuba: the inaugural year of Series competition. The dozen years that comprised the first stage of Caribbean Series action saw a lopsided domination by Cuban teams featuring not only dark-skinned Cuban stars but also a stellar assortment of Negro and white North American big leaguers. The pattern was set with the very first tourney, when the Almendares club, representing the host country and managed by native son and Philadelphia Athletics catcher Fermín "Mike" Guerra, swept through its entire six games undefeated and scarcely breaking a sweat.

Starring for the locals were outfielders Al Gionfriddo (still being cheered for his 1947 World Series catch in Yankee Stadium), Monte Irvin (longtime Negro leaguer and current star of the New York Giants), and Boston Braves rookie sensation Sam Jethroe. Philadelphia Phillies second sacker Granny Hamner (soon to earn fame as one of the 1950 Phillies Whiz Kids) anchored the infield, along with Brooklyn first baseman Chuck "Rifleman" Connors (also a talented pro basketballer before baseball and then later a television actor), and sure-handed Cuban third base defender Héctor Rodríguez. Washington Senators moundsman Connie Marrero was the winning pitcher in the opening game for Almendares, and another Almendares pitcher, Eddie Wright, hurled the first shutout of inaugural Caribbean Series play.

Without question, the biggest story of the opening Caribbean Series was Cuban hurler Agapito Mayor. In his three outings, the slender right-hander proved largely unhittable as he cruised to three consecutive victories (one as a starter and two in relief). Mayor thus established a mark of three Series victories that would still stand fifty-five seasons later, despite subsequent challenges by such talented Caribbean Series pitchers as Camilo Pascual, Juan Pizarro, and Pedro Borbón (each of whom dominated later individual tournaments). Mayor himself had already established a solid Caribbean reputation by the late 1940s (he twice led the Cuban winter league in victories during that decade, in 1941–1942 and 1946–1947) but would never find his way onto a big league diamond.

Several other years from early Series play stand out for thrilling, stellar individual feats of landmark proportion. During the 1951 round-robin, Cuba's Jesús Lorenzo Cabrera would post his sensational .619 batting mark by socking thirteen base hits in his twenty-one trips to the plate. It was a sweet performance for the often overshadowed Negro first baseman for the Havana Reds. Cabrera had recently recorded three seasons of excellent batting marks (.322 in 1949, .330 in 1950, .342 in 1951) in Cuban Winter League play only to narrowly lose out for the batting title (to Alejandro Crespo, Pedro Formental, and Silvio García) all three winters.

A mere season later, in 1952, Tommy Fine would provide the only no-hitter of Caribbean Series competition.

In 1954, pitching mastery took a back seat to record-breaking long-ball slugging as North American Willard "Ese Hombre" Brown hammered a record four round-trippers while leading Santurce to the first repeat title in tournament history. And in 1955 big league star Willie Mays (fresh off a National League batting title the previous fall) would clinch yet another flag for Santurce by stroking perhaps the most dramatic home run ever blasted in championship-level Latin American competition. Mays's circuit blast (with Roberto Clemente on base) came in the bottom of the eleventh frame of a tense 2–2 tie game between Puerto Rico and Venezuela (Magallanes). The dramatic hit was ironically registered against Mays's summertime New York Giants teammate Ray Monzant and also put a resounding end to Willie's 0-for-12 slump. With Mays registering fourteen hits over his final nineteen trips to the plate (.469), the Santurce Crabbers ball club waltzed to a fourth Puerto Rican championship in the first seven years of CWS play.

But even the memorable Willie Mays homer does not enjoy quite the legendary status of Tommy Fine's unique 1952 no-hit effort. Fine would twirl his masterpiece for the title-winning Havana ball club of manager Mike González and against the Venezuelan entry, Cervecería Caracas. Another North American, knuckleballer Al Papai, would be the losing hurler, himself allowing a single run and but four hits across seven stellar innings of work. It would be future Brooklyn World Series hero Sandy Amoros who would single home

Tommy Fine with the game's only tally in the sixth inning. Fine struck out four and walked three during his masterpiece, with two additional Caracas base runners reaching on errors and with defensive gems by third baseman Vern Benson (later Atlanta Braves manager) and center fielder Pedro Formental robbing opposing hitters of two seemingly certain base hits.

Papai would enjoy only a brief and undistinguished big league career (9–14 lifetime mark) with the Cardinals, Browns, Red Sox, and White Sox. Fine was even less distinguished as a major leaguer, appearing in but 23 games over two seasons with the Red Sox and St. Louis Browns and gaining just one major league victory. On February 21, 1952, however, these two diminutive right-handers teamed up for a display of championship pitching that will long be remembered fondly by those for whom not the summer months but the winter season is the largest storehouse of hometown ballpark thrills.

Sometimes the Caribbean World Series has been seemingly owned by one man alone, and that was clearly the case during 1958 in San Juan, Puerto Rico. Hometown hero Juan Pizarro, soon to earn his full measure of big league fame with the Milwaukee Braves and Chicago White Sox, would that year put on a one-day display never seen before or since in the countless dramatic clashes of winter-ball legend. The tenth annual CWS was a tourney crammed full of outstanding individual performances: Pedro Ramos won two games on the mound for the Cuban champions (Marianao); Panama's first big leaguer, Humberto Robinson (Pizarro's teammate in Milwaukee) also won two contests and even blanked the victorious Cubans; Victor Pollet Power batted .458 for Puerto Rico; and Chicago White Sox ace Bob Shaw hurled a title-clinching shutout for the Cubans. Yet none escaped the shadow of Pizarro. A big league 131-game winner, the Puerto Rican lefty was never better than on February 8, 1958, when his dominant fastball struck out 17 batters in the Panama (Carta Vieja) lineup. Pizarro allowed but two harmless safeties (a single and double) and walked a mere three in one of the most dominant CWS pitching performances ever witnessed. An additional thirty-five CWS competitions have yet to bring a serious challenge to this 1-game strikeout record.

Two years after Pizarro, still another hurler with established big league credentials etched his name permanently into Caribbean winter-ball legend. Cuba's Camilo Pascual would win two games within a single Series play-down for the third time in 1960, thus establishing an all-time career best Series record of six victories without a single defeat. Pascual's 1956 CWS performance brought two complete games, one a shutout. The last of his six victories, in 1960, was again a shutout. Over the three tourneys, Camilo Pascual would fail to complete only one of his six outings; four times he allowed only two or fewer runs, posting an overall ERA of 1.90 (see Table on p. 520). All this came on the eve of a dramatic upswing in Pascual's big league career as well, with a franchise shift of his club from Washington to Minnesota and a sudden emergence of the Cuban as the most dominant American League right-hander of the early 1960s.

When the Series resumed after its long hiatus (1961–1969), new legends would be built during the 1970s. Suddenly, the Dominicans and Puerto Ricans were vying for total domination of a competition once seemingly owned by the powerhouse teams from pre-Castro Cuba. Nowhere was Dominican power more in evidence than in Caracas in 1977, when 14-year big league veteran Rico Carty pounded out five round-trippers to pace the Licey ball club to their third CWS title in the span of seven years. But it was not all island power across the decade. During the 1979 series, U.S. import Mitchell Page unleashed fire power of his own—he had been author of 21 rookie homers with Oakland's Athletics in 1977. Behind a ninth-inning game-winning round-tripper by Page in San Juan's Hiram Bithorn Stadium, the Venezuelan ball club (Magallanes) earned only the second title for that country in three decades of Caribbean Series play.

For a great display of home run firepower, however, no account of Caribbean Series highlights could overlook the contingent of Puerto Rican bombers in 1987, at the Héctor Espino Stadium in Hermosillo, Mexico. Team Caguas would establish a lofty standard that year by smacking 8 homers in a single contest. The round-trippers came off the bats of six different men in the power-packed Caguas lineup: Hedi Vargas (2), Carmelo Martínez (2), Germán Rivera, Candy Maldonado, Bobby Bonilla, and Henry Cotto. Though Caguas eventually emerged as Series champions, they would nonetheless lose that fan-pleasing slugfest to the Dominicans (Aguilas), falling by a memorable 14–13 count.

FAILED EXPERIMENTS AT AMERICANIZING LATIN WINTER BASEBALL

Despite so rich a past, all has not gone well for winter ball in recent times. First, there is the matter of media and fan exposure. For literate baseball fans the world over, a spate of articles and books (especially Robert Whiting's best-selling *You Gotta Have Wa*, published in 1989) have successfully spread the word far and wide about Japanese professional baseball, and recent televised tours by teams of big league all-stars to the novel Tokyo Dome and other Japanese pro ballparks have increased interest tenfold in the distant Japanese league. By contrast, Latin American professional play has remained, to date, largely relegated to the world of trivia and obscurity, buried deep in the back pages of *Baseball America* or *USA Today Baseball Weekly*—reserved for only a select (but therefore also miniscule) baseball audience.

This is true despite obvious long-standing big league ties for Winter League competition over the past 40 years and more, as well as the undeniable impact of Caribbean-born players on the major league games being played stateside. Almost any U.S. fan worth his mettle can tell you everything about the diamond talent font for shortstops that has sprung forth in tiny San Pedro de Macorís—but few can name a single Winter League ball club based in the Dominican Republic or even tell you what league champion copped last winter's Caribbean Series title.

It is not entirely surprising, then, that when Winter League play was first launched on North American soil in February 1990 the landmark event went largely unnoticed in the nation's baseball press, as well as among the nation's hard-core fandom. North American fans, faced with an impending spring training lockout and likely suspension of major league play in April, were for the first time being offered a rare glimpse at the showcase of Caribbean winter ball. A set of most discouraging economic circumstances had suddenly meant that for the first time the sponsors of Latin baseball's prime showcase would have to court U.S. television and advertising money. The Caribbean Series, hoping to overcome or evade severe economic problems at home on the island circuit, was now picking up the thirty-third renewal of its annual spectacle and transporting it whole into Miami's Orange Bowl. The pioneering one-week engagement was aimed at attracting a North American audience, one with much larger supplies of expendable income. With sparse advance publicity, however, and attended by even less apparent interest than the moribund Senior Professional Baseball League (which had played out its own final winter of discontent to empty stadiums and indifferent fans throughout the Florida State League ballparks only weeks earlier), the first-ever North American version of the Caribbean Series would quickly prove itself a mammoth public relations boondoggle and an unparalleled show business disaster.

The baseball action that unfolded before empty grandstands within the hastily revamped Orange Bowl Stadium on February 5th to 11th lived up to every on-field expectation of the devoted winter league ballpark fan. But overambitious promoters, hoping to grab North American exposure, perhaps secure a lucrative television package, and thus rescue the financially troubled Winter League circuit had suffered a rude setback at the hands of inexcusably bad planning. They had also fallen victim to the naïve notion that Hispanic-flavored Miami (and Southern Florida in general, with its huge Spanish-speaking population) would bring an automatic and inevitable rush of fans to glimpse firsthand Caribbean baseball's wintertime glory.

The Caribbean Series was admittedly embarking on treacherous new grounds with its first-ever North American visit in 1990. North American appeal for such an event was both unmeasured and untapped; in contrast, enthusiastic crowds had always filled Mexican and Dominican stadiums to overflowing. The week-long Caribbean Series was, furthermore, an established national tradition throughout the Winter League nations themselves. Yet the move seemed to have indisputable economic logic, backed by an indisputable chain of events. Major league stars on the order of Willie Mays or Roberto Clemente or Steve Garvey had long since abandoned the Caribbean ballpark circuit for the North American hot stove banquet circuit. Lofty modern player salaries ruled out the need for income-producing extra games, and guaranteed contracts preclude exhibition appearances that might result in career-threatening injury. Without celebrity big league ballplayers, attendance had dropped dramatically during the recent ten-week regular season winter league schedules. Political haggling in the Dominican Republic had even literally short-circuited electric power to ballparks in Santo Domingo and Santiago during late 1989, and hurricane damage had killed attendance that same fall in the Puerto Rican venues as well. Low ticket prices (an unavoidable economic reality in Latin countries with starvation wages) and lack of corporate sponsorship had conspired to make Caribbean Series competition itself a losing proposition in recent years, despite packed stadiums and leather-lunged crowds of fanatical patrons.

Once underway, the unprecedented yet underpublicized 1990 Miami Series provided a stirring weeklong baseball festival marked with its full share of controversy and contention. Hoping to draw large throngs from the local Hispanic (especially Cuban American) population, a hastily formed partnership between local Miami sports promoters and the Venezuelan firm ProEventos Deportivos had just as hastily selected the 55,000-seat Orange Bowl Stadium as temporary home for the first American-based Series. There had been surprisingly little uproar on the Caribbean sporting scene when it was first announced that the vaunted Series would leave its traditional home for Florida dates in 1990 and 1991. (Mexico was again penciled in for 1992, but it was hoped that a planned return to Miami in 1993 would at long last provide a permanent home for the struggling event.) Promotions mogul Juan Morales, president of Pro-Eventos Deportivos, had invested $1.5 million to acquire rights to the languishing Series and move it (lock, stock, and batting cages) from its Caribbean homeland into the lucrative stateside venue. It was assumed that four teams of (mostly) Latin ballplayers and a huge supply of seats was all that it would take to bring Caribbean baseball fervor into Miami.

From the very beginning, however, it was not at all a happy marriage of north and south. Miami's Orange Bowl had not housed baseball since 52,000 turned out to witness a 1956 Miami Marlins exhibition game featuring the legendary Negro leaguer Satchel Paige. The playing conditions seemed to prove that North American promoters (led by Senior League President Rick Horrow) did not take at all seriously the existing tradition of first-class ballpark conditions regularly found throughout island winter league play. Flustered by reported criticism of the site selection, especially by the Dominican and Venezuela team delegations, the baseball-naïve Horrow responded with *gringo* tact. Quoted in published reports by *USA Today*, Horrow snapped angrily that Caribbean ballplayers ought to be happy enough with the Orange Bowl facilities, since they all played on "rock piles" and "cow pastures" back home in Venezuela and the Dominican Republic.

Horrow's ill-conceived remarks almost sent the Dominican and Venezuelan delegations packing at the end of but two days of roughshod competition. Once the dust and controversy had settled and fastballs began to fly, however, the landmark series proved one of the most dramatic and hotly contested in years. Records fell and good baseball abounded as the Dominican team (Leones de Escogido) triumphed for the second time in three years, paced by the bats of big leaguers Junior Felix, Nelson Liriano, and Geronimo Berroa, and hot-prospect Moises Alou. Among plentiful highlights, Atlanta farmhand Barry Jones slugged his way to a record-tying 5 homers (matching Rico Carty's 1977 output) and kept an undermanned Puerto Rican team in contention until the final day of the tourney, and two marvelous pitching performances (under the adverse conditions of a bad-hop infield and the Orange Bowl's Chinese Wall) were crafted by minor league hurlers Doug Linton (Toronto Blue Jays) and Bob Patterson (Pittsburgh Pirates). Several fan-pleasing slugfests featured a cloudburst of homers and ground-rule doubles, as well as astronomical scores of 20–8 and 10–8 in the first days of play. A memorable old-timers' game featured Caribbean immortals Tony Oliva (author of a gigantic 350-foot homer in his first at-bat), Juan Marichal, José Tartabull, Camilo Pascual, and Bobby Ávila (Latin America's first big league batting champ). It was the old-timers' match-up, in fact, which best reminded Orange Bowl patrons of the unique blend of past and present that is the lifeblood of Caribbean baseball; it drew the largest paying crowd in an otherwise sparsely attended week.

Perhaps more than anything else, the inaugural Caribbean Series held on North American soil fell victim to atrociously bad timing. The 1990 spring season was hardly a lucky one for the national pastime, with a big league players union labor action looming on the horizon. Spring training would be delayed by an ownership lockout of the major league ballplayers. Caribbean Series play in Miami was itself unfortunately surrounded with every bit as much bad planning, off-field bickering and contentiousness, and generalized confusion as were the abortive 1990 Grapefruit and Cactus League seasons that followed only a month later.

Promoter Horrow's off-the-cuff comments about Caribbean playing conditions piqued the ire of all four visiting delegations and required a hasty press conference and formal public apology from Horrow to placate the proud Latin visitors. The worst thing about this inaugural Miami Series, however, had to be the playing locale itself. Miami's antiquated Orange Bowl Stadium (home to the University of Miami footballers, and earlier to the NFL Miami Dolphins) held an eerie resemblance to the legendary Los Angeles Coliseum that had greeted Walter O'Malley's renegade Dodgers in 1958. The strange configuration carved out of a football oval featured a 200-foot deep and 60-foot high wire left field fence exactly like the one that three decades earlier found Gil Hodges, Charlie Neal, and Carl Furillo (as well as every visiting right-handed slugger) salivating in Los Angeles. Miami's newfangled Orange Monster even necessitated a unique set of ground rules: balls hit over the wall were counted only as doubles, unless reaching the second tier of grandstand seats, in which case they were allowed as homers. The right field fence was itself only a declared 315 feet from home plate—yet hitters pacing off the distances to both left field and right field barriers reported finding them closer to 180 feet and 300 feet. Infield conditions were more troublesome still: a sea of dips, rocks, and soft spots. Whatever conceivable measure you chose, the hastily constructed diamond was hardly up to big league or even minor league or collegiate standards.

The questionable stadium conditions did not mar some skilled pitching performances, however. Venezuela's top U.S. import, Doug Linton of the Toronto Blue Jays, hurled a masterful five-hit shutout (featuring 11 strikeouts) at Puerto Rico's San Juan team during game eight of the tourney, and Pittsburgh Pirate lefty Bob Patterson (with relief aid from Ramón Peña) shut down Caracas 2–1 with yet another masterful piece of moundsmanship in game three. It was not quality baseball that was missing from the 1990 Orange Bowl competition but rather the anticipated throngs of enthusiastic Latino fans. High ticket prices and poor promotion of the event, as well as the reputation of a crime-ridden neighborhood surrounding the ramshackle Orange Bowl, conspired to keep crowds in the neighborhood of only 2,000 per game. To the dismay of the promoters, it was quickly discovered that Puerto Rican or Venezuelan or Dominican expatriates in South Florida might indeed show up in modest numbers to watch their own national representative in one game of an evening doubleheader but would quickly depart when their countrymen were not on the field.

The first stateside Caribbean Series departed Miami after a week of exciting if sparsely attended baseball and with many questions still hanging tenuously in the balance. What would be the venue for this proud Series when the next winter season rolled around? Would a return to Miami duplicate the 1990 failures at both the ticket gate and the drawing board? And if Miami, in what ballpark? Could Harrow and ProEventos Deportivos, the current promoters, be foolish enough to again risk injury to budding major league prospects and unleash the anger of traditional fans by staging their event in the makeshift, creaky, and misshapen Orange Bowl? Might Bobby Maduro Stadium, longtime spring training home to the Baltimore Orioles, provide a more attractive setting, despite its similar location in a reputedly unsafe low-income Hispanic neighborhood?

And what about the sagging status of the economically depressed Winter Leagues themselves? Rob Ruck has succinctly captured the issues surrounding a depressed winter league scene in an excellent assessment of Caribbean baseball economics (printed in the February 25, 1990, issue of *Baseball America*). Can Winter League seasonal play survive the economic disasters brought by such taxing local conditions as Hurricane Hugo (which flooded Puerto Rican ballparks and severely damaged Dominican electrical hookups in 1989) and the continued absence of yesteryear's superstar big league players (now too wealthy to covet off-season employment) who in past campaigns filled the local stadiums with enthusiastic *fanáticos* panting to see the legendary North American ballplayers? Given the current economics of big league baseball, Ruck sees bleak prospects for any strong revival of a healthy and star-filled Dominican or Venezuelan or Puerto Rico winter league. Major League Baseball's own sponsored Arizona Fall League player development circuit (implemented in 1992) seems a further threat to a long-standing Caribbean baseball tradition.

Fortunately for the Series and its backers, the worst fears generated by the disappointing 1990 CWS were never realized during the second season of stateside play. Luckily, the Orange Bowl had indeed been abandoned and, although attendance was still sparse in 1991, at least the venue of Bobby Maduro Stadium provided the familiar spectacle of real baseball. New corporate sponsorship also meant a healthier financial result, even if the short-sighted corporate decision to rename the tournament "Winterball I" could not have sat well with tradition-minded fans throughout any of the Caribbean winter league countries. Bobby Maduro had been spiced up for the 1991 renewal of CWS play with a display of outfield billboard ads (Coors Light Beer, Diet Pepsi, American Airlines, and several Hispanic magazines) and the stadium infield conditions, outfield dimensions, sound system, and electronic scoreboard all now reflected major league playing conditions. Perhaps the biggest blow to traditionalists, however, was not a new corporate name for the event but rather a novel playoff structure for this thirty-third Series. A 6-game round-robin was now in effect, designed to eliminate two countries, followed by a best-of-three matchup among the two survivors. Little embarrassment resulted from the revised format, fortunately, as for the second straight year in Miami the Dominican entrant proved clearly dominant over the field. This time it was Licey that captured all three of its first-round games and then slaughtered Venezuela 13–4 and 13–1 in the two championship-round contests.

If the 1991 Miami tournament was clearly better than the first attempt, buoyed by a new stadium venue and a new sense of pride and organization, the real Caribbean World Series revival came only when play returned to its rightful home on Latin soil in 1992. Fans once again flocked to Héctor Espino Stadium in Hermosillo, Mexico, this time to the tune of 15,000 and more per contest. (This better than threefold attendance upswing from the Miami years suggests that low ticket prices and baseball-hungry Caribbean fans are the true touchstone of ongoing CWS success.) The Mexican throngs who turned out at Hermosillo were fittingly rewarded with one of the best Series ever contested. The double round-robin format now in effect left two clubs—Mayagüez of Puerto Rico and Zulia of Venezuela—with identical 4–2 records. The final contest of the final night was played for all the marbles—something rare in CWS history—and saw Mayagüez crush Zulia 8–0 behind the three-hit shutout pitching of Roberto Hernández and two relievers and the home run slugging of Cleveland Indians star Carlos Baerga. A special footnote to the 1992 play-down was the dramatic story of catcher Chad Kreuter, who had entered winter league play without a 1992 big league contract but subsequently earned a Detroit Tigers roster spot on the basis of his outstanding Puerto Rican League and Caribbean World Series MVP performances.

In all, however, a bleak future seems still to hang over the horizon of Caribbean winter championship playoffs. The future is uncertain regarding both the economically unstable Caribbean winter leagues themselves and the constantly evolving tournament that still follows them. With an Arizona Fall League now in place and even televised on cable networks, even more talent is now siphoned off from the player-thin Caribbean winter circuits—and without top-flight ballplayers, Caribbean fans simply won't come to the now less popular Winter League games. Latin crowds, after all, have been spoiled by a half-century of baseball at the highest professional levels possible. Their own parks seem to offer only double-A prospects, while at the same time television now brings the real big league games from Chicago and New York and Los Angeles straight into their own homes. These most fanatical of America's ballpark fans are used to cheering for stars, after all, and not merely unheralded prospects.

However, these mounting problems are addressed, colorful and frenetic Winter League baseball will likely continue producing its excitement for at least several more seasons during the otherwise dormant hot stove months of December and January. For at least a few more February seasons, a handful of true *fanáticos* will count themselves among the privileged (alongside an army of professional scouts and journalists) and will again cast their joyous glances southward to witness professional baseball's least-known celebration of the impending rites of spring.

CARIBBEAN SERIES ACTION IN THE NEW MILLENNIUM

Throughout the 1990s, the biggest stories involving Caribbean World Series action were the continued domination by Dominican teams (usually Aguilas; occasionally Licey), the surprise showing of two separate underdog Mexican entries, and the widely different results that greeted bold experiments by both Puerto Rico and the Dominicans to field high-profile Dream Team rosters laced with renowned big league stars. Better timing their efforts, the Puerto Ricans succeeded spectacularly in this move toward regenerating both fan interest and gate receipts, but the copycat Dominicans misfired and failed badly. The usually timid Mexicans somehow managed to breathe some life into the faltering tournament on two separate occasions, but their overall poor performances year after year also revealed the growing imbalance within the four historic Caribbean winter circuits.

Mexico's first surprising victory came in 1996 on unfriendly Dominican soil and stole the thunder of the Dominicans' half-hearted efforts to duplicate Puerto Rico's previous-year ploy of instilling interest back into the tournament with big-name gate attractions and a home club loaded up with superstars and the promise of runaway victories. The upset championship earned instead by Mexico's Culiacán club, managed by Paquín Estrada (catcher on Mexico's last winner, in 1986), not only turned heads but also continued a rather bizarre pattern of producing once-a-decade uprisings exactly ten years apart: 1976 Hermosillo, 1986 Mexicali, and 1996 Culiacán. The high-profile Dominican squad pasted together under frustrated manager Terry Francona was totally without chemistry—but it didn't lack for celebrities: Pedro Martínez, José Mesa, Mel Rojas, Julio Franco, Raúl Mondesi, Juan Guzmán. It seemed a minor miracle that such a lineup could limp off with only a pair of game victories. The Mexicans were obviously simply much hungrier, and they played far over their heads for the overjoyed Estrada. To add to the total unpredictability of it all, their leading star was an American mystery man, one of the most surprising luminaries of recent CWS history. Mexican Pacific League veteran David Brinkley had served in pro leagues in Holland, Italy, and Canada but never back home in the United States. Once unleashed on the CWS, Brinkley sprayed hits at a .350 clip and walked off with the year's MVP honors. Estrada in the end had the most poetic if not most analytical explanation. "The ugly ducklings are the belle of the ball," he crowed; Estrada was also quick to observe that the Mexican entry—whoever it might be—would be a good bet once the odd cycle rolled around again in 2006.

Puerto Rico's own Dream Team a year earlier had been a much more rousing success—at the gate and certainly on the field of play. There was no slacking off for the celebrity lineup of Roberto Alomar, Juan González, Carlos Baerga, Edgar Martínez, Rubén Sierra, Ricky Bones, Rey Sánchez, Bernie Williams and company. The virtual all-star team in Santurce Crabbers uniform ran up relatively easy victories, six in a row. If there was any surprise, it was that some of the top performances for the winners were turned in not by million-dollar megastars on paid holiday but instead by some of Puerto Rico's lesser lights—lower-profile big league veterans struggling to earn next year's job. Doug Brocail and Eric Gunderson from the United States and island native José Alberro rang up the lowest ERAs for the mound corps. But the big names did produce most of the heavy artillery. Alomar was series MVP and batting champ; Williams and González were among the top five batsmen; and Williams poked 3 homers out of the leadoff slot. The rationale for such a team was abundantly clear. The Puerto Rican winter baseball enterprise had long needed some type of kick-start, and it all had worked precisely as planned. The big on-field success was making the locals a huge box office sensation. An overflow throng of 22,000 attended the deciding match with the Dominicans, and television coverage electrified the entire island. The situation had also been just right for enticing top native stars into uniform, because the ongoing big league players strike had left most ballplayers primed for action simply to stay in shape. The 1995 Caribbean series was one of the most successful since the 1950s. It also quickly proved to be a hard act to follow.

The Mexicans' second surprise outing didn't have to wait a decade but came instead in Venezuela in 2002; once again it featured Culiacán's Tomateros directed by the unflappable Francisco Estrada. This time, there was another underappreciated journeyman in the Mexican lineup who, like Brinkley several years earlier, set out to make the tournament his personal stage for hawking his wares to big league bird dogs. Mazatlán-native Adán Amezcua, a castoff catcher from the Baltimore organization, found new life in the 2002 Mexican Pacific League season and then put on one of the best CWS performances of the entire decade. Already a Culiacán hero after his playoff-winning homer ended the League season, Amezcua pushed home eight RBI in Culiacán's fast 3-game start out of the gate and maintained his momentum with a .455 batting average that was second in the tournament. Three homers and nine total RBI clinched the MVP trophy. The Mexican squads of 1996 and 2002 had demonstrated the exciting element of unpredictability that might still fan the fires of winter league baseball—but these exceptions seemed only to highlight the overall weakness of Mexican Pacific League baseball. In 1998, 1999, and 2000 the Mexican contingents (Mazatlán, Mexicali, and Navojoa) looked far more like their familiar inept selves, all finishing dead last.

In the most recent CWS reunion (February 2003 in Carolina, Puerto Rico), the constantly revamping Dominicans—Aguilas again—finally caught up with the Puerto Ricans in the number of total tournaments won down through the years. Dominican forces had been slowly gaining ground for the past ten years. Six of the last dozen crowns have been Dominican; four belonged to Puerto Rico, and Mexico owns the remaining two. The apex for the Dominican teams came with the final three seasons of the 1990s. Aguila was the main force, with back-to-back first-place finishes in Hermosillo (1997) and Puerto la Cruz (1998); however, the perennial powerhouse Licey franchise also made their contribution in the last season of the old millennium (San Juan, 1999). Licey is in fact still the winningest individual team in CWS history, having captured three crowns in the 1970s, two more in the 1980s, and three in the 1990s.

Venezuela was the odd league out throughout the 1990s, just as they have been for most of three decades. Venezuelan teams haven't captured a single CWS banner in nearly fifteen years now. To find a victorious team from the nation of coastal oil fields one has to reach back to 1989, in Mazatlán, and the upset triumph of a Zulia team that had finished only second in its own league but rode the hefty power hitting of Chicago Cubs property Phil Stephenson (a near triple-crown winner in Venezuela that year). Most of the time, recent Venezuelan entries haven't even been very close—last or tied for last in 1999, 2000, and 2002. This low level of performance is surprising, against the backdrop of fresh talent constantly streaming from the country. Of late, matters outside of baseball have made things even worse. Political unrest was so bad in 2003 that Venezuela had to shut down its league in midseason and miss out on the annual CWS event altogether.

For now, the Caribbean Series rolls on as it has for forty-odd years. Winter League baseball has been seriously threatened for more than a decade by a number of factors—mostly economic and mostly flowing from the drastically altered salary structures of U.S. organized baseball. At times it seems that major league baseball is as bent on shutting down Caribbean-based winter operations as it is in sabotaging historically independent amateur world tournament play. Natural disasters (in the form of severe tropical storms and floods in the Dominican and Puerto Rico) and seething political turmoil (in Venezuela) have also had substantial negative impact on struggling pro franchises in San Juan, San Pedro, Santo Domingo, Caracas, and surrounding ports of call. But traditions of winter baseball on the professional level are not yet dead, nor even quite on life support. In fact, the Caribbean World Series continues to be one of baseball's best-kept secrets for true *fanáticos* looking to get back to the very roots of a shared Pan-American national pastime.

CAPSULE HISTORY OF THE CARIBBEAN WORLD SERIES

1949, Havana (Cuba)—Series I

February 20–25, 1949

Champion: Almendares Alacranes (Cuba), managed by Fermín Guerra.

Highlights: Cuban ace Agapito Mayor provides a stellar performance and leads his Almendares club to victory in the first Caribbean Series, also becoming the only pitcher to win three games in a single tourney. Two victories come in short relief stints and the third in an 11–4 romp over Puerto Rico, in which the Cuban starter hurls seven successful frames.

Outstanding Players: Brooklyn's 1947 World Series hero Al Gionfriddo paces all batters with his .533 average (8 for 15), but Negro leaguer and Winter League legend Wilmer Fields (Puerto Rico) turns in an even more outstanding all-around performance, finishing third in hitting (.450), first in runs scored (8), third in hits (9), second in both doubles and homers, and third in RBI (6), while also pitching one game.

Team Standings (Managers): Almendares (Cuba, Fermín Guerra) 6–0; Cervecería Caracas (Venezuela, José Casanova) 3–3; Spur Cola (Panama, Leon Treadway) 2–4; Mayagüez (Puerto Rico, Artie Wilson) 1–5.

1950, San Juan (Puerto Rico)—Series II

February 21–26, 1950

Champion: Carta Vieja (Panama), managed by Wayne Blackburn.

Highlights: Panama's Carta Vieja club wins that country's only CWS title and the only championship triumph of the Primera Etapa not registered by either Cuba or Puerto Rico. Fine relief work by Negro leaguer Chet Brewer leads Carta Vieja to a title-clinching 9–3 over Puerto Rico, with the Panamanians pounding two top Caguas pitchers (Dan Bankhead and Rubén Gómez) in the process.

Outstanding Players: Dan Bankhead (first big league black pitcher) and Washington Senators' Cuban ace Conrado Marrero (Almendares) hook up in an outstanding duel, finally won by Bankhead 1–0 on a five-hitter. Dan Bankhead (Brooklyn) thus authors the second Series shutout, the first having come a year earlier in form of an eight-hitter thrown by Eddie Wright of Cuba versus Panama.

Team Standings (Managers): Carta Vieja (Panama, Wayne Blackburn) 5–2; Caguas (Puerto Rico, Luis Rodríguez Olmo) 4–3; Almendares (Cuba, Fermín Guerra) 3–3; Magallanes (Venezuela, Vidal López) 1–5.

1951, Caracas (Venezuela)—Series III

February 22–25, 1951

Champion: Santurce Cangrejeros (Puerto Rico), managed by George Scales.

Highlights: Puerto Rico registers its first championship victory, setting the tone early with an opening 13–1 spanking of Cuba. Luis Olmo slugs 2 homers for the Puerto Rican team and José "Pantalones" Santiago proves to be the staff ace by winning two games on the hill. Cuba, behind the stellar pitching of Hoyt Wilhelm, hands Santurce its only defeat by a count of 2–1.

Outstanding Player: Stellar Cuban first baseman Jesús Lorenzo "Chiquitín" Cabrera of the Havana Reds establishes a long-lasting (and perhaps unchallengeable) hitting mark by batting a stratospheric .619 on 13 safeties in 21 official at-bats.

Team Standings (Managers): Santurce (Puerto Rico, George Scales) 5–1; Havana (Cuba, Mike González) 4–2; Magallanes (Venezuela, Lázaro Salazar) 2–4; Spur Cola (Panama, Leon Kellman) 1–5.

1952, Panama City (Panama)—Series IV

February 20–26, 1952

Champion: Habana Leones (Cuba), managed by Mike González.

Highlights: Cuba becomes the first repeat champion, under the direction of Latin America's first-ever big league manager, Mike González. A tie with Puerto Rico, however, prevents González's team from becoming the second club to record an unblemished tournament record. Future major league World Series hero Edmundo "Sandy" Amoros (Brooklyn) is the year's batting star (.450 BA) for the Cubans.

Outstanding Player: Texas-born hurler Tommy Fine (a lifetime 1–3 major leaguer) pitches for Havana and hurls the first and only no-hit, no-run game in Series history, a 1–0 blanking of Cervecería Caracas. The veteran right-hander walks three and strikes out four along the way to his rare and unexpected once-in-a-lifetime masterpiece.

Team Standings (Managers): Havana (Cuba, Mike González) 5–0–1; Cervecería Caracas (Venezuela, José Casanova) 3–3; Carta Vieja (Panama, Al Leap) 3–3; San Juan (Puerto Rico, Freddie Thon) 0–5–1.

1953, Havana (Cuba)—Series V

February 20–25, 1953

Champion: Santurce Cangrejeros (Puerto Rico), managed by Buster Clarkson.

Highlights: The Santurce Crabbers become the second club to repeat as champions, thus also allowing Puerto Rico to become the second country to garner multiple team

Jim Gilliam with champion Santurce Crabbers at the 1953 Caribbean World Series, Havana. [Author's Cuban Collection]

Cuba's Pedro Formental (right) poses in Havana's Cerro Stadium with Camilo Pascual. Formental batted .560 in the 1953 Caribbean World Series, a mark surpassed only twice in thirty years. [Transcendental Graphics]

titles. Santurce is also only the second team to post an unblemished 6-game record. Bobo Holloman (on the eve of his one major league season with the St. Louis Browns) wins two games on the hill for the talented Santurce team managed by James "Buster" Clarkson.

Outstanding Players: Willard "Ese Hombre" Brown establishes a record with 4 homers. Cuban center fielder Pedro Formental bats .560, a level surpassed only twice in thirty-plus years (by Jesús Lorenzo Cabrera in 1951 and Manny Mota in 1971).

Team Standings (Managers): Santurce (Puerto Rico, Buster Clarkson) 6–0; Havana (Cuba, Mike González) 3–3; Chesterfield (Panama, Graham Stanford) 2–4; Caracas (Venezuela, Martín Dihigo) 1–5.

1954, San Juan (Puerto Rico)—Series VI

February 18–23, 1954

Champion: Caguas Criollos (Puerto Rico), managed by Mickey Owen.

Highlights: Puerto Rico becomes the first three-time champion as Caguas repeats Santurce's two earlier triumphs. Mickey Owen, a goat of the 1941 World Series in Brooklyn but an astute baseball man nonetheless, is the successful Puerto Rican skipper. "Jungle Jim" Rivera of the Chicago White Sox (.450 BA) paces the Puerto Ricans at the plate.

Outstanding Players: Ray Orteig (Cuba) becomes only the third player to slug 2 homers in a single game, accomplishing the feat (which also gave him the home run title) against Panama. Russian-born pitcher Victor Strizka (raised in Panama) leads the pitchers with a perfect 2–0 mark.

Team Standings (Managers): Caguas (Puerto Rico, Mickey Owen) 4–2; Almendares (Cuba, Bob Bragan) 3–3; Carta Vieja (Panama, Joseph Tuminelli) 3–3; Pastora (Venezuela, Napoleón Reyes) 2–4.

1955, Caracas (Venezuela)—Series VII

February 10–15, 1955

Champion: Santurce Cangrejeros (Puerto Rico), managed by Herman Franks.

Highlights: Willie Mays, fresh off his 1954 National League batting title and memorable World Series catch against Vic Wertz, strokes an eleventh-inning home run off Giants teammate Ramón Monzant (pitching for Magallanes of Venezuela). Mays's smash, with Roberto Clemente on base, earns an important 4–2 victory for Santurce (Puerto Rico), the eventual 1955 champion. Mays's gigantic home run also breaks up a nagging 0-for-12 slump for the future Hall of Famer and remains one of the most dramatic clouts of Caribbean series history. Puerto Rico reigns as champion for the third straight year.

Outstanding Players: Never known as a power hitter, diminutive shortstop and future big league manager Don Zimmer (Brooklyn) becomes the third player in Series history to smack three round-trippers in a single tournament. More muscular slugger Rocky Nelson (also Brooklyn) takes the batting title with a .471 average.

Team Standings (Managers): Santurce (Puerto Rico, Herman Franks) 5–1; Magallanes (Venezuela, Lázaro Salazar) 4–2; Almendares (Cuba, Bob Bragan) 2–4; Carta Vieja (Panama, Al Kubski) 1–5.

1956, Panama City (Panama)—Series VIII

February 10–15, 1956

Champion: Cienfuegos Elefantes (Cuba), managed by Oscar Rodríguez.

Highlights: Cuba claims its third title and thus launches a string of victories that will stretch out over five winters and reach throughout the remainder of Phase One tournament play. Cienfuegos will eventually capture two of those five titles, as will Marianao. Dick Farrell of Venezuela (Philadelphia Phillies) narrowly misses repeating Tommy Fine's no-hit masterpiece of 1952 but loses both his no-hitter and his shutout on Ramón Maldonado's late-inning round-tripper for Puerto Rico.

Outstanding Players: Camilo Pascual records the first of what will over the next five years become three 2–0 marks. Pascual (Cuba), in his first CWS appearance, establishes himself as the most effective pitcher (at least in terms of wins and losses) in Series history. Catcher Rafael "Ray" Noble (Cuba and New York Giants) becomes the fourth batsman to hit .500 (10 for 20) for the week-long tournament.

Team Standings (Managers): Cienfuegos (Cuba, Oscar Rodríguez) 5–1; Chesterfield (Panama, Graham Stanford) 3–3; Caguas (Puerto Rico, Ben Geraghty) 3–3; Valencia (Venezuela, Regino Otero) 1–5.

1957, Havana (Cuba)—Series IX

February 9–14, 1957

Champion: Marianao Tigres (Cuba), managed by Napoleón Reyes.

Highlights: Marianao captures its first of two straight titles under manager Napoleón Reyes. While native Cuban Minnie Miñoso is a prominent batting star for the victorious Marianao club, big league import Jim Bunning (Detroit Tigers) is the mound standout with a 2–0 record. Cuba's only loss comes in a 6–0 whitewashing at the hands of Puerto Rico and former Cleveland Indians hurler José "Pantalones" Santiago.

Outstanding Players: Big league outfielder Sammy Drake (Chicago Cubs) hits .500 (10 for 20) for Cuba, the fifth player to reach the magic .500 level. José Santiago (Mayagüez over Marianao), George Brunet (Balboa over Mayagüez), and Winston Brown (Balboa over Caracas) all throw complete-game shutouts.

Team Standings (Managers): Marianao (Cuba, Napoleón Reyes) 5–1; Club Balboa (Panama, Leon Kellman) 3–3; Mayagüez (Puerto Rico, Mickey Owen) 2–4; Caracas (Venezuela, Bryant Clay) 2–4.

1958, San Juan (Puerto Rico)—Series X

February 8–13, 1958

Champion: Marianao Tigres (Cuba), managed by Napoleón Reyes.

Highlights: Marianao completes its two-year domination under manager Napoleón Reyes,

Cuban League MVP Minnie Miñoso, Marianao hero during the third Havana Caribbean World Series, 1957. [Author's Cuban Collection]

Nap Reyes managed back-to-back Caribbean World Series champions for Marianao in 1957 and 1958. [Author's Cuban Collection]

this time barely edging out both Panama and Puerto Rico by a single game. Marianao clinches the title with a clutch 2–0 three-hit shutout of Puerto Rico, thrown by right-hander Bob Shaw of the Chicago White Sox.

Outstanding Player: Striking out at least one batter in every inning, lefty big league star Juan Pizarro (Puerto Rico) fans an incredible 17 hitters against the Carta Vieja club of Panama City, a record which still stands today. Pizarro allows but two scratch hits and walks only three batters in an 8–0 Puerto Rican victory.

Team Standings (Managers): Marianao (Cuba, Napoleón Reyes) 4–2; Carta Vieja (Panama, Wilmer Shantz) 3–3; Caguas (Puerto Rico, Ted Norbert) 3–3; Valencia (Venezuela, Regino Otero) 2–4.

1959, Caracas (Venezuela)—Series XI

February 10–15, 1959

Champion: Almendares Alacranes (Cuba), managed by Clemente Carreras.

Highlights: Cuba threatens to turn the annual Series into a full-blown sham with a fourth straight triumph. This year at least the team is new, however, as Almendares returns to the scene under rookie skipper Clemente Carreras. Cuba is the obvious best team, but Venezuela dominates the individual statistics, at least those for hitting. Jesús Mora of Oriente wins the batting title (.417) and Oriente's Norm Cash (Chicago White Sox and later Detroit Tigers) blasts out the most homers (2) and knocks in the most runs (8).

Outstanding Players: Camilo Pascual (Cuba) wins two games without a defeat for the second time. Orlando Peña also provides marvelous hurling for Cuba's Almendares, hooking up in two great mound duels against the Puerto Rican ball club. Peña is defeated by National League rival Rubén Gómez in a first contest but blanks Santurce 1–0 in a rematch meeting.

Team Standings (Managers): Almendares (Cuba, Clemente Carreras) 5–1; Oriente (Venezuela, Kerby Farrell) 4–2; Santurce (Puerto Rico, Moses Concepción) 3–3; Cocle (Panama, Lester Peden) 0–6.

1960, Panama City (Panama)—Series XII

February 10–15, 1960

Champion: Cienfuegos Elefantes (Cuba), managed by Antonio Castaños.

Highlights: Cuba makes it five in a row, this time leaving no suspense from the outset by sweeping all six of its contests. Stan Palys (Panama) sets an RBI record of 12, which stands for 33 years. Two other prominent major leaguers also enjoy a fine tournament as Tommy Davis (Dodgers) wins the batting title for Puerto Rico and infielder Héctor López (Yankees) slams 3 home runs for his native Panama.

Outstanding Player: Veteran major leaguer Camilo Pascual (Cuba) wins two games in a single Series for a record third time, establishing an all-time best career Series record of six victories without a single defeat.

Team Standings (Managers): Cienfuegos (Cuba, Antonio Castaños) 6–0; Marlboro (Panama, Wilmer Shantz) 3–3; Caguas (Puerto Rico, Vic Pollet Power) 2–4; Rapiños (Venezuela, Les Moss) 1–5.

1970, Caracas (Venezuela)—Series XIII

February 5–10, 1970

Champion: Magallanes Navegantes (Venezuela), managed by Carlos Pascual.

Highlights: The only country not to win a title in the CWS First Phase play, Venezuela celebrates the tournament's revival with its own initial championship banner. Ponce (Puerto Rico) and Licey (Dominican Republic) are the only invited opposition, yet it is a handful of Cuban expatriates who remind all in attendance of previous Cuban domination in CWS contests. In a crucial early game, Cuban hurler Orlando Peña (Venezuela) outduels fellow-Cuban Mike Cuéllar (Puerto Rico) by a 3–1 count. Peña and still another Cuban moundsman, Aurelio Monteagudo, each hurl two victories for title-bound Magallanes.

Outstanding Players: Catcher Ray Fosse, outfielders César Tóvar and Gonzalo Márquez (the batting champ at .478), and pitchers Larry Jaster (1–0) and Jay Ritchie (1–0) all contribute heavily to a first-ever Venezuelan team title.

Team Standings (Managers): Magallanes (Venezuela, Carlos Pascual) 7–1; Ponce (Puerto Rico, Jim Fregosi) 4–4; Licey (Dominican Republic, Manny Mota) 1–7. No Mexican entry.

Big leaguer Román Mejías played on the final Cuban Caribbean World Series champion Cienfuegos team in 1960. [Author's Cuban Collection]

1971, San Juan (Puerto Rico)—Series XIV

February 6–11, 1971

Champion: Licey Tigres (Dominican Republic), managed by Manny Mota.

Camilo Pascual, Pete Ramos, and Raúl Sánchez: Cienfuegos aces during the 1960 Caribbean World Series. [Author's Cuban Collection]

Highlights: A powerful Dominican team becomes the fourth undefeated and untied squad and the first in Second Phase play. All three opponents finish with identical marks of 2–4, never challenging Manny Mota's juggernaut. Chris Zachary wins two games on the hill for Licey, retiring eleven straight batters at one point during his first outing.

Outstanding Players: Manny Mota not only manages Licey to an undefeated sweep of tourney play but himself leads all hitters with a stratospheric .579 average (11 for 19), the second highest batting average of Series history. Manny Mota's amazing hitting even overshadows the power display of Mexico's Celerino Sánchez, who paces the tournament in both homers (3) and RBI (9).

Team Standings (Managers): Licey (Dominican Republic, Manny Mota) 6–0; Hermosillo (Mexico, Maurice "Maury" Wills) 2–4; Santurce (Puerto Rico, Frank Robinson) 2–4; La Guaira (Venezuela, Graciano Ravelo) 2–4.

1972, Santo Domingo (Dominican Republic)—Series XV

February 1–6, 1972

Champion: Ponce Leones (Puerto Rico), managed by Frank Verdi.

Highlights: Venezuelan champion Aragua features a double-play combination of future Hall of Famers (with playing manager Rod Carew at second base and Davy Concepción at shortstop), but it is not nearly enough to prevent Puerto Rico from running away from the pack with five straight opening victories. This is the first CWS tournament hosted by the Dominican Republic, and enthusiastic Dominican *fanáticos* cheer their own Cibao team on toward a respectable second-place finish.

Outstanding Players: Big leaguers Sandy Alomar, Don Baylor, Pat Corrales, Bernie Carbo, and Carlos May provide the heavy hitting for Ponce, while the Puerto Rican team also features a rare trio of native-son brothers, major league reserve outfielders José, Tommy, and Héctor Cruz.

Team Standings (Managers): Ponce (Puerto Rico, Frank Verdi) 5–1; Cibao (Dominican Republic, Osvaldo "Ozzie" Virgil) 3–3; Aragua (Venezuela, Rod Carew) 3–3; Guasave (Mexico, Vinicio García) 1–5.

1973, Caracas (Venezuela)—Series XVI

February 1–6, 1973

Champion: Licey Tigres (Dominican Republic), managed by Tommy Lasorda.

Highlights: Future longtime Los Angeles Dodgers manager Tommy Lasorda provides leadership in Licey's runaway championship campaign. Caracas gets two shutouts from its pitchers (Milt Wilcox and Diego Seguí) in its first three games but then falters and drops three straight. Lasorda's team already sports a Dodgers flavor with Steve Garvey at first base and Manny Mota at third, and also features Bobby Valentine (ex-Dodger) at shortstop and Jesús Alou (Houston Astros) in the outfield.

Outstanding Players: Pedro Borbón wins two starts for Licey, the second and third victories of his eventual 5–0 lifetime win–loss mark. Jesús Alou also joins the select circle of six (at that time) batsman hitting .500 or better for a single CWS.

Team Standings (Managers): Licey (Dominican Republic, Tommy Lasorda) 5–1; Caracas (Venezuela, Osvaldo "Ozzie" Virgil) 3–3; Santurce (Puerto Rico, Frank Robinson) 3–3; Obregón (Mexico, Dave García) 1–5.

1974, Hermosillo (Mexico)—Series XVII

February 1–6, 1974

Champion: Caguas Criollos (Puerto Rico), managed by Bobby Wine.

Highlights: Puerto Rico proves a penchant for winning on new grounds by copping the first tournament ever held in Mexico (the Puerto Ricans having also won the inaugural CWS on Dominican soil two seasons earlier). A players strike keeps the Venezuelan entry at home and host Mexico therefore provides two entrants—Obregón (1973 Mexican League winner) and Mazatlán (1974 Mexican champion).

Outstanding Players: Two likely Cooperstown Hall of Famers pace Caguas to the title— Mike Schmidt at third base and Gary Carter catching. Mexican legend Héctor Espino (Obregón) wins the batting title (.429), however, in his first hometown performance during CWS play.

Team Standings (Managers): Caguas (Puerto Rico, Bobby Wine) 4–2; Licey (Dominican Republic, Tommy Lasorda) 3–3; Obregón (Mexico, Mike Alejandro) 3–3; Mazatlán (Mexico, Ramon Camacho) 2–4. Two Mexican teams and no Venezuelan entry.

1975, San Juan (Puerto Rico)—Series XVIII

February 1–6, 1975

Champion: Bayamón Vaqueros (Puerto Rico), managed by José Pagán.

Highlights: Puerto Rico (this time the Bayamón team) garners the first back-to-back championships of Phase Two as play returns to San Juan for the first time since 1971 and for the fifth time overall. Ken Griffey paces the batters, and first baseman Willie Montañez provides much of the Puerto Rican firepower by blasting home 10 crucial runs, 2 short of the CWS RBI record (12 in 1960) by Stan Palys.

Outstanding Players: Ken Griffey becomes the eighth player to bat .500 (12 for 24) or better during CWS play (six more would reach the threshold by 2003). Héctor Espino (Mexico) slugs 2 of his eventual 6 CWS homers, both in a single contest versus Aragua of Venezuela.

Team Standings (Managers): Bayamón (Puerto Rico, José Pagán) 5–1; Hermosillo (Mexico, Benjamin Reyes) 3–3; Cibao (Dominican Republic, Al Widmar) 3–3; Aragua (Venezuela, Ozzie Virgil) 1–5.

1976, Santo Domingo (Dominican Republic)—Series XIX

February 4–9, 1976

Champion: Hermosillo Naranjeros (Mexico), managed by Benjamin Reyes.

Highlights: Hermosillo drops its opener to a Cibao team playing in its own ballpark, then rallies for five straight victories and the first-ever Mexican team title. Veteran hurler George Brunet tosses the clinching victory for the Mexicans while slugging star Héctor Espino provides the batting power with his fourth lifetime CWS homer and a year's-best 7 RBI.

Outstanding Player: Juan Pizarro (Puerto Rico) hurls his second CWS shutout (his first was recorded in 1958) and thus becomes only the second hurler (Camilo Pascual was first) to author two shutouts in lifetime Series play.

Team Standings (Managers): Hermosillo (Mexico, Benjamin Reyes) 5–1; Aragua (Venezuela, Osvaldo "Ozzie" Virgil) 3–3; Bayamón (Puerto Rico, José Pagán) 2–4; Cibao (Dominican Republic, Tim Murtaugh) 2–4.

1977, Caracas (Venezuela)—Series XX

February 4–9, 1977

Champion: Licey Tigres (Dominican Republic), managed by Bob Rodgers.

Highlights: Licey sweeps all six games and posts a 45–7 scoring margin over its opponents in the most one-sided tourney yet. Licey thus becomes the second undefeated team in Phase Two and the fifth in CWS history. Pedro Borbón (Cincinnati Reds) posts a shutout for the champions and thus increases his overall Series record to 5–0, second only to Camilo Pascual's 6–0 as the best lifetime pitching mark.

Outstanding Player: Rico Carty (Licey) pounds out five round-trippers to lead his Dominican countrymen to their third title in seven years, thus also establishing the new milepost for home runs in a single CWS tournament. Carty also knocks in ten runs and posts a batting average of .476 and a slugging mark of 1.333, perhaps the greatest all-around batting performance of any single Winter League finale.

Team Standings (Managers): Licey (Dominican Republic, Bob Rodgers) 6–0; Magallanes (Venezuela, Don Leppert) 3–3; Mazatlán (Mexico, Alfredo Ortiz) 2–4; Caguas (Puerto Rico, Doc Edwards) 1–5.

1978, Mazatlán (Mexico)—Series XXI

February 4–9, 1978

Champion: Mayagüez Indios (Puerto Rico), managed by Rene Lachemann.

Highlights: Mexico returns to the role of host and Puerto Rico returns to the role of champion (having also won in Mexico in 1974). Mayagüez opens with five quick victories and is never headed, although both Cibao and Caracas manage three wins apiece. Puerto Rico's José Morales is the batting champion (.421) while Venezuela's Leon Roberts (Seattle Mariners) leads in HRs (2) and paces the tourney in RBI (6).

Outstanding Player: Nicaraguan hurler Tony Chávez (Caracas) strikes out six straight batters to establish a new CWS record. In still another remarkable mound performance, 42-year-old former big leaguer George Brunet returns to CWS play and loses twice for Culiacán. Brunet, who pitched for Panama in the 1950s, thus finishes his lengthy career with a 3–4 CWS record.

Team Standings (Managers): Mayagüez (Puerto Rico, Rene Lachemann) 5–1; Cibao (Dominican Republic, Johnny Lipon) 3–3; Caracas (Venezuela, Felipe Alou) 3–3; Culiacán (Mexico, Raúl Cano) 1–5.

1979, San Juan (Puerto Rico)—Series XXII

February 4–9, 1979

Champion: Magallanes Navegantes (Venezuela), managed by Willie Horton.

Highlights: Big league outfielder Mitchell Page (Oakland Athletics) smashes a hefty 450-foot home run in the penultimate Series game to clinch the team championship for Magallanes, only the second championship title earned by a Venezuelan ball club in three decades of Caribbean Series play. The Magallanes triumph ends a nine-year drought for Venezuela, and thus the Magallanes ball club gains bookend CWS titles for the 1970s.

Outstanding Player: Magallanes is sparked by several outstanding individual performances. Mike Norris hurls a one-hitter (11–0) against Caguas; outfielder Jerry White paces all hitters at .522, and first baseman Mitchell Page hits .417 and leads with 2 homers. Mexican shortstop Mario Mendoza bats a lofty .286 in his fifth and final CWS yet still finishes with a career CWS average of .159, far south of his own famous Mendoza-line standard (.200 BA) for offensive futility.

Team Standings (Managers): Magallanes (Venezuela, Willie Horton) 5–1; Cibao (Dominican Republic, Johnny Lipon) 4–2; Caguas (Puerto Rico, Félix Millán) 2–4; Navojoa (Mexico, Chuck Coggins) 1–5.

1980, Santo Domingo (Dominican Republic)—Series XXIII

February 2–7, 1980

Champion: Licey Tigres (Dominican Republic), managed by Del Crandall.

Highlights: Licey's fourth CWS crown comes on home turf as the Dominicans win their first four contests and then watch as Mexico eliminates Caracas from title contention on the final day. Licey pitchers toss two shutouts (Gerald Hannahs and Dennis Lewallyn), and Joaquín Andújar also twirls a masterful 3–1 triumph over runner-up Venezuela. Lewallyn's ten-inning blanking of Bayamón is the first extra-inning shutout in Series history.

Outstanding Player: CWS home run king Tony Armas powers a grand slam (the tenth in tourney history) to provide all the runs in a 4–2 Caracas defeat of Licey, postponing by one day the Dominicans' eventual tournament title clincher.

Team Standings (Managers): Licey (Dominican Republic, Del Crandall) 5–1; Caracas (Venezuela, Felipe Alou) 3–3; Bayamón (Puerto Rico, Art Howe) 2–4; Hermosillo (Mexico, Benjamin Reyes) 2–4.

1982, Hermosillo (Mexico)—Series XXIV

February 4–9, 1982

Champion: Leones de Caracas (Venezuela), managed by Alfonso Carrasquel.

Highlights: Play resumes after a players strike forces cancellation of 1981 CWS action. Under manager Chico Carrasquel, Caracas cruises to victory on the strength of productive hitting, paced by 2 Bo Díaz homers (.400 BA) and six well-timed Tony Armas RBI (with a. 375 BA). Fernando Valenzuela makes his only CWS appearance, earning one of two victories registered by host team Hermosillo.

Outstanding Player: Mexican hitting legend Héctor Espino plays his fifth and final CWS with Hermosillo, extending his career totals to 46 hits, 6 homers, and a .297 batting average. Fittingly, this year's tourney is played in renamed Héctor Espino Stadium.

Team Standings (Managers): Caracas (Venezuela, Alfonso "Chico" Carrasquel) 5–1; Ponce (Puerto Rico, Edward Nottle) 3–3; Hermosillo (Mexico, Tom Harmon) 2–4; Escogido (Dominican Republic, Felipe Alou) 2–4.

1983, Caracas (Venezuela)—Series XXV

February 4–9, 1983

Champion: Arecibo Lobos (Puerto Rico), managed by Ron Clark.

Highlights: Arecibo is crushed 17–2 by Licey in their opener yet the Lobos rebound immediately to win five straight on their way to a ninth pennant for Puerto Rico. Hometown Venezuela (La Guaira) features a power-packed lineup spotted with big league stars like Dave Concepción at shortstop, Tony Armas and Luis Salazar in the outfield, and catcher Bo Díaz, who extends his own record CWS consecutive appearances streak to thirty games. Mexico's Culiacán Tomato Pickers become the first ball club to lose all their games since Panama did so in 1959.

Outstanding Players: Venezuela's Tony Armas launches his 1980s CWS home run on-slaught with three round-trippers, the first of his two such CWS performances. Minor leaguer Rick Anderson (New York Mets) pitches a five-hit shutout for La Guaira versus punchless Culiacán.

Team Standings (Managers): Arecibo (Puerto Rico, Ron Clark) 5–1; La Guaira (Venezuela, Ozzie Virgil) 4–2; Licey (Dominican Republic, Manny Mota) 3–3; Culiacán (Mexico, Francisco Estrada) 0–6.

1984, San Juan (Puerto Rico)—Series XXVI

February 4–9, 1984

Champion: Zulia Aguilas (Venezuela), managed by Rubén Amaro.

Highlights: Poor attendance does little to inspire the host Mayagüez team, which manages only one win and one tie for a last-place deadlock with the Dominicans. Big league star third sacker Aurelio Rodríguez makes his final CWS appearance and inspires Los Mochis to a fast second-place finish at 4–2. Zulia takes the title with top performances from catcher Bobby Ramos, third baseman Luis Sálazar, and batting leader (.529) Leo Carrión.

Outstanding Players: Toronto Blue Jays slugger George Bell does most of the heavy hitting, with 3 homers and 6 RBI. Venezuelan Luis Leál and Nicaraguan Porfi Altamirano (Los Mochis) turn in the top pitching performances.

Team Standings (Managers): Zulia (Venezuela, Rubén Amaro) 5–1; Los Mochis (Mexico, Vinicio García) 4–2; Mayagüez (Puerto Rico, Frank Verdi) 1–4–1; Licey (Dominican Republic, Manny Mota) 1–4–1.

1985, Mazatlán (Mexico)—Series XXVII

February 2–7, 1985

Champion: Licey Tigres (Dominican Republic), managed by Terry Collins.

Highlights: Licey grabs its fifth CWS team crown and thus cements itself as all-time club champion. Four solo homers (including two by import Glenn Davis and one by native George Bell) spark an opening 4–2 victory over La Guaira. After a tight second game loss against Mexico, the Dominicans take four straight (including a combined shutout by Mike Torrez and José Rijo) to lock up the title.

Outstanding Player: Glenn Davis wins the home run title while becoming only the eleventh player to sock 3 or more homers in a single CWS tournament, the twelfth to blast two in one game.

Team Standings (Managers): Licey (Dominican Republic, Terry Collins) 5–1; Culiacán (Mexico, Francisco Estrada) 3–3; San Juan (Puerto Rico, Mako Olivares) 2–4; La Guaira (Venezuela, Aurelio Monteagudo) 2–4.

1986, Maracaibo (Venezuela)—Series XXVIII

February 4–9, 1986

Champion: Mexicali Aguilas (Mexico), managed by Benjamin Reyes.

Highlights: Ten years after their first triumph, Mexico wins its first repeat CWS flag, again under veteran skipper Benjamin Reyes. Mexico is actually shut out twice (11–0 and 6–0) in its first three games, but after four contests all four teams are tied at 2–2 for the first time ever. Mexicali finishes strong and backs into the title when host Venezuela is stopped by Cibao in the final contest. Mexicali's 14–0 triumph over La Guaira is the second most lopsided single-game affair in tourney history.

Outstanding Players: Manager Benjamin Reyes joins Cuban skipper Napoleón Reyes as the only bench bosses to win two CWS titles. Luis DeLeón of Mayagüez hurls a two-hit complete-game shutout (6–0) against the eventual champions.

Team Standings (Managers): Mexicali (Mexico, Benjamin Reyes) 4–2; Cibao (Dominican Republic, Winston Llenas) 3–3; La Guaira (Venezuela, José Martínez) 3–3; Mayagüez (Puerto Rico, Nick Leyva) 2–4.

1987, Hermosillo (Mexico)—Series XXIX

February 3–8, 1987

Champion: Caguas Criollos (Puerto Rico), managed by Ramón Aviles.

Highlights: Caguas (the eventual champion) establishes a lofty team standard by smacking 8 home runs in a single contest against the outmanned Dominicans; nevertheless, Puerto Rico falls in this strange game by a close 14–13 score. Puerto Rico falls victim to another unique event, as well, when manager Tim Foli is removed from his post after three contests (1–2), thus becoming the only manager ever fired in the midst of CWS play.

Outstanding Player: Journeyman big league outfielder Carmelo Martínez (Puerto Rico) smacks 3 homers (his third multiple-homer Series) to secure the second spot on the all-time CWS round-tripper list (with 8). Martínez also captures this year's batting title with a .556 average.

Team Standings (Managers): Caguas (Puerto Rico, Tim Foli, Ramón Aviles) 5–2; Cibao (Dominican Republic, Winston Llenas) 4–3; Mazatlán (Mexico, Carlos Paz) 2–4; Caracas (Venezuela, Bill Plummer) 2–4.

1988, Santo Domingo (Dominican Republic)—Series XXX

February 4–9, 1988

Champion: Escogido Leones (Dominican Republic), managed by Phil Regan.

Highlights: Host club Escogido rides to victory on the arms of its strong pitching staff (Jose DeLeón, José Núñez, Luis Encarnación) and clinches the 1988 flag in its fifth contest with a 2–1 victory over Caracas. This is the sixth Dominican title, but the first won by a team other than Licey. Phil Regan (former Cubs and Dodgers relief ace) skippers the Escogido Lions in his first-ever pro managerial assignment.

Outstanding Players: Former cup-of-coffee big leaguer and Dominican legend Rufino Linares enjoys another fine winter as the Series MVP, batting .389 and knocking in five runs. Cardinals catching prospect Tom Pagnozzi (Puerto Rico) is the leading hitter (.474) in the tournament; DeLeón and Encarnación, along with Ramón de los Santos, pace the standout Dominican staff to a combined 1.80 ERA. But the final hour of glory belongs to Tony Armas (Venezuela), who cements his career Series home run lead (11) with two final CWS round-trippers.

Team Standings (Managers): Escogido (Dominican Republic, Phil Regan) 4–2; Mayagüez (Puerto Rico, Jim Riggleman) 3–3; Tijuana (Mexico, George Ficht) 3–3; Caracas (Venezuela, Bill Robinson) 2–4.

1989, Mazatlán (Mexico)—Series XXXI

February 2–7, 1989

Champion: Zulia Aguilas (Venezuela), managed by Pete McKannin.

Highlights: A surprise entry that had only finished second in the Venezuelan Winter League, Zulia comes on strong at tournament time with four opening wins plus a thirteen-inning 8–7 fifth-game victory over Escogido in the clincher. An earlier sixteen-inning match between these same two teams lasts a record 5 hours and 23 minutes.

Outstanding Players: Career minor league first baseman Phil Stephenson (Chicago Cubs) narrowly misses a Venezuelan League triple crown, then continues his hot hitting with a Caribbean Series MVP performance (3 HRs, 7 RBI, .385 BA). Dale Polley (Braves) and Leonard Damian (Cubs) also lead a Zulia pitching corps, which registers a sizzling 1.68 staff ERA over the first five contests of the 6-game Series. Zulia is later blown out 11–1 by Mayagüez in a meaningless final game.

Team Standings (Managers): Zulia (Venezuela, Pete McKannin) 5–1; Mayagüez (Puerto Rico, Tomás Gomboa) 4–2; Mexicali (Mexico, David Machemer) 2–4; Escogido (Dominican Republic, Phil Regan) 1–5.

1990, Miami (USA)—Series XXXII

February 5–11, 1990

Champion: Escogido Leones (Dominican Republic), managed by Felipe Alou.

Highlights: Caribbean Series play moves to foreign soil for the first time in the tourney's 32-year history and the results are both a baseball travesty and a public relations disaster. Makeshift conditions in Miami's Orange Bowl result in poor infield play, a bevy of cheap homers and high-scoring contests, and almost nonexistent fan support.

Outstanding Players: Muscular Atlanta Braves outfield prospect Barry Jones ties Rico Carty's single Series home run mark with five long circuit blows for the San Juan Metros. A lefty pull hitter, Jones thus achieves his record without any assist from the controversial shortened left field fence (188 feet) required by the patchwork Orange Bowl diamond.

Team Standings (Managers): Escogido (Dominican Republic, Felipe Alou) 5–1; San Juan (Puerto Rico, Mako Oliveras) 3–3; Caracas (Venezuela, Phil Regan) 3–3; Hermosillo (Mexico, Tim Johnson) 1–5.

1991, Miami (USA)—Series XXXIII

February 2–9, 1991

Champion: Licey Tigres (Dominican Republic), managed by John Roseboro.

Highlights: Licey's Tigers prove dominant by outscoring the opposition 50–8 over five games and slaughtering Lara of Venezuela 13–4 and 13–1 in the best-of-three final round. This second U.S.-based tourney enjoys a new short-lived corporate name (Winterball I) and a new baseball-friendly home (Bobby Maduro Stadium), and attendance thus increases moderately over 1990 (six of eleven games draw 5,000-plus fans).

Outstanding Players: Two Licey sluggers, both owned by the Los Angeles Dodgers, share MVP honors: first sacker Henry Rodríguez hits .458 with 6 RBI to cop preliminary round MVP honors; outfielder James Brooks bats .473 and records 6 RBI in the opening championship game, earning final-round MVP status.

Team Standings (Managers): Licey (Dominican Republic, John Roseboro) 5–0; Lara (Venezuela, Domingo Carrasquel) 3–4; Tijuana (Mexico, Joel Serna) 1–3; Santurce (Puerto Rico, Mako Oliveras) 1–3.

1992, Hermosillo (Mexico)—Series XXXIV

February 4–9, 1992

Champion: Mayagüez Indios (Puerto Rico), managed by Patrick Kelly.

Highlights: Mayagüez and Zulia complete the double-round elimination portion of the schedule with identical records, forcing a single head-to-head playoff contest. Paced by Carlos Baerga's (Cleveland Indians) two-run homer and the strong pitching of Roberto Hernández (Chicago White Sox), Puerto Rico breezes through the playoff game, 8–0, capturing the island's first Caribbean title since 1987. Crowds of 15,000 and up jam Héctor Espino Stadium throughout the six-day tournament.

Outstanding Players: Detroit Tigers catcher Chad Kreuter (Puerto Rico) climaxes a hot winter season with 3 homers, 4 RBI, and a .391 average to grab MVP honors in Hermosillo. Wilson Álvarez (Chicago White Sox) wins his only Series decision and is tabbed Winter League Player of the Year on the strength of his brilliant 13–0 (including playoffs) Venezuelan League record.

Team Standings (Managers): Mayagüez (Puerto Rico, Patrick Kelly) 5–2; Zulia (Venezuela, Rubén Amaro) 4–3; Hermosillo (Mexico, Tim Johnson) 3–3; Escogido (Dominican Republic, Felipe Alou) 1–5.

1993, Mazatlán (Mexico)—Series XXXV

February 4–9, 1993

Champion: Santurce Cangrejeros (Puerto Rico), managed by Max Oliveras.

Highlights: Puerto Rico repeats as champion, this time on the strength of Santurce's 9–5 victory over Aguilas in a 1-game tie-breaker. Both teams had completed the round-robin at 4–2, with both Santurce losses coming at the hands of the Dominican club. Paced by infielders Dickie Thon (Brewers) and Eric Fox (Athletics), Santurce won its first-ever crown during the Second Phase that had begun in 1970. Controversy surrounded the final day when Aguilas defeated Santurce to force the extra playoff contest and officials then wrangled over whether or not to hold a meaningless second game between Mexico and Venezuela. More than 12,000 had packed the stadium for the day's final match, since national hero Fernando Valenzuela was scheduled to hurl for also-ran Mazatlán. The unpopular forfeit leaves a bitter taste with local fans.

Outstanding Players: Santurce first baseman Héctor Villanueva (Cardinals) hits successfully in 9 of 18 at-bats and slugs 2 homers along with 9 RBI to earn MVP honors. Baltimore Orioles right-hander Mike Cook also does yeoman service out of the Santurce bull pen with two wins and 11 scoreless innings. Dickie Thon's two-run homer in the sixth proves the crucial clinching blow in the extra playoff game.

Team Standings: Santurce (Puerto Rico) 4–2; Aguilas (Dominican Republic) 4–2; Zulia (Venezuela) 2–4; Mazatlán (Mexico) 2–4.

1994, Puerto la Cruz (Venezuela)—Series XXXVI

February 3–9, 1994

Champion: Licey Tigres (Dominican Republic), managed by Casey Parsons.

Highlights: Licey breaks a Puerto Rican stranglehold on recent tournaments by breezing through five of six contests and edging Venezuela's Magallanes club by a single game. Magallanes ace Jim Waring claims two one-run victories, including the tournament's finale against Licey, which trims the Dominicans' lead to its final slim margin. The championship is the seventh title for Licey and extends the Tigers' record for first place finishes, also running the team's overall win–loss mark through eleven series to 44–22.

Outstanding Players: Jim Waring's two victories highlight the week's pitching, while Licey's Jim Bowie and San Juan's Carlos Delgado each smack a pair of homers and Licey's Raúl Mondesi is the batting champion. Juan Carlos Pulido, hurling for Magallanes, earns a negative slot in tournament record books when he yields homers to three Licey sluggers (Bowie, Junior Noboa, and Alex Arias) in the same inning.

Team Standings: Licey (Dominican Republic) 5–1; Magallanes (Venezuela) 4–2; San Juan (Puerto Rico) 3–3; Hermosillo (Mexico) 0–6.

1995, San Juan (Puerto Rico)—Series XXXVII

February 4–9, 1995

Champion: San Juan Senators (Puerto Rico), managed by Luis Meléndez.

Highlights: With major leaguers still on strike and organized baseball crippled during the off-season, Puerto Rican League officials seize full advantage and put together a powerful San Juan roster of willing participants that includes Roberto Alomar, Carlos Baerga, Juan González, Edgar Martínez, Rubén Sierra, and Bernie Williams. This Puerto Rican Dream Team sweeps the opposition but needs a final win against the Dominican Azucareros to clinch first-place honors. The home forces win the deciding match on the strength of two Bernie Williams homers before an overflow crowd of better than 22,000 in Hiram Bithorn Stadium.

Outstanding Players: Ricky Bones limits the Dominicans to two safeties over six innings in the one-sided deciding contest, and Bernie Williams blasts a third round-tripper to capture the home run hitting honors, but the biggest star is Roberto Alomar, who earns the Series MVP by batting .560 (14 for 25) and ties the CWS record for base hits (first set by Cuba's Pedro Formental back in 1953 and subsequently tied in 1986 by Randy Ready).

Team Standings: San Juan (Puerto Rico) 6–0; Azucareros (Dominican Republic) 4–2; Caracas (Venezuela) 1–5; Hermosillo (Mexico) 1–5.

1996, Santo Domingo (Dominican Republic)—Series XXXVIII

February 3–8, 1996

Champion: Culiacán Tomateros (Mexico), managed by Francisco Estrada.

Highlights: The Dominicans attempted to match Puerto Rico's Dream Team of the previous year with one of their own making, but the experiment proved an utter failure when the squad of big leaguers representing Aguilas collapsed on home turf and limped home third, with only two wins to show for their modest efforts. The home club roster included Pedro Martínez, Juan Guzmán, José Mesa, Julio Franco, and Raúl Mondesi but displayed little in the way of chemistry. Mexico's unheralded Culiacán Tomato Pickers seize the opportunity and win five of six. Managing the winners was Francisco "Paquín" Estrada, catcher on the last Mexican club (1986) to win the CWS title.

Outstanding Player: Despite all the high-priced talent filling the Aguilas bench and lineup, the surprise star proved to be American journeyman Darrel Brinkley (Mexico) who had earlier played professionally only in Holland, Italy, Canada, and Mexico but never back home in the United States. Brinkley paced a Culiacán attack that boasted only two big leaguers (Benji Gil and pitcher Ésteban Loaiza); the American outfielder hit .350 for the series, scored five times and knocked in five more, and was an easy choice for series MVP honors.

Team Standings: Culiacán (Mexico) 5–1; Arecibo (Puerto Rico) 4–2; Aguilas (Dominican Republic) 2–4; Magallanes (Venezuela) 1–5.

1997, Hermosillo (Mexico)—Series XXXIX

February 4–9, 1997

Champion: Aguilas Cibaeñas (Dominican Republic), managed by Mike Quade.

Highlights: Taking to heart the lesson of a failed Dream Team effort one winter earlier, Dominican representative Aguilas launched a new strategy of "more with less" by featuring a no-name lineup with the likes of Oakland shortstop Tony Batista, Red Sox outfielder Jesús Tavárez, and journeymen pitchers Elvin Hernández and Félix Heredia on the hill. It was a winning combination for manager Mike Quade as Aguilas edged defending champ Culiacán 4–3 in the title game. Batista's three-run homer in the first was the eventual difference. That final showdown game between the Dominicans and host Culiacán nearly caused a riot, as thousands without tickets were turned away from the match by police and many of the 16,000 with legitimate tickets couldn't manage to force their way into Héctor Espino Stadium until the final two innings.

Outstanding Players: Canadian journeyman outfielder Matt Stark—a longtime Mexican Pacific League fixture—captured MVP honors in a heroic losing effort, including a two-run homer that sparked a nearly successful comeback for the Mexican forces in the eighth inning of the championship game. Venezuela's Bobby Abreu also provided some serious thunder, with the second highest individual batting average (.588) in CWS history. José Offerman generated most of the offensive fireworks for the victors with a .480 batting average that trailed only Abreu and Mexico's Ever Magallanes (.526).

Team Standings: Aguilas (Dominican Republic) 4–2; Culiacán (Mexico) 3–3; Magallanes (Venezuela) 3–3; Mayagüez (Puerto Rico) 2–4.

1998, Puerto la Cruz (Venezuela)—Series XL

February 5–10, 1998

Champion: Aguilas Cibaeñas (Dominican Republic), managed by Tony Peña.

Highlights: There were plenty of nip-and-tuck games this time around but the standings were pretty much one-sided, with Aguila notching a repeat Dominican crown with a perfect 6–0 ledger. A 3–0 Aguilas win over Lara assured the title on day five. It also ran the club's individual-game winning string to ten. But it was a hard-earned unblemished record in the final analysis. It took fourteen frames to triumph over Mayagüez on opening night. Night two witnessed a gift final-inning win, when Lara closer Oscar Hernández converted an easy game-ending double-play comeback into a disastrous base-clearing throwing error. In the third and fourth contests, victory for Aguilas came only after Tony Peña's shaky club nearly blew late-inning 5–0 leads on both occasions. Peña was a playing manager during the Dominican League season itself and hit the decisive single in that circuit's title game before deactivating himself for CWS play.

Outstanding Players: Neifi Pérez dominated rival pitching (12 for 27, with 5 RBI and 6 doubles) and also the MVP ballot box. Puerto Rican League MVP José Hernández smacked his 24th homer of the long winter in a game with Aguilas. The feat was enough to clinch his selection as *Baseball America*'s winter league Player of the Year but not enough to wrench CWS honors from Pérez, who himself stroked a two-run dinger in the second frame of the clinching game versus Lara, providing the victory margin to support Julián Tavárez's shutout pitching.

Team Standings: Aguilas (Dominican Republic) 6–0; Mayagüez (Puerto Rico) 4–2; Lara (Venezuela) 1–5; Mazatlán (Mexico) 1–5.

1999, San Juan (Puerto Rico)—Series XLI

February 2–8, 1999

Champion: Licey Tigres (Dominican Republic), managed by Dave Jauss.

Highlights: San Juan fans had the dubious distinction of watching the latest Dominican League champion run that country's CWS victory string to three—but they almost had something to cheer about when Licey blew a golden opportunity to close out the title on the final day and thus backed into a bonus extra tie-breaker showdown with host Mayagüez. The Tigers were clubbing the Indians 5–0 in the eighth but then collapsed with three vital errors and promptly kicked away the clinching game. Another Puerto Rico rally was capped by Wil Cordero's ninth-inning homer off Manny Aybar to deadlock the deciding match. In the end Licey prevailed, nonetheless, with comeback heroics of their own: Boi Rodríguez pulled Mayagüez on top with a tenth-inning solo shot, but it was soon forgotten when David Ortiz singled home the tying and winning markers a half-inning later.

Outstanding Players: Neifi Pérez (Colorado Rockies shortstop serving with Licey) lost out on repeating as batting champ, despite slugging at a .400 clip, but maintained his grip on a second straight MVP trophy. Pérez's award was earned on solid consistency, not any last-minute heroics. While Twins first sacker David Ortiz stroked the series-winning hit on the final day (and also blasted a homer in that game), Ortiz had slumped at 4 for 21 during the tournament's opening five games. On the whole, Dave Jauss's Licey club earned a championship banner by traveling the route of a total team effort.

Team Standings: Licey (Dominican Republic) 5–2; Mayagüez (Puerto Rico) 4–3; Lara (Venezuela) 2–4; Mexicali (Mexico) 2–4.

2000, Santo Domingo (Dominican Republic)—Series XLII

February 1–6, 2000

Champion: Santurce Cangrejeros (Puerto Rico), managed by Max Oliveras.

Highlights: Santurce posted a perfect record and from afar looked like an easy victor, but in the end the triumph wasn't as much of a cakewalk as it looked. The Puerto Rican champs almost wore goat horns when they blew a six-run cushion in the final two innings of a deciding game versus Aguilas (Dominican victory would have forced a tie-breaker). Shortstop José Valentin was able to rescue the Crabbers in the end with an eleventh-inning homer to salvage the title effort. The victory slowed the momentum of the Dominican forces, who had won three straight championships, and it also preserved for the moment Puerto Rico's increasingly slim advantage in the overall series standings.

Outstanding Players: Series MVP José Cruz Jr. had 3 hits and 3 runs scored in the extra-inning deciding game and rounded out the top ten in batting with his .385 batting average. But it was the 10 RBI contributed by the Blue Jays outfielder that carried the measure of his contribution. The entire Santurce team seemingly had on their hitting shoes and posted new all-time CWS records with their 86 safeties and 24 doubles, and a hefty club .365 batting average.

Team Standings: Santurce (Puerto Rico) 6–0; Aguilas (Dominican Republic) 4–2; Zulia (Venezuela) 1–5; Navojoa (Mexico) 1–5.

2001, Culiacán (Mexico)—Series XLIII

February 2–7, 2001

Champion: Aguilas Cibaeñas (Dominican Republic), managed by Tony Peña.

Highlights: Hermosillo rode the enthusiastic support of hometown Mexican crowds to bounce back from two early losses and earn its way into the showdown final-day match with the Dominican Aguilas club. Here the gritty Mexicans ran out of steam and lost 4–2 in a deciding match that handed the Dominicans their sixth first-place banner in eleven tries. The strong Mexican showing was a rare reversal of form from the often inept play that has cemented Mexican teams in last place for 14 of 30 Phase Two CWS tournaments. The Hermosillo roster for this renewal was one of the strongest ever with Vinny Castilla and Erubiel Durazo in the middle of the batting order, big league veterans Trenidad Hubbard and Warren Newson adding further punch, and 41-year-old Fernando Valenzuela providing mound savvy as well as a top gate attraction.

Outstanding Players: If the host Mexicans were not quite up to a championship challenge, they were able to provide the festival's top individual performer in MVP slugger Erubiel Durazo. The Diamondbacks left-handed swinger topped all batters in batting average and homers—but teammate Hubbard nearly stole the show in a thrilling game versus Caguas when his 2 long homers spelled the entire margin of a 6–4 ten-inning comeback victory.

Team Standings: Aguilas (Dominican Republic) 4–2; Lara (Venezuela) 3–3; Hermosillo (Mexico) 3–3; Caguas (Puerto Rico) 2–4.

2002, Caracas (Venezuela)—Series XLIV

February 2–8, 2002

Champion: Culiacán Tomateros (Mexico), managed by Francisco Estrada.

Highlights: On the surface, Mexico's entry from Culiacán should have been little match for the strong Dominicans, whose Licey lineup was stocked with veteran big leaguers Miguel Tejada and Vladimir Guerrero in the heart of the batting order and Dodgers lefty Odalis Pérez at the top of the mound rotation. The Tomateros had only one big leaguer in their lineup (Detroit outfielder Jacob Cruz). Tradition was also stacked against the Mexicans, whose countrymen had won only once since joining the fray in 1970. But short-series baseball has a way of spawning unlikely heroes, out of nowhere, and this time around it was an unknown aging catcher named Adán Amezcua from Mexico's Pacific League. Amezcua himself was on a personal mission to salvage his stalled career by grabbing notice from an expected overflow crowd of MLB scouts.

Outstanding Player: Amezcua hit well above .400 and drove home 9 runs, 8 of them in Culiacán's opening three victories. It was a spectacular encore for a player who was coming off a true career moment when he slugged the series-clinching homer to lift his Tomateros over Mazatlán in the Pacific League playoffs and thrust them straight into the CWS limelight. Amezcua's late-inning homers with men on base next sparked two early wins over Licey and Bayamón that lifted Culiacán into CWS contention. In game four with Venezuela the overachieving catcher homered once more to knot the contest in the seventh, after his earlier defensive gem had kept the game tight. Amezcua had spread his heroics around democratically, striking crucial blows against all three other contending clubs.

Team Standings: Culiacán (Mexico) 5–1; Licey (Dominican Republic) 3–3; Bayamón (Puerto Rico) 2–4; Magallanes (Venezuela) 2–4.

2003, Carolina (Puerto Rico)—Series XLV

February 1–8, 2003

Champion: Aguilas Cibaeñas (Dominican Republic), managed by Tony Peña.

Highlights: A national strike aimed at forcing the resignation of Venezuelan President Hugo Chávez (ironically once himself a crack amateur baseball pitcher) paralyzed that country in mid-December and also affected winter baseball throughout the region. With the Venezuelan season ultimately canceled, Puerto Rico (as host country) was permitted two CWS entries to round out the field. It was a compromise that cost Puerto Rican forces dearly, because with the runner-up Criollos now also in the tournament field the league champ Mayagüez could no longer draw reinforcements from Caguas. The Dominican victory was their second in a row on Puerto Rican turf and served to knot up the overall CWS championship totals at 14 apiece.

Outstanding Players: Boston Red Sox slugging first baseman David Ortiz reprised his CWS heroics of 1999 (when his eleventh-inning double had decided the decisive game). Ortiz's offensive barrage contributed decisively to Aguilas victories in the final pair of games and keyed that club's fourth trip into the winner's circle in seven years. Ortiz finished the week with an overall .462 batting average, 2 homers, 11 RBI, and 8 tallies; he also claimed MVP honors in a tight contest with teammate Miguel Tejada (2003 American League MVP with the Athletics), who matched Ortiz with an equal batting average on an identical number of base knocks.

Team Standings: Aguilas (Dominican Republic) 6–1; Mayagüez (Puerto Rico) 5–2; Caguas (Puerto Rico) 2–4; Los Mochis (Mexico) 0–6. Two Puerto Rican teams and no Venezuelan entry.

SELECTED CARIBBEAN SERIES RECORDS AND STATISTICS
Caribbean Series Championship Summaries

A major change in the makeup of teams representing four competing nations occurred between the Phase One (1949–1960) and Phase Two (1970 onward) versions of the otherwise consistent Caribbean World Series. The earliest version of competition featured actual championship teams (with their regular winter league rosters) from the four existing Caribbean circuits (Cuba, Puerto Rico, Panama, and Venezuela). With the 1970 revival of play (minus Cuba and Panama but with the addition of Mexico and the Dominican Republic), the tourney format was slightly altered. Winning ball clubs from the four winter league postseason tournaments are still the Caribbean Series entrants, but these clubs are now allowed to reinforce their rosters with a select number of stars (including North Americans) from other league teams. CWS play now more closely resembles a playoff among league all-star squads than between true league champions.

First Phase–*Primera Etapa* (1949–1960)

Year	Location	Championship Team	Country	Winning Team Manager
1949	Havana, Cuba	Almendares Alacranes	Cuba	Fermín Guerra
1950	San Juan, Puerto Rico	Carta Vieja	Panama	Wayne Blackburn
1951	Caracas, Venezuela	Santurce Cangrejeros	Puerto Rico	George Scales
1952	Panama City, Panama	Habana Leones	Cuba	Mike González
1953	Havana, Cuba	Santurce Cangrejeros	Puerto Rico	Buster Clarkson
1954	San Juan, Puerto Rico	Caguas Criollos	Puerto Rico	Mickey Owen
1955	Caracas, Venezuela	Santurce Cangrejeros	Puerto Rico	Herman Franks
1956	Panama City, Panama	Cienfuegos Elefantes	Cuba	Oscar Rodríguez
1957	Havana, Cuba	Marianao Tigres	Cuba	Napoleón Reyes
1958	San Juan, Puerto Rico	Marianao Tigres	Cuba	Napoleón Reyes
1959	Caracas, Venezuela	Almendares Alacranes	Cuba	Clemente Carreras
1960	Panama City, Panama	Cienfuegos Elefantes	Cuba	Antonio Castaños

Composite Standings in First Phase (1949–1960)

Country	Games	W	L	T	PCT	Championships
Cuba*	72	51	20	1	.718	7
Puerto Rico	73	38	34	1	.528	4
Panama†	73	29	44	0	.397	1
Venezuela	72	26	46	0	.361	0

* Cuba was replaced by the Dominican Republic in Second Phase play.
† Panama was replaced by Mexico in Second Phase play.

Second Phase–*Segunda Etapa* (1970–2003)

Year	Location	Championship Team	Country	Winning Team Manager
1970	Caracas, Venezuela	Magallanes Navegantes	Venezuela	Carlos Pascual
1971	San Juan, Puerto Rico	Licey Tigres	Dominican Republic	Manny Mota

Year	Location	Championship Team	Country	Winning Team Manager
1972	Santo Domingo, DR	Ponce Leones	Puerto Rico	Frank Verdi
1973	Caracas, Venezuela	Licey Tigres	Dominican Republic	Tommy Lasorda
1974	Hermosillo, Mexico	Caguas Criollos	Puerto Rico	Bobby Wine
1975	San Juan, Puerto Rico	Bayamón Vaqueros	Puerto Rico	José Pagán
1976	Santo Domingo, DR	Hermosillo Naranjeros	Mexico	Benjamin Reyes
1977	Caracas, Venezuela	Licey Tigres	Dominican Republic	Bob Rodgers
1978	Mazatlán, Mexico	Mayagüez Indios	Puerto Rico	Rene Lachemann
1979	San Juan, Puerto Rico	Magallanes Navegantes	Venezuela	Willie Horton
1980	Santo Domingo, DR	Licey Tigres	Dominican Republic	Del Crandall
1981	*Series Canceled*			
1982	Hermosillo, Mexico	Caracas Leones	Venezuela	Alfonso Carrasquel
1983	Caracas, Venezuela	Arecibo Lobos	Puerto Rico	Ron Clark
1984	San Juan, Puerto Rico	Zulia Aguilas	Venezuela	Rubén Amaro
1985	Mazatlán, Mexico	Licey Tigres	Dominican Republic	Terry Collins
1986	Maracaibo, Venezuela	Mexicali Aguilas	Mexico	Benjamin Reyes
1987	Hermosillo, Mexico	Caguas Criollos	Puerto Rico	Ramón Aviles
1988	Santo Domingo, DR	Escogido Leones	Dominican Republic	Phil Regan
1989	Mazatlán, Mexico	Zulia Aguilas	Venezuela	Pete McKannin
1990	Miami, USA	Escogido Leones	Dominican Republic	Felipe Alou
1991	Miami, USA	Licey Tigres	Dominican Republic	John Roseboro
1992	Hermosillo, Mexico	Mayagüez Indios	Puerto Rico	Patrick Kelly
1993	Mazatlán, Mexico	Santurce Cangrejeros	Puerto Rico	Max Oliveras
1994	Puerto la Cruz, Venezuela	Licey Tigres	Dominican Republic	Casey Parsons
1995	San Juan, Puerto Rico	San Juan Senators	Puerto Rico	Luís Meléndez
1996	Santo Domingo, DR	Culiacán Tomateros	Mexico	Francisco Estrada
1997	Hermosillo, Mexico	Aguilas Cibaeñas	Dominican Republic	Mike Quade
1998	Puerto la Cruz, Venezuela	Aguilas Cibaeñas	Dominican Republic	Tony Peña
1999	San Juan, Puerto Rico	Licey Tigres	Dominican Republic	Dave Jauss
2000	Santo Domingo, DR	Santurce Cangrejeros	Puerto Rico	Max Oliveras
2001	Culiacán, Mexico	Aguilas Cibaeñas	Dominican Republic	Tony Peña
2002	Caracas, Venezuela	Culiacán Tomateros	Mexico	Francisco Estrada
2003	Carolina, Puerto Rico	Aguilas Cibaeñas	Dominican Republic	Tony Peña

Composite Standings in Second Phase (1970–2003)

Country	Games	W	L	T	PCT	Championships
Dominican Republic*	202	121	80	1	.602	14
Puerto Rico[†]	208	114	93	1	.551	10
Venezuela	189	90	99	0	.476	5
Mexico[‡]	191	69	122	0	.361	4

* The Dominican Republic replaced Cuba in Second Phase play.
[†] Puerto Rico entered two teams in 2003; Venezuela had no 2003 entrant.
[‡] Mexico replaced Panama in Second Phase play.

All-Time Composite Standings in Caribbean Series (1949–1960; 1970–2003)

Country	Games	W	L	T	PCT	Championships
Cuba*	72	51	20	1	.718	7
Dominican Republic[†]	202	121	80	1	.602	14
Puerto Rico[‡]	281	152	127	2	.545	14
Venezuela[‡]	261	116	145	0	.444	5

(continued)

(continued)

Country	Games	W	L	T	PCT	Championships
Panama*	73	29	44	0	.397	1
Mexico†‡	191	69	122	0	.361	4

* Cuba and Panama participated only in First Phase play.
† The Dominican Republic and Mexico participated only in Second Phase play.
‡ Puerto Rico entered two teams in 2003; Venezuela did not enter in 1974 or 2003; Mexico did not enter in 1970 and entered two teams in 1974.

Composite Championships in Caribbean Series (1949–1960; 1970–2003)

Country	First Phase		Second Phase		Total Titles
	Titles	Years	Titles	Years	
Puerto Rico	4	1951, 1953, 1954, 1955	10	1972, 1974, 1975, 1978, 1983, 1987, 1992, 1993, 1995, 2000	14
Dominican Republic	0	—	14	1971, 1973, 1977, 1980, 1985, 1988, 1990, 1991, 1994, 1997, 1998, 1999, 2001, 2003	14
Cuba*	7	1949, 1952, 1956, 1957, 1958, 1959, 1960	0	—	7
Venezuela	0	—	5	1970, 1979, 1982, 1984, 1989	5
Mexico	0	—	4	1976, 1986, 1996, 2002	4
Panama†	1	1950	0	—	1

Two Caribbean Series were played on neutral territory in Miami, FL (1990, 1991).
* Cuba was replaced by the Dominican Republic in Second Phase play (1970–1992).
† Panama was replaced by Mexico in Second Phase play (1970–2003).

Caribbean Series Records and Milestones

Caribbean World Series Record of Camilo Pascual Pitching for Cuba

Year	Opponent	Score	W–L for Series	IP	H	R	ER	BB	SO
1956	Panama	13–5 Cuba		9	6	5	4	3	6
	Venezuela	7–0 Cuba	2–0	9	4	0	0	0	7
1959	Panama	4–1 Cuba		9	6	1	1	2	7
	Venezuela	8–2 Cuba	2–0	9	4	2	2	0	9
1960	Venezuela	8–5 Cuba		7.1	11	5	4	4	8
	Puerto Rico	4–0 Cuba	2–0	9	1	0	0	1	7
Overall			6–0	52.1	32	13	11	10	44

Milestone Events of Caribbean Series History (1949–2003)

Category	Name	Country	Record	Notes
Most Total Series Played	Tony Armas	Venezuela	9	1973, 1978, 1980, 1982, 1983, 1986, 1987, 1988, 1990
Most Series Games Played	Luis García	Venezuela	46	8 total series
	Vic Power [Pollet]	Puerto Rico	46	8 total series
	Tony Armas	Venezuela	46	9 total series

Category	Name	Country	Record	Notes
Team Championship Leader	Licey Tigres	Dominican Republic	8	1971, 1973, 1977, 1980, 1985, 1991, 1994, 1999
All-Time Series Career Records				
At-Bats Leader	Tony Armas	Venezuela	174	9 total series
Hits Leader	Vic Power [Pollet]	Puerto Rico	50	8 total series
Home Run Leader	Tony Armas	Venezuela	11	
Triples Leader	Manny Mota	Dominican Republic	6	6 total series
Doubles Leader	Luis García	Venezuela	23	8 total series
	Manny Mota	Dominican Republic	23	6 total series
Runs Scored Leader	Luis García	Venezuela	11	8 total series
Strikeout Leader, Pitchers	Juan Pizarro	Puerto Rico	61	
Single-Series Records				
Most Home Runs	Rico Carty	Dominican Republic	5	1977
	Barry Jones	Puerto Rico	5	1990
Highest Batting Average	Lorenzo Cabrera	Cuba	.619	13 Hits, 21 At-Bats (1951)
Most Base Hits	Pedro Formental	Cuba	14	25 At-Bats, .560 BA (1953)
	Randy Ready	Puerto Rico	14	1986
	Roberto Alomar	Puerto Rico	14	1995
Most Runs Batted In	Willard Brown	Puerto Rico	13	1953
Most Runs Scored	Chico Fernández	Cuba	10	1956
Lifetime (Career) Series Records				
Most Pitching Victories	Camilo Pascual	Cuba	6	6–0, 1.000 PCT (1956, 1959, 1960)
	Rubén Gómez	Puerto Rico	6	6–2, .750 (1950, 1951, 1953, 1954, 1955, 1959, 1971)
	José "Carracho" Bracho	Venezuela	6*	6–4, .600 (1949, 1951, 1952, 1953, 1955, 1958)
Most Pitching Appearances	Rubén Gómez	Puerto Rico	17	7 total series
Most Complete Games Pitched	Camilo Pascual	Cuba	5	3 total series
Best Pitching Record[‡]	Pedro Borbón	Dominican Republic	5–0 W–L	1971, 1973, 1974, 1977, 1984
	Orlando Peña	Cuba, Venezuela	5–1 W–L	1959, 1960, 1970, 1971
Best Earned Run Average	Francisco Oliveras	Puerto Rico	1.00	36 innings pitched
	Odell Jones	Dominican Republic, Venezuela	1.38	52 innings pitched
	Camilo Pascual	Cuba	1.90	52.1 innings pitched
Best Lifetime Strikeout Ratio, Pitchers[†]	José Rijo	Dominican Republic	1.45	38 strikeouts in 26.2 innings pitched
Best Managerial Record	James "Buster" Clarkson	Puerto Rico (Santurce)	6–0 W–L	1953
	Antonio Castaños	Cuba (Cienfuegos)	6–0 W–L	1960
	Bob Rodgers	Dominican Republic (Licey)	6–0 W–L	1977
Most Managerial Victories	Benjamin Reyes	Mexico	14	14–10, .583 PCT (1975, 1976, 1980, 1986)
	Ozzie Virgil	Dominican Republic	14	14–16, .467 PCT (1972, 1973, 1975, 1976, 1983)

* Also Series record for most pitching decisions.
[†] Calculated as strikeouts per innings pitched, based on a minimum of 24 innings.
[‡] Based on four or more series.

Series-by-Series Individual Leaders (1949–2003)

Year	Batting Champion	Team	BA	Home Run Leader		HR	Pitching Champion		W–L
1949	Al Gionfriddo	Cuba	.533	Monte Irvin	Cuba	2	Agapito Mayor	Cuba	3–0
1950	Héctor Rodríguez	Cuba	.474	Joe Tuminelli	Pan	2	Bob Hooper	Cuba	2–0
1951	Lorenzo Cabrera	Cuba	.619	Luis Olmo	PR	3	José Santiago	PR	2–0
1952	Sandy Amoros	Cuba	.450	Wilmer Fields	Ven	2	Thomas Fine	Cuba	2–0
1953	Pedro Formental	Cuba	.560	Willard Brown	PR	4	Bob Holloman	PR	2–0
1954	Jim Rivera	PR	.450	Ray Orteig	Cuba	2	Vic Strizka	Pan	2–0
1955	Rocky Nelson	Cuba	.471	Don Zimmer	PR	3	Bill Greason	PR	2–0
1956	Rafael Noble	Cuba	.500	Elias Osorio	Pan	3	Camilo Pascual	Cuba	2–0
1957	Sammy Drake	Cuba	.500	Luís Márquez	PR	2	Jim Bunning	Cuba	2–0
1958	Bob Wilson	Ven	.400	Lou Limmer	Ven	2	Bert Robinson	Pan	2–0
1959	Jesús Mora	Ven	.417	Norm Cash	Ven	2	Camilo Pascual	Cuba	2–0
1960	Tommy Davis	PR	.409	Héctor López	Panama	3	Camilo Pascual	Cuba	2–0
Caribbean Series Not Held (1961–1969)									
1970	Gonzalo Márquez	Ven	.478	*Six Tied*		2	*Three Tied at*		1–0
1971	Manny Mota	Dom	.579	Celerino Sánchez	Mex	3	Chris Zachery	Dom	2–0
1972	Carlos May	PR	.455	*Four Tied*		1	Gaby Jones	PR	2–0
1973	Jesús Alou	Dom	.500	*Fourteen Tied*		1	Pedro Borbón	Dom	2–0
1974	Héctor Espino	Mex	.429	Darrel Thomas	Mex	2	*Two Tied at*		1–0
1975	Ken Griffey	PR	.500	*Four Tied*		2	Charlie Hough	Dom	2–0
1976	Enos Cabell	Ven	.400	*Seven Tied*		1	Mark Wiley	Ven	2–0
1977	Félix Rodríguez	Ven	.522	Rico Carty	Dom	5	*Three Tied at*		2–0
1978	José Morales	PR	.421	Leon Roberts	Ven	2	*Three Tied at*		2–0
1979	Jerry White	Ven	.522	Mitchell Page	Ven	2	Mike Norris	Ven	2–0
1980	Jaime Rosario	PR	.417	*Five Tied*		1	Dave Smith	PR	2–0
1981	*Series Canceled*								
1982	Baudilio Díaz	Ven	.412	Baudilio Díaz	Ven	2	Luís Leál	Ven	2–0
1983	Darrel Thomas	Ven	.476	Tony Armas	Ven	3	*Eleven Tied at*		1–0
1984	Leonel Carrión	Ven	.529	George Bell	Dom	3	*Eight Tied at*		1–0
1985	Juan Navarrete	Mex	.533	Glenn Davis	Dom	3	Tom Brennan	Dom	2–0
1986	Randy Ready	PR	.467	Andrés Galarraga	Ven	2	Jaime Orozco	Mex	2–0
1987	Carmelo Martínez	PR	.556	Candy Maldonado	PR	4	Francis Oliveras	PR	2–0
1988	Tom Pagnozzi	PR	.474	Tony Armas	Ven	2	*Ten Tied at*		1–0
1989	Matías Carrillo	Mex	.500	Phil Stephenson	Ven	3	Dale Polley	Ven	2–0
1990	Cornelio García	Mex	.520	Barry Jones	PR	5	Mel Rojas	Dom	2–0
1991	Edwin Alicea	PR	.500	*Seven Tied*		1	Melido Pérez	Dom	2–0
1992	Chad Kreuter	PR	.450	Chad Kreuter	PR	3	*Six Tied at*		1–0
1993	Héctor Villanueva	PR	.500	*Three Tied*		2	Mike Cook	PR	2–0
1994	Raúl Mondesi	Dom	.450	Carlos Delgado	PR	3	Jim Waring	Ven	2–0
1995	Roberto Alomar	PR	.560	Bernie Williams	PR	3	*Seven Tied at*		1–0
1996	Tony Barron	PR	.500	Leo Gómez	PR	3	Felipe Murillo	Mex	2–0
1997	Bobby Abreu	Ven	.588	Guillermo García	Dom	3	*Six Tied at*		1–0
1998	Nefei Pérez	Dom	.444	José Hernández	PR	4	*Four Tied at*		1–0
1999	Carlos Mendoza	Ven	.500	Boi Rodríguez	PR	3	Anthony Chávez	Dom	2–0
2000	Marcos Scutaro	Ven	.480	Alonzo Powell	PR	2	Stevenson Agosto	PR	2–0
2001	Erubiel Durazo	Mex	.455	Erubiel Durazo	Mex	3	*Four Tied at*		1–0
2002	Ramón Hernández	Ven	.474	Vladimir Guerrero	Dom	4	*Six Tied at*		1–0
2003	Miguel Tejada	Dom	.462	Orlando Merced	PR	3	Hipólito Pichardo	Dom	2–0

Abbreviations: Dom, Dominican Republic; Mex, Mexico; Pan, Panama; PR, Puerto Rico; Ven, Venezuela.

Baseball America **Winter League Player of the Year (1986–2003)**

Season	Name	Position	Team	League
1985–1986	Wally Joyner	1B	Mayagüez Indios	Puerto Rico
1986–1987	Vicente Palacios	RHP	Mexicali Aguilas	Mexico
1987–1988	José Núñez	RHP	Escogido Leones	Dominican Republic
1988–1989	Phil Stephenson	1B	Zulia Aguilas	Venezuela
1989–1990	Edgar Martínez	3B	San Juan Senators	Puerto Rico
1990–1991	Henry Rodríqüez	OF	Licey Tigres	Dominican Republic
1991–1992	Wilson Álvarez	LHP	Zulia Aguiles	Venezuela
1992–1993	Matías Carrillo	OF	Mexicali Aguilas	Mexico
1993–1994	John Hudek	RHP	Magallanes Navegantes	Venezuela
1994–1995	Carlos Delgado	C	San Juan Senators	Puerto Rico
1995–1996	Darryl Brinkley	OF	Mexicali Aguilas	Mexico
1996–1997	Bartolo Colón	RHP	Aguilas Cibaeñas	Dominican Republic
1997–1998	José Hernández	SS	Mayagüez Indios	Puerto Rico
1998–1999	Bobby Abreu	OF	Caracas Leones	Venezuela
1999–2000	Morgan Burkhart	1B	Navojoa Mayos	Mexican Pacific
2000–2001	Courtney Duncan	RHP	Caguas Criollos	Puerto Rico
2001–2002	Ramón Hernández	C	Occidente Pastora	Venezuela
2002–2003	Arnie Múñoz	RHP	Aguilas Cibaeñas	Dominican Republic

NOTE

1. Few English-language records exist for the well-established Caribbean Series and its most notable baseball moments, but several fine Spanish-language chronicles have been published treating winter ball and Caribbean Series play. See especially the two books by José Antero Nuñez in the chapter bibliography.

BIBLIOGRAPHY

Books

Antero Nuñez, José. *Serie del Caribe 1988* (Tomo II). Caracas, Venezuela: Impresos Urbina, 1988.
Antero Nuñez, José. *Serie del Caribe 1989* (Tomo III). Caracas, Venezuela: Impresos Urbina, 1989.
Piña Campora, Tony. *Los Grandes Finales.* Santo Domingo, Dominican Republic: Editora Colegial, 1981.
Salas, Alexis. *Momentos Inolvidables del Béisbol Profesional Venezolano, 1946–1984.* Caracas, Venezuela: Miguel Angel García, 1985.

International Baseball Timeline

Greatest Moments in World Baseball History

•••

Baseball emerged as a national pastime throughout Caribbean island nations from as early as the 1860s, the same decade that witnessed the bat-and-ball sport's first explosion of popularity on North American diamonds. For more than a century and a quarter, baseball heroics have been regularly performed on dusty Latin American pastures in Cuba, Puerto Rico, Venezuela, Mexico, Panama, and the Dominican Republic. Since the birth of organized baseball's lively-ball era during the early 1920s, Latin-born ballplayers have been performing big league feats of note with an ever-increasing frequency. Through the bleak years of American baseball's noxious era of racial segregation, dark-skinned Cuban superstars Martín Dihigo, José Méndez, Alejandro Oms, and dozens more wrote some of Negro league baseball's most colorful chapters all across North America. In the same period, American black stars with once-forgotten names like Oscar Charleston, Josh Gibson, and Satchel Paige migrated annually to color-blind winter leagues in Cuba, the Dominican Republic, and Mexico to display their incomparable diamond talents. Jackie Robinson's heroic toppling of baseball's racial barriers in 1947 would soon release a flood-tide of dark-skinned, Spanish-speaking talent upon major league diamonds across a midcentury golden age featuring Minnie Miñoso, Vic Power, Juan Marichal, and Roberto Clemente—on down to the present-day era boasting Sammy Sosa, Juan González, Pedro Martínez, and Albert Pujols.

Baseball can claim roots nearly as ancient in Australia (where the sport was first introduced in 1857) and in Japan (where it was imported by American professor Horace Wilson in 1872), and has also long enjoyed substantial popularity in Taiwan, Korea, and even a scattered handful of European nations. On the world amateur baseball stage, it has always been the Cubans and Japanese (occasionally the Koreans)—not the Americans or Canadians—who have since the 1930s dominated all comers year after year in prestigious international tournament competitions.

The following chronology provides a simple capsule history of important international baseball events, featuring landmark moments in the development of baseball at widely scattered points around the globe as well as historic contributions of international players performing on the major league and minor league diamonds of North America's organized baseball.

1838

June 4, Canada. The first bat-and-ball game resembling modern-day baseball is played in Beachville, Ontario, and later described by witness Adam Ford in a letter to *Sporting Life* (published May 5, 1886). This contest had many characteristics of the sport later known in America as baseball, yet was quite distinct in appearance from the popular New York game, soon to be invented by New York Knickerbocker Club at Hoboken, NJ; among other differences, the Ontario game used five bases instead of four.

1846

June 19, USA. The Knickerbocker Club holds its first game of "baseball" at Hoboken's Elysian Fields, playing by New York rules and thus giving formal birth to baseball largely as we know it today. Credit is usually assigned to Alexander Joy Cartwright as the Knickerbocker Club member who drew up playing rules substantially different from the formalities of rounders, town ball, or other forms of bat-and-ball sport based on ancient British schoolyard games.

1856

September, USA. British-born Henry Chadwick, already a newspaper commentator on the sport of cricket, discovers baseball on New York sandlots and soon becomes the game's most renowned early proselytizer. Chadwick in a few short years will develop and polish the baseball box score as the game's unique method of detailed record keeping.

1857

February 28, Australia. Homesick Americans had staged first known Australian baseball matches on Ballarat gold rush fields before 1855, but the first reported game between native Australians is a three-inning contest in which Collingwood defeated Richmond, 350–230. The incredibly high score is due to awarding runs for each individual base secured during the match.

1866

June, Cuba. Caribbean baseball is reputedly born when U.S. sailors from an American naval ship anchored at pierside in Matanzas Bay demonstrate diamond play for a crowd of Cuban dockhands loading sugarcane onto North American vessels. Cubans reportedly joke that the American instructors seemed highly motivated by a desire to sell baseball equipment to their raw diamond recruits. One competing account of baseball's Cuban origins suggests it was actually teenager Nemesio Guilló (sometimes spelled Guillót)—an upper-class youth educated in the United States—who (along with his older brother Ernesto) introduced equipment and demonstrations of the new Yankee sport upon his return from Alabama's Spring Hill College (a secondary school) to his native Havana in 1864.

1870

Dominican Republic. Baseball makes its first reported appearance in the Dominican Republic, presumably brought there by Cuban settlers escaping that country's Ten Year War against Spanish colonial rule. Cubans were thus early established as baseball's first true apostles involved in actively spreading the game throughout the rest of Latin America.

1871
April, USA. Cuban-born Ésteban "Steve" Bellán mans third base for the Troy Haymakers during an inaugural season for the National Association, pro baseball's first recognized big league circuit. Bellán, who honed his baseball skills while studying at Fordham University in New York and later hit .236 in 59 games over a three-year professional career, thus becomes the first official Latin American big league ballplayer, appearing a century ahead of the modern-era Latin Invasion.

1872 (date sometimes also given as 1873 or 1874)
Japan. American professor and Christian missionary Horace Wilson introduces baseball to Japan by teaching rudiments of the sport to university students in Tokyo. Japan thus enjoys one of the earliest introductions to the new pastime, which had already caught on like wildfire throughout both North America and the Caribbean island of Cuba.

1874
England. Baseball makes an early appearance in England when pitcher and promoter A. G. Spalding visits with two crack professional squads (Boston and Philadelphia) and holds exhibitions of the new American sport at Lord's Cricket Grounds outside London.
December 27, Cuba. Only eight years after baseball's reported introduction in Matanzas, that city—known as the "Athens of Cuba"—hosts a visiting Habana nine in the first recorded organized ball game between native Cuban teams. Playing for Club Habana are two early giants of Cuban pro baseball, ex–big leaguer Steve Bellán and patriot–athlete Emilio Sabourín, himself later one of the organizing geniuses behind Cuba's new professional league. Bellán catches and socks three homers and Sabourín scores eight runs for Club Habana during its 51–9 rout of the talent-thin Matanzas nine. The game lasts but seven innings, when it is ended by darkness.

1878
December 29, Cuba. The Cuban Professional Baseball League (*"Liga de Base Ball"*) launches play in Havana, thus making the Cuban League the world's second oldest professional baseball organization, trailing North America's National League in seniority by a mere two seasons. Habana wins the first game, 21–20 over Almendares, in a contest featuring ten men to a side (the extra position was "right short field"). The inaugural Cuban championship—ending February 16, 1879—consists of only three ball clubs (Habana, Matanzas, and Almendares) and Habana wins the trophy with a perfect 4–0–1 record behind the leadership of team manager and playing captain Ésteban "Steve" Bellán.

1882
January 21, Cuba. In an apparent single-game world record, 60 errors are committed in a Cuban semi-pro contest between Club Caridad (with 39 miscues) and Club Ultimatum (with 21). It seems safe to assume that ballplayers at this sloppy Havana spectacle had not even primitive fielding gloves for their crude ragtag match.

1887
Mexico. The "Mexico Club" team is organized in Mexico City. Various sources report that baseball was first played in Mexico sometime in the late 1870s and that the first notable game likely took place in Nuevo Laredo during that same period.
February 13, Cuba. The first professional league no-hitter in Cuba is pitched by Carlos Maciá, as Almendares defeats Carmelita with a one-sided 38–0 margin. This may, in fact, have been the first no-hit, no-run game pitched anywhere in Latin America, although existing historical records remain altogether cloudy on this matter.

1888

December, Australia. A world tour organized by Al Spalding visits Australia and stages matches with his two clubs known as White Sox and All-Americans. American squads made up of seasoned professionals battled each other and also played against teams representing several Australian cricket clubs.

1889

Nicaragua. Two baseball clubs, known as Club Southern and White Rose, are reportedly organized in Nicaragua. It remains unknown who first imported the spreading game into this coastal Central American country.

Cuba. Wenceslao Gálvez y Delmonte, a superior shortstop and manager during first decade of professional play in Cuba—also later enshrined in the Cuban Baseball Hall of Fame and noted as both novelist and journalist—publishes his book *El baseball en Cuba* in Havana. This is undoubtedly the first formal history of baseball ever published in any country.

July 14, Cuba. The second professional no-hit, no-run game in Cuba is pitched by Eugenio de Rosas, hurler for Club Progreso, during an 8–0 victory over Club Cárdenas. The game's highly unusual line score shows Cárdenas with no runs or hits, yet an astronomical total of 14 errors. This will be the last Cuban no-hitter for the next forty-seven seasons, and only four more such flawless masterpieces will be tossed by Cuban hurlers during the pre-Castro decades of twentieth-century Cuban play.

1895

August, Cuba. Visiting Cuban businessman Emilio Cramer reportedly first demonstrates the playing of baseball in Venezuela, again affirming the spread of baseball play in the Caribbean region as having Cuban roots. Few additional details remain about the earliest baseball play in Venezuela, but the first references to the sport in the Venezuelan press appear that same year, on August 5, 1895.

1896

Japan. A first game is played between Japanese and American teams when Tokyo university students challenge the American Athletic Club of Yokohama and walk off with an embarrassingly easy 29–4 victory. After demanding a rematch, the Americans recruit better players from U.S. battleships stationed in the harbor but lose again by an almost equally lopsided score.

1897

April, USA. A barnstorming Australian team makes what is billed as the first visit by a foreign club to U.S. soil, playing exhibition matches around the country until late July. One of the tour's most unique games is played versus the Boston old-timers team, a contest in which Henry Chadwick threw out a ceremonial first ball, Al Spalding played for the Boston nine, and former Cincinnati Red Stockings shortstop George Wright (brother of baseball pioneer Harry Wright) organized a postgame banquet, held after the Aussies won handily by a 27–13 count.

1898

January 9, Puerto Rico. A first formal reported baseball game takes place on the island of Puerto Rico; it is held on a bicycle racing course in the capital city of San Juan. This inaugural game was called off because of rain showers, then again postponed during a first attempt to reschedule, so Puerto Rico's first baseball game actually took three weeks to complete. The sport had apparently been first brought to the island by a Spanish diplomat who had earlier been exposed to baseball matches while on assignment in Cuba.

1901

The Netherlands. Baseball is reportedly played for first time in Holland, thus giving the Netherlands bragging rights for the first organized baseball activity anywhere on the European continent. The sport is reportedly first introduced by J. C. G. Grassé, a Hollander who returned from a U.S. visit as a converted baseball enthusiast and soon translated playing rules into Dutch for the first time.

1905

June, USA. A Waseda University team from Tokyo tours the U.S. West Coast to play American college and high school teams in Los Angeles, San Francisco, and Seattle. In a game against Stanford University, the Japanese team dons spiked shoes for the first time, but the game is delayed considerably because Japanese players had attached the unfamiliar cleats backwards on their makeshift shoes. By tour's end, the Japanese students have claimed seven victories but also lose to American host teams nineteen times.

1908

October, Japan. Reach All-Americans (barnstormers that include a handful of bench-warmer big leaguers and mostly Pacific Coast League regulars) become the first U.S. professional team to tour Japan, playing a series of games versus Japanese college nines and winning all of the seventeen matches played.

November, Cuba. Cuban baseball makes it onto the North American map when Matanzas-born hurler José Méndez—a Cuban League rookie with the Almendares team—unleashes a string of impressive outings versus touring Cincinnati Reds. The slightly-built 20-year-old fastballer blanks the National Leaguers with a sterling 1–0 one-hitter, then follows up two weeks later with a 7-inning shutout relief outing and second nine-inning whitewash start. The surprise ace, whom John McGraw eventually dubbed "Cuba's Black Diamond," continued his mastery with a 44–2 mark versus U.S. Negro leaguers during a 1909 North American barnstorming tour.

1909

Japan. A University of Wisconsin baseball team visits Japan as guests of the Keio University Athletic Association and promptly loses three straight to the host squad. Wisconsin nonetheless rebounds to defeat a Tokyo college all-star team by scores of 10–0 and 8–7 before departing for home.

1911

July 4, USA. Outfielders Armando Marsans and Rafael Almeida debut with the Cincinnati Reds, becoming the first twentieth-century Cubans and the first modern-day Latin Americans to appear in major league action. Complaints about the dark skin color of both ballplayers are met by an official Cincinnati club press release stating that these were "two of the purest bars of Castilian soap ever floated to these shores."

1912

July 15, Sweden. Baseball debuts as an Olympic demonstration sport in Stockholm, with an exhibition staged between teams representing the United States and Sweden. The Americans (a team of volunteers from a U.S. track and field squad) triumph 13–3 over the outmanned Swedes, who themselves employ a pitching battery consisting of another pair of U.S. track stars on loan for the occasion.

1913

October, Japan. The Chicago White Sox and New York Giants play a brief three-game exhibition series in Tokyo, Japan, during a whirlwind world tour by the big league barnstormers. After two games head to head, the major leaguers combine into one team and easily paste the Keio University team, 12–3.

1914

January, Australia. New York Giants and Chicago White Sox (carrying all-stars from other teams on their rosters) arrive in Brisbane, Australia, for a week of exhibitions that includes five games between the major league outfits and four games (two by each club) against teams representing Victoria and New South Wales. Big leaguers on the tour include Buck Weaver, Tris Speaker, Sam Crawford, Fred Merkle, Germany Schaefer, and Olympic track and field hero Jim Thorpe. During the tour, games are also played in Sydney and Melbourne.

1919

October 3, USA. Cuban Adolfo Luque becomes the first Latin American major leaguer to appear in a World Series game, pitching one inning of relief for the Cincinnati Reds in game three against Charlie Comiskey's infamous "Black Sox" team in Chicago. Luque, who will later win 27 National League games during the 1923 season for Cincinnati, also pitched four relief innings in game seven, at Cincinnati's Redland Field, on October 8th.

1922

Japan. The first Japanese victory over a touring U.S. big league team comes when the Japanese pitcher—identified in local press accounts only as Ono—leads his amateur Mita Club of Shibaura to a surprising 9–3 victory over the New York Yankees squad and ace pitcher and future major league Hall of Famer Waite Hoyt.

1923

October, USA. At season's end, Cincinnati Reds hurler Adolfo "Dolf" Luque of Cuba posts a major league–leading win–loss record of 27–8 and an ERA mark of 1.93, today still the best single-season performance ever posted by a Latin American big league pitcher. Luque during this season earns his moniker, "The Pride of Havana."

1925

Japan. College baseball shows increased popularity in Japan, and the Tokyo Six University League is formed by Waseda, Keio, Meiji, Hosei, Rikkyo, and Tokyo universities. The league will soon hold popular annual collegiate championship tournaments to rival the fan-favorite nationwide high school tournaments that still continue today.

1926

October–November, Mexico. The first edition of the Central American and Caribbean Games is staged in Mexico City and includes a baseball tournament that features only the host country and Cuba. Cuba wins all three matches in the event, which launches the concept of international amateur baseball competitions between national all-star teams.

1929

January 1, Cuba. Outfielder James "Cool Papa" Bell, famed North American Negro leaguer playing for Cienfuegos, becomes the first slugger to connect for three homers within a single game during Cuban professional league play. Bell's feat occurs at Aida Park in a 15–11 slugfest victory over Habana. Bell's three homers are struck against Oscar Levis, "Campanita" Bell, and Hall of Famer Martín Dihigo—although Bell himself will later claim that all three came off American black-ball ace Johnny Allen.

1930

March–April, Cuba. The first full-scale Central American Games baseball tournament is held in Havana, with Cuba winning five of six contests to earn the gold medal position. Mexico (4–2), Panama (3–3), Guatemala (0–3), and El Salvador (0–3) are also participants.

1931

October, Japan. A big league all-star contingent with Lefty O'Doul and Lou Gehrig tours Japan and sweeps seventeen games played against university nines, commercial league teams, and Japanese all-star squads. Accompanying the Americans are Hall of Famers Robert (Lefty) Grove, Mickey Cochrane, Frankie Frisch, Rabbit Maranville, George Kelly, and Al Simmons. Gehrig is hit by a pitch in the seventh game of tour and breaks two bones in his hand, an injury that fortunately heals in time for him to continue his big league iron-man streak with the New York Yankees.

1932

October, Japan. Lefty O'Doul visits Japan with Chicago White Sox pitcher Ted Lyons and Washington Senators catcher Moe Berg to coach Big Six university teams in Tokyo. Apparently multilingual Berg, later reported to have been moonlighting as a U.S. government spy, secretly took photos from the roof of St. Luke's International Hospital in downtown Tokyo, photos that may have been used to plan U.S. bombing raids during World War II.

1933

October 7, USA. Cuban Dolf Luque provides four and one third innings of stellar relief to gain championship-clinching victory in game five of the 1933 World Series. In notching the fall classic title for the New York Giants against the Washington Senators, Luque becomes the first Latin American to post a World Series pitching victory.

1934

Japan. Professional baseball begins in Japan with the founding of the Tokyo Kyojin (Yomiuri Giants) team by Matsutaro Shoriki, president of the Yomiuri newspaper group. The tradition thus also begins of naming Japanese pro teams for their sponsoring corporations and not for home cities (Hanshin Tigers represent the Hanshin railway company and Chunichi Dragons represent the Chunichi newspaper chain). A full-fledged Japanese professional league with seven original teams will begin play two summers later.

November, Japan. Babe Ruth tours Japan with Lefty O'Doul's big league all-stars and gives a huge lift to American-style baseball all across the island nation. The touring big league squad also includes such stars as Lou Gehrig, Charlie Gehringer, Earl Averill, Connie Mack, Lefty Gomez and Jimmy Foxx. One game in Tokyo draws a crowd in excess of 100,000 to Meiji Stadium, Americans win all eighteen games, and Babe Ruth thrills fans by smacking thirteen home runs, but the true highlight for Japanese fans comes when 18-year-old Eiji Sawamura pitches brilliantly against the major leaguers, striking out Gehringer, Ruth, Gehrig, and Foxx in succession before losing, 1–0, on a seventh-inning homer by Lou Gehrig.

1936

October, Japan. The first season of Japanese professional baseball is highlighted by 20-year-old Eiji Sawamura of the Tokyo Kyojin (aka Yomiuri Giants), who posts a 13–2 mound record and strikes out 112 in 120 innings. Sawamura, who so impressed U.S. barnstormers two seasons earlier, will establish 63–22 career pitching record before being killed in action during World War II.

November 7, Cuba. American Negro leaguer Raymond "Jabao" Brown with Santa Clara hurls the first twentieth century no-hitter in Cuba, a 7–0 victory over Habana.

1937

September 16, Mexico. Black Cuban Hall of Famer Martín Dihigo pitches the first professional no-hit, no-run game on Mexican soil in a 4–0 victory over Nogales at Veracruz.

1938

June 5, Venezuela. In one of the most incredible pitching duels found anywhere in organized baseball history, semi-pro Venezuelan hurler Andrés Julio Báez (Club Pastora) and Cuban Lázaro Salazar (Gavilanes) battle for twenty innings in a game played at Maracaibo. With the game lasting an incredible six hours and thirty minutes, Pastora emerges victorious by a 1–0 count, with Báez facing 65 batters and Salazar facing 67.

September 18, Mexico. Cuban star Martín Dihigo, earlier the author of the first Mexican League no-hitter (September 16, 1937), also becomes the first Mexican League hitter to register six hits in six at-bats (while playing for Veracruz against Agrario).

October, Puerto Rico. The Puerto Rican Winter League's inaugural season opens with six teams that include Ponce, Guayama, Humacao, San Juan, Caguas, and Mayagüez. Guayama captures the split-season first half and San Juan leads the field in the second round. With a 27–12 overall mark, Guayama is the season's best team and also captures a year-end playoff with San Juan.

Japan. Haruyasu Nakajima with the Tokyo Kyojin, playing in the Japanese Fall League, becomes the first Japanese pro baseball triple crown winner, slugging 10 homers, knocking home 38 runs, and batting a lofty .361.

1939

August, Cuba. The first full-fledged Amateur World Series is staged in Havana, inaugurating the event that will eventually develop into the Baseball World Cup.[1] Only three teams participate, and Cuba wins all six of its matches to earn the champion's trophy. Nicaragua splits its three matches, losing thrice to Cuba but defeating Team USA in all three contests between runner-up teams.

Japan. Russian-born Victor Starffin wins 42 games for the Tokyo Kyojin in Japanese League, also striking out 282 in 458 innings. Considered the greatest pitcher in Japanese professional history, the right-hander had also claimed 33 victories a single season earlier and will capture 38 games during the coming campaign.

1940

September–October, Cuba. The United States, Hawaii Territory (not yet a state), Cuba, Mexico, Puerto Rico, Nicaragua, and Venezuela meet in the third annual World Amateur Baseball Championship tournament, the first championship series featuring more than three participants and the second held on Latin American soil. Cuba, the host country, is an easy victor for the second year in a row.

1942

Japan. Yasuo Hayashi sets an all-time durability standard by pitching record 541 innings during a 105-game Japanese League schedule. Hurling for the Asahi team, Hayashi posts a 32–22 win–loss mark; his amazing 1.01 mark also captures the league ERA crown.

1943

December 11, Cuba. Negro league Cuban ace Manuel "Cocaína" García of Club Habana pitches the fourth no-hit, no-run game in Cuban League history, besting Club Marianao, 5–0.

1944

September 6, USA. Tommy de la Cruz, Cuban-born right-hander with the Cincinnati Reds, pitches the first one-hitter by a Latin American in big league annals. De la Cruz pitches just this single wartime season, with a 9–9 record and an ERA of 3.25. The Cuban pitcher was very dark in skin color, which hastened his release from the still-segregated majors.

December 3, Puerto Rico. The first no-hitter in the Puerto Rico Winter League is pitched by Tomás Quiñónez of Ponce, who bests the rival Mayagüez Indians, 8–0. Puerto Rican hitting legend Perucho Cepeda (father of future major leaguer and Cooperstown Hall of Famer Orlando Cepeda) is in the lineup for the whitewashed Mayagüez team.

1945

January 3, Cuba. Cuban professional baseball witnesses a fifth no-hit, no-run game, pitched by former big leaguer Tommy de la Cruz of Almendares against rival Habana, 7–0.

January 7, Cuba. The most violent incident in Cuban baseball history transpires when outfielder Roberto Ortiz of Almendares attacks umpire Bernardino Rodríguez during a wild home plate dispute and knocks the umpire unconscious.

May 6, Mexico. Monterrey establishes a new Mexican League record for lopsided wins by pounding Puebla 21–0. The previous record was 19–0 (Mexico City versus Carta Blanca; August 31, 1941).

December 8, Venezuela. Venezuelan leaguer Rafael Gallis Tello connects for the first home run ever hit in Estadio Olímpico of Maracaibo. His fifth-inning blow propels Club Gavilanes to a 5–2 victory over semi-pro rival Pastora before 10,000 thrilled spectators during the inaugural game at one of Venezuela's most famous and tradition-rich ballparks.

1946

January 12, Venezuela. A game between Club Venezuela and Magallanes launches the newly constituted four-team *Liga be Béisbol Profesional de Venezuela* (aka Venezuelan Baseball League). The game, played in Cervecería Caracas Stadium, is won by Magallanes, 5–2, with Luis Aparicio Sr. ("El Grande"), father of future Cooperstown Hall of Famer Luis Aparicio Jr. ("Junior"), starting at shortstop for the victors.

January 13, Venezuela. The second professional game in Venezuela sees Vargas routing Cervecería Caracas, 12–1, behind the stellar play of North American Negro league stars Roy Welmaker (the winning pitcher), outfielder Sam Jethroe (later with the National League Boston Braves), and future Brooklyn Dodger catching great Roy Campanella.

January 17, Venezuela. Venezuelan great Alfonso "Chico" Carrasquel, future star of the American League Chicago White Sox, makes his professional baseball debut at age 17 in a Venezuelan League game between Club Venezuela and Cervecería Caracas. Carrasquel, later considered the most popular all-time player by Venezuelan fans (edging Hall of Famer Luis Aparicio for the honor), achieves lasting fame by hitting the first home run ever registered in Venezuelan League play, which provides the game-winning run in the top of the seventh inning for Cervecería Caracas.

January 20, Venezuela. Venezuelan pitching great Alejandro Carrasquel (ten-year major leaguer with 1940s-era Senators and White Sox) and Negro league star Roy Welmaker face-off in a sensational pitching duel still considered the greatest in Venezuelan professional baseball history. Carrasquel of Magallanes defeats Welmaker, 3–2, during a seventeen-inning contest that sees both hurlers go the full distance.

March 7, Venezuela. American Negro league star second baseman Marvin Williams, playing for Vargas team against Magallanes, enjoys his finest career day and sets a Venezuelan League single-game batting record that still stands. Williams registers eight RBI, with two homers and two singles, in leading his team to a 16–9 triumph at Caracas.

April, Mexico. Millionaire Mexican businessman Jorge Pasquel creates the first serious competition against big league monopoly since the long-defunct Federal League, causing a small defection of major league players to "south of the border" with his offers of huge salaries for Mexican League contracts. A total of twenty-six players defect (seventeen National Leaguers and nine American Leaguers), including Dodgers catcher Mickey Owen, Giants pitcher Sal Maglie and outfielder Danny Gardella, Cardinals pitcher Max Lanier, and St. Louis Browns infielder Vern "Junior" Stephens. Commissioner Happy Chandler announces lifetime suspension for defecting players, but this ban is later reduced to only five years.

October 9, Cuba. A team of National League All-Stars begins a seven-game exhibition schedule against the Cuban National All-Star team in Havana. The National League team, featuring Buddy Kerr and Sid Gordon of New York Giants and Brooklyn Dodgers regulars Eddie Stanky and Ralph Branca (who five years later yielded Bobby Thomson's "Shot Heard Round the World" pennant-winning homer in the Polo Grounds), wins the opening game of the tour, 3–2.

October 26, Cuba. A record crowd estimated at 31,000 fans attends the inaugural game at new Estadio del Cerro (Gran Stadium) in Havana, watching Almendares defeat Cienfuegos, 9–1. At the time, this was the largest crowd ever to see a professional baseball game in Cuba.

1947

October 16, Venezuela. Don Newcombe makes a sensational winter league debut with a 4–0 complete game victory for Club Vargas against Club Venezuela at Caracas. Newcombe, who will soon enjoy a major league debut with Brooklyn in 1949 (the first black big league pitching star of that era), dominates the 1947–1948 Venezuelan League season, capturing the triple crown of pitching with league-leading figures for wins (10), ERA (2.13), and strikeouts (94).

November 30, Venezuela. Guillermo Vento, a little-known left fielder for Cervecería Caracas team, establishes a still unbroken Venezuelan League record, recording six hits (five singles and a double) in six at-bats during a 12–6 rout of Magallanes in Cervecería Stadium at Caracas.

December 26, Venezuela. Luis "Mono" Zuloaga, legendary Venezuelan pitching immortal, hurls finest single game of Venezuelan League history, a one-hit 5–0 masterpiece for Cervecería Caracas against Club Venezuela, during which he registers 10 strikeouts and permits no runner to reach second base.

1948

January 4, Venezuela. One of most bizarre moments in professional baseball history occurs during Venezuelan League game in Caracas, when Club Venezuela pitcher "Tuerto" Arrieta yields an eleventh-inning base on balls to Cervecería Caracas batter Benítez Redondo with bases filled, and yet no run scores. This unprecedented set of circumstances is set in motion when third base runner Luis Romero Petit delays in coming home on the fourth ball, seeing that batter Redondo has not started toward first. When Romero finally approaches the plate he is tagged by catcher Humberto Leál, who completes his clever decoy by shouting, "You're out!" The enraged and confused Romero then commits baseball's greatest bonehead play, grabbing the ball from the rival catcher's mitt and heaving it toward the backstop. Umpire Henry Tatler immediately rules Romero out—on perhaps the rarest interference play of all time.

June 5, Venezuela. Venezuelan League teams Gavilanes and Pastora begin an unprecedented string of five consecutive extra-innings games against each other, a record perhaps never duplicated by any other two teams anywhere in organized baseball. The final game of this rare string is won, 5–4, by Pastora in eleven innings at Maracaibo on June 26th.

July 10, Venezuela. In still another of the bizarre events found in the annals of organized baseball, Venezuelan first base umpire Robinson Pirale is arrested by police during a thirty-minute suspension of play which features an ugly rock-throwing incident between the panicked arbiter and unruly spectators. This event occurs during an emotional 5–3 victory by Pastora over Gavilanes at Maracaibo. The incarcerated umpire is eventually released by authorities later that evening, after signing an agreement to engage in no further public rock throwing.

July 25, Venezuela. Luis "El Grande" Aparicio (father of the famed major leaguer) achieves the rare feat of hitting three triples in a single game, for Gavilanes versus Pastora during Venezuelan League play. Such a feat is indeed rare (though not unprecedented) for modern-day major league play, but the Venezuelan League will see it repeated several times in subsequent years.

August 21, Cuba. Representatives of Cuba, Panama, Puerto Rico, and Venezuela meet in Havana and agree to stage a four-country round-robin twelve-game tournament to be known as the *Serie del Caribe* (Caribbean series) and to be launched in Cuba during February 1949. The series, the future highlight of winter league play, will continue uninterrupted through 1960 (later known as Phase One, or *Primera Etapa*). Reinstituted in 1970 with Series 13, Phase Two (*Segunda Etapa*) continues on down to the present. In Second Phase play, the Dominican Republic replaces Cuba and Mexico replaces Panama.

1949

February 20, Cuba. Panama (behind the pitching of major leaguer Pat Scantlebury) defeats Puerto Rico 13–9 in the first-ever game of the professional winter league championship Caribbean series. The event is staged at Gran Stadium in Havana, and the host Cubans roll over Venezuela 16–0 in the second contest of the evening. Future big leaguer and longtime amateur star Connie Marrero is the victorious pitcher for the eventual champion Cubans (represented by the pennant-winning Almendares Cuban League team).

February 25, Cuba. Agapito Mayor wins his third individual game during the first annual Caribbean series—pitching for Almendares (Cuba) against Spur Cola (Panama)—thus becoming the first and only pitcher to win three games in a Caribbean series.

February 25, Cuba. Al Gionfriddo, 1947 Brooklyn Dodgers World Series hero with his miraculous catch of Joe DiMaggio's near home run during game six, completes a three-game eight-for-fifteen batting rampage that makes him the first Caribbean series batting champion, sporting a .533 average. Gionfriddo plays for Almendares (Cuba) in the first *Serie del Caribe*, staged in Havana's Gran Stadium.

November 17, Venezuela. Luis "Camaleón" García, third baseman for Magallanes of the Venezuelan League, begins a record 518 consecutive-game playing streak that doesn't end until October 26, 1960. This record for longevity has yet to be surpassed during winter league play.

1950

February 6, Cuba. The sixth no-hitter in the history of Cuban League baseball is pitched by Rogelio "Limonar" Martínez as he leads Marianao to victory, 3–0, over Almendares.

December 6, Venezuela. Cuban catcher Carlos Colás provides one of the greatest single-game batting displays ever witnessed in winter league play. Colás registers five hits in five at-bats for Club Venezuela during 10–9 loss to Venezuelan League rival Vargas. In this game, Colás also performs the rare feat of three triples in a single contest.

1951

January 14, Venezuela. Incomparable Venezuelan pitching star José de la Trinidad "Carrao" Bracho enjoys his finest single game, a Venezuelan League 10–0 one-hitter for Cervecería Caracas against Club Venezuela. During his illustrious career, Bracho leads all Venezuelan pitchers in victories four times, compiles the most single-season wins (15 in 1961–1962), most lifetime victories (110), most games started (192), most years pitched (23), most games completed (93), and also most innings pitched (1758).

February–March, Argentina. The first Pan American Games (including baseball tournament) are staged in Buenos Aires, with Cuba dominating the baseball action. Cuba wins all but one match; the U.S. team takes up the silver medal slot, losing twice. Other participants include Mexico (bronze), Nicaragua, Venezuela, Colombia, Brazil, and Argentina.

July 10, USA. Briggs Stadium in Detroit hosts the eighteenth annual major league All-Star game, with the National Leaguers victorious, 8–3. History is made when Venezuelan shortstop Alfonso "Chico" Carrasquel, of the Chicago White Sox, becomes the first Latin American player to appear in the famed big league midsummer classic.

September 15, Dominican Republic. The opening game of the first Dominican Finals series ("*Los Grandes Finales*") played between Licey and Escogido in Santiago. Behind stellar hitting of American Alonzo Perry (.400 series average) and clutch pitching of Marion "Sugar" Caine, Licey wins the lidlifter, 8–0, and goes on to take the full series, 4–1, becoming the first champion of Dominican professional baseball. The first four years of Dominican League play are held during summer months; winter league play is introduced during the 1955–1956 campaign.

October 3, USA. Scotland-born Bobby Thomson, a New York Giants outfielder, strokes his dramatic "Shot Heard Round the World" home run to conclude highly memorable National League pennant playoff game between Giants and rival Brooklyn Dodgers; Thomson's miracle homer earns instant canonization as organized baseball's most famous base hit ever.

November 18, Venezuela. League champion Cervecería Caracas sets a winter league record that still stands today, winning the league's seventeenth consecutive game, a 4–3 triumph in Caracas against Vargas. This incredible streak actually consisted of eighteen straight games without a loss, one contest having ended in a suspended-game tie.

1952

January 31, Venezuela. What is believed to be the shortest game in winter league history transpires in Venezuelan League play at Caracas. Club Venezuela edges Cervecería Caracas, 2–1, in night-game action that lasts only one hour and thirteen minutes.

February 7, Venezuela. North American pitcher Bill Samson achieves an unwanted winter league record by walking 14 Vargas batters in six innings while pitching for Cervecería Caracas of the Venezuelan League. This negative feat also matches a big league record set by Henry Mathewson (Christy Mathewson's little-known brother) in 1906 with the New York Giants—but Mathewson needed nine full innings for his display of equal wildness.

February 14, Venezuela. The longest game in winter league history is played in Venezuela when Magallanes and Cervecería Caracas battle to a 3–3 eighteen-inning tie in a game that lasts three hours and ten minutes. Two other notable feats also occur during this game: American Johnny Hetki pitches all eighteen innings for Magallanes, and teammate Jesús "Chucho" Ramos handles a record twenty-one putouts at first base without a single miscue.

February 21, Panama. Tommy Fine, a North American right-hander with only four major league decisions for the Boston Red Sox and St. Louis Browns, achieves immortality by pitching the only no-hit, no-run game in the long history of the Caribbean series. Fine hurls for Club Habana (Cuba) against Cervecería Caracas (Venezuela), striking out three and walking three in the 1–0 victory, which occurs during the fourth *Serie del Caribe* (Series IV) at Panama City.

September 2, USA. Mike Fornieles, Cuban-born right-hander toiling with the Washington Senators, makes a sensational major league debut by becoming the first Latin-born pitcher and only the second American Leaguer to toss a one-hitter in his first big league outing. The American League pitcher preceding Fornieles with this same feat was Addie Joss (Cleveland in 1902), and the achievement has been duplicated only once since, by William Rohr (Boston in 1967). The only National League hurlers to duplicate Fornieles' rare debut were also Latin American pitchers, Juan Marichal (with San Francisco in 1960) and Silvio Martínez (with St. Louis in 1978).

October 19, Venezuela. North American John Mackinson makes his Venezuelan League debut one of the most spectacular in pro baseball history, pitching ten and two thirds innings of no-hit, no-run ball before allowing three singles in the twelfth and thirteenth innings. Mackinson's Magallanes team defeats Caracas 10–1, with nine runs scored in the top of the thirteenth.

October 21, Venezuela. Pedro "Pajita" Rodríguez of Vargas makes Venezuelan League history by stealing three bases in a single inning against Club Caracas at Ciudad Universitaria Stadium.

October 23, Venezuela. Henry Schenz, a veteran of six years of major league play with the Cubs and the Pirates, begins a batting onslaught that will eclipse the Venezuelan League hitting-streak record held by fellow American Sammy Hairston. Playing for Club Venezuela, Schenz launches his own streak on October 23rd against Caracas with two hits, and the hitting string continues through December 19th, reaching a total of twenty-seven consecutive games.

1953

January 8, Venezuela. American Negro leaguer Quincy Trouppe, star catcher for Magallanes of the Venezuelan League, records the improbable feat of six bases on balls in six at-bats during a game against Caracas in Ciudad Universitaria Stadium. Trouppe thus scores three runs without a single official plate appearance.

October 14, Venezuela. Club Magallanes establishes a winter league record with six home runs in a single contest against Pastora at Olympic Stadium at Maracaibo. Major leaguers Foster Castleman and Billy Gardner record two of the round-trippers during the 8–3 Magallanes victory.

November 18, Venezuela. Future Hall of Famer Luis Aparicio (Junior) makes his Venezuelan pro baseball debut for Gavilanes versus Pastora at Olympic Stadium in his hometown of Maracaibo. The following night, the promising 19-year-old short-stop records his first winter league base hit, earned against big league hurler Ralph Beard.

1954

May 5, Mexico. Leon Edrick Kellman, playing for Laredo against Mexico City, becomes the first batter in Mexican League history to connect for two grand slams in a single game, a record that will later be tied by Arnoldo Castro of the Mexico City Tigers on June 18, 1967.

June 26, Belgium. Italy defeats Belgium, 6–1, and Spain blasts Germany, 10–4, in opening day action of the first-ever European Amateur Baseball Championships. These games are held in Antwerp (Belgium), and Italy walks off with the gold medal by also besting Spain on the second day of competition. The first Asian championships are held later this same year in Manila, and the host Philippines team is victorious over Japan, Korea, and Chinese Taipei.

September 30, USA. Roberto "Beto" Ávila, second baseman for the Cleveland Indians, becomes the first Mexican and the first Latin-born player to win a major league batting championship, leading the American League with his .341 mark. This was Ávila's only season to bat above .304, and he finishes his 11-year major league career with a lifetime .281 average.

September 30, USA. Cuban Sandy Consuegra of the Chicago White Sox becomes the second Latin American pitcher to lead his league in winning percentage, completing the year with a sparkling 16–3 mark (.842). Fellow Cuban Dolf Luque, 27–8 with the Cincinnati Reds in 1923, was the first "south of the border" pitcher to gain such a memorable distinction.

October 1, USA. Puerto Rico's Rubén Gómez becomes the second Latin American pitcher to win a World Series contest, gaining a 6–2 victory over the American League Indians in game three at Cleveland's Municipal Stadium. Four seasons later, Gómez will also become the first pitcher to win a West Coast game, when baseball expansion by the Los Angeles Dodgers and San Francisco Giants brought a first summer of coast-to-coast play to the majors.

1955

February 11, Venezuela. Perhaps the most emotional and memorable game in Caribbean series history is played in University Stadium at Caracas. Emilio Cueche, legendary Venezuelan pitcher, throws a brilliant two-hitter for Magallanes (Venezuela) yet loses, 1–0, to Club Almendares (Cuba). A near-riot in the grandstand, in dispute of a close call on the basepaths, delays this game for more than forty-five minutes as spectators throw objects onto the field. Major leaguers Vern Rapp, Román Mejías, Rocky Nelson, Gus Triandos, and Willie Miranda are featured in the Cuban starting lineup during this famous game.

February 12, Venezuela. In a second consecutive memorable night of Caribbean series play in Venezuela, Willie Mays and Roberto Clemente belt crucial home runs to lead Santurce (Puerto Rico) to a 4–2 win over Magallanes (Venezuela) in eleven innings, the second heartbreaking loss for the host Venezuelans in as many nights. Mays's eleventh-inning homer is still celebrated as the most dramatic circuit blast in Venezuelan baseball history.

October 4, USA. Brooklyn defeats the New York Yankees, 2–0, in game seven to capture the Dodgers' first-ever World Championship. Cuban journeyman outfielder Sandy Amoros is the ultimate Brooklyn hero, with his miraculous left field catch of Yogi Berra's line drive—a brilliant one-handed grab at the fence—and toss to Pee Wee Reese at short (relayed to Gil Hodges at first) for a game-saving 7–6–3 double play.

October 30, Venezuela. American Ron Mrozinski completes the most sensational winter league pitching debut on record, hurling a third consecutive shutout in Venezuelan League play for Club Valencia. Mrozinski establishes a string of twenty-seven consecutive shutout innings with victories on October 14th (against Caracas), 22nd (versus Magallanes), and 30th (over Pampero).

December 8, Venezuela. Hurling for Club Caracas, journeyman American Leonard Yochim pitches the first no-hit, no-run game in the history of the nine-year-old Venezuelan League, defeating Magallanes, 3–0, at Caracas.

December 15, Venezuela. Stanley Jok, playing for Caracas against Pampero, achieves winter league immortality by becoming the first player in Venezuelan League history to sock three home runs in a single game. Jok earlier appeared in only 12 major league games with the Philadelphia Phillies and Chicago White Sox.

Japan. Despite suffering an embarrassing 7–21 win–loss mark in his final campaign, Japanese league pitching legend Victor Starffin wins game number 300 while laboring for the last-place Tombo Unions in the Japanese Pacific League. Russian-born Starffin, the first Japanese 300-game winner, completes his brilliant 19-year career with a lifetime 303–175 ledger.

1956

January 8, Venezuela. Stanley Jok's single-game Venezuelan record of three home runs is shattered by Russell Rac, who hits four round-trippers for Pastora against Cabimas. At the time, Rac was only the eighth player in professional baseball history to achieve this rare feat of four homers during a single game.

January 16, Venezuela. Clarence "Buddy" Hicks, shortstop for Pampero of the Venezuelan League, socks three triples in a single game, thus joining Luis Aparicio (July 25, 1948) and Carlos Colás (December 1950).

January 28, Dominican Republic. Playoff finals open between Aguilas and Escogido in the first postseason tournament of new Dominican Winter League, which had begun play in October 1955 on the heels of four Dominican summer seasons. Escogido, with three pitching victories by American import Jim Hughes, will eventually capture the tense series with a 9–4 victory (earned by Hughes) in the seventh and deciding contest.

July 17, USA. One of baseball's most memorable bean-ball incidents (second in infamy perhaps only to the Marichal–Roseboro incident of 1965) occurs in Milwaukee, when Puerto Rican pitcher Rubén Gómez of the New York Giants unfortunately reinforces stereotypes about hot-blooded Latin players. Having hit Braves slugger Joe Adcock on the wrist with an errant fastball, Gómez fires the ball at Adcock a second time as the angry Milwaukee batsman charges the mound. A panic-stricken Gómez flees to the Giants dugout, with the enraged Adcock in hot pursuit. Gómez races straight to the Giants club-house, where he obtains a lethal ice-pick and attempts to return onto the field for further battle with the willing Adcock. Gómez is finally restrained by Giants teammates and ejected from the contest.

October, USA. Venezuelan Luis Aparicio, having replaced countryman "Chico" Carrasquel as Chicago White Sox shortstop and champion base-stealer, becomes the first Latin American player to claim Rookie of the Year honors when he receives the American League trophy. Aparicio will eventually be inducted into the Hall of Fame at Cooperstown in 1984.

1958

April 15, USA. A historic opening game for major league baseball on the West Coast has a decidedly Latin American flavor. The San Francisco Giants defeat the Los Angeles Dodgers, 8–0, before 23,449 in Seals Stadium, with veteran Puerto Rican hurler Rubén Gómez pitching the six-hit shutout for the Giants and rookie Puerto Rican slugger Orlando Cepeda leading the attack with his first major league homer. The first big league pitcher to record a West Coast victory is thus a Latin American, but Cepeda comes in second in the Latino home run department, his own four-bagger following Daryl Spencer's earlier historic blast for the Giants.

August 14, USA. Flamboyant Puerto Rican infielder Vic Power (Victor Pellot) scores the winning run with a steal of home in the tenth inning as the Indians defeat Detroit, 10–9, in Cleveland. Power had also stolen home in the eighth inning, thus becoming only the ninth player in major league history—the first since 1927—to steal home twice in a single game. Power was also the first Latin-born player to accomplish this exotic base-running feat.

November 10, USA. San Francisco Giants slugger Orlando Cepeda is named National League Rookie of the Year, after leading senior circuit in doubles with thirty-eight and blasting out twenty-five round-trippers. The Puerto Rican first baseman thus becomes the first Latin American to capture this distinction as a National Leaguer.

1959

July 25, Cuba. Fidel Castro supporters, enjoying a raucous celebration at Gran Stadium in downtown Havana, bring to a halt the International League contest between Rochester Red Wings and Cuban Sugar Kings with numerous random gunshots fired from the grandstand and surrounding streets. Rochester third base coach Frank Verdi and Sugar Kings shortstop Leo Cárdenas are both grazed but not injured during this infamous incident, which causes Red Wings manager Cot Deal to pull his team from the field and retreat to the team's nearby hotel. International League officials promptly cancel the remainder of the Havana team's current home stand. This little-reported event marks the beginning of the end for Cuba's long-standing participation in professional organized baseball.

1960

June, Cuba and USA. The International League suddenly pulls the plug on the Havana-based Cuban Sugar Kings franchise, relocating the team overnight to Jersey City, NJ. Some Cuban players return home while others remain in the United States to pursue professional careers. This event marks the official closing of the Cuban borders to organized baseball.

July 19, USA. "Dominican Dandy" Juan Marichal, arguably the greatest Latin American hurler in major league history, enjoys an incredible big league debut, becoming only the second Latin pitcher and the first National Leaguer ever to toss a one-hitter in his initial game. Defeating the Philadelphia Phillies, 2–0, at Candlestick Park, Marichal retires the first nineteen batters, strikes out twelve, and finally gives up a pinch-hit two-out single to Clay Dalrymple in the seventh. Latin pitcher Mike Fornieles of the Washington Senators preceded Marichal (September 2, 1952) and Silvio Martínez of the St. Louis Cardinals followed (May 30, 1978) in duplicating this feat.

1961

January 6, Venezuela. In one of the most legendary pitching performances of winter league play, American Gary Peters (a big leaguer with Chicago White Sox) of Rapinos and Julián Ladera of Valencia duel for seventeen innings in a Venezuelan League game at Maracaibo, with Peters emerging as the victor by a score of 2–1.

February, Cuba. The last season of Cuban League play winds down to close the ledger on Cuban professional baseball. Cienfuegos wins the final Cuban winter league pennant in a campaign during which only native Cuban players participated.

September 25, USA. Puerto Rican first sacker Orlando Cepeda has four RBI in a 10–2 Giants rout of Philadelphia, raising his season's total to 140 and establishing himself as the greatest slugging Latin American major leaguer up to that time. Cepeda's 142 RBI lead the National League (and break the Giants club record for first basemen of 138, set by Hall of Famer Johnny Mize in 1947), as do his 46 round-trippers. Cepeda thus becomes both the first Latin American to lead his league in RBI totals and also the first Latin home run champion.

September 30, USA. Roberto Clemente of the Pittsburgh Pirates closes the season with a .351 batting average, thus becoming the first Latin American player to win the senior circuit batting title.

1962

January, Cuba. The Cuban League is revived as a four-team amateur circuit after professional sports are banned in Cuba. The league will slowly expand in size over the next two decades, with a true national league finally emerging during the 1980s and containing teams representing all Cuban provinces.

January 25, Venezuela. Venezuelan immortal José de la Trinidad "Carrao" Bracho establishes a still-standing Venezuelan League record for single-season victories at 15, with a 7–1 victory for Club Oriente over Pampero. In his previous start, four nights earlier, Bracho barely missed what would have been his only career no-hitter, allowing only two tame ninth-inning singles.

July 10, USA. Dominican Juan Marichal becomes the first Latin American pitcher to win a major league All-Star game, emerging as victor in the 3–1 National League win during the first of two 1962 classics, this one held in Washington's District of Columbia Stadium. Ironically, the game's loser is Senators Cuban ace Camilo Pascual. The 1962 Washington All-Star game thus sees Latin American firsts on both sides of the All-Star victory ledger.

August 13, USA. Cuban Bert Campaneris pitches two relief innings for Daytona of the Florida State League against Fort Lauderdale, throwing as both a right-hander and left-hander and allowing only one run while striking out four batters during this unusual stunt. (See also September 8, 1965; September 22, 1968.)

1962–1963

Venezuela. Victor Davalillo becomes the first hitter to bat .400 for the complete Venezuelan Winter League season. Davalillo accomplishes his feat playing for the Caracas Lions.

1963

May 19, Mexico. Scoring in every inning, the Monterrey Sultanes equal their own Mexican League record with a 21–0 conquest of Reynosa; their first such lopsided victory had been against Puebla, on May 6, 1945.

June 15, USA. Juan Marichal becomes the first Latin American hurler to toss a major league no-hitter, with his brilliant 1–0 victory at San Francisco over the Houston Colt 45s. This season, perhaps Marichal's finest, sees the Dominican Dandy record 25 victories, strike out 248 batters while walking only 61, and lead the majors with 321 innings pitched, overall the best single-season pitching performance ever recorded by a Latin American big leaguer.

September 3, USA. Dominican Juan Marichal defeats the Chicago Cubs, 16–3, to become the first Latin American pitcher to win twenty games in a major league season since Dolf Luque (the only previous Latin American 20-game-winner, with 27 victories for Cincinnati in 1923).

September 10, USA. For the first time ever in major league history, three brothers appear in same starting lineup. In a game at New York's Polo Grounds, won by the Giants over the Mets, 4–2, San Francisco features an improbable outfield of three brothers, Dominicans Jesús, Matty, and Felipe Alou. This Giants tandem does not last long, however, as Felipe departs to the Milwaukee Braves in time for the 1964 season opener.

November 18, Venezuela. American Mel Nelson, laboring for Orientales against Caracas, pitches the second no-hitter in Venezuelan League history. Nelson won only four games during an undistinguished major league career spanning parts of six seasons.

1964

January 6, Venezuela. José de la Trinidad "Carrao" Bracho becomes the first pitcher in Venezuelan League history to record a hundred career victories. Bracho achieves the feat with a 5–0 three-hit shutout for Orientales versus La Guaira in Caracas.

May 2, USA. Cuban rookie sensation Tony Oliva of the Minnesota Twins blasts the first of a big league record-tying four consecutive Twins homers in the eleventh inning, pacing the team's 7–4 victory at Kansas City. Following Oliva with round-trippers were Bob Allison, Jimmie Hall, and Harmon Killebrew, the quartet equaling a feat earlier performed by the Milwaukee Braves in 1961 and by Cleveland in 1963. (This is Oliva's first full campaign in the big leagues, and he will lead the junior circuit in hitting. See entry for October.)

May 3, Mexico. Monterrey batter Saul Villegas slugs his second grand slam in as many days against Pericos in Puebla, in the process becoming the first and only player in Mexican League history to accomplish such a feat.

May 10, Mexico. Monterrey's Héctor Espino makes Mexican League history by belting four home runs (two in each game) and producing 10 RBI as the Sultanes post double-header victories over Poza Rica, 5–4 and 8–5. Espino also homers twice more in his next two outings, achieving an incredible six circuit blasts in a brief span of three days.

May 20, Mexico. Cuban-born pitcher José Ramón López of Monterrey records sixteen strikeouts, nine in succession, in a 5–2 victory over the Diablos Rojos team, thus tying a short-lived Mexican League record set in 1959 by Dominican Diómedes "Guayubín" Olivo with Poza Rica.

July 7, USA. San Francisco Giants Dominican ace Juan Marichal is the pitcher of record in the National League's 7–4 All-Star game victory at New York's Shea Stadium, thus becoming the first and only Latin American pitcher to record two All-Star game victories.

July 23, USA. Cuban rookie Bert Campaneris of Kansas City Athletics becomes the second man in baseball history to hit two homers in his inaugural big league appearance, the first round-tripper coming on the initial pitch served by Twins hurler Jim Kaat. Bob Nieman of the St. Louis Browns earlier homered in his first two big league at-bats in 1951; Campaneris accomplishes this feat with his first and fourth trips to the plate.

September 1, USA. Masanori Murakami becomes the first Japanese big leaguer by debuting with San Francisco Giants. Murakami originally pitched for the Nankai Hawks of the Japanese Pacific League. When that club protested his big league contract after his 1964 brief debut with the Giants, an agreement was reached with Major League Baseball to allow the Japanese star to appear once more in National League during 1965, before returning permanently to Japanese League action. Overall, southpaw Murakami pitched in 54 games with San Francisco, posting a solid 5–1 record and an impressive 3.43 ERA.

October, USA. Minnesota Twins Cuban slugger Tony Oliva becomes the first black ballplayer to garner both a batting title and Rookie of the Year honors in the same season. By pacing the American League with a sparkling .323 average, the Cuban stand-out becomes only the third Latino to win a major league batting championship—and the first American League rookie ever to gain the batting title.

October, Japan. Yomiuri Giants slugger Sadaharu Oh establishes a new Japanese League home run mark by slugging 55 round-trippers during 140-game Central League season. Oh's performance surpasses the record 52 homers slugged by Katsuya Nomura of Nankai Hawks in Pacific League one season earlier.

1965

January 25, Venezuela. Eventual all-time major league base hits leader Pete Rose (Cincinnati Reds) enjoys his greatest day in winter league play, going five for six for Caracas against Magallanes (Venezuelan League), with five runs scored, one home run, two doubles, and four RBI.

August 22, USA. In what is referred to as "Bloody Sunday at Candlestick" and will live among baseball's most infamous incidents, temperamental San Francisco Giants pitcher Juan Marichal strikes the helpless Dodgers catcher John Roseboro on the head with his bat, in a violent dispute over a Sandy Koufax pitch that Marichal thought was aimed at his own head. The ensuing ugly brawl takes fourteen minutes to calm and results in a nine-day suspension and then-huge $1,750 fine for the flamboyant Dominican pitcher. This display of outrageously poor sportsmanship was later believed to have considerably delayed Marichal's eventual election into the Hall of Fame (see July 31, 1983).

September 8, USA. Infielder Bert Campaneris of the Kansas City Athletics becomes the first player in major league history to field all nine positions in a single contest. The versatile Cuban plays one position per inning against the Los Angeles Angels, recording a single error (in right field), allowing one run and two hits while on the mound, and catching the final inning, during which he is injured in a home plate collision with Ed Kirkpatrick and forced to leave the game. Campaneris will later also be the first batter to face Venezuelan utility man César Tóvar when he duplicates this amazing display of versatility (see September 22, 1968).

October, USA. Cuban infielder Zoilo Versalles of the American League champion Minnesota Twins blazes new trails when he becomes the first Latin American ball player ever to earn league Most Valuable Player honors.

November 3, Venezuela. Kansas City A's right-hander Lew Krausse enjoys one of the finest pitching performances in winter league history, throwing a one-hitter for Caracas against Lara and establishing three still unsurpassed standards: most strikeouts in a nine-inning game (21), most consecutive strikeouts (10), and most strikeouts in two consecutive games (33).

1966

January 16 and 25, Cuba. One of the most overlooked performances in international baseball history occurs in Cuban League National Series when diminutive right-hander Aquino Abreu (Centrales) hurls back-to-back no-hit games (beating Occidentales 11–0 and Industriales 7–0), thus matching Johnny Vander Meer's more recognized big league feat. These are also the first two no-hit, no-run games ever pitched in the postrevolution amateur Cuban League, then in its fifth season.

January 21, Venezuela. Dominican slugger and 1970 National League batting champion Rico Carty sets a single-season Venezuelan League home run record of 13 dingers in thirty-two games. Playing for Aragua, Carty blasts two homers against Magallanes on January 12th and two more against La Guaira on the 21st to obtain his record.

August 13, Mexico. Cuban-born Mexican League strikeout king José Ramón López establishes an all-time standard of 309 strikeouts for a single season, reaching 309 while hurling for Monterrey versus Reynosa. Striking out a dozen batters, López still loses the contest, 2–0.

October 25, Venezuela. Luis "Camaleón" García, third baseman playing for Magallanes, becomes the first player in Venezuela League history to achieve the plateau of 1,000 career base hits. Stroking two singles against Cardenales, García reaches his 1,000-hit total in only 864 games and 3,304 official at-bats.

1967

January 22, Venezuela. Eugene Brabender, a pitcher for the Baltimore Orioles, achieves a rare distinction in winter league play. Hurling for La Guaira against Caracas, Brabender wins both ends of a doubleheader, thus achieving two victories on a single day. Brabender's first-game victory comes in a starting role against big league rival Luis Tiant; his second is earned in three innings of relief.

May 26, USA. Juan Marichal defeats the Los Angeles Dodgers, 4–1, in Candlestick Park, upping his career record against Los Angeles to 14–0 at Candlestick and also surpassing Whitey Ford's major league record career winning percentage of .690 for pitchers with over 100 victories. Marichal, whose record was 138–61 (.693) at the time, will hover under but close to this standard but finally will finish his career in 1975 at 243–142 (.631), considerably below Ford's still-standing mark.

July 11, USA. Cincinnati Reds Cuban third baseman Tony Pérez hits a dramatic fifteenth-inning home run off Jim "Catfish" Hunter to give the National Leaguers a 2–1 victory in the midsummer classic at Anaheim. The hitting heroics of the Cuban slugger not only ended the longest contest in All-Star game history but also capped one of the odder games of the long series: third basemen accounted for all three runs in this contest, with Dick Allen of the Phillies and Brooks Robinson of the Orioles also homering for the game's only other tallies.

October 4, USA. Puerto Rican hurler José Santiago of the Boston Red Sox becomes the only pitcher in major league World Series history to lose a game (2–1 to St. Louis Cardinals) in which he also hit a home run. Santiago homered off St. Louis ace Bob Gibson in his first World Series at-bat.

1968

September 20, USA. Dominican Juan Marichal records his 26th victory (with 8 defeats) in a 9–1 San Francisco win over Atlanta, thus recording the most single-season victories in Giants history since Carl Hubbell's 26 in 1936 and Christy Mathewson's 27 in 1910. This is also the second most victories in a single campaign recorded by a Latin American major league hurler, surpassed only by Dolf Luque's 27 victories for Cincinnati in 1923.

September 22, USA. Venezuelan utility player César "Pepe" Tóvar of the Minnesota Twins writes his name forever in the baseball trivia books by becoming the second man to play all nine positions in a single game during a 2–1 victory over the Oakland A's.

Tóvar starts with a one-inning stint on the mound, striking out Reggie Jackson, and then rotates through the other positions, one per inning. The only other player ever to attempt this feat is also a Latin American, Kansas City's Bert Campaneris (see September 8, 1965); oddly enough, Campaneris is the first Oakland batter to face Tóvar during his one-inning mound stint.

October 14, Canada. Dominican outfielder Manny Mota is selected by the Montreal Expos (off the roster of the Pittsburgh Pirates) as the first player taken in the 1968 National League expansion draft. Mota thus becomes the first official player on the roster of a Canadian major league team: the first non-U.S.-based team selects as its first player a non-U.S.-born athlete.

October 24, Venezuela. Howie Reed, journeyman pitcher with four major league clubs, hurls the third no-hitter in Venezuelan League history, a 5–0 masterpiece for Caracas against Magallanes. Reed faces only one batter over the minimum, allowing but a single base on balls.

1969

April 8, Canada. Canada's expansion Montreal Expos win their first National League opener, besting the eventual league champion New York Mets on the road at Shea Stadium. Bob Shaw is the winning pitcher in the 11–10 inaugural slugfest, and Jim "Mudcat" Grant makes history as the first Montreal pitcher to take the mound.

April 8, USA. Dominican outfielder Jesús Alou, member of the Houston Astros, is the first hitter in the grand opening of San Diego's Jack Murphy Stadium, completing the Alou family's one-per-brother string of stadium-opening leadoff appearances. Matty, with the Pittsburgh Pirates, had been the first batter to the plate on April 12, 1966, in the inaugural game at Fulton County Stadium in Atlanta. Felipe, of the Atlanta Braves, performed the same honor a month later for the opening in St. Louis of Busch Memorial Stadium, on May 12, 1966.

April 14, Canada. The first National league game on Canadian soil, at Jarry Park in Montreal, sees the Expos defeat the St. Louis Cardinals, 8–7, with Dan McGinn earning credit for the pitching victory. A capacity crowd of 29,184 witnesses the historic, chilly event.

April 27, Mexico. Monterrey slugger Héctor Espino enjoys the rare experience of receiving four consecutive intentional walks during a Mexican League game against Mexico City. Over the previous two days, Espino had connected for four home runs in six trips to the plate. In the second game of this memorable doubleheader, Espino homers for hit number 1,000 of his illustrious Mexican League career.

May 19, Mexico. Incomparable Mexican League slugging star Héctor Espino of Monterrey belts two homers against Aguila, his seventh and eighth over a period of six consecutive games. This establishes a new Mexican League record, surpassing the mark of six homers in six games set by Cuban Witty Quintana during the 1961 league campaign.

June 16, USA. Panamanian native Rod Carew of the Minnesota Twins ties an American League season record with six successful steals of home, a mark held jointly by Ty Cobb and Bobby "Braggo" Roth and untouched for fifty-two seasons. Carew's landmark steal occurs in Minnesota and comes against right-hander Tom Murphy of the California Angels.

July 16, USA. In the first game of a doubleheader in Bloomington, MN, versus the Chicago White Sox, Panamanian-born Rod Carew establishes major league record with his seventh steal of home, eclipsing the single-season American League mark held by Ty Cobb and Bobby Roth and tying a major league standard set in 1946 by Pete Reiser. The record steal comes off Sox rookie right-hander Jerry Nyman, occurs in the 74th game of Carew's third major league season, and completes a string of home-base steals begun on April 9th in Kansas City. Carew's string of seven steals came on only

seven attempts, and an injury that sidelined him for over a month late in the season may well have kept Carew from ultimately breaking Pete Reiser's still-standing mark.
October 2, USA. Puerto Rican relief pitcher Miguel Fuentes closes his brief one-year major league career by pitching the final inning of the final game for the Seattle Pilots (versus the Oakland A's), thus bringing to conclusion the shortest franchise history in modern major league play.
October 2, USA. Rod Carew of the Minnesota Twins wins an American League batting title with his .332 average, earning the first of seven batting championships over the next ten seasons. Although incidentally born in the U.S. territory of the Panama Canal Zone, Carew is widely recognized over the next decade as the greatest Latin American hitter ever to perform in the big leagues.
November 11, Venezuela. Completing a streak which began back on October 13th, La Guaira hurler Mike Hedlund establishes the Venezuelan League record with 38 consecutive scoreless innings pitched. Hedlund's unprecedented streak extends over five games and now comes to a sudden end in a game against Caracas, a heartbreaker in which Hedlund is rudely knocked out of the box with a three-run ninth-inning rally by the home team.
November 11, USA. Cuba's Mike Cuéllar is the first Latin American winner of the coveted Cy Young Award, leading a powerhouse Baltimore Orioles staff (2.83 team ERA, plus 20 staff shutouts) with an outstanding 23–11 record and 2.38 ERA.

1970
June 21, USA. Diminutive 5'8", 150-pound Venezuelan infielder César Gutiérrez, playing for the Tigers at Cleveland's Municipal Stadium, goes seven for seven at the plate, the first major leaguer to do so since before the modern era (Wilbert Robinson, a catcher with the Baltimore Orioles, did it in 1892). Gutiérrez's heroics occur in the twelve-inning second game of a Sunday doubleheader, when the sparsely used utility player records six singles and a double. The feat boosts his batting average by 38 points, to .249, and earns him a starting shortstop position for the remainder of the season. (Another Latin player will become the first to go seven for seven in a nine-inning game; see September 16, 1975.)
August 22–23, USA. Pittsburgh Pirates Hall of Fame outfielder (and perhaps the greatest right fielder in baseball history) Roberto Clemente enjoys the finest two-day performance by any modern-era player while rapping out ten base hits in two consecutive games versus the Los Angeles Dodgers. Clemente's onslaught, at age 36, is all the more re-markable for the fact that his August 22nd five-hit day occurs in a marathon 15-inning 2–1 Pirate triumph which does not end until an hour after midnight. Although he might have rested on the bench the following day, an injury to Willie Stargell keeps Clemente's bat in the lineup, and Roberto responds with another five-hit outing, climaxed by an eighth-inning homer off Dodger rookie Charlie Hough in an 11–0 Pittsburgh victory.
August 28, USA. Juan Marichal, battling back from a slow start in the 1970 season due to negative reactions to penicillin injections, defeats the Pirates, 5–1, for his 200th career victory, thus becoming the first post–World War II pitcher to reach the 200-victory plateau in as little as 11 seasons. Marichal also becomes the first-ever Latin American 200-game winner.
October 1, USA. Dominican slugger Rico Carty of the Atlanta Braves wins National League batting race with an outstanding .366 average, a feat all the more remarkable considering that Carty missed the entire 1968 season due to a life-threatening battle with tuberculosis.

1971
April 8, Mexico. Three pitchers for Mexico City's Tigers—Enrique Icedo, José Lyva, and Nicolas García—combine for first multiple-pitcher no-hit, no-run game in Mexican

League history. This feat is accomplished during a 3–0 seven-inning victory over Mexico City.

May 19, Mexico. Martín Dihigo, Cuba's greatest baseball legend, dies in Cienfuegos from cerebral thrombosis. Six years later, the Negro league great will be elected to Cooperstown by the Veterans Committee, as Cuba's first U.S. Hall of Famer (see August 8, 1977).

1972

September 30, USA. Roberto Clemente culminates the 1972 season with his 3,000th hit, making him the eleventh man (and only the third active player, along with Hank Aaron and Willie Mays) to reach this exalted level of hitting performance. Clemente's milestone base hit is a double to center field off New York Mets southpaw Jon Matlack during a 5–0 Pirate victory at Three Rivers Stadium. It will prove also to be his final career hit. Clemente will die in an off-season plane crash only three months later (see December 31, 1972).

November 4, Venezuela. Antonio "Tony" Armas, a Venezuelan-born slugger who will later become the second Latin player (1981) to lead the American League in homers, hits his first winter league round-tripper. Armas connects against big league hurler Ken Forsch, while playing for Caracas against La Guaira.

November 22, Venezuela. Dámaso Blanco, shortstop for Magallanes of the Venezuelan League, achieves a rare distinction in winter league play by performing an unassisted triple play, the first in the history of Venezuelan professional baseball.

December 31, Puerto Rico. Roberto Clemente, perhaps the greatest Latin American player ever to appear in the major leagues, is tragically killed at age 38 in his native Puerto Rico. An overloaded cargo plane carrying Clemente, tons of supplies, and two other volunteers on a mercy mission to aid thousands left homeless by a devastating earthquake in Nicaragua, goes down off the coast of San Juan, killing all three passengers. Puerto Rico declares three days of national mourning.

1973

January 6, Venezuela. Urbano Lugo, pitching for Caracas against La Guaira, becomes the first native Venezuelan to pitch a no-hit, no-run game in Venezuelan League play, the fourth such game in the brief history of the second youngest winter circuit. Lugo gives up only one walk and allows but one outfield fly ball during his 6–0 masterpiece.

August 6, USA. Roberto Clemente, in the wake of his tragic premature death the previous December, is voted into Cooperstown Hall of Fame with special dispensation, waiving the normal five-year waiting period. Clemente is thus the first Latin American player to achieve permanent enshrinement at Cooperstown.

September, Italy. The first Intercontinental Cup baseball championship staged at Parma and Rimini, in northern Italy, between teams representing Japan (gold medal), Puerto Rico (silver), the United States (bronze), Nicaragua, Canada, Italy, Chinese Taipei, and Argentina. With Cuba not entered, Japan (6–1 W–L) trips Canada, 1–0, in its final outing to claim a first title in the FEMBA event (Federación Mundial de Béisbol Amateur; World Federation of Amateur Baseball), originally planned for alternate years.

November 27, Venezuela. Teolindo Acosta, nicknamed "Inventor del Hit" and one of Venezuela's top batting stars, becomes the second player to post 1,000 career base hits in Venezuelan League play. Acosta, outfielder for Aragua, gains the distinction over 18 seasons and in 3,254 career at-bats.

1974

June 1, Japan and USA. The *New York Times* reports Sadaharu Oh's 600th career homer in Japan. The left-handed first baseman will eventually slug 154 more homers than Babe Ruth and 113 more than Aaron, while playing 467 fewer games than Hammerin' Hank.

This notice in the U.S. press first calls Sadaharu Oh to the attention of American fans, who previously knew almost nothing of players in Japanese professional baseball.
December 5, Venezuela. Victor Davalillo, a Caracas first baseman who also played 17 seasons in the major leagues, becomes the third player in Venezuelan League history to record 1,000 base hits, achieving this cherished plateau over seventeen seasons, 792 games, and 2,906 at-bats.

1975

September 16, USA. With four singles, two doubles, and a triple in seven at-bats, Panamanian infielder Rennie Stennett of the Pittsburgh Pirates becomes the first and only player in major league history to collect seven hits in a nine-inning game. The Pirates 22–0 rout of the Chicago Cubs is also the most lopsided shutout in big league history. Stennett then collects three hits the following night, to become only player ever to register ten hits in two consecutive nine-inning games. Stennett's feat is further highlighted by the tying of a third major league record, his recording of two hits in each of two separate innings within the same game.

1976

January 4, Mexico. Executives of the International Amateur Baseball Association (IABA) meet in Mexico City to end a long-standing feud among delegations, creating in the process a new organization named the *Asociación Internacional de Béisbol Amateur* (AINBA). With the United States returning to the IABA fold for these meetings (after an absence of several years), the first AINBA World Championships is announced for Cartagena, Colombia, and Cuban delegate Manuel González Guerra is named as the first AINBA President.
July 28, USA. Mexican journeyman pitcher Francisco Barrios of Chicago White Sox combines with American Johnny Lee "Blue Moon" Odom to become the first Latin American pitcher to hurl part of a multipitcher no-hitter in the major leagues. The rare feat is accomplished during a 2–1 victory over the Oakland Athletics.
September 12, USA. Orestes "Minnie" Miñoso becomes the oldest player to record a base hit in major league play, singling off Sid Monge in the first game of a doubleheader against the California Angels. Seeing limited duty as the designated hitter, this is the Cuban star's only hit during eight 1976 plate appearances. Miñoso is nine months past his 53rd birthday at the time, thus eclipsing a mark set in 1929 by pitcher and outfielder Nick Altrock, who collected his final base hit for the Washington Senators only days after turning 53.
November 13, Venezuela. César Tóvar, Minnesota Twins infielder and outfielder playing with Aragua, becomes the fourth man in Venezuelan League play to achieve the 1,000-hit plateau. Tóvar reaches the milestone during his 18th season of winter league play.
November 26, Venezuela. Adrian Garrett, an eight-year major leaguer, hits safely in his 28th consecutive game with Caracas, breaking the long-standing Venezuelan League mark owned by Henry Schenz and established back in 1952.

1977

April 7, Canada. Arctic temperatures and intermittent snow squalls provide the ideal setting for a first American League game in Canada as the Toronto Blue Jays outlast the Chicago White Sox before 44,649 thrilled faithful at Exhibition Stadium. Rookies Doug Ault (with two) and Al Woods are Toronto Blue Jays batting heroes with crucial home runs; right-hander Jerry Johnson is the historic winning pitcher.
June 27, USA. Héctor Torres, Mexican-born outfielder with the Toronto Blue Jays, homers with the bases full against New York Yankees in Toronto's Exhibition Stadium, providing the first grand slam home run hit on Canadian soil in American League history.

August 8, USA. Black Cuban star Martín Dihigo, known as "El Inmortal" (The Immortal) and considered by most to be greatest all-around performer in Negro league history, is voted into Cooperstown by the Baseball Writers Association of America (BBWAA) Veterans Committee. Dihigo is the second Latin player (and the first Cuban) to make it into the U.S. Hall of Fame and the first player ever enshrined in three different national baseball halls of fame, those of Cuba, Mexico, and the United States. Dihigo was a top pitcher and also a standout at every position on the diamond save catcher. He was batting and home run champion several times in Negro league play, and pitched the first no-hitter in Mexican League history (see September 16, 1937).

1978
December 26, Venezuela. Designated hitter Ángel Bravo of La Guaira connects for a fifth-inning single against Club Zulia and thus becomes the fifth player in Venezuelan League history to register 1,000 hits. Bravo earlier appeared in three brief seasons of major league play with the Chicago White Sox and Cincinnati Reds, appearing also in the 1970 World Series for Cincinnati.

1979
August 14, Mexico. Leonardo Valenzuela of Monterrey establishes an unprecedented all-time Mexican League mark by connecting for his 19th triple of the season in a game against Tampico.

December, Cuba. The fourth Intercontinental Cup tournament, staged in Havana, marks Cuba's first entry in this event. The host country sweeps the competition with a perfect 10-0 record for an easy first-place finish. Cuba will quickly come to dominate this prestigious event, as it has all other world tournaments; Cubans will win eight of the next eleven Intercontinental Cup titles.

1980
January 12, Venezuela. Baudilio "Bo" Díaz, major league catcher with Philadelphia Phillies and Cincinnati Reds, becomes the first Venezuelan League slugger to register 20 home runs in a single winter campaign, breaking American Bobby Darwin's mark of 19 and earning the lasting title in Venezuela of "*Rey del Jonrón*" (Home Run King).

January 13, Venezuela. Victor Davalillo of Club Aragua establishes a new all-time single-season mark for base hits in the Venezuelan League, stroking his hundredth of the 1979–1980 campaign. On January 9th, Davalillo had surpassed the old mark of 95 set by former Cleveland Indian and Baltimore Oriole Dave Pope in 1953–1954.

October 4, USA. After nearly four seasons as first coach and later ball club public relations representative, at age 57 Cuban Orestes "Minnie" Miñoso makes a last token 0-for-1 pinch-hitting appearance for the Chicago White Sox. Miñoso thus becomes only the second player in big league history to appear in official league play during five different decades. The popular Miñoso had enjoyed four earlier stints with the White Sox (1951–1957, 1960–1961, 1964, and 1976), and this fifth-decade appearance is largely a happy promotional stunt orchestrated by White Sox owner and ultimate baseball showman Bill Veeck.

October 4, USA. Panama's Ben Oglivie posts 41 round-trippers for the Milwaukee Brewers by season's end to become the first Latin American junior circuit home run champion.

October, Japan. First baseman Sadaharu Oh, star slugger of the Yomiuri Giants in the Japanese Central League, retires from active play with a record 868 career homers, bringing to a close the 22-year career that began in 1959. Though his single-season Japanese record of 55 home runs will be tied and passed in the next century, Oh's career mark is 113 more than the lifetime major league standard set by Hank Aaron (755) and may well stand forever as an overall world record for professional baseball.

October, Japan. A second Japanese milestone is set this same season by Nankai Hawks (Japanese Pacific League) catcher Katsuya Nomura, who retires from active play with 2,918 games played as a receiver. Nomura also finishes second to Oh on the all-time home run list in Japan with 657 round-trippers over his productive 27-season career.

1981

October, Mexico. Sensational Mexican rookie hurler Fernando Valenzuela completes his dazzling first big league campaign and a summer of fever-pitch "Fernandomania" throughout Los Angeles and southern California by capturing both the Cy Young trophy and Rookie of the Year accolades in baseball's senior circuit. Valenzuela thus becomes the first Latino winner of Cy Young honors in the National League.

November 10, Venezuela. Major league hurler Eric Rasmussen throws the sixth no-hit, no-run game in Venezuelan League history, a 3–0 victory for Lara over La Guaira. Two runners reach base for La Guaira on errors by Lara shortstop Fred Manrique, himself later a defensive stalwart for the Montreal Expos and Chicago White Sox.

1982

October, Korea. Professional baseball debuts in South Korea with the opening season of the Korean Baseball Organization, a six-team circuit featuring a 70-game schedule. The October close of the season finds the OB Bears winning the first Korean League pennant with a 56–24 win–loss mark. Foreign players are not admitted into this league until the 1998 season.

1983

January 16, Venezuela. Future Houston Astros slugger Kevin Bass establishes a winter league mark in Venezuelan League play, accounting for eight RBI during a single game for Caracas against rival Lara. Bass slugs two homers and a single in five at-bats, including a culminating mammoth grand slam homer in the eighth inning.

July 31, USA. Juan Marichal becomes the first and only pitcher of Latin American birthright elected into major league baseball's Hall of Fame in Cooperstown. Marichal is actually the first Latino player elected to Cooperstown under regular voting procedures, Roberto Clemente having received an exemption to the normal five-year wait owing to his tragic death, and Negro leaguer Martín Dihigo having been selected by the Hall's Veterans Committee. The infamous "Roseboro incident" of 1965, however, stood out for many balloters as a substantial blemish on Marichal's otherwise brilliant career and likely delayed his Cooperstown enshrinement (which came only after Roseboro's public reconciliation and forgiveness).

1984

January 7, Venezuela. Future major leaguer Jeff Stone (he will be a Philadelphia Phillies rookie later in the year), playing for Zulia Eagles, pilfers three bases against Magallanes to establish a new Venezuelan single-season mark of 43 steals.

August 12, USA. Venezuelan Luis "Little Looie" Aparicio, considered by many observers as the finest defensive shortstop in the history of the game, becomes only the second Latin American player to be voted into baseball's ultimate shrine at Cooperstown via the regular BBWAA voting procedures. Aparicio enjoyed a marvelous 18-year big league career for Chicago's White Sox (twice), Baltimore, and Boston, all in the American League.

October 2, USA. Venezuelan Tony Armas becomes the second Latin to win an American League home run title outright, slugging 43 homers for the Boston Red Sox. Armas had also earlier shared the junior circuit title with Dwight Evans (Boston), Bobby Grich (California), and Eddie Murray (Baltimore) during a strike-shortened 1981 campaign, each then connecting for 22 round-trippers.

1985

May 14, Mexico. Derek Bryant of Tamaulipas becomes the first player in Mexican League history to connect for four homers in a nine-inning game. Bryant launches a memorable home run streak, having also hit a record five dingers in three consecutive games only one week earlier (May 9, 11, 12).

1987

October 3, USA. San Diego Padres catcher Benito Santiago closes out the season with a 34-game hitting streak. The string is the longest ever by a rookie, a catcher, or a Latin American player in the big leagues, and thus earns the 22-year-old Puerto Rican backstop coveted National League Rookie of the Year honors.

October 3, USA. Dominican Jorge (George) Bell wins American League Most Valuable Player honors for his hefty slugging (47 homers, 134 RBI, .308 BA), despite slumping badly in the week's final season as the Toronto Blue Jays drop their final seven games to blow a seemingly certain Eastern Division championship. Bell is the fourth Latino, but the first Dominican, to win MVP honors in the junior circuit.

October 22, Japan. Third baseman and outfielder Sachio Kinugasa of the Hiroshima Carp in the Japanese Central League ends a streak of 2,215 consecutive games played that had begun on October 19, 1970. Kinugasa thus sets a world iron-man record that will last until Cal Ripken Jr. of the Baltimore Orioles stretches his own string to 2,632 games in the big leagues during 1998.

1988

February 9, Dominican Republic. Tony Armas, California Angels slugger, homers off Jesse Orosco of Tijuana (Mexico) while playing for Caracas (Venezuela) in the 30th Caribbean series, his 11th career homer in the winter league classic. Armas becomes the only player to hit more than 10 homers in Series play, followed on the all-time list by Carmelo Martínez (with eight) and Rico Carty (with seven).

February 9, Dominican Republic. Escogido (Dominican Republic) loses 5–1 to Mayagüez (Puerto Rico) in the final game of the 30th *Serie del Caribe* (Caribbean series), staged in Santo Domingo. The final-game loss, however, does not prevent the host club from reigning as champions, because Escogido (managed by American Phil Regan) emerges in first place with a 4–2 record over the five-day, four-country round-robin tournament. Mexico and Puerto Rico tie for second (3–3) and Venezuela finishes dead last (2–4).

April 4, USA. Dominican slugger George Bell of the Toronto Blue Jays becomes the first player in major league annals to connect for three homers on opening day, stroking three round-trippers versus the Kansas City Royals at Royals Stadium.

September, Korea. The Olympic baseball movement gains steam with a competitive demonstration tournament during the Summer Games in Seoul, South Korea. Coached by Mark Marquess of Stanford University and featuring top pro prospects Jim Abbott, Ben McDonald, and Andy Benes as a starting pitching rotation, Team USA triumphs over Japan, 5–3, in the gold medal showdown, largely on the strength of Abbott's brilliant pitching and a pair of homers by another future big leaguer, Tino Martínez. Cuba chose to boycott the Seoul Games, however, taking some of the shine off the U.S. victory. The much-anticipated showdown match between Cuba's perennial world champions and a fresh and talent-loaded Team USA never materialized.

September 24, USA. Dominican hurler Pascual Pérez of the Montreal Expos pitches a rain-shortened no-hitter in a 1–0 victory over the Philadelphia Phillies. This is the first abbreviated no-hitter by a Latin American pitcher in major league history, as well as being the first no-hitter in the history of Philadelphia's seventeen-year-old Veterans Stadium.

October, Japan. Fleet-footed outfielder Yutaka Fukumoto (Hankyu Braves, Japanese Pacific League) completes his Japanese league career with 1,065 stolen bases, setting a world standard that will stand until broken in the big leagues by Rickey Henderson in 1993. Fukumoto earlier captured a Japanese league-record thirteen consecutive stolen base crowns and pilfered 106 bases in a single season (1972).

1990

February, USA. The Escogido Lions (Dominican Republic) ride the slugging of Moises Alou (7 RBI), the pitching of Mel Rojas (2–0, 1.69 ERA), and the managing skills of Felipe Alou to post a 5–1 record and capture the 1990 Caribbean series title. San Juan's Metros (Puerto Rico) and the Caracas Lions (Venezuela) tie for second place with identical 3–3 records before sparse crowds at the Miami Orange Bowl Stadium during the first Caribbean series tournament ever staged on North American soil.

March, Taiwan. Professional baseball debuts in Taiwan with the Chinese Professional Baseball League's first season, a small circuit of only four teams: President Lions, Brother Elephants, Weichuan Dragons, and Mercury Tigers. These teams barnstorm across the island nation between March and October with a 90-game schedule; they draw 900,000-plus paying fans for league games.

June 29, USA. In a final glory moment with the Dodgers, Fernando Valenzuela pitches the seventh no-hitter in Los Angeles club history. Valenzuela's no-hitter comes against St. Louis Cardinals (6–0) at Dodger Stadium, on the same night as one pitched by Oakland's Dave Stewart in Toronto, and also the day before a rare losing no-hit effort by Yankee Andy Hawkins in Chicago.

1991

January 8, USA. Canada's greatest-ever ballplayer, pitcher Ferguson Jenkins of Chatham, Ontario, takes his place in Cooperstown as Canada's first (and so far only) elected member of major league baseball's Hall of Fame. Jenkins posted 284 wins and struck out 3,192 batters in his marvelous big league career, split between the American League's Texas Rangers and National League's Chicago Cubs.

July 28, USA. Dennis Martínez pitches a perfect game for the Montreal Expos at Dodger Stadium (2–0 final score), thus becoming the first Latin American hurler ever to toss a big league perfect game.

August, USA. Rod Carew of Panama (fortuitously born in the Canal Zone) is inducted into National Baseball Hall of Fame in Cooperstown, becoming only the fifth Latin American Hall of Famer (including Cuba's Negro leaguer Martín Dihigo) and only the fourth Latin genuine big leaguer to be so honored.

August 11, USA. Venezuelan rookie Wilson Álvarez, making his hurling debut for the Chicago White Sox against the Orioles in Baltimore's Memorial Stadium, becomes the eighth youngest pitcher in major league history to hurl a no-hit, no-run game. At age 21 years and 4 months old at the time of his masterpiece, Álvarez also becomes both the first Venezuelan and the first Chicago White Sox left-hander ever to pitch a hitless and scoreless game.

September 11, USA. Dominican relief pitcher Alejandro Peña of the Atlanta Braves teams with starter Kent Mercker and fellow reliever Mark Wohlers for a rare combined no-hit, no-run game against the San Diego Padres in Atlanta. Peña also registers 14 saves over the course of the same season for the pennant-winning Atlanta team.

October, USA. Julio Franco (Dominican Republic) of the Texas Rangers captures an American League batting title with his .341 season's mark. The right-handed hitting second baseman thus becomes the first Latino batting champion since Rod Carew's final title in 1978, thirteen seasons earlier.

October, USA. Franco's Texas Rangers teammate, strapping rookie outfielder Juan González of Puerto Rico, knocks in 102 runs while also belting 27 homers and stroking 34 doubles and thus establishes himself as one of the true upcoming slugging stars in the major leagues.

October 22, Puerto Rico. The newly formed Hall of Fame of Puerto Rican Professional Baseball holds its inaugural induction ceremonies at the Interamerican University in Ponce. A first class of inductees features Negro league and winter league stars Luis Ángel "Canena" Márquez, Francisco "Pancho" Coimbre, Pedro "Perucho" Cepeda, Robert "El Múcaro" Thurman, and Willard "Ese Hombre" Brown. Also included in the first Puerto Rican Hall of Fame induction ceremonies are big leaguers Roberto Clemente, Orlando Cepeda, Victor (Pellot) Power, Rubén Gómez, and Juan "Terín" Pizarro.

December 10, Mexico. Benjamín "Cananea" Reyes, the winningest manager in Mexican baseball history, dies at age 54 after an extended bout with cancer. In addition to winning 14 Mexican League titles, Reyes also piloted Hermosillo and Mexicali to Caribbean series championships in 1976 and 1986, the only two Caribbean titles ever claimed by Mexico.

1992

July, Canada. Felipe Alou takes over managerial reins of the Montreal Expos, thus becoming the first Dominican big league manager. During Felipe's debut managerial summer, his son, Moises, is one of the Expos star players, happily creating the first-ever Latin father–son, manager–ballplayer combo.

August 5, Spain. Cuba coasts to victory in the first official Olympics baseball tournament at Barcelona, Spain. The gold medal victory comes with an easy 11–1 romp over Chinese Taipei, with Japan posting an 8–3 bronze medal victory versus Team USA. Victor Mesa was the batting hero for the champion Cubans during an important 6–1 semifinal win against the disappointed American squad.

August 31, USA. The Texas Rangers and Oakland Athletics swap Latin American sluggers José Canseco and Rubén Sierra in the most sensational player trade ever involving Hispanic superstars. Canseco joins Texas in exchange for the switch-hitting Sierra, as well as relief ace Jeff Russell and starting hurler Bobby Witt. With Canseco now in the same lineup alongside junior circuit home run leader Juan González, potent Cuban slugger Rafael Palmeiro, and former batting champ Julio Franco, the Texas Rangers will boast the most awesome Latin slugging knockout punch ever assembled on major league diamonds.

October, USA. Puerto Rico's Juan González clinches an American League home run title with 43 circuit blasts in just his second full-time season. González also sets the Texas Rangers team standard for round-trippers and becomes the third youngest (at 21 years, 11 months, 19 days) to hit 40-plus homers during a big league season. Only Mel Ott and Eddie Mathews (twice) previously reached the 40-homer level at an earlier age than González.

October 14, USA. Dominican utility man Francisco Cabrera becomes a household name by striking the pennant-winning hit for Atlanta's Braves in a crucial seventh game of National League Championship Series action. Cabrera's dramatic pinch-hit blow came with two outs in the bottom of the ninth to snatch an emotional comeback 3–2 victory and a National League pennant from the Eastern Division champion Pittsburgh Pirates. A crucial ninth-inning error by Pittsburgh's gold glove second baseman José "Chico" Lind (Puerto Rico) is also significant in opening the door for this dramatic Atlanta pennant-winning rally.

October 20, Canada. The first-ever World Series game played outside the United States takes place in Toronto, Canada, and matches the Atlanta Braves against the hometown Blue Jays. Toronto catapults the entire Canadian countryside into celebration with a 3–2 victory before a throng of 51,813 Ontario partisans.

November 8, Puerto Rico. Puerto Rico's Professional Baseball Hall of Fame conducts its second formal induction ceremonies at the Interamerican University in Ponce. Second-year inductees include ex-major leaguers Luis Arroyo, Carlos Bernier, Luis Rodríguez

Olmo, and Saturnino "Nino" Escalera. Also inducted are Negro leaguers Juan Ésteban "Tetelo" Vargas, José Antonio Figueroa, and Rafael "Rafaelito" Ortiz, plus local island figures and nonplayers (scouts, writers and owners) Jorge "Griffin" Tirado, Pedro Miguel Caratini, Ceferino Conde y Faria, Juan Guilbe, Rafael Pont Flores, Pedro "Pedrín" Zorrilla, Pedro Vázquez, and Emilio "Millito" Navarro.

1993

April, USA. Tony Pérez debuts as manager of the Cincinnati Reds but is fired only 44 games into the 1993 season. Hopes were high in Cincinnati for a Reds pennant challenge, and when the local ball club floundered early in the season (20–24 on May 24th, the date of Pérez's firing), even future Hall of Famer Pérez's stature as a revered star of the 1970s Big Red Machine teams was not enough to save the popular Cuban's slow-starting managerial career.

April 8, USA. Carlos Baerga, switch-hitting Puerto Rican second baseman with the Cleveland Indians, achieves the rarest of feats when he becomes the first player in major league history to homer from both sides of the plate during the same inning. Baerga's two circuit blasts come in the opening frame of a 15–5 rout over the New York Yankees at Cleveland's Municipal Stadium.

April 9, USA. José Canseco (Cuba) of the Texas Rangers becomes the first player since Ted Williams (1947) and the seventeenth in baseball history to reach the 750 career RBI plateau in 1,000 games or less. Canseco's milestone RBI hit comes in a game (his 999th career contest) against the Royals in Kansas City.

April 9, USA. Former Cuban national team ace René Arocha debuts in the National League with the St. Louis Cardinals, after defecting from his homeland back in 1991. Arocha represents the first slow trickle of a significant string of Cuban defectors to appear in the majors throughout the 1990s and the first decade of the new century.

June 7, Japan. MVP Omar Linares smacks a homer, a double, and a sacrifice fly in three at-bats as Cuba defeats the IBA World All-Star squad, 8–2, in Tokyo Dome. IBA World All-Star game three is the first match-up of Olympic champions and all-stars from all other competing nations.

June 17, USA. Carlos Baerga becomes the twelfth Latin American slugger to pound three homers in a single contest. His predecessors in achieving the feat were Bobby Ávila (1951), Héctor López (1958), Manny Jiménez (1964), Tony Oliva (1973), Ben Oglivie (1979, 1982 and 1983), Otto Velez (1980), Juan Beníquez (1986), George Bell (1988), José Canseco (1988), Danny Tartabull (1991), and Juan González (1992).

June 18, Canada. Montreal Expos ace right-hander Dennis Martínez wins his 200th career game (200–161), becoming the 92nd hurler overall, and only the third Latin American, to reach this coveted milestone for career victories. With his fifth-straight win of the young season, by a 2–1 count over the Atlanta Braves, the Nicaraguan pitcher joins Juan Marichal (243) and Luis Tiant (229) as the only Latin Americans ever to reach the charmed 200-victory plateau.

June 20, USA. Dominican slugger George Bell hits his tenth career grand slam homer for the Chicago White Sox in a game against the California Angels at Anaheim Stadium. This round-tripper moved Bell into the all-time lead for bases-loaded homers among Latin American batsmen, surpassing Orlando Cepeda and Danny Tartabull, who had each previously stroked nine. Bell's 13 homers during the 1993 season will also move him into third place on the all-time Latin list, with 265.

July, USA. Launching one of the great personal comebacks in recent baseball history, first baseman Andrés Galarraga smacks the ball at a torrid .400-plus pace for almost the entire first half of the 1993 season, maintaining a .401 batting average for the expansion Colorado Rockies as late as the season's halfway point (July 6th, the club's 82nd game). Galarraga had hit only .256, .219, and .243 over the previous three campaigns, causing first the Montreal Expos and later the St. Louis Cardinals to give up altogether on this Venezuelan slugger's sagging career. Galarraga battles injuries throughout the season but maintains his torrid hitting pace to become the National League's Comeback Player of the Year.

October 3, USA. The Texas Rangers play their final game in Arlington Stadium, losing to the Kansas City Royals. Puerto Rican slugger Juan González, the last batter in the ballpark's history, flies out to left field. Fittingly, another Puerto Rican native, California Angels second baseman Sandy Alomar (Sr.), was the first official batter in Stadium history, back on April 21, 1972.

October, USA. The Milwaukee Brewers add Ángel Miranda and Rafael Novoa to the club's starting rotation in late season, marking the first time that four Latin hurlers (in this case all Puerto Ricans) comprise the starting rotation of a big league ball club. Jaime Navarro and Ricky Bones are also members of the Milwaukee Brewers' starting staff during the final month of the season.

October, USA. Venezuela's Andrés Galarraga reaches the minimum qualification number in official plate appearances with the Colorado Rockies during the season's final week and thus becomes the first expansion team player ever to win a major league batting crown, pacing the National League with a .370 average in 120 games, 470 at-bats.

October, USA. Puerto Rico's Juan González with the Texas Rangers powers past the 40-homer plateau for his second campaign in a row, thus becoming the first Latin slugger ever to post back-to-back 40-homer seasons in the big leagues. At season's end, González leads the American League in homers with 46, his second consecutive home run title. González thus also becomes the third Latin batter (after Tony Armas in 1981 and 1984, and José Canseco in 1988 and 1991) to garner two home run crowns, and the first to accomplish the feat in consecutive seasons.

October, USA. The Texas Rangers announce an "All-Time Rangers All-Star Team" covering the first twenty-two seasons (1972–1993) of ball club history (to correspond with the closing of the original Arlington Stadium). This mythical team includes five Latin American players: Rafael Palmeiro, first base; Julio Franco, second base; Juan González and Rubén Sierra, outfielders; and Iván Rodríguez, catcher. González was the second highest vote-getter (84% of ballots cast), surpassed only by pitcher Nolan Ryan (94%). Cuban-born Palmeiro (68%) ranked fourth.

1994

March, Cuba. Lázaro Junco, Cuba's all-time long ball slugger, wins his eighth Cuban League home run crown. Junco (who played for Citricultores, Henequeneros, and Matanzas) retires with Cuba's career home run record (later passed by Orestes Kindelán) of 405 round-trippers.

October, USA. Cuban-born José Canseco is tabbed the American League Comeback Player of the Year after a stellar season (his last with Texas Rangers ball club) in which he slugs 31 homers, drives in 90 runs, and bats a respectable .282.

1995

May 2, USA. Hideo Nomo debuts with the Los Angeles Dodgers and almost immediately becomes the first Japanese sensation in major league baseball, posting a phenomenal rookie season, running up a 13–6 record, and also appearing in the midsummer All-Star game hosted by the Texas Rangers. The National League's Rookie of the Year is only the second former Japanese Leaguer to make it into the U.S. majors (see September 1, 1964).

August 31, Japan. Pedro Luis Lazo tosses a no-hitter and strikes out 17 as Cuba defeats the United States, 5–0, in the semifinals of the World University Games at Fukuoka, Japan. Lazo had pitched another brilliant six-inning 12–1 one-hit win earlier in same tourney versus Taiwan (Chinese Taipei), striking out 11.

October, USA. José Canseco, now with the Boston Red Sox, finishes the season with 300 career round-trippers, becoming only the third Latin player to reach the 300-homer plateau. Canseco thus stands only 79 circuit blasts behind Tany Pérez and Orlando Cepeda for the all-time top spot among Latin American sluggers.

1996

July, USA. Cuba (9–0 for tournament) again dominates international amateur scene by breezing to victory in Summer Olympics at Atlanta's Fulton County Stadium. Cuba defeats Japan 13–9 in the gold medal game. Omar Linares (with eight home runs) and Orestes Kindelán (with nine) perform an awesome two-week display of aluminum-bat slugging. First baseman and designated hitter Kindelán blasts the longest third-deck four-bagger ever witnessed in Fulton County Stadium.

September 17, USA. Hideo Nomo pitches the twentieth no-hitter in Los Angeles (Brooklyn) Dodgers franchise history and also the first ever by a Japanese major league import. Nomo's masterpiece is especially remarkable for being performed in Denver's Coors Field, a stadium widely known as a true hitter's paradise because of its high-altitude location and inviting configuration of outfield fences.

1997

April 8, Cuba. Omar Linares of Pinar del Río slugs four homers in one game at hometown Captain San Luis Stadium, becoming only the third player to accomplish this rare feat at any level in more than a full century of Cuban amateur league or professional baseball. Linares also matches Leonel Moa (with Camagüey, on December 10, 1989) and Alberto Díaz (with Matanzas, on December 17, 1995) with his four round-trippers. Coinciden-tally, veteran Cuban umpire Nelson Díaz works all three of these games—at second base in the first two and behind the plate for the third historic contest.

August 10, Spain. Japan surprises Cuba 11–2 in the finals of Intercontinental Cup play at Barcelona, Spain, thus ending a ten-year Cuban domination of senior-level international tourneys, as well as the string of seven straight titles for Cuba in Inter-continental Cup competitions. This loss, hardly expected on the heels of the 1996 Olympic victory over Japan, shocks both Cuban fans and the country's INDER officials and leads to dramatic changes in both the Cuban League National Series format and the leadership of Cuba's national team. The following Cuban League season will fea-ture a single National Series of 90 games (dropping the 54-game Selective Series), and Jorge Fuentes is replaced as manager of both Pinar del Río and Cuba's embarrassed national team.

September 8, USA. One year after his remarkable no-hitter in Colorado, Japanese star Hideo Nomo, still toiling for the Los Angeles Dodgers, records career big league strike-out number 1,000 during only his 146th career game. Only Hall of Fame–bound Roger Clemens and New York Mets standout Dwight Gooden ever reached the plateau more quickly.

October, USA. Cuban League defector Liván Hernández stars in World Series play for the National League Florida Marlins and thus refocuses attention of U.S. fans on the long and proud legacy of Cuban baseball. The high-powered memorable World Series MVP performance by 22-year-old Hernández also creates considerable stir among diehard fans back home in Cuba.

1998

April, Cuba. Veteran José Ibar wins 20 games on the mound for Habana Province and becomes the first pitcher in modern-era Cuban League play to post 20 victories in a single National Series season. Pinar del Río, featuring superstar slugger Omar Linares and mound aces José Contreras and Pedro Luis Lazo, captures the Cuban League championship for the second straight year.

June 3, USA. Orlando "El Duque" Hernández makes his major league debut with world champion New York Yankees. Half-brother of 1997 World Series hero Liván Hernández, "El Duque" defected from Cuba in December 1997 and signed with the New York club in February 1998 after a much-publicized open tryout session held during the winter league Caribbean series in Caracas, Venezuela.

July, USA. José Canseco surpasses Cuban Tany Pérez and Puerto Rican Orlando Cepeda (379 each) to become Latin America's all-time career leader in big league home runs. Regla-born and Miami-raised Canseco approaches 400 career homers before the season's end, yet will soon be easily overtaken in the slugging department by another Cuban-born but Miami-raised player, Rafael Palmeiro (see May 11, 2003).

August, Italy. Cuba recaptures its long-standing reputation for international domination by winning the IBA world championships in Italy, posting a perfect 9–0 tournament record and defeating South Korea 7–1 in the one-sided finals. Cuba's stars again are ageless Omar Linares (.500 BA), veteran slugger Orestes Kindelán (also above .500, and the tournament's leading hitter), and power pitcher José Contreras, who hurls a title game five-hitter. Cuba also beats Nicaragua (14–2) in semifinals and the Netherlands (12–1) in quarterfinals to capture its 25th overall senior-level world title in 27 outings since 1952 (the string including both IBA world championships and Intercontinental Cup tournaments).

September–October, USA. Dominican Republic slugger Sammy Sosa of Chicago Cubs creates fan sensation across North America as well as in his Caribbean homeland as his season-long home run duel with St. Louis slugger Mark McGwire continues to season's end. Sosa blasts 66 round-trippers (behind McGwire's 70) for an all-time record for Latin American big leaguers.

October 18, Cuba. The Cuban National Series season (number XXXVIII) opens on a dramatic note when popular star shortstop Germán Mesa makes his emotional return to action in Estadio Latinoamericano after serving a two-year league suspension. High drama thus surrounds the opening inning of a game between Industriales and defending champion Pinar del Río; ballplayers from both teams jog onto the field to shake Mesa's hand as he takes his position for the first time since his controversial banning.

1999

January 23, Cuba. Up-and-coming young Cuban outfield star Yasser Gómez slugs three triples during same game in Havana's Estadio Latinoamericano versus Holguín. Industriales veteran shortstop Germán Mesa joins Gómez in mad dashes around the base paths when the two teammates hit back-to-back three-baggers during the same inning.

March 28, Cuba. Major leaguers appear on Cuban soil for the first time in 40 years for a historic meeting between the American League Baltimore Orioles and the Cuban national team, played before 55,000 frenzied fans in Estadio Latinoamericano. Omar Linares singles home a tying run in the eighth, but the major leaguers finally prevail, 3–2, after eleven thrill-packed innings. Catcher Charles Johnson homers in the second frame for Baltimore and José Contreras pitches eight dominant innings of relief for Cuba.

April, Cuba. During the week following Orioles' historic visit, baseball interest is further stoked in Havana by a return trip of local favorite Industriales to the National Series finals. Industriales takes a commanding early 3–0 series lead before cross-island rival Santiago de Cuba sweeps the final four games to earn the National Series XXXVIII championship.

April 4, Mexico. The San Diego Padres and Colorado Rockies play a historic major league season opener in Monterrey, Mexico. Colorado wins the landmark National League contest by an 8–2 score before a Mexican throng of 60,021 spectators.

May 3, USA. Two triples by shortstop Danel Castro, a dramatic ninth-inning round-tripper with a joyous dance around basepaths by designated hitter (and future defector)

Andy Morales, and six and two thirds innings of hitless relief hurling by Norge Vera all highlight a stunning 12–6 romp by the Cuban national team in their rematch with the Baltimore Orioles at Camden Yards. The game—a first-ever meeting on U.S. soil between a Castro-era Cuban team and a big league club—establishes Cuban League credibility and sets off wild celebrations in Havana and everywhere else across Cuba.

July, Canada. Cuba wins the Pan American Games tournament in Winnipeg and thus qualifies for upcoming 2000 Olympics in Sydney, Australia. The Pan American tournament makes history as the first international competition matching teams using professional players (mostly AAA minor leaguers). A dramatic final round of games provides perhaps the most exciting competition in international baseball annals, as Cuba rebounds from two preliminary-round losses to take three straight from the Dominican Republic, Canada, and the United States. José Contreras pitches brilliantly in quarterfinals and finals with only a single day's rest between must-win games.

November, Australia. Cuba is rudely upset in the gold medal showdown at the Intercontinental Cup tournament, played in Sydney, thus losing the championship game of an ICC tournament for the second straight time after seven consecutive victories dating back to 1983. A surprise loss to host Australia, 4–3 in eleven innings, again shakes the Cuban baseball establishment back home, even though Cuba had not sent many veteran national team players to this tune-up event for 2000 Sydney Olympics.

December, Cuba. A rare unassisted triple play occurs in Cuban League action when Villa Clara's third baseman Rafael Acebey tags two Industriales baserunners along with the batter on a slow roller off the bat of Juan Padilla. Padilla himself facilitates the unusual play when he remains at home plate to argue with the umpire that his weak roller had first hit him in the batter's box and was thus a foul ball.

December 8, Cuba. Maels Rodríguez cracks the 100 miles per hour barrier on a speed gun in a National Series game at Sancti Spíritus. It is the first time that any Cuban League hurler has reached this ultimate three-figure standard for measuring pitching speed.

December 22, Cuba. Maels Rodríguez throws the first perfect game in Cuban League history when he blanks Las Tunas, 1–0, on his home field in Sancti Spíritus. This game, along with the remarkable 100 miles per hour speed clocked only two weeks earlier, establishes 19-year-old phenom Rodríguez as Cuba's brightest new pitching prospect.

2000

March 28, Japan. The New York Mets and the Chicago Cubs open the National League season with a ground-breaking two-game set in Japan's Tokyo Dome. The unprecedented event marks the first major league opener outside of North America. The teams split the historic series when Benny Agbayani (Hawaiian-born New York outfielder) smacks a dramatic eleventh-inning grand slam homer to cap the second contest.

April, Cuba. Norge Vera, Santiago ace right-hander, completes the year with a sterling 0.97 ERA and leads a host of pitchers who dominate the first Cuban League season in 23 winters played with wooden bats. Other sterling performances are turned in by José Contreras (1.24 ERA) and Maels Rodríguez (177 strikeouts in 139 innings); ten different starting pitchers all record ERAs of 1.75 or less.

July, USA. Atanasio "Tany" Pérez becomes the first Cuban major leaguer inducted into the major league baseball Hall of Fame in Cooperstown. Pérez joins Martín Dihigo as the only other Cuban in Cooperstown. With the two Cubans, Puerto Rico's Roberto Clemente and Orlando "Baby Bull" Cepeda, the Dominican Republic's Juan Marichal, and Venezuela's Luis Aparicio, there are now a half-dozen Latin Americans enshrined in baseball's most exclusive Valhalla.

September 27, Australia. Cuba is shocked by Team USA during the Olympic gold medal match in Sydney. The U.S. starter, Ben Sheets (Milwaukee Brewers), hurls a brilliant three-hit shutout in a 4–0 American victory that stops Cuba's Olympic baseball domination. Cubans had earlier defeated the Americans by a 6–1 score in preliminary round action behind José Ibar's hurling and the timely hitting of Oscar Macías and Miguel Caldés. Veteran Cuban manager Servio Borges likely committed a crucial tactical error by deciding to start ace José Ariel Contreras in semifinal showdown versus Japan (a 3–0 Cuban victory) in order to save Pedro Luis Lazo for the gold medal match-up.

December, Cuba. Cuban Olympic team headliner and longtime national team out-fielder Miguel Caldés—star player for Camagüey and former Cuban League home run champion—is killed instantly in an automobile accident outside his home town of Camagüey.

2001

January 21, Cuba. Santiago de Cuba ace Norge Vera hurls a no-hit, no-run game against Habana Province during a Sunday doubleheader at Nelson Fernández Stadium in San José de las Lajas. This first-ever no-hitter by a Santiago de Cuba pitcher is also the 43rd such masterpiece of postrevolution Cuban League history and number 36 during National Series seasons.

May, Cuba. Twenty-year-old Maels Rodríguez shatters a Cuban League strikeout record that had stood since 1969 (208 by Santiago "Changa" Mederos) and also posts circuit's top ERA. Maels' performance highlights the most exciting Cuban League season in years, with Santiago de Cuba capturing their third straight pennant, and with several other individual records and performances of note being recorded. Record-breakers include Alex Ramos (whose unmatched consecutive games streak extends to 712), Lázaro de la Torre (fourth Cuban League pitcher to post 200 career wins), Eduardo Paret (with a new league high of 99 runs scored), Orlis Díaz (who ties Oscar Machado's RBI mark at 87), and Antonio Pacheco and Orestes Kindelán (who extend their respective career marks for base hits and home runs).

October, USA. Six-time Japanese League batting champion Ichiro Suzuki completes his sensational big league debut season as the American League batting champion with a .350 average. Suzuki also leads the Seattle Mariners to a 116-win season, which ties the major league mark set back in 1906 by the Chicago Cubs. Suzuki also finishes second in *Baseball America*'s Rookie of the Year balloting, where he is barely edged out by sensational Dominican outfielder Albert Pujols, who himself batted .329 and slugged 37 homers.

November, Taiwan. Cuba reclaims the top slot in world amateur baseball with an impressive gold medal victory in the 34th World Cup (aka Amateur World Series) staged in Taiwan. The sweet championship game victory comes against Team USA (by a 5–3 score), which avenges the Olympics loss in Sydney a year earlier. Veteran outfielder Luis Ulacia—38 years old—enjoys a career swan song as tournament MVP. This World Cup outing also marks the likely final international appearance of longtime Team Cuba stars Omar Linares (all-time Cuban League batting leader), Orestes Kindelán (career home run leader), and Antonio Pacheco (career base hits pacesetter).

2002

January, Cuba. The opening of Cuba's 41st annual National Series is postponed until January, due to world championship tournament action staged in Taiwan during November and also to damage inflicted by a severe hurricane which swept the island in late October. The new Cuban season also marks a renewal of the suspended short-season Selective Series (renamed the Super League and featuring thirty games and four teams named Occidentales, Habaneros, Centrales, and Orientales) at the conclusion of National Series playoffs in late June.

February, USA. Dominican-born and New York-raised Omar Minaya blazes trails as the first Latin American general manager in major league baseball. Minaya takes the reins of the financially troubled Montreal Expos, a team now owned jointly by all twenty-nine other major league clubs. Montreal surprises under Minaya and field manager Frank Robinson, posting an 83–79 record to finish second in the National League East.

June, Cuba. A surprising Cuban National Series XLI concludes with western provincial winner Holguín defeating eastern provincial champ Sancti Spíritus in a hotly contested seven-game finale. The unexpected match-up marked a first-ever championship-series appearance for Holguín and only the second for Sancti Spíritus. Ace Maels Rodríguez performs yeoman service in the final playoff round as both a starter and reliever but suffers defeat three separate times.

July, Cuba. New ground is broken for Cuban baseball with the surprise announcement that five top stars will officially "retire" from league play and immediately join Japanese amateur and professional leagues as "rented" players and coaches. Longtime national team star Omar Linares is loaned to the pro Chunichi Dragons; Orestes Kindelán and Antonio Pacheco sign on with the amateur Sidas club; outfielder Luis Ulacia (MVP of the 2001 World Championships in Taipei) and shortstop Germán Mesa are designated as Japanese coaches.

September, Cuba and Mexico and USA. Cuban National team ace hurler José Ariel Contreras (sporting a perfect 13–0 record for major international tournaments) departs from the Cuban squad in Mexico and later turns up in the United States, having defected from Cuban baseball alongside longtime team technical director (general manager) Miguel Valdés. Contreras will eventually sign a lucrative $30 million long-term contract with the New York Yankees and appear in the major leagues, as well as at the AAA level (Columbus), during the 2003 season.

November, Cuba. Cuba breezes with a perfect 10–0 record to another Intercontinental Cup championship on home turf in Havana and Matanzas. Pinar del Río's Yobal Dueñas is the batting hero with a dramatic game-deciding home run in a 2–1 gold medal win versus South Korea.

2003

April 11, Puerto Rico. The Montreal Expos host the New York Mets at Hiram Bithorn Stadium in San Juan, Puerto Rico. It is the first of 22 regularly scheduled Montreal games played in Puerto Rico during the 2003 National League season.

May, Cuba. Led by slugging third baseman and outfielder Kendry Morales and hard-hitting catcher Bárbaro Cañizares, Industriales captures the Cuban National Series for the first time in seven seasons with a four-game rout of Villa Clara in the playoff finals. Fan interest again peaks with the achievements of the island's most popular team representing the capital city of Havana.

May 11, USA. Cuban-born Rafael Palmeiro slugs career homer number 500 for the Texas Rangers, becoming the second Latin ballplayer to reach the Hall-of-Fame–qualifying landmark milestone. (Sammy Sosa had hit his 500th earlier this year, on April 4.)

October, Cuba. Oblivious to recent defections by headliners Maels Rodríguez and Yobal Dueñas, a young Cuban squad fronted by new leaders Yulieski Gourriel and Frederich Cepeda reemerges at the forefront of international competition by sweeping all opposition during a gold medal win in the World Cup tournament in Havana. Kendry Morales slugs a dramatic ninth-inning homer to rescue Cuban hopes in the quarterfinals and avert a defeat at the hands of upstart Brazil. One of the surprises of the event is the quarterfinal loss to Chinese Taipei by a U.S. team that had dominated its group in preliminary round action. Norge Vera of Cuba makes history as the first pitcher ever to win both the semifinal and final games of a World Cup event.

November, Panama. At the Olympic Qualifier in Panama City, Cuba again rides its young bats and arms to sweep the competition easily and earn an Olympic berth in Athens for 2004. A strong U.S. team managed by Hall of Famer Frank Robinson is shocked in the quarterfinals by a Mexico club that had lost all three of its preliminary-round games. Losing in the finals, 5–0, to the invincible Cubans, Canada earns the second North American Olympic berth.

2004

August 23, USA. Dominican infielder Julio Franco celebrates his 46th birthday on the field with the Atlanta Braves, thus becoming the oldest nonpitching everyday ballplayer in major league history. Franco was playing his 20th big leaguer campaign in a career that also saw stints in the Mexican and Japanese leagues.

August, USA. Seattle Mariners Japanese superstar Ichiro Suzuki crosses yet another milestone in his brief whirlwind big league career as the first-ever player to collect 200-plus hits in each of his first four major league campaigns.

August, Athens, Greece. Cuba recaptures its seat atop the international baseball world with a third Olympic gold medal victory in four tries. Rebounding from a disappointing silver medal finish in Sydney four years earlier, Cuba brings its youngest and most inexperienced squad yet to the Olympic battleground and still manages to march through the nine-game event with only a single preliminary-round loss to third-place Japan. Cuba's surprise win is highlighted by a gutsy eight-inning six-run comeback against Team Canada in the semifinal and a hard-fought 6–2 victory over upstart Australia in the finale. Top Cuban stars are catcher Ariel Pestano (the tournament batting champion) and southpaw Adiel Palma (the event's top pitcher). The tournament's biggest story, however, is the collapse of the favored Japanese team, which unaccountably suffers an upset 1–0 semifinal loss to Australia that dashes gold medal hopes for a Japanese Dream Team composed of top all-stars from the professional Japanese Pacific League and Japanese Central League.

NOTE

1. Strictly speaking, the 1939 tourney is World Cup II. An initial tournament had been held in England in 1938, with American soldiers comprising a majority of the players on both teams. See Chapter 10.

International Baseball Federation

2003 Membership Roster

• •

HEADQUARTERS

International Baseball Federation (IBAF)
Federación Internacional de Béisbol (FIBA)
Avenue de Mon Repos 24
Case Postale 131
1000 Lausanne 5, Switzerland
Telephone: +41 21 318-8240
Fax: +41 21 318-8242
E-mail: ibaf@baseball.ch
Website: www.baseball.ch
Executive Director: Miquel Ortín
Communications Manager: Enzo Di Gesù
Note: The IBAF Website maintains current
information for all member countries.

CONTINENTAL CONFEDERATIONS

African Baseball and Softball
Association (ABSA)
Paiko Road, Changaga, Minna,
Niger State
PMB 150, Nigeria
Telephone: +234 66 224-555
Fax: +234 66 224-555
E-mail: absasec@yahoo.com
President: Ishola Williams (Ivory Coast)
Secretary General: Fridah Shiroya (Kenya)

Confederación Panamericana de Béisbol
(COPABE)
Calle 3, Francisco Filos, Vista Hermosa

Edificio 74 Primer Alto,
Local no. 2,
Panamá Ciudad, Panama
Telephone: +507 2361-5677
Fax: +507 261-5215
E-mail: copabe@sinfo.net
President: Eduardo De Bello (Panama)
Secretary General: Héctor Pereyra
(Dominican Republic)

Baseball Federation of Asia (BFA)
Mainichi Palaceside Building 1-1-1,
Hitotsubashi, Chiyoda-ku

Tokyo 100, Japan
Telephone: +81 3 3201-1155; 3213-6776
Fax: +81 3 3201-0707
President: Eiichiro Yamamoto (Japan)
Secretary General: Yukichi Maeda
(Japan)

Confédération Européene de Baseball (CEB)

Baseball Confederation of Europe (CEB)
Avenue de Mon Repos 24
Case Postale 131
1000 Lausanne 5, Switzerland
Telephone: +32 3 219-0440 (Belgium)
Fax: +32 3 772-7727 (Belgium)

E-mail: ibaf@baseballeurope.com
Website: www.baseballeurope.com
President: Aldo Notari (Italy)
Secretary General: Gaston Panaye
(Belgium)

Baseball Confederation of Oceania (BCO)

48 Partridge Way, Mooroolbark
Victoria 3138, Australia
Telephone: +61 3 9727-1779
Fax: +61 3 9727-5959
E-mail: chetg@ozemail.com.au
President: Mark Peters (Australia)
Secretary General: Chet Gray (Australia)

MEMBER COUNTRIES

American Samoa (ASA)

American Samoa Baseball Association
(ASBA)
PO Box 3807
Pago Pago, 96799
Telephone: +684 699-6000
Fax: +684 699-6005
E-mail: rcoulter@yahoo.com;
peni49@hotmail.com
President: Bob Coulter
Secretary General: Chris King

Argentina (ARG)

Federación Argentina de Béisbol (FAB)
Baseball Federation of Argentina
Presidencia Calle 11 Nro 275
1900 La Plata, Prov. de Bs. As.
Telephone: +54 221 423-1330
E-mail: presidenciafab@hotmail.com
Website: www.beisbolargentina.com.ar
President: Oscar Trombetta
Secretary General: José Ramón Majul

Armenia (ARM)

Baseball Federation of Armenia (ABF)
G. Lousavorich Str. 32/18
Vanadzor 377200
Telephone: +374 514-2352
Fax: +374 514-2123
E-mail: armbf@mail.ru
President: Sergey Sargsyan
Secretary General: Karen Ayvazyan

Aruba (ARU)

Amateur Baseball Bond Aruba (ABBA)
Sabana Grandi 39, Sta. Cruz
Telephone: +297 5 821-100
Fax: +297 5 835-171
E-mail: arubabaseball_2000@yahoo.com
President: Lucien Mohamed
Secretary General: Rudolfo Wester

Australia (AUS)

Australian Baseball Federation (ABF)
Level One, 7 Short Street
PO Box 10468
Southport, Queensland 4215
Telephone: +61 7 5564-0144
Fax: +61 7 5564-0155
E-mail: ausbaseball@baseball.org.au
Website: www.baseball.org.au
President: Ron Finlay
Executive Director: Chris White

Austria (AUT)

Österreichischer Baseball-
undSoftballverband (ÖBSV)
Austrian Baseball-Softball Federation
Baumgasse 28/1
A-1030 Vienna
Telephone: +43 1 774-4114
Fax: +43 1 774-4115
E-mail: office@baseballaustria.com
Website: www.baseballaustria.com
President: Joerg Breyer
Secretary General: Joerg Wachter

Bahamas (BAH)
Bahamas Baseball Association
(BBA)
Ministry of Local Government, Sport
and Culture
PO Box N-1747
Nassau 10114
Telephone: +1 242 364-7540
Fax: +1 242 392-6573
E-mail: rodgerssamuel@hotmail.com
President: James Franklin Wood
Secretary General: Oria Maria Wood

Belarus (BLR)
Belarus Baseball and Softball Federation
(BBSF)
Kirova str. 8/2
220600 Minsk, Belarus
Telephone: +375 17 226-1058
Fax: +375 17 227-7622
E-mail: belarus_baseball@yahoo.com
Website: www.belarusbaseball.com
President: Boris Mitckevich
Secretary General: Alexei Sechka

Belgium (BEL)
Koninklijke Belgische Baseball en
Softball Federatie (KBBSF)
Federation Royale Belge de Baseball et
de Softball (FRBBS)
Belgian Baseball and Softball Federation
(KBBSF)
Boulevard d'Avroy 192/12
B-4000 Liège
Telephone: +32 4 250-0600
Fax: +32 4 250-0606
E-mail: lucien.destexhe@belgacom.net
Website: www.lfbbs.be
President: Lucien Destexhe
Secretary General: Christophe Lacrosse

Bolivia (BOL)
Federación Boliviana de Béisbol y
Softbol (ABS)
Bolivian Baseball and Softball
Federation
Avenida Heroínas No. 0-686, PO Box 89
Cochabamba
Telephone: +591 4 425-9400
Fax: +591 4 425-9427
E-mail: agga_beisbol@hotmail.com

Website: www.beisbolenbolivia.com
President: Antonio Gaete Argote
Secretary General: Marcelo Gómez
Rodrigo

Brazil (BRA)
Confederação Brasileira de Beisebol e
Softbol (CBBS)
Brazilian Baseball and Softball
Federation
Rua Visconde de Ouros 161,
Jardim Aeroporto
São Paulo, 04632-020 SP
Telephone: +55 11 5034-9904; 5034-2512
Fax: +55 11 5034-0262
E-mail: secretaria@cbbs.com.br
Website: www.cbbs.com.br
President: Jorge Otsuka
Secretary General: Alexandre Nita

British Virgin Islands (IVB)
British Virgin Islands Baseball
Federation
Road Town, PO Box 231, Tortola
Telephone: +1 284 494-4706
Fax: +1 284 494-4706
President: Derry Fahie
Secretary General: None

Brunei Darussalam (BRU)
Brunei Amateur Softball and Baseball
Association (BASBA)
No. 23 Simp. 1747, Kgrig Nangka Jl.
PO Box 2442, Tutong KM-19
Telephone: +673 2 660-900
Fax: +673 2 671-717
President: Pehin Brigen Hj. Ja'afar Aziz
Secretary General: P. J. Sulaiman

Bulgaria (BUL)
Bulgarian Baseball Federation (BBF)
kv. "Geo Milev", Studentski
Obshtezhitia, bl.3-B
Sofia 1111
Telephone: +359 2 971-4767
Fax: +359 2 971-4767
E-mail: baseball@olympic.bg
Website: www.hup.bg/baseball
President: Mario Primdjanov
Secretary General: Yassen Nedelchev

Cameroon (CMR)
Cameroon Baseball and Softball
Federation (CBSF)
Avenue Charles de Gaulle 1069,
PO Box 7399
Yaoundé
Telephone: +237 223-2373
Fax: +237 233-5262
E-mail: fecabaseball@hotmail.com
President: Sone Winslow
Secretary General: Charles Bayemi

Canada (CAN)
Canadian Federation of Amateur
Baseball (BC)
2212 Gladwin Crescent, Unit A-7
Ottawa, Ontario K1B 5N1
Telephone: +1 613 748-5606
Fax: +1 613 748-5767
E-mail: info@baseball.ca
Website: www.baseball.ca
President: Raymond Carter
Executive Director: Jim Baba

Chile (CHI)
Federación de Béisbol de Chile
(FECHIBEIS)
Baseball Federation of Chile
Avenida Vicuña MacKenna 40, Of. 13
Santiago de Chile
Telephone: +56 2 635-9453
Fax: +56 2 222-9968
E-mail: fechibeis@beisbolchile.cl
Website: www.beisbolchile.cl
President: Aldo Picozzi Bilbao
Secretary General: Roberto Kohan
Hurtado

People's Republic of China (CHN)
Chinese Baseball Association (CBA)
5, Tiyuguan Road
Beijing 100763
Telephone: +86 10 8582-6001
Fax: +86 10 8582-5994
E-mail: cga_cra@263.net
President: Hu Jianguo
Secretary General: Shen Wei

Colombia (COL)
Federación Colombiana de Béisbol
(FEDEBEISBOL)
Colombian Baseball Federation

La Matuna, Edificio Concasa, Oficina 404
Cartagena de Indias 2253
Telephone: 57 5 664-2384
Fax: +57 5 664-2566
E-mail: redsis@enred.com
President: Ramón León Hernández
Secretary General: René Ayub Batrouni

Cook Islands (COK)
Baseball and Softball Cook Islands
Association (BSCIA)
Ministry of Education, PO Box 97
Rarotonga
Telephone: +682 25270
Fax: +682 25864
E-mail: joel@education.gov.ck
President: Joel Pokura
Secretary General: None

Costa Rica (CRC)
Federación Costarricense de Béisbol
Aficionado (FECOBEISA)
Costa Rican Amateur Baseball
Federation
Calle 5 y 7 Ave. 2426
Bº. San Cayetano, San José
Telephone: +506 373-5173
Fax: +506 223-2560
E-mail: fecobeisa@yahoo.com
President: Rodrigo Vargas Castaing
Secretary General: Francisco Vargas
Arias

Croatia (CRO)
Hrvatski Baseball Savez (HBS)
Croatian Baseball Association (CBA)
Trg sportova No. 11
10000 Zagreb
Telephone: +385 1 301-2355
Fax: +385 1 6636-277
E-mail: info@baseball-cro.hr;
hrvatski.baseball.savez@zg.htnet.hr
Website: www.baseball-cro.hr
President: Osvaldo Vavra
Secretary General: Karin Krunoslav

Cuba (CUB)
Federación Cubana de Béisbol
Aficionado (FCBA)
Cuban Amateur Baseball Federation
Estadio Latinoamerica, Calle Pedro Pérez
No. 302

Cerro, Habana
Telephone: +53 7 878-6882; 873-2527
Fax: +53 7 878-1662; 833-5310
E-mail: latino@inder.co.cu
President: Carlos Rodríguez Acosta
Secretary General: Humberto Arrieta
Villate

Cyprus (CYP)
Cyprus Amateur Baseball Federation
(CABF)
PO Box 777, Larnaca
Telephone: +357 24 620-460
Fax: +357 24 660-870
President: Nicos Mannouris
Secretary General: Stelios Stylianou

Czech Republic (CZE)
České Baseballové Asociace (CBA)
Czech Baseball Association (CBA)
POP Box 40, Atleticka 100/2
16017 Praha 6
Telephone: +420 2 205-13290
Fax: +420 2 205-13290
E-mail: baseball@cstv.cz
Website: www.baseball.cz
President: Petr Ditrich
Executive Director: Jiri Votinsky

Denmark (DEN)
Dansk Baseball Softball Forbund (DBSF)
Danish Baseball Softball Federation
(DBSF)
Idraettens Hus, Broendby Stadion 20
2605 Broendby
Telephone: +45 43 262-437
Fax: +45 43 262-176
E-mail: sekretariatet@softball.dk
Website: www.dbasof.dk
President: Bo Oria-Jensen
Secretary General: Frants Gufler

Dominican Republic (DOM)
Federación Dominicana de Béisbol
Aficionado (FEDOBE)
Dominican Amateur Baseball Federation
Calle Ortega y Gasset Esq. Avenida
John F. Kennedy
Estadio de Béisbol #2, Centro Olympico
Juan Pablo Duarte
Distrito Nacional
Telephone: +1 809 562-4641; 562-4771

Fax: +1 809 562-4708
E-mail: hectorpereyra@hotmail.com
President: Héctor Manuel Pereyra Checo
Secretary General: Juan Núñez
Nepomuceno

Ecuador (ECU)
Federación Ecuatoriana de Béisbol
(FECUABEIS)
Ecuadoran Baseball Federation
Ciudadela Kennedy, Calle G y la 7 Oeste
Guayaquil, Guayas 09-04-351-P
Telephone: +593 4 269-2834
Fax: +593 4 269-2834
E-mail: Johnny-quintana@hotmail.com
President: Ernesto Pólit Ycasa
Secretary General: Juan Quintana
Andrade

El Salvador (ESA)
Federación Salvadoreña de Béisbol
(FSB)
Salvadoran Baseball Federation
Alameda Dr. Manuel Enrique Araujo,
Km. 5
Carretera a Santa Tecula
Parque de Pelota "Saturnino Bengoa"
San Salvador
Telephone: +503 224-5669
Fax: +503 279-2476
E-mail: beisbol_elsalvador@hotmail.com
President: Pablo Enrique Ventura Julián
Secretary General: César Edgardo
Martínez

Estonia (EST)
Estonian Baseball & Softball Federation
(EBSF)
Pohja 31-6, Keila 76610
Telephone: +372 604-5472
Fax: +372 678-0303
President: Jaanus Väljamäe

Fiji Islands (FJI)
Fiji Islands Baseball Association (FIJ)
FASANC, Suva Apartments Complex
17 Bau strett, Flagstaff, Suva
Telephone: +679 3 303-525; 309-866
Fax: +679 3 305-421; 301-647
E-mail: etuiloma@govnet.gov.fj
President: Eliesa B. Tuiloma
Secretary General: Ronald Seeto

Finland (FIN)
Suomen Baseball ja Softball Liitto (SBSL)
Finnish Baseball & Softball Federation
(FBSA)
SBSL Radiokatu 20
00093 SLU
Telephone: +358 9 3481-3135
Fax: +358 9 3481-2411
E-mail: federation@baseballfinland.com
Website: www.baseballfinland.com
President: Simopekka Vänskä

France (FRA)
Fédération Française de Baseball-Softball
et Cricket (FFBSC)
French Federation of Baseball, Softball
and Cricket
41, Rue de Fécamp
75012 Paris
Telephone: +33 1 446-88930
Fax: +33 1 446-89600
E-mail: FFBSC@FFBSC.org
Website: www.ffbsc.org
President: Eric-Pierre Dufour
Secretary General: André Parker

Georgia (GEO)
Baseball Federation of Georgia (BFG)
49a Chavchavadze Avenue
Tbilisi 380062
Telephone: +995 32 230-279
Fax: +995 32 230-279
E-mail: gelac@caucasus.net
President: Ramaz Goglidze
Secretary General: Gela Chikhradze

Germany (GER)
Deutscher Baseball und Softball Verband
e.v. (DBV)
German Baseball and Softball Federation
Feldbergstrasse 20-22
55118 Mainz
Telephone: +49 6131 618-250
Fax: +49 6131 618-650
E-mail: info@dbvnet.de
Website: www.baseball.de
President: Frank Wagner
Secretary General: Dirk Brennecke

Ghana (GHA)
Ghana Baseball and Softball Association
(GHABSA)

Central Secretariat Sports Stadium
PO Box 1272, Accra
Telephone: +233 2166-1510; 2166-3926
Fax: +233 2166-2281
E-mail: ghabsa42@yahoo.com
President: George O. Asubonteng
Secretary General: George Billings
Awuakye

Great Britain (GBR)
British Baseball Federation (BBF)
Ariel House, 74a Charlotte Street
London W1T 4QJ
Telephone: +44 20 7453-7055
Fax: +44 20 7453-7007
E-mail: info@BaseballSoftballUK.com
Website: www.BaseballSoftballUK.com
President: Kevin Macadam
Secretary General: Simon Gordon

Greece (GRE)
Hellenic Amateur Baseball Federation
(HABF)
Entrance A West Airport
Hellinikon D.C. 16777 Athens
Telephone: +30 210 985-9031; 985-9032
Fax: +30 210 985-9815
E-mail: info@baseballhellas.gr
Website: www.baseballhellas.gr
President: Panagiotis Mitsiopoulos
Secretary General: Ilias Koutroumani

Guam (GUM)
Guam Baseball Federation (GBF)
Bank of Guam, 111 Chalan Santo Papa,
Suite 137
Agana 96910
Telephone: +1 671 479-2265; 479-2267
Fax: +1 671 479-2266
E-mail: bgi@ite.net
Commissioner: Francis E. Santos

Guatemala (GUA)
Federación Nacional de Béisbol
Aficionado de Guatemala (FEDEBEIS)
National Amateur Baseball Federation
of Guatemala
Avenida Simeón Cañas,
Final Hipodromo del Norte
Zona 2, Guatemala Ciudad 01002
Telephone: +502 254-0858
Fax: +502 254-1119

E-mail: dmolina@fedebeis.org
President: David Molina Cassiano
Secretary General: Dagoberto Vásquez
Grajeda

Honduras (HON)
Federación Hondureña de Baseball
Aficionado (FEHBA)
Honduran Amateur Baseball
Federation
Complejo Deportivo "José Simon Azcona
del Hoyo"
Villa Olimpica, Tegucigalpa
Telephone: +504 221-0124
Fax: +504 232-1539
President: Conrado Rivera
Secretary General: Gustavo González

Hong Kong China (HKG)
Hong Kong Chinese Baseball Association
(HKBA)
Room 1003, Sports House
1 Stadium Path, Causeway Bay
Telephone: +852 2504-8330
Fax: +852 2504-4663
E-mail: hkbsa@hksdb.org.hk
Website: www.hkbaseball.org
President: Laurence Lee
Secretary General: Allan Mak Nin-fung

Hungary (HUN)
Magyar Országos Baseball és Softball
Szövetség (MOBSSz)
Hungarian National Baseball & Softball
Federation
PO Box 760
Budapest 1535
Telephone: +36 30 212-7827
Fax: +36 1 350-0415
E-mail: mobssz@posta.net
Website: www.baseball.hu
President: Attila Borbély
Secretary General: György Huszti

India (IND)
Amateur Baseball Federation of India
(ABFI)
Pocket E-19/12-13, Sector-3
Rohini, Delhi-110085
Telephone: +91 11 2006-2030
Fax: +91 11 2751-9327
E-mail: pc_bhardwaj@yahoo.com

Website: www.indiabaseball.com
President: Pius Pandarwani
Secretary General: Sudhanshu Roy

Indonesia (INA)
Perserikatan Baseball dan Softball
Amatir Seluruh Indonesia (PERBASASI)
Indonesia Amateur Baseball & Softball
Federation
Wisma Kosgoro Building, 14th Floor,
Jl.M.H. Thamrin 53
Jakarta 10350
Telephone: +62 21 230-0988
Fax: +62 21 230-0988
E-mail: basesoft@indo.net.id
Website: www.perbasasi.org
President: Abbas Adhar
Secretary General: Suryo Adi Prasetyo

Iran (IRI)
Baseball Federation, Islamic Republic of
Iran (BFI)
Varzandeh 51, Mofateh Avenue
Tehran 15815/1881
Telephone: +98 21 830-7813
Fax: +98 21 882-4014
E-mail: mbz.baseballir@hotmail.com
President: Mohammed Bacher
Zolfagharian
Secretary General: Mohammed Reza
Kashani

Ireland (IRL)
Baseball Ireland (BI)
Highfield, Pluckhimin Cross, Garristown
Co. Dublin 6
Telephone: +353 87 283-7494
Fax: +353 1 402-5850
E-mail: sean@baseballireland.com
Website: www.baseballireland.com
President: Sean Mitchell
Secretary General: Ann Flynn

Israel (ISR)
Israel Association of Baseball
(IAB)
Judith Fortis, PO Box 16t3
Kfar Saba 44101
Telephone: +972 9 765-7448
Fax: +972 9 792-0059
E-mail: isbasebl@zahav.ndt.il
Website: www.iab.org.il

President: Jay Zauderer
Secretary General: Ephraim Keren

Italia (ITA)
Federazione Italiana Baseball & Softball (FIBS)
Italian Baseball and Softball Federation
Viale Tiziano 70/74
00196 Roma
Telephone: +39 06 3685-8297; 3685-8337
Fax: +39 06 3685-8201; 323-3752
E-mail: info@baseball-softball.it
Website: www.baseball-softball.it
President: Riccardo Fraccari
Secretary General: Marcelo Standoli

Ivory Coast (CIV)
Fédération Ivoirienne de Baseball & Softball (FIBS)
Ivoirian Federation of Baseball and Softball
Immeuble EECI, Equipe Houdaille 3éme d.
Avenue Houdaille, Abidjan
Telephone: +225 20 206-252; 22 471-131
Fax: +225 20 322-471
E-mail: nketn@africaonline.co.ci
President: Etienne N'Guessan
Secretary General: Bilé Tanoe

Jamaica (JAM)
Jamaica Baseball Association
c/o Office of the Parliamentary Ombudsman
78 Harbor Street, PO Box 695, Kingston, West Indies
Telephone: +1 876 922-4882; 927-7742
Fax: +1 876 922-9830
President: Elouisa Sinclair

Japan (JPN)
Baseball Federation of Japan (BFJ)
Mainchi Palaceside Building 4F,
1-1-1, Hitosubashi
Chiyoda-ku, Tokyo 1000-0003
Telephone: +81 3 320-11155
Fax: +81 3 320-10707
E-mail: baseball@jaba.or.jp
Website: www.jaba.or.jp
President: Eiichiro Yamamoto
Secretary General: Masaru Ushiro

Kazakhstan (KAZ)
Baseball and Softball Federation of the Republic of Kazakhstan
56-156, Kazyibek Bi str. 156, apt. 56
Almaty
Telephone: +7 327 2 680-033
Fax: +7 327 2 686-305
Note: The country code 7 is temporarily the same as for Russia; it will eventually become 584 for Kazakhstan alone.
President: Zhan Kanapyanov
Secretary General: Mansur Yarullin

Kenya (KEN)
Baseball Federation of Kenya (BFK)
Association of Evangelicals of Africa and Madagascar
PO Box 50242
Nairobi
Telephone: +254 2 722-769; 714-977
Fax: +254 2 710-254
E-mail: aea@maf.org
President: Solomon Gacece
Secretary General: Hudson A. Liyai

Democratic Peoples Republic of Korea (PRK)
Baseball and Softball Association of DPR Korea
PO Box 56 Kumsongdong-2,
Kwangbok Street
Mangyondae District
Pyongyang City
Telephone: +850 2 181-11-ext.8164
Fax: +850 2 381-4403
President: Kim Su Hak
Secretary General: Ko Choi Ho

South Korea (KOR)
Korean Baseball Association (KBA)
4th Floor, Hall of Baseball, 946-16
Dogok-dong
Kangnam-gu, Seoul
Telephone: +82 2 572-8411
Fax: +82 2 572-7041
E-mail: baseball@koreabaseball.or.kr
Website: www.koreabaseball.or.kr/
President: Nae-Heun Lee
Secretary General: Sang-Hyun Lee

Lesotho (LES)
Lesotho Baseball and Softball
Association (LBSA)
PO Box 1319
Maseru 100
Telephone: +266 22 311-366
Fax: +266 22 310-494
President: Putsoa Moroke
Secretary General: Shelile Teboho

Liberia (LBR)
Liberia Baseball & Softball Association
c/o Charles Potter
PO Box 10-6473, Monrovia
Telephone: +231 227-176; 226-656
Fax: +231 226-007
President: Christian King
Secretary General: Fred J.A. Pratt

Lithuania (LTU)
Lietuvos Beisbolo Asociacija (LBA)
Lithuanian Baseball Association
Raudondvario 93
LT-3026 Kaunas
Telephone: +370 37 360-322
Fax: +370 37 360-323
E-mail: petras@lycos.com;
petras.v@mailcity.com
Website: www.beisbolas.lt
President: Jonas Kronkaitis
Secretary General: Petras Vilčinskas

Malaysia (MAS)
Federation of Baseball Malaysia (FBM)
N 6, Lorong Dugun, Damansara Heights
50490 Kuala Lumpur
Telephone: +603 252-2004
Fax: +603 252-5490; 958-3380
E-mail: nah49@pd.jaring.my
President: Abdullah Dato' Noh
Secretary General: Ibrahim Ramlay

Mali (MLI)
Fédération Malienne de Base-Ball et de
Softball (FMBS)
Malian Federation of Baseball and Softball
B.P. 1929
Bamako
Telephone: +223 297-478
Fax: +223 297-478
E-mail: traorefr3@afribane.net.mi
President: Lassana Traore

Malta (MLT)
Maltese Association Baseball Softball
(MABS)
2 Trig Ir-Rignu
Qormi QRM 10
Telephone: +356 2124-9626
E-mail: mariodebono@maltabaseball.org
President: Anthony Ghio
Secretary General: Mario Debono

Mexico (MEX)
Federación Mexicana de Béisbol
(FEMEBE)
Mexican Baseball Federation
Calle Berlin 15, 1er piso, Col. Juárez
Caja Postal 06600, México, D.F.
Telephone: +52 55 5546-1030
Fax: +52 55 5546-1031
E-mail: femebe@codeme.org.mx
Website: www.femebe.galeon.com
President: Carlos Buenrostro Avila
Secretary General: Enrique Mayorga
Betancourt

Micronesia (MCR)
Federated States of Micronesia Baseball
Federation
PO Box PS 319
Palikir, Pohnpei FM 96941
Telephone: +691 320-8914
Fax: +691 320-8915
E-mail: fsmnoc@mail.fm
President: Eliuel K. Pretrick
Secretary General: Jim Tobin

Moldova (MDA)
Association of Baseball & Softball of the
Republic of Moldova (BSFM)
Chetatia Alba s. 17
277002 Kishinev, MD 2002
Telephone: +373 2 527-184; 276-605
Fax: +373 2 275-216
E-mail: orgcomitee@yahoo.com;
baseball_md@mail.ru
President: Vladimir Rotari
Secretary General: Roman Ostapenco

Mongolia (MGL)
Mongolian National Federation of
Baseball (MBF)
"Tavan Erdene" Company Building,
Chinggis Khan Avenue, Khan-Uul
District

PO Box 357, Ulaanbaatar 210136
Telephone: +976 11 342-275; 342-210
Fax: +976 11 344-432
E-mail: chono@magicnet.mn
President: Enkhbold Tumurkhuyag
Secretary General: Tumendelger
Tsenddorj

Morocco (MAR)

Morocco Baseball Federation
55 Cité Es-Safadi, Villa Es-Saada
Rabat, Aviation
Telephone: +212 3 323-818
Fax: +212 3 310-691
President: Hamid Rachdi Alami

Namibia (NAM)

Namibia Baseball Association (NBA)
PO Box 32035
Windhoek
Telephone: +264 61 238-550
Fax: +264 61 238-553
E-mail: hankey@namibnet.com
President: Trevor Dawson

Netherlands (NED)

Koninklijke Nederlandse Baseball en
Softball Bond (KNBSB)
Royal Netherlands Baseball and
Softball Association
Perkinsbaan 15
3439 ND Nieuwegein
Telephone: +31 30 607-6070
Fax: +31 30 294-3043
E-mail: baseball.softball@knbsb.nl
Website: www.knbsb.nl
President: Theo Reitsma
Secretary General: Ruud van Zetten

Netherlands Antilles (AHO)

Netherlands Antillean Baseball
Federation (NABAFE)
Dr. W.P. Maalweg 40
Curaçao
Telephone: +599 9 465-5359; 463-7885
Fax: +599 9 463-7885
E-mail: FPH.Coronel@mindef.nl;
febeko@curinfo.an
Website: www.curinfo.com/febeko/
index.html
President: Kenneth Gijsbertha
Secretary General: Fermin Coronel

New Zealand (NZL)

New Zealand Baseball Federation
(NZBF)
PO Box 91035, Auckland Mail Center
14 Gibson Place, Howick, Auckland
Telephone: +64 9 634-2079
Fax: +64 9 634-5090
E-mail: nzbaseball@hotmail.com;
info@baseballnz.co.nz
Website: www.baseballnz.co.nz/
President: Glenn Campbell

Nicaragua (NCA)

Federación Nicaragüense de Béisbol
Asociada (FENIBA)
Nicaraguan Baseball Federation
Estadio "Dennis Martínez"
Apartado Postal 2443, Managua
Telephone: +505 222-2021; 222-7794
Fax: +505 268-0702
E-mail: gonzarm@ibw.com.ni
President: Bob Carlos García Solórzano
Secretary General: Edgard Martínez

Nigeria (NGR)

Nigerian Baseball & Softball Association
(NBSA)
302, Lju Waterworks Road, Ishaga
Agege, Lagos
Telephone: +234 1 492-5535; 266-8545
Fax: +234 1 492-5535
E-mail: tin@alpha.linkserve.com;
afstrag@cyberspace.net.ng
President: Ishola Williams
Secretary General: William Boyd

Norway (NOR)

Norges Soft og Baseball Forbund (NSBF)
Norwegian Softball and Baseball
Federation
Serviceboks 1, Ullevål Stadion
0840 Oslo
Telephone: +47 21 029-855
Fax: +47 21 029-003
E-mail: baseball@nif.idrett.no
Website: www.soft-baseball.no
President: Magnus Blom
Secretary General: Bjorn Christian Thode

Pakistan (PAK)

Pakistan Federation Baseball Softball
National Hockey Stadium

Ferozepur Road, Lahore
Telephone: +92 42 575-3928
Fax: +92 42 571-1828
E-mail: fakhar_shah@hotmail.com
President: Shaukat Javed
Secretary General: Khawar Shah

Palau (PLW)
Palau Major League
PO Box 155
Koror 96940
Telephone: +680 488-6562; 488-2577
Fax: +680 488-6563; 488-2862
E-mail: pnoc@palaunet.com
President: Alexander R. Merep
Secretary General: Elbuchel Sadang

Panamá (PAN)
Federación Panameña de Béisbol
Aficionado (FEDEBEIS)
Panamanian Amateur Baseball
Federation
Estadio Nacional, Avenida Cerro
Patacón
Kilómetro 3, Apartado 9664, Zona 4,
Panamá
Telephone: +507 230-4524; 230-5399
Fax: +507 230-4525; 230-5399
E-mail: fedebeis@cwpanama.net
President: Franz Wever
Secretary General: Eduardo Alfaro

Papua New Guinea (PNG)
Papua New Guinea Baseball Federation
PO Box 1096
Boroko NCD
Telephone: +675 323-6974
Fax: +675 323-6974
E-mail: wpp@datec.com.pg
President: Wesley Pailkolus

Peru (PER)
Federación Peruana de Béisbol (FDMBP)
Avenida Canadá, Cuadra 30
San Luis, Lima 30
Telephone: +51 1 473-2870
Fax: +51 1 473-2870
E-mail: fpb@ec-red.com
President: Gerardo Maury Takayama
Secretary General: Juan Palomino
Yamamoto

Philippines (PHI)
Philippine Amateur Baseball Association
(PABA)
7487 Bagtikan Street, SAV, Makati 1203
Metro Manila
Telephone: +63 2 890-8277; 896-7218
Fax: +63 2 897-7732
E-mail: 618hcn@itextron.com
President: Héctor Cruz Navasero
Secretary General: Ernesto P. Abarientos

Poland (POL)
Polski Zwiazek Baseballu i Softballu
(PZBS)
Polish Baseball & Softball Federation
ul. Sygnaly 62, 44-251 Rybnik 9
woj Slaskie
Telephone: +48 32 421-8822
Fax: +48 32 421-8822
E-mail: pzball-rybnik@wp.pl
Website: www.baseball.com.pl/
President: Jan Liszka
Secretary General: Jan Smolka

Portugal (POR)
Federação Portuguesa de Beisebol e
Softbol (FPBS)
Portuguese Baseball and Softball
Federation
Rua Padre António Vieira,
C.C. Charlot 2
Loja 36 Cave – 8100-611 Loulé
Telephone: +351 28 941-3838
Fax: +351 28 941-3518
E-mail: f.p.baseball@mail.telepac.pt
President: José Gonçalves
Secretary General: Ricardo Panuzzio

Puerto Rico (PUR)
Federación de Béisbol Aficionado de
Puerto Rico (FBAPR)
Amateur Baseball Federation of
Puerto Rico
PO Box 7707 Carolina 000986-7707
Plazoleto Edificio Jesús T. Piñero,
Calle Fernández
Juncos Esq. Molinillo, Carolina 00985
Telephone: +1 787 768-8540; 776-8060
Fax: +1 787 752-7729
President: Israel Roldán González
Secretary General: José Martínez

Romania (ROM)
Federación Rumana de Béisbol y Softbol
(FRBS)
Romanian Baseball and Softball
Federation (RBSF)
B-dul Basarabiei 37-39, Sector 2
Bucaresti cod 73403
Telephone: +40 21 324-9106
Fax: +40 21 324-9106
E-mail: frbs@go.ro
President: Vasile Molan
Secretary General: Cristian Costescu

Russia (RUS)
Russian Baseball Federation (RBF)
8, Luzhnetskaya nab. 8
Moscow, GSP 119992
Telephone: +7-095 725-4549
Fax: +7-095 248-3434
*Note: Any leading zero before city codes is
usually omitted in international dialing, but
is required for Moscow regardless of the
caller's location.*
E-mail: rusbaseball@roc.ru
Website: www.geocities.com/rusbaseball
President: Yuri Kopilov
Secretary General: Vladimir Telkov

San Marino (SMR)
Federazione Sammarinese
Baseball-Softball (FSBS)
San Marino Federation Baseball Softball
Via Rancaglia 30
47899 Serravalle
Telephone: +378 901-211; 906-488
Fax: +378 906-468
E-mail: fsbs@omniway.sm
President: Maurizio Gasperoni
Secretary General: Fabrizia Giuccioli

Serbia-Montenegro *(see Yugoslavia)*

Singapore (SIN)
Singapore Baseball & Softball
Association (SBSA)
722 North Bridge Road
Singapore 198690
Telephone: +65 6345-0646
Fax: +65 6299-1343
E-mail: abdulazi@cyberway.com.sg
President: Johnny Goh

Secretary General: Abdul Aziz Bin Abu
Talib

Slovakia (SVK)
Slovenská Baseballová Federácia
(SBF)
Slovak Baseball Federation
Junácka 6
Bratislava 832 80
Telephone: +421 2 4924-9547
Fax: +421 2 4924-9547
E-mail: sbf@sztk.sk
Website: www.sbf.sk
President: Stanislav Horacek
Secretary General: Frantisek Bunta

Slovenia (SLO)
Zveza za Baseball in Softball Slovenije
(ZBSS)
Baseball and Softball Association of
Slovenia (BSAS)
Savlje 6, P.P. 3722
1001 Ljubljana
Telephone: +386 40 614-026
Fax: +386 1 786-4202
E-mail: zbss@siol.net
Website: www.baseball-softball-zveza.si
President: Igor Veselinovic
Secretary General: Egon Süssinger

South Africa (RSA)
South African Baseball Union
(SABU)
PO Box 2398, Highlands North
Johannesburg 2037
Telephone: +27 83 453-4211
Fax: +27 11 443-9960
E-mail: baseball@icon.co.za
President: Mark Alexander
Secretary General: Moira Dempsey

Spain (ESP)
Real Federación Española de Béisbol y
Sófbol (RFEBS)
Spanish Royal Federation of Baseball
and Softball
Calle Coslada 10-4 Izda
28028 Madrid
Telephone: +34 91 355-2844
Fax: +34 91 355-1206
E-mail: rfebsm@arrakis.es
Website: rfebeisbolsofbol.com

President: Julio Pernas López
Secretary General: Luis Angel Melero
Martín

Sri Lanka (SRI)
Sri Lanka Amateur Baseball & Softball
Association
c/o 55, Janadhipathi Mawatha
Colombo 1
Telephone: +94 1 722-658; 724-254
Fax: +94 1 501-934
President: A.M. Moragosa

Sweden (SWE)
Svenska Baseboll och Softboll Förbundet
(SBSF)
Swedish Baseball and Softball Federation
Idrottshuset, Mårbackagatan 19SE 123 43
Farsta
Telephone: +46 8 605-6288; 605-6000;
683-3028
Fax: +46 8 605-6287; 683-3029
E-mail: basesoft@swipnet.se;
info@baseboll-softboll.se
Website: www.baseboll-softboll.se
President: Mats Fransson
Secretary General: Kristian Palvia

Switzerland (SUI)
Suisse Baseball & Softball Federation (SBSF)
Swiss Baseball & Softball Association
Birsmatt str. 21
4106 Therwil
Telephone: +41 61 721-5463
Fax: +41 61 723-8191
E-mail: jmsschmitt@datacomm.ch
Website: www.swiss-baseball.ch
President: Carmen Schwab
Secretary General: Monique Schmitt

Chinese Taipei (TPE)
Chinese Taipei Baseball Association
(CTBA)
16 Floor, 270 Chung Hsiao East Road, sec. 4
Taipei City 106
Telephone: +886 2 2711-8128 ext. 152
Fax: +886 2 2711-5487
E-mail: ctba@ctba.org.tw
Website: www.ctba.org.tw
President: Tom C. H. Peng
Secretary General: Richard C. Lin

Thailand (THA)
Amateur Baseball Association of
Thailand (ABAT)
No. 1 Moo 7, Phaholyyothin Road, Km. 51
Tambol Chiang Rak-Noi, Ayutthaya 13180
Telephone: +66 35 361-439
Fax: +66 35 361-477
E-mail: abat@minebea.co.th
President: Tienchai Sirisumpan
Secretary General: Vutichai
Udomkarnjananan

Togo (TOG)
Fédération Togolaise de Baseball et
Softball (FTBS)
Togo Federation of Baseball and Softball
57 Rue de l'Ogou
B.P. 330, Lomé
Telephone: +228 21 2390; 21 2391
Fax: +228 21 5165
E-mail: ftgtt@yahoo.com
President: Koshi Djodji Tamakloe
Secretary General: Agbogbankou
Anoumou Drackey

Tunisia (TUN)
Fédération Tunisienne de Baseball et
Softball (FTBS)
Tunisian Federation of Baseball and
Softball
5 Rue Bab Souika – 1006 Tunis
B.P. No. 61 – 1059 Tunis, Hafsia
Telephone: +216 71 565-486
Fax: +216 71 565-486
President: Mohamed Ben Guiza
Secretary General: Naoufel Kaddour

Uganda (UGA)
Uganda Baseball and Softball
Association
PO Box 30034
Kampala
Telephone: +256 41 285-861
Fax: +256 41 285-861
E-mail: somuganda@yahoo.com
President: Shilla Agonzibwe
Secretary General: Barnabas Mwesiga

Ukraine (UKR)
Ukraine Baseball Softball Federation
Kropyvnytskogo st. 14
Kiev 01004

Telephone: +380 44 490-3973
Fax: +380 44 490-3973
E-mail: kostyuk17@mail.ru
President: Olexander Nikulin
Executive Director: Vitaly Lizogubenko

United States of America (USA)
USA Baseball
Overlook Building, 4825 Creekstone
Drive, Suite 200
Durham, NC 27703
Telephone: +1 919 474-8721
Fax: +1 919 474-8822
E-mail: info@usabaseball.com
Website: www.usabaseball.com
President: Mike Gaski
Executive Director: Paul Seiler

U.S. Virgin islands (ISV)
Virgin Islands Baseball Federation (VIBF)
Innovative Business Center
4006 Estate Diamond, St. Croix 00820
Telephone: +1 340 773-4425
Fax: +1 340 773-4425
President: Thomas A. Johnson
Secretary General: Morgan D. Quigley

Uzbekistan (UZB)
Uzbekistan Baseball Federation (UZBF)
15/1, Almazar str.
70003 Tashkent
Telephone: +998 712 306-630; 712 455-254
Fax: +998 712 459-609; 711 207-444
E-mail: uzbfed@yahoo.com
President: Fazlitdin Najimitdinov
Secretary General: Rustam Abdukadyrov

Venezuela (VEN)
Federación Venezolana de Béisbol (FVB)
Venezuelan Baseball Federation
Avenida Urdaneta, Animas a Platanal,
Edificio Las Marias
Piso 4, Oficina 401, Caracas
Telephone: +58 212 563-5919; 564-2316
Fax: +58 212 563-5919
E-mail: fserrano@fedebeisbol.org.ve

President: Francisco José Serrano
Secretary General: Oscar Antonio Izaguirre

Western Samoa (SAM)
Western Samoa Baseball Association
c/o-Samoa NOC & Sports Federation
Private Bag, Apia
Telephone: +685 25-033
Fax: +685 26-701; 26-675
President: Niko Palamo
Secretary General: Henry Taefu

Yugoslavia (YUG)
Yugoslav Baseball Association (YBA)
Serbia-Montenegro Baseball Federation
(SMBF)
29, Novembra 39a
Belgrade 11000
Telephone: +381 11 323-6364
Fax: +381 11 311-6286
E-mail: chipper@yubc.net;
yuba@yubc.net
President: Milan Zonic
Secretary General: Nikola Vucevic

Zambia (ZAM)
Zambia Softball & Baseball Association
(ZSBA)
PO Box 70561
Ndola
Telephone: +260 221-7149
Fax: +260 222-6706
President: Raymond Pitcher
Secretary General: Fred Mulenga

Zimbabwe (ZIM)
Zimbabwe Baseball & Softball
Association (ZBSA)
PO Box 6539
Harare
Telephone: +263 4 773-725
Fax: +263 4 773-725
E-mail: aoa@ecoweb.co.zw
President: Mtasa Mandishona
Secretary General: Violet Soko

PROVISIONAL MEMBER COUNTRIES

Luxembourg (LUX)
Luxembourg Baseball Federation
212, rte de Burange
B.P. 272, 3429 Dudelange, Luxembourg

Telephone: +352 2651-3960
Fax: +352 2651-3960
E-mail: baseball@pt.lu
President: Serge Jetzen

Marshall Islands (IMA)
Republic of Marshall Islands Baseball
Federation
Ministry of Social Services
PO Box 1138, Majuro 96960
Telephone: +692 625-3422; 625-3384
Fax: +692 625-3902
President: Danny Wase
Secretary General: Jeimata Kabua

Saipan (NMI)
Saipan Major League Baseball
Association
c/o KMCV News, Nauru Building
Susupe MP 96950
Telephone: +1 670 664-8887;
234-5498

Fax: +1 670 664-8889; 235-4966
E-mail: rosei@nmcet.edu;
rligitol@gtepacifica.net
President: Tom B. Pangelinan
Secretary General: Rose L. Igitol

Turkey (TUR)
Turkiye Beyzbol Federasyonu
Ulus Iş Hani A Blok Kat. 5
No. 507
Ulus Ankara
Telephone: +90 312 309-8646
Fax: +90 312 312-3992
E-mail: beyzbolfed@mynet.com
Website: www.tbsf.org.tr
President: Kamil Kehale
Secretary General: Fikret Bulutgu

IBAF Annual Awards

Year	Coach of the Year	Umpire of the Year	Executive of the Year
1982	Servio Borges (CUB)	Tom Ravashiere (USA)	Bruno Beneck (ITA)
1983	V.R. Woo-Hung (KOR)	Alfredo Paz (CUB)	Miguel Oropeza (MEX)
1984	Reiichi Matsunaga (JPN)	Riccardo Fraccari (ITA)	Manuel González (CUB)
1985	Juan Delís (CUB)	Howard Chapman (CAN)	Casmer Pielak (CAN)
1986	Wu Hsiang Mu (TPE)	Chris Pieters (NED)	Guus van der Heijden (NED)
1987	Ron Fraser (USA)	Ivan Davis (CUB)	Eiichiro Yamamoto (JPN)
1988	Lin Chia-Hsiang (TPE)	Roberto Marchi (ITA)	Aldo Notari (ITA)
1989	Mark Marquess (USA)	Anibal Rosario (PUR)	Jang Nak Kim (KOR)
1990	José Carradero (PUR)	Jim Cressman (CAN)	P. P. Tang (TPE)
1991	Todashi Watanabe (JPN)	Javier Pallarés (ESP)	Neville Pratt (AUS)
1992	John Haar (CAN)	Kao Chuen-Yon (TPE)	Miguel Ortín (ESP)
1993	Jorge Fuentes (CUB)	Katshisa Fuse (JPN)	Robert E. Smith (USA)
1994	Kim Dae Kwen (KOR)	Nelson Díaz (CUB)	Jorge Otsuka (BRA)
1995	Steve Cohen (USA)	Yoshikazu Tanaka (JPN)	Reynaldo González (CUB)
1996	Jorge Fuentes (CUB)	Juan Hernández Reyes (MEX)	Tsutomu Shida (JPN)
1997	Michael Young (AUS)	Richard Fetchiet (USA)	Miguel Angel Pozueta (ESP)
1998	Silvano Ambrosioni (ITA)	Gustavo Rodríguez (USA)	Marlene Campbell (AUT)
1999	Michael Young (AUS)	Dave Yeast (USA)	Mark Alexander (RSA)
2000	Eung-Yong Kim (KOR)	Anibal Rosario (PUR)	Osvaldo Gil (PUR)
2001	Higinio Vélez (CUB)	Joe Burleson (USA)	Tom C. H. Peng (TPE)
2002	Seong Ro Joo (KOR)	Wiilie Rodríguez (PUR)	Carlos Rodríguez Acosta (CUB)

Annotated Bibliography

• •

This brief and highly selective bibliography offers annotations for major works valuable in the pursuit of world baseball history, followed by a list of further less primary resources (without annotation). Many of these materials were invaluable in producing the current volume. Others are offered to guide researchers and readers wishing to delve more deeply into baseball's infrequently told international saga.

MAJOR RESOURCES: ANNOTATED BIBLIOGRAPHY

General Works

Baldassaro, Lawrence, and Richard A. Johnson, eds. *The American Game: Baseball and Ethnicity*. Carbondale, IL: Southern Illinois University Press, 2002.

Nine scholarly essays tracing cultural and racial influences of distinct major ethnic or immigrant groups on major league baseball from the 1870s down to the present and thus also offering a valuable one-volume ethnic and racial profile of the American national sport. Ethnic groups covered include British, German, Irish, Afro-American, Italian, Jewish, Slavic (Eastern European), Latin American, and Asian-Pacific (Japanese and Hawaiian).

Bjarkman, Peter C. *Baseball with a Latin Beat: A History of the Latin American Game*. Jefferson, NC: McFarland, 1994.

Pioneering scholarly study of Latin American baseball culture and history, treating both the saga of Latinos in the major leagues and the origins and development of baseball in Latin America and the Caribbean island nations (Cuba, Mexico, the Dominican Republic, Panama, Puerto Rico, Venezuela, Nicaragua, and additional Caribbean outposts). Detailed player stats, history of the winter leagues, and an extensive Latin American baseball chronology.

———, ed. "An Olympic-Year Appreciation of Baseball around the Globe." Special issue, *The National Pastime: A Review of Baseball History* 12 (Fall 1992).

Special issue of the annual baseball journal published by the Society for American Baseball Research (SABR). Wide-ranging essays on international baseball themes published in conjunction with the first official Olympic medal competitions in baseball. Topics include Mexico's 1946 recruiting war with the majors, Puerto Rico's winter league as launching pad for future hall of famers, Russian (Japanese League) pitching star Victor Starffin, Latino blacks in the majors before Jackie Robinson, Canadian baseball pioneers, Sadaharu Oh's true legacy, and emerging Soviet baseball.

García, Carlos J. *Baseball Forever! (Béisbol Para Siempre!)* Mexico City, Mexico; privately printed, ca. 1978.

Invaluable if hard-to-find source outlining baseball origins in numerous nations around the globe. Contains chronologies for both organized baseball and international amateur baseball, numerous black-and-white photos, and notes on the origin and development of major international amateur tournaments. Includes baseball's roots, deep or superficial, in some fifty different countries, and also features a broad history of the international amateur baseball movement.

Humber, William. *Let's Play Ball: Inside the Perfect Game*. Toronto: Lester & Orpen Dennys Publishers, 1989.

Published in conjunction with a March–October 1989 baseball history and culture exhibit at Toronto's Royal Ontario Museum and written by Canada's leading baseball historian. Traces the origins, development, and appeal of the sport both inside and outside the U.S. major leagues. Contains a superb chapter on international competition ("Baseball Around the World"), as well as numerous black-and-white photos and a useful reading list emphasizing baseball's cultural appeal.

Jiménez, José de Jesús. *Archivo de Béisbol (The Baseball Archive)*. Santo Domingo, Dominican Republic: privately printed, 1977.

Heavy emphasis on major league history (interestingly told from the perspective of a Dominican fan), but also contains valuable if dated information on the Latinos and Dominicans performing in organized baseball. Photos and complete major and minor league career stats (to 1977) for top Latin American big league stars. Special achievement here is integration of the saga of Latin stars into a backdrop of comprehensive big league history.

Krich, John. *El Béisbol: Travels through the Pan-American Pastime*. New York: Atlantic Monthly Press, 1989.

Flowery and sometimes pompous account of one author's travels in Spanish-speaking baseball countries in search of the true local flavor of a shared national sport. Entertaining often culturally biased portraits of Latino appreciation for baseball, and also of Caribbean and Latin adaptations of baseball culture. Cuba (baseball's main Latin outpost) is omitted from Krich's treatment, a fact which diminishes the scope of his analysis.

Latino Baseball Magazine. Ninth Edition. New York: King Paniagua Publications, 1999. (Spanish–English bilingual edition) (Published in annual editions, 1991–1999)

Published annually through the 1990s in near-identical format. Celebrates the role of Latin Americans and U.S. Hispanics in major league baseball. Each edition features a selection of some of the following: sharp color photos and graphics, feature stories on individual Latino big league stars, treatments of baseball's origins in individual Latin countries, accounts of the year's winter league or Caribbean series action, country-by-country lists of Latins who played in the big leagues.

McNeil, William F. *Baseball's Other All-Stars*. Jefferson, NC: McFarland, 2000.

Attempt at resurrecting careers of baseball's forgotten stars from outside the major leagues (the winter leagues, Cuban and Japanese pro leagues, Mexican League, Negro leagues). Player portraits are largely superficial and not based on any original research; meaningless comparisons are drawn by projecting big league season parameters (550 at-bats per season) for shorter foreign seasons; many errors in the historical summaries for Cuba and Mexico. There is little redeeming about this volume and it is included here only to warn readers away from an entirely misleading resource.

Oleksak, Michael M., and Mary Adams Oleksak. *Béisbol: Latin Americans and the Grand Old Game*. Grand Rapids, Michigan: Masters Press, 1991.

Early treatment of Latin American baseball history heavily focused on Latino ballplayers reaching the U.S. majors; outstripped by more recent treatments. Helpful bibliography and now outdated major league player list, along with some very readable portraits on top Latino stars. The volume is marred by numerous typographical and historical errors which weaken scholarly value.

Regalado, Samuel O. *Viva Baseball! Latin Major Leaguers and Their Special Hunger*. Urbana and Chicago: University of Illinois Press, 1998.

Story of Latin American and Caribbean baseball history, focused on Latino contributions to the majors, but also featuring brief accounts of baseball origins in most Latin outposts. Regalado's approach is largely anecdotal and emphasizes the special struggles of Latin ballplayers to adjust to North American culture and customs, racial prejudices, and the English language. Useful bibliography and extensive footnotes accompany the lively text.

Canada

Cauz, Louis. *Baseball's Back in Town: From the Don to the Blue Jays, a History of Baseball in Toronto*. Toronto: Controlled Media Corporation, 1977.

Celebratory historical account of Toronto-area baseball published on the occasion of big league expansion into the Ontario city. Most notable for enthralling rare photographs. Heavy emphasis is naturally on Toronto's previous rich International League history, but much valuable detail is also provided concerning the off-field story of the birth of the American League Blue Jays.

Humber, William. *Diamonds of the North: A Concise History of Baseball in Canada*. Toronto; New York: Oxford University Press, 1995.

Most exhaustive history of baseball played in Canada and one of the best and most thoroughgoing histories of baseball outside of the big leagues. Rare details of baseball's amateur and professional evolution in each Canadian province, hundreds of black-and-white archive photos, extensive listings of all Canadian major leaguers and all Canadian minor league affiliations, racial integration in Canada, and the arrival of major leaguers.

———. *Cheering for the Home Team: The Story of Baseball in Canada*. Erin, Ontario: The Boston Mill Press, 1983.

Humber's earlier and briefer but nonetheless equally impressive history of Canada's baseball pageant. Likewise notable for its stunning (if fewer) photographs, this treatment lacks only the details of baseball evolution in western and central provinces during the late nineteenth and early twentieth centuries. Contains a useful statistical chart of Canadian big leaguers.

Shearon, Jim. *Canada's Baseball Legends: True Stories of Canadians in the Big Leagues Since 1879*. Kanata, Ontario: Malin Head Press, 1994.

Rather prosaic portraits of Canada's more historically significant or better-known major leaguers. Best feature is the choice of player photographs, alongside several entertaining anecdotes not likely found elsewhere. Divided into five sections: The Pioneers (1879–1925), the Golden Age (1930–1950), the 1950s and 1960s, the 1970s and 1980s, and Stars of Today and Tomorrow. Records section contains Canadian career leaders for pitching and batting.

Turner, Dan. *Heroes, Bums and Ordinary Men: Profiles in Canadian Baseball*. Toronto: Doubleday Canada, 1988.

Charming and literate profiles of some of Canada's leading baseball names, including big leaguers (among them stars such as Larry Walker, Fergie Jenkins, Terry Puhl; plus also-rans such as Reno Bertoia, Goody Rosen, Ted Bowsfield), founders, women ballplayers, and even Canada's 1987 national team. Personalities are captured in off-beat photo portraits.

Caribbean Series

Araujo Bojórquez, Alfonso. *Guías de las Series del Caribe, 1949–1995 (Guides to the Caribbean Series, 1949–1995)*. Obregón, Sonora, Mexico: privately printed, 1995.

Year-by-year statistical companion to Caribbean series competitions through the mid-1990s. Special features include lists of yearly team champions and individual batting and pitching leaders for all major categories; game-by-game scores (with winning and losing pitchers) for every Series; single-game, single-year, and all-time records for individual and team performances; and lifetime Series-by-Series batting and pitching totals for important ballplayers appearing in this event. Some black-and-white photos are included.

Nuñez, José Antero. *El Serie del Caribe, 1949–1995 (The Caribbean Series, 1949–1995)*. Volume V: *De La Habana a Quisqueya (From Havana to Quisqueya Stadium)*. Caracas, Venezuela: Impresos Urbina, 1995.

This fifth volume of Nuñez's Series coverage offers historical reviews of significant pre-Series Latin American tournaments of 1930s; chapters devoted to pioneering individual ballplayer batting achievements; all-time offense, defense, and pitching records; detailed game-by-game summaries of the 1995 Series in Puerto Rico; and an all-time records section.

———. *El Serie del Caribe, 1989 (The Caribbean Series, 1989)*. Caracas, Venezuela: Impresos Urbina, 1988.

Nuñez's third volume provides a detailed summary chapter on the inaugural 1949 Havana event; a section dedicated to seventeen unforgettable moments from past Series history; detailed game-by-game accounts (with box scores) of the 1989 tournament in Mazatlán, Mexico. Also separate chapters detailing offense and defense leaders for all past years; the top pitching performances of past seasons; and past home run leaders, managers, and umpires.

———. *El Serie del Caribe, 1988 (The Caribbean Series, 1988)*. Caracas, Venezuela: Impresos Urbina, 1988.

Second volume in the collection of annual Nuñez guides sets the format for following issues. Black-and-white photos and crude ink-sketched cartoons are interspersed with historical summaries, details of the 1988 (Series XXX) Dominican-based championships (with box scores and game-by-game summaries); tributes to memorable past ballplayers and managers; and the standard section summarizing year-by-year individual leaders and all-time Series records.

Cuba

Bjarkman, Peter C. *Baseball's Mysterious Island: A True History of Baseball in Fidel Castro's Cuba*. Jefferson, NC: McFarland, forthcoming.

Most extensive account of Cuban baseball history currently available, featuring narrative text, detailed statistics, and numerous rare black-and-white photographs. Unique among all Cuban baseball histories for its balanced reviews of both the prerevolution and postrevolution Cuban leagues, as well as of Cuba's impressive century-long amateur baseball tradition. Bibliography and statistical appendices, along with a thorough Cuban baseball chronology.

Casa, Edel, Jorge Alfonso, and Alberto Pestana. *Viva y en juego (Alive and playing)*. Havana, Cuba: Editorial Científico Técnica, 1986.

Only extensive history of island baseball published within Cuba during the postrevolution period. Limited photos but valuable detail on world amateur tournaments, National Series seasons, Selective Series seasons, and chronology of early Cuban professional baseball. Oriented toward trumpeting the achievements and values of postrevolution amateur play.

González Echevarría, Roberto. *The Pride of Havana: A History of Cuban Baseball*. New York: Oxford University Press, 1999.

An exhaustive narrative history of Cuban baseball before the revolution, with superficial treatment of post-1961 era. Unmatched explanations of Cuban baseball origins, off-the-field evolutions of Cuban League in the early twentieth century, and the connection between baseball and Cuban concepts of nationality. Disappointing on baseball tradition under Fidel Castro.

Guía Oficial: Béisbol (Official Cuban League Baseball Guide). Havana, Cuba: Editorial Deportes, 2003. (Published in annual editions after 1998)

Invaluable statistical guides to Cuban League baseball, begun in the 1960s with several handsome editions but then dropped until their reappearance in the mid-1990s. Exhaustive stats on yearly National Series and Selective Series seasons, including individual leaders in batting and pitching categories, team records, and career stats for all past Cuban Leaguers.

Jamail, Milton. *Full Count: Inside Cuban Baseball.* Carbondale, IL: The Southern Illinois University Press, 2000.

Rationale and support for opening up the Cuban League as a new and valued source for replenishing waning big league talent. Jamail only superficially outlines Cuba's extensive baseball history but provides best existing account of how the state-run Cuban baseball machinery operates. A generally negative portrait of Cuban baseball in its present form.

Pettavino, Paula J., and Geralyn Pye. *Sport in Cuba: A Diamond in the Rough.* Pittsburgh, PA: University of Pittsburgh Press, 1994.

Scholarly analysis of the motives, structure, development, triumphs, and failures of state-controlled sports under the communist government of Fidel Castro. Loaded with charts and statistics, this treatment covers all sports activities and explains most thoroughly the political and social roles for athletics in Cuban society. Baseball is a primary focus throughout.

Price, S.L. *Pitching Around Fidel: A Journey into the Heart of Cuban Sports.* New York: The Ecco Press, 2000.

Sports Illustrated writer travels around Cuba to interview both well-known and obscure Cuban athletes, drawing out their guarded opinions on the pros and cons of the athlete's life on the communist island. Baseball is not a sole focus, but nonetheless a central one, and big league defectors Rey Ordóñez and Duque Hernández are profiled alongside island loyalist (and 1990s pitching star) Lázaro Valle.

Rucker, Mark, and Peter C. Bjarkman. *Smoke: The Romance and Lore of Cuban Baseball.* New York: Total Sports Illustrated, 1999.

Unparalleled photographic record of Cuban baseball (1860s–present) with stunning color and black-and-white photos collected from all corners of the island. Rucker and Bjarkman traveled widely in Cuba during four baseball seasons and enjoyed total access and full cooperation from INDER (Cuban Sports Ministry) and Cuban League officials.

Santana Alonso, Alfredo. *El Inmortal del Béisbol: Martín Dihigo (Baseball's Immortal: Martín Dihigo).* Havana, Cuba: Editorial Científico Técnica, 1998.

The only full (if brief) biography of Cuba's legendary diamond star, Negro league immortal, and Cooperstown hall of famer. Many helpful details of Dihigo's early life and lengthy ballplaying career are included, along with lifetime statistics, winter-ball feats, and details of the star athlete's postcareer life and much-lamented death. Numerous photos, but most are of poor quality.

Torres, Angel. *La Leyenda del Béisbol Cubano, 1878–1997 (The Legend of Cuban Baseball, 1878–1997).* Miami, Florida: Review Printers [privately printed], 1996.

Inaccurately titled volume, which extends its treatment of Cuba's baseball story only up to the shutdown of Cuban pro winter seasons after 1961. Valuable nonetheless for season-by-season summaries, team rosters, listings of league leaders, many black-and-white newsprint photos, individual ballplayer portraits, and nuggets of trivia covering the full scope of pre-1961 Cuban baseball.

Dominican Republic

Alou, Felipe (with Herm Weiskopf). *Felipe Alou . . . My Life in Baseball*. Waco, TX: Word Books, 1967.

> One of the most readable and informative among such standard player autobiographies, published at the height of Alou's successful playing career and especially valuable here for its revealing portrait of life as a youth in the Dominican Republic and frank opinions on the roles and experiences of Latinos (especially black Latinos) in organized baseball.

Joyce, Gare. *The Only Ticket off the Island*. Toronto: Lester & Orpen Dennys Publishers, 1990.

> Toronto journalist spends a winter wandering the Dominican baseball beat in attempt to explain Dominican love for the game and to understand the impact of Dominican players on the majors (especially on the hometown American League Blue Jays). Entertaining portrait of winter baseball, but lacking the sophistication and insights of Ruck or Klein.

Klein, Alan M. *Sugarball: The American Game, the Dominican Dream*. New Haven, CT: Yale University Press, 1991.

> Klein's take on the Dominican baseball phenomena and explanations for the productive Dominican big league talent pipeline. Klein's treatment (like many of his ideas) parallels Ruck's, but lacks much of the latter's intimate first-hand appreciation for the actual Dominican baseball experience. Like Ruck, Klein sees baseball as defining past and present Dominican–U.S. political relations.

La Pelota Nuestra–Revista Annual del Béisbol Invernal Dominicano (Our Baseball—Dominican Winter League Baseball Annual Magazine). Santo Domingo, Dominican Republic: Editora Doble A, 1994.

> Most attractive and utilitarian among several Dominican winter league guidebooks. Crammed with numerous top-quality color and black-and-white photos, informative player profiles and event summaries, and reams of statistical info (including career stats for all active ballplayers, plus useful lists of imported major league stars who earlier performed in the Dominican Republic).

Piña, Tony. *Presencia Dominicana (The Dominican Presence)*. Santo Domingo: Editoria Colegial Quisqueyana, 1988.

> Treatment of Dominican Republic's major leaguers through final seasons of the 1980s. Piña includes career stats and personal data for all past Dominican big leaguers, career summaries of then-current players, a detailed chronology of events involving Dominicans in the majors, landmark achievements (such as one-hitters for pitchers), and black-and-white player photos consisting in large part of Xerox reproductions of Topps bubblegum trading cards.

———. *Los Grandes Finales (The Grand Finals)*. Santo Domingo: Editoria Colegial Quisqueyana, 1981.

> Complete season-by-season history (1951–1981) of the championship finals (best-of-nine series after 1972) in Dominican winter league. Each chapter (each year) includes detailed narrative history, complete box scores for all games, and valuable composite summaries of all individual batting and pitching data. Photos are limited, however, to one star player portrait (often a Topps bubblegum card reproduction) for each season summary section.

———. *Guía del Béisbol Profesional Dominicano (Official Guidebook of the Dominican Professional Baseball League)*. Eighth Edition. Santo Domingo: Editorama, 1989. (Published in annual editions, 1982–1989)

> These encyclopedic annual guidebooks feature all relevant statistical data for Dominican League winter seasons. Each volume summarizes the previous season and updates annual data on individual pitching and batting league leaders; individual records for career totals, single games and single seasons; and total career statistics for all currently active players.

Ruck, Rob. *The Tropic of Baseball: Baseball and the Dominican Republic.* Westport, CT: Meckler Publishers, 1991.

Intimate historical and contemporary portrait of baseball in the Dominican Republic and persuasive explanation for the sport's central role in Dominican cultural and national life. Ruck aims to explain why Dominicans have in recent decades provided the biggest influx of major leaguers from outside U.S. borders and also how baseball shapes both Dominican consciousness as well as the nation's highly ambivalent attitude toward the United States.

Sánchez Peralta, Luichy. *Cronologia Dominicana en Grandes Ligas, 1995 (Dominican Major League Chronology, 1995).* Santiago, Dominican Republic: Impresora Editora Teófilo, 1995.

Statistical handbook providing valuable data on Dominican big leaguers through the mid-1990s. Tables and lists include personal data on all players, yearly lists of Dominicans currently in the majors, complete lifetime individual player statistics, big league leaders among Dominicans, and Dominicans in All-Star games and big league postseason play.

Japan

Johnson, Daniel E. *Japanese Baseball: A Statistical Handbook.* Jefferson, NC: McFarland, 1999.

First English-language source containing extensive Japanese baseball data, covering all pro seasons from 1936 until 1997. Season-by-season team standings, individual leaders for batting and pitching, and All-Star game and postseason playoff results (Central League and Pacific League). Career and single-season individual records also included.

Maitland, Brian. *Japanese Baseball: A Fan's Guide.* Rutland, VT: Charles E. Tuttle, 1991.

Hard-to-find overview of Japanese pro league history containing stats, player profiles, and accounts of baseball's early development in the island nation. Maitland contrasts big league play with Japanese baseball and offers both his assessments of Japanese playing styles and his ratings of major league potential among the top Japanese professionals.

Oh, Sadaharu, and David Falkner. *Sadaharu Oh: A Zen Way of Baseball.* New York: Vintage Books (Random House), 1984.

Still unrivaled explanation of Japanese baseball culture, revealed with intimate portrait of Japan's greatest-ever baseball hero. Oh lays out his own and his country's approach to baseball as a paternalistic management system built on notions of collective responsibility and paralleling the world of corporate big business. As much a guide to controlling the secrets of our human spirit as it is a book about perfecting foolproof batting techniques.

Whiting, Robert. *You Gotta Have Wa: When Two Cultures Collide on the Baseball Diamond.* New York and London: Collier Macmillan Publishers, 1989.

Celebrated award-winning study of contrasting American and Japanese approaches to the joint national game of baseball. Crucial to understanding Japan's pastime is the concept of *wa*, or "perfect harmony found in team unity." Whiting's true subject is a larger Japanese culture, which he sees as best understood through unique Japanese approaches to baseball.

Mexico

Araujo Bojórquez, Alfonso. *Historia de la Liga de la Costa Pacifico, 1945–1958 (History of the Pacific Coast League, 1945–1958).* Mexico City: privately printed, n.d.

Brief narrative history of the original Mexican Pacific Coast League wintertime circuit that operated from the end of World War II through the late 1950s. Individual chapters are devoted to each of fourteen seasons, with final league standings and team win–loss records. Some black-and-white photos are included, as well as a limited statistical summary section with individual batting and pitching leaders plus the league's MVPs.

Cisneros, Pedro Treto, ed. *The Mexican League: Comprehensive Player Statistics, 1937–2001*. Jefferson, NC: McFarland, 2002. (English-Spanish bilingual edition)

Complete statistic record of Mexican (Summer) League play from origins in the 1930s on to the present (2001). Yearly and career leaders in all batting and pitching categories are included, along with complete individual player statistics and such features as a no-hitter list and Mexican hall of fame register. Drawbacks include numerous typographical errors, absence of win–loss records for pennant winners, and slim accounts of the nonstatistical history.

Lara, Joaquín. *Historia del Béisbol en Yucatán, I: 1890–1906 (The History of Yucatán Baseball, Part I:, 1890–1906)*. Mérida, Yucatán, Mexico: Editorial Zamma, 1954.

The Yucatán peninsula region of southeastern Mexico stands out as both the country's foremost baseball hotbed and also the locale for the earliest importation of the "American" game by Cuban settlers. Lara traces the earliest baseball roots in this region at the close of the nineteenth century among wealthy Cuban settlers escaping a war for independence from Spain.

León Lerma, Arturo. *Arriba . . . Mayos . . . Arriba—30 Temporadas de Béisbol Profesional, 1959–1994 (On, Mayos, On—30 Seasons of Professional Baseball, 1959–1994)*. Mexico City: Revistas Deportivas, 1994.

Restricted to a single Mexican pro ball club, this history of the Navojoa Mayos covers action over six seasons in the Sonora Winter League (1959–1966) and twenty-four campaigns in the wintertime Mexican Pacific League (1970–1994). Season recaps, league standings, rosters, player photos, and individual player statistics offer not only a detailed account of the Navojoa franchise but also a valuable summary of Mexican Pacific League baseball.

Phillips, John. *The Mexican Jumping Beans: The Story of the Baseball War of 1946*. Perry, GA: Capital Publishing Company, 1997.

Most extensive and useful account of background and details concerning Jorge Pasquel's 1946 attempts to raid U.S. big league talent for Mexican League team rosters. Details of the fateful 1946 season, on and off the field, are supplemented with accounts of follow-up events over the next ten years, including the impact of these events not only on the contract-jumping players but also on the fate of Pasquel and the health of the Mexican League itself.

Puerto Rico

Béisbol Profesional de Puerto Rico, Recuento Temporada 1998–1999 (Puerto Rican Professional Baseball, 1998–1999 Season Recap). San Juan, Puerto Rico: *El Nuevo Dia* Magazine, 1999. (Published in annual editions, 1993–2000)

Sixty-year league anniversary statistical guide covering both the 1998–1999 winter season and the 1999 Caribbean series hosted by San Juan. Featured is an extensive interview section and career summary for 1950s-era big leaguer Vic Power, and career stats for all active league players.

Costa, Rafael. *Enciclopedia Béisbol, Ponce Leones, 1938–1987 (Baseball Encyclopedia, Ponce Lions, 1938–1987)*. Santo Domingo, Dominican Republic: Editora Corripio, 1989.

Exhaustive single-team statistical encyclopedia covering one of the top Caribbean winter league franchises. Complete year-by-year team and player statistics and all-time ball club records are supplemented with some black-and-white photos and additional illustrations. Lifetime batting and pitching records for Puerto Rican and imported players up to the 1986–1987 season.

Van Hyning, Thomas E. *The Santurce Crabbers: Sixty Seasons of Puerto Rican Winter League Baseball*. Jefferson, NC: McFarland, 1999.

Intimate if prosaically written history of one of Caribbean winter league baseball's most storied franchises. Emphasis falls on the visionary role of first owner Pedrín Zorilla across the decade of the 1940s, which established the colorful Crabbers (featuring big league heroes Roberto

Clemente and Willie Mays) as the league's most dominant force throughout the decade of the 1950s.

————. *Puerto Rico's Winter League: A History of Major League Baseball's Launching Pad.* Jefferson, NC: McFarland, 1995.

Overview of once-thriving Puerto Rican winter baseball from the perspective of its role as stepping stone to prosperous big league careers for both imported Americans and native island prospects. Puerto Ricans among those whose careers were launched on the island include Vic Power, Rubén Gómez, Jerry Morales, Orlando Cepeda, and the immortal Roberto Clemente.

Venezuela

Gutiérrez, Daniel. *50 Años de Big Leaguers Venezolanos, 1939–1989 (Fifty Years of Venezuelan Big Leaguers, 1939–1989).* Caracas, Venezuela: Distribuidora Continental [privately printed], 1990.

Brief career summaries and major league stats for all Venezuelans playing in the major leagues through the end of the 1980s. Useful supplemental materials include a comparative chart of Venezuelan big leaguers' career stats, year-by-year listing of Venezuelan debuts, annual lists of Venezuelans currently in the big time, major league teams for individual Venezuelan big leaguers, and the author's all-time all-star team of Venezuela's major leaguers.

Mijares, Rubén. *Béisbol por Dentro (Inside Baseball).* Mérida, Venezuela: Editorial Alfa, n.d. (circa 1989).

Brief portraits of highlight moments and memorable players drawn from the author's quarter-century of covering Venezuelan winter league baseball and the U.S. major leagues. Black-and-white photos support the lively (if sometimes superficial) text recounting cherished memories of the Venezuelan national game. Focus is mostly on native Venezuelan stars, but portraits include Mexican (Fernando Valenzuela), Dominican (Pedro Guerrero), and American (Pete Rose, Dave Parker, Kirk Gibson) big leaguers.

Salas, Alexis. *Los Eternos Rivales: Caracas–Magallanes, Pastora–Gavilanes, 1908–1988 (The Eternal Rivals: Caracas–Magallanes, Pastora–Gavilanes, 1908–1988).* Caracas, Venezuela: Grupo Editorial C.A., 1988.

Thorough review of highlight moments marking the eight-decade rivalries between two pairs of historic Venezuelan ball clubs, whose sagas together cover almost the entire twentieth century. Numerous box scores plus historic photographs enliven capsule reports treating significant individual contests played throughout the long history of Venezuelan summer and winter baseball.

————. *Momentos Inolvidables del Béisbol Profesional Venezolano, 1946–1984 (Unforgettable Moments in Venezuelan Professional Baseball, 1946–1984).* Caracas, Venezuela: Miguel Angel García and Sons, 1985.

Arranged chronologically by important dates in the country's pro baseball history, Salas's text captures Venezuela's greatest winter league legends, stars, and events with photos, box scores, and brief summaries for more than 150 unforgettable games. Many photos are of inferior newsprint quality, but full box scores add valuable historic data for each game.

Other Countries

Clark, Joe. *A History of Australian Baseball: Time and Game.* Lincoln: University of Nebraska Press, 2003.

Academic history of rise in stature for Australian baseball from nineteenth-century grudging acceptance as an off-season substitute for the more popular cricket through some brief late-twentieth-century gains in world tournament play. Both shortcomings and strengths of Australia's baseball experience are examined. Highlights include an Intercontinental Cup gold medal win (1999) over Cuba at Sydney and the role in hosting the 2000 Olympic baseball competitions.

Costello, Rory S. *Baseball in the Virgin Islands*. New York: Hungry Joe Publishing, 2000. Available at http://members.aol.com/vibaseball.

Delightful brief account of contributions by Virgin Islands ballplayers to the major leagues, minor leagues, winter ball, and Negro leagues scenes. Individual career portraits and photos of a dozen top island players (including Valmy Thomas, Joe Christopher, Horace Clarke, José Morales, and Elrod Hendricks), plus brief accounts of baseball's origins in the Virgin Islands and the role of pioneering Pittsburgh scout Howie Haak in mining local island talent.

Pastrian, Héctor. *Béisbol: Reseña histórica internacional y argentina (Historical Review and Outline of International and Argentinean Baseball)*. Buenos Aires: Argentinean Baseball Federation, 1977.

Thorough history of the game's origins in Argentina and all levels of amateur league play and provincial and national tournaments, beginning in 1933. Details on Argentina's few appearances in international tournament play including the 1973 Intercontinental Cup in Italy. Newspaper-quality black-and-white photos of top players and teams, plus tournament action.

Riley, James A. *The Biographical Encyclopedia of the Negro Baseball Leagues*. New York: Carroll & Graf Publishers, 1994.

Some details on individual black-ball stars from Cuba and elsewhere in the Caribbean, plus the playing records of American blacks in Caribbean winter leagues. The volume is greatly hampered by repeated misspellings of Latino player and team names and numerous factual errors concerning career details for important black Latino ballplayers.

ADDITIONAL RESOURCES

The following list of journal and magazine articles includes sources relied upon for the current volume, as well as valuable background reading on aspects of international baseball competitions and on the emergence of baseball as an international sport. Only English-language materials are included.

Ardolino, Frank. "The Hawaii Winter League, 1993–1997." *The National Pastime: A Review of Baseball History* 20 (2000): 42–45.
———. "Wally Yonamine: From Hawaiian plantation to the Japanese Baseball Hall of Fame." *The National Pastime: A Review of Baseball History* 19 (1999): 10–11.
Atchison, Lewis F. "How Mexican Raids Threatened to Ruin Majors 25 Years Ago." *Baseball Digest* 30.7 (July 1971): 72–75.
Barney, Robert Knight. "In Search of a Canadian Cooperstown: The Future of the Canadian Baseball Hall of Fame." *Nine: A Journal of Baseball History and Social Policy Perspectives* 1.1 (Fall 1992): 61–78.
Barthel, Tom. "Ducky and the Lip in Italy." *The National Pastime: A Review of Baseball History* 23 (2003): 115–121.
Beezley, William. "The Rise of Baseball in Mexico and the First Valenzuela." *Studies in Latin American Popular Culture* 4 (1985): 3–23.
Bjarkman, Peter C. "Waiting for Che—Chasing Illusions in the Modern-Era Cuban Ballpark." *Elysian Fields Quarterly* 21:2 (Spring 2004), 6–17.
———. "Adolfo Luque: The Original 'Pride of Havana'." *Elysian Fields Quarterly* 20:1 (Winter 2003): 21–38.
———. "The Cuban Comet (Minnie Miñoso)." *Elysian Fields Quarterly* 19:1 (Winter 2002): 22–36.

———. "Martín Dihigo: Baseball's Least-Known Hall of Famer." *Elysian Fields Quarterly* 18:2 (Spring 2001): 22–39.

———. "Latin America's Game—History and the Latin Age: Exclusion, prejudice yield to a Latin Age." *Devil Ray's Magazine* 3:3 (May–July 2000): 38–39, 40, 42, 44, 46, 48, 50.

———. "The Baseball Half-Century of Conrado Marrero." *Elysian Fields Quarterly* 17:1 (Winter 2000): 27–44.

———. "Fidel on the Mound: Baseball Myth and History in Castro's Cuba." *Elysian Fields Quarterly* 16:3 (Summer 1999): 31–41.

———. "Baseball and Fidel Castro: The Maximum Leader affected baseball in Cuba, but he was never a big league pitching prospect." *The National Pastime: A Review of Baseball History* 18 (1998): 64–68.

———. "The Real World Series—Cubans again dominate Olympic action." *The Baseball Research Journal* 26 (1997): 28–29.

———. "Lifting the Iron Curtain of Cuban Baseball: Mystery and change surround the island's national pastime." *The National Pastime: A Review of Baseball History* 17 (1997): 31–35.

Bouchier, Nancy, and Robert Knight Barney. "A Critical Examination of a Source on Early Ontario Baseball: The Reminiscence of Robert E. Ford." *Journal of Sport History* 15.1 (Spring 1998): 75–90.

Boyle, Robert H. "The Latins Storm Las Grandes Ligas." *Sports Illustrated* 23.6 (August 9, 1965): 24–30.

Brown, Bruce. "Cuban Baseball." *Atlantic Monthly* 253.6 (June 1984): 109–114.

Cantwell, Robert Francis. "Invasion from Santo Domingo: Dominican Big Leaguers." *Sports Illustrated* 18.8 (February 25 1963): 54–61.

Cava, Pete. "Baseball in the Olympics." *The National Pastime: A Review of Baseball History* 12 (1992): 2–28.

Clifton, Merritt. "Where the Twain Shall Meet: What baseball means to Japan—and humanity." *The National Pastime: A Review of Baseball History* 4:1 (Spring 1985): 12–22.

Costello, Rory S. "Baseball in the Virgin Islands." *The Baseball Research Journal* 28 (1999): 33–40.

Feldman, Jay. "In Holland, Honk if You Love Baseball: Green grass and fine art in the Netherlands." *The National Pastime: A Review of Baseball History* 13 (1993): 50–52.

———. "Baseball in Nicaragua." *Whole Earth Review* (Fall 1987): 40–45.

———. "The Hidden Ball Trick: Nicaragua and Me." *The National Pastime: A Review of Baseball History* 6:1 (Winter 1987): 2–4.

Field, Russell. "World Ball: Just whose pastime is it anyway?" *Play Ball! Celebrating 150 Years of Baseball*. Clearwater, Florida: Storm Publications, 1996, 108–117.

Fimrite, Ronald. "In Cuba, It's Viva El Grand Old Game." *Sports Illustrated* (June 6, 1977): 69–80.

Frio, Daniel C., and Marc Onigman. "Good Field No Hit: The Image of Latin American Players in the American Press, 1871–1946." *Revista-Review Interamericana* 9:2 (Summer 1979): 192–208.

Hoekstra, Dave. "Cuban Game is a Study in Socialism." *Chicago Sun-Times* (February 4, 1990): 20–21, 24.

Holway, John B. "Taiwan Little Leaguers Grow Into Big Leaguers." *The National Pastime: A Review of Baseball History* 12 (1992): 48–50.

Hoose, Philip G. "Hot Blood: The Latin American Baseball Player." *Necessities: Racial Barriers in America Sports* 12. New York: Random House, 1989, 90–122.

Humber, William. "The Story of Canadian Ballplayers." *The National Pastime: A Review of Baseball History* 12 (1992): 26–29.

Ivor-Campbell, Frederick. "Sadaharu Oh's Place in Baseball's Pantheon." *The National Pastime: A Review of Baseball History* 12 (1992): 35–36.

Jamail, Milton. "Béisbol: Competition is fierce and Loyalties strong in the Caribbean Series." *Diamondbacks Quarterly* 2:1 (Spring 1997): 29.

———. "Latin America's Winter World Series: Baseball goes salsa as teams from south of the border meet in Miami." *Diversion* (Spring 1997): 151–157.

Joseph, Gilbert. "Documenting a Regional Pastime: Baseball in Yucatán." *Windows on Latin America: Understanding Society Through Photographs.* Miami, Florida: The University of Miami Press, 1987, 77–89.

Kirwin, Bill. "The Mysterious Case of Dick Brookins: Jim Crow crosses the border." *The National Pastime: A Review of Baseball History* 19 (1999): 38–43.

Kuenster, John. "Latin American Quality Players Abound in the Majors." *Baseball Digest* 42:7 (July 1983): 17–21.

LaFrance, David G. "Labor, the State, and Professional Baseball in Mexico in the 1980s." *Journal of Sport History* 22:2 (Summer 1995): 111–134.

———. "A Mexican Popular Image of the United States through the Baseball Hero, Fernando Valenzuela." *Studies in Latin American Popular Culture* 4 (1985): 14–23.

Leutzinger, Richard. "Lefty O'Doul and the Development of Japanese Baseball." *The National Pastime: A Review of Baseball History* 12 (1992): 30–34.

Mandt, Edward. "Latin American All-Stars: Los Niños de Otono." *The Baseball Research Journal* 17 (1988): 23–24.

Obojski, Robert. "Baseball Latin Style." *The Baseball Research Journal* 6 (1977): 104–110.

Prentice, Bruce, and Merritt Clifton. "Baseball in Canada." *Total Baseball: The Official Encyclopedia of Major League Baseball.* Sixth Edition. New York: Total Sports, 1999, 544–548.

Puff, Richard. "The Amazing Story of Victor Starffin." *The National Pastime: A Review of Baseball History* 12 (1992): 17–19.

Rondon, Tito. "The Pan-American Series of 1958: A Latin Series that happened only once." *The National Pastime: A Review of Baseball History* 14 (1994): 70–71.

Rosenthal, Harold. "The War with Mexico." *Baseball Digest* 22:10 (December 1963–January 1964): 53–56.

Ruck, Rob. "The Crisis in Winter Baseball—Can It Survive?" *Baseball America* 10 (February 25–March 9, 1990): 8–9.

———. "Chicos and Gringos of Béisbol Venezolana." *The Baseball Research Journal* 15 (1986): 75–78.

Sheer, Harry. "Cuban Ballplayers in the Majors." *Baseball Digest* 30:11 (November 1971): 72–74.

Tiemann, Robert. "Join the Majors, See the World: Baseball on Tour." *The National Pastime: A Review of Baseball History* 10 (Fall 1990): 43–48.

Travaglini, M.E. "Olympic Baseball 1936: Was es Das?" *The National Pastime: A Review of Baseball History* 4:2 (Winter 1985): 46–55.

Van Hyning, Thomas E. "The Santurce Crabbers: From Josh Gibson to Juan González." *The National Pastime: A Review of Baseball History* 19 (1999): 49–52.

Vaughn, Gerald F. "Jorge Pasquel and the Evolution of the Mexican League." *The National Pastime: A Review of Baseball History* 12 (1992): 9–13.

———. "George Hausmann Recalls the Mexican League of 1946–47." *The Baseball Research Journal* 19 (1990): 59–63.

Wagner, Eric A. "Baseball in Cuba." *Journal of Popular Culture* 18:1 (Summer 1984): 113–120.

Whiting, Robert. "East meets West in the Japanese game of 'besuboru'." *Smithsonian* 17:6 (September 1986): 108, 120–38.

Wilson, Lyle. "The Harlem Globetrotters Baseball Team: Straight baseball with lots of hustle." *The National Pastime: A Review of Baseball History* 17 (1997): 77–80.

Index

· ·

About the Author

PETER C. BJARKMAN writes extensively about baseball, basketball, and travel-related topics. He has published two previous books on Cuban baseball, plus a history of baseball in Latin America and more than three dozen other titles treating major league baseball, NBA basketball, and NCAA basketball. His recent work includes team history encyclopedias on the New York Mets, Cincinnati Reds, Boston Celtics, and New York Knicks. A fluent Spanish speaker, Bjarkman has twice been featured on Cuban national television discussing Cuban League baseball and the Cuban national team, the only American to claim this distinction during the 40-plus years of the Cuban Revolution.